Encyclopedia of
Information Systems and Technology

Volume II

GIS–XML

Encyclopedias from the Taylor & Francis Group

Agropedia

Encyclopedia of Agricultural, Food, and Biological Engineering, Second Ed. (2 Vols.)
Edited by Dennis R. Heldman and Carmen I. Moraru   *Published 10/21/10*
Print: K10554 (978-1-4398-1111-5)   Online: K11382 (978-1-4398-2806-9)

Encyclopedia of Animal Science, Second Ed. (2 Vols.)
Edited by Duane E. Ullrey, Charlotte Kirk Baer, and Wilson G. Pond   *Published 2/1/11*
Print: K10463 (978-1-4398-0932-7)   Online: K10528 (978-0-415-80286-4)

Encyclopedia of Biotechnology in Agriculture and Food (1 Vol.)
Edited by Dennis R. Heldman, Dallas G. Hoover, and Matthew B. Wheeler   *Published 7/16/10*
Print: DK271X (978-0-8493-5027-6) Online: DKE5044 (978-0-8493-5044-3)

Encyclopedia of Pest Management (1 Vol.)
Edited by David Pimentel, Ph.D.   *Published 5/9/02*
Print: DK6323 (978-0-8247-0632-6) Online: DKE517X (978-0-8247-0517-6)

Encyclopedia of Plant and Crop Science (1 Vol.)
Edited by Robert M. Goodman   *Published 2/27/04*
Print: DK1190 (978-0-8247-0944-0) Online: DKE9438 (978-0-8247-0943-3)

Encyclopedia of Soil Science, Second Ed. (2 Vols.)
Edited by Rattan Lal   *Published 12/22/05*
Print: DK830X (978-0-8493-3830-4) Online: DKE5051 (978-0-8493-5051-1)

Encyclopedia of Water Science, Second Ed. (2 Vols.)
Edited by Stanley W. Trimble   *Published 12/26/07*
Print: DK9627 (978-0-8493-9627-4) Online: DKE9619 (978-0-8493-9619-9)

Business and Public Administration

Encyclopedia of Public Administration and Public Policy, Third Ed. (5 Vols.)
Edited by Melvin J. Dubnick and Domonic Bearfield   *Published 7/15/15*
Print: K16418 (978-1-4665-6909-6)   Online: K16434 (978-1-4665-6936-2)

Encyclopedia of Supply Chain Management (2 Vols.)
Edited by James B. Ayers   *Published 12/21/11*
Print: K12842 (978-1-4398-6148-6)   Online: K12843 (978-1-4398-6152-3)

Encyclopedia of U.S. Intelligence (2 Vols.)
Edited by Gregory Moore   *Published 12/19/14*
Print: AU8957 (978-1-4200-8957-8) Online: AUE8957 (978-1-4200-8958-5)

Chemistry, Materials, and Chemical Engineering

Encyclopedia of Chemical Processing (5 Vols.)
Edited by Sunggyu Lee   *Published 11/1/05*
Print: DK2243 (978-0-8247-5563-8) Online: DKE499X (978-0-8247-5499-0)

Encyclopedia of Chromatography, Third Ed. (3 Vols.)
Edited by Jack Cazes   *Published 10/12/09*
Print: 84593 (978-1-4200-8459-7)   Online: 84836 (978-1-4200-8483-2)

Encyclopedia of Iron, Steel, and Their Alloys (5 Vols.)
Edited by George E. Totten and Rafael Colas   *Published 9/15/15*
Print: K14814 (978-1-4665-1104-0)   Online: K14815 (978-1-4665-1105-7)

Encyclopedia of Supramolecular Chemistry (2 Vols.)
Edited by Jerry L. Atwood and Jonathan W. Steed   *Published 5/5/04*
Print: DK056X (978-0-8247-5056-5) Online: DKE7259 (978-0-8247-4725-1)

Encyclopedia of Surface and Colloid Science, Third Ed. (10 Vols.)
Edited by P. Somasundaran   *Published 5/8/15*
Print: K20465 (978-1-4665-9045-8)   Online: K20478 (978-1-4665-9061-8)

Environment

Encyclopedia of Environmental Management (4 Vols.)
Edited by Sven Erik Jorgensen   *Published 12/13/12*
Print: K11434 (978-1-4398-2927-1)   Online: K11440 (978-1-4398-2933-2)

Encyclopedia of Natural Resources (2 Vols.)
Edited by Yeqiao Wang   *Published 7/23/14*
Print: K12418 (978-1-4398-5258-3) Online: KE12440 (978-1-4398-5283-5)

Engineering

Dekker Encyclopedia of Nanoscience and Nanotechnology, Third Ed. (7 Vols.)
Edited by Sergey Edward Lyshevski   *Published 3/20/14*
Print: K14119 (978-1-4398-9134-6)   Online: K14120 (978-1-4398-9135-3)

Encyclopedia of Energy Engineering and Technology, Second Ed. (4 Vols.)
Edited by Sohail Anwar   *Published 12/1/14*
Print: K14633 (978-1-4665-0673-2)   Online: KE16142 (978-1-4665-0674-9)

Encyclopedia of Optical and Photonic Engineering, Second Ed. (3 Vols.)
Edited by Craig Hoffman and Ronald Driggers   *Published 6/1/15*
Print: K12323 (978-1-4398-5097-8)   Online: K12325 (978-1-4398-5099-2)

Medicine

Encyclopedia of Biomaterials and Biomedical Engineering, Second Ed. (4 Vols.)
Edited by Gary E. Wnek and Gary L. Bowlin   *Published 5/28/08*
Print: H7802 (978-1-4200-7802-2)   Online: HE7803 (978-1-4200-7803-9)

Encyclopedia of Biomedical Polymers and Polymeric Biomaterials (11 Vol.)
Edited by Munmaya Mishra   *Published 3/12/15*
Print: K14324 (978-1-4398-9879-6)   Online: K14404 (978-1-4665-0179-9)

Encyclopedia of Biopharmaceutical Statistics, Third Ed. (3 Vols.)
Edited by Shein-Chung Chow   *Published 5/20/10*
Print: H100102 (978-1-4398-2245-6) Online: HE10326 (978-1-4398-2246-3)

Encyclopedia of Clinical Pharmacy (1 Vol.)
Edited by Joseph T. DiPiro   *Published 11/14/02*
Print: DK7524 (978-0-8247-0752-1) Online: DKE6080 (978-0-8247-0608-1)

Encyclopedia of Dietary Supplements, Second Ed. (1 Vol.)
Edited by Paul M. Coates, Joseph M. Betz, Marc R. Blackman, Gordon M. Cragg, Mark Levine, Joel Moss, and Jeffrey D. White   *Published 6/25/10*
Print: H100094 (978-1-4398-1928-9) Online: HE10315 (978-1-4398-1929-6)

Encyclopedia of Medical Genomics and Proteomics (2 Vols.)
Edited by Jürgen Fuchs and Maurizio Podda   *Published 12/29/04*
Print: DK2208 (978-0-8247-5564-5) Online: DK501X (978-0-8247-5501-0)

Encyclopedia of Pharmaceutical Science and Technology, Fourth Ed. (6 Vols.)
Edited by James Swarbrick   *Published 7/1/13*
Print: H100233 (978-1-84184-819-8) Online: HE10420 (978-1-84184-820-4)

Software, Networking, and Security

Encyclopedia of Information Assurance (4 Vols.)
Edited by Rebecca Herold and Marcus K. Rogers   *Published 12/21/10*
Print: AU6620 (978-1-4200-6620-3) Online: AUE6620 (978-1-4200-6622-7)

Encyclopedia of Information Systems and Technology (2 Vol.)
Edited by Phillip A. Laplante   *Published 10/15/15*
Print: K15911 (978-1-4665-6077-2)   Online: K21745 (978-1-4822-1432-1)

Encyclopedia of Library and Information Sciences, Third Ed. (7 Vols.)
Edited by Marcia J. Bates and Mary Niles Maack   *Published 12/17/09*
Print: DK9712 (978-0-8493-9712-7) Online: DKE9711 (978-0-8493-9711-0)

Encyclopedia of Software Engineering (2 Vols.)
Edited by Phillip A. Laplante   *Published 11/24/10*
Print: AU5977 (978-1-4200-5977-9) Online: AUE5977 (978-1-4200-5978-6)

Encyclopedia of Wireless and Mobile Communications, Second Ed. (3 Vols.)
Edited by Borko Furht   *Published 12/18/12*
Print: K14731 (978-1-4665-0956-6)   Online: KE16352 (978-1-4665-0969-6)

Encyclopedia of
Information
Systems and
Technology

Volume II

GIS–XML

Edited by Phillip A. Laplante

CRC Press
Taylor & Francis Group
Boca Raton London New York

CRC Press is an imprint of the
Taylor & Francis Group, an **informa** business

AN AUERBACH BOOK

CRC Press
Taylor & Francis Group
6000 Broken Sound Parkway NW, Suite 300
Boca Raton, FL 33487-2742

© 2016 by Taylor & Francis Group, LLC
CRC Press is an imprint of Taylor & Francis Group, an Informa business

No claim to original U.S. Government works

Printed on acid-free paper
Version Date: 20151030

International Standard Book Number-13: 978-1-4987-5786-7 (Hardback)

Visit the Taylor & Francis Web site at
http://www.taylorandfrancis.com

and the CRC Press Web site at
http://www.crcpress.com

Encyclopedia of Information Systems and Technology

To the beloved dogs that I have had in my life: Ginger, Francis, Maggie, Teddy, and Henry, and those yet to come.

Encyclopedia of Information Systems and Technology

Editor-in-Chief
Phillip A. Laplante
Professor of Software Engineering, Great Valley School of Graduate Professional Studies,
Pennsylvania State University, Malvern, Pennsylvania, U.S.A.

Editorial Advisory Board

Contributors

Azad Adam / *London, U.K.*

Ali Naser Al-Khwildi / *Commission of Media and Communications (CMC), Jadreiah, Iraq*

Sven Axsðter / *Department of Industrial Management and Logistics, Lund University, Lund, Sweden*

Mohamad Badra / *College of Technological Innovation, Zayed University, Dubai, United Arab Emirates*

Ricardo Baeza-Yates / *Barcelona Media Innovation Centre, Yahoo! Research, Barcelona, Spain*

Robert B. Batie Jr. / *Cyber Defense Solutions, Network Centric Systems, Raytheon Company, Largo, Florida, U.S.A.*

A. R. Bednarek / *University of Florida, Gainesville, Florida, U.S.A.*

Chuck Bianco / *IT Examination Manager, Office of Thrift Supervision, Department of the Treasury, Dallas, Texas, U.S.A.*

Galina Bogdanova / *Department of Mathematical Foundations of Informatics, Institute of Mathematics and Informatics, Bulgarian Academy of Sciences, Veliko Tarnovo, Bulgaria*

Gloria Bordogna / *Italian National Research Council, Institute for the Dynamics of Environmental Processes, Dalmine, Italy*

Terrence Brooks / *iSchool, University of Washington, Seattle, Washington, U.S.A.*

Christopher Brown-Syed / *Faculty of Continuing Education and Training, Seneca College, Burlington, Ontario, Canada*

Jason Burke / *SAS Institute, Cary, North Carolina, U.S.A.*

Carlos Castillo / *Yahoo! Research, Barcelona, Spain*

Glenn Cater / *Director, IT Risk Consulting, Aon Consulting, Inc., Freehold, New Jersey, U.S.A.*

Ranganai Chaparadza / *IPV6 Forum, ETSI-AFI, Berlin, Germany*

Ansuman Chattopadhyay / *Health Sciences Library System, University of Pittsburgh, Pittsburgh, Pennsylvania, U.S.A.*

Brian J.S. Chee / *School of Ocean and Earth Sciences and Technology (SOEST), University of Hawaii, Honolulu, Hawaii, U.S.A.*

Hsinchun Chen / *Department of Management Information Systems, University of Arizona, Tucson, Arizona, U.S.A.*

Jianhua Chen / *Computer Science Department, Louisiana State University, Baton Rouge, Louisiana, U.S.A.*

Marco Conti / *National Research Council (CNR), Pisa, Italy*

Marcelo Nogueira Cortimiglia / *Industrial Engineering Department, Federal University of Rio Grande do Sul, Porto Alegre, Brazil*

Kimiz Dalkir / *Graduate School of Library and Information Studies, McGill University, Montreal, Quebec, Canada*

Yan Dang / *Department of Management Information Systems, University of Arizona, Tucson, Arizona, U.S.A.*

Joanna F. DeFranco / *Pennsylvania State University, Malvern, Pennsylvania, U.S.A.*

Harry B. DeMaio / *Cincinnati, Ohio, U.S.A.*

Brian Detlor / *DeGroote School of Business, McMaster University, Hamilton, Ontario, Canada*

Andrew Dillon / *School of Information, University of Texas at Austin, Austin, Texas, U.S.A.*

Jianguo Ding / *School of Informatics, University of Skovde, Skovde, Sweden*

G. Reza Djavanshir / *Carey Business School, Johns Hopkins University, Baltimore, Maryland, U.S.A.*

Matt Dobra / *Department of Economics, Methodist University, Fayetteville, North Carolina, U.S.A.*

Marek J. Druzdzel / *School of Information Sciences and Intelligent Systems Program, University of Pittsburgh, Pittsburgh, Pennsylvania, U.S.A.*

Artur Dubrawski / *Robotics Institute, Carnegie Mellon University, Pittsburgh, Pennsylvania, U.S.A.*

Mark Edmead / *President, MTE Software, Inc., Escondido, California, U.S.A.*

Scott Erkonen / *Hot skills Inc., Minneapolis, Minnesota, U.S.A.*

Ben Falchuk / *Telcordia Technologies, Inc., Piscataway, New Jersey, U.S.A.*

Dave Famolari / *Telcordia Technologies, Inc., Piscataway, New Jersey, U.S.A.*

Roger R. Flynn / *School of Information Sciences and Intelligent Systems Program, University of Pittsburgh, Pittsburgh, Pennsylvania, U.S.A.*

Park Foreman / *Austin, Texas, U.S.A.*

Alejandro Germán Frank / *Industrial Engineering Department, Federal University of Rio Grande do Sul, Porto Alegre, Brazil*

Ulrik Franke / *Department of Information and Aeronautical Systems, Swedish Defense Research Agency (FOI), Stockholm, Sweden*

Curtis Franklin Jr. / *Senior Writer, NetWitness, Gainsville, Florida, U.S.A.*

José Antonio Garcia-Macias / *CICESE Research Center, Esenada, Mexico*

Antonio Ghezzi / *Department of Management, Economics and Industrial Engineering, Milan Polytechnic, Milan, Italy*

Lal C. Godara / *Australian Defence Force Academy, School of Electrical Engineering University College, University of New South Wales, Canberra, Australian Capital Territory, Australia*

Tandy Gold / *Independent Executive Consultant, Sanford, Florida, U.S.A.*

Steven D. Gray / *Nokia Research Center, Espoo, Finland*

Wendy Hall / *Intelligence, Agents, Multimedia Group, University of Southampton, Southampton, U.K.*

Monte F. Hancock Jr. / *Chief Scientist, Celestech, Inc., Melbourne, Florida, U.S.A.*

Chris Hare / *Information Systems Auditor, Nortel, Dallas, Texas, U.S.A.*

Kirk Hausman / *Assistant Commandant, Texas A&M University, College Station, Texas, U.S.A.*

Gilbert Held / *4-Degree Consulting, Macon, Georgia, U.S.A.*

Markus Helfert / *School of Computing, Dublin City University, Dublin, Ireland*

Paul A. Henry / *Senior Vice President, CyberGuard Corporation, Ocala, Florida, U.S.A.*

Rebecca Herold / *Information Privacy, Security and Compliance Consultant, Rebecca Herold and Associates LLC, Van Meter, Iowa, U.S.A.*

Francis Heylighen / *Free University of Brussels, Brussels, Belgium*

Randolph Hock / *Online Strategies, Vienna, Virginia, U.S.A.*

Javek Ikbal / *Director, IT Security, Major Financial Services Company, Reading, Massachusetts, U.S.A.*

Carrie L. Iwema / *Health Sciences Library System, University of Pittsburgh, Pittsburgh, Pennsylvania, U.S.A.*

Valentina Janev / *Mihajlo Pupin Institute, Belgrade, Serbia*

Gary G. Jing / *TE Connectivity, Shakopee, Minnesota, U.S.A.*

Leighton Johnson III / *Chief Operating Officer and Senior Consultant, Information Security and Forensics Management Team (ISFMT), Bath, South Carolina, U.S.A.*

Keith Jones / *Annapolis, Maryland, U.S.A.*

Paul B. Kantor / *School of Communication, Information and Library Studies, Rutgers University, New Brunswick, New Jersey, U.S.A.*

Leon Kappelman / *Information Technology and Decision Sciences Department, University of North Texas, Denton, Texas, U.S.A.*

Jessica Keyes / *New Art Technologies, Inc., New York, New York, U.S.A.*

Shafiullah Khan / *School of Engineering and Information Sciences, Computer Communications Department, Middlesex University, London, U.K.*

Joshua L. Kissee / *Instructional Technology Services, Information Technology Division, Texas A&M University, College Station, Texas, U.S.A.*

Walter S. Kobus Jr. / *Vice President, Security Consulting Services, Total Enterprise Security Solutions, LLC, Raleigh, North Carolina, U.S.A.*

Donald Kraft / *Department of Computer Science, U.S. Air Force Academy, Colorado Springs, Colorado, U.S.A.*

Mollie E. Krehnke / *Senior Information Security Consultant, Insight Global, Inc., Raleigh, North Carolina, U.S.A.*

Stephan Kudyba / *New Jersey Institute of Technology, Newark, New Jersey, U.S.A.*

Matthew Kwatinetz / *QBL Partners, New York, New York, U.S.A.*

Zhenhua Lai / *Department of Management Information Systems, University of Arizona, Tucson, Arizona, U.S.A.*

Sian Lun Lau / *Department of Computer Science and Networked Systems, Sunway University, Subang Jaya, Malaysia*

Ross A. Leo / *Professional Training and Development, University of Houston-Clear Lake, CyberSecurity Institute, Houston, Texas, U.S.A.*

Timothy F. Leslie / *Department of Geography and Geoinformation Science, George Mason University, Fairfax, Virginia, U.S.A.*

Shoshana Loeb / *Telcordia Technologies, Inc., Piscataway, New Jersey, U.S.A.*

Jonathan Loo / *School of Engineering and Information Sciences, Computer Communications Department, Middlesex University, London, U.K.*

Phillip Q. Maier / *Vice President, Information Security Emerging Technology & Network Group, Inovant, San Ramon, California, U.S.A.*

Franjo Majstor / *EMEA Senior Technical Director, CipherOptics Inc., Raleigh, North Carolina, U.S.A.*

Arun K. Majumdar / *VivoMind Research, Rockville, Maryland, U.S.A.*

Katherine Marconi / *Health Care Administration and Health Administration Informatics, University of Maryland, Adelphi, Maryland, U.S.A.*

Johan Marklund / *Department of Industrial Management and Logistics, Lund University, Lund, Sweden*

George G. McBride / *Senior Manager, Security and Privacy Services (SPS), Deloitte & Touche LLP, Princeton, New Jersey, U.S.A.*

Lowell Bruce McCulley / *IT Security Professional, Troy, New Hampshire, U.S.A.*

Lynda L. McGhie / *Information Security Officer (ISO)/Risk Manager, Private Client Services (PCS), Wells Fargo Bank, Cameron Park, California, U.S.A.*

Hermann Moisl / *Center for Research in Linguistics, University of Newcastle upon Tyne, Newcastle Upon Tyne, U.K.*

William Hugh Murray / *Executive Consultant, TruSecure Corporation, New Canaan, Connecticut, U.S.A.*

Nikolay Noev / *Department of Mathematical Foundations of Informatics, Institute of Mathematics and Informatics, Bulgarian Academy of Sciences, Veliko Tarnovo, Bulgaria*

David O'Berry / *Director of Information Technology Systems and Services, South Carolina Department of Probation, Parole and Pardon Services (SCDPPPS), Columbia, South Carolina, U.S.A.*

Kieron O'Hara / *Intelligence, Agents, Multimedia Group, University of Southampton, Southampton, U.K.*

Tero Ojanperä / *Nokia Research Center, Espoo, Finland*

Gabriella Pasi / *Department of Informatics, Systems and Communication, University of Studies of Milano Bicocca, Milan, Italy*

Keith Pasley / *PGP Security, Boonsboro, Maryland, U.S.A.*

Bonnie A. Goins Pilewski / *Senior Security Strategist, Isthmus Group, Inc., Aurora, Illinois, U.S.A.*

Christopher A. Pilewski / *Senior Security Strategist, Isthmus Group, Inc., Aurora, Illinois, U.S.A.*

Sean M. Price / *Independent Information Security Consultant, Sentinel Consulting, Washington, District of Columbia, U.S.A.*

Bernice M. Purcell / *School of Business Administration and Extended Learning, Holy Family University, Philadelphia, Pennsylvania, U.S.A.*

Viju Raghupathi / *Brooklyn College, City University of New York, New York, New York, U.S.A.*

Wullianallur Raghupathi / *Fordham University, New York, New York, U.S.A.*

James F. Ransome / *Cisco Systems, Santa Clara, California, U.S.A.*

John W. Rittinghouse / *Tomball, Texas, U.S.A.*

Ben Rothke / *International Network Services (INS), New York, New York, U.S.A.*

Jason W. Rupe / *Polar Star Consulting, LLC, Lafayette, Colorado, U.S.A.*

John C. Russ / *Department of Materials Science and Engineering, College of Engineering, North Carolina State University, Raleigh, North Carolina, U.S.A.*

Tefko Saracevic / *School of Communication and Information, Rutgers University, New Brunswick, New Jersey, U.S.A.*

Greg Schulz / *StorageIO Group, Stillwater, Minnesota, U.S.A.*

Suresh Singh / *Portland State University, Portland, Oregon, U.S.A.*

Ed Skoudis / *Senior Security Consultant, Intelguardians Network Intelligence, Howell, New Jersey, U.S.A.*

Floyd (Bud) E. Smith / *Writer, Oakland, California, U.S.A.*

John F. Sowa / *VivoMind Research, Rockville, Maryland, U.S.A.*

Dick Stenmark / *Department of Applied IT, IT University of Gothenburg, Gothenburg, Sweden*

D.E. Stevenson / *School of Computing, Clemson University, Clemson, South Carolina, U.S.A.*

E. Burton Swanson / *Anderson School of Management, University of California—Los Angeles, Los Angeles, California, U.S.A.*

M. Jafar Tarokh / *K.N. Toosi University of Technology, Tehran, Iran*

Christine B. Tayntor / *Writer, Cheyenne, Wyoming, U.S.A.*

Richard Temple / *AristaCare Health Services, South Plainfield, New Jersey, U.S.A.*

Charles Thompson / *Research Triangle Institute (RTI) International, Washington, District of Columbia, U.S.A.*

Wayne Thompson / *SAS Institute, Cary, North Carolina, U.S.A.*

James S. Tiller / *Chief Security Officer and Managing Vice President of Security Services, International Network Services (INS), Raleigh, North Carolina, U.S.A.*

Harold F. Tipton / *HFT Associates, Villa Park, California, U.S.A.*

Todor Todorov / *St. Cyril and St. Methodius University of Veliko Turnovo, and Department of Mathematical Foundations of Informatics, Institute of Mathematics and Informatics, Bulgarian Academy of Sciences, Veliko Tarnovo, Bulgaria*

Leyla Toumi / *Software Systems Research Laboratory (LSR-IMAG), National Center for Scientific Research (CNRS)/National Polytechnic Institute of Grenoble (INPG), Grenoble, France*

Don Turnbull / *School of Information, University of Texas at Austin, Austin, Texas, U.S.A.*

Sanja Vrane / *Mihajlo Pupin Institute, Belgrade, Serbia*

Nigel M. Waters / *Department of Geography and Geoinformation Science, George Mason University, Fairfax, Virginia, U.S.A.*

Jana Zabinski / *American National Standards Institute, New York, New York, U.S.A.*

Sherali Zeadally / *College of Communication and Information, University of Kentucky, Lexington, Kentucky, U.S.A.*

Yulei Zhang / *Department of Management Information Systems, University of Arizona, Tucson, Arizona, U.S.A.*

Encyclopedia of Information Systems and Technology

Contents

Volume I

Volume II

Encyclopedia of Information Systems and Technology

Topical Table of Contents

5. Integrative Programming and Technologies

6. Mathematics and Statistics for IT

7. Networking

13. Web Systems and Technologies

Preface

So, how does one go about building an encyclopedia? First you need a framework or body of knowledge to guide the commissioning of entries. There are several bodies of knowledge related to Information Systems and Technology that could have been used in organizing this *Encyclopedia*. But a consensus body of knowledge based on several of these was developed by Bill Agresti at Johns Hopkins University.[1] This body of knowledge is the one used in this encyclopedia. It defines the following key areas:

1. IT fundamentals,
2. human-computer interaction,
3. information assurance and security, IT as a profession,
4. information management,
5. integrative programming and technologies,
6. mathematics and statistics for IT,
7. networking,
8. programming fundamentals,
9. platform technologies,
10. systems administration and maintenance,
11. system integration and architecture,
12. social and professional issues, and
13. Web systems and technologies.

These areas, then, provide the organizational structure for this Encyclopedia.

Next is the formation of an Editorial Advisory Board. I am delighted and lucky to have recruited a Board who are both experts in their respective fields and friends. Together we identified and recruited expert authors to write these entries.

The task of finding authors was not easy. Teasing small entries for a dictionary is much easier than extracting substantial entries for an encyclopedia, and experts are always busy. Therefore, there were many false starts and stops, searches for new authors when necessary, and the need for constant encouragements. As the entries began to be delivered by the authors, peer reviews for the entries needed to be organized. Finding expert peer reviewers, who are also busy, wasn't always easy. The entries and review reports were then returned to the authors for revision, and in many cases, another round of reviews. The process was not dissimilar to editing a special issue of a scholarly journal, only magnified by a factor of 20. The final entries then needed to be edited by expert copy editors, then returned to the authors for another check. The editor-in-chief conducted one final check. It should be no surprise, then, the process from start to finish took four years.

I hope you are pleased with the result. This Encyclopedia is the result of the work of more than 200 expert contributors and reviewers from industry and academia across the globe. We tried to be as correct and comprehensive as possible, but of course, in a work of this grand scope, there are bound to be holes in coverage, as well as typographical, possibly even factual errors. I take full responsibility for these errors, and hope that you will contact me at eit@taylorandfrancis.com to notify me of any. The good news is that this Encyclopedia is a perpetual project – the online version will be updated regularly, and new print editions are anticipated. These updated versions allow for ongoing correction and augmentation of the Encyclopedia, and to keep pace with the rapid changes in Information Systems and Technology. My intention is to keep this Encyclopedia as relevant and fresh as possible.

The target readership for this Encyclopedia includes Information Systems and Technology professionals, managers, software professionals, and other technology professionals. I also expect the Encyclopedia to find its way into many library databases. Finally, I hope that this Encyclopedia will be added to the reading list for Information Science undergraduate and graduate students.

Phillip A. Laplante, Editor-in-Chief

Reference

1. Agresti, William W. An IT Body of Knowledge: The Key to an Emerging Profession, *IT Professional*, pp. 18–22, November/December, 2008.

Acknowledgments

Compiling an Encyclopedia is a massive effort, and the role of Editor-In-Chief is similar to that of the captain of an aircraft carrier – the captain merely articulates the mission of the ship and its destination and provides general guidance along the way – hundreds of others do the real work. This encyclopedia really did involve hundreds of people: contributors, reviewers, editors, production staff and more, so I cannot thank everyone personally. But some special kudos are required.

Collectively, I thank the authors of the entries and the reviewers – without them, of course, there would be no Encyclopedia. Members of the Editorial Advisory Board also provided a great deal of advice, encouragement, and hard work, and I am grateful to them for those. And there are many staff at Taylor & Francis in the acquisitions, editing, production, marketing, and sales departments who deserve credit. But I must call out some key individuals who guided me through this journey.

First, I want to thank senior acquisitions editor, John Wyzalek and production supervisor Claire Miller – I have worked with John and Claire on many projects and they have always provided wise guidance and kept me on task. Over the four years that were needed to solicit, develop, review, revise, and edit the entries, my development editor, Molly Pohlig has been my eyes, ears and hands. I am grateful for her enthusiasm and counsel. Finally, I have to, once again, thank my family for putting up with my physical presence but mental absence as I worked on this project in our family room over many days and evenings.

About the Editors

Phillip A. Laplante

Dr. Phillip A. Laplante is professor of Software and Systems Engineering at Penn State Universitys Great Valley School of Graduate Professional Studies. Previously, he was a professor and academic administrator at several colleges and universities. Prior to his academic experiences, Dr. Laplante worked as a professional software engineer for almost eight years. He was involved in requirements engineering and software delivery for such projects as the Space Shuttle Inertial Measurement Unit, commercial CAD software, and major projects for Bell Laboratories.

Dr. Laplante's research, teaching, and consulting focus on the areas of requirements engineering, software testing, project management, and embedded systems. He serves on a number of corporate and professional boards and is a widely sought speaker and consultant.

Dr. Laplante has written or edited 30 books, including three dictionaries and the *Encyclopedia of Software Engineering*, published by CRC Press/Taylor & Francis. He also edits the following Taylor & Francis Book Series: Applied Software Engineering, Image Processing, and What Every Engineer Should Know About.

He holds a BS degree in Systems Planning and Management, a Masters degree in Electrical Engineering, and a PhD in Computer Science, all from Stevens Institute of Technology. He also holds an MBA from University of Colorado. He is a Fellow of the IEEE and SPIE.

Encyclopedia of Information Systems and Technology

Volume II
GIS–XML
Pages 551–1178

GIS–

HIPAA–

Information

Knowledge–

Network–

Resources–

SOA–

W3C–

GIS: Geographic Information Systems

Timothy F. Leslie
Nigel M. Waters
Department of Geography and Geoinformation Science, George Mason University, Fairfax, Virginia, U.S.A.

Abstract

This entry, describing the world of geographic information systems (GIS), begins with a synopsis of the considerable academic debate over the classification of GIS as a tool or a science. The state of the art for GIS technology is described along with the concern over the teaching of spatial thinking, a necessary prerequisite for the successful use of GIS. The importance of spatial autocorrelation in the statistical analysis of geographic data is explained. Recent developments including public participation GIS and volunteer geographic information are recounted. The second part of the entry describes GIS applications and software packages along with the anticipated future for GIS. This entry concludes with a resource section that includes information on GIS Day and GIS conferences, journals, books, and organizations.

INTRODUCTION AND OVERVIEW

In 1998, *The Encyclopedia of Library and Information Science* published an entry on geographic information systems (GIS)[11] that reviewed both the history and the body of knowledge associated with GIS. A sequel in 2001[2] documented the progress made by the community during the following 3 years, with particular detail given to the "systems versus science" debate. For the sake of completeness and self-containment, this overview of the subject again begins with formal definitions of GIS. Next, the state of the art as it existed in 2008 is described. This is followed by a discussion of spatial thinking as conceptualized within the (generally American) educational system.

GIS has come to represent a synthesis of science and application. The "systems versus science" debate has become passé. Internet applications have flourished, with many users unaware they were using GIS technology to create maps or obtain driving directions. This entry concludes with an overview of the near-term future of GIS and with a list of GIS resources, both online and traditional print materials. The present account does not provide a complete and comprehensive introduction to GIS, and readers wishing to learn the basics before consulting the rest of the entry are advised to go to the following online tutorials: the U.S. Geological Survey GIS education Web site at http://education. usgs.gov/common/lessons/gis.html and the Environmental Systems Research Institute (ESRI) discussion of GIS presented at http://www.gis.com/whatisgis/. A comprehensive description of those topics belonging to the body of knowledge associated with GIS may be found in DiBiase et al.[3]

In addition, this entry does not review the history of GIS. The reader may consult the extensive discussion in Waters[11] or in Clarke.[4] A complete review may be found in Foresman[5] and comprehensive online resources are maintained with The GIS History Project (http://www.ncgia.buffalo.edu/gishist/). Chrisman[6] has described the transformation of computer mapping software into GIS at the Harvard Laboratory for Computer Graphics and Spatial Analysis during the 1960s and 1970s.

MODERN DEFINITIONS OF GIS

A terse, useful definition of GIS continues to elude the community. Two views of GIS pervade the literature, differing largely because of the difference in the "S" in the acronym. Those scholars that represent the "S" as systems include Clarke,[4] who provides a number of definitions of GIS. Clarke begins by stating that a GIS is a computer-based system for linking attribute data from a database with spatial information. He notes that a GIS can be described in various ways. Thus some authors have referred to GIS as a toolbox. Similarly, Burrough and McDonnell[7] state that GIS is a "a powerful set of tools for storing and retrieving at will, transforming and displaying spatial data from the real world for a particular set of purposes." Longley et al.[8] review definitions that describe GIS as both data analysis–data display tools and as map-making tools. These definitions emphasize the applied nature of GIS and are generally used by practitioners in the field, such as the government and related industry contractors. These definitions have become more entrenched with the

Encyclopedia of Information Systems and Technology, DOI: 10.1081/E-EIST-120043922

increasing use of software programming packages and languages (e.g., Visual Basic, Python, and Java, among others) to create sets of procedures that specialized user groups can employ (e.g., transportation planners, see Kang and Scott[9]).

Alternatively, the "S" in GIS can be taken to represent Science (Mark[10]). This approach has been advocated by scholars who are actively developing new methods and who view themselves as more than simple toolmakers. Goodchild provides an overview of the differences between GISystems, GIScience, and GIStudies at http://www.ncgia.ucsb.edu/giscc/units/u002/u002.html. According to Goodchild, GIScience is the science behind the technology of GIS. It is also the science that keeps GIS at the research frontier. GIScience is thus a multidisciplinary field in which cartography, cognitive psychology, computer science, geodesy, geography, photogrammetry, and spatial statistics are all important contributors.

The tool versus science debate has been reviewed by Wright et al.[11] It has been resolved largely by the acceptance of both terms and an increased vagueness in the use of the GIS acronym. Within universities this dichotomy is evident in the number of "professional master's" programs available largely to fill the market for increased application courses and community-based GIS funding in the vein of GISystems. GIScience remains as a realm for continued research and software development, and is popular as a specialization, minor, or additional certificate in degree programs. Academic units with a mix of GIScience and GISystems activity remain healthy.

Finally, Chrisman[12] has defined GIS as an "organized activity by which people measure and represent geographic phenomena then transform these representations into other forms while interacting with social structures." This definition reflects the increased interest in the use of GIS for community planning and advocacy. It is such an important new trend that it has been variously referred to as community-based GIS and Public Participation GIS (PPGIS) and more recently as VGIS where the "V" in the acronym indicates volunteer involvement. These developments are described in further detail below.

GIS: THE STATE OF THE ART IN 2008

In 2008, GIS software packages for making maps and for displaying and analyzing spatial data in a variety of ways was commonplace. Large price differences existed, with GIS software packages ranging in cost from free [for the geographic resources analysis support system (GRASS) and other open source initiatives] to a few hundred dollars (for Idrisi, MapInfo, and Maptitude) to tens of thousands of dollars (for enterprise versions of

TransCAD and ArcServer). These packages generally come with a graphical interface and run on the Windows operating system, although Unix-friendly server editions are becoming common. Mac OS X and Linux are poorly represented, and can only run a subset of existing GIS software without a Windows emulator or interpreter. Open source software has been particularly successful with these operating systems, to the point that dedicated teams focus on GIS-specific Linux distributions (see information on DebianGIS at http://wiki.debian.org/DebianGis).

Conducting analysis with GIS software still requires extensive training and this is especially so if it is to be used for decision making and policy implementation. Most GIS education and training is completed in university undergraduate programs. Postdegree diploma programs are also popular as are graduate level master's degree programs, and employers frequently pay for such education for their employees.

Web-based GIS applications and the use of software and data online are becoming increasingly common. Many of these Web-based devices are lowering the technical know-how necessary to interact with spatial data. GPS units are capable of calculating driving directions as well as tracking traffic information from a server and rerouting the user on the fly. Cell phones, such as the iPhone, can track their location, navigate users, and check the weather with a few touches of the screen.

Spatial data is still extremely costly in most countries where cost-recovery models are often used by government agencies (see Taylor[13] for an exhaustive discussion of this topic for various countries around the world). The United States is almost the lone exception to this approach to the provision of spatial data, and it is arguable that this has done much to spawn the world's most active and innovative GIS industry.

Although GIS, even today, cannot be considered more than a niche application, it is now a common place subject in university curricula and is frequently used as a research tool by a large number of university disciplines.[1] In addition, it is being taught more and more in the K-12 curriculum in schools and is being used in an increasingly extensive number of applications in both the public and private sectors.

Public Participation GIS and Volunteered Geographic Information

During the last decade, GIS has been used more and more for community planning and social advocacy. Such developments have been variously described as Public Participation GIS and Participatory GIS with the acronyms PPGIS and PGIS, respectively, in common use. The most extensive set of resources for participatory GIS may be found at the portal Web site maintained by the integrated approaches to participatory development (IAPAD) organization at http://www.iapad. org/. IAPAD maintains a list for those interested in PGIS research and also stores numerous case studies which may be downloaded. It has been promoted as participatory three-dimensional modeling (P3DM) of physical environments and the ethically responsible use of GIS to protect lands belonging to indigenous communities.

PGIS has now been well accepted by mainstream GIS researchers with highly regarded texts such as that by Craig et al.[14] devoted to this topic. For a number of years PGIS had its own series of conferences sponsored by the Urban and Regional Information Systems Association (URISA) although during 2006 and 2007 PGIS was again merged into URISA's main, annual conference. The PPGIS Web site (http://www.ppgis.net/) maintains an open forum on Participatory GIS and associated technologies.

Volunteered geographic information is an increasingly important and associated development. Software developments that include Google Earth, Google SketchUp, Wikimapia, and OpenStreetMap have allowed citizens with limited or indeed no specialized knowledge of GIS to upload their geographic knowledge to publicly accessible Web sites. This process of "geotagging" and its impact on the future of GIS is discussed by Goodchild.[15] The Geography Network (http://www. geographynetwork.com/) supports project Globe (http:// www.globe.gov/GaN/analyze.html) which allows students in elementary schools to observe data, for example, the brilliance of the night sky. It is easy for these students to record their observations and upload them to a map where they can become part of a network of thousands of observations from schoolchildren around the world. As Goodchild notes, the children have become geographic sensors.

TEACHING SPATIAL THINKING

GIS Education continues to progress as spatial thinking has received attention at all educational levels. Many vendors of GIS software offer reduced or free versions of their packages for education institutions, and resource materials including data sets and lesson plans are widely available.

Schools

The National Research Council has produced a major study[16] advocating the teaching of spatial thinking and GIS across the K-12 curriculum. The authors of the report argue that spatial thinking is a constructive mix of three elements: spatial concepts, methods of representation, and spatial reasoning. Indeed the Association of American Geographers has argued (http://aag. org/nclb/nclb.pdf) for changes to the U.S. No Child Left Behind Legislation that would see an appropriation of funding in this legislation for the teaching of geography and GIS.

It can be argued that GIS should be incorporated into the K-12 curriculum for several reasons. First, it helps with the teaching of geography, a core academic discipline. Major software manufacturers such as ESRI (http://www.esri.com) have made available at no cost software such as ArcGIS Explorer which, at the time of writing is available with seven worldwide coverages that include various themes such as physical relief and political boundaries. Second, spatial thinking is advocated because it helps with other disciplines such as the physical, mathematical, and environmental sciences. Third, it prepares students to be better citizens in that the data embedded within a GIS provides them with an understanding of other regions of their country and of other countries within the world. A GIS also prepares them to interact with the world in a more effective manner as an entrepreneur or merely as someone who can use an in-car navigation system more resourcefully.

Evidence to support improved spatial thinking and education in the National Research Council Report is contained in Chapter 4 and Appendix C of the study. Unfortunately, most of this research is dated and will have to be revisited if the council is to succeed in its goal of developing new GIS software that is age appropriate in its design, scope, and sequence.

Information on geographic information technology for teachers and the lay person may be found at http:// geography.about.com/od/geographictechnology/ Geographic_Technology.htm. A complete set of links summarizing articles, lesson plans, and software for teaching GIS in the K-12 curriculum is available at http://www.esi.utexas.edu/gk12/lessons.php.

GIS and geography teaching in elementary and secondary schools has moved forward quickly since 1990. Bednarz and Bednarz[17] take an optimistic view of the progress that has been made and how future challenges may be addressed. Doering (http://gis2.esri.com/library/ userconf/educ02/pap5039/p5039.htm) has analyzed the effectiveness of various strategies for teaching about GIS in the K-12 curriculum.[18].

Simply put, GIS is a highly effective way of teaching schoolchildren about their world. There is, however, a steep learning curve for teachers and professional development resources constantly need to be upgraded.[19] Others have argued for a minimal GIS software package that increases in complexity with grade level and focuses on the introduction of geographical concepts appropriate to a child's intellectual development.[20]

Resources for teachers may be found at a link on the ESRI Web site at http://www.esri.com/industries/k-12/

education/teaching.html. These resources include lesson plans for a variety of ages and skill levels. A list of resources for teachers including annotated bibliographies of the use of GIS in the K-12 system may be found at the Web site http://gislounge.com/k-12-education-in-gis/. Links to resources on best practices and "white papers" discussing the future of GIS in school education may be found at this link on the ESRI Web site: http://www.esri.com/library/whitepapers/pdfs/higher_ed.pdf.

The work of the National Center for Geographic Information and Analysis (NCGIA) at the University of California at Santa Barbara in supporting the integration of GIS into the secondary school curriculum may be seen at the following Web site: http://www.ncgia.ucsb.edu/education/projects/SEP/sep.html. This Web site also contains links to other sites providing resources and support for K-12 GIS initiatives. Resources for schools in the United Kingdom and a sourcebook that may be ordered online can both be found at http://www.abdn.ac.uk/gis_school/.

A new trend is the linking of qualitative geography to GIS.[21]. This development may also unite interest in another new area of research, Children's Geographies (see the new journal of that name and introductory editorial by Matthews[22]). Children and youths may be used to supply volunteer information that can be incorporated into GIS (see discussion above and Dennis[23]).

Despite all these developments, the reality is that in the year 2008 many schools still do not have the computers or the teacher expertise to take advantage of the resources that are available to them on the Internet. It can only be hoped that this will change in the coming years.

Universities

University education in GIS grew substantially after the introduction of the core curriculum in GIS by the NCGIA in 1990. The original core curriculum was designed to provide university faculty with notes for 75 lectures that represented a year-long introduction to the fundamental issues and concepts in GIS. This curriculum was remarkably successful and about 2000 copies were distributed to over 70 countries after being translated into at least eight languages (including Portuguese, Chinese, Hungarian, Japanese, Korean, Polish, Russian, and French). It may still be found at http://www.geog.ubc.ca/courses/klink/gis.notes/ncgia/toc.html.

The new Core Curriculum in GIScience may be found at http://www.ncgia.ucsb.edu/education/curricula/giscc/ and is still under development. It includes two sets of lecture notes specifically on teaching GIS within a university setting http://www.ncgia.ucsb.edu/education/curricula/giscc/units/u158/u158_f.html. A core curriculum for the closely related field of remote sensing may be found at http://userpages.umbc.edu/~tbenja1/umbc7/.

A related occurrence has been the NCGIA's development of CSISS (The Center for Spatially Integrated Social Science http://www.csiss.org/index.html).

GIS research and teaching in Universities in the United States has been substantially stimulated through the creation of the University Consortium for Geographic Information Science (UCGIS; http://www.ucgis.org/). The UCGIS defines its mission to be "an effective, unified voice for the geographic information science research community." A listing of university-based, GIS courses in the United Kingdom may be found at http://www.agi.org.uk/ under the Education Link. University-based GIS research in the UK was also supported by the Regional Research Laboratory initiative.[1] Canadian GIS degree programs may be accessed at http://www.canadian-universities.net/Universities/Programs/Geography_and_GIS.html.

Masters courses

In recent years, master's degrees have proliferated at universities in the United States and in many other countries around the world. A listing of these programs, including distance-based offerings, may be found at http://www.ucgis.org/priorities/education/GIS_Cert + Masters_Prog/certificates.htm. Many of these master's degree programs now include modules on programming in GIS. Popular choices for programming languages include Visual Basic, Java, C, C#, and C++. Students find these courses most attractive and often feel that their education in the GISciences is not complete without some basic training in programming. The more important software vendors such as ESRI (see below) are moving away from their own, proprietary scripting languages toward industry standard languages such as Visual Basic.

In some cases these masters programs have been seen as terminal, professional degree programs which supply a need generated by the GIS industry. Others have seen them as the ideal "springboard" into Ph.D. research in Geography and other disciplines such as Archaeology that use spatially distributed data (see the Web site at http://www.le.ac.uk/geography/postgraduate/msc_gis_hg.html which discusses the Master of Science degree in GIS at the University of Leicester).

Colleges

The NCGIA has developed a core curriculum for technical programs taught in colleges and this may be accessed at http://www.ncgia.ucsb.edu/education/curricula/cctp/Welcome.html. GIS has found a particularly successful niche in technical colleges that offer postgraduate diploma programs. One of the oldest and most successful of these programs has been taught at the College of Geographic Sciences in Nova Scotia,

Canada, since the early 1980s. A description of this program may be found at http://www.cogs.ns.ca/Programs/ Geomatics/. A partial listing of some of the better known college programs in GIS may be found at http:// www.ncgia.ucsb.edu/education/curricula/cctp/resources/ example_courses/examples_f.html.

Virtual Campuses

Distance education is a well-established method of instruction in GIS and is sponsored by the UCGIS organization among others. A "white paper" on this topic may be found at (http://dusk.geo.orst.edu/disted/). Links to many U.S. sites that offer distance education may be found at this location together with a link to the UNIGIS International site (http://www.unigis.org/) which has offices in 10 separate countries around the world. Perhaps one of the most outstandingly successful attempts at distance education is ESRI's virtual campus which may be found at http://training.esri.com/gateway/ index.cfm?fa = trainingOptions.gateway. These courses may be either self-study or instructor led.

While distance-based education represents an affordable and convenient way of learning about GIS or indeed any other subject it is not without its critics such as Noble.[24]

SOFTWARE PACKAGES

Software vendors have done much to popularize the use of GIS in academia, government, and industry. This they have achieved by sponsoring software distribution, conferences, Web sites, Web services, and trade newsletters. Here the activities of a number of the more important vendors and software developers are described. Most software vendors now support their own online listserves, Web knowledge banks, and other interactive communities in order to resolve problems for their user base. Information on Open Source GIS software may be found at the Open Source Geospatial Foundation Web site (http://www.osgeo.org/) and is discussed in more detail in the following sections. A survey of this software undertaken in late 2007 is available at http://www.foss4g2007.org/presentations/view. php?abstract_id=136. The rest of this section lists the leading commercial GIS software.

ESRI

Founded in 1969, ESRI (http://www.esri.com/) continues to dominate the industry as the GIS market leader. ESRI offers various configurations of its ArcGIS software. The current version of the ArcGIS software is 9.3 but new releases occur about every 6 months. The Desktop

configuration has three components: ArcGIS Desktop, ArcGIS Engine, and ArcGIS Explorer (http://www.esri. com/products.html#arcgis). The Desktop product allows for the creation, editing, and analysis of geographic data and the development of professional, publication-quality maps. ESRI provides a server configuration for delivering maps and geographic data across an organization and over the Web. This configuration requires their ArcGIS Server and Image Server products. ESRI's Mobile GIS products include ArcGIS Mobile and ArcPad, products that allow the development of GIS products in the field and full use by clients with mobile devices including phones. ESRI offers data in various formats to populate these GIS products and also as Web services that are available online (http://www.esri.com/software/ arcwebservices/index.html). Other organizations that offer Web services include GIS factory (http://gisfactory. com/webservices.html) where the services include address finders, district finders, and route finders (http:// gisfactory.com/whitepapers/wp_giswebservices.pdf).

ESRI sponsors the ArcWatch e-mail newsletter, the ArcUser magazine, and the ArcNews publication. In 2008 it will hold its 28th annual user conference (http:// www.esri.com/events/uc/index.html), one of the most popular and enduring of all the yearly GIS conferences. Attendance at this premier, vendor-sponsored conference has been around 14,000 attendees. The functionality of the ESRI ArcGIS software has been augmented by a series of extensions that can be deployed to perform specific functions. For ArcGIS these include extensions for analysis, such as Spatial Analyst and Network Analyst, for productivity including, Publisher and Street Map, and solution-based software such as Business Analyst and Military Analyst and, finally, Web services. A complete list of ESRI supported extensions may be found at http://www.esri.com/software/arcgis/about/ desktop_extensions.html. Extensions developed by their partners may be found at http://gis.esri.com/partners/ partners-user/index.cfm. A review of these extensions, organized by application type, is provided by Limp,[25] an article which may be accessed by registering at the GeoPlace Web site (http://www.geoplace.com), a GIS industry Web portal. Some extensions are packaged in the form of toolboxes that perform specific GIS operations that are often missing from the standard GIS packages. A prototypical example is Hawth's Tools that provides functionality for a variety of spatial, sampling, and animal movement operations and may be found at the spatial ecology Web site (http://www.spatialecology. com/htools/tooldesc.php).

IDRISI

One of the most popular, affordably priced, GIS products is Idrisi which was developed in 1987 by Ron

Eastman and is now supported by Clark Labs at Clark University in Worcester, Massachusetts (http://www. clarklabs.org/). Idrisi's roots are as a raster GIS and as such it has been most widely used in resource management, land use change, and image processing applications. At the time of writing, the Andes Edition, the 15th major release, was the current version of this enormously popular GIS software package. The unusual name of the software owes its origins to the famed, twelfth century, Moroccan cartographer, Muhammad al-Idrisi. The Idrisi software is a fully functional GIS and image processing package that is now used in more than 175 countries. It has an especially rich and diverse set of processing modules for analytical research that include the first ever machine learning algorithms for use in a GIS and image processing system, soft classifiers, multicriteria and multiobjective decision making that provided the first GIS implementation of Saaty's Analytical Hierarchy Process,[26] sophisticated geospatial statistics, and a dynamic modeling routine that is implemented through a graphical interface.

Intergraph

Intergraph is ESRI's chief competitor for the title of GIS market leader and has been providing GIS and related software for 35 years. Intergraph has a suite of GIS-related products including its GeoMedia products (http://www.intergraph.com/geomediasuite/). Intergraph also sponsors its own annual user's conference and publications including the trade publication, Insight, which is available online together with Intergraph's e-Connection Newsletter. Intergraph works with business partners such as Hansen Information Technologies (http://www. hansen.com/) to provide additional geospatial functionality, in this case for asset management and transportation and related solutions.

MAPINFO

Since 1986 MapInfo Corporation, Troy, New York (http://www.mapinfo.com/) has been producing affordable GIS software that is eminently suited to desktop mapping and such applications as geodemographics and target marketing. MapInfo emphasizes location-based intelligence especially in the field of business planning and analysis. It too supports an annual conference, the MapWorld Global User Conference, and provides customer support through online user groups.

Caliper Corporation

Caliper Corporation, Newton, Massachusetts (http:// www.caliper.com/), produces one of the most sophisticated low-cost GIS desktop mapping products available,

Maptitude. This software comes complete with extensive data sets from the U.S. Bureau of the Census and is an ideal software for many GIS applications and has been favorably reviewed. A special version of Maptitude is available for building and analyzing political and other redistricting plans. Caliper Corporation's flagship product is TransCAD, a transportation GIS package that has the most complete set of transportation planning and related routines available in any GIS package. The latest release of this software, Version 5, is also produced as a Web mapping package that may be used for developing online transportation planning applications. One suggestion is that this software could be used to do online travel surveys greatly reducing the cost of traditional in-house, paper-based surveys (http://www.caliper.com/ web/gist2002.pdf). Caliper Corporation is now marketing a GIS-based traffic simulation package, TransModeler.

Autodesk

Autodesk, San Rafael, California (http://www.autodesk. com), is the major software developer in the Computer Assisted Drafting market with its AutoCAD product. In recent years it has also added desktop mapping and GIS to its product line with its Map 3D product.

Bentley

In a 2006 study the Daratech organization (http://www. daratech.com/) rated Bentley Systems, Inc., as the number two provider of GIS systems worldwide. Their flagship GIS/CAD product, Microstation, was originally developed for Intergraph. It is now available as Bentley Map.

Manifold

Manifold (http://www.manifold.net/index.shtml), manufactured by CDA International Ltd., is a low cost GIS that is highly popular with organizations that have limited budgets and lack the technical expertise to work with open source software. It has an online users' support group (http://forum.manifold.net/forum/). It is a full featured GIS that in its release of 8.0 offers 64 bit processing, an Internet map server, and is available in personal and enterprise editions.

Free and Open Source Software

There are numerous GIS packages now available in various amounts of free and open-source packages. GRASS has made large strides in development since its release under the open source GPL license in 1999 (http://grass. itc.it/). It is designed primarily to work on Linux and other operating systems that use X windows (not to be confused with Microsoft Windows).

GeoDA is a specialized analysis tool used to examine spatial autocorrelation and related spatial regression analyses implemented on Windows. PySal (python spatial analysis library) is a shared set of libraries for both GeoDA and the STARS software that is available at the Regional Analysis Laboratory at San Diego State University (http://regionalanalysislab.org/).

Software, such as the crime analysis package, Crimestat (http://www.icpsr.umich.edu/CRIMESTAT/), are free and used frequently in the professional world, although they are not truly open source. GIS also shares a great deal of overlap with the postgreSQL and mySQL server backends, and postgis serves as "spatially-enabled" upgrade for postgreSQL and has been implemented in both the U.S. and U.K. Programs such as terraview (http://www.terralib.org/), and mapserver (http://mapserver.gis.umn.edu/) have more niche audiences but are also growing in popularity.

Geoexploration Systems

There now exist a number of competing technologies that have been described as geographic exploration systems[27] or geoexploration systems. These technologies include Google Earth, Microsoft's Virtual Earth, NASA WorldWind, and ESRI's ArcGIS Explorer among others. They have become extremely popular since the introduction of "mashup" technology that allows even the neophyte user to combine their spatial data with real world environments across a nation or indeed across the globe. Visualization software such as GeoFusion (http://www.geofusion.com/) has been developed to improve download times, allow the integration of multiple data sets, and enhance the interface of these systems. Geoexploration systems have proved extremely useful in aiding the development of participatory GIS where non-specialists use GIS technology for advocacy planning or to protect the rights of indigenous populations (see discussion above). Volunteer geographic information has been made far more effective by the ease of use of this new type of GIS.

Geographic social networking is a new development that represents the integration of social network technology such as MySpace, video technology such as YouTube, and geoexploration systems like Virtual Earth. This approach is being pioneered by The Carbon Project (http://www.thecarbonproject.com/).

SPATIAL AUTOCORRELATION

Spatial analysis continues to be the crux of GIScience's growth. The forms of analysis special to geographic

information have continued to be developed and remain unique to the discipline.[28] Spatial autocorrelation, the problem of observations near each other having correlated regression residuals, and related analysis has become ubiquitous in the geography literature. Increases in computational resources have allowed for most desktop computers to be able to create weight matrices, calculate spatial autocorrelation, and map significance scores.[29–31] These tools were originally implemented in stand-alone software, but are increasingly part of commercial software such as Idrisi and ArcMap.

For more sophisticated forms of analysis, researchers are still forced to use packages such as SpaceStat (http://www.spacestat.com/) or the spatial statistics routines in S-Plus (http://insightful.com). Modern spatial analysis continues to focus on local models of spatial association.[32] These Local Indicators of Spatial Association statistics, such as Local Moran's I, are frequent in the literature. Anselin's GeoDA software is the most frequently used software employed to examine these local autocorrelation statistics. GeoDA allows for the creation and analysis of weight matrices, as well as the use of them to account for spatial autocorrelation in modified regression analysis. Another approach has been to allow the coefficients within regressions to vary over space. This method, termed geographically weighted regression, is promoted by Fotheringham and has received a mixed reception in the literature.

Markup Languages

Markup languages are the *lingua franca* of the Internet. Since its inception, hypertext markup language (HTML) has been the dominant method for encoding information for text that is transmitted over the Internet. Essentially HTML does little more than provide a "picture" of a document for the Web user. All markup languages seek to provide information about the data that is transmitted over the Internet. When that data has unique characteristics, as is the case with spatial or geographical data, it requires its own markup language.

Geography markup language has been in development since 1998 and this has been largely due to the efforts of Ron Lake and his company, Galdos Systems (http://www.galdosinc.com/). GML v3.0 was released as ISO Standard 19136 for the storage and transport of geographic data. GML is now the standard for the GeoWeb (http://www.geoweb.org/). It thus allows devices that are connected to the Internet to store and transmit geographical data across the Internet, permitting the efficient use of Web services. Like XML, it has also spawned other related markup languages including CityGML which enables the storage and exchange of three dimensional objects that describe urban infrastructure (http://www.citygml.org/). In late 2007, CityGML was officially adopted by the Open Geospatial

Consortium as the preferred markup language for urban infrastructure.

More commonly, GIS data on a server is accessed through flash and JavaScript applets that do not require the screen to refresh every time the user makes a change but instead the onscreen image will change "on the fly." This has vastly increased the usability of many online GIS applications. However, it also has made it far more difficult to create these GIS systems, with more advanced training required for these software and database packages.

GIS AND ITS APPLICATIONS

A major strength of GIS has been its ability to prove itself useful in a great many application areas. The reader may find detailed discussions of the use of GIS in the management of utilities, telecommunications, emergency management, land administration, urban planning, military applications, library management, health care, political redistricting, geodemographics and target marketing, agriculture, and environmental monitoring in Longley et al.[8] Each of these application areas has an extensive literature of its own and these are described in the various chapters included in comprehensive review of the discipline by Longley et al.

CERTIFICATION OF GIS PROFESSIONALS

An ongoing concern for GIS professionals has been the need for certification. Many individuals and organizations have argued that GIS professionals should be certified in a manner similar to the certification of engineers, geologists, psychologists, and others in professional disciplines. In 1998, the Urban and Regional Information Systems Association (URISA: http://www.urisa.org/) created a Certification Committee. After extensive industry-wide debate, the finalized portfolio-based certification program was established in 2003. This certification process was adopted and administered by the newly established GIS Certification Institute (http://www.gisci.org/). Certification involves establishing evidence of professional competence and ethical conduct. Until January 1, 2009, a "grandfathering" process was also permitted. At the end of 2007, almost 2000 individuals have availed themselves of the certification process.

GIS AND THE FUTURE

Judging the future of the discipline is difficult, as rapid advancements make such statements outdated by the

time of publishing. Such is the case in the work by Reuter and Zipf (http://www.i3mainz.fh-mainz.de/publicat/ zipf05/gis.where.next-reuter-zipf.pdf) that predicts the trajectory of a device to support trip planning that is partially implemented in a new release of the iPhone. As GIS presses onward, it will continue to be embedded within more and more electronics. While appliances such as refrigerators and stoves do not generally need location information, most devices that move today already have some sort of location-finding mechanism inside them. The future of these devices may rely on the ability to more precisely locate themselves, particularly inside buildings. Reuter and Zipf suggest this may come in a ground-based GPS system they term a "Global Universal Computer."

The amount of spatial data is blossoming and will likely continue to do so. As users mark important personal events and places linked to particular places, storage and retrieval of this data will become increasingly important. Reuter and Zipf suggest it is the storage and search of these items that will be most important. This technology may be crucial to historians and psychologists working to understand the reasons for individual behavior.

At some point, the lack of widespread spatial education will segment the population further, based on those who can use new integrated devices and those who cannot. Technological advances will make up for some of this digital divide by simplifying interfaces. However, these new interfaces generally cannot wholly account for such differences and maintain full functionality without a significant paradigm shift.

Finally, it may be noted that GIS in the future will become more involved with the third and fourth dimensions. The third dimension is already being implemented in geographic exploration systems and the integration of products such as Google SketchUp (http:// sketchup.google.com/) into Google Earth. The fourth dimension is time, a difficult concept to incorporate into traditional GIS software structures. Peuquet[33] has provided part of the theoretical paradigm for this new implementation and new versions of commercial software such as ESRI's ArcGIS 9.3 make it easier to create animated visualizations of geodatabases. 3-D/4-D GIS will be the new frontier.

BIBLIOGRAPHY AND ADDITIONAL RELATED RESOURCES

GIS Day

On November 14, 2007, GIS Day was held in over 80 countries around the World and in all 50 states in the United States. GIS Day is a grassroots movement in which GIS users and vendors (academics, government employees, and entrepreneurs) open their doors to school-children and all members of the general public in order to showcase the capabilities of GIS projects which they have developed (http://www.gisday.com/). The event is sponsored principally by the National Geographic Society, the Association of American Geographers, the University Consortium for Geographic Information Science, the United States Geological Survey, The Library of Congress, Sun Microsystems, and Hewlett-Packard and ESRI, and by local GIS organizations. The next GIS Day will be held on November 18 and 17 in 2009 and 2010, respectively. The event is usually held as part of Geography Awareness Week, which has been sponsored by the National Geographic Society since 1987. The U.S. e-Government Web site using data from Daratech estimates that there are 1,000,000 users of GIS worldwide, half of whom are in the United States (http://www.whitehouse.gov/omb/egov/c-7-10-b-geospatial.html).

Books

The most important reference works for GIS are the so-called "Big-Books" of GIS. The first edition of this huge, two-volume review of the state of the art in GIS was edited by Maguire et al.[34] and published in 1991, while the second edition was edited by Longley et al.[35] in 1999. More recently, the second volume has been published in a paperback edition with editorial updates based on input from the individual chapter authors, various additional chapters, and a CD featuring all the chapters from the second edition.[36] Popular textbooks discussing the concepts behind GIS include Longley et al.[37] and Clarke.[4] The latter author provides an extensive list of GIS books, magazines, and journals, conference proceedings, and professional organizations. Price's[38] text is a guide to operating the industry leading ArcGIS 9.2 software and includes a series of hands-on tutorials to aid the novice user.

A searchable GIS bibliography may be found at ESRI's Web site: http://training.esri.com/campus/library/index.cfm. Important publishers of GIS texts include ESRI (http://store.esri.com/esri/category.cfm?SID = 2&Category_ID = 35) and Taylor & Francis (http://gis.tandf.co.uk/). Longley et al.[37] provide a list of major GIS textbooks while Chrisman[6] describes the earliest days of the discipline. Vendor publications have been discussed above. Suffice it to note that most major vendors have a company publication designed to inform their user base of the latest developments in their software products and many of these are now available online.

Journals and Magazines

Some of the main academic journals in which GIS research is published include

- Annals of the Association of American Geographers (http://www.aag.org/).
- Canadian Geographer (http://www.blackwellpublishing.com/CG).
- Cartographica (http://www.utpjournals.com/carto/carto.html).
- Cartographic Perspectives (http://www.nacis.org/index.cfm?x = 5).
- Cartography and GIS (http://www.cartogis.org/).
- Computers, Environment, and Urban Systems (http://www.elsevier.com/locate/compenvurbsys).
- Computers and Geosciences (http://www.elsevier.com/locate/cageo).
- Conference Papers in GIS (http://srmwww.gov.bc.ca/gis/papers/index.html).
- ESRI User Conference Proceedings (http://gis.esri.com/library/userconf/index.html).
- Geocarto International (http://www.geocarto.com/geocarto.html).
- Geographical Systems (http://link.springer.de/link/service/journals//10109/).
- GeoInformatica (http://www.wkap.nl/journalhome.htm/1384-6175).
- Geoscience E-Journals (http://paleopolis.rediris.es/geosciences/).
- Geographical Journal (http://www.ingentaconnect.com/content/bpl/geoj/latest).
- GeoJournal (http://www.ingentaconnect.com/content/klu/gejo/latest).
- GIS Law.
- IEEE Transactions on Computer Graphics and Applications (http://ieeexplore.ieee.org/xpl/RecentIssue.jsp?punumber = 38).
- IEEE Transactions on Geoscience and Remote Sensing (http://ieeexplore.ieee.org/xpl/RecentIssue.jsp?punumber = 36).
- International Journal of Geographical Information Science (http://www.tandf.co.uk/journals/titles/13658816.asp).
- International Journal of Remote Sensing (http://www.tandf.co.uk/journals/frameloader.html?http://www.tandf.co.uk/journals/tf/01431161.html).
- International Journal of Mapping Sciences and Remote Sensing (http://www.ingentaconnect.com/content/bell/msrs/latest).
- Journal of Geographical Systems (http://link.springer.de/link/service/journals/10109/index.htm).
- Photogrammetric Engineering and Remote Sensing (http://www.asprs.org/publications/pers/www.asprs.org/publications/pers/).
- Public Health GIS News and Information (http://www.cdc.gov/nchs/about/otheract/gis/gis_publichealthinfo.htm).
- Remote Sensing Reviews (http://www.tandf.co.uk/journals/online/0275–7257.asp).

- Transactions in GIS (http://www.blackwellpublishing. com/journals/tgis/).
- The Spatial Odyssey Website also has a list of GIS Journal Abstracts and Citations (http://libraries.maine. edu/Spatial/gisweb/journals/journals.html).

Many **magazines** are available in both an online and a paper version. Some of the more notable examples are

- ArcNews Online (http://www.esri.com/news/arcnews/ arcnews.html).
- ArcUser Online (http://www.esri.com/news/arcuser/ index.html).
- Challenges: A newsletter from UCGIS (http://dusk2. geo.orst.edu/ucgis/news/).
- Asian surveying and mapping (http://www.asmmag. com/).
- GEOWorld (http://www.geoplace.com/).

Other online GIS-oriented magazines include

- Directions Magazine (http://www.directionsmag. com/).
- Earth Observing Magazine (http://www.eomonline. com/).
- GeoCommunity (http://www.geocomm.com/).
- Geomatics Information and Trading Centre (http:// www.gitc.nl/).
- GeoSpatial Solutions (http://www.geospatial-online. com/).
- GeoVision (http://www.gisvisionmag.com/).
- Geomatics Info Magazine International (http://www. reedbusiness-geo.nl/Home.asp).
- GPS World (http://www.gpsworld.com/).
- Spatial News (http://spatialnews.geocomm.com/).
- Mentor Software (http://www.mentorsoftwareinc.com/ cc/ccdir.htm).
- Position Magazine (http://www.positionmag.com.au/).
- Professional Surveyor Magazine Online (http://www. profsurv.com/).
- The CADD/GIS Technology Center CADD/GIS Bulletins Page (https://tsc.wes.army.mil/news/bulletins/).

Organizations

The following are some of the better known organizations with a strong interest in GIS:

- The American Congress on Surveying and Mapping (ACSM) (http://www.acsm.net/).
- The American Society for Photogrammetry and Remote Sensing (ASPRS) (http://www.asprs.org/).
- The Association for Geographic Information (AGI) (http://www.agi.org.uk/).

- The Association of American Geographers (AAG) (http://www.aag.org/ this organization has a specialty group devoted to GIS) (http://geography.sdsu.edu/ aaggis/).
- The International Geographical Union which has a Commission on Geographical Information Science (http://www.hku.hk/cupem/igugisc/).
- The North American Cartographic Information Society (NACIS) (http://www.nacis.org/).
- Geospatial Information and technology Association (http://www.gita.org/).
- The Urban and Regional Information Systems Association (URISA) (http://www.urisa.org/).

Conferences

This section lists a number of the more important conferences other that the vendor-specific conferences mentioned above. Many of the general, omnibus GIS Conferences have in recent years folded as more specialized offerings take their place. These conferences have usually produced either print proceedings or proceedings on CD-ROM.

Most of the major GIS organizations such as URISA will also have annual and even regional GIS conferences. Some conferences are strictly devoted to a single theme and are strongly oriented toward training. This is true of the Web mapping conferences (http://www.gis-conferences.com/). In 2007, the following was a selection of the conferences held across the globe:

- ACM GIS conference in Bellevue, Washington
- Africa GIS conference in Ouagadougou, Burkina Fasa
- AGIC (Arizona Geographic Information Council); GIS conference in Prescott, Arizona
- AGILE (Association Geographic Information Laboratories Europe); conference on GIS in Aalborg, Denmark
- Annual CA Geographic Information Association conference in Cypress, California
- Annual GIS conference, ASPRS and URISA in Vancouver, Washington
- Annual GIS for Oil & Gas Conference in Aurora, Colorado
- Annual International airport GIS conference in Budapest, Hungary
- Annual Minnesota GIS conference in Rochester, Minnesota
- Annual Missouri GIS conference in Osage Beach, Missouri
- Annual NC GIS conference in Winston-Salem, North Carolina
- Annual Ohio GIS conference in Columbus, Ohio

- Annual Virginia GIS conference in Virginia Beach, Virginia
- Arc GIS conference in Biloxi, Mississippi
- Biennial GIS conference, Iowa Geographic Council in Sioux City, Iowa
- California GIS conference in Oakland, California
- Croatian GIS Association conference in Sinj, Croatia
- Delaware GIS conference in Dover, Delaware
- East Tennessee GIS conference in Pigeon Forge, Tennessee
- Eastern Montana GIS conference in Miles City, Missouri
- ESRI Asia-Pacific User Conference in New Delhi, India
- ESRI Australia: GIS user conference in Sydney, Australia
- ESRI Eastern Africa: GIS user conference in Kampala, Uganda
- ESRI Federal Users GIS conference in Washington, District of Columbia
- ESRI GIS solution expo in Danvers, Massachusetts
- ESRI Health GIS conference in Scottsdale, Arizona
- ESRI International User conference in San Diego, California
- ESRI New Zealand: GIS user conference in New Zealand
- ESRI South Asia user conference in Novotel Clarke Quay, Singapore
- EUC (European User Conference) in Stockholm, Sweden
- The GeoTec Event in Ottawa, Ontario, Canada
- GI and GIS conference in Porto, Portugal
- GIS conference, Office of Lt Governor, U.S. Virgin Islands
- GIS Engineers Society conference in Trivandrum, India
- GIS for public sector conference in London, U.K.
- GIS for Urban Environmental summit in Johannesburg, South Africa
- GIS in Rockies conference in Denver, Colorado
- GIS in Transit in Tampa, Florida
- GIS South Africa conference in Umhlanga Rocks, Durban
- Historical GIS conference in Nagoya, Japan
- Homeland Security GIS summit in Denver, Colorado
- Illinois GIS conference (ILGISA) in Oak Brook, Illinois
- Indiana GIS conference in Indianapolis, Indiana
- Indonesian Geospatial Technology Exhibition in Jakarta, Indonesia
- Intermountain GIS conference in Donnelly, Idaho
- International conference of GIS/RS in Hydrology in Guangzhou, China
- International conference on Health GIS in Bangkok, Thailand
- International GIS crime mapping conference in Brussels, Belgium
- Ireland GIS conference in Dublin, Ireland
- Kentucky GIS conference in Louville, Kentucky
- Kuwait GIS conference in Kuwait
- Map Asia in Kulamanpur, Malaysia
- Memphis Area Geographic Information Council GIS conference in Memphis, Tennessee
- National GIS symposium in Saudi Arabia in Khobar, Saudi Arabia
- Nebraska GIS Symposium in Omaha, Nebraska
- Nordic GIS conference in Herning, Denmark
- North Dakota GIS user conference in Bismarck, North Dakota
- North Western PA GIS conference in Clarion, Pennsylvania
- Northeast Arc Users Group: GIS conference in Burlington, Vermont
- NSGIC (National States Geographic Information Council); in Madison, Wisconsin
- NYS GIS conference in Liverpool, New York
- PA GIS conference in Harrisburg, Pennsylvania
- Pacific Islands GIS/RS conference in Suva, Fiji
- Real estate GIS user conference in Scottsdale, Arizona
- Rhode Island GIS conference in Narragansett, Rhode Island
- ScanGIS—Scandinavian GIS Conference in As, Norway
- Southern Forestry and Natural Resources Management GIS conferences in Kissimmee, Florida
- Super map GIS conference in Beijing, China
- Towson GIS conference in Towson, Maryland
- UGIC (Utah Geographic Information Council)—GIS conference in Salt Lake City, Utah
- URISA & IAAO 11th Annual GIS conference in Las Vegas, Nevada
- URISA (urban regional information systems association)
- VIGIC (Virgin Islands Geospatial Information Council)
- Washington GIS conference in Lynnwood, Washington

GIS Dictionaries

The Association for Geographic Information has an online dictionary at http://www.geo.ed.ac.uk/agidict/welcome.html. For a published GIS dictionary McDonnell and Kemp's[39] International GIS Dictionary can be referred to.

GIS–
Healthcare

ACKNOWLEDGMENT

The authors would like to thank Matt Ball for comments on an earlier draft.

REFERENCES

1. Waters, N.M. Geographic information systems. In *Encyclopedia of Library and Information Science*; Marcel Dekker Inc.: New York, NY, 1998; Vol. 63, 98–125, Supplement 26.

2. Waters, N.M. Geographic information systems. In *Encyclopedia of Library and Information Science*; 2nd Ed.; Drake, M., Ed.; Marcel Dekker, Inc.: New York, NY, 2003; 1106–1115.

3. DiBiase, D.; Demers, M.; Johnson, A.; Kamp, K.; Taylor Luck, A.; Plewe, B.; Wentz, E. In *Geographic Information Science and Technology Body of Knowledge*; Association of American Geographers: Washington, DC, 2006.

4. Clarke, K.C. *Getting Started with Geographic Information Systems*; 4th Ed.; Prentice Hall: Upper Saddle River, NJ, 2003.

5. *The History of Geographic Information Systems: Perspectives from the Pioneers*; Foresman, T. W., Ed.; Prentice Hall: Upper Saddle River, NJ, 1997.

6. Chrisman, N. *Charting the Unknown: How Computer Mapping at Harvard Became GIS*; ESRI Press: Redlands, CA, 2006.

7. Burrough, P.; McDonnell, R. In *Principles of Geographical Information Systems*; 2nd Ed.; Oxford University Press: New York, NY, 1998.

8. Longley, P.; Goodchild, M.F.; Maguire, D.J.; Rhind, D. W. Introduction. In *Geographical Information Systems, Vol. 1, Principles and Technical Issues*; Longley, P., Goodchild, M. F., Maguire, D. J., Rhind, D. W., Eds.; Wiley: New York, NY, 1999; 1–16.

9. Kang, H.; Scott, D.M. An integrated spatio-temporal GIS toolkit for exploring intra-household interactions. Transportation **2008,** *35* (2), 253–268.

10. Mark, D.M. Geographic information science: defining the field. In *Foundations of Geographic Information Science*; Duckham, M., Goodchild, M. F., Worboys, M. F., Eds.; Taylor & Francis: New York, NY, 2003; 3–18.

11. Wright, D.J.; Goodchild, M.F.; Proctor, J.D. Demystifying the persistent ambiguity of GIS as 'tool' versus 'science.' Ann. Assoc. Am. Geogr. **1997,** *87* (2), 346–362.

12. Chrisman, N.R. What does GIS mean? Trans. GIS **1999,** *3* (2), 175–186.

13. *Policy Issues in Modern Cartography*; Taylor, D. R. F., Ed.; Elsevier Science: Oxford, 1998.

14. Craig, W.J.; Harris, T.M.; Weiner, D. *Community Participation and Geographical Information Systems*; CRC Press: Boca Raton, FL, 2002.

15. Goodchild, M.F. Citizens as sensors: the world of volunteered geography. GeoJournal **2007,** *69* (4), 211–221.

16. National Research Council, *Learning to Think Spatially*; The National Academies Press: Washington, DC, 2006.

17. Bednarz, S.W.; Bednarz, R.S. Geography education: The glass is half full and its getting fuller. Prof. Geogr. **2004,** *56*, 22–27.

18. Doering, A.; Veletsianos, G. An investigation of the use of real-time, authentic geospatial data in the K-12 classroom. J. Geogr. **2007,** *106*, 217–225.

19. McClurg, P.A.; Buss, A. Professional development: teachers use of GIS to enhance student learning. J. Geogr. **2007,** *106* (2), 79–87.

20. Marsh, M.; Golledge, R.; Battersby, S.E. Geospatial concept understanding and recognition in G6-college students: a preliminary argument for minimal GIS. Ann. Assoc. Am. Geogr. **2007,** *97* (4), 696–712.

21. Kwan, M.P.; Knigge, L. Guest editorial: doing qualitative research using GIS: an oxymoronic endeavor? Environ. Plann. A **2006,** *38* (11), 1999–2002.

22. Matthews, H. Inaugural editorial: coming of age for children's geographies. Child. Geogr. **2003,** *1* (1), 3–5.

23. Dennis, S. Prospects for qualitative GIS at the intersection of youth development and participatory urban planning. Environ. Plann. A **2006,** *38* (11), 2039–2002.

24. Noble, D. *Digital Diploma Mills*; Monthly Review Press: New York, NY, 2003.

25. Limp, W.F. ArcGIS extensions: quick take review. GeoWorld **2005,** *18* (7), 54–58.

26. Saaty, T.L. *Theory and Applications of the Analytic Network Process: Decision Making with Benefits, Opportunities, Costs, and Risks*; RWS Publishers: Artarmon, Australia, 2005.

27. Ball, M. *Digital Reality: Comparing Geographic Exploration Systems,* 2006 http://www.geoplace.com.

28. Gould, P.R. Is Statistix Inferens the geographical name for a wild goose? Econ. Geogr. **1970,** *46*, 439–448.

29. Anselin, L. *Spatial Econometrics*; Kluwer: Dordrecht, 1988.

30. Anselin, L. Local indicators of spatial autocorrelation. Geogr. Anal. **1995,** *27* (2), 93–115.

31. Anselin, L.; Florax, R. *New Directions in Spatial Econometrics*; Springer-Verlag: Berlin, 1995.

32. Fotheringham, A.S.; Brunsdon, C.; Charlton, M. *Quantitative Geography: Perspectives on Spatial Analysis*; Sage: London, 2000.

33. Peuquet, D. *Representations of Space and Time*; Guilford: New York, NY, 2002.

34. *Geographical Information Systems,* Maguire, D. J., Goodchild, M. F., Rhind, D. W., Eds.; Longman: London, 1991.

35. *Geographical Information Systems,* Longley, P., Goodchild, M. F., Maguire, D. J., Rhind, D. W., Eds.; Wiley: New York, NY, 1999.

36. *Geographical Information Systems,* 2nd Ed.; Longley, P. A., Goodchild, M. F., Maguire, D. J., Rhind, D. W., Eds.; Wiley: New York, NY, 2005 abridged Ed.

37. Longley, P.A.; Goodchild, M.F.; Maguire, D.J.; Rhind, D.W. In *Geographic Information Systems and Science*; 2nd Ed; Wiley: New York, NY, 2005.

38. Price, M. *Mastering ArcGIS 9.2*; McGraw-Hill: New York, NY, 2008.

39. McDonnell, R.; Kemp, K. *International GIS Dictionary*; Longman: London, 1995.

Green Computing: Data Centers

Greg Schulz
StorageIO Group, Stillwater, Minnesota, U.S.A.

Abstract

By understanding fundamentals and background information about electricity usage as well as options and alternatives including rebates or incentives, information technology (IT) data centers can deploy strategies to become more energy-efficient without degrading service delivery. Reducing carbon footprint is a popular and trendy topic, but addressing energy efficiency—that is, doing more work with less energy—addresses both environmental and business economic issues. The importance of this entry is that near-term economic as well as environmental gains can be realized by making more efficient use of energy. By reducing energy consumption or shifting to a more energy-efficient IT model, businesses can reduce their operating expenses and enable more useful work to be done per dollar spent while improving service delivery. This entry looks at challenges with electrical power for IT data centers as well as background information to help formulate effective strategies to become energy efficient.

In this entry you will learn:

- How to identify issues that affect the availability of power, cooling, and floor space
- Why achieving energy efficiency is important to sustain growth and business productivity
- How electrical power is generated, transmitted, and used in typical data centers
- How electrical power is measured and charges determined

ELECTRIC POWER AND COOLING CHALLENGES

Asking the right questions can help you to close the "green gap" and address power, cooling, floor space, and environmental (PCFE) issues. That is, insight into how infrastructure resources are being used to meet delivery and service levels is critical. For example, instead of asking whether there is a green mandate or initiative, try asking the following questions:

- Does the data center have a power issue or anticipate one in the next 18–24 months?
- Does the IT data center have enough primary and backup power capacity?
- Is there enough cooling capacity and floor space to support near-term growth?
- How much power does the data center consume?
- How much of that power goes for cooling, lighting, and other facility overhead items?

- How much power is used by servers, storage, and networking components?
- Is power constrained by facility, local substation, or generating capability limits?
- What floor space constraints exist, and is there adequate cooling capabilities for growth?
- Can energy usage be aligned with the level of service delivered or amount of data stored?
- What hazardous substances and materials exist in the data center?

Closing the green gap is important in that core IT PCFE issues can be addressed with positive environmental and economic benefits. For example, building on the previous questions, common PCFE-related pain points for many IT data centers include:

- A growing awareness of green and environmentally friendly issues and topics
- The need to remove heat from IT equipment and the power required for this cooling
- Excessive power consumption by older, less energy-efficient technology
- Insufficient primary or standby power
- Rising energy costs and insufficient availability of power
- Lack of sufficient floor space to support growth and use of heavier and denser equipment
- Aging and limited heating, ventilating, and air conditioning (HVAC) capabilities
- Disposing of older technology in compliance with recycling regulations

Encyclopedia of Information Systems and Technology, DOI: 10.1081/E-EIST-120053839

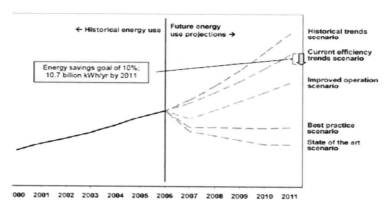

Fig. 1 Projected electricity use, 2007–2011.
Source: From U.S. environmental protection agency.

- Complying with environmental health and safety mandates
- Improving infrastructure and application service delivery and enhancing productivity
- Doing more with less—less budget, less head count, and more IT equipment to support
- Support applications and changing workloads with adaptive capabilities

The available supply of electricity is being impacted by aging and limited generating and transmission (G&T) capabilities as well as rising fuel costs. While industries such as manufacturing consume ever more electrical power, IT data centers and the IT equipment housed in those habitats require continued and reliable power.

IT data centers rely on available power and transmission capabilities, which are being affected by rising fuel costs and increasing demands as shown in Fig. 1. The U.S. Environmental Protection Agency (EPA) estimates that with no changes, U.S. IT data center electric power consumption will jump to 3% of the U.S. total by 2010–2012. IT data centers require ever more power, cooling, and physical floor space to accommodate the servers, storage, and network components necessary to support growing application demands. In an era of growing environmental awareness, IT data centers, information factories of all sizes, and enterprise data centers in particular have issues and challenges pertaining to power, cooling, floor space, and greenhouse gas emissions as well as "clean" disposal of IT equipment.

Data center demand for electrical power is also in competition with other power consumers, leading to shortages and outages during peak usage periods. There are also increasing physical requirements for growing data centers in the form of more servers, storage, and network components to support more IT and related services for business needs. Other pressing issues for IT data centers are cooling and floor space to support more

performance and storage capacity without compromising availability and data protection.

Thus, if a data center is at its limit of power, and if the data center needs to increase processing and storage capabilities by 10% per year, a corresponding improvement in efficiency of at least the same amount is required. Since the 1990s, capacity planning has been eliminated in many organizations because of the lowering cost of hardware; however, there is an opportunity to resurrect the art and science of capacity planning to tie power and cooling needs with hardware growth and to implement data center power demand-side management to ensure sustained growth.

Fig. 2 shows typical power consumption and energy usage of typical data center components. With present focus on boosting performance and reducing power consumption for servers and their subsequent cooling requirements, the PCFE focus will shift to storage. Even with denser equipment that can do more work and store more information in a given footprint, continued demand for more computing, networking, and storage capability will keep pressure on available PCFE resources. Consequently, addressing PCFE issues will remain an ongoing issue, and, thus, performance and capacity considerations for servers, storage, and networks need to include PCFE aspects and vice versa.

ELECTRICAL POWER—SUPPLY AND DEMAND DISTRIBUTION

Adequate electrical power is often cited as an important IT data center issue. The reasons for lack of available electrical power can vary greatly. Like data networks, electrical power transmission networks, also known as the power grid, can bottleneck. For example, there may be sufficient power or generating capabilities in your area, but transmission and substation bottlenecks may

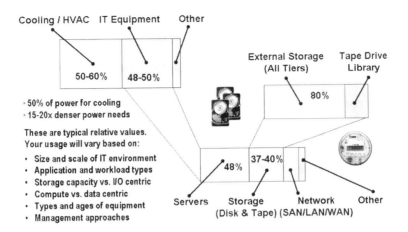

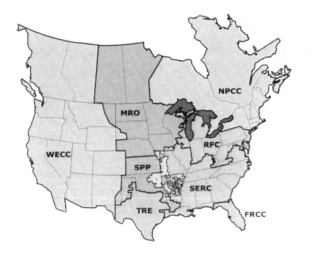

Fig. 2   Average IT data PCFE consumption.
Source: From http://www.storageio.com.

prevent available power from getting where it is needed. For example, consider the following scenarios:

- Power is available to the facility, but the facility's power distribution infrastructure is constrained.
- Power is available to the facility, but standby or backup power is insufficient for growth.
- Power is available in the general area, but utility constraints prevent delivery to the facility.
- Power costs are excessive in the region in which the IT equipment and facilities are located.

General factors that affect PCFE resource consumption include:

- Performance, availability, capacity, and energy efficiency (PACE) of IT resources
- Efficiency of HVAC and power distribution technologies

Fig. 3   North American electrical power grid.
Source: From http://www.nerc.com.

- The general age of the equipment—older items are usually less efficient
- The balance between high resource utilization and required response time
- Number and type of servers, type of storage, and disk drives being used
- Server and storage configuration to meet PACE service-level requirements

There is a correlation between how IT organizations balance server, storage, and networking resources with performance and capacity planning and what electrical G&T utilities do. That correlation is capacity and demand management. For G&T utilities, building or expanding existing G&T facilities are cost- and time-consuming activities, so G&Ts need to manage the efficient use of resources just as IT managers must. G&Ts rely on supervisory control and data acquisition management systems to collect data on G&T components and to enable real-time management of these resources.

Thus, there are many similarities between how IT centers manage resources using simple network management protocol traps and alerts together with capacity planning and how the G&T industry manages its resources. Think of the power plants as servers and the transmission grid as a network. Like IT data centers, which have historically used performance and capacity planning to maximize their resources versus the expense of buying new technologies, the power companies do so on an even larger scale. Power companies have a finite ceiling to the amount of power they can provide, and data centers have a ceiling on the amount of power they can consume based on available supply.

Fig. 3 shows how electrical power is managed in different regions of the United States (U.S.) as part of the North American electrical power grid. The U.S. power grid is, as is the case in other parts of the world, a network of different G&T facilities that is able to shift

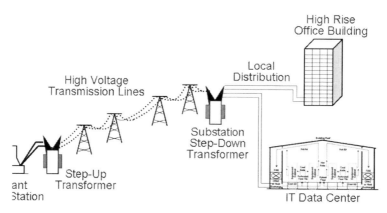

Fig. 4   Electrical power G&T distribution.

available power to different areas within a region as needed.

Fig. 4 shows a simplified example of how the G&T power grid works, including generation facilities (power plants), high-voltage distribution lines, and lower-voltage distribution from local substations. IT data centers typically receive electric power via local distribution from one or more substation power feeds. As in an IT data network, there are many points for possible bottlenecks and contention within the G&T infrastructure. As a result, additional power may not be available at a secondary customer location; however, there may be power available at a primary substation or at a different substation on the G&T grid.

Once electricity is supplied to an IT data center, various devices, some of which are shown in Fig. 5, consume the power. Additional items not shown in Fig. 5 that consume power include HVAC or computer room air conditioning, power conversion, and distribution, along with general facility components such as battery chargers and lights.

DETERMINING YOUR ENERGY USAGE

When was the last time you looked at your business energy bill or your home electric bill? If you have not done so, look at or ask someone about what your facilities' energy bill looks like. Also, look at your home energy bill and see how many kilowatt-hours you used, what the base energy rates are, what surcharges and other fees are assessed, and other information. Once you have reviewed your energy bill, can you determine where, when, and how electrical power is being used?

There are different approaches to determining energy usage. One is to take a macro view, looking at how much energy a data center consumes in total and working down to individual devices. The opposite approach is to work backwards from a micro view of components in a device and total the results across the various devices. Measured electricity usage can be obtained from utility bills, meters, or facilities management software tools, depending on what is available. Sources for estimating power consumption on a device or component level are vendor-supplied information, including equipment faceplates, and site planning guides. Other sources

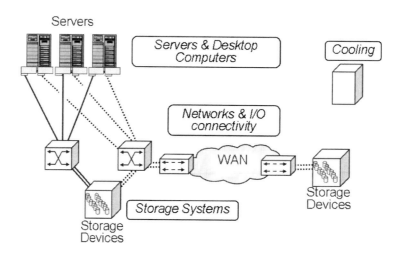

Fig. 5   IT Data center consumers of power.

for determining energy usage are power meters and analyzers as well as power distribution devices that can also measure and report on power usage.

Electrical power is typically charged by utilities based on the number of kilowatt-hours used or the number of 1000 Watt (W) of electricity used. For example, a server that draws 500 W consumes 0.5 kWh, or a storage device that consumes 3500 W when being actively used consumes 3.5 kWh. Note that while energy usage varies over time and is cumulative, energy from a utility billing standpoint is based on what is used as of an hour. That is, if a server draws 500 W, its hourly energy bill will be 500 W or 0.5 kWh, as opposed to 500 × 60 seconds × 60 minutes. Likewise, electrical power generation is quoted in terms of kilowatt-hours or mega (million) watt-hours (MWh) as of a given point in time. For example, an 11MW power plant is capable of producing 11,000 kWh at a given point in time, and if usage is constant, the energy is billed as 11,000 kWh.

Typically, energy usage is based on metered readings, either someone from the utility company physically reading the meter, remote reading of the meter, or, perhaps, estimated usage based on historical usage patterns, or some combination. Electric power is charged at a base rate (which may vary by location, supply, and demand fuel sources, among other factors) per kilowatt-hour plus fuel surcharges, peak demand usage surcharges, special fees, applicable commercial volume peak usage minus any applicable energy saver discounts. For example, for voluntarily reducing power consumption or switching to standby power generation during peak usage periods, utilities may offer incentives, rebates, or discounts.

IT technology manufacturers provide information about electrical energy consumption and/or heat (Btu per hour) generated under a given scenario. Some vendors provide more information, including worst-case and best-case consumption information, while others provide only basic maximum breaker size information. Examples of metrics published by vendors and that should be visible on equipment include kilowatts, kilovolts, amperage, volts AC or Btu.

To calculate simple energy usage, use the values in Table 1, selecting the energy costs for your location and the number of kilowatt-hours required to power the device for 1 hour. For example, if a server or storage device consumes 100 kWh of power and the average energy cost is 8¢/kWh, energy cost is $70,100 annually.

As another example, a base rate for 1 kWh might be 12¢/kWh but 20¢/kWh for usage over 1000 kWh per month. Note that this simple model does not take into consideration regional differences in cost, demand, or availability, nor does it include surcharges, peak demand differentials, or other factors. The model also does not differentiate between energy usage for IT equipment operation and power required for cooling. The annual kWh is calculated as the number of kWh × 24 × 365.

A more thorough analysis can be done in conjunction with a vendor environment assessment service, with a consultant, or with your energy provider. As a start, if you are not in the habit of reading your monthly home energy bill, look to see how much energy you use and the associated costs, including surcharges and fees.

FROM ENERGY AVOIDANCE TO EFFICIENCY

Given specific goals, requirements, or objectives, shifting to an energy-efficient model can either reduce costs or enable new IT resources to be installed within an existing PCFE footprint. Cost reductions can be in the form of reducing the number of new servers and associated power and cooling costs. An enabling growth and productivity example is to increase the performance and capacity, or the ability to do more work faster and store more information in the same PCFE footprint. Depending on present or anticipated power and/or cooling challenges, several approaches can be used to maximize what is presently in place for short-term or possibly even long-term relief. Three general approaches are usually applied to meet the various objectives of data center PCFE aims:

- Improve power usage via energy efficiency or power avoidance.
- Maximize the use of power—do more with already available resources.
- Add additional power, build new facilities, and shift application workload.

Other approaches can also be used or combined with short-term solutions to enable longer-term relief, including:

- Establish new facilities or obtain additional power and cooling capacity.

Table 1 Example annual costs for various levels of energy consumption

Hourly Power Use (kWh)	5¢/kWh	8¢/kWh	10¢/kWh	12¢/kWh	15¢/kWh	20¢/kWh
1 kWh	$438	$701	$806	$1,051	$1,314	$1,752
10 kWh	$4,380	$7,010	$8,060	$10,510	$13,140	$17,520
100 kWh	$43,800	$70,100	$80,600	$105,100	$131,400	$175,200

- Apply technology refresh and automated provisioning tools.
- Use virtualization to consolidate servers and storage, including thin provisioning.
- Assess and enhance HVAC, cooling, and general facility requirements.
- Reduce your data footprint using archiving, real-time compression and de-duplication.
- Follow best practices for storage and data management, including reducing data sprawl.
- Leverage intelligent power management such as MAID 2.0-enabled data storage.
- Use servers with adaptive power management and 80% plus efficient power supplies.

Virtualization is a popular means of consolidating and eliminating underutilized servers and storage to reduce cost, electricity consumption, and cooling requirements. In their place, power-efficient and enhanced-performance servers and storage, including blade centers, are being deployed to support consolidated workloads; this is similar to what has historically been done in enterprise environments with IBM mainframe systems. However, for a variety of reasons, not all servers, storage, or networking devices lend themselves to being consolidated.

Some servers and storage as well as network devices need to be kept separate to isolate different clients or customers, different applications or types of data, development and test from production, online customer-facing systems from back-end office systems, or for political and financial reasons. For example, if a certain group or department bought an application and the associated hardware, that may prevent those items from being consolidated. Department turf wars can also preclude servers and storage from being consolidated.

Two other factors that can impede consolidation are security and performance. Security can be tied to the examples previously given, while application performance and size can have requirements that conflict with those of applications and servers being consolidated. Typically, servers with applications that do not fully utilize a server are candidates for consolidation. However, applications that are growing beyond the limits of a single dual-, quad-, or multi-core processor or even cluster of servers do not lend themselves to consolidation. Instead, this latter category of servers and applications need to scale up and out to support growth.

Industry estimates and consensus vary from as low as 15% to over 85% in terms of actual typical storage space allocation and usage for open systems or non-mainframe-based storage, depending on environment, application, storage systems, and customer service-level requirements. Low storage space capacity usage is typically the result of one or more factors, including the need to maintain a given level of performance to avoid

performance bottlenecks, over-allocation to support dynamic data growth, and sparse data placement because of the need to isolate applications, users, or customers from each other on the same storage device. Limited or no insight as to where and how storage is being used, not knowing where orphaned or unallocated storage is stranded, and buying storage based on low cost per capacity also contribute to low storage space capacity utilization.

The next phase of server virtualization will be to enhance productivity and application agility in order to scale on a massive basis. Combined with clustering and other technologies, server virtualization is evolving to support scaling beyond the limits of a single server—the opposite of the server consolidation value proposition. Similarly, server virtualization is also extending to the desktop to facilitate productivity and ease of management. In both of these latter cases, transparency, emulation, and abstraction for improved management and productivity are the benefits of virtualization.

ENERGY EFFICIENCY INCENTIVES, REBATES, AND ALTERNATIVE ENERGY SOURCES

Carbon offsets and emissions taxes have their place, particularly in regions where legislation or regulations require meeting certain footprints. In such locations, a business decision can be to do an analysis of paying the emissions tax fee to comply near term versus cost to comply long term. In other words, pay carbon offsets or get money back and achieve efficiency.

Some U.S. energy utilities provide incentives and rebates for energy efficiency and/or use of renewable energy. The programs vary by utility, with some being more advanced than others, some more defined, and some more customer oriented. Some programs provide rebates or energy savings, while others provide grants or funding to conduct energy efficiency assessments or make infrastructure and facilities changes. In general, utilities do not differentiate between an IT data center and vendor development and testing lab facilities or consider the size of the data center.

Pacific Gas and Electric (PG&E) has been a pioneer in energy rebates incentives for IT data centers. PG&E has programs targeted toward energy demand-side management for various localities and industry sectors. Other energy utilities also leverage demand-side management as part of their capacity planning and performance management of their resources: energy generation via their G&T facilities. A group of utilities led by PG&E has created a Consortium for Energy Efficiency to exchange and coordinate ideas and to further develop specific programs to address IT data center power issues. Another venue is Database of State

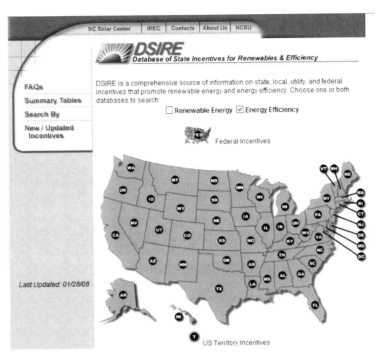

Fig. 6 Database of state incentives for renewables & efficiency (DSIRE).

Incentives for Renewables & Efficiency, which is a portal that provides information on various available energy efficiency as well as renewable energy programs across the U.S. As shown in Fig. 6, additional information about such incentives on a state-by-state basis can be found at ww.dsireusa.org.

The EPA has many programs associated with power and energy that combine an environmental viewpoint with a perspective on sustaining supply to meet demand. Examples of EPA programs include Energy Star, Green Power (http://www.epa.gov/grnpower), and others. The EPA Green Power portal shown in Fig. 7 provides information on various programs, including alternative and green power sources, on a state-by-state basis. Other

agencies in different countries also have programs and sources of information, for example, the Department for Environment, Food and Rural Affairs (DEFRA; http://www.defra.gov.uk), in the United Kingdom. In Canada, Bullfrog Power has a portal (http://www.bullfrogpower.com) that provides information on green and alternative power for homes and businesses.

Fossil fuels for primary and secondary electric power generation are coal, oil and gas (natural gas, liquefied propane [LP] gas, gasoline or aviation fuel, diesel). Alternative and renewable sources for electricity generation include biomass (burning of waste material), geothermal, hydro, nuclear, solar, wave and tidal action, and wind. Part of creating an energy-efficient and

Fig. 7 The EPA power portal.
Source: From U.S. environmental protection agency.

Table 2 Some relevant standards, regulations, and initiatives

Abbreviation or Acronym	Description
DOE FEMP	U.S. Department of Energy Federal Energy Management Program
ECCJ	Energy Conservation Center Japan (http://www.eccj.or.jp)
ELV	End of Life Vehicle Directive (European Union)
Energy Star	U.S. EPA Energy Star program (http://www.energystar.gov/datacenters)
EPEAT	Electronic Product Environmental Assessment Tool (http://www.epeat.net)
ISO 14001	Environmental management standards
JEDEC	Joint Electronic Device Engineering Council (http://www.jedec.org)
JEITA	Japan Electronics IT Industry Association (http://www.jeita.or.jp)
J-MOSS	Japanese program for removal of hazardous substances
LEED	Leadership in Energy Efficiency Design
MSDS	Material Safety Data Sheet for products
NRDC	Natural Resources Defense Council (http://www.nrdc.org)
REACH	Registration, Evaluation, Authorization and Restriction of Chemicals
RoHS	Restriction of Hazardous Substances (http://www.rohsguide.com)
SB20/50	California Electronics Waste Recycling Act of 2003
USGBC	U.S. Green Building Council (http://www.usgbc.org)
WEEE	Waste from Electrical and Electronic Equipment
WGBC	World Green Building Council (http://www.worldgbc.org)

environmentally friendly data center involves leveraging different energy sources for electricity. For example, a local power utility can provide a primary source for electric power, leveraging the lowest-cost, most effectively available power presently available in the power grid. As a standby power source, backup generators fueled by diesel, propane, or LP gas can be used.

From an economic standpoint, working with local and regional utilities to improve electrical efficiency and obtain rebates and other incentives should all be considered. For example, during nonpeak hours, electrical power from the local power grid can be used; during peak demand periods, backup standby generators can be used in exchange for reduced energy fees and avoiding peak demand surcharges. Another economic consideration, however, is the cost to run on standby generator power

sources. These costs, including fuel and generator wear and tear, should be analyzed with respect to peak-demand utility surcharges and any incentives for saving energy. For organizations that have surplus self-generated power, whether from solar, wind, or generators, some utilities or other organizations will buy excess power for distribution to others, providing cash, rebates, or discounts on regular energy consumption. Learn more about electrical energy fuel sources, usage, and related statics for the U.S. and other countries at the energy information administration website http://www.eia.doe.gov/emeu/aer/elect.html.

PCFE AND ENVIRONMENTAL HEALTH AND SAFETY STANDARDS

The green supply chain consists of product design, manufacture, distribution, and retirement, along with energy production, deliver, and consumption. Table 2 provides a sampling of initiatives relating to PCFE and environmental health and safety.

SUMMARY

Action items suggested in this entry include:

- Gain insight into how electrical power is used to determine an energy efficiency baseline.
- Investigate rebates and incentives available from utilities and other sources.
- Explore incentives for conducting data center energy efficiency assessments.
- Understand where PCFE issues and bottlenecks exist and how to address them.
- Investigate alternative energy options, balancing economic and environmental concerns.
- Review your home and business electric utility bills to learn about power usage and costs.
- Learn more about the various regulations related to environmental health and safety.

Other takeaways from this entry include:

- Energy avoidance may involve powering down equipment
- Energy efficiency equals more useful work and storing more data per unit of energy.
- Virtualization today is for consolidation
- Virtualization will be used tomorrow to enhance productivity.

Green Computing: Devices

Floyd (Bud) E. Smith
Writer, Oakland, California, U.S.A.

Abstract

This entry describes what to look for from specific kinds of devices. It summarizes green buying criteria for devices; suggests green buying criteria for suppliers; showcases Hewlett Packard and Dell's green claims; describes how to give feedback to suppliers; and discusses purchase considerations for desktops, laptops, and tablets.

KEY CONCEPTS

This entry describes what to look for from specific kinds of devices:

- Summarizing green buying criteria for devices
- Reviewing green buying criteria for suppliers
- Comparing Hewlett Packard and Dell
- Giving feedback to suppliers and vendors
- Looking at purchase considerations for desktops, laptops, and tablets

WHAT MAKES A DEVICE GREEN?

This entry will help you answer questions, such as: Once you've decided you need to buy a bunch of laptops, how to pick the greenest model?

The buying criteria for a device are mixed up with the selection criteria for suppliers. I've provided buying criteria for devices in this section and selection criteria for suppliers in the next section. If you have a formal supplier selection and approval process, use the criteria for choosing suppliers first, then use the device-specific criteria for choosing devices. The greenest suppliers will, of course, usually produce the greenest devices.

If your purchasing process is a mix of supplier and device selection, use both lists at once. A lot of what a supplier does in making a device green is infrastructure work, which is unlikely to happen just for one isolated device. For instance, a supplier is more likely to have product take back at the end of a device's useful life for all of their products (or for most of them), than for just one or two.

There are exceptions, of course. I have a Samsung Replenish cell phone that's largely made with recycled plastics—a very green choice. But Samsung only ranks in the middle of the pack in the latest Greenpeace Guide

to Greener Electronics, below Sony Ericsson and Nokia, among others (http://www.greenpeace.org/international/en/Guide-to-Greener-Electronics/18th-Edition/). And Samsung ranks 22nd among technology companies in the latest Newsweek Green 500 rankings (http://www.thedailybeast.com/newsweek/2012/10/22/newsweek-green-rankings-2012-u-s-500-list.html).

With all this in mind, you need to look at the supplier as well as specific devices every time you make a purchasing decision. Let's sum up green buying criteria in a checklist:

- **Smallest class of device** that will do the job. (Be creative!)
- **Smaller size** for a device of its class.
- **Lower weight** for a device of its class.
- **Longer battery life** (especially where the battery size is the same as a competing device, which means the device itself runs lean).
- **Lower power usage per hour.** (Criteria on this can vary, so don't decide based on manufacturer's assertions alone.)
- **Green packaging**—for instance, plain cardboard printed with bio-friendly black ink, rather than plastic-sheathed cardboard in multiple colors.
- **Slimline packaging**—standard, or as an option.
- **Slimline or electronic documentation**—standard, or as an option.
- **Volume purchase options** for minimal packaging, documentation per shipment rather than per device, etc.
- Meets or exceeds **Energy Star** standards. (This is almost de rigeur these days.)
- Products **free of hazardous substances**: polyvinyl chloride plastic, brominated flame retardants, antimony, beryllium, and phthalates.
- **Use of recycled plastics.** Evaluate this for specific products, and as a percentage of plastics in all products from a given manufacturer.

Encyclopedia of Information Systems and Technology, DOI: 10.1081/E-EIST-120053841

- **Durability.** Look for statements about, and evidence of, a product being more durable than competitors.
- **Ease of repair.** Look for evidence of, and statements about, a product being easier to repair than competitors. Are spare parts available? Will a manufacturer support on-site repair against large purchases of a specific device?
- **Product take back.** Is the manufacturer willing to cheerfully take back anything they've sold you at the end of its life cycle? Do they publicize this energetically? Do they share how they put returned devices back to use, either as complete devices or as components? Does the manufacturer sell previously used— and, hopefully, refurbished—devices?
- **Reusability.** Look for efforts by the manufacturer to put returned devices back to use—through refurbished product sales, donations, and donations of refurbished components.
- **Supplier green goodness.** Even if you're considering a purchase on device-specific grounds, sum up supplier goodness and add it to the criteria for the specific device.

For additional criteria, and specifics on these criteria, see the Greenpeace ranking guide. The latest version can be found at the following: http://www.greenpeace.org/rankingguide.

Take these criteria, Greenpeace's criteria, and your own concerns and create your own evaluation ranking system. Include standard business concerns, such as cost, supplier reliability, and past performance of a device and/or supplier.

When in doubt, keep it simple; a few criteria can stand in for a longer list (as with the "supplier green goodness" bullet above).

Apply the system to all device purchases. It will quickly become second nature and will contribute strongly to your green computing efforts.

WHAT MAKES A SUPPLIER GREEN?

The first thing that makes a supplier green is making green products, as per the criteria above. Avoid suppliers who make "feel-good" statements about the environment, or one-off efforts such as product donations to environmental groups. (This is a notorious practice by software vendors who make donations valued at millions of dollars when the product cost to them for CDs and manuals might be pennies on the dollar.)

A positive example of a financial donation is an effort a few years ago by leading global bank HSBC. One year, HSBC donated $50 million (!) to a coalition of green groups, such as the World Wildlife Federation. The partnership was called Investing in Nature, and it focused on environmental research (http://www.hsbcusa.com/ourcompany/bankarchives/bk2002/news_-hbarch022102.html).

This is, of course, impressive. But by itself, it might have been merely a particularly expensive form of greenwashing. HSBC, however, has a strong commitment to green causes and sustainability. HSBC is "the world's first carbon-neutral bank" and has made reasonably strong efforts to introduce green and sustainability criteria into its lending policies as well (http://news.bbc.co.uk/2/hi/business/4071503.stm).

All this makes for a good example of what is, and isn't, greenwashing. Bold statements about what a company is going to do, or exaggerated descriptions of what a company has done, fall into the greenwashing bucket. Reasoned descriptions and case studies of what a company has already done tend to be taken as evidence of a serious commitment, especially when supported by third-party verification, such as the Greenpeace Guide and the Newsweek Green 500.

You need to be especially careful to not give the appearance of greenwashing if you're a "sinner" by nature of the business you're in. Tobacco companies, arms dealers, and furriers are going to suffer disapproval from most of the activist community, and many from the public at large. Such companies can recoup somewhat by "going green," but strong efforts with measurable results have to lead, and exceed, generic statements about your commitment to the environment.

So look out for greenwashing when evaluating suppliers—and apply the same criteria to your own green efforts, and the way that you talk about them in public.

Here are some of the key criteria for selecting green suppliers:

1. **Leadership commitment.** "The fish rots from the head," as the saying goes, and the opposite is true as well. You want to hear from the top about a company's green commitment—and, hopefully, see signs in leaders' resumes that they've been onto this for a while. (The long-time Chairman of the Board of HSBC Bank was also a part-time pastor and had been speaking out about corporate social responsibility for decades.)

2. **Company-wide commitment.** As you'll find in implementing green computing, you need the commitment of the whole company to get very far. Look first for a company-wide commitment to sustainability and low environmental impact.

3. **Long-standing commitment.** Pressure to go green is increasing, so commitments might be more reactive than sincere. Companies that made the commitment earlier, saw the problem earlier, and have had more opportunity to get at least some things right.

4. **Green supply chain.** You can't go very green all by yourself. A company that's greening its supply

chain—not just its upstream suppliers, but its partners, distributors, and customers—is starting to do the hard work of becoming green for the long term.

5. **Leading point in marketing.** Marketing green credentials before you have any is a huge problem, and not marketing them once you do have them is a problem as well. Truly sustainable sustainability efforts make up a virtuous circle, including innovative efforts, cost savings, promotion, and ongoing improvements in the organization's efforts.

6. **Promotion to employees, new hires, and other audiences.** College graduates are a discerning audience. A company that can, and does, credibly market its green efforts to the most exciting college graduates has accomplished something and is hiring the very people who will help it accomplish more. Look for the use of sustainability in the company's hiring efforts.

7. **Case studies.** Look for published case studies of sustainability efforts that are spaced out over a period of time, described in detail, and build on each other. Few companies get this right; those that do are highly likely to be reflecting a sustained commitment.

8. **Carbon footprint assessment.** "That which gets measured gets done," says management guru Peter Drucker, yet there are few hard measures for green computing and overall sustainability. For example, a carbon footprint assessment is hard to do, so doing it is a sign of seriousness. Tracking and improving the numbers over time is a strong validation of long-term commitment.

9. **Industry leadership.** Look for an organization to assert industry leadership on sustainability in groups of like-minded organizations, professional bodies, at trade shows and conferences, and in other venues. If there's truly good news here, it will be repeated to small, focused groups as well as to the public at large.

10. **External verification.** Look for awards earned by the company. Two excellent resources are the Newsweek Green 500, shown in Fig. 1, which ranks the Fortune 500 by green-related criteria, and the aforementioned Greenpeace Guide to Greener Electronics. These are two resources that cut through the blather by clearly stating their criteria, stack ranking the companies involved—not everyone gets to be above average—and repeating the exercise over and over again. If a given supplier isn't included in the published rankings, use the same criteria that Greenpeace and Newsweek use to assess the company yourself.

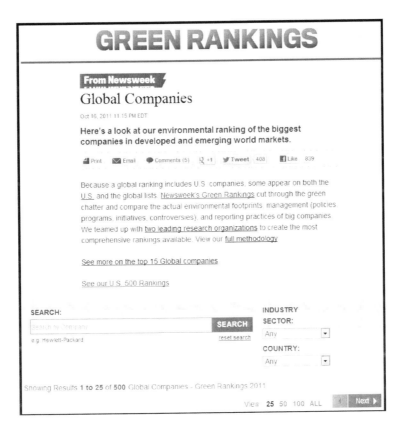

Fig. 1 Newsweek Green 500.
Source: From http://www.thedailybeast.com/newsweek/2011/10/16/green-rankings-2011.html.

I don't mean to suggest that you are going to build the perfect green supply chain, green company, or green computing effort. The supply chain effort, for instance, is generally referred to as "greening the supply chain," suggesting an ongoing process. You do want to achieve steady improvement.

Use other criteria to narrow down the list before applying green criteria. Your company has external commitments that require it to meet many specifications, while seeking out the lowest cost (even if the lowest cost supplier doesn't always win). Use green criteria to reward potential suppliers who get all the basics right— and manage to meet green criteria as well.

Of course, these are not mutually exclusive. Greener companies tend to be better suppliers for three major reasons:

1. **The peacock effect.** Male peacocks with dramatic tail feather arrays are attractive to females because only a healthy male can afford the resources to grow such a striking display. Only a healthy company can meet green criteria while also being fully competitive on traditional criteria as well. Hewlett Packard (HP), for instance, is the world's largest vendor of personal computers (PCs)—and a perennial leader in green assessments.

2. **The serendipity effect.** Green efforts are costly at first, taking up time, effort, and management attention. However, they often yield surprising savings while also helping attract and retain top employees, executives, business partners, and supply chain partners. So the green company gradually finds it easier to excel on traditional criteria as well (not the least of which is price competitiveness).

3. **Longer-term orientation.** Green concerns reflect an interest in the longevity of an organization and the systems in which it plays a part. These concerns suggest that the company will also take its relationship with you as a customer more seriously, investing the extra effort needed to create a sustainable "win-win."

As you implement green computing, and green your own supply chain, you'll benefit from these effects as well.

Create a supplier checklist for all aspects of your selection criteria, nongreen as well as green. Then rank suppliers on it. Build and deepen relationships with the best of them, entering into long-term supply contracts, seeking large volume discounts, and helping them understand your business. For other purchasing decisions, use the supplier checklist as a short-term tool. You'll steadily green your supply chain.

CASE STUDY: HP VS. DELL

Two of the biggest suppliers of PCs are HP and Dell. Let's take a quick look at some of the supplier-level considerations for choosing one over another. The following comparison holds as of mid-2012:

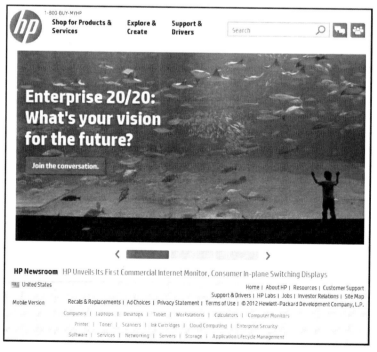

Fig. 2 HP's website is sparse, but dramatic.
Source: From http://www.hp.com.

- **Greenpeace Guide rating.** The Greenpeace Guide to Greener Electronics ranks HP #1 overall, with a ranking of nearly 6 out of 10; Dell is #2, with a ranking of just over 5 out of 10. (Apple is third among computer vendors, with a ranking somewhat below 5 out of 10.) It's no accident that the leading vendors are also green leaders (http://www.greenpeace.org/international/en/Guide-to-Greener-Electronics/18th-Edition/).
- **Newsweek Green 500 ranking.** The Newsweek Green 500 ranking ranks HP #2 in its segment, Technology Equipment, and Dell #5. Apple, by contrast, is #50 (!) (http://www.thedailybeast.com/newsweek/2012/10/22/newsweek-green-rankings-2012-u-s-500-list.html).
- **Website review.** HP has a simplistic website (see Fig. 2). Searching in the About section yields an Environment mini-site, including information on recycling, carbon footprint, and more. Dell has a much richer site, but Environment is pushed down a level to a heading under Corporate Responsibility in the About Dell section of the site. The Dell Environment area is somewhat richer, with areas of focus including recycling, energy efficiency, and green information technology (IT), with case studies. Both seem representative of a solid green commitment.
- **Classes of devices.** Both companies offer a full range of desktop and laptop computers. Both are weaker in tablets (neither offers the leading device, the iPad), and neither offers much in the smartphone arena.

Clearly, both companies are leaders; and clearly, HP has the overall edge on green criteria. You would, of course, complement the company-level study with a look at specific computers that meet your criteria, and Dell might win at that level. You'd then have to compare the vendors on having the products you want, support, price, and other factors.

If you go through this process, make the purchase decision, and let the vendors know why, you'll contribute quite a bit to the green computing cause.

GIVING SUPPLIERS AND VENDORS FEEDBACK

Choosing green suppliers helps green your own organization. Giving feedback to suppliers helps green every organization.

When you buy a green or greener device, no one knows why you did it—unless you tell them. Not only do you need to tell them, you need to make sure you're heard. There are two main ways to do that. The first is to use the old model that speakers use to organize their talks:

1. Tell them what you're going to tell them.
2. Tell them.
3. Tell them what you've told them.

This means a lot of repetition. Here's one way to implement this model:

1. **Tell them what you're going to tell them.** Create a statement of principles as to how you buy, including green principles that you rely on. Put it on your website. Vendors research potential customers; they're likely to see this statement. If not, direct them to it.
2. **Tell them.** When you create a request for quotation, include your principles. Raise them in conversations with vendors. Note what they tell you and use it in your buying decision.
3. **Tell them what you've told them.** When you make a purchase, let the winning and losing vendors know why, at the same time as you tell each vendor "yes" or "no." Refer back to your statement of principles. You'll give your vendors powerful incentives to do better with the next customer—and with you, the next time around.

Another way to make sure you're heard is to ask vendors to repeat back what you've told them. You can do this literally, and in person: Describe your buying criteria and ask vendors to repeat the key points back to you. Also, in quotations, ask vendors to spell out how they meet—or don't meet—each of your key criteria.

This can be an eye-opening experience for vendors. I know from experience that there's not much worse than having nothing to say when a potential customer asks you about one of their key criteria. If several of your key points have to do with green computing, you'll make a powerful and lasting impression on vendors.

Even when you say "no" to most vendors, it may still not be the end of the story. Don't be surprised if vendors who lose out on one purchasing decision start keeping you up to date on their green efforts, with their eyes on your next request.

You can also take advantage of the dynamic summed up in the old expression, "A rising tide lifts all boats." Share your approach with other companies—even competitors. If your industry segment gets a strong reputation with vendors for using green criteria, you'll all get better offers. If your industry segment gets a strong reputation with customers for using green criteria, you'll all get more sales.

Ironically, your communications around your green buying principles may make as much, or more, of a difference than the simple fact of having and using them, because good examples can resonate far and wide. So pay attention to all parts of the process.

PUBLICIZING YOUR SELECTION PROCESS AND THE WINNER

You have many degrees of freedom in how much you publicize all your green computing efforts, and device purchases are part of it. There are some special considerations around device purchases, though, that are worth thinking about.

You can actually do marketing and PR around a purchasing process, especially if (1) it's a relatively large purchase (or a supplier review); and (2) there's a "hook" that the public at large can get interested in—like, say, green computing!

The normal urge is to go through the purchase process and then share the results, not only with internal audiences and vendors, but with the world. However, doing your first publicity at the end of the process is likely to come across as self-congratulatory. Green marketing about an event like this is likely to work better if it ties into an ongoing story. And you can create that story yourself. Consider publicizing the entire process, creating an arc of interesting and engaging communications along the way.

What might be the benefits of such a process? Here are a few:

- **Enhanced vendor participation.** Your business might be valued more highly by suppliers if they're going to get good publicity as well as money from a win. And suppliers who see you being thoughtful will also conclude that they might be able to build a longer-term relationship, not just make a one-off sale.
- **A greener offer.** Highly motivated vendors will go the extra mile to win your business. For instance, they might offer you specialized packaging options and product take back that might not otherwise have been forthcoming.
- **Better financial terms.** Vendors will sharpen their pencils while creating your quote if there's a lot at stake for them in a win. Not only lower prices but better financing terms and "extras" included for free might be part of a deal.
- **Better support.** You may well receive better support after the completion of the deal if the vendor perceives that there's benefit in keeping you saying good things about them.
- **Better products.** A vendor might offer you early access to products after development, or give you early input into an upcoming generation of devices that you might consider in a future deal.

Note that I'm not recommending you pursue green devices just to get these benefits; it's unlikely to work. But if you are making a sincere effort, which will cost some money (at least up front) and management time,

you might as well get all the benefits you can from it. The benefits you create for yourself will serve as an incentive to do even more on later rounds of purchases, and on other parts of your green computing effort.

Here's an example of how to publicize a major purchasing event. Let's assume that you're going to take a year to go through the whole purchasing cycle, for a purchase process that starts in the spring and needs to be budgeted in the fall, for delivery in January of the following year:

- **Spring:** Decide what you need. Do you want to buy specific equipment, create a flexible master purchase agreement, create an approved vendors list? Decide on your overall goal. Share what you're doing—including the use of green criteria—internally. You might consider a small, low-key press release describing the overall process you're entering into, just to lay the groundwork.
- **Early summer:** Get details for the initial purchase. Survey affected departments about their needs. Work with them to meet needs with a smaller class of devices, where possible. For example, some departments might get inspired about having fewer support costs and hassles by having some employees use smartphones or tablets instead of full computers.
- **Late summer:** Send out a Request for Proposal. Now's the time to kick the publicity machine into gear. Consider creating a news release, with supporting web content, about your green computing focus. Include early wins, such as choosing smaller-footprint devices. Publicize your criteria. Don't be surprised if a better class of vendors than usual responds!
- **Fall:** Get proposals and quotations back from vendors. Have vendors come in to present. Stick with all your criteria—cost and other suitability requirements, as well as green requirements. Without naming names, you can challenge each vendor to match the best aspects of other vendors' proposals. You can also rough out your budget for the purchase using the information you've gathered.
- **Winter:** Winnow quotations down to finalists and decide. Consider having you and the winning vendor issue separate, but complementary, press releases. (Joint press releases raise too many issues for most companies.) Highlight traditional criteria—cost, performance, etc.—as well as green criteria. You can also include the process as a case study in your annual report or other communications.
- **January:** Receive the shipment—or the initial, partial shipment of devices. Consider a small press release to mark the occasion and finish your messaging.

Here are a few suggestions to follow in publicity efforts of this sort:

- **Keep it low key.** It might have taken a lot of effort for your organization to start adopting green computing, but that's "inside baseball" that no one outside cares about (or needs to know about). Be businesslike and matter-of-fact in your announcements and statements.
- **Keep it positive.** Don't say anything bad about anyone in your communications. Talk about how you want to "improve" the environment and "reduce" negative side effects. Focus on the good qualities of the winning vendor; don't mention the bad qualities of the losing ones. (Keep in mind that you may be buying from one or more of them at a later date.)
- **Measure success.** Note the public impact of your announcements—web page hits, media mentions, and so on. Write an after-action report describing the positives and negatives of the effort. This will prove invaluable for colleagues in your organization seeking to make similar efforts of their own.

A SAMPLE STATEMENT OF GREEN BUYING PRINCIPLES

It's much easier to create any kind of marketing or purchasing statement if you have an example to work with, so I'm providing one here. You don't have to use the example as is—heck, you might go in an entirely different direction. But having something to start with will save you a lot of time, even if it only serves as a model of what you don't want to do.

So the following is an example statement, incorporating the major points from the Greenpeace Guide to Greener Electronics:

> We at Bud Smith Consulting have incorporated green computing principles into our IT buying process. We have made a commitment to pursue green computing, and that includes buying the lowest-impact devices that meet our needs.

> Our criteria reflect a wide variety of business needs as well as green-specific requirements. They include the following eight points:

1. **Supplier commitment.** We want to buy from suppliers who have made an ongoing, visible, and long-standing commitment to green computing, in their own operations and products. We particularly value efforts suppliers make to measure, publicize, and reduce their carbon footprint.
2. **Smaller classes of devices.** We use the smallest class of device that will do the job. We won't buy a laptop if a tablet can do the job, and we won't buy a tablet if a smartphone can do the job.
3. **Smaller devices within a class; recycled materials.** When we do buy a laptop, for example, we lean toward smaller and lighter ones. And we lean toward devices that include recycled materials.
4. **Battery life.** Other things being equal, we prefer devices with longer battery life.
5. **Rare earth and other hazardous materials usage.** We ask that you avoid or minimize use of rare earth minerals and other materials that are hazardous, or that generate hazardous waste in their production.
6. **Light packaging and documentation.** We prefer that standard packaging and documentation be as small and low-impact as possible, and that lighter packaging and documentation options be available, especially for bulk purchases.
7. **Labor and legal issues.** We prefer that suppliers treat workers fairly and well within the bounds of locally applicable laws and internationally accepted principles.
8. **Take-back policy.** Please include product take back in your proposal for our purchase requirements. This should include take back for complementary products, such as additional batteries or power cords for laptops, even if not made by you. We prefer that you have a uniform product take-back policy for all your customers.

For a much more detailed plan that we use as a model in our purchasing decisions, please see the Greenpeace Guide to Greener Electronics ranking criteria. The latest version of the ranking criteria is available as a PDF, which you can access at the following URL: http://www.greenpeace.org/international/en/campaigns/toxics/electronics/Guide-to-Greener-Electronics/.

DESKTOP COMPUTERS

Desktop computers are now a minority when it comes to computer purchases; laptops sales comprise more than half of computer sales worldwide.

Desktop computers can, however, be workhorses. A desktop computer typically has a larger power supply, more slots for add-in cards, and connectors for multiple monitors. It's not by accident that many of the remaining customers for desktop computers are hard-core computer game players.

Desktop computers can also be inherently more secure: A computer that doesn't leave the premises is far easier to protect from loss or theft than one that does.

One problem with buying desktop computers, however, is that employees will then ask for a laptop to complement the desktop machine. If you don't give them one, they'll keep sensitive company data on their

Fig. 3 Planet green highlights green desktop computers.
Source: From http://planetgreen.discovery.com/buying-guides/buy-green-desktop-computers.html.

own computer, or on several of their own computers. All the cost, support, and security problems you solved by getting a desktop machine in the first place open up again if the desktop computer doesn't really meet employees' needs.

Another problem with buying desktop computers is that the advantages of a desktop machine militate against green computing principles. A desktop machine has more capacity and is more flexible—that's because it has more electronic and physical "stuff" in it. Vendors who are creating a machine that never has to run on battery power can waste power freely without anyone noticing.

There are several steps you can take in "greening" your desktop computing purchases:

- **Get your specs right.** Take the time up front to understand the likely needs of each computer user you're buying for. This will give you far more flexibility in planning your purchases.
- **Look at laptops first.** Try to downsize your desktop computing purchases to laptops, where possible.
- **Look at specialized "green" desktops.** Many vendors now make specialized "green" desktops. These are small and boast reduced power consumption. Some include recycled materials. They are almost as portable as laptops, making it easier to work at home, for instance.

The Planet Green website, shown in Fig. 3, highlights several green desktop computers: HP, Dell, Apple, and Lenovo are among the companies represented. One featured computer, the Zonbu Desktop Mini, from specialty maker Zonbu, is entirely cloud based and comes with carbon offsets to make the whole operation carbon neutral.

The Mac Mini is the most senior of major green desktop computers; Apple's made them since 2005. That means you can get really good at buying and supporting them. It's worth reading the history of the Mac Mini on Wikipedia (see Fig. 4) to get a sense of how general computer trends, as well as green computer trends, have shifted in the recent years or so. Along with standard computer uses, Mac Minis are often used as media servers in homes and as web servers by businesses.

LAPTOPS

Laptops are becoming the workhorse computers for most businesses. Many of them, ironically, rarely leave the desktop. Others travel regularly to meetings, to employees' homes, and on business trips.

In my current workplace, most people have laptops in docking stations with at least one large-screen monitor attached. Some laptops are Macs (most of which also run Windows, using special software as a bridge);

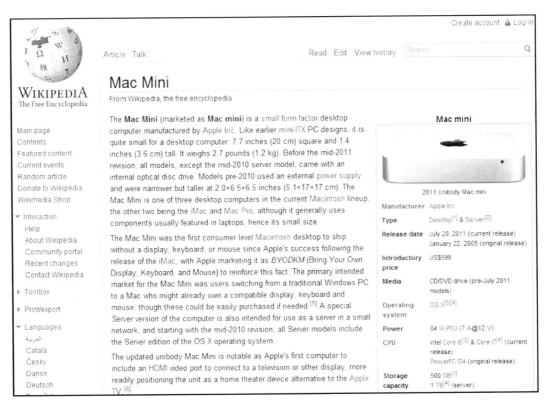

Fig. 4 Wikipedia goes deep on the Mac Mini.
Source: From http://en.wikipedia.org/wiki/Mac_Mini.

the rest are Windows laptops. The laptops often accompany people to meetings and out of the office. There's hardly a desktop computer in the building of this 5-year-old company.

Many employees, at my workplace and in many others, have their laptops in a holder that puts them in a strange-looking, wide-open, upright position, so the screen is at eye level, but the keyboard is nearly unusable. A separate keyboard is plugged into the base station for desktop use; some people also use a mouse. When the laptop goes with the employee, the laptop keyboard and trackpad are used.

Before you buy a laptop, consider several other possibilities:

- **Desktops.** A green desktop may do the job and can be greener (and cheaper) than some laptops. This is especially true for employees who can use tablets for meetings and short trips. Get in a few green desktops as examples, then ask employees to compare before deciding.
- **Tablets.** A tablet can replace a desktop or laptop, but you may need custom software development to make company-specific applications run on the tablet. A tablet's footprint is far less than a laptop's. Even using a tablet part-time results in savings, as hours of very low-power usage of the tablet replace hours of higher-power usage of the laptop or desktop.

- **"Dumb" terminals and stripped-down PCs.** If everything is in the cloud, a bare-bones machine may do the job. Many companies offer ways to run Windows on a server and mirror it on a tablet or dumb terminal. A stripped-down PC running Windows, or a Mac, may do the job if software and data are all, or almost all, in the cloud.

These many uses give rise to many needs for laptops, including specific twists on the green-related needs shared by all IT devices:

- **Low power use.** Laptops have to be efficient in their power use because they have to be able to run a long time on batteries—and battery life is one of the most-watched laptop specifications. So it's easy to compare power use and weight of laptops.
- **Small screen size.** Check with your users as to what screen size they prefer; they might like a smaller model, as it's easier to carry. When the laptop is used on the desktop, external monitors can carry the load for display power when needed.
- **Sufficiency.** Today's laptops have to do a lot. They should be as small and as low-powered as possible, but not offer less capability than needed.
- **Durability.** A laptop that lasts twice as long means a lot less embedded energy gets thrown away. Use external reviews and other sources to identify makers

and models of laptops that are more likely to last a long time.

- **Maintainability.** A laptop that's easy to clean up after spills and easy to repair after, say, a drop may serve you better than a more disposable model.
- **Connectivity.** Laptops serve as hubs for numerous other devices. They need a strong assortment of ports and an excellent connection to a durable dock. The laptop and dock need to survive and thrive through potentially thousands of docking/undocking repetitions (some of which might be rough).
- **Safety.** Engineers push the limits of technology to make laptops work, and some laptops develop dangerous "hot spots" on the bottom or edges, or even burst into flames occasionally. Pay close attention to problem reports, and to whether manufacturers respond effectively to problems that do arise. (Safety is also green, as having to suddenly replace a bunch of new-ish laptops, among other problems, is not very sustainable.)
- **Home office and road usability.** Consider whether a laptop can easily support work-at-home days and travel. Consider making additional peripherals, such as docks and monitors, available to employees, so they can create consistent work and home-working environments while carrying the laptop back and forth.

Put a lot of time and energy into deciding when a laptop is the right choice and picking the right suppliers and models. Keep buying the same model, where possible, so as to negotiate a lower purchase price and keep accessory, maintenance, and support costs under control.

SUSTAINABILITY AND FAILURE TO SUPPLY

"Failure to supply" is a way of describing a surprisingly persistent phenomenon: Customers often don't leave suppliers; instead, suppliers, in effect, leave their customers. That is, customers, out of habit or laziness, will often stick with a supplier, or at least a type of solution, for a very long time, indeed. But if the supplier ever—even briefly—fails to supply the expected product, the customer can quickly, and permanently, go away.

A version of "failure to supply" is that the market can subtly shift away from a vendor or a type of solution. For instance, customers have gradually moved sustainability from a nice extra to a necessity. Their definition of an acceptable product has changed. (Laptops used to have red on black or green on black displays, and color screens became a necessity, in a similar shift.) Any vendor who wasn't ready with reasonably sustainable products as this shift is occurring will have been caught out, and replaced by vendors who are ready.

Look out for this phenomenon with vendors, especially with regard to sustainability. It's no accident that the two biggest Windows PC makers worldwide, HP and Dell, are the top two in the Greenpeace Guide to Greener Electronics. They see that the definition of a "standard" PC is changing, and that the new definition includes sustainability, so they're leading the charge.

Actually, a similar definitional shift is happening to you with regard to your organization's upper management and stakeholders. The definition of what an IT department provides an organization is changing to include at least a reasonable effort toward green computing. The definition of "reasonable" depends on many factors, including your competitors' actions and the predilections of your upper management and Board of Directors. Exceeding these steadily rising expectations is likely to be rewarded; falling short of them, not so much.

THE CASE OF WINDOWS 8

A potential future business school case study around "failure to supply" seems to be germinating in the market for Windows-compatible computers.

Since its launch in January 2010, the iPad has taken the tablet market by storm. Competitors have tried, and largely failed, to establish viable alternatives. At this writing, in mid-2012, the iPad is on its third generation—and Microsoft has just announced its first tablet—the Surface, and Windows 8—a new version of Windows for tablets and PCs. For the first time, Microsoft was selling a tablet—the Surface—directly. According to *ComputerWorld's* Preston Gralla, after the first few months, Windows 8 sales were said to be sluggish. Partners were said to be concerned about the situation (http://blogs.computerworld.com/windows/21721/new-report-shows-windows-8-sales-remain-sluggish-no-significant-growth-sight).

Windows 8 offers a new interface, called the Metro UI, based on tiles (see Fig. 5). For Microsoft's new Surface tablet, it's an attractive interface, and a first-time tablet buyer might consider it over an iPad. (The initial Windows 8 tablet, though, is behind the iPad on important specifications, such as screen resolution.)

Except for Microsoft and Windows 8, no other major vendor tries to have the same interface from the smartphone all the way up to the desktop. Apple has one operating system (OS) for PCs—OS X, and one for tablets and smartphones—iOS; Google offers Android for smartphones and tablets and doesn't have a strong PC entry. Unix is available for PCs, but not for smartphones or tablets.

In fact, no other vendor differentiates the user interface (UI) from the underlying OS the way Microsoft is

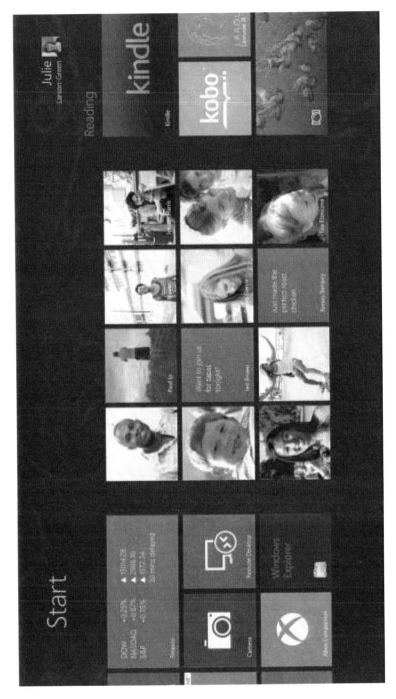

Fig. 5 Microsoft Windows 8 in action.
Source: From http://www.microsoft.com/en-us/news/presskits/windows/videogallery2.aspx.

trying to do. All the other vendors have a different UI for different OSs. (While it's true that there's some blurring between versions of Apple's OS X and iOS, that's "blurring," not "the same as," and Apple users are far more used to change than Microsoft users.)

Let me summarize the "use case" for the Metro UI, on two different OS's, on different platforms:

- **Smartphones** (Windows Phone OS plus Metro): Strong entry, almost no one uses it.

- **Microsoft's Surface tablet** (Windows 8 for tablets plus Metro): The Surface line of tablets has received mixed reviews and is not yet a rival to the iPad, the market leader.
- **Laptops and desktops** (Windows 8 with Metro): Windows 8 is a big change from Windows 7 and earlier versions of Windows, presenting challenges for adoption.

TABLETS

Buying tablets is a *good thing*. They cost much less than PCs and are easier to use, more portable, and far less impactful environmentally. It's worth buying tablets instead of PCs, whenever it is possible to do so. It's even worth buying tablets in addition to PCs, because they cost less, there is less software to purchase, and much less per hour to run (environmentally and in terms of power usage).

There are a few things to look out for, though, with tablets:

- **Obsolescence.** A tablet's battery(ies) may wear out after as little as 18 months of heavy use. Look for longevity in the product descriptions and reviews of tablets you're considering.
- **Durability.** The iPad, the industry standard, seems pretty rough and tough. I've almost managed to break my iPad 1: It developed an ugly bulge around the volume rocker after I dropped it, and steam got in there while I was taking a bath and shorted it out for a while. It still works, though. So durability is an important issue.
- **Scrubbing and finding.** It's very easy for tablets to be lost or stolen; make sure a tablet can be easily "wiped" and locked remotely, and that it has a remote findability service. The iPad has all of this; if you consider competing tablets, they should too.
- **Connectivity.** Tablets are very low on connection options, both for physically plugging things in, and software drivers for making them work once you do. One of the main advantages of a noniPad solution may be enhanced connectivity.
- **Accessories.** Carefully consider tablet accessories. I'm one of the millions of people, for instance, who bought a Bluetooth keyboard for my iPad, and now rarely use it.
- **Custom software development.** Employees are going to want to use their iPad to get through short trips. Make certain they can access e-mail and their calendar, and be aggressive about giving them at least partial access to other applications as well.

An example of partial access to an application is the development by cloud marketing software vendor Marketo of a check-in app for the iPad. You can't, at this writing, run the Marketo interface on an iPad; what you can do is run a special iPad app that helps check people into an event, such as a tradeshow. The app then synchronizes with Marketo software in the cloud to update the records of these present and potential customers with their check-in status.

Salesforce, which makes cloud software for salespeople, offers more—a version of their software with fairly full capability for the iPhone and iPad. Use these considerations in your hardware as well as your software choices.

"LESS COMPUTER" AND "COMPUTER-LESS" SOLUTIONS

It sounds radical, but some employees won't need a computer at all—and some won't even need a tablet. A smartphone can be used as a Personal Digital Assistant to automate many tasks.

Also consider a smartphone capability that many people overlook—the phone part. If you can avoid giving tablets and/or laptops to 20 or 40 field employees by having them call into or text one or two internal phone support people for updates, you're ahead of the game. (And, you can train the phone support people to use your full array of software.)

There are also exciting options around using "dumb" terminals and accessing a Windows interface from an iPad or Android tablet.

Be creative. People weren't created to use computers and consumer electronics devices; computers and consumer electronics devices are there to help people. Helping people help themselves using a minimal device, or even no additional device, has the potential to be the greenest solution of all.

SUMMARY

This entry described what to look for from specific kinds of devices. It summarized green buying criteria for devices; suggested green buying criteria for suppliers; showcased HP and Dell's green claims; described how to give feedback to suppliers; and discussed purchase considerations for desktops, laptops, and tablets.

Hackers: Attacks and Defenses

Ed Skoudis
Senior Security Consultant, Intelguardians Network Intelligence, Howell, New Jersey, U.S.A.

Abstract

Computer attackers continue to hone their techniques, getting ever better at undermining our systems and networks. As the computer technologies we use advance, these attackers find new and nastier ways to achieve their goals—unauthorized system access, theft of sensitive data, and alteration of information. This entry explores some trends in computer attacks and presents tips for securing your systems. To create effective defenses, we need to understand the latest tools and techniques our adversaries are throwing at our networks. With that in mind, we will analyze four areas of computer attack that have received significant attention: wireless LAN attacks, active and passive operating system fingerprinting, worms, and sniffing backdoors.

WIRELESS LAN ATTACKS (WAR DRIVING)

A very large number of companies have deployed wireless LANs, using technology based on the IEEE 802.11b protocol, informally known as *Wi-Fi*. Wireless LANs offer tremendous benefits from a usability and productivity perspective: A user can access the network from a conference room, while sitting in an associate's cubicle, or while wandering the halls. Unfortunately, wireless LANs are often one of the least secure methods of accessing an organization's network. The technology is becoming very inexpensive, with a decent access points and wireless cards for a laptop or PC at very reasonable prices. In addition to affordability, setting up an access point is remarkably simple (i.e., if security is ignored). Most access points can be plugged into the corporate network and configured in a minute by a completely inexperienced user. Because of their low cost and ease of (insecure) use, wireless LANs are in rapid deployment in most networks today, whether upper management or even IT personnel realize or admit it. These wireless LANs are usually completely unsecure because the inexperienced employees setting them up have no idea of or interest in activating security features of their wireless LANs.

In our consulting services, we often meet with Chief Information Officers (CIOs) or Information Security Officers to discuss issues associated with information security. Given the widespread use of wireless LANs, we usually ask these upper-level managers what their organization is doing to secure its wireless infrastructure. We are often given the answer, "We don't have to worry about it because we haven't yet deployed a wireless infrastructure." After hearing that stock answer, we conduct a simple wireless LAN assessment (with the CIO's permission, of course). We walk down a hall with a wireless card, laptop, and wireless LAN detection software. Almost always we find renegade, completely unsecure wireless networks in use that were set up by employees outside of formal IT roles. The situation is similar to what we saw with Internet technology at the turn of the century. Back then, we would ask corporate officers what their organizations were doing to secure their Internet gateways. They would say that they did not have one, but we would quickly discover that the organization was laced with homegrown Internet

Network Stumbling, War Driving, and War Walking

Attackers have taken to the streets in their search for convenient ways to gain access to organizations' wireless networks. By getting within a few hundred yards of a wireless access point, an attacker can detect its presence and, if the access point has not been properly secured, possibly gain access to the target network. The process of searching for wireless access points is known in some circles as *network stumbling*. Alternatively, using an automobile to drive around town looking for wireless access points is known as *war driving*. As you might guess, the phrases *war walking* and even *war biking* have been coined to describe the search for wireless access points using other modes of transportation. I suppose it is only a matter of time before someone attempts *war hang-gliding*.

When network stumbling, attackers set up a rig consisting of a laptop PC, wireless card, and antenna for discovering wireless access points. Additionally, a global positioning system unit can help record the geographic location of discovered access points for later attack. Numerous software tools are available for this task as well. One of the most popular is NetStumbler (available

Encyclopedia of Information Systems and Technology, DOI: 10.1081/E-EIST-120046285

at http://www.netstumbler.com), an easy-to-use GUI - based tool written by Marius Milner. NetStumbler runs on Windows systems, including Win95, 98, and 2000, and a PocketPC version called *Mini-Stumbler* has been released. For UNIX, several war-driving scripts have been released, with Wi-scan (available at http://www.dis. org) among the most popular.

This wireless LAN discovery process works because most access points respond, indicating their presence and their services set identifier (SSID) to a broadcast request from a wireless card. The SSID acts like a name for the wireless access point so that users can differentiate between different wireless LANs in close proximity. However, the SSID provides no real security. Some users think that a difficult-to-guess SSID will get them extra security. They are wrong. Even if the access point is configured not to respond to a broadcast request for an SSID, the SSIDs are sent in cleartext and can be intercepted.

In a war-driving trip in a taxi in Manhattan, an attacker discovered 455 access points in 1 hour. Some of these access points had their SSIDs set to the name of the company using the access point, gaining the attention of attackers focusing on juicy targets.

After discovering target networks, many attackers will attempt to get an IP address on the network, using the Dynamic Host Configuration Protocol (DHCP). Most wireless LANs freely give out addresses to anyone asking for them. After getting an address via DHCP, the attacker will attempt to access the LAN itself. Some LANs use the Wired Equivalent Privacy (WEP) protocol to provide cryptographic authentication and confidentiality. While WEP greatly improves the security of a wireless LAN, it has some significant vulnerabilities that could allow an attacker to determine an access point's keys. An attacker can crack WEP keys by gathering a significant amount of traffic (usually over 500 MB) using a tool such as Airsnort (available at airsnort. shmoo.com/).

Defending against Wireless LAN Attacks

So, how do you defend against wireless LAN attacks in your environment? There are several levels of security that you could implement for your wireless LAN, ranging from totally unsecure to a strong level of protection. Techniques for securing your wireless LAN include the following:

- *Set the SSID to an obscure value.* As described earlier, SSIDs are not a security feature and should not be treated as such. Setting the SSID to an obscure value adds very little from a security perspective. However, some access points can be configured to prohibit responses to SSID broadcast requests. If

your access point offers that capability, you should activate it.
- *Use media access control (MAC) address filtering.* Each wireless card has a unique hardware-level address called the MAC address. A wireless access point can be configured so that it will allow traffic only from specific MAC addresses. While this MAC filtering does improve security a bit, it is important to note that an attacker can spoof wireless card MAC addresses.
- *Use WEP, with periodic rekeying.* While WEP keys can be broken using Airsnort, the technology significantly improves the security of a wireless LAN. Some vendors even support periodic generation of new WEP keys after a given timeout. If an attacker does crack a WEP key, it is likely that they break the old key, while a newer key is in use on the network. If your access points support dynamic rotating of WEP keys, such as Cisco's Aironet security solution, activate this feature.
- *Use a virtual private network (VPN).* Because SSID, MAC, and even WEP solutions have various vulnerabilities as highlighted earlier, the best method for securing wireless LANs is to use a VPN. VPNs provide end-to-end security without regard to the unsecured wireless network used for transporting the communication. The VPN client encrypts all data sent from the PC before it gets sent into the air. The wireless access point simply collects encrypted streams of bits and forwards them to a VPN gateway before they can get access to the internal network. In this way, the VPN ensures that all data is strongly encrypted and authenticated before entering the internal network.

Of course, before implementing these technical solutions, you should establish specific policies for the use of wireless LANs in your environment. The particular wireless LAN security policies followed by an organization depend heavily on the need for security in that organization. The following list, which I wrote with John Burgess of Predictive Systems, contains recommended security policies that could apply in many organizations. This list can be used as a starting point, and pared down or built up to meet specific needs.

- All wireless access points/base stations connected to the corporate network must be registered and approved by the organization's computer security team. These access points/base stations are subject to periodic penetration tests and audits. Unregistered access points/base stations on the corporate network are strictly forbidden.
- All wireless network interface cards (i.e., PC cards) used in corporate laptop or desktop computers must be registered with the corporate security team.

- All wireless LAN access must use corporate-approved vendor products and security configurations.
- All computers with wireless LAN devices must utilize a corporate-approved VPN for communication across the wireless link. The VPN will authenticate users and encrypt all network traffic.
- Wireless access points/base stations must be deployed so that all wireless traffic is directed through a VPN device before entering the corporate network. The VPN device should be configured to drop all unauthenticated and unencrypted traffic.

While the policies listed earlier fit the majority of organizations, the policies listed in the following text may or may not fit, depending on the technical level of employees and how detailed an organizations' security policy and guidelines are:

- The wireless SSID provides no security and should not be used as a password. Furthermore, wireless card MAC addresses can be easily gathered and spoofed by an attacker. Therefore, security schemes should not be based solely on filtering wireless MAC addresses because they do not provide adequate protection for most uses.
- WEP keys can be broken. WEP may be used to identify users, but only together with a VPN solution.
- The transmit power for access points/base stations near a building's perimeter (such as near exterior walls or top floors) should be turned down. Alternatively, wireless systems in these areas could use directional antennas to control signal bleed out of the building.

With these types of policies in place and a suitable VPN solution securing all traffic, the security of an organization's wireless infrastructure can be vastly increased.

ACTIVE AND PASSIVE OPERATING SYSTEM FINGERPRINTING

Once access is gained to a network (through network stumbling, a renegade unsecured modem, or a weakness in an application or firewall), attackers usually attempt to learn about the target environment so they can hone their attacks. In particular, attackers often focus on discovering the operating system (OS) type of their targets. Armed with the OS type, attackers can search for specific vulnerabilities of those operating systems to maximize the effectiveness of their attacks.

To determine OS types across a network, attackers use two techniques: 1) the familiar, time-tested approach called active OS fingerprinting and 2) a technique with new-found popularity, passive OS fingerprinting. We will explore each technique in more detail.

Active OS Fingerprinting

The Internet Engineering Task Force (IETF) defines how TCP/IP and related protocols should work. In an ever-growing list of requests for comment (RFCs), this group specifies how systems should respond when specific types of packets are sent to them. For example, if someone sends a TCP SYN packet to a listening port, the IETF says that a SYN ACK packet should be sent in response. While the IETF has done an amazing job of defining how the protocols we use every day should work, it has not thoroughly defined every case of how the protocols should fail. In other words, the RFCs defining TCP/IP do not handle all of the meaningless or perverse cases of packets that can be sent in TCP/IP. For example, what should a system do if it receives a TCP packet with the code bits SYN-FIN-URG-PUSH all set? I presume such a packet means to SYNchronize a new connection, FINish the connection, do this URGently, and PUSH it quickly through the TCP stack. That is nonsense, and a standard response to such a packet has not been devised.

Because there is no standard response to this and other malformed packets, different vendors have built their OSs to respond differently to such bizarre cases. For example, a Cisco router will likely send a different response than a Windows NT server for some of these unexpected packets. By sending a variety of malformed packets to a target system and carefully analyzing the responses, an attacker can determine which OS it is running.

An active OS fingerprinting capability has been built into the Nmap port scanner (available at http://www.insecure.org/nmap). If the OS detection capability is activated, Nmap will send a barrage of unusual packets to the target to see how it responds. Based on this response, Nmap checks a user-customizable database of known signatures to determine the target OS type. Currently, this database houses over 500 known system types.

A more recent addition to the active OS fingerprinting realm is the Xprobe tool by Fyodor Yarochkin and Ofir Arkin. Rather than manipulating the TCP code bit options like Nmap, Xprobe focuses exclusively on the Internet Control Message Protocol (ICMP). ICMP is used to send information associated with an IP-based network, such as ping requests and responses, port unreachable messages, and instructions to quench the rate of packets sent. Xprobe sends between one and four specially crafted ICMP messages to the target system. Based on a very carefully constructed logic tree on the sending side, Xprobe can determine the OS type. Xprobe is stealthier than the Nmap active OS fingerprinting capability because it sends far fewer packets.

Passive OS Fingerprinting

While active OS fingerprinting involves sending packets to a target and analyzing the response, passive OS fingerprinting does not send any traffic while determining a target's OS type. Instead, passive OS fingerprinting tools include a sniffer to gather data from a network. Then, by analyzing the particular packet settings captured from the network and consulting a local database, the tool can determine what OS type sent that traffic. This technique is far stealthier than active OS fingerprinting because the attacker sends no data to the target machine. However, the attacker must be in a position to analyze traffic sent from the target system, such as on the same LAN or on a network where the target frequently sends packets.

One of the best passive OS fingerprinting tools is p0f (available at http://www.stearns.org/p0f/), originally written by Michal Zalewski and now maintained by William Stearns. P0f determines the OS type by analyzing several fields sent in TCP and IP traffic, including the rounded-up initial time-to-live, window size, maximum segment size, don't fragment flag, window scaling option, and initial packet size. Because different OSs set these initial values to varying levels, p0f can differentiate between 149 different system types.

Defending against Operating System Fingerprinting

To minimize the impact an attacker can have using knowledge of your OS types, you should have a defined program for notification, testing, and implementation of system patches. If you keep your systems patched with the latest security fixes, an attacker will be far less likely to compromise your machines even if they know which OS you are running. One or more people in your organization should have assigned tasks of monitoring vendor bulletins and security lists to determine when new patches are released. Furthermore, once patches are identified, they should be thoroughly but quickly tested in a quality assurance environment. After the full functionality of the tested system is verified, the patches should be rolled into production.

While a solid patching process is a must for defending your systems, you may also want to analyze some of the work in progress to defeat active OS fingerprinting. Gaël Roualland and Jean-Marc Saffroy wrote the IP personality patch for Linux systems, available at ippersonality.sourceforge.net/. This tool allows a system administrator to configure a Linux system running

kernel version 2.4 so that it will have any response of the administrator's choosing for Nmap OS detection. Using this patch, you could make your Linux machine look like a Solaris system, a Macintosh, or even an old Windows machine during an Nmap scan. Although you may not want to put such a patch onto your production systems due to potential interference with critical processes, the technique is certainly worth investigating.

To foil passive OS fingerprinting, you may want to consider the use of a proxy-style firewall. Proxy firewalls do not route packets, so all information about the OS type transmitted in the packet headers is destroyed by the proxy. Proxy firewalls accept a connection from a client, and then start a new connection to the server on behalf of that client. All packets on the outside of the firewall will have the OS fingerprints of the firewall itself. Therefore, the OS type of all systems inside the firewall will be masked. Note that this technique does not work for most packet filter firewalls because packet filters route packets and, therefore, transmit the fingerprint information stored in the packet headers.

RECENT WORM ADVANCES

A computer worm is a self-replicating computer attack tool that propagates across a network, spreading from vulnerable system to vulnerable system. Because they use one set of victim machines to scan for and exploit new victims, worms spread on an exponential basis. In recent times, we have seen a veritable zoo of computer worms with names like Ramen, L10n, Cheese, Code Red, and Nimda. New worms are being released at a dizzying rate, with a new generation of worm hitting the Internet every 2–6 months. Worm developers are learning lessons from the successes of each generation of worms and expanding upon them in subsequent attacks. With this evolutionary loop, we are rapidly approaching an era of super-worms. Based on advances in worm functions and predictions for the future, we will analyze the characteristics of the coming super-worms that we will likely see in the next 6 months.

Rapidly Spreading Worms

Many of the worms have spread fairly quickly throughout the Internet. In July 2001, Code Red was estimated to have spread to 250,000 systems in about 6 hours. Fortunately, recent worms have had rather inefficient targeting mechanisms, a weakness that actually impeded their speeds. By randomly generating addresses and not taking into account the accurate distribution of systems in the Internet address space, these worms often wasted time looking for nonexistent systems or scanning machines that were already conquered.

After Code Red, several articles appeared on the Internet describing more efficient techniques for rapid worm distribution. These entries, by Nicholas C. Weaver and the team of Stuart Staniford, Gary Grim, and Roelof Jonkman, described the hypothetical Warhol and Flash worms, which theoretically could take over all vulnerable systems on the Internet in 15 minutes or even less. Warhol and Flash, which are only mathematical models and not actual worms (yet), are based on the idea of fast-forwarding through an exponential spread. Looking at a graph of infected victims over time for a conventional worm, a hockey-stick pattern appears. Things start out slowly as the initial victims succumb to the worm. Only after a critical mass of victims succumbs to the attack does the worm rapidly spread. Warhol and Flash jump past this initial slow spread by prescanning the Internet for vulnerable systems. Through automated scanning techniques from static machines, an attacker can find 100,000 or more vulnerable systems before ever releasing the worm. The attacker then loads these known vulnerable addresses into the worm. As the worm spreads, the addresses of these prescanned vulnerable systems would be split up among the segments of the worm propagating across the network. By using this initial set of vulnerable systems, an attacker could easily infect 99% of vulnerable systems on the Internet in less than an hour. Such a worm could conquer the Internet before most people have even heard of the problem.

MultiPlatform Worms

The vast majority of worms we have seen to date focused on a single platform, often Windows or Linux. For example, Nimda simply ripped apart as many Microsoft products as it could, exploiting Internet Explorer, the IIS Web server, Outlook, and Windows file sharing. While it certainly was challenging, Nimda's Windows-centric approach actually limited its spread. The security community implemented defenses by focusing on repairing Windows systems.

While single-platform worms can cause trouble, be on the lookout for worms that are far less discriminating from a platform perspective. New worms will contain exploits for Windows, Solaris, Linux, BSD, HP-UX, AIX, and other operating systems, all built into a single worm. Such worms are even more difficult to eradicate because security personnel and system administrators will have to apply patches in a coordinated fashion to many types of machines. The defense job will be more complex and require more time, allowing the worm to cause more damage.

Morphing and Disguised Worms

Recent worms have been relatively easy to detect. Once spotted, the computer security community has been able to quickly determine their functionalities. Once a worm has been isolated in the lab, some brilliant folks have been able to rapidly reverse-engineer each worm's operation to determine how best to defend against it.

In the very near future, we will face new worms that are far stealthier and more difficult to analyze. We will see polymorphic worms, which change their patterns every time they run and spread to a new system. Detection becomes more difficult because the worm essentially recodes itself each time it runs. Additionally, these new worms will encrypt or otherwise obscure much of their own payloads, hiding their functionalities until a later time. Reverse-engineering to determine the worm's true functions and purpose will become more difficult because investigators will have to extract the crypto keys or overcome the obfuscation mechanisms before they can really figure out what the worm can do. This time lag for the analysis will allow the worm to conquer more systems before adequate defenses are devised.

Zero-Day Exploit Worms

The vast majority of worms encountered so far are based on old, off-the-shelf exploits to attack systems. Because they have used old attacks, a patch has been readily available for administrators to fix their machines quickly after infection or to prevent infection in the first place. Using our familiar example, Code Red exploited systems using a flaw in Microsoft's IIS web server that had been known for over a month and for which a patch had already been published.

In the near future, we are likely going to see a worm that uses brand-new exploits for which no patch exists. Because they are brand new, such attacks are sometimes referred to as *zero-day exploits*. New vulnerabilities are discovered practically every day. Oftentimes, these problems are communicated to a vendor, who releases a patch. Unfortunately, these vulnerabilities are all too easy to discover, and it is only a matter of time before a worm writer discovers a major hole and first devises a worm that exploits it. Only after the worm has propagated across the Internet will the computer security community be capable of analyzing how it spreads so that a patch can be developed.

More Damaging Attacks

So far, worms have caused damage by consuming resources and creating nuisances. The worms we have seen to date have not really had a malicious payload. Once they take over hundreds of thousands of systems, they simply continue to spread without actually doing something nasty. Do not get me wrong; fighting Code Red and Nimda consumed much time and many resources. However, these attacks did not really do anything *beyond* simply consuming resources.

Soon, we may see worms that carry out some plan once they have spread. Such a malicious worm may be released in conjunction with a terrorist attack or other plot. Consider a worm that rapidly spreads using a zero-day exploit and then deletes the hard drives of 10 million victim machines. Or, perhaps worse, a worm could spread and then transfer the financial records of millions of victims to a country's adversaries. Such scenarios are not very far-fetched, and even nastier ones could be easily devised.

Worm Defenses

All of the pieces are available for a moderately skilled attacker to create a truly devastating worm. We may soon see rapidly spreading, multi platform, morphing worms using zero-day exploits to conduct very damaging attacks. So, what can you do to get ready? You need to establish both reactive and proactive defenses.

Incident response preparation

From a reactive perspective, your organization must establish a capability for determining when new vulnerabilities are discovered, as well as rapidly testing patches and moving them into production. As described earlier, your security team should subscribe to various security mailing lists, such as Bugtraq (available at http://www.securityfocus.com), to help alert you to such vulnerabilities and the release of patches. Furthermore, you must create an incident response team with the skills and resources necessary to discover and contain a worm attack.

Vigorously patch and harden your systems

From the proactive side, your organization must carefully harden your systems to prevent attacks. For each platform type, your organization should have documentation describing to system administrators how to build the machine to prevent attacks. Furthermore, you should periodically test your systems to ensure they are secure.

Block unnecessary outbound connections

Once a worm takes over a system, it attempts to spread by making outgoing connections to scan for other potential victims. You should help stop worms in their tracks by severely limiting all outgoing connections on your publicly available systems (such as your Web, Domain Name System (DNS), e-mail, and FTP servers). You should use a border router or external firewall to block all outgoing connections from such servers, unless there

is a specific business need for outgoing connections. If you do need some outgoing connections, allow them only to those IP addresses that are absolutely critical. For example, your web server needs to send responses to users requesting web pages, of course. But does your web server ever need to *initiate* connections to the Internet? Likely, the answer is no. So, do yourself and the rest of the Internet a favor by blocking such outgoing connections from your Internet servers.

Nonexecutable system stack can help stop some worms

In addition to overall system hardening, one particular step can help stop many worms. A large number of worms utilize buffer overflow exploits to compromise their victims. By sending more data than the program developer allocated space for a buffer overflow attack allows an attacker to get code entered as user input to run on the target system. Most operating systems can be inoculated against simple stack-based buffer overflow exploits by being configured with nonexecutable system stacks. Keep in mind that nonexecutable stacks can break some programs (so test these fixes before implementing them), and they do not provide a bulletproof shield against all buffer overflow attacks. Still, preventing the execution of code from the stack will stop a huge number of both known and as-yet-undiscovered vulnerabilities in their tracks. Up to 90% of buffer overflows can be prevented using this technique. To create a nonexecutable stack on a Linux system, you can use the free kernel patch at http://www.openwall.com/linux. On a Solaris machine, you can configure the system to stop the execution of code from the stack by adding the following lines to the/etc/system file:

```
set noexec_user_stack = 1
set noexec_user_stack_log = 1
```

On a Windows NT/2000 machine, you can achieve the same goal by deploying the commercial program SecureStack, available at http://www.securewave.com.

SNIFFING BACKDOORS

Once attackers compromise a system, they usually install a backdoor tool to allow them to access the machine repeatedly. A backdoor is a program that lets attackers access the machine on their own terms. Normal users are required to type in a password or use a cryptographic token; attackers use a backdoor to bypass these normal security controls. Traditionally, backdoors have listened on a TCP or UDP port, silently waiting in the background for a connection from the attacker. The

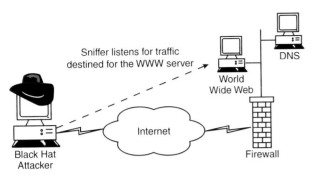

Fig. 1 A promiscuous sniffing backdoor.

attacker uses a client tool to connect to these backdoor servers on the proper TCP or UDP port to issue commands.

These traditional backdoors can be discovered by looking at the listening ports on a system. From the command prompt of a UNIX or Windows NT/2000/XP machine, a user can type "netstat -na" to see which TCP and UDP ports on the local machine have programs listening on them. Of course, normal usage of a machine will cause some TCP and UDP ports to be listening, such as TCP port 80 for Web servers, TCP port 25 for mail servers, and UDP port 53 for DNS servers. Beyond these expected ports based on specific server types, a suspicious port turned up by the netstat command could indicate a backdoor listener. Alternatively, a system or security administrator could remotely scan the ports of the system, using a port-scanning tool such as Nmap (available at http://www.insecure.org/nmap). If Nmap's output indicates an unexpected listening port, an attacker may have installed a backdoor.

Because attackers know that we are looking for their illicit backdoors listening on ports, a major trend in the attacker community is to avoid listening ports altogether for backdoors. You may ask, "How can they communicate with their backdoors if they aren't listening on a port?" To accomplish this, attackers are integrating sniffing technology into their backdoors to create sniffing backdoors. Rather than configuring a process to listen on a port, a sniffing backdoor uses a sniffer to grab traffic from the network. The sniffer then analyzes the traffic to determine which packets are supposed to go to the backdoor. Instead of listening on a port, the sniffer employs pattern matching on the network traffic to determine what to scoop up and pass to the backdoor. The backdoor then executes the commands and sends responses to the attacker. An excellent example of a sniffing backdoor is the Cd00r program written by FX. Cd00r is available at http://www.phenoelit.de/stuff/cd00r.c.

There are two general ways of running a sniffing backdoor, based on the mode used by the sniffer program to gather traffic: the so-called nonpromiscuous and promiscuous modes. A sniffer that puts an Ethernet

interface in promiscuous mode gathers all data from the LAN without regard to the actual destination address of the traffic. If the traffic passes by the interface, the Ethernet card in promiscuous mode will suck in the traffic and pass it to the backdoor. Alternatively, a non-promiscuous sniffer gathers traffic destined only for the machine on which the sniffer runs. Because these differences in sniffer types have significant implications on how attackers can use sniffing backdoors, we will explore non-promiscuous and promiscuous backdoors separately in the following text.

Nonpromiscuous Sniffing Backdoors

As their name implies, nonpromiscuous sniffing backdoors do not put the Ethernet interface into promiscuous mode. The sniffer sees only traffic going to and from the single machine where the sniffing backdoor is installed. When attackers use a nonpromiscuous sniffing backdoor, they do not have to worry about a system administrator detecting the interface in promiscuous mode.

In operation, the nonpromiscuous backdoor scours the traffic going to the victim machine looking for specific ports or other fields (such as a cryptographically derived value) included in the traffic. When the special traffic is detected, the backdoor wakes up and interacts with the attacker.

Promiscuous Sniffing Backdoors

By putting the Ethernet interface into promiscuous mode to gather all traffic from the LAN, promiscuous sniffing backdoors can make an investigation even more difficult. To understand why, consider the scenario shown in Fig. 1. This network uses a tri-homed firewall to separate the DMZ and internal network from the Internet. Suppose an attacker takes over the DNS server on the DMZ and installs a promiscuous sniffing backdoor. Because this backdoor uses a sniffer in promiscuous mode, it can gather all traffic from the LAN. The attacker configures the sniffing backdoor to listen in on all traffic with a destination address of the Web server (not the DNS server) to retrieve commands from the attacker to execute. In our scenario, the attacker does not install a backdoor or any other software on the web server. Only the DNS server is compromised.

Now the attacker formulates packets with commands for the backdoor. These packets are all sent with a destination address of the web server (*not* the DNS server). The web server does not know what to do with these commands, so it will either discard them or send a RESET or related message to the attacker. However, the DNS server with the sniffing backdoor will see the commands on the LAN. The sniffer will gather these commands and forward them to the backdoor where they will be executed. To further obfuscate the situation, the attacker can send all responses from the backdoor using the spoofed source address of the web server.

Given this scenario, consider the dilemma faced by the investigator. The system administrator or an intrusion detection system complains that there is suspicious traffic going to and from the web server. The investigator conducts a detailed and thorough analysis of the web server. After a painstaking process to verify the integrity of the applications, operating system programs, and kernel on the web server machine, the investigator determines that this system is intact. Yet backdoor commands continue to be sent to this machine. The investigator would only discover what is really going on by analyzing other systems connected to the LAN, such as the DNS server. The investigative process is significantly slowed down by the promiscuous sniffing backdoor.

Defending against Sniffing Backdoor Attacks

It is important to note that the use of a switch on the DMZ network between the web server and DNS server does not eliminate this dilemma. Attackers can use active sniffers to conduct Address Resolution Protocol (ARP) cache poisoning attacks and successfully sniff a switched environment. An active sniffer such as Dsniff (available at http://www.monkey.org) married to a sniffing backdoor can implement this type of attack in a switched environment.

So if a switch does not eliminate this problem, how can you defend against this kind of attack? First, as with most backdoors, system and security administrators must know what is supposed to be running on their systems, especially processes running with root or system-level privileges. Keeping up with this information is not a trivial task, but it is especially important for all publicly available servers such as systems on a DMZ. If a security or system administrator notices a new process running with escalated privileges, the process should be investigated immediately. Tools such as lsof for UNIX

(available at ftp://vic.cc.purdue.edu/pub/tools/unix/lsof/) or Inzider for Windows NT/2000 (available at http://ntsecurity.nu/toolbox/inzider/) can help to indicate the files and ports used by any process. Keep in mind that most attackers will not name their backdoors "cd00r" or "backdoor," but instead will use less obvious names to camouflage their activities. In my experience, attackers like to name their backdoors "SCSI" or "UPS" to prevent a curious system administrator from questioning or shutting off the attackers' processes.

Also, while switches do not eliminate attacks with sniffers, a switched environment can help to limit an attacker's options, especially if it is carefully configured. For your DMZs and other critical networks, you should use a switch and hard-code all ARP entries in each host on the LAN. Each system on your LAN has an ARP cache holding information about the IP and MAC addresses of other machines on the LAN. By hard-coding all ARP entries on your sensitive LANs so that they are static, you minimize the possibility of ARP cached poisoning. Additionally, implement port-level security on your switch so that only specific Ethernet MAC addresses can communicate with the switch.

CONCLUSIONS

The computer underground and information security research fields remain highly active in refining existing methods and defining completely new ways to attack and compromise computer systems. Advances in our networking infrastructures, especially wireless LANs, are not only giving attackers new avenues into our systems, but they are also often riddled with security vulnerabilities. With this dynamic environment, defending against attacks is certainly a challenge. However, these constantly evolving attacks can be frustrating and exciting at the same time, while certainly providing job security to solid information security practitioners. While we need to work diligently in securing our systems, our reward is a significant intellectual challenge and decent employment in a challenging economy.

Hackers: Tools and Techniques

Ed Skoudis
Senior Security Consultant, Intelguardians Network Intelligence, Howell, New Jersey, U.S.A.

Abstract

Many of the tools described in this entry have dual personalities; they can be used for good or evil. When used by malicious individuals, the tools allow a motivated attacker to gain access to a network, mask the fact that a compromise occurred, or even bring down service, thereby impacting large masses of users. When used by security practitioners with proper authorization, some tools can be used to measure the security stance of their own organizations, by conducting ethical hacking tests to find vulnerabilities before attackers do.

Headlines demonstrate that the latest crop of hacker tools and techniques can be highly damaging to an organization's sensitive information and reputation. With the rise of powerful, easy-to-use, and widely distributed hacker tools, many in the security industry have observed that today is the golden age of hacking. The purpose of this entry is to describe the tools in wide-spread use today for compromising computer and network security. Additionally, for each tool and technique described, the entry presents practical advice on defending against each type of attack.

The terminology applied to these tools and their users has caused some controversy, particularly in the computer underground. Traditionally, and particularly in the computer underground, the term hacker is a benign word, referring to an individual who is focused on determining how things work and devising innovative approaches to addressing computer problems. To differentiate these noble individuals from a nasty attacker, this school of thought labels malicious attackers as crackers. While hackers are out to make the world a better place, crackers want to cause damage and mayhem. To avoid the confusion often associated with these terms, in this entry the terms system and security administrator and security practitioner will be used to indicate an individual who has a legitimate and authorized purpose for running these tools. The term attacker will be used for those individuals who seek to cause damage to systems or who are not authorized to run such tools.

CAVEAT

The purpose of this entry is to explain the various computer underground tools in use today and to discuss defensive techniques for addressing each type of tool. This entry is *not* designed to encourage attacks.

Furthermore, the tools described in the following text are for illustration purposes only, and mention in this entry is *not* an endorsement. If readers feel compelled to experiment with these tools, they should do so at their own risk, realizing that such tools frequently have viruses or other undocumented features that could damage networks and information systems. Curious readers who want to use these tools should conduct a thorough review of the source code, or at least install the tools on a separate, air-gapped network to protect sensitive production systems.

GENERAL TRENDS IN THE COMPUTER UNDERGROUND

The Smart Get Smarter, and the Rise of the Script Kiddie

The best and brightest minds in the computer underground are conducting probing research and finding new vulnerabilities and powerful, novel attacks on a daily basis. The ideas and deep research done by supersmart attackers and security practitioners are being implemented in software programs and scripts. Months of research on how a particular operating system implements its password scheme are being rendered in code, so even a clueless attacker (often called a script kiddie) can conduct a highly sophisticated attack with just a point-and-click. Although the script kiddie may not understand the tools' true function and nuances, most of the attack is automated.

In this environment, security practitioners must be careful not to underestimate their adversaries' capabilities. Often, security and system administrators think of their potential attackers as mere teenage kids cruising the Internet looking for easy prey. While this assessment is sometimes accurate, it masks two major concerns.

Encyclopedia of Information Systems and Technology, DOI: 10.1081/E-EIST-120046287

First, some of these teenage kids are amazingly intelligent and can wreak havoc on a network. Second, attackers may not be just kids; organized crime, terrorists, and even foreign governments have taken to sponsoring cyberattacks.

Wide Distribution of High-Quality Tools

Another trend in the computing underground involves the widespread distribution of tools. In the past, powerful attack tools were limited to a core group of elites in the computer underground. Today, hundreds of websites are devoted to the sharing of tools for every attacker (and security practitioner) on the planet. Frequently asked questions abound describing how to penetrate any type of operating system. These overall trends converge in a world where smart attackers have detailed knowledge of undermining our systems, while the not-so-smart attackers grow more and more plentiful. To address this increasing threat, system administrators and security practitioners must understand these tools and how to defend against them. The remainder of this entry describes many of these very powerful tools in widespread use today, together with practical defensive tips for protecting one's network from each type of attack.

NETWORK MAPPING AND PORT SCANNING

When launching an attack across a TCP/IP network (such as the Internet or a corporate intranet), an attacker needs to know what addresses are active, how the network topology is constructed, and which services are available. A network mapper identifies systems that are connected to the target network. Given a network address range, the network mapper will send packets to each possible address to determine which addresses have machines.

By sending a simple Internet Control Message Protocol (ICMP) packet to a server (a ping), the mapping tool can discover if a server is connected to the network. For those networks that block incoming pings, many of the mapping tools available today can send a single SYN packet to attempt to open a connection to a server. If a server is listening, the SYN packet will trigger an ACK if the port is open, and potentially a Port Unreachable message if the port is closed. Regardless of whether the port is open or closed, the response indicates that the address has a machine listening. With this list of addresses, an attacker can refine the attack and focus on these listening systems.

A port scanner identifies open ports on a system. There are 65,535 TCP ports and 65,535 UDP ports, some of which are open on a system, but most of which

are closed. Common services are associated with certain ports. For example, TCP Port 8 is most often used by web servers, TCP Port 23 is used by Telnet daemons, and TCP Port 25 is used for server-to-server mail exchange across the Internet. By conducting a port scan, an attacker will send packets to each and every port. Essentially, ports are rather like doors on a machine. At any one of the thousands of doors available, common services will be listening. A port scanning tool allows an attacker to knock on every one of those doors to see who answers.

Some scanning tools include TCP fingerprinting capabilities. While the Internet Engineering Task Force has carefully specified TCP and IP in various requests for comments (RFCs), not all packet options have standards associated with them. Without standards for how systems should respond to illegal packet formats, different vendors' TCP/IP stacks respond differently to illegal packets. By sending various combinations of illegal packet options (such as initiating a connection with an RST packet, or combining other odd and illegal TCP code bits), an attacker can determine what type of operating system is running on the target machine. For example, by conducting a TCP fingerprinting scan, an attacker can determine if a machine is running Cisco IOS, Sun Solaris, or Microsoft Windows 2000. In some cases, even the particular version or service pack level can be determined using this technique.

After utilizing network mapping tools and port scanners, an attacker will know which addresses on the target network have listening machines, which ports are open on those machines (and therefore which services are running), and which operating system platforms are in use. This treasure trove of information is useful to the attacker in refining the attack. With this data, the attacker can search for vulnerabilities on the particular services and systems in an attempt to gain access.

Nmap, written by Fyodor, is one of the most full-featured mapping and scanning tools available today. Nmap, which supports network mapping, port scanning, and TCP fingerprinting, can be found at http://www.insecure.org/nmap.

Network Mapping and Port Scanning Defenses

To defend against network mapping and port scans, the administrator should remove all unnecessary systems and close all unused ports. To accomplish this, the administrator must disable and remove unneeded services from the machine. Only those services that have an absolute, defined business need should be running. A security administrator should also periodically scan the systems to determine if any unneeded ports are open. When discovered, these unneeded ports must be disabled.

VULNERABILITY SCANNING

Once the target systems are identified with a port scanner and network mapper, an attacker will search to determine if any vulnerabilities are present on the victim machines. Thousands of vulnerabilities have been discovered, allowing a remote attacker to gain a toehold on a machine or to take complete administrative control. An attacker could try each of these vulnerabilities on each system by entering individual commands to test for every vulnerability, but conducting an exhaustive search could take years. To speed up the process, attackers use automated scanning tools to quickly search for vulnerabilities on the target.

These automated vulnerability scanning tools are essentially databases of well-known vulnerabilities with an engine that can read the database, connect to a machine, and check to see if it is vulnerable to the exploit. The effectiveness of the tool in discovering vulnerabilities depends on the quality and thoroughness of its vulnerability database. For this reason, the best vulnerability scanners support the rapid release and update of the vulnerability database and the ability to create new checks using a scripting language.

High-quality commercial vulnerability scanning tools are widely available, and are often used by security practitioners and attackers to search for vulnerabilities. On the freeware front, SATAN (the Security Administrator Tool for Analyzing Network) was one of the first widely distributed automated vulnerability scanners, introduced in 1995. Nessus has been introduced as a free, open-source vulnerability scanner available at http://www.nessus.org. The Nessus project, which is led by Renaud Deraison, provides a full-featured scanner for identifying vulnerabilities on remote systems. It includes source code and a scripting language for writing new vulnerability checks, allowing it to be highly customized by security practitioners and attackers alike.

While Nessus is a general-purpose vulnerability scanner, looking for holes in numerous types of systems and platforms, some vulnerability scanners are much more focused on particular types of systems. For example, Whisker is a full-feature vulnerability scanning tool focusing on web server CGI scripts. Written by Rain Forest Puppy, Whisker can be found at http://www.wiretrip.net/rfp.

Vulnerability Scanning Defenses

As described earlier, the administrator must close unused ports. Additionally, to eliminate the vast majority of system vulnerabilities, system patches must be applied in a timely fashion. All organizations using computers should have a defined change control procedure that specifies when and how system patches will be kept up-to-date.

Security practitioners should also conduct periodic vulnerability scans of their own networks to find vulnerabilities before attackers do. These scans should be conducted on a regular basis (such as quarterly or even monthly for sensitive networks), or when major network changes are implemented. The discovered vulnerabilities must be addressed in a timely fashion by updating system configurations or applying patches.

WARDIALING

A cousin of the network mapper and scanner, a wardialing tool is used to discover target systems across a telephone network. Organizations often spend large amounts of money in securing their network from a full, frontal assault over the Internet by implementing a firewall, intrusion detection system, and secure DMZ. Unfortunately, many attackers avoid this route and instead look for other ways into the network. Modems left on users' desktops or old, forgotten machines often provide the simplest way into a target network.

Wardialers, also known as demon dialers, dial a series of telephone numbers, attempting to locate modems on the victim network. An attacker will determine the telephone extensions associated with the target organization. This information is often gleaned from a website listing telephone contacts, employee newsgroup postings with telephone contact information in the signature line, or even general employee e-mail. Armed with one or a series of telephone numbers, the attacker will enter into the wardialing tool ranges of numbers associated with the original number (e.g., if an employee's telephone number in a newsgroup posting is listed as 555-1212, the attacker will dial 555-XXXX). The wardialer will automatically dial each number, listen for the familiar wail of a modem carrier tone, and make a list of all telephone numbers with modems listening.

With the list of modems generated by the wardialer, the attacker will dial each discovered modem using a terminal program or other client. Upon connecting to the modem, the attacker will attempt to identify the system based on its banner information and see if a password is required. Often, no password is required, because the modem was put in place by a clueless user requiring after-hours access and not wanting to bother using approved methods. If a password is required, the attacker will attempt to guess passwords commonly associated with the platform or company.

Some wardialing tools also support the capability of locating a repeat dial-tone, in addition to the ability to detect modems. The repeat dial-tone is a great find for the attacker, as it could allow for unrestricted dialing from a victim's PBX system to anywhere in the world. If an attacker finds a line on PBX supporting repeat dial-tone in the same local dialing exchange, the attacker can conduct international wardialing, with all phone bills paid for by the victim with the misconfigured PBX.

The most fully functional wardialing tool available today is distributed by The Hacker's Choice (THC) group. Known as THC-Scan, the tool was written by Van Hauser and can be found at http://inferno.tusculum. edu/thc. THC-Scan 2.0 supports many advanced features, including sequential or randomized dialing, dialing through a network out-dial, modem carrier and repeat dial-tone detection, and rudimentary detection avoidance capabilities.

Wardialing Defenses

The best defense against wardialing attacks is a strong modem policy that prohibits the use of modems and incoming lines without a defined business need. The policy should also require the registration of all modems with a business need in a centralized database only accessible by a security or system administrator.

Additionally, security personnel should conduct periodic wardialing exercises of their own networks to find the modems before the attackers do. When a phone number with an unregistered modem is discovered, the physical device must be located and deactivated. While finding such devices can be difficult, network defenses depend on finding these renegade modems before an attacker does.

NETWORK EXPLOITS: SNIFFING, SPOOFING, AND SESSION HIJACKING

TCP/IP, the underlying protocol suite that makes up the Internet, was not originally designed to provide security services. Likewise, the most common data-link type used with TCP/IP, Ethernet, is fundamentally unsecure. A whole series of attacks are possible given these vulnerabilities of the underlying protocols. The most widely used and potentially damaging attacks based on these network vulnerabilities are sniffing, spoofing, and session hijacking.

Sniffing

Sniffers are extremely useful tools for an attacker and are therefore a fundamental element of an attacker's toolchest. Sniffers allow an attacker to monitor data passing across a network. Given their capability to monitor network traffic, sniffers are also useful for security practitioners and network administrators in troubleshooting networks and conducting investigations. Sniffers

exploit characteristics of several data-link technologies, including Token Ring and especially Ethernet.

Ethernet, the most common LAN technology, is essentially a broadcast technology. When Ethernet LANs are constructed using hubs, all machines connected to the LAN can monitor all data on the LAN segment. If userIDs, passwords, or other sensitive information are sent from one machine (e.g., a client) to another machine (e.g., a server or router) on the same LAN, all other systems connected to the LAN could monitor the data. A sniffer is a hardware or software tool that gathers all data on a LAN segment. When a sniffer is running on a machine gathering all network traffic that passes by the system, the Ethernet interface and the machine itself are said to be in promiscuous mode.

Many commonly used applications, such as Telnet, FTP, POP (the Post Office Protocol used for e-mail), and even some web applications, transmit their passwords and sensitive data without any encryption. Any attacker on a broadcast Ethernet segment can use a sniffer to gather these passwords and data.

Attackers who take over a system often install a software sniffer on the compromised machine. This sniffer acts as a sentinel for the attacker, gathering sensitive data that moves by the compromised system. The sniffer gathers this data, including passwords, and stores it in a local file or transmits it to the attacker. The attacker then uses this information to compromise more and more systems. The attack methodology of installing a sniffer on one compromised machine, gathering data passing that machine, and using the sniffed information to take over other systems is referred to as an island-hopping attack.

Numerous sniffing tools are available across the Internet. The most fully functional sniffing tools include Sniffit (by Brecht Claerhout, available at http://reptile. rug.ac.be/coder/sniffit/sniffit.html) and Snort (by Martin Roesch, available at http://www.clark.net/roesch/security. html). Some operating systems ship with their own sniffers installed by default, notably Solaris (with the snoop tool) and some varieties of Linux (which ship with tcpdump). Other commercial sniffers are also available from a variety of vendors.

Sniffing defenses

The best defense against sniffing attacks is to encrypt the data in transit. Instead of sending passwords or other sensitive data in cleartext, the application or network should encrypt the data (secure shell (SSH), secure Telnet, etc.).

Another defense against sniffers is to eliminate the broadcast nature of Ethernet. By utilizing a switch instead of a hub to create a LAN, the damage that can

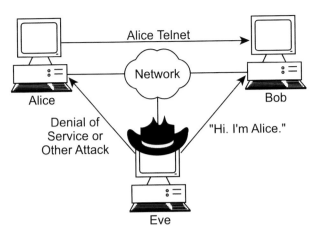

Fig. 1 Eve hijacks the session between Alice and Bob.

be done with a sniffer is limited. A switch can be configured so that only the required source and destination ports on the switch carry the traffic. Although they are on the same LAN, all other ports on the switch (and the machines connected to those ports) do not see this data. Therefore, if one system is compromised on a LAN, a sniffer installed on this machine will not be capable of seeing data exchanged between other machines on the LAN. Switches are therefore useful in improving security by minimizing the data a sniffer can gather, and also help to improve network performance.

IP Spoofing

Another network-based attack involves altering the source address of a computer to disguise the attacker and exploit weak authentication methods. IP address spoofing allows an attacker to use the IP address of another machine to conduct an attack. If the target machines rely on the IP address to authenticate, IP spoofing can give an attacker access to the systems. Additionally, IP spoofing can make it very difficult to apprehend an attacker, because logs will contain decoy addresses and not the real source of the attack. Many of the tools described in other sections of this entry rely on IP spoofing to hide the true origin of the attack.

Spoofing defenses

Systems should not use IP addresses for authentication. Any functions or applications that rely solely on IP address for authentication should be disabled or replaced. In UNIX, the **r**-commands (**rlogin, rsh, rexec,** and **rcp**) are notoriously subject to IP spoofing attacks. UNIX trust relationships allow an administrator to manage systems using the **r**-commands without providing a password. Instead of a password, the IP address of the system is used for authentication. This major weakness should be avoided by replacing the **r**-commands with administration tools that

utilize strong authentication. One such tool, SSH, uses strong cryptography to replace the weak authentication of the **r**-commands. Similarly, all other applications that rely on IP addresses for critical security and administration functions should be replaced.

Additionally, an organization should deploy antispoof filters on its perimeter networks that connect the organization to the Internet and business partners. Antispoof filters drop all traffic coming from outside the network claiming to come from the inside. With this capability, such filters can prevent some types of spoofing attacks and these should be implemented on all perimeter network routers.

Session Hijacking

While sniffing allows an attacker to view data associated with network connections, a session hijack tool allows an attacker to take over network connections, kicking off the legitimate user or sharing a login. Session hijacking tools are used against services with persistent login sessions, such as Telnet, rlogin, or FTP. For any of these services, an attacker can hijack a session and cause a great deal of damage.

A common scenario illustrating session hijacking involves a machine, Alice, with a user logged in to remotely administer another system, Bob, using Telnet. Eve, the attacker, sits on a network segment between Alice and Bob (either Alice's LAN, Bob's LAN, or between any of the routers between Alice's and Bob's LANs). Fig. 1 illustrates this scenario in more detail.

Using a session hijacking tool, Eve can do any of the following:

- *Monitor Alice's session.* Most session hijacking tools allow attackers to monitor all connections available on the network and select which connections they want to hijack.
- *Insert commands into the session.* An attacker may just need to add one or two commands into the stream to reconfigure Bob. In this type of hijack, the attacker never takes full control of the session. Instead, Alice's login session to Bob has a small number of commands inserted, which will be executed on Bob as though Alice had typed them.
- *Steal the session.* This feature of most session hijacking tools allows an attacker to grab the session from Alice, and directly control it. Essentially, the Telnet client control is shifted from Alice to Eve, without Bob's knowing.
- *Give the session back.* Some session hijacking tools allow the attacker to steal a session, interact with the server, and then smoothly give the session back to the user. While the session is stolen, Alice is put on hold while Eve controls the session. With Alice on

hold, all commands typed by Alice are displayed on Eve's screen, but not transmitted to Bob. When Eve is finished making modifications on Bob, Eve transfers control back to Alice.

For a successful hijack to occur, the attacker must be on a LAN segment between Alice and Bob. A session hijacking tool monitors the connection using an integrate sniffer, observing the TCP sequence numbers of the packets going each direction. Each packet sent from Alice to Bob has a unique TCP sequence number used by Bob to verify that all packets are received and put in proper order. Likewise, all packets going back from Bob to Alice have sequence numbers. A session hijacking tool sniffs the packets to determine these sequence numbers. When a session is hijacked (through command insertion or session stealing), the hijacking tool automatically uses the appropriate sequence numbers and spoofs Alice's address, taking over the conversation with Bob where Alice left off.

One of the most fully functional session hijacking tools available today is Hunt, written by Kra and available at http://www.cri.cz/kra/index.html. Hunt allows an attacker to monitor and steal sessions, insert single commands, and even give a session back to the user.

Session hijacking defenses

The best defense against session hijacking is to avoid the use of insecure protocols and applications for sensitive sessions. Instead of using the easy-to-hijack (and easy-to-sniff) Telnet application, a more secure, encrypted session tool should be used. Because the attacker does not have the session encryption keys, an encrypted session cannot be hijacked. The attacker will simply see encrypted gibberish using Hunt, and will only be able to reset the connection, not take it over or insert commands.

SSH offers strong authentication and encrypted sessions, providing a highly secure alternative to Telnet and rlogin. Furthermore, SSH includes a secure file transfer capability to replace traditional FTP. Other alternatives are available, including secure, encrypted Telnet, or a virtual private network established between the source and destination.

DENIAL-OF-SERVICE ATTACKS

Denial-of-service attacks are among the most common exploits available today. As their name implies, a denial-of-service attack prevents legitimate users from being able to access a system. With E-commerce applications constituting the lifeblood of many organizations and a growing piece of the world economy, a well-timed denial-of-service attack can cause a great deal of damage. By bringing down servers that control sensitive machinery or other functions, these attacks could also present a real physical threat to life and limb. An attacker could cause the service denial by flooding a system with bogus traffic, or even purposely causing the server to crash. Countless denial-of-service attacks are in widespread use today, and can be found at http://packetstorm.securify.com/exploits/DoS. The most often used network-based denial-of-service attacks fall into two categories: malformed packet attacks and packet floods.

Malformed Packet Attacks

This type of attack usually involves one or two packets that are formatted in an unexpected way. Many vendor product implementations do not take into account all variations of user entries or packet types. If the software handles such errors poorly, the system may crash when it receives such packets. A classic example of this type of attack involves sending IP fragments to a system that overlap with each other (the fragment offset values are incorrectly set). Some unpatched Windows and Linux systems will crash when they encounter such packets. The teardrop attack is an example of a tool that exploits this IP fragmentation handling vulnerability. Other malformed packet attacks that exploit other weaknesses in TCP/IP implementations include the colorfully named WinNuke, Land, LaTierra, NewTear, Bonk, Boink, etc.

Packet Flood Attacks

Packet flood denial-of-service tools send a deluge of traffic to a system on the network, overwhelming its capability to respond to legitimate users. Attackers have devised numerous techniques for creating such floods, with the most popular being SYN floods, directed broadcast attacks, and distributed denial-of-service tools.

SYN flood tools initiate a large number of half-open connections with a system by sending a series of SYN packets. When any TCP connection is established, a three-way handshake occurs. The initiating system (usually the client) sends a SYN packet to the destination to establish a sequence number for all packets going from source to destination in that session. The destination responds with a SYN-ACK packet, which acknowledges the sequence number for packets going from source to destination, and establishes an initial sequence number for packets going the opposite direction. The source completes the three-way handshake by sending an ACK to the destination. The three-way handshake is completed, and communication (actual data transfer) can occur.

SYN floods take advantage of a weakness in TCP's three-way handshake. By sending only spoofed SYN packets and never responding to the SYN-ACK, an attacker can exhaust a server's ability to maintain the state of all the initiated sessions. With a huge number of so-called half-open connections, a server cannot handle any new, legitimate traffic. Rather than filling up all of the pipe bandwidth to a server, only the server's capacity to handle session initiations needs to be overwhelmed (in most network configurations, a server's ability to handle SYNs is lower than the total bandwidth to the site). For this reason, SYN flooding is the most popular packet flood attack. Other tools are also available that flood systems with ICMP and UDP packets, but they merely consume bandwidth, so an attacker would require a bigger connection than the victim to cut off all service.

Another type of packet flood that allows attackers to amplify their bandwidth is the directed broadcast attack. Often called a smurf attack, named after the first tool to exploit this technique, directed broadcast attacks utilize a third-party's network as an amplifier for the packet flood. In a smurf attack, the attacker locates a network on the Internet that will respond to a broadcast ICMP message (essentially a ping to the network's broadcast address). If the network is configured to allow broadcast requests and responses, all machines on the network will send a response to the ping. By spoofing the ICMP request, the attacker can have all machines on the third-party network send responses to the victim. For example, if an organization has 3 hosts on a single DMZ network connected to the Internet, an attacker can send a spoofed network broadcast ping to the DMZ. All 30 hosts will send a response to the spoofed address, which would be the ultimate victim. By sending repeated messages to the broadcast network, the attacker has amplified bandwidth by a factor of 30. Even an attacker with only a 56-kbps dial-up line could fill up a T1 line (1.54 Mbps) with that level of amplification. Other directed broadcast attack tools include Fraggle and Papasmurf.

A final type of denial-of-service that has received considerable press is the distributed denial-of-service attack. Essentially based on standard packet flood concepts, distributed denial-of-service attacks were used to cripple many major Internet sites in February 2000. Tools such as Trin00, Tribe Flood Network 2000 (TFN2K), and Stacheldraht all support this type of attack. To conduct a distributed denial-of-service attack, an attacker must find numerous vulnerable systems on the Internet. Usually, a remote buffer overflow attack (described in the following text) is used to take over a dozen, a hundred, or even thousands of machines. Simple daemon processes, called zombies, are installed on these machines taken over by the attacker. The attacker communicates with this network of zombies using a control program. The control program is used to send commands to the hundreds or thousands of zombies, requesting them to take uniform action simultaneously.

The most common action to be taken is to simultaneously launch a packet flood against a target. While a traditional SYN flood would deluge a target with packets from one host, a distributed denial-of-service attack would send packets from large numbers of zombies, rapidly exhausting the capacity of even very high-bandwidth, well-designed sites. Many distributed denial-of-service attack tools support SYN, UDP, and ICMP flooding, smurf attacks, as well as some malformed packet attacks. Any one or all of these options can be selected by the attacker using the control program.

Denial-of-Service Attack Defenses

To defend against malformed packet attacks, system patches and security fixes must be regularly applied. Vendors frequently update their systems with patches to handle a new flavor of denial-of-service attack. An organization must have a program for monitoring vendor and industry security bulletins for security fixes, and a controlled method for implementing these fixes soon after they are announced and tested.

For packet flood attacks, critical systems should have underlying network architectures with multiple, redundant paths, eliminating a single point of failure. Furthermore, adequate bandwidth is a must. Also, some routers and firewalls support traffic flow control to help ease the burden of a SYN flood.

Finally, by configuring an Internet-accessible network appropriately, an organization can minimize the possibility that it will be used as a jumping-off point for smurf and distributed denial-of-service attacks. To prevent the possibility of being used as a smurf amplifier, the external router or firewall should be configured to drop all directed broadcast requests from the Internet. To lower the chance of being used in a distributed denial-of-service attack, an organization should implement anti-spoof filters on external routers and firewalls to make sure that all outgoing traffic has a source IP address of the site. This egress filtering prevents an attacker from sending spoofed packets from a zombie or other denial-of-service tool located on the network. Antispoof ingress filters, which drop all packets from the Internet claiming to come from one's internal network, are also useful in preventing some denial-of-service attacks.

STACK-BASED BUFFER OVERFLOWS

Stack-based buffer overflow attacks are commonly used by an attacker to take over a system remotely across a network. Additionally, buffer overflows can be

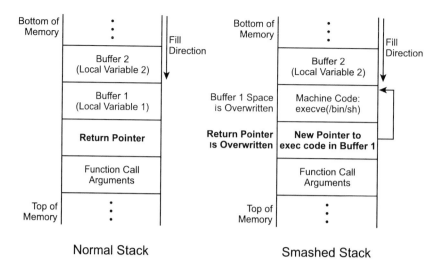

Fig. 2 A normal stack and a stack with a buffer overflow.

employed by local malicious users to elevate their privileges and gain superuser access to a system. Stack-based buffer overflow attacks exploit the way many operating systems handle their stack, an internal data structure used by running programs to store data temporarily. When a function call is made, the present state of the executing program and variables to be passed to the function are pushed on the stack. New local variables used by the function are also allocated space on the stack. Additionally, the stack stores the return address of the code calling the function. This return address will be accessed from the stack once the function call is complete. The system uses this address to resume execution of the calling program at the appropriate place. Fig. 2 shows how a stack is constructed.

Most UNIX and all Windows systems have a stack that can hold data and executable code. Because local variables are stored on the stack when a function is called, poor code can be exploited to overrun the boundaries of these variables on the stack. If user input length is not examined by the code, a particular variable on the stack may exceed the memory allocated to it on the stack, overwriting all variables and even the return address for where execution should resume after the function is complete. This operation, called smashing the stack, allows an attacker to overflow the local variables to insert executable code and another return address on the stack. Fig. 2 also shows a stack that has been smashed with a buffer overflow.

The attacker will overflow the buffer on the stack with machine-specific bytecodes that consist of executable commands (usually a shell routine), and a return pointer to begin the execution of these inserted commands. Therefore, with very carefully constructed binary code, the attacker can actually enter information as a user into a program that consists of executable code and a new return address. The buggy program will not analyze the length of this input, but will place it on

the stack, and actually begin to execute the attacker's code. Such vulnerabilities allow an attacker to break out of the application code, and access any system components with the permissions of the broken program. If the broken program is running with superuser privileges (e.g., SUID root on a UNIX system), the attacker has taken over the machine with a buffer overflow.

Stack-Based Buffer Overflow Defenses

The most thorough defense against buffer overflow attacks is to properly code software so that it cannot be used to smash the stack. All programs should validate all input from users and other programs, ensuring that it fits into allocated memory structures. Each variable should be checked (including user input, variables from other functions, input from other programs, and even environment variables) to ensure that allocated buffers are adequate to hold the data. Unfortunately, this ultimate solution is only available to individuals who write the programs and those with source code.

Additionally, security practitioners and system administrators should carefully control and minimize the number of SUID programs on a system that users can run and have permissions of other users (such as root). Only SUID programs with an explicit business need should be installed on sensitive systems.

Finally, many stack-based buffer overflow attacks can be avoided by configuring the systems to not execute code from the stack. Notably, Solaris and Linux offer this option. For example, to secure a Solaris system against stack-based buffer overflows, the following lines should be added:

```
/etc/system:
set noexec_user_stack = 1
set noexec_user_stack_log = 1
```

The first line will prevent execution on a stack, and the second line will log any attempt to do so. Unfortunately, some programs legitimately try to run code off the stack. Such programs will crash if this option is implemented. Generally, if the system is single purpose and needs to be secure (e.g., a web server), this option should be used to prevent stack-based buffer overflow.

ART AND SCIENCE OF PASSWORD CRACKING

The vast majority of systems today authenticate users with a static password. When a user logs in, the password is transmitted to the system, which checks the password to make the decision whether to let the user log in. To make this decision, the system must have a mechanism to compare the user's input with the actual password. Of course, the system could just store all of the passwords locally and compare from this file. Such a file of cleartext passwords, however, would provide a very juicy target for an attacker. To make the target less useful for attackers, most modern operating systems use a one-way hash or encryption mechanism to protect the stored passwords. When a user types in a password, the system hashes the user's entry and compares it to the stored hash. If the two hashes match, the password is correct and the user can login.

Password cracking tools are used to attack this method of password protection. An attacker will use some exploit (often a buffer overflow) to gather the encrypted or hashed password file from a system (on a UNIX system without password shadowing, any user can read the hashed password file). After downloading the hashed password file, the attacker uses a password cracking tool to determine users' passwords. The cracking tool operates using a loop: it guesses a password, hashes or encrypts the password, and compares it to the hashed password from the stolen file. If the hashes match, the attacker has the password. If the hashes do not match, the loop begins again with another password guess.

Password cracking tools base their password guesses on a dictionary or a complete brute-force attack, attempting every possible password. Dozens of dictionaries are available online, in a multitude of languages, including English, French, German, Klingon, etc.

Numerous password-cracking tools are available. The most popular and full-functional password crackers include:

- John-the-Ripper, by Solar Designer, focuses on cracking UNIX passwords, and is available at http://www.openwall.com/john/.
- L0phtCrack, used to crack Windows NT passwords, is available at http://www.l0pht.com.

Password Cracking Defenses

The first defense against password cracking is to minimize the exposure of the encrypted/hashed password file. On UNIX systems, shadow password files should be used, which allow only the superuser to read the password file. On Windows NT systems, the SYSKEY feature available in NT 4.0 SP 3 and later should be installed and enabled. Furthermore, all backups and system recovery disks should be stored in physically secured locations and possibly even encrypted.

A strong password policy is a crucial element in ensuring a secure network. A password policy should require password lengths greater than eight characters, require the use of alphanumeric *and* special characters in every password, and force users to have passwords with mixed-case letters. Users must be aware of the issue of weak passwords and be trained in creating memorable, yet difficult-to-guess passwords.

To ensure that passwords are secure and to identify weak passwords, security practitioners should check system passwords on a periodic basis using password cracking tools. When weak passwords are discovered, the security group should have a defined procedure for interacting with users whose passwords can be easily guessed.

Finally, several software packages are available that prevent users from setting their passwords to easily guessed values. When a user establishes a new password, these filtering programs check the password to make sure that it is sufficiently complex and is not just a variation of the user name or a dictionary word. With this kind of tool, users are simply unable to create passwords that are easily guessed, eliminating a significant security issue. For filtering software to be effective, it must be installed on all servers where users establish passwords, including UNIX servers, Windows NT Primary and Back-up Domain Controllers, and Novell servers.

BACKDOORS

Backdoors are programs that bypass traditional security checks on a system, allowing an attacker to gain access to a machine without providing a system password and getting logged. Attackers install backdoors on a machine (or dupe a user into installing one for them) to ensure they will be able to gain access to the system at a later time. Once installed, most backdoors listen on special ports for incoming connections from the attacker across the network. When the attacker connects to the backdoor listener, the traditional userID and password or other forms of authentication are bypassed. Instead, the attacker can gain access to the system without providing a password, or by using a special password used only to enter the backdoor.

Netcat is an incredibly flexible tool written for UNIX by Hobbit and for Windows NT by Weld Pond (both versions are available at http://www.l0pht.com/weld/net-cat/). Among its numerous other uses, Netcat can be used to create a backdoor listener with a superuser-level shell on any TCP or UDP port. For Windows systems, an enormous number of backdoor applications are available, including Back Orifice 2000 (called BO2K for short, and available at http://www.bo2k.com) and hack-a-tack (available at http://www.hack-atack.com).

Backdoor Defenses

The best defense against backdoor programs is for system and security administrators to know what is running on their machines, particularly sensitive systems storing critical information or processing high-value transactions. If a process suddenly appears running as the superuser listening on a port, the administrator needs to investigate. Backdoors listening on various ports can be discovered using the **netstatna** command on UNIX and Windows NT systems.

Additionally, many backdoor programs (such as BO2K) can be discovered by an anti-virus program, which should be installed on all users' desktops, as well as on servers throughout an organization.

TROJAN HORSES AND ROOTKITS

Another fundamental element of an attacker's toolchest is the Trojan horse program. Like the Trojan horse of ancient Greece, these new Trojan horses appear to have some useful function, but in reality are just disguising some malicious activity. For example, a user may receive an executable birthday card program in electronic mail. When the unsuspecting user activates the birthday card program and watches birthday cakes dance across the screen, the program secretly installs a backdoor or perhaps deletes the users' hard drive. As illustrated in this example, Trojan horses rely on deception. They trick a user or system administrator into running them for their (apparent) usefulness, but their true purpose is to attack the user's machine.

Traditional Trojan Horses

A traditional Trojan horse is simply an independent program that can be run by a user or administrator. Numerous traditional Trojan horse programs have been devised, including:

- The familiar birthday card or holiday greeting e-mail attachment described earlier.
- A software program that claims to be able to turn CD-ROM readers into CD writing devices. Although this feat is impossible to accomplish in software, many users have been duped into downloading this tool, which promptly deletes their hard drives upon activation.
- A security vulnerability scanner, WinSATAN. This tool claims to provide a convenient security vulnerability scan for system and security administrators using a Windows NT system. Unfortunately, an unsuspecting user running this program will also have a deleted hard drive.

Countless other examples exist. While conceptually unglamorous, traditional Trojan horses can be a major problem if users are not careful and run untrusted programs on their machines.

RootKits

A RootKit takes the concept of a Trojan horse to a much more powerful level. Although the name implies otherwise, RootKits do not allow an attacker to gain root (superuser) access to a system. Instead, RootKits allow an attacker who already has superuser access to keep that access by foiling all attempts of an administrator to detect the invasion. RootKits consist of an entire suite of Trojan horse programs that replace or patch critical system programs. The various tools used by administrators to detect attackers on their machines are routinely undermined with RootKits.

Most RootKits include a Trojan horse backdoor program (in UNIX, the /bin/login routine). The attacker will install a new Trojan horse version of /bin/login, overwriting the previous version. The RootKit /bin/login routine includes a special backdoor userID and password so that the attacker can access the system at later times.

Additionally, RootKits include a sniffer and a program to hide the sniffer. An administrator can detect a sniffer on a system by running the **ifconfig** command. If a sniffer is running, the **ifconfig** output will contain the PROMISC flag, an indication that the Ethernet card is in promiscuous mode and therefore is sniffing. RootKit contains a Trojan horse version of **ifconfig** that does not display the PROMISC flag, allowing an attacker to avoid detection.

UNIX-based RootKits also replace other critical system executables, including **ps** and **du**. The **ps** command, employed by users and administrators to determine which processes are running, is modified so that an attacker can hide processes. The **du** command, which shows disk utilization, is altered so that the file space taken up by RootKit and the attacker's other programs can be masked.

By replacing programs like /bin/login, ifconfig, ps, du, and numerous others, these RootKit tools become part of the operating system itself. Therefore, RootKits are used to cover the eyes and ears of an administrator. They create a virtual world on the computer that appears benign to the system administrator, when in actuality, an attacker can log in and move around the system with impunity. RootKits have been developed for most major UNIX systems and Windows NT. A whole variety of UNIX RootKits can be found at http://packetstorm. securify.com/UNIX/penetration/rootkits, while an NT RootKit is available at http://www.rootkit.com.

One of the developments in this arena is the release of kernel-level RootKits. These RootKits act at the most fundamental levels of an operating system. Rather than replacing application programs such as /bin/login and ifconfig, kernel-level RootKits actually patch the kernel to provide very low-level access to the system. These tools rely on the loadable kernel modules that many new UNIX variants support, including Linux and Solaris. Loadable kernel modules let an administrator add functionality to the kernel on-the-fly, without even rebooting the system. An attacker with superuser access can install a kernel-level RootKit that will allow for the remapping of execution of programs.

When an administrator tries to run a program, the Trojanized kernel will remap the execution request to the attacker's program, which could be a backdoor offering access or other Trojan horse. Because the kernel does the remapping of execution requests, this type of activity is very difficult to detect. If the administrator attempts to look at the remapped file or check its integrity, the program will appear unaltered, because the program's image *is* unaltered. However, when executed, the unaltered program is skipped, and a malicious program is substituted by the kernel. Knark, written by Creed, is a kernel-level RootKit that can be found at http://packetstorm.securify.com/UNIX/penetration/ rootkits.

Trojan Horses and RootKit Defenses

To protect against traditional Trojan horses, user awareness is key. Users must understand the risks associated with downloading untrusted programs and running them. They must also be made aware of the problems of running executable attachments in e-mail from untrusted sources.

Additionally, some traditional Trojan horses can be detected and eliminated by antivirus programs. Every end-user computer system (and even servers) should have an effective and up-to-date antivirus program installed.

To defend against RootKits, system and security administrators must use integrity checking programs for critical system files. Numerous tools are available, including the venerable Tripwire, that generate a hash of the executables commonly altered when a RootKit is installed. The administrator should store these hashes on a protected medium (such as a write-protected floppy disk) and periodically check the veracity of the programs on the machine with the protected hashes. Commonly, this type of check is done at least weekly, depending on the sensitivity of the machine. The administrator must reconcile any changes discovered in these critical system files with recent patches. If system files have been altered, and no patches were installed by the administrator, a malicious user or outside attacker may have installed a RootKit. If a RootKit is detected, the safest way to ensure its complete removal is to rebuild the entire operating system and even critical applications.

Unfortunately, kernel-level RootKits cannot be detected with integrity check programs because the integrity checker relies on the underlying kernel to do its work. If the kernel lies to the integrity checker, the results will not show the RootKit installation. The best defense against the kernel-level RootKit is a monolithic kernel that does not support loadable kernel modules. On critical systems (such as firewalls, Internet web servers, Domain Name System (DNS) servers, mail servers), administrators should build the systems with complete kernels without support for loadable kernel modules. With this configuration, the system will prevent an attacker from gaining root-level access and patching the kernel in realtime.

OVERALL DEFENSES: INTRUSION DETECTION AND INCIDENT RESPONSE PROCEDURES

Each of the defensive strategies described in this entry deals with particular tools and attacks. In addition to employing each of those strategies, organizations must also be capable of detecting and responding to an attack. These capabilities are realized through the deployment of intrusion detection systems (IDSs) and the implementation of incident response procedures.

IDSs act as burglar alarms on the network. With a database of known attack signatures, IDSs can determine when an attack is underway and alert security and system administration personnel. Acting as early warning systems, IDSs allow an organization to detect an attack in its early stages and minimize the damage that may be caused.

Perhaps even more important than IDSs, documented incident response procedures are among the most critical elements of an effective security program.

Unfortunately, even with industry-best defenses, a sufficiently motivated attacker can penetrate the network. To address this possibility, an organization must have procedures defined in advance describing how the organization will react to the attack. These incident response procedures should specify the roles of individuals in the organization during an attack. The chain of command and escalation procedures should be spelled out in advance. Creating these items during a crisis will lead to costly mistakes.

Truly effective incident response procedures should also be multidisciplinary, not focusing only on information technology. Instead, the roles, responsibilities, and communication channels for the Legal, Human Resources, Media Relations, Information Technology, and Security organizations should all be documented and communicated. Specific members of these organizations should be identified as the core of a Security Incident Response Team (SIRT), to be called together to address an incident when one occurs. Additionally, the SIRT should conduct periodic exercises of the incident response capability to ensure that team members are effective in their roles.

Additionally, with a large number of organizations outsourcing their information technology infrastructure by utilizing web hosting, desktop management, e-mail, data storage, and other services, the extension of the incident response procedures to these outside organizations can be critical. The contract established with the outsourcing company should carefully state the obligations of the service provider in intrusion detection, incident notification, and participation in incident response. A specific service-level agreement for handling security incidents and the time needed to pull together members of the service company's staff in a SIRT should also be agreed upon.

CONCLUSIONS

While the number and power of these attack tools continues to escalate, system administrators and security personnel should not give up the fight. All of the defensive strategies discussed throughout this entry boil down to doing a thorough and professional job of administering systems: know what is running on the system, keep it patched, ensure appropriate bandwidth is available, utilize IDSs, and prepare a SIRT. Although these activities are not easy and can involve a great deal of effort, through diligence, an organization can keep its systems secured and minimize the chance of an attack. By employing IDSs and sound incident response procedures, even those highly sophisticated attacks that do get through can be discovered and contained, minimizing the impact on the organization. By creating an effective security program with sound defensive strategies, critical systems and information can be protected.

Hash Algorithms

Keith Pasley
PGP Security, Boonsboro, Maryland, U.S.A.

Abstract

Hash algorithms have existed in many forms at least since the 1950s. As a result of the increased value of data interactions and the increased motivation of attackers seeking to exploit electronic communications, the requirements for hash algorithms have changed. At one time, hashing was used to detect inadvertent errors generated by data processing equipment and poor communication lines. Now, secure hash algorithms are used to associate source of origin with data integrity, thus tightening the bonds of data and originator of data. So-called hashed message authentication codes (HMACs) facilitate this bonding through the use of public–private cryptography. Protocols such as transport layer security (TLS) and Internet Protocol Security (IPSec) use HMACs extensively. Over time, weaknesses in algorithms have been discovered and hash algorithms have improved in reliability and speed. The present digital economy finds that hash algorithms are useful for creating message digests and digital signatures.

There are many information-sharing applications that are in use on modern networks today. Concurrently, there are a growing number of users sharing data of increasing value to both the sender and the recipient. As the value of data increases among users of information-sharing systems, the risks of unauthorized data modification, user identity theft, fraud, unauthorized access to data, data corruption, and a host of other business-related problems mainly dealing with data integrity and user authentication are introduced. The issues of integrity and authentication play an important part in the economic systems of human society. Few would do business with companies and organizations that do not prove trustworthy or competent.

For example, the sentence "I owe Alice US$500" has a hash result of "gCWXVcL3fPV8VrJNajm8JKA ==," while the sentence "I owe Alice US$5000" has a hash result of "DSAyXRTza2bHLH46IPMrSq ==." As can be seen, there is a big difference in hash results between the two sentences. If an attacker were trying to misappropriate the $4500 difference, hashing would allow detection.

WHY HASH ALGORITHMS ARE NEEDED AND THE PROBLEMS THEY SOLVE

- Is the e-mail you received really from who it says it is?
- Can you ensure the credit card details you submit are going to the site you expected?

- Can you be sure the latest anti-virus, firewall, or operating system software upgrade you install is really from the vendor?
- Do you know if the web link you click on is genuine?
- Does the program hash the password when performing authentication or just pass it in the clear?
- Is there a way to know who you are really dealing with when disclosing your personal details over the Internet?
- Are you really you?
- Has someone modified a web page or file without authorization?
- Can you verify that your routers are forwarding data only to authorized peer routers?
- Has any of the data been modified in route to its destination?
- Can hash algorithms help answer these questions?

WHAT ARE HASH ALGORITHMS?

A hash algorithm is a one-way mathematical function that is used to compress a large block of data into a smaller, fixed-size representation of that data.

To understand the concept of hash functions, it is helpful to review some underlying mathematical structures. One such structure is called a function. When hash functions were first introduced in the 1950s, the goal was to map a message into a smaller message called a message digest. This smaller message was used as a sort of shorthand of the original message. The digest was used originally for detection of random and

Table 1 The hash function

4 * 3	12
Drop the first digit (1) leaves	2
2 * next number (3)	6
6 * next number (7)	42
Drop the first digit (4) leaves	2
2 * next number (3)	6
6 * next number (8)	48
Drop the first digit (4)	8

unintended errors in processing and transmission by data processing equipment.

Functions

A function is a mathematical structure that takes one or more variables and outputs a variable. To illustrate how scientists think about functions, one can think of a function in terms of a machine (see Table 1). The machine in this illustration has two openings. In this case the input opening is labeled x and the output opening is labeled y. These are considered traditional names for input and output. The following are the basic processing steps of mathematical functions:

1. A number goes in.
2. Something is done to it.
3. The resulting number is the output.

The same thing is done to every number input into the function machine. Step 2 earlier describes the actual mathematical transformation done to the input value, or hashed value, which yields the resulting output, or hash result. In this illustration, Step 2 can be described as a mathematical rule as follows: x + 3 = y. In the language of mathematics, if x is equal to 1, then y equals 4. Similarly, if x is equal to 2, then y equals 5. In this illustration the function, or mathematical structure, called an algorithm is: for every number x, add 3 to the number. The result, y, is dependent on what is input, x.

As another example, suppose that, to indicate an internal company product shipment, the number 43,738 is exchanged. The hash function, or algorithm, is described as: multiply each number from left to right, and the first digit of any multiplied product above 9 is dropped. The hash function could be illustrated in mathematical notation as: x * the number to the right = y (see Table 1).

The input into a hash algorithm can be of variable length, but the output is usually of fixed length and somewhat shorter in length than the original message. The output of a hash function is called a message digest. In the case of the preceding, the hash input was of arbitrary (and variable) length; but the hash result, or message digest, was of a fixed length of 1 digit, 8. As

can be seen, a hash function provides a shorthand representation of the original message. This is also the concept behind error checking (checksums) done on data transmitted across communication links. Checksums provide a nonsecure method to check for message accuracy or message integrity. It is easy to see how the relatively weak mathematical functions described earlier could be manipulated by an intruder to change the hash output. Such weak algorithms could result in the successful alteration of message content leading to inaccurate messages. If you can understand the concept of what a function is and does, you are on your way to understanding the basic concepts embodied in hash functions. Providing data integrity and authentication for such applications requires reliable, secure hash algorithms.

Secure Hash Algorithms

A hash algorithm was defined earlier as a one-way mathematical function that is used to compress a large block of data into a smaller, fixed size representation of that data. An early application for hashing was in detecting unintentional errors in data processing. However, due to the critical nature of their use in the high-security environments of today, hash algorithms must now also be resilient to deliberate and malicious attempts to break secure applications by highly motivated human attackers—more so than by erroneous data processing. The one-way nature of hash algorithms is one of the reasons they are used in public key cryptography. A one-way hash function processes a bit stream in a manner that makes it highly unlikely that the original message can be deduced by the output value. This property of a secure hash algorithm has significance in situations where there is zero tolerance for unauthorized data modification or if the identity of an object needs to be validated with a high assurance of accuracy. Applications such as user authentication and financial transactions are made more trustworthy by the use of hash algorithms.

Hash algorithms are called secure if they have the following properties:

- The hash result should not be predictable. It should be computationally impractical to recover the original message from the message digest (one-way property).
- No two different messages, over which a hash algorithm is applied, will result in the same digest (collision-free property).

Secure hash algorithms are designed so that any change to a message will have a high probability of resulting in a different message digest. As such, the message alteration can be detected by comparing hash

Table 2 Output bit lengths

Hash algorithm	Output bit length
SHA-1	160
SHA-256	256
SHA-384	384
SHA-512	512

results before and after hashing. The receiver can tell that a message has suspect validity by the fact that the message digest computed by the sender does not match the message digest computed by the receiver, assuming both parties are using the same hash algorithm. The most common hash algorithms as of this writing are based on Secure Hash Algorithm-1 (SHA-1) and Message Digest 5 (MD5).

Secure Hash Algorithm-1

SHA-1, part of the Secure Hash Standard (SHS), was one of the earliest hash algorithms specified for use by the U.S. federal government (see Table 2). SHA-1 was developed by the National Institute of Standards and Technology (NIST) and the National Security Agency. SHA-1 was published as a federal government standard in 1995. SHA-1 was an update to the SHA, which was published in 1993.

How SHA-1 Works. Think of SHA-1 as a hash machine that has two openings, input and output. The input value is called the hashed value, and the output is called the hash result. The hashed values are the bit streams that represent an electronic message or other data object. The SHA-1 hash function, or algorithm, transforms the hashed value by performing a mathematical operation on the input data. The length of the message is the same as the number of bits in the message. The SHA-1 algorithm processes blocks of 512 bits in sequence when computing the message digest. SHA-1 produces a 160-bit message digest. SHA-1 has a limitation on input message size of less than 18 quintillion (i.e., 2^{64} or 18,446,744,073,709,551,616) bits in length.

SHA-1 has five steps to produce a message digest:

1. Append padding to make message length 64 bits less than a multiple of 512.
2. Append a 64-bit block representing the length of the message before padding out.
3. Initialize message digest buffer with five hexadecimal numbers. These numbers are specified in the FIPS 180-1 publication.
4. The message is processed in 512-bit blocks. This process consists of 80 steps of processing (four rounds of 20 operations), reusing four different

hexadecimal constants, and some shifting and adding functions.
5. Output blocks are processed into a 160-bit message digest.

MD5

SHA was derived from the secure hash algorithms MD4 and MD5, developed by Professor Ronald L. Rivest of MIT in the early 1990s. As can be expected, SHA and MD5 work in a similar fashion. While SHA-1 yields a 160-bit message digest, MD5 yields a 128-bit message digest. SHA-1, with its longer message digest, is considered more secure than MD5 by modern cryptography experts, due in part to the longer output bit length and resulting increased collision resistance. However, MD5 is still in common use as of this writing.

Keyed Hash (HMAC)

Modern cryptographers have found the hash algorithms discussed earlier to be insufficient for extensive use in commercial cryptographic systems or in private electronic communications, digital signatures, electronic mail, electronic funds transfer, software distribution, data storage, and other applications that require data integrity assurance, data origin authentication, and the like. The use of asymmetric cryptography and, in some cases, symmetric cryptography has extended the usefulness of hashing by associating identity with a hash result. The structure used to convey the property of identity (data origin) with a data object's integrity is the hashed message authentication code (HMAC), or keyed hash.

For example, how does one know if the message and the message digest have not been tampered with? One way to provide a higher degree of assurance of identity and integrity is by incorporating a cryptographic key into the hash operation. This is the basis of the keyed hash or HMAC. The purpose of a message authentication code (MAC) is to provide verification of the source of a message and integrity of the message without using additional mechanisms. Other goals of HMAC are as follows:

- To use available cryptographic hash functions without modification
- To preserve the original performance of the selected hash without significant degradation
- To use and handle keys in a simple way
- To have a well-understood cryptographic analysis of the strength of the mechanism based on reasonable assumptions about the underlying hash function
- To enable easy replacement of the hash function in case a faster or stronger hash is found or required

To create an HMAC, an asymmetric (public/private) or a symmetric cryptographic key can be appended to a message and then processed through a hash function to derive the HMAC. In mathematical terms, if x = (key + message) and f = SHA-1, then f(x) = HMAC. Any hash function can be used, depending on the protocol defined, to compute the type of message digest called an HMAC. The two most common hash functions are based on MD5 and SHA. The message data and HMAC (message digest of a secret key and message) are sent to the receiver. The receiver processes the message and the HMAC using the shared key and the same hash function as that used by the originator. The receiver compares the results with the HMAC included with the message. If the two results match, then the receiver is assured that the message is authentic and came from a member of the community that shares the key.

Other examples of HMAC usage include challenge–response authentication protocols such as the Challenge Handshake Authentication Protocol (CHAP, RFC 1994). CHAP is defined as a peer entity authentication method for Point-to-Point Protocol (PPP), using a randomly generated challenge and requiring a matching response that depends on a cryptographic hash of the challenge and a secret key. Challenge–Response Authentication Mechanism (CRAM, RFC 2195), which specifies an HMAC using MD5, is a mechanism for authenticating Internet Mail Access Protocol (IMAP4) users. Digital signatures, used to authenticate data origin and integrity, employ HMAC functions as part of the "signing" process. A digital signature is created as follows:

1. A message (or some other data object) is input into a hash function (i.e., SHA-1, MD5, etc.).
2. The hash result is encrypted by the private key of the sender.

The result of these two steps yields what is called a *digital signature* of the message or data object. The properties of a cryptographic hash ensure that, if the data object is changed, the digital signature will no longer match it. There is a difference between a digital signature and an HMAC. An HMAC uses a shared secret key (symmetric cryptography) to "sign" the data object, whereas a digital signature is created by using a private key from a private–public key pair (asymmetric cryptography) to sign the data object. The strengths of digital signatures lend themselves to use in high-value

applications that require protection against forgery and fraud.

See Table 3 for other hash algorithms.

HOW HASH ALGORITHMS ARE USED IN MODERN CRYPTOGRAPHIC SYSTEMS

In the past, hash algorithms were used for rudimentary data integrity and user authentication; today hash algorithms are incorporated into other protocols—digital signatures, virtual private network (VPN) protocols, software distribution and license control, web page file modification detection, database file system integrity, and software update integrity verification are just a few. Hash algorithms used in hybrid cryptosystems are discussed next.

Transport Layer Security

Transport layer security (TLS) is a network security protocol that is designed to provide data privacy and data integrity between two communicating applications. TLS was derived from the earlier Secure Sockets Layer (SSL) protocol developed by Netscape in the early 1990s. TLS is defined in IETF RFC 2246. TLS and SSL do not interoperate due to differences between the protocols. However, TLS 1.0 does have the ability to drop down to the SSL protocol during initial session negotiations with an SSL client. Deference is given to TLS by developers of most modern security applications. The security features designed into the TLS protocol include hashing.

The TLS protocol is composed of two layers:

1. The Record Protocol provides in-transit data privacy by specifying that symmetric cryptography be used in TLS connections. Connection reliability is accomplished by the Record Protocol through the use of HMACs.
2. TLS Handshake Protocol (really a suite of three subprotocols). The Handshake Protocol is encapsulated within the Record Protocol. The TLS Handshake Protocol handles connection parameter establishment. The Handshake Protocol also provides for peer identity verification in TLS through the use of asymmetric (public/private) cryptography.

Table 3 Other hash algorithms

Hash algorithm	Output bit length	Country
RIPEMD (160,256,320)	160, 256, 320	Germany, Belgium
HAS-160	160	Korea
Tiger	128, 160, 192	United Kingdom

There are several uses of keyed hash algorithms (HMAC) within the TLS protocol.

TLS uses HMAC in a conservative fashion. The TLS specification calls for the use of both HMAC MD5 and HMAC SHA-1 during the Handshake Protocol negotiation. Throughout the protocol, two hash algorithms are used to increase the security of various parameters:

- Pseudorandom number function
- Protect record payload data
- Protect symmetric cryptographic keys (used for bulk data encrypt/decrypt)
- Part of the mandatory cipher suite of TLS

If any of the preceding parameters were not protected by security mechanisms such as HMACs, an attacker could thwart the electronic transaction between two or more parties. The TLS protocol is the basis for most web-based in-transit security schemes. As can be seen by this example, hash algorithms provide an intrinsic security value to applications that require secure in-transit communication using the TLS protocol.

IPSec

The Internet Protocol Security (IPSec) protocol was designed as the packet-level security layer included in IPv6. IPv6 is a replacement TCP/IP protocol suite for IPv4. IPSec itself is flexible and modular in design, which allows the protocol to be used in IPv4 implementations. Unlike the session-level security of TLS, IPSec provides packet-level security. VPN applications such as intranet and remote access use IPSec for communications security.

Two protocols are used in IPSec operations: Authentication Header (AH) and Encapsulating Security Payload (ESP). Among other things, ESP is used to provide data origin authentication and connectionless integrity. Data origin authentication and connectionless integrity are joint services and are offered as an option in the implementation of the ESP. RFC 2406, which defines the ESP used in IPSec, states that either HMAC or one-way hash algorithms may be used in implementations. The authentication algorithms are used to create the integrity check value (ICV) used to authenticate an ESP packet of data. HMACs ensure the rapid detection and rejection of bogus or replayed packets. Also, because the authentication value is passed in the clear, HMACs are mandatory if the data authentication feature of ESP is used. If data authentication is used, the sender computes the integrity check value (ICV) over the ESP packet contents minus the authentication data. After receiving an IPSec data packet, the receiver computes and compares the ICV of the received datagrams. If they are the same, then the datagram is authentic; if not, then

the data is not valid, it is discarded, and the event can be logged. MD5 and SHA-1 are the supported authentication algorithms.

The AH protocol provides data authentication for as much of the IP header as possible. Portions of the IP header are not authenticated due to changes to the fields that are made as a matter of routing the packet to its destination. The use of HMAC by the ESP has, according to IPSec VPN vendors, negated the need for AH.

Digital Signatures

Digital signatures serve a similar purpose as those of written signatures on paper—to prove the authenticity of a document. Unlike a pen-and-paper signature, a digital signature can also prove that a message has not been modified. HMACs play an important role in providing the property of integrity to electronic documents and transactions. Briefly, the process for creating a digital signature is very much like creating an HMAC. A message is created, and the message and the sender's private key (asymmetric cryptography) serve as inputs to a hash algorithm. The hash result is attached to the message. The sender creates a symmetric session encryption key to optionally encrypt the document. The sender then encrypts the session key with the sender's private key, re-encrypts it with the receiver's public key to ensure that only the receiver can decrypt the session key, and attaches the signed session key to the document. The sender then sends the digital envelope (keyed hash value, encrypted session key, and the encrypted message) to the intended receiver. The receiver performs the entire process in reverse order. If the results match when the receiver decrypts the document and combines the sender's public key with the document through the specified hash algorithm, the receiver is assured that: 1) the message came from the original sender; and 2) the message has not been altered. The first case is due to use of the sender's private key as part of the hashed value. In asymmetric cryptography, a mathematical relationship exists between the public and private keys such that either can encrypt and decrypt; but the same key cannot both encrypt and decrypt the same item. The private key is known only to its owner. As such, only the owner of the private key could have used it to develop the HMAC.

Other Applications

HMACs are useful when there is a need to validate software that is downloaded from download sites. HMACs are used in logging onto various operating systems, including UNIX. When the user enters a password, the password is usually run through a hash algorithm; and the hashed result is compared to a user database or password file.

An interesting use of hash algorithms to prevent software piracy is in the Windows XP registration process. SHA-1 is used to develop the installation ID used to register the software with Microsoft.

During installation of Windows XP, the computer hardware is identified, reduced to binary representation, and hashed using MD5. The hardware hash is an eight-byte value that is created by running 10 different pieces of information from the PC's hardware components through the MD5 algorithm. This means that the resultant hash value cannot be backward-calculated to determine the original values. Further, only a portion of the resulting hash value is used in the hardware hash to ensure complete anonymity.

Unauthorized file modification such as web page defacement, system file modification, virus signature update, signing XML documents, and signing database keys are all applications for which various forms of hashing can increase security levels.

PROBLEMS WITH HASH ALGORITHMS

Flaws have been discovered in various hash algorithms. One such basic flaw is called the birthday attack.

Birthday Attack

This attack's name comes from the world of probability theory that out of any random group of 23 people, it is probable that at least two share a birthday. Finding two numbers that have the same hash result is known as the birthday attack. If hash function f maps into message digests of length 60 bits, then an attacker can find a collision using only 230 inputs ($2^{f/2}$). Differential cryptanalysis has proven to be effective against one round of MD5. (There are four rounds of transformation defined in the MD5 algorithm.) When choosing a hash algorithm, the speed of operation is often a priority. For example, in asymmetric (public/private) cryptography, a message may be hashed into a message digest as a data integrity enhancement. However, if the message is large, it can take some time to compute a hash result. In consideration of this, a review of speed benchmarks would give a basis for choosing one algorithm over another. Of course, implementation in hardware is usually faster than in a software-based algorithm.

LOOKING TO THE FUTURE

SHA-256, -384, and -512

In the summer of 2001, NIST published for public comment a proposed update to the SHS used by the U.S. government. Although SHA-1 appears to still be part of SHS, the update includes the recommendation to use hash algorithms with longer hash results. Longer hash results increase the work factor needed to break cryptographic hashing. This update of the Secure Hash Standard coincides with another NIST update—selection of the Rijndael symmetric cryptography algorithm for U.S. government use for encrypting data. According to NIST, it is thought that the cryptographic strength of Rijndael requires the higher strength of the new SHS algorithms. The new SHS algorithms feature similar functions but different structures. Newer and more secure algorithms, such as SHA-256, -384, and -512, may be integrated into the IPSec specification in the future to complement the Advanced Encryption Standard (AES), Rijndael. In May 2002, NIST announced that the Rijndael algorithm had been selected as the AES standard, FIPS 197.

SUMMARY

Hash algorithms have existed in many forms at least since the 1950s. As a result of the increased value of data interactions and the increased motivation of attackers seeking to exploit electronic communications, the requirements for hash algorithms have changed. At one time, hashing was used to detect inadvertent errors generated by data processing equipment and poor communication lines. Now, secure hash algorithms are used to associate the source of origin with data integrity, thus tightening the bonds of data and originator of data. So-called hashed message authentication codes (HMACs) facilitate this bonding through the use of public–private cryptography. Protocols such as transport layer security (TLS) and Internet Protocol Security (IPSec) use HMACs extensively. Over time, weaknesses in algorithms have been discovered and hash algorithms have improved in reliability and speed. The present digital economy finds that hash algorithms are useful for creating message digests and digital signatures.

BIBLIOGRAPHY

1. http://www.deja.com/group/sci.crypt.

Healthcare Informatics

Stephan Kudyba
New Jersey Institute of Technology, Newark, New Jersey, U.S.A.

Richard Temple
AristaCare Health Services, South Plainfield, New Jersey, U.S.A.

Abstract

The healthcare industry is in the unique position of holding a wealth of personal information, bound by strict privacy requirements. One way to better manage the complex nature of this industry is through the incorporation of information technologies. More and more, informatics can and does provide value in a multitude of different care settings and in a number of different operational processes. Organizations invariably will derive significant benefits from having a mechanism to generate an accurate read of data on all fronts and being able to turn that data into actionable information.

Healthcare is probably one of the most complex business models in American industry given the uniqueness of the marketplace in which it operates. It is perhaps the only industry where the consumer does not necessarily pay for the service he or she receives, but rather third parties (in this case, insurance companies) negotiate arrangements with service providers to determine payment rates and types of service that are to be paid on the consumer's behalf. The nature of the services required corresponds to a variety of ailments that are attributed to vast numbers of patients—factors that add to the mix of issues to manage. Complexities for healthcare organizations are heightened when considering the numerous data exchanges that are involved with services provided to patients. Data exchanges can be plagued by myriad formats, captured, and stored in a variety of repositories. These exchanges introduce further complexities in the form of "vocabularies," or in other words, the coding languages that are required to identify types of services that vary considerably from payer to payer, state to state, and service type to service type. Also, data in general come from a multitude of different "niche" systems and are presented in many different ways (e.g., text reports, spreadsheets, ANSI X12 formats, etc.) and need to be integrated and presented to a caregiver or analyst in a consistent and coherent manner. It is the combination of all these factors that begins to describe the underpinnings of the spectrum of healthcare informatics.

Data provide the building blocks to information, a vital resource to administrators, practitioners, and decision makers in healthcare organizations. The process of transforming data into information is a daunting task, and given the complexities described earlier, the task is particularly challenging in this unique industry. This challenge must be managed, as healthcare is one segment of American industry where incorrect decisions or errors can cost lives or put innocent people in significant danger. The need to understand what patterns of treatment for a variety of different conditions will produce the best outcomes is profound. Adding to the challenge are the financial burdens healthcare providers are experiencing, as reimbursements are being cut and more and more conditions are being mandated in order to pay for services rendered. Healthcare organizations invariably lose money on certain classes of patients, and it is critical to understand where those areas are and how to address them.

INFORMATION TECHNOLOGY, INFORMATICS, AND HEALTHCARE PRODUCTIVITY

One way to better manage the complex nature of this industry is through the incorporation of information technologies. Web platforms, data storage, analytic software, telecom and wireless communications systems, etc., can help provide critical information and speed information dissemination to those who require it, when they require it.

During the mid-1990s, organizations across industry sectors retooled their information technology infrastructures in response to dramatic innovations in storage, processing, analytics, and bandwidth (see Table 1). The enhanced capabilities facilitated by these technologies offered organizations opportunities to increase productivity in a variety of ways. Factors such as the dissemination of critical information to decision makers

Encyclopedia of Information Systems and Technology, DOI: 10.1081/E-EIST-120053823

Table 1 Growth in investment in information technologies

Year	Investment in Information Technology as a Proportion of Industrial Equipment and Software (%)
1980	30.7
1990	41.1
1999	47.2

Source: From Economic Report of the President 2001, Table B-18, p. 296.

regarding process performance; the ability to communicate within organizations, across industry sectors, and on the global spectrum; and simplifying procedures, to name a few, enabled organizations to better manage available resources in providing a good or service to the ultimate consumer.

The significant investment in information technologies was initially questioned by many as to the payoff or gains from these dollar outlays for hardware, software, telecom platforms, etc. This debate sparked myriad research from the academic and private sector arenas to investigate the potential gains to IT. Resulting studies illustrated positive returns to investment in information technologies by firms operating across industry sectors.[1–3] On a macroeconomic perspective, U. S. productivity grew dramatically from levels achieved over the previous decade (see Fig. 1).

This jump in productivity enabled the U. S. economy to grow at a robust pace without experiencing a noteworthy acceleration to price inflation as gains in efficiency helped reduce costs throughout the economic system (see Fig. 2). These productivity gains have been maintained as companies continue to invest in and apply information technologies in a variety of process-enhancing ways.

One industry, however, lagged behind the strong pulse in leveraging information technology, and this involved healthcare organizations. The fragmented nature of the industry is often cited as a reason for the lag in technological implementations along with the adherence to traditional paper-based procedural modes of operations.

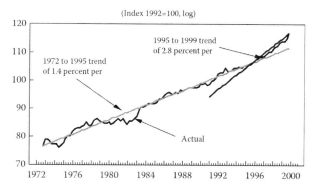

Fig. 1 The trend rate of nonfarm productivity growth accelerated.
Source: From U.S. Department of Labor, Bureau of Labor.

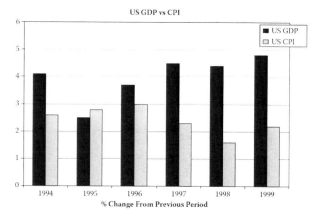

Fig. 2 U.S. GDP data: U.S. Commerce Department Bureau of Economic Analysis; U.S. Consumer Price Index: U.S. Department of Labor, Bureau of Labor Statistics.

The structure of the industry involving numerous individual hospitals and health-related entities created a dichotomous environment that involved diverse naming procedures and formatting standards of and breakdowns in the ability to share critical data resources. Paper-based methods of operations (e.g., charting by physicians and nurses) limited the creation of vital data resources that describe critical treatment activities of patients.

These factors reduced gains in efficiency that otherwise could be achieved based on network effects of information sharing. In other words, the lack of data resources and the existence of disparate data resources involving diverse naming conventions existing in a variety of storage devices corresponding to separate providers of health services (e.g., hospitals, clinics, and private practices) deter the ability of healthcare organizations to create robust information resources from available data. With only pieces of the puzzle (e.g., data existing in isolated systems, information in paper-based form), healthcare providers are limited in the amount of information available to them when attempting to enhance their knowledge regarding service effectiveness and efficiency.

To further clarify this point, we need to turn to the evolution of the Internet. Forms of the Internet were actually in existence well before the information boom of the 1990s (e.g., the government ARPANET was in existence in the 1970s). However, the true gains in efficiency resulting from utilization of the Internet for consumers and businesses alike were not achieved until network effects took hold. This refers to the fact that the network of users who had access to the Internet needed to reach critical mass.[4] As more and more consumers and businesses had access to the Internet, it became a viable mechanism to communicate and conduct commerce. In comparison, as data resources in the healthcare industry become more standardized and integrated within health organizations and across systems of corresponding service providers, the ability to extract information from and generate knowledge regarding better allocating resources to enhance process efficiencies in financial, clinical, and administrative activities should increase dramatically. The result should be less wasted resources, enhanced process performance, and a lower-cost operating environment.[5]

Given the consolidation of individual providers into systems of providers (e.g., healthcare systems); advancements in hardware, software, telecom, and Internet-based technologies; the ability of treatment and diagnosis-based technologies to help enhance data capture; the creation of digital data resources from paper-based procedures; and enhanced data input and communication of information, healthcare providers are on the cusp of experiencing increased operational efficiencies that will enable them to manage their cost structure while providing the best care possible to patients. The incorporation of billing and financial-related technologies, decision support systems, data management, and analytic capabilities enables healthcare providers to enhance their ability to identify misallocations of resources and increase the effectiveness and speed of processes in administrative, financial, and clinical activities.

Enhanced efficiencies made possible by investment in information technologies could result in significant cost savings to healthcare providers. These gains are critical in addressing the ongoing growth in healthcare expenditures in the United States, which now account for roughly 17% of GDP. If productivity gains from investment in information technologies experienced in other industries are achieved in the healthcare sector, savings in the form of reduced expenditures could exceed $300 billion.[6] Investment in technologies that seek to promote a more automated delivery system through workflow and medical records systems, evidenced-based decision support systems, integration of information between healthcare providers, and streamlining the claims-based transactions billing system to an all-electronic payment at point of service system can yield substantial savings to healthcare providers and ultimately the consumer/patient.[7]

PRODUCTIVITY, EFFICIENCY, AND THE UNIQUENESS OF HEALTHCARE

Despite the fact that the healthcare industry possesses unique characteristics from those of other sectors (e.g., doctor–patient relationships and the ultimate objective of providing the best quality of care to patients that can override established business profit optimization goals), healthcare still entails procedures and processes that can be made more efficient.

Technologies can help providers discover more effective treatment tactics that may reduce ineffective, redundant, and unnecessary tests and procedures that inconvenience the patient and the provider and increase costs. They can reduce bottlenecks in administrative processes that can alleviate waiting times for patients and direct them to the most appropriate areas to address their problems. They can alleviate complexities in billing activities that can result in overbilling recipients. Technologies can help enhance preemptive treatment to mitigate illnesses from developing into fully developed chronic diseases.

Some critics of applying management and business concepts in the healthcare sector argue that treating patients should not be considered a business. They argue that these initiatives could adversely affect patient treatment and care as the quest for achieving enhanced operational performance may dictate procedures. The answer to this critique lies in monitoring the overall activities of health providers, and this process includes enhancing the patient experience. The bottom line to all these capabilities is helping allocate the correct resources to the demand for those resources. Accomplishing this helps preserve the essence of healthcare organizations and those individuals involved in providing treatment for patients. With the aid of accurate and timely information, and the ability to communicate and apply that information, physicians, nurses, technicians, and administrators can improve the process of caring for those in need in a more efficient, less costly manner. Techniques and methodologies that create, disseminate, and analyze data comprise the realm of informatics. Two basic definitions of informatics are provided to clarify what is meant by this concept.

Informatics: The sciences concerned with gathering, manipulating, storing, retrieving, and classifying recorded information.

   Source: From http://wordnetweb.princeton.edu/perl/webwn

Health informatics or medical informatics is the intersection of information science, computer science, and health care. It deals with the resources, devices, and methods required to optimize the acquisition, storage, retrieval, and use of information in health and biomedicine. Health informatics tools include not only computers but also clinical guidelines, formal medical terminologies, and information and communication systems.

   Source: Wikipedia

EFFECTIVE INFORMATICS THROUGH MANAGEMENT THEORY

Pure investment in information technologies is not the final solution to enabling providers to operate more productively. Applications in management theory are essential to ensure effective implementation and utilization of these technologies to best leverage their capabilities to increase labor and process productivity. Management theory that must be considered includes strategic management, management information systems, project management, knowledge management (KM) and organizational behavioral, quantitative techniques, and decision support theory, to name a few. These management concepts focus on the acquisition of technologies that provide the correct functionality to facilitate a particular process and proper implementation of the technology to ensure its proper utilization (this includes creating a receptive culture within the organization by users to adopt the platform as an essential tool to enhance their daily routines). Theoretical concepts also address analyzing, communicating, and best utilization of the results and outputs of systems that are used.

Project and KM

Project management addresses methods that support successful implementations of information technologies. It addresses the incorporation of correct tactics to acquire the most appropriate technology platform to facilitate an organizational need in the most seamless way possible. For example, when a healthcare provider wants to implement a new database system that facilitates the conversion of paper-based routines into digital assets for clinical and treatment activities, the organization must consider which technology best offers the most feasible functionality corresponding to the operational structure of the organization. This includes the cost of the technology, scalability, ability to integrate with existing systems, and user friendliness. Once the technology is chosen, factors to promote the most seamless integration into the work environment must be considered. This includes timing schedules, training for users, and eventual complete rollout to the workforce. KM theory overlaps project management to some extent when considering the implementation stages of new technologies. It addresses the additional critical factors of ensuring the system's adoption by users with the ultimate goal that it becomes a key component to the everyday activities of its users and stakeholders. KM also addresses those factors that support leveraging the output produced by users working with systems and the dissemination and collaboration of corresponding information among individuals connected to processes and procedures. In other works, KM theory promotes the active utilization of information and creation of knowledge within an organization, concepts that drive best practices, and innovation.[8,9]

Other management-related concepts also must be considered in attempting to best leverage information technologies, and these involve such strategic initiatives as Six Sigma, total quality management, supply chain management, and workflow optimization, and advanced analytics such as data mining. The process of treating a patient incorporates a network of activities that are complementary and interdependent in nature, where breakdowns in aspects of one operational entity can cause disruptions to the overall process of patient care. The patient treatment process can include diagnosis, prescription of medications, radiology and lab tests, administration of treatment procedures, monitoring of results and outcomes, etc. These activities include input from numerous personnel in corresponding operational departments in the healthcare organization. Workflow analytic methodologies must be considered to better understand the efficiencies of the entire treatment process. The overall process can be compared to managing a supply chain or supply network of activities that are complementary and interdependent with the ultimate objective of achieving the best allocation of available resources to provide the best care to corresponding patients. These management methodologies can be augmented with the incorporation of statistical and quantitative-based analytics such as the Six Sigma approach.

Six Sigma and Data Mining

Six Sigma is an analytic method that leverages available data resources and incorporates statistical applications and visual capabilities to monitor process variance and efficiencies. By analyzing data resources corresponding to various operational processes with the utilization of statistical techniques, analysts can better determine which types of practices result in unacceptable variances in performance metrics.[10] For example, are there bottlenecks in the network of activities in the radiology department that produce high time delay variances in getting x-ray results back to an attending physician? More robust and sophisticated techniques to analyze data involve the utilization of quantitative methods to process data and statistical testing to determine patterns and trends that may exist in particular service activities. Traditional regression methods and data mining methodologies enable analysts to better identify reoccurring trends in the various activities of healthcare services. Resulting models can determine whether particular treatment procedures result in enhanced health outcomes according to patient populations, whether particular procedural activities result in unacceptable outcome measures, etc.

Business Intelligence and Decision Support Systems

Other methods of data analysis that can help increase the knowledge of healthcare practitioners involves the more simple creation and presentation of reports and graphics through online analytic processing and dashboards. The advantage of these methods is that they focus on presenting data in a timely and understandable manner, where decision makers can quickly view these analytic platforms to identify factors impacting operational performances.

These various data-driven software technologies and initiatives comprise the realm of decision support systems and business intelligence. The functionalities of the components, including report generation, trend and pattern detection, quantitative and statistical-based analytics, complemented with graphical interfaces provide users/decision makers in various functional areas of healthcare organizations with timely, actionable information to enhance strategizing. Informatics to improve efficiencies includes optimizing resource allocations corresponding to a variety of activities and procedures. The utilization of decision support systems and business intelligence that leverage essential data resources can ultimately help reduce lag times in patients waiting for treatment, adjust treatment procedures to enhance outcomes, reduce inefficiencies in billing, reduce lag times in lab and radiology exam completion and reporting times, etc. The ultimate result is better management of healthcare operations and costs and care effectiveness and outcomes for patients.

FOUR AREAS OF FOCUS FOR HEALTHCARE EFFICIENCIES

With all of the turbulence existing in the healthcare landscape, it is little wonder that healthcare organizations are embracing the potential of leveraging information technologies and informatics and their ability to enhance efficiencies. Informatics applications and capabilities within the healthcare spectrum can be categorized into four discrete areas:

- Financial: Tracking activity-based costing, ensuring that services rendered are properly billed and compensated, and that expenses stay within acceptable budgetary parameters.
- Clinical compliance: Ensuring that the appropriate procedures are applied to the right patient at the right time, making sure that staffing patterns and other reportable parameters are within acceptable mandated bounds, and alerting as quickly as possible when they are not.

- Quality improvement: Analyzing clinical data to see which treatment protocols provide the best outcomes in an economically sustainable way.
- Patient satisfaction/marketing: What aspects of a patient's stay were problematic—how are those measured, identified, and remedied for the future?

The following sections will take a quick look at each of these areas to give a broader sense of just how informatics can be so important in managing the critical factors that healthcare leadership needs to better understand in order to properly manage their respective organizations.

FINANCIAL ACTIVITIES

Hospitals and many other healthcare providers have undergone a drastic transformation during the last 15–20 years. This transformation is characterized by the change in environment, as is evidenced by organizations who saw their role almost as benevolent charities whose mission it was to provide care to all without particular regard to reimbursement (the guiding assumption was "if you bill it, they will pay"), to rough-and-tumble competitive businesses who needed to track all aspects of financial performance to satisfy their boards, shareholders, and other organizational stakeholders. Over this period of time, large public companies or large organizations have invested significant sums and acquired many healthcare organizations with the expectation of receiving an aggressive return on their investments. Also, during this time, regulations on healthcare payers were loosened, which helped spark the managed care (Health Maintenance Organization) and "capitated payment" (fixed monthly payment to providers not directly tied to specific visits) movements. As more players entered the healthcare space with specific bottom-line interests, reimbursement schemas became increasingly more complex; more entities needed to be measured (e.g., are we getting more in monthly capitated payments than we are paying out in actual patient encounters?). With all this going on, one can only imagine how critical it became to understand in great detail what one's reimbursement and cost foundation was, where timeliness and accuracy of information describing these activities were critical to determine potential trends over time. Modeling capabilities needed to be generated to analyze corresponding data, and alert mechanisms needed to be incorporated to highlight what key indicators breached certain predetermined levels.

Computerized financial systems have been in existence in healthcare for decades. Their ability to generate data and report-driven balance sheets, profit-and-loss statements, and other relevant accounting reports points to an acute need for informatics—for instance, many hospitals, especially not-for-profit systems, finance growth and other capital initiatives through the use of fixed income securities (e.g., bonds), many of which may be guaranteed by a governmental or quasi-governmental authority. There are conditions attached to many of these securities that if certain key financial indicators breach agreed-upon values, sanctions may be invoked that may include deeming these bonds as in "technical default." This can have far-reaching implications for organizations in terms of ongoing financial viability, future access to credit, and changes in administrative personnel or on board membership in impacted organizations. It is critical for an organization to be able to, at the very least, access vital information that would indicate whether variances in financial metrics exceeded pre-established thresholds of acceptance and, also, to know *in advance* that trends among various other key indicators may be leading the organization to this precipice.

There are also financial metrics that are unique to healthcare that speak of how efficiently the organization is being run and, indirectly, what the quality of care is likely to be based on, important factors such as staffing patterns. Some of the metrics that are typically tracked include "full-time equivalent employees per occupied bed" (e.g., is the organization staffing its units commensurate with the patient volume on those units?), "net revenue" versus "net cash collected" (is the organization getting properly reimbursed for what it thinks it is rightfully owed for the services it renders?), and productive hours and agency hours (e.g., is the organization having to rely on expensive and less predictable agency nursing to fulfill its regulated staffing requirements), to name a few.

With the advent of managed care and capitated contracts with payers, a whole new realm of tracking becomes critical. These types of contracts have become increasingly more complicated over the years, and it can be a challenge for an organization to have an accurate sense of the correct monetary allocation for particular types of services. Issues such as what services may not be reimbursable, what services may qualify as "outliers," and under what circumstances "extraordinary" services would entitle the organization to reimbursement over and above the agreed upon base rate from the payer may need to be considered. Contract management systems surfaced during the 1990s to address this new paradigm and have, over the years, become a much more important part of a healthcare organization's informatics tool kit. Combining information from contract management systems, such as gauging receipts for particular services by particular payers with financial decision support systems, becomes strategic for healthcare providers. Tracking both revenue as a whole and costs per different types of services

(e.g., activity-based costing) and disseminating profitability information of different aspects of managed care contracts to decision makers provide the strategic information to implementing more effective initiatives.

COMPLIANCE ISSUES

The next area in which informatics could yield significant efficiencies involves the realm of clinical compliance. There are important regulations that can impact an institution's accreditation status if procedures are not strictly adhered to.

Organizations such as the Joint Commission or the Department of Health have very stringent and detailed regulations as to the exact protocols that need to be followed under different care circumstances. Also, governmental entities are reporting on websites accessible to the public the different levels of compliance of organizations to protocol standards. This can translate into lost revenue, lost market share, or diminished stature for those who underperform their competitors by registering subpar results of relevant indicators. For instance, at a relatively basic level, any patient who enters a facility exhibiting signs of respiratory problems is supposed to be given smoking cessation counseling. Another example is that any patient presenting at a hospital with signs of a cardiac event is to be given an aspirin right away. These are basic care guidelines that are universally recognized as being important in ensuring that a patient has a desired health outcome. The challenge, however, arises when considering how an entity can capture this type of data and disseminate reports that indicate whether rules are complied with or not. With this information, organizations can take strategic initiatives to mitigate any undesirable performance variances.

There are also important factors to consider regarding the time and allocation of resources to minimize the risk of complications to certain classes of patients. For instance, certain patients can be identified as having an elevated risk of skin integrity issues (pressure ulcers, etc.) based on a test that yields what is referred to as a Braden score. Patients with a Braden score in excess of a certain threshold must have their caregivers turn them in their beds once every 2 hours in order to avoid negative health outcomes resulting from staying in one position for too long. Best-of-class healthcare providers are going to want to know: (1) Did they properly identify all patients who were at risk for pressure ulcers; and (2) did they administer the correct procedure to those patients once identified as an at-risk population candidate?

Another commonly tracked factor in a patient population is individuals that are classified in the "falls risk" category. In other words, based on one or two different scales used by providers, patients can be identified as having a greater risk of falling, which means more risk of complications, longer (unreimbursed) lengths of stay, broken limbs, and ultimately perhaps, increased legal liability exposure for the organization. Informatics, at an operational level, identifies falls risk patients and facilitates analysis of other aspects of electronic medical records (EMRs) to ensure that proper protocols are in place to mitigate the negative ramifications of falls risk.

Individuals often think of informatics as management reporting—something that is reported after the fact and is based on a particular retrospective point of view. While this aspect of informatics is necessary, its real incremental power is to provide timely information to individuals who can proactively implement initiatives to mitigate negative outcomes. For example, a charge nurse on a given unit can have access to data quickly showing that 3 hours (instead of two) have elapsed since a patient with skin integrity issues was turned. He or she can then address the situation right away, before complications set in. This most certainly saves lives, improves outcomes, and enhances financial controls.

Regulatory mandates govern areas such as medication reconciliation and pain assessments as well, where, once again, informatics enables organizations to better identify breakdowns in processes and procedures that cause subpar performance results, so appropriate steps can be taken to adjust resource allocations such as staffing to mitigate negative outcomes. When addressing the issue of optimizing staffing resources within the organization, there exist a number of complicated factors to consider. The notion of "acuity tracking," or matching the severity of the conditions in a particular hospital unit with staffing allocations, should be considered. Also, since staffing schedules tend to be projected a number of weeks into the future, census trends need to be analyzed. Factors such as day of week or time of year (e.g., winter months involving snow and ice could result in increased injuries and demand for healthcare services) must be considered. Proper staffing in light of these various factors can contribute to improved and more comprehensive care, which in turn will contribute to better outcomes, fewer complications, fewer medical errors, etc. However, as noted, because staffing decisions are made based on best estimates of what may happen in the future, it becomes all the more important to have the best data available to ideally model what these needs will be. Informatics can synthesize data from myriad different systems, such as EMRs, financial systems, and even external web-based systems that can provide information on factors outside the hospital walls, such as temperature or perhaps the severity of the flu season in the area, and can enhance the understanding of potential demand for staffing resources.

QUALITY IMPROVEMENT IN CLINICAL AND OPERATIONAL ACTIVITIES

Another area that is rapidly maturing in the healthcare provider arena involves the growing utilization of devices that can interface directly with an EMR system and, ultimately, an informatics system. Ventilators, "smart" pumps, IVs, vital sign tracking monitors, and other devices like these can "talk" to EMRs and populate data directly into an EMR. Some EMRs, facilitated by information technologies, offer a capability to page a clinician or otherwise provide a real-time alert if a certain clinical value is outside accepted medical bounds. These technologies also add to existing data elements to enhance the overall data resources for more advanced analytics.

Statistically based analytics such as correlations can help providers identify the best possible order sets to use for a given condition (in conjunction with evidence-based medicine protocols). Informatics incorporating statistical correlations and causation can identify that individuals who receive a certain type of specialized therapy have much shorter lengths of stay and lower rates of readmission than those who do not. Analytics can also allow for comparing different clinical regimens to factors such as "patient satisfaction survey" scores. It can identify whether certain high-priced medications or medical devices may provide a less desirable outcome than lower-priced medications, and can identify which doctors have a predisposition to order those medications or devices. Looking at physician comparisons, informatics will enable hospitals and other organizations to compare physician ordering patterns with desired outcomes such as reduced length of stay, lower readmissions, fewer complications or comorbidities, and revenue generation metrics. This provides a key level of accountability for all involved in the interdisciplinary plan of care of a patient to ensure that the right people are doing the right things at the right time.

Many factors affiliated with clinical compliance apply to our third area of focus: quality improvement programs. At the end of the day, all healthcare providers certainly strive to provide the highest quality of care possible at all times. However, attempting to define what constitutes quality can be elusive. Regulatory agencies and payers have offered their own parameters as to what constitutes quality care. So-called pay for performance programs and never event prohibitions have helped crystallize much of what providers need to measure in order to demonstrate to appropriate agencies or payers that they are adopting the correct procedures for their patients. Pay-for-performance programs specify that there will be either incentives or penalties based on a provider's demonstrated compliance with a certain set of quality protocols. If the provider complies effectively, incentive payments are provided. If not, differing levels of reduction of payment come into play. Never events are significant medical errors that can cause grave patient harm, and Medicare and other payers have made it a policy that they will not reimburse providers for costs incurred from provider events that should *never* happen—hence the name never events. Not only does pay-for-performance and never event tracking impact the long-term financial viability of healthcare organizations, but these types of statistics now are among those that typically are compiled by governmental agencies, benchmarked, and posted on websites, where consumers (potential customers) can view them and compare them with those of a provider's competition.

Other indicators that are being tracked and reported via the web include hospital-acquired infection rates, readmissions, and average waits to see a doctor in an emergency department. It becomes imperative that healthcare organizations develop the wherewithal to track these types of metrics accurately, and in ways that allow for interceding proactively to address procedural issues to manage negative outcomes in the pipeline. Benchmarking, or comparing an organization against its peers and against what is considered to be acceptable performance, is becoming increasingly common and increasingly visible to larger sections of the public. For a provider, knowing where its performance *should* be early in the game allows for more aggressive programs to be designed and deployed to ensure that the organization is applying the most optimal procedures.

The concept of quality improvement can also be articulated in a somewhat different but extremely important way as well. While, as noted earlier, there are a multitude of clinical metrics that often can and should be shared both internally and externally, quality improvement can also be construed as using data to improve business processes in general and enforce accountability for appropriate and acceptable performance. Informatics can be used, for instance, to compare the length of time it takes physicians in an emergency room to see a patient. This can be a significant motivating factor to enhance performance by comparing individuals to their peers. In general, informatics enables healthcare providers to aggregate and analyze data in constructive and actionable ways, the results of which are continuous improvement in various procedures throughout the organization.

CUSTOMER RELATIONSHIP MANAGEMENT IN HEALTHCARE

Our final aspect of healthcare operations that can benefit immensely from informatics is the realm of patient satisfaction. As noted earlier, healthcare institutions increasingly have to view themselves as businesses, and part of maintaining a viable business is producing positive experiences for your customers. In the healthcare industry, customers can take on a number of forms, ranging from patients to patients' families to doctors. Providing an exceptional experience for customers remains a significant goal for healthcare organizations, as it promotes repeat visits from individuals in need of services. Happy customers also provide good word-of-mouth recommendations of their experiences that help rein in new customers, which maintains positive demand and, hopefully, increased revenue. Much of this is intuitive, certainly, but what is not so intuitive is how a healthcare institution gauges the satisfaction rates of its customers.

Measuring patient satisfaction in a healthcare setting can take on two separate forms. One form, and perhaps the most common, involves the process of having an unbiased, objective third-party organization send out a survey to patients soon after they have left the facility. This third-party organization (PressGaney and Health-Stream are two such noteworthy players) sends out a survey with a standard set of questions to recently discharged patients from all of its facilities. Some percentage of the patients respond, and the responses are tabulated and trended over time and broken out by parameters that the organizations generally make available. An added bonus of working through these third-party organizations is that participating healthcare institutions get an extra benefit of being able to benchmark how their responses fare against those of a wide array of similar peer organizations. These kinds of data can point to areas where an organization needs to fine-tune certain operational processes that are resulting in patient dissatisfaction. These surveys offer the patient the opportunity to add comments to his or her response, where proactive healthcare organizations can build systems to automatically route these comments to the appropriate decision makers in the organization and track the timeliness of issue resolution. Medicare regulations spell out a formal procedure for what are called grievances, which have mandates attached to them about how facilities need to address them. Clearly tracking these to ensure the responses to these grievances stay within the bounds of the regulations is most important for the organization in order for it to avoid falling out of Medicare compliance parameters, which may lead to financial or other, perhaps more severe, sanctions.

The second type of patient satisfaction issues can be gleaned from surveys that are administered directly to the patient while he or she remains in the facility. These surveys allow for an organization to receive more timely feedback of issues as they are occurring and take steps to address them and, if necessary, initiate a formal "service recovery" procedure for particular types of unfortunate customer service situations. The general process for how this type of survey works involves interviewing patients (assuming they are fit to be interviewed) at certain time intervals and asking them questions regarding issues, such as their perception of the food they received, the demeanor of nurses, etc. Responses can be entered into a database and tracked and trended over time through the utilization of informatics methods, which can also drilldown to identify if particular areas are problematic. Furthermore, certain types of responses and comments can be routed automatically to key individuals, and processes can be built to track the timeliness and completeness of responses to these issues. The main advantage about this type of survey is the rapid response capability it offers. The organization can find out right away if something is wrong and can react and correspond directly with the individual to ensure that the remedy to the problem was effective. This can transform a dissatisfied customer to a satisfied one.

More and more, informatics can and does provide value in a multitude of different care settings and in a number of different operational processes. Organizations invariably will derive significant benefits from having a mechanism to generate an accurate read of data on all fronts and being able to turn that data into actionable information. This information enhances the knowledge of service providers who can implement appropriate strategic initiatives to enhance efficiencies throughout the organization.

CLOSING COMMENTS ON THE ISSUE OF DATA PRIVACY

A critical element that needs to be maintained, preserved, and perhaps strengthened refers to the privacy safeguards of healthcare-related data of individuals. The integration of data resources from various healthcare providers and databases no doubt enhances efficiencies from analytics capabilities and information generation. As the process of developing more robust data resources enhances efficiencies, it also introduces the requirement for well-defined and strictly enforced standards to protect the privacy rights of individuals regarding health-related data. New privacy policies (mentioned in the following text) need to be designed to address any changes that transpire within the realm of data access and exchanges in the evolving healthcare system. The U. S. Department of Health and Human Services issued a privacy rule to implement the requirement for the Health Insurance Portability and Accountability Act of 1996, which addresses the use and disclosure of individuals' health information. A major goal of the privacy rule is to ensure that individuals' health information is properly

protected while allowing the flow of health information needed to provide and promote high-quality healthcare and to protect the public's health and well-being. The rule strikes a balance that permits important uses of information while protecting the privacy of people who seek care and healing.[11] New initiatives are addressing privacy requirements in this evolving data-intensive environment. The American Recovery and Reinvestment Act of 2009 incorporates improvements to existing law, covered entities, business associates, and other entities that will soon be subject to more rigorous standards when it comes to protected health information.[12] Data resources become more comprehensive, so too should policies that safeguard individual privacy rights.

REFERENCES

1. Lehr, W.; Lichtenberg, F. Computer use and productivity growth in U.S. federal government agencies, 1987–1992. J. Ind. Econ. **1998**, *46* (2), 257–279.
2. Brynjolfsson, E.; Hitt, L. Beyond computation: Information technology, organizational transformation, and business performance. J. Econ. Perspect. **2002**, *14* (4).
3. Kudyba, S.; Diwan, R. Increasing returns to information technology. Infor. Syst. Res. March **2002**, 104–111.
4. Shaprio, C.; Varian, H. *Information Rules: A Strategic Guide to the Network Economy*; Harvard Business Press: Boston, MA, 1998.
5. Kudyba, S.; Diwan, R. *Information Technology, Corporate Productivity and The New Economy*; Greenwood Publishing: Westport, CT, 2002.
6. Hillestad, R.; Bigelow, J.; Bower, A.; Girosi, F.; Meili, R.; Scoville, R.; Taylor, R. Can electronic medical record systems transform health care? Potential health benefits, savings, and costs. Health Aff. **2005**, *24* (5) September–October, 1103–1117.
7. Patterson, N. The ABCs of systemic healthcare reform: A plan for driving $500 billion in annual savings out of the U.S. healthcare system. Healthcare Industry Brief. Cerner Corporation. 2009, http://www.cerner.com/ABCs.
8. Davenport, T.; Prusak, L. *Working knowledge*; Harvard Business Press: Boston, MA, 2000.
9. Davenport, T.; Harris, J.; DeLong, D.; Jacobson, A. Data to knowledge to results: Building an analytic capability. Calif. Manag. Rev. **2001**, *43*, 117–138.
10. Pande, P.; Neuman, R.; Cavanagh, R. *The Six Sigma Way: How GE, Motorola, and Other Top Companies Are Honing Their Performance*; McGraw-Hill: New York, NY, 2000.
11. U.S. Department of Health and Human Services. *Summary of the HIPAA privacy rule*. http://www.hhs.gov/ocr/privacy/hipaa/understanding/summary/privacysummary.pdf.
12. American Recovery and Reinvestment Act of 2009. http://frwebgate.access.gpo.gov/cgi-bin/getdoc.cgi?dbname = 111_cong_bills&docid = f:h1enr.pdf.

Healthcare Informatics: Analytics

Jason Burke
SAS Institute, Cary, North Carolina, U.S.A.

Abstract

In healthcare, we are just at the beginning of seeing how analytics—whether biased toward the business or clinical sides of the spectrum—can transform our ecosystem. Analytics will give us better guidance on how to control costs—not just line items, but the hidden and true costs of healthcare. Analytics will help us identify and dismantle old assumptions about the way healthcare is delivered—not relying on gut instincts and hearsay, but real evidence. Analytics will allow us to determine not only the treatments that produce the best outcomes, but the real factors that determine optimum treatment efficacy and cost. The hidden gems in healthcare will surface, and with them will come better lives for patients everywhere.

INTRODUCTION

Evidence-based medicine. Personal electronic health records. Disease management. Personalized medicine. These terms, among many others, reflect a rapidly growing change within the health sciences ecosystem—a transformative shift toward more information-based decision making related to patient care and healthcare cost management. For decades, the efficiencies and improvements attained in other industries through the adoption of information technology have largely been missing in healthcare, an ecosystem mired in paper records, administrative overhead, and labor-intensive business processes.

But that is all changing. The sustained rise in healthcare costs, consistent problems in patient safety, highly expensive prescription drugs, and inconsistent treatment outcomes have all contributed to a new drive toward making better use of the tremendous volumes of information flowing through the ecosystem. Whereas, historically hospitals have looked to expansions in service lines and facilities to drive top-line revenue growth, analytics that provide business opportunities in utilization, cost containment, and quality control are now seen as critical enablers of bottom-line financial performance. Health plans that have relied on relatively simple business rules to determine the appropriateness of reimbursements are now looking to advanced analytical models to identify previously undetected fraudulent claims activities and patterns. Drug researchers, struggling to find ways to bring innovative and safe therapies to market faster and cheaper, are aggregating tremendous volumes of data covering many years of research to look for biomarkers that can accurately predict drug safety and efficacy in named patient populations. Across

the board, electronic data, whether business based or science based, are now seen as the fuel to power the engines of business and clinical analytics driving the evolution of patient outcomes and wellness.

But those growing volumes of data contain a hidden burden: How can we efficiently and effectively manage such large and disparate volumes of information? How do we make it useful? With information flowing from every corner of the healthcare ecosystem, how do we prioritize which data are most important, and how can we simplify the inherent complexity down to something with which educated human beings can make rational decisions? Anyone seeking an easy answer to this dilemma will be disappointed.

Modern information technology, especially in the areas of data integration, data quality, data management, and advanced analytics, holds the key to unlocking the power of this information and the corresponding business and scientific transformation contained within. Advanced analytics and information management sit at the center of the new health enterprise—an information-driven business and science-informed medical practice that can dramatically reduce healthcare costs and improve health outcomes for all patients. But only if organizations embrace them.

ANALYSIS PARALYSIS

The healthcare industry is no stranger to technology—hospitals have invested millions in medical devices for decades, for example. But capabilities with respect to information technology—electronic data collection, management, quality, analysis, and reporting—are reasonably new. Extensive paper-based forms, change-

Encyclopedia of Information Systems and Technology, DOI: 10.1081/E-EIST-120053824

averse physicians, tightly controlled business processes, overtaxed nurses, and business demands on self-funding investments have conspired to inhibit the proliferation of information technology in much of the healthcare sector. But as the industry has sought to better understand its deep-rooted problems in cost, quality, safety, and outcomes, a growing recognition has emerged that information technology must be a priority for every health enterprise.

And yet, when we speak of advanced analytics in healthcare, it is not uncommon to hear a list of excuses why the industry is not ready for them:

- **More technology.** Many people argue that until the industry has had more time to implement more technology that collects information electronically, there is little use in investing in advanced analytics.
- **More integration and standards.** Some people argue that, because the industry has historically lacked data standards that facilitate information aggregation and sharing, any insights that might be derived from their existing data would be of questionable value.
- **Data privacy.** Inevitably, some people will question the appropriateness of using personal medical information outside the context of care for that particular patient; Health Insurance Portability and Accountability Act is usually cited.

As organizations consider analytics-oriented projects and hear these concerns, it is quite easy to fall into "analysis paralysis"—continuously trying to find ways to overcome issues that cannot be overcome without doing the projects that elicited the issues in the first place. Organizations will always need more technology, but we have a lot today. We will always need better integration and deeper support in standards, but we have standards and integration models that are proven today. We should always be holding patient data privacy at the forefront of our minds, but we have many ways of protecting patient privacy, while also allowing us to pursue improvements that will inevitably benefit those patients.

The question should not be whether to take on analytics as a corporate priority; the question should be how. And the answer is surprisingly simple, residing in the neonatal and pediatric units of every hospital in the world. Newborn babies, infants, and toddlers physiologically develop along a predefined biological path, one that serves to gradually bring new biological systems online and grow the systems already online until the person reaches adulthood. It is a long-term process, but one with clearly defined steps and associated personal abilities. Such is this case with analytics, as they are born and grown inside companies.

ANALYTICAL MATURITY AND OBJECTIVES

The term *analytics* may be one of the most overused and misunderstood terms in the business community today, with the possible exception of *business intelligence*. Every software application that has the ability to run reports with numbers in them also has the capability of providing analytics. Any person who has taken a statistics course is absolutely capable of performing whatever analytics are needed for an organization. Even the definition of the term *analytics* is used in one context to describe web reporting, while in another context it describes the most obscure statistical methodology imaginable.

When we use the term *analytics* in healthcare, we are using it to mean something very specific:

> Analytics are the complete series of integrated capabilities needed to provide progressively deeper statistical insights into health-related information.

We are describing capabilities—a capacity that can be found or learned within organizations and individuals. Those capabilities should be complete, meaning they cover all of the needed areas of information access, integration, quality, storage, management, interpretation, and governance. Those capabilities are also progressive, meaning that the simpler capabilities need to be in place to enable the more sophisticated capabilities to operate. They are statistical in nature, not merely mathematical. And they are progressively deeper, meaning the insights derived from higher-order analytical capabilities offer greater value than those of lower-order capabilities.

THE EIGHT LEVELS OF ANALYTICS

So what are these capabilities that organizations and individuals need to have? There are eight levels of analytical capabilities that any organization or person needs in order to fully address the challenges in healthcare (Fig. 1):

1. **Standard reports.** Answer the questions: What happened? When did it happen?
2. **Ad hoc reports.** Answer the questions: How many? How often? Where?
3. **Query drilldown.** Answer the questions: Where exactly is the problem? How do I find the answers?
4. **Alerts.** Answer the questions: When should I react? What actions are needed now?
5. **Statistical analysis.** Answer the questions: Why is it happening? What opportunities am I missing?
6. **Forecasting.** Answer the questions: What if these trends continue? How much is needed? When will it be needed?

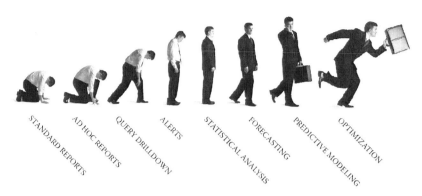

Fig. 1 Evolution of analytical capabilities.

7. **Predictive modeling.** Answer the questions: What will happen next? How will it affect my business?

8. **Optimization.** Answer the questions: How do we do things better? What is the best decision for a complex problem?

Let's use a hypothetical example to illustrate how these various capabilities are developed and used. Christopher Regional Hospital is struggling to understand why its operating margins are decreasing. In particular, the cardiac service line, typically associated with a good contribution margin, has seen a decline over the last six months. Hospital administrators decide to undertake an analytics initiative in order to understand what is causing the decline in contribution margin.

1. **Standard reports.** The problem was identified when the administrators consulted a series of standard reports that the hospital uses on a monthly basis. They realized the cardiac service line's contribution margin was down from the same period last year.

2. **Ad hoc reports.** These standard reports did not show all of the performance indicators the administrators needed to understand the issues, so they asked for a few specific reports related to the inpatient and outpatient volumes, as well as statistics trending by fiscal period over the last year. These reports showed that patient visits were not down, and the service line was fairly busy, and so the problems were not simply a matter of getting more patients. The administrators asked that these *ad hoc* reports become a part of the hospital's standard reporting environment.

3. **Query drilldown.** To explore the problem further, hospital administrators asked the head of the cardiac service line to investigate the problem and report back at the next service line committee meeting. He formed a series of hypotheses about potential causes, and then explored a number of other factors related to contribution margin, such as length of stay, payer, and service utilization. The reporting

environment allowed him to use a web browser to dynamically divide, subset, and report on these business metrics. During his query drilldown work, the administrator noticed something peculiar—there were a lot of reimbursement denials for patients having a "rule out myocardial infarction (MI)" code. The director checked with the billing department and was told that they are being denied because the hospital will not receive payment for "rule out MI" patients unless they are coded as an observation status and not as an inpatient.

4. **Alerting.** In order to understand what was happening with these patients, the director set up an alert that was sent each time a patient received the "rule out MI" code and had a status of an inpatient. Those alerts were sent to the case manager and the nurse manager of the cardiac unit so that they could monitor the care, to understand what was happening.

5. **Statistical analysis.** The director then decided to analyze the data for this particular diagnostic code. Running a series of statistical analyses on this patient population, he found a correlation between inpatient status, longer lengths of stay, and days of the week the patient arrived in the emergency room. In particular, he noticed that patients who were admitted in an inpatient status, with lengths of stay between 3 and 4 days, who had come to the emergency room with chest pain on a Friday or a Saturday were most of the denials. This finding was reaffirmed when following up on the alerting procedure: the nurse manager of the cardiac unit knew that these patients required a stress test, and stress tests were not performed in the hospital on Saturdays or Sundays. Patients were admitted to stay through the weekend to receive their stress tests on Monday; standard procedure was to schedule the stress test within 24 hours, allowing the patients to be placed in a cardiac Intensive Care Unit (ICU) bed and not be admitted. The director also realized when speaking with the nurse manager that more and more "rule out MIs" were taking up beds in the cardiac ICU.

6. **Forecasting.** After hearing the findings in the service line committee meeting, the administrators wanted to know what the impact of this trend would be over a longer time horizon. They constructed a forecast of patient admission, diagnosis, length of stay, and payments over the next 24 months based on the past 4 years of hospital data, census data for their region, and projections from several medical institutions. The forecast showed that their hospital's patient admissions around this condition were expected to grow 56% each year for the next 2 years due to the recent closing of area hospitals. It also showed that their relatively small drop in contribution margin today could easily grow into a bigger problem in the next 18 months unless they found a way to address both the availability of stress testing on weekends and the problem this condition presents on utilization of beds in the cardiac ICU. This analysis highlighted the patient throughput issues that were just starting to develop, affecting the quality of care for the cardiac patients.

7. **Predictive modeling.** The hospital leaders now wanted to understand the value of more timely treatments and care focused on acuity. The administrators wanted to know whether receiving stress tests within 24 hours, and removing cardiac rule-outs from the emergency room to an observation unit, were beneficial from a quality, safety, and financial perspective. They had staff construct a statistical model that could predict patient outcomes. By using historical patient information, the statistical model could predict the likelihood of death, readmission, disease progression, and long-term costs based on the timing and the treatment that was administered. This model showed opening an observation unit and staffing stress testing on weekends could decrease this condition's returns to the emergency room visits; reduce medical errors and negative outcomes, including death; and create more cardiac ICU beds, increasing throughput for critical cardiac patients and reducing expenses by staffing by acuity. They also found out something else.

8. **Optimization.** During the predictive modeling exercise, the hospital analysts used data mining software to look for trends in the electronic medical records that might have an impact on outcomes. They uncovered a previously unknown trend: patients under the care of one physician in the hospital were 32% less likely to be readmitted after a cardiac catheterization. The administrators contacted the clinical chief of cardiology and informed him of the analysis. When the clinical chief questioned the physician about her treatment strategies, she indicated that she required her patients to follow up with a cardiovascular exercise and diet program. She had her staff follow up on her patients to make

sure they completed the program. Predictive modeling showed that patients that participated in that program, as well as received timely treatment, had 61% fewer admissions in the following 2-year period.

The preceding example illustrates how health insights are derived through a successive series of steps. Each step provides vital information needed to make the next step feasible and effective. It would have been quite difficult, for example, to know what statistical analyses needed to be run if the organization did not already have some direction from the query drilldown. Each step is also more complex than the former, requiring deeper analytical skills, better data, and more coordinated engagement within the organization.

BUSINESS VS. CLINICAL ANALYTICS

The numbers and types of analytics that can be applied to healthcare are practically endless, constrained only by the creativity of the human mind to ask intelligent questions and define mathematical inferences. When comparing health and life sciences to other industries' use of analytics, one characteristic stands out as somewhat unique: the questions, data, and decisions involved include traditional types of business information—sales, operations, etc.—but also include scientific information and interpretation. This distinction brings an additional level of complexity to looking at analytics as a transformative engine for healthcare. Whereas many software tools and people skills applicable to other businesses can be applied equally to health and life sciences, there are a variety of science-oriented capabilities, Fig. 2, that are not as broadly available. And for many business insights in healthcare, it is the combined view of both business and scientific information that enables more educated decisions.

Any analytical solution in health and life sciences exists on a continuum of business-focused to clinically focused analytics (Fig. 2). Some types of insights—assessing profitability of a business unit or providing a standardized financial reporting environment—mainly involve the use of information from business units, systems, and knowledge workers. Other insights, such as the safety dimensions of a drug therapy or the outcomes of a clinical research study, reside more clearly in the realm of patient information and scientific interpretation. Between these two extremes lies an entire continuum of analytical applications that provide a unique view into the operations of a health enterprise, the management of patient populations and diseases, and the primary determinants of costs, quality, and outcomes.

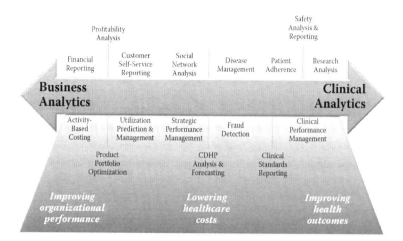

Fig. 2 Continuum of business-focused to clinically focused analytics.

With such diversity and breadth of scope, it is difficult to develop any taxonomy of analytical capabilities that adequately conveys all of the various analytical dimensions of the ecosystem. However, at the highest level, any healthcare-related analytical application can be said to target at least one of three main business imperatives:

1. **Improving organizational performance.** These analytics focus on the financial and commercial performance of the organization. Profitability and performance management are commonly cited issues in this area.
2. **Lowering healthcare costs.** These analytics focus on cost avoidance, active cost management, cost reduction through improvements in efficiency, and other aspects of operational improvement. Detection and prevention of healthcare fraud, as well as activity-based costing initiatives, often fall into this area.
3. **Improving health outcomes.** These analytics focus on improved patient outcomes, including areas of patient safety and treatment efficacy. Clinical research of novel drugs and therapies can be considered a component of this area.

Obviously, there is a close interdependency between these three business imperatives, and it is not uncommon for improvements in one area to impact the other areas. But for an organization considering a new analytics project, these imperatives represent a critical aspect of project scoping. For an analytics program to be successful, absolute clarity needs to exist in the program's intended objectives. Programs with scopes intending to cover all three imperatives are unlikely to be successful; the data, objective measures, people, and impacted business processes are dramatically different. But for targeted analytical programs, the impact to each of these imperatives can be equally dramatic.

With these imperatives and the business-clinical continuum as context, let us look more deeply into some representative programs.

IMPROVING ORGANIZATIONAL PERFORMANCE

At its core, healthcare is a business just like any other industry. Profitability is linked to efficiency and competitive differentiation. Innovation breeds opportunity. Quality can command premium pricing. Customer relationships determine long-term revenue potential. These and many other business principles serve as the underpinning for a portfolio of analytical capabilities that can have a tremendous impact on the quality, safety, and cost of healthcare delivery.

Aside from issues related to clinical outcomes (considered separately in a subsequent section), there are three general categories of organizational performance analytics:

- Financial: Analytical capabilities related to revenue, operating costs, and investments. Typical topics include financial management, revenue cycle optimization, and profitability analysis.
- Operational: Analytical capabilities related to the way an organization operates internally. Typical topics include utilization management, human resources, and other enterprise-wide competencies.
- Commercial: Analytical capabilities related to the way an organization sells, markets, and interacts with its customer and partner base. Typical topics include customer targeting, retention, and sales and marketing effectiveness.

The following table highlights some of the more common performance-oriented analytical scenarios found across the healthcare ecosystem today.

Financial	• Financial management	• Expense management
	• Revenue management and cycle optimization	• Contribution margin analysis
		• Provider profitability analysis
Operational	• Human resource performance management and optimization	• Strategic performance management
	• Reporting standards and requirements	• Operational performance management and monitoring
	• Utilization prediction, management, and analysis	• Inventory management
Commercial	• Cross-selling	• Customer satisfaction
	• Member/customer campaign management	• Health plan reporting
	• Multichannel relationship marketing	• Customer/group defection
	• Physician targeting	• Customer experience analytics
	• Provider/customer selection, retention, and acquisition	• Provider/customer self-service reporting and explanation of benefits
	• Sales force and territory optimization	• Risk stratification
	• Sales force effectiveness	

Let us look at one real-world example of an organization using analytics in this way. A large, nonprofit teaching hospital cares for over 40,000 inpatients and 750,000 outpatients every year. Like any large hospital, its databases and reports are incredibly diverse, covering financial, quality, and patient satisfaction information. But it was quite difficult for executives to see the information in a way that would facilitate better decision making. For example, what was the relationship between patient-related services and productivity in the different care units?

The hospital developed a performance management system utilizing balanced scorecard concepts to draw correlations between measurements from the different areas of their organization. By combining data relating to 50,000 patient encounters a year from 29 different sources, the system analyzes and distributes operational metrics to executive management, physicians, and front-line employees throughout the hospital. Whether in a patient care setting or in the business office, about 900 employees at all levels can see how their actions, individually and as a whole, affect the organization and its patients. Over thirty metrics detail key financial information, length of stay, and patient satisfaction measures. Select physicians and nurses even have their own score-cards, enabling them to share information relating to finance, productivity, workload, and quality indicators with their colleagues.

Some department heads now routinely use the system to gauge hospital performance, and spot anomalies relating to length of stay, spikes in certain diagnosis-related groups, and procedural delays. As an example, operating room efficiency and productivity are impacted significantly by start times. If more cases start on time in the morning, then efficiency and productivity increase. So by identifying patterns relating to delays in operating room start times, physicians can have a better understanding of the impact of specific test orders and procedures. Using this approach, the hospital can also identify best practices.

The key to unlocking the value of performance solutions is in the identification and measurement of key performance indicators (KPIs). In this area, healthcare actually has a fair amount of information already available from which to draw. Organizations such as the Joint Commission (http://www.jointcommission.org), the Agency for Healthcare Research and Quality (http://www.ahrq.gov), and the National Quality Forum (http://www.qualityforum.org) have completed extensive work in identifying critical healthcare KPIs, which every healthcare enterprise should monitor. These measures cover the gamut of business and clinical analytics, and are themselves the subjects of entire books. The following table gives a small sample of these types of KPIs:

When considering a performance management program and its associated KPIs, it is important to keep several things in mind:

1. KPIs should be empirically measurable. The idea in performance management is to make better decisions based on real data.
2. KPIs should be linked directly to a business objective. Simply measuring performance with no intended action based on the measurement is a waste of effort.
3. KPIs are the indicator, not the problem or the solution. The goal in performance management is to use KPIs as a detection tool for the business; the root cause analysis of a failing indicator is a separate process often involving different analytical techniques.
4. Measuring and reporting are not the end goal. The reason to use analytics in performance management is not to create easy-to-read dashboards (though good reporting is required). Rather, the end goal is to be able to *predict* and *optimize* performance along those specific performance dimensions.

As you might imagine, one of the more significant areas to predict and optimize is costs.

Financial

- Net revenue, profit/loss, and contribution margin per health system, facility, service line, condition, and physician
- Actual and overtime expenses to budgeted per health system, facility, service line, and department
- Cost per service line, condition, physician
- Nursing travelers' expense per health system, facility, service line, and department
- Ambulatory surgeries per health system, facility, and surgeon
- Clinic and Emergency Room visits per health system, facility, and clinic

Operational

- Nurse-to-bed ratio overall and per nursing unit
- Attrition overall, per role, and per department
- Throughput red alerts per health system and facility
- Length of stay per health system, facility, service line, condition, and physician
- Percentage of 11 A.M. discharges per health system, facility, service line, nursing unit, and physician
- Number of tests performed by test, health system, facility, service line, condition, and physician
- Door to bed time
- Registration to triage time
- Days to appointment
- Physician order entry compliance
- Registration to triage time
- Days to appointment
- Physician order entry compliance

Quality and Safety

- Percent of patients who received recommended care, and percent of process measures met for specific conditions by health system, facility, service line, nursing unit, physician, etc.
- Percent of patients who received recommended surgical infection prevention, and percent of process measures met by health system, facility, service line, nursing unit, physician, etc.
- Infection rates for specific conditions by health system, facility, service line, nursing unit, physician, etc.
- Medication errors per 1,000 orders
- Pediatric IV infiltration rates
- Psychiatric patient assault rate
- Percent of major surgical inpatients with a hospital-acquired complication and death
- Inpatient falls per inpatient days with and without injuries

Nursing Care

- Percent of inpatients with a hospital-acquired pressure ulcer
- Rate of urinary tract infections with catheters
- Rate of bloodstream infections with catheters
- Ventilator-associated pneumonia
- Smoking cessation counseling for acute myocardial infarction, heart failure, and pneumonia
- Number of registered nurses per patient day and number of nursing staff hours (registered nurse, licensed vocational/practical nurse, and unlicensed assistive personnel) per patient day
- Nursing work life scores related to participation in hospital affairs, foundations for quality of care, manager ability, staffing and resource adequacy, and collegiality of nurse–physician relations

LOWERING HEALTHCARE COSTS

Many people would argue that the concept of lowering healthcare costs is a measure and benefit as opposed to a business imperative. In some sense, this is probably true. Many analytics initiatives related to organizational performance or healthcare outcomes are justified by illustrating the impact on health-related expenditures in R&D, marketing, reimbursements, and other sources. But considering the central role that rising costs are playing in healthcare market dynamics, it is also useful to consider cost reduction programs as a separate topic in its own right. In fact, many organizations place a greater emphasis on cost management initiatives than performance or outcomes, as the organizational "pain" is so acute.

One example of analytics applied in this way pertains to healthcare fraud. Historically, an organization's ability to detect abusive or fraudulent activity has been limited to solutions that are called rules engines. Rules engines—a simplification of the "alerting" tier in our taxonomy—maintain an inventory of known fraud and

abuse schemes, and can draw a sample from the collection of all healthcare transactions to look for situations that violate the rules. There are problems here, though:

1. The rules engine is usually only collecting a sample of records; it is not looking at every transaction. So low-volume fraud transactions are likely to slip through undetected.
2. When a rules engine detects a deviation, it is only detecting a violation of a rule. There are countless reasons why that rule violation might occur that are perfectly legitimate. There is little ability to understand the actual likelihood a given incident is indeed fraudulent, or what the real financial impact of that violation might mean for the organization. As such, fraud investigators spend time investigating a large number of incidents that waste time and money.
3. The volume of false positives (transactions that are identified as fraudulent but actually are not) creates a situation where investigators have very limited bandwidth to investigate fraudulent activities. As such, they tend to focus their efforts on high-dollar

transactions. Fraud and abuse schemes consisting of low-dollar transactions are unlikely to trigger an investigation.

4. In order for a rules engine to know about a fraudulent activity, the activity must have been previously detected and codified into a rule. So rules engines always suffer from a delay between someone finding a fraud scheme, someone else coding into a rules system, and when organizations then start implementing the updated rules. These delays can span from months to years. And even a slight modification to an existing fraud scheme can render its existing rule useless.

5. Generally speaking, there is a complexity ceiling for rules engines. Abuse patterns that do not easily lend themselves to the relatively simple structure of a codified rule—for example, a complex matrix of collusion—are not easily detectable by rules engines.

So the smart fraudster is one that generates low-dollar transactions at a relatively low and distributed volume so as to not show up in the rules engine sampling. Of course, there will always be a pattern to the activity, but as long as the volume doesn't look suspicious and the dollar value is low, the likelihood of detection remains small. Even if the fraudulent scheme is detected, by the time it becomes a rule deployed within healthcare institutions, the fraudster will be already working the next scheme.

The use of analytics for fraud detection is not encumbered by these shortcomings. An analytical model looks for patterns, not rule deviations. As opposed to sampling a small group of transactions, an analytical model can be applied to every single transaction flowing through a healthcare system, even in real time. It is less likely to produce false positives, because the detection is not based on some arbitrary comparison criteria, but rather on a model. Indeed, an analytical model can even be applied to the targets identified by rules engines to help separate the real signals from the noise. Note also that the delay between fraud identification and deployment of a detection process is much lower, because the analytical model can be "tuned" in real time based on real-world experience.

Analytical fraud models also offer the ability to detect fraudulent or abusive patterns, whose complexity is larger than what can easily be understood by the human mind. For example, a collusion scheme might actually involve three people working in four different organizations and generating six different types of claims. It is quite difficult for an investigator to ascertain a pattern across so many variables and permutations. But by applying data mining algorithms that examine each of the variables, relationships, and interdependencies, a pattern of social "connectedness"

between these three people can emerge that is markedly different from those of their cohorts.

Fraud is only one example of the potential contribution of analytics to cost management and reduction. Other examples include:

• Portfolio optimization—Ensuring that high-value products and services are progressed, and stopping investments in products and services predicted to be unviable or unprofitable.
• Product development and pricing—Balancing market opportunity to pricing strategy in order to maximize profit (not necessarily price), minimize leakage, and ensure competitiveness.
• Case management/readmission prediction—Identifying and targeting patient cost factors and proactively introducing interventions to avoid the costs.
• Activity-based costing and management—Understanding where an enterprise is actually incurring costs in specific activities, as well as identifying and predicting the outcome of potential changes.

Regardless of the specific focus area, all of these analytical opportunities revolve around a common concept of using prediction to maximize investments in the right areas of the business, and minimize exposure to areas that extend costs without sufficient upside.

Let's look at another real-world example. One of the Blue Cross and Blue Shield insurance providers in the United States sought to gain a better understanding of costs and cost overruns within its organization. Traditional accounting systems provide departmental budgets, but beyond budget line items, those systems typically lack the analytical sophistication needed to look at financial information along different cost dimensions: corporate vs. departmental processes, predicted vs. accrued costs, etc. In this particular case, the company's finance managers could perform basic budget variance at the corporate and department levels, but they could not break out costs by product or individual lines of business, or even scrutinize contributions to activity costs at the program level.

The lack of process-oriented insights, which is far from unique to this particular insurer, has several ramifications. First, there is no way of ensuring that a given customer contract would be profitable. In one case, executives believed the company was losing money on a particular contract, but had no comprehensive way to evaluate all of the costs that supported this agreement. Profitability calculations can be very complex, as the way that costs are accrued (i.e., by individuals) differs significantly from the way that pricing is structured (e.g., by family, employee, child, etc.). Second, this lack of visibility at the contract level is further complicated by the fact that the administrative costs of plans differ between large group plans, small group plans, individual products, and government plans. And third, even if a single contract is unprofitable, unless there is a mechanism to ensure cost management on an ongoing basis, future contracts will suffer similar problems.

To address these concerns, the insurer adopted a particular analytical framework focused on activity-based costing and management. This solution pulls data from its corporate and departmental account systems, enabling planners to explore and predict cost data at all different levels of the business. For many programs, budgets need to actually be set at the individual business activity level. As opposed to simply watching budget reports for cost deviations, the analytical solution allows them to actively monitor projected costs and compare actual costs with the allowable rates for each activity. It becomes much easier to recognize that potential cost overruns and institute changes to the company's activities fall within acceptable cost parameters.

Moving from reactive to proactive, this same approach is also used to help managers decide when to modify the pricing plans for contracts, or when to restructure expenses by outsourcing or consolidating tasks. This concept provides real value when considered at the enterprise level. Departmental budgets often mask the costs associated with cross-functional business activities such as corporate sustaining activities, sales and marketing, and product service and support. Using this approach, an organization can even establish and measure corporate benchmarks as part of a broader transformational strategy.

Ultimately, the solution allows the company to evaluate costs for every business process and to identify areas for implementing cost-saving measures and company-wide process improvements. Marketing and underwriting can see how product costs vary depending on the size and type of the group plan; department managers can see what activities performed truly at cost; and executives can look at administrative costs for specific lines of business as a ratio to revenue, claims paid, or other financial metrics.

In this scenario, notice the many different levels of costs being impacted:

- Budget management—Ensuring programs and business units stay to budget.
- Activity management—Ensuring efficiency and consistency in execution.
- Work reduction—Spending less time manipulating data, improving decision speed.
- Profitability—Ensuring that contracts and pricing are actually profitable.
- Cost arbitrage—Facilitating outsourcing to lower-cost fulfillment options.

The breadth of scope and impact is one reason why reducing healthcare costs can stand on its own as a business imperative, and not simply reflect the outcome of other improvement programs.

IMPROVING HEALTHCARE OUTCOMES

Beyond any of the organizational productivity or cost issues presented so far, the Holy Grail in healthcare analytics is all about improving the health of patients. Though providers, payers, researchers, manufacturers, and policy makers can disagree on most other aspects of the healthcare ecosystem, everyone can agree that we need more health in healthcare. Analytics provide the means of finding that health, and bringing it to scale.

Health-oriented analytics are not new. Every prescription drug discovered and marketed was required to demonstrate safety and efficacy via statistical models before being approved for use. Epidemiologists rely on computational methods in studying the progression of diseases in populations. Analytical models and methods are used to explore the estimated 3 billion chemical base pairs and 20,000 genes in the human genome. In truth, advanced analytics have been a long-standing tool in understanding the scientific bases of biology and medicine.

Despite this analytical heritage, the hardest health-related questions—the ones that will likely have the biggest impact toward the lives of patients—are just now rising to the surface. Why? There are several reasons:

1. Scientific advancement. Our understanding of the fundamental nature of human physiology, genetics, and disease is reaching a point where we can more directly apply the learnings toward making patients better.
2. Convergence. The health-related improvements needed in any one health market—providers, payers, researchers—require access to information in the other markets. As greater transparency and openness to collaboration unfold, new opportunities to apply advanced analytics arise as well.
3. Cost. The dramatically rising costs of healthcare around the world have brought a new level of discrimination in treatment efficiency and effectiveness. Rather than continuing to fund expensive treatments with unclear outcomes, a better fiscal policy would focus on funding the best treatments with the best cost structures.

So what types of opportunities exist now? The following table highlights some of the main categories of outcomes-oriented analytics. It is important to note that this list is just a sampling. The ability to positively impact the treatment programs and corresponding patient outcomes is limited only by the creativity of the

Prospective Performance and Intervention	Optimized and Targeted Treatments	Adverse Event Avoidance
• Disease and population management • Expedited research • Member and patient programs • Pay for performance • Provider performance • Provider/physician profiling	• Biomedical informatics • Clinical and patient decision support • Clinical program compliance • Clinical research analysis • Evidence-based clinical decision support • Clinical performance management • Patient adherence	• Adverse event detection and prediction • Biosurveillance • Clinical alerting • Clinical quality performance analysis and reporting

human mind to develop novel ideas and test them. As you will see in the examples that follow, there are many different ways to look at health outcomes.

Consider the following real-world example. A professor of epidemiology at a large Canadian university is studying the risk factors and relationships between cardiovascular disease and cholesterol levels, lifestyle, diet, childhood experiences, and environmental factors. The research includes studying the incidence and distribution of diseases by combining massive amounts of data from many disparate sources: nutrition databases, healthcare delivery data, community demographic information, national patient surveys, and information supplied by Health Canada and the U. S. Centers for Disease Control and Prevention. By bringing these large, disparate information resources together, the professor has been able to develop statistical models that establish the relationship between high cholesterol intake at an early age and chronic diseases later in life. For example, the evidence indicates that cardiovascular disease has a long latency time, and that problems begin in early childhood. By looking at a variety of factors such as cholesterol intake, height, weight, and level of physical activity, the professor can predict childhood risks of adult cardiovascular illness and death.

So how can analytics like that be put into action? In one case, a large U. S. health services company uses data mining to help identify people who would benefit from preventive care services. The data mining software predicts hidden relationships in millions of member records to 1) determine patient risk levels; and 2) develop more targeted intervention and prevention plans. Large volumes of clinical and operational data are applied in statistical models that can predict the members in greatest need of support programs. In addition, by identifying high-risk patients and implementing preventative actions against future conditions, health problems and treatments can actually be avoided.

In another case, a western European health research institute sought a way for doctors and patients to predict the effects of drugs, other treatments, and lifestyle factors on patients with rheumatoid arthritis. To do this, they developed two analytics-based solutions: one

enables rheumatism patients to examine the factors that affect their health, and the other helps rheumatologists select the best treatment for each patient. A statistical methodology called factor analysis is used to test various treatment hypotheses with the support of randomized trials. The goal is to find the scientifically best combination of various lifestyle factors for each individual case. Patients choose what they would prefer to improve, such as pain, and up to four independent lifestyle factors, such as exercise, diet, and sleeping habits, which might conceivably reduce pain. The system then generates a test plan that the patient prints out as a diary of what should be tested each day. At the end of the period, the program calculates which combination of factors provided the best lifestyle impact.

Over 50 clinics have been involved in the collection of these data from patients and physicians: more than 26,500 patients and 144,000 consultations have been collected and analyzed. The predictive model uses patient data as the basis for predicting the results of various treatments such as different drugs and drug combinations. In other words, instead of a physician relying on a generic treatment plan that may or may not be the best option for a particular patient, the system assists doctors in choosing the best treatment for each patient based on that patient's profile. This approach has the added benefit of avoiding the costs associated with expensive treatments or drugs that are unlikely to be a good fit for a given patient.

Unfortunately, in many cases, humankind has yet to find cures or even strong treatments for diseases. It is in these areas where analytics can have a dramatic impact. For pharmaceutical and biotechnology companies, the development of a new medicine can take more than a decade—a decade of great expense for the developer and of prolonged anxiety for patients in need of new treatments. Meanwhile, the escalating cost of research and development, accompanied by the increasing complexity and expense of human clinical trials, threatens pharmaceutical innovation and drives up healthcare costs.

Using analytics, it is possible to develop simulations of human clinical research (clinical trials simulations) that can considerably expedite the development of novel therapies, and save millions of development dollars. Simulated clinical trials are virtual replicas of actual clinical trials. The simulations take data models developed from actual clinical trials and develop clinical scenarios and putative trial results that take into account variability caused by treatment effects, survival times, adverse events such as the occurrence of headaches or nausea, and other events that occur during trials. Researchers might perform 10,000 simulations of a single scenario, which means an entire trial can generate millions of observations. Using this approach, a U. S. biotechnology company is actively exploring new treatments for HIV infection, hepatitis, various forms of cancer, inflammatory diseases such as rheumatoid arthritis, and many others. Its solution, which also takes advantage of grid computing technology, can produce as many as 1 million patients for 2 terabytes of data in a single simulation. The company has the ability to do over 10,000 replicates in an hour, and that rate is growing.

SUMMARY

With all of the different dimensions of analytics covered so far, it is logical to ask where an organization begins in its journey toward deeper insights. As you might expect, there is no single correct answer—the journey depends on the traveler and the desired destination. In watching many organizations move through their analytical maturity process, one key theme emerges among successful companies: start where you are. As mentioned earlier, it is easy to fall prey to analysis paralysis, constantly evaluating abilities instead of instituting programs to change those abilities. You will never have enough electronic data, it will never be clean enough, there will always be conflicting priorities, and you will never have enough of the right resources to focus on the project. But in all likelihood, you have enough of all of the above to get started.

Another trap some organizations fall into is "boiling the ocean." It is impossible to take on all of these analytical challenges and opportunities at the same time. And even if you could, it would not be advisable. Organizations and their knowledge workers need time to learn, determine what makes sense for their company, find the pitfalls and build bridges over them, and institutionalize those learnings for future projects. The intelligent enterprise identifies a significant, clearly defined business challenge and puts an agile team together to demonstrate success. With a successful project completed, the ability to launch the next initiative is much easier, and the people involved in the first project are now tour guides on the journey.

Using this approach, leading organizations often create an analytical center of excellence (ACE) within their enterprise. An ACE consists of a small, cross-functional group of people who help the many different parts of the company successfully leverage analytics. ACEs provide several benefits:

- Provide internal consulting and training on how to apply analytics to business problems
- Serve as business sponsors in the identification and management of data integration, quality, and management activities that support analytics
- Establish clear accountability for the advancement of analytical competencies within the enterprise
- Ensure consistency in the selection and use of enterprise architecture, analytical tools, and solutions to support analytics across the enterprise

Whether you are starting your first analytics initiative or finishing your 100th project, you hopefully are getting a sense of the curiosity and excitement many people feel about analytics: there is always another question to ask with hidden gems in the answers. In healthcare, we are just at the beginning of seeing how analytics—whether biased toward the business or clinical sides of the spectrum—can transform our ecosystem. Analytics will give us better guidance on how to control costs—not just line items, but the hidden and true costs of healthcare. Analytics will help us identify and dismantle old assumptions about the way healthcare is delivered—not relying on gut instincts and hearsay, but real evidence. Analytics will allow us to determine not only the treatments that produce the best outcomes, but the real factors that determine optimum treatment efficacy and cost. The hidden gems in healthcare will surface, and with them will come better lives for patients everywhere.

ACKNOWLEDGMENT

I am grateful for the contributions of Cindy Berry and Rick Pro, both from SAS's Health and Life Sciences organization, to the content and review of this entry.

Healthcare Informatics: Data Mining

Wullianallur Raghupathi
Fordham University, New York, New York, U.S.A.

Abstract
With the development and maintenance of large health data repositories of structured and unstructured data, health organizations are increasingly using data analytics, including data mining, to analyze and utilize the patterns and relationships found in the data to make improved clinical and other health-related decisions. This entry discusses the potential of data mining in healthcare and describes the various applications of data mining methods and techniques. A brief review of examples of data mining in healthcare is also offered. An ongoing project in the mining of the unstructured information in cancer blogs is also described. Conclusions are then offered.

INTRODUCTION

Health data, including general patient profiles, clinical data, insurance data, and other medical data, are being created for various purposes, including regulatory compliance, public health policy analysis and research, and diagnosis and treatment.[1] The data include both structured data (e.g., patient histories as records in a database) and unstructured data[2] (e.g., audio/video clips, textual information such as in blogs or physician's notes). Data mining methods can be applied to search and analyze these large repositories to shed light on a wide range of health issues, including drug reactions, side effects, and other issues. For example, data mining techniques revealed the association between Vioxx, the arthritis drug, and increased risk of heart attack and stroke. The drug was withdrawn from the market (http://www.informationweek.com/news/business_intelligence/mining/showArticle.jhtml?articleID = 207300005).

In another example, IBM has been working with the Mayo Clinic for mining the data of millions of patient records to "analyze the information, look for similarities from one patient and another, and identify patterns" (http://www.healthcareitnews.com/news/data-mining-key-phase-2-ibm-mayo-partnership).

Healthcare organizations, including hospitals, health maintenance organizations (HMOs), and government entities such as the Centers for Disease Control, are establishing numerous health data repositories. These are typically large, relational databases that store different types of clinical and administrative data from primary electronic health sources such as hospital admission records. These repositories collect comprehensive data on large patient groups in longitudinal fashion, thereby permitting the examination and analysis of patterns and trends over time.[1] Tasks include utilization statistics and outcomes. The data can be used for quality assurance and

clinical management queries.[3,4] Although the breadth and depth of the repositories include a variety of health and medical data, including genetic data, biomedical data, and data for general health issues such as quality control (e.g., medical error patterns), data mining applications are relatively new.[5–8] Additionally, challenges are also foreseen. For example, large repositories may lead to a combinatorial explosion of alternatives. On the other hand, the multiple dimensions of the data for very complex relationships are typically rarely available because the relationships are spread thinly across the several dimensions.[1] Fortunately, the developing large medical and health repositories can alleviate these challenges to an extent. These are providing integrated views of the patient encounters. Data mining of these quantitative and qualitative data has great potential for improving the quality of healthcare and reducing the costs of healthcare delivery.

In this entry we discuss the potential of data mining in healthcare. An outline and discussion of the steps involved is also provided. Our ongoing research in the data mining of health-related blogs using the Unstructured Information Management Architecture is then described. Finally, conclusions are offered.

DATA MINING IN HEALTHCARE

The Value of Data Mining

Data mining is defined as "the nontrivial extraction of implicit previously unknown and potentially useful information from data."[9] The value for healthcare delivery is enhanced when the data mining has specific purposes and health/medical questions to answer. Typically, the healthcare process being data rich, many potential patterns can be discovered by the use of different types of algorithms. However, the patterns have

Encyclopedia of Information Systems and Technology, DOI: 10.1081/E-EIST-120053825

value for enhancing the quality of the healthcare delivery process only when specifically addressing a particular issue or question. For example, using a data mining method involving clustering, a user can automatically discover distinct patient sets classified by one or more variables. It is not necessary to hypothesize a solution or delve into the details of the clustering. An application with a well-defined user interface has the potential to make the mining process transparent and seamless.[10] The application with the underlying algorithm works on the data repository to enable the user to find solutions (e.g., categorizing patients, grouping patients by drug reactions, profile of emergency visit patients) in the most promising way. The data themselves become an active part of the solution. To this end, data mining is data driven. As Mullins et al. suggest, it is pertinent as a strategy to "discover" patterns already known to be true in the preliminary stages of the health data mining task. It is important to confirm the tool, build confidence in the approach, and often, serendipitously, revelations may occur.[1]

In healthcare, therefore, pattern-discovering algorithms in the data mining process can transform raw data into useful decision-making information with minimal intervention by the user, be it a physician or a hospital administrator. The data repositories created by health delivery organizations and health insurance companies are not in vain as the role of the data is enhanced. These organizations can tap into the discovery role of data mining, just as the financial services industry has done, and provide higher-quality healthcare as participants in the healthcare delivery process are empowered with useful information.

In the healthcare domain encompassing bioinformatics, medical informatics, and health informatics, data mining offers many new opportunities for practitioners and researchers. Some of the more significant ones include:[10]

- Discovery of previously unknown facts (e.g., correlation between a drug and side effect). In this situation the application learns associations and flags the user, or the application facilitates the health data to identify value (e.g., potential drug discovery).
- Organization of large repositories of health and medical data for very complex problems (e.g., pandemic patterns and clusters). In this regard, the application can provide real-time alerts as to particular situations that require immediate attention, as well as provide insight into what might occur next.
- Prediction of the future in various situations and scenarios (e.g., what-if analysis in clinical trials, consequences of certain actions on public health policy). Data mining can help forecast trends (as in epidemics) and threats as well as opportunities, thereby enabling the organization, be it for profit or

nonprofit, to deal with the future effectively with knowledge.[10]

Data Mining as a Process in Healthcare

The typical types of healthcare questions that are solvable by data mining techniques can be divided into two main categories: those that are solved by discovery techniques and those solved by predictive techniques.[10] If the healthcare problem requires the researcher to find useful patterns and relationships in the data (e.g., relationship between a particular diet and blood pressure), that problem will lead the researcher to a discovery method. On the other hand, if the healthcare problem requires the researcher to predict some type of value (e.g., the radiation dosage for a particular profile of cancer patients), that problem would obviously lead the researcher to a predictive method. In the pharmaceutical industry, for example, a range of methods, including associations, sequences, and predictive methods for clinical disease management, associations and prediction for cost/quality management, and segmentation and clustering for patient groupings in clinical trials, have tremendous potential.

Typical questions include:

- What do my patients look like?
- What is the drug dosage–patient profile association?
- With which other drugs does the new drug interact negatively?
- What effect does use of a particular drug for a disease have on other conditions?
- Does the drug cause side effects, and if so, what?

Many of the typical problems and questions can be resolved by one of a few data mining techniques.[10] They include three discovery techniques (clustering, associations, and sequences) and two predictive techniques (classification and regression).[10]

Discovery techniques

The data mining techniques based on this method find health or medical patterns that preexist in the data, but with no *a priori* knowledge of what those patterns may be. One could think of these patterns as serendipitously discovered, although the goals are inherently present in the data themselves. Three of the popular discovery techniques include:

1. The *clustering technique* groups health/medical records into segments by how similar they are based on the characteristics under study. Clustering could be used, for example, to find distinct symptoms of

diseases with similar characteristics to create a disease/patient segmentation model.

2. *Association* is a type of relationship analysis that finds relationships or associations among the health/medical records of single transactions. A potential use of the association method is for health group analysis, that is, to find out what diseases tend together to form a group, such as viral or bacterial (or patient groups), which is quite useful in epidemic/pandemic surveillance and identifying cause-treatment protocols for particular diseases.

3. The *sequential* pattern discovers associations among health/medical records, but across sequential transactions. A hospital could use sequential patterns (longitudinal studies) to analyze admissions over time, and to provide customized patient care.[10]

Predictive techniques

The predictive techniques of classification and regression are data mining techniques that can help forecast some type of categorical or numerical value (e.g., optimal dosage of a drug, drug pricing, etc.).

1. The technique of *classification* can be used to forecast the value that would fall into predefined grouping or categories. For example, it can predict whether a particular treatment will cure, harm, or have no effect on a particular patient.

2. On the other hand, the technique of *regression* is used to predict a numerical value on a continuous scale, for example, predicting the expected number of admissions each hospital will make in a year. In contrast, if the range of values is between 0 and 1, then this becomes a probability of an event occurring, such as the likelihood of a patient dying (repeat visits) or getting well, for example.[10]

In many instances a combination of data mining techniques is necessary (e.g., first perform patient segmentation using the clustering technique to identify a target group of patients); this is followed by a grouping analysis using the associations technique with the transactions (data) only for the target group to find drug affinities on which to base treatments.[10]

Mining and scoring

The five mining techniques outlined above are used against current health/medical data to create a data mining model. The process of applying an existing mining model against new data is called scoring.[10] Each of the five techniques has an associated scoring method that is used to apply against new data. Cluster scoring can be used, for example, to assign a new patient to the

appropriate clinical trial based on the existing cluster model (or a drug for treatment).

In order to select the initial mining technique, one may develop a short list of typical health questions that the most common mining method or combination of methods may help answer. For example:

1. What do my patients look like? Clustering
2. Which patients should be targeted for drug (treatment) promotion (trial)? Clustering
3. Which drugs should I use for the trial (treatment)? Association or sequential patterns
4. Which drugs should I replenish in anticipation of an epidemic? Associations
5. Which of my patients are most likely to get well (based on a protocol)? Classification or regression
6. How can I identify high-risk patients? Clustering
7. When one drug fails, which others are most likely to fail too? Sequential patterns
8. Who is most likely to have another heart attack? Classification or Regression
9. How can I improve quality of care (or patient satisfaction)? Clustering plus associations

Build and deploy data mining application

The process of building and deploying a data mining application is highly iterative.[10] This process may include three specific steps:

1. Health/medical data preparation
2. Creation and verification of the particular mining model
3. Deployment of the model in some way

The process of data preparation involves finding and organizing the health/medical data for the chosen mining technique. Once the data are ready for use, the mining technique can be involved in the development of the mining model, which is then confirmed by the developer. It is possible that the process goes through several iterations until one obtains a refined data model. After confirmation, the model is ready to be deployed for use. Generally speaking, the data preparation step comprises the identification of the specific data requirements, the appropriate location of the data, and the extraction and transformation of the data into the appropriate format for the chosen mining technique.[10]

The data mining model is created once the data are transformed and ready for use. The particular application/tool is used on the data set after choosing the technique and providing the parameters. Multiple algorithms may be used with the input parameters. In predictive techniques additional steps may be involved, including a training phase and a testing phase. The resulting model can be stored and possibly viewed using an appropriate visualization tool in the application.[10] The visualization process plays a critical role in presenting information about model quality, specific results such as associations, rules, or clusters, and other information about the data and results pertinent to the particular model. This information enables the data mining analyst to evaluate the model quality and determine whether the model fulfills its healthcare purpose. If need be, improvements to the input data, model parameters, and modeling technique can then be made to obtain a good model that reflects the healthcare objective.[10] In the final step, the data mining results are deployed in the healthcare organization as part of a business intelligence (data analytics) solution. Data mining results can be deployed by several means:

1. *Ad hoc* decision support: Use data mining on an *ad hoc* basis to address a specific nonrecurring question. For example, a pharmaceutical researcher may use data mining techniques to discover a relationship between gene counts and disease state for a cancer research project.
2. Interactive decision support: Incorporate data mining into a larger health intelligence application for ongoing interactive analysis.
3. Scoring: Apply a data mining model to generate some sort of prediction for each health/medical record, depending on model type. For example, for a clustering model, the score is the best-fit cluster for each patient. For the association model, the score is the highest-affinity item (variable), given other items (variables). For a sequence model, the score is the most likely action to occur next. For a typical predictive model, the score is the predicted value or response.[10]

EXAMPLES

Mullins et al.[1] report on the application of Health Miner to a large group of 667,000 inpatient and outpatient digital records from an academic medical system. They used three unsupervised methods: Clici mines, predictive analysis, and pattern discovery. The initial results from their study suggested that these approaches had the potential to expand research capabilities through identification of potentially novel clinical disease associations. In other examples, the prior analyses using large clinical data sets have typically focused on specific treatment or disease objects.[1] Most have examined specific treatment procedures, for example, cesarean delivery rate,[11] coronary artery bypass graft (CABG) surgery volume,[12] routine chemistry panel testing,[13] patient care, cancer risk for nonaspirin nonsteroidal/anti-

inflammatory drugs users,[14] preoperative beta-blocker use and mortality and morbidity following CABG surgery,[15] and incidence and mortality rate of acute (adult) respiratory distress syndrome,[16] to name a few. These studies have several factors in common: large sample size, clinical information source, and they support or build upon preestablished hypotheses or defined research paradigms that use specific procedures or disease data. Clinical outcome algorithms have also been applied to harness large health information databases in order to generate models directly applicable to clinical treatment. These models have been used successfully to create mortality risk assessments for adults[17–19] and pediatric intensive care units.[20]

In other studies, Uramoto et al. describe the application of IBM Text Analysis and Knowledge Mining (TAKMI) for biomedical documents to facilitate knowledge discovery from the very large text databases characteristic of life science and healthcare applications. MedTAKMI dynamically and interactively mines a collection of documents to obtain characteristic features within them.[21] By using multifaceted mining of these documents together with biomedically motivated categories for term extraction and a series of drill-down queries, users can obtain knowledge about a specific topic after seeing only a few key documents.

Inokuchi et al.[22] and Wang et al.[23] describe Med-TAKMI-clinical decision intelligence (CDI), an online analytical processing system that enables the interactive discovery of knowledge for CDI. CDI supports decision making by providing in-depth analysis of clinical data from multiple sources.[22,23] These and other examples indicate the potential and promise of data mining in healthcare.

MINING OF CANCER BLOGS WITH THE UNSTRUCTURED INFORMATION MANAGEMENT ARCHITECTURE (UIMA)

In this section we describe our ongoing research project in the use of the UIMA in mining textual information in cancer blogs. Health organizations and individuals such as patients are using information in blogs for various purposes. Medical blogs are rich in information for decision making. Current software such as web crawlers and blog analysis are good at generating statistics about the number of blogs, top ten, etc., but they are not advanced/useful computationally to help with analysis and understanding of the social networks that form in healthcare and medical blogs, the process of diffusion of ideas (e.g., the commonality of symptoms and disease management), and the sharing of ideas and feelings (support and treatment options, what worked). Therefore, there is a critical need for sophisticated tools to fill this gap. Furthermore, there are hardly any studies or applications in the content analysis of blogs.

There has been an exponential increase in the number of blogs in the healthcare area, as patients find them useful in disease management and developing support groups. Alternatively, healthcare providers such as physicians have started to use blogs to communicate and discuss medical information. Examples of useful information include alternative medicine and treatment, health condition management, diagnosis-treatment information, and support group resources. This rapid proliferation in health- and medical-related blogs has resulted in huge amounts of unstructured yet potentially valuable information being available for analysis and use.[2] Statistics indicate health-related bloggers are very consistent at posting to blogs.

The analysis and interpretation of health-related blogs are not trivial tasks. Unlike many of the blogs in various corporate domains, health blogs are far more complex and unstructured. The postings reflect two important facets of the bloggers: the feeling and the mind of the patient (e.g., an individual suffering from breast cancer but managing it). How does one parse and extract the deep semantic meanings in this environment? Mere syntactic analysis would not do.

The UIMA defines a framework for implementing systems for the analysis of unstructured data.[2,24–26] In contrast to structured information, whose meaning is expressed by the structure or the format of the data, the meaning of unstructured information cannot be so inferred.[2] Examples of data that carry unstructured information include natural language text and data from audio or video sources. More specifically, an audio stream has a well-defined syntax and semantics for rendering the stream on an audio device, but its music score is not directly represented.[27] The UIMA is sufficiently advanced and sophisticated computationally to aid in the analysis and understanding of the content of the health-related blogs. At the individual level (document-level analysis) one can perform analysis and gain insight into the patient in longitudinal studies. At the group level (collection-level analysis) one can gain insight into the patterns of the groups (network behavior, e.g., assessing the influence within the social group), for example, in a particular disease group, the community of participants in an HMO or hospital setting, or even in the global community of patients (ethnic stratification). The results of these analyses can be generalized. While the blogs enable the formation of social networks of patients and providers, the uniqueness of the health/medical terminology comingled with the subjective vocabulary of the patient compounds the challenge of interpretation. Taking the discussion to a more general level, while blogs have emerged as contemporary modes of communication within a social network context, hardly any research or insight exists in the content

analysis of blogs. The blog world is characterized by a lack of particular rules on format, how to post, and the structure of the content itself. Questions arise: How do we make sense of the aggregate content? How does one interpret and generalize? In health blogs in particular, what patterns of diagnosis, treatment, management, and support might emerge from a meta-analysis of a large pool of blog postings? The overall goal, then, is to enhance the quality of health by reducing errors and assisting in clinical decision making.

Additionally, one can reduce the cost of healthcare delivery by the use of these types of advanced health information technology.

Therefore, the *objectives* of our project include:

1. To use UIMA to mine a set of cancer blog postings from http://www. thecancerblog.com
2. To develop a parsing algorithm and clustering technique for the analysis of cancer blogs
3. To develop a vocabulary and taxonomy of keywords (based on existing medical nomenclature)
4. To build a prototype interface with Eclipse (based on our existing work in the use of Eclipse in the development of an electronic health record system)
5. To contribute to social networks in the semantic web by generalizing the models from cancer blogs

The following levels of development are envisaged:

- First level: Patterns of symptoms, management (diagnosis/treatment)
- Second level: Glean insight into disease management at individual/group levels
- Third level: Clinical decision support (e.g., generalization of patterns, syntactic to semantic)

Typically, the unstructured information in blogs comprises:

- Blog topic (posting)—What issue or question does the blogger (and comments) discuss?
  ○ Disease and treatment (not limited to)—What cancer type and treatment (other issues) are identified and discussed?
- Other information—What other related topics are discussed? What links are provided?

What Can We Learn from Blog Postings?

Unstructured information related to blog postings (bloggers), including responses/comments, can provide insight into "diseases" (cancer), "treatment" (e.g., alternative medicine, therapy), support links, etc.

1. What are the most common issues patients have (bloggers/responses)?
2. What are the cancer types (conditions) most discussed? Why?
3. What therapies and treatments are being discussed? What medical and nonmedical information is provided?
4. Which blogs and bloggers are doing a good job of providing relevant and correct information?
5. What are the major motivations for the postings (comments)? Profession (e.g., doctor) or patient?
6. What are the emerging trends in disease (symptoms), treatment and therapy (e.g., alternative medicine), support systems, and information sources (links, clinical trials)?

What Are the Phases and Milestones?

This project envisions the use of UIMA and supporting plug-ins to develop an application tool to analyze health-related blogs. The project is scoped to content analysis of the domain of cancer blogs at http://www.thecancerblog. com. Additional open-source plug-ins and an Eclipse development environment with Java/Extensible Markup Language plug-ins, limited AJAX capability, and a social network analysis tool such as Apache Agora would provide the desired capabilities. In a typical scenario, the cancer blogs can be stored in an open-source Derby database application.

- Phase 1 involved the collection of blog postings from http://www.thecancerblog.com into a Derby application.
- Phase 2 consisted of the development and configuration of the architecture—and taxonomy, clustering, correlations, keywords.
- Phase 3 entailed the analysis and integration of extracted information in the cancer blogs; preliminary results of initial analysis (e.g., patterns that are identified).
- Phase 4 involved the development of taxonomy.
- Phase 5 proposes to test the mining model and develop the user interface for deployment.

We propose to develop a comprehensive text mining system that integrates several mining techniques, including association and clustering, to effectively organize the blog information and provide decision support in terms of search by keywords.

CONCLUSIONS

The development and application of large repositories of patient-specific clinical, medical, and health data generated during patient encounters in the routine delivery of healthcare was, until recently, limited to static uses of utilization management, quality assurance, and cost management.[1] However, with the focus on reducing medical errors through evidence-based health management, these repositories are being subjected to more sophisticated analyses using data mining techniques. These techniques offer numerous opportunities to perform in-depth analysis of the data to gain new insights into the healthcare process with the resultant decision support for a range of tasks. In the future, we will see not only an increased use of data mining techniques in healthcare but also their integration with health intelligence and health organization strategy. The overall goals include the delivery of quality care with a simultaneous decrease in costs.

REFERENCES

1. Mullins, I.M.; Siadaty, M.S.; Lyman, J.; Scully, K.; Garrett, C.T.; Miller, W.G.; Muller, R.; Robson, B.; Apte, C.; Weiss, S.; Rigoutsos, I.; Platt, D.; Cohen, S.; Knaus, W.A. Data mining and clinical data repositories: Insights from a 667,000 patient data set. Comp. Biol. Med. **2006**, *36* (12), 1351–1377.
2. Spangler, S.; Kreulen, J. *Mining the Talk—Unlocking the Business Value in Unstructured Information*; IBM Press: Upper Saddle River, NJ, 2008.
3. Einbinder, J.S.; Scully, K. Using a clinical data repository to estimate the frequency and costs of adverse drug events. J. Am. Med. Inform. Assoc. **2002**, Suppl. S, S34–S38.
4. Scully, K.W.; Pates, R.D.; Desper, G.S.; Connors, A.F.; Harrell, F.E.; Pieper, K.S.; Hannan, R.L.; Reynolds, R.E. Development of an enterprise-wide clinical repository: Merging multiple legacy databases. J. Am. Med. Inform. Assoc. **1997**, Suppl. S, 32–36.
5. Brosette, S.E.; Sprague, A.P.; Hardin, J.M.; Jones, W.T.; Moser, S.A. Association rules and data mining in hospital infection control and public health surveillance. J. Am. Med. Inform. Assoc. **1998**, *5* (4), 373–381.
6. Downs, S.M.; Wallace, M.Y. Mining association rules from a pediatric primary care decision support system. Proc. AMIA Symp. 2000, 200–204.
7. Holmes, J.H.; Durbin, D.R.; Winston, F.K. Discovery of predictive models in an injury surveillance database: An application of data mining in clinical research. Proc. AMIA Symp. 2000, 359–363.
8. Prather, J.C.; Lobach, D.F.; Goodwin, L.K.; Hales, J.W.; Hage, M.L.; Hammond, W.E. Medical data mining: Knowledge discovery in a clinical data warehouse. Proc. AMIA Symp. 1997, 101–105.
9. Frawley, W.; Piatetsky-Shapiro, G.; Mathews, C. Knowledge discovery in databases: An overview. AI Magaz. 1992, 213–228.
10. Ballard, C.; Rollins, J.; Ramos, J.; Perkins, A.; Hale, R.; Dorneich, A.; Milner, E.C.; Chodagam, J. *Dynamic*

Warehousing: Data Mining Made Easy; IBM Redbook: Los Angeles, CA, 2007, http://www.redbooks.ibm.com.

11. Lin, H.-C.; Xirasagar, S. Institutional factors in cesarean delivery rates: Policy and research implications. Obstet. Gynecol. **2004**, *103* (1), 128–136.

12. Peterson, E.D.; Coombs, L.P.; DeLong, E.R.; Haan, C. K.; Ferguson, T.B. Procedural volume as a marker of quality for CABG surgery. JAMA **2004**, *291* (2), 195–201.

13. Bock, B.J.; Dolan, C.T.; Miller, G.C.; Fitter, W.F.; Hartsell, B.D.; Crowson, A.N.; Sheehan, W.W.; Williams, J. D. The data warehouse as a foundation for population-based reference intervals. Am. J. Clin. Pathol. **2003**, *120* (5), 662–670.

14. Sorensen, H.T.; Friis, S.; Norgard, B.; Mellemkjaer, W. J.; Blot, J.K.; McLaughlin, A.; Ekbom, J.A.B. Risk of cancer in a large cohort of nonaspirin NSAID users: A population-based study. Br. J. Cancer **2003**, *88* (11), 1687–1692.

15. Ferguson Jr., T.B.; Coombs, L.P.; Peterson, E.D. Preoperative beta-blocker use and mortality and morbidity following CABG surgery in North America. J. Am. Med. Assoc. **2002**, *287* (17), 2221–2227.

16. Reynolds, H.N.; McCunn, M.; Borg, U.; Habashi, C.; Cottingham, C.; Bar-Lavi, Y. Acute respiratory distress syndrome: Estimated incidence and mortality rate in a 5 million-person population base. Crit. Care **1998**, *2* (1), 29–34.

17. Knaus, W.A.; Wagner, D.P.; Lynn, J. Short-term mortality predictions for critically ill hospitalized adults: Science and ethics. Science **1991**, *18*, 389–394.

18. LeGall, J.R.; Lemeshow, S.; Saulnier, F. A new Simplified Acute Physiology Score (SAPS II) based on a European/North American multicenter study. JAMA **1993**, *270* (24), 2957–2963.

19. Lemeshow, S.; Teres, D.; Klar, J.S.; Avrunin, S.H.; Gehlbach, J.R. Mortality probability models based on an international cohort of intensive care unit patients. JAMA **1993**, *270* (20), 2478–2486.

20. Pollack, M.M.; Patel, K.M.; Ruttimann, U.E. PRISM III: An updated pediatric risk of mortality score. Crit. Care Med. **1996**, *24*, 743–752.

21. Uramoto, N.; Matsuzawa, H.; Nagano, T.; Murakami, A.; Takeuchi, H.; Takeda, K. A text-mining system for knowledge discovery from biomedical documents. IBM Syst. J. **2004**, *43* (3), 516–533.

22. Inokuchi, A.; Takeda, K.; Inaoka, N.; Wakao, F. Med-TAKMI-CDI: Interactive knowledge discovery for clinical decision intelligence. IBM Syst. J. **2007**, *46* (1), 115–133.

23. Wang, X.S.; Nayda, L.; Dettinger, R. Infrastructure for a clinical-decision intelligence system. IBM Syst. J. **2007**, *46*, 151–169.

24. Ferrucci, D.; Lally, A. Building an example application with the unstructured information management architecture. IBM Syst. J. **2004**, *43* (3), 455–475.

25. Mack, R.; Mukherjea, S.; Soffer, A.; Uramoto, N.; Brown, E.; Coden, A.; Cooper, J.; Inokuchi, A.; Iyer, B.; Mass, Y.; Matsuzawa, H.; Subramaniam, L.V. Text analytics for life science using the unstructured information management architecture. IBM Syst. J. **2004**, *43* (3), 490–515.

26. Nasukawa, T.; Nagano, T. Text analysis and knowledge system mining. IBM Syst. J. **2001**, *40* (4), 967–984.

27. Gotz, T.; Suhre, O. Design and implementation of the UIMA common analysis system. IBM Syst. J. **2004**, *43* (3), 476–489.

Healthcare Information Technology

Bernice M. Purcell
School of Business Administration and Extended Learning, Holy Family University, Philadelphia, Pennsylvania, U.S.A.

Abstract

Healthcare information technologies (HITs) encompass a growing range of data collection, processing, and analyzing devices and procedures. The healthcare industry in general is a highly regulated field, and at times agencies impose regulations on healthcare technology and data use can conflict with each other as well as with healthcare and computer industry standards. The field of HIT emerged slowly beginning in the 1960s, but advances in computer technology and declines in technology costs accelerated growth. Technologies include electronic health records, e-prescribing, computerized physician order entry, and clinical decision support systems. Beyond use for data storage and analysis are technologies such as radiological scans, robotics, and lasers, which use data to deliver healthcare services. Big data plays a growing role in the HIT area, and data governance gains importance due to the need to ensure accurate and secure data on demand.

INTRODUCTION

The article covers the growing field of healthcare information technology (HIT). Healthcare professionals use HIT extensively in providing services to patients. Hospital workers, primary care physicians, pharmaceutical researchers, and medical insurance providers are using HIT in a growing number of ways. HIT first emerged in the 1960s with the creation of electronic health record (EHR) systems. Concurrent with the establishment of the first EHR systems was the development of standards for the systems to ensure safe and effective use. Further uses of HIT including personal health records (PHR), computerization physician order entry (CPOE), and clinical decision support systems (CDSS) developed as computer use increased and technology costs declined. As the use of HIT evolved, government regulation and further standardization arose to provide a framework for usage.[1,2] Healthcare professionals now use HIT in the fields of radiology, surgery, and public health; the technologies range from computers to handheld scanners to robotics to environmental sensors.[3]

HISTORY OF HEALTH INFORMATION TECHNOLOGY

The development of first health information systems occurred in the 1960s. Early projects included a health information system at LDS Hospital in Utah, the Computer Stored Ambulatory Record System at Massachusetts General Hospital, the Regenstrief Medical Record System, the Department of Defense's Composite Health Care System, and the Veteran's Administration's De-Centralized Hospital Computer Program. Concurrent with the development of EHR systems, the World Health Organization began promoting healthcare doctrine worldwide. The International Classification of Diseases (ICD) program started an international disease tracking system. The American Medical Association developed the Current Procedural Terminology (CPT) to describe surgical procedures following the ICD system. The ICD and CPT coding systems expanded to all categories of health maintenance, enabling a standard EHR system. The development of the Uniform Billing System made a reimbursement system for medical claims possible using the EHR.[1,2]

The twofold goal of health information systems was an improvement of clinical decisions and reduction of medical errors. However, use of the technology was limited due to reluctance of physicians to use slow, expensive, unproven technologies, the reticence of administrators to invest in technology with no financial advantage, and lack of integration of the technology with hospital systems in general. The situation began to change in the 1980s with advances in computer technology that led to reduction in computing costs, introduction of large-scale microcomputer networking, and the development of data interchange protocols.[1]

Since the 1980s, the emergence of Internet technologies has spurred the growth of HIT. Many countries have adopted national healthcare systems. Healthcare professionals have grown more accustomed to using technology on a daily basis and are thus less reluctant to use systems on the job.[1]

The study "To Err is Human" published by the Institute of Medicine in 1999 motivated the public health professionals to action regarding HIT. The researchers

Encyclopedia of Information Systems and Technology, DOI: 10.1081/E-EIST-120053801

reported that as many as 98,000 people die each year in U.S. hospitals due to preventable mistakes, and recommended the use of EHR in part to remedy the problem. However, 10 years later the adoption rates of EHR systems were only 17% for physician's offices and 12% for hospitals. Government regulation influenced greater adoption of HIT in general and EHR systems in particular.[2]

REGULATIONS

U.S. government intervention in the realm of HIT extends back to the enactment of the Health Insurance Portability and Accountability Act (HIPAA) of 1996. With HIPAA, legislators mandated security and privacy measures for healthcare information systems. The Medicare Modernization Act of 2003 requires a prescription drug benefit for Medicare beneficiaries (Part D) that depends upon the support of an electronic prescription program for providers and pharmacies voluntarily using computer systems for prescriptions. The Bush Administration stressed the necessity of interoperability of health information technology infrastructure in Executive Order 13335 in 2004 and promoted quality healthcare through the use of health information technology in Executive Order 13410 in 2006. Both the Patient Protection and Affordable Care Act of 2010 and Health Care and Education Reconciliation Act of 2010 stipulated the development of interoperability and security standards and protocols in federal and state health and human service program providers.[1]

The legislation with the greatest influence on recent adoption of EHR is the Health Information Technology for Economic and Clinical Health (HITECH) Act, which is part of the American Recovery and Reinvestment Act (ARRA) of 2009. The HITECH Act established the Office of the National Coordinator and charged the office with the development of a national HIT infrastructure. The HITECH Act emphasized the importance of information security and privacy as part of the infrastructure. The HITECH Act also authorized monetary provisions for EHR-related training and HIT improvements. In conjunction with the HITECH mandate, the ARRA set requirements for EHR adoption and use by healthcare providers.[1,4]

STANDARDS

HITs are subject to sometimes conflicting standards in healthcare and in technology. The Joint Commission, the Utilization Review Accreditation Commission (URAC), and the National Committee for Quality Assurance set healthcare-related standards. Standards development organizations including the Institute of Electrical and Electronics Engineers (IEEE), the American National Standards Institute (ANSI), the National Institute of Standards and Technology (NIST), and the World Wide Web Consortium (W3C) establish, examine, and revise technology standards. The Certification Commission for Health Information Technology and the Healthcare Information Technology Standards Panel influence standards specific to healthcare technologies. Major standards in the healthcare area are ICD, Health Level Seven (HL7), and Digital Imaging and Communication in Medicine (DICOM).[1,3]

The Joint Commission is an independent, not-for-profit organization responsible for the accreditation and certification of healthcare organizations and programs in the United States. The mission of URAC focuses on determining whether healthcare and related service functions are medically necessary. The National Committee for Quality Assurance uses many approaches, including surveys, audits, and clinical performance measurement to accredit, certify, or recognize healthcare organizations.[1]

The IEEE, ANSI, NIST, and W3C establish standards for all technology use. The most important technology standard is the Open-Systems Interconnection/Internet Protocol (OSI/IP), which affects transfer of data from one system to another and provides the basis for Internet communication. The protocol includes seven layers for communications: physical, data link, network, transport, session, presentation, and application. The physical layer deals with the characteristics of the local network. The data link layer involves transferring data node-to-node within the immediate subnet. The network layer routes data across all necessary subnets. The transport layer checks for data integrity and prepares the data for transfer to another network. The session layer establishes communication between two systems. The presentation layer encodes the data for ultimate display. The application layer is the user interface, which is the ultimate means of displaying the data.[3]

Healthcare data standards regulate both coding and communications. The ICD classification system extends back to the 1960s and 1970s, with the most current revision being ICD-10. The ICD classification system encompasses several terminology–vocabulary standards: Medicare Severity Diagnosis-Related Groups (MS-DRG), CPT, Logical Observation Identifiers Names and Codes (LOINC), Systematized Nomenclature of Medicine Reference Terminology (SNOMED), Clinical Care Classification (CCC), and International Classification of Primary Care (ICPC). The MS-DRG standard affects payment services and Medicare and Medicaid billing. The CPT contains standard procedure codes for reimbursement and billing. The LOINC identifies laboratory results and clinical observations. The SNOMED integrates data from multiprovider care processes through mapping with other ICD coding standards. The CCC provides the framework for documenting holistically hospital-based patient care processes. The ICPC encompasses severity of illness checklists as well as functional status assessment charts.[3]

HL7, the standard related to management, processing, integration, and exchange of electronic healthcare data, receives its name from the OSI application layer (level 7). HL7 is currently the most widely implemented data-messaging standard in healthcare. Several core clinical standards are available through HL7 including order entry, scheduling, radiographic reports, and examination findings. HL7 establishes strategies to help healthcare agencies achieve compliance with its regulations:

1. HL7 will maintain the meaning and/or semantics of nomenclature of health-related knowledge and will promote the development of relevant and compatible standards that would support the efficient transfer and sharing of healthcare knowledge and information between computers.
2. It will evolve a formal methodology to support the creation of HL7 standards from the HL7 Reference Information Model.
3. It will disseminate information on the benefits of healthcare information standardization to academic institutions, healthcare management organizations, healthcare service providers, policy makers, and the public at large.
4. It will encourage the adoption and diffusion of HL7 standards worldwide through the efforts of HL7 international affiliate organizations, which will be formed to participate in developing and localizing HL7 standards.
5. It will bring together domain experts from academic institutions, healthcare service provider organizations, and healthcare management organizations to collaborate and develop standards for HL7 inclusion in various specialty areas.
6. HL7 will join with other Standards Development Organizations and national and international sanctioning bodies such as ANSI and International Organization for Standardization to promote the mutual exchange and use of compatible and other healthcare information standards.
7. HL7 will ensure that current propagate standards fulfill the diverse requirements of the present era and will initiate effort to meet the emergent requirements.
8. HL7 will institute membership policies to ensure that all requirements are met uniformly and equitably with quality and consistency.[3]

The DICOM standard addresses the transfer of digital images in a variety of formats between diverse devices and systems. The level of transferability bridges gaps in interoperability among different hardware systems and platforms. Healthcare areas that use DICOM standards include cardiology, dentistry, endoscopy, mammography, ophthalmology, orthopedics, pathology, radiation therapy, radiology, surgery, and even veterinary science. The DICOM standards committee has numerous working groups that concentrate efforts in five general application areas: network image management, network image interpretation management, network print management, imaging procedure management, and offline storage media management.[3]

TECHNOLOGIES

A number of computerized technologies exist in the health information area. Most HIT systems either interact with or act as part of an EHR system. Other forms of HIT include PHR, CPOE, CDSS, picture archiving and communication systems (PACS), regional health information organizations (RHIOs), and the Nationwide Health Information Network (NwHIN).

Electronic Health Records

Healthcare practitioners use EHR systems to collect, store, and retrieve patient data. The systems allow health information professionals to view patient data upon request, enter patient care orders, and receive advice in making healthcare decisions.[11] An EHR system seeks to improve healthcare provider access to all relevant patient health data enabling the diagnosis and treatment of both injuries and diseases.

Researchers classify EHR systems as either basic or comprehensive. Basic EHR systems have 10 clinical functions used in at least one hospital unit, while comprehensive EHR systems have 24 clinical functions used throughout all hospital units. Four groups of clinical functions are clinical documentation, test and imaging results, computerized provider-order entry, and decision support. Clinical documentation functions include physicians' notes, nursing assessments, problem lists, medication lists, discharge summaries, demographic characteristics of patients, and advanced directives. Test and imaging results include laboratory reports, radiologic reports, radiologic images, diagnostic test results, diagnostic test images, and consultant reports. Computerized provider-order entry functions are laboratory tests, radiologic tests, medications, consultation requests, and nursing orders. Decision support functions include clinical guidelines, clinical reminders, drug allergy alerts, drug–drug interaction alerts, drug–laboratory interaction alerts, and drug–dose support.[5] Basic and comprehensive EHR systems are both able to meet all legislated requirements. While adoption of comprehensive systems provides the greater benefits, the financial cost and time to implement greatly reduce the range of clinical systems a healthcare provider ultimately selects.

Lack of widespread EHR implementation motivated legislators to enact ARRA in 2009. The ARRA has best encouraged EHR system establishment through incentives, including the U.S. Department of Health and Human Services-sponsored Medicare and Medicaid Incentive Programs. The key provision of both incentive programs is documentation of meaningful use of an EHR system.

To document meaningful use, the programs designate required reporting objectives that include core objectives, nine menu objectives, and clinical quality measures (CQM). Healthcare providers must report all of the core objectives and five of the menu objectives; there is no specific threshold for reporting CQM. The core objectives are CPOE, drug–drug and drug–allergy checks, maintenance of an up-to-date problem list of current and active diagnoses, E-Prescribing (eRx), maintenance of an active medication list, maintenance of an active medication allergy list, maintenance of recording demographics, maintenance of recording and charting changes in vital signs, maintenance of recording of smoking status for patients 13 years or older, implementation of clinical decision support, provision to patients of the ability to view, download, or transmit their health information online, provision of clinical summaries for patients for each office visit, and protection of electronic health information.

The first two menu objectives are a submission of electronic data to immunization registries or the submission of electronic syndromic surveillance data to public health agencies; it is required that one of these two is fulfilled. The remaining menu objectives are drug formulary checks, incorporating of clinical lab test results, generation of lists of patients by specific conditions, sending reminders to patients for preventive follow-up care, use of patient-specific education resources, electronic access to health information for patients, medication reconciliation, and summary of care record for transitions of care. Two sets of CQM exist, one for adult patients (both Medicare and Medicaid) and one for pediatric patients (Medicaid only). The CQM for adults are controlling high blood pressure, use of high-risk medications in the elderly, preventive care and screening for tobacco use, screening and cessation intervention, use of imaging studies for low back pain, preventive care and screening (including screening for clinical depression) and developing related follow-up plan, documentation of current medications in the medical record, preventive care and screening including body mass index screening and follow-up, closing the referral loop through receipt of specialist reports, and functional status assessment for complex chronic conditions. The CQM for pediatric patients are appropriate testing for children with pharyngitis, weight assessment and counseling for nutrition and physical activity for children and adolescents, chlamydia screening for women, use of appropriate medications for asthma, childhood immunization status, appropriate treatment for children with upper respiratory infection, attention-deficit/hyperactivity disorder (ADHD) treatment notation including follow-up care for children prescribed ADHD medication, preventive care and screening and screening for clinical depression and follow-up plan, and notation of children who have dental decay or cavities. Each of the incentive programs had slightly different levels of reimbursement for EHR implementation. The Medicaid incentive program reimburses up to $63,700 and the Medicare incentive program reimburses up to $43,700.[6–9] With the advent of ARRA and the meaningful use directives, EHR adoption became a necessity for healthcare practitioners. The mandated systems fulfill meaningful use reporting requirements but cause a major change in workflow. The goal of EHR implementation is to reduce medical errors. Increased legibility, access to information, and standardization of data entry and display are factors influencing the realization of the goal. The outcome of the goal is overall improvement in the healthcare system in the United States.

Increased revenue and avoided costs are two financial benefits of EHR adoption. One means of increasing revenue is the shortening of visit times due to more efficient records. Improvements in medical billing also increased revenue. Fewer rejected claims and more accurate coding of work performed generated the medical billing revenue increase. Avoidance of dictation and external billing are cost-avoidance benefits, as is staff reductions.[10] Doctors are able to attend to more patients on any given day because of shortened visit time for each patient. Medical office staffs have the potential to work more efficiently; filing duties are greatly reduced if not eliminated.

Several obstacles need to be overcome before EHR systems maximize potential benefits. Even with existing incentive programs, cost and uncertainty of return on investment predominate as the main obstacles to EHR adoption. One study of physicians' offices in Massachusetts indicated that of the survey respondents, only 27% experienced a positive return on investment over a 5-year period.[10] Not all physicians' offices experience all of the potential benefits; some actually have longer visits due to lack of physician or staff capability with the technology. Costs can be greater than anticipated and budgeted.

Lack of interoperability continues to be an issue with EHR systems. In 2012, 700 EHR vendors sold over 1,700 highly proprietary products.[11] While coding standards exist to allow similarities in recording of medical data hardware or software, differences impede the ability to share the data among different healthcare providers' systems.

Personal Health Record Systems

PHR empower patients to play a more active role in their healthcare. Through the ability to view healthcare data, obtain referrals, schedule appointments, obtain prescription refills, and e-mail physicians using PHR, patients can be more active and knowledgeable participants in their healthcare. Researchers note that major capabilities of PHR systems include quality, completeness, depth, and accessibility of personal health data; better communication; better access to health knowledge; portability; and self-entry of data.[1]

Major means of PHR implementation are stand-alone PHR, patient portals, and integrated PHR. Stand-alone PHR programs are home-use systems for patients that allow the patients to manually enter and organize their own data. Patient portals allow users to connect to their primary care physicians' records for limited information. Integrated PHR systems use network or Internet connections to allow patients to directly log into health records systems of their primary physicians; some hospitals also have PHR systems integrated into the institution's EHR system.[1]

Stand-alone PHR programs, which include Dr. Koop, HealthCentral, and Revolution Health, have extremely limited capabilities. The stand-alone PHR programs do not have the ability to connect with physician records, so the onus falls entirely on the patient to maintain and update data.[1,3] Potential inaccuracy of the data entered and lack of review by knowledgeable healthcare professionals impair the usefulness of stand-alone PHR programs.

Patient portals are a step further than stand-alone PHR programs in that portals allow the patient access to their primary care physician's records. Patient portals, however, lack full integration; data comes only from the primary care physician's office and does not incorporate tests or lab results from other sources. Also, patient portals are not connected with hospitals.[1] One patient portal that differs from the model of connection to the physician's office is Google Health, a web-based patient portal which allows patients to request healthcare providers to send electronically captured treatment data to Google's site for collection into a patient's record. Participating care providers that would send the data to the Google Health portal include Cleveland Clinic, PatientSite (an integrated PHR system), Beth Israel Deaconess Medical Center, Minute Clinic/CVS, Quest Laboratories, RxAmerica, and Walgreens. Rather than the patient accessing the provider's system, the patient requests that the provider send the requested health data to the Google Health portal. While it does overcome the limitation

of the patient only accessing data from the primary care provider, Google Health presents issues with security, privacy, and ownership of the data.[10]

Integrated PHR systems provide the greatest benefit to patients, as they provide access to healthcare provider-maintained data. Often integrated PHR systems are an aspect of EHR systems in physician offices in which the PHR allow the patients password-protected restricted access to the physician's data as well as test and lab results. Data available to patients can include clinical data, claims data, interpretations of technical data in the record, screening and appointment alerts, and information about their health concerns.[1]

Researchers have conducted studies of success of PHR systems including both vendor-created and institution-created integrated PHR systems. MyChart by Epic Systems is one vendor-created PHR system studied. The PHR system allows patients to view most of the contents of their medical records (except for progress notes), diagnoses, active medications, allergies, health maintenance schedules, immunizations, test results, radiology results, appointments, and demographics. The overall system provides improved patient–physician communication. The PatientSite system at Beth Israel Deaconess Medical Center is a self-built system which provides patients full access to problem lists, medications, allergies, visits, laboratory results, results of diagnostic tests, and microbiology results as well as the ability to access personal health information from any of three hospitals and 72 ambulatory care facilities. Patients could also use the PatientSite system to update information including home glucometer readings, over-the-counter medications, and personal notes themselves. Indivo is a self-built, institution-neutral open-source personally controlled health record. A personally controlled health record is a subset of PHR in which a patient can designate who can read, write, or modify his or her health records. Patients can also grant consent or restrict permission to use the health information for research studies. Other PHR systems include Dossia, a web-based framework for sharing personal health data through open-source structures, and Microsoft HealthVault which enables Internet-based users to search for health-related information and to store their personal health data in a secure online environment.[1] An overall analysis of the PHR systems indicate an increase in the patient's knowledge regarding his or her health situation and better communications between the physician and patient.

A major benefit of integrated PHR systems is an improved patient–physician relationship. Many patients want a more active role in their healthcare, and PHR enable the patients to view the accumulation of records about themselves and to actively manage their health information. Both parties have access to information used to determine healthcare solutions, which improves patient–physician interaction. Physicians see PHR as a way to improve intervention planning and patient education.[10] Improved patient–physician relationships and better patient education promotes a higher level of patient empowerment in healthcare.

Challenges with PHR implementation stem from patient concerns regarding privacy and security of data and lack of technical standards. Interoperability remains an issue with PHR for the same reasons cited in the EHR section. Important hurdles include the authentication of the user (ensuring that the person attempting to access the data is indeed the patient), integration of Internet knowledge sources, and security of messaging.[11] Technical standardization of PHR and EHR systems can mitigate the challenges cited.

eRx Systems

The Medicare Modernization Act of 2003 provided a major stimulus for increased use of electronic prescribing (eRx) systems. eRx systems can either be stand-alone or integrated, where the stand-alone systems support only eRx and integrated systems are part of a comprehensive EHR system. Due to the incorporation into EHR systems, the integrated systems predominate. Five major functions performed using eRx systems are computerized prescribing associated with clinical decision support, pharmacy benefit eligibility checking, formulary compliance, medical history reporting, and prescription routing to the pharmacy.[11] When a healthcare provider enters a prescription into an eRx system, the system records the prescription and checks against both the diagnosis and patient history, including other current prescriptions. The checks reduce the possibility of adverse drug events (ADEs), which are basically side effects of a prescription due to interaction with another prescription or incorrect dosage. Once checks of the prescription are complete, the system sends prescription electronically to the patient's pharmacy. The transmission of an electronically prepared prescription reduces the pharmacy's need to check patient prescription plan eligibility or to call to verify the prescription due to illegible handwriting.

Patient safety is the primary benefit of eRx systems.[11] The functions of the system ensure fewer adverse drug interactions and pharmacy fulfillment errors. The entire prescribing process is more efficient, with both reconciliation of prescriptions being quicker to perform and reduction of a pharmacist's time and effort spent on difficult-to-read prescriptions.

A number of barriers to implementation exist for eRx systems. The barriers include the need to overcome previous negative technology experiences, initial and long range costs, lost productivity at implementation time, competing priorities, change management issues, confusion about competing products, information technology

requirements, interoperability limitations, and standards limitations.[11] However, with the mandate to install eRx systems and the incentives to do so in conjunction with EHR systems, the benefits realized reduce the impact of the barriers. Upon full implementation of eRx systems few problems were noted.

Computerized Physician Order Entry Systems

CPOE systems are often a subset of EHR systems. The ARRA makes CPOE system activity a requirement of EHR systems in order to fulfill meaningful use criteria. A CPOE system allows the physician to enter medication, diagnostic testing, and ancillary service orders.[1,11]

Benefits of CPOE include increased efficiency through use of medication and lab ordering functionality, potential reduction in medication errors and ADEs, and improvement in the quality of prescribing. Of particular importance is the reduction of ADEs. Most preventable ADEs result from errors at the physician ordering stage. System efficiencies as well as the elimination of problems resulting from both illegible writing and lack of structure generate the benefits of the systems. Overall the benefits improve patient care and safety.[11–13] The use of CPOE standardizes the entry of physician orders. The standardization improves understandability due to better and more uniform structure. Since many medications have names that differ by a few letters, or have long names that physicians abbreviate, handwritten prescribing was a major threat to patient safety. Ready access to data about both drug interactions and adverse effects within the system provides the physician better information to make an informed decision about medication.

Safety issues attributed to CPOE systems are a major concern. A study divided safety issues related to CPOE into five distinct areas: people, process, organization, environment, and technology. Safety issues in the people area involve the user's lack of clinical knowledge or technical expertise, level of critical thinking ability, or negative emotions arising from using the system. Safety issues arising from process relate to the change in communication patterns and workflow that occur when adopting CPOE. Changes in power structure and organizational culture resulting from CPOE adoption are organizational safety issues. Distractions in the work environment were the main environmental issue. Inherit technology problems, such as data entry failures and crashes, are the final class of issues.[14]

Other barriers exist to the adoption of CPOE. High installation and operating costs, disruptions to operating procedures, organizational and clinical work practice issues, and uncertainty about governmental requirements related to HIT are major issues. Also, several researchers fear that a rush to adopt CPOE could adversely affect the quality of the design and implementation of the system, thus negating the system's benefits.[12] Healthcare providers need to treat CPOE technology adoption as a major undertaking. Fast-tracking installation can lead to poor system quality decreasing physician use and thus reducing the benefit of the system overall.

Clinical Decision Support Systems

CDSS aid healthcare professionals in a clinical setting with evaluating decisions. Typical decisions made with the use of CDSS include decisions regarding patient transfer to or from an intensive care unit, use of ventilation and drugs, and discharge home or to a skilled nursing facility. While CDSS can be nonknowledge based with use of machine learning and statistical pattern recognition, typical systems are knowledge based. Knowledge-based CDSS are comprised of a knowledge base, an inference engine, and a user interface. The knowledge base contains information gathered from healthcare professionals formatted as if–then rules. The inference engine combines the necessary rules from the knowledge base with the patient data. The CDSS enables capture as well as reuse of clinical data and optimization of problem solving and decision making.[1]

Different benefits of CDSS emerge from system use by different clinical users. Studies found that nurses and doctors use the systems differently, with nurses using system-generated information to strengthen their patient advocacy position in coordinating care with physicians whereas physicians use the systems to compare with their own clinical judgment.[1] Nurses provide direct care for the patients and are able to observe the patients more closely. Based upon their own observations and CDSS use, nurses can raise concerns to the doctors, thus improving patient care. Doctors supplement their own knowledge with the information the CDSS provides. The CDSS output may offer the doctor alternative diagnoses or offer new treatment methodologies.

Some safety issues exist with the use of CDSS. The safety issues include false expectations of the system or incorrect perception of accuracy, deficit of either clinical knowledge or clinical judgment on part of the user, missing data, and lack of patient-specific decision support.[1] Users can become over-reliant upon the CDSS or use the system to rush decisions. When creating the knowledge base, developers could fail to enter important information into the system due to carelessness or misjudgment, rendering the CDSS output less than optimal or even wholly incorrect. Combinations of conditions of a specific patient may not be available in the knowledge base, also making the decision less accurate.

Regional Health Information Organizations

RHIOs are local groups of physicians' offices, hospitals, health insurance providers, employers, pharmacies, consumer groups, and government officials that work together to establish a local infrastructure for HIT interoperability.[1] Members of an RHIO meet to agree upon standards and technology that all members will adopt. Use of common standards and technologies enable interoperability of the systems. While a trade-off of less freedom of choice in system adoption exists, the benefit of interoperability outweighs the cost.

The Massachusetts eHealth Collaborative (MAeHC) provides an instructive example of an RHIO. Members of the MAeHC agreed on a standard architecture and a limited number of vendors. Factors determining the architecture and vendors include security, cost, implementation complexity, performance, measurement of quality of care, strategic goals, trust in the medical community, and the stakeholders' desire for independence. The participants enjoyed the benefits of increased quality, safety, and efficiency in the regional system. However, members found barriers during the implementation of the RHIO that included inadequate standards for data representation and vocabulary, vendor and system obsolescence concerns, and privacy and security issues.[1] Even so, a recent survey of participants in the MAeHC found that just over a quarter of the respondents experienced a 5-year return on investment on the technology expenditure.[10]

Nationwide Health Information Network

The NwHIN is the proposed infrastructure for sharing health data across the United States. The Office of the National Coordinator of Health Information (ONC) established the initial plan for the infrastructure during the Bush Administration. The ONC proposed a model with a network of health information organizations exchanging data with other such organizations. The plan was essentially a decentralized network, possibly built of RHIOs. However the ONC now recommends a centralized, point-to-point information exchange enabled by Internet technologies.[1,15] Change in staffing in the ONC during the Obama Administration likely caused the change in strategy.

At this point, politicians and healthcare practitioners debate the infrastructure of the NwHIN. Advantages and disadvantages exist under both a decentralized RHIO-based infrastructure and the centralized Internet-based counterpart. The RHIO-based infrastructure could potentially optimize existing resources while preserving local autonomy. The functions of RHIOs depend on the community's need and RHIOs serving the need through health information exchange across the community. The

RHIO model is difficult to sustain due to lack of return on investment and funding cuts under the Obama Administration. Most other countries with health information sharing infrastructures have adopted models that are consistent with the centralized architecture. However, current technology makes implementation at the nationwide scale impractical.[15] Further examination of infrastructure options and technologies could result in a compromise between the proponents of each model or creation of a radically different model as new technologies develop.

OTHER IMPLEMENTATIONS OF HEALTH INFORMATION TECHNOLOGIES

Health information technology encompasses more than the storage and transmission of patient health information. A wide range of technologies exist to aid in diagnostic and surgical procedures. Technologies allow practitioners to perform new procedures and to process data in new ways that lead to improvements in public health.

Radiology

Several health information technologies exist in the field of radiology. The older technologies in the field are x-ray and ultrasound, and newer computer-aided technologies include computed tomography (CT) scan, magnetic resonance imaging (MRI), single-photon emission computed tomography (SPECT) scan, positron emission tomography (PET) scan, and dual x-ray absorptiometry (DEXA) scan. Computer-aided detection capabilities integrated into the technologies allow users to automatically read the scan. In addition to these diagnostic technologies, PACS enable electronic storage and communication of scans and tests.[16]

x-Ray technology has evolved in recent years with the introduction of digital x-rays. One advantage of digital x-rays is that technicians do not need to develop the images, so images are available immediately for viewing and sharing. Additionally, practitioners can easily share the digital images over a network for consultation, and several consulting healthcare professionals can view the images simultaneously in consultation. Users can enhance, highlight, and resize digital x-ray images; technologists are exploring the concept of three-dimensional digital x-rays based upon multiple images. Digital x-rays also use less radiation than traditional x-rays, making the process safer for patients and practitioners. Healthcare workers use x-rays prevalently in cases of broken bones and in the fields of dentistry and mammography.[16]

Ultrasound makes use of high-frequency sound waves and the echoes produced when the waves hit an object. Computer technology has enhanced ultrasound technology by enabling users to view two-dimensional moving pictures onscreen during the imaging. Surgeons use three-dimensional ultrasonic endoscopes for minimally invasive surgery. Uses of ultrasound extend from the study of blood flow to treatment of prostate disease and diagnosis of breast cancer.[16]

Health information technologies that are specifically based upon digital imaging techniques include CT scans, MRIs, PET scans, SPECT scans, and DEXA scans. CT scans incorporate the use of x-rays and digital technology in the generation of cross-sectional images of a patient's body. Exams using CT scans can contain thousands of images and are better than x-rays alone in distinguishing soft tissue. Practitioners also use CT scans to locate nerve centers when dealing with pain. Enhanced CT scans use special dyes to aid in diagnosing brain tumors. Virtual cystoscopy and colonoscopy use CT scans and reduce the need for invasive surgery.[16]

The scientific visualization technique in MRI enables the MRI machines to use computers combined with strong magnetic fields and radio waves to produce images from mathematically generated data. The images are accurate pictures of body or brain structures aiding in the diagnosis of strokes, brain tumors, and multiple sclerosis. Practitioners use functional MRIs (fMRIs) to identify brain activity through the measurement of metabolic changes in active parts of the brain. The fMRI aids in the diagnosis and treatment of strokes, brain tumors, and other brain injuries. Neurosurgeons use the MRI technique of diffusion tensor imaging as a surgical aid.[16]

Healthcare professionals use radioisotope technology in PET scans to create images of the body in action. Computers construct images from the positive electrons (positrons) emitted by radioactive substances technicians administer to patients prior to testing. The images a PET scan produces show how the body works rather than how it looks. Doctors use PET scans to detect changes in cell function that indicate conditions such as Alzheimer's disease, Parkinson's disease, epilepsy, learning disabilities, bipolar disorder, and cancer. Neuroimaging techniques show the chemical and physiological processes taking place in the brain, allowing doctors to diagnose schizophrenia, main depression, post-traumatic stress disorder, and obsessive–compulsive disorder. Single-photon emission computer tomography scans are similar to PET scans, but the equipment is less expensive. The SPECT scan uses gamma radiation in image creation. Doctors can diagnose osteoporosis through the use of DEXA scans, which use low-radiation x-rays to show changes in intensity after passing through bone, which indicate changes in bone density.[16]

A PACS is an electronic system to acquire, store, display, and transmit medical images. The PACS allows users to quickly and easily share images with authorized practitioners through the use of the DICOM standard protocol. Radiology information systems often integrate PACS to facilitate the sharing of images.[16]

Surgery

Information technologies in surgery include computer-aided surgery, robotics, and laser surgery. The technologies continue to advance, and practitioners look to use nanotechnology in the future. Computer technology can assist in surgery in several ways. Use of enhanced images and an endoscope, a thin tube connected to a microcamera, enables minimally invasion surgery. Computer-assisted surgical planning makes use of a virtual environment to provide realistic models on which to teach and plan surgical operations.[16]

Several different robotic devises exist to aid in surgery. Robots provide several advantages in the surgical process: robots hold instruments for long periods of time without becoming tired or unsteady, determine proper pressure and tension when manipulating instruments, and can scale down surgical motions. ROBODOC, the first robot used in surgery, performed a hip replacement in 1992. Technologists developed an automated endoscopic system for optimal positioning for the space program, but it now assists in endoscopic surgical procedures. Surgeons use the ZEUS robotic surgical system for minimally invasive microsurgery; ZEUS's computer-controlled arms scale back the surgeon's movements and filter out hand tremors. Developers created daVinci for use in endoscopic cardiac bypass surgery, mitral value repairs, and coronary bypass procedures. Other robots surgeons use are MINERVA for stereotactic neurosurgical procedures and ARTEMIS for minimally invasive surgeries. These and other robots aid in a variety of surgical techniques. The main problem with robots is the large size of the units, leading to current development of portable sensor-driven robots.[16]

Surgeons use laser surgery to cut, vaporize tumors, and seal small blood vessels. LASIK, a laser surgery technique, corrects vision through reshaping the cornea.[16] Use of computer-aided surgery, robots, and lasers help surgeons perform operations in smaller areas with greater precision and increased patient safety.

Public Health

Public health informatics is the use of technology to research and inform the practice of public health. In particular, epidemiologists, who use statistical data collection and analysis to study public health, can perform research more efficiently and effectively. One means of study involves the use of computer simulations such as the Models of Infectious Disease Agent Study to study influenza outbreaks. Syndromic surveillance is a modeling approach aimed at the containment of infectious diseases through the use of healthcare data that can indicate probable cases or outbreaks. The National Electronic Disease Surveillance System is part of the public health information network in the United States that uses health data in the prediction of possible epidemics. The Joint United Nations Programme on HIV/AIDS is an epidemiologic software tool researchers use to map and predict the spread of HIV/AIDS.[16]

DATA STEWARDSHIP

An important issue healthcare professionals need to address is data stewardship. In the context of healthcare, data stewardship pertains to balancing the rights of patients to have their data protected with improvements in effectiveness of the health system. Data stewardship encompasses all activities related to collection, use, disclosure, management, and security of health information.[17] Essentially a data steward has the role of maintaining the accuracy, security, and availability of data. As diverse entities share health data, several data stewards will be responsible for the data; in fact, one site may require multiple data stewards. For example, the data for one patient may be under the control of a data steward at the primary care office, multiple data stewards at a hospital (admissions office, laboratory, and radiology department), a data steward at the health insurer, and a data steward at the pharmacy. An important area of consideration related to data stewardship is the reuse of health data. Researchers access health data to perform studies and generate information used for improvement of public health.

Researchers have established principles related to data stewardship: accountability, transparency, notice to patients, technical issues, patient consent, permitted use and disclosures, and enforcement and remedies. Accountability entails the application of and adherence to government or healthcare agency regulations. Transparency is the existence of clear, understandable policies and procedures for storage, processing, and delivery of data as well as related business processes and practices. Notice to patients relates to permitted use and disclosures, which involve the use of patient data for studies. The patients must give consent for researchers to use healthcare data for studies (known as secondary use of data) and must receive notice whenever researchers use the data. Technical issues involve the maintenance of quality and security of data as well as deidentification of data earmarked for secondary use. Administrators need to establish methods to enforce policies and procedures related to the quality, security, and privacy of data and establish remedies regarding problems pertaining to the data quality, security, or privacy.[1,17]

Several areas for improvement exist in the data governance area in healthcare. Healthcare professionals need to establish and monitor data ownership and security policies. System developers need to design data architecture and governance models to ensure improved management and sharing of healthcare data within organizations. Data models need to comply with all relevant standards.[4]

BIG DATA AND HEALTHCARE

The current phenomenon of big data also has a tremendous positive effect on the healthcare industry. The term big data comes from the fact that the datasets stored and analyzed are huge. The data exist in nontraditional forms such as multimedia and unstructured text data. The nontraditional sources generating the data include environmental sensors and the Internet. Advances in data storage technology and processing enabled the development of a variety of big data technologies.[18]

The collection of healthcare data from sensors, surveys, and other big data-related sources enables the study of health data through the development of data analytics engines. Data analytics allows such activities as the comparison of data between healthcare providers and health insurer networks, determination of factors driving the performance of health insurers, and improvement of healthcare through the use of the best-performing providers.[4]

Google Flu Trends, an example of big data's use in healthcare, is a query model aimed at predicting and estimating the intensity of influenza epidemics. Google started using the query model based upon Internet search terms to estimate national, regional, and state influenza like illness (ILI) activity. Researchers derived the model by fitting linear regression models to weekly counts of search queries related to ILI activity submitted between 2003 and 2007. The emergence of a pandemic influenza virus in 2009 that researchers did not detect using the system led the researchers to revise the algorithm. The new Google Flu Trends model used retrospective estimates from the revised algorithm. Both the original and the updated Google Flu Trends models demonstrate a high retrospective correlation with national and regional ILI surveillance data at the respective levels. Google Flu Trends also indicated a strong correlation with emergency department influenza cases at the local level.[9,19]

The ability of Google Flu Trends to forecast influenza epidemics is questionable. Researchers have found problems with both the original and the modified models. Researchers hypothesized that the problems could stem from changes in internet search activity and differences found in epidemics between the development and use of the models. Differences in epidemics include seasonality, geographical heterogeneity, and age distribution. Researchers concluded that the Google Flu Trends data should be interpreted with caution until developers further refine the algorithm. However, the use of near-real time electronic health data and refined computational methods for model fitting could have a positive impact on the development of influenza surveillance systems.[9]

Several current big data initiatives in healthcare aim to increase the value of healthcare. Kaiser Permanente, a major healthcare system, has implemented an extensively integrated EHR system called HealthConnect across all of its facilities. Analysis of operation of the HealthConnect system indicates a reduction of office visits by 26.2% and an eightfold increase in scheduled telephone visits.[4] Due to the sharing of data among all of the facilities in Kaiser Permanente, physicians are able to conduct telephone consultations with patients rather than needing to schedule office visits for follow-up appointments after tests.

Sanofi, as major pharmaceutical firm, used big data to reverse the rejection by G-BA, a German payor, for coverage of its product Lantus, a form of insulin. Big data research allowed Sanofi to prove that Lantus use resulted in a 17% higher persistence, delaying possible need for expensive conventional therapy. Blue Shield of California is partnering with Nant Health to use big data in advancement of care delivery through improved evidence-based personal health care. AstraZeneca and HealthCore, a subsidiary of WellPoint, are conducting studies to find the most effective and economical treatments for both chronic diseases and common ailments. Employers such as Providence Everett Medical Center conduct programs offering financial rewards or other incentives to employees meeting designated wellness criteria. Providence Everett Medical Center documented a 14% reduction in employee health cost and a 20% decrease in sick leave.[4]

Big data has spurred several healthcare innovations. Asthmopolis developed a GPS-enabled tracking system that monitors when asthmatics use inhalers. Researchers store and analyze the tracking information in conjunction with data related to known asthma catalysts from the Centers for Disease Control. The goal is to aid physicians in developing treatment plans for asthmatics. Ginger.io has developed a smartphone application that integrates data obtained from the app and cellphone sensors with publicly available research by the National Institutes of Health and other such sources of behavioral health data. The goal of the app is to monitor activity that could indicate illness or anxiety. mHealthCoach uses data to provide education about the patients' conditions and to aid the patients in following the prescribed treatments. The Healthcare Cost and Utilization Project, sponsored by the Agency for Healthcare Research and Quality, as well as numerous clinical trials are the sources of data for mHealthCoach. Rise Health has developed a dashboard for healthcare providers to improve collection, storage, and exchange of information.[4]

As the use of big data increases in healthcare, developers must address several concerns. Data governance efforts must increase and become more standardized. Developers must design mechanisms for sharing data that maintain patient privacy and security. Industry analysts must develop better overall capabilities in the areas of data analysis, data management, and system management.[4]

CONCLUSION

HITs play a pivotal role in delivering healthcare services and conducting research in pharmacology, epidemiology, and public health. Regulations and standards provide a framework for HIT usage and operation, but, unfortunately, at times contradict each other, hampering efforts to effectively use and share data. HITs are subject to standards pertaining to both healthcare and computing. Initial HIT use involved data collection and storage in the form of EHR. With advances in computing technology, HIT expanded to include PHR, eRx, CPOE, and CDSS. A proposed national infrastructure for health data sharing in the United States, the NwHIN, is still under development. Two different models currently exist for the NwHIN expansion: decentralized through the use of RHIOs, or centralized under government management.

HITs enable the delivery of modern healthcare services. Radiology practitioners use ultrasound, CT scans, MRIs, PET scans, SPECT scans, and DEXA scans regularly. Professionals store and share radiological data using PACS, which are often integrated with EHR systems. Surgeons frequently use computer-aided surgery, robotics, or lasers to either aid or perform operations and procedures.

The dependence upon HIT-generated data leads to the increased vigilance regarding accuracy, privacy, and security. Data governance is a growing area that addresses issues related to data accuracy, privacy, and security. The role of the data steward is a key aspect in data governance and employees with the designation of data stewards have a crucial role in ensuring accuracy, availability, and security of healthcare data.

The term "big data" refers to the collection and use of data from a variety of sources in the decision making and research processes. Healthcare professionals acquire data through the use of a plethora of scanners in the environment or the Internet. Pharmaceutical researchers and medical researchers use big data to create the next generation of drugs, medical devices, and procedures.

The use of HIT and related data will continue to grow as new computing-related technologies develop further. Standards and regulations have an important influence on HIT use, and therefore agencies must examine and refine these codes to ensure compatibility with one another. The dual promises of HIT are the improvement of healthcare and simultaneous decrease in associated costs.

REFERENCES

1. Purcell, B.M. *Examining the Relationship Between Electronic Health Record Interoperability and Quality Management in School of Business and Technology Management;* Northcentral University, UMI Dissertation Publishing: Ann Arbor, MI, 2013.
2. Malhotra, N.; Lassiter, M. The coming age of electronic medical records: From paper to electronic. Intl J. Manag. Inform. Syst. **2014**, *18* (2), 117.
3. Tan, J.; Fay, C.P.Ed., *Adaptive Health Management Information Systems,* 3rd Ed.; Jones and Bartlett: Gaithersburg, MD, 201; p. 413.
4. Groves, P.; Kayyali, B.; Knott, D.; Van Kuiken, S. *The "Big Data" Revolution in Healthcare: Accelerating Value and Innovation;* McKinsy & Company, 2013.
5. Jha, A.K.; DesRoches, C.M.; Campbell, E.G.; Donelan, K.; Rao, S.R.; Ferris, T.G.; Shields, A.; Rosenbaum, S.; Blumenthal, D. Use of electronic health records in U. S. hospitals. N Engl J. Med. **2009**, *36* (16), 1628–1638.
6. *An Introduction to the Medicaid EHR Incentive Program for Eligible Professionals.* Center for Medicare and Medicaid Services, Department of Health and Human Services: Washington, D. C., April 2014 (updated).
7. *An Introduction to the Medicare EHR Incentive Program for Eligible Professionals.* Center for Medicare and Medicaid Services, Department of Health and Human Services: Washington, D. C., April 2014 (updated).
8. Adler-Milstein, J.; Green, C.E.; Bates, D.W. A survey analysis suggests that electronic health records will yield revenue gains for some practices and losses for many. Health Affairs **2013**, *32* (3), 562–57.
9. Olson, D.R.; Konty, K.J.; Paladini, M.; Viboud, C.; Simonsen, L. Reassessing google flu trends data for detection of seasonal and pandemic influenza: A comparative epidemiological study at three geographic scales. PLoS Comp. Biol. **2013**, *9* (1), e1002356.
10. Huba, N.; Zhang, Y. Designing patient-centered personal health records (PHRs): Health care professionals' perspective on patient-generated data. J. Med. Syst. **2012**, *36* (6), 3893–3905.

11. Spaulding, T.J.P.; Raghu, T.S.P. Impact of CPOE usage on medication management process costs and quality outcomes. Inquiry—Excellus Health Plan, **2013**, *5* (3), 229–247.

12. Ford, E.W.; Huerta, T.R.; Thompson, M.A.; Patry, R. The impact of accelerating electronic prescribing on hospitals' productivity levels: Can health information technology bend the curve? Inquiry **2011**, *48* (4), 304–312.

13. Leung, A.A.; Keohane, C.; Amato, M.; Simon, S.R.; Coffey, M.; Kaufman, N.; Cadet, B.; Schiff, G.; Zimlichman, E.; Seger, D.L.; Yoon, C.; Song, P.; Bates, D.W. Impact of vendor computerized physician order entry in community hospitals. J. Gen. Intern. Med. **2012**, *27* (7), 801–807.

14. Harrington, L.; Kennerly, D.; Johnson, C.; Snyder, D.A. Safety issues related to the electronic medical record (EMR): Synthesis of the literature from the last decade, 2000–2009. J. Healthcare Manag. **2011**, *56*, 31–44.

15. Lenert, L.; Sundwall, D.; Lenert, M.E. Shifts in the architecture of the Nationwide Health Information Network. J. Am. Med. Inform. Assoc. **2012**, *19* (4), 498–502.

16. Burke, L.; Weill, B. *Information Technology for the Heatlh Professions*, 4th Ed.; *Pearson Education INc.*: Boston, 2013.

17. Bloomrosen, M.; Detmer, D. Advancing the framework: Use of health data—A Report of a Working Conference of the American Medical Informatics Association. J. Am. Med. Inform. Assoc. **2008**, *15* (6), 715–722.

18. Purcell, B.M. Emergence of 'big data' technology and analytics. J. Technol. Res. **2013**, *4*, 1–7.

19. Dugas, A.F.; Jalalpur, M.; Gel, Y.; Levin, S.; Torcaso, F.; Igusa, T.; Rothman, R.E. Influenza forecasting with Google Flu Trends. PLoS ONE, **2013**, *8* (2), e56176.

HIPAA: Health Insurance Portability and Accountability Act

Professional Training and Development, University of Houston-Clear Lake, CyberSecurity Institute, Houston, Texas, U.S.A.

HIPAA–Information Protection

Abstract

The "Health Insurance Portability and Accountability Act," commonly referred to as HIPAA, and its amendment known as "Health Information Technology for Economic and Clinical Health (HITECH)," have been heralded as bringing vital attention to the matters or the privacy and security to patient information. They have also brought controversy to the general discussion of information protection, its cost, the associated burden of program management, breach reporting, and related topics. Over time, much has been clarified but much remains to be clarified before truly effective and cost-efficient programs can be designed and institutionalized. This entry will address these issues and provide more clarity on how to achieve the objective for protecting the privacy and security of patient information. It will lay the foundation for defining IT controls, the objective of each, implementation and operational guidance, and the interdependence of them. It will provide examples of effective options to achieve the goals without breaking the bank or adversely impacting the delivery of timely, appropriate, and high-quality healthcare. It will enlarge on the requirements of these important laws, their impacts on the IT portions of an affected enterprise, and will elaborate on the manner in which they must be addressed so that this vital program of protection can be brought about quickly and efficiently, without excessive cost or adding unacceptable overhead, in an evolutionary, not revolutionary manner.

OVERVIEW

This entry will discuss the "Health Insurance Portability and Accountability Act," commonly referred to as HIPAA (Public Law 104191, 1996), including the amendment known as "HITECH," which is a specific portion (Title XIII, Subpart D) of the American Recovery and Reinvestment Act of 2009 (ARRA), and the Omnibus Rule issued in January of 2013.

The entry will enlarge on the requirements of these important laws, their impacts on the IT portions of an affected enterprise, and will elaborate on the manner in which they must be addressed when an entity works to comply with them. All security measures, concepts, functions, and controls reflect current best practice endorsed by all certification bodies and government organizations.

Within this legislation are four primary categories of controls: Administrative, Physical, Technical, and Organizational. This entry focuses on those related to the Information Systems processing the covered data types, but will address the Physical and the Organizational as well in terms of their impact on these systems and data.

BACKGROUND OF THE LEGISLATION

This legislation was signed into law by President William J. Clinton in August of 1996. Its intended goals included:

a. Administrative simplification in the processes used in handling healthcare information by creating types and functions of "transactions," standardizing messaging formats, exchange mechanisms, and process participants;

b. Combat fraud, waste, and abuse of the claims process which often resulted from millions to billions of dollars in payments on fraudulent or duplicate claims, unnecessary tests and treatments, and other forms of waste;

c. Formalizing and adopting rules by which protection of patient information privacy would be implemented and assured;

d. Setting security standards through which the privacy protections would be implemented in technical and nontechnical methods and systems.

Most of the focus of the attention paid to this large and broadly-sweeping act has been on the changes it directs onto the first two of the three classes of entities:

Encyclopedia of Information Systems and Technology, DOI: 10.1081/E-EIST-120048630
Copyright © 2015 by Taylor & Francis. All rights reserved.

1. **Covered Entities (CE):** plans, providers, and clearing house functions, each and all of which create, transmit, receive, and process a variety of electronic messages known collectively as "transactions," which carry information, bill encoding, and other data elements (defined below). CE includes both institutions and individuals.

2. **Business Associates (BA):** a wide spectrum of business types that support the operations of CE in a variety of areas, including accounting, administration, nursing registries, and others, all of which involve handling the same sensitive information on behalf of the CE. This category includes **subcontractors** to BA's as well as the BAs themselves.

3. **Couriers or Conduits:** this very narrowly defined category includes two basic types of service providers best regarded as a common carrier (Telephone Company) or a typical delivery service (United Parcel Service or United States Postal Service). This category is very sparingly applied, and those entities that qualify are all but completely exempt from these requirements.

The program that these entities must design and implement is based on risk management, that is, a program that quantitatively, qualitatively, or in combination:

a. Identifies and categorizes organization assets, and then prioritizes them by their relative importance to the operation in order to guide mitigation activities;

b. Determines the existence of vulnerabilities in those assets that, should the threats materialize, would allow, enable, or amplify the adverse impacts to the assets' normal functioning;

c. Identifies and categorizes relevant threats to their assets (inclusive of information, systems, facilities, and personnel) that have a meaningful probability of occurrence and a measurably material adverse impact to the assets;

d. Evaluates the existence and effectiveness of countermeasures to prevent, minimize, or compensate for the impacts;

e. Selects and implements effective mitigations that have a positive cost-benefit ratio when compared to the value of the asset or the estimated overall cost of the compromise.

The requirements, called "Standards" that these entities must adhere to also fall into two classes:

1. **Required:** these often dictate "what" must be done, "why" it must be done, and are often self-describing as to the "how" it must be accomplished as well.

2. **Addressable:** those so designated also describe what must be accomplished, but allow the entity some latitude or creativity with regard to the form

and manner of implementation used to achieve the intended goal. This quality enables the CE or BA to choose effective methods that fit the infrastructure or culture of the entity, rather than attempting to force-fit a predefined solution.

In many cases, there are "Implementation Specifications" that accompany the standards. Each of these identifies specific elements that must be addressed in order to achieve the goal of the standard. Both the Standards and the Specifications are described in greater detail later. Neither the Standards nor the Implementation Specifications are optional, but rather may be nonapplicable depending upon the type of entity or operation in question.

The information that these entities handle is known variously as "Individually Identifiable Health Information (IIHI)"; "Patient Identifiable Information (PII)"; and "Protected Health Information (PHI)". The term "IIHI" is the most comprehensive of these and includes all types, elements, and forms of this information.

While there is indeed a difference in a legalistic sense between the definitions and the specific elements of each one, there is no effective difference between these type-labels from an operational or programmatic implementation perspective with regard to how they will be secured and protected. However, the most commonly used term is PHI, despite its strictest application is to this sensitive information being originated, handled, or otherwise manipulated by a Covered Entity, usually in electronic form. Consequently, for ease of understanding, this article will refer to them by the more common PHI.

Bearing the above in mind, all the standards and specifications reflected here are intended to be flexible and scalable so as to fit within the operations of nearly any CE or BA. They are intended to be technologically neutral, and as such to be widely implementable across the many structure and system types currently in use. Thus, these control elements will facilitate reasonable and sufficient protection in all three in which PHI will be found: expressed verbally, expressed on paper (by hand or machine printout), or in any way electronically ("at rest," "in motion," or in process).

It will be seen that there is a very noticeable emphasis throughout the law, its Code of Federal Regulations (CFRs) and rules that Management is actively involved and cognizant of all actions. This aligns with the companion thread of individual accountability. Within the body, HIPAA makes it very clear that the required documentation must be present and current, as well as being followed in practice. It also makes clear the necessity to ensure all parties to whom such guides apply are fully informed. As a capstone to these, the law states plainly that all parties will be held accountable for their behavior and adherence to the regulations. This reflects the same approach to full disclosure as the Medical profession has had for decades through "informed consent."

A HIPAA compliance program therefore is very "front-loaded," as can be seen from the considerable amount of documentation required from which it is formed. The hazard in this is that a compliance audit will find that, while practice complies, the written guidance is often informal, out of date, or lacking entirely. While daily performance is clearly the proof of compliance, both are required for the program to conform, for a number of reasons:

a. Policy is the law of the organization, and is often driven by actual laws. The presence of policy illustrates awareness and enactment of that law within the organization.
b. The written policy makes clear what is required, and removes the potential to debate what would otherwise be verbal direction; hearsay, open to wide interpretation.
c. The written policy enables consistent and uniform enforcement along with metrics; again, removing the aspects of hearsay and general vagueness.

IMPLEMENTATION AND GUIDANCE

Taken directly, laws are difficult to implement as they give only indications of "what" result is expected when whatever modifications discernible from its text are accomplished, and "why" those to whom it applies are to do them. The institutional (the CE and BA) equivalent to a law is the policy.

Implementation instructions and supporting descriptive explanations therefore must be provided to enable affected parties to attain the desired results. For laws, these are given in the CFRs. For institutions, such instructions and supporting descriptions have their analogues in procedures, standards, and guidelines, each defined fully later.

This body of documentation enables compliant performance and sustains an ongoing program of maintenance of the compliant state. As such, they form a framework that serves as the primary basis of becoming and remaining compliant with both the law and the regulations that derive from it as may be written by the staff of the Department of Health and Human Services, the regulatory body that is the "owner" and enforcer of HIPAA. Getting compliant is often easier than remaining so over an extended period, but both are essential.

Adding somewhat to this difficulty is the "nonprescriptive" nature of HIPAA. It directs the impacted entities to perform a best-effort risk management approach to create and implement their privacy and security compliance programs. One result is that

such a program at a given entity may vary greatly in its implemented form from that found at another entity. Another result is that the impacted entities are able to follow the guidance to achieve the compliance requirements in a manner consistent with the characteristics of the given entity. This approach enables compliance attainment across the widely varying landscape of entity-business types, and avoids the poor fit and even impedimentary outcomes of the traditional "one-size-fits-all" prescriptive approach found in other laws.

Thus, setting a program in place that facilitates evolutionary changes, as opposed to revolutionary changes, will add new task performance and modify existing practices with only minor disruption to workflow and will keep the additional administrative burden to an acceptable minimum. This "continuous process improvement" approach, versus the common "repetitive remediation and repair" approach, provides improved and more cost-effective outcomes over the long term in these programs.

STRUCTURE OF CONTROL CATEGORIES

The compliance requirements of HIPAA are expressed in terms of "Standards" and "Implementation Specifications." The former is the directive regarding an area of coverage or a specific action (the "what" is to be complied with, and the "why" of the necessary objective), while the latter adds details regarding individual points requiring attention and action. To satisfy these, the structure of such a program has been broken down into four different and complementary controls categories:

1. **Administrative:** these are the paper-based documents that outline and guide performance and achievement of the goals, as described previously.
2. **Physical:** controls in this category are those that provide safety and security for facilities, rooms, and grounds, and guide performance of specific functions.
3. **Technical:** these are best thought of as implementations in hardware and software to enable security and privacy protections within computers, workstations, and networks, and specific steps regarding user behaviors.
4. **Organizational:** this category reflects the program of managing and controlling the contracts, records retention, and other processes that both CE and BA must perform periodically to ensure their attention to these requirements does not waver so that compliance is maintained long-term.

Individual control functions within each of these larger categories will vary depending upon what control is selected and what desired effect is to be achieved. These functions are:

1. **Preventive:** a control that prevents undesired actions or results.
2. **Detective**: a control that alerts when an undesired or unauthorized action has been attempted (and may have succeeded).
3. **Corrective:** a control that enables reconfiguration of some feature or parameter to enable an authorized user to perform proper actions.
4. **Deterrent:** control that discourages some unwanted behavior.
5. **Recovery:** a control that enables restorative action to be taken to put a compromised system back into correct, usable condition.
6. **Compensating:** an approach that may use a variety of technical and nontechnical components to achieve the desired result without producing undesirable affects that a direct approach or control might cause.

Within each of the major categories there exists some example of each type of control function: some are technical, some are nontechnical, and some are process-based, while others are simply the consequence of a binary decision.

Throughout the body of the regulations appear the words "reasonable" and "appropriate." The former means that, when correctly implemented and operated, the given measure does not create a situation of impaired operation, reduced care quality, undue administrative burden, excessive cost, technological fragility, excessive complexity, or other undesirable outcome. In other words, the concepts enable the CE or BA some latitude in seeking the remedy by emphasizing the achievement of the goal, and not a specific method to attain it. The latter refers to something "fit for use" such that when it is employed it is sufficient and correct in its application.

Compliance with HIPAA in the technology infrastructure of a CE or BA requires the assessment of conditions extant in that environment, an analysis of controls that are applicable to each use-case defined, and is accomplished through an informed selection process followed by a well-reasoned and skilled implementation of those controls and components chosen as fit for the given purpose.

Ultimately, a successful program will employ selected elements performing the desired functions from all categories. This program, as stated in the law itself, is intended to achieve security and privacy protections that are both effective and reasonable; that is, protective measures that accomplish the compliance requirement, in proportion to the quantified risks present and that ultimately do not interfere with the CE or BA's ability to deliver quality patient care.

Thus, such a program must begin by assessing both the operational environment and the risks within it through the process of risk analysis, and an on-going program of risk management, which are two of the primary requirements laid out in the law. Such an analysis must assess both the technical and nontechnical aspects of the environment so that initial mitigating actions can be undertaken to establish compliant operations, and to enable the program of continuous awareness and management of risk to maintain the compliant state to become institutionalized.

The next sections will discuss and elaborate on the standards and implementations that are to be evaluated and employed to meet the objectives specified by the regulations. The sections will also define and discuss the terms "Required" and "Addressable" with regard to practical applications to meet HIPAA requirements.

ADMINISTRATIVE CONTROLS FRAMEWORK

This control category acts as a general repository of the documentation that will be used as the guidance for implementations intended to satisfy the specified requirements. In it are defined policies, procedures, responsibilities, and other programmatic elements for the various roles involved in achieving the ultimate compliance posture. Outlining the various processes, they fall into the following types:

1. **Policies:** spawned by the external regulations, these are the "laws" internal to the organization that state basis of "what" is to be complied with, and the "why" must it happen. Also stated in the policy is that any records not containing PHI are considered "operational" in nature and carry a 6-year retention requirement (health records containing PHI require a minimum of 7 years retention).
2. **Procedures:** these outline the "how-to" steps of the processes to accomplish the objectives described in the policies.
3. **Standards:** often defined as targets, these are products, services, methods, and configurations that are chosen as benchmarks or preferences that will be used or set to enable achievement of the compliance goal. In HIPAA, these are also the descriptions of what the CE or BA is directed to do to comply.
4. **Guidelines:** these may be best regarded as "preferred" practices to be employed in cases where implementing specific standards is not practicable. In cases where standards or specifications are termed "Addressable," guidelines will outline considerations and approaches to be used to best meet the need, even though actual implementation outcomes might vary from case to case.

5. **Baselines:** these are defined minimums quantifying desired performance, benchmarks, or configuration from which variance will be measured.

In some cases, the stated standard may describe a process to be defined and implemented. Other cases may require a binary decision to be made to satisfy the requirement. The following outlines how in each case each of the above fits together with the others to provide a complete approach to each requirement and implementation specification.

The record types outlined here are regarded as "operational records": that is, they constitute a body of records about IIHI describing its history, its evolution and so on. This body of records, however, does not itself contain any IIHI. As such, HIPAA specifies it is subject to a minimum 6-year retention period (states may independently lengthen this period), where patient records must be retained for a minimum of 7 years, unless lengthened by state law augmentation.

The following sections will outline each requirement, and detail an approach to each one, providing specific examples of how each may be successfully accomplished to secure the systems, data, and facilities in accordance with the regulatory requirement.

Standard: Security Management Process (from 45 CFR § 164.308(a)(1))

This standard states that a security management process must be defined and implemented to ensure that certain perpetual activities are in place, are clearly outlined and embodied in the five document types noted above, are performed periodically, and are supported and enforced by Management. The goal and intent of the standard is to ensure the CE or BA implement policies and procedures to prevent, detect, contain, and correct security violations. Within this standard are four Implementation Specifications:

Specification—Risk analysis (required): this specification means that a risk analysis process will be defined and adopted by the CE or BA, typically involving quantitative and qualitative methods, and will be employed consistently to evaluate asset-risk-threat relationships as they are found in the environment. "Assets" may be system, physical, human, or information in nature, but all must be evaluated in their operational context. The "Required" aspect means that a method of doing this must be chosen, validated, and consistently followed: it does not direct the precise method the entity will use. The process and methods used will be described in the document types noted above in sufficient detail that they can be competently employed by the appointed staff members, and the documentation generated by its performance will be comprised of

1. A comprehensive Risk Analysis report detailing and discussing all asset-risk-threat scenarios, the expected negative effect on the confidentiality, integrity, or availability of that asset, and the anticipated monetary value of the loss and associated recovery.

2. A Corrective Action Plan (CAP) that offers options and recommendations to: a) preventing the loss where and as possible and cost-effective; and b) describes contingency plan steps in the event of its loss to address the need to respond to incidents with or without a privacy breach.

Specification—Risk management (required): this particular specification is the primary element that will frame a program that will achieve the essential goal of the standard. This specification regards design and construction of processes that will enable the entity to manage its environment and operations such that risks are identified in a timely manner and mitigated. It implies a general risk identification and reduction program throughout the operation in administrative, physical, technical and, organizational areas, and requires this be a regular part of the operation to first achieve reasonable reductions and then to maintain that level. Meeting this requirement takes this form:

1. Policy: this would state that Management will implement and pursue a program of risk analysis in order to meet HIPAA requirements. It would specify the basic philosophy of risk management (risk-averse, risk-accepting, scenario specific), who shall be designated to perform these, the periodicity on which they will be performed, specify and define what metrics will be used, any sort of severity scale to be employed, decision criteria and acceptable variances to be employed.

2. Standard: this document would outline in sufficient detail what the chosen risk method is, its source and validity, and all necessary definitions and metrics.

3. Procedure: how the method is to be followed, step-by-step, and what items are to be used or examined. This would include calculations, evidence sources, interviews, and other items and actions to complete the process.

4. Guidelines: these would describe considerations, examples, and other recommendations for dealing with encountered situations and conditions that do not neatly fit models or assumptions.

5. Baseline: these would specify acceptable minimums and maximums for performance, variances, and similar boundaries and qualities.

As a general rule, standards and baselines would normally be included in the associated policy documents themselves, where procedures and guidelines would be attachments to them.

Specification—Sanction policy (required): this particular specification regards creating a new or modifying the organization's existing general disciplinary policy to include the specific details of the types of infractions and their potential consequences under HIPAA. As such, it is derived directly from the law itself, and is more or less the essential points expressed unmodified in the entity's policy style. Meeting this requirement takes this form:

1. Policy: Management would redraft the disciplinary policy to include the descriptions of the Tier I through Tier IV civil violations and possible consequences to the organization if such were committed and discovered (normally through periodic audit, complaints investigation, or other external exposing event). This would also include the same information for the Tier I through Tier III criminal violations and the related consequences to the individuals involved.
2. Standard: this describes a standard of behavior and as such would very likely be included in the policy document and require 100% adherence.
3. Procedure: this would describe how the entity will conduct routine audits of a technical (systems) and nontechnical nature, what evidence would be sought and used in doing so, and what it considers a qualifying violation. Typically this would also cover the results assessment process in order to determine appropriate courses of action.
4. Guidelines: these would typically take two forms. The first would be instructive guidance for the workforce members for avoiding violations and how to report them if found. The second would be for those performing the audits and would be derived from the Audit Protocols from the Department of Human Health and Services (DHHS) and the standard practices of the entity.
5. Baseline: As before, this would typically describe a 100% compliance posture.

Specification—Information system activity review (required): this particular specification regards creating a new or modifying the organization's existing general disciplinary policy to include the specific details of the types of infractions and their potential consequences under HIPAA. As such, it is derived directly from the law itself, and is more or less the essential points expressed unmodified in the entity's policy style. Meeting this requirement takes this form:

1. Policy: Management would redraft the disciplinary policy to include the descriptions of the Tier I through Tier IV civil violations and possible

consequences to the organization if such were committed and discovered (normally through periodic audit, complaints investigation, or other external exposing event). This would also include the same information for the Tier I through Tier III criminal violations and the related consequences to the individuals involved.
2. Standard: This describes a standard of behavior and as such would very likely be included in the policy document and require 100% adherence.
3. Procedure: These describe the methodology to be used. As the law itself proscribes no specific method, this could be a derivation from the CoBIT standard, from JCAHO protocols, or from the issued protocols from DHHS itself (recommended source). The goal is to implement processes and procedures to regularly review records of information system activity, such as audit logs, access reports, and security incident tracking reports, or a variety of other sources as appropriate.
4. Guidelines: For this specification, these would outline the specific types of informational evidence to be acquired, with guidance on how to extract, format, and interpret the contents.
5. Baseline: Most likely specified in the policy, the baseline would outline the periodicity, records selection modeling, and timelines.

Standard: Assigned Security Responsibility (from 45 CFR § 164.308(a)(2))

This standard mandates the appointment of a staff member who will be responsible for the development and implementation of the policies and procedures required to accomplish the program objectives: i.e., the achievement of compliance. This particular standard has no associated Implementation Specification; the member is appointed to act in the role (compliant) or not (noncompliant).

This is an example of a binary decision. The CE and the BA must each appoint someone, with the appropriate qualifications and experience, who will undertake these efforts to lay the groundwork for attaining the objectives. This would typically be a senior person with holding a Certified Information Systems Security Professional, a Ceritified Information Security Manager or other professional credential indicating they are technically qualified to perform this work. They must also be informed of and sensitive to the organization continuing to meet its operational objectives as well; in other words, they must work with Staff and Management to balance these potentially competing priorities and have the authority to perform this role. Often they will hold the title of Chief Information Security Officer (CISO).

To effectively act in this role, the CISO must gain a full understanding of the requirements, the operational issues, the culture, and find the balance among them to be successful. This requires a detailed approach in collaboration with the IT staff and representatives of Management and the User Community in order to facilitate acceptance and compliant performance of all parties. They must likewise appreciate the complementary nature of the controls in the technical and physical areas such that they are able to choose appropriate implementations that do not adversely impact business success.

Standard: Workforce Security (from 45 CFR § 164.308(a)(3)(i))

This standard requires that various policies and procedures be constructed and enforced to ensure that all workforce members are authorized access to PHI commensurate with their job requirements. It goes on to require preventive measures be put in place to protect against inappropriate or unauthorized access. In general, accomplishment of the intent of this standard requires a well-formed, documented access control policy and procedure to lay the foundation, and an Acceptable Use Policy and End-User Access Agreement (for each user to sign) to implement and enforce it.

This standard has three Implementation Specifications:

Specification 1: Authorization or Supervision (Addressable)—This is a straightforward requirement but an important one because it reflects the critical need for Management to be activity involved in the approval and monitoring of all workforce members accessing protected information. This represents a process type of requirement, considered addressable as it must conform to the culture of the entity even while it satisfies the requirement.

This involves the need for Management to review staff roles and take decisions about what access and what level of privilege is appropriate for each member in a given role. It also reinforces the fact that, ultimately, Management is accountable for such access and any deviations from policy or violations of such access or privileges by workforce members using their accounts. If Management delegates this responsibility, there must be a memorandum so noting on file, and they must still review the activity periodically themselves.

The process involves the specific steps:

1. Assessment of role and access levels and needs for it
2. Formal authorization, followed by provisioning activities

   a. This will include items such as User Agreement signing and training
   b. It will also include awareness briefings and advising users that their actions will be subject to periodic review and monitoring
3. Regular generation of auditing reports showing what users are doing with an assessment of the actions as appropriate or not
4. Periodic review of assigned privileges to ensure they are only what has been approved, and to prevent unintended "privilege creep"–the unintended accumulation of privileges beyond the minimum necessary in accordance with the practice of "Least Privilege"
5. All violations are documented and corrected, along with any disciplinary consequences deemed necessary, with a record placed in the employee file

Proof of compliance would normally be established through the presence of and examination of audit reports accompanied by documented corrective actions and their results.

This process will also satisfy the "Access Authorization Requirement" defined in 164.308(b)(4), and the "Access Establishment and Modification" noted in 164.308(c)(4).

Specification 2: Workforce clearance procedure (addressable)—This requirement relates particularly to how each member is placed in a role and how their information system access is defined appropriately for that role. Background checks and other clearance steps would normally be completed through the Human Resources function.

The basic principles at work involve the members "Need to Know" and "Least Privilege." These take the role and translate it into role definitions and access control rules for data that enable access to all pertinent systems and information but only to the lowest level possible. The role of "Nurse" would provide access to patient records but would exclude all data not defined as a part of the patient record. The same would be true of a "Staff Doc;" however the latter would likely differ in actual access to that of "Associate Doc" that might have access only to those patients they have been referred from their outside practices.

The roles and rules would be defined in Policy and implemented by provisioning Procedures. The Standards applied would describe the construction, aging, change intervals, and other specifics of passwords members are to use. Guidelines would be provided to all members to enable them to comply with the policies and construct proper passwords. All of these are **addressable**, in part because the current standards used by industry are continuously evolving and improving, and in part because each organization is operationally unique.

Specification 3: Workforce Termination Procedure (Addressable)—This requirement relates particularly to how each member will be processed out of the organization, and applies whether the separation is voluntary or involuntary. The primary objective is to ensure specific, procedural steps are routinely taken in order to reclaim all company property (access keys, tools, etc.), recover any information assets acquired by the workforce member, and to hold an exit interview during which the member should be reminded that HIPAA requirements to safeguard patient privacy remain in force following termination.

STANDARD: Information Access Management (from 45 CFR § 164.308(a)(3)(i))

This Standard requires the entity (CE or BA) to create a control framework that enables it to validate and authorize access to electronic PHI for any party requesting or claiming that such access is needed.

Specification: Isolation of healthcare clearinghouse (required)—This requirement addresses the need for clearly delineating access to information to: 1) avoid conflicts of interest (COI); 2) set a specific process in place to characterize access requirements by role; and 3) ensure that Management is directly and actively involved in the routine oversight of these processes. The latter two requirements are Addressable for the same reasons noted above.

The first of these implementation specifications (Required) regards a CE functioning in part as a Healthcare Clearinghouse (HCCH): an entity that acts to process nonstandard format covered transactions into the required standard form prior to submission for acceptance and adjudication. The COI element addresses the situation where a CE that may in the main be a provider organization, but contains a unit that performs HCCH activities, because such an arrangement without proper separation and controls enables the potential for the creation of fraudulent transactions.

In such CE, proper implementation requires two basic things: 1) identification of the HCCH component and creating an "arm's length" legal separation between it and other units of the containing CE such that any input from them is subjected to processing in a fashion identical to input submitted from an outside CE with all associated controls; and 2) the creation of a role that creates full logical isolation for the HCCH and its workforce, and enforces all applicable controls to ensure full auditing capability to validate that this isolation is complete and verifiable.

Specification: Access authorization (addressable)—This requirement carries with it the need to construct the electronic data access control framework that entails establishing and enforcing the following elements:

1. Policy: Management prepares a statement that lays out the regulatory requirements, and drafts a policy that takes the form of an "Acceptable Use Policy." This document describes the various allowed and disallowed behaviors that all authorized users must abide by when granted access to systems housing sensitive information. It would also include descriptions of how access requests would be validated, approving authorities, appropriate role creation or assignment, and disciplinary consequences for violations discovered during auditing. This document would ensure that workforce members are made aware of the following conditions of use (displayed in the required Login Banner):

   a. Users shall have no expectation of privacy, to include e-mail usage.

   b. That the system and its contents are corporate property and as such they will be auditing and monitored, even to include Law Enforcement access should circumstances warrant.

   c. That any unauthorized use may constitute a federal crime, which is under the jurisdiction of the FBI.

   d. That all information accessed is considered sensitive and is protected by rules of nondisclosure as well as state and federal regulations.

2. Standard: This describes a standard of behavior and as such would very likely be included in the policy document and require 100% adherence.

3. Procedure: These describe the validation methodology to be used, evidence required, and any necessary documentation. This would also apply in case of escalation, de-escalation, or other alterations in access types and levels.

4. Guidelines: If present, guidelines would normally recommend considerations that would modify access request evidence requirements, provide temporary access and levels when and if required, and how to handle violations.

5. Baseline: Typically not necessary in this case.

As an addressable requirement, this one recognizes the necessity to scale and adapt to the particular system architecture features used by the CE or BA, as there are many and they vary widely in the capabilities and sophistication. The objective is to configure the available features to meet the required details and performance, within the system's capability envelope. In cases where certain aspects cannot be configured to precisely meet a requirement, compensating controls (usually closest approximation in configuration coupled with increased monitoring) must be designed and implemented. This situation may also result in unmitigated risk, which must be documented with a narrative describing how this risk will be monitored to prevent any unknown and adverse change in its character.

Specification: Access establishment and modification (addressable)—In practice this requirement is met through diligent performance of the above. It underscores the emphasis mentioned earlier that Management should be directly involved in any material change in access levels and types granted workforce members or other authorized entities. It further requires that there should be an auditable trail of documentation to validate any change performed.

STANDARD: SECURITY AWARENESS AND TRAINING (FROM 45 CFR § 164.308(A)(5))

This standard includes four **Addressable** implementation specifications:

1. Security Reminders
2. Protection from Malicious Software
3. Login monitoring
4. Password Management

Successful implementation of this standard begins with a basic awareness briefing that must be delivered to all workforce members at all levels and of all types that will be handling PHI to set the baseline for the CE or BA by informing all members of the basic requirements for secure and proper handling of this sensitive information. Specific subgroups with particular roles should also receive training in topics pertinent to such roles. Following the establishment of such a baseline, ongoing training should be provided as an integral part of New Employee Orientation (NEO) delivered by HR. The CISO would participate with HR to set the topics and their coverage.

The four items listed above would be covered at sufficiently detailed levels to ensure the workforce is properly informed about the given issue, and that they are reminded periodically of the importance of adhering to policy: frequent enough but not so frequent or of a kind that they build up a "psychological callous" to the message.

"Protection from malicious software" would discuss, in layman's terms computer viruses and other malware, how to recognize these threats, and the dos and don'ts (i.e., don't open e-mails from unknown sources, do ensure your antivirus software is always running and up to date).

"Login Monitoring" is a briefing topic through which the CE or BA informs its staff that all computer activity is monitored and recorded. Though a potentially sensitive subject, all workforce members must be enlightened that this is constant and universal. In addition, the staff should likewise be informed that audit reports are generated from this system log and are reviewed regularly for anomalous or inappropriate activity.

In support of this policy, every CE and BA should have implemented a "Login Warning Banner" adapted from the basic text provided by the Department of Justice as a deterrent control—the first thing all staff see at login. In effect, it begins their awareness training by informing at every login of the conditions for its use. It should inform them of the following (an expansion of the above):

1. The system is a business asset to be used for business purposes only. As such, the organization reserves the right to periodically audit system or user activities to ensure that these resources are being used only for such purposes.
2. Users should have no expectation of privacy when using these information systems.
3. Logging in to the system gives the users' consent to having their activity monitored and potentially recorded.
4. Any attempt to login by unauthorized users is a federal crime and therefore no such attempt should be made.
5. The information in this system contains sensitive and private elements and must never be disclosed by any means to any unauthorized party.
6. Users will exercise their assigned levels of access and privilege in the performance of the assigned roles, and should at no time attempt to perform unapproved activities that diverge from or exceed these levels.

STANDARD: SECURITY INCIDENT PROCEDURES (FROM 45 CFR § 164.308(A)(6))

This **required** standard has no implementation specifications associated with it, but is one of the more important compliance program elements.

With the very common condition that most CE or BA operations have live Internet connections that in some way interact with their business or PHI-handling systems, each has assumed the risk that this global and untrusted network can and will at some stage convey a threat agent or electronically-borne attack vector to their system and will thus cause a material and potentially devastating impact. Notwithstanding the fact that most, if not all have already implemented protective countermeasures against these agents and vectors, every CE and BA must have a proven plan to respond to these events and take every reasonable and possible action to contain and minimize the effects of them.

Guidance on how to undertake a program of Incident Response, Analysis, and Reporting was issued by Centers for Medicare & Medicaid Services (CMS) internally, and to its contractors in 2008 (Version 2.1).

The National Institute of Standards and Technology (NIST) has also published a guide on Security Incident Handling (Special Publication Series 800-61), which describes in sufficient detail the construction of a capability and steps to effectively prepare, identify, respond, contain, and recover from these adverse events, regardless of type. The CMS guide was derived from this, and both are applicable to either security or privacy compromise events.

For the CE or BA undertaking to construct a response team, it should begin with its risk assessment (RA) and a business impact analysis (BIA) to clearly identify areas where these agents are most likely to enter or arise, and assess the potential type and magnitude of such an event. This will permit focus on areas needing the greatest and most immediate attention; areas that when struck will impart the highest and most costly impact. At this stage, the entity must consider the skills and experience required by the prospective team members, whether it desires to create this capability internally or outsource it (the law makes no comment on either being preferred, only that the capability must be created and be effective).

Normally, the responses to be employed are characterized by scenarios, and the steps of response are defined appropriate to each context. Following this, the steps to perform are:

1. Prepare: this phase uses the RA and the BIA as guides to employ when selecting controls and countermeasures to offset areas of weakness, to strengthen it against compromise through procedures and technologies and to enhance its resilience, resistance, and recoverability.
2. Identification: using alert mechanisms, monitoring, auditing, and other detection methods, the entity must find and validate the seminal event indicators as early as possible. HIPAA considers the "day of discovery" of an event as Day 1, regardless of when the compromising agent now identified actually occurred.
3. Response: through-out the event, every person involved must keep a record of all steps taken and their outcomes. Chain of Custody must be observed by all at all times. Each type defined in reference to the type of incident or agent (malware, hack, internal, external, etc.), the response must be commensurate in type and effort to that agent, and should be proceduralized in steps:
    a. Investigation and Analysis (critical to determining the next course of action of response type)
    b. Containment (damage control activities)
    c. Eradication (clearing and verification activities)
4. Recovery and Restoration: These steps are vital to heal the compromised elements and restore normal (or as near to normal as possible) operation.

5. Review and reporting: Once the crisis has been reduced and normal operations resumed, the after-action review will be conducted to evaluate the process, the outcome, and next steps, which may include breach notification activities (must be performed as soon as possible, but not later than 60 after Day 1). This phase is vital to continuing to improve the quality of this capability.

Incidents are very costly, and are unavoidable over the long-term. These are made even more costly when associated with breaches of unsecured (unencrypted) PHI. Effective response is also often greatly impeded by ineffective investigation and analysis techniques.

However, these cost factors and management aspects must be compared to the negative impacts that will be suffered without this capability in place to prepare for and respond to these events, in addition to a failure to comply with the requirement. A business case will most often show that the offset is in favor of having the capability in place even without the requirement as the force behind having it.

Standard: Contingency Planning (from 45 CFR § 164.308(a)(7))

This requirement is intended to establish and implement policies and procedures for responding to an emergency or other occurrence (for example, fire, vandalism, system failure, and natural disaster) that damages systems that contain electronic protected health information. It is one of several requirements within HIPAA that addresses business continuity and disaster recovery planning activities. This particular entry has five implementation specifications within it. The NIST Guide (Special Publication 800-34) provides the basis for the CMS guidance on contingency planning and is itself an excellent guide to this topic.

Specification: Data backup plan (required)—The purpose of this requirement is to establish and implement procedures to create and maintain retrievable exact copies of electronic PHI.

The practical implementation of this requirement is the composition of operational procedures to identify and categorize data based on type, frequency of change, and other parameters so that a schedule of backup processing is constructed and regularly performed. Most organizations have already performed this action, and make daily-use and archival backups. It makes no reference to business operations data, only to PHI and claims history. The regulations also take no notice of whether the backups are made to disk or to tape, although the language seems to assume that the latter is the customary form.

HIPAA has added some significant details to this activity however in light of the sensitivity of the data involved:

- The first is that samples are pulled from selected backup runs, and test restores are performed. This action is to provide assurance that the backups can in fact be restored in usable form.
- The second (derived from the CMS guidance following the HITECH passage) is that backups should be encrypted if the system possesses the capability to do so. This renders the data "secured PHI" since the media is movable/removable and enables it to be moved safely offsite as "data in motion" as well.

Specification: Disaster recovery plan (required)— The purpose of this requirement is to establish, implement, and periodically test plans and procedures to restore the information systems capability to an operative condition in the event of some magnitude of outage-causing event. Plans of this type address the needs of both business continuity and disaster recovery. In both cases, the plans developed are location and entity specific.

The continuity portion focuses on the business operations and directs planning and preparation actions to first, make the operation more resistant and resilient in the face of adverse events, and second, to create responses that will enable the business to restore operations to a minimum survival level as quickly as possible following the outage event.

The disaster recovery portion of the overall plan regards the event itself and directs focused, scenario-based activities to stabilize the circumstances, assess the damage, and set about to recover and restore operable IT services as quickly as possible through a variety of means and methods.

The requirement here is to ensure that an appropriate planning effort is conducted and that a viable, actionable plan is produced, tested, and implemented. The requirement includes annual testing and updating to ensure the plan stays current and relevant in the face of potential organizational or structural changes to the entity and its facilities. All tests must be documented and are auditable records.

Specification: Emergency mode operations plan (required)— The purpose of this requirement is to establish and implement procedures to enable continuation of critical business processes for protection of the security of electronic PHI while operating in emergency mode. This then is the very essence of the business continuity portion of the overall Disaster Recovery plan.

Specification: Testing and revision procedures (addressable)— The purpose of this requirement is to define and implement a process for the periodic testing and revising of the continuity and disaster recovery

plans procedures. This activity requires that the CE or BA perform annual (at a minimum) testing of these plans and capture both the performance and results of the test. It also requires that the test type and its results be documented as auditable records, and subsequently be applied to modify the existing plan to ensure its continuing appropriateness and relevance to the operation.

A variety of methods are available for application: checklist, structured walk-through, simulation, parallel, and full interruption. While the regulation here is addressable in its formation and execution, the conduct of the test and the subsequent updating of the plans and procedures is not. The regulation does not require the entity assume the risk of the full interruption type test (this type can precipitate a major outage if preparations are inadequate), but it does require that whatever form the test takes, that the results are applied to proper effect when incorporated into the plan.

Specification: Applications and data criticality analysis (addressable)– This requirement is intended to assess the relative criticality of specific applications and data in support of other contingency plan components. The output from this process will produce required audit evidence documentation.

The conduct of this activity is required during a BIA to determine the character of the systems, applications, and associated data in order that a priority order can be established to facilitate the recovery effort. A NIST guide exists that can assist with performing this: Special Publication Series 800-60.

Though potentially tedious to perform, the output from its application will enable the CE or BA to determine which IT elements and data are of greatest importance to the operation so that a restoration order based on priority can be set to make the overall restoration more efficient. More importantly, the output from this process is often very revealing to Management by identifying previously unknown crucial areas of systems and data that have direct bearing on organizational survivability and possible exposure to data breach or unavailability, and the consequences to operations.

Standard: Evaluation (from 45 CFR § 164.308(a) (8))

This standard embodies the periodic (annual) reperformance of the original RA and addressing any changes in risk posture from existing sources, and any new risks that have become evident. This is required for both CE and BA entities.

This reperformance includes all the technical and nontechnical aspects, based initially upon the standards implemented under this rule and subsequently, in response to environmental or operational changes affecting the security of electronic PHI, which establishes the extent to which an entity's security policies and procedures meet the compliance requirements then in force.

Standard: Business associate contracts (from 45 CFR § 164.308(b)(1) and. 314)

This standard specifies the drafting and execution of a business associate contract (BAC) that describes in detail all terms and conditions that the Covered Entity will expect the BA to perform. The BAC is thus a reflection of the BA's duties and requirements under HIPAA to do all things necessary to perform its contractual obligations for services, as well as to perform (as the CE is required to do) to process and safeguard the PHI it will handle on that CE's behalf.

The BAC also directs the BA to enforce the same conditions and requirements on any subcontractor it may engage to perform its duties in response to the primary BA's contractual requirements to the CE.

Under the original legislation, it was assumed the BA would receive the BAC from the CE, and that the language would read as indicated above. Subsequent analysis proved that many BAs were operating without a BAC in force, never having gotten such from the CE. The remedy applied by the passage of HITECH was to formally require all BAs to be subject to the same privacy and security requirements already enforced upon CEs, and that the BAC could originate with either party, so long as one existed and was enforced by the CE.

An additional change in the HIPAA definitions (45 CFR § 160.103) came in the form of a clarification through the Omnibus Rule issued by DHHS in January of 2013. This clarification stated that subcontractors to BAs are themselves BAs, and are therefore subject to all the same requirements historically accorded to both CE and BA, so long as the functions the subcontractor performs in its contractual duties supporting the BA, conform to the same criteria, as do those of the BA itself in support of the CE.

Standard: Documentation (from 45 CFR § 164.316(a) and 170.210(d))

The required standard in §164.316 embodies the directive to maintain as current the documentation prepared (as described above) and proscribes these specifications:

Specification: Time limit (required)—This requirement establishes the 6 year records retention cycle period for these operational (no contained PHI) records: from the date of their most recent retirement and replacement by a superseding version. There must be a policy setting this forth, accompanied by a procedure

outlining the review, updating, and re-issuance process. All of these elements are auditable.

Specification: Availability (required)—This requirement directs that all persons involved in this maintenance process have access to all guidance in order to carry out their duties.

Specification: Updates (required)—This requirement directs that all documentation created in this program must be reviewed no less often than annually, or as circumstances or changes warrant, and that updates (as required) to them will be issued accordingly. It necessarily follows that all procedures affected by changes in policy must likewise be updated. All superseded versions then go into the retention program, and all new versions are reissued and covered with all affected parties in briefing sessions.

Specification: Disclosure accounting (required)—This requirement comes directly from HITECH, and directs that specific data elements (date, time, patient identification, user identification, and a description of the disclosure) must be recorded for disclosures for treatment, payment, and health care operations, as these terms are defined at 45 CFR § 164.501.

This requirement has been changed to mandate that all electronic health record (EMR/EHR) software be capable by January 2014 of keeping records of any disclosures made beyond those made for treatment, payment, and healthcare operations ("TPO") purposes. The Omnibus Rule also required that the default form of the record requested should be offered as electronic. Hardcopy versions would serve as the alternate form.

PHYSICAL CONTROLS FRAMEWORK

No program such as this can succeed without a complete program of guidance documentation properly implemented. If the Administrative controls framework forms the basis of a HIPAA compliance program, the Physical controls section of the requirements complements this as an implementation derived from it. This section of the regulation presents four Standards, and within them a total of ten Implementation Specifications.

The physical controls set forth in this section embody those determined by the regulatory authors as being those with the most relevant and important effect–positive if present, negative if absent–on overall program success in safeguarding PHI (in all forms) from compromise while enabling appropriate access and use. These choices then reflect the continuing emphasis on positive control and protection without creating undue hardship or excessive administrative burden on the CE or BA implementing them.

Standard: Facility Access Controls (from 45 CFR § 164.310(a))

The required standard in 164.316 embodies the directive to implement policies and procedures to limit physical access to its electronic information systems and the facility or facilities in which they are housed, while ensuring that properly authorized access is allowed. The process reflected here is identical to the process used to enable system access, and emphasizes the same "need-to-know" and "least privilege" requirements on everyone to whom access is granted.

Thus reinforced, this general approach then becomes embedded within the organization's methods and decision-making logic: grant access and level to all requiring it commensurate with their role and defined need. Restrictive but appropriate, such practices enable a general evolutionary systematic reduction in risk throughout the entity by contracting its exposure to both internal and external sources of risk while continuing to enable workforce performance and success.

This standard proscribes these specifications:

Specification: Contingency operations (addressable)—This requirement mandates that the CE or BA create and implement procedures that allow facility access in support of restoration of lost data under the disaster recovery plan and emergency mode operations plan. This means that official members of the Continuity and Recovery teams are authorized to re-enter the facility (when deemed safe) and begin recovery and restoration operations.

This specification would describe site assessment and damage control measures to be used by the teams to evaluate whether reoccupation is advisable, criteria to apply regarding whether to activate the entity's DR plan (or portion of it), what steps are to be followed to restore operations, and precautions to be employed to minimize further disruption and damage. These procedures describe marginal conditions that would dictate activating the offsite recovery capability in the event (regardless of cause) that reoccupation is infeasible. All of these elements are auditable through document examination and performance observation.

Specification: Facility security plan (addressable)—The plan itself is one typically found in most organizations, whether they are located in single or multitenant facilities. In that each organization's circumstances will be unique, this element directs that policies and procedures be implemented to ensure the safeguarding of the location, its physical assets, the information and systems, and the workforce members from unauthorized physical access, tampering, theft, and potentially hazardous conditions.

Plans such as these will contain programmatic elements that address both safety and security concerns. They typically contain procedures for handling disruptions, vandalism, bomb threats, forcible invasion, environmental events (gas leaks, flooding, HAZMAT, etc.), fire and other nonnormal occurrences.

This plan would include elements that would describe any periodic testing of fire suppression and alarming systems, emergency power generation equipment, fire drills, emergency response drills with police, EMS and fire units in the area, mock disaster events, and other activities that provide assurance of adequacy of the procedures and readiness of the staff. All records of these activities must be retained for audit purposes and are subject to the 6-year retention requirement.

Specification: Access control and validation procedures (addressable)–Here again is a programmatic element that emphasizes the appropriateness of access requested and the necessity of Management's involvement in its evaluation and approval. The process defined under this requirement is applicable to both workforce members (CE or BA) and to visitors. All aspects of these procedures would normally be covered in awareness briefings and during NEO.

Specification: Maintenance records (addressable)– This requirement relates to those specific records generated through the installation, maintenance, repair, and decommissioning of any system that has anything to do with facility or data center safety and security. These records are also subject to the 6-year retention period to maintain congruence with similar operational records, and to map to the 7-year retention cycle for PHI records.

While most organizations are already retaining such records for purely business reasons, the HIPAA requirement reflects an appreciation of the impact of the physical upon the technological. Many cases of disasters, whether accidental or intentionally caused, can be attributed to poor maintenance practices, or to tampering and sabotage. These records may contribute important information to investigations of facility or systems events and breaches, and as such they constitute a vital part of the overall security program.

Standards: Workstation Use (164.310(b)) and Workstation Security (164.310(c))

These two **required** standards together lay out the principles behind how workstations will be deployed and used through the facility. They also contain environmental elements complementary to the "Acceptable Use Policy" that guide user behavior.

The **Workstation Use** standard requires drafting policies and procedures that specify the proper functions to be performed, the manner in which those functions are to be performed, and the physical attributes of the surroundings of a specific workstation or class of workstation that can access electronic PHI.

The practical implementation result is a general directive stating that workstations in a given area, such as Patient Care, Administration, or the ER, are to be used solely for the normal functions of that area. The technical implementation of this policy would involve defined security policies on servers and hosts that enable users to sign into the systems and perform their normal role in their home area, but not in others.

The **Workstation Security** standard requires that physical safeguards for all workstations that access electronic PHI, to restrict access to authorized users. Implementation of this standard typically involves the use of physical anti-theft measures, tamper detection devices and seals, and various forms of "lock-downs" such as cable locks (normally for laptops), locking cabinetry, and other methods.

The combination of these two standards will produce an environment where the workstations are:

1. Configured such that only functions of a given area can be performed on the workstation, and then only by authorized workforce members;
2. Arranged in such a manner that will allow them to be used by authorized uses, while making it difficult or obvious should an unauthorized person attempt to do so;
3. Positioned such that any person in the area cannot observe PHI displayed on the screen except from the users primary position;
4. Secured by such cabinets, locking devices, and detection mechanisms possibly including CCTV.

The point of these standards is to restrict system user activities to appropriate areas in order to minimize the incidental disclosure of PHI to the workforce within the facility, and to reasonably eliminate the opportunities for unauthorized parties to observe (without being obvious in the attempt) PHI displayed on computer screens.

Standards: Device and Media Controls (164.310 (d))

This standard regards the use of any and all media and devices that may or will hold PHI of any kind. These devices are typically laptops, removable storage media (USB memory, CD, DVD, floppy disc, tape, and similar media), mobile phones, and tablets such as IPad, Droids, and their variants. Also included but often overlooked are the storage devices found within copiers and facsimile machines. Within the standard are four implementation specifications.

The first two specifications reflect an awareness that using such removable or transportable media raises high the risk that the loss of such a device, whether memory only or an actual computing device, will allow PHI to become exposed under uncontrolled, unauthorized condition and thus result in a breach, at a minimum. As can be gleaned from many news sources, such events are quite common and many thousands of records are compromised in this way annually. Consequently, these two required specifications are intended to effectively address these concerns.

The HITECH Amendment and rules guidance from DHHS-CMS adds important definition to these specifications also. No particular mention was made in the original legislation of how this data was to be protected; meaning that no specific discussion regarding the use of encryption technology was presented. Laws normally attempt to remain technologically neutral, and in 1996 these technologies were not as widespread, as low-cost, or as conveniently usable as they have become since.

The HITECH Amendment added the language that defined "secure" PHI: PHI that had been rendered "unusable, unreadable, or indecipherable to an unauthorized party" through the employment of a suitably sophisticated technological transformational method.

It further included that PHI had to receive such protection whether "at rest" (in storage, not in direct use), or "in motion" (in transmission through transport or tunneling methods). Rules issued by DHHS in August of 2009 following HITECH's passage in February further clarified this, and stated that encryption technology, compliant with NIST proscribed standards, would in fact be required. This was further reinforced and clarified by the Omnibus Rule issued in 2013.

These rules specified algorithmic systems using components of cipher strength at least equivalent to AES-128 (minimum) for crypto-processing (confidentiality assurance), and MD5-128 (minimum) for hash-processing (integrity assurance). Evidence indicates that AES-256 and SHA (160/384 bit) are in more common usage as they provide greater protective strength and longer survivability against attack or when stored.

Specification: Disposal (required)—This requirement directs that when an entity elects to dispose of a particular device it must use a method that provides very high assurance that any reasonable attempt to reclaim the information previously stored on the device will be unsuccessful. Prior to taking this irreversible step, however, there exists the requirement to ensure that the data on such devices has been accounted for within the official records so that it is not lost to the authorized users and patients.

The law does not prevent an entity using an outside contracted service for the purpose, and such providers are commonly engaged. Doing so involves executing a services contract, inclusive of a Business Associate

Agreement/Addendum since the contractor and its personnel may well come into direct contact with PHI when performing their services. Such contracts normally cover the destruction processing of paper and electronic media. All processing is done onsite and Certificates of Destruction are to be provided before the contractor departs.

Specification: Media re-use (required)—This requirement directs that when an entity elects to re-use a particular device it must use a method that provides very high assurance that any reasonable attempt to reclaim the information previously stored on the device will be unsuccessful. Prior to taking this irreversible step, however, there exists the requirement to ensure that the data on such devices has been accounted for within the official records so that it is not lost to the authorized users and patients.

No mention is made that the final disposition must be destruction; the final disposition could be redeployment within the organization or an external donation of a computing device. Given that these options are equally possible, the CE or BA is expected to judge exposure potential and take appropriately strong, assured methods to reasonably ensure that no exposure (i.e., breach) can result.

Achieving this result can be done internally so long as the entity selects appropriately effective physical and logical means of destroying the information contained on the media. These methods would include (separately or in combination) binary over-writing, complete format (low-level or multiple passes), or strong magnetic erasure (degaussing). Actual physical destruction will provide positive assurance as well, but obviously renders the media nonreusable.

One source of guidance on methods acceptable for use would be the Department of Defense Guide known as the "National Industrial Security Program Operations Manual (DoDM 5220.22M)," which proscribes rules for both clearing (applicable for internal re-use) and sanitization (for media used externally). This guide is publicly available, but an extract of it and the specific methods described is provided in Appendix A.

Specification: Accountability (addressable)—This specification directs that an inventory tracking system be designed and implemented that: 1) identifies the device or media and labels it in some way (if feasible); 2) monitors its movements regularly; and 3) assigns a workforce member responsibility for that device. Most organizations of all types already have in place such a system, and continuously monitor device assignments and movement, as would be found when devices are installed, relocated within facilities, or decommissioned.

What makes the healthcare setting unique, however, is that the need of movement of data onto removable storage (beyond routine backups) would be a rare occurrence. Typically this type of PHI movement would not be permitted as such data is not used outside of a CE or

BA facility. While certainly there would be exceptions to this, the standard policy for such actions would be a preventive control placed on USB ports and CD/DVD drives rendering them as Read Only devices or disabling their use for memory media entirely. Such action would not affect the use of headphones, webcams, or other nonmemory devices.

Specification: Data backup and storage (addressable)—This specification directs that whenever devices possessing local storage (harddrives) and are slated to be relocated or possibly decommissioned, that a backup be taken of the drive to ensure no data is lost.

The manner by which this is performed is not described in the rules, but could take the form of a remote backup done over its network connection, or a local backup performed using a portable backup drive (tape or disk). If the CE or BA employs the use of diskless workstations known as "Thin Clients," no backup would be required as there is no permanent local storage of any kind.

TECHNICAL CONTROLS FRAMEWORK

The Technical Controls standards and specifications of the HIPAA/HITECH regulations outline areas of the IT infrastructure of particular importance and impact on the security and privacy of PHI.

Many things could be said to be at the heart of a HIPAA compliance program: the transaction automation, the privacy controls, or improved insurance portability. While good choices, none of them work as intended if the secure electronic information formats and processing requirements that underpin them are not effectively addressed. Thus it is to complete the protective envelope surrounding this sensitive information that the Technology Standards must be selected and implemented.

The technical controls described in this section are commonly accepted and used in most sectors of the American economy. While not an exhaustive set of controls, the ones proscribed by the regulations present a minimum set that will implement a cost-effective program that safeguards against the most commonly occurring threats that produce the highest amount of losses and privacy compromises of PHI. As one of the seventeen sectors identified as Critical Infrastructure by the Department of Homeland Security (DHS), the directive to adopt these controls brings healthcare into alignment with all other sectors, and with American commerce generally.

Standard: Access control (from 45 CFR § 164.312(a))

This standard, which contains five specifications, requires that a CE or BA implement technical policies and procedures that will provide protection for electronic PHI and the systems housing it so that only authorized individuals, systems, programs, and other external entities are allowed access to it, regardless of the means of such access.

Implemented through the specifications, this standard ensures that Management is actively and directly involved in the details and oversight of validating access requests, actions taken when anomalous or unauthorized actions appear on audit reports. Ultimately these elements create a program of access protections that is designed, implemented, and operated appropriately to achieve the overall objective of assuring only authorized entities can access the information, only through authorized means, and then perform only authorized actions on that information.

Specification: Unique user identification (required)—A straightforward requirement, this specification directs that all authorized users be assigned a login identifier that is uniquely theirs. Though already a very common practice in many organizations, the nature of healthcare is such that systems may be built and deployed that do not carry this capability (if they are old enough). They may also enable the use of generic or group logins. Virtually no system sold today omits the capability to assign and monitor the individually assigned user login, but many still allow the creation and use of the generic types.

The fundamental principle here is "individual identifiability and accountability." As in all other areas of these regulations, all entities having access to PHI must have a valid need-to-know, and the law enforces accountability on every individual and entity commensurate with such access. To make this possible, the system must be able to clearly and precisely identify and track each user or entity and their actions. Otherwise accountability and thus disciplinary action is unenforceable, and the sanctions policy or legal action all but pointless.

While there is not particular required format for the identifiers themselves, this policy will contain the specifications of their associated validating credentials:

1. Type I Authenticators—something the user "knows": a password or PIN code.
   a. Complexity and content (length, mixed case, inclusion of numbers and special characters)
   b. Normal expiration periods
   c. History-generations precluding re-use
   d. Pattern prevention rules
   e. Dictionaries of denied words and combinations
   f. Minimum effective life, maximum usage period
2. Type II Authenticators—something the user "has": a token device or card-key.
   a. A badge-card that also functions as a system access key by embedding credential-validation coding

   b. A token device that generates a one-time use challenge-response code in either synchronous (time driven) or asynchronous (even-driven) mode
3. Type III Authenticators—something a user "is or does": a biometric marker or action.
   a. Any one of a number of biometric traits that in real-time use are matched to a stored template. Examples include fingerprints, retina blood-vessel patterns, iris color/reflectivity patterns, or other passive characteristics.
   b. Any one of specific actions performed by the user during real-time authentication: spoken phrase voice prints, typing actions, or other user-unique actions.

Current regulatory requirements specify only Type I Authenticators as only these are built into virtually every computing environment, and as such require no additional software to provide the specified security features. If, however, the RA of the CE or the BA should indicate a type or level of threat that is unacceptable in this aspect of the system in use, the entity would be expected to evaluate this situation and develop a countermeasure for it (though not necessarily requiring the addition of Type II or III Authenticators). As no entity would be compensated by government funding to meet this additional risk, the actual solution deployed would be the most cost-effective possible, regardless of the technological solution chosen.

The audit records produced from this requirement are derived from the raw system logs and capture for all user activity:

1. Login/logout (data, time, originating address, and possibly other attributes)
2. Password change
3. Password mis-entry
4. Username suspension due to mis-entry or other reason (i.e., termination)
5. Change of privilege level (requires paper-trail authorizing this)
6. Transaction and file manipulation activities
7. Errors, violations, or other anomalies appearing during user sessions

The frequency of generation and review is described in the regulations as "periodic," leaving it to the entities to define it precisely. This information is most usable and revealing when obtained daily, though weekly may be often enough for smaller, less active entities. Any less often and the information mass may be too great to evaluate in a meaningfully short period of time (more than a full day), or may miss certain activities. The raw logs do not have a records retention requirement on them, but the extracted reports are operational records that are under the 6-year retention rule.

Specification: Emergency Access Procedure (Required)—A straightforward requirement, this specification directs that an all-powerful, nonsuspendable username and password be created, the sole purpose of which is to enable an authorized administrator access to a compromised system to perform recovery activities, while ensuring that protection of the resident PHI will continue uninterrupted. The pre-packaged "Admin" loginid is often configured to this use.

The implementation of this requirement is a procedure involving at least three staff members: an administrator, a member of Management and a selected other member of the workforce. This process applies the principle of Separation of Duties-Dual Control to ensure no inappropriate use is made of this access:

1. Administrator: has the technical skill to use the username, but cannot access it as it is in the custody of the second workforce member and access to it must be approved by Management each time
2. Second workforce member: is the keeper of the username, but does not possess the technical skill to make any use of it
3. Management: must personally approve the username's use every time it is required, review the transcript of all actions it is used to perform while out, and must sign off when it is refreshed and replaced in storage

All those involved in this process are formally assigned and are individually accountable for all actions taken during its invocation. All records generated through this are required to be retained as auditable for the 6-year period.

Specification: Automatic logoff (addressable)— This specification directs that either a full system logoff/logout is forced by the system's security settings, or if this feature does not exist, that an acceptable alternative is for the system to force a screensaver to activate: in either case the feature is to activate after a preset time interval of user inactivity expires.

It is a normal part of Acceptable Use or Password policies as mandatory that users are to never leave their workstation sessions logged on if they step away from it for any length of time (an obvious exposure to misuse by another). This particular feature also ensures that a session times-out due to inactivity even if the user is present. The regulation originally required a full, forced logout, but Microsoft systems did not and do not support this. The HITECH amendment modified the requirement to allow the use of password-protected screensavers as an alternative. No specification was made as to the expiration period length (most use the system default of 30 minutes), but universal enforcement

of the feature and the chosen duration are required (validated by technical compliance systems audit).

Specification: Encryption and decryption (addressable)—The origin specification from HIPAA [(164.312.(a)(iv)]required only that a suitable method to encrypt and decrypt PHI was found and implemented. While certainly a vital part of the over security program, no mention was made as the type or strength of the cipher to be employed to accomplish this. As with all addressable requirements, the law left the selection process to the CE or BA, so long as it was done, universally deployed on PHI-containing volumes and repositories, and that its use was consistent and of reasonably sufficient strength.

Specification: Encryption and decryption (required)—This added specification from HITECH [170.210(a)] extended the original and set strength and performance minimums for qualifying technologies and products considered for use. The HITECH version stated that:

1. Encryption and decryption operations were to use a symmetric (secret) key cipher 128 bit fixed-block cipher algorithm capable of using a 128, 192, or 256 bit key strength. (This describes the Advance Encryption Standard (AES) in everything but name.)
2. Operations for key or information exchange require that an encrypted and integrity protected link must be implemented.

In the case of point b, this describes a public key (PKI) exchange involving the use of encryption for content confidentiality (symmetric keys themselves or PHI) and hashing for content integrity assurance. This applies equally to tunneling at setup or in normal use, or to message (transport mode) communications involving data "in motion," whether actual PHI or cryptographic materials.

Standard: Audit Controls (from 45 CFR § 164.312(b))

This standard requires that a CE or BA implement technical policies and procedures that will enable a detailed and thorough examination of the logs and records produced by a system housing or processing PHI in order to make an accurate determination about the: 1) correct performance of the system such that information integrity is assured; 2) that authorized user activity can be shown in sufficient detail to determine policy compliance (or its lack); and 3) to provide supporting formation validating the overall management of the system such that these traits are observed and maintained through continuous and diligent performance of these processes.

Specification: Audit controls (required)—No additional detail is added by the original specification [(164.312(b)] except to restate the standard itself.

The specification for audit controls added by HITECH [170.210(B)] added a lot of detail to the standard, now requiring that the system log (from which audit reports are extracted) must record actions related to electronic health information. The date, time, patient identification, and user identification must be recorded when electronic health information is created, modified, deleted, or printed; and an indication of which action (s) occurred must also be recorded.

There is no indication, even in the added details from HITECH, if there is a particular audit protocol to be employed. There is the Control Objectives for IT (CoBIT) standard that is widespread use, but it does not focus on healthcare systems or PHI. There is also the ISO 27000 series of security and audit standards, but this course is valid only if the ISO itself has been implemented and validated as having met HIPAA requirements. (Despite its globally recognized quality as a security framework, there is no mandate or reference within the regulations or CFR's regarding its use).

The Office of Civil Rights (DHHS-OCR) has itself issued audit protocols for both privacy and security, and each Privacy Officer and Security Officer for each CE or BA should evaluate these as the applicable metrics to certify their own performance and preparedness for an official audit, or readiness for a complaints investigation.

Standard: Integrity (from 45 CFR § 164.312(c))

This addressable standard requires that a CE or BA implement policies and procedures that will direct selection and implementation of technical mechanisms that will protect electronic protected health information from improper alteration or destruction. There are no additional specifications for this standard.

Typical implementations for this standard involve the application of protective mechanisms that prevent editing or deletion of files even by those granted access to them. Coresident with these access controls are often integrity assurance mechanisms that record all changes, both authorized and unauthorized. Such mechanisms typically alert the file owners of attempts but do not act preventatively.

There will often be a variable level of detail these detection records provide as well: sometimes to the file level and other times to the field level. The regulations do not make clear which is preferable, but more detail is preferable to less, within reason.

Standard: Person or Entity Authentication (from 45 CFR § 164.312(d))

This standard requires that any entity, whether person or organization, granted access or to be provided any PHI

be positively identified. This means that a combination of electronic and procedural controls must be implemented to: 1) first establish the entity's need to know and authorization for acquiring the information; and 2) re-verify that the same entity is the intended recipient each time before a transmission of PHI is made. The controls employed must include provisions for transmission of PHI whether through a network, via facsimile, or mail.

Standard: Transmission Security (from 45 CFR § 164.312(e) and 170.210(C))

This standard requires that any form of PHI transmission must be protected against violations of its confidentiality and its integrity. The transmission types include tunneling (VPN), transport (message-based or e-mail), and facsimile.

Specification: Integrity controls (addressable)—The method used here would typically employ hashing as the assurance mechanism for detection of any alterations while in transit.

Specification: Encryption (required)—Specifies that a hashing algorithm of 160 bit strength or greater be used as the integrity assurance mechanism (equivalent to or greater than the Secure Hash Algorithm (SHA) certified by NIST.)

Specification: Encryption (addressable)—Added by HITECH and clarified by rules from OCR, this indicates that symmetric encryption at a minimum 128 bit strength must be used to sufficiently protect the confidentiality of PHI in transit regardless of transmission method.

THE OMNIBUS RULE

This was issued in January 2013 and extends the original HIPAA law and it's HITECH Amendment. Rules provide clarification and refinement to the interpretation of the law to facilitate better understanding and implementation of the regulations.

Of the 64 total entries addressed by the Omnibus Rule, a careful analysis shows that only eight of these are in fact changes to the original legislation. Of these eight, two concern the breach notification process, three affect the patient's ability to opt-out of various activities, and one deals with the clarification of a subcontractor (to a BA) as being a BA itself.

With respect to impact on the information systems function in particular, Omnibus has little if any direct effect. All indirect effects have already been noted above.

BIBLIOGRAPHY

1. Leo, R.A.Ed. *The HIPAA Program Reference Handbook*; Auerbach Publishing: 2005, ISBN 0-8493-2211-1
2. Herrold, R.; Beaver, K. *The Practical Guide to HIPAA Privacy and Security Compliance*; Auerbach Publishing: 2004, ISBN 0-8493-1953-6.
3. The Health Insurance Portability and Accountability Act of 1996 ("HIPAA"), Public Law 104-191.
4. The American Recover and Reinvestment Act of 2009 ("ARRA"), Public Law 111-5.
5. The HITECH Act of 2009, (ARRA, Division A, Title XIII, Subpart D, and Division B, Title IV).
6. The Omnibus Rule, Department of Health and Human Services (DHHS), January 23, **2013**.
7. DoD Manual 5220.22M, "The National Industrial Security Program Operations Manual," U. S. Department of Defense: 1997.
8. Centers for Medicare and Medicaid Services (CMS) CIO Directive 07-03, August 13, **2007**: "Mandatory Encryption on all Removable Storage Devices".

HIPAA–
Information
Protection

Image Processing and Measurement

John C. Russ
Department of Materials Science and Engineering, College of Engineering, North Carolina State University, Raleigh, North Carolina, U.S.A.

Abstract

Images provide important information in scientific, technical, and forensic situations, in addition to their role in everyday life. Extracting information from images acquired by digital cameras involves image processing to correct colors, reduce noise, and correct for nonuniform illumination or nonplanar views. Enhancement of image details is generally accomplished by reducing the contrast of other information in the image, so that,for example, lines and edges that make measurements of structure are more accessible. The processing steps use a variety of computer algorithms and may be performed on the pixel array, or in a different space, for example, by using a Fourier transform. Some applications, especially forensic ones, require simple comparisons, but for object identification, classification, or correlations, quantitative measurements of color or density, position, size, and shape are needed. Several possible measurement quantities are available for each category, particularly shape, for which a variety of dimensionless ratios, Fourier or wavelet coefficients, and invariant moments may be used. Interpretation of the measurements depends on the nature of the image and of the specimen or scene, for instance, whether it consists of discrete objects on a surface, a section through a complex structure, or a projection through a three-dimensional space.

INTRODUCTION

Humans depend to a high degree on images to gather information about their world, and to organize and understand that information. This dependence extends to scientific, technical, and forensic analysis as well, and to scales that include the microscopic and astronomical, aided by a broad variety of instruments designed to use infrared light, X-rays, radar, sound waves, and so on.

Human vision is not a quantitative tool, and is easily fooled by illusions and distracted by extraneous or random background features. Measurement requires direct comparison to appropriate standards (rulers, protractors, color scales, etc.). Consequently, the design of instruments and computer algorithms that collect, process, and analyze images is a key part of acquiring quantitative data for many scientific, technical, and forensic activities.

Image processing is done for two principal reasons: to improve visual appearance for a human observer, including printing and transmission, and to prepare images for measurement and analysis of the features and structures which they reveal. Image processing methods can be considered in two principal categories: the correction of defects or limitations in acquisition, and the enhancement of important details. Image processing may alter the values or locations of pixels (picture elements) to produce another image. Image analysis, on the other hand, extracts numerical measurement information from the picture.

It is important to understand that the scale of an image (μm, feet, miles, or light years) matters little, as does the type of signal used to form the image. Most processing and measurement tools are equally applicable to a broad variety of images, and may be used in a very wide range of applications.

Correction of Defects 1: Color Adjustment

Digital cameras, and earth-observing satellites, capture color images. Color correction should be the first operation performed if it is required. Compensation for variations in illumination can be made in several ways. The best results require capturing an image of known color standards under the same lighting, or having sufficient independent knowledge of the characteristics of the light source and the physics of the instrumentation.

With standards, a tristimulus matrix can be calculated that corrects for the overlap in the wavelength ranges of the filters used to form the red, green, and blue (RGB) signals that are typically stored. In some cases, a simpler and more approximate approach is used in which neutral gray objects are located and the RGB values adjusted to be equal. This constructs adjustment curves for each color channel which are then applied throughout the image.

Encyclopedia of Information Systems and Technology, DOI: 10.1081/E-EIST-120052401

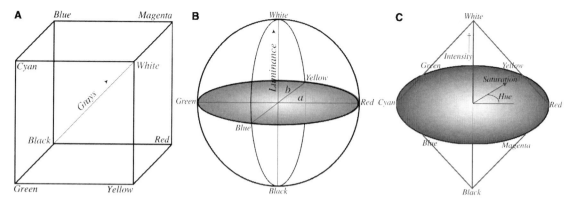

Fig. 1 Color spaces: (A) cubic RGB; (B) spherical L•a•b; (C) biconic HSI.

Most cameras and computers store and display color images as RGB values for each pixel, but for most processing and measurement purposes other color spaces are more useful. L•a•b and HSI color coordinates are often used as shown in Fig. 1. In the L•a•b space, which may be represented as a sphere with orthogonal axes, L is the luminance, or brightness, while the "a" and "b" axes are red–green and blue–yellow.

HSI space is more complicated, with H or hue represented as an angle on the color wheel from red to yellow, green, cyan, blue, magenta, and back to red, while S is saturation, or the amount of color (e.g., the difference between gray, pink, and red), and I (also called V for value or B for brightness) is the intensity. This space may be represented as a cylinder, cone, or bi-cone. In the bi-cone shown in the figure, saturation is reduced to zero at the ends. The color saturation at maximum intensity can be increased only by reducing some color contribution, and likewise at the dark end saturation can be increased only be increasing intensity. Conversion from one color space to another is performed in software as necessary.

Correction of Defects 2: Noise Reduction

Noise is generally any part of the image that does not represent the actual scene, but arises from other sources. These may include the statistics of charge production in the detector, thermal or electronic noise in the amplifier and digitization process, electrical interference in transmission, vibration of the camera or flickering of the light source, and so on. The two principal kinds of noise are random and periodic; they are treated in different ways, under the assumption that they can be distinguished from the important details. Random or speckle noise usually appears as fluctuations in the brightness of neighboring pixels and is treated in the spatial domain of the pixels, while periodic noise involves larger-scale variations and is best dealt with using the Fourier transform of the image.

Fig. 2 shows an image with significant random noise, visible as variations in the pixels in the uniform background above the cat's head. It arises primarily from the amplification required, because the photo was taken in dim light. The most common, but generally poor, approach used for random noise reduction is a Gaussian blur, which replaces each pixel value with the weighted average of the pixels in a small neighborhood. This reduces the noise as shown, but also blurs detail and shifts edges. It is identical to a low-pass filter in Fourier space that keeps low frequencies and reduces the high frequencies (variations over a short distance) that constitute the pixel-to-pixel noise variations, but which are also needed to define edges, lines, and boundaries. Extensions of the Gaussian model may adjust the weights applied to neighboring pixels based on their difference in value or the direction of the local brightness gradient.

Fig. 2 Random noise reduction: (**A**) original; (**B**) Gaussian smooth; (**C**) median filter; (**D**) nonlocal means filter.

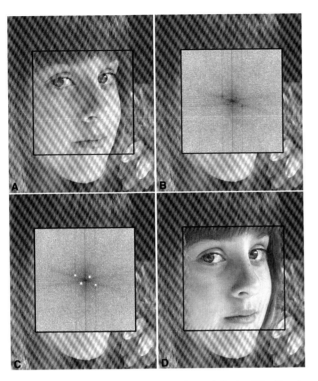

Fig. 3 Periodic noise removal: (A) original; (B) Fourier power spectrum of outlined region; (C) removal of spikes; (D) re-transformed result.

Median filters replace each pixel with the mean value found by ranking the pixel values in the neighborhood according to brightness (all of the examples in the figure use a neighborhood with a radius of three pixels). The median filter is a nonlinear operation that has no equivalent in Fourier space. This filter, and variations that combine partial results from multiple neighborhoods, or use vectors for color images, are widely used and do a better job of preserving details such as lines and edges while reducing random noise. More computationally complex filters such as the nonlocal means filter[1] produce even better results. This works by replacing each pixel with a weighted average of all pixels in the image, based on the similarity of their neighborhoods.

Fig. 3 shows an example of periodic noise. In the Fourier transform, this appears as "spikes" at radii

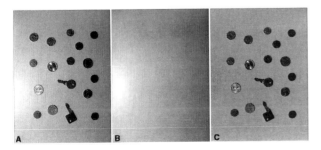

Fig. 4 Correction of nonuniform illumination: (A) original image; (B) image of the background with the objects removed; (C) after subtracting the background.

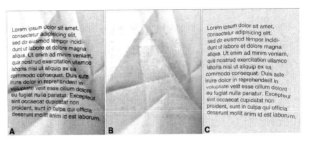

Fig. 5 Generating a background by morphological opening: (A) original; (B) removal of the letters; (C) subtracted result.

corresponding to the frequency (inverse of the spacing of the lines) and at angles that correspond to their orientation. Removal of the spikes and calculating the inverse Fourier transform restores the image with the noise removed but all other information, which is composed of different frequencies and orientations, intact.

Correction of Defects 3: Nonuniform Illumination

A key assumption behind most methods for selecting features for measurement is that an object should have the same color and brightness wherever it happens to lie in the field of view. In some controlled situations, such as microscopy and laboratory setups, uniform illumination can be achieved. In real world imagery, including crime scene photos and satellite imaging of a curved planet, it may be difficult or impossible to do so. There are several ways to adjust the resulting image to correct the nonuniformity.

Fig. 4 shows the preferred approach—recording an image of the background or substrate with the objects of interest removed. This background can then be subtracted or divided into the original to remove the variation. The choice of subtraction or division depends on how the camera recorded the brightness, as explained in the section Detail Enhancement 7: Image Combinations. When recording a background image is not practical, it may be possible to model the background by fitting a smooth function, typically a polynomial, to multiple points in the image that are known or assumed to be the same, or in some cases to calculate a background based on independent knowledge of the circumstances (such as the lighting of a spherical planet by the sun).

In other cases, it may be possible to "remove" the objects of interest by a morphological procedure called an opening. As shown in Fig. 5, replacing each pixel by its brightest neighbor, and repeating the operation until the dark letters are removed, and then reversing the operation and replacing each pixel by its darkest neighbor to restore the position of the edges and creases, produces a background image that can be subtracted.

Fig. 6 Geometric correction of the original image (**A**) produces a normal view (**B**) in which measurement of wear marks can be made to identify the individual tire. Similar procedures are used for footprints.

Correction of Defects 4: Geometric Distortion

Measurements are most straightforwardly performed when the image shows the subjects of interest in a normal view of a flat surface. Transforming an image taken at an angle, or of a curved surface, requires knowing the geometry and performing a correction as shown in Fig. 6. Including rulers in images, and locating fiducial marks, is a critical step to enable this procedure and is standard practice for forensic imaging. Pixel values are interpolated from those in the original to generate the corrected image.

Enhancement 1: Histogram Adjustments

After the corrective steps shown earlier, it is often useful to make adjustments to contrast and brightness. This is done by referring to the image histogram, a plot showing

Fig. 7 Histogram modification: (**A**) original image with limited brightness range; (**B**) linear stretch; (**C**) inverting the range to produce a negative image; (**D**) adjusting gamma to stretch the dark range and compress the bright values; (**E**) histogram equalization; (**F**) homomorphic compression.

the number of pixels as a function of brightness. For color images, there may be a histogram for each channel, but adjustments, like all of the enhancement operations, should be performed on the brightness, luminance, or intensity values leaving the color information unchanged. Attempting to make adjustments to the RGB channels, for example, would alter the relative amounts producing new and strange colors in the resulting image.

When the brightness range captured in the image does not cover the full available dynamic range, a linear stretch of the values can be applied (Fig. 7b). It is important not to push pixel values beyond the black and white limits, causing them to be clipped to those values and data to be irretrievably lost. After the contrast expansion, there are just as many possible brightness values that have no pixels, as shown by the gaps in the histogram, but they are uniformly distributed across the brightness range rather than being collected at one or both ends of the histogram. Linear stretching is not the only possibility. Fig. 7 shows several other possibilities, with the resulting histogram shown for each case.

Adjusting the "gamma" value (Fig. 7d) changes the mid-gray point in the histogram and can expand the contrast for either the bright or dark portion of the image by compressing the values at the opposite end of the range. Rather than this manual adjustment, applying histogram equalization (Fig. 7e) adjusts values so that the histogram is as nearly uniform as possible, and all levels of brightness are represented by equal areas of the image. This is shown in the cumulative histogram, shown in Fig. 7e, which becomes a straight line. Equalization is often useful for comparing images taken under different lighting conditions. A more computationally intensive approach is the homomorphic transformation, which is applied in Fourier space by adjusting the amplitudes of dominant frequencies. In Fig. 7f, details in both the bright and dark regions are clearly evident.

Enhancement 2: Sharpening Detail

Human vision locates lines and edges in images as places where the brightness changes abruptly, and from these forms a mental sketch of the scene. Increasing the local contrast at steps, or narrowing the distance over which the change occurs, makes the image appear sharper. The simplest approach to this is the Laplacian filter, which calculates the difference between each pixel and the average value of its neighbors. A more flexible routine, called the unsharp mask and implemented in many programs, subtracts a Gaussian smoothed copy of the image from the original. This is a high-pass filter (it removes low frequencies or gradual variations in brightness, and "passes" or keeps the high frequencies) and may equivalently be performed using the Fourier transform. The results of all

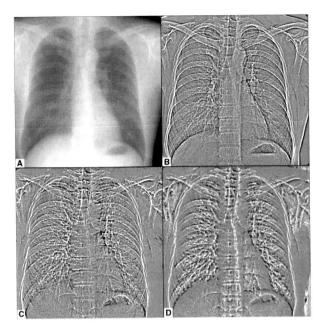

Fig. 8 Local detail enhancement: (**A**) original; (**B**) difference of Gaussians; (**C**) difference of medians; (**D**) local equalization.

these "detail extracting" routines are typically added back to the original for viewing.

The most flexible such approach is the difference of Gaussians or DoG filter, which calculates the difference between two copies of the image which have been smoothed with Gaussians having different radii.[2] This is a band-pass filter that selects a range of frequencies and can enhance detail while suppressing high frequency noise as well as low frequency variations. It is shown in Fig. 8b. Using similar logic but calculating the difference between median values in different size neighborhoods (Fig. 8c) requires more computation but is superior in its ability to avoid haloes around edges. Local equalization (Fig. 8d) performs histogram equalization within a local neighborhood and keeps the new value only for each central pixel; this emphasizes fine

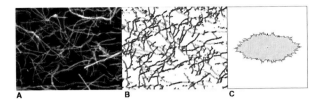

Fig. 10 Measuring fiber orientations: (**A**) original; (**B**) gray values along each fiber indicate the local compass angle; (**C**) rose plot of values shows a nearly 3:1 preferred orientation in the horizontal direction.

detail by increasing the difference, either positive or negative, between each pixel and local neighbors.

Detail Enhancement 3: Defining edges

In addition to the visual enhancement of images, edges and boundaries are important for the measurement of features. Defining their position may be performed using several different approaches. The most common, the Sobel filter,[3] replaces the value of each pixel with the magnitude of the local gradient of pixel brightness, as shown in Fig. 9b. A different approach, the variance filter (Fig. 9c), calculates the statistical variance of pixel values in a neighborhood, responding strongly to local changes. Both of these produce broad lines because of the size of the neighborhood used for the calculation. The Canny filter (Fig. 9d) begins with the gradient but keeps only those pixels with the maximum value in the gradient direction, producing single-pixel-wide lines that mark the most probable location of the boundary.[4]

In addition to marking the location of boundaries, the brightness gradient vector has a direction that can be used to measure the orientation of edges. Fig. 10 shows the use of the Sobel gradient vector to mark cellulose fibers used in papermaking with gray values proportional to the local angle. A histogram of values, shown as a compass plot, indicates the nonisotropic distribution of fiber orientations.

Detail Enhancement 4: Revealing Texture

Features in images are not always distinguished by differences in brightness or color, or by outlined boundaries.

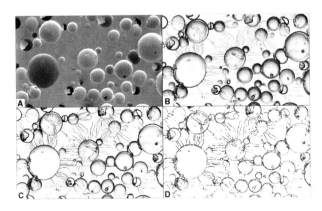

Fig. 9 Section through bubbles in a polymer: (**A**) original; (**B**) Sobel filter; (**C**) variance filter; (**D**) Canny filter.

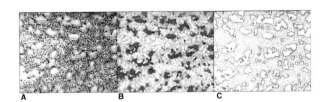

Fig. 11 Microscope image of a section through cheese, showing the smooth curds: (A) original; (B) fractal dimension as described in the text; (C) resulting outlines superimposed on the curds for measurement of volume and surface area.

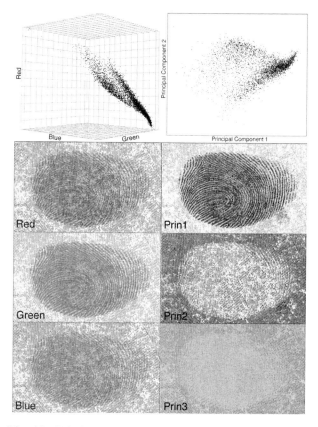

Fig. 12 Principal components: the RGB channels of the original image do not distinguish the fingerprint; the images formed using the principal components values separate the fingerprint from the printed background.

Another criterion can be texture, which can be understood as a local variation in brightness or color. Fig. 11 shows an example: the curds in the cheese do not have a distinct brightness, but have a "smooth" appearance while the surrounding matrix is highly textured.

Processing the image to replace each pixel value with the result from calculating various statistical properties of the local neighborhood can convert the image to one in which the regions have a unique brightness and can be isolated for measurement. The most commonly used properties are the range (difference between the brightest and darkest value) or the variance of the pixel values. In the figure, the fractal dimension has been calculated; this is a more complex calculation that fits the slope (on log-log axes) of the variance as a function of the size of the neighborhood. The resulting difference in brightness allows outlining the boundaries of the curds, so that their volume fraction and surface area can be determined using stereological relationships as explained in the section Measurements 2: Stereology.

Detail Enhancement 5: Principal Components

RGB color images, and satellite images covering multiple wavelengths, may be processed using principal components analysis (also known as the Hotelling or Karhunen–Loève transform) to obtain one or more new color channels as a combination of the existing ones, which can provide optimum contrast for the details in a particular image.

This can be visualized as a rotation of the color coordinate axes as shown in Fig. 12. The original image is a fingerprint on a check which has an imprinted texture pattern. In the original RGB channels, the minutiae in the print are difficult to discern. Plotting each pixel's RGB values in a three-dimensional graph shows correlation, and fitting a plane to the data produces the maximum dispersion of the values and hence the greatest contrast.

Using the position of each pixel's point along the new principal components axes results in the images shown that separate the fingerprint from the printed background pattern. The third axis, which is perpendicular to the plane, generates an image with little contrast, containing primarily the random noise in the original image.

Detail Enhancement 7: Image Combinations

The example of subtracting a recorded background image is shown in the section Correction of Defects 3: Nonuniform Illumination. There are other situations in which two or more images of the same scene may be acquired, for instance using different wavelength bands, or different lighting, or different camera focus. Processing an image may also produce an additional representation (e.g., the Gaussian blurred copy that is subtracted to produce the unsharp mask result).

Arithmetic operations between images are performed pixel-by-pixel, with scaling and offset applied to keep the resulting values within the permitted range (for single-byte images this is 0...255, but some programs accommodate many different bit depths and normalize all of them to 0...1 using real numbers rather than integers).

Either subtraction or division is used for removing background, depending on whether the acquisition device responds logarithmically (like film and vidicon cameras) or linearly (solid state detectors, but the electronics may convert the result to logarithmic in order to mimic film). Division is used to ratio one wavelength band to another, compensating for variations in illumination and, for example, the curvature of the earth. Addition may be used to superimpose difference-of-Gaussian or edge-delineation results on the original image for visual enhancement. Multiplication is less often employed, but is used in graphics applications, for example, to superimpose texture on smooth regions. In addition, mathematical operations include keeping whichever pixel value is greater or smaller, and for

Fig. 13 A series of images taken with different focal settings, the extended focus composite produced by selecting the pixel with the greatest local variance, and a map showing the source of each pixel.

black and white or "binary" thresholded images the various Boolean operations (AND, OR, Exclusive-OR, and their combinations) are useful for combining various selections and information.

When a series of images acquired with different focal planes are captured, they can be combined to keep whichever pixel value at each location gives the sharpest focus, resulting in an extended focal depth. The pixel value selected may be the one with the highest local contrast or variance in its neighborhood. Fig. 13 shows an example, with a map indicating from which original image each pixel in the composite was selected.

DETAIL ENHANCEMENT 8: DECONVOLUTION

When the Hubble telescope was first launched, a fabrication error in the curvature of the primary mirror

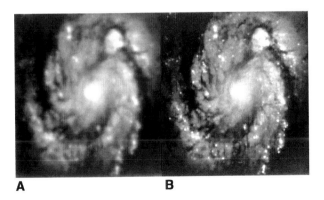

Fig. 14 Deconvolution: (**A**) original blurred image; (**B**) deconvolved result, which reveals fine detail.

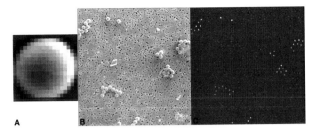

Fig. 15 Cross-correlation: (**A**) enlarged target image showing individual pixels; (**B**) image of filter with particles on a complex background; (**C**) cross-correlation result marking the particle locations.

caused the images to be out-of-focus. Several years later a replacement secondary mirror was installed that compensated for the incorrect primary curvature, restored the focal sharpness, and increased the amount of light directed to the instrument package. But in the interim, sharp images were obtained by deconvolution using computer software. If the point-spread-function (PSF) of the optics, which is simply the recorded image produced by point of light like a star, can be either calculated or measured, it can be used to remove much of the blur introduced in image capture, either due to the optics or to motion.

Fig. 14 shows an example. The process is usually performed in Fourier space, with the most basic algorithm (Wiener deconvolution) dividing the transform of the blurred image by that of the PSF, plus a small scalar constant that depends on the amount of noise present.[5] Other methods include iterative techniques that may try to determine the PSF from the image itself (e.g., Lucy-Richardson deconvolution).[6,7] The results are never as good as a perfectly focused original image, because the noise is increased and not all of the blur can be removed. But the improvement over the original blurred image can be great, and for images such as forensic evidence may be critical.

Detail Enhancement 8: Cross-Correlation

Cross-correlation is used to align images, and also to locate a target in a scene. It is often used for aerial surveillance, machine and robotics vision, and finding faces in images. It is frequently carried out using Fourier transforms, but for small targets may be applied in the spatial or pixel domain. It is easy to visualize the process as having the target image on a transparent film and sliding it across all locations in the scene image to find a match. The result is another image in which each pixel records a measure of the similarity of that location to the target. Fig. 15 shows an example. Searching for the target particle shape finds all of the occurrences with high matching scores, in spite of the different contrast for single particles versus those in groups, while

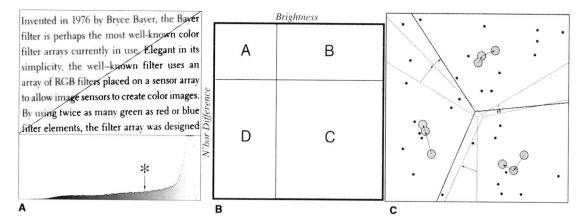

Fig. 16 Methods for automatic thresholding: (**A**) based on histogram statistics; (**B**) using a co-occurrence matrix; (**C**) iterative *k*-means cluster analysis.

ignoring the background texture of the filter and objects present with other sizes or shapes.

Binary Images 1: Thresholding (Automatic)

Except for manual measurements on images, in which a human marks points using a mouse and the computer reports distances, most image measurements are performed after thresholding or segmentation to delineate the objects, structures, or other features of interest. Manual measurements are generally suspect, because of nonreproducibility and the possible influence of expectation or desire. For the same reason, manual thresholding, although often used, is not a preferred approach.

Thresholding selects pixels based on some defining characteristics as belonging to the features of interest. The process may identify all pixels at once as part of one or another of several classes of structure, or simply erase as background those which are not part of the structure of current interest. The simplest of all types of thresholding is based on the brightness histogram of the image, as shown in Fig. 16a.

A peak in the histogram indicates that many pixels have similar brightnesses, which may indicate that they represent the same type of structure. Placing thresholds "between peaks" may distinguish the features of current interest. In the example in the figure, the bright peak corresponds to the paper but there is no dark peak representing the ink. Instead, a statistical test is used to select the threshold value (marked with an arrow) that is used to (hopefully) isolate the printed characters for measurement and ultimately identification.

The test illustrated is one of the most widely used, producing often satisfactory and at least reproducible results. It uses the Student's t-test to compare the values of pixels above and below each possible threshold setting and selects the one that produces the greatest value of t. This indicates that the two groups are most

different and distinguishable.[8,9] However, the statistical test makes the tacit assumption that the two populations have Gaussian or normal distributions, which is rarely the case. There are a variety of other statistical tests, which use entropy, fuzzy weighting of values, and other means, and which produce somewhat different threshold settings.

A different approach to automatic threshold setting uses not only the value of the pixels, but also those of their immediate neighbors. The logic behind the test is that pixels within features, or within background, should be similar to their neighbors, while those along borders should not. A co-occurrence matrix that counts the number of pixels with each value along one direction and the number with each average neighbor value along the other is used, as indicated schematically in Fig. 16b. In the figure, the areas marked A and C are the more uniform regions, corresponding to features and background in which pixels are similar to their neighbors. Those marked B and D represent the borders where they are different. Iteratively adjusting thresholds to maximize the total counts or the entropy in A and C and minimize those in B and D is a more computer intensive approach, but is superior in performance.[10]

Another powerful method is indicated in Fig. 16c. The *k*-means procedure[11] is particularly appropriate for color or multichannel images (the figure shows just two dimensions, but the method generalizes directly to any number). The values of all pixels are plotted and the method searches for clusters. An initial set of *k* locations are selected arbitrarily, and all pixel points that are closest to each location are temporarily given that class identity. The mean of each class is then used as the next proposed cluster center, and the procedure is repeated. This causes some points to change identity, and the cluster boundaries and cluster means to change. The procedure continues until no further changes take place.

Fig. 17 Additional segmentation methods: (**A**) edge delineation; (**B**) region growing; (**C**) active contours.

BINARY IMAGES 2: THRESHOLDING (INTERACTIVE)

Other approaches to thresholding or segmentation are sometimes useful, and may involve some degree of human interaction. Fig. 17a shows the use of an edge-marking procedure as described in the section Detail Enhancement 3: Defining Edges to outline each object. Since there are also some lines and edges drawn within the objects (e.g., the pumpkin ridges and stems), it becomes necessary for the operator to select those lines that are the object boundaries, but which have been located automatically.

Human selection also operates in the seed-fill or region-growing approach, shown in Fig. 17b. Marking an initial point (indicated by an asterisk in the figure) begins the process. Then every neighboring point is examined and ones that are similar are added to the growing region. This continues until no further neighboring points are added. The resulting selection is outlined in the figure. The test for similarity can be a fixed range of color or brightness, or it may be based on the statistics of the growing region, or may be weighted toward the values of the pixels near the local expanding boundary. The most common problem with region growing is that it may "escape" from the feature and become free to spread across background or other objects.

Fig. 17c illustrates the active contour approach. It begins with a manually drawn outline, which then contracts until it is stopped by the borders of the object (active contours that expand from an inner outline can also be used). The stopping may be based on color or brightness, gradient, or other criterion. Active contours can bridge over gaps where the border is indistinct because the shrinking criterion seeks to minimize the energy in the boundary, based on its length and curvature.[12] Active contours may be called "snakes," and when applied in three dimensions (3D) are referred to as "balloons."

These are not the only approaches used for thresholding and segmentation. Top-down split and merge segmentation examines the histogram for the image, and if it is not uniform by some statistical test it divides the area into parts. Each of these is examined similarly and divided, and the process continues. At each iteration, adjacent regions with different previous parents are compared and joined if they are similar. The final result reaches the level of individual pixels and produces a set of regions. Other computer-intensive methods include fuzzy approaches to cluster analysis that weight pixels by how different they are from the cluster mean, and neural net approaches which begin with the entire array of pixel values as input.

Binary Images 3: Morphological Processing

Thresholded images are often imperfect delineation of the features or structures of interest. Random variations in pixel values may cause some individual errors, boundaries may be poorly defined if the finite size of pixels straddle them and have intermediate values, and some pixels may have values that are the same as those within the structures of interest. These flaws are usually small in dimension (often single pixels) and are dealt with by morphological operations of erosion and dilation, which remove or add pixels according to the identity of their neighbors.

Dilation in its simplest form adds background pixels that are adjacent to a feature boundary, and erosion removes feature pixels that are adjacent to background. Since each of these changes the size of the object, they are usually used in combination. Fig. 18 shows an example, in which a closing (the sequence of dilation followed by erosion) is able to fill internal gaps without changing the external dimensions of the fibers. The opposite sequence, erosion followed by dilation, is called an opening and is used to remove background noise or speckle.

Continued erosion with a rule that a pixel may not be removed if it causes an object to divide into two parts generates the feature skeleton. An alternative method assigns to each pixel within a feature a value that measures its straight line distance to the nearest background point. The ridges in this Euclidean distance map (EDM) define the skeleton and their values form the medial axis transform, which is often useful for measurement purposes.

In the example in Fig. 19, the number of end points in the skeleton (pixels with only one neighbor) identifies the number of teeth in the gear. In other cases, the number of node points (pixels with more than two neighbors) measure network connectivity. Euler's rule

Fig. 18 Applying a closing: (**A**) original image showing cross-sections of glass fibers; (**B**) thresholded image showing cracks; (**C**) filling the cracks with a closing.

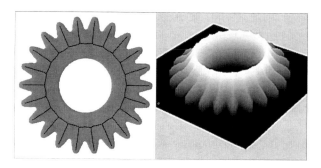

Fig. 19 A gear, with its skeleton superimposed, and the EDM.

for the topology of skeletons in two-dimensional images is (Number of Loops – Number of Segments + Number of Ends + Number of Nodes = 1).

The EDM is also used to separate touching features, as shown in Fig. 20. The watershed segmentation method considers "rain" falling on the EDM and proceeds downhill from the peaks to locate points that would receive runoff from more than one initial peak. These locations mark watershed boundaries and are removed, leaving separated features for measurement. The method works for mostly convex features that have only a single peak in their EDM, with overlaps less than their radii.

Measurements 1: Photogrammetry

Dimensions and spatial arrangements of objects in 3D scenes can be determined from measurements on images. In some cases, such as accident reconstruction, image measurements are used to construct detailed 3D models. Sometimes measurement is based on multiple images taken from different positions, for example, stereo pair images, employing trigonometry. But even single images often can be accurately interpreted to determine 3D information.

For example, knowing the location and lens specification of a surveillance camera makes it possible to determine the height of a person from the image. This can be done trigonometrically, but a scaled drawing of the geometry also provides a solution and is easier to explain, for instance to a nontechnical jury. An even

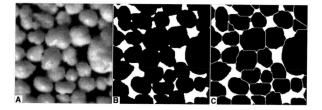

Fig. 20 Watershed segmentation: (**A**) original image of touching sand grains; (**B**) thresholded image; (**C**) after watershed segmentation.

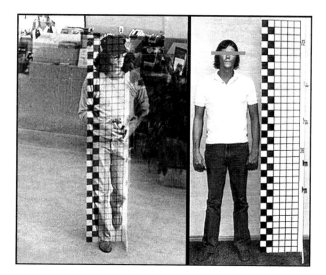

Fig. 21 Reverse projection measurement used to measure the height of a bank robber.
Source: Courtesy of George Pearl, Atlanta Legal Photo Services, Atlanta, GA.

simpler method, called "reverse projection," requires taking a suitable measuring ruler to the scene and recording its image using the same camera and geometry, and then superimposing the two images as shown in Fig. 21 so that the height or other dimension can be read directly.

Another forensic example is the measurement of a blood spatter pattern. The elongation of each droplet gives the angle and direction from which it arrived at the surface (a wall, floor, table, etc.). The intersection point of lines projected back in the indicated directions locates the point in space where the droplets originated, which is the exit wound from a gunshot and hence determines the location of the victim when shot.

Measurements 2: Stereology

Sections through 3D samples are typically imaged in various kinds of light and electron microscopes, and are also produced by tomographic imaging using light, X-rays, sound, neutrons, and many other signals. The features revealed in these section images do not directly show the size or even the number of objects present in the space, because the sampling plane may pass through any portion of the object, not necessarily showing its full extent. However, it is possible using rules derived from geometric probability to infer many important structural parameters including the volume fraction, surface area, length, curvature, number, and connectivity of the objects.

This field is known as stereology (from the Greek for study of three-dimensional space). Many of the rules and procedures are simple to apply and involve counting of "events"—the intersection of the structure(s) of

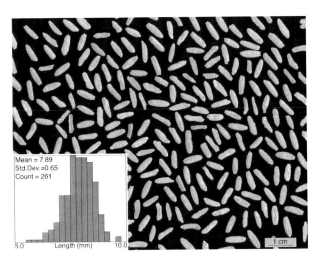

Fig. 22 Measurement of the distribution of lengths of rice grains.

interest with properly designed grids of lines or points—rather than the measurement of dimensions. The key to using stereological relationships is understanding that a section plane intersects a volume to produce an area, intersects a surface to generate a line, and intersects a linear feature producing points. In all cases, the dimension of the structure of interest is one greater than the evidence found in the image.

For example, the volume fraction of a structure is measured by the fraction of points in a regular or random grid that fall on the structure. The surface area per unit volume is equal to two times the number of intersections that a line grid makes with the surface, divided by the total length of the line, or to $(4\pi/3)$ times the length of the boundary line divided by the image area. The length of a linear structure per unit volume is two times the number of intersection points divided by the image area. In all cases, care is needed in the design of grids and the sectioning techniques used in order to produce unbiased results. This somewhat specialized topic is well covered in texts such as Baddeley and Vedel Jensen.[13]

Measurements 3: Feature Brightness, Size, and Location

The measurements of individual features in images fall generally into four groups: brightness or color, location, size, and shape. It is also important in many cases to count the number of features present. Fig. 22 shows an image of rice grains captured using a desktop flatbed scanner. Some of the rice grains intersect the edges of the image, indicating that this is a sample of a larger field of objects. One unbiased procedure for counting the number per unit area is to count as one-half those grains that intersect the edges, since the other "half"

count would be obtained if the adjacent field of view was measured.

For measurement purposes, the edge-intersecting grains cannot be used, as their dimension is unknown. Since large objects are more likely to intersect an edge, the bias in a measured size distribution such as the one shown in the figure can be compensated by counting each measurable grain with a weighting function equal to $(Wx–Fx)\bullet(Wy–Fy)/(Wx\bullet Wy)$, where Wx and Wy are the dimensions of the image in the x and y directions, and Fx and Fy are the projected or box dimensions of each object in those directions. For very small features, this weight is nearly 1, but for large features it is greater than one to compensate for other similar size objects that would have intersected the borders of the image and been excluded from the measurements.

The distribution of the length of the rice grains is used, for example, to determine that the sampled rice has a small percentage of short grains and can be sold as "long grain" rice. There are many other useful measures of size, such as area (which may or may not include internal holes and peripheral indentations), the radii of the maximum inscribed and minimum circumscribed circles, and the perimeter.

Perimeter is the most difficult measurement to determine properly. It may be calculated using the center-to-center path through the boundary pixels, or along their outer edges, or by fitting smooth curves, and these all give slightly different results. More important, the perimeter depends on the pixel size and resolution of the original image, and in many cases as magnification increases the resolution reveals more and more irregularities, so that the perimeter is not a well-defined concept. Indeed, the rate at which perimeter varies with resolution is one of the ways to determine the fractal dimension of a shape.[14]

Pixel brightness values can be calibrated to measure density and other object parameters, but the values recorded in the RGB channels cannot be used to measure color in the sense of a spectrophotometer. This is because the filters used in cameras cover ranges of wavelengths so that different combinations of intensity and wavelength can produce identical results. This is also true for satellite images, which record many bands with each one covering a range of visible or infrared wavelengths.

The location of objects can be determined as their centroids, which may be weighted by density determined from the pixel values. Location may also be based on the center of the circumscribed or inscribed circles in some cases; the latter location is the only one guaranteed to lie within the boundary of the object. One use of location data for a collection of objects is determining whether the objects are clustered, randomly arranged, or self-avoiding. Cacti in the desert are

Table 1 A few dimensionless ratios that may be used to describe shape

$$Radius\ Ratio = \frac{Inscribed\ Diameter}{Circumscribed\ Diameter}$$

$$Roundness = \frac{4 \cdot Area}{\pi \cdot Max\ Diameter^2}$$

$$Formfactor = \frac{4\pi \cdot Area}{Perimeter^2}$$

$$Aspect\ Ratio = \frac{Max\ Caliper\ Dimension}{Min\ Caliper\ Dimension}$$

$$Solidity = \frac{Area}{Convex\ Area}$$

naturally self-avoiding, as they compete for water and nutrients. People cluster in cities (and stars cluster in galaxies). Raindrops fall as separate events and their impacts are random. Comparison of the mean nearest neighbor distance between features to the square root of (image area/number of features) reveals these trends.[15] The measured value is less than the calculated test value for clustering, greater for self-avoidance.

Measurements 4: Feature Shape

Shape is a difficult concept to describe, and humans generally resort to nouns rather than adjectives ("... shaped like a ..."). "Round" may mean "like a circle" (or a sphere or cylinder) but might also mean without indentations and sharp corners. "Skinny" and "bent" generally have meaning only by comparison to other forms. Putting numbers to shape description is complicated as well. The simplest and most widely used approach to measuring shape uses dimensionless ratios of size measurements. Table 1 lists a few as examples, but it should be understood that various names are assigned to these relationships with no consistency, and that it is possible to have shapes that are visually entirely different that share values for one or several of these ratios.

To illustrate the use of dimensionless ratios, a collection of leaves from various trees were used.[16] Fig. 23 shows representative examples (not at the same scale), with a plot of the values for three of the shape factors that are able to identify the various species based on shape alone. The regions occupied by the points in each class are irregular, and improved results can be obtained by using linear discriminant analysis to calculate canonical variables, which are linear combinations of the measured parameters. This produces the plot shown in the figure, in which each class is represented by a spherical region centered on the mean value with a radius of two standard deviations.

Other methods for shape description can also distinguish all of these classes. The principal ones in use are harmonic coefficients and moments. The former is based on the periphery of the feature, for example, expressing the point coordinates along the boundary in complex form (x + iy). A Fourier transform of the boundary then represents the shape as a series of terms, and the amplitudes can be used as numeric shape descriptors.[16,17] Instead of a Fourier transform, a wavelet transform may also be used.

Moments, on the other hand, use all of the interior pixel coordinates as well, which can be an advantage if the boundary is poorly defined, or when the shape consists of multiple parts (e.g., an animal paw print). There are invariant moments[18,19] that may be used to describe shape. Both the harmonic coefficients and the moment values can be used in subsequent statistical analysis for comparison and correlation.

MEASUREMENTS 5: DATA ANALYSIS

Measurements on objects and structures obtained from images are typically used for descriptive statistics and classification, and for correlation with object history or function. The common statistical parameters (mean, standard deviation, etc.) are convenient but make the tacit assumption that the values are normally distributed, which is not always the case (especially rarely so for shape parameters).

Nonparametric comparisons between data sets using Mann–Whitney or Kolmogorov–Smirnov statistics are preferred, as they yield meaningful probabilities whether the data are normal or not. Likewise, correlation based on rank order (Spearman correlation) is preferred over the usual Pearson correlation if relationships may be nonlinear. The interpretation of the r-squared value is the same in both cases.

Classification based on measurements such as those shown in Fig. 23 may use linear discriminant analysis, neural nets, fuzzy cluster analysis, or k-nearest neighbor tests. These are standard tools for treating data, not limited to measurements from images, and are well covered in most statistics texts.

A particular interest for image analysis is database searching. Landmark methods, such as the Automated Fingerprint Identification System, work by using the relative location of multiple points. For fingerprints, these are minutiae such as the gaps, ends, and bifurcations of the ridge lines in the print. A list of 12–16 such landmarks can call up the 10 or so most similar fingerprints on file, for a human to compare. Similar use of human judgment of a small number of "most like" selections found by automatic search algorithms is used in medical

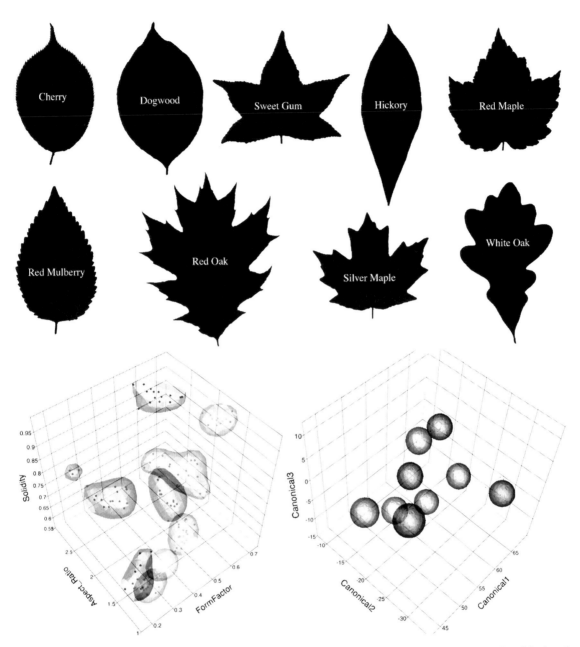

Fig. 23 Measurement of shape using leaves: several dimensionless shape factors are shown that can distinguish the classes, as well as the canonical parameters calculated by linear discriminant analysis.

diagnosis, such as the analysis of Pap smears and mammograms.

An elusive goal for image analysis is "query by example" in which the presentation of an image is used to locate other images of similar objects. The problem is that with a few exceptions such as finding paintings with the same predominant color(s), it is not easy for computer algorithms to decide what it is that the presenter believes to be the important characteristics of the example image. Online Internet searches for images work using the words in accompanying text, not the contents of the images themselves.

ACKNOWLEDGMENT

The explanations and topics covered, and the examples shown, are from The Image Processing Handbook (John C. Russ, CRC Press, 2011). More detailed information, additional examples and comparisons of algorithms, and extended references are available there.

REFERENCES

1. Buades, A.; Coll, B.; Morel, J.M. A non-local algorithm for image denoising. Comp. Vision Pattern Recogn. **2005**, *2*, 60–65.

2. Marr, D.; Hildreth, E. Theory of edge detection. Proc. R Soc. London **1980**, *207* (1167), 187–217.

3. Sobel, I.E. Camera models and machine perception. Ph. D. thesis, publ. AIM-121, Stanford University Electrical Engin. Dept., 1970.

4. Canny, J. A computational approach to edge detection. IEEE Trans. Pattern Anal. Mach. Intel., **1986**, *PAMI-6*, 679–698.

5. Pratt, W.K. Generalized wiener filter computation techniques. IEEE Trans. Comput. **1972**, *C-21*, 636–641.

6. Richardson, W.H. Bayesian-based iterative method of image restoration. J. Opt. Soc. Am. **1972**, *62*, 55–59.

7. Lucy, L.B. An iterative technique for the rectification of observed distributions. Astron. J. **1974**, *79*, 745.

8. Otsu, N. A threshold selection method from gray-level histograms. IEEE Trans. Syst. Man Cyber. **1979**, *SMC-9*, 62–69, 377–393.

9. Trussell, J. Comments on picture thresholding using an iterative selection method. IEEE Trans. Syst. Man Cybern. **1979**, *SMC-9* (5), 311.

10. Pal, N.R.; Pal, S.K. Entropic thresholding. Signal Process. **1989**, *16*, 97–108.

11. Hartigan, J.A. *Clustering Algorithms*; John Wiley & Sons: New York, 1975.

12. Mumford, D.; Shah, J. Optimal approximation by piecewise smooth functions and associated variational problems. Commun. Pure Appl. Math. **1989**, *42*, 577–685.

13. Baddeley, A.; Vedel Jensen, E. B. *Stereology for Statisticians*; Chapman and Hall/CRC: Boca Raton FL, 2005.

14. Mandelbrot, B.B. *The Fractal Geometry of Nature*; W. H. Freeman: San Francisco CA, 1982.

15. Schwarz, H.; Exner, H.E. The characterization of the arrangement of feature centroids in planes and volumes. J. Microsc. **1983**, *129*, 155.

16. Neal, F.B.; Russ, J.C. *Measuring Shape*; CRC Press: Boca Raton FL, 2012,

17. Lestrel, P.E. Ed. *Fourier Descriptors and Their Applications in Biology*; Cambridge Univ. Press: Cambridge, 1997.

18. Hu, M.K. Visual pattern recognition by moment invariants. IEEE Trans. Inform. Theo. **1962**, *IT-8*, 179–187.

19. Flusser, J.; Suk, T. Pattern recognition by affine moment invariants. Pattern Recognit. **1993**, *26* (1), 167–174.

Incident Response and Digital Forensics

Joanna F. DeFranco
Pennsylvania State University, Malvern, Pennsylvania, U.S.A.

Abstract

This entry contains explanations of both the incident response (IR) and digital forensic processes. Most major enterprises, well aware of the cyberthreats to their critical assets, maintain a significant focus on the IR and digital forensic processes. The goal of the IR process includes the detection, containment, and recovery from security incidents. An effective execution of the IR process will increase the chances of business continuity when a security incident occurs. The goal of the digital forensic process is to collect and analyze evidence in a manner that ensures the integrity of the data while also assisting in the determination of system vulnerabilities and/or crimes committed. The handling of digital evidence is a complex process that if not done correctly can easily destroy valuable evidence.

INTRODUCTION

As we have all heard before, *efficiency is doing things right* and *effectiveness is doing the right things.* Both incident response (IR) and digital forensics (DF) need efficiency as well as effectiveness because if they are not done correctly, your efforts will be futile. In this entry, the fundamental processes for IR and DF analysis will be discussed. Just today, an *incident* occurred on my laptop, no less. Similar to every other day, I dock my laptop upon my arrival and start checking my—e-mail. Within a few minutes, the IT admin is at my door and announces that we have a problem. He said he received a message from the main IT office—over 300 miles away and monitoring over 20 locations and thousands of computers—that my laptop has been compromised. He was instructed to remove it from the network and begin the analysis process by scanning it for any personal information that may have been accessed by a hacker. This is a great example of an incident; as small as it sounds, it is, in fact, an incident. The official definition of an incident is a situation that has compromised the integrity, confidentiality, or availability of an enterprise network, host, or data. Other incident examples include attempting to gain unauthorized access to a system, a distributed denial of service (DDOS) attack, unauthorized use of a system, website defacement, etc.

Generally, the IR process is to detect, contain, and eradicate the incident, and the DF process is to collect, analyze, and report the evidence. In other words, once the incident is contained and eradicated, the DF professional begins the evidence collection process. The goal of the analysis is to determine[1] what happened so that the reoccurrence of the incident can be avoided and[2] also to determine if this is a criminal case.

The cases where electronic evidence is critical are not always action-packed with computer break-ins, Structured Query Language injections, DDOS, malware, phishing attempts, or company web page defacement. Some cases requiring electronic evidence are disloyal employees who are suspected of industrial espionage (an attempt to gain access to trade secrets), breached contracts, an employee disputing their dismissal, theft of company documents, inappropriately using company resources (e.g., possession of pornography), copyright infringement (music illegally traded over the Internet), harassment (e-mail based stalking), and identity theft.

INCIDENT RESPONSE

Be prepared. We have all heard that before. It can be applied to almost every aspect of our lives. For example, financial experts tell us to prepare for job loss by having three to 6 months of savings available. In a poor economy we should have even more saved but the point is that we are taught to prepare for that rainy day. When an incident occurs on your system it may be more of a hurricane. If you are prepared and monitor anything that could impede success, when something unplanned occurs, you are prepared to deal with the issue in order to get your system back up and running. It's like buying a generator to prepare for a power loss or installing a house alarm system that calls the police. Even if you never use the generator or the alarm is never triggered, you did everything you could if something unexpected does occur.

National Institute of Standards and Technology (NIST)[1] has provided a baseline for IR. Table 1 shows the simplified view of their *priority one* recommendations. This entry will address these controls.

Encyclopedia of Information Systems and Technology, DOI: 10.1081/E-EIST-120051029

Table 1 NIST's priority one recommendations

CONTROL NAME	IMPACT LEVEL		
	LOW	MODERATE	HIGH
Formal documentation of the IR policy and procedures	✓	✓	✓
Incident handling capability to include preparation, detection and analysis, containment, eradication, and recovery	✓	✓	✓
Implement monitoring and documentation of incidents	✓	✓	✓
Require incident reporting within a defined time period	✓	✓	✓
IR plan that is a roadmap for response capability as well as describes the structure and org of the IR capability	✓	✓	✓

IR is a life cycle of stages shown in Fig. 1. *Preparing* for IR is a topic that deserves its own entry in that there are many things that need to be implemented to facilitate success when running through the IR life cycle. The next stage, *detection/identification*, is more difficult to address because incidents aren't always apparent; hence, constant monitoring (using tools acquired during the prep stage) of the assets is required to detect an incident. If an anomaly is detected, the situation is analyzed to confirm an incident is occurring. If the incident is confirmed, it needs to be *contained* (to not infect other parts of the system) and *eradicated*. And, finally the *recovery* process will bring the system back to working order.

Preparation

Being prepared for IR has two goals:

1. To contain and eradicate the incident to enable recovering and continuation of business as usual.
2. Be able to gather information, in a forensically sound manner so that it will help to determine and

Fig. 1 IR life cycle.

secure the vulnerability that was exploited as well as be valid evidence in the event that the incident is a legal issue (Forensically, sound refers to the manner in which the electronic information was acquired. The process ensures that the acquired information is as it was originally discovered, and thus reliable enough to be evidence in a court proceeding).

A summarized list of means to the goal:

1. *Identify risk*: To be sufficiently prepared, an organization should first evaluate their risk. For example, a risk evaluation may include determining the critical assets, security threats and vulnerabilities, and who has access to mission critical data.
2. *Preparing individual host computers*: The host computers are connected to the network and have access to a lot of sensitive data. Thus, user privileges need to be limited, passwords and default settings need to be evaluated, warning banners for unauthorized use need to be displayed, and logging of significant security-related events needs to be enabled.[2]
3. *Preparing the network:* Network vulnerabilities need to be assessed as nearly all incidents involving vulnerability exploits could have been avoided.[3] Networks also need to be prepared to protect our data privacy, integrity, and availability. One example would be encrypting, backing up, and inspecting all communication and network traffic. Another example would be monitoring access to sensitive data as well as user status.
4. *Establishing appropriate policies and procedures*: Policies and procedures would include, documenting rules and restrictions of network use, policies to mitigate malware and which assets need to be monitored in the organization.
5. *Creating/preparing a response tool kit*: A response toolkit contains all of the necessary hardware and software needed to acquire evidence and protect it from contamination in the event of an incident.
6. *Establishing an IR team*: This team is the point of contact when an incident occurs. They can help to determine the incident's impact on the organization as well as perform tasks that can mitigate the damage and get the organization up and running again.
7. *Training*: Users should be informed about the appropriate use of networks, hosts, and the applications they use. Training should also include guidance about malware incident prevention which can mitigate incidents.[4]

Detection/Identification

In this stage, the monitoring has produced an inconsistency or alarm that needs to be investigated to determine if an incident actually occurred. Incidents may also be discovered by a system administrator or even an end user. In any case, the first step is to verify that the "incident" isn't actually an error. For example, a user error, a system/software configuration, or a hardware failure could present itself as an incident. Ways to confirm an incident include analyzing the technical details such as reports and logs, interviewing any personnel who may have insight, and reviewing the access control lists of the network topology.[5] If it is concluded upon analysis that the incident is not an error, the type of incident needs to be determined. There are two types of incidents: 1) a precursor that an incident is imminent; and 2) an indicator that the incident is occurring or has occurred.[6] An *incident precursor*, for example, could be server entries of a vulnerability scanner, knowledge of a new mail server exploit, or a directed threat at the organization. Some possible *incident indicators* are, for example, Intrusion Detection and Prevention System (IDPS) or antivirus alerts, a logged configuration change, failed login attempts, a large quantity of bounced emails, or unusual network traffic. It is not an easy process to validate an incident since an alert can be a false positive. In order to perform an effective analysis when an incident occurs, NIST[6] recommends the following items be in place in order to more efficiently determine the scope of the incident (or precursor):

- Have the networks and systems profiled for normal use so file integrity and changes can easily be identified.
- Understand normal behaviors of networks, systems, and applications by reviewing log entries and security alerts so abnormalities can be easily identified.
- Create a log retention policy to determine how long log data from firewalls, IDPSs, and applications should be stored. Log data is helpful in the analysis of an incident.
- Perform event correlation between all of the available logs (e.g., firewall, IDPS, application) as they all record different aspects of the attack.
- Keep all host clocks synchronized. It is important during an investigation that all of the logs show the same time that an attack occurred.
- Maintain a knowledge base of searchable information related to incidents and the IR process.
- Use a separate work station for web research on unusual activity.
- Run packet sniffers (configured to specified criteria) to collect additional network traffic.

- Have a strategy in place to filter the data on categories of indicators that are of high significance to the organization's situation.
- Have plan B in place. If the incident scope is larger than can be handled by your team, seek assistance from external resources.

Finally, if an incident is a reality and the containment process is started, make sure any evidence is documented, a chain of custody is in maintained of any evidence collected, and the incident is reported to the appropriate officials within a defined time period.

Containment

The goal of the containment stage is to minimize the scope and damage of the incident. The containment strategy will depend on certain aspects of the incident such as the damage/theft of resources, the need for evidence preservation, service availability, time and resources available to implement the strategy, and duration of the solution.[6] For example, in a DDOS attack, shown in Fig. 2, the attacker is attempting to make the resource unavailable to the users by sending a flood of messages from compromised computers, which the attacker is controlling, to a network. Essentially, it is more traffic than it can handle, which means it will be inaccessible to a legitimate user.

These types of attacks can bring your favorite social networking website to a standstill for hours until the attack on the website stops. One containment strategy for DDOS is filtering the traffic directed at the victim host, then locating the machines doing the attacking. This is obviously more easily said than done because there could be 300 to 400 unique IP addresses doing the attacking. DDOS attacks are not uncommon. If you think your assets are at risk for a DDOS, then contracting with a DDOS mitigation firm—before the attack occurs, of course—may be a good idea. If you are under attack, there are DDOS mitigation firms that will help, but that's like calling on the (Heating Ventilation and Air) HVAC service when your air conditioner doesn't work during a heat wave.

Containment strategies for other incidents include maintaining a low profile (so the attacker is not tipped off), avoiding potentially compromised code (some hackers like to install their own versions of system utilities), backing up the system (in the event evidence is needed), and changing the passwords on any of the compromised systems.[7]

Eradication

The goal of the eradication phase is to remove the cause of the incident. In addition to determining the type of

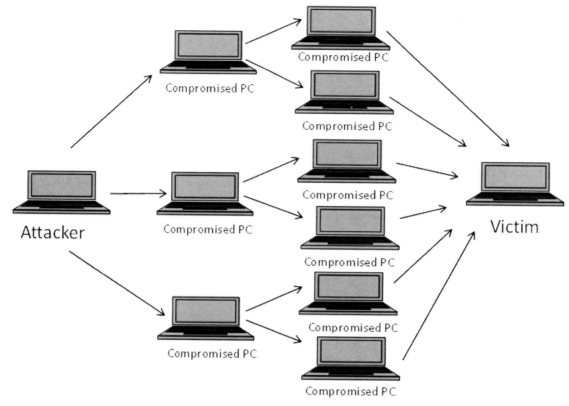

Fig. 2 DDOS attack.

attack, the containment phase hopefully provided insight into how the attack was executed—information that may help in determining an effective eradication strategy. For example, eliminating the cause of the incident may involve removing viruses or deactivating accounts that may have been breached as well as securing the vulnerability that facilitated the attack. Therefore, a clean back up to reimage the system will be needed to ensure that malicious content is gone and that any problems cannot be spread. Then, the appropriate protection to secure the system will be implemented.

Recovery

The goal of the recovery phase is to get the system back up to normal operation. The system should also be validated. Validation means that the system is in fact operating normally after the restoration. The system should also be monitored for reinfection and for anything that was not detected originally. Once the system is back up and running, a follow-up analysis on the incident would be effective. Some aspects of the analysis should be:[8]

• **Damage assessment:** Determine the systems, networks, and data affected; then, identify possible remediation steps.

• **Reverse damage:** Attempt to minimize the costs associated with the incident by restoring compromised data from a backup and consulting with public relations on situations that may have had an effect on any customer base.
• **Nullify the source of the incident:** After the vulnerabilities are addressed, further incidents can be prevented through improvements to access controls.
• **Review the incident:** It is always effective to perform a post-mortem on an incident to learn from any mistakes made during the response life cycle and to determine the risk level of a similar incident to other company assets.

EXAMPLE

It is important to note that even though an incident may appear to be innocuous you can never be too careful. That said; let's go through the IR life cycle using the laptop incident mentioned earlier in this entry. First, the problem was detected by a network intrusion detection system. Once the alert from the intrusion detection system was triggered, the logs were viewed by the IT administrator. Here is an excerpt of the log from this particular incident:

```
———————————All logs are
EST——————————— Snort Logs
= = = = = = = = = = Feb 20 09:28:56 ET TROJAN
Backdoor. Win32. Pushdo.s Checkin
[Classification: A Network Trojan was detected]
{TCP}
1XX.1XX.1XX.1XX:58989 - > 213.182.5.:80 Feb 20
09:28:56 ET TROJAN
Backdoor. Win32. Pushdo.s Checkin.................
............................................. .....................
```

Note: Backdoor. Win32. Pushdo.s is a Trojan that allows unauthorized access and control of an affected computer.

To contain the incident, the laptop was immediately taken off the network (and out of my office). Eradication primarily consisted of removing the Trojan; however, the network traffic was also analyzed for any communication of the laptop with any malicious websites, as well as for any network vulnerabilities that were not known prior to the incident. Recovery consisted of patching any vulnerabilities that were determined based on log analysis, blocking the IP address of any malicious websites that were communicating with the laptop, and rebuilding the laptop by backing up personal files and reinstalling the Operating System, user applications, and personal files. Finally, if any personal information was compromised, those individuals will be notified.

THE INTERNET CRIME COMPLAINT CENTER (IC3)

If you believe you are the victim of an Internet crime, or if you are aware of an attempted Internet crime, you should file a complaint with the IC3. The IC3 is an alliance between the National White Collar Crime Center and the Federal Bureau of Investigation (FBI). The IC3's mission is to reduce economic crimes committed over the Internet. Internet crime is defined as "any illegal activity involving one or more components of the Internet, such as websites, chat rooms, and/or emaile-mail. Internet crime involves the use of the Internet to communicate false or fraudulent representations to consumers. These crimes may include, but are not limited to, advance-fee schemes, non-delivery of goods or services, computer hacking, or employment/business opportunity schemes."

The IC3 crime repository not only benefits the consumer, but also helps law enforcement to reduce Internet crime by providing training in being able to identify Internet crime issues. It is also an effective way for different law enforcement and regulatory agencies to share data.

Once a complaint is submitted, the IC3's trained analysts review and research each complaint, then disseminate the information to the appropriate federal, state, local, or international law enforcement agency. To file an Internet crime complaint, visit the IC3 Web site at http://www.ic3.gov.

IR FOR CLOUD COMPUTING

If you are thinking about utilizing cloud computing, it is imperative that the IR procedure of the cloud provider be understood before any commitments are made. An organization utilizing cloud computing should consider the following in an IR plan:[9]

- Event data must be available in order to detect an incident. Depending on what type of cloud service is being provided (Information as a Service (IaaS), Platform as a Service, Software as a Service (SaaS), or Infrastructure as a Service, Platform as a Service, Software as a Service), event logs may or may not be available to the customer. IaaS customers have the most access to event sources.
- The scope of the incident needs to be determined quickly. It should include a forensic copy of the incident in the event legal proceedings are necessary.
- Containment will again depend on the cloud service provided. For example if SaaS is the cloud service, containment may mean taking the software off-line.

TOP 10 *THREAT ACTIONS* (WHAT THE HACKER DID TO CAUSE THE BREACH) FROM VERIZON'S 2012[10] DATA BREACH INVESTIGATIONS REPORT:

1. Keylogger (Spyware that captures data from user activity)
2. Guessing login credentials
3. Stolen login credentials
4. Sending data to external sites
5. Brute force and dictionary attacks (hacking by systematically using an exhaustive word list)
6. Using backdoors malware
7. Hacking the backdoor (gaining unauthorized access to a network)
8. Manipulating the security controls
9. Tampering
10. Exploiting insufficient authentication

Some of those are easy fixes. In addition, they also analyzed dates and locations of incidents and determined that hackers do most of their work Saturday through Monday where Monday is the most productive. Good to know!

DIGITAL FORENSICS

Crimes occur and the investigations hit a dead end because there appears to be no witness or evidence; that is, until DF comes into play. The FBI solved a case using computer forensics in 2008 where a tip was received regarding two children being sexually abused at a hotel.[11] Unfortunately, by the time the tip was received, the crime had occurred. It appeared there was no evidence to charge anyone until the computer of the accused was analyzed. The evidence on the computer, a deleted e-mail with directions to the hotel where the abuse occurred, was enough to charge three adults, who are now serving life sentences in prison.

There are also times where you don't know a crime was committed until a forensic analysis is performed. For example, determining a trade secret was accessed by an executive after the executive quit and before the executive went to work for a competitor. The point is that an incident may appear to be innocuous until the situation is analyzed. For example, in a situation where the server seemingly went off line for no reason, after analyzing the log files you may determine that the cause was malware installed after an intrusion. If a crime has been committed or even suspected, it is of the utmost importance that the investigator has collected and documented the evidence in a forensically sound manner because the next step would be to hand all of the evidence off to law enforcement.

Another application for DF is evidence gathering for e-discovery. E-discovery is the pre-trial phase where electronic evidence is collected. For example, a lawyer may want to prove a spouse's infidelity and may use a forensic analysis of e-mail files to prove the accusation. In evidence gathering, technique and accuracy is critical to ensure the authenticity of the data collected when an incident occurs. The forensic investigator needs to always keep in mind that he or she may be called on to defend the techniques utilized to gather the evidence.

Handling digital evidence is a complex process that should be handled by a professional. If not handled with care, it can be easily destroyed and rendered inadmissible if a court case ensues. There is evidence that can be easily found but other evidence may have been hidden, deleted, or encrypted. Adding to the complexity, if the evidence is not handled properly, it will be thrown out or the case will be lost. The four main stages of the DF lifecycle (Fig. 3) provide guidance for a forensic expert.

Fig. 3 DF life cycle.

The remainder of this section will review the tasks involved in each stage.

Preparation

Being prepared to perform a forensic investigation involving digital evidence will save a lot of time and effort in the long run. This includes having all of the tools and equipment needed as well as understanding how to effectively use those tools to collect and analyze the evidence. In addition, there should be a plan in place as to where the evidence will be stored securely to prevent contamination or data destruction.

Generally, these are the types of software and hardware needed to perform a forensic investigation: software to duplicate evidence in a forensically sound manner (that doesn't alter the evidence), software to analyze the drive space that was duplicated (including at a minimum features to identify deleted files and filter through keyword searches), and a write blocker to show the disk copy did not modify the evidence. For example, the write blocker shown in Fig. 4 is designed to allow forensically sound images on a Universal Serial Bus (USB) to be extracted without fear that the data on the USB will be modified during the process.

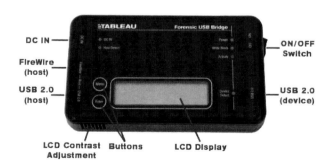

Fig. 4 Tableau T-8 write blocker.
Source: From guidance software, http://www.tableau.com.

Other items that may be useful during an investigation are notebooks, evidence bags, tape, labels, pens, cameras, anti-static bags (to transport electronic components), faraday bags (bags to shield a device from signals that may modify evidence), and clean drives (wiped of all other data) to store the duplicated drive image. To wipe a drive, disk sanitation software is used to write zeros over every bit of a drive (as an example: Electronic Data Disposal—DOD Compliant Disk Sanitation Software). This is not an exhaustive list of items, but it gives you an idea of what types of things need to be considered when preparing for a digital forensic investigation.

Collection

Part of the evidence collection is to document the scene. This includes documenting things like the model and make of the devices under investigation as well as photographing the surroundings. For example, the investigator may take a photo of the screen to show what was happening when they entered the scene. In addition, they may check out the task bar and take a photo of the maximized applications running. If the investigator is subpoenaed to come to court, one of the things the lawyer may do is put some doubt into his or her credibility. The lawyer may ask the color was the door to the office where the computer resided. If you say brown and it was dark blue, that will be strike one.

Once the scene is documented, the electronic data needs to be dealt with. In the 80's, when responding to an incident, a forensic investigator wouldn't think twice about the "pull the plug" method which means shutting it down, bringing it back to a lab, and duplicating the hard drive. Due to the increase in complexity in today's computing, the investigator's response is not the same for every incident, thus powering it down right away may not be in the best interest for this investigation (note: taking it off the network is a good idea to avoid further damage). The reason that the computer should not be turned off is because the volatile data (e.g., running processes or network connections) is lost. In addition, there is a risk that a rogue application may start a malicious attack when a shutdown is detected. Even the duplication step has changed. Not only have hard drive sizes increased considerably, but the server that needs to be analyzed may be on the other side of the world! I am not saying that the plug is never pulled—it's that the decision is not black and white any more. Accordingly, there are a few ways to respond to live data collection: focusing on the collection of the volatile data, collecting volatile data AND log files (e.g., IDPS, router, firewall), or conducting a full investigation by collecting everything (a forensic duplication where every bit of data is copied). A duplication (or disk image) is necessary if court proceedings are imminent. The image is stored either on an external drive, or you may send it over the network using a network utility such as netcat or cryptcat. Netcat is a networking utility that reads and writes data across a network connection. Cryptcat is Netcat with encryption. Never use the suspect system to do any analysis. Doing so will overwrite evidence.

For example, if the incident merits collecting the volatile data, the investigator may run a script from a USB drive on the suspect machine. The script will run different commands to determine the following: open ports, who is logged on to the system, dates/times, running processes, applications running on certain ports, unauthorized user accounts and privileges, etc. Then, the script output is directed to a file stored on your USB drive. For example, a script called volatile collection would look like this:

E:\ > volatile_collection > volatile_data_case101.txt where, the output from volatile collection script would be stored in the file volatile_dat_case101.txt.

Network data, routers, firewalls, IDPS logs, and servers may also need to be analyzed (via network logs) for anything suspicious to determine the scope of the incident, who was involved, and a timeline of events. And finally, the investigator must identify other sources of data which could go beyond a hard drive such as a USB drive or mobile phone.

All of this digital evidence collected must be preserved to be suitable in court. Digital evidence is very fragile, like footprints in snow or sand, because it is easily destroyed or changed. The FBI suggests having a secure location for storage (locked up), having sufficient backup copies (two suggested), having proof that the data has not been altered (hash algorithm), and establishing a *chain of custody*, which is a written log (a.k.a. evidence log) to document when media goes in or out of storage.[12] (Hash functions are mostly used to confirm data integrity (that the data has not changed). There are many hash algorithms used. One of the widely used hash algorithms is Message Digest Algorithm 5. A good algorithm is determined by having a limited number (e.g., 1 in 1 billion) of collisions (two distinct files resulting with the same hash value). When the hash algorithm is performed on the plaintext, a hash value is created. If the plaintext changes so will the hash value.) In order for the data to be admissible, it has to be proven that it has not been tampered with; therefore, you should be able to trace the location of the evidence from the moment it was collected to the moment it appears in court. If there is a time period that is unaccounted for, there is a chance that changes could have been made to the data. One way to preserve evidence is to transfer digital information on to a read-only, nonrewritable CD-ROM and/or uploading the data onto a secure server and hashing the file to ensure the data's integrity.

Analysis

Following data collection is data analysis. The image of the suspect machine (s) need to be restored so the analysis of the evidence can begin. The image should be either restored on a clean (wiped) drive that is slightly larger or restored to a clean destination drive that was made by the same manufacturer to ensure the image will fit. Next, the review process begins by using one of the forensic tools such as EnCase, FTK (Forensic Toolkit), P2 by Paraben, or Helix 3, etc. To recover deleted files, the unallocated space of the image needs to be reviewed. The investigator may find whole files or file fragments—since files are never removed from the hard drive when the delete feature is utilized. What is deleted is the pointer the operating system used to build the directory tree structure. Once that pointer is gone, the operating system won't be able to find the file—but the investigator can! Keep in mind, however, that when new files are created, a memory spot is chosen, so there is a chance that the file is written over or at least part of the file. Here is why:

All data is arranged on a hard drive into *allocation units* called *clusters*. If the data being stored requires less storage than a cluster size, the entire cluster is still reserved for that file. The unused space in that cluster is call *slack space*. Fig. 5 shows an example.

But, deleting that 20K file frees up the space for a new file. If that cluster is chosen, the new file is going to be written on top of the old file. If the new file is smaller than 20K, then part of that 20K file will be retrievable (Fig. 6).

Evaluating every file on the restored image can be an arduous task; thus, one trick a forensic examiner will use is identifying files with known hashed values. Known file hashes can be files that are received from a manufacturer for popular software applications. Other known hashes can be from movies, cracking tools, music files, and images. The National Software Reference Library (http://www.nsrl.nist.gov) provides hash values for common software applications. An investigator may be able to reduce the number of files needed to be analyzed by 90% by using the "hashkeeper

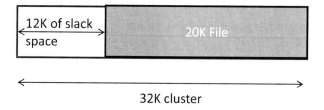

Fig. 5 Slack space.

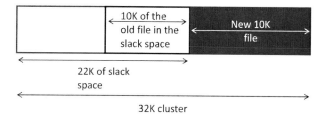

Fig. 6 Slack space with a partial life.

paradigm" which assumes that two similar files produce the same hash value:[13]

1. Obtain a list of hash values of "known" files.
2. Obtain the hashes of the suspect files.
3. Compare the two hash lists to match the known files or identify the unknown files.
4. Eliminate the "known" files from the search.
5. Identify and review the unknown files.

For string searches within the data, the drive needs to have all compressed files decompressed and all encrypted files unencrypted. Then, just as you do with web searches, you should use effective key words to pare down results. The exact search methodology used depends on the forensic software tool you are using, what you are the looking for (e.g., files, web browser history, or e-mails), the format of the data, and your time constraints, and whether the suspect is aware of the investigation. If so, they may have deleted some files.

A common investigation is an Internet usage analysis that monitors inappropriate usage at work where, for example, an employee is gambling, or viewing pornography. Divorce lawyers may use this type of analysis to prove infidelity by showing evidence on a social networking site or proving a spouse was on a blog website looking for advice on how to get an easy divorce. An anonymous blog posting can be attributed to a spouse by showing that he or she made purchases with their credit card before and after the post on the blog. Web browsers store multiple pieces of information such as history of pages visited, recently typed URLS, cached versions of previously viewed pages, and favorites. The challenge is also showing that the accused was actually the one using that computer at the time of the incident. For example, if pornography was viewed on a particular employee's computer, the investigator has to make sure that employee wasn't on vacation or in meetings all day when the abuse occurred. When doing this type of analysis, a.k.a. a *temporal analysis*, the investigator may want to reconstruct the webpage. The web page can be reconstructed by searching the index.dat file for files that are associated with a given URL. Then, the investigator can look for those files in the cache and copy them to a temporary directory. The reconstructed page should be viewed in a browser that is offline so the browser does not access the Internet. If the reconstructed page accesses the Internet it may follow the URL and download the latest version of the page from the server and won't be the version of the web page that the suspect viewed at the time of the incident. Note that the presence of a single image file does not indicate the individual visited a website. Because there are times images are a result of a pop-up or redirect it is important that the investigator also determine which sites were visited prior to the site in question. These are just a few of the many techniques an investigator could utilize for an effective and forensically sound Internet usage analysis.

E-mail analysis is also very common. The investigator may be tasked to prove a certain policy violations, harassment or impersonation. It may be as simple as finding the e-mail and determining who sent and who received it, or as complicated as reconstructing the entire e-mail chain. This is also an analysis that should be done offline so no e-mails are sent or received inadvertently during the analysis.

Reporting

The final stage in the DF lifecycle is reporting the results of the analysis in the previous stage as well as describing reasoning behind actions, tool choices, and procedures. NIST[14] describes three main factors that affect reporting: *alternative explanations, audience consideration*, and *actionable information.*

Alternative explanations back up the conclusions of the incident by including all plausible explanations for what happened. In a case involving a substitute teacher that was convicted (later overturned) of viewing pornography on a school computer in front of minors, the investigators did NOT look for alternative explanations. Had they done that, they would have figured out that the pornography websites viewed were caused by spyware. Instead, the clearly ignorant original investigators mislead the jury by only presenting evidence in the temporary Internet files directory and the school firewall logs showing that pornography websites were accessed. They missed the alternative explanation and caused her to be unfairly convicted because their findings (temporary Internet Files and firewall logs) do not demonstrate a user's intent. Upon reanalysis by expert forensic investigators,[15] it was discovered that the antivirus software was an out-of-date trial version, that there was no antispyware software (software designed to detect and remove malicious applications from a computer) installed on the system, and that the spyware was definitely installed prior to the incident. The original investigators also misled the jury by informing them that spyware is not capable of spawning popups (not true), that popups cannot be in an endless loop (not

true), and that the red link color used for some of the text on the porn website (that they showed the jury) indicated the substitute teacher clicked on the links (the link visits, whether intentional or not, are shown in the visited color, which they indicated was red). In this particular case, the link was red; however, if the original investigators had opened the browser preferences, they would have noted a few things: 1) the links were selected to be green if a site was visited; and 2) the html source code changed the font color to red. The investigators also misled the jury by telling them that the only way spyware is installed on a computer was by actually visiting a pornographic site (not true). Eckelberry et al. determined that this particular spyware was installed right after a Halloween screen saver was downloaded. There were multiple inconsistencies with the original investigation. I encourage you to read this case (listed in the reference section of this entry) as it illustrates very clearly what NOT to do in a forensic investigation.

Reports on the results of a forensics analysis will vary in content and detail based on the incident. Just as in any writing, *audience consideration* is important. Thus, the level of detail of a forensic analysis report is determined by the audience who needs the report. If the analysis resulted in a noncriminal case, the executives or management may want a simple overview of the incident, how it was resolved, and how another occurrence will be prevented. A system administrator may need details regarding network traffic. Or, if it is criminal case, law enforcement will require a very detailed report. In all cases, the report should be accurate, concise, and complete. Nelson et al.[16] suggest the report should include supporting material, an explanation of the examination and data collection methods, calculations (e.g., MD5 hash), an explanation of any uncertainty and possible errors, and an explanation of the results found and references utilized for the content of the report.

The third report factor is *actionable information,* where the information provided may lead to another source of information and/or information that will help to prevent future similar incidents.

Another type of report is an *after action report* that in addition to identifying issues that need to be improved upon for future incidents, may also include improvements to the team or process. For example, team members may decide to improve their skills using the forensic software, fix the acceptable use policy for the organization, or modify the IR procedure. This will, of course, help in staying current with the changes in law, technology, and the latest cyber issues.

A GREAT EXAMPLE OF SECURITY THROUGH OBSCURITY (AND DF)

Security through obscurity is a derogatory term that implies that secrecy or hiding something makes it secure. It's similar to when I put my laptop on the front seat of my car and cover it with a blanket while parked in a public parking lot. If it is discovered, there is nothing really protecting it from getting stolen.

If you have an e-mail account that you think is anonymous, think again. An anonymous e-mail account is an account that is created without revealing any personal information. However, that alone does not guarantee anonymity. An anonymous e-mail account, when used with mail clients such as Outlook, appends the IP address information to each e-mail's metadata that is sent—which is a great clue for a forensic investigator. Therefore, if the e-mails are investigated, the IP address can help pinpoint the sender. You may be wondering who is looking at your e-mail. Due to the Provisions of 1986s Stored Communications Act (SCA), the government can access e-mails stored by a third-party service provider. However, there are a few caveats to that access. If the e-mail is in "electronic storage" AND less than 180 days old, a warrant needs to be obtained to access the e-mails. E-mails not in "electronic storage" OR in "electronic storage" more than 180 days can be accessed with a subpoena. Electronic storage is defined as e-mail that has been received by the Internet Service Provider (ISP), but has not been opened by the recipient.[17]

The way to make your Internet and e-mail activity really anonymous is to use software such as Tor (Tor (https://www.torproject.org/) is software that was developed originally to protect government communication. Now it is used by people as a safeguard to their privacy (not anonymity). It is used to safeguard your behavior and interests. One of the examples on the Tor website is when traveling abroad, Tor can hide your connection to your employer's computer so your national origin is not revealed) that conceals a user's location even if the e-mails are accessed. This type of software is often used by journalists, military, and activists to protect research and investigations etc. Hence, Tor needs to be running in order to make an anonymous e-mail account actually anonymous. Unfortunately for a recent Central Intelligence Agency (CIA) director and his girlfriend, this software was not used and their extramarital affair was revealed by piecing together the e-mail trail left by the girlfriend—even though anonymous e-mail accounts were utilized by both of them.

The investigation began due to harassing e-mails sent to another woman.[18] The FBI analyzed the logs from the e-mail provider to determine who sent the harassing e-mails. They specifically looked at the metadata from the e-mails to determine the locations from which the e-mails were sent. By comparing the e-mail metadata from the e-mail providers, guest lists from hotels, and IP login records (hotel WiFi), the FBI put the puzzle together and discovered the identity of the sender of the harassing e-mails as well as her affair with the CIA director.[19] This discovery led to the CIA director's resignation.

MOBILE PHONE FORENSICS

Mobile phone forensics is the science of recovering digital evidence from a mobile phone. Mobile phones, being much more than a communication tool, retain a substantial amount of data: calendars, photos, call logs, text messages, web history etc. The cellular network also retains data regarding location. Mobile phone data has helped convict many criminals. A man was convicted of the murder of a college student with the help of cellular phone network data.[20] The killer was actually helping the police locate the college student by showing them around the college campus. At the same time, the police were analyzing the cellular network data. When the victim's phone was turned off, it disengaged itself from a specific cellular tower near the killer's home who eventually admitted the crime due to the mounting evidence.

Mobile phone forensics uses the DF lifecycle just described. The challenge with mobile phone forensics is the frequent release of new phone models, often making cables and accessories obsolete, as well as the lack of a standard for where mobile phones store messages. The upside is that the puzzle can be more easily solved because of all of the information stored on cell phones: calls (incoming, outgoing, missed), address books, texts, e-mail, chat, Internet use, photos, videos, calendars, music, voice records, notes—the list could go on forever with all the apps available, as well.

A brief overview of NIST[21] recommendations to seize mobile phones in an investigation will be presented in this section. For further details, please download the special publication listed in the reference section of this entry. First, consider all of the types of evidence needed from the phone. For example, if fingerprints are needed, follow the appropriate handling procedures for acquiring fingerprints. The investigator may also want to record any viewable information from the phone. It is advisable to leave the phone off for a two reasons: first, there is a potential for data loss if the battery expires and second, data may be overwritten if network activity occurs. If the phone must remain on for some reason, the phone should be placed in a container that blocks radio frequency or in airplane mode. Finally, that container should be placed into a labeled evidence bag that is then sealed to restrict access. Before leaving the scene, collect all related phone hardware such as cradles, cables, manuals, and packaging—anything you find related to the phone.

To collect the evidence from the mobile phone, NIST[21] also recommends isolating the phone from all other devices used for data synchronization. Imaging the device at the scene is the best option if battery depletion is an issue. If not, bring it back to a lab to acquire the data. There are many memory categories as well as various memory structures that vary among manufacturers. Sometimes it is just call log data, so it may not be necessary to recover all of the data on the phone. If not familiar with acquiring data from a particular phone, it is best to seek the assistance from another digital forensic professional.

INFRAGARD

A great organization for security professionals is InfraGard. InfraGard is a not for profit organization that is a partnership between the private sector and the FBI. The members of InfraGard are individuals from businesses, academic institutions, state and local law enforcement, and any person that wants to participate in sharing information and intelligence that may prevent hostile acts against the U.S. (http://www.infragard.net). For example, a university professor (and his class) helped the FBI catch criminals involved in a case called "Trident Breach." In this case, the criminals infected computers (via an e-mail link or attachment) with the ZeuS virus that is essentially a key logger application that logged the user's banking information. Then, the criminals were able to lure other people (a.k.a. money mules) into "work-at-home" schemes where their "job" was completing banking transactions. The banking transaction went as follows: the mule opens the bank account; the money is deposited from the Zeus infected computer user's account into the mule's account; and then the mule withdraws the cash and sends it to the criminals. Gary Warner, professor at the University of Alabama at Birmingham (and member of InfraGard) used data mining techniques to establish the links between the ZeuS infected computers and the origin of the mass infector. Most of the hackers and the "mules" were caught. There were still 18 mules at large who were found by his students using computer forensic investigation techniques such as crawling social networking sights to identify the remaining suspects.[22]

To apply for membership to InfraGard, fill out the online application (http://www.infragard.net/member.php), read and sign the "Rules of Behavior" form, and submit. Once accepted, find your local chapter and attend any meetings of interest.

CONCLUSION

Security incidents include everything from the misuse of company resources, to stolen data, to a distributed denial of service attack. Preparation for security incidents assists in an effective response that enables business continuity and minimizes damage to critical assets. The Digital forensic process occurs post incident with the goal of collecting and analyzing evidence. The depth of collection and analysis is situation dependent—but always utilizes a process that keeps the integrity of the evidence intact.

REFERENCES

1. NIST, *Recommended Security Controls for Federal Information Systems and Organizations*, Special Publication 800-53, 2009.
2. Grance, T.; Kent, K.; Kim, B. *Computer Security Incident Handling Guide, National Institute of Standards and Technology*, Special Publication 800-61, 2004, http://www.csrc.nist.gov/publications/nistpubs/800-61/sp800-61.pdf,(accessed January 2013).
3. NTT, *Communications White Paper, 8 Elements of Complete Vulnerability Management*, September 2009.
4. Brownlee, N.; Guttman, E. *Expectations for Computer Security Incident Response*, Network Working Group RFC 2350, June 1998.
5. Mandia, K.; Prosise, C.; Pepe, M. *Incident Response & Computer Forensics*, 2nd Ed.; McGraw-Hill: 2003.
6. Cichonski, P.; Millar, T.; Grance, T.; Scarfone, K. *Computer Security Incident Handling Guide*, NIST Special Publication 800-61 Revision 2, August 2012.
7. Federal Communications Commission, *FCC Computer Security Incident Response Guide*. December 2001.
8. Lynch, W. *Writing an Incident Handling and Recovery Plan*, http://www.net-security.org/article.php?id=775&p=3, (accessed Febraury 2013).
9. Jansen, W.; Grance, T. *Guidelines on Security and Privacy in Public Cloud Computing*, NIST SP800-144, December 2011.
10. Verizon, *Data Breach Investigations Report*, 2012, http://www.indefenseofdata.com/data-breach-trends-stats/, (accessed Febraury 2013).
11. FBI, *Regional Labs Help Solve Local Crimes*, http://www.fbi.gov/news/stories/2011/may/forensics_053111, (accessed Febraury 2013).

12. Cameron, S. *Digital Evidence, FBI Law Enforcement Bulletin*, August 2011.

13. Mares, D. Using file hashes to reduce forensic analysis, SC Mag. May **2002**.

14. Kent, K.; Chevalier, S.; Grance, T.; Dang, H. *Guide to Integrating Forensic Techniques Into Incident Response*. NIST Special Publication 800-86, August 2006.

15. Eckelberry, A.; Dardick, G.; Folkerts, J.; Shipp, A.; Sites, E.; Stewart, J.; Stuart, R. *Technical review of the Trial Testimony State of Connecticut vs. Julie Amero*, March 21, 2007, http://www.sunbelt-software.com/ihs/alex/julieamerosummary.pdf (accessed March 2013).

16. Nelson, B.; Phillips, A.; Steuart, C. *Guide to Computer Forensics and Investigations*, 4E, Course Technoloy, Cengage Learning, 2010.

17. Jarrett, H.; Bailie, M.; Hagen, E.; Judish, N. *Searching and Seizing Computers and Obtaining Electronic Evidence in Criminal Investigations*. The U.S. Department of Justice, 2009, http://www.justice.gov/criminal/cybercrime/docs/ssmanual2009.pdf (accessed March 2013).

18. Perez, E.; Gorman, S.; Barrett, D. FBI Scrutinized on Petraeus. Wall St. J. November 12, **2012**.

19. Isikoff, M.; Sullivan, B. Emails on 'coming and goings' of Petraeus, other military officials escalated FBI concerns. NBC News November 12, **2012**, http://openchannel.nbcnews.com/_news/2012/11/12/15119872-emails-on-coming-and-goings-of-petraeus-other-military-officials-escalated-fbi-concerns?lite (accessed March 2013).

20. Summers, C. Mobile Phones—The new fingerprints. BBC News (accessed December 2003).

21. Jansen, W.; Ayers, R. *Guidelines on Cell Phone Forensics*, NIST Special Publication 800-101, May 2007.

22. Engel, R. *University professor helps FBI crack $70 million cybercrime ring*, http://rockcenter.nbcnews.com/_news/2012/03/21/10792287-university-professor-helps-fbi-crack-70-million-cybercrime-ring (accessed August 2012).

HIPAA– Information Protection

Information Architecture

Andrew Dillon
Don Turnbull
School of Information, University of Texas at Austin, Austin, Texas, U.S.A.

Abstract

Information architecture has become one of the latest areas of excitement within the library and information science community, largely resulting from the recognition it garners from those outside of the field for the methods and practices of information design and management long seen as core to information science. The term information architecture (IA) was coined by Richard Wurman in 1975 to describe the need to transform data into meaningful information for people to use, a not entirely original idea, but certainly a first-time conjunction of the terms into the now common IA label. Building on concepts in architecture, information design, typography, and graphic design, Wurman's vision of a new field lay dormant for the most part until the emergence of the World Wide Web in the 1990s, when interest in information organization and structures became widespread. The term came into vogue among the broad web design community as a result of the need to find a way of communicating shared interests in the underlying organization of digitally accessed information.

BACKGROUND INFORMATION

Two seminal events serve as milestones in the emergence of this discipline or community of practice: the publication of a book on the topic by Rosenfeld and Morville in 1998 and the organization of a preliminary summit by the American Society for Information Science and Technology (ASIS&T) in May 2000 on the theme of Defining Information Architecture. The Rosenfeld and Morville text was aimed at, in its own words, "applying the principles of architecture and library science to Web site design," an ambition that is simultaneously broad in its coverage of issues but narrow in its application domain, implying that information architecture (IA) has no role in non-Web environments, which has largely been taken as a given by most people in IA since. Now in its second edition, this text is often referred to as the "bible" of IA, but its focus is on the practical rather than theoretical domain, with guidance on how to implement Web sites and intranets that support management and growth of information.

The original IA Summit, part of the normal, one-off mid-year series run by ASIS&T, was so successful that it has been repeated annually since. The summits are now considered the primary annual conference for professionals in this area. While the first summit sought to define the field, it never actually succeeded in doing so. Instead, it brought together almost 400 library and information scientists, usability and user experience professionals, information designers, and company web masters; all of whom recognized a shared interest and a need for broader dialog. A resulting special issue of the *ASIS&T Bulletin* (vol. 25, part 5) (http://www.asist.org/) did its best to make sense of the process. In addition to launching a series of summits, while writing part number six, ASIS&T launched the SIGIA-L listserv to provide a forum for continuing discussions in the field. This list remains, in 2005, the most active of ASIS&T discussion lists and has many subscribers who are not even members of the parent organization.

Other groups have followed. A dedicated IA professional collective, the Asimolar Institute for Information Architecture (AIfIA), was formed in 2003 (see http://www.aifia.org) by a self-identified group of information architects dedicated to advancing and promoting the field. It was renamed "The IA Institute" in early 2005 and at this time has 500 members in 40 countries. There is a considerable overlap between the ASIS&T and AIfIA groups, though the former is largely populated with academics.

Further signs of progress can be observed in academia. There are now dedicated degree programs in IA at universities such as Kent State and Baltimore, with many IA programs and courses offered through graduate programs in library and information studies across the nation. The establishment of such programs in such a short period of time within a slow-moving university system is testimony to the interest that has been created for IA.

Despite the advent of formal education in IA, a majority of professionals in the field are self-identified as information architects on the basis of their work or job title. No formal credentials are required to become an IA, though it is probable that a majority of people

Encyclopedia of Information Systems and Technology, DOI: 10.1081/E-EIST-120017582

using that title have received some education or training in library and information science (LIS). Perhaps not surprisingly, LIS programs are also the most likely home for courses and degrees in IA.

There are other routes into the profession however. A large number of IA practitioners have backgrounds in technical writing and graphic design. Skills in clear communication of ideas, structuring information flow, representing information, etc. all prove extremely valuable for the work of IA. Yet another group of IAs came from a user experience or usability background, though there remains some disagreement about the boundaries between these roles.

DEFINING IA

Formal definitions of IA tend to vary from the general to the multiple. Rosenfield and Morville offer a variety of definitions as candidates:[1]

1. The combination of organization, labeling, and navigation schemes within an information system.
2. The structural design of an information space to facilitate task completion and intuitive access to content.
3. The art and science of structuring and classifying Web sites and intranets to help people find and manage information.
4. An emerging discipline and community of practice focusing on bringing principles of design and architecture to the digital landscape.

Central to this mix is the idea of structuring information spaces for management and use, which can be interpreted in several ways, either as a relatively narrow concern with labeling, as in (1), or more broadly as a concern with facilitating interaction, as in (2). For this study, we emphasize the larger or broader perspective.

Other definitions abound, but it is clear that the precise wording of any one has failed to capture the terrain in such a way as to be taken as definitive. Even Wurman, in his original conception of the field, left scope for interpretation in his definition of the information architect as "the emerging 21st century professional ... focused upon clarity, human understanding, and the science of the organization of information."[2]

In as much as there is or could be a science of information organization, other disciplines may lay justifiable claim to the territory: library and information scientists who have long dealt with classification and categorization of recorded knowledge; cognitive psychologists who have contributed to our understanding of information use, comprehension, and problem solving; anthropologists and sociologists who analyze cultural constructions of meaning, to name but a few. To this extent, IA is an interdisciplinary field of practice and research, borrowing heavily from these domains.

Dillon offered a broad definition that attempted to accommodate the diversity of approaches by defining IA as "the process of designing, implementing, and evaluating information spaces that are humanly and socially acceptable to their intended stakeholders."[3] This not only aimed at inclusion, but also bypassed any reference to IA as a discipline or field of its own, likening it more to human activities such as design or creative writing, which of necessity draw on disciplines to support process and education.

Furthermore, Dillon advocated a view of IA as craft rather than engineering, a distinction based on the lack of separation within IA between the design and the manufacture of the resulting application.[3] As craft, IA creates as it produces, often reacting to emerging elements of its own design to drive subsequent modifications. Craft-based disciplines are less amenable to formal methodological abstraction for management and instructional purposes, which can result in them shifting or being altered radically by outside forces. One problem facing the IA community in its drive to professional status is the need to overcome abstraction and education problems in order to provide the field with the legitimacy accorded to related fields within information science.

Big IA vs. Little IA?

In the absence of formal definition, a line of division has been drawn between two competing views of the field, known generally as the Big IA vs. Little IA perspectives. Big IA is used to describe those who practice or believe in IA as an all-encompassing term for the process of designing and building information resources that are useful, usable, and acceptable. From this perspective IA must cover user experience and even organizational acceptance of the resource. By contrast, Little IA refers to those who practice or believe that IA is a far more constrained activity that deals with information organization and maintenance, but does not involve itself in analyzing the user response or the graphical design of the information space. Big IA tends to be seen as top-down, conceiving the full product and its human or organizational impact; Little IA is viewed as more bottom-up, addressing the metadata and controlled vocabulary aspects of information organization, without dealing directly with, and certainly never evaluating formally, the user experience of the resulting space.

For the purposes of this study, we adopt the view that IA is an umbrella term for the process of designing interactive information spaces, and it is likely then that within its ranks will be advocates of specific styles, and practitioners focusing on specific architectural issues to the exclusion of others. Reconciling these niche perspectives within a unified field remains the major challenge.

WHAT DO INFORMATION ARCHITECTS DO?

One can gain an appreciation of the process of IA by examining what practitioners actually do. An incomplete list would include:

- Illustrating key concepts or steps through graphics.
- Designing site maps.
- Creating metaphors to brand content and promote navigation.
- Developing style and formatting templates for elements of information.
- Conducting user analyses.
- Creating scenarios and storyboards.
- Building taxonomies and indices.
- Testing user experience.

Engineering approaches to the building of the IA include: programming and database design, content and source code management, functional evaluation (including usability testing), and final information deployment and versioning.

The breadth of these IA activities suggests that most information architects perform only a few of these tasks, owing to either skill limitations or the constraints of the IA project. Generally, IA tasks revolve around four major areas of effort. The first involves understanding the information as content and shaping its organization and access; the second includes building the abstract associations between units of content; the third focuses on developing browsing and searching functionality; and the fourth is designing the graphics, interfaces, and interaction techniques to allow users to access the body of information.

Creating Content Organization Systems

A content inventory involves identifying, collecting, and cataloging the project's content to establish the scope of materials involved, often requiring a meeting with all of the project stakeholders and initially planning out the other IA tasks. An initial information taxonomy (sometimes called a hierarchy) is also prepared by sorting the information into common, subjectively derived sets such as alphabetical, chronological, geographical, or topical among others. Derived from this taxonomy, a set of term names or labels is established to provide naming consistency when both organizing the information and describing or representing the topics. Classifying content

types and formats to provide the basis for presentation (markup) standards is also important to keep the content organized and presented consistently throughout the project, and for user consumption.

Creating Semantic Organization Systems

A semantic (logical and associative) organization of the information is created to represent the complex, objectively derived relationships that can be further understood after the project's content has been inventoried. This process may involve coding a set of data with a set of overlapping or multifaceted conceptual organizational schemes, such as those required for browsing, searching, learning a concept embedded in the information, or performing a task based on the information. In many cases, this conceptual organization has been mapped out in a content inventory, but no additional data have been added to express the more complex, often multifaceted, relationships in the information. This semantic organization would be used when accessing information via a search function and could be used to suggest alternate searches or different types of search results. These relationships are coded with metadata (information about the content such as creation date, author, location, intended use, or language) by using schemas (specific types of formal, descriptive specifications to convey syntax and structure) that can be used by machines, authors, and sometimes users to promote access for each type of information. Popular metadata schemas include the Dublin Core Metadata Initiative, which utilizes the Resource Description Framework syntax for representing this metadata in the Web.[4,5]

Other conceptual IAs needed include thesauri (synonyms, antonyms as words or phrases) and indices (terms and phrases with links to their location in the information space), which provide users with paths for browsing through information or an array of possible keywords to be found while searching the information space. These thesauri and indices are populated by controlled vocabularies (subject domain-specific sets of terms—e.g., medical) and synonym rings (groups of words not strictly equivalent) that provide a (potentially comprehensive) variety of language to enable users to locate sought-after information.[1]

Creating Navigation Systems

The user's view of an information space is influenced significantly by the navigation systems that provide points of access to associated information via any interaction method from simple Web links to more complex animations, dynamic lists, or software application–like functional menus. Navigation can be globally and locally based, each form with specific functions. Global navigation systems serve to keep a user oriented in the information space and provide easy access to all of the main sections or functions of an information space. Typical global navigation aids could be site maps (sometimes called blueprints or flow charts when initially designed) that display graphically how the information is organized. Other textually based navigation methods can include site indices that appear as keyword organized lists (with links). Customized, application-driven dynamic systems, such as intranet portals, are used as global navigational hubs, which are especially useful for dynamically changing information. Local navigation systems focus on only a small subset of the total information, arranged around a specific topic or task such as an e-commerce checkout, or feature tutorial, or guide. Other local navigation may simply be a set of links embedded in content to supply supplementary information or to aid in scrolling or zooming through large units of information or graphics.

In some cases, a combination of global and local navigation systems are specifically designed to support the hierarchical or semantic relationships of the information, giving users the ability to "drill down" or quickly subdivide all of the possible information into a small, more viewable set. One example of this is faceted browsing where users can rapidly navigate to a subset of information by choosing links or specifying search terms in succession to find the closest fit for their information requirement.[6] There is a significant body of research literature on user navigation of digital spaces that informs IA practice.[7,8]

Creating Interaction Designs

The visual appearance, or interface to the information, is also often a responsibility for the information architect to create or advise on during development. Initially, simple wire frames (sketches and mockups of common information layouts) (see Fig. 1) are designed to show how content will be displayed, including text flow, locations of menus, sizes of buttons, and other common features of the web page or information display. These wire frames are then adapted to more specific templates that are tailored to the required displays, applications, and platforms that the information will be accessed from. The templates give a baseline for populating individual pages or documents of content into a few standard layouts and organization schemes, often each representing the variety of semantic and content-related units of information defined earlier in the IA process. Style sheets are also developed to consistently control the actual text and graphical layout of the content for each type of display or task, including fonts, lists, tables, and text flow (borders, indentation, column widths, etc.), among others. The styles can also be set to describe image sizing, text colors, and basic link behavior.

Basic interfaces may also be designed by the information architect, including prototypes that may include dynamic pull-down menus, scrolling timelines, and interactive search interfaces. It is also possible to quickly build and test application-like functionality, such as item selection or interactive survey forms that can be mocked-up using lightweight scripting languages such as JavaScript or visual interaction toolkits, including Flash or ActiveX technology. By focusing on the interface as part of the overall IA, the context of the information can be kept conceptually in synchronization with the purpose of the information content, setting up the IA as a critical participant in the progressively complex development of applications or features that require heavy programming to interact with or utilize the core information of a project.

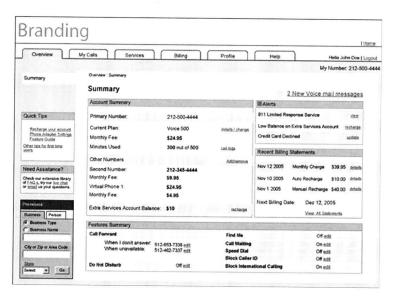

Fig. 1 A typical wire frame outlining the basic layout of navigation and design essentials.

Progressive, Big IA involvement in the application development process may also include focusing on the specific IA of database design, such as the types and labels used to collect and display information with users, as well as the fine-grained selection of specific vocabulary and icons to describe application functionality and enable the navigation and use of software more usable and consistent for users. Again, there is a significant body of literature on interaction design from the field of human computer interaction (HCI) that can be employed within IA to guide this process.[9]

Information Architecture as Process

It is worth noting that even while we can isolate categories of activities generally conducted under the heading of IA, the term itself can be used to describe the whole process of information systems creation. In other words, IA refers to the complete process of design with specific methodologies for managing the deployment of resources and sequencing of deliverables. There are two main approaches to architecting information spaces, which can be grossly characterized as "top-down" and "bottom-up." Each method is more suited to certain situations and applications.

Top-down designs rely on process-driven stages that are often thought to follow sequentially, as with the classic "waterfall" approach of software engineering. The process allows for formalized tracking of deliverables and progress. Often a central design specification is used as the reference point for all involved, and is continually updated to serve as a progress report and checklist. Such a methodology is often deemed advantageous for managers seeking to ensure process completion and budgetary controls, particularly where many participants are involved. Within this process, it is more typical to see the practice of IA structured around the specialized activities outlined herein.

Bottom-up methodologies focus more on the end product of the design and engage in a series of iterative design proposals, each of which can be refined over time to meet known or emerging targets. This approach may be more suitable for smaller-scale projects with fewer team members. Bottom-up IA methods take more from software engineering than product design—as more Web sites include application functionality, these bottom-up, prototype-driven methods are becoming more applicable to IA processes. Within this process, the practice of IA blends more seamlessly with related aspects of design such as user experience testing, scenario development, and interface design, leading to a sense of IA as the complete set of activities involved in creating a final product.

It should be noted that few design processes slavishly follow one or the other approach, and may blend parts of each according to resources, available time, competing demands, and skills of the participants. However, as IA becomes seen as a larger term for the overall process, we can anticipate greater management skill sets being required of practitioners, and fewer jobs for those with only one specific niche role.

Research Issues in IA

Pure research in IA is rare, the field borrowing more from outside as needed than tackling research questions directly. However, as the process of IA has become structured and recognized, dedicated research for IA is beginning to take form, driven largely by practitioners seeking answers to design questions.

The major theme in IA research is the study of navigation and how people find what they are looking for in an information space. From concerns with labeling and menu structures to the development of models of navigation behavior, there are now significant research publications dealing with topics of direct relevance to IA.[10,11] True, most of this work is still borrowed from outside, but this is subject to change as more academic researchers become involved in the field.

There is also significant work that extends examinations of navigation into areas such as the perception of information shape or the emergence of web genres and their exploitation for design.[7,12] This research aims to uncover the interaction between various structural forms of information space and the user, employing a socio-cognitive-based analytical approach to explaining and predicting use.

Another central theme for IA research is search behavior and the underlying design of efficient search mechanisms. Again, this research not only draws on the history of such work for information retrieval but also contains new contributions dealing with faceted metadata and image databases.[13–15]

Indeed, it is difficult to bound work exclusively as the province of IA because concerns with organization of information and user search and navigation of information spaces have such a long history. It is likely that for the foreseeable future, IA will remain a net borrower of intellectual research from other disciplines until such time as dedicated venues for IA research publications emerge. That said, the need to understand how best to design and implement IAs will remain an important driver of research work.

APPLICATION OF IA

As with any information technology–related discipline, the domain of IA is heavily influenced by the technologies that create content and permit access. In most cases, a Web browser is the primary application and interface for accessing IAs, but differences in types of users, tasks, and information content can shape IA efforts in myriad ways.

World Wide Web

The advent of the graphical Web browser and the near ubiquity of Hypertext Transfer Protocol (http) Web servers have fueled the growth of Web page development from basic home pages to complex ecommerce sites.[16] The majority of the Web consists of these common types of Web information, which share the common properties of providing links to other Web resources and are searchable via standard Web search engines.

Information architects designing these most common, now almost prosaic, sites can fit their work into certain known genres of Web sites such as news, e-commerce, entertainment, and corporate. However, not all IA is focused on these general Web sites. In fact other, more user-specific domains are the areas where IA is only beginning to make an impact. In most cases, these more focused Web sites use the Internet as a backbone of access, but often provide functionality beyond the typical Web browsing and information access paradigms. Each additional type of IA has its own specific set of users, use cases, and access environments.

Intranets

The use of Web standard technologies to help an organization communicate and work together has steadily increased with information technology developments. Leveraging the ubiquity and ease of use in Web site design and use, organizations are primarily turning to using Web sites both internally and externally to achieve business goals. Standard IAs on a corporate intranet would include company directories, policy guidelines, procedural information, and document workflow access. Increased use of application-level technology has transformed the organizational intranet into a knowledge management tool with repositories of institutional knowledge being created and accessed online. The design of these information systems is becoming the responsibility of information architects, often under the aegis of the management information system efforts. Portals (placeholders for new information to flow into them), often from corporate databases or external information feeds, are commonplace. The challenges of designing access methods and organizational schemes to deal with dynamically changing information are not unique to intranet applications, but lately have been the primary focus of intranet and portal IAs.

Interestingly, the advent of user-driven IAs as seen in the use of webblogs (blogs) and wikis (two technology

platforms that enable easy, rapid Web content development and organization) to facilitate communication among a group of similar users (or those with similar interests) may place new responsibilities on information architects as coordinators and meta-designers for these ad hoc, dynamic elements of information. The development of information taxonomies for this dynamically created information through the use of soundly designed templates may prove to increase the reach of finely architected information beyond those that IAs must explicitly manage and create themselves.

Vertical Markets

Some IAs are focused on specific industries or vertical markets. These areas can include government, healthcare, manufacturing, education, retail, and finance— each with their own characteristics for content, organization, and intended use. All of these markets require the organization of information assets and design of interaction interfaces that traditionally were developed within organizations. However, as the varieties of information access and functionality among these applications increase, so do the complexities of the information organization and user interfaces that are possible. Because of this, information architects are becoming progressively involved in these vertical application development efforts to both design and implement specific architectures to support users as well as grow organically as functionality increases.

In some cases, vertical IAs may primarily be carefully organized, task-based interfaces to databases or traditional end-user applications accessed via a Web browser and tailored to each industry, purpose, and activity. The most common example may be retail (e-commerce) applications within commercial Web sites such as shopping carts, merchandise hierarchies for browsing, and specific term creation to support searching. Also included are financial management interfaces to view and select stock market information, as well as track news related to certain stocks or economic issues. For other vertical markets, IA may be crafted to provide a directory of support information and promote discussion among members in specially organized forums. Each of these domains requires a unique set of information organization, understanding of user needs, and a facility with existing application technology. The size of any of these vertical markets is such that information architects can build on specialized knowledge and experience to work successfully and persistently in these fields.

Digital Libraries

The volume and variety of information now digitally accessible in libraries of all kinds have led to significant growth in search engines, primarily because of the lack of structured access methods to get to the bulk of information being produced and provided in digital form. In some ways, any repository of digital information can be thought of as a library of sorts, and requires a set of organizational schemas and interfaces to provide access for users. However, even traditional libraries and information providers are seeing a massive shift by users to on-line, often Web browser-accessible, repositories. Projects as large as the Internet Archive and search engines such as Google are the primary ways users are accessing information.[17] In most cases, this information is loosely organized, if at all, and users are in need of structures and paths through the volumes of information they are accessing.

Standards for organizing digital libraries are in place, including initiatives from both the public and the private sectors, and mostly concern the overall organization of the information along traditional dimensions, such as the consideration of digital information as an object for cataloging, preserving, and archiving. Information architecture in digital libraries will grow beyond this traditional organization, but still benefit from the approaches to collection and management, possibly to the extent that digital librarianship may be thought of as IA. The growth of multimedia information also pushes digital library research and development toward practicing IA to provide a set of best practices methods for displaying and organizing video and audio. Additional digital library responsibilities may involve the creation of collection-specific metadata as well as understanding ownership and copyright in a digital age.

Semantic Web

Information architecture may be the first profession that focuses on what many call the Semantic Web of information. Semantic Web spaces represent deeper, more meaningful relationships among discrete units of information that have "well-defined meaning, better enabling computers, and people to work in cooperation," often according to user-driven tasks or taxonomies.[18] Semantic Web information is, in some proposed cases, semantically structured IAs that will be acted on automatically by groups of software agents empowered to act on behalf of individual users or organizations.[18] In this case, IA will include a more complex analysis of the information elements themselves, with a perhaps less overt focus on the interfaces for interacting with the information. As Semantic Web applications emerge, programmatic interaction will be more commonplace, which increases the importance of highly structured units of information with rich, descriptive metadata that will control its display and use.

THE FUTURE OF INFORMATION ARCHITECTURE

Information architecture seems assured of a long future, even if the term itself ceases to gain formal agreement. A world of digital information will always need people to architect spaces for sharing, collecting, and organizing documents and resources. The existing understanding of IA as a discipline is likely to evolve as the profession grows and formal education takes shape.

Technical and theoretical advances are likely to yield new opportunities for tailoring information for personal use. The dynamic structuring of information in response to user activity is likely to offer increasing challenges for research to understand how people construct meaning and navigate through fluid information environments. Present discussions talk of a movement toward design "beyond the page," where the structures of the paper world are no longer applied to new information spaces. Under these circumstances we will likely witness the emergence of new information genres that cannot easily (or ever) be instantiated in anything other than digital form.

On the practical side, IA is likely to develop a set of roles that will offer an identity to the profession that is shared by more than the rather limited number of people with that job title at present. For this to occur, it is likely that a more formal educational path will need to emerge for this profession. Information architecture is not unique in this regard. There are many parallel roles within the information design community that are constantly being named and recruited, even if formal educational qualifications for them have yet to emerge (e.g., user experience designer, interaction designer, and digital librarian). The term IA appropriately covers this terrain and we should not expect rapid formalism of credential or educational path to emerge. However, the trend to date indicates that IA has made impressive progress down the path to recognizable status as a professional role and this is likely to continue in the near future.

CONCLUSIONS

Information architecture has grown steadily and securely from a hot topic term to a credible application and research area within the library and information science disciplines, though formal definition of its meaning and boundaries is yet to be agreed. A growing group of professionals now use the term to describe their work, formal degree programs have emerged, and the annual ASIS&T Summit has established itself as the core venue for sharing ideas and findings among this community.

Core competencies in IA include the semantic organization of information, the creation of navigation systems, and the design of user interfaces, with any individual professional tending to have greater interest or strengths in one or other of these areas. These skills are applied to the design of websites, intranets, and digital libraries in multiple environments and markets.

As research into user search behavior, navigation, content management, and information structures continues, it provides IA with a growing body of findings on which to create a more formal knowledge base, though the categorization of IA as a craft discipline that extends beyond the LIS world is likely to remain.

REFERENCES

1. Rosenfield, L.; Peter, M. *Inform ation Architecture for the World Wide Web: Designing Large-Scale Web Sites*; O'Reilly & Associates, Inc.: Sebastopol, CA, 2002.
2. Wurman, R. S.; Bradford, P. Eds.; *Information Architects;* Graphis Press: Zurich, Switzerland, 1996.
3. Dillon, A. Information architecture in JASIST? J. Am. Soc. Inf. Sci. Technol. **2002**, *53* (10), 821–823.
4. Weibel, S.L. The Dublin Core: A simple content description model for electronic resources. Bull. Am. Soc. Inf. Sci. Technol. **1997**, *24* (1).
5. Beckett, D.; McBride, B., Eds.; *RDF/XML Syntax Specification (Revised): W3C Recommendation* World Wide Web Consortium, Cambridge, MA, http://www.w3.org/TR/2004/REC-rdf-syntax-grammar-20040210/ (accessed 10 February 2004).
6. Instone, K. Fun with faceted browsing. American Society of Information Science and Technology Information Architecture Summit, Austin, TX, February, 28, 2004.
7. Dillon, A. Spatial semantics: How users derive shape from information spaces. J. Am. Soc. Inf. Sci. **2000**, *51* (6), 521–528.
8. Nielsen, J. *Designing Web Usability*; New Riders: Indianapolis, IN, 2000.
9. Helander, M.; Landauer, T.; Prabhu, P.V. *Handbook of Human Computer Interaction*; North-Holland: Amsterdam, Kingdom of the Netherlands, 1997.
10. Jacko, J.A.; Slavendy, G. Hierarchical menu design: Breadth, depth and task complexity. Percept. Motor Skills **1996**, *82*, 1187–1201.
11. Pirolli, P.L.; Fu, W. SNIF-ACT: A model of information foraging on the World Wide Web. 9th International Conference on User Modeling, Johnstown, PA, June, 22–26, 2003.
12. Kwasnik, B.; Crowston, K. A framework for creating a faceted classification for genres. Hawaii International Conference on Systems Science (HICSS 04), Los Alamitos, CA, January, 2004.
13. Bates, M.J. The design of browsing and berrypicking techniques for the on-line search interface. Online Rev. **1989**, *13*, 407–424.
14. Yee, K.; Swearingen, K.; Li, K.; Hearst, M. Faceted metadata for image search and browsing. Proceedings of CHI'03, Annual Conference of the ACM SIGCHI, New York, April, 2003; ACM Press: New York, 401–408.
15. Wildemuth, B.; Marchionini, G.; Yang, M.; Geisler, G.; Wilkens, T.; Hughes, A.; Gruss, R. How fast is too fast? Evaluating fast forward surrogates for digital video. ACM/IEEE Joint Conference on Digital Libraries, Los Alamitos, CA, June, 2003; 221–230.
16. Berners-Lee, T. The World-Wide Web. Commun. ACM **1994**, *37* (8), 76–82.
17. Lyman, P.; Kahle, B. Archiving digital cultural artifacts: Organizing an agenda for action. D-Lib Mag. **1998**, *4* (7), http://www.dlib.org/dlib/july98/07lyman.html.
18. Berners-Lee, T.; Hendler, J.; Lassila, O. The Semantic Web. Sci. Am. **2001**, *284* (5), 34–43.

Information Flow

Sean M. Price
Independent Information Security Consultant, Sentinel Consulting, Washington, District of Columbia, U.S.A.

Abstract

Modern IT systems facilitate information flows at many levels. At the microlevel, data moves between software and hardware components within a single machine. Macrolevel flows involve information movement between discrete system components up to intrasystem transfers of information.

INTRODUCTION

Information is the essence of IT systems. Most modern systems exist primarily to store, process, and share information. We consider information flow to include the aforementioned activities associated with information. These activities can be highly dynamic and complex. Some of the information flowing within an IT system requires appropriate security measures and controls. Information security practitioners must understand the dynamic nature of information flows within a system to be able to determine if the appropriate controls are in place and functioning as intended.

Understanding information flow paths is an important aspect of information assurance (IA). The overall goal of an IA program is to ensure that appropriate controls are in place to protect a system and its information. When actual and theoretical information flow paths are identified, then it becomes possible to identify the associated threats. Knowing the flow of information is also essential when evaluating newly discovered vulnerabilities and their potential impact on the information. Knowledge of the path of information as well as the associated threats and vulnerabilities provides the capability to assess the risk for each path. This provides information and system owners with the ability to select the most appropriate controls to counteract the identified risk. Thus, the selection of controls can be weighed against risk and cost associated with a control. Finally, the identification of information flows within a system aids the continuous monitoring process that might identify information flows that are new, unintended, or are unauthorized.

Data can be defined as individual elements that comprise information. The differences between data and information are sometimes ambiguous. What is data for one person or group may be information for yet another. Therefore, we will consider the terms "data" and "information" to be interchangeable in this entry.

CONCEPTUAL OVERVIEW

In the context of this entry, information flow is defined as the movement of information at the micro- and macrolevels. Microlevel movements of information include all aspects of information access within a computer, including system calls, file system actions, as well as data input and output. Macrolevel movements involve intrasystem and intersystem movements. Intrasystem movements include information flows between workstations and servers on an organizational system. Intersystem movements involve the flow of information between organizations, such as sending an e-mail from an organization's system to that of its customer.

The classical view of computing consists of input, processing, memory, local storage, and output. Fig. 1 provides a graphical image of the classical view. Information flows from input, such as a keyboard, into the central processor. Inside the processor, information is acted upon through slice-of-time increments that handle information for various tasks. This involves frequent exchanges and refreshing of information between the processor and memory. Occasionally, information is also communicated between the processor and local storage. At some point, information is ready for output. The processor pushes information to the appropriate output devices such as monitors and printers. This view of a computer system provides a high-level understanding of its basic functions and the fundamental paths for information to flow.

The emergence of distributed computing and the client/server paradigm complicates information flows. Information may exist in different states on multiple machines simultaneously. We can see in Fig. 2 that the classical view is expanded to incorporate communication aspects allowing information to flow through other devices and systems. The advent of communication interfaces expands the number of possible routes for information to travel. Inputs, outputs, storage, and other processors are available through the communications

Encyclopedia of Information Systems and Technology, DOI: 10.1081/E-EIST-120046872

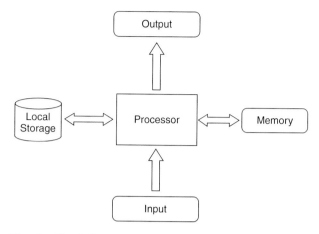

Fig. 1 Classical computing view.

interface. Information may now exist in multiple states and at multiple locations. Establishing assurance for the information flow at each point becomes a significant challenge.

INFORMATION ASSURANCE

Information exists in three possible states according to the IA model:[3] storage, processing, and transmission. Each state is best understood by assuming each represents a potential location for information. In this regard, storage refers to a static location such as fixed or removable media. Processing includes information that resides in memory or the CPU. We note that transmission is the location of information in a communication path such as network media. Information could reside in any one or all three states. For example, a word processing document in the storage state could be stored on a hard drive or on removable media. The same document

could be opened for editing, which exemplifies the processing state, while maintaining the storage state. Finally, the opened document could be sent to a colleague via e-mail, which would cause it to enter the transmission state. Protecting information in each of these states may require the use of different countermeasures.

The IA model identifies five security services: confidentiality, integrity, availability, authentication, and nonrepudiation. Confidentiality protects information from unauthorized disclosure. Integrity is used to protect information from unauthorized modification or destruction. Availability ensures resources can be accessed when needed. Authentication identifies the validity of a message, a transmission, or an originator. Nonrepudiation provides proof that precludes a sender or recipient from denying not having processed a message. In this entry, we will focus our attention on the first three security services and refer to them jointly as "CIA."

Models are a useful technique to explain information flow in a system. In this respect, we may consider the movement of information from one place to another to represent a change of state in the system. Computer scientists consider finite state autonoma (FSA) an empirical means to evaluate state changes. This view of information flow provides a formal (mathematical) means to represent information flows. This provides the computer scientist with the means to evaluate information flow through the use of mathematical proofs. FSA proofs can be very complex to construct, but when done correctly, have the ability to properly analyze state changes to information. Rather than rely upon FSA, security practitioners embrace more informal views of information flow through frameworks such as the IA model. This entry will make use of the informal attributes of the IA model to make observations and draw conclusions.

DATA LINEAGE

Most information has a lineage, i.e., some information is derived from a collection of sources. One document may include information that is replicated from other documents, reports, or raw data. Some researchers also refer to this concept as data provenance.[1] Knowing the origination of information is very important in some communities. For instance, the scientific community must know where certain data is derived from so they can accurately interpret the results of their experiments. Many organizations also face this issue when they simply want to identify document versions in a collaboration environment. This situation has given rise to a plethora of document management solutions. As opposed to the use of expensive tools, a simple process for implementing version control that achieves a similar

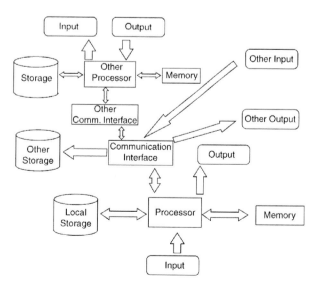

Fig. 2 Expanded computing view.

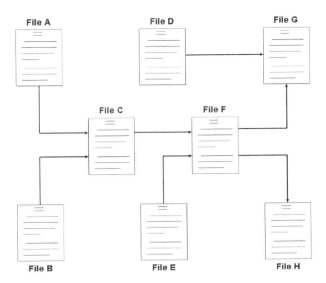

Fig. 3 Information lineage.

effect has been proposed by Price.[2] However, these solutions do not always provide exact details of who changed what and from where the information might have been derived.

Tracking information lineage can be a daunting task. Fig. 3 is an example of information lineage as it flows from one file into another. Given files A through H in the figure, let us assume that the information in files A, B, D, and E are mutually exclusive of each other. Note in the figure that an arrow from one file to the next represents a one-way flow of information. We will also assume that any new file may contain original information exclusive of the information flowing into it. We can, therefore, interpret that file C is derived from files A and B. It is also conceivable that file C contains original information not found in files A or B. When we consider file F, it is apparent that it contains information from files C and E, but it is not immediately apparent

whether it contains flows from files A and B. File G contains information from files D and F, but it is difficult to know whether information flowed into it from files A, B, or C. File H is derived from F. Because we may not know exactly what information flowed from file F into files G and H, it is problematic to say that G and H are mutually exclusive or that they are related. Both situations are possible. Files G and H can be mutually exclusive if each file is derived from different parts of file H, which do not have overlapping lineage from files A, B, C, and E. If any information from files A, B, C, E, or F exists in both files G and H, then they will not be mutually exclusive, but rather have a relation to each other and a similar lineage. Considering the scenario exhibited in Fig. 3, the difficulty in assessing data lineage as it relates to information flows is apparent.

The diagram in Fig. 3 is a simplistic representation of information flow. However, it does not consider more common and complicated scenarios that are likely to occur in the real world. Information flow can take compound and circular routes. Consider the data flow depicted in Fig. 4. Information is flowing from file D directly into file G. It is also possible that information is flowing from file D into file G via files C and F. This depicts a compound information flow because information in a file may emerge from a root source over multiple routes. Another possibility is that information may flow circularly between files as can be seen between files C and F. The same information may flow between these files, which may frustrate attempts to determine where an aspect of information originated. We also note that it is possible now for file C to have data flowing into it from file E from file F. Thus, information lineage and the identification of data flows can be further complicated when compound and circular routes are present.

TRACKING INFORMATION FLOWS

Knowing information flows helps to identify violations of separation of duties or least privilege. Consider the information flow depicted in Fig. 5. In this figure, we have users 1, 2, and 3. We assume the duties of users 1 and 3 are mutually exclusive. User 3 depends on some information from user 1 to accomplish their duties. Information not explicitly shared should not be readable by other users. Files completely within the area of a user are not shared between users. At the discretion of a user, information within a nonshared file may flow to those that are shared. For example, user 3 has complete control over files G and H. Files on the broken line are shared between users. For instance, files D and F are shared between users 2 and 3. If we were implementing discretionary access control (DAC), we might say that

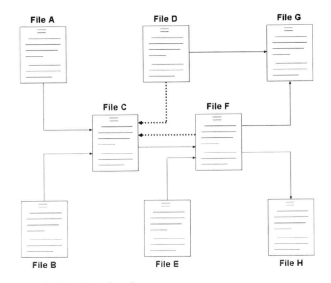

Fig. 4 Complex data flow.

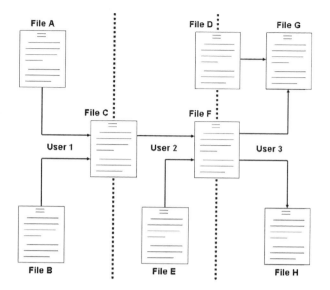

Fig. 5 Data flows and users.

user 2 has the right to modify file D while user 3 should only have the capability to read it. The arrows indicate the authorized flow of information from one file to the next. However, it is important to note that this does not mean that all information must flow from one file to the next. For instance, not all information from file A needs to flow to file C. It is up to the discretion of user 1 to determine what information must flow from file A to file C and still not violate least privilege or separation of duties.

Now suppose that the access controls on the shared files allow read and write privileges to those who are authorized access. A situation may arise similar to that depicted in Fig. 6. This figure demonstrates a breakdown in least privilege and separation of duties due to inappropriate information flows. We can see that information is now allowed to flow from file G to D.

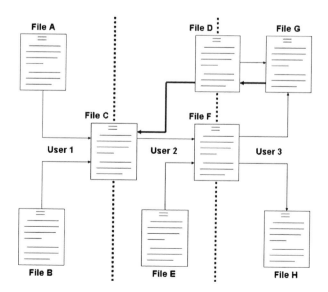

Fig. 6 Data flow violations.

Assuming user 2 is not authorized access to this information, we have a situation where least privilege is violated. Now suppose user 2 copies this information from file D to C. This also violates least privilege because user 1 now has unauthorized access to the copied information. If this information has the potential to allow user 1 to perpetrate a fraud, then we will also realize a violation of separation of duties. This scenario demonstrates a method by which inappropriate flows of information can cause violations to the concepts of least privilege and separation of duties. If the authorized paths of information flow are known, then it would be possible to identify these potential or actual violations due to the inappropriate access controls.

FLOWS WITHIN A SYSTEM

Information flow within an operating system does not flow immediately from one point to another as depicted in Fig. 1. Information is often handled by a variety of execution threads as it travels from one point to another. Fig. 7 depicts a high-level overview of some of these interactions as they might be observed in an operating system such as Microsoft Windows XP. Operating systems of this type enable separation between user and kernel activities. The kernel implements services for user applications such as interfaces for input, output, and storage. It also provides mechanisms for processes to communicate with each other as well as with those on other systems. Fig. 7 extends the basic elements seen in Fig. 2 by providing more fundamental detail on how information flows in the system. It is evident from Fig. 7 that information flow can have multiple intermediate handling points in a system.

Each of the intermediate points seen in Fig. 7 enables specialized handling of information. Device drivers are the interfaces between hardware and software. They ensure that information flows correctly between the device and the operating system. Most device drivers execute in kernel mode and are controlled by the operating system. System calls are functions provided by the operating system that are made available for user processes and other kernel threads. System calls are usually intermediate communications between a thread, device drivers, and other threads. When a process makes a system call, it typically causes information to flow. Examples of information flow-related system calls include reading a file, writing a file to storage, sending data to a printer or the network, and interprocess communication (IPC).

Perhaps the most powerful aspect of modern operating systems is their ability to allow separate threads of execution to communicate. This ability is what provides most of the rich system capabilities users experience

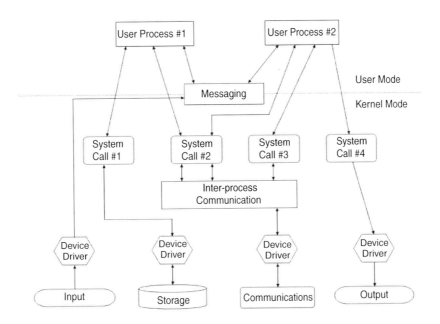

Fig. 7 Operating system information flows.

when they interact with a modern IT system. Enormous amounts of information flow between communicating processes and threads. Allowing individual processes to communicate enables the sharing of tasks and information. As such, work can be spread out among several processes. This sharing of information and work is an essential aspect of what enables rapid software development through reusable code. Some processes are dedicated to a particular task and handle specific types of information. Processes dedicated to a particular task provide a service to other processes, which shortens development cycles. This provides efficiency to software development efforts. The ability of processes to participate in information flow is a fundamental aspect of modern operating systems.

Within modern Windows operating systems, there are principally two services that allow processes to communicate: the Windows messaging subsystem and IPC. Windows messaging is essentially a service available to all processes executing in the context of the user interacting at the console. This service allows threads, or more generally windows, to send messages back and forth. Some of the types of messages sent through Windows messaging include keystrokes, commands to close a window, terminate requests, and window resizing. The Windows messaging system also provides a way to pass data between threads. In contrast, IPC allows communication between processes that are not executing in the same context. Thus, a user process can communicate with other processes at the kernel level or even on a physically separate machine. IPC provides the ability for processes to communicate by using a particular protocol or service. Some of the more common IPC

protocols include pipes, mail slots, remote procedure calls, and sockets. The Windows clipboard is an example of an IPC service. Windows messaging and IPC are backbone services for information flow between local processes as well as intrasystem and intersystem processes.

The emergence of reusable code, system services, IPC, and publication of application programming interfaces (APIs) by product vendors enables an open architecture system. Reusable code shortens development life cycles and allows more effort to be put into new concepts as opposed to recreating the previous functionality. Most of the reusable code is packaged as statically or dynamically linked libraries. System services might be viewed as reusable processes. As opposed to sharing libraries, a service provides a way to share information processing power and perform tasks on behalf of other processes. We can consider IPC an important conduit for information flow between processes. APIs are the glue facilitating an open architecture system. Through an API, vendors publish the functions, methods, events, and data structures that are related to their proprietary libraries and services. Developers use published and proprietary APIs to send data and make requests between processes. Published APIs allow the sharing and reuse of proprietary code. Within an open architecture, APIs are the essential element facilitating the flow of information between processes.

We can see the various points in Fig. 7 that handle and process information as it flows through the system. For instance, information traveling through the input, such as a keyboard, is intercepted by a device driver that passes it along to the messaging subsystem. Processes retrieve messages directed to them from the messaging subsystem. User process #1 uses system call #1 to read and write information to local storage. It also uses system call #2 to communicate with user process #2. Communication with external processes is occurring with user process #2 through system call #3. Data is also being sent to an output device through system call #4 by user process #2. It is evident from this example that there are many possible paths for information to flow within a modern operating system.

Unfortunately, the open architecture of modern operating systems has a downside. The rich extensibility and reusability of code has made it easy for malevolent individuals to produce malicious code. The sinister processes concocted by social deviants, political rivals, and criminals exploit aspects of an open architecture to subvert the security services of the system. We can observe in Fig. 8 some of the more common uses of malicious code to compromise a system. A Trojan horse executing as its own process in the context of a user has access to all of the same objects and services available to the user. If the user has sufficient privileges, a Trojan could create and load new services or device drivers. For instance, an evil device driver could be installed to intercept all communications between the keyboard device and the messaging subsystem, compromising all keystrokes, including passwords and other sensitive information. The Trojan could also create its own information flows by accessing stored data through system call #1 and sending it on to the attacker through the communications interface via system call #2. Most viruses are associated with an infected process. Typically, they propagate by infecting other files. In the diagram, we can see that a virus could infect other files

using system call #1 to read and write data. A virus causes information to flow from itself, which also happens to look like itself, into other executable files. Spyware is a special type of malicious code that is most interested in capturing user activity. One of the most notorious features of spyware is its ability to capture passwords. On Windows systems, this is usually accomplished through a special system call that allows a thread to receive all keystroke activity that passes through the messaging subsystem. Although it is not depicted, spyware typically causes captured information to flow to the file system or the communications interface, or both. Vulnerabilities are sometimes present in applications. The most notorious of these is the buffer overflow. This type of vulnerability is often exploited by causing the vulnerable process to execute a new process or thread within its context. In either of these cases, the new thread has the same contextual privileges as the vulnerable process. Worms have been known to leverage vulnerabilities by creating new threads within a process. The new evil thread, resulting from a buffer overflow in user process #2, can seek out other victims through the communications interface via system call #3. Clearly, malicious software leverage published interfaces as well as weaknesses within an open architecture to accomplish devious tasks.

COMPLICATIONS

Information can be fragile. It can be impacted within any of the processing states noted in the IA model.[3] Actions that impact information flow can result in

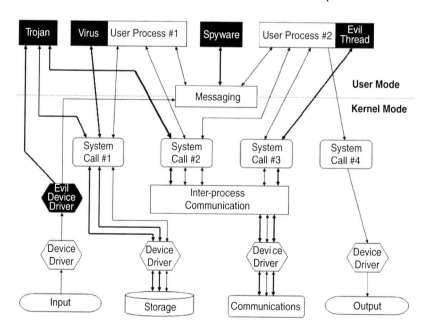

Fig. 8 Compromised operating system.

compromises to the CIA of the affected data. The movement of information is so pervasive within a system that there are numerous places where information flow can be compromised. Confidentiality of information flows can be compromised through malicious acts of surreptitious data capture. Similarly, confidentiality can also be compromised through unencrypted network communications. Data integrity is vulnerable to changes during any of the information states. Given the integrity is not assured, it becomes apparent that availability is also jeopardized. Consider the situation where a message in transit is overwritten with a repeating character. This violation to the message's integrity also impacts its availability. In modern operating systems, the problem of information fragility can be attributed to weaknesses inherent in today's predominant access control methods.

DAC is known to have weaknesses that affect the CIA of the system or application where it is used.[4] This is related to the attributes of DAC and is manifested through the Trojan horse threat. The underlying premise of DAC is that an object owner retains the discretion to identify who (subject) may have what (privilege) access to the object. An object owner first identifies other subjects who are authorized access to their object. Then the owner specifies what privileges are permitted on the object. Some of the more common privileges include read, append, modify (or write), delete, and execute. The read privilege permits a subject the ability to access the object and read its contents. Append allows a subject to add information to an object. The modify privilege enables any change to information in the object. The delete privilege grants the

subject the right to remove pointers to the object. A subject with the execute privilege is allowed to invoke the object as a process. The read privilege is the most problematic privilege regarding information flows. This privilege essentially allows the subject to create a copy of the object in memory. As such, it must be understood that the read privilege does not imply read-only; rather, it really means the right to make a copy of the object. As such, information can easily flow from one object to another even if this was not the intent of the owner of the original object.

Fig. 9 provides a scenario that describes the aforementioned weaknesses in DAC. We see in the figure that Alice has created document A and allowed Bob the privilege to read it and write to (modify) it. Unbeknown to Bob, a Trojan horse is running in his context. It has all of the same rights and privileges as Bob. Bob was duped by Troy to run the malicious code. Troy now has unauthorized access to document A through the Trojan horse, which he controls remotely. Troy uses the malicious code along with Bob's privileges to read document A and makes a copy of it. This violates the confidentiality of the document. Troy then directs his malicious code to overwrite the contents of document A with the phrase, "I WIN!!" With one fatal command, Troy has compromised the integrity of the document and has made the information unavailable. He completes his devious scheme by providing a copy of document A to Mallory, who pays handsomely for the exact information originally contained in document A. From this scenario, it is easy to understand how the weaknesses of DAC impact information flow assurances.

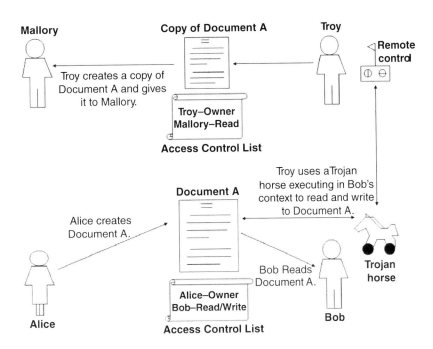

Fig. 9 Weaknesses of DAC exemplified.

HIPAA– Information Protection

Table 1 Directed attacks

	Physical	Logical
Confidentiality (theft)	Media theft	Malicious code
	System component theft	Removable media
	Physical keystroke logger	Printouts
	Network traffic interception	Network transmission
	Dumpster diving	Backdoors
	Social engineering	Covert channels
		Privilege escalation
Integrity (manipulation)	Network traffic interception	Malicious code
	Direct storage access	Abuse of privileges
	Information warfare	Backdoors
		Privilege escalation
Availability (obstruction)	Network traffic interception	Malicious code
	System destruction	Bots and zombies
	Component theft	Abuse of privileges
	Media destruction	Backdoors
	Media overwrite	Privilege escalation

ATTACK METHODS

Directed attacks against information flows can be broadly categorized as physical or logical. Physical attacks involve actions that require physical human intervention to disrupt or intercept information flows. Logical attacks are those that use manual or automated techniques to compromise the security service most often through DAC weaknesses. Within each of these categories, we can further classify attacks based on their circumvention of the CIA security services. Table 1 provides an overview of some of the possible attacks against information flows.

With respect to confidentiality, a directed attack is most likely concerned with capturing information for illicit purposes. Physical approaches attempt to intercept information flows to capture the desired information directly. Outright theft of media and system components is the obvious course of action. Theft of system backups can provide instant access to an organization's most sensitive information. Keystroke loggers placed inline with keyboards can capture sensitive information as it is typed. The most likely motive of the physical keystroke logger is to capture passwords that enable the attacker to masquerade as the affected authorized user. Sensitive information commonly traverses organizational internal networks and is subject to interception. An attacker may use specialized tools to intercept network traffic passing a particular node in the network. Physical access to network backbone media provides an attacker with the opportunity to intercept most, if not all, traffic within an organization. This is possible when the attacker either splices the cable or uses inductive methods to intercept the traffic. Dumpster diving and social engineering rely on the mistakes of others to gain access to sensitive information. Logical attacks are primarily manifested as

an abuse or unauthorized use of system credentials. Malicious software, backdoors, and covert channels provide automated means to compromise information confidentiality. Malicious software running in the context of the user can compromise information in files accessible to the user. These can also capture other activity, such as keystrokes or screen images, as a way to steal information as well. Backdoors may provide a means to circumvent existing controls allowing unauthorized or unaccounted access to information processed. Covert channels enable the surreptitious transfer of information through innocuous methods. Inappropriate diversions of sensitive information by authorized users are commonly accomplished by printing, removable media, or through network transmissions such as e-mails and peer-to-peer networking. Insiders with special rights, such as administrators, may give themselves inappropriate access to information through privilege escalation. Compromise of information flow confidentiality can be difficult to detect. When a compromise is detected, the results can be devastating to the organization.

Attacks directed at information flow integrity seek to alter the original data. Some aspects of IT have inherent integrity mechanisms to assure or detect changes to data integrity. Cyclic redundancy checks are commonly used in network protocols to detect changes to data. Hashing techniques are employed with cryptographic measures to detect unauthorized changes to data. Transaction processing assures only valid data is written to a file system or database. Aside from hashing, most of the IT integrity mechanisms are designed to detect or correct errors during processing. In many cases, the error detection mechanisms are of no consequence when the data is manipulated prior to or after the integrity check. Although the IA model includes integrity as an important aspect, it is seldom given the necessary attention by system owners and security professionals. Physical attacks against integrity involve the unauthorized manipulation of data from its original form. Data traversing a network is vulnerable to interception and manipulation. A malicious router could be used to alter data packets in transit. Physical access to storage media allows an attacker to alter any file it contains. This is easily accomplished for removable media. System media, such as hard drives, can either be removed or the system booted to an alternate operating system that mounts the target media, allowing file manipulation. Information warfare involves changes to specific information within a system to achieve a desired effect on the target organization. An attacker using information warfare tactics may involve small changes to information, causing the organization to make decisions that benefit the attacker.[5] Logical attacks to integrity generally leverage the credentials of authorized users to change information. Malicious code executing in the context of a user could make any change normally authorized for the user. The most likely change would be file corruption. Insiders may abuse their authorized access and change information in a system. They may make unauthorized changes to important documents, web content, or database fields. Organizations seldom institute appropriate integrity validation checks to assure that changes made to important information are appropriate or authorized. At best, fields in a database may have some auditing enabled to identify who made the changes. Backdoors allow an attacker to change information surreptitiously and may even avoid audit detection mechanisms. An authorized user with the capability to escalate their privileges could make changes to information that may go unnoticed. Undetected changes to information integrity may cause an organization to make poor decisions. Attackers can take advantage of a lack of integrity change detection in information flows to manipulate organizational actions to their benefit.

Availability could be referred to as the mantra of IT professionals and managers. It is a goal equally shared by security and operations professionals. The availability of an information flow is commonly affected by obstruction techniques such as data destruction and denial-of-service attacks. These types of attacks can be perpetrated through a variety of physical and logical techniques. Physical availability attacks attempt to disrupt system components. This includes severing network connections and damaging hardware components.

Critical system components, such as routers and switches, could also be stolen from the premises. Although this involves severing a network connection, it is more problematic as a necessary component of the network is now missing. Storage media may also be subjected to attack. Backups could be physically damaged. Exposing magnetic media to strong magnetic fields could alter the stored data and prevent recovery. Similarly, malicious individuals could use overwrite utilities coupled with their physical access to deny access to stored information. Logical attacks against availability are well known. Viruses have been known to corrupt or encrypt files preventing access to its contents. Worms have caused systems and services to become unavailable for use. Bots and zombies have been used to launch distributed denial-of-service attacks against a selected target, preventing others from accessing the system resources. Insiders have been known to delete or corrupt critical files. Backdoors provide another means to damage or remove information surreptitiously, making it unavailable. Insiders with the ability to elevate their privileges could also damage or remove selected files, denying authorized users access to the information. Given the commonality of the availability security service, attacks against it will likely be reacted to by the operations and security staff. However, such attacks can still be difficult to detect in some cases and problematic to counter in others.

REFERENCES

1. Bose, R. A conceptual framework for composing and managing scientific data lineage. Proceedings of the 14th International Conference on Scientific and Statistical Database Management, 2002; 15–19.
2. Price, S.M. Supporting resource-constrained collaboration environments. Computer **2007**, *406*, 108–107.
3. Maconachy, W.V.; Schou, C.D.; Ragsdale, D.; Welch, D. A model for information assurance: An integrated approach. Proceedings of the 2001 Information Assurance Workshop, West Point, NY, June 5–6, **2001**; 306–310.
4. Downs, D.D.; Rub, J.R.; Kung, K.C.; Jordan, C.S. Issues in discretionary access control. Proceedings of the IEEE Symposium on Security and Privacy, Kluwer, **1985**; 208–218.
5. Waltz, E. *Information Warfare Principles and Operations*; Artech House: Boston, MA, 1998.

Information Management

Brian Detlor
DeGroote School of Business, McMaster University, Hamilton, Ontario, Canada

Abstract

Information management (IM) concerns the control over how information is created, acquired, organized, stored, distributed, and used as a means of promoting efficient and effective information access, processing, and use by people and organizations. Various perspectives of IM exist. For this entry, three are presented: the organizational, library, and personal perspectives. Each deals with the management of some or all of the processes involved in the information life cycle. Each concerns itself with the management of different types of information resources. The purpose of this entry is to clearly describe what "information management" is and to clarify how IM differs with regard to closely related terms.

INTRODUCTION

Information management (IM) is a broad conceptual term that has various meanings and interpretations among different constituencies. Often the term is used interchangeably with others. For instance, IM is often equated with the management of information resources, the management of information technology (IT), or the management of information policies or standards.[1] Some suggest that IM draws upon ideas from both librarianship and information science.[2] The purpose of this entry is to clarify the meaning of the term "information management," to showcase its major perspectives, and to illustrate how it relates to associated terms.

What is IM? IM is the management of the processes and systems that create, acquire, organize, store, distribute, and use information. The goal of IM is to help people and organizations access, process, and use information efficiently and effectively. Doing so helps organizations operate more competitively and strategically, and helps people better accomplish their tasks and become better informed.

This entry adopts a process orientation toward IM where IM is viewed as the control over the information life cycle. Various models of information processes exist; some of the major processes involved in information life cycle concern those that create, acquire, organize, store, distribute, and use information.

Importantly, this entry recognizes three major perspectives of IM: the organizational, library, and personal perspectives. By far, the organizational perspective is the most predominant and popular. In a nutshell, this perspective deals with the management of all information processes involved in the information life cycle with the goal of helping an organization reach its competitive and strategic objectives. A variety of information resources are managed by organizations. These include transactional information stored in databases, summarized information found in data warehouses, and unstructured information content found in documents and reports. From the organizational perspective, the management of IT is a major component of any IM plan. It is with this perspective where associated terms like information systems management, IT management, data management, business intelligence, competitive intelligence, content management, and records management have relevance.

The library perspective of IM recognizes the unique role of information provision organizations, such as libraries, whose central mandate is to provide their clientele with access to information resources and services. As such, these types of organizations view IM primarily as the management of information collections, such as books and journals. With respect to information collections, libraries are neither the creators nor the users of this information. As such, this perspective deals with the management of a subset of information processes involved in the information life cycle with the goal of helping library patrons access and borrow information items held in the collection. It is with the library perspective where associated terms like knowledge organization, classification, cataloging, digital libraries, indexes, and information retrieval systems have relevance.

The personal perspective of IM, though not strong, is similar to the organizational perspective in that it involves the management of all information processes in the information life cycle. The major difference, however, is that the organizational perspective concerns the management of information of interest to the success and well-being of an organization, while the personal

Encyclopedia of Information Systems and Technology, DOI: 10.1081/E-EIST-120043257

perspective deals with the management of information of relevance and concern to the individual.

In terms of this entry's organization, the remainder is structured to further explain the major points just described. First, description is given on the information life cycle and the process view of IM. This is followed by a detailed discussion on each of the three major perspectives of IM: the organizational, library, and personal perspectives. Last, concluding remarks are made.

A PROCESS VIEW OF IM

Leading IM scholars and organizations purport a process-driven view of IM. For example, Wilson defines IM as "the application of management principles to the acquisition, organization, control, dissemination and use of information relevant to the effective operation of organizations of all kinds."[3] Similarly, Choo defines IM as the management of processes that acquire, create, organize, distribute, and use information.[1] Likewise, the U.S. Government Accountability Office defines IM as "the planning, budgeting, manipulating, and controlling of information throughout its life cycle."[4]

The conceptualization of IM from a process perspective emerged in the early 1990s.[5,6] Advocates of this approach stress that a process model of IM should encompass all or some parts of the information value chain or life cycle. Choo proposes six discrete information-related processes or activities that need to be managed: 1) identification of information needs; 2) acquisition of information to address those needs; 3) organization and storage of information; 4) design and development of information products; 5) distribution of information; and 6) information use.[1] Wilson positions the creation and use of information outside the IM rubric and purports the following six information-related processes pertaining to IM: 1) acquisition; 2) organization; 3) storage; 4) retrieval; 5) access/lending; and 6) dissemination.[7] Not all IM frameworks include information needs identification and information use as processes to be managed. However, many see the most critical issue facing information managers is eliciting information requirements and matching those information needs in the design and delivery of information systems to promote effective and efficient information use.[1,8,9]

With respect to this entry, the following are considered to be the predominant information processes to be managed in IM: information creation, acquisition, organization, storage, distribution, and use. Information creation is the process where individuals and organizations generate and produce new information artifacts and items. Information acquisition is the process where information items are obtained from external sources.

Information organization is the process of indexing or classifying information in ways that support easy retrieval at later points in time. Information storage is the process of physically housing information content in structures such as databases or file systems. Information distribution is the process of disseminating, transporting, or sharing information. Information use is the process where individuals and organizations utilize and apply information made available to them. Effectively managing these information processes helps get the right information to the right people in the right forms at the right times and at reasonable costs.[1,10]

THE ORGANIZATIONAL PERSPECTIVE

The organizational perspective is the most predominant perspective of IM. Under the organizational perspective, IM concerns the management and control over the full life cycle of information processes ranging from creation to use for the betterment of the organization itself. In this sense, the management of information processes is seen as a strategic advantage that affords four kinds of benefits to an organization: 1) a reduction of costs; 2) a reduction of uncertainty or risks; 3) added value to existing products and services; and 4) the creation of new value through the introduction of new information-based products and services.[11]

Information as a Resource

Fundamental to the organizational perspective of IM is the view and treatment of information as a strategic resource—one that needs to be managed like any other critical organizational resource, such as people, equipment, and capital. Many organizations recognize the potential value of information and the need to be aware of what information resources exist in an organization, and the costs associated with acquiring, storing, processing, and using that information. Forward-looking companies consider information as a strategic asset that can be leveraged into a competitive advantage in the markets served by the company.[8]

The concept of managing information as an organizational resource emerged in the late 1970s with the creation of the U.S. Paperwork Reduction Act that was established to resolve the huge costs of managing and handling information by bidders for government contracts.[12] It was at this time that the term information resources management (IRM) became popular and was used to signify the management of both information and information technologies.[13,14] In reality though, the IRM concept was more about the management of data than it was about the management of other types of information, such as documents or reports. Case in point, an empirical assessment of the IRM construct defines IRM as "a comprehensive approach to planning, organizing, budgeting, directing, monitoring and controlling the people, funding, technologies and activities associated with acquiring, storing, processing and distributing data to meet a business need for the benefit of the enterprise"—not other types of information.[15]

This entry suggests that within the organizational perspective of information management, IM is more than just the management of data (e.g., raw facts stored in transactional databases). Rather, IM in organizations involves the management of a varied set of information resources, ranging from data to information.[16]

Data can be considered as "raw facts" that reflect the characteristics of an event or entity. Examples of data items held in an organization would be a customer name, an order quantity, or a unit price. The management of data in organizations traditionally belonged to the "Data Management" function or "Data Resource Management" department. Data management deals with the storage and processing of low-level data items found in transaction processing systems. The focus of data management is to maximize the speed, accuracy, and efficiency of processing and maintaining transactions or records.[1] Data management is concerned with the creation and "acquisition of data, its storage in databases, its manipulation or processing to produce new (value-added) data and reports via application programs, and the transmission (communication) of the data or resulting reports."[8]

Information can be viewed as "meaningful data" where data have been converted into a meaningful and useful context, such as in the identification of a best-selling or worst-selling product item from historical sales data for a company. Examples of information items managed in a company would be summarized information pulled from transactional database systems and stored in data warehouses and/or data marts. Such "business intelligent" systems support decision making, and allow for the slicing-and-dicing of summarized transactional information to find patterns and trends in operational data (e.g., sales data, supplier data, and customer profile data) of importance and relevance to the organization. For example, the mining of summarized transactional data stored in a data warehouse could be used to justify the promotion of a product or service to an untapped market segment, or to measure the effectiveness of a marketing campaign in a certain geographical area.[16]

Though more emphasis in organizations is placed on the management of data and information that is structured and formalized (i.e., data neatly contained within a transactional database or summarized information stored in a data warehouse), the amount of unstructured information that is created, acquired, organized, stored, distributed, and used within an organization usually far exceeds the amount of structured data and information an organization manages.

Unstructured information is the type of information that can be found in reports, documents, e-mail messages, and PowerPoint presentations, among others. This includes reports and documentation generated internally with a company and outside the enterprise as well. For example, managing information concerning industry trends, legislative regulations, competitor happenings, news bulletins, etc., is key to helping an organization stay abreast and to react to competitor threats and environmental concerns. This is where IM intersects with a company's "competitive intelligence" initiatives and "environmental scanning" activities. Competitive intelligence refers to the analysis of information about competitors and competitive conditions in particular industries or regions.[17] Environmental scanning refers to the analysis of information about every sector of the external environment that can help an organization plan for its future.[18,19]

Often document management systems, also known as content management systems, help manage unstructured information that is created, acquired, organized, stored, distributed, and used within an organization. These systems support the electronic capture, storage, distribution, archiving, and accessing of documents. These systems typically provide a document repository where documents can be housed, indexed, and accessed. In these repositories, metadata information is maintained about each document that tracks each document's editorial history and relationships to other documents. Indexing of documents within these systems, through both manual keyword classifications and automatic indexing techniques, facilitates easy document retrieval by organizational workers at later points in time.[16]

Unstructured information also includes records of transactional information processing such as invoices, contracts, order requisitions, bills of lading, and financial statements. The actual data may be resident in a transaction database and managed elsewhere, but the entire record of the event, often with signatures, are handled as a complete entity that must be generated, stored, processed, retrieved, and archived. The management of such information is referred to as "records management" and involves the application of systematic and scientific control to all recorded information that an organization needs to do business.[20]

Managing Information Processes

A good IM program in an organization will manage the full life cycle of information ranging from creation to use. For example:

- When generating transactional data, steps will be taken to ensure that the data will be stored following database "normalization rules" to promote data integrity, the single sourcing of data, the reduction of wasted database space, and fast transaction processing.
- When acquiring information, such as the purchase of market research data or competitor intelligence information, steps will be taken to reduce duplicate purchases and to increase the accessibility of any purchased data and information across the enterprise.
- Any data or information that is stored will be adequately protected against unauthorized access, as security, privacy, and copyright concerns exist.
- Data and information stewardship programs will be set up to identify those organizational workers or units who are responsible for the quality and management of certain data and information items.
- Data and information will be regularly backed up for recovery purposes.
- Duplicate or mirror copies of data and information items will be created to facilitate access, and reduce network congestion and/or an overload of requests on the servers on which the data and information reside.
- Old data and outdated information will be archived and/or deleted.[16]

Information Technology's Role

Information technology plays a critical role in the management of information in organizations. However, having said that, it should be understood that IT is the technical medium upon which information is housed, accessed, retrieved, distributed, and used, and not the primary entity that is being managed under the IM rubric. Information processes are.

Nevertheless, much confusion exists over the role IT plays in the management of information in organizations, with some equating IM primarily to the management of IT itself. For example, the mission of the Society for Information Management, a professional society for chief information officers and senior IT leaders based in the United States, is "to provide international leadership and education in the successful management and use of IT to achieve business objectives."[21] Likewise, Davis and Hamilton define IM as "the management of information systems and information resources by an individual, a group, or an organization" and describe IM as a "new business function with responsibility to define organizational informational requirements, plan, and build an information infrastructure and information systems applications, operate the system, and organize, staff, and manage these activities."[22]

This entry suggests that such descriptions of the IM function in organizations are inappropriate and are better served by alternate terms such as information systems management or IT management. Information systems management refers to the control over the development, design, rollout, and support of information systems applications that support business processes and workflow. Information technology management refers to the management and control over IT (e.g., hardware and software).

A variety of factors need to be considered when managing technology in organizations. The appropriate hardware and software need to be installed and implemented. Repair and maintenance of hardware and software systems must be done. Licensing concerns must be taken into consideration. Information systems professionals (e.g., programmers, network specialists, database administrators, and systems analysts) need to be hired and trained.[16]

Information technology is very important to how information is managed in organizations, and the management of IT should be an integral part of any IM plan.[11] After all, IT facilitates the ability to support information creation, acquisition, organization, storage, distribution, and use in both efficient and effective manners.

Organizational Information Processing

IM is concerned with organizational information processing. Two broad orientations exist in the organizational information processing literature that have implications on IM.[23]

The first, mainly developed at Carnegie Mellon University and represented by Herbert Simon, James March, and Richard Cyert, sees an organization's ability to process information as the core of managerial and organizational competencies and organizations as bounded, rational systems.[24] Here, strategies to improve information processing capabilities concern increasing an organization's information processing capacity and reducing an organization's need for information processing.[25]

The second, represented by Karl Weick and Richard Daft, sees organizations as loosely coupled systems where individual participants collectively develop shared interpretations of the environment and then act on the basis of this interpretation. In this sense, information processing is about reducing the equivocality or ambiguousness of information about the organization's external environment.[26]

Taking these two orientations of organizational information processing together, IM then is about increasing an organization's information processing capacity and reducing both information processing needs and information equivocality.

THE LIBRARY PERSPECTIVE

Outside of the organizational context, IM also has meaning in the library world and to other information provision organizations whose central mandate is to provide clientele with access to information resources and services. IM is of concern to all kinds of libraries, such as public libraries and academic and research libraries. This includes corporate libraries that manage serial subscriptions and electronic access to industry reports and electronic databases for workers and employees in their organizations.

From a library perspective, IM concerns the management of information collections, such as books and journals. The goal of IM from a library perspective is to help library patrons access and borrow information items held in the collection. A variety of activities surround the management of a library collection, including the development of collection policies and materials budgets, the selection of collection items, the analysis of collection usage and end-user collection needs, training of collection staff, preservation of collection items, and the development of cooperative collections with other institutions.[27]

Since libraries are neither the creators nor the users of information, this perspective deals with the management of a subset of information processes involved in the information life cycle. For example, Wilson identifies six information-related processes pertaining to IM that are applicable to the library perspective: 1) acquisition; 2) organization; 3) storage; 4) retrieval; 5) access/lending; and 6) dissemination.[7]

Information acquisition involves the process of buying or securing information from sources external to the library for the collection. Care must be taken to ensure that the correct information items are acquired (those that match the information needs of end users) and at reasonable costs.

Information organization pertains to the process of indexing or classifying information housed in the collection to support easy retrieval at later points in time. Today, this process is sometimes referred to as "knowledge organization" in the library world. For example, the International Society for Knowledge Organization (ISKO) utilizes the term "knowledge organization" to represent the process of how documents, document representations (such as bibliographic records), and concepts (keywords, constructs) are ordered and classified.[28] Likewise, Anderson defines knowledge organization as "the description of documents, their contents, features and purposes, and the organization of these

descriptions so as to make these documents and their parts accessible to persons seeking them or the messages that they contain" and describes how knowledge organization encompasses "every type and method of indexing, abstracting, cataloging, classification, records management, bibliography and the creation of textual or bibliographic databases for information retrieval."[29] In this sense, knowledge organization deals with both processes and systems.[30] With respect to IM, this entry suggests that the use of the "knowledge organization" label is misleading. In actuality, information items (such as documents and document representations) are being organized or ordered (i.e., indexed, classified, and cataloged) rather than knowledge items (concepts, constructs) per se. As such, "information organization" is suggested to be a better label to use when talking about the indexing and classification of items held in a collection, at least from a library perspective of IM.

Information storage refers to physically housing items in the collection. This encompasses the housing of both paper and electronic documents (and their document representations). This could be accomplished by storing books and journals in physical stacks in the library or storing full-text electronic versions of documents in an electronic or digital library.

Information retrieval involves the process of searching and finding information in the collection. Typically, end users will conduct a search query using electronic tools that are Webbased to find items of interest in the collection. In the information retrieval process, end users themselves, or information search intermediaries (librarians) working on the behalf of end users, "pull" the information that is needed from the collection.

Information access/lending involves the process of providing physical or electronic access to the collection and the ability to check out information items of interest. For paper-based documents, this may involve signing out and borrowing a physical information item. For information in electronic form, this may involve viewing the information item online and/or downloading a copy of the information item from the collection.

Information dissemination is the process of circulating physical information items of interest from the collection to end users. Traditionally, methods of dissemination involve the distribution of photocopied journal content pages, or the circulation of documents. Today, this has largely been replaced with electronic alert services that "push" information items in the collection of interest to specific users based on stored end-user profiles.

The management of library information collections is a complex and ever-evolving process.[31] The extensive digitization of information resources has placed new pressures on libraries to respond to securing the requisite skills, resources, and competencies to successfully manage digital library collections.[32] In order to manage the transition and reliance on digital information collections, it is important more than ever for libraries to consider the expectations and needs of end users, as well as limitations in library staff and budget adaptability.[31] These are critical factors in rolling out any successful IM program from a library perspective.

THE PERSONAL PERSPECTIVE

IM from the personal perspective refers to how individuals create, acquire, organize, store, distribute, and use information for personal purposes. This can concern the management of information for everyday use (e.g., personal calendars, schedules, diaries, and news items) or work-related reasons (e.g., work schedules, things to do, and project files). As such, personal information management involves the handling and processing of information over the entire information life cycle, just as in the case of the organizational perspective. However, the personal information management perspective differs from the organizational perspective of IM in that personal information management concerns items of interest to the individual, not the organization.

Central to the personal perspective of IM is the need to manage the information processes of information creation, acquisition, organization, distribution, and use so that the right information is accessible and available in the right place, in the right form, and of sufficient completeness and quality to meet personal information needs. A variety of information items are created, acquired, organized, stored, distributed, and used by people for personal purposes. These include personal notes, personal journals, Web pages, e-mail messages, news articles, address books, calendar dates, reminders, and fax communications.

Technologies and tools, such as electronic personal information managers like PDAs, help people carry out these processes more efficiently and effectively.[33] Cheap and fast search and storage technologies bring stability and order to people's often chaotic and messy personal information environments, and facilitate making the most of people's personal information collections.[34] Despite the benefits of these technological tools, there is some evidence to suggest that technological advances are less important in determining how individuals organize and use information than are the tasks that people perform.[35]

It is interesting to note that the phrase "personal information management" was first used in the 1980s with the advent of personal computers and their capacity to process and manage information.[36] However, the concept of "personal information management" was most likely first implied back in 1945 by Vannevar Bush when he envisioned using the "Memex" machine for personal information management—a machine that allowed an individual to store all his or her books, records, and communications and consult those personal information sources with great speed and flexibility.[37]

As the proliferation of personal computing devices and the explosion of the amount of information that is created, generated, and used continues to increase, the relevance of IM from the personal perspective will likely gain more attention and importance from both researchers and practitioners alike.

CONCLUSION

This entry provided a review and discussion of the IM concept. Importantly, a process-oriented definition of IM was proposed and three distinct perspectives of IM were described: the organizational, library, and personal perspectives. It was suggested that the organizational perspective was the most predominant, though the other two were shown to have relevance and meaning in today's world.

This entry emphasized the importance of IM. IM allows organizations to reach strategic goals and make sound decisions. IM enables libraries and other information provision organizations to manage information collections effectively and efficiently. IM helps people manage their own personal information collections.

This entry also described how IM is not so much about the management of technology, but rather more about the management of the processes of IM, specifically the creation, acquisition, organization, storage, distribution, and usage of information.

According to the prevalent scope of the *International Journal of Information Management*, the challenge for IM now is less about managing activities that collect, store, and disseminate information, and more about placing greater focus on managing activities that make changes in patterns of behavior of customers, people, and organizations, and information that leads to changes in the way people use information.[38] This may not be such an easy task. People and their information behaviors are hard to change. So are organizational cultures.[11] IM is less about solving technical problems and more about addressing the human side of IM. Humans add the context, meaning, and value to information, and it is humans who benefit and use this information. As such, "mastering information management is an essentially human task."[39]

REFERENCES

1. Choo, C.W. In *Information Management for the Intelligent Organization: The Art of Environmental Scanning*; 3rd Ed.; Learned Information: Medford, NJ, 2002.

2. Macevičiūtė, E.; Wilson, T.D. The development of the information management research area. Inform. Res. **2002**, 7 (3), http://InformationR.net/ir/7-3/paper133.html (accessed July 2008).

3. Wilson, T.D. Information management. In *International Encyclopedia of Information and Library Science*; Routledge: London, 2003; 263–278.

4. http://www. GAO.gov.

5. Davenport, T.H. In *Process Innovation: Reengineering Work Through Information Technology*; Harvard Business School Press: Boston, MA, 1993.

6. McGee, J.V.; Prusak, L. In *Managing Information Strategically*; John Wiley & Sons: Toronto, ON, 1993.

7. Wilson, T.D. 'The nonsense of knowledge management' revisited. In *Introducing Information Management*; Macevičiūtė, E., Wilson, T.D., Eds.; Facet Publishing: London, 2005; 151–164.

8. Karim, N.S.A.; Hussein, R. Managers' perception of information management and the role of information and knowledge managers: The Malaysian perspectives. Int. J. Inform. Manage. **2008**, 28 (2), 114–127.

9. Detlor, B. In *Towards Knowledge Portals: From Human Issues to Intelligent Agents*; Kluwer Academic Publishers: Dordrecht, The Netherlands, 2004.

10. Robertson, J. Ten principles of effective information management. KM Column 2005, November http://www. steptwo.com.au/papers/kmc_effectiveim/index.html (accessed July 2008).

11. http://choo.fis.utoronto.ca/Imfaq/

12. Commission on Federal Paperwork, In *Information Resources Management*; U.S. Government Printing Office: Washington, DC, 1977.

13. Horton, F.W. In *Information Resources Management: Concept and Cases*; Association for Systems Management: Cleveland, OH, 1979.

14. Horton, F.W. In *The Information Management Workbook: IRM Made Simple*; Information Management Press: Washington, DC, 1982.

15. Lewis, B.R.; Snyder, C.A.; Rainer, R.K., Jr. An empirical assessment of the information resource management construct. J. Manage. Inform. Syst. **1995**, 12 (1), 199–223.

16. Baltzan, P.; Phillips, A.; Detlor, B. In *Business-Driven Information Systems*; 1st Canadian Ed.; McGraw-Hill Ryerson: Whitby, ON, 2008.

17. Sutton, H. In *Competitive Intelligence*; The Conference Board Inc.: New York, NY, 1988.

18. Aguilar, F.J. In *Scanning the Business Environment*; MacMillan Co.: New York, NY, 1967.

19. Choo, C.W.; Auster, E. Scanning the business environment: Acquisition and use of information by managers. In *Annual Review of Information Science and Technology*; Williams, M.E., Ed.; Learned Information: Medford, NJ, 1993.

20. Robek, M.F.; Brown, G.F.; Wilmer, O.M. In *Information and Records Management*; 3rd Ed.; Glencoe Publishing: Encino, CA, 1987.

21. http://www.simnet.org.

22. Davis, G.B.; Hamilton, S. In *Managing Information: How Information Systems Impact Organizational Strategy*; Business One Irwin: Homewood, IL, 1993.

23. Choo, C.W. Towards an informational model of organizations. Can. J. Inform. Sci. **1991**, 16 (3), 32–62.

24. Simon, H. In *Administrative Behavior: A Study of Decision-Making Processes in Administrative Organization*; 3rd Ed.; The Free Press: New York, NY, 1976.

25. Galbraith, J.R. In *Organization Design*; Addison-Wesley: Reading, MA, 1977.

26. Weick, K.E.; Daft, R.L. The effectiveness of interpretation systems. In *Organizational Effectiveness: A Comparison of Multiple Models,* Cameron, K.S., Whetten, D.A., Eds.; Academic Press: New York, NY, 1983; 71–93.

27. In *Collection Management in the 1990s,* Branin, J.J., Ed.; American Library Association: Chicago, IL, 1993.

28. http://www.isko.org/ko.html.

29. Anderson, J.D. Organization of knowledge. In *International Encyclopedia of Information and Library Science*, Feather, J., Sturges, P., Eds.; Routledge: London, U.K., 1996; 336–353.

30. http://www.db.dk/bh/lifeboat_ko/CONCEPTS/ knowledge_organization.htm.

31. Branin, J.; Groen, F.; Thorin, S. The changing nature of collection management in research libraries. Libr. Resour. Tech. Serv. **2000**, 44 (1), 23–32.

32. Sreenivasulu, V. The role of a digital librarian in the management of digital information systems (DIS). Electron. Libr. **2000**, 18 (1), 12–20.

33. Jones, W. In *Keeping Found Things Found: The Study and Practice of Personal Information Management*; Morgan Kaufmann Publishers: Burlington, MA, 2008.

34. Teevan, J.; Jones, W.; Bederson, B.B. Personal information management. Commun. ACM **2006**, 49 (1), 40–43.

35. Barreau, D. The persistence of behavior and form in the organization of personal information. J. Am. Soc. Inform. Sci. Technol. **2008**, 59 (2), 307–317.

36. Lansdale, M. The psychology of personal information management. Appl. Ergon. **1988**, 19 (1), 55–66.

37. Bush, V. As we may think. The Atlantic Monthly **1945**, July, 176 (1), 101–108.

38. http://www.elsevier.com/wps/find/journaldescription.cws_ home/30434/description#description.

39. Davenport, T. Putting the I in IT. *Mastering Information Management*; Pearson Education: London, U.K., 2000.

Information Protection

Rebecca Herold
Information Privacy, Security and Compliance Consultant, Rebecca Herold and Associates LLC, Van Meter, Iowa, U.S.A.

Abstract

Successful information protection and security requires the participation, compliance, and support of all personnel within an organization, regardless of their positions, locations, or relationships with the company. This includes any person who has been granted access to the organization's extended enterprise information, and any employee, contractor, vendor, or business associate of the company who uses information systems resources as part of the job. A brief overview of the information protection and security responsibilities for various groups within an organization follows.

ALL PERSONNEL WITHIN THE ORGANIZATION

All personnel have an obligation to use the information according to the specific protection requirements established by an organization's information owner or information security delegate. A few of the basic obligations include, but are not limited to, the following:

- Maintaining confidentiality of log-on passwords
- Ensuring the security of information entrusted to their care
- Using the organization's business assets and information resources for approved purposes only
- Adhering to all information security policies, procedures, standards, and guidelines
- Promptly reporting security incidents to the appropriate management area

Information Security Oversight Committee

An information protection and/or security oversight committee comprising representatives from various areas of an organization should exist or be created if not already in existence. The members should include high-level representatives from each of the revenue business units, as well as a representative from the organization's legal, corporate auditing, human resources, physical and facilities management, and finance and accounting areas. The oversight committee should be responsible for ensuring and supporting the establishment, implementation, and maintenance of information protection awareness and training programs to assist management in the security of corporate information assets. Additionally, the committee should be kept informed of all information security-related issues, new technologies, and provide input for information security, protection costs, and budget approvals.

Corporate Auditing

The corporate auditing department should be responsible for ensuring compliance with information protection and security policies, standards, procedures, and guidelines. They should ensure that the organizational business units are operating in a manner consistent with policies and standards, and ensure any audit plan includes a compliance review of applicable information protection policies and standards that are related to the audit topic. Additionally, a high-level management member of the corporate auditing department should play an active role in the organization's information security oversight committee.

Human Resources

The human resources department of an organization should be responsible for providing timely information to the centrally managed information protection department, as well as the enterprise and division systems managers and application administrators, about corporate personnel terminations or transfers. They should also enforce the stated consequences of non-compliance with the corporate policies, and a high-level member of the human resources department should play an active role in the organization's information security oversight committee.

Law

The law department should assign to someone the responsibility for reviewing the enterprise security policies and standards for legal and regulatory compliance and enforceability. The law department should also be advised of and responsible for addressing legal issues arising from security incidents. Additionally, a high-

Encyclopedia of Information Systems and Technology, DOI: 10.1081/E-EIST-120046578

level member of the law department should play an active role in the organization's information security oversight committee. This person should be savvy with computer and information technology (IT) and related issues; otherwise, the person will not make a positive contribution to the oversight committee, and could, in fact, create unnecessary roadblocks or stop necessary progress owing to lack of knowledge of the issues.

Managers

The organization's line management should retain primary responsibility for identifying and protecting information and computer assets within their assigned areas of management control. When talking about a manager, one is referring to any person who has been specifically given responsibility for directing the actions of others and overseeing their work—basically, the immediate manager or supervisor of an employee. Managers have ultimate responsibility for all user identity documents (IDs) and information owned by company employees in the areas of their control. In the case of nonemployee individuals, such as contractors, consultants, and so on, managers are responsible for the activity and the company assets used by these individuals. These managers are the ones usually responsible for hiring the outside party. Managers have additional information protection and security responsibilities including, but not limited to, the following:

* Continually monitor the practices of employees and consultants under their control and take necessary corrective actions to ensure compliance with the organization's policies and standards.
* Inform the appropriate security administration department of the termination of any employee so that the user ID owned by that individual can be revoked, suspended, or made inaccessible in a timely manner.
* Inform the appropriate security administration department of the transfer of any employee if the transfer involves the change of access rights or privileges.
* Report any security incident or suspected incident to the centralized information protection department.
* Ensure the currency of user ID information (e.g., employee identification number and account information of the user ID owner).
* Educate the employees in their area of the organization's security policies, procedures, and standards for which they are accountable.

IT Administrators (Information Delegates)

A person, organization, or process that implements or administers security controls for the information owners is referred to as an information delegate. Such information delegates typically (but not always) are part of the IT departments with primary responsibilities for dealing with backup and recovery of the business information, applying and updating information access controls, installing and maintaining information security technology, and systems and so on.

An information delegate is also any company employee who owns a user ID that has been assigned attributes or privileges associated with access control systems, such as Top Secret, RACF, ACF2 and so on. This user ID allows them to set system-wide security controls or administrator user IDs and information resource access rights. These security and systems administrators may report to either a business division or the central information protection department.

Information delegates are also responsible for implementing and administering security controls for corporate extended enterprise information as instructed by the information owner or delegate. Some of the responsibilities of information delegates include, but are not limited to, the following:

* Perform backups according to the backup requirements established by the information owner.
* Document backup schedule, backup intervals, storage locations, and number of backup generation copies.
* Regularly test backups to ensure they can be used successfully to restore data.
* When necessary, restore lost or corrupted information from backup media to return the application to production status.
* Perform related tape and direct access storage device management functions as required to ensure availability of the information to the business.
* Ensure record retention requirements are met based on the information owner's analysis.
* Implement and administer security controls for corporate extended enterprise information as instructed by the information owner or delegate.
* Electronically store information in locations based on classification.
* Specifically identify the privileges associated with each system, and categorize the staff allocated to these privileges.
* Produce security log reports that will report applications and system violations and incidents to the central information protection department.
* Understand the different data environments and the impact of granting access to them.
* Ensure access requests are consistent with the information directions and security guidelines.
* Administer access rights according to criteria established by the information owners.
* Create and remove user IDs as directed by the appropriate managers.

- Administer the system within the scope of the job description and functional responsibilities.
- Distribute and follow up on security violation reports.
- Report suspected security breaches to your central information protection department.
- Give passwords of newly created user IDs to the user ID owner only.
- Maintain responsibility for day-to-day security of information.

Information Asset and Systems Owners

The information asset owner for a specific data item is a management position within the business area facing the greatest negative impact from disclosure or loss of that information. The information asset owner is ultimately responsible for ensuring that appropriate protection requirements for the information assets are defined and implemented. The information owner responsibilities include, but are not limited to, the following:

- Assign initial information classification and periodically review the classification to ensure it still meets the business needs.
- Ensure security controls are in place and commensurate with the information classification.
- Review and ensure currency of the access rights associated with information assets they own.
- Determine security requirements, access criteria, and backup requirements for the information assets they own.
- Report suspected security breaches to corporate security.
- Perform, or delegate if desired, the following:
  ○ Approval authority for access requests from other business units or assign a delegate in the same business unit as the executive or manager owner.
  ○ Backup and recovery duties or assign to the information custodian.
  ○ Approval of the disclosure of information.
  ○ Act on notifications received concerning security violations against their information assets.
  ○ Determine information availability requirements.
  ○ Assess information risks.

Systems owners must consider three fundamental security areas: management controls, operational controls, and technical controls. They must follow the direction and requests of the information owners when establishing access controls in these three areas.

Information Protection

An area should exist that is responsible for determining your organization's information protection and security

directions (strategies, procedures, guidelines), as approved or suggested by the information protection oversight committee, to ensure information is controlled and secured based on its value, risk of loss or compromise, and ease of recoverability. As a very high overview, some of the responsibilities of an information protection department include, but are not limited to, the following:

- Provide information security guidelines to the information management process.
- Develop a basic understanding of your organization's information to ensure proper controls are implemented.
- Provide information security design input, consulting, and review.
- Ensure appropriate security controls are built into new applications.
- Provide information security expertise and support for electronic interchange.
- Create information protection audit standards and baselines.
- Help reduce the organization's liability by demonstrating a standard of due care or diligence by following general standards or practices of professional care.
- Help ensure awareness of information protection and security issues throughout the entire organization and act as internal information security consultants to project members.
- Promote and evaluate information and computer security in IT products and services.
- Advise others within the organization of information security needs and requirements.

The remainder of this entry includes a full discussion of the roles and related issues of the information protection department.

WHAT IS THE ROLE OF INFORMATION PROTECTION?

Secure information and network systems are essential to providing high-quality services to customers, avoiding fraud and disclosure of sensitive information, promoting efficient business operations, and complying with laws and regulations. The organization must make information protection a visible, integral component of all business operations. The best way to accomplish this is to establish a department dedicated to ensuring the protection of all the information assets of the organization throughout every department and process. Information protection, or information security, is a very broad discipline.

The information protection department should fulfill five basic roles:

1. Support information risk management processes.
2. Create corporate information protection policies and procedures.
3. Ensure information protection awareness and training.
4. Ensure the integration of information protection into all management practices.
5. Support the organization's business objectives.

Risk Management

Risk management is a necessary element of a comprehensive information protection and security program. What is risk management? The General Accounting Office (GAO) has a good, high-level definition: risk management is the process of assessing risk, taking steps to reduce risk to an acceptable level, and maintaining that level of risk. There are four basic principles of effective risk management.

Assess risk and determine needs

The organization must recognize that information is an essential asset that must be protected. When high-level executives understand and demonstrate that managing risks is important and necessary, it will help to ensure that security is taken seriously at lower levels in the organization and that security programs have adequate resources.

The organization must develop practical risk assessment procedures that clearly link security to business needs. However, spend too much time must not be spent trying to quantify the risks precisely—the difficulty in identifying such data makes the task inefficient and overly time consuming.

The organization must hold program and business managers accountable for ensuring compliance with information protection policies, procedures, and standards. The accountability factor will help ensure that managers understand the importance of information protection and not dismiss it, considering it a hindrance.

The risks must be managed on a continuing basis. As new technologies evolve, one must stay abreast of the associated risks to information assets. And, as new information protection tools become available, one must know how such tools can help mitigate risks within the organization.

Establish a central information protection and risk management focus

The information protection department will focus on central information protection and risk management.

Key information protection risk management activities must be carried out. The information protection department will serve as a catalyst for ensuring that information security risks are considered in planned and ongoing operations. There is a need to provide advice and expertise to all organizational levels and keep managers informed about security issues. Information protection should research potential threats, vulnerabilities, and control techniques, and test controls, assess risks, and identify needed policies.

The information protection department must have ready and independent access to senior executives. Security concerns can often be at odds with the desires of business managers and system developers when they are developing new computer applications—they want to do so quickly and want to avoid controls that they view as impeding efficiency and convenience. By elevating security concerns to higher management levels, it helps ensure that the risks are understood by those with the most to lose from information security incidents and that information security is taken into account when decisions are made.

The information protection department must have dedicated funding and staff. Information protection budgets need to cover central staff salaries, training and awareness costs, and security software and hardware.

The central information protection department must strive to enhance the professionalism and technical skills of the staff. It is important in fulfilling one's role as a trusted information security advisor to be informed on new information security vulnerabilities as well as new information security tools and practices.

Information and systems security must be cost-effective

The costs and benefits of security must be carefully examined in both monetary and nonmonetary terms to ensure that the cost of controls does not exceed expected benefits. Security benefits have direct and indirect costs. Direct costs include purchasing, installing, and administering security measures, such as access control software or fire-suppression systems. Indirect costs include system performance, employee morale, and retraining requirements.

Information and systems security must be periodically reassessed

Security is never perfect when a system is implemented. Systems users and operators discover new vulnerabilities or ways to intentionally or accidentally circumvent security. Changes in the system or the environment can also create new vulnerabilities. Procedures become outdated over time. All these issues make it necessary to periodically reassess the effectiveness of the organization's security.

Information Protection Policies, Procedures, Standards, and Guidelines

The information protection department must create corporate information protection policies with business unit input and support. Additionally, they must provide guidance and training to help the individual business units create their own procedures, standards, and guidelines that support the corporate information protection policies.

Information protection department must create and implement appropriate policies and related controls

There is a need to link the information protection policies created to the business risks of the organization. The information protection policies must be adjusted on a continuing basis to respond to newly identified risks. Paying particular attention to addressing user behavior within the information protection policies must be ensured.

Distinguish between information protection policies and guidelines or standards. Policies generally outline fundamental requirements that managers consider mandatory. Guidelines and standards contain more detailed rules on how to implement the policies.

It is vital to the success of the information protection policies for the oversight group and executive management to visibly support the organization's information protection policies.

Information and systems security is often constrained by societal factors

The ability of the information protection department to support the mission of the organization may be limited by various social factors depending upon the country in which its offices are located, or the laws and regulations that exist within certain locations where the organization does business. The information protection department must know the operating environments and ensure the organization's policies are in sync with these environments.

Awareness and Training

The information protection department must make the organization aware of information protection policies, related issues, and news on an ongoing basis. Additionally, adequate training must be provided—not only to help ensure personnel know how to address information security risks and threats, but also to keep the information protection department personnel up-to-date on the most appropriate methods of ensuring information security.

An information protection department must promote awareness of information protection issues and concerns throughout your entire organization

The information protection department must continually educate users and others on risks and related policies. Merely sending out a memo to the management once every year or two is not sufficient. Use attention-getting and user-friendly techniques to promote awareness of information protection issues. Awareness techniques do not need to be dry or boring—they should not be, or the personnel will not take notice of the message one is trying to send.

An information protection department must monitor and evaluate policy and control effectiveness of the policies

The information protection department needs to monitor factors that affect risk and indicate security effectiveness. One key to success is to keep summary records of actual security incidents within the organization to measure the types of violations and the damage suffered from the incidents. These records will be valuable input for risk assessments and budget decisions. The results of monitoring and record keeping can help to determine subsequent information protection efforts and hold managers accountable for the activities and incidents that occur. Staying aware of new information protection and security monitoring tools and techniques is must to address the issues found during monitoring.

An information protection department must extend security responsibilities to those outside the organization

The organization and the systems owners have security responsibilities outside the organization. They have a responsibility to share appropriate knowledge about the existence and extent of security measures with the external users (e.g., customers, business partners and so on) for them to be confident that the systems are adequately secured and can help to address any risks that is communicated to them.

An information protection department must make security responsibilities explicit

Information and systems security responsibilities and accountability must be clearly and explicitly documented and communicated. The information security responsibilities of all groups and audiences within the organization must be communicated to them, using effective methods and on an ongoing basis.

Management Practices

Information and systems security must be an integral element of sound management practices. Ultimately, managers of the areas owning the information must decide what level of risk they are willing to accept, taking into account the cost of security controls as well as the potential financial impact of not having the security controls. The information protection department must help the management understand the risks and associated costs. Information and systems security requires a comprehensive approach that is integrated within the organization's management practices. The information protection department also needs to work with traditional security disciplines, such as physical and personnel security. To help integrate information protection within the management practices, use the following:

- Establish a process to coordinate implementation of information security measures. The process should coordinate specific information security roles and responsibilities organization-wide, and it should aid agreement about specific information security methods and processes, such as risk assessment and a security classification system. Additionally, the process should facilitate coordination of organization-wide security initiatives and promote integration of security into the organizational information planning process. The process should call for implementation of specific security measures for new systems or services and include guidelines for reviewing information security incidents. Also, the process should promote visible business support for information security throughout the organization.
- Establish a management approval process to centrally authorize new IT facilities from both a business and technical standpoint.
- Make managers responsible for maintaining the local information system security environment and supporting the corporate information protection policies when they approve new facilities, systems, and applications.
- Establish procedures to check hardware and software to ensure compatibility with other system components before implementing them into the corporate systems environment.
- Create a centralized process for authorizing the use of personal information processing systems and facilities for use in processing business information. Include processes to ensure necessary controls are

implemented. In conjunction with this, ensure the vulnerabilities inherent in using personal information processing systems and facilities for business purposes have been assessed.

- Ensure management uses the information protection department for specialized information security advice and guidance.
- Create a liaison between the information protection department and external information security organizations, including industry and government security specialists, law enforcement authorities, IT service providers, and telecommunications authorities, to stay abreast with new information security threats and technologies and to learn from the experiences of others.
- Establish management procedures to ensure that the exchange of security information with outside entities is restricted so that confidential organizational information is not divulged to unauthorized persons.
- Ensure information protection policies and practices throughout the organization are independently reviewed to ensure feasibility, effectiveness, and compliance with written policies.

Business Objectives

Information protection must support the business needs, objectives, and mission statement of the organization.

Information and systems security practices must support the mission of the organization. Through the selection and application of appropriate safeguards, the information protection department will help the organization's mission by protecting its physical and electronic information and financial resources, reputation, legal position, employees, and other tangible and intangible assets. Well-chosen information security policies and procedures do not exist for their own sake—they are put in place to protect the organization's assets and support the organizational mission. Information security is a means to an end, and not an end in itself. In a private-sector business, having good security is usually secondary to the need to make a profit. With this in mind, security ought to be seen as a way to increase the firm's ability to make a profit. In a public sector agency, security is usually secondary to the agency's provision of services to citizens. Security, in this case then, ought to be considered as a way to help improve the service provided to the public.

So, what is a good mission statement for the information protection department? It really depends upon the business, environment, company size, industry, and several other factors. To determine the information protection department's mission statement, ask yourself these questions:

- What do the personnel, systems users, and customers expect with regard to information and systems security controls and procedures?
- Will the organization lose valued staff or customers if information and systems security is not taken seriously enough, or if it is implemented in such a manner that functionality is noticeably impaired?
- Has any downtime or monetary loss occurred within the organization as a result of security incidents?
- Is the organization concerned about insider threats? Does it trust its users? Are most of the systems users local or remote?
- Does the organization keep non-public information online? What is the loss to the organization if this information is compromised or stolen?
- What would be the impact of negative publicity if the organization suffered an information security incident?
- Are there security guidelines, regulations, or laws the organization is required to meet?
- How important are confidentiality, integrity, and availability to the overall operation of the organization?
- Have the information and network security decisions that have been made been consistent with the business needs and economic stance of the organization?

To help get started with creating an information protection department mission statement, here is an example to use in conjunction with considering the previous questions:

> The mission of the information protection department is to ensure the confidentiality, integrity, and availability of the organization's information; provide information protection guidance to the organization's personnel; and help ensure compliance with information security laws and regulations while promoting the organization's mission statement, business initiatives, and objectives.

Information Protection Budgeting

What should be the organization's budget for information protection? One will not like the answer; however, there is no benchmark for what information protection and security could or should cost within organizations. The variables from organization to organization are too great for such a number. Plus, it really depends upon how information protection and security costs are spread throughout the organization and where the information protection department is located within the organization.

Most information and network security spending recommendations are in extremes. The Gartner Group research in 2000 showed that government agencies spent 3.3% of their IT budgets on security—a significantly

higher average percentage than all organizations as a whole spent on security (2.6%). Both numbers represent a very low amount to spend to protect an organization's information assets. Then there is the opinion of a former chief security officer (CSO) at an online trading firm who believes the information security budget should be 4–10% of *total company revenues* and not part of the IT budget at all. An October 2001, *Computerworld*/J.P. Morgan security poll had showed that companies with annual revenues of more than $500 million were expected to spend the most on security in 2002, when security-related investments would have accounted for 11.2% of total IT budgets on average, compared with an average of 10.3% for all the users that responded to the poll. However, there are other polls, such as a 2001 survey from Metricnet, that showed that only 33% of companies polled after September 11, 2001, had spent more than 5% of their IT budgets on security. What is probably the most realistic target for information security spending is the one given by eSecurityOnline.com, which indicates information protection should be 3–5% of the company's total revenue.

Unfortunately, it has been documented in more than one news report that some CIOs do not consider information security a normal or prudent business expense. Some CFOs and CEOs have been quoted as saying information security expenses were "nuisance protection." Some decision makers need hard evidence of a security threat to their companies before they will respond. But doing nothing is not a viable option. It only takes one significant security incident to bring down a company.

When budgeting for information protection, keep in mind the facts and experiences of others. As the San Francisco-based Computer Security Institute found in its 2001 annual Computer Crime and Security Survey, 85% of the respondents admitted they had detected computer security breaches during the year. Although only 35% of the respondents admitted to being able to quantify the losses, the total financial impact from these incidents was a staggering $378 million in losses.

The CIO of the Department of Energy's Lawrence Livermore National Laboratory in Livermore, California, indicated in 2001 that security incidents had risen steadily by about 20% a year. Security of information is not a declining issue; it is an increasingly significant issue to address. Basically, security is a matter of existence or nonexistence for data.

So, to help establish the information protection budget:

- *Establish need before cost.* If the organization knows money is going to be a stumbling block, then it must not lead with a budget request. Instead, a break down of the company's functions by business process will illustrate how these processes are tied to the company's information and network. Ask executive management, "What do you want to protect?" and then show them, "This is what it will cost to do it."

- *Show them numbers.* It is not enough to talk about information security threats in broad terms. The point must be made with numbers. Track the number of attempted intrusions, security incidents, and viruses within the organization. Document them in reports and plot them on graphs. Present them monthly to the executive management. This will provide evidence of the growing information security threat.
- *Use others' losses to one's own advantage.* One must show them what has happened to other companies. Use the annual Computer Security Institute/Federal Bureau of Investigation computer crime and security statistics. Give the executive managers copies of *Tangled Web* by Richard Power to show them narratives of exactly what has happened to other companies.
- *Put it in legal terms.* Corporate officers are not only accountable for protecting their businesses' financial assets, but are also responsible for maintaining critical information. The executive management must be reminded that it has a fiduciary responsibility to detect and protect areas where information assets might be exposed.
- *Keep it simple.* Divide the budget into categories and indicate needed budgets within each. Suggested categories include:
  ○ Personnel
  ○ Software systems
  ○ Hardware systems
  ○ Awareness and training
  ○ Law and regulation compliance
  ○ Emerging technology research
  ○ Business continuity
- *Show them where it hurts.* Simply state the impact of not implementing or funding security.

EXECUTIVE MANAGEMENT MUST SPONSOR AND SUPPORT INFORMATION PROTECTION

Executive management must clearly and unequivocally support information protection and security initiatives. It must provide a role model for the rest of the organization that adhering to information protection policies and practices is the right thing to do. It must ensure information protection is built into the management framework. The management framework should be established to initiate and control the implementation of information security within the organization. Ideally, the structure of a security program should result from the implementation of a planned and integrated management philosophy. Managing computer security at multiple levels brings many benefits. The higher levels (such as the

headquarters or unit levels) must understand the organization as a whole, exercise more authority, set policy, and enforce compliance with applicable policies and procedures. On the other hand, the systems levels (such as the computer facility and applications levels) know the technical and procedural requirements and problems. The information protection department addresses the overall management of security within the organization as well as corporate activities such as policy development and oversight. The system-level security program can then focus on the management of security for a particular information processing system. A central information protection department can disseminate security-related information throughout the organization in an efficient and cost-effective manner. A central information protection department has an increased ability to influence external and internal policy decisions. A central information protection department can help ensure spending its scarce security dollars more efficiently. Another advantage of a centralized program is its ability to negotiate discounts based on volume purchasing of security hardware and software.

Where Does the Information Security Role Best Fit within the Organization?

Information security should be separated from operations. When the security program is embedded in IT operations, the security program often lacks independence, exercises minimal authority, receives little management attention, and lacks resources. In fact, the GAO identified this type of organizational mode (information security as part of IT operations) as a principal basic weakness in federal agency IT security programs.

The location of the information protection department needs to be based on the organization's goals, structure, and culture. To be effective, a central information protection department must be an established part of organization management.

Should information protection be a separate business unit reporting to the CEO?

This is the ideal situation. Korn/Ferry's Jim Bock, a recruiter who specializes in IT and information security placements, has noticed that more CSOs are starting to report directly to the CEO, on a peer level to the CIO. This provides information protection with a direct line to executive management and demonstrates the importance of information security to the rest of the organization.

Should information protection be a separate business unit reporting to the CIO?

This is becoming more commonplace. This could be an effective area for the information protection group. However, there exists conflict of interest in this position. Additionally, security budgets may get cut to increase spending in the other IT areas for which the CIO has responsibility. Based upon latter-day history and published reports, CIOs tend to focus more on technology and security; they may not understand the diverse information protection needs that extend beyond the IT arena.

Should information protection be a separate business unit reporting to the CFO?

This could possibly work if the CFO also understands the information security finance issues. However, it is not likely because it is difficult (if not impossible) to show a return on investment for information security costs; so this may not be a good location for the information protection department.

Should information protection exist as a department within IT reporting to the IT VP?

This is generally not a good idea. Not only does this create a true conflict of interest, but it also demonstrates to the rest of the organization an attitude of decreased importance of information security within the organization. It creates a competition of security dollars with other IT dollars. Additionally, it sends the message that information protection is only a technical matter and does not extend to all areas of business processes (such as hard-copy protection, voice, fax, mail, etc.).

Should information protection exist as a group within corporate auditing reporting to the corporate auditor?

This has been attempted within several large organizations, and none have had success with this arrangement. Not only does this create a huge conflict of interest—auditors cannot objectively audit and evaluate the same security practices the people within their same area created—but it also sends the message to the rest of the organization that information security professionals fill the same role as auditors.

Should information protection exist as a group within human resources reporting to the HR VP?

This could work. One advantage of this arrangement is that the area creating the information protection policies would be within the same area as the people who enforce the policies from a disciplinary aspect. However, this could also create a conflict of interest. Also, by placing information protection within the HR area, you could send the message to the rest of the organization that information protection is a type of police unit; and it could also place it too far from executive management.

Should information protection exist within facilities management reporting to the risk management director?

This does place all types of risk functions together, making it easier to link physical and personnel security with information security. However, this could be too far removed from executive management to be effective.

Should information protection exist as a group within IT reporting to middle management?

This is probably the worst place to put the information protection group. Not only is this too far removed from executive management, but this also creates a conflict of interest with the IT processes to which information security practices apply. It also sends a message to the rest of the organization that information protection is not of significant importance to the entire organization and that it only applies to the organization's computer systems.

What Security Positions Should Exist, and What are the Roles, Requirements, and Job Descriptions for Each?

Responsibilities for accomplishing information security requirements must be clearly defined. The information security policy should provide general guidance on the allocation of security roles and responsibilities within the organization. General information security roles and responsibilities must be supplemented with a more detailed local interpretation for specific sites, systems, and services. The security of an information system must be made the responsibility of the owner of that system. To avoid any misunderstanding about individual responsibilities, assets and security processes associated with each individual must be clearly defined. To avoid misunderstanding individual responsibilities, the manager responsible for each asset or security process must be assigned and documented and alsoauthorization levels must be defined and documented. Multiple levels of dedicated information security positions must exist to ensure full and successful integration of information protection into all aspects of the organization's business processes. So what positions are going to accomplish all these tasks? A few example job descriptions can be found in Table 1. The following are some suggestions of

Table 1 Example job descriptions

The following job descriptions should provide a reference to help create unique job descriptions for information security-related positions based upon the organization's needs.

Compliance officer

Job description

A regulatory/compliance attorney to monitor, interpret, and communicate laws and legislation impacting regulation. Such laws and legislation include Health Insurance Portability and Accountability Act of 1996 (HIPAA) regulations. The compliance officer will be responsible for compliance and quality control covering all areas within the IT and operations areas. Responsibilities include:

- Quality assurance
- Approval and release of all personal health information
- HIPAA compliance oversight and implementation
- Ensuring all records and activities are maintained acceptably in accordance with health and regulatory authorities

Qualifications

- J. D. with outstanding academics and a minimum of 10 years of experience
- Three to five years' existing experience with healthcare compliance and regulatory issues
- In-depth familiarity with federal and state regulatory matters (Medicare, Medicaid, fraud, privacy, abuse, etc.)

Chief security officer

Job description:

The role of the information security department is primarily to safeguard the confidential information, assets, and intellectual property that belongs to or is processed by the organization. The scope of this position primarily involves computer security but also covers physical security as it relates to the safeguarding of information and assets. The CSO is responsible for enforcing the information security policy, creating new procedures, and reviewing existing procedures to ensure that information is handled in an appropriate manner and meets all legislative requirements, such as those set by the HIPAA security and privacy standards. The security officer must also be very familiar with antivirus software, internet protocol firewalls, virtual private network (VPN) devices, cryptographic ciphers, and other aspects of computer security

Requirement:

- Experience with systems and networking security
- Experience with implementing and auditing security measures in a multiprocessor environment
- Experience with data center security
- Experience with business resumption planning
- Experience with firewalls, VPNs, and other security devices
- Good communication skills, both verbal and written
- Good understanding of security- and privacy-related legislation as it applies to the Maintenance Management Information System (MMIS)
- Basic knowledge of cryptography as it relates to computer security
- CISSP certification

Duties and responsibilities:

The information security department has the following responsibilities:

- Create and implement information security policies and procedures
- Ensure that procedures adhere to the security policies
- Ensure that network security devices exist and are functioning correctly where they are required (such as firewalls and software tools such as antivirus software, intrusion detection software, log analysis software, etc.)
- Keep up-to-date on known computer security issues and ensure that all security devices and software are continuously updated as problems are found
- Assist the operations team in establishing procedures and documentation pertaining to network security
- Assist the engineering team to ensure that infrastructure design does not contain security weaknesses
- Assist the facilities department to ensure that physical security is adequate to protect critical information and assets
- Assist the customer systems administration and the professional services groups in advising clients on network security issues

(Continued)

- Provide basic security training programs for all employees, and—when they access information—partners, business associates, and customers
- In the event of a security incident, work with the appropriate authorities as directed by the executive
- Work with external auditors to ensure that information security is adequate and evaluate external auditors to ensure that external auditors meet proper qualifications

The CSO has the following responsibilities:

- Ensure that the information security department is able to fulfill the above mandate
- Hire personnel for the information security department
- Hold regular meetings and set goals for information security personnel
- Perform employee evaluations of information security personnel as directed by human resources
- Ensure that information security staff receives proper training and certification where required
- Participate in setting information security policies and procedures
- Review all company procedures that involve information security
- Manage the corporate information security policies and make recommendations for modifications as the needs arise

Information security administrator

Job specifications

The information security administrator will:

- Work with security analysts and application developers to code and develop information security rules, roles, policies, standards and so on.
- Analyze existing security rules to ensure no problems will occur as new rules are defined, objects added and so on.
- Work with other administrative areas in information security activities
- Troubleshoot problems when they occur in the test and production environments
- Define and implement access control requirements and processes to ensure appropriate information access authorization across the organizations
- Plan and develop user administration and security awareness measures to safeguard information against accidental or unauthorized modification, destruction, or disclosure
- Manage the overall functions of user account administration and the company-wide information security awareness training program according to corporate policies and federal regulations
- Define relevant data security objectives, goals, and procedures
- Evaluate data security user administration, resource protection, and security awareness training effectiveness
- Evaluate and select security software products to support the assigned functions
- Coordinate security software installation
- Meet with senior management regarding data security issues
- Participate in designing and implementing an overall data security program
- Work with internal and external auditors as required
- Ensure that user administration and information security awareness training programs adhere to HIPAA and other regulations

Qualifications

- Human relations and communication skills to effectively interact with personnel from technical areas, internal auditors, and end users, promoting information security as an enabler and not as an inhibitor
- Decision-making ability to define data security policies, goals, and tactics, and to accurately measure these practices as well as risk assessments and selection of security devices including software tools
- Ability to organize and prioritize work to balance cost and risk factors and bring adequate data security measures to the IT environments
- Ability to jointly establish measurable goals and objectives with staff, monitor progress on attainment of them, and adjust as required
- Ability to work collaboratively with IT and business unit management
- Ability to relate business requirements and risks to technology implementation for security-related issues
- Knowledge of role-based authorization methodologies and authentication technologies
- Knowledge of generally accepted security practices such as ISO 17799 standards
- Security administration experience
- Good communication skills
- Two to four years of security administration experience
- SSCP or CISSP certification a plus, but not required

positions for to consider establishing within an organization:

- *Chief Security Officer.* The CSO must raise security issues and help to develop solutions. This position must communicate directly with executive management and effectively communicate information security concerns and needs. The CSO will ensure security management is integrated into the management of all corporate systems and processes to assure that system managers and data owners consider security in the planning and operation of the system. This position establishes liaisons with external groups to take advantage of external information sources and to improve the dissemination of this information throughout the organization.

- *Information Protection Director.* This position oversees the information protection department and staff. This position communicates significant issues to the CSO, sets goals, and creates plans for the information protection department, including budget development. This position establishes liaisons that should be established with internal groups, including the information resources management office and traditional security offices.

- *Information Protection Awareness and Training Manager.* This position oversees all awareness and training activities within the organization. This position communicates with all areas of the organization about information protection issues and policies on an ongoing basis. This position ensures that all personnel and parties involved with outsourcing and customer communications are aware of their security responsibilities.

- *Information Protection Technical/Network Manager.* This position works directly with the IT areas to analyze and assess risks within the IT systems and functions. This position stays abreast of new information security risks as well as new and effective information security tools. This position also analyzes third-party connection risks and establishes requirements for the identified risks.

- *Information Protection Administration Manager.* This position oversees user account and access control practices. This person should have a wide experience range over many different security areas.

- *Privacy Officer.* This position ensures the organization addresses new and emerging privacy regulations and concerns.

- *Internal Auditor.* This position performs audits within the corporate auditing area in such a way as to ensure compliance with corporate information protection policies, procedures, and standards.

- *Security Administrator.* The systems security administrator should participate in the selection and implementation of appropriate technical controls and

security procedures, understand system vulnerabilities, and be able to respond quickly to system security problems. The security administrator is responsible for the daily administration of user IDs and system controls, and works primarily with the user community.

- *Information Security Oversight Committee.* This is a management information security forum established to provide direction and promote information protection visibility. The committee is responsible for review and approval of information security policy and overall responsibilities. Additionally, this committee is responsible for monitoring exposure to major threats to information assets, for reviewing and monitoring security incidents, and for approving major initiatives to enhance information security.

How Do You Effectively Maintain Separation of Duties?

When considering quality assurance for computer program code development, the principles of separation of duty are well established. For example, the person who designs or codes a program must not be the only one to test the design or the code. There is a need for similar separation of duties for information protection responsibilities to reduce the likelihood of accidental compromise or fraud. A good example is the 1996 Omega case where the network administrator, Tim Lloyd, was an employee who was responsible for everything to do with the manufacturing of computers. As a result, when Lloyd was terminated, he was able to add a line of program code to a major manufacturing program that ultimately deleted and purged all the programs in the system. Lloyd also had erased all the backup tapes, for which he also had complete control. Ultimately, the company suffered $12 million in damages, lost its competitive footing in the high-tech instrument and measurement market, and 80 employees lost their jobs as a result. If separation of duties had been in place, this could have been avoided.

Management must be active in hiring practices (ensuring background checks) bonding individuals (which should be routine for individuals in all critical areas) and auditing and monitoring, which should be routine practices. Users should be recertified to resources, and resources to users, at least annually to ensure proper access controls are in place. Because the system administration group is probably placed within the confines of the computer room, an audit of physical and logical controls also needs to be performed by a third party.

Certain information protection duties must not be performed by the same person or within one area. For example, there should be separation of roles of systems operators, systems administrators, and security

Table 2 Application roles and privileges worksheet

Application System			
Purpose/Description			
Information Owner			
Application/System Owner			
Implementation Date			
Role/Function	**Group/Persons**	**Access Rights**	**Comments**
User Account Creation			
Backups			
Testing			
Production Change Approvals			
Disaster Recovery Plans			
Disable User Accounts			
Incident Response			
Error Correction			
End-User Training			
Application Documentation			
Quality Assurance			
User Access Approvals			

administrators, and separation of security-relevant functions from others. Admittedly, ideal separation can be costly in time and money, and often possible only within large staffs. There is a need to make information security responsibilities dependent upon the business, organization size, and associated risks. One must perform risk assessment to determine what information protection tasks should be centralized and what should be distributed. When considering separation of duties for information security roles, it is helpful to use a tool similar to the one in Table 2.

How Large Should the Information Protection/Security Department Be?

If only there was one easy answer to the question of how large an information protection department should be. This is one of the most commonly asked questions raised at information security conferences over the previous several years, and asked regularly within all the major information security companies. There is no "best practice" magic number or ratio. The size of an information protection department depends on many factors. These include, but are not limited to, the following:

- Industry
- Organization size
- Network diversification and size
- Number of network users
- Geographical locations
- Outsourced functions

Whatever size one determines is best for the organization, there is a need to ensure the staff choosen has a security background or, at least, has some basic security training.

SUMMARY

This entry reviewed a wide range of issues involved in creating an information protection program and department. Specifically:

- Organizational information protection responsibilities
- Roles of an information protection department
- Information protection budgeting
- Executive management support of information protection
- Where to place the information protection department within an organization
- Separation of information security duties
- Descriptions of information protection responsibilities

Accompanying this entry is a tool to help determine separation of information security duties (Table 2) and some examples of information protection job descriptions to help in getting one written (Table 1).

BIBLIOGRAPHY

1. National Institute of Standards and Technology (NIST) publication, *Management of Risks in Information Systems: Practices of Successful Organizations.*

2. NIST publication, *CSL Bulletin. Security Program Management:* August 1993.

3. NIST, *Generally Accepted System Security Principles (GSSPs).*

4. ISO 17799. http://www.iso.org/iso/catalogue_detail?csnumber=39612.

5. Organization for Economic Cooperation and Development's (OECD), *Guidelines for the Security of Information Systems.*

6. Computer Security Institute (CSI) and FBI joint annual, *Computer Crime and Security Survey.*

7. Berinato, S. The security spending mystery. CIO Magazine, January 1, **2002**.

8. Scalet, S.D. Will security make a 360-degree turn? CIO Magazine, December 6, 2001.

9. Scalet, S.D. Another chair at the table. CIO Magazine, August 9, 2001.

10. Field, T. Protection money. CIO Magazine, October 1, **2000**.

Information Science

Tefko Saracevic
School of Communication and Information, Rutgers University, New Brunswick, New Jersey, U.S.A.

Abstract
The purpose of this entry is to provide an overview of information science as a field or discipline, including a historical perspective to illustrate the events and forces that shaped it. Information science is a field of professional practice and scientific inquiry dealing with effective communication of information and information objects, particularly knowledge records, among humans in the context of social, organizational, and individual need for and use of information. Information science emerged in the aftermath of World War II, as did a number of other fields, addressing the problem of information explosion and using technology as a solution. Presently, information science deals with the same problems in the Web and digital environments. This entry covers problems addressed by information science, the intellectual structure of the field, and the description of main areas—information retrieval, human information behavior, metric studies, and digital libraries. This entry also includes an account of education related to information science and conclusions about major characteristics.

INTRODUCTION

The purpose of this entry is to provide an overview of information science as a field or discipline, including a historical perspective to illustrate the events and forces that shaped it.

Information science is the science and practice dealing with the effective collection, storage, retrieval, and use of information. It is concerned with recordable information and knowledge, and the technologies and related services that facilitate their management and use. More specifically, information science is a field of professional practice and scientific inquiry addressing the effective communication of information and information objects, particularly knowledge records, among humans in the context of social, organizational, and individual need for and use of information.[1] The domain of information science is the transmission of the universe of human knowledge in recorded form, centering on manipulation (representation, organization, and retrieval) of information, rather than knowing information.[2]

There are two key orientations: toward the hu
man and social need for and use of information pertaining to knowledge records, on the one hand, and toward specific information techniques, systems, and technologies (covered under the name of *information retrieval*) to satisfy that need and provide for effective organization and retrieval of information, on the other hand. From the outset, information science had these two orientations: one that deals with information need, or more broadly human information behavior, and the other that deals with information retrieval techniques and systems.

Information science is a field that emerged in the aftermath of the World War II, along with a number of new fields, with computer science being but one example. While developments and activities associated with information science already started by the end of 1940s, the very term "information science" came into full use only at the start of the 1960s. A significant impetus for the coalescence of the field was the *International Conference on Scientific Information*, held in Washington, DC, November 16–21, 1958, sponsored by the National Science Foundation (NSF) in the United States, the National Academy of Sciences—National Research Council, and the American Documentation Institute, and attended by some 1000 delegates from 25 countries. The conference was meticulously planned for over 3 years and attracted wide international attention. The 75 papers and lively discussions that followed, all recorded in the *Proceedings* of over 1600 pages, affected the direction of research, development, and professional practice in the field for at least a decade if not longer.[3] It also affected the internationalization of the field and the approaches used. They became global.

This entry covers problems addressed by information science, the intellectual structure of the field, and the further description of main areas—information retrieval, human information behavior studies, metric studies, and digital libraries. At the end, the entry includes an account of education related to information science and conclusions about major trends.

Encyclopedia of Information Systems and Technology. DOI: 10.1081/E-EIST-120043704

PROBLEMS ADDRESSED

To understand information science, as with any other field, a description of problems addressed and methods used in their solution is crucial. Generally, information science addressed the problem of information explosion and used information technology as a solution.

The rapid pace of scientific and technical advances that were accumulating since the start of the 20th century produced by mid-century a scientific and technical revolution. A most visible manifestation of this revolution was the phenomenon of "information explosion," referring to the unabated, exponential growth of scientific and technical publications and information records of all kinds. The term "information explosion" is a metaphor (as is "population explosion") because nothing really exploded but just grew at a high rate, even exponentially at times. Simply put, information explosion is information and information objects piling up at a high rate. The problem this presents is getting to the right information as needed at a given time.

A number of scientists documented this growth, but none better and more vividly than Derek de Solla Price (1922–1983, British and American physicist, historian of science and information scientist), recognized as the father of scientometrics. In his seminal works, S*cience since Babylon* followed by *Little Science, Big Science*, Price documented the exponential and logistical growth of scientific publications linking them with the growth of the number of scientists. The logistical growth started slow right after the appearance of the first scientific journals in the seventeenth century, accelerated by the start of the twentieth century and became explosive after the World War II.[4,5]

The impetus for the development of information science, and even for its very origin and agenda, can be traced to a 1945 article, "As We May Think" by Vannevar Bush (1890–1974), a respected MIT scientist and, even more importantly, the head of the U.S. scientific effort during World War II.[6] In this influential article, Bush did two things: 1) he succinctly defined the critical and strategic problem of information explosion in science and technology that was on the minds of many and 2) proposed a solution that was a "technological fix," and thus in tune with the spirit of the time. Both had wide appeal. Bush was neither the first nor the only one that addressed these issues, but he was listened to because of his stature. He defined the problem in almost poetic terms as "The summation of human experience is being expanded at a prodigious rate, and the means we use for threading through the consequent maze to the momentarily important item is the same as was used in the days of square-rigged ships." In other words, Bush addressed the problem of information explosion and the associated methods for finding relevant information.

As a solution, Bush proposed a machine, dubbed Memex, incorporating (in his words) a capability for "association of ideas," and the duplication of "mental processes artificially." A prescient anticipation of information science and artificial intelligence is evident. Memex, needless to say, was never built, but to this day is considered an ideal, a wish list, an agenda, and, some think, a utopia. Information science is still challenged by the ever-worsening problem of information explosion, now universal and in a variety of digital formats, and the field is still trying to fix things technologically.

A number of scientists and professionals in many fields around the globe listened and took up Bush's challenge. Most importantly, governments listened, as well, and provided funding. The reasoning went something like this: Because science and technology are strategically important for society, efforts that help them, information activities in particular, are also important and need support. In the United States, the United Kingdom, and other countries, this led to the support of research and development related to information problems and solutions. By the end of the 1940s, information science was well on its way.

Bush also participated in the establishment of the NSF. The National Science Foundation Act of 1950 (P. L. 81-507) provided a number of mandates, among them "to foster the interchange of scientific information among scientists in the U.S. and foreign countries" [Section 3(a)3] and "to further the full dissemination of [scientific and technical] information of scientific value consistent with the national interest" [Section 11(g)]. The 1958 National Defense Education Act (P.L. 85-864) (the "Sputnik act") enlarged the mandate: "The National Science Foundation shall [among others].undertake programs to develop new or improved methods, including mechanized systems, for making scientific information available" (Title IX, Section 901). By those mandates, an NSF division, which after a number of name and direction changes is now called the Division of Information and Intelligent Systems (IIS), has supported research in these areas since the 1950s. Information science evolution, at least in the United States, was greatly affected by the support of the U.S. government. In this respect it was not an exception. For instance, artificial intelligence, among others, was for decades supported by the U.S. government starting in the 1950s and ending by the 1990s.

Historically, one force affecting government support of information science, as of many other fields in the United States and a number of European countries, had to do with the cold war. Among others, one impetus was the establishment in 1952 of the All-Union Scientific and Technical Information Institute of the Academy of Sciences of the USSR (Russian acronym: VINITI). VINITI implemented a massive gathering and bibliographic control of scientific and technical information from around the world, eventually covering some 130 countries in 66 languages; it employed thousands of scientists and engineers full- and part-time. In the framework of the Cold War, VINITI was repeatedly brought up as a challenge needing a response.

At the start, information science was directed solely toward information explosion in science and technology. However soon it expanded to other areas, including business, humanities, law, and eventually any area of human endeavor. In all areas, the phenomenon of information explosion is continuing and even accelerating to this day, particularly in the digital and Web environments. Addressing the problems of dealing with information explosion in any human area where information and knowledge records are overbearing is at the heart of information science. The approach to these problems involves a number of disciplines; in other words, information science, as many other modern fields, is interdisciplinary in nature.

In its goals and activities, information science established early, and maintains prominently, a social and human function—not only a technological one. On the social level, it participates actively, with many other fields, in the evolution of information society around the globe. Yet information science also has an individual human function. It relates to searching for and use of information as done by (or on behalf of) individuals. People individually search for and use relevant information. For information science, managing information is a global, social function, while providing and using information is an intense individual function.

INTELLECTUAL STRUCTURE

Information science, like any other field, has a dynamic intellectual structure; the objects of study and practice appear, change, disappear, or are emphasized, realized, and interwoven in different ways over time. A general framework for the intellectual structure for the field can be derived from the Three Big Questions for information science as identified by Bates[2]:

1. The physical question: What are the features and laws of the recorded information universe?
2. The social question: How do people relate to, seek, and use information?
3. The design question: How can access to recorded information be made most rapid and effective?

Indeed, when looking at the literature of information science since its emergence to this day, the general structure can be discerned from these questions in both research and practice reported. While they can be approached individually, the three questions are not independent but interdependent. Effective design is highly dependent on the consideration of social and physical features. Over time, details in the answers differed greatly. But, as is seen from three examples below, the general structure stands.

Three examples illustrating the intellectual structure of information science spanning some five decades are presented here. The first one is the enumeration of topics in the proceedings of the mentioned 1959 *International Conference on Scientific Information*.[3] The second one is an author cocitation analysis mapping information science for the years 1972–1995.[7] And the third one is a similar analysis, using the same methods, mapping information science for the years 1996–2005.[8] Author cocitation analysis is a statistical and visualization method developed in information science that allows for mapping of connections between authors in a given domain and identifying clusters or oeuvres of work in that domain. The raw data reflects the number of times selected author pairs are cited together in papers, regardless of which of their work is cited.

The 1959 Proceedings had seven areas covering the research, practice, and interests of information science at the time and illustrating the intellectual structure of the field by the end of 1950s. These were

1. *Literature and reference needs of scientists.* An example of a title of a paper in the area: An Operations Research Study of the Dissemination of Scientific Information.
2. *The function and effectiveness of abstracting and indexing services.* A paper example: All-Union Institute for Scientific and Technical Information (VINITI).
3. *Effectiveness of monographs, compendia, and specialized centers. Present trends and new and proposed techniques and types of services.* A paper example: Scientific, Technical, and Economic Information in a Research Organization.
4. *Organization of information for storage and search. Comparative characteristics of existing systems.* A paper example: The Evaluation of Systems Used in Information Retrieval.
5. *Organization of information for storage and retrospective search. Intellectual problems and equipment considerations in the design of new systems.* A paper example: Linguistic Transformations for Information Retrieval.
6. *Organization of information for storage and retrospective search. Possibility for a general theory.* A paper example: The Structure of Information Retrieval Systems.
7. *Responsibilities of government, professional societies, universities, and industry for improved information services and research.* A paper example: Differences in International Arrangements for Financial Support of Information Services.

Table 1 Intellectual structure of information science as presented in studies of two time periods (labels provided by authors of respective studies)

1972–1995	1996–2006
1. Experimental retrieval (design and evaluation of IR systems)	1. User studies (information seeking/searching behavior, user-centered approach to IR, users and use)
2. Citation analysis (interconnectedness of scientific and scholarly literatures)	2. Citation analysis (scientometrics; evaluative bibliometrics)
3. Practical retrieval (applications in "real world")	3. Experimental retrieval (algorithms, models, systems, evaluation of IR)
4. Bibliometrics (statistical distributions of texts and mathematical modeling)	4. Webometrics
	5. Visualization of knowledge domains (author cocitation analysis)
5. General library systems (library automation, library operations research, services)	6. Science communication
6. Science communication (including social sciences)	7. Users' judgment of relevance (situational relevance)
7. User theory (information needs and users)	8. Information seeking and context
8. Online Public Access Catalogs (OPACs) (design, subject searching)	9. Children's information searching behavior (usability, interface design)
9. Imported ideas (information theory, cognitive science, etc.)	10. Metadata and digital resources
10. Indexing theory	11. Bibliometric models and distributions
11. Citation theory	12. Structured abstracts (academic writing)
12. Communication theory	

Results from the next two studies are comparable—they used the same set of basic data (major journals in information science) and the same method (author cocitation analysis and mapping).[7,8] The authors of both studies mapped clusters of authors, classifying their areas of publications in a number of categories—they labeled the categories—and showing the relation or lack thereof between categories. The categories reflecting clusters of work in the two studies, as labeled by the authors, are shown in Table 1.

Some of the areas in the three examples remain the same over time, showing an overall stability of general interests and foci of information science from its emergence to this day. The three areas of major and continuing interest are *information retrieval, user and use studies, and metric studies*. They correspond to the Three Big Questions for information science listed at the start of this section. Naturally, the variety and type of work in these three areas has changed and evolved over time, as elaborated below, but the general thrust and emphasis stayed stable.

Some areas have disappeared. The interest in the functioning of abstracting and indexing services, specialized information centers, and the responsibilities of different agencies for improved information services, so prominent in the 1959 Proceedings, are not prominent at all in later periods. Online Public Access Catalogs (OPACs) were prominent as an area cluster in the period 1971–1995 but did not appear in the 1996–2005 period; research in this area waned. The same holds for general library systems, covering library automation; the area was prominent during 1971–1995, but not anymore. The field had a prominent area of imported ideas between 1971–1995, covering the deliberations of adaptation and the application of various theories from information theory (Shannon), sociology (Merton), and other fields, but not anymore. Theory importing is not a major area any longer in information science. However, there is a significant exception. A major trend is evident in the incorporation of ideas, theories, and methods from the social sciences into many studies related to human information behavior to such an extent that they are not considered as imported any more.

In the Web age, covering the period 1996–2005, new areas have appeared. Not surprisingly, one of them is webometrics, extending the metric studies to the Web. Another new area is the visualization of knowledge domains, providing a new method of presenting retrieval processes and results and also extending citation and metric analyses.

The intellectual structure of information science also covers two camps of authors concentrating in different areas. White and McCain called them "retrieval people" and "literature people."[7] The first group congregates in the area of information retrieval; the second in the area of human information behavior and metric studies. They represent two broad branches of information science, one system-oriented and the other user-oriented. They are relatively isolated from each other. In the words of White and McCain again: "As it turns out, information science looks rather like Australia: Heavily coastal in its development, with a sparsely settled interior." The relative isolation is conceived as unproductive for all areas. There were a number of calls for collaboration, some quite impatient, and a few efforts at actually bridging the gap, but the gap has yet to be effectively bridged.

INFORMATION RETRIEVAL

Considering the Three Big Questions for information science, stated above, this section addresses the design question: *How can access to recorded information be made most rapid and effective?* The area is concentrated on systems and technology.

Right after World War II, a variety of projects started applying a variety of technologies to the problem of controlling information explosion, particularly in science and technology. In the beginning the technologies were punched cards and microfilm, but soon after computers became available, the technology shifted to, and stayed with, computers. Originally, many activities involved specific fields of application, such as chemistry. By the mid-1960s computer science joined the efforts in a big way.

Various names were applied to these efforts, such as "*machine literature searching,*" or "*mechanical organization of knowledge,*" but by the mid-1950s "*information retrieval*" prevailed. Actually, the term "*information retrieval*" (IR) was coined by mathematician and physicist Calvin N. Mooers (1919–1994), a computing and IR pioneer, just as the activity started to expand from its beginnings after World War II. He posited that:

> Information retrieval is ... the finding or discovery process with respect to stored information ... useful to [a user]. Information retrieval embraces the intellectual aspects of the description of information and its specification for search, and also whatever systems, technique, or machines that are employed to carry out the operation.[9]

Over the next half century, information retrieval evolved and expanded widely. In the beginning IR was static. Now it is highly interactive. Earlier it dealt only with representations—indexes, abstracts—now it deals with full texts as well. It concentrated on print only, now it covers every medium, ..., and so on. Advances in the field are impressive, now covering the Web, and still go on. Contemporary search engines are about information retrieval. But in a basic sense, IR still continues to concentrate on the same fundamental things Mooers described. Searching was and still is about retrieval of relevant (useful) information or information objects.

It is of interest to note what made IR different, compared to many other techniques, applied to the control of information records over a long period of time. The key difference between IR and related methods and systems that long preceded it—such as classifications, subject headings, various indexing methods, or bibliographic descriptions, including the contemporary Functional Requirements for Bibliographic Records—is that IR specifically included "specification for search." The others did not. Since the days of the pioneers in bibliographic organization in the United States, Charles Ammi Cutter (1837–1903) and Melvil Dewey (1851–1931), the emphasis was on the creation of systems for bibliographic representation and control. In these long-standing techniques, what users' needs are and should be fulfilled was specified in detail. Following that, the representation of information objects was also prescribed in detail. In other words, data about information objects (books, articles, etc.) in bibliographic records are organized in a way to fulfill the specified needs. However, how the search ought to be done was not specified or addressed at all. Searching was assumed and left to itself—it just happens. In IR, users' needs are assumed as well, but the search process is specified in algorithmic detail and data is organized to enable the search. Search engines are about searching to start with; everything else is subsumed to that function.

Relevance

The fundamental notion used in bibliographic description and in all types of classification or categorization, including those used in contemporary databases, is *aboutness*. Cataloging and classification describe what the documents were all about with an implied idea that *about*, among others, may facilitate searching. Machine Readable Cataloging (MARC) that was developed by Henriette Avram (1919–2006) at the Library of Congress beginning in the 1960s follows the same principle. OPACs that emerged more than a decade later are based on MARC. They include various search mechanisms, but are relatively difficult and ineffective as search tools. While implying searching *aboutness* does not really facilitate it.

The fundamental notion used in IR is *relevance*. Retrieval is not about any kind of information, and there are a great many, but about *relevant* information (or as Mooers called it *useful to a user* or Bush *momentarily important*). Basically, relevant information is that which pertains to the matter or problem at hand. Fundamentally, bibliographic description and classification concentrate on describing and categorizing information objects. IR is also about that, but in addition IR is about searching, and searching is about relevance. Very often, the differences between databases and IR are discussed in terms of differences between structured and unstructured data, which is OK, but the fundamental difference is in the basic notion used: *aboutness* in the former and *relevance* in the latter. The two notions are not at all equivalent. Relevance entered as a basic notion through the specific concentration on searching. True, searching for relevant information precedes IR by centuries, if not millennia, but in IR the process was adapted as primary orientation.

By choosing relevance as a basic, underlying notion of IR, related information systems, services, and activities—and with it, the whole field of information science—went in a direction that differed from approaches taken in librarianship, documentation, and related information services, and even in expert systems and contemporary databases in computer science.

In this sense, information science is on the one hand connected to relevance and on the other hand to technologies and techniques that enhance probability of the retrieval of relevant and the suppression of non-relevant information. Relevance, as a basic notion in information science, is a human notion, widely understood in similar ways from one end of the globe to the other. This affected the widespread acceptance of information retrieval techniques globally. However, relevance, and with it information retrieval, involves a number of complexities: linguistic, cognitive, psychological, social, and technological, requiring different solutions. But the basic idea that searching is for relevant information does not.

As mentioned, relevance is a human notion. In human applications, relevance judgments exhibit inconsistencies, situational and dynamic changes, differences in cognitive interpretations and criteria, and other untidy properties common to human notions. This stimulated theoretical and experimental investigations about the notion and applications of relevance in information science. The experiments, mostly connected to relevance judgments and clues (what affected the judgments, what are people using in judgments), started already in the 1960s and continue to this day. The idea was and still is that findings may affect development of more effective retrieval algorithms. This is still more of a goal; actual translations from research results to development and practical applications were meager, if attempted at all.

Algorithms

IR systems and techniques, no matter in what form and including contemporary search engines, are geared toward retrieval of relevant information. To achieve that, they use algorithms—logical step-by-step procedures—for the organization, searching, and retrieval of information and information objects. Contemporary algorithms are complex and in a never-ending process of improvement, but they started simple and still incorporate those simple roots.

The first and simple algorithm (although at the time it was not called that) applied in the 1940s and early 1950s was aimed at searching and retrieving from edge-notched punch cards using the operation of Boolean algebra. In the early 1950s Mortimer Taube (1910–1965), another IR pioneer and entrepreneur, founded a company named Documentation Inc. devoted to the development and operation of systems for the organization and retrieval of scientific and technical information. Taube broke away from the then-standard methods of subject headings and classification, by developing Uniterms and coordinate indexing. Uniterms were keywords extracted from documents; a card for a given Uniterm

listed the documents that were indexed by that Uniterm. Coordinate indexing was actually a search and retrieval method for comparing (coordinating) document numbers appearing on different Uniterm cards by using a logical AND, OR, or NOT operation. Although at the time the algorithm was not recognized as Boolean algebra by name, the operation was in effect the first application of a Boolean algorithm for information retrieval. Uniterms and coordinate indexing were controversial for a time but soon it was recognized that the technique was a natural for use as a base for computerized search and retrieval. All IR systems built in the next few decades incorporated Boolean algebra as a search algorithm and most have it under the hood today, along with other algorithms. All search engines offer, among others, Boolean search capabilities.

At the start of IR, and for a long time to come, the input—indexes and abstracts in particular—was constructed manually. Professionals indexed, abstracted, classified, and assigned other identifiers to information objects in a variety of fields. Input was manual; output—searching—was automated. Big online systems and databases, such as Medline and Dialog, which came about respectively in 1971 and 1972 and operate to this day, were based on that paradigm. Efforts to automate input, as well, commenced in the 1950s by the development of various algorithms for handling of texts. They took much longer to be developed and adopted more operationally than searching algorithms—the problem was and still is much tougher.

Hans Peter Luhn (1896–1964), a prodigious inventor with a broad range of patents joined IBM in 1941 and became a pioneer in development of computerized methods for handling texts and other IR methods in the 1950s. Luhn pioneered many of the basic techniques now common to IR in general. Among others, he invented the automatic production of indexes from titles and texts—Key Words in Context (KWIC) indexing that lead to automatic indexing from full texts; automatic abstracting that lead to summarization efforts; and Selective Dissemination of Information (SDI) to provide present awareness services that led to a number of variations, including today's RSS (Really Simple Syndication). The demonstration of automatic KWIC indexing was the sensation at the aforementioned 1959 International Conference on Scientific Information.

Luhn's basic idea to use various properties of texts, including statistical ones, was critical in opening the handling of input by computers for IR. Automatic input joined the already automated output. Of course, Luhn was not the only one who addressed the problems of deriving representations from full texts. In the same period of the 1950s for instance, Phyllis Baxendale developed methods of linguistic analysis for automatic phrase detection and syntactic manipulations and Eugene Garfield was among the first, if not even the first, to join automated input and output in an operational system, that of citation indexing and searching.

Further advances that eventually defined modern IR came about in the 1960s. Statistical properties of texts—frequency and distribution of words in individual documents and in a corpus or collection of documents—were expressed in terms of probabilities that allowed for a variety of algorithms not only to extract index terms, but also to indicate term relations, distances, and clusters. The relations are inferred by probability or degree of certainty. They are inductive not deductive. The assumption, traced to Luhn, was that frequency data can be used to extract significant words to represent the content of a document and the relation among words. The goal was to find a match between queries and potentially relevant documents, based on a probability of documents being relevant. Once expressed in terms of probabilities, documents can be ranked from those that have a higher probability to those that have a lower probability of a match. There are many methods for doing this. The basic plan was to search for underlying mathematical structures to guide computation. These were powerful ideas that led to an ever-expanding array of new and improved algorithms for indexing and other information organization methods, along with the associated search and retrieval. Moreover, they lend themselves to experimentation.

A towering figure in advancing experimentation with algorithms for IR was Gerard (Gerry) Salton (1927–1995), a computer scientist and academic (Harvard and Cornell Universities) who firmly connected IR with computer science. Within a framework of a laboratory he established, (entitled the SMART project) Salton and collaborators, mostly his students, ran IR experiments from the mid-1960s to the time of his death in 1995. Many new IR algorithms and approaches were developed and tested; they inspired practical IR developments and further IR research in many countries around the world. Many of his students became leaders in the IR community. Salton was very active nationally and internationally in the promotion of IR; he is the founder of the Special Interest Group on Information Retrieval (SIGIR) of the Association of Computing Machinery (ACM). SIGIR became the preeminent international organization in IR with annual conferences that are the main event for reporting advances in IR research. As a result of global interest in IR, these conferences now alternate between continents. While Salton's research group started in the United States, today many similar groups operate in academic and commercial environments around the globe.

Contemporary IR has spread to many domains. Originally, IR concentrated on texts. This has expanded to any and all other media. Now there are research and pragmatic efforts devoted to IR in music, spoken words, video, still and moving images, and multimedia. While originally IR was monolingual, now many efforts are devoted to cross-lingual IR. Other efforts include IR connected with Extensible Markup Language (XML), software reuse, restriction to novelty, adversarial conditions, social tagging, and a number of special applications.

With the appearance and rapid growth of the Web starting in the mid-1990s, many new applications or adaptations of IR sprouted, as well. The most prominent are search engines. While a few large search engines dominate the scene globally, practically, there is no nation that does not have its own versions tailored to its own populace and interests. While practical IR was always connected with commercial concerns and information industry, the appearance, massive deployment and use of search engines pushed IR into a major role commercially, politically, and socially. It produced another effect, as well. Most, if not all, search engines use many well-known IR algorithms and techniques. But many search engines, particularly the major ones, in addition have developed and deployed their own IR algorithms and techniques, not known in detail and not shared with the IR community. They support aggressive efforts in IR research and development, mostly in-house. Contemporary IR also includes a proprietary branch, like many other industries.

Testing

Very soon after IR systems appeared, a number of claims and counterclaims were made about the superiority of various IR methods and systems, without supporting evidence. In response, the perennial questions asked of all systems were raised: *What is the effectiveness and performance of given IR approaches? How do they compare?* It is not surprising that these questions were raised in IR. At the time; most developers, funders, and users associated with IR were engineers, scientists, or worked in related areas where the question of testing was natural, even obligatory.

By the mid-1950s suggestions for two measures for evaluation of effectiveness of IR systems were made; they were precision and recall. Precision measures how many of *retrieved* items (let's say documents) were relevant or conversely how many were noise. Recall measures how many of the *potentially relevant items in a given file or system* were actually retrieved, or conversely how many were not retrieved even though they were relevant. The measures were widely adopted and used in most evaluation efforts since. Even today, the two measures, with some variation, are at the base for evaluation of the effectiveness of output using given retrieval algorithms and systems. It is significant to note that the two measures are based on the comparison of human (user or user surrogate) judgments of relevance with IR algorithms' or systems' retrieval of what it considered as relevant, where human judgment is the gold standard.

A pioneer in IR testing was Cyril Cleverdon (1914–1997), a librarian at the Cranfield Institute of Technology (now Cranfield University) in the United Kingdom. From the late-1950s until the mid-1970s Cleverdon conducted a series of IR tests under the name "Cranfield tests." Most famous were the tests sponsored by the NSF from 1961 to 1966 that established a model of IR systems (the so-called traditional model that concentrates on query on the one end and matched with static retrieval from an IR system or algorithm on the other end), and a methodology for testing that is still in use. One of the significant and surprising finding from Cranfield tests was that uncontrolled vocabularies based on natural language (such as keywords picked by a computer algorithm) achieve retrieval effectiveness comparable to vocabularies with elaborate controls (such as those using thesaurus, descriptors, or classification assigned by indexers). The findings, as expected, drew skepticism and strong critique, but were confirmed later by Salton and others. Not surprisingly, these conclusions caused a huge controversy. But they also provided recognition of automatic indexing as an effective approach to IR.

Salton coupled development of IR algorithms and approaches with testing; he enlarged on Cranfield approaches and reaches. Everything that Salton and his group proposed and developed was mandatorily tested. The norm was established: No new algorithms or approaches were accepted without testing. In other words, testing became mandatory for any and all efforts that propose new algorithms and methods. It became synonymous with experimentation in IR.

After Salton, contemporary IR tests and experiments are conducted under the umbrella of the Text REtrieval Conference (TREC). TREC, started in 1992 and continuing to date, is a long-term effort at the (U.S.) National Institute for Standards and Technology, that brings various IR teams together annually to compare results from different IR approaches under laboratory conditions. Over the years, hundreds of teams from dozens of countries participated in TREC covering a large number of topics. TREC is dynamic: As areas of IR research change, so do the topics in TREC. Results are at the forefront of IR research.[10]

In many respects, IR is the main activity in information science. It has proved to be a dynamic and ever-growing area of research, development, and practice, with strong commercial interest and global use. Rigorous adherence to testing contributed to the maturing of information retrieval.

HUMAN INFORMATION BEHAVIOR

Considering the Three Big Questions for information science stated above, this section addresses the social and individual question: *How do people relate to, seek, and use information?* While often connected with

systems, the emphasis in this area of information science is on people rather than systems.

Human information behavior refers to a wide range of processes which people employ when engaged with information and to related cognitive and social states and effects. In his book that comprehensively covers research on information behavior (with over 1100 documents cited, most since 1980), Case defines that information behavior:

> encompasses information seeking as well as the totality of other *unintentional* or *passive* behaviors (such as glimpsing or encountering information), as well as purposive behaviors that do not involve seeking, such as actively *avoiding* information (p. 5).[11] (emphasis in the original).

As can be imagined, human information behavior, as with many other human behaviors, is complex, not fully understood, and of interest in a number of fields. A great many studies and a number of theories address various aspects related to human information behavior in psychology, cognitive science, brain sciences, communication, sociology, philosophy, and related fields, at times using different terminology and classifications. Under various names, scholarly curiosity about human information behavior is longstanding, going back to antiquity.

Of particular interest in information science are processes, states, and effects that involve *information needs and use* and *information seeking and searching*. The order in which these two major areas of human information behavior studies are listed, represents their historic emergence and emphasis over time.

Historically, the study of information needs and use preceded information science. Many relevant studies were done during the 1930s and 1940s in librarianship, communication, and specific fields, such as chemistry, concentrating on use of sources, media, systems, and channels. Already by the 1950s this area of study was well developed in information science—for instance, the aforementioned 1959 *Proceedings of the International Conference on Scientific Information*[3] had a whole area with a number of papers devoted to the topic. The *Annual Review of Information Science and Technology* had regular annual chapters on "information needs and use" starting with the first volume in 1966 and ongoing through 1978. Thereafter, chapters covering this area were broadened to cover in addition various aspects or contexts of information behavior, including information seeking. This change illustrates how the emphasis in topics studied significantly changed over time. Studies in human information behavior are evolving and slowly maturing.

Information Needs and Use

Over the years "information needs and use" was used as a phrase. However, while related information need and information use are distinct concepts. *Information need* refers to a cognitive or even a social state and *information use* to a process.

For decades, *information need* was used as a primitive concept on two levels: on an individual level it signified a cognitive state which underlies questions posed to information systems and requests for information in general; on a social level it signified information required for functioning and keeping abreast of a whole group, such as chemists. On the first, or cognitive, level it was assumed that individuals ask questions and request information because of a recognition that the knowledge one has is inadequate for a given problem or situation; it is subjective as represented by individuals; it is in the head of a user. On the second, or social level, it was assumed that a social group with common characteristics, goals, or tasks shares common information requirements that may be satisfied by specific information sources; it is more objective as determined by a group of individuals on the basis of some consensus or by experts based on experience. In general, information need was considered as instrumental in reaching a desired informational goal.

The concept of *information need* was entrenched until the start of the 1980s. Slowly, critiques of the concept gained ground by pointing out that it is nebulous, as are most other "need" concepts in every field where they are used; that it is often substituted for "information demand," which is a very different process and not a state; that it is associated with behaviorism, which in itself fell out of favor; that it is a subjective experience in the mind of a person and therefore not accessible for observation; and that it ignores wider social aspects and realities. Moreover, underlying assumptions were challenged. By the end of the decade, information need was largely abandoned as a subject of study or explanation of underlying information processes. Instead, studies of information seeking and other aspects of information behavior gained ground. However, information need is still represented in the traditional IR model (mentioned above) as the source of questions that are submitted to retrieval systems. It is not further elaborated in that framework, just listed as a primitive concept.

The concept of *information use* is more precise and it is operationally observable. Studies of information use were done for a long time and in many fields. For instance, use of libraries or use of literature in a given area was investigated long before information science emerged and before information use became one of the major topics of information science research. In information science, information use refers to a process in which information, information objects, or information channels are drawn on by information users for whatever informational purpose. The process is goal-directed. Questions are asked: *Who are the users of a given information system or resource? What information objects do they use? What information channels are used to gather information?* Or in other words: *Who uses what? How? For what purpose?*

The studies addressing these questions were, and still are, pragmatic, retrospective, and descriptive. Historically, as they emerged in the early 1950s, they were directed toward fields and users in science and technology. This is not surprising. As mentioned, information science emerged as a response to the problem of information explosion in science and technology thus the use studies were in those areas. Regarding topics, many early studies addressed users' distribution of time and resources over different kinds of documents: scientific journals, books, patents, abstracting and indexing services, and so on. As the realm of information science expanded to cover other areas and populations, use studies expanded their coverage as well. By the 1990s, studies emerged that also covered information use in many populations and activities, including the small worlds of everyday living.

The early motivation for user studies was pragmatic: to discover guidelines for the improvement of practice. This was of great concern to practitioners, and consequently most such studies were done by practitioners. By 1970 or so there was a move toward academic studies of information use motivated by a desire to understand the process better and provide models and theories. By 2008 there were still two worlds of user studies: one more pragmatic, but now with the goal of providing the basis for designing more effective and usable contemporary IR and Web systems, including search engines, and the other more academic, still with the goal of expanding understanding and providing more plausible theories and models. The two worlds do not interact well.

Information Seeking and Searching

Information seeking refers to a set of processes and strategies dynamically employed by people in their quest for and pursuit of information. Information seeking also refers to the progression of stages in those processes. In majority of theories and investigations about information seeking, the processes are assumed to be goal directed. In his aforementioned book, Case defines information seeking as:

> "a conscious effort to acquire information in response to a need or gap in your knowledge." (p. 5).[11]

Not surprisingly, information seeking is of interest in a number of fields from psychology, sociology, and political science to specific disciplines and professions, often under different names and classifications, such as information gathering or information foraging. The literature on the theme is large, spanning many decades. Historically, information-seeking concerns and studies in information science emerged by the late 1970s in academic rather than pragmatic environments. Only lately have they turned toward pragmatic concerns, as well. It was recognized that information use was the end process, preceded by quite different, elaborate, and most importantly, dynamic behavior and processes not well understood. The studies began in large part by trying to observe and explain what people do when they search and retrieve information from various retrieval systems, to expand fast to involving a number of different contexts, sources—formal and informal—and situations or tasks. The dynamic nature of information-seeking became the prime focus in observations, experiments, models, and theories. Questions are asked: *What do people actually do when they are in a quest for and pursuit of information? How are they going about and how are they changing paths as they go about? What are they going through on a personal level? What information channels are used to gather information? How?*

Information seeking, as is the case with most human information behavior, is highly dependent on context. While context may be everything, the very concept of context is ill defined, or taken as primitive and not defined. The contexts may involve various motivations for information seeking, various cognitive and affective states, various social, cultural, or organizational environments, various demographic characteristics, values, ways of life, and so on. A number of information-seeking studies were indeed directed toward various contexts. Thus, there is a wide range of such studies regarding context, accompanied by difficulties toward generalization.

To deal with more defined contexts, and enable specific observation, task-oriented information-seeking studies emerged in the 1990s. And they are going strong up to this day. Task studies deal with specific goals, mostly related to assignments in defined circumstances, time periods, or degree of difficulty. They represent a step in the ongoing evolution, not only of information-seeking studies in particular but also in information behavior research in general. By the 2000s we also see the emergence of studies in collaborating behaviors, also related to given tasks.

Information searching is a subset of information seeking, and in the context of information science, it refers to processes used for interrogating different information systems and channels in order to retrieve information. It is the most empirical and pragmatic part of information-seeking studies. Originally, search studies concentrated on observation and modeling of processes in the interrogation of IR systems. With the advent of digital environments, the focus shifted toward Web searching by Web users. New observational and experimental methods emerged, becoming a part of exploding Web research. Such search studies have a strong pragmatic orientation in that many are oriented toward improving search engines and interfaces, and enhancing human–computer interactions.

Models and Theories

The research area and accompanying literature of information behavior in information science is strong on models and theories. It follows a tradition and direction of such research in many other disciplines, particularly psychology, communication, and philosophy. Being primarily pragmatic and retrospective, information use studies were not a great source for models and theories. In contrast, broader studies of information behavior, and particularly of information seeking, are brimming with them. Numerous models and theories emerged, some with more, others with less staying power. The extent of this work is exemplified in a compilation *Theories of Information Behavior,*"[12] where some 70 different (or differing) theories and models are synthesized. To illustrate, we should sample three well-known theories, each in one of the three areas of human information behavior described above. Each of them is widely accepted and cited, and tested, as well.

What is behind an information need? Why do people seek information in the first place? Starting in late 1970s and for the next two decades or so, Nicholas Belkin and his colleagues addressed this question by considering that the basic motivation for seeking information is what they called "anomalous state of knowledge" (ASK), thus the "ASK theory," or as they called it, "ASK hypothesis" (described among others in Belkin, Oddy, and Brooks).[13] Explicitly following a cognitive viewpoint, they suggest that the reason for initiating an information-seeking process could be best understood at the cognitive level, as a user (information seeker) recognizes that the state of his/her knowledge is in some way inadequate (anomalous) with respect to the ability to resolve a problematic situation and achieve some goal. Anomaly was used explicitly, not only to indicate inadequacy due to lack of knowledge, but also due to other problems, such as uncertainty of application to a given problem or situation. ASK theory is an attempt to provide an explicit cognitive explanation of information need or gap by proposing specific reasons why people engage in information seeking. It also suggests that anomalous states could be of different types. One of the strengths of ASK theory is that, unlike many other similar theories, it was successfully tested in a few experiments. One of the weaknesses is that it rests solely on a cognitive basis, using the problem or situation toward which the whole process is oriented as a primitive term.

What is behind the information search process? How is it constructed? Carol Collier Kuhlthau addressed these questions in a series of empirically grounded studies through a period of 20 years starting in the early 1980s.[14] Her model and theory, called the Kuhlthau Information Search Model, provides a conceptual and relatively detailed framework of the information-seeking and search process. It is based on the personal construct theory in psychology that views learning as a process of testing constructs; consequently it views the search as a dynamic process of progressive construction. The model describes common patterns in the process of information seeking for complex tasks that have a discrete beginning and ending over time and that require construction and learning. The innovative part of the model is that it integrates thoughts, feelings, and actions in a set of stages from initiation to presentation of the search process. Not only cognitive, but also affective aspects, such as uncertainty connected with anxiety, are brought in the explanation of the process. The work started within learning context in schools, continued with a series of longitudinal studies, and moved on to a series of case studies in a number of fields. The strength of the model is that it incorporates affective factors that play a great role not only in searching but in human information behavior at large; furthermore it was extensively verified and revised over time. The weakness is that its educational roots are still recognizable—many search processes have different goals and contexts, thus the model may not fit.

What types of activities are involved in information seeking in general and information retrieval searching in particular? What is the relation between different activities? Starting in the mid-1980s and continuing for close to two decades, David Ellis and his colleagues addressed these questions in a series of empirical studies that led to the formulation and continuing refinement of a model known as Ellis's Model of Information-Seeking Behavior, primarily oriented toward behavior in information retrieval.[15] The model is based on a theoretical premise that the study of behavior presents a more tractable and observable focus for study than cognitive approaches. Consequently, its base is behavioral rather than cognitive. The model incorporates a premise that the complex process of information seeking, particularly as related to information retrieval, rests on a relatively small and finite number of different types of interacting activities, these include starting, chaining, browsing, differentiating, monitoring, and extracting. The explicit goal of studies associated with Ellis' model was pragmatic: to inform design and operations of IR systems. The strength of the model is in the reduction of a complex process to a relatively small set of distinct and dynamically interacting processes. The weakness is that it does not address cognitive and affective aspects, shown to be of importance.

The three models can be considered also as theories of information behavior. In turn, each of them is based on a different approach and theory. The first one is related to cognition as treated in cognitive science, the second to personal construct theory in psychology, and the third to behaviorism in psychology. This illustrates different approaches and multidisciplinary connections of human information behavior studies in information science. As yet, they have not found a common ground.

METRICS

Considering the Three Big Questions for information science, stated above, this section addresses the physical question: *What are the features and laws of the recorded information universe?* While often connected with systems, the emphasis in this area of information science is on information objects or artifacts rather than systems; these are the content of the systems. It is about characterizing content objects.

Metrics, such as econometrics, biometrics, sociometrics, etc., are important components in many fields; they deal with statistical properties, relations, and principles of a variety of entities in their domain. Metric studies in information science follow these by concentrating on statistical properties and the discovery of associated relations and principles of information objects, structures, and processes. The goals of metric studies in information science, as in other fields, are to characterize statistically, entities under study and more ambitiously to discover regularities and relations in their distributions and dynamics, in order to observe predictive regularities and formulate laws.

The metric studies in information science concentrate on a number of different entities. To denote a given entity under study over time, these studies were labeled by different names. The oldest and most widely used is *bibliometrics*—the quantitative study of the properties of literature, or more specifically of documents, and document-related processes. Bibliometric studies in information science emerged in the 1950s right after the start of the field. *Scientometrics*, which came about in the 1960s, refers to bibliometric and other metric studies specifically concentrating on science. *Informetrics*, emerging in the 1990s, refers to the quantitative study of properties of all kinds of information entities in addition to documents, subsuming bibliometrics. *Webometrics*, which came about at the end of the 1990s, concentrates, as the name implies, on Web-related entities. *E-Metrics*, which emerged around 2000, are measures of electronic resources, particularly in libraries.

Studies that preceded bibliometrics in information science emerged in the 1920s and 1930s; they were related to authors and literature in science and technology. A number of studies went beyond reporting statistical distributions, concentrating on relations between a quantity and the related yield of entities under study. Here are two significant studies that subsequently greatly affected development of bibliometrics. In the 1920s, Alfred Lotka (1880–1949, American mathematician, chemist, and statistician) reported on the distribution of productivity of authors in chemistry and physics in terms of articles published. He found a regular pattern where a large proportion of the total literature is actually produced by a small proportion of the total number of authors, falling down in a regular pattern, where the majority of authors produce but one paper—after generalization this became known as Lotka's law. In the 1930s, Samuel Bradford (1878–1948, British mathematician and librarian), using relatively complete subject bibliographies, studied the scatter of articles relevant to a subject among journals. He found that a small number of journals produce a large proportion of articles on the subject and that the distribution falls regularly to a point where a large number of journals produce but one article on the same subject—after generalization this became known as Bradford's law or Bradford's distribution. Similar quantity-yield patterns were found in a number of fields and are generally known as Pareto distributions (after Italian economist Vilfredo Pareto, 1848–1923). Lotka's and Bradford's distributions were confirmed many times over in subsequent bibliometric studies starting in the 1950s. They inspired further study and moreover set a general approach in bibliometric studies that was followed for decades.

Data Sources

All metric studies start from and depend on data sources from which statistics can be extracted. Originally, Lotka used, among others, Chemical Abstracts, and Bradford used bibliographies in applied geophysics and in lubrication. These were printed sources and analysis was manual. For a great many years, the same kind of print sources and manual analysis methods were used.

The advent of digital technology vastly changed the range of sources, as well as significantly enlarged the type and method of analysis in bibliometrics, or as Thelwall put it, in a historical synthesis of the topic, "bibliometrics has changed out of all recognition since 1958."[16] This is primarily because sources of data for bibliometric analyses proliferated (and keep proliferating), inviting new analysis methods and uses of results.

In 1960 Eugene Garfield (U.S. chemist, information scientist, and entrepreneur) established the Institute for Scientific Information (ISI), which became a major innovative company in the creation of a number of

information tools and in bibliometric research. In 1964, ISI started publishing the *Science Citation Index*, created by use of computers. Citation indexes in social sciences and in art and humanities followed. While citation indexes in various subjects, law in particular, existed long before Garfield applied them in science, the way they were produced and used was innovative. Besides being a commercial product, citation indexes became a major data source for bibliometric research. They revolutionized bibliometrics.

In addition to publication sources—journal articles and citations—de Solla Price pioneered the use of a range of statistics from science records, economics, social sciences, history, international reports, and other sources to derive generalizations about the growth of science and the factors that affected information explosion.[5] Use of diverse sources became a trademark of scientometrics.

As the Web became the fastest growing and spreading technology in history it also became a new source of data for ever-growing types of bibliometric-like analyses, organized under the common name of webometrics. The Web has a number of unique entities that can be statistically analyzed, such as links, which have dynamic distributions and behavior. Thus, webometrics started covering quite different grounds.

As more and more publications, particularly journals and more books, became digital they also became a rich source for bibliometric analyses. Libraries and other institutions are incorporating these digital resources in their collections, providing a way for various analyses of their use and other aspects. Digital libraries have become a new source of analysis for they are producing massive evidence of the usage patterns of library contents, such as journal articles, for the first time. Thus the emergence of e-metrics.

[From now on all the metric studies in information science (bibliometrics, scientometrics, informetrics, webometrics, and e-metrics) for brevity will be collectively referred to as *bibliometrics*.]

In the digital age, sources for bibliometric analyses are becoming more diversified, complex, and richer. They have become a challenge for developing new methods and refining existing methods and types of analysis.

Types and Application of Results

Lotka showed distribution of publication regarding authors and Bradford distribution of articles regarding journals. In seeking generalization, both formulated respective numerical distributions in a mathematical form. The generalizations sought a scientific law-like predictive power, with full realization that social science laws are not at all like natural science laws. In turn, mathematical expressions of Lotka's and Bradford's laws were refined, enlarged, and corrected in numerous subsequent mathematical papers; the process is still going on. This set the stage for the development of a branch of bibliometrics that is heavily mathematical and theoretical; it is still growing and continuously encompassing new entities and relations as data becomes available. Bradford also illustrated the results graphically. This set the stage for the development of visualization methods for showing distributions and relations; the efforts evolved to become quite sophisticated using the latest methods and tools for data visualization to show patterns and structures.

Over the years, bibliometric studies showed many features of the ever-growing number of entities related to information. Some were already mentioned, here is a sample of others: frequency and distribution analysis of words; co-words; citations; co-citations; e-mails; links; etc., and quite a few others.

Until the appearance of citation indexes, bibliometric studies in information science were geared to analysis of relations; many present studies continue with the same purpose and are geared toward relational applications. But with the appearance of citation data, a second application emerged: evaluative.[16]

Relational applications seek to explicate relationships that are results of research. Examples are emergence of research fronts; institutional, national, and international authorship productivity and patterns; intellectual structure of research fields or domains; and the like.

Evaluative applications seek to assess or evaluate the impact of research, or more broadly, scholarly work in general. Examples are use of citations in promotion and tenure deliberations; ranking or comparison of scholarly productivity; relative contribution of individuals, groups, institutions, or nations; relative standing of journals; and the like.

Evaluative indicators were developed to numerically express the impact of given entities. Here are two of the most widely used indicators. The first deals with journals, the second with authors. *Journal Impact Factor*, devised in the 1960s by Garfield and his colleagues, provides a numerical value to how often a given journal is included in citations in all journals over a given period of time, normalized for the number of articles appearing in a journal. Originally, it was developed as a tool to help selection of journals in *Science Citation Index* but it morphed into a widely used tool for ranking and comparing the impact of journals. The second indicator deals with authors. A most influential new indicator of impact is the *h-index* (proposed in 2005 by Jorge Hirsh, a U.S. physicist). It quantifies and unifies both an author's scientific productivity (number of papers published by an author) and the apparent scientific impact of a scientist (number of citations received)—it unifies how much was published with how

much was cited. Both of the indices are continuously discussed, mathematically elaborated, and criticized.

Evaluative studies are controversial at times. By and large, evaluative applications rest on citations. The central assumption here is that citation counts can be used as an indicator of value because the most influential works are most frequently cited. This assumption is questioned at times, thus it is at the heart of controversies and skepticism about evaluative approaches.

Evaluative applications are used at times in support of decisions related to tenure and promotion processes; academic performance evaluations of individuals and units in universities; periodic national research evaluations; grant applications; direction of research funding; support for journals; setting science policies; and other decisions involving science. Several countries have procedures in place that mandate bibliometric indicators for the evaluation of scientific activities, education, and institutions. They are also used in the search of factors influencing excellence.

The present and widening range of bibliometric studies is furthering understanding of a number of scholarly activities, structures, and communication processes. They are involved in the measuring and mapping of science. In addition, they have a serious impact on evaluation, policy formulation, and decision making in a number of areas outside of information science.

DIGITAL LIBRARIES

Long before digital libraries emerged in the mid-1990s, J.C.R. Licklider (1915–1990, U.S. computer scientist) in a prescient 1965 book *Libraries of the Future* envisioned many of the features of present digital libraries, with some still to come.[17] While Licklider was a technology enthusiast and formulated his vision of the library in a technological context, he also foresaw the handling of content in cognitive, semantic, and interactive ways.

Many of the components were in place quite some time before they were shaped and unified operationally into digital libraries. For instance, online searching of abstracting and indexing databases; a number of network information services; library automation systems; document structuring and manipulation procedures based on metadata; digitized documents; human computer interfaces; and others. With the advent of the Web, many of these older components were refined as needed and amalgamated with a number of new ones to form digital libraries as we know them today.

From the outset, people from a number of fields and backgrounds got involved in the development of digital libraries. Thus various conceptions were derived. Two viewpoints crystallized, one more technological the other more organizational. From the first point of view, a digital library is a managed collection of digital information with associated services, accessible over a network. From the second point of view, a digital library is that, but in addition it involves organizations that provide resources to select, structure, and offer intellectual access to collections of digital works for use by defined communities, and to preserve integrity and ensure persistence of collections and services. The first viewpoint comes mostly from computer science and the second from libraries and other organizations that house and provide digital library services. Digital libraries continue this dual orientation, technological and organizational, because, yes, they are indeed completely dependent on technology but by their purpose and functions they are social systems in the first place.

Many organizations other than libraries enthusiastically started developing and operating digital libraries—museums, historical societies, academic departments, governments, professional organizations, publishers, nonprofit organizations, and so on. As a result, digital libraries take many shapes and forms. They involve a variety of contexts, media, and contents. Many are oriented toward a specific subject. Most importantly, they are used by a variety of users and for a variety of uses. Digital libraries are a highly diverse lot.

The wide and constantly increasing diversity of digital libraries and related collections and portals suggest several issues: traditional libraries are not traditional any more, but hybrid and coming in many digital library forms; many new players have entered the arena, particularly in subject areas; and many new types of uses have emerged in addition to the traditional use of libraries. Digital libraries are truly interdisciplinary. Information science was one of the fields that actively participated in digital library formation, development, and research.

Through NSF and other agencies, the U.S. government funded research in digital libraries through Digital Library Initiatives; European Union and other governments funded similar research and development programs. Governmental funding started around 1995 and lasted about a decade. Most of the funding went toward technological aspects and demonstrations. An important by-product of this funding was the creation of a strong international community of digital library researchers from a number of fields, information science included. Here is another by-product often mentioned: Google was initially developed at Stanford University under an NSF grant in the Digital Library Initiatives program.

From the outset, information science was involved with digital libraries in a number of ways. Professionally, many information scientists work in digital libraries, particularly in relation to their architecture, systems operations, and services. A diverse number of topics were addressed in research covering the whole life-cycle of digital libraries as reflected in numerous reports, journals, proceedings, and books. Here is a sample: development and testing of digital library architecture; development of appropriate metadata; digitization of a variety of media; preservation of digital objects; searching of digital library contents; evaluation of digital libraries; access to digital libraries; security and privacy issues; study of digital libraries as a place and space; study of users, use, and interactions in digital libraries; effect of digital libraries on educational and other social institutions; impact of digital libraries on scholarship and other endeavors; and policy issues. New research topics are coming along at a brisk pace.

The rapid development and widespread deployment of digital libraries became a force that is determining not only the future of libraries but also of many other organizations as social, cultural, and community institutions. It is instrumental in the development of e-science. It is also affecting the direction of information science in that the domain of problems addressed has been significantly enlarged.

EDUCATION

The fact that education is critical for any field is a truism that hardly needs to be stated. Information science education began slowly in the 1950s and 1960s. Two educational models evolved over time and were followed for decades to come: For brevity, they should be referred to as the Shera and Salton models, after those that pioneered them. Both have strengths and weaknesses. A third model is presently emerging, under the label of i-Schools.

Jesse H. Shera (1903–1982, librarian and library educator) was a library school dean at Western Reserve University (later Case Western Reserve) from 1952 to 1970. Among others, he was instrumental in starting the Center for Documentation and Communication Research at the library school there in 1955. The Center was oriented toward research and development in IR. Shortly thereafter, the library school curriculum started to include courses such as "machine literature searching" (later to become "information retrieval"), and a few other more advanced courses and laboratories on the topics of research in the Center. The basic approach was to append those courses, mostly as electives, to the existing library school curriculum, without modifications of the curriculum as a whole, and particularly not the required core courses. Information science (or information retrieval) became one of the specialty areas of library science. The base or core courses that students were taking rested in the traditional library curriculum. Information science education was an appendage to library science. Library schools in the United States and in many other countries imitated Shera's model. They used the same approach and started incorporating information science courses in their existing curriculum as a specialty.

The strength of the Shera model is that it posits education within a service framework, connects the education to professional practice and a broader and user-oriented frame of a number of other information services, and relates it to a great diversity of information resources. The weakness is a lack of a broader theoretical framework, and a lack of teaching of formalism related to systems, such as the development and understanding of algorithms. A majority of researchers in the human information behavior and user-centered approach are associated with this educational environment. Out of this was born the widely used designation, *library and information science.*

Shera's model, with contemporary modifications is still the prevalent approach in a majority of schools of library and information science. Some schools evolved to include a major in information science, or reoriented the curriculum toward some of the aspects of information science, or even provided a separate degree. The changes in curricula are accelerating. Dissatisfaction with the model as not in synch with contemporary developments related to information-spurred development of i-Schools discussed below.

Gerard Salton (already mentioned above) was first and foremost a scientist, and a computer scientist at that. As such, he pioneered the incorporation into IR research a whole array of formal and experimental methods from science, as modified for algorithmic and other approaches used so successfully in computer science. His primary orientation was research. For education, he took the time-honored approach of a close involvement with research. The Salton model was a laboratory and research approach to education related to IR. As Shera's model resulted in information science education being an appendage to library science education, Salton's model of IR education resulted in being a specialty of and an appendage to computer science education. Computer science students that were already well-grounded in the discipline got involved in SMART and other projects directed by Salton, worked and did research in the laboratory, completed their theses in areas related to IR, and participated in the legendary IR seminars. They also published widely with Salton and with each other and participated with high visibility in national and international conferences. From Harvard and Cornell, his students went to a number of computer science departments where they replicated Salton's model. Many other computer science departments in the United States and abroad took the same approach. The strength of Salton's model is that it: 1) starts from a base of a firm grounding in formal mathematical and

other methods and 2) relates directly to research. The weakness is in that it: 1) ignores the broader aspects of information science, as well as any other disciplines and approaches dealing with the human aspects, that have great relevance to both outcomes of IR research and research itself and 2) does not incorporate professional practice where these systems are realized and used. It loses users. Consequently, this is a successful, but narrowly concentrated education in IR as a specialty of computer science, rather than in information science. Not surprisingly, the researchers in the systems-centered approach came out of this tradition.

The two educational approaches are completely independent of each other. Neither reflects fully what is going on in the field. While in each model there is an increase in cognizance of the other, there is no educational integration of the systems- and user-centered approaches. The evident strengths that are provided by Shera's and Salton's model are not put together.

The late 1990s and early 2000s saw a movement to broaden and reorient information science education, spearheaded by a number of deans of schools with strong information science educations. Some library and information science schools were renamed into Information Schools or i-Schools. An informal i-School Caucus was formed in 2005. By 2008, the Caucus included over 20 schools quite diverse in origin. They include schools of: information; library and information science; information systems; informatics; public policy and management; information and computer sciences; and computing. The i-Schools are primarily interested in educational and research programs addressing the relationship between information, technology, and people and understanding the role of information in human endeavors. While the i-School movement was originally restricted to the United States, some schools outside the United States are joining. The movement is attracting wide international interest.

The i-Schools represent an innovative, new approach to information science education, with some true interdisciplinary connections. As the millennial decade draws toward an end, it is also signifying a new direction to information science education.

CONCLUSIONS

It was mentioned that information science has two orientations: one that deals with information retrieval techniques and systems and the other that deals with information needs and uses, or more broadly with human information behavior. One is technical and system-oriented, the other individual and social and user-oriented. In pursuing these orientations, certain characteristics of the field emerged.

Information science has several general characteristics that are the leitmotif of its evolution and existence. These are shared with many modern fields.

- First, information science is interdisciplinary in nature. However, with various advances, relations with various disciplines are changing over time. The interdisciplinary evolution is far from over.
- Second, information science is inexorably connected to information technology. A technological imperative is compelling and encouraging the evolution of information science, as is the evolution of a number of other fields, and moreover, of the information society as a whole.
- Third, information science is, with many other fields, an active participant in the evolution of the information society. Information science has a strong social and human dimension, above and beyond technology.
- Fourth, while information science has a strong research component that drives advances in the field, it also has an equally strong, if not an even stronger, professional component oriented toward information services in a number of environments. Many innovations come from professionals in the field.
- Fifth, information science is also connected with information industry, a vital, highly diversified, and global branch of the economy.

With accelerating changes in all these characteristics, information science is a field in a constant flux. So are many other fields. The steady aspect is in its general orientation toward information, people, and technology.

REFERENCES

1. Saracevic, T. Information science. J. Am. Soc. Info. Sci. **1999**, *50* (12), 1051–1063.
2. Bates, M.J. The invisible substrate of information science. J. Am. Soc. Info. Sci. **1999**, *50* (12), 1043–1050.
3. National Science Foundation, National Academy of Sciences, American Documentation Institute, National Research Council, In *Proceedings of the International Conference on Scientific Information*; The National Academies Press: Washington, DC, 1959; Vol. 2 http://books.nap.edu/openbook.php?isbn=NI000518&page=R19 (accessed April 2008).
4. Price, D.J.; de, S. In *Science Since Babylon*; Yale University Press: New Haven, CT, 1961.
5. Price, D.J.; de, S. In *Little Science Big Science*; Columbia University Press: New York, 1963.
6. Bush, V. As we may think. Atlantic Mon. **1945**, *176* (11), 101–108 http://www.theatlantic.com/doc/194507/bush (accessed April 2008).
7. White, H.D.; McCain, K.W. Visualizing a discipline: An author cocitation analysis of information science. 1972–1995. J. Am. Soc. Info. Sci. **1998**, *49* (4), 327–355.
8. Zhao, D.; Strotmann, A. Information science during the first decade of the Web: An enriched cocitation analysis. J. Am. Soc. Info. Sci. Technol. **2008**, *59* (6), 916–937.
9. Mooers, C.N. Zatocoding applied to mechanical organization of knowledge. Am. Doc. **1951**, *2* (1), 20–32.
10. In *TREC. Experiment and Evaluation in Information Retrieval*; Voorhees, E.M., Harman, D.K., Eds.; MIT Press: Cambridge, MA, 2005.
11. Case, D.O. In *Looking for Information: A Survey of Research on Information Seeking, Needs, and Behavior*, 2nd Ed.; Academic Press, Elsevier: New York, NY, 2007.
12. Fisher, K.E.; Erdelez, S.; McKechnie, L.E.F. In *Theories of Information Behavior*; American Society for Information Science and Technology: Washington DC, 2005.
13. Belkin, N.J.; Oddy, R.N.; Brooks, H.M. ASK for information retrieval. Parts 1 and 2. J. Doc. **1986**, *28* (2), 61–71, 145–164.
14. Kuhlthau, C.C. In *Seeking Meaning: A Process Approach to Library and Information Services*, 2nd Ed.; Libraries Unlimited: Westport, CT, 2004.
15. Ellis, D. A behavioral model for information retrieval system design. J. Doc. **1989**, *45* (3), 171–212.
16. Thelwall, M. Bibliometrics to webometrics. J. Info. Sci. **2008**, *34* (4), 605–621.
17. Licklider, J.C.R. *Libraries of the Future*; The MIT Press: Cambridge, MA, 1965.

Information Security Controls: Types

Harold F. Tipton
HFT Associates, Villa Park, California, U.S.A.

Abstract

Security is generally defined as the freedom from danger or as the condition of safety. Computer security, specifically, is the protection of data in a system against unauthorized disclosure, modification, or destruction and protection of the computer system itself against unauthorized use, modification, or denial of service. Because certain computer security controls inhibit productivity, security is typically a compromise toward which security practitioners, system users, and system operations and administrative personnel work to achieve a satisfactory balance between security and productivity.

Controls for providing information security can be physical, technical, or administrative. These three categories of controls can be further classified as either preventive or detective. Preventive controls attempt to avoid the occurrence of unwanted events, whereas detective controls attempt to identify unwanted events after they have occurred. Preventive controls inhibit the free use of computing resources and therefore can be applied only to the degree that the users are willing to accept. Effective security awareness programs can help increase users' level of tolerance for preventive controls by helping them understand how such controls enable them to trust their computing systems. Common detective controls include audit trails, intrusion detection methods, and checksums.

Three other types of controls supplement preventive and detective controls. They are usually described as deterrent, corrective, and recovery. Deterrent controls are intended to discourage individuals from intentionally violating information security policies or procedures. These usually take the form of constraints that make it difficult or undesirable to perform unauthorized activities or threats of consequences that influence a potential intruder to not violate security (e.g., threats ranging from embarrassment to severe punishment).

Corrective controls either remedy the circumstances that allowed the unauthorized activity or return conditions to what they were before the violation. The execution of corrective controls could result in changes to existing physical, technical, and administrative controls. Recovery controls restore lost computing resources or capabilities and help the organization recover monetary losses caused by a security violation.

Deterrent, corrective, and recovery controls are considered to be special cases within the major categories of physical, technical, and administrative controls; they do not clearly belong in either preventive or detective categories. For example, it could be argued that deterrence is a form of prevention because it can cause an intruder to turn away; however, deterrence also involves detecting violations, which may be what the intruder fears most. Corrective controls, by contrast, are not preventive or detective, but they are clearly linked with technical controls when antiviral software eradicates a virus or with administrative controls when backup procedures enable restoring a damaged database. Finally, recovery controls are neither preventive nor detective but are included in administrative controls as disaster recovery or contingency plans.

Because of these overlaps with physical, technical, and administrative controls, the deterrent, corrective, and recovery controls are not discussed in this entry. Instead, the preventive and detective controls within the three major categories are examined.

PHYSICAL CONTROLS

Physical security is the use of locks, security guards, badges, alarms, and similar measures to control access to computers, related equipment (including utilities), and the processing facility itself. In addition, measures are required for protecting computers, related equipment, and their contents from espionage, theft, and destruction or damage by accident, fire, or natural disaster (e.g., floods and earthquakes).

Preventive Physical Controls

Preventive physical controls are employed to prevent unauthorized personnel from entering computing facilities (i.e., locations housing computing resources, supporting utilities, computer hard copy, and input data media) and to help protect against natural disasters. Examples of these controls include:

Encyclopedia of Information Systems and Technology, DOI: 10.1081/E-EIST-120046292

Information Science—ITIL

- Backup files and documentation
- Fences
- Security guards
- Badge systems
- Double door systems
- Locks and keys
- Backup power
- Biometric access controls
- Site selection
- Fire extinguishers

Backup files and documentation

Should an accident or intruder destroy active data files or documentation, it is essential that backup copies be readily available. Backup files should be stored far enough away from the active data or documentation to avoid destruction by the same incident that destroyed the original. Backup material should be stored in a secure location constructed of noncombustible materials, including 2-hour-rated fire walls. Backups of sensitive information should have the same level of protection as the active files of this information; it is senseless to provide tight security for data on the system but lax security for the same data in a backup location.

Fences

Although fences around the perimeter of the building do not provide much protection against a determined intruder, they do establish a formal no trespassing line and can dissuade the simply curious person. Fences should have alarms or should be under continuous surveillance by guards, dogs, or TV monitors.

Security guards

Security guards are often stationed at the entrances of facilities to intercept intruders and ensure that only authorized persons are allowed to enter. Guards are effective in inspecting packages or other hand-carried items to ensure that only authorized, properly described articles are taken into or out of the facility. The effectiveness of stationary guards can be greatly enhanced if the building is wired with appropriate electronic detectors with alarms or other warning indicators terminating at the guard station. In addition, guards are often used to patrol unattended spaces inside buildings after normal working hours to deter intruders from obtaining or profiting from unauthorized access.

Badge systems

Physical access to computing areas can be effectively controlled using a badge system. With this method of control, employees and visitors must wear appropriate badges whenever they are in access-controlled areas. Badge-reading systems programmed to allow entrance only to authorized persons can then easily identify intruders.

Double door systems

Double door systems can be used at entrances to restricted areas (e.g., computing facilities) to force people to identify themselves to the guard before they can be released into the secured area. Double doors are an excellent way to prevent intruders from following closely behind authorized persons and slipping into restricted areas.

Locks and keys

Locks and keys are commonly used for controlling access to restricted areas. Because it is difficult to control copying of keys, many installations use cipher locks (i.e., combination locks containing buttons that open the lock when pushed in the proper sequence). With cipher locks, care must be taken to conceal which buttons are being pushed to avoid a compromise of the combination.

Backup power

Backup power is necessary to ensure that computer services are in a constant state of readiness and to help avoid damage to equipment if normal power is lost. For short periods of power loss, backup power is usually provided by batteries. In areas susceptible to outages of more than 15–30 minutes, diesel generators are usually recommended.

Biometric access controls

Biometric identification is a more sophisticated method of controlling access to computing facilities than badge readers, but the two methods operate in much the same way. Biometrics used for identification includes fingerprints, handprints, voice patterns, signature samples, and retinal scans. Because biometrics cannot be lost, stolen, or shared, they provide a higher level of security than badges. Biometric identification is recommended for high-security, low-traffic entrance control.

Site selection

The site for the building that houses the computing facilities should be carefully chosen to avoid obvious risks. For example, wooded areas can pose a fire hazard, areas on or adjacent to an earthquake fault can be dangerous, and sites located in a flood plain are susceptible to water damage. In addition, locations under an aircraft approach or departure route are risky, and locations adjacent to railroad tracks can be susceptible to vibrations that can precipitate equipment problems.

Fire extinguishers

The control of fire is important to prevent an emergency from turning into a disaster that seriously interrupts data processing. Computing facilities should be located far away from potential fire sources (e.g., kitchens or cafeterias) and should be constructed of noncombustible materials. Furnishings should also be noncombustible. It is important that appropriate types of fire extinguishers be conveniently located for easy access. Employees must be trained in the proper use of fire extinguishers and in the procedures to follow should a fire break out.

Automatic sprinklers are essential in computer rooms and surrounding spaces and when expensive equipment is located on raised floors. Sprinklers are usually specified by insurance companies for the protection of any computer room that contains combustible materials. However, the risk of water damage to computing equipment is often greater than the risk of fire damage. Therefore, carbon dioxide extinguishing systems were developed; these systems flood an area threatened by fire with carbon dioxide, which suppresses fire by removing oxygen from the air. Although carbon dioxide does not cause water damage, it is potentially lethal to people in the area and is now used only in unattended areas.

Existing extinguishing systems flood the area with Halon, which is usually harmless to equipment and less dangerous to personnel than carbon dioxide. At a concentration of about 10%, Halon extinguishes fire and can be safely breathed by humans. However, higher concentrations can eventually be a health hazard. In addition, the blast from releasing Halon under pressure can blow loose objects around and can be a danger to equipment and personnel. For these reasons and because of the high cost of Halon, it is typically used only under raised floors in computer rooms. Because it contains chlorofluorocarbons, it will soon be phased out in favor of a gas that is less hazardous to the environment.

Detective Physical Controls

Detective physical controls warn protective services personnel that physical security measures are being violated. Examples of these controls include:

- Motion detectors
- Smoke and fire detectors
- Closed-circuit television monitors
- Sensors and alarms

Motion detectors

In computing facilities that usually do not have people in them, motion detectors are useful for calling attention to potential intrusions. Motion detectors must be constantly monitored by guards.

Fire and smoke detectors

Fire and smoke detectors should be strategically located to provide early warning of a fire. All fire detection equipment should be tested periodically to ensure that it is in working condition.

Closed-circuit television monitors

Closed-circuit televisions can be used to monitor the activities in computing areas where users or operators are frequently absent. This method helps detect individuals behaving suspiciously.

Sensors and alarms

Sensors and alarms monitor the environment surrounding the equipment to ensure that air and cooling water temperatures remain within the levels specified by equipment design. If proper conditions are not maintained, the alarms summon operations and maintenance personnel to correct the situation before a business interruption occurs.

TECHNICAL CONTROLS

Technical security involves the use of safeguards incorporated in computer hardware, operations or applications software, communications hardware and software, and related devices. Technical controls are sometimes referred to as logical controls.

Preventive Technical Controls

Preventive technical controls are used to prevent unauthorized personnel or programs from gaining remote access to computing resources. Examples of these controls include:

- Access control software
- Antivirus software
- Library control systems
- Passwords
- Smart cards
- Encryption
- Dial-up access control and callback systems

Access control software

The purpose of access control software is to control sharing of data and programs between users. In many computer systems, access to data and programs is implemented by access control lists that designate which users are allowed access. Access control software provides the ability to control access to the system by establishing that only registered users with an authorized log-on ID and password can gain access to the computer system.

After access to the system has been granted, the next step is to control access to the data and programs residing in the system. The data or program owner can establish rules that designate who is authorized to use the data or program.

Antivirus software

Viruses have reached epidemic proportions throughout the microcomputing world and can cause processing disruptions and loss of data as well as significant loss of productivity while cleanup is conducted. In addition, new viruses are emerging at an ever-increasing rate—about one every 48 hours. It is recommended that antivirus software be installed on all microcomputers to detect, identify, isolate, and eradicate viruses. This software must be updated frequently to help fight new viruses. In addition, to help ensure that viruses are intercepted as early as possible, antivirus software should be kept active on a system, not used intermittently at the discretion of users.

Library control systems

These systems require that all changes to production programs be implemented by library control personnel instead of the programmers who created the changes. This practice ensures separation of duties, which helps prevent unauthorized changes to production programs.

Passwords

Passwords are used to verify that the user of an ID is the owner of the ID. The ID–password combination is unique to each user and therefore provides a means of holding users accountable for their activity on the system.

Fixed passwords that are used for a defined period of time are often easy for hackers to compromise; therefore, great care must be exercised to ensure that these passwords do not appear in any dictionary. Fixed passwords are often used to control access to specific databases. In this use, however, all persons who have authorized access to the database use the same password; therefore, no accountability can be achieved.

Dynamic or one-time passwords, which are different for each log-on, are preferred over fixed passwords. Dynamic passwords are created by a token that is programmed to generate passwords randomly.

Smart cards

Smart cards are usually about the size of a credit card and contain a chip with logic functions and information that can be read at a remote terminal to identify a specific user's privileges. Smart cards carry prerecorded, usually encrypted access control information that is compared with the data that the user provides (e.g., a personal ID number or biometric data) to verify authorization to access the computer or network.

Encryption

Encryption is defined as the transformation of plaintext (i.e., readable data) into ciphertext (i.e., unreadable data) by cryptographic techniques. Encryption is presently considered to be the only sure way of protecting data from disclosure during network transmissions.

Encryption can be implemented with either hardware or software. Software-based encryption is the least expensive method and is suitable for applications involving low-volume transmissions; the use of software for large volumes of data results in an unacceptable increase in processing costs. Because there is no overhead cost associated with hardware encryption, this method is preferred when large volumes of data are involved.

Dial-up access control and callback systems

Dial-up access to a computer system increases the risk of intrusion by hackers. In networks that contain personal computers or are connected to other networks, it is difficult to determine whether dial-up access is available or not because of the ease with which a modem can be added to a personal computer to turn it into a dial-up access point. Known dial-up access points should be controlled so that only authorized dial-up users can get through.

The best dial-up access controls use a microcomputer to intercept calls, verify the identity of the caller (using a dynamic password mechanism), and switch the user to authorized computing resources as requested. Previously, call-back systems had intercepted dial-up callers, verified their authorization, and called them back at their registered number, which at first proved effective; however, sophisticated hackers have learned how to defeat this control using call-forwarding techniques.

Detective Technical Controls

Detective technical controls warn personnel of violations or attempted violations of preventive technical controls. Examples of these include audit trails and intrusion detection expert systems, which are discussed in the following sections.

Audit trails

An audit trail is a record of system activities that enables the reconstruction and examination of the sequence of events of a transaction, from its inception to output of final results. Violation reports present significant, security-oriented events that may indicate either actual or attempted policy transgressions reflected in the audit trail. Violation reports should be frequently and regularly reviewed by security officers and database owners to identify and investigate successful or unsuccessful unauthorized accesses.

Intrusion detection systems

These expert systems track users (on the basis of their personal profiles) while they are using the system to determine whether their ongoing activities are consistent with an established norm. If not, the user's session can be terminated or a security officer can be called to investigate. Intrusion detection can be especially effective in cases in which intruders are pretending to be authorized users or when authorized users are involved in unauthorized activities.

ADMINISTRATIVE CONTROLS

Administrative, or personnel, security consists of management constraints, operational procedures, accountability procedures, and supplemental administrative controls established to provide an acceptable level of protection for computing resources. In addition, administrative controls include procedures established to ensure that all personnel who have access to computing resources have the required authorizations and appropriate security clearances.

Preventive Administrative Controls

Preventive administrative controls are personnel-oriented techniques for controlling peoples' behavior to ensure the confidentiality, integrity, and availability of computing data and programs. Examples of preventive administrative controls include:

- Security awareness and technical training
- Separation of duties

- Procedures for recruiting and terminating employees
- Security policies and procedures
- Supervision
- Disaster recovery, contingency, and emergency plans
- User registration for computer access

Security awareness and technical training

Security awareness training is a preventive measure that helps users to understand the benefits of security practices. If employees do not understand the need for the controls being imposed, they may eventually circumvent them and thereby weaken the security program or render it ineffective.

Technical training can help users prevent the most common security problem—errors and omissions—as well as ensure that they understand how to make appropriate backup files and detect and control viruses. Technical training in the form of emergency and fire drills for operations personnel can ensure that proper action will be taken to prevent such events from escalating into disasters.

Separation of duties

This administrative control separates a process into component parts, with different users responsible for different parts of the process. Judicious separation of duties prevents one individual from obtaining control of an entire process and forces collusion with others in order to manipulate the process for personal gain.

Recruitment and termination procedures

Appropriate recruitment procedures can prevent the hiring of people who are likely to violate security policies. A thorough background investigation should be conducted, including checking on the applicant's criminal history and references. Although this does not necessarily screen individuals for honesty and integrity, it can help identify areas that should be investigated further.

Three types of references should be obtained: 1) employment; 2) character; and 3) credit. Employment references can help estimate an individual's competence to perform, or be trained to perform, the tasks required on the job. Character references can help determine qualities, such as trustworthiness, reliability, and ability to get along with others. Credit references can indicate a person's financial habits, which in turn can be an indication of maturity and willingness to assume responsibility for one's own actions.

In addition, certain procedures should be followed when any employee leaves the company, regardless of the conditions of termination. Any employee being involuntarily terminated should be asked to leave the premises

Information Science–ITIL

immediately upon notification, to prevent further access to computing resources. Voluntary terminations may be handled differently, depending on the judgment of the employee's supervisors, to enable the employee to complete work in process or train a replacement.

All authorizations that have been granted to an employee should be revoked upon departure. If the departing employee has the authority to grant authorizations to others, these other authorizations should also be reviewed. All keys, badges, and other devices used to gain access to premises, information, or equipment should be retrieved from the departing employee. The combinations of all locks known to a departing employee should be changed immediately. In addition, the employee's log-on IDs and passwords should be canceled, and the related active and backup files should be either deleted or reassigned to a replacement employee.

Any special conditions to the termination (e.g., denial of the right to use certain information) should be reviewed with the departing employee; in addition, a document stating these conditions should be signed by the employee. All terminations should be routed through the computer security representative for the facility where the terminated employee works to ensure that all information system access authority has been revoked.

Security policies and procedures

Appropriate policies and procedures are key to the establishment of an effective information security program. Policies and procedures should reflect the general policies of the organization as regards the protection of information and computing resources. Policies should cover the use of computing resources, marking of sensitive information, movement of computing resources outside the facility, introduction of personal computing equipment and media into the facility, disposal of sensitive waste, and computer and data security incident reporting. Enforcement of these policies is essential to their effectiveness.

Supervision

Often, an alert supervisor is the first person to notice a change in an employee's attitude. Early signs of job dissatisfaction or personal distress should prompt supervisors to consider subtly moving the employee out of a critical or sensitive position.

Supervisors must be thoroughly familiar with the policies and procedures related to the responsibilities of their department. Supervisors should require that their staff members comply with pertinent policies and procedures and should observe the effectiveness of these guidelines. If the objectives of the policies and procedures can be accomplished more effectively, the

supervisor should recommend appropriate improvements. Job assignments should be reviewed regularly to ensure that an appropriate separation of duties is maintained, that employees in sensitive positions are occasionally removed from a complete processing cycle without prior announcement, and that critical or sensitive jobs are rotated periodically among qualified personnel.

Disaster recovery, contingency, and emergency plans

The disaster recovery plan is a document containing procedures for emergency response, extended backup operations, and recovery should a computer installation experience a partial or total loss of computing resources or physical facilities (or of access to such facilities). The primary objective of this plan, used in conjunction with the contingency plans, is to provide reasonable assurance that a computing installation can recover from disasters, continue to process critical applications in a degraded mode, and return to a normal mode of operation within a reasonable time. A key part of disaster recovery planning is to provide for processing at an alternative site during the time that the original facility is unavailable.

Contingency and emergency plans establish recovery procedures that address specific threats. These plans help prevent minor incidents from escalating into disasters. For example, a contingency plan might provide a set of procedures that defines the condition and response required to return a computing capability to nominal operation; an emergency plan might be a specific procedure for shutting down equipment in the event of a fire or for evacuating a facility in the event of an earthquake.

User registration for computer access

Formal user registration ensures that all users are properly authorized for system and service access. In addition, it provides the opportunity to acquaint users with their responsibilities for the security of computing resources and obtain their agreement to comply with related policies and procedures.

Detective Administrative Controls

Detective administrative controls are used to determine how well security policies and procedures are complied with, to detect fraud, and to avoid employing persons who represent an unacceptable security risk. This type of control includes:

- Security reviews and audits
- Performance evaluations

- Required vacations
- Background investigations
- Rotation of duties

Security reviews and audits

Reviews and audits can identify instances in which policies and procedures are not being followed satisfactorily. Management involvement in correcting deficiencies can be a significant factor in obtaining user support for the computer security program.

Performance evaluations

Regularly conducted performance evaluations are an important element in encouraging quality performance. In addition, they can be an effective forum for reinforcing management's support of information security principles.

Required vacations

Tense employees are more likely to have accidents or make errors and omissions while performing their duties. Vacations contribute to the health of employees by relieving the tensions and anxieties that typically develop from long periods of work. In addition, if all employees in critical or sensitive positions are forced to take vacations, there will be less opportunity for an employee to set up a fraudulent scheme that depends on the employee's presence (e.g., to maintain the fraud's continuity or secrecy). Even if the employee's presence is not necessary to the scheme, required vacations can be a deterrent to embezzlement because the employee may fear discovery during his or her absence.

Background investigations

Background investigations may disclose past performances that might indicate the potential risks of future performance. Background investigations should be conducted on all employees being considered for promotion or transfer into a position of trust; such investigations should be completed before the employee is actually placed in a sensitive position. Job applicants being considered for sensitive positions should also be investigated for potential problems. Companies involved in government-classified projects should conduct these investigations while obtaining the required security clearance for the employee.

Rotation of duties

Similar to required vacations, rotation of duties (i.e., moving employees from one job to another at random intervals) helps deter fraud. An additional benefit is that as a result of rotating duties, employees are cross-trained to perform each other's functions in case of illness, vacation, or termination.

SUMMARY

Information security controls can be classified as physical, technical, or administrative. These are further divided into preventive and detective controls. Fig. 1 lists the controls discussed in this entry.

The organization's security policy should be reviewed to determine the confidentiality, integrity, and availability needs of the organization. The appropriate physical,

Physical Controls	Technical Controls	Administrative Controls
Preventative	**Preventative**	**Preventative**
• Backup files and documentation	• Access control software	• Security awareness and technical training
• Fences	• Antivirus software	• Separation of duties
• Security guards	• Library control systems	• Procedures for recruiting and terminating employees
• Badge systems	• Passwords	• Security policies and procedures
• Locks and keys	• Smart cards	• Supervision
• Backup power	• Encryption	• Disaster recovery and contingency plans
• Biometric access controls	• Dial-up access control and callback systems	• User registration for computer access
• Site selection		
• Fire extinguishers		
Detective	**Detective**	**Detective**
• Motion detectors	• Audit trails	• Security reviews and audits
• Smoke and fire detectors	• Intrusion-detection expert systems	• Performance evaluations
• Closed-circuit television monitoring		• Required vacations
• Sensors and alarms		• Background investigations
		• Rotation of duties

Fig. 1 Information security controls.

technical, and administrative controls can then be selected to provide the required level of information protection, as stated in the security policy.

A careful balance between preventive and detective control measures is needed to ensure that users consider the security controls reasonable and to ensure that the controls do not overly inhibit productivity. The combination of physical, technical, and administrative controls best suited for a specific computing environment can be identified by completing a quantitative risk analysis. Because this is usually an expensive, tedious, and subjective process, however, an alternative approach— referred to as meeting the standard of due care—is often used. Controls that meet a standard of due care are those that would be considered prudent by most organizations in similar circumstances or environments. Controls that meet the standard of due care generally are readily available for a reasonable cost and support the security policy of the organization; they include, at the least, controls that provide individual accountability, auditability, and separation of duties.

Information Systems

E. Burton Swanson
Anderson School of Management, University of California—Los Angeles, Los Angeles, California, U.S.A.

Abstract

An information system provides information to help guide organizational actions. It typically features substantial human–computer interaction. Application software and a data base form the digital content around which a system is built. Among the different types are transaction-processing systems, management information systems, decision support systems, group support systems, and enterprise systems.

INTRODUCTION

An information system is commonly a computer-based system for providing information to an organization to help guide its actions.[1] The term "information system" is also sometimes used in information science to refer to information retrieval systems based more on documents than on data, an application domain familiar to libraries, in particular. The term is sometimes also used very generally and informally, without reference to either computers or organizations. People sometimes refer to their own personal information systems, for instance. In this entry, we take the organizational perspective, which has its origins in business, but applies to organizations of every kind, including libraries.

In an organization, an information system typically features people working interactively with computers to accomplish a particular task. Human–computer interaction (HCI) enables both people and their machine extensions to be informed via the system. Where decisions are routine and highly structured, they may sometimes be automated and relegated to the machine.[2] Often, the information provided serves to coordinate workers' specialized but necessarily collective efforts. The varieties of information systems are many, reflecting the diversity of organizations and tasks to be accomplished. A typical large business firm has information systems to support its accounting and finance, operations, supply chain management, sales and marketing, customer service, human resource management, and research and development. But information systems are found everywhere, in organizations of all kinds and sizes, public as well as private.

This entry discusses information systems both as a subject and as a field of study and practice. In the sections to follow, information systems are first described in terms of their 1) origins; 2) varieties; and 3) practices. As information systems also constitute 4) an evolving field of study and practice with; 5) attendant social issues, these aspects too are considered.

ORIGINS

Modern information systems have emerged with the rise and spread of digital computing in the 1950s, although punched card tabulating equipment was in use for data processing in organizations before then. The stored-program computer itself was initially viewed as a high-powered calculating device, suitable primarily for numerical and other sophisticated analyses. Such "scientific computing" was distinguished from what was termed "electronic data processing", which emerged about the same time to support the more prosaic work of business, such as accounting.[3] In the 1960s, computers came to be designed and marketed specifically for business purposes, eventually displacing the tabulating equipment. Notably, a high-level programming language for business applications, Common Business-Oriented Language (COBOL), was also developed, which emphasized data and file structures, and deemphasized the computational features found in FORmula TRANslation (FORTRAN), the language most commonly used in scientific computing. COBOL ultimately became the most widely used programming language for the development of application software for information systems on mainframe computers. As much of this code remains in use, the language persists even today.

Beyond business-oriented application software, the emergence of data base technology in the late 1960s was central to the rapid rise and spread of large-scale information systems among firms. A data base is an organized collection of related data files.[4] A data base management system (DBMS) is system software that enables data bases to be managed as integrated wholes, where relationships among files are clearly delineated. With a DBMS, data can be defined via a data dictionary

Encyclopedia of Information Systems and Technology, DOI: 10.1081/E-EIST-120043700

Information
Science—
ITIL

and managed separately from the different software which access it. Finally, the articulation of the relational data model as a foundation for data bases spurred the development of relational data bases in the 1970s, which came to dominate the field.[5] Today, Oracle provides the leading relational data base software for medium to large firms, while Microsoft's Access is well established among small businesses.

Together, application software and a related data base have come to form the digital content around which any modern information system is now built. Typically, the application software incorporates the "business rules" to be followed, while the data base incorporates the "business facts" that shape the data processing, for instance, in processing a business payroll, or in selling seats to a concert, or in managing the circulation of a library's holdings, or in almost any other endeavor in which carefully informed organizational actions are routinely taken. While the business facts and data base will typically be specific to the enterprise, the business rules and application software may be either specific or generic, i.e., commonly used, as with accounting systems that incorporate professionally mandated rules and principles. Where the business rules and application software is specific to the organization, it may underpin the unique capabilities of the enterprise, in which case it may be strategic.[6] Today, people in a wide variety of occupations and in organizations large and small are likely to work interactively with information systems to accomplish much of their work. Through networks and the Web and Internet, in particular, and through the use of laptops and mobile devices they engage in this HCI from wherever they happen to be and at whatever times they choose or are called upon to be available.

VARIETIES

Information systems come in a wide variety, reflecting the diversity in the organizations that employ them. Among business firms, some information systems will be characteristic of the industry, in particular, as with process control systems in chemical and refining enterprises, or electronic funds transfer (EFT) systems in banks and other financial services firms. However, certain basic types are found in enterprises of all kinds, reflecting both their historical origins based in then-new technologies and the nature of organization itself. These include transaction-processing systems; management information systems (MIS); decision support systems (DSS); group support systems; and enterprise systems. These are not pure types; actual systems may combine features of two or more basic types.

Transaction-Processing Systems

Transaction-processing systems support an enterprise in its transactions with others, such as customers, suppliers, and employees.[7] Every business transaction involves an exchange of goods, services, money, and information in some combination between the parties. Transaction-processing systems exist to ensure the integrity of these transactions. In today's world, each time a consumer makes a purchase with a credit card, withdraws cash from an account, or books an airline ticket, the consumer likely engages the other party's transaction-processing systems. Increasingly, a consumer does this directly, by swiping a bank card at a point-of-sale (POS) device or employing an automated teller machine (ATM) or initiating a purchase from the Web.

Beyond their primary function, transaction-processing systems also enable a business to coordinate its internal operations among units, especially in the making of goods, where parts are withdrawn from inventory and a manufactured item is assembled in a series of operations, and the final product eventually distributed from one location to another, for instance. Here and elsewhere, transaction-processing systems are basically event driven, and are often engaged to authorize formal actions, such as accepting a customer order or authorizing a credit purchase. The business rules for such data processing may be quite sophisticated, as in credit authorization that incorporates rules aimed at fraud detection, for instance. The data pertaining to these events will ultimately serve to update a data base that is typically drawn upon in processing and is relied upon to give the existing status of the organization's affairs. Where the data base is immediately updated as events happen, the system is said to operate in "real time." In the case of firms, basic transaction data will further feed the accounting systems that provide a formal financial picture of the ongoing business.

Where firms do business with each other, for instance, within a supply chain, their transaction-processing systems are also sometimes tied together by means of an interorganizational system that enables them to communicate directly with each other.[8] For such machine-to-machine communication, this necessitates resolution of disparities in how the data themselves are defined by the communicating parties. The interorganizational system may be based on electronic data interchange (EDI) arrangements or increasingly on eXtensible Markup Language (XML) standards for exchange over the Web. The concept of Web services envisions a world of business services and firm transactions seamlessly tied together via standards for business data of all kinds.[9]

Management Information Systems

Management information systems support an organization's hierarchical structure and are targeted to management at all levels. MIS aim to support every manager's need to know within his or her scope of responsibility, typically by extracting important performance information from data gathered from the organization's transaction-processing and operational systems and presenting it efficiently in tabular or graphical form. The concept of an MIS emerged in the 1960s and signaled an important transition in information systems, from traditional EDP to systems that served more sophisticated purposes.[10] In the United States, both practitioners and educators embraced the MIS concept and many business schools originated programs of study under this banner. Today the term continues to be widely used, although the more generic term "information systems" has become more common.

Executive information systems (EIS) were founded in the 1980s as a new form of MIS aimed at top management.[11] The early EIS featured access to news external to the business, in addition to traditional performance metrics, and further employed new graphics and communications technologies. Lately, executive support systems have been developed that provide a personalized Web page and "executive dashboard" of up-to-the-minute information with which the manager is to engage and steer the enterprise. These systems are now also popularly referred to as "business intelligence systems," reflecting the sophisticated analytics that may lie behind the dashboard metrics.[12]

Decision Support Systems

Decision support systems emerged in the 1970s as interactive systems that supported managers and other "knowledge workers" in tasks that were semi-structured, where decisions could be aided by analytical computer-based means.[13] These systems shifted the original MIS focus from information to decisions. Early DSS featured innovative HCI employing graphics, formal models, and heuristics or algorithms as means of support. A pioneering example was IBM's Geodata Analysis and Display Systems (GADS), which supported organizational decisions related to urban geography, such as arranging police beats and assigning school district boundaries.[14] Today, the concept of geographical information systems (GIS) continues in this tradition as a major area of application supported by new technologies such as remote sensing, geographical positioning, graphical analytics, and visualization. The firm ESRI is the leading provider of GIS software.

The concept of group decision support systems (GDSS) extended the basic DSS concept in the 1980s.

Substantial research led to the development of decision rooms equipped with systems that facilitated complex, interactive group decision making in a particular location.[15] The early focus was typically on largely unstructured problems, with tools provided to support collective brainstorming and idea evaluation, for instance, while further capturing a record of the group meeting. With advances in communications technologies, the GDSS concept soon evolved into one that supported group work more broadly, where group members could be at multiple locations and could also meet asynchronously as needed.

Group Support Systems

Beyond the informational and decisional needs of managers, it is well understood that communication and cooperation more broadly in the organization is required to coordinate the work undertaken within and across units. Certain of this communication and cooperation can be built into the work systems themselves; however, other organizational means such as cross-functional teams can also facilitate lateral communication, cooperation, and coordination, thus moderating the burden on the management hierarchy.[16] Not surprisingly, given the ubiquity of group work in organizations, a wide variety of systems have been originated to support group work, in particular.

The concept of computer-supported collaborative work (CSCW) originated in the 1980s to characterize designs for computer-enabled group work, understood to require substantial communication and coordination, typically over time and across locations.[17] Lotus Notes exemplified the software then deployed in these new systems and remains in wide use today. Existing groupware in support of group work is diverse and includes, e.g., that which provides for electronic meetings, electronic mail and messaging, calendar management, project and document management, knowledge sharing, workflow management, and collaborative design. Today, group work can also be organized and conducted on the Web, making use of a commercially available service.

Enterprise Systems

Enterprise systems emerged in the 1990s with the rise of enterprise resource planning (ERP), a concept for integrating the major functional systems of the enterprise, in particular, the organization's financial, human resource, and operational systems around a common data base.[18] The principal means of integration was typically a software package provided by a vendor such as SAP or Oracle. Firms sought to replace their older and disparate home-grown legacy systems, which required high maintenance, with standard off-the-shelf software that promised an integrated solution to relieve them of this burden. ERP basically incorporated the firm's major transaction-processing and operational systems. Its adoption was further given a large boost by concerns related to the millennium bug and the threat it posed at the time to vulnerable legacy systems. Today, most large firms have adopted and implemented ERP in the form of packaged software provided by one or more leading suppliers.

A second type of enterprise system termed customer relationship management (CRM) has also become popular, focusing on the "front office" of a firm, beyond the already heavily computerized "back office."[19] A central CRM aim is to provide the firm with a "unified view" of its customers, who might otherwise engage in separate transactions with different business units, each in the absence of full customer information. Just as it promises better customer service, CRM also typically supports a firm's sales force and enables it to be better managed. Still another CRM aim is to help the firm assess the profitability of its different customer segments, in the interest of focusing marketing and customer retention initiatives on achieving higher overall profits.

PRACTICE

Information systems practice rests on four closely intertwined bodies of professional knowledge: 1) application knowledge; 2) technology knowledge; 3) development knowledge; and 4) management knowledge. Each is associated with job specialties in the field.

Application Knowledge

Application knowledge refers to the domain in which the information system supports work within the organization. The system's users are of course expected to be knowledgeable in this domain, first and foremost. So too are the systems analysts who aid in specifying the requirements for any new system. The required knowledge may be relatively broad or narrow, shallow or deep, according to the work supported, which often involves multiple individuals in different roles. The purpose of the information system is typically to inform its various users within such a work system, in support of their decisions and actions.[20] Beyond their domain knowledge, users are typically trained in their interactive use of any new system, such that they understand how to navigate it, interpret its displays or other output, and provide needed data or other input. Ease of use is a major issue in successful implementation.

Notwithstanding such training, research suggests that new information systems are unlikely to deliver full

value to organizations and their users until they have been assimilated into the work practices they support.[21] Repeated "learning by doing" is needed before users "appropriate" a system into their preferred work practices. Moreover, with such assimilation, certain application knowledge will be tacit on the part of users, demonstrated primarily in their competently doing the needed work. Users will also typically find new uses of information systems, beyond those envisioned by system designers. Systems are thus substantially "reinvented" through their use. Importantly, then, application knowledge is ultimately inseparable from the work practice that gives it meaning.

Technology Knowledge

Technology knowledge pertains to the computer-based platforms on which applications are built. This includes the computers, communications, storage and other devices, and the system software that operates these resources. Among the jobs associated with building and maintaining these platforms are those of the system programmer, the network manager, the data base administrator, and the Web master. Technology knowledge also pertains to basic tools and resources drawn on by those engaged directly in application development; these are sometimes integrated and provided in the form of a "work bench."

The most basic aspects of a computer-based platform are its suitability, capacity, and reliability in supporting applications. Growth in firms and their information systems makes capacity planning a vital task. Also important are standards.[22] Where the platforms are in wide use by organizations, the associated technology knowledge is similarly widespread and more easily acquired in the marketplace when needed. Even more significantly, widely used platforms attract their own extensions, as vendors build new features for them roughly according to the potential market reached. This advantage extends to the application software employed in system building, where a wider variety of packaged systems will be readily available for standard platforms.

Development Knowledge

Development knowledge pertains to the application software, data model, Web or other interface, and human procedures that are specified, built or otherwise acquired, documented, tested, installed, and maintained over the life of an information system. It pertains further to the methodology used in this particular work.[23] Principal jobs include those of the systems analyst, who in collaboration with prospective users specifies the functional requirements for the system, and the applications programmer, who in consultation with the systems analyst designs and codes the software to meet these specifications. Within the user community, "lead users" often represent the interest of their peers in the development activity, helping in particular with system implementation and needed training.

Project management knowledge for guiding implementation of systems is especially important, as system development work tends to be organized as projects. Senior developers of individual systems often work as project managers. Projects are typically managed according to their associated deliverables, schedule, and budget. Because of characteristic pressures on schedule and budget, a particularly important aspect of project management is attention to the quality of the deliverables as well as the avoidance of their expensive elaboration through "feature creep." While these issues have long been well known among professionals, they continue to bedevil most of those engaged in the work.[24]

Management Knowledge

Management knowledge pertains to the management of information systems activities within the enterprise. Depending on the size of the organization, managers may include the data center or operations manager, the network manager, the applications development manager, the applications maintenance manager, and the executive in charge of the function as a whole, who in a large organization sometimes has the title of chief information officer (CIO). A primary responsibility of the CIO is the alignment of the information systems strategy with the broader firm strategy.[25] Another is the staffing and organization of the function and the building of its expertise, as well as setting policy and contracting for external services. A third is the building of a reliable and adaptable network and technological infrastructure.[26] Still another is the management of the application systems portfolio, and the allocation of resources between maintenance of existing systems and the development of new or replacement systems.[27]

One highly visible issue of late has been the outsourcing of the information systems function, in whole or in part. "Off-shoring" is much discussed, in particular. Much system development work in the most developed nations is now carried out in countries with more attractive wage rates and growing technical competencies, such as India and China, and certain eastern European states. Exactly which work should be outsourced and which should not remains controversial.[28] The data center itself is a prime candidate for outsourcing. In general, programming is more easily outsourced than is systems analysis, which requires a deep grasp of the work context. The long-run implications of this shift in work are globally significant for the world economy,

beyond the immediate challenges and choices faced by today's managers.

AN EVOLVING FIELD

Today, the information systems field of study and practice remains an evolving one marked by continuous change. Notwithstanding its accomplishments to date, the field faces numerous challenges. Its various professional associations, publications, and research firms and consultancies will play important roles in guiding future information systems developments.

Professional Associations

The International Federation for Information Processing (IFIP), founded by 13 national computer societies in 1960, established Technical Committee 8 (TC8) on Information Systems in 1966. TC8's aims are "to promote and encourage interactions among professionals from practice and research and advancement of investigation of concepts, methods, techniques, tools, and issues related to information systems in organizations."[29] TC8 now includes eight working groups, the first of which, WG8.1, Design and Evaluation of Information Systems, was established in 1976, and the second of which, WG8.2, The Interaction of Information Systems and the Organization, was established in 1977.

The International Conference on Information Systems (ICIS) is the premier academic research conference in the field, held annually since 1980. The Association for Information Systems (AIS) is the leading academic association, established in 1994 to bring IS academics together from around the world. It sponsors ICIS and three regional conferences annually: the Americas Conference on Information Systems (AMCIS); the European Conference on Information Systems (ECIS); and the Pacific Asia Conference on Information Systems (PACIS). Among its other activities, AIS publishes the *Journal of AIS* and *Communications of AIS*, and sponsors AIS World, an important Web resource for IS scholars.

The IS field today also maintains its important roots in the allied fields of computer science, operations research, and management. The Association for Computing Machinery (ACM), founded in 1947, claims to be the world's oldest educational and scientific computing society and now serves professionals in more than 100 countries. Its many publications include the widely read *Communications of the ACM*, which features many articles of interest to IS professionals. Its interest groups include the Special Interest Group on Management Information Systems (SIGMIS). Among ACM's most important contributions has been its issuance since

Information Science–ITIL

1972–1973 of curriculum recommendations for academic programs of study in information systems.[30]

The Institute for Operations Research and Management Science (INFORMS), formed in 1995 from two earlier societies, is now an umbrella association of operations for research-oriented academics and practitioners that includes an Information Systems Society among its 10 societies. It also publishes the leading journal, *Information Systems Research*, begun in 1990.

The Academy of Management includes an Organizational Communications and Information Systems Division among its some two dozen interest groups and divisions.

Among practitioners, the Society for Information Management (SIM), originally founded as the Society for Management Information Systems (SMIS) in 1969, serves IS executives and professionals through a series of chapters located primarily in North America. In its early years, SIM was instrumental in advancing the MIS concept among executives.[31] It also established the leading journal, *MIS Quarterly*, in 1977, in cooperation with the Management Information Systems Research Center (MISRC) of the University of Minnesota, which now publishes it exclusively, while SIM members receive it as a membership option.

Publications

Today, a wide variety of publications reaching both general and specialized audiences feature articles on information systems. Business periodicals such as *The Economist, Business Week*, and the *Wall Street Journal* provide good coverage for the general reader. In addition to those already mentioned, other notable academic journals devoted to information systems include the *Journal of Management Information Systems*, the *Journal of Information Technology, Information and Organization*, and the *European Journal of Information Systems*. Practitioners in the field find the periodicals *Information Week, CIO Magazine*, and *Computerworld* important for following events in the fast-changing technology industry.

Research Firms and Consultancies

Practitioners are also served by a number of market research and analysis firms such as Gartner Group and Forrester Research, which offer assessments of new technologies and their markets, as well as international consultancies such as Accenture, Deloitte, Tata Consulting, and IBM Business Services, which are widely engaged in "system integration" activities, and which further help to spread "best practices" in information systems among firms. These research firms and consultancies also serve as "thought leaders" in the

institutional environment within which "organizing visions" for the application of new technologies originate and serve to guide adoption and diffusion.[32]

SOCIAL ISSUES

Information systems are associated with several ethical and social issues inherent to their nature, design, and use.[33] The authors Kenneth and Jane Laudon identify five moral dimensions to the Information Age: information rights and obligations; property rights and obligations; accountability and control; system quality; and quality of life.[34] We consider each briefly.

Information Rights and Obligations

Every information system poses questions of information rights and obligations, often for both persons and organizations. Rights to individual privacy are particularly salient in an age where much organizational data are gathered about customers, employees, and others, and too where those who do business on the Internet can easily gather individual data generated through Web site visits, for subsequent use in targeted advertising, for instance. Throughout the world, businesses thus now operate under various laws intended to safeguard individual privacy. In Europe, privacy protection is stronger than in the United States, as businesses there are generally prohibited from using information about persons without their prior consent. In the United States, most businesses make their privacy policy known to their customers, who must typically then "opt out" if they wish to avoid having certain of their data shared with others for marketing purposes. As many U.S. customers do not take this opt-out step, nor do many probably even consider it, their individual data are widely shared in marketing.

Privacy concerns are of course also inherent to surveillance schemes which employ information systems. Firms may closely monitor the work of their employees, sometimes stepping over the line into private lives. Governments of all kinds are notoriously tempted to keep more than close track of their citizens as well as others, as they seek to repel threats both real and imagined.

Property Rights and Obligations

Information systems also pose challenges to certain intellectual property, which increasingly is represented in digital form, and which a firm may seek to protect as a trade secret, or through copyright or patent. Both the software and the data associated with information systems are likely to be associated with property rights, as are other digital products such as music or video or text recordings that offer entertainment and education, and which are commonly organized, managed, and distributed via information systems. An interesting illustration today is Apple's i-Tunes business, which is entirely digital in nature, and which distributes music for download by consumers on demand, much of it under protection of Apple digital rights management (DRM) software that is itself a protected asset, with several different parties sharing in the resulting revenues.[35]

Accountability and Liability

Information systems also pose new issues of accountability as well as liability, where harm results from their employment. When things go massively wrong, e.g., when an operating error at a bank results in failure to automatically deposit customer paychecks in a timely manner, it may be difficult to disentangle the reasons behind the debacle. Often we are told that a software bug was the problem, and indeed this is often the case. But because information systems are based substantially in HCI, whether it was human error or a software bug or a problem in data exchanged or the interaction itself, or more broadly a problem in the design or execution of the work being carried out, or a failure in the oversight and management of overall system quality, blame can be difficult to fix and hence may sometimes be misplaced to avoid accountability and in some cases liability.

System Quality

As just suggested, system quality is a broader issue than one of minimizing the bugs in software. Organizations bear a responsibility to attend to the broader quality of their information systems. Research suggests that notwithstanding this responsibility, few firms systematically assess the quality of the data associated with their systems, for instance, even though data errors are known to be rather commonplace.[36] One area where attention to data quality is typically enforced is in business accounting, where external auditors provide independent oversight. However, even here, where the financial stakes may be high, system quality may be compromised through inattention or misguided cost-cutting measures. The reality is that system quality is achieved only at the cost of means that ensure it.

Quality of Life

Lastly, information systems have long been associated with a variety of quality-of-life issues, especially as they pertain to system users.[37] Among ongoing issues are the extent to which power is centralized or decentralized through systems, the increased difficulty in maintaining

a balance between individuals' working and private lives, new vulnerabilities to crime and abuse such as spam, the reengineering of work and its consequences for job skills needed, characteristic health problems such as repetitive stress injury (RSI), the problem of electronic trash disposal, and social inequities in access to technology, as illustrated by the much discussed problem of the "digital divide" in U.S. schools. In short, information systems have come to have pervasive consequences for the quality of our individual and social, and private and public lives.

CONCLUSION

In the relatively short span of several decades, information systems have emerged to be a dominant feature of modern organizational life, with broad implications for people everywhere. The future promises to extend this story. Organizations throughout the world are rapidly building their presence on the Web, and moving from merely offering certain published content, sometimes disparagingly referred to as "brochure ware," to engaging in basic transactions with their customers, suppliers, and other partners. In short, more organizations are doing everyday business on the Web, popularly termed "electronic commerce," underpinned by information systems that make this possible. New businesses are at the same time originating everywhere on the Web to provide the basic infrastructure for doing this business (Google, eBay, and Amazon.com are widely known examples), as well as to offer new distribution for digital content in the realms of education and entertainment, in particular, attracting more traffic to the Web and thus broadening and deepening its user base, making it more appealing for social networking and advertising. As of this writing, the concept of "Web 2.0" as a social space that enables new forms of organizing is the latest new vision to capture the fancy of the field.[38]

ACKNOWLEDGMENTS

I have benefited from several excellent textbooks in preparing this entry and have incorporated them in the references section. They provide good resources for additional reading. I am also grateful to Ephraim R. McLean and an anonymous reviewer for their comments on an earlier prepared version.

REFERENCES

1. Langefors, B. Information systems theory. Inform. Syst. **1977**, 2, 207–219.

2. Simon, H. *The New Science of Management Decision*; Harper & Row: New York, 1960.

3. Canning, R. *Electronic Data Processing for Business and Industry*; Wiley: New York, 1956.

4. Date, C.J. *An Introduction to Data Base Systems*; 3rd Ed.; Addison-Wesley: Reading, MA, 1981.

5. Codd, E.F. A relational model of data for large shared banks. Commun. ACM **1972**, *13* (6), 377–387.

6. Porter, M.E.; Millar, V.E. How information gives you competitive advantage. Harvard Bus. Rev. **1985**, *63* (4), 149–160.

7. Zwass, V. *Foundations of Information Systems*; Irwin/McGraw-Hill: Boston, MA, 1998 Chapter 9.

8. Johnston, R.; Vitale, M.J. Creating competitive advantage with interorganizational information systems. MIS Quart. **1988**, *12* (2), 153–165.

9. Hagel, J., III; Brown, J.S. Your next IT strategy. Harvard Bus. Rev. **2001**, *79* (10), 105–113.

10. Dickson, G.W. Management information systems: Evolution and status. Adv. Comput. **1981**, *20*, 1–37.

11. Watson, H.J.; Rainer, K.; Koh, C. Executive information systems: A framework for development and a survey of current practice. MIS Quart. **1991**, *15* (1), 13–30.

12. Gray, P. *Manager's Guide to Making Decisions about Information Systems*; Wiley: New York, NY, 2006 Chapter 8.

13. Keen, P.G.W.; Scott Morton, M.S. *Decision Support Systems: An Organizational Perspective*; Addison-Wesley: Reading, MA, 1978.

14. Sprague, R.H., Jr.; Carlson, E.D. *Building Effective Decision Support Systems*; Prentice-Hall: Englewood Cliffs, NJ, 1982; 41–54.

15. Dennis, A.R.; George, J.F.; Jessup, L.M.; Nunamker, J. F., Jr.; Vogel, D.R. Information technology to support meetings. MIS Quart. **1988**, *12* (4), 591–624.

16. Galbraith, J. *Designing Complex Organizations*; Addison-Wesley: Reading, MA, 1973.

17. Grudin, J. Computer-supported cooperative work: Its history and participation. IEEE Comput. **1994**, *27* (5), 19–26.

18. Davenport, T.H. Putting the enterprise into enterprise systems. Harvard Bus. Rev. **1998**, *76* (4), 121–131.

19. Winer, R.S. A framework for customer relationship management. Calif. Manage. Rev. **2001**, *43* (4), 89–105.

20. Alter, S. *Information Systems*; 4th Ed.; Prentice-Hall: Upper Saddle River, NJ, 2002.

21. Orlikowski, W.J. Improvising organizational transformation over time: A situated change perspective. Inform. Syst. Res. **1996**, *7* (1), 63–92.

22. Shapiro, C.; Varian, H.R. *Information Rules*; Harvard Business School Press: Cambridge, MA, 1999.

23. Davis, G.B.; Olson, M.H. *Management Information Systems*; 2nd Ed.; McGraw-Hill: New York, NY, 1985, Chapter 18.

24. Keil, M.; Robey, D. Blowing the whistle on troubled software projects. Commun. ACM **2001**, *44* (4), 87–93.

25. *Competing in the Information Age: Strategic Alignment in Practice*; Luftman, J. N., Ed.; Oxford University Press: New York, NY, 1996.

26. Weill, P.; Broadbent, M. *Leveraging the New Infrastructure: How Market Leaders Capitalize on IT*; Harvard Business School Press: Boston, MA, 1998.

27. McFarlan, F.W. Portfolio approach to information systems. Harvard Bus. Rev. **1981**, *59* (5), 142–150.

28. Lacity, M.C.; Willcocks, L.P.; Feeny, D.F. IT outsourcing: Maximize flexibility and control. Harvard Bus. Rev. **1995**, *73* (3), 84–93.

29. Information bulletin, *International Federation for Information Processing*, January, 2007; *37*, 82.

30. Information systems curriculum recommendations for the 80s: Undergraduate and graduate programs. In *Commun. ACM*; Nunamaker, J. F., Jr., Couger, J. D., Davis, G. B., Eds.; 1982; *25* (11), 781–805.

31. *What is a management information system? Research report no. 1*; Society for Management Information Systems: Chicago, IL, 1970.

32. Swanson, E.B.; Ramiller, N. The organizing vision in information systems innovation. Organ. Sci. **1997**, *8* (5), 458–474.

33. Mason, R.O. Four ethical issues of the information age. MIS Quart. **1986**, *10* (1), 5–12.

34. Laudon, K.C.; Laudon, J.P. *Essentials of Business Information Systems*; 7th Ed.; Prentice-Hall: Upper Saddle River, NJ, 2007; 405.

35. *iTunes: How copyright, contract, and technology shape the business of digital media—A case study*; Digital Media Project. The Berkman Center for Internet & Society: Harvard Law School, March 2004.

36. Strong, D.M.; Lee, Y.W.; Wang, R.Y. Data quality in context. Commun. ACM **1997**, *40* (5), 103–110.

37. Mumford, E.; Weir, M. *Computer Systems in Work Design—The ETHICS Method*; Wiley: New York, NY, 1979.

38. McAfee, A. Enterprise 2.0: The dawn of emergent collaboration. MIT Sloan Manage. Rev. **2006**, *47* (3), 21–28.

Information
Science–
ITIL

Information Theory

Paul B. Kantor
School of Communication, Information and Library Studies, Rutgers University, New Brunswick, New Jersey, U.S.A.

Abstract

Information theory "measures quantity of information" and is that branch of applied mathematics that deals with the efficient transmission of messages in an encoded language. It is fundamental to modern methods of telecommunication, image compression, and security. Its relation to library information science (LIS) is less direct. More relevant to the LIS conception of "quantity of information" is economic concepts related to the expected value of a decision, and the influence of imperfect information on that expected value.

THE FUNDAMENTALS OF INFORMATION THEORY

Information theory traces its origin to technical work done by Claude Shannon of Bell Laboratories, in the late 1940s.[1] Communication engineers wanted to determine the largest amount of information that could be transmitted when noise on the "channel" (which was, at the time, a cable carrying electrical waves) made the signal at the receiving end different from what was originally sent.

Shannon introduced measures of the amount of information, of the capacity of a channel, and of the noisiness of the channel, and by combining them was able to prove important mathematical results relating the "rate of transmission of information" to the "capacity of the channel" and the amount of "noise."

Unpredictability, Random Variables, and Information

The capacity required to transmit a message, even through a channel that has no noise in it at all, depends on the unpredictability of the characters in the message.

The discussion of unpredictable messages requires the mathematical concept of a "random variable." An entity is represented mathematically as a random variable when it may take any one of a specified set of values, and, over the long term, the relative frequencies of those alternatives remain steady. The frequencies will then converge to numbers that represent the probabilities of the several alternatives. The choice among them is (subject to these probabilities) not controlled by any known forces, and thus is regarded as random. As an example, the result of a coin toss can be represented by a random variable. In the field of economics, the concept is extended to events that do not repeat many times, and one speaks of "the probability of a nuclear reactor accident" or similar rare events.

A random variable is completely characterized by specifying the allowed set of values, and the probability that it takes on each of its possible values. We can represent this by displaying the alternatives and the probabilities together in an array, as shown in Eq. 1:

$$FairCoin = \begin{bmatrix} .5 & .5 \\ head & tail \end{bmatrix}; BiasedCoin = \begin{bmatrix} .8 & .2 \\ head & tail \end{bmatrix}$$

$$(1)$$

The expression in brackets corresponding to the random variable *FairCoin* means that the event "head" occurs with probability 0.5 or 50%. So does the complementary event "tail." The second expression represents a random variable, *BiasedCoin*, which assumes the value "head" 80% of the time and the value "tail" only 20% of the time.

Equally Probable Alternatives

Shannon showed that the relation between the amount of information in a message and the number of different possible values that the message might have is a logarithmic one. This can be understood in an intuitive way by the following simple argument. Suppose that we have to send a message about which of three alternatives, let us say {A, B, or C}, is true. And we also have to send a message about which of some other four alternatives, let us call them {1, 2, 3, 4}, is true. For example, suppose we want to specify that we will meet for one of three meals, {breakfast, lunch, or dinner} = {A,B,C}, and will do so on one of four days: {Monday, Tuesday, Wednesday, or Thursday} = {1,2,3,4}.

Whatever the amount of information required to specify one out of three alternatives is, and whatever the amount of information required to specify one out of

Encyclopedia of Information Systems and Technology. DOI: 10.1081/E-EIST-120043262

four alternatives is, taken together, the amount of information that they provide is enough to specify one out of 12 alternatives, as there are $12 = 4 \times 3$ possible combinations. The only continuous function that has the required property—that it be additive when its arguments are multiplied—is the logarithm.

Therefore, when there are N equally possible alternatives, the "amount of information" required to specify one of them should be related directly to the logarithm of N. Logarithms may be computed to any base. It is customary in communication to compute the logarithm to the base 2. The resulting number is measured in "bits" (binary digits). For example, $\log_2(8) = 3$ bits.

Varying Probabilities and the Entropy Measure

The situation is more complicated when the alternatives are not equally probable, which leads to the very important concept of entropy. The entropy, or amount of disorder, is a concept previously known for physical systems, which Shannon used very effectively in the discussion of messages.

Shannon showed that this unpredictability could be characterized by a numerical function, which is called the entropy of the message. The higher the entropy of the message, the longer the string (or the larger the "alphabet") required to transmit it accurately, and the more "information" it carries.

The entropy is a mathematical function that represents the amount of uncertainty presented by a random variable, in terms of the set of probabilities of the outcomes. If the values of a particular random variable whose name is X are represented by the numbers $1, 2, 3, \ldots, n$, and their corresponding probabilities are represented as $p_1, p_2, p_3, \ldots, p_n$, then the entire random variable can be represented, in the notation of Eq. 1, as

$$X = \begin{bmatrix} p_1 & p_2 & p_3 & & p_n \\ & & & \cdots & \\ 1 & 2 & 3 & & n \end{bmatrix}. \tag{2}$$

The entropy of this random variable, $H(X)$, is defined by the equation:

$$H(X) = -\sum_{i=1}^{n} p_i \log_2(p_i) \tag{3}$$

If a particular alternative cannot occur, the corresponding term in the sum is 0. If, for example, there are 16 alternatives, and each of them is equally likely, then each of the probabilities $p_i = 1/16 = 2^{-4}$. Thus $-\log_2(p_i) = 4$. The whole sum consists of 16 identical terms, each equal to $-p_i \log_2(p_i) = 1/16 \times 4$, and thus the sum (the entropy) is equal to 4. This is precisely the logarithm to the base 2, of the number of equally probable alternatives. It can be shown mathematically that this is the

largest value that the entropy can have, when there are 16 possible alternatives. If, for example, one of them were enormously more probable than the others, one of the terms in the sum would have the value $-(1-\delta) \log_2(1-\delta)$ (where δ is a very small positive number). This number becomes proportional to δ when δ is small, and vanishes as δ goes to zero. At the same time, all of the other terms in the sum vanish because they have vanishingly small probability. So when one of the possible outcomes is nearly certain, the entropy is nearly 0. The entropy formula can be shown to satisfy all other requirements of a "reasonable" measure of the quantity of information, and it is unique, up to a constant factor. We have, in effect, selected that constant factor by choosing to use logarithms to the base 2, rather than to the base 10, or the base of natural logarithms, e.

The Entropy of a String of Characters

The entropy can be defined for any situation in which there is a series of events or symbols, which are determined to some degree, by those that precede them. As a concrete example, we might consider an alphabet containing only the three letters a, b, c. From these three letters we can form 9 ($= 3 \times 3$) two letter "words": *aa, ab, ac, ba, bb, bc, ca, cb, cc*. Similarly we can form 27 ($= 3 \times 3 \times 3$) three letter "words": *aaa, aab, aac, aba, abb, abc, aca, acb, acc, baa, bab, bac, bba, bbb, bbc, bca, bcb, bcc, caa, cab, cac, cba, cbb, cbc, cca, ccb, ccc*. Thus, it would appear that when we specify which one of those three-letter sequences occurs, we have specified 1 out of 27 possibilities. If they are equally likely, then the entropy, or amount of information, will be given (to three decimal places) by $\log_2(27) = 4.755$. However, if we know in advance that the three letters will *form a complete word in the English language*, there is only one possibility, and the amount of information conveyed when we see the string *cab* is, in the sense of information theory, 0. Finally, if we know only that the string will be the whole or a part of an English word, then there are several more possibilities, including *acc, bab, bac*, and perhaps others. In this case, the amount of information conveyed when we see the string is greater than 0, but less than 4.755. Thus, in the sense of Information Theory, the amount of information conveyed by a message is related to the number of possible messages that might have been received.

This concept has been applied, on a character-by-character basis, to compute the entropy of the English alphabet, given that the 26 letters (and the space character) are being used to form (possibly meaningless) English expressions. The result is usually given as about 1.5 bits per letter.[2] (Luenberger[2] is an excellent introduction for a reader comfortable with elementary

Table 1 The information in joint variables and in the variables separately

Case I
Probabilities

	Breakfast	Lunch	Dinner	Which day (1)	Logarithms (4)
Monday	10%	30%	10%	50%	−1.00
Tuesday	0%	15%	0%	15%	−2.74
Wednesday	5%	0%	10%	15%	−2.74
Thursday	5%	10%	5%	20%	−2.32
Which meal (2)	20%	55%	25%	100%	H(days) = 1.79
Logarithms (5)	−2.32	−0.86	−2.00	*1.44 = H(meals)*	

The numbers in the cells represent the probability that my lunch meeting falls on each specified meal and day. Let us say that I meet only once per week. Thus, there is a 30% chance that the meeting, in a particular week, is Monday lunch. There is only a 5% chance that the meeting of the week, for me, is Thursday dinner. Of course, these numbers add up to 100%, as shown in the lower corner of the table. We can also compute the probability that I meet on each particular day (1), or that I meet for each particular meal (2). These sets of numbers themselves each sum to 100% separately. Using an additional column (4) to record the logarithms (to the base 2) of the "by day probabilities" I have enough information to compute the entropy of the "by day" information. It is 1.79 bits. (Each logarithm is multiplied by the probability to its left, and the products are summed). This is the amount of information conveyed, or the amount of uncertainty resolved, by determining on which of the 4 days I meet for a meal. Note that although there are four possible days, this amount of information is less than 2 = Log(4) because the days are not equally likely. Similarly, I could work with the totals in the columns, multiplying them each by their logarithms, and summing the results to yield the entropy of the "which meal" information, which is 1.44 bits. This is less than 1.58 = Log (3), again because the meals are not equally likely.

Logarithms	Breakfast	Lunch	Dinner	
Monday	−3.32	−1.74	−3.32	
Tuesday	0.00	−2.74	0.00	
Wednesday	−4.32	0.00	−3.32	
Thursday	−4.32	−3.32	−4.32	H(meals, days) = **2.91**

Mutual Information = 1.44 + 1.79 − 2.91 = 0.32

Finally, we can calculate the information in the array of information about days and meals. To see how this works, we display the logarithms of the probabilities in this small table (Table 1). Multiplying each logarithm by its corresponding probability, and summing the numbers, yields the entropy of the joint distribution. This is the number, 2.91, referenced in the text.

algebra, elementary calculus, and elementary probability.)

The Mutual Information in a Pair of Random Variables

When there are two random variables that have some relation to each other, the strength of that relation can be measured in many ways. Shannon approached this problem by considering the amount of information in the pair of random variables (observed together) and comparing that to the amount of information in observation of each of the variables separately. Specifically, using the definition of entropy as given earlier, we can calculate the entropy of each variable separately, and of the two variables together. This is somewhat complicated, and example calculations are shown in Table 1.

Combining the information in Table 1, we calculate the Mutual Information $M(X,Y)$ of the two random variables X and Y according to the formula of Eq. 4.

$$M(X,Y) = H(X) + H(Y) - H(X,Y)$$
$$M(meals, days) = 1.44 + 1.79 - 2.91 \qquad (4)$$
$$M(meals, days) = 0.32 \text{ bits}$$

This is a relatively weak relationship. A stronger one is shown in Table 2. The mutual information in that case is, in fact, precisely equal to the information about which meal I designate. The joint information is precisely equal to the information about the day on which I meet. This is because, when the day is specified, with these probabilities, the meal is completely determined, and knowing the meal in addition to the day, adds no information. Note that although the day determines the meal, and the meal does not determine the day, the mutual information is symmetric.

This is because, if we want to convey information about the meals, by reporting only the days, we can cleverly choose the "days" to remove the ambiguity. Note that we have moved here from describing a "real world" to a situation where we are trying to exploit the probabilistic relation between meals and days to convey information about one of the two, when it is expressed in terms of the other. So the connection to the Shannon theory is to imagine that, for example, we want to tell

Table 2 A stronger information relation

Probabilities

	Breakfast	Lunch	Dinner	Which day	Logarithms
Monday	10%	0%	0%	10%	−3.32
Tuesday	0%	35%	0%	35%	−1.51
Wednesday	0%	0%	45%	45%	−1.15
Thursday	0%	10%	0%	10%	−3.32
Which meal:	10%	45%	45%	100%	H(days) = **1.71**
Logarithms	−3.32	−1.15	−1.15	*1.37* = H(meals)	

The numbers in Table 2 could represent the fact that if I send a message such as "Monday," it will **definitely** arrive as "Breakfast."

Logarithms	Breakfast	Lunch	Dinner	
Monday	−3.32	0.00	0.00	
Tuesday	0.00	−1.51	0.00	
Wednesday	0.00	0.00	−1.15	
Thursday	0.00	−3.32	0.00	H(meals, days) = **1.71**

Mutual Information = 1.71 + 1.37 − 1.71 = 1.37

someone about the day, but the nature of our "communication channel" is such that when we choose a day, the recipient is told the name of a meal, according to the probabilities specified.

The situation in Information Theory has some additional freedom for the sender of the message. I could choose to use the "days" as a kind of code. For example, I might represent the letter *P* by the code string *{Monday, Thursday, Tuesday}*. The situation becomes quite complex, and this entry provides only a brief introduction.

The reader may verify, by detailed calculations, that if there is a one-to-one correspondence between the two variables, the mutual information is equal to the information in either of them separately.

Communication and Mutual Information

Being employed by the telephone company, Shannon was concerned with the real-world situation in which the signals initially sent over a telephone cable could be distorted or affected by "noise," with the result that the signal received at the other end of the cable is not precisely the one that was transmitted. To address this problem, he defined two concepts: *the rate of information transfer* and the *capacity of the channel* (or cable) itself.

As suggested earlier, suppose that we wish to send information as to which specific day we have in mind. But we are constrained to do this not by naming the *day*, but by, instead, "transmitting" specific information about *which meal* we ate, and asking the recipient to decode that information, and decide which *day* we mean. To be specific, in Table 3, we show a relationship in which only the day "Tuesday" corresponds to more than one meal. If we avoid "Tuesday" then the message that he receives will be unambiguous. For example, if

we want to indicate "Monday" he will receive the message "Breakfast." And he will know that this corresponds only to Monday. But we have to avoid Tuesday because in that case the message could be either "Breakfast" or "Dinner" and this will introduce ambiguity into the decoding.

We can choose how often we send the message corresponding to each particular day. As we have mentioned earlier, balancing them equally will transmit the largest amount of information, provided that we never choose Tuesday. This is because Tuesday sends an ambiguous message: the meal might be breakfast or dinner. If we choose among the remaining days in an unbalanced way, we decrease the amount of information that we can transmit.

Using these ideas, Shannon was able to establish his Second Theorem of communication. This expresses the amount of information that can be communicated. The highest possible amount is called the capacity of the channel. In its most fundamental form this is given in terms of maximizing the mutual information, as described earlier.

$$Capacity \begin{Bmatrix} When\ a\ message \\ about\ X\ is\ received\ it \\ terms\ of\ signals\ Y \end{Bmatrix} = \underset{all\ distributions\ of\ X}{maximum} M(X, Y) \quad (5)$$

Here, the maximum means that we choose how often each message X is sent, in order to get the best possible communication. Strictly speaking, as was articulated by subsequent research, this is the limiting rate when the source of the message is "ergodic," which means, roughly, unpredictable, or having maximum entropy

Table 3 Another relation between the intended message (the day) and the code used to represent it (the meal). The entry is the probability that a given message is received, given what message is sent

| | Message received | | | | |
Intended message	Breakfast	Lunch	Dinner	$P(X)$	$-\text{Log}\ (P)$
Monday	100.0%	0.0%	0.0%	33%	1.58
Tuesday	50.0%	50.0%	0.0%	0%	0.00
Wednesday	0.0%	0.0%	100.0%	33%	1.58
Thursday	0.0%	100.0%	0.0%	33%	1.58
$P(Y)$	33.3%	33.3%	33.3%	33%	
$-\text{Log}\ (P)$	1.58	1.58	1.58	100.0%	

Here we represent the fact that if I send the message "Monday" the recipient is certain (100%) to get the message "Breakfast." Alternatively, we might say that I am "encoding" "Monday" by sending the message "Breakfast." However (perhaps due to noise in the transmission process), when I encode "Tuesday" the recipient gets the message "Breakfast" 50% of the time and "Lunch" 50% of the time. This introduces ambiguity. We can think of it as noise in the transmission process. If I insist on sometimes sending the message "Tuesday," then I cannot achieve the full channel capacity.

Probabilities $P(X,Y)$

	33.33%	0.00%	0.00%		
	0.00%	0.00%	0.00%		
	0.00%	0.00%	33.33%		
	0.00%	33.33%	0.00%		
				100.00%	
$E(Y)$	1.5850				
$E(X)$	1.5850				

Note: 1.05850 = log$_2$3

Logarithms of $P(X, Y)$

	1.58	0.00	0.00
	0.00	0.00	0.00
	0.00	0.00	1.58
	0.00	1.58	0.00
$E(X, Y)$	1.5850		
$M = E(X) + E(Y)$			
$-E(X, Y)$	1.5850		

when viewed as a sequence of characters in whatever alphabet is being used.[3] There are many implications of this formula. Some variants deal with the specific case where the values assumed by the variables X and Y are both binary. Other variations take account of the entropy of the message to be sent.

In all real cases, the difficult technical problem is to find a scheme for encoding that comes as close as possible to the theoretical limiting rate. This involves considerable ingenuity, and there are many open problems.

In addition to this mathematical and engineering focus of Information Theory, the book by Shannon and Weaver,[1] included a speculative essay by Weaver on the possible general implications of these results for behavioral sciences in general, and opened other worlds for exploration.

INFORMATION THEORY TODAY

Sixty years later, the field of Information Theory, whose central professional society is the IEEE Society for

Information Theory, is flourishing. The problem of finding the actual encoding that will come close to the Shannon theoretical limit is a difficult one, leading into complex fields of mathematics.

The corresponding methods for the compression of information are part of our everyday lives, especially for users of the Internet. They range from the use of zipped compression to reduce the size of files, to the complex compressions involved in the jpeg and mpeg conventions for static and moving images.

Progress on the social science side has also been energetic, but has not proceeded in the directions anticipated in Weaver's essay.

Human Communication

Scholars in the field called Communication (e.g., the National Communication Association, NCA, of the United States) concern themselves primarily with the social contexts and functional roles of communication. In their analysis it is never important to attempt to quantify the "amount of information" that is being

Table 4 Specific choices for the utility function of a decision maker

Utilities of the decision maker

	Action	
State	Not carry	Carry
No rain	0	2
Rain	2	−1

communicated. Thus, the approaches pioneered by Shannon have only rhetorical impact in that field.

Library and Information Science

In the field of LIS, it has seemed that one might want to know something about the relation between the "amount of information" and something else, which Brookes[4] has called the "increase in knowledge." Brookes proposed that the phenomenon of importance to information science is that the transmission of information *to a suitable recipient* results in an increase in the amount of knowledge "held by" that recipient. The idea, while often referenced, does not seem to have led to any serious attempt to provide a measurement of either the "amount of information" or the "increase in quantity of knowledge."

Economics

The third social scientific discipline that concerns itself with information is Economics. In Economics there has been an effective effort to quantify the notion of the value of information. It is clear that information has economic value, since, for example, information about tomorrow's stock prices could be immediately converted into economic gain. Economic theory has further developed, drawing upon the von Neumann and Morgenstern theory of games[5] and economic behavior, a concrete way of measuring the economic value of information, which is uncertain or noisy, in precisely the way that the channels described by Shannon are.

Utility theory

However, the detailed theory works out rather differently. The essential concept is "utility," an abstract measure of worth that behaves in a very specific way with respect to uncertain situations. In particular, the utility measure of an uncertain event, or "lottery," L, such as

$$L = \begin{bmatrix} p & 1-p \\ A & B \end{bmatrix}, \tag{6}$$

which is represented by the expression $u(L)$, is required to satisfy the equation

$$u(L) = pu(A) + (1-p)u(B) \tag{7}$$

This equation will continue to be satisfied if the utility is transformed to any new scale of the form: $u_{new}(X) = b^2 u(X) + c$, for any real numbers b and c. This means that the utility is measured on an interval scale, whose zero point and unit of measure may be set at any convenient values.

Utility theory applies to decision makers, who are assumed to be able to (perhaps implicitly) assign a utility value to every situation that they might need to consider. This assignment is called the decisionmaker's "utility function": $u_{decision-maker}(X)$. Utility theory is related to observable behavior by the requirement that a "rational" decision maker who values specific situations X,Y, according to a specific utility function for which $u_{decision-maker}(X) > u_{decision-maker}(Y)$ will definitely prefer to be in situation X, rather than in situation Y. It can be shown that a decision maker who does not follow Eq. 7 when making decisions about lottery can be systematically caused to make decisions, which, over the long run, will reduce his cumulated utility. This is the specific sense in which Eq. 7 is interpreted as representing rationality.

A decision may depend on the existing estimates of probability

The application of utility theory for measuring the value of information is made clear by a simple example of a twofold decision involving an uncertain outcome. Suppose, for example, a decision maker must decide whether or not to carry an umbrella, and assigns the following utilities to the four possible alternative situations:

A = carry an umbrella and have it rain.
B = carry an umbrella and not have it rain.
C = not carry an umbrella and have it rain.
D = not carry an umbrella and not have it rain.

Specific values for these parameters are shown in Table 4.

This information can be used to create a graph as shown in Fig. 1A, where the abscissa is the probability that it will in fact rain, and the ordinate is the utility value to the decision maker. The two straight lines on the graph represent the expected utility of the two possible actions, both of which depend on the probability that it will rain. The value of the choice or action "carry

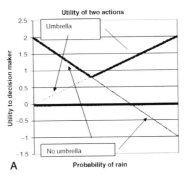

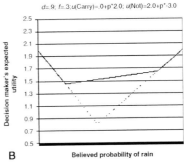

Fig. 1 (A) As the probability of rain increases, the utility of not carrying an umbrella decreases. Correspondingly, the utility of carrying an umbrella increases. In this case they cross at 40%, the critical probability. The decision maker, according to his estimate of the probability, chooses the action corresponding to the higher line. His expected utility, as a function of the probability, never falls below the crossing value. (B) With an imperfect predictor of rain, the decision maker can still improve his expectation, in some situations, but not all. The "bridge" in this diagram shows the higher utility that can be achieved if: 1) his estimate is close enough to the critical point; and 2) he makes use of the prediction. The expected utility increase, due to using the prediction, is the rational basis for assigning "value" to the prediction. Note that the same prediction will have a higher value for a decision maker whose original estimate of the probability is closer to the critical value. This is quite different from entropy measures, which increase as the probability nears 50%.

an umbrella" is low when the probability of rain is low, but increases as the probability of rain increases. The value of "not carrying the umbrella" is high for low probabilities of rain, and decreases as the probability of rain increases. An important feature of this situation is the value of the probability at which the two lines cross, which we call the "critical probability" for this utility function. According to the principles of utility theory, the decision maker will not carry an umbrella if the probability is less than this value, will carry an umbrella if it is greater than this value, and is indifferent when the probability of rain is equal to the critical value.

Imperfect information can improve the expected utility of a situation

The preceding discussion describes the situation, without any information, or the "prior situation." Suppose now that the decision maker is offered an imperfect or "noisy" prediction of whether it will rain. We can calculate the expected value of "being in the situation of having this information" and compare it to the expected value in the present situation. The difference can, of course, be interpreted as the "value of the information." The mathematics is somewhat complicated. To begin

with, an imperfect prediction can be imperfect in two distinct ways: failing to predict rain, on rainy days, and predicting rain on days when there is no rain. These two numbers are independent of each other, and both are needed to complete the calculation. We denote the first probability by "t" for true alarm or warning, and the second by "f" for "false warning." The information can be summarized as in Table 5 or Table 6.

The second complexity comes in interpreting a prediction that is known to be inaccurate in this way. This is accomplished using Bayes' rule,[6] which relates the probability of rain, given the imperfect information, p_1, to the prior probability of rain p_0. That equation is given in terms of odds ratios as

$$\frac{p_1}{1-p_1} = \frac{t}{1-t}\frac{p_0}{1-p_0} \text{ if the prediction is "rain'}$$

$$\frac{p_1}{1-p_1} = \frac{f}{1-f}\frac{p_0}{1-p_0} \text{ if the prediction is "not rain'} \tag{8}$$

For a reasonable weather predictor, the first of the numbers p_1, found by solving these equations, will be higher than the second; that is, it is more likely to rain if the prediction is "rain" than if it is "not rain." Let us refer to them as p_H and p_L, respectively (H for high; L for low). Having this prediction, the decision maker will then refer to his personal utility diagram. If the result of the prediction leaves the probability below p_C, he will

Table 5 Specific performance characteristics of an imperfect predictor of rain

Performance of the predictor		
	Truth	
Predict	**Rain**	**Not**
Rain	0.9	0.3
Not	0.1	0.7

Table 6 The accuracy of a prediction of rain

	Truth	
Prediction	**Truth = rain**	**Truth = not rain**
Rain	T	F
Not rain	$1-t$	$1-f$

not carry an umbrella. If the result falls above the critical probability, he will carry an umbrella. But the results of these calculations depend on the prior probability estimate: p_0. If the prior estimate is very low, both P_H and P_L fall below p_C, and he will not carry an umbrella. If the prior estimate is very high, both P_H and P_L fall above p_C, and he will carry an umbrella, with or without the prediction. In those two situations, the information has no value to him, since he will do precisely what he would have done without the information. The value of the information is, therefore, 0.

However, for a certain range of the prior probability, spanning the critical value, the information will cause him to change his behavior. Therefore, it has some potential value. The calculation of this value depends on the principle of expected utility. In particular, it depends on the chance that the prediction is "rain." This, as we see from Eq. 8, depends on prior estimate of the probability. One might ask: "Doesn't it really depend on the chance of rain?". But there is no way the decision maker can know the truth. He is restricted to choosing between his prior belief and the available imperfect prediction. In other words, if he buys the information, he will face a lottery where the outcomes are "predictions he receives" and he must compute the probability that each will occur.

$$\begin{bmatrix} \text{probability prediction} & \text{probability prediction is "} \\ \text{is "rain'} & \text{not rain'} \\ p_H & p_L \end{bmatrix} \quad (9)$$

Note that for any given belief about p, the probability of rain, the computed probability of the prediction "rain" contains two terms, corresponding to the true and false predictions. Thus:

$$p_H = tp + f(1-p)$$
$$p_L = (1-t)p + (1-f)(1-p) \quad (10)$$

Note that the sum of these two probabilities is 1, since the predictor must make *some* prediction.

The decision maker can then apply Eq. 7, carrying through the calculations. The result is a third line segment on the graph of expected utility, as shown in Fig. 1B. It forms a "bridge" above the intersection at the critical probability. The left-hand end of the bridge falls at the lowest prior probability for which the information has a nonzero value. The right-hand end of the bridge falls at the highest prior probability for which the information has a nonzero value. The expected value of the information, in units of the decisionmaker's utility, is the vertical distance between the bridge and the higher of the original two lines, at the specific value of the prior probability. For further details see, for example, Hirshleifer and Riley.[7]

Thus we see that the expected value of the information depends not only on the unreliability of the prediction (that is, on the numbers t and f) but also on the decision maker's own prior estimate of the probability of rain. While the first two parameters represent the kind of information about uncertainty that is addressed by Information Theory, the dependence on the prior probability is quite a different matter. This complexity has prevented the development of any accepted theory that relates the expected value of information, in a decision situation, to computations of the type introduced by Shannon. Some efforts to develop an alternative to the Shannon formulation are discussed by Rényi.[8]

Behavior beyond Expected Utility Theory

The field called Behavioral Economics addresses the many ways in which observed human behavior does not easily fit with the specific assumptions of utility theory. For example, if there is a set of possible situations, then the decision maker should be able to select one of them, or be indifferent among two or more. But experiments showed[9] that if the set is not small (i.e., contains more than six or seven alternatives) decision makers will report pair preferences that are not transitive, which is inconsistent with the notion that preferences correspond to inequalities relating real numbers (the values of the utility function). Leaders in behavioral economics include Daniel Kahneman[10] and Amos Tversky.[11]

The question of whether the notion of utility can be broadened beyond the formulation given here, to accommodate apparently irrational human preferences, remains open. An interesting discussion, from the perspective of a philosopher, has been given by Nozick.[12] He proposes that, in addition to economic utility, dealt with as above, human decision makers base their actions on a separate property of actions, which he calls "symbolic utility." There is no conversion between these two utilities, and so, the model does not make specific predictions about behavior.

The study of behavior in the context of the theory of evolution suggests that actions that do not provide calculable utility gain for the individual decision maker may be the result of complex evolved behavior. which has net utility for the genome of which the individual is a particular instance. ("A person is the gene's way of making a new gene.") This is an area of intense study, but no irrefutable demonstrations of the principle have been shown, for human behavior. It has been reported that the *Toxoplasma gondii* protozoan affects the brains of infected rodents in such a way as to decrease their innate fear of cats, enabling the parasite to progress to its next reproductive stage, which takes place in cats.[13] One possible example in humans is infection with the thirst for education, which causes young adults to sacrifice productive and child-bearing years to the pursuit of academic degrees, and thus perpetuate the academy.

SURPRISE AND IDENTIFICATION

There are some relatively new streams of research that show promise of beginning to capture the element of information that is most salient from the perspective of library information science: the degree to which the message received causes a change in what the recipient already knows or believes.

Surprise

The computer scientist Pierre Baldi[14] has proposed that messages can be judged on a scale that measures their "surprise" value. The analysis is based in part on measures related to the entropy. Specifically, he uses a measure called the Kullback-Leibler[15] measure, which assesses the difference between one probability distribution and another, when both describe the same basic set of outcomes. The analysis adds the notion of Bayesian updating, as discussed in economics section. When information is received, the recipient is presumed to alter his prior beliefs about the probability distribution, to yield a new distribution. The "distance" (the Kulback-Leibler measure is not a proper metric in the geometric sense, but could be converted to one if needed) of the new distribution from the old is a measure of the "surprise" that the information represents to the recipient.

Identification

The information scientist Rudolf Ahlswede[16] has developed a line of research that is somewhat dual to classical Shannon theory. He considers the problem of a recipient who knows in advance the list of messages that might be sent and wishes to determine, with at least a specified probability of being correct, which of the messages has, in fact, been sent to him. The capacity of channels, measured against this criterion, becomes different (and, roughly speaking, higher). At a very superficial level, it appears that this line of thinking might eventually develop into a convergence between the Library/Information Science view of the problem (in which the possible messages are constrained by language, social roles, customs of expression, etc.), and the more rigorous theory that has produced so many striking improvements in the storage and transmission of the messages themselves.

CONCLUSION

In addition to its own practical contributions to our lives, it appears that the most concrete translation of the original hope that information theory might contribute to the social sciences is in the field of economics. However, in that setting, rigorous analysis shows that the value of information is not in any simple way functionally determined by the quantity of information as it was defined by Shannon. Developments in this field may eventuate in a convergence of the problems, but the path to solution is not yet clear.

There are excellent sources on the Web for information about these topics, from many perspectives, and this rich field is very much open for exciting prospective developments.

SCHOLARLY AND SCIENTIFIC ORGANIZATIONS (WEB SITES)

American Economic Association. http://www.vanderbilt.edu/AEA/

American Society for Information Science and Technology. http://www.asis.org/

IEEE Information Theory Society. http://www.itsoc.org/

Institute for Operations Research and Management Sciences. http://www.informs.org/

The National Communication Association. http://www.natcom.org/nca/

REFERENCES

1. Shannon, C.; Weaver, W. *The Mathematical Theory of Communication*; University of Illinois Press: Urbana, IL, 1949.
2. Luenberger, D. *Information Science*; Princeton University Press: Princeton, NJ, 2006.
3. http://en.wikipedia.org/wiki/Shannon_limit
4. Brookes, B.C. The foundations of information science. Part II. Quantitative aspects: classes of things and the challenge of human individuality. J. Info. Sci. **1980**, *2* (5), 209–221.
5. von Neumann, J.; Morganstern, O. In *Theory of Games and Economic Behavior with an Introduction by Harold W. Kuhn and an Afterword by Ariel Rubinstein*; 60th Anniversary Ed.; Princeton University Press: Princeton, NJ, 1944.
6. Bayeshttp://en.wikipedia.org/wiki/Bayes'_theorem
7. Hirshleifer, J.; Riley, J.G. In *The Analytics of Uncertainty and Information (Cambridge Surveys of Economic Literature)*; Cambridge University Press: New York, 1992; 9.
8. Rényi, A. On measures of information and entropy. Proc. 4th Berkeley Symp. Math. Stat. Probability **1960**, 547–561.
9. Luce, R.D.; Raiffa, H. Games and decisions: Introduction and critical survey. In *A Study of the Behavioral Models Project, Bureau of Applied Social Research, Columbia University*; Wiley: New York, NY, 1957.

10. Kahneman, D. Maps of bounded rationality: A perspective on intuitive judgment and choice prize lecture. December 8, 2002, http://nobelprize.org/nobel_prizes/economics/laureates/2002/kahnemann-lecture.pdf.

11. In *Choices, Values, and Frames*; Kahneman, D., Tversky, A., Eds.; Cambridge University Press: New York, NY, 2000.

12. Nozick, R. In *The Nature of Rationality*; Princeton University Press: Princeton, NJ, 1993.

13. Berdoy, M.; Webster, J.; Macdonald, D. Fatal attraction in rats infected with *Toxoplasma gondii*. Proc. R. Soc. Lond. **2000**, *B268*, 1591–1594.

14. Itti, L.; Baldi, P. Bayesian surprise attracts human attention. Adv. Neural Inform. Process. Syst. NIPS **2005**, *18* http://ilab.usc.edu/publications/doc/Itti_Baldi06nips.pdf

15. Kullback, S. The Kullback-Leibler distance. Am. Stat **1987**, *41*, 340–341.

16. Ahlswede, R. *Towards a general theory of information transfer, Shannon Lecture at ISIT*; Seattle, WA, July 13, 2006, http://www.itsoc.org/publications/nltr/itNL0907.pdf.

Information
Science–
ITIL

Intelligence and Security Informatics

Hsinchun Chen
Zhenhua Lai
Yan Dang
Yulei Zhang
Department of Management Information Systems, University of Arizona, Tucson, Arizona, U.S.A.

Abstract

The tragic events of September 11, 2001, have had far-reaching effects on many aspects of U.S. society. Six critical mission areas, as suggested in the "National Strategy for Homeland Security" report, have been identified where information technology can contribute to safeguarding our national security. These areas include *intelligence and warning, border and transportation security, domestic counterterrorism, protecting critical infrastructure, defending against catastrophic terrorism,* and *emergency preparedness and responses.* Intelligence and Security Informatics (ISI) encompasses the development of advanced and socially responsible information technologies, systems, algorithms, and databases for national security–related applications, through an integrated technological, organizational, policy-based, and privacy-preserving approach. This entry reviews ISI research challenges and presents a research framework with a primary focus on knowledge discovery from databases (KDD) technologies. The framework is discussed in the context of crime types and security implications. In addition to the technical discussions, caveats for data mining and civil liberties concerns are also considered.

INTRODUCTION

The tragic events of September 11 have caused far-reaching changes to many aspects of society. Terrorism is one of the most significant threats to national security due to its potential of bringing massive damage to our infrastructure, economy, and people. In response to this challenge, federal authorities are actively implementing comprehensive strategies and measures in order to achieve the three objectives identified in the "National Strategy for Homeland Security" report:[1] 1) preventing future terrorist attacks; 2) reducing the nation's vulnerability; and 3) minimizing the damage and enabling recovery from attacks that occur. State and local law enforcement agencies, likewise, are becoming more vigilant about criminal activities, which can harm public safety and threaten national security.

Academics in the fields of natural sciences, computational science, information science, social sciences, engineering, medicine, and many others have also been called upon to help enhance the government's abilities to fight terrorism and other crimes. Science and technology have been identified in the "National Strategy for Homeland Security" report as the keys to win the new counterterrorism war.[1] Especially, it is believed that information technology will play an indispensable role in making our nation safer,[2] by supporting intelligence and knowledge discovery through collecting, processing, analyzing, and utilizing terrorism- and crime-related data.[3,4] Based on the crime and intelligence knowledge discovered, federal, state, and local authorities can make timely decisions in selecting effective strategies and tactics as well as allocate the appropriate amount of resources to detect, prevent, and respond to future attacks.

PRIVACY VS. INFORMATION SHARING: A BROADER SOCIETAL ISSUE

To protect the United States from future terrorist attacks, various law enforcement and homeland security agencies must act proactively and collaboratively to thwart planned or future acts of aggression. Most government agencies involved in safeguarding national security create their own databases and other stores of information that relate to potential sources of threats. The sharing of such data stores has been widely proposed as a method for leveraging existing knowledge to better forecast possible attacks. However, these shared databases may be misused, and may violate the privacy rights and civil liberties of innocent citizens. Privacy is the ability of an individual or group to keep their lives and personal affairs out of public view, or to control the flow of information about them. It is considered by many to be one of the most fundamental rights of citizens in a modern society.

Encyclopedia of Information Systems and Technology, DOI: 10.1081/E-EIST-120043514

More than ever, information technologies have become more prevalent and overreaching in modern day, post-Internet society. Companies, organizations, and governments are using better databases, Internet applications, and information technologies to collect information about their customers, employees, and citizens. Advanced data mining techniques have also been increasingly used by companies and governments to better understand their customers or citizens. These pervasive and powerful technologies are also beginning to adversely affect individual privacy. How can one tell what kind of data is being collected by whom, and for what purposes? How can one ensure that data are collected and used for, and only for, the intended purposes?

Many information misuses have been reported in popular news sources (e.g., identity theft reported in http://law.jrank.org/pages/7469/Identity-Theft.html). In one federal prosecution, the defendants allegedly obtained the names and social security numbers of U.S. military officers from a Web site. The defendants used more than 100 of those names and social security numbers to apply for a Delaware Bank credit card. The fraudulent credit card transaction cost the Delaware Bank millions of dollars in 2000. In another reported case in the Central District of California, a woman pleaded guilty for using a stolen social security number and filing for bankruptcy in the name of her victim. Because (digital) information can be easily collected, copied, transmitted, and (potentially) misused, information collectors' abilities to safeguard the data they collect is even more critical now.

Despite the clear need for maintaining individual privacy, governments and businesses may have reasons for accessing and sharing customer or citizen information. Many previous court cases have supported such uses. For example, in *Davis versus Freedom of Information Commission*, 259 Conn. 45 (2001), The Connecticut Supreme Court declared that the Drivers Privacy Protection Act (DPPA) does not prohibit other government agencies from receiving personal information from the State DMV in the course of their normal government functions. Similarly, in 2002, Nevada's highest court ruled that the incoming and outgoing calls on the public telephones are not considered to be protected information and may be used for other purposes. Clearly, privacy and information sharing will continue to raise serious debates for the foreseeable future.

INFORMATION TECHNOLOGIES AND NATIONAL SECURITY

As part of the post-9/11 national security programs in the United States, six critical mission areas have been identified where information technology can contribute to the accomplishment of the strategic national security objectives identified in the "National Strategy for Homeland Security" report:[1]

- *Intelligence and warning.* Although terrorism depends on surprise to bring damage to targets,[1] terrorist activities are neither random nor impossible to track. Terrorists must plan and prepare before the execution of an attack by selecting a target, recruiting, and training executors, acquiring financial support, and traveling to the country where the target is located.[5] To avoid being preempted by authorities they may hide their true identities and disguise attack-related activities. Similarly, criminals may use falsified identities during police contacts.[6] Although it is difficult, detecting potential terrorist attacks or crimes is possible and feasible with the help of information technology. By analyzing the communication and activity patterns among terrorists and their contacts (i.e., terrorist networks), detecting deceptive identities, or employing other surveillance and monitoring techniques, intelligence and warning systems may issue timely, critical alerts and warnings to prevent attacks or crimes from occurring.

- *Border and transportation security.* Terrorists enter a targeted country through an air, land, or sea port of entry. Criminals in narcotics rings travel across borders to purchase, carry, distribute, and sell drugs. Information, such as travelers' identities, images, fingerprints, vehicles used, and other characteristics, is collected from customs, borders, and immigration authorities on a daily basis. The collection can greatly improve the capabilities of counterterrorism and crime-fighting capabilities by creating a "smart border" where information from multiple sources is shared and analyzed to help locate wanted terrorists or criminals. Technologies such as information sharing and integration, collaboration and communication, biometrics, and image and speech recognition will be greatly needed to create smart borders across all ports of entry.

- *Domestic counterterrorism.* Because both international and domestic terrorists may be involved in local crimes, state and local law enforcement agencies are also investigating and prosecuting terrorism-related crimes. Terrorism, like gangs and narcotics trafficking, is regarded as a type of organized crime in which multiple offenders cooperate to carry out offenses. Information technologies that help find cooperative relationships between criminals and their interactive patterns are also helpful for analyzing terrorism. Monitoring activities of domestic terrorist and extremist groups using advanced information technologies will also likely to be helpful to public safety personnel and policy makers.

- *Protecting critical infrastructure and key assets.* Roads, bridges, water suppliers, and many other physical service systems are critical infrastructure and are key assets of a nation. They may become the target of terrorist attacks because of their vulnerabilities.[1] Moreover, virtual (cyber) infrastructure such as the Internet may also be vulnerable to intrusions and inside threats.[7] Criminals and terrorists are increasingly using cyberspace to conduct illegal activities, share ideology, solicit funding, and recruit. In addition to physical devices such as sensors and detectors, advanced information technologies are needed to model the normal behaviors of the usage of these systems and then use the models to distinguish abnormal behaviors from normal behaviors. Protective or reactive measures can be selected based on the results to secure these assets from attacks.

- *Defending against catastrophic terrorism.* Terrorist attacks can cause devastating damage through the use of chemical, biological, or radiological weapons. Biological attacks, for example, may cause contamination, infectious disease outbreaks, and significant loss of life. Information systems that can efficiently and effectively collect, access, analyze, and report data about catastrophe-leading events can help prevent, detect, respond to, and manage these attacks.[8]

- *Emergency preparedness and responses.* In case of a national emergency, prompt and effective responses are critical to reducing the damage resulting from an attack. In addition to the systems that are prepared to defend against catastrophes, information technologies that help design and experiment optimized response plans,[9] identify experts, train response professionals, and manage consequences are beneficial for both planning and emergency response. Moreover, information systems that facilitate social and psychological support to the victims of terrorist attacks can also assist disaster recovery efforts.

PROBLEMS AND CHALLENGES

Although it is important for the critical missions of national security, the development of information technology for counterterrorism and crime-fighting applications faces many problems and challenges. Presently, intelligence and security agencies are gathering large amounts of data from various sources. Processing and analyzing such data, however, have become increasingly difficult tasks. Treating terrorism as a form of organized crime allows the categorization of these challenges into the following types:

- *Characteristics of criminals and crimes.* Crimes can be geographically diffused and temporally dispersed. In organized crimes such as transnational narcotics, the trafficking criminals often live in different cities,

states, or even countries. Drug distribution and sales occur in different places at different times. Similar situations exist in other organized crimes (e.g., terrorism, armed robbery, and gang-related crime). As a result, investigations must cover multiple offenders who commit criminal activities in different places at different times. This can be fairly difficult, given the limited resources that most intelligence and security agencies have. Moreover, as computer and Internet technologies advance, criminals are utilizing cyberspace to commit various types of cyber-crimes under the disguise of ordinary online transactions and communications.

- *Characteristics of crime and intelligence-related data.* A significant source of challenge is information stovepipe and overload resulting from diverse data sources, multiple data formats, and large data volumes. Unlike other domains such as marketing, finance, and medicine in which data can be collected from particular sources (e.g., sales records from companies and patient medical history from hospitals), the intelligence and security domain does not have a well-defined data source. Both authoritative information (e.g., crime incident reports, telephone records, financial statements, and immigration and custom records) and open-source information (e.g., news stories, journal articles, books, and Web pages) need to be gathered for investigative purposes. Data collected from these different sources often are in different formats, ranging from structured database records to unstructured text, image, audio, and video files. Important information such as criminal associations may be available but contained in unstructured, multilingual texts and can therefore remain difficult to access and retrieve. Moreover, as data volumes continue to grow, extracting valuable and credible intelligence and knowledge becomes a difficult problem.

- *Characteristics of crime and intelligence analysis techniques.* Ongoing research on the technologies for counterterrorism and crime-fighting applications lacks a consistent framework for addressing the major challenges. Some information technologies including data integration, data analysis, text mining, image and video processing, and evidence combination have been identified as being particularly helpful.[2] However, the question of how to employ them in the intelligence and security domain and use them to effectively address the critical mission areas of national security (with proper protection of privacy and civil liberties) remains unanswered and requires further research.

AN ISI RESEARCH FRAMEWORK

"Intelligence and Security Informatics" (ISI)[3,4,10] is a multidisciplinary science, with its main objective being

Table 1 Crime types and security concerns

	Crime types	
Type	**Local law enforcement level**	**National security level**
Traffic violations	Driving under influence (DUI), fatal/personal injury/property damage, traffic accident, road rage	—
Sex crime	Sexual offenses, sexual assaults, child molesting	Organized prostitution, people smuggling
Theft	Robbery, burglary, larceny, motor vehicle theft, stolen property	Theft of national secrets or weapon information
Fraud	Forgery and counterfeiting, fraud, embezzlement, identity deception	Transnational money laundering, identity fraud, transnational financial fraud
Arson	Arson on buildings, apartments	
Organized crime	Narcotic drug offenses (sales or possession), gang-related offenses	Transnational drug trafficking, terrorism (bioterrorism, bombing, hijacking, etc.)
Violent crime	Criminal homicide, armed robbery, aggravated assault, other assaults	Terrorism
Cyber crime	Internet fraud (e.g., credit card fraud, advance fee fraud, and fraudulent Web sites), illegal trading, network intrusion/hacking, virus spreading, hate crimes, cyber-piracy, cyber-pornography, cyber-terrorism, theft of confidential information	

Information Science–ITIL

the "development of advanced and socially responsible information technologies, systems, algorithms, and databases for national security-related applications, through an integrated technological, organizational, policy-based, and privacy-preserving approach." ISI has at its core a focus on developing and employing computationally intensive techniques with the goal of increasing existing levels of national security through an integrated approach that takes into account organizational considerations; national security priorities; laws, regulations, and policies; and privacy protection. This next section presents a research framework with a primary focus on knowledge discovery from databases (KDD) technologies, and is discussed in the context of crime types and security implications.

Crime is an act or the commission of an act that is forbidden, or the omission of a duty that is commanded by a public law and that makes the offender liable to punishment by that law. The more threat a crime type poses to public safety, the more likely it is to be of national security concern. Some crimes, such as traffic violations, theft, and homicide, are primarily in the jurisdiction of local law enforcement agencies. Other crimes need to be dealt with by both local law enforcement and national security authorities. Identity theft and fraud, for instance, is relevant at both the local and national levels—criminals may escape arrest by using false identities, or drug smugglers may enter the United States by holding counterfeited passports or visas. Organized crimes such as terrorism and narcotics trafficking often diffuse geographically, resulting in common security concerns across cities, states, and countries. Cybercrimes can pose threats to public safety across multiple jurisdictional areas due to the widespread nature of computer networks. Table 1 summarizes the different types of crimes sorted by the degree of their respective public

influence.[4] International and domestic terrorism, in particular, often involves multiple crime types (e.g., identity theft, money laundering, arson and bombing, organized and violent activities, and cyber-terrorism) and has the potential to cause enormous damage.

KDD techniques can play an important role in improving counterterrorism and crime-fighting capabilities of intelligence, security, and law enforcement agencies by reducing cognitive and information overload that results from dealing with massive amounts of data. Knowledge discovery refers to the nontrivial extraction of implicit, previously unknown, and potentially useful knowledge from data. Knowledge discovery techniques promise easier, more convenient, and practical exploration of very large collections of data for organizations and users, and have been applied in marketing, finance, manufacturing, biology, and many other domains (e.g., predicting consumer behaviors, detecting credit card frauds, or clustering genes that have similar biological functions).[11] Traditional knowledge discovery techniques include association rule mining, classification and prediction, cluster analysis, and outlier analysis.[12] As natural language processing (NLP) research advances, text mining approaches that automatically extract, summarize, categorize, and translate text documents have also been widely used.

Many of these KDD technologies can be applied in ISI studies.[3,4] Existing ISI technologies can be categorized into six classes: *information sharing and collaboration, crime association mining, crime classification and clustering, intelligence text mining, spatial and temporal crime mining,* and *criminal network mining.* These six classes are grounded on traditional knowledge discovery technologies, but with new approaches added, including spatial and temporal crime pattern mining and criminal network analysis, which are

	Crime Types							
Crime Data Mining Techniques	Traffic Violation	Sex Offense	Theft	Fraud	Arson	Organized Crime	Violent Crime	Cyber Crime
Criminal Network Analysis						X	X	X
Spatial and Temporal Pattern Mining				X		X	X	X
Text Mining		X	X	X	X	X	X	X
Classification & Clustering	X	X	X	X	X	X	X	X
Association	X	X	X	X	X	X	X	X

(Analysis Capability ↑) (Public Harm →)

Fig. 1 A knowledge discovery research framework for ISI.

more relevant to counterterrorism and crime investigation. In addition, new research has begun in the areas of privacy-preserving, security-aware data integration, and data mining. Although information sharing and collaboration are not data mining per se, they help prepare, normalize, warehouse, and integrate data for knowledge discovery and thus are included in the framework.

Fig. 1 presents the proposed research framework, showing crime types and the six classes of techniques useful for (or showing the promise of utility to) the investigation of the various crime types.[4] The crime data mining techniques are listed, from bottom to top, in an increasing scale of analysis capability. Note that more serious crimes—those inducing greater public harm—may require a more complete set of knowledge discovery techniques. For example, the investigation of organized crimes such as terrorism may depend on criminal network analysis technology, which requires the use of other knowledge discovery techniques such as association mining and clustering. An important observation about this framework is that the high-frequency occurrences and strong association patterns of severe and organized crimes such as terrorism and narcotics trafficking present a unique opportunity and potentially high rewards for adopting such a knowledge discovery framework.

Some of these classes of data mining techniques are of great relevance to ISI research. *Text mining* is critical for extracting key entities (people, places, narcotics, weapons, time, etc.) and their relationships presented in voluminous police incident reports, intelligence reports, open-source news clips, etc. Some of these techniques need to be multilingual in nature, including the abilities to employ machine translation and cross-lingual information retrieval (CLIR). *Spatial and temporal mining and visualization* is often needed for geographic information systems (GIS) and temporal analysis of criminal and terrorist events. Most crime analysts are well trained in GIS-based crime mapping tools; however, automated spatial and temporal pattern mining techniques (e.g., hot-spot analysis) have not been widely adopted in intelligence and security applications. Organized criminals (e.g., gangs and narcotics) and terrorists often form interconnected covert networks to carry out illegal activities. Often referred to as "dark networks," these

organizations exhibit unique structures, communication channels, and resilience to attack and disruption. New computational techniques including social network analysis, network learning, and network topological analysis (e.g., random network, small-world network, and scale-free network) are needed for the systematic study of those complex and covert networks. These techniques are classified under *criminal network analysis* in Fig. 1.

ISI, CIVIL LIBERTIES, AND DATA MINING

The U.S. Constitution and its Bill of Rights were drafted in part to define and protect the civil liberties of United States citizens and to set limits on the government's power. Important civil liberties include freedom of association, freedom of assembly, freedom of speech, and the right to privacy. In the United States, the American Civil Liberties Union (ACLU) is a powerful advocacy group that aims to ensure the protection of free speech, privacy, and other fundamental human rights.

The potential negative effects of intelligence gathering and analysis on the privacy and civil liberties of the public have been well publicized.[13] There exist many laws, regulations, and agreements governing data collection, confidentiality, and reporting, which could directly impact the development and application of ISI technologies. Intelligence and security agencies and ISI researchers must be aware of these laws and regulations in research and practice. The use of a hypothesis-guided, evidence-based approach in crime and intelligence analysis research can also help assure that privacy is appropriately respected. For example, there should be probable and reasonable causes and evidence for targeting particular individuals or data sets for analysis. Proper investigative and legal procedures need to be strictly followed. It is neither ethical nor legal to "fish" for potential criminals from diverse and mixed crime, intelligence, and civilian-related data sources. The well-publicized Defense Advanced Research Program Agency (DARPA), Total Information Awareness (TIA) program, and the Multi-State Anti-Terrorism Information Exchange (MATRIX) system, for example, have been shut down by the U.S. Congress due to their potential misuse of citizen data and impairment of civil liberties.[14]

Information Science–ITIL

However, other initiatives have been maintained, as the catastrophic 9/11 events had a profound impact on the way the U.S. government acts on security concerns. In response to the attacks, for example, the U.S. government enacted the USA PATRIOT Act, created the Department of Homeland Security (DHS), increased security efforts and airports and other ports of call, etc.

The PATRIOT Act expands the government's ability to examine records on an individual's activity whether those records are being held by third parties or were acquired by secret searches and/or wiretap surveillance. The Act expands a narrow exception to the Fourth Amendment that had been created for the collection of foreign intelligence information and also expands another Fourth Amendment exception for spying that collects "addressing" information about the origin and destination of communications. An immediate result of the events of September 11, 2001, was the extraordinarily rapid passage of the USA PATRIOT Act in late 2001. The legislation was passed by the Senate on October 11, 2001, and by the House on October 24, 2001; it was signed by the president on October 26, 2001, with some revisions following in 2005 and 2006. But the continuing legacy of the then-existing consensus and the lack of detailed debate and considerations have created an ongoing national argument as to the proper balance between national security and civil liberties.

FUTURE DIRECTIONS

National security research poses unique challenges and opportunities. Much of the established data mining and knowledge discovery literature, findings, and techniques need to be reexamined in light of the unique data and problem characteristics in the law enforcement and intelligence community. New text mining, spatial and temporal pattern mining, privacy-preserving data mining, and criminal network analysis of relevance to national security are among some of the most pressing research areas. However, researchers cannot conduct research in a vacuum. Partnerships with local, state, and federal agencies need to be formed to obtain relevant test data and necessary domain expertise and feedback for ISI research.

ACKNOWLEDGMENTS

We would like to acknowledge the funding support of NSF and other agencies:

- NSF, Knowledge Discovery and Dissemination (KDD) Program, "Detecting Identity Concealment," September 2004–August 2005.

- NSF, Digital Government Program, "COPLINK Center: Social Network Analysis and Identity Deception Detection for Law Enforcement and Homeland Security," September 2003–August 2006.
- NSF, Information Technology Research (ITR) Program, "COPLINK Center for Intelligence and Security Informatics—A Crime Data Mining Approach to Developing Border Safe Research," September 2003–August 2005.
- NSF, Community Resource Development (CRD) Program, "Developing a Dark Web Collection and Infrastructure for Computational and Social Sciences," September 2007–August 2010.

REFERENCES

1. Office of Homeland Security, *National Strategy for Homeland Security*; Office of Homeland Security: Washington, DC, 2002.
2. National Research Council, *Making the Nation Safer: The Role of Science and Technology in Countering Terrorism*; National Academies Press: Washington, DC, 2002.
3. *Intelligence and Security Informatics*; Chen, H., Miranda, R., Zeng, D.D., Demchak, C., Schroeder, J., Madhusudan, T., Eds.; Springer: Berlin, 2003 Proceedings of the First NSF/NIJ Symposium on Intelligence and Security Informatics.
4. *Intelligence and Security Informatics*; Chen, H., Moore, R., Zeng, D., Leavitt, J., Eds.; Springer: Berlin, 2004 Proceedings of the Second Symposium on Intelligence and Security Informatics.
5. Sageman, M. *Understanding Terror Networks*; University of Pennsylvania Press: Philadelphia, PA, 2004.
6. Wang, G.; Chen, H.; Atabakhsh, H. Automatically detecting deceptive criminal identities. Commun. ACM **2004**, *47* (3), 71–76.
7. Lee, W.; Stolfo, S. Data mining approaches for intrusion detection. In Proceedings of the 7th USENIX Security Symposium, San Antonio, TX, January, 26–29, 1998; USENIX: Berkeley, CA, 1998.
8. Damianos, L.; Ponte, J.; Wohlever, S.; Reeder, F.; Day, D.; Wilson, G.; Hirschman, L. MiTAP for bio-security: A case study. AI Mag. **2002**, *23* (4), 13–29.
9. Lu, Q.; Huang, Y.; Shekhar, S. Evacuation planning: A capacity constrained routing approach. In Proceedings of the First NSF/NIJ Symposium on Intelligence and Security Informatics, Tucson, AZ, June, 2003; Chen, H., Miranda, R., Zeng, D., Demchak, C., Schroeder, J., Madhusudan, T., Eds.; Springer: Berlin, 2003 LNCS 2665.
10. Chen, H. In *Intelligence and Security Informatics for International Security: Information Sharing and Data Mining*; Springer: New York, NY, 2006.
11. Fayyad, U.; Uthurusamy, R. Evolving data mining into solutions for insights. Commun. ACM **2002**, *45* (8), 28–31.
12. Han, J.; Kamber, M. In *Data Mining: Concepts and Techniques*; 2nd Ed.; Morgan Kaufmann: San Francisco, CA, 2005.

13. Cook, J.S.; Cook, L.L. Social, ethical and legal issues of data mining. In *Data Mining: Opportunities and Challenges*; Wang, J., Ed.; Idea Group Publishing: Hershey, PA, 2003; 395–420.

14. American Civil Liberties Union. MATRIX: Myths and reality, http://www.aclu.org/Privacy/Privacy.cfm?ID = 14894&c=130.

IPv6: Expanding Internet Support

Gilbert Held
4-Degree Consulting, Macon, Georgia, U.S.A.

Abstract

The next-generation Internet Protocol will significantly enhance the ability of the Internet in terms of device addressing, router efficiency, and security. Although the actual implementation of IPv6 is still a few years away, most network managers and administrators will eventually be tasked with planning migration strategies that will enable their organizations to move from the existing version of the Internet Protocol to the next-generation Internet Protocol, IPv6. Therefore, it is important to obtain an appreciation for the major characteristics of IPv6, which will then serve as a foundation for discussing migration methods that can be considered to take advantage of the enhanced functionality of the next-generation Internet Protocol.

OVERVIEW

The ability to obtain an appreciation for the functionality of IPv6 is best obtained by comparing its header to the IPv4 header. Fig. 1 provides this comparison, showing the IPv4 header at the top of the illustration, with the IPv6 header below.

In comparing the two headers shown in Fig. 1, one notes that IPv6 includes six less fields than the existing version of the Internet Protocol. Although at first glance this appears to make an IPv6 header simpler, in actuality the IPv6 header includes a Next Header field that enables one header to point to a following header, in effect, resulting in a daisy chain of headers. While the daisy chain adds complexity, only certain routers need to examine the contents of different headers, facilitating router processing. Thus, an IPv6 header, which can consist of a sequence of headers in a daisy chain, enables routers to process information directly applicable to their routing requirements. This makes IPv6 packet processing much more efficient for intermediate routers when data flows between two Internet locations, enabling those routers to process more packets per second than when the data flow consists of IPv4 headers.

A close examination of the two IP headers reveals that only one field kept the same meaning and position. That field is the Version field, which is encoded in the first four bits of each header as a binary value, with 0100 used for IPv4 and 0110 for IPv6.

Continuing the comparison of the two headers, note that IPv6 does away with seven IPv4 fields. Those fields include the Type of Service, Identification, Flags, Fragment Offset, Checksum, Options, and Padding. Because headers can be daisy chained and separate headers now identify specific services, the Type of Service field is no longer necessary. Another significant change between IPv4 and IPv6 concerns fragmentation, which enables senders to transmit large packets without worrying about the capabilities of intermediate routers. Under IPv4, fragmentation required the use of Identification, Flags, and Fragment Offset fields. Under IPv6, hosts learn the maximum acceptable segment size through a process referred to as path maximum transmission unit discovery. Thus, this enabled the IPv6 designers to remove those three fields from the new header.

Another difference between IPv4 and IPv6 headers involves the removal of the Header Checksum. In an era of fiber backbones, it was thought that the advantage obtained from eliminating the processing associated with performing the header checksum at each router was considerably more than the possibility that transmission errors would go undetected. In addition, since the higher layer (transport layer) and lower layer (IEEE 802 networks) perform checksum operations, the risk of undetected error at the network layer adversely affecting operations is minimal. Two more omissions from the IPv4 header are the Options and Padding fields. Both fields are not necessary in IPv6 because the use of optional headers enables additional functions to be specified as separate entities. Since each header follows a fixed format, there is also no need for a variable Padding field, as was the case under IPv4.

Perhaps, the change that obtains the most publicity is the increase in source and destination addresses from 32-bit fields to 128-bit fields. Through the use of 128-bit addressing fields, IPv6 provides the potential to supply unique addresses for every two- and four-footed creature on Earth and still have enough addresses left over to assign a unique address to every past, present, and future appliance. Thus, the extra 96-bit positions virtually ensures that one will not experience another IP

Encyclopedia of Information Systems and Technology, DOI: 10.1081/E-EIST-120046373

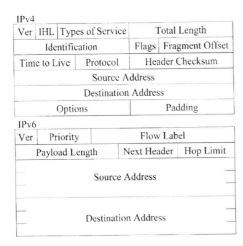

Fig. 1 Comparing IPv4 and IPv6.

Table 2 IPv6 extension headers

Extension header	Description
Hop-by-hop options	Passes information to all routers in a path
Routing	Defines the route through which a packet flows
Fragment	Provides information that enables destination address to concatenate fragments
Authentication	Verifies the originator
Encrypted security payload	Defines the algorithm and keys necessary to decrypt a previously encrypted payload
Destination options	Defines a generic header that can obtain one or more options identified by options type that can define new extensions on an as-required basis

address crunch such as the one now being experienced with IPv4.

NEW AND RENAMED IPv6 FIELDS

IPv6 adds three new fields while relabeling and slightly modifying the use of Total Length and Time to Live fields in Ipv4. Concerning the renamed and revised fields, the Total Length field in IPv4 was changed to a Payload Length. This subtle difference is important, as the use of a payload length now specifies the length of the data carried after the header instead of the length of the sum of both the header and data. The second revision represents the recognition of the fact that the Time to Live field under IPv4, which could be specified in seconds, was difficult—if not impossible—to use due to a lack of time-stamping on packets. Instead, the value used in that field was decremented at each router hop as a mechanism to ensure that packets did not endlessly flow over the Internet, since they are discarded when the value of that field reaches zero. In recognition of the actual manner by which that field is used, it was renamed the Hop Limit field under IPv6.

The Priority field is 4 bits wide, enabling 16 possible values. This field enables packets to be distinguished from one another based on their need for processing

Table 1 Recommended congestion-controlled priorities

Priority	Type of traffic
0	Uncharacterized traffic
1	Filter traffic, such as Netnews
2	Unattended data transfer (i.e., e-mail)
3	Reserved
4	Attended bulk transfer (i.e., FTP and HTTP)
5	Reserved
6	Interactive traffic (i.e., telnet)
7	Internet-controlled traffic (i.e., SNMP)

precedence. Thus, file transfers would be assigned a low priority, while real-time audio or video would be assigned a higher priority.

Under IPv6, priority field values of 0 to 7 are used for traffic that is not adversely affected by backing off in response to network congestion. In comparison, values 8 to 15 are used for traffic that would be adversely affected by backing off when congestion occurs, such as real-time audio packets being transmitted at a constant rate. Table 1 lists the priority values recommended for different types of congestion-controlled traffic.

Priorities 8 to 15 are used for traffic that would be adversely affected by backing off when network congestion occurs. The lowest priority value in this group, 8, should be used for packets one is most willing to discard under congestion conditions. In comparison, the highest priority, 15, should be used for packets one is least willing to have discarded.

The Flow Label field, also new to IPv6, allows packets that require the same treatment to be identified. For example, a real-time video transmission that consists of a long sequence of packets would more than likely use a Flow Label identifier as well as a high-priority value so that all packets that make up the video are treated the same, even if other packets with the same priority arrive at the same time at intermediate routers.

HEADER CHAINS

The ability to chain headers is obtained through the use of the IPv6 Next Header field. The IPv6 specification designates six extension headers. Those headers and a brief description of the functions they perform are listed in Table 2.

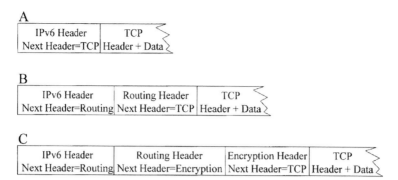

Fig. 2 Creating a daisy chain of headers.

To illustrate how the Next Header field in IPv6 is actually used, one can use a few of the headers listed in Fig. 2 to create a few examples. First, assume that an IPv6 header is followed directly by a Transmission Control Protocol (TCP) header and data, with no optional extension headers. Then, the Next Header field in the IPv6 header would indicate that the TCP header follows as indicated in Fig. 2A.

For a second example, assume that one wants to specify a path or route the packet will follow. To do so, one would add a Routing Header, with the IPv6's Next Header field containing a value that specifies that the Routing Header follows. Then, the Routing Header's Next Header field would contain an appropriate value that specifies that the TCP header follows. This header chain is illustrated in Fig. 2B.

As a third example, assume one wants to both specify a route for each packet as well as encrypt the payload. To accomplish this, one would change the TCP Header's Next Header field value from the previous example where it indicates that there are no additional headers in the header chain, to a value that serves to identify the Encryption Header as the next header.

Fig. 2C illustrates the daisy chain of IPv6 headers that would specify that a specific route is to be followed and the information required to decrypt an encrypted payload. Now that one has an appreciation for the general format of the IPv6 header, the use of its header fields, and how headers can be chained to obtain additional functionality, one can focus attention on addressing under IPv6.

ADDRESSING

Under IPv6, there are three types of addresses supported: unicast, multicast, and anycast. The key difference between IPv6 and IPv4 with respect to addressing involves the addition of an anycast type address and the use of 128-bit source and destination addresses.

An anycast address represents a special type of multicast address. Like a multicast address, an anycast address identifies a group of stations that can receive a packet. However, under an anycast address, only the nearest member of a group receives the packet instead of all members. It is expected that the use of anycast addressing will facilitate passing packets from network to network as it allows packets to be forwarded to a group of routers without having to know which is the one nearest to the source. Concerning the actual 128-bit address used under IPv6, its expansion by a factor of four over IPv4 resulted in the necessity to introduce methods to facilitate the notation of this expanded address. Thus, the methods by which IPv6 addresses can be noted can be examined.

IPv6 ADDRESS NOTATION

Under IPv4, a 32-bit IP address can be encoded as eight hexadecimal digits. The expansion of the IP address fields to 128 bits results in a requirement to use 32 hexadecimal digits. However, because it is fairly easy to make a mistake that can go undetected by simply entering a long sequence of 32 digits, IPv6 allows each 128-bit address to be represented as eight 16-bit integers separated by colons (:). Thus, under IPv6 notation, one can represent each integer as four hexadecimal digits, enabling a 128-bit address to be encoded or noted as a sequence of eight groups of four hexadecimal digits separated from one another by a colon. An example of an IPv6 address follows:

AB01:0000:OO1A:000C:0000:0000:3A1C:1B1F

Two methods are supported by IPv6 addressing that can be expected to be frequently used by network managers and administrators when configuring network devices. The first method is zero suppression, which allows leading zeros in each of the eight hexadecimal groups to be suppressed. Thus, the application of zero suppression would reduce the previous IPv6 address as follows:

AB01:0:1A:C:0:0:3A1C:1B1E

Table 3 Initial IPv6 address space allocation

Address space allocation	(Binary)	Prefix fraction of address space
Reserved	0000 0000	1/256
Unassigned 0000	0000 0001	1/256
Reserved for Network Service Access Point allocation	0000 001	1/128
Reserved for Internetwork Packet Exchange allocation	0000 010	1/128
Unassigned	0000 011	1/128
Unassigned	0000 1	1/32
Unassigned	0001	1/16
Unassigned	001	1/8
Provider-based unicast address	010	1/8
Unassigned	011	1/8
Reserved for geographic-based unicast addresses	100	1/8
Unassigned	101	1/8
Unassigned	110	1/8
Unassigned	1110	1/16
Unassigned	1111 0	1/32
Unassigned	1111 10	1/64
Unassigned	1111 110	1/128
Unassigned	1111 1110 0	1/512
Link local use addresses	1111 1110 10	1/1024
Site local use addresses	1111 1110 11	1/1024
Multicast addresses	1111 1111	1/256

A second method supported by IPv6 to facilitate the use of 128-bit addresses recognizes that during a migration process, many IPv4 addresses carried within an IPv6 address field will result in a considerable sequence of zero-bit positions that cross colon boundaries. This zero-density situation can be simplified by the use of a double colon (::), which can replace a single run of consecutive zeros. Thus, one can further simplify the previously zero-suppressed IPv6 address as follows:

AB01:0:1A:C::3A1C:1B1E

Note that the use of the double colon can only occur once in an IPv6 address. Otherwise, its use would produce an ambiguous result because there would be no way to tell how many groups of four hexadecimal zeros a double colon represents.

ADDRESS ASSIGNMENTS

With 2^{128} addresses available for assignment, IPv6 designers broke the address space into an initial sequence of 21 address blocks, based on the use of binary address prefixes. As one might surmise, most of the address blocks are either reserved for future use or unassigned because even a small fraction of IPv6 address space is significantly larger than all of the IPv4 address space. Table 3 provides a list of the initial IPv6 address space allocation. Of the initial allocation of IPv6 address space, probably the most important will be the provider-based unicast address. As noted in Table 3, the prefix for this allocated address block is binary 010 and it represents one-eighth (1/8) of the total IPv6 address space. The provider-based unicast address space enables the registry that allocates the address, the Internet service provider (ISP), and the subscriber to be identified. In addition, a subscriber can subdivide his address into a subnetwork and interface or host identifiers similar to the manner by which IPv4 class A through class C addresses can be subdivided into host and network identifiers. The key difference between the two is the fact that an extension to 128 bits enables an IPv6 address to identify organizations that assigned the address to include the registry and ISP. Concerning the registry, in North America, the Internet Network Information Center (Internet NIC) is tasked with distributing IPv4 addresses and can be expected to distribute IPv6 addresses. The European registry is the Réseaux IP Européens Network Coordination Centre, while the APNIC is responsible for distributing addresses for networks in Asian and Pacific countries.

MIGRATION ISSUES

After a considerable amount of deliberation by the Internet community, it was decided that the installed base of approximately 20 million computers using IPv4 would require a dual-stack migration strategy. Instead of one giant cutover sometime in the future, it was recognized that a considerable amount of existing equipment would be incapable of migrating to IPv6. Thus, an IPv6 Internet will be deployed in parallel to IPv4, and all IPv6 hosts will be capable of supporting IPv4. This means that network managers can decide both if and when they should consider upgrading to IPv6. Perhaps, the best strategy is that, when in doubt, to obtain equipment capable of operating a dual stack, such as the one shown in Table 3. In addition to operating dual stacks, one must consider the relationship of one's network with other networks with respect to the version of IP supported. For example, if an organization migrates to IPv6, but its ISP does not, one will have to encapsulate IPv6 through IPv4 to use the transmission services of the ISP to reach other IPv6 networks. Fortunately, two types of tunneling—configured and automatic—have been proposed to allow IPv6 hosts to reach other IPv6 hosts via IPv4-based networks. Thus, between the use of dual-stack architecture and configured and automatic tunneling, one will be able to continue to use IPv4 as the commercial use of IPv6 begins, as well as plan for an orderly migration.

RECOMMENDED COURSE OF ACTION

Although the first commercial use of IPv6 is still a few years away, an organization can prepare itself for Ipv6 use by ensuring that acquired hosts, workstations, and routers can be upgraded to support IPv6. In addition, one must consider the fact that the existing Domain Name Server (DNS) will need to be upgraded to support IPv6 addresses, and one must contact the DNS software vendor to determine how and when to implement IPv6 addressing support. By carefully determining the software and possible hardware upgrades, and by keeping abreast of Internet IPv6-related Request for Comments, one can plan a migration strategy that will allow an organization to benefit from the enhanced router performance afforded by IPv6 addressing.

ISO Standards and Certification

Scott Erkonen
Hot skills Inc., Minneapolis, Minnesota, U.S.A.

Abstract

This entry discusses the International Organization for Standardization (ISO) standards and how to become certified. After giving a history and background of ISO standards, the author discusses ISO 27001, 27002, and 27000 series as well as the standards that accompany them. The entry also details the relationship to other standards and why a new ISO standard, ISO 27001, is being considered for implementation. The author discusses what the future may hold for ISO standards in the United States and concludes that security managers should take the time to explore ISO 27001 and the ISO 27000 series as important tools that can help strengthen their ability to manage information security.

INTRODUCTION

The development of information security standards on an international level involves the International Organization for Standardization (ISO) and the International Electronics Consortium (IEC). Although other bodies provide sector-specific standards, they are often derived from or refer to the "ISO" standards (commonly referred to as ISO/IEC). In the United States, this work is managed through the American National Standards Institute and the International Committee for Information Technology Standards (INCITS). The group directly responsible for developing, contributing to, and managing this work is INCITS CS/1, cyber security. This group, CS/1, is also responsible for standards work in the areas of information technology (IT) security, privacy, identity management, and biometric security. One major area of focus for CS/1 involves the information security standards known as ISO/IEC 27001: 2005 [information security–information security management system (ISMS) requirements] and ISO/IEC 17799: 2005 (specification for information security management). For the sake of keeping things simplified as much as possible, these will be referred to as "ISO 17799" and "ISO 27001," respectively. It is also important to note that, effective April 2007, ISO 17799 has undergone a numbering change and is renumbered to ISO 27002.

ISO 27001, ISO 27002, AND THE ISO 27000 SERIES

So what are these standards and what are the differences between them? ISO 27001 is the standard for ISMS. Most people are more familiar with ISO 17799 (now ISO 27002), which is the code of practice for information security. Although it may seem confusing at first, the relationship is not difficult to understand. Many people confuse ISO 27001 and ISO 27002 with British Standard (BS) 7799; although they are similar, they are not 100% equal. It is important to acknowledge that much of the work in this area was initiated by, and developed from, BS 7799 prior to it being modified and approved as an ISO standard, ISO 17799. What we have today is the result of that initial work combined with the input and participation of multiple nations. This entry is not designed to serve as implementation guidance, but to educate you on the topic of ISMS, specifically as it pertains to ISO 27001. Implementation guidance is best left where it belongs, in ISO 27003.

ISO/IEC 27001 is the international standard that provides requirements for the creation, structure, and management of an ISMS. It contains five major areas, often referred to as "Sections 4 through 8." These areas are ISMS, management responsibility, internal ISMS audits, management review of the ISMS, and ISMS improvement. These four sections are what allow an organization to create a program structure, or ISMS. Most information security practitioners are familiar with or have heard of ISO 9001, which deals with quality management systems. Think of ISO 27001 as having a similar structure, but dealing with this in the context of information security. One way to visualize this is as an umbrella. ISO 27001 provides the top layer defining how you document, organize, empower, audit, manage, and improve your information security program. In other words, an ISMS is an organization's structure for managing its people, processes, and technology. This entry will provide you with information about the standards, but will not go into line-by-line descriptions or list the control objectives. It is highly recommended, if you are considering going down this path or would like to learn more, that you pick up a copy of the ISO standards.

Encyclopedia of Information Systems and Technology, DOI: 10.1081/E-EIST-120046779

ISO/IEC 17799 provides the control objectives, along with the legal, regulatory, or business requirements, that are relevant to an information security practitioner's organization. There are 10 different areas that are covered in ISO 17799. These should look familiar as you are reading this book:

1. Security policy
2. Security organization
3. Asset classification and control
4. Personnel security
5. Physical and environmental security
6. Communications and operations management
7. Access control
8. Systems development and maintenance
9. Business continuity management
10. Compliance

Together with an organization's legal, regulatory, and business requirements, these control objectives provide the foundation of an ISO 27001 ISMS. Examine Annex A of ISO 27001 and you will notice that the control objectives in ISO 17799 are replicated there. When a security manager or practitioner wants to certify his or her organization's program as conforming to ISO 17799, it is actually done through certifying against the criteria defined in ISO 27001. This could seem confusing, but understand that the objective is to prove implementation of applicable controls from ISO 17799 (also Annex A of ISO 27001), and the ISMS developed from ISO 27001 (general requirements) provides the method by which this is accomplished.

So what are the requirements of ISO 27001? Sections 4 through 8 are often referred to as "general requirements."

Section 4 covers the requirements for development, implementation, management, and improvement of an ISMS. One of the first steps in the development of an ISMS is to define the scope. This scope can be based upon physical location, function, organizational culture, environment, or logical boundaries. Many organizations use physical or logical boundaries to simplify things. A scope includes physical, technical, information, and program elements and human assets. We will go a little deeper than normal regarding the concept of scoping, as it is a critical concept in information security and audit.

When you are developing an information security program based on ISO 27001, without the goal of certification, your scope would be where you have determined that your information security program is applicable. For example, you may work for a company with multiple divisions. Your scope may include the division that you are responsible for, but not the others or the overlying corporate structure. Think of scope in terms of span of control, which is critical for any program to be successful. You may choose to leverage

building a program based on ISO 27001 to expand the span of control to drive consistency or manage risk.

If creating a scope for certification purposes, there are several important things to consider:

1. What is the value of the contents of the domain defined by the scope of the organization?
2. Do you have the span of control over the domain?
3. What roles and responsibilities are performed by the people associated with the domain?
4. What are the logical or physical boundaries that can be used to define the domain?
5. What exceptions exist?
6. Is the desired scope reasonable for a certification effort?

When determining the value of the contents, there are many formulas that are available for you to use. Some are based on tangible values such as the dollar value of equipment. Others are based upon risk or business impact (potential for major disruption to the business caused by lack of availability, etc.). Oftentimes, a combination of these approaches proves to be the most successful. This entry does not go into risk-management approaches, but will discuss the ISO risk requirements later.

Span of control is a critical concept in regard to successful scoping. You need to analyze what you have direct control over, can influence, or have no say in. Certification scopes typically deal with these areas of no control or limited influence through service-level agreements, memorandums of understanding, responsibility documents, or other methods. Trying to create a scope with little or no span of control may not be a wise idea and may end in the frustration of an ineffective program or failed certification attempt.

Roles and responsibilities exist within the scope and should be defined and understood so as to eliminate overlap and duplication. Responsibility for the management of the ISMS needs to be defined as well as the responsibility for those activities that make up the day-to-day operations of the system. A great way to keep all this information straight is through the use of RACI diagrams (in which tasks are split into four types of roles: Responsible, Accountable, Consulted, Informed), or responsibility matrices.

Physical and logical boundaries can be used to help define where a scope exists and can also help clarify the span of control. These boundaries can be walls, floors, fences, etc., for the physical and virtual local area networks, segments, or even filtered ports for the logical boundaries. This is particularly valuable when preparing a scope for a data center, for example. Ingress and egress points, both physical and logical, can be identified and should be examined and documented.

Another important step in creating a scope is documenting exceptions. Exceptions are anything that is not applicable from the control objectives in Annex A. The requirements in Sections 4 through 8 are just that—required. You cannot document exceptions to those areas. One way to handle this is to create a list as you go or utilize a process that keeps these exceptions organized. You may need to defend your rationale for exceptions during an audit.

OK, so we have covered most of the items to be considered (granted, at a high level) when creating a scope. The most important question that needs to be answered is the last question that was asked earlier. Is the scope reasonable for attempting a certification audit? Many organizations, when first deciding whether to go down this road, choose to certify an entire organization (often referred to by consultants as "boiling the ocean"). Although this may be successful in smaller organizations with a strong span of control, it may not be reasonable for most. Experience has shown that successful certification is based upon a program that is designed and implemented enterprise-wide, but in which certification specifics are applied to the assets that are of the highest value to the organization. What you end up with is a situation in which the organization is able to benefit from the information security program that you developed (your ISMS) and from a certification that is internationally recognized and applied to your highest-value assets or services. My advice to you would be not to try to boil the ocean, but to look at a certification scope that makes sense for you. Are you a service provider? Consider certifying the portions of your organization that provide those services for your customers. Are you a financial institution? Consider certifying the services or centers where your customer information is stored, used, and retained. If you have a desire for enterprise-wide certification, break your efforts up into manageable domains and apply the same scoping process to those domains.

Getting back to the rest of this section, defining an ISMS policy is just what it sounds like, writing a policy. Policy templates are popular starting points, but beware trying to use a canned document if you are going for certification or trying to build a truly effective program. Any good policy should be well thought out and be exactly that—a policy. Too often people put components of specifications (i.e., 128-bit encryption minimums) into policy. This prevents you from exercising the span of control. Who wants to go to the board of directors every time you need to update a technical setting? The best advice to give here is to make sure that your "policy" fits the culture and environment of your organization. Take the time to be sure that you are not setting yourself up for failure by creating an unrealistic policy that you cannot live up to.

Risk management means different things to different people, but anyone should like the flexibility and business-friendly approach that the ISO standards take. If you are looking for a "how to" document, you will be disappointed. From the ISO standard perspective, they are more concerned that you have an organizational approach to risk, criteria or thresholds, and a repeatable methodology.

Informative references (optional, informational) exist that are directly applicable. Two of them are the following:

- *ISO/IEC 27005 Information Technology—Security Techniques—Information Security Risk Management.*
- *ISO/IEC TR 13335-3, Information Technology— Guidelines for the Management of IT Security—Techniques for the Management of IT Security.*

I strongly recommend using these documents as resources. At the end of performing a solid risk assessment, you should have a very good idea where your risks exist, what controls are there, and what your residual risk is. Remember, acceptance or transference are also approved methods for dealing with risk.

Monitoring and reviewing the ISMS—these requirements ensure that you are actively "managing" the ISMS. You not only have to understand what you have, but you need to be reviewing for errors or security events, reviewing effectiveness, and checking to see if you are still on track with your objectives. Time should be spent on looking forward to improve the ISMS, while making sure that any identified problems or observations are acted upon.

Documents and records need to be maintained, as the remainder of the Section 4 requirements discuss. For this, certain types of documents and document control requirements are outlined. Keep all the applicable documentation in an environment that is easy to access and work with and that maintains the integrity of this information. Oftentimes, people have a content management system, portal, or web server that can serve this purpose. However, there is no requirement that says these records need to be electronic. Pay attention to Section 4.3.1 if you are going for certification, as you will need to have those items on hand and ready for the auditors. These are the core categories of the actual documents that make up an ISMS.

Section 5 is the area of the ISMS requirements that talks about management involvement and responsibility. The support of management is critical to any program, not just an ISMS. Proof of this commitment comes in many ways, including documented responsibilities, approval of policy, funding, and active involvement with the appropriate levels of ISMS activities. Other examples of management's commitment are the hiring, training, and empowerment of staff.

Internal audits are another required function, and the requirements are described in Section 6. Internal audit is the function that reviews whether your ISMS is meeting your requirements and functioning properly. What is covered here is what you would expect regarding audit considerations, including scheduling, performance, and remediation requirements. Internal audit is an important process, as it allows for the identification and resolution of issues between registrar audit cycles. If you find a problem, you can fix it—but be aware that major problems or "non-conformities" must be reported.

Management review is the subject of Section 7. This section correlates directly with the PDCA (Plan, Do, Check, Act) model, which is a foundation for all the ISO ISMS standards. Here, you review your actions, changes in the environment, and measurements among other things. There are two parts, one that deals with "inputs" and one that deals with "outputs." The "outputs" portion helps you document your actions, considerations, and outcomes. These types of records are important to show the active management of the ISMS.

The last section, Section 8, deals with ISMS improvement. This is often compared to continuous process improvement, which, in effect, it is. Section 8 can be simplified in the following manner: "corrective" actions, which focus on problems that have been identified, and "preventative" actions taken to avoid negative events and impacts. Oftentimes, these preventative actions are the result of a review of corrective actions.

That should give you a basic understanding of what is covered in the general requirements of ISO 27001. As

you can see, there are various other standards and documents that work together to make an ISMS effective.

27000 SERIES OF ISO STANDARDS

Various other documents in the 27000 series are under development. The main purpose of these developing standards is to support organizations in their efforts to implement an ISMS based on ISO 27001.

- ISO 27000 is a standard designed to educate and inform people of what the 27000 series of documents is and how they interrelate. It will also contain vocabulary and concepts that are not specifically contained in the other 27000 series of documents.
- ISO 27002 (effective April 2007) is what is known as ISO 17799.
- ISO 27003 is implementation guidance for ISO 27001, focusing on the general requirements (Sections 4 through 8).
- ISO 27004 deals with how to gather measurements and metrics from an ISMS.
- ISO 27005 covers risk management in regard to ISO 27001 and ISMS.
- ISO 27006 deals with the requirements for accreditation bodies (the people who actually perform the registration audits).

Additional standards in the 27000 series will be added as needed, in support of the overall ISMS standards.

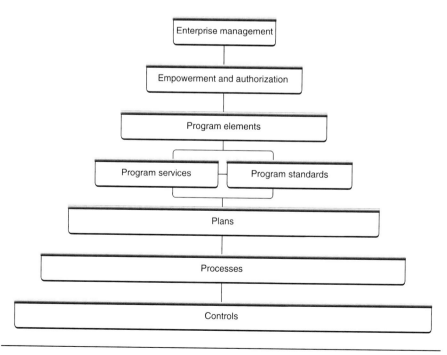

Fig. 1 Information security management reference model.

Fig. 1 explains the relationships and functions of these standards.

RELATIONSHIPS TO OTHER STANDARDS

Although these standards focus on information security, they do not exist in a vacuum. There are various other standards, such as ISO 20000 (IT service management) that complement and interface with ISO 27001 and ISO 17799. Consider ISO 20000 as the mechanism to deal with the IT infrastructure and ISO 27001 as the mechanism to deal with the information security program and requirements. IT service management can help organizations define how to deal with areas such as change management and release management, which are both important from an information security standpoint as well.

Security managers often ask how standards such as COBIT (Control Objectives for Information and related Technology) and the National Institute of Standards and Technology standards relate to ISO standards. Although ISO 27001 will not direct someone to block a certain port on a firewall, it will require an understanding of the risk environment and the application of what is determined to be an appropriate control, that is, blocking that port. The important thing to understand is that where other standards are more operational, ISO standards deal with the issues of how security managers actually manage information security. This assists at a tactical and strategic level, while forming the processes for "informed decision," which impacts the operational level. These operational requirements are derived from legal, regulatory, or business requirements. When these elements are combined correctly, the result is a comprehensive information security program.

WHY DO PEOPLE LOOK TO IMPLEMENT AN ISO 27001 ISMS?

There are many reasons information security practitioners and organizations are looking to implement or have implemented ISO 27001 ISMS. These reasons include looking for a way to provide proof of activities, due care, due diligence, and regulatory compliance. An ISO 27001 ISMS clearly meets the rigors of the Sarbanes–Oxley Act and other similar legislation in the United States or worldwide through the process of identifying and meeting requirements. Others see this as a road map into the future, understanding where future requirements may be met more easily by having a proven, flexible structure in place. Clear demonstration of industry leadership drives some, such as Fujitsu, PREMIER Bankcard, and the Federal Reserve Bank of New York, who were among the first worldwide to certify to ISO 27001 when it was published in November 2005. Various organizations have leveraged ISMS efforts to accelerate maturity in their organization while maintaining flexibility.

One differentiator with the ISO 27001 standard is that it is risk based and, therefore, "business friendly." Security managers get to choose which control objectives apply to them based on their risk, legal, regulatory, and business requirements. There are many additional benefits that have been experienced firsthand, but to list them all here would be too lengthy.

HOW DOES ONE BECOME CERTIFIED?

One potential advantage of building an information security program based on ISO 27001 is that you can achieve certification. Although there are many industry- or technology-specific certification schemes, none offer the level of international recognition that the ISO ISMS certification does. The actual certification audit is performed by an accredited registrar, working with a certification body (CB). Several of the best-known registrars include British Standards Institution (BSI) and Bureau Veritas Certification (BVQI), but American-based companies such as SRI Quality System Registrar and Cotecna are now beginning to offer services in this area. Globally, there are many CBs (also known as accreditation services). Several have been very active in ISMS activities. The best known of these is the United Kingdom Accreditation Service. In America, the American National Accreditation Body has expanded its existing quality management system offerings to include ISO 27001. This is an important step toward increased adoption of the ISO standards in the United States. If someone is looking to become certified, or is interested, a program analysis is a good way to start. These can either be performed internally or with the help of an experienced partner. Following this, you should be able to have a good feel for where you sit, and what it will take to achieve your goal. Even if you are not interested in certification, the ISO standards provide a sound, accepted measuring stick against which you can examine your information security program. One last word of assistance to those who seek certification—train and educate those involved with the process. There are lead auditor and implementer courses available that should be considered. These can shorten your learning curve and bring better results in the long run.

WHAT IS THE FUTURE?

The use of the ISO standards continues to grow in the United States. Many private and public sector organizations have information security programs built on components of ISO 17799. Although there were under 25 organizations certified to BS 7799 (in the United States), this number has already nearly doubled since the publication of ISO 27001. As awareness of the standards and the benefits of implementing ISMS continues to grow, it is estimated that the United States will begin to surpass many countries and become more on the level of the United Kingdom, Japan, and India, countries with registrations numbering in the hundreds. Security managers should take the time to explore ISO 27001 and the ISO 27000 series as important tools that can help strengthen their ability to manage information security.

ISSEP: Information Systems Security Engineering Professional

Robert B. Batie, Jr.
Cyber Defense Solutions, Network Centric Systems, Raytheon Company, Largo, Florida, U.S.A.

Abstract

The Information Systems Security Engineering Professional (ISSEP) credential was developed as an advanced area of concentration to the Certified Information Systems Security Professional (CISSP) credential by the International Information Systems Security Certification Consortium (ISC)^2 in 2004. This advanced concentration provides a systems security engineering professional with the tools needed to develop secure systems using the CISSP-ISSEP Common Body of Knowledge (CBK®) as a guide for incorporating systems security engineering (SSE) into projects, applications, business processes, and information systems. The ISSEP security professional understands the SSE methodologies and best practices to integrate security into all facets of information systems, being development as well as business operations. The ISSEP certification was sponsored by the U.S. National Security Agency (NSA) and developed by (ISC)^2. There are four domains and six process steps that make up the content of the ISSEP certification. The domains include Information Systems Security Engineering, Technical Management, Certification and Accreditation, and U.S. Government Information Assurance Regulations. The six process steps include discover the information protection needs; define the system security requirements; define system security architecture; develop detailed security design; implement the design; and continuously assess the effectiveness of the security services, features, and functionality. The entry goes on to discuss the certification examination, recertification considerations and provides an explanation of how to earn the Continuing Professional Education (CPE) to maintain the certification.

INTRODUCTION

The Information Systems Security Engineering Professional (ISSEP) credential was developed as an advanced area of concentration to the Certified Information Systems Security Professional (CISSP) credential by the International Information Systems Security Certification Consortium (ISC)^2 in 2004. The ISSEP certification was sponsored by the U.S. National Security Agency (NSA) and developed by (ISC)^{2}.[1]

This advanced concentration provides an invaluable tool for any systems security engineering professional. CISSP-ISSEP Common Body of Knowledge (CBK®)[1] is the guide for incorporating information systems (IS) security into projects, applications, business processes, and information systems. The ISSEP is expected to understand and use systems security engineering (SSE) methodologies and best practices to integrate security into all facets of information systems development and business operations. The SSE model used in the ISSEP concentration is based on the Information Assurance Technical Framework (IATF) SSE model and is a guiding light in the field of information security for the incorporation of security into information systems.

The ISSEP credential was designed to recognize mastery of national standards for information security

engineering, including an understanding of the ISSEP CBK. Certification can enhance a professional's career and provide added information systems credibility. The potential candidate must already be a CISSP in good standing, pass a written examination, subscribe to the (ISC)^2 code of ethics, and be endorsed by another certified ISSEP in good standing.[1]

COMMON BODY OF KNOWLEDGE

ISSEP SSE model is based on the traditional systems engineering model with the purpose of focusing on the security requirements, services, policies, and procedures needed to design, implement, certify, and accredit security in the information systems. The ISSEP CBK consists of four advance security-related domains on which the foundation of the ISSEP certification is built. The CISSP-ISSEP CBK domains are as follows (see Fig. 1):

- Domain 1—Systems Security Engineering
- Domain 2—Technical Management
- Domain 3—Certification and Accreditation
- Domain 4—U.S. Government Information Assurance Regulations

Encyclopedia of Information Systems and Technology, DOI: 10.1081/E-EIST-120045495

Information Science– ITIL

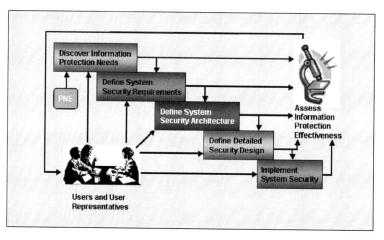

Fig. 1 Systems security engineering process.

For each of the four domains, a fairly thorough list of subdomain topics has been developed to identify tasks the ISSEP should be familiar with to attain this advanced security credential. The four domains and sub-domain topics are reviewed and updated periodically to ensure they are addressing the relevant security topics of the day.

Domain 1

SSE focuses on the activities of the process as defined in the IATF 3.1SSE model and aligns with normal systems engineering activities. The steps of the SSE model process are listed and also shown in Fig. 1:

1. *Discover information protection needs.* Ascertain why the system needs to be built and what information needs to be protected.
2. *Define system security requirements.* Define the system in terms of what security is needed.
3. *Define system security architecture.* Define the security functions needed to meet the specific security requirements. This process is the core of designing the security architecture.
4. *Develop detailed security design.* Based on the security architecture, design and develop the detailed security functions and features for the system.
5. *Implement system security.* Following the documented detailed security design, build and implement the security functions and features for the system.
6. *Assess security effectiveness.* Assess the degree to which the system, as it is defined, designed, and implemented, meets the security needs. This assessment activity occurs continuously during all the activities in the SSE process.

Domain 2

Technical Management consists of activities needed to manage the technical security-related aspect of a program or project. It includes development of security architecture models using standard system engineering models such as waterfall model, spiral development model, and the VEE model. Other architectural development models and methods that are discussed include statistical process control, linear and dynamic programming economic analysis methods, rapid prototyping, analytical methods, and mock-ups and scaled models.

Other activities in this Technical Management domain consist of an understanding of technical management roles and responsibilities such as program managers, personnel development and training, and configuration management. Technical documentation such as systems engineering management plans, statement of work, project schedule, and cost projections must be understood by the ISSEP practitioner. Finally, in this domain, the use of technical management tools such as PERT and Gantt charts, requirements traceability, and analysis are discussed.

Domains 3 and 4

Domains 3 and 4 discuss the various U.S. government certification and accreditation (C&A) processes and national security policy standards and directives. Domain 3 describes the C&A process in both the National Institute of Standards and Technology (NIST) SP 800-37 for most federal information systems and the Department of Defense (DoD) 8500.1 for defense information systems. Some of the professionals engage in self-study by reviewing books, U.S. government policies, standards regulations, and other materials that make up ISSEP common body of knowledge.

Table 1 Group A and B credits for recertification

Qualifying activities	
Direct information systems (IS) security activities Group A credits	Professional skills activities Group B credits
• Access control systems and methodology	• Organizational behavior
• Telecommunications and network security	• Strategic planning
• Security management practices	• Programming languages
• Applications and system development security	• Programming techniques
• Cryptology	• Tools and techniques
• Security architecture and models	• Interpersonal communications skills
• Operations security	• Interviewing techniques
• Business continuity planning (BCP) and disaster recovery planning (DRP)	• Team development skills
• Law, investigation, and ethics	

CERTIFICATION EXAMINATION

The candidate seeking to become an ISSEP must pass a rigorous examination that consists of 125 questions composed from the four security domains in the CISSP-ISSEP CBK. Candidates are allotted up to 3 hours to complete this examination. The objective of the examination is to pass the most qualified candidate based on their knowledge of the CBK. Candidates prepare for the examination in various ways. Some perform self-study by reviewing reference books, U.S. government policies, standards regulations, and other materials that cover the four domains. Others attend training sessions, boot camps, and review seminars in order to help prepare for the examination. The examination is administered by a certified professional who is trained in test administration. The examinations are scheduled in various public forums and often during security conferences and in venues around the world.

The candidate receives an e-mail after completing the examination notifying the result. If the candidate has failed, a breakdown of the areas of weakness is included along with a score. If the candidate has passed the examination, the e-mail congratulates the candidate and provides the next steps that must be taken to complete the certification process. The candidate must be endorsed by an ISSEP in good standing and provide a copy of their resume.

The recertification of the ISSEP is in conjunction with the CISSP certification, which is good for 3 years, at which time one must recertify by accumulating at least 40 ISSEP-related Continuing Professional Education (CPE) credits out of the 120 hours of credits required for the CISSP certification or retaking the examination. An annual maintenance fee (AMF) is charged to each certified practitioner to manage administratively the individual certifications. Payment of the AMF ensures that the $(ISC)^2$ organization has the necessary financial resources to maintain member records, the certification continues to meet the needs and requirements of the market, and the organization will continue to be a functional, dynamic entity in the long run.[1]

Table 2 CPE activities and credits

CPE activities	Number of CPEs per activity
Professional association chapter meetings	1 CPE credit for each hour of attendance at a professional association chapter meeting
Vendor presentation	1 CPE credit for each hour of attendance at a vendor meeting or presentation
Approved item writing (examination questions)	1 CPE for each approved item
Security training provided	4 CPE credits for each hour spent per subject teaching a new subject, lecturing, or presenting security-related training
University/college course completed	12 CPE credits per semester credit with a passing grade from an accredited college or university
Published a security book	40 CPE credits for publishing a security-related book
Published a security magazine article	10 CPE credits for publishing a security-related article

RECERTIFICATION

The ISSEP professionals must certify as both a CISSP and an ISSEP during the 3-year certification cycle and must earn 120 CPEs. These CPEs are classified as either Group A credits, which are focused on the 10 domains, or Group B credits, which cover other types of security professional skills activities. These CPEs may be earned in a variety of ways, although two-thirds (80 credits) must be Group A credits and one-third (40 credits) may be Group B credits. Those with ISSEP concentrations[2] require 20 additional credits per concentration as part of the total 120. Table 1 shows the list of Group A and Group B credits. As per $(ISC)^2$ policy, the certified professional must accumulate a minimum of 20 CPEs per year.

A certified professional can also earn CPEs in the manner shown in Table 2.

CONCLUSION

The CISSP credential is a vendor-neutral information security certification that has been referred to as the gold standard for information security certification. The reputation of the CISSP is built on trust, integrity, and professionalism with an elite membership and network of nearly 60,000 certified industry professionals in 135 countries worldwide. The CISSP-ISSEP certification was designed to recognize mastery of a U.S. national standard for information systems security engineering and understanding of a CISSP-ISSEP CBK. The candidate seeking to become a CISSP-ISSEP must pass a rigorous examination that consists of 125 questions composed from the four security domains in the CISSP-ISSEP CBK. During the 3-year certification cycle, certified professionals must earn 120 CPEs; of which, 20 must address the CISSP-ISSEP concentration to maintain their credentials or retake the examination. CPEs may be earned in a variety of ways such as Group A credits or Group B credits. The requirement for more certified engineering security professionals is expected to continue as national policies, standards, and regulations require protection of the nation's most valuable resource: information.

ACKNOWLEDGMENTS

The author thanks the $(ISC)^2$ family of professionals for access to their web site and information regarding this certification.

REFERENCES

1. $(ISC)^2$, Inc., https://www.isc2.org/cissp/default.aspx.
2. $(ISC)^2$, Inc., http://www.isc2.org/concentrations/default.aspx.

BIBLIOGRAPHY

1. Tipton, H.F.; Henry, K. In *Official (ISC)$^{2®}$ Guide to the CISSP-ISSEP® CBK®* ($(ISC)^2$ Press Series). Auerbach Publication: New York, 2009.
2. Hansche, S. *Official (ISC)$^{2®}$ Guide to the CISSP-ISSEP CBK®* ($(ISC)^2$ Press Series). Auerbach Publication: New York, 2006.

ITGI: IT Governance Institute

Mollie E. Krehnke
Senior Information Security Consultant, Insight Global, Inc., Raleigh, North Carolina, U.S.A.

Abstract
The perspectives and actions of information technology (IT) professionals, information security professionals, and auditors will impact the IT stance of an organization and the ability of IT to securely and consistently meet and exceed the objectives of an enterprise in a global community. The IT Governance Institute has become a strategic force and a leading reference on IT-enabled business systems governance for the global business community.

PURPOSE

Federal regulations, business competition, complex information and communication technologies, and expanded worldwide connectivity increase the risks associated with doing business. The information technology Governance Institute (ITGI) was established to:

- Raise awareness and understanding of enterprise business and technology risks
- Provide guidance and tools to those responsible for IT at all levels
- Enable those professionals to conduct their responsibilities in such a manner that IT meets and exceeds internal (business) and external (federal) requirements
- Empower those professionals in the mitigation of their business process-related risks through the provision of pertinent publications based on extensive, focused, applied (as opposed to basic) research.[1]

HUMBLE BEGINNINGS

The ITGI was established by the Information Systems Audit and Control Association (ISACA) in 1976 as the Information Systems Audit and Control Foundation.[1] ISACA was formed in 1967 and incorporated in 1969 as the Electronic Data Processing Auditors Association by a group of professionals who audited controls in the computer systems in their respective companies. In 2003, the ITGI was established to undertake large-scale research efforts to expand the knowledge and value of the IT governance and control field.

The new name reflects the expanded role of IT in the support of business enterprises—the enablement and transformation—of enterprise growth and (even) survival, and further embraces the many disciplines that are responsible for IT governance within the business enterprises such as audit, assurance, information security, control, and privacy.

OPERATIONS AND FUNDING

ITGI accomplishes its objective as a 501(c)3 not-for-profit and vendor-neutral organization. Volunteers use their personal time to create, review, and publish the deliverables that are made available under the ITGI cognizance. No Information ISACA member dues are used to support the activities of ITGI. Personal and corporate contributions can be made to ITGI to offset the institute costs, and gifts of over U.S. $25 are acknowledged as a contribution in the ISACA/ITGI annual report.[1] The various opportunities for contributions (affiliates, sponsors, and donors) are described on the ITGI website.

RESEARCH FOCUS AND ASSOCIATED DELIVERABLES

The research conducted by ITGI "contributes to a new level of excellence in practices worldwide, by evaluating and analyzing emerging guidelines for implementation and control of new technologies and applications, capitalizing on technological advances to help enterprises achieve competitive advantage, bringing a global perspective to the critical issues facing senior management, and providing practitioners a specialized viewpoint."[1]

The ITGI "strives to assist enterprise leadership in ensuring long-term, sustainable enterprise success and increased stakeholder value by expanding awareness of the need for and benefits of effective IT governance. The institute develops and advances understanding of the vital link between IT and enterprise governance, and offers best practice guidance on the management of IT-related risks".[2]

Information Science–ITIL

Encyclopedia of Information Systems and Technology. DOI: 10.1081/E-EIST-120046531

By conducting original research on IT governance and related topics, ITGI helps enterprise leaders understand the relationship of IT to business objectives and have the tools to ensure effective governance over IT within their enterprises. The resource center on the ITGI website includes articles, white papers, slide presentations, survey results, links, and other resources. Many publications are available in downloadable form, and hard copies are available from the ISACA bookstore. The major categories for the ITGI research are:

- Security control and assurance
- Accounting, finance, and economics
- Business, management, and governance
- Contingency planning and disaster recovery
- IT
- Risk management.[3]

ISACA members are granted a discount on the publications (generally $10–100 per item) that, over time, can result in substantial savings to an individual or an organization. Academic and bulk discounts are also available to those who qualify. ISACA journals have a section in the back entitled *The ISACA Bookstore* that lists new products and a description of those products and a bookstore price list for several hundred deliverables. The website provides a complete description for all deliverables at http://www.isaca.org/bookstore.

The content and scope of ITGI deliverables is continually expanding, and past research is enhanced to reflect new regulations, technologies, and changed business processes. An example of this would be the newest Control Objectives for Information and related Technology (CobiT®) 4. (Trademark registered by ISACA.) This version "emphasizes regulatory compliance, helps organizations to increase the value attained from IT, and enables and simplifies implementation of the CobiT Framework."[4]

USING ITGI PRODUCTS TO GUIDE AND SUPPORT INITIATIVES

The number of ITGI products continues to expand, and the focus of many research deliverables is international in scope (and in language, including Japanese, German, and French). For example, a deliverable from the *CobiT Mapping* research project is *CobiT Mapping: Overview of International IT Guidance* that focuses on the business drivers for implementing international IT guidance documents and the risks of non-compliance. Another available resource is *A Guide to Cross-Border Privacy Impact Assessment* that addresses principles and questions associated with the collection, use, and disclosure of personally identifiable information that may be

subject to regulation. The ITGI landmark study in 2003 and follow up survey in 2005 present IT governance perceptions and activities worldwide, as noted by senior IT executives and enterprise executives, entitled the *IT Governance Global Status Report*.

The best way to learn what is available is to routinely visit the ITGI and ISACA web sites. However, some product reviews are listed below to present a more detailed sampling of the offerings. ITGI makes excerpts available for review, so the reader can make a determination as to the usefulness of a product before purchasing it.

Members of the ISACA can read the book reviews in the *Information Systems Control Journal* to see if a particular product would be beneficial to their work. Examples of reviews of ITGI products are summarized below.

Information Security Governance

The Information Security Governance: Guidance for Boards of Directors and Executive Management document presents a big punch in a small package. The document defines management-level actions that ensure information security addresses the IT structure and the needs of the business and presents questions for directors and management, best practices, and critical success factors to facilitate the deployment of the desired actions. The document also provides an information security governance maturity model that can be used to define an organization's security ranking. The ranking can then be used as the focal point for determining subsequent strategies for the improvement of the security of the organization.[5]

International Information Governance Practices

Strategies for IT Governance is a collection of research articles on IT governance written by academics and practitioners from different countries with a message of IT governance as a business imperative and a top management priority. The book presents case studies that show how IT governance can work in practice.[6] In addition, *CobiT* is considered to be a valuable resource in many countries as an organizational standard or guideline for multiple topics, including IT management, IT governance, and auditing. This is well presented in the text and figures in the article, "The Value to IT of Using International Standards," by Ernst Jan Oud.[7] The article also discusses the value associated with the implementation of a *de facto* standard, or set of best practices, rather than developing standards from scratch; although, the need for customizing the practices to meet company objectives is strongly emphasized.

Network Security for Business Processes Governed by Federal Regulations

Network Security: The Complete Reference presents a broad spectrum of security topics, including return on security investment; security strategy and risk analysis; security policy development and security organizations; access control and physical security; biometrics; e-mail; network architecture; firewalls and Intrusion Detection Systems; Virtual Private Network; wireless security; disaster recovery; Windows, Linux, UNIX, and Novell; application and database security; and incident response. The book will be useful to security professionals, IT administrators, and software developers who are writing secure code for the J2EE and .NET platforms.[8]

Secure Outsourcing of IT Functions

Outsourcing Information Security by C. Warren Axelrod is a risk-based approach to outsourcing according to the reviewer, Sarathy Emani, an IT professional with international experience. The book "explains the issues one needs to identify, quantify, and analyze to make the right outsourcing decisions without sacrificing security." Topics included in the book are, the history of IT outsourcing, internal and external security risks associated with outsourcing, motivations and justifications behind outsourcing, objectives of outsourcing, tangible and intangible costs and benefits, the outsourcing evaluation and decision process, and candidate security services for outsourcing. The book will be useful to managers, information security, and IT senior management professionals who are directly involved in outsourcing or business partner relationships.[9]

Business Impacts for an Unavailable e-Commerce Service

The e-Commerce Security series, particularly *e-Commerce Security—Business Continuity Planning*, provides guidance to businesses and organizations in the creation of a plan to reduce the risk associated with such an event and to recover more quickly if resources are unavailable. The book addresses:

- Business continuity planning and evaluation
- Business assessment
- Strategy selection
- Plan development
- Testing and maintenance.

According to Linda Kinczkowski, it will be useful to business managers, security and audit professionals, and educators and students who have to address business continuity and disaster planning. The book also presents precautions and procedures that apply specifically to the e-commerce business component.[10]

Financial Audit Processes

Auditing: A Risk Analysis Approach, Fifth Edition, "offers an in-depth framework that addresses the relationships among audit evidence, materiality, audit risk and their concrete applications." In addition, the book provides resources that would be useful for anyone studying for the Certified Public Accountant (CPA) and Certified Internal Auditor exams based on the review questions and essays provided at the end of each entry and the computer audit practice case. Students, accountants, chief financial officers (CFOs), CPAs, IT auditors, and faculty members teaching financial audit will find this to be a useful resource.[11]

Internal Audit Processes

The book, *Managing the Audit Function: A Corporate Audit Department Procedures Guide*, Third Edition, is very comprehensive, addressing all aspects of the internal auditing function. The procedural format provides a resource that could be used as a starting point for many organizations and includes audit plans, work papers, and descriptions of the roles and responsibilities for the audit team. The third edition, with its expanded focus on internal auditing, is applicable for internal audit managers and management for large and small businesses. The book also includes a discussion of other factors that impact corporate business processes, including the United States' Sarbanes–Oxley Act of 2002 and the Foreign Corrupt Practices Act. The reviewers felt that this book is an essential resource for every audit department.[12]

Risk-Based Auditing Processes

Auditor's Risk Management Guide—Integrating Auditing and Enterprise Resource Management (ERM) is a guide for conducting a risk management-based auditing methodology and provides case studies that utilize the concepts presented. Topics include an overview of ERM; control-based, process-based, risk-based, and risk management-based auditing approaches; an integration of strategy into risk management-based auditing; and risk assessment quantification techniques. The book also includes a CD-ROM containing electronic versions of work programs, checklists, and other tools. The reviewer felt that this book is "outstanding in the way it is organized and the extent of details it covers and the presentation from generalities to specifics aids the reader in understanding the concepts being presented."[13]

Information Science–ITIL

Oracle® Database Security, Privacy, and Auditing Requirements

Oracle Security Privacy Auditing addresses HIPAA technical requirements but is also "an excellent primer on Oracle database security, describing what is arguably best practice, which is why it is assessed as valuable even to a reader who is not specifically concerned with Health Insurance Portability and Accountability Act." The authors are distinguished Oracle professionals, and the presentation enables the reader to skim through the text and read only the portions that are pertinent for a particular concern. However, the book is addressed to database administrators, architects, system developers, and designers, and the reader must be familiar with basic Oracle database concepts and Structured Query Language.[14]

IT Audit Tools for New Auditors

CobiT 4.0 is considered to be a vital tool for IT auditors, particularly in the "strong linkages to business objectives and goals to provide the drivers and rationale for the IT supporting process." The text, illustrations, and diagrams have been updated from earlier editions, and these changes have greatly enhanced the usability of the document, and the appendices provide additional IT governance processes and references.[15] In an article by Tommie Singleton, "CobiT is the most effective auditing tool available today, which can be applied to a variety of IT audit-related functions." In support of this perspective, numerous process models (such as Committee of Sponsoring Organization of the Treadway Commission, Information Technology Infrastructure Library, British Standard 1500, and Capability Maturity Model) have been mapped to CobiT, at least in part because of the guidance it provides in assessing IT controls.[16]

ITGI: A LEADER AND A RESOURCE

The perspectives and actions of IT professionals, information security professionals, and auditors will impact the IT stance of an organization and the ability of IT to securely and consistently meet and exceed the objectives of an enterprise in a global community. ITGI has become a strategic force and a leading reference on IT-enabled business systems governance for the global business community. A corresponding effort relates to the ISACA perspective regarding the responsibilities of auditors or information security practitioners—those individuals are going to be required to support and become experts in IT governance. As a result, ITGI

stands ready and continues in its research endeavors to support corporate enterprise in the utilization and protection of information resources to obtain business objectives. ISACA is prepared to provide resources to empower those individuals who must implement the enterprise objectives in their current (and in time to come) job responsibilities.[17]

REFERENCES

1. IT Governance Institute, In *IT Governance Institute Brochure*; Rolling Meadows, IL, 2–4.
2. IT Governance Institute , In *Information Security Governance: Guidance for Boards of Directors and Executive Management*; IT Governance Institute: Rolling Meadows, IL, 2001; 2.
3. IT Governance Institute (ITGI). Resources Center web page sidebar, http://www.itgi.org/ResourceCenter
4. IT Governance Institute, In *CobiT® 4.0 Brochure*; IT Governance Institute: Rolling Meadows, IL, 2.
5. IT Governance Institute, In *Information Security Governance: Guidance for Boards of Directors and Executive Management 17–19, and 21–23, Brochure*; IT Governance Institute: Rolling Meadows, IL, 2001; 14, ISBN1-893209-28-8.
6. Tsang-Reveche, C. Book review: Strategies for information technology governance by Wim Van Grembergen. Inform. Syst. Control J. **2004**, *3*, 9.
7. Oud, E. The value to IT using international standards. Inform. Syst. Control J. **2005**, *3* (35), 9.
8. Parmar, K. Book review, network security: The complete reference by Roberta Bragg, Mark Rhodes-Oulsey, and Keith Strassberg. Inform. Syst. Control J. **2004**, *3*, 11.
9. Emani, S. Book review, outsourcing information security. Inform. Syst. Control J. **2006**, *1*, 21.
10. Kinczkowksi, L. Book review, e-commerce security—Business continuity planning. Inform. Syst. Control J. **2003**, *4*, 11.
11. Bettex, E. Auditing: A risk analysis approach. Inform. Syst. Control J. **2003**, *4*, 13.
12. McMinn, J.; Simon, M. Managing the audit function: A corporate audit department procedures guide. Inform. Syst. Control J. **2003**, *6*, 13.
13. Sobel, R. Book review, auditor's risk management guide—Integrating auditing and ERM. Inform. Syst. Control J. **2003**, *6*, 15.
14. Nanda, A.; Burleson, D. Book review, oracle security privacy auditing. Inform. Syst. Control J. **2005**, *1*, 20.
15. Singh-Latulipe, R. Book review: CobiT 4.0. Inform. Syst. Control J. **2006**, *1*, 20.
16. Singleton, T. CobiT—A key to success as an IT auditor. Inform. Syst. Control J. **2006**, *1*, 11.
17. Everett, C.J. President's message. *A Newsletter for Members about Entry and International Events and Programs*; ISACA GLOBAL COMMUNIQUÉ, 2006, *1*, 2.

ITIL: IT Infrastructure Library: Operational Excellence Framework

Joshua L. Kissee
Instructional Technology Services, Information Technology Division, Texas A&M University, College Station, Texas, U.S.A.

Abstract

Contemporary information technology (IT) operations generally require the management of numerous systems composed of infrastructure elements, software applications, client-side devices, and external vendor-hosted applications. Effectively managing the processes, functions, inputs, outputs, and transitions between systems requires a consistent, repeatable, best-practice framework that organizations may adapt in total or in part. The Information Technology Infrastructure Library (ITIL) is suitable for addressing the modern management dilemmas within the IT field. The ITIL framework contains generalized models that may be adapted to fit any IT environment regardless of industry or internal structure. This entry decree's the imperative for IT organizational adoption of a best-practice framework, namely, the ITIL framework, to enable business-driven IT operation. Illustrative examples of specific components within the ITIL framework will be applied in an effort to highlight realistic benefits of leveraging ITIL. The five core service lifecycles within ITIL will be explored and justified through explanation and illustrative examples.

INTRODUCTION

The Information Technology Infrastructure Library (ITIL) framework is a widely recognized and scalable model for addressing the numerous challenges associated with the management of complex information technology (IT) operations. While a variety of IT Service Management models may be leveraged for addressing IT operational problems, the ITIL model is comprehensive in coverage of the IT operational landscape.

The ITIL framework is composed of five stages as part of the lifecycle and these stages are known as Service Strategy, Service Design, Service Transition, Service Operation, and Continual Service Improvement (CSI). Each stage is composed of multiple processes that contain inputs, outputs, roles for process management, functions, challenges, critical success factors, and a variety of best-practice discussions.

This entry will present a persuasive argument for leveraging one or more of the five stages and one or more process within a stage for the purpose of improving IT operations. Selected processes and lifecycle stage references will be included, though not exhaustive of the scope of ITIL process coverage. The term businesses will be used as a representation of any organization regardless of industry or scope of services.

THE ARGUMENT FOR OPERATIONAL EXCELLENCE USING ITIL

IT Driven by the Business

The degree to which IT organizations enable a business to reach its strategic and organizational goals is the foundation for the justification of existence. IT organizations work in the foreboding shadow of outsourcing all or parts of the supported IT services as external pressures from globalization, rapidly changing market structures, and the age of *do more with less* strain operations and budgets.

Upper-level executives have many choices in the marketplace for outsourcing IT components in the modern landscape of IT service providers, in part from the extensive marketing in place that transmits a message of low-cost, high-reliability, exemplary services. When examining IT from a cost perspective, and if a relatively low knowledge of how IT systems function is apparent, upper-level executives may be easily tempted to seek the acquisition of outsourcing systems. This scenario is plausible when coupled with executive IT leaders who fail to communicate or deliver on the value of their organizations' IT services. Further, the absence of a reliable framework for IT operational excellence creates a reactive environment that is subjected to the personal leadership style of executive IT personnel.

IT organizations must take the actions necessary to integrate fully from a focus and priority perspective with the business, ensuring that all decisions are taken

Encyclopedia of Information Systems and Technology, DOI: 10.1081/E-EIST-120049052

Information Science— ITIL

with business context in mind. This is the heart of a business-driven approach—the ultimate expression of a service mindset.[1] IT organizations driven by the business may be exemplified through a multitude of best practices and in part by:

- Provisioning IT services based on the mission and strategic goals of an organization
- Ensuring that IT operations and their management align with core values
- Validating that autonomous, lower-level IT units coordinate initiatives with executive-level goals
- Maintain agility and scalability within the IT service portfolio for the addition of new services and systems
- Practicing proactive operational measures as opposed to reactive, short-duration operations known as *firefighting*
- Protecting an appropriately balanced governance structure to ensure that flexibility is equally yoked with control
- Conserving IT capital for strategic imperatives as opposed to allotting funding primarily to operations
- Purging systems that have lost the minimum acceptable level of business value to the organization
- Guarding IT talent through leadership, professional organization engagement, training, and financial incentives
- Leading the IT human resources through a culture of reward and recognition as opposed to allowing non-IT leaders to assume the role in an ad-hoc manner

Numerous examples, buzz phrases, and leadership methods exist on implementing or maintaining an IT organization that is aligned and driven by the business at executive or intermediate levels. Given the diversity in approaches, adopting a common framework that is ethical, repeatable, and practical is important when creating common standards across IT organizations. The ITIL framework is capable of providing guidance toward business alignment at strategic levels through the Service Strategy stage processes, key performance indicators, demand management practices, and financial management.

IT Driven by the Customer

The customer is not always right, but the customer is always the customer. Businesses exist for the purpose of creating a value and accepting the risk that customers are unable to achieve on their own. Higher education organizations, as an example, offer an assortment of degrees as a core business offering that allow a customer (student) to select a degree (product) for the purpose of qualified entry into the workforce (value). IT services, with the exception of fully online degree programs, act primarily as a supporting and enabling function to the customer as opposed to the business service itself. Therefore, all IT services must be aligned with business imperatives that produce and support activities that create customer value.

When IT is driven by the customer, gauging customer satisfaction is required through a variety of measures. The end and chief result among those measures is the ability to determine if IT services are providing value to the customer or functions that support customers.

> "Companies that sell products or services requiring technical support realize the importance of assessing customer satisfaction with the support service as only a small percentage (5%) report that they are not measuring any satisfaction indicators."[2]

The importance of IT driven by the customer is linked to revenue. Customer service indicators have a direct correlation with the likelihood of the continued customer base size and forecast the growth or decline of the customer base. In some organizations, customer service ratings are tied to compensation and incentives. IT organizations in general leverage one to many IT services that support all or portions of the organization and the related customer service metrics.

To support the business and promote operational excellence, IT organizations should leverage a variety of ITIL-aligned customer service metrics found through the Service Operations stage. The customer service metrics presented are not based on ITIL; rather, they are aligned with ITIL and could come from a variety of sources. Customer-driven IT service metrics may include:

- *First Call Resolution.* The rate at which issues are resolved on the first contact to the service center.
- *Average Incident Response Time.* The average time for the service center to respond to customer support incidents where a technology component is not functioning correctly.
- *Average Support Request Response Time.* The average time for the service center to respond to customer support requests. Examples may include requests for a new printer, monitor, account change, or similar demand on IT services.
- *Percentage System Availability.* The rate at which key business systems are available to customers, excluding legitimate maintenance periods.
- *Percentage Satisfaction of Systems.* The generalized satisfaction and experience by customers of IT systems based on qualitative psychological perception.

Numerous customer satisfaction metrics exist and should be adjusted to meet the needs of the IT industry. The practicality of ITIL is related to providing a standard baseline of processes and metrics that may be transformed to fit the model of the organization. ITIL offers universal terms that are comprehensive in application to all IT components and may be effectively used for customer-driven IT initiatives.

IT Driven by Excellence

The core purpose of ITIL is to drive operational excellence through the leveraging of best-practice frameworks that are meant for IT service management. Modern IT services are generally complex in architecture, integration, infrastructure, and dependencies. This requires deep knowledge and specialized training to support such services.

IT professionals frequently receive specialized training to support a variety of services in the organization. However, it is not common for IT professionals to receive training on managing IT service operations using a framework while leveraging a variety of metrics to gauge performance. Professional IT positions generally require a Baccalaureate degree from an accredited institution. Common majors for computing and information system professionals include computer science, software engineering, engineering, management of information systems, mathematics, and information science.[3] IT degrees provide adequate preparation to analyze, design, implement, and support IT services. Unfortunately, these degrees normally do not contain course (s) that provide a robust survey of best-practice frameworks that may be leveraged for IT operations such as ITIL, International Organization for Standardization (ISO) 2001, Microsoft Operations Framework (MOF), or Control Objectives for Information and Related Technology (COBIT). This dilemma is producing an IT workforce that is not adequately prepared for delivering operational excellence.

Professional adults are motivated through excellence among other incentives. "The vast majority of poor performance is not due to poor skills or lack of knowledge; it's a result of other causes such as process problem, motivation, incentive issues, resources, or unclear standards."[4]

ITIL is valuable in addressing performance issues through providing clear processes that may be modified while providing foundational standards that may be adapted for any business environment. A common framework of practices unites all areas of IT service management toward the goal of delivering value and thus increases the likelihood for highperformance, resulting in rewards and recognition for IT professionals. Further, ITIL drives excellence through providing information resources for managing risk, knowledge, strategy, and optimizing costs. These factors create cultures of excellence and minimize the likelihood of outsourcing all or some of the organization's IT service

assets. Essentially, ITIL has the potential to not only excel the business as it relates to IT services, but also provide employment security for the professionals working within the framework.

SERVICE STRATEGY

Service Strategy Overview

IT Service Management leverages the unique capabilities of the IT organization in an effort to provide value through services. Changing those capabilities normally begins at the executive level of the organization. The Service Strategy stage focuses on the broad, enterprise-wide actions and outputs that generate these changes.

Roles within the IT organization that generally leverage the Service Strategy processes and practices include chief information officer, chief technology officers, vice-presidents for IT, directors, and senior-level IT managers. These roles are tasked with providing organizational change and interfacing with customers of the business through managing demand for IT services. Processes within Service Strategy offer insights into strategic IT management that are not found through a Master of Business Administration (MBA) program or other graduate education programs. IT roles responsible for strategy rely on their years of experience from lower levels in the organization once in their strategic role. This may not provide the most effective strategic manager as their previous roles in the IT organization did not require the extent of strategic planning, execution, validation, and measurement.

ITIL Service Strategy is an IT executive's micro-MBA program that can serve as a great jumpstart to strategic management within IT. ITIL Service Strategy training typically lasts for 24–40 hours of instruction and is completed within a week. This compression allows an executive-level IT role to receive directed education that may be immediately applied to daily work routines without delay while supplementing other executive education and experience-related competencies under development. This is an attractive offer given that IT executives generally do not have excess time due to the often fast-paced nature of their role. ITIL Service Strategy provides a much needed boost to an IT executive's overall portfolio of knowledge and competency-based education.

The ITIL Service Strategy stage contains numerous core processes and related considerations as shown in Table 1.[5]

Service Portfolio Management

The sum of all services offered through an IT organization that are being planned for delivery, now being

Table 1 Service strategy select processes and considerations

Process Area	Considerations
Strategy Management for IT Services	• What business outcomes must be supported • What markets are served by the organization • What constraints are now impacting the IT organization • Who are the internal and external customers/stakeholders • What IT standards or frameworks are in place across the organization • What governance structure is in place for managing IT strategy
Service Portfolio Management	• When should the service portfolio be reviewed • Who maintains the existing business relationships for each IT service offered • What inputs feed changes to the service portfolio • How is business value calculated for each service • Are all services accurately defined and displayed to customers
Financial Management for IT Services	• What is the existing IT cost model • Who determines the approval of IT budgeting and policies • What charging policies exist for the IT organization • When are financial compliance issues reviewed for validation • How are IT contracts managed and cost forecasting conducted
Demand Management	• How are demands for new services estimated • Does the appropriate capacity exist for managing the existing services and scaling to select new services • Who defines and monitors PBA used for forecasting demand • Why are services delivered at their existing capacity
Business Relationship Management	• How are customer needs identified • Who is responsible for establishing and maintaining business relationships between the IT organization and customers • What value is provided for IT services from the customer perspective • What levels of customer satisfaction with IT services exist

Source: From Joshua.[5]

offered, or retired from service comprises the service portfolio. The right composition of IT services that create value for the cost investment into the IT organization is the primary duty of service portfolio management.

The analyses of all IT services in the organization, when executed with a consistent method through ITIL, produce service definitions, service costs, illustration of alignment to business goals, and financial analysis creating data for common metrics such as return on investment (ROI). Objectives of service portfolio management include, but are not limited to:

• Analysis of services that should remain in operation without adjustment, be changed, or be transferred to a legacy service (retirement of service)
• Governance of which services are offered through an executive decision structure with specific financial investment return thresholds
• Providing an easy-to-understand and consolidated outline of IT services so that customers and employees of the organization are able to clearly discern what services are available
• Implementation of the organization's risk tolerance levels through risk analysis against IT services offered or being considered
• Calculation of ROI on select IT services

At the core, the purpose of this process is to monitor the changing environment of the organization and adjust the portfolio of IT services with respect to financial factors, volatility of the service, risk tolerance, and strategic imperatives. A financial portfolio of stocks, bonds, mutual funds, or other investment instruments are managed under similar influences. IT executives are wise in managing IT services and demands with the same tenacity and scrutiny of financial investment managers monitoring an investment portfolio. Most IT executives are likely conducting service portfolio management, yet they are not doing so with ascendency toward a framework that provides a consistent decision-making structure with the tools and processes for generating excellence. Adopting service portfolio management provides a clear existing state measurement of IT services and long-term strategy planning and positioning to support impending business imperatives.

Demand Management

Understanding, influencing, and preparing for inevitable customer requests for new or changed services is part of IT service portfolio management. Having too much excess capacity through over-preparation creates costs that may not be recovered, given the rapidly changing nature of the technological landscape. Having too little capacity for new or changed services increases risk, limits organizational agility, and may frustrate customers when demands are not realized. This balancing act is the magic wand that executive IT leaders must yield as they walk the tightrope of IT service management.

Demand management may be practiced within any of the ITIL stages. A large demand for support services related to wireless devices would commonly be found within the Service Operations stage. Yet, demand management leverages, at its most basic definition, supply and demand. If the demand for wireless device support is 1000 support requests and the service center has capacity for 200 support requests per day, then demand is not adequately met. In this example, demand management principles transcend across ITIL stages. However, the majority of demand management, given its complexity and financial relationships, is practiced at the executive level within Service Strategy.

Words such as anticipation, patterns, analysis, identification, and utilization are common within the demand management process family. These words imply a proactive manager who monitors, measures, and takes action before realization of the demand. These activities reduce risk and optimize cost structures. Demand management is not a panacea and learning comes through experience after risks are realized in many cases. In any case, proactive identification and survey of the IT landscape allows for an improved potential of meeting business demand for IT services.

Monitoring for repeated patterns of business activity (PBAs) is the primary tool of demand management. "PBAs represent the dynamics of the business and include interactions with customers, suppliers, partnerships, and other stakeholders. Once a PBA has been identified, a profile may be drawn and documented".[5] These profiles display patterns that aid the IT executive in making decisions related to budget requests, staffing, project or program management, and reporting.

An example of PBA applied through demand management may come through multiple reports or data sources that trickle in over a three-month period. The first being a balanced scorecard report from the service center indicating the increase of service requests for new or changed mobile devices that contain applications (apps) that provide access to an inventory management system within the IT organization as one of numerous reportable items. A second report contains customer service feedback through a third-party survey vendor containing numerous survey responses indicating a lack of mobile access to the inventory management system. When reading an IT industry-related publication, a featured article references transition statistics related to decreasing access of business data via desktop computers and increasing access requests through mobile apps and devices. The IT executive then reads a business

case for a new project request to upgrade the existing inventory management system without adding new features. Finally, a memorandum from the chief executive officer channeled through the vice president for Human Resources states that an initiative is underway for increasing the number of telecommuters who will work from their home or a remote location.

When reviewing the previous example, the reader has the luxury of seeing the facts in a single paragraph that subtly proposes the idea that a mobile app containing inventory management data should be considered as an additional IT service. The project to upgrade the inventory management system would be delayed unless it could directly support the implementation of the mobile app's new feature. This is a reader luxury. IT executives are bombarded with large quantities of data in a three-month period and could easily overlook the relationships between these data sources. Enter ITIL demand management. Through practicing a periodic approach that reviews the service portfolio of new services and existing services against specific criteria amid established PBAs, there is an opportunity for identification. When using this information with profiles of customers and/or business users, these patterns will be addressed proactively as opposed to reactively.

"Being proactive is about taking responsibility. Between the stimulus and the response is your greatest power—you have the freedom to choose your response."[6] The core of demand management is not to reduce risk and optimize cost alone. These are symptoms of the true opportunity that demand management presents; proactive identification and the relative freedom of our actions as it relates to IT Service Management.

SERVICE DESIGN

Service Design Overview

Processes occur within the organization whether designed by IT leaders or not. The question for IT staff is whether they want to be in control or allow the processes to develop from the lower levels of the organization and upward. Processes that occur without careful design tend to be more prone to error, less holistic, and inefficient in nearly every case, reducing the intended value of the IT service.

The Service Design stage captures the new or changed business requirements from the Service Strategy stage. The new or changed service is then analyzed and evaluated with the ultimate intended output of a new service that is ready to begin transition into a live environment. An example of a new or changed service moving through the Service Design stage could come in the form of a significant new feature within a mobile app based on the previous example. The existing mobile app contained four core features. Through the Service Strategy stage, it was determined that adding a fifth core feature to support inventory management would fit within the overall service portfolio and support the existing PBAs.

A project manager or one in a similar role is notified of the changed service structure through the addition of the fifth core feature. Teams or functional groups would then be gathered to design and build the new feature, most likely under the guidance of a project management framework such as the Project Management Body of Knowledge (PMBOK). These teams would then analyze, design, and build the new feature. During the architecture of the service, the team would address the following Service Design stage processes:

- Where does this service fit within the *service catalog*?
- What are the appropriate *service levels* that should be provided when supporting this new service and are the existing support functions capable of supporting the service?
- When should the service be *available* with respect to dates and times? What are the appropriate time periods for conducting maintenance activities?
- How much *capacity* or transactions for a specified time period should the service be able to accommodate?
- Who and how will we ensure *service continuity* in the event of a disaster or system failure?
- What *information security* practices must be followed and designed into the service to ensure security policy compliance?
- Are there any *third-party vendors or suppliers* who must be managed as part of the long-term support of the service and who will execute the management?

Once these questions have been identified and included within the design and development of the service, it is ready for moving to the Service Transition stage. It is important to note that other frameworks such as the PMBOK for project management, ISO 27001 for information security, or the open group architecture framework for system architecture may be used in conjunction with ITIL. The ITIL framework provides a holistic view in an effort to ensure that important service considerations are not overlooked while allowing for inclusion of other frameworks to cooperate with ITIL to produce a comprehensive service that creates the intended customer value.

Roles within the IT organization that generally leverage the Service Design processes and practices include directors, project managers, senior-level IT managers, business analysts, systems analysts, developers (programming), system architects, and other analysis- and design-related IT roles.

The Service Catalog

The ITIL-based service catalog is one of the most customer-visible components of any process within the ITIL stages. The service catalog presents a consolidated view of all IT services available to customers presently or available through imminent deployment. Within the catalog, every service contains detailed information that describes the service, prices, how to request the service, how to request support for the service, support levels available, and practical uses of the service. The service catalog is intended to be available publicly to customers or internally within the IT organization and available through an intranet or private cloud.

An analogy of the service catalog is like a well-designed menu at a premier restaurant. Numerous dishes are available and some dishes contain supplemental items. An entrée of peppered steak includes a baked potato, broccoli, and carrots. The peppered steak entrée contains a thorough description and has a price of $44.95. A statement next to the steak indicates that "45 minutes should be allowed for preparation" and that customers normally enjoy "red wine" as a supplemental item, though it is not included in the peppered steak entrée. Finally, the instruction to "see your service attendant for ordering information and questions" is appended to the end of the entrée description. This menu item description would provide the customer with adequate information to make a basic decision on whether to order the entrée. Unique questions based on the customers dining preferences would be addressed by the service attendant.

An IT service catalog is intended to provide a similar experience for customers as there should be enough information to make basic decisions without the need to contact an IT representative. Some services may have relationships with others and when described on the service catalog, the customer is able to bundle services and see a total expected costs and wait time for delivery of the service. This works to set customer expectations as opposed to having ambiguous service expectations that lead to customer frustration. Without an idea of costs, time to receive service, or fully understanding what will be received there could be some shock on the customer side. In our previous example of the entrée, if the customer had only seen a peppered steak being listed, the person could be frustration when asked to wait for nearly an hour, pay more than what was intended, and then had received broccoli instead of spinach that was hoped for. Table 2 provides a service catalog entry example. This single example would be one of possible

Table 2 Service catalog example

Service	Vendors Available	Minutes	Cost	Ordering Information	Support
Mobile Telephone (Receive and transmit cellular calls with a data plan)	AT&T Wireless	1,000 Unlimited Data	$199.99 Device $30 Monthly	Fill out the online order form	Monday–Saturday 8 am to 8 pm Eastern time U.S.
	Verizon Wireless	2,000 Unlimited Data	$299.99 Device $45 Monthly	Fill out the online order form	Monday–Friday 8 am to 5 pmCentral time U.S.

Source: From Joshua.[5]

hundreds within a service catalog with robust explanations and examples for customer review.

Service-Level Management

The service-level management (SLM) process includes the administration of numerous service-level agreements (SLAs). The SLA is effectively a level of assurance or warranty with regard to the level of service quality delivered by the service provider for each of the services delivered to the business.[7] SLAs serve as a core measurement that may be used by IT organizations for evaluating service goals and making adjustments based on how well the goals are being reached. SLAs provide a metric for having open discussions that lead into continuous improvement activities to improve a service once it is in operation.

The term *agreement* in SLA implies that two parties have reached consensus. This is certainly true in the case of an SLA. The IT organization develops the baseline SLAs either alone or with customers who will use the SLA and then meets with a customer representative to reach consensus. In the case of our new mobile application feature for inventory management, an SLA would be developed by IT representatives that outlined categories of response time for service based on impact and urgency. For example, an issue that impacted fewer customers with high urgency may be considered a medium priority. This priority level provides a four-hour response time from the service center and a two-day resolution time. Response time would require definition and resolution time would require definition as would any terms that describe actions to be taken by IT representatives. Once the priority levels, term definitions, response times, and resolutions times were documented the process would move forward.

A committee, focus group, or executive level process owner would meet to review the proposed SLA and offer feedback. Modifications would be negotiated, and once completed, an executive-level role would approve the SLA for the service. Later in the ITIL lifecycle, the service will be in operations and the metrics developed in the SLA tracked through the service management application. These metrics will be included in service management reporting and reviewed by the parties who agreed to the SLA. The core value provided to customers through this process is not to hold IT organizations accountable, but to identify if the value intended for the business is being reached. If the resolution time for a medium priority issue is three days and reports indicate that it takes four days to resolve the issue, then the underlying impact of not reaching the agreement should be examined. If a customer using the mobile app feature is completing a process that has a short time period for resolution, such as two days, then solving the problem in four days would not be an acceptable target. The SLA would require review and a new agreement reached for establishing a two-day resolution time for that priority. If the IT organization does not have the resources or capacity to hold to that service level, these data provide the justification for requesting additional resources or shifting resources away from other obligations to meet the business requirement.

Without SLAs, IT organizations are unable to quantitatively gauge how well the service is being supported for the purpose of providing the intended value to the business. While hallway discussions, complaint boxes, service center surveys, and other feedback channels may offer insight into service quality, they generally provide qualitative measures alone. It is in the best interest of the IT organization to quantitatively measure as much as possible to provide a holistic viewpoint as opposed to qualitative measures that may only listen to the *loudest voices* or *angry customers* who could inaccurately represent the service quality as a whole. SLAs eliminate dependency on these reactive measures and promote operational excellence, open discussions, and justification for the acquisition of new or shifted IT resources.

Numerous SLAs could exist in an IT organization depending upon how many critical services and business processes have been identified. Data from these SLAs are generally reported from the service center as captured through service management software. In large enterprises or cases where a significant number of SLAs are present, it is strongly recommended that a service-level manager role be assigned to a senior IT manager role or to a higher level. Clear assignment of this duty provides accountability to periodically monitor the

Information Science– ITIL

service portfolio of SLAs for the purpose of identifying patterns of success or weakness. In cases of success, these should be communicated to the business in an effort to show IT organizational value and capability for supporting new services. In cases of weakness, root-cause analysis should be performed with the expectation of performance intervention to improve services to their defined SLAs or modification of the original SLA.

Availability Management

SLM requires frequent, periodic attention and evaluation at a high rate, as much as weekly in some cases. Availability management is normally included in the planning and design of a new or changed service and then reviewed annually or semiannually, barring critical events or outages that prompt immediate review.

Availability management is primarily concerned with the service being accessible to customers. If the service cannot be accessed, then it is of no use to customers or the business. The most ambitious of all availability goals is the offering of a 24-hour, 7-days a week, 365 days a year (24/7/365) approach. Essentially, this equates to promising customers that the service will always be available with no exception. IT organization providers generally attempt this goal by default without considering realistic targets and appropriate maintenance periods that minimize business impact. Rates of availability then become skewed when maintenances occur and result in less than 100% availability, implying performance problems even in the most mature IT organization.

Business representatives should first be consulted to determine what time periods are appropriate for conducting maintenance activities along with calendar periods where service availability is critical. For example, an electronics retailer would likely desire minimal service unavailability, if any at all, during the major holidays in November and December. The business may also recognize that the weekends are the busiest days of the week, as such, maintenances would not be allowed on weekends and an alternative time chosen where the lowest amount of service traffic is observable. Understanding this information allows the availability manager to develop an agreed service time (AST) metric that includes these periods.

An AST metric is intended to produce an availability percentage. If the service was agreed to be in operation for 5020 hours in a year (AST), the amount of service unavailability would be subtracted from the AST, then divided by the AST and multiplied by 100 to reach the percentage rate. This metric would accurately evaluate the percentage of availability.

Additional metrics may include the reliability measure of mean time between service incidents (MTBSI), the maintainability measure of mean time to restore service (MTRS), and the reliability measure of mean time between service failures (MTBSF).

The MTBSI seeks to determine how reliable the service is to customers. The purpose is to make improvements to specific components of the service that produce incidents or problems. The measure is quantified by using the available time of the service in hours and dividing by the number of breaks in service. The MTBSF is a similar reliability measure that is more robust in that the total downtime in hours is included, thus more preferable for determining availability. MTBSF is determined by identifying the available time of the service in hours and subtracting the total downtime in hours, then dividing by the number of breaks in service. The maintainability measure of MTRS uses the total downtime in hours divided by the number of breaks in service.

Using measures to identify reliability and maintainability within availability management removes the dependency of reactive approaches and listening only to qualitative feedback sources for determining the availability metrics of an IT service.

SERVICE TRANSITION

Service Transition Overview

A service that has been identified, designed, and developed is now ready for transition into the live service environment. The Service Transition stage contains the most commonly used processes of all the IT stages as they serve to reduce risk of technical failure and increase the likelihood of customer satisfaction with the new or changed service.

All planning, architecture, and development may be undermined through a poorly managed transition into a live environment. Service Transition may be compared to the last segment of a marathon. The race may have been identified through careful planning and analysis well in advance. The runner in the race came healthy, ran with great strides, and used consistent running principles. Yet, when the runner was preparing to cross the finish line, she stopped all of those positive practices and started walking in circles to take a break. As a result, the runners passed her and she did not finish well. Service Transition is dedicated to ensuring that the last mile is run well and that mistakes from the earlier portion of the race are discovered, mitigated, and resolved.

During the transition of the service into the live environment, the questions that would be covered within the Service Transition stage include:

- What *testing and validation* plans have been executed or will be executed for determining if the service meets the agreed level of quality?
- Has the *change advisory board (CAB)* received all necessary information to make an accurate decision?
- How will the change be *communicated* to customers?
- How will the change be *communicated* to support and IT stakeholders?
- Is the service center prepared to *support* the new feature once available?
- What *technical documentation* exists or should exist for support personnel to provide acceptable levels of technical support?
- What *customer documentation* exists or should exist for customers to learn and utilize the feature as needed on their own?
- What available *release* dates will provide the best transition into the live environment with minimal interruption to customers?
- Do customers require *training* to use the tool and how will that training be executed?

These questions are not inclusive of all possible questions and roles that would benefit the team in transitioning the service into the live production environment. Roles within the IT organization that generally leverage the Service Transition processes and practices include project managers, change managers, release and deployment managers (RDMs), quality managers, developers, mid-level IT managers, systems analysts, technical writers, marketing and communication professionals, knowledge managers, IT system trainers, knowledge managers, and other IT service implementation roles.

Returning to our previous example of a mobile application with a fifth core feature, we find a finished feature ready for transition into the live production environment. The project manager contacts the service testing and validation team for final quality control. Once completed with quality control and related corrections, a CAB reviews a request for change (RFC) to deploy the new feature. The CAB analyzes the request containing all of the details provided from the previous ITIL processes used, namely, service testing, and determines if there are any factors that would cause the change to be rejected for further development or quality analysis. If approved, the RDM reviews the change. The RMD then contacts the marketing and communications team, technical documentation team, training team, service center, change deployment team, and other stakeholders interested in the deployment. The RMD negotiates a finalized date for entry into the live environment among the teams and coordinates the change through to successful completion. The teams should have ideally been a part of the release planning throughout the service transition process so that no surprises or frustration at the upcoming event will be experienced. Early on, the testing and validation processes in non-production environments should create awareness of the impending release that brings the service transition stakeholders into the discussion.

At a set number of days following the change, the RMD reconvenes the change implementers and determines if the change was successful. If successful, it is allowed to remain in the live environment. The RMD then finalizes the change-related documentation and closes the RFC or bundle of RFCs used to deploy the fifth core feature.

Change Management

ITIL has received notoriety and attention from the IT world primarily from the change management processes available. Numerous IT service management software companies and consulting firms are quick to highlight their change management features or skills in an effort to attract IT professionals. A brief glance at top IT service management websites will display the strength of their change management suite of tools.[7]

The emphasis on change management originates from the conception that IT organizations lack a framework or coordinated method for managing services. This may create a perception that a lack of control and visibility exists in the operations of the IT organization. Authorized developers, system administrators, webmasters, support personnel, and any variety of IT representatives have the capability of making changes to the configuration of an IT service. The question then becomes "was the change executed and defined in such a way that it would have been approved by a superior in the IT organization?" This does not mean that the issue is founded in trust to execute a task. Rather, the problem lies in taking a holistic, coordinated, risk-minded approach to introducing a change that provides the maximum potential value to customers. To gain this perspective, teams of IT representatives using a standardized approach are required. Change management is seen as the primary process to implement in an effort to *stop the bleeding* of individual approaches and replace with a team-based holistic approach. The crux of the change debate then centers on the definition of change to avoid certain systems falling within the reach of the CAB.

Change management has not only gained notoriety from the benefits that come from providing this holistic approach to changes, but has also received negative attention as it is frequently recognized as a method of control being placed on lower-level IT representatives by upper-level IT executives or leaders. ITIL defines a change as the addition, modification, or removal of anything that could have an effect on IT services.[8] A definition written with

Information Science–ITIL

such generality leaves little room for exclusion from the change management process and may become a source of frustration for certain IT roles that now fall under its governance. Therefore, numerous change management implementations have failed or experienced strong rejection from the IT organization. "Every organization struggles with the question of exactly which activities need to be controlled with a change record. After establishing the highest-level flow, you should try to get agreement about the policy of when a change record is needed. This is the first, and perhaps most important, policy to define."[9]

Once the selected services and activities that fall within the control of a CAB have been identified, the development of templates, risk matrices, process maps, and key performance indicators are documented within a change management plan. The CAB itself must be named and a voting structure determined for different types of changes to include normal, standard, emergency, or any other definition of change. A change manager must also be named so that deadlocks on the CAB may be broken and authority of change execution granted. A software application is configured using the change management plan and those who are responsible, accountable, consulted, and informed are given various roles and privileges within the software. After executive communication and rollout of the process, the CAB is then able to begin evaluating changes with an open mindset to CSI to address problems with the process or tools.

Unique books on the subject of change management alone have been developed to address the positive potential and variety of negative problems that result from change management implementation. Readers are urged to consider further research into the change management process upon a full survey of ITIL as this is the second most commonly implemented ITIL process, with 57.3% of all ITIL-practicing organizations having implemented this process in 2013.[10]

SERVICE OPERATIONS

Service Operations Overview

A service that has been transitioned into the live environment falls to the service center as the first line of interaction between the customer and the IT organization. The Service Operations stage contains guidance for how to address service requests, incidents, problems, events, and access management. Any customer interaction regarding the service may flow through the service center against the ITIL Service Operations framework serving as a feedback mechanism to internal divisions of the IT organization. At its core, "the support center exists to professionally manage, coordinate and resolve

incidents as quickly as possible and to ensure that no request is lost, forgotten, or ignored."[11]

Roles within the IT organization that generally leverage the Service Operation processes and practices include service desk managers, access managers, technical support consultants, incident managers, problem managers, support engineers, and other IT support-related roles.

Incident Management

An incident may be defined as an unplanned interruption to an IT service or reduction in the quality of an IT service or failure from an IT service that has not yet impacted the live environment.[12] The intention of incident management in the case of an unplanned interruption is to restore service to the customer through resolution or a workaround.

Returning to our mobile application feature that has now been deployed, a customer contacted the service center via telephone to request assistance with an error message that was presented when accessing some portion of the feature. The IT support consultant (ITSC) used a variety of technical tools to reproduce the error as described by the customer to validate the incident. The ITSC would then research the available technical documentation to determine if instructions existed for resolving the issue. If instructions existed, she would employ the instructions and resolve the issue, restoring service to the customer. If instructions did not exist, she would attempt to provide a workaround to the customer. A workaround is intended to restore normal service operation as close as possible to the original service while minimizing the impact to the business. In the mobile application example, a potential workaround may be to use a different path for accessing the same feature or some other alternative that would produce the same or closely similar result as the original service. A common example for explaining incident management relates to a printer that will not print. The customer contacts the ITSC, who attempts to resolve the problem and restore service. When unable, the ITSC maps the customer to another printer down the hall to restoring the service of printing until the failed printer is able to be fully restored.

Table 3 depicts a sample template for incident management fields used when gathering data to assess the incident, develop a workaround, and pass the information to problem management.

Incident management is the most customer-visible process within the IT organization once a service has been released into the live environment. This process directly interacts with customers and either provides a positive experience (restoration or workaround) or a negative experience (no restoration or no workaround).

Table 3 Incident management template fields

Incident Field	Sample Description
Name of the IT service experience the interruption of service	*Inventory management consolidation feature*
Date, time, and customer experiencing the interruption	*10/21/2013, 8:52 p.m. Central time, Susan Smith—Inventory manager*
Configuration of device used to access the IT service	*iPhone 4S, iOS 7.1, Inventory mobile app version 1.2.7.514*
Steps to repeat	1. Open the inventory mobile app. 2. Press the Consolidation tab. 3. Select the Alpha-Omega fields. 4. Press the Run option. 5. Error 123.XYZ.567 is presented
Workaround provided	*Instructed the customer to use the **Management** tab followed by the R2D2 option to print a full report.*
Screenshots of the error	*Attached to the support record*
Priority rating	*High*

IT leaders should focus on incident management with careful attention as this process provides a direct reflection on customer satisfaction metrics and the overall image of an IT organization's ability to support a service.

PROBLEM MANAGEMENT

Where incident management is concerned with restoring service or providing a workaround, problem management is exclusively focused upon identifying the rootcause of a problem. Incident management is temporary; problem management is longterm and critical to addressing incident recurrence.

The customer who experienced an error and received a workaround is most likely not the only customer who will experience the same issue. As a result, the underlying problem will continue to aggravate the live production environment causing frustration to other customers and increasing the number of people complaining to the service center. The more significant the issue, the higher the rate of recurrence. Problem management then becomes a crucial process where advanced ITSCs with higher-tier knowledge are able to use ITIL problem management processes and references for identifying the rootcause of the problem and proposing a solution to system administrators, developers, webmasters, or other IT roles responsible for resolving problems. The speed at which root-cause analysis may be conducted becomes critical as it is a feeder process to other ITIL Service Transition processes necessary for moving the change through to production. Customers are impacted negatively each day that passes from the first day the error was observed. In cases where the workaround provided in incident management is poor or

unacceptable to customers, immense pressure forms to complete problem resolution.

Once the problem is resolved in a non-live environment, the Service Transition processes repeat through testing, change management, release coordination, communication, and documentation. These processes take time to complete separately from problem management. The severity of the problem has a direct impact on the amount of time and planning that is required to move the problem resolution through Service Transition and back into the live environment. Creating an effective, efficient, and energetic incident-problem-testing-change-release process provides a positive reputation to the IT organization as the ability to support the services is directly visible to the customer. When these processes are not organized, customers may experience:

- Incidents that receive no workaround or an unacceptable workaround
- Problems that go unresolved or do not find rootcause in an acceptable time
- Problems that are not researched consistently, yielding inaccurate information to the testing function for determining if the problem is resolved
- A slow or dysfunctional CAB may bottleneck numerous changes that includes problems and add unnecessary delays to deploying the feature
- A release manager lacks the skills to understand the change and does not coordinate the various IT stakeholders and customers. Once the problem is resolved, customers may never be notified and continue using the same workaround for an extended period
- Technical documents may not be created and cause support representatives to be unaware of how to support the newly changed service related to the error

Service Operations inherit the mistakes and successes of all the previous ITIL processes or lack thereof. Once a service has been transitioned to the live production environment, it is easy for the previous processes to neglect support of the service center and the related Service Operations processes as it would seem that the project or development sprint is over. It is critical for the service center to be in direct contact and receive close support from the previous processes well beyond the initial deployment of the service for success. Service center managers should be in weekly contact with Service Transition process owners to maintain effective service support.

CONTINUAL SERVICE IMPROVEMENT

CSI Overview

There is always room for improvement to any IT service that is leveraged by a business. The CSI stage, as the name implies, focuses on increasing the efficiency and effectiveness of the IT service management processes that are leveraged by the organization.[13] Once a service has transitioned into operations, the typical IT organizational response is to focus on incident and problem management–related activities. Once a process is in place and the roles are identified, the process will carry forward indefinitely in the absence of a major event that prompts investigation.

CSI seeks to find ways to improve a service regardless of how well it is performing using the existing metrics for monitoring the service. IT organizations can never claim that there is an absence of work available when leveraging the CSI stage processes as any process may undergo analysis at any time.

The ITIL CSI stage has strength through assigning process owners to each process leveraged in the Service Strategy, Service Design, Service Transition, and Service Operations stages. These process owners are responsible for executing continuous service improvement on the services related to their process. For example, Susan Smith is assigned as the process owner for the problem management of three features within the mobile application used for inventory management. In the absence of a CSI functional group exercising CSI governance, Susan is responsible for initiating improvement activities. The ITIL CSI stage provides a variety of tools and techniques for executing this responsibility.

Tools and Techniques of CSI

The strength of ITIL CSI, as related to tools and techniques, is the absence of dependency upon a single framework. Rather, any preferred method for conducting continuous improvement may be leveraged as there is no rigidity or requirement to use a specific method. A suggested approach is to harness the best-practice frameworks such as Capability Maturity Model Integration, Control Objectives for Information and related Technology (COBIT), ISO/IEC 20000, or the process maturity framework.[12] ITIL is more focused on the act of ensuring repeated and structured CSI events than the method used to conduct the event itself.

ITIL does provide the Plan-Do-Check-Act cycle along with a variety of process considerations, key performance indicators, challenges, risks, and planning templates for implementing a CSI event. The tools and techniques within CSI are relatively week in comparison to other best-practice framework offerings.

CONCLUSION

The ITIL framework provides a suite of best-practice processes that give IT professionals the guidance needed to create, modify, and sustain the operational excellence required of the modern IT organization. ITIL is not a standard by which an organization receives a certification. IT professionals may seek certification, but the organization is never certified in the way that the ISO suite of certifications offer. This is an added strength of ITIL, in that an IT professional may use a little, a lot, or whatever mix of ITIL-aligned processes that are needed without the often arduous requirements of organization certification. ITIL is essentially the MBA for IT professionals without several years of graduate school and may be applied to what the business needs the most.

While ITIL contains five stages, there are truly four stages that are followed on a routine basis to include Service Strategy, Service Design, Service Transition, and Service Operations. New or changed services follow this general path from Strategy to Operations using various other best-practice frameworks along the way. CSI acts like an umbrella stretched out across the four previous stages seeking to provide continuous operational excellence.

ITIL is an active framework with worldwide usage. Major refreshes of the framework occur every 3–5 years in Her Majesty's Government of the United Kingdom, which licenses the core material. Given the government adoption of the framework, worldwide process usage, numerous consulting firms leveraging ITIL processes, IT professional job descriptions containing ITIL knowledge requirements, IT service management software application development, professional certifications available, and executive propulsion for IT driven by the business, ITIL will likely remain a strong framework.

From January 1 to July 1, 2013, approximately 148,847 ITIL—Foundation certifications were achieved in all seven continents of the world. Of those, 22,199 were ITIL Experts who have received a minimum of 22 credits and passed seven certification examinations with over 168 hours of classroom instruction.[14]

REFERENCES

1. Hunnebeck, L. *Business-Driven IT: The Pursuit of Excellence in Outcome-Based Services*; Third-Sky Publications: Alameda, CA, Vol. 1; 2013.
2. Atkinson, R.; Hanson, M. *HDI Research Corner: Pearls of Wisdom*; UBM, LLC: Colorado Springs, CO, 2013.
3. Bureau of Labor Statistics, U. S. Department of Labor, *Occupational Outlook Handbook, 2012–13 Edition; Computer and Information Systems Managers*, http://www.bls.gov/ooh/management/computer-and-information-systems-managers.htm (accessed October 2013).
4. Willmore, J. *Performance Basics*; ASTD Press: Alexandria, VA, 2004.
5. Cabinet Office of Her Majesty's Government. *ITIL Service Strategy*, ISBN 9780113313044, The Stationary Office of the United Kingdom: London, England, 2011.
6. Covey, S.R. *The Seven Habits of Highly Successful People*; Simon and Schuster: New York, NY, 1989.
7. BMC Change Management Suite, http://www.bmc.com/products/offering/itil-change-configuration-release-management-software.html (last accessed October 2013)
8. Cabinet Office of Her Majesty's Government. *ITIL Service Transition*, ISBN 9780113313068, The Stationary Office of the United Kingdom: London, England, 2011.
9. Klosterboer, L. *Implementing ITIL Change and Release Management;* Pearson Education: Boston, MA, 2008.
10. Rains, J. *HDI 2013 Support Desk Practices Report*; UBM, LLC: Colorado Springs, CO, 2013.
11. Higday-Kalmanowitz, C.; Simpson, S.E. *Implementing Service and Support Management Processes: A Practical Guide*; Van Haren Publishing: Netherlands, 2005; 172.
12. Cabinet Office of Her Majesty's Government. *ITIL Service Operations*, ISBN 9780113313075, The Stationary Office of the United Kingdom; London, England, 2011.
13. Cabinet Office of Her Majesty's Government. *ITIL Continual Service Improvement*, ISBN 9780113313082, The Stationary Office of the United Kingdom; London, England, 2011.
14. Montgomery, J. *ITIL Certification Pass Rates*, July 2013, http://info.plexent.com/itil-pass-rates (accessed October 2013).

Knowledge Management

Kimiz Dalkir
Graduate School of Library and Information Studies, McGill University, Montreal, Quebec, Canada

Abstract

Knowledge management (KM) is defined as a deliberate and systematic coordination of an organization's people, technology, processes, and organizational structure in order to add value through reuse and innovation. There is a lack of consensus on clearly defining KM partly due to the multidisciplinary origins of the concept, ranging from organizational science, to cognitive science, to library, and information science. Core management concepts include the notion of difficult-to-articulate tacit knowledge, documented tangible or explicit knowledge, organizational learning as encapsulated in the form of best practices (successes) and lessons learned (failures), and preservation of this content in an organizational memory system. The knowledge processing life cycle then consists of creating new knowledge, capturing existing knowledge, contributing knowledge for reuse by others, documenting knowledge, reconstructing, refining, and sharing knowledge as well as continually evaluating the value of each knowledge resource in order to decide whether to keep it in circulation or to retire it from "active duty." The Nonaka and Takeuchi knowledge spiral model is used to illustrate how knowledge is transformed from one form to the other. A brief historical overview of KM is presented to show the evolution from a management fad to a scholarly discipline of study and research. Finally, the emerging roles for information professionals in this field are briefly described, outlining some of the key roles such as Chief Knowledge Officer, Knowledge Manager, Content Editor, and Knowledge Journalist.

INTRODUCTION

This entry provides an overview of knowledge management (KM), both as a scholarly discipline and a professional field of practice. Key terms such as "knowledge" and "knowledge management" are defined. Core concepts such as intellectual capital, lessons learned, best practices, and value-added knowledge reuse are introduced and defined. Key stages in the knowledge processing cycle are defined and described. A brief historical chronology of KM is outlined to show the multidisciplinary roots and the evolution that has taken place to date. The emerging roles for information professionals in KM are presented and the links to information studies are emphasized. The primary goal of this entry is to illustrate how KM that rests on a solid foundation of information management emerges as a stronger and more rigorous field of study and practice.

DEFINITION OF KNOWLEDGE MANAGEMENT

There is no universally accepted definition of KM. Part of this stems from the fact that there is a lack of consensus in defining knowledge. A sample dictionary definition of knowledge is:

The fact or condition of knowing something with familiarity gained through experience or association; acquaintance with or understanding of a science, art, or technique; the fact or condition of being aware of something; the range of one's information or understanding (e.g. answered to the best of my *knowledge*); the circumstance or condition of apprehending truth or fact through reasoning; the sum of what is known: the body of truth, information, and principles acquired by humankind; cognizance, awareness, learning.[1]

It is useful to view the knowledge in KM as being composed primarily of experiential knowledge that is highly subjective in nature. This can be contrasted with information that, although subject to different interpretations, is typically thought of as having a more neutral and verifiable nature. The same dictionary defines information as:

Knowledge obtained from investigation, study, or instruction; intelligence, news data or facts; the attribute inherent in and communicated by one of two or more alternative sequences or arrangements of something (as nucleotides in DNA or binary digits in a computer program) that produce specific effects **c** (1): a signal or character (as in a communication system or computer) representing data (2): something (as a message, experimental data, or a picture) which justifies change in a construct (as a plan or theory) that represents physical or mental experience or another construct.[1]

Encyclopedia of Information Systems and Technology, DOI: 10.1081/E-EIST-120043816

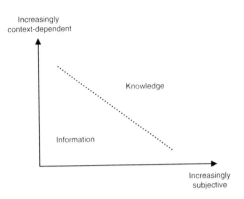

Fig. 1 Key attributes of knowledge assets.

Other definitions from the KM literature include

Knowledge is a subset of information: it is subjective; it is linked to meaningful behavior; and it has tacit elements born of experience (p. 113).[2]

Knowledge is always recreated in the present moment. Most of us cannot articulate what we know. It is largely invisible, and often comes to mind when we need it to answer a question or solve a problem.[3]

Knowledge is a fluid mix of framed experience, values, contextual information, and expert insight that provides a framework for evaluating and incorporating new experiences and information. It originates and is applied in the minds of those who know. In organizations, it often becomes embedded not only in documents or repositories but also in organizational routines, processes, practices and norms (p. 5).[4]

A typical example of information would be to read the listings of movies being shown on a given week,

Table 1 Diverse disciplines that contribute to knowledge management

1. Organizational development, organizational science, and organizational learning
2. Cognitive science, individual learning, and mental models
3. Linguistics and computational linguistics
4. Design of information technologies such as knowledge-based systems, document and information management, electronic performance support systems, and database technologies
5. Information and library science, classification, and taxonomy
6. Technical writing and journalism
7. Anthropology and sociology, sociograms, and social network analysis
8. Education and training
9. Storytelling and communication studies
10. Collaborative technologies such as Computer Supported Cooperative Work (CSCW) and groupware as well as intranets, extranets, portals, and other Web technologies

reading the reviews, and consulting the times and places the film will be showing at. An example of knowledge would be calling on a friend who has, in the past, demonstrated an uncanny inverse relationship with respect to likes and dislikes: if this person liked a movie, experience has shown that one would hate it and vice versa. Knowledge is also brought into play in making a decision to drive or take public transport, given the time of the year, possibility of inclement weather, and the rapid trend analysis that concludes that it has never been possible to find parking in time to see a movie being shown downtown.

A key point is that not all information is of value to a given individual, group, or organization. A knowledge asset is defined as knowledge that is of value, which is more context dependent and more subjective in nature, as illustrated in Fig. 1.

The Multidisciplinary Nature of KM

There is a great diversity to be found in KM definitions. This is due to the multidisciplinary nature of the field. In fact, most definitions appear to provide only one piece of the KM definition puzzle, as they are heavily influenced by their particular discipline. Table 1 lists some of the different disciplines and specialties that have contributed to and that make use of KM.

Here are a few sample definitions from the business perspective:

Knowledge management is a business activity with two primary aspects: treating the knowledge component of business activities as an explicit concern of business reflected in strategy, policy, and practice at all levels of the organization; and, making a direct connection between an organization's intellectual assets—both explicit (recorded) and tacit (personal know-how)—and positive business results.[5]

Knowledge management is a collaborative and integrated approach to the creation, capture, organization, access and use of an enterprise's intellectual assets.[6]

There is much more to knowledge management than technology alone. Management is a business process (p. 95).[7]

Some definitions from the cognitive science or knowledge science perspective:

Knowledge—the insights, understandings, and practical know-how that we all possess—is the fundamental resource that allows us to function intelligently.

Over time, considerable knowledge is also transformed to other manifestations – such as books, technology, practices, and traditions – within organizations of all kinds and in society in general. These transformations result in cumulated expertise and, when used appropriately, increased effectiveness. Knowledge is one, if not THE, principal factor that makes personal, organizational, and societal intelligent behavior possible.[8]

Some sample definitions from the process/technology perspective:

Knowledge Management (KM) was initially defined as the process of applying a systematic approach to the capture, structuring, management and dissemination of knowledge throughout an organization to work faster, reuse best practices, and reduce costly rework from project to project.[9–12]

American Productivity and Quality Center (APQC)[13] defines knowledge management as:

KM is the managing of knowledge through systematic sharing. Even in highly sophisticated modern knowledge organizations, the most valuable knowledge—the know-how in terms of what really gets results and what mistakes to avoid—often resides mainly in people's minds. Knowledge Management works towards migrating that knowledge from one person to a wide-range of individuals within an organization.

Some "people-oriented" definitions:

Knowledge management is not seen as a matter of building up a large electronic library, but by connecting people so they can think together (p. 104).[3]

Most executives seem to understand that knowledge is highly people-based, but they are stuck with an investment model that is geared primarily toward technology implementations (p. 86).[12]

Knowledge management and its varied definitions need to achieve a balance: there cannot be an overemphasis on any one of the key dimensions, such as technology.[14] Effective KM (and comprehensive KM definitions) should include people, process, technology, culture, and measurable organizational objectives.[15,16]

Wiig[8] also emphasizes that given the importance of knowledge in virtually all areas of daily and commercial life, two knowledge-related aspects are vital for viability and success at any level. These are knowledge *assets* that must be applied, nurtured, preserved, and used to the largest extent possible by both individuals and organizations; and knowledge-related *processes* to create, build, compile, organize, transform, transfer, pool, apply, and safeguard knowledge. They must be carefully and explicitly managed in all affected areas.

Historically, knowledge has always been managed, at least implicitly. However, effective and active knowledge management requires new perspectives and techniques and touches on almost all facets of an organization. We need to develop a new discipline and prepare a cadre of knowledge professionals with a blend of expertise that we have not previously seen. This is our challenge! (Wiig, in Grey).[6]

The Intellectual Capital Perspective

The focus of intellectual capital management (ICM), on the other hand, is on those pieces of knowledge that are of *business value* to the organization—referred to as intellectual capital or assets.[17] While some of these are more visible (e.g., patents, intellectual property), the majority consists of know-how, know-why, experience, and expertise that tend to reside within the head of one or a few employees.[18,19]

Knowledge management is often characterized by a "pack rat" approach to content: "save it, it may prove useful sometime in the future." Many documents tend to be warehoused, sophisticated search engines are then used to try to retrieve some of this content, and fairly large-scale and costly KM systems are built. Knowledge management solutions have proven to be most successful in the capture, storage, and subsequent dissemination of knowledge that has been rendered explicit—particularly lessons learned and best practices.

Intellectual capital management is characterized by less content—because content is filtered, judged, and only the best is inventoried (the "top ten"). Intellectual capital management content tends to be more representative of peoples' real thinking (contextual information, opinions, stories) due to its focus on actionable knowledge and know-how, with the result that less costly endeavors and a focus on learning (at the individual, community, and organizational level) results, rather than on the building of systems.

It is essential to identify that knowledge which is of value and is also at risk of being lost to the organization, through retirement, turnover, and competition. The best way to retain valuable knowledge is to identify intellectual assets and then ensure legacy materials are produced, and subsequently stored in such a way as to make their future retrieval and reuse as easy as possible.[20] These tangible by-products need to flow from individual to individual, between community of practice (CoP) members and, of course, back to the organization itself, in the form of lessons learned, best practices, and corporate memory.

The knowledge capture and transfer approaches described here help to:

- Facilitate a smooth transition from those retiring to their successors who are recruited to fill their positions.

Fig. 2 The iceberg metaphor used to show the respective proportions of tacit and explicit knowledge.

- Minimize loss of corporate memory due to attrition and retirement.
- Identify critical resources and critical areas of knowledge so that the corporation "knows what it knows and does well—and why."
- Build up a toolkit of methods that can be used with individuals, with groups, and with the organization to stem the potential loss of intellectual capital.

Knowledge management is often mistakenly perceived as a process of documenting knowledge held in people's minds, then storing or archiving this knowledge.[21] In fact, it is better to view KM in a broader context, one that encompasses all the processes used to generate value from knowledge-based assets. Knowledge management is facilitated by technology and by the culture of an organization. A good way of defining KM is:

> ...the deliberate and systematic coordination of an organization's people, technology, processes and organizational structure in order to add value through reuse and innovation. This is achieved through the promotion of creating, sharing and applying knowledge as well as through the feeding of valuable lessons learned and best practices into corporate memory in order to foster continued organizational learning (p. 3).[22]

CORE KM CONCEPTS

Kransdorff[23] coined the term "corporate amnesia" to refer to the loss of accumulated expertise and know-how due to employee turnover as people take what they know with them when they leave. The costs of employee turnover to the organization have been well documented (e.g., separation costs, recruitment and selection costs, training of replacements, initial lack of productivity of new hire, and the loss of productivity of coworkers during the transition). Far less research attention has been paid to the cost to the firm of losing know-how that resides within the minds of individual employees who depart. In an era of knowledge workers, learning

organizations, and service economies, individuals are increasingly responsible for value creation. Although many organizations have succession plans in place, the process usually involves transferring know-how from the departing employee to their successor but the whole process has to be repeated again for the next departure. Organizations need to "capture" this know-how and transfer it to a stable, easily accessible, cumulative knowledge base—an organizational memory—to retain and make accessible valuable knowledge gained through the experiences of all knowledge in a continuous and uninterrupted manner.

Organizations need to effectively manage their organizational memory in order to prevent the loss of essential knowledge, particularly knowledge that resides predominantly in the heads of their knowledge workers ("tacit knowledge") and less in documents, procedures, and other tangible forms ("explicit knowledge").[24] More often than not, it is this difficult-to-articulate "know-how" that is of greatest value in organizational competitiveness and viability and which represents the vast majority of experiential know-how. Fig. 2 shows how the metaphor of an iceberg is often used to depict tacit and explicit knowledge forms.

The National Aeronautics and Space Administration (NASA), for example, has publicly admitted that the knowledge of how to put a man on the moon has been lost.[25] The lessons that were learned and the innovations that were sparked cannot be found in the collective organizational memory of NASA. This means that NASA's organizational memory cannot be used as a resource to plan a more effective mission to send another manned flight to the moon or to Mars. A well-designed and well-managed organizational memory does not only combat corporate amnesia, but it ensures knowledge continuity—the effective transfer of know-how amongst peers and to future generations of knowledge workers. A better understanding of the nature of organizational memory, what it should include (content), how it can best be retained (technological containers), and how the accumulated lessons learned and best practices can be used by newcomers (connections), will help mitigate the cost of lost, forgotten, or un-transferred knowledge and know-how.

Organizations today face escalating risks of losing strategic knowledge and know-how and face incredible difficulties in recruiting and retaining skilled employees. Many industries face astounding rates of high and constant turnover. In addition, we are experiencing a demographic pressure as baby boomers rapidly approach retirement age, which means that a "critical mass" of knowledge will literally walk out the door over the next 5–10 years. Approximately, 11,000 baby boomers are turning 50 years old every day.[26] Over 80% of Canadian government federal executives will be eligible to retire by 2010 and 53% of U.S. federal civil servants

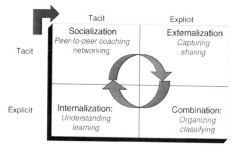

Fig. 3 The Nonaka and Takeuchi knowledge spiral model of knowledge management.

will be eligible to retire within the next 2 years.[27] The number of workers age 55 and over is expected to increase by 47% during the year 2010.[28] Other vulnerable organizations include high technology companies with very high turnover rates and the military or banking, where constant turnover is the norm given rotational postings.

Most successful organizations will state that their two greatest assets are the people who work for them and the knowledge they possess. The imminent turnover signals a potential for the loss of valuable accumulated knowledge and know-how in the form of the competence and expertise possessed by the departing individuals. This valuable knowledge and know-how exists in both formal and tangible forms, such as documents, but also in less visible forms—often referred to as tacit or difficult-to-articulate knowledge. Particular emphasis must be placed on the tacit form as this often resides within a given individual or group and is therefore more easily and completely lost when the people leave the organization.[29]

The typical technological tools used in KM are some form of centralized database system, an intranet or Web portal, to access the database content as well as other organizational knowledge, some type of messaging system (typically e-mail and discussion groups), some content management tools to organize the knowledge resources (e.g., content management software, taxonomy software), and some form of collaborative software (e.g., virtual meeting tools, groupware).

The essential elements that go into organizational memory include best practices, which are innovations or improved practices, processes, and so forth; together with the flip side of the coin: lessons learned, outcomes that were not desirable, or errors that should not be repeated. By carefully capturing, documenting, organizing, and making available accumulated experiential knowledge in the form of best practices and lessons learned, KM can provide a framework within which we can process knowledge throughout its useful life cycle.

Knowledge management typically addresses three levels within an organization: the individual, the group, and the organization. Organizational memory resides at the level of the organization and this is the preservation layer of KM. Innovation and knowledge creation occurs at the individual level while knowledge dissemination and sharing occur at the group level. In KM, groups of a particular nature, called "communities of practice" (CoPs) are often key elements in ensuring that valuable knowledge flows or moves around appropriately. These CoPs are essentially thematic networks of like-minded individuals who share a common purpose, a common professional zeal, and agree to mutually help out one another to achieve some strategic goals for the organization.[30,31]

Szulanski[32] introduced the notion of knowledge "stickiness" to refer to knowledge that was difficult to move around, and thus could provide little in the way of value to individuals, groups, or the organization as a whole. The knowledge processing cycle is used to describe the various stages a particular knowledge resource goes through during the course of its "lifespan" within an organization.

THE KNOWLEDGE PROCESSING CYCLE

Nonaka and Takeuchi described how knowledge was disseminated and transformed as it made its way around an organization in their Knowledge Spiral Model.[9] Essentially, knowledge is created by an individual (an innovative idea for example), but remains initially tacit. This innovation or idea is typically shared only with trusted friends and colleagues at first ("socialization"). With time, others may be aware of the innovation and the knowledge may be transformed from its tacit state to an explicit one ("externalization"), by documenting it in the form of text, audio, or other formats. Once explicit, it is easier to disseminate more widely and to preserve in an organizational memory system. At this stage ("combination"), the content may be organized and reworked (e.g., addition of an abstract or executive summary). In the final stage ("internalization"), explicit knowledge once again becomes tacit as an individual learns, understands, and "buys into" a knowledge resource (e.g., sees its value and decides to apply this new knowledge). The knowledge resource then continues cycling through the four quadrants in a "knowledge spiral." Fig. 3 outlines the major stages in the Nonaka and Takeuchi KM model, as knowledge is transformed, disseminated, and applied within an organization.

As knowledge resources circulate throughout an organization, value can be added at each step. A more detailed view of what happens to knowledge as it undergoes transformation from tacit to explicit and back again is provided in the form of a knowledge life cycle. The first stage is to either capture existing knowledge (e.g., already existing in tangible form such as project

Table 2 Key steps in knowledge processing cycle

Step number	Description
1.	Knowledge capture
2.	Knowledge creation
3.	Knowledge contribution
4.	Knowledge codification
5.	Knowledge refinement (including sanitize) and reconstruction (e.g., synthesis)
6.	Knowledge selection—filter contributions
7.	Knowledge sharing and pooling
8.	Knowledge organization and access
9.	Knowledge learning and application
10.	Knowledge evaluation and reuse or divest (e.g., destroy, archive)

reports, conference reports, or other documents), or to create knowledge that does not yet exist in documented form (e.g., by interviewing subject matter experts to document a particular procedure). This knowledge resource can then be contributed to or made available for reuse by others. Knowledge is then codified by the addition of sufficient descriptive information about both the content and the format it is in (e.g., metadata describing theme, whether it is a text or also available as a short video clip). At this point, knowledge is further refined by sanitization (removing all sensitive information that may identify a person, place, or event, or other confidential content) and reconstruction (e.g., recombining or synthesizing in a new version). Contributions that have been refined and reconstructed are then subjected to a selective filtering process and those that are deemed to be valuable are made available for knowledge sharing.

Knowledge sharing involves the pooling and distribution of valuable content, either globally (e.g., a "broadcast" mode) or selectively (e.g., targeted to specific users, communities, or based on user profiles, subscriptions, etc.). The knowledge is better organized (classified using a taxonomic scheme) and access is typically provided through an intranet or portal interface. These valuable knowledge resources are then learned and applied by knowledge workers. Each knowledge

resource is evaluated periodically in order to ensure continued relevance and to decide whether to discard or to archive at the appropriate time. Table 2 lists the key phases in knowledge processing that occurs during the useful life cycle of a knowledge resource, such as a best practice or lesson learned.

HISTORY AND EVOLUTION OF KM

Knowledge and management are concepts that have obviously been around for some time—the combination, "knowledge management," however, is fairly new. The emergence of communication technologies that create real-time networks such as the Internet, intranets, e-mail, and so forth have made KM easier to implement.[33]

A number of management theories have contributed to the definition of KM. Two KM gurus were responsible for establishing the field as a serious target for scholarly study: Peter Drucker,[34] who coined the term "knowledge worker" and who wrote about KM from a management perspective in the 1970s and Nonaka and Takeuchi, who wrote the seminal book *The Knowledge Creating Company* in the 1990s.[9] Others such as Peter Senge[35] and Chris Argyris[36,37] have focused on the "learning organization" and cultural dimensions of managing knowledge. The notion of knowledge as an asset became more widely adopted by the mid-1980s. Early pioneers in information technologies from artificial intelligence and expert systems at Carnegie Mellon University (CMU) and Digital Equipment Corporation (DEC) developed hypertext and groupware tools that allow information to be better shared and organized. Knowledge management-related articles began appearing in prestigious journals such as the *Harvard Business Review* and *Organizational Science* and a number of foundational books were published such as *The Fifth Discipline* and *The Knowledge-Creating Company*. Table 3 illustrates the major milestones in KM history.

In 1989, the International Knowledge Management Network (IKMN) was founded in Europe and was

Table 3 Major milestones in KM history

Year	Source	Event
1980	DEC, CMU	XCON Expert System
1986	Dr. K. Wiig	Coined KM concept at UN
1989	Consulting firms	Start internal KM projects
1991	HBR article	Nonaka & Takeuchi
1993	Dr. K. Wiig	First KM book published
1994	KM network	First KM conference
Mid-1990s	Consulting firms	Start offering KM services
Late 1990s	Key vertical industries	Implement KM and start seeing benefits
2000–2003	Academia	KM courses/programs in universities with KM texts

Table 4 Major peer-reviewed KM journals

Journal title	Year founded
IBM Systems Journal	1962
Journal of Managerial and Organizational Learning	1970
Journal of Management Information Systems	1984
Journal of Organizational Change Management	1989
Knowledge and Process Management	1996
Journal of Knowledge Management	1997
Journal of Management Studies	1997
Journal of Knowledge Management Practice	1998
Journal of Intellectual Capital	2000
E-Journal of Organizational Learning and Leadership	2002
Journal of Information and Knowledge Management (JIKM)	2002
Electronic Journal of Knowledge Management	2003
International Journal of Knowledge, Culture and Change Management	2003
Knowledge Management Research and Practice	2003
Interdisciplinary Journal of Storytelling Studies	2004
International Journal of Nuclear Knowledge Management (IJNKM)	2004
International Journal of Knowledge Management	2005
Knowledge Management for Development Journal	2005
International Journal of Knowledge Management Studies	2006
Interdisciplinary Journal of Information, Knowledge and Management (IJIKM)	2007

joined by the U.S.-based Knowledge Management Forum in 1994.

Businesses began implementing KM solutions in earnest in the 1990s. At first, projects tended to be technological implementations, mostly portals and knowledge repositories. This was followed by a wave of "people not technology" emphasis that led to the popularity of thematic networks or CoPs. A third wave emerged as knowledge workers, much like information workers, found themselves faced with "content overload" which in turn led to a number of content management, knowledge organization, or taxonomic classification projects to make the knowledge more readily accessible to users.

With the new millennium, KM faded a bit from public view, likely due to disappointment, the result of expectations having been raised too much by "KM hype" and focusing too much on technologies that were largely left untouched. Practitioners and researchers came to the realization that converting theory into practice was more challenging than previously thought. Among the missing elements were ensuring that KM was not being done for KM's sake but that there was a clear link to organizational objectives and that all participants saw value in KM (incentives for knowledge sharing, for example). By 2004, the field had finally shaken its burden of being yet another management fad. Organizations appreciated the holistic nature of KM and paid attention not only to tools but also to organizational culture requirements for successful KM solutions.

In parallel, the nature of work evolved, with collaboration becoming the default rather than the exception, not only for our professional lives but social interactions and learning objectives. Knowledge sharing with a group of trusted peers has become the de facto way of working, learning, and living. Knowledge management found itself in tune with these changes that greatly facilitated its adoption as a philosophy, a mindset, a strategic perspective, and a way of interacting to create, share, and use valuable content.

Knowledge management today is being taught in universities around the world, typically in business, computer science, education, and information studies departments. Doctoral students are completing Ph.D. theses on KM topics. International conferences are being held around the world, with both practitioner and researcher tracks. A number of consortia and KM professional organizations have been established. The number and type of KM journals have also changed. While at first publications were primarily authored by KM tool vendors and practitioners, and in more general management, computer science and organizational science journalists, there has been a significant shift to more scholarly venues and publications that represent KM research rather than KM project mandates. Along with the proliferation in the number of journals, there has also been increasing specialization (e.g., *International Journal of Nuclear Knowledge Management*), more interdisciplinary journals (e.g., *Interdisciplinary Journal of Information, Knowledge and Management*), and more emphasis on international KM (e.g., *International Journal of Knowledge Management*). Up until about the year 2000, only non-peer reviewed journals were available (e.g., *KM World, KM Review*). Some of the major peer-reviewed KM journals available today are shown in Table 4, ordered by the first year of publication.

Knowledge management is found in all vertical industry sectors (e.g., banking, pharmaceutical); in all sizes of organizations (including volunteer-run associations with less than 10 full-time employees); profit and nonprofit organizations and organizations with a strong hierarchical structure (for example, the U.S. military was one of the early pioneers of KM). Organizations today are defining and staffing KM positions.

Knowledge management is increasingly perceived as an element that cuts across organizational structures, projects, and silos—it enjoys a status similar to that of "quality assurance" or "ethics" and it has become a critical element of organizational viability. Knowledge management is no longer something interesting to explore—it has become subsumed in the way in which individuals, groups, and organizations work, learn, and remember.

EMERGING ROLES FOR INFORMATION PROFESSIONALS

The KM field has transformed from one led primarily by consultants and other KM practitioners to a bona fide discipline, with a distinct body of knowledge. This has been paralleled by the growing number of academic programs that offer KM as compared to the predominately private sector training that had been the only way to learn about KM up until now.[38] TFPL[39] is a specialist recruitment, advisory, training, and research services company with offices in London focusing on KM, library and information management, records management, and Web and content management. Since 1987, TFPL has worked with organizations in both public and private sectors to help them develop and implement knowledge and information strategies and to recruit and train information and knowledge leaders and their teams. TFPL has drafted a KM skills and competencies guide to provide a clear and practical overview of KM skills and competencies that draws on the practical experience of organizations in a wide range of sectors and with varying approaches to KM.

In general, these KM skills include:

- Time management to use their time and energy effectively for acquiring knowledge (spending all day surfing the Net is probably counterproductive).
- Use of different learning techniques to absorb key knowledge and learning quickly.
- Effective skills of advocacy and inquiry to present knowledge to, and gather knowledge from, others.
- Informal networking skills to build influence to gain access to people with knowledge.
- Resource investigation skills.
- Effective information technology skills for recording and disseminating information.
- Skills of cooperative problem solving.
- Open dialogue skills.
- Flexibility and willingness to try new things and take educated risks.
- Active review of learning from mistakes, risks, opportunities, and successes.

The TFPL KM skills inventory[40] is based on an extensive international research. The project team contacted over 500 organizations involved in implementing KM, and identified the roles that they had created, the skills that were needed in those roles, and the additional skills that were required across the organization. These key skills included an understanding of the KM concept—the philosophy and theory—and an awareness of the experience of other organizations in developing KM solutions and approaches; an understanding of, and the ability to, identify the business value of KM activities to the organization; an appreciation of the range of activities, initiatives, and labels which are employed to create an environment in which knowledge is effectively created, shared, and used to increase competitive advantage and customer satisfaction.

Knowledge management roles are quite diverse and include such categories as senior and middle management roles—Chief Knowledge Officer (CKO) who ensures that KM goals are in line with organizational strategies and objectives; Chief Learning Officer (CLO) who ensures that the organization acts like a learning organization, improving over time with the help of accumulated best practices and lessons learned; Knowledge Managers who are typically responsible for the acquisition and management of internal and external knowledge. Other roles include:

- Knowledge navigators, responsible for knowing where knowledge can be located, also called knowledge brokers.
- Knowledge synthesizers, responsible for facilitating the recording of significant knowledge to organizational memory, also called Knowledge Stewards.
- Content editors, responsible for codifying and structuring content, also called content managers; roles involving capturing and documenting knowledge—researchers, writers, editors.
- Web developers, electronic publishers, intranet managers, content managers.
- Learning-oriented roles such as trainers, facilitators, mentors, coaches—including those with responsibility for developing information and knowledge skills.
- Human resources roles with specific responsibility for developing programs and processes that encourage knowledge-oriented cultures and behaviors.
- Knowledge publishers, responsible for internal publishing functions, usually on an intranet, also called Webmasters, knowledge architects, Knowledge editors.
- Coaches and mentors, responsible for assisting individuals throughout the business unit or practice to develop and learn KM activities and disciplines.
- Help desk activities, including the delivery of KM and information related to training, also called Knowledge Support Office (KSO).

Knowledge management professionals require a multidisciplinary skill-set that consists of such competencies as finding, appraising, and using knowledge, beginning to be able to reformulate questions, navigating through content, evaluating the relevance of content, filtering out what is not needed, and synthesizing from diverse sources in order to apply the knowledge (e.g., to make a decision). Last but not least, they must contribute to the recording of such valuable experiences to organizational memory systems.[41]

CONCLUSION

Knowledge management has assumed a greater priority due to the demographic pressures created by retiring baby boomers. Retirement en masse means a loss of valuable knowledge and know-how that has been accumulated by experience over the years. All organizations, regardless of type of industry, size, country, and so forth will have to face the issue of knowledge continuity. Knowledge continuity is analogous to business continuity: while the latter targets data loss prevention due to disasters, the former targets knowledge loss due to turnover in personnel. Valuable knowledge must not only be preserved and transferred to future workers, but also transferred across geographical and temporal boundaries due to the fact that work today is spread out over networks that may extend beyond organizational boundaries. Knowledge management is the discipline and field of practice that will equip us with the necessary tools, processes, and skill-sets to ensure that knowledge reaches all knowledge workers so that they can carry out their work more efficiently and more effectively.

REFERENCES

1. Merriam-Webster Dictionary Online. http://www.m-w.com/dictionary/knowledge (accessed November 2008).
2. Leonard, D.; Sensiper, S. The role of tacit knowledge in group innovation. Calif. Manage. Rev. **1998**, *40* (3), 112–132.
3. McDermott, R. Why information technology inspired but cannot deliver knowledge management. Calif. Manage. Rev. **1999**, *41* (4), 103–117.
4. Davenport, T.; Prusak, L. *Working Knowledge*; Harvard Business School Press: Boston, MA, 1998.
5. Barclay, R.; Murray, P. What is knowledge management? Knowledge Praxis. http://www.media-access.com/whatis.html (accessed November 2008).
6. Grey, D. What is knowledge management? Knowl. Manage. Forum March 1996.
7. Sarvary, M. Knowledge management and competition in the consulting industry. Calif. Manage. Rev. **1999**, *41* (2), 95–107.
8. Wiig, K. *Knowledge Management Foundations*; Schema Press: Arlington, TX, 1993.
9. Nonaka, I.; Takeuchi, H. *The Knowledge-Creating Company: How Japanese Companies Create the Dynamics of Innovation*; Oxford University Press: New York, NY, 1995.
10. Pasternack, B.; Viscio, A. *The Centerless Corporation*; Simon and Schuster: New York, NY, 1998.
11. Pfeffer, J.; Sutton, R. *The Knowing-Doing Gap: How Smart Companies Turn Knowledge into Action*; Harvard Business School Press: New York, NY, 1999.
12. Ruggles, R.; Holtshouse, D. *The Knowledge Advantage*; Capstone Publishers: Dover, NH, 1999.
13. APQC (The American Productivity and Quality Centre). What is KM? From the APQC knowledge base. http://www.apqc.org/portal/apqc/ksn?paf_gear_id=contentgearhome&paf_dm=full&pageselect=detail&docid=101261 (accessed November 2008).
14. Hibbard, J. Knowledge tools debate. http://www.informationweek.com/673/73iudeb.htm Information Week (accessed March 1998).
15. Frappaolo, C. Knowledge management: A 2001 perspective. http://www.kwork.org/Stars/KM_perspective.pdf
16. Levinson, M. The ABCs of knowledge management. CIO Magazine. http://www.cio.com/article/40343/ABC_An_Introduction_to_KM/40343/40343/1#1
17. Bontis, N.; Nikitopoulos, D. Thought leadership on intellectual capital. J. Intel. Capital **2001**, *2* (3), 183–191.
18. Klein, D. *The Strategic Management of Intellectual Capital*; Butterworth-Heineman: Oxford, U.K., 1998.
19. Stewart, T. *Intellectual Capital*; Doubleday: New York, NY, 1997.
20. Stewart, T.A. Software preserves knowledge, people pass it on. Fortune **2000**, *142* (5), 390–392.
21. Rothberg, H.; Erickson, G. In *From Knowledge to Intelligence. Creating Competitive Advantage in the New Economy*; Butterworth-Heinemann: Boston, MA, 2005.
22. Dalkir, K. *Knowledge Management Theory and Practice*; Butterworth-Heinemann: Boston, MA, 2005.
23. Kransdorff, A. *Corporate Amnesia: Keeping Know-How in the Company*; Butterworth-Heinemann: Oxford, U.K., 1998.
24. Polanyi, M. *The Tacit Dimension*; Peter Smith: Gloucester, MA, 1966.
25. Glesinger, J. The not-so-hidden cost of lost knowledge. Energy Press J. September 2, **2008**, http://energy.pressandjournal.co.uk/Article.aspx/800114/?UserKey = (accessed November 2008).
26. Hutchison, L. Phased retirement saves intellectual capital. St. Louis Commerce Magazine **2001** http://www.stlcommercemagazine (accessed November 2008).
27. Liu, S.; Fidel, R. Managing aging workforce: Filling the gap between what we know and what is in the system. Proceedings of the 1st International Conference on Theory and Practice of Electronic Governance, Macao, China, December, 10–13, 2007; (ICEGOV 2007) ACM: New York, 2007; Vol. 232, 121–128 http://doi.acm.org/10.1145/1328057.1328084
28. Liebowitz, J. Bridging the knowledge and skills gap: tapping federal retirees. Public Personnel Manage. **2004**, *33* (4), 421–447.

29. LaBarre, P. People go, knowledge stays. Fast Company **2001**, *17* (4), http://www.fastcompany.com/magazine/17/wyp17.html (accessed November 2008).

30. Wenger, E.; Snyder, W. Communities of practice: The organizational frontier. Harvard Bus. Rev. **2000**, January–February, 139–145.

31. Wenger, E.; McDermott, R.; Snyder, W. In *Cultivating Communities of Practice: A Guide to Managing Knowledge*; Harvard Business School: Cambridge, MA, 2002.

32. Szulanski, G. *Sticky Knowledge—Barriers to Knowing in a Firm*; Sage: Thousand Oaks, CA, 2003.

33. Alvesson, M.; Karreman, D. Odd couple: Making sense of the curious concept of knowledge management. J. Manage. Stud. **2001**, *38* (7), 995–1018.

34. Drucker, P. *Management: Tasks, Responsibilities, Practices*; Harper & Row: New York, NY, 1973.

35. Senge, P. *The Fifth Discipline: The Art and Practice of the Learning Organization*; Doubleday: New York, NY, 1990.

36. Argyris, M.; Schön, D. *Theory in Practice. Increasing Professional Effectiveness*; Jossey-Bass: San Francisco, CA, 1974.

37. Argyris, C. *Knowledge for Action. A Guide to Overcoming Barriers to Organizational Change*; Jossey-Bass: San Francisco, CA, 1993.

38. Al-Hawamdeh, S. *Knowledge Management: Cultivating Knowledge Professionals*; Chandos Publishing: Rollinsford, NH, 2003.

39. TFPL website. http://www.tfpl.com.

40. TFPL Ltd.: London, 1999 TFPL Skills for knowledge management, a briefing paper by TFPL Ltd: Based on research undertaken by TFPL on behalf of the Library and Information Commission.

41. Henzcel, S. Supporting the KM environment: The roles, responsibilities, and rights of information professionals; Constructive thoughts on knowledge management. Information Outlook **2004**, *8* (1), 14–19.

Knowledge Management Systems

Dick Stenmark
Department of Applied IT, IT University of Gothenburg, Gothenburg, Sweden

Abstract

Knowledge management systems (KMS) are loosely understood as a type of information technology (IT) to support organizational knowledge management (KM) work. The challenge here is to understand first what KM is and then figure out how it can be supported by IT. This entry first provides a review of KM work and the critique it received. Then KMS are defined and analyzed through various well-used theoretical frameworks. The major challenges KMS are facing today are discussed and the entry ends with some hints on what may lie ahead.

INTRODUCTION

Knowledge management systems (KMS) refers to a class of information systems (IS) that is used to enhance knowledge and information transfer within an organization and to manage organizational knowledge.[1] Although this statement seems straightforward, it is rather difficult to define what a KMS is, since it is still unclear exactly what should be included in the concept of knowledge management (KM). What is the difference between knowledge and information and can computer applications really deal with knowledge? Some have argued that computers can only process data, and certainly not knowledge.[2] What, then, is a KMS and what role does it play in KM work? Before we can talk about *systems* for KM, we need a shared view of KM itself.

Is KM an emerging new discipline of its own or is it a topic that runs across several existing scholarly discourses? Throughout the years, there have been advocates of both positions. There are also commentators arguing that organizations have always been practicing KM-related activities so there is essentially nothing new to KM. This is no uncommon phenomenon but something that happens whenever new terminology is introduced. In the 1980s, Cronin asked whether information management had something new to offer or if it was just a new label for librarianship.[3] Twenty or so years later, people ask the same thing about KM and KMS.

Whilst several voices claim that there is no consensus regarding what exactly knowledge management is or how it differs from information management, Davenport and Grover in their editorial comment on the 2001 Special KM issue of Journal of Management Information Systems (JMIS) concluded that KM as a *practical* phenomenon was here to stay but that *formal research* on the topic was lacking.[4] A couple of years have passed since Davenport and Grover made this observation and

today it is fair to say that KM has established itself as a research topic, as reported elsewhere in this encyclopedia. Davenport and Grover continued by observing that IT support for KM, i.e., KMS, was seen as a useful but far from required resource by practitioners and scholars alike.

In the following text, we shall first look briefly at the history of KM and KMS before turning to the various theories underpinning this field. Thereafter, some of the most well-cited frameworks for KMS found in the IS literature are introduced to help the reader see what *types* of KMS are available. The ontological aspects of KMS are touched upon before finally discussing the challenges KMS are facing today.

ROOTS OF KM

It can be debated when and where KM started, since it depends on what discipline you examine. A large number of fields have clearly influenced the emerging KM discourse—e.g., sociology, human resource management, organization science, and IS research to name a few. Many commentators would probably hold organizational learning as the one discipline that has had perhaps the most profound effect on the KM field.[5,6] When it comes to KMS, though, the IS discipline has taken a leading role, since the development, implementation, and use of systems to informate and automate are central to the IS field.[7]

Tiwana[8] places the roots of KM in the 1950s management literature, whereas Maier[6] traces the first instances of KM back to the studies of societal application of knowledge in the late 1960s and early 1970s. However, it was not until the late 1980s, through the writings of, e.g., Sveiby and Lloyd[9] and Wiig,[10] that the phenomenon started to receive more widespread attention. Nonaka and Takeuchi's book "The Knowledge

Encyclopedia of Information Systems and Technology, DOI: 10.1081/E-EIST-120043724

Creating Company"[11] is also an early landmark in organizational KM literature and one of the most cited sources with almost 10,000 references in Google Scholar.

What propelled the development of KM as a new research discipline was the growing emphasis on knowledge work and knowledge workers as the primary source of productivity as opposed to assets such as land or capital.[11] This view paved way for the knowledge-based perspective of the firm[12] that suggests that the tangible resources of an organization generate value dependent on how they are combined and applied, which in turn depends on the organization's knowledge. This knowledge is deeply permeated in culture, procedures, routines, systems, and minds of the individual employees.

In the introduction of their 2001 paper, Alavi and Leidner note that it is not the existence of this knowledge per se that matters, but the ability to apply it and put it to use. To that end, advanced information technologies can be instrumental in effectuating the knowledge-based view of the firm by systemizing, enhancing, and expediting large-scale knowledge management.[13]

CRITIQUE OF KM

Knowledge management as a research discipline has also received critique. Some have argued that it is no more than yet another exemplar in a long list of management fads that have come and gone over the years.[2,14] In his critical analysis of KM, Wilson concludes:

> [Knowledge management] is, in large part, a management fad, promulgated mainly by certain consultancy companies, and the probability is that it will fade away like previous fads.[14]

Much of this skepticism stems from the fact that many consultancy firms and software vendors simply seemed to have renamed their old services and products, replacing the term "information" with the term "knowledge." Therefore, says Wilson:

> [T]he confusion of 'knowledge' as a synonym for 'information' is one of the most common effects of the 'knowledge management' fad.[14]

In addition to the fad debate, the KM discourse was also criticized for being "technology-driven." Comparing and contrasting the KM literature to that of organizational learning (OL), Swan et al. found that although the two disciplines are concerned with the improvement of organizational performance through knowledge development, i.e., human issues, only the OL literature focused on humans whereas the KM literature was predominantly occupied with tools and techniques.[5] The emphasis on information technology in the KM literature resulted in people being marginalized to either "inputs to KM [...] or as constraints on its effectiveness [...]" (p. 673).[5] Swan and colleagues argue that much of the richness of human relations is lost when KM is reduced to merely technology.

This distinction between technology-oriented and human-oriented approaches has a long tradition in organization science and goes back to at least the early 1980s. However, a more holistic understanding of KM that encompasses both these stances has developed, and much of the turf wars from the late 1990s have now abated.

THEORETICAL FOUNDATION

Much of the epistemology used in KM literature has been influenced by the separation of knowledge in a tacit and an explicit component. The notion of tacit knowing is attributed to philosopher Michael Polanyi but was introduced to the KM discourse by Nonaka and Takeuchi.[11] Interestingly, the commonly used tacit–explicit distinction is not directly derived from Polanyi's work. Most commentators see explicit knowledge as knowledge that has been captured and codified into manuals, procedures, and rules, and is easy to disseminate. Tacit knowledge, on the other hand, is then knowledge that cannot be easily articulated and thus only exists in people's hands and minds, and manifests itself through their actions. In contrast, Polanyi does not make such a distinction. Instead, he envisions tacit knowing as the backdrop against which all understanding is distinguished.

While Polanyi speaks of tacit *knowing*, i.e., the verb, as a backdrop against which all actions are understood, Nonaka and Takeuchi use the term tacit *knowledge*, i.e., the noun, to denote particular type of knowledge that is difficult to express. This view has been criticized but due to the strong influence of Nonaka and Takeuchi's writings on the knowledge management discourse, this interpretation has been widely adopted. Amongst the critics is Tsoukas, who argues that tacit knowledge is *not* explicit knowledge internalized. Instead, tacit knowledge is inseparable from explicit knowledge since "[t]acit knowledge is the necessary component of all knowledge" (p. 14).[15] According to Tsoukas the two are so inseparately related that to even try to separate the two would be to "miss the point." There had perhaps been less confusion had Nonaka instead used the term "implicit knowledge."

Tsoukas recognizes that the dichotomy between tacit and explicit knowledge and the taxonomies derived from this duality have advanced our understanding of organizational knowledge by showing its multifaceted nature. However, such typologies also limit our understanding by the inherent formalism that accompanies them. "The conceptual categories along which the phenomena are classified must be assumed to be discrete, separate, and stable. The problem is that they hardly ever are" (p. 14).[15]

The tacit–explicit dichotomy has also taken other expressions. Choo suggests a differentiation between tacit, explicit, and cultural knowledge,[16] and Spender suggests, in addition to tacit and explicit knowledge, individual and collective knowing.[12] Blackler speaks of embodied, embedded, embrained, encultured, and encoded knowledge.[17] Yet another derivative is the distinction between the community view and the commodity view. The community view sees knowledge as socially constructed and inseparable from the knower, whereas the commodity view holds knowledge as a universal truth, and as facts and collectable objects.[18] Though several other ways to classify knowledge exist and have been suggested, they all, more or less, build on the tacit–explicit dichotomy.

DEFINITION OF KM SYSTEMS

Whereas most people agree that data and information may exist outside humans, supporters of the community view of knowledge have argued that knowledge can never be separated from the knower and thus never stored digitally.[2,13] Computer support for knowledge management would thus be, in a sense, impossible. How can we then talk about KMS?

KMS is often employed as a catalyst or enabler of KM but such implementations should not be carried out without careful coordination with the required people-oriented activities needed. Alavi and Leidner note that while KM initiatives may not *require* tools, IT can certainly support KM in many ways, in particular in firms where the ratio of *knowledge workers* is high.[13] Schultze defines a knowledge worker as someone who interacts knowledgeable with information and sees information not only as something derived from knowledge but as something that changes knowledge.[19] There is thus a tight relationship between information and knowledge and it seems that any knowledge work needs to be supported by information technology.

As stated in the introduction, a KMS is an IS and IS and knowledge systems are thus not radically different; instead, there is a subtle yet important difference in the *attitude* towards and the *purpose* of the systems. While an IS processes information without engaging the users, a KMS must be geared towards helping the users to understand and assign *meaning* to the information.[13]

The value of any given piece of information resides in the relationship between the information and the user's knowledge. This means that design of KMS should be based on an understanding not only of the information per se, but also of the context where the user develops the information need, and the analysis of the usage of the same information once it has been obtained and interpreted by the user.[20]

Following Alavi and Leidner,[13] a KMS should thus be understood as *a particular class of information systems developed specifically to support organizations in their attempt to create, codify, collect, store, integrate, share, and apply knowledge.*

KMS THEORY

The theoretical foundation underpinning KMS vary considerably and is not easily detected but we can get a reasonably good picture by looking at Schultze and Leidner's classification of theoretical perspectives in KM-related IS research. Having reviewed six leading IS journals and thoroughly analyzed nearly 100 articles from 1990 to 2000, Schultze and Leidner showed that a vast majority or 70% belonged to the Normative Discourse, 25% could be labeled as Interpretative Discourse and only a handful of papers represented a Critical (or Dialogic) Discourse.[21]

According to Schultze and Leidner's analysis, the normative discourse, which is characterized by a strive towards consensus from an a priori understanding of what the research problems are, typically assumes progressive enlightenment and increasing rationalization, management, and control. IS research representing the normative discourse are thus concerned with "codification, normalization of experience, and the search for law-like relationships" (pp. 216–217).[21] Much of the research focuses on problem solving, and it creates "a problem space that can be decomposed in a logical, top-down fashion" (p. 221).[21] Although both the research topics and the way knowledge is operationalized show great diversity, a common metaphor used within the normative discourse is that of knowledge as an asset. Researchers in this category typically view knowledge as a key driver of organizational efficiency and performance. Amongst the theories underpinning normative research, Schultze and Leidner mention innovation diffusion theory, absorptive capacity theory, and management cognition theory (p. 222).[21]

The interpretative discourse, which also opts for consensus but from an emergent understanding of the organizational situation, emphasizes the social aspects of organizational life that has not been rationalized or systematized. IS research representing the interpretative discourse thus aims "to create a coherent, consensual, and unified representation of what the organizational reality is 'actually' like" (p. 217),[21] and is typically targeted on work situations and organizational practices. Knowledge is therefore studied indirectly via its role in organizational transformation and how it is supported by various types of KMS. In this discourse, knowledge, technology, and organizational practice are all seen as socially constructed and dynamic, and the theories upon which interpretive research rests include organizational learning, communities of practice, activity theory, and bricolage (pp. 224–225).[21]

It is evident that almost all KM-related IS research is consensus-oriented. There are, however, also those who apply a dissensus-oriented approach. Although Schultze and Leidner treat critical and dialogic as two separate discourses, one can here use the critical discourse label to include both these perspectives, since both understand struggle, conflict, and tension as natural organizational states. Seen from this perspective, organizations are "sites of political struggle and fields of continuous conflict" (p. 217)[21] and the objective of the research is thus to show that there is no coherent reality but different forms of domination and distortions. KMS (and other IT tools) are thus not to be understood as neutral, according to this perspective, but should be seen as instruments to make invisible work visible or to actively change social conditions. Schultze and Leidner call for more research in the critical discourse since this perspective allows the highlighting of the social inequities underpinning the distinction between service and knowledge work and the examination of contradictions in managing knowledge.[21] The direct implications for KMS, however, are less obvious.

TYPES OF KMS AND ITS APPLICATIONS

As we saw earlier, many vendors tried to repackage their applications under the KM label at the end of the last millennium and a list of different KMS can therefore be made arbitrarily long. Instead of presenting a list of software that not all would agree upon, and, in addition, soon would be dated, it is more useful to examine three of the most referenced classification schemes for KMS and let them define the *various types of applications* that are possible. The frameworks are Hansen et al.'s *Codification vs. Personalization* from *Harvard Business Review* in 1999,[22] Hahn and Subramani's *Knowledge Residence and Level of Structure* from ICIS 2000,[23] and finally Alavi and Leidner's scheme from MISQ in 2001.[13]

Codification vs. Personalization

An early framework for KM work (and hence for KMS to support that work) is found in Hansen et al.'s well-referred article from *Harvard Business Review*. Based on their studies of management consultancy firms, and implicitly building on Nonaka's dichotomy of explicit and tacit knowledge, Hansen et al. divide knowledge management efforts into two different strategies; codification and personalization.[22]

Companies where the KM strategy centers on codifying and storing knowledge into databases for easy dissemination and retrieval, is said to follow a codification strategy. In such companies, computers have a central role in the strategy, as carriers of knowledge. Hansen et al. point to Ernst and Young as a company following a codification strategy. Knowledge is harvested and coded into documents or other "knowledge objects" as an informant called them (p. 108),[22] and these are thereafter stored in electronic repositories for later retrieval. Even though the codification process is laborious, Ernst and Young has dedicated staff members doing nothing else but codifying knowledge into documents—this approach allows for scaling up since the repositories are accessible for all employees worldwide and available round the clock. Once the object is put into the repository it can be used over and over again at a very low cost, provided it does not have to be modified. Companies using the codification strategy thus typically deal with problems where the same solution can be applied many times. The "economics of reuse" is what motivates the KM efforts in these companies, and the KMS used are typically document management systems and databases.[22]

In contrast, when knowledge is tied to the individual that developed it and thus cannot be stored in a database, it has to be shared through face-to-face interactions. The role of the computers is thus to facilitate communication between people. Companies with this approach are said to follow a personalization strategy, and Hansen et al. mention McKinsey as a company in this category. In their company, knowledge emerges out of dialogues between individuals and their IT focus is thus to enable interactions between employees. Part of McKinsey's KM strategy is to move people between offices to expand their networks. Even though face-to-face meetings are unequalled for sharing tacit knowledge, space and time distances may sometime prevent people from physical meetings. McKinsey thus engage e-mail and video conferencing equipment to communicate and allow employees tap into the expertise of their peers. Companies following a personalization strategy typically deal with unique problems that do not have clear solutions and where customized answers must be provided. In "experts economics" knowledge is tacit and cannot be systematized and made efficient. Instead, these companies charge much higher prices, and KMS used are expert finder systems and communications software.[22]

Hansen et al. stress that companies should not try to combine these two strategies but, based on their business strategy, select one as their main KM strategy and merely use the other as a complementary strategy.

Knowledge Residence and Level of Structure

Adding another dimension to the tacit–explicit dichotomy, Hahn and Subramani present a framework for KMS by looking on the one hand at where the knowledge is said to reside (i.e., in artifacts or in people) and on the other hand to the extent to which knowledge is said to impose or require a priori structure. These axes form a two-by-two matrix hosting four different classes of KMS.[23]

- One is where the system manages knowledge artifacts that has an inherent structure or where the system imposes a structure on the artifacts. Formal document repositories and data warehouses belong to this class.
- A second class also requires a priori structure but manages links to knowledgeable people. A competence database intended to let employees find colleagues with specific skills falls into this class.
- A third class does not impose any structure in particular and assumes that knowledge is codified into artifacts. Intranets where Web pages and documents are found through full-text indexing search engines belong to this class.
- Finally, a fourth class again requires no structure but provides means for employees to identify and communicate with local experts. Discussion forums and e-mail Listservs are systems in this class.

Hahn and Subramani identify three interesting challenges regarding KMS. First, balancing information overload and potential useful content involves the size and diversity of both the users and the content. When the knowledge resides in artifacts, more items mean higher chances of being able to find what you need. Also when human resources are required, more users increase the possibilities of finding a knowledgeable coworker. The down side is that more information also means more unrelated or useless information, and more users typically generate more interactions and more e-mails, which blurs the picture. For the same reason is diversity useful, and no problem in highly structured environments, but when structures and shared vocabularies are lacking, diversity can easily get overwhelming.[23]

Second, balancing additional workload and accurate content addresses the issue of keeping KMS updated. Highly structured environments require considerable efforts to ensure the appropriateness of the structure,

and this work often comes on top of the employees' ordinary work tasks. In more loosely structured systems motivation to share knowledge often comes in the form of higher social status. The downside is that those who contribute and earn a reputation may end up being occupied answering people's questions and helping colleagues instead of doing their jobs.[23]

Third, balancing exploitation and exploration means being aware of the fact that reliance on existing solutions only may result in a competency trap.[24] A system that supports the exploitation of existing knowledge may provide short-term benefits but in the long run be detrimental to the organization. At the same time, a system preoccupied with generating new knowledge may prevent organizational members from learning and adding to the collective experience that exists in the organization.

Hahn and Subramani suggest the KMS should consider including agent technology, collaborative filtering methods, and advanced visualization tools, in order to address the above challenges.[23]

Alavi and Leidner's Scheme

Without suggesting an explicit framework, Alavi and Leidner in their review of the literature discussing applications of IT to knowledge management efforts, identify three common approaches: Coding and sharing of best practice, Creation of knowledge directories, and Creation of knowledge networks[13], [p. 114].

Coding and sharing of best practice is one of the most common applications of KMS, according to Alavi and Leidner. The term "best practice" is typically used to refer to a superior or exemplary practice that leads to superior performance. By collecting and codifying stories that mediate such practice, organizations can build KMS that stores and disseminates these experiences within the organization.

Creation of knowledge directories forms a second common class of KMS. Knowledge directories are also known as expert finder systems and aim at mapping the internal expertise of the organization. Alavi and Leidner report that 74% of the respondents in Gazeau's survey believed that their organization's most useful knowledge was not available in explicit form. When knowledge cannot be codified into artifacts, creating knowledge directories allows organizational members to benefit from the knowledge by being able to find and subsequently talk to the knowledgeable coworker.

Creation of knowledge networks is the third commonly used approach to KMS. Applications to first identify and then bring together (virtually or face-to-face) people from the same community of practice or those who share an interest has proven useful in many organizations. Ford Motor Company found that by sharing knowledge in networks the development, time for cars was reduced by 33%. Online forums belong to the technology used in this approach.[13]

We have seen that KMS can either be used to support a commodity view of KM, where the explication of knowledge is assumed not only to be possible but also necessary, or a community view of KM, where the implicit nature of knowing puts people in focus. The success of KMS (as with most IS) depends on the extent of use, which in turn depends on a number of factors. In their concluding discussion, Alavi and Leidner point to a set of research questions concerning the application of IT to KM. In sum, they ask what effect an increased breadth and depth of knowledge via KMS would have on organizational performance; how to ensure that knowledge in a KMS can be modified (if necessary) prior to being used, and how these modifications too can be captured; how anonymized knowledge in a KMS can be trusted; and what are the quality and usefulness factors of KMS.[13] The answers to many of these questions are still pending.

ONTOLOGICAL ASPECTS

It has often been argued that only individuals can think and act—not organizations. At the same time, as human beings we are social creatures and we tend to seek, and benefit from, each other's company. Inputs from colleagues and the surrounding context greatly affect our ability to create and use knowledge because the individual and the collective interact in fruitful ways. Focusing primarily on how new knowledge emerges, Nonaka and Takeuchi stress the fact that knowledge creation initiates from the individual but is a process that moves through expanding communities of interaction, crossing group, division, and, finally, organizational boundaries.[11] Other scholars have made similar comments about other KM processes.

Still, IT support for KM has traditionally focused on organizational-wide systems, possibly due to the acknowledged fact that the usefulness of a KMS grows exponentially with the size of the organization. Much of the IS research has thus had a macro-level focus, but also applications supporting organizational learning and organizational memory are common in the KMS repertoire. The challenge associated with organizational KMS is that individuals often have to provide input without getting much back in return. This problem, often referred to as the maintenance problem seriously threatens the quality and usefulness of these systems.

Another category of KMS are the groupware systems targeting smaller subsets of the organization, typically aiming for management. This category includes various types of Decision Support Systems (DSS). Many KMS in this category can also be related to the field of Computer-Supported Collaborative Work (CSCW). Typical applications here include Helpdesk applications and expert finder systems within specific subgroups. The maintenance problem continues to be a challenge also at this level.

When it comes to the individual, there has—until recently—not been equally much support. Some argue that this situation is about to change. One of the problems here is that not all of the applications used at an individual level are officially labeled KMS. For example, the information retrieval (IR) field has provided the knowledge worker with search engines and other tools to help locate information, but not all would agree that a search engine is a KMS. Another noticeable trend is the growth of social media. These applications exploit the individual–collective relationship and are able to provide the individual with added value through the actions of the collective relationship and vice versa. It will be interesting to follow this development to see whether social media will provide a means to avoid, if not solve, the maintenance problem.

THE KMS CHALLENGES

A number of KMS challenges can be identified in the KM literature. One issue is that of dispersion of work. It is argued that knowledge workers are increasingly dispersed—spatial as well as contractual.[25] Organizational members work outside the physical boundaries of the firm and/or change positions within the firm, often including geographical changes. This, it is argued, makes them less exposed to colleagues with similar functional skills.

There is also the contractual dispersion, i.e., the provisional nature of employment and the higher level of partial or temporary involvement in the firm that many knowledge workers experience. In addition, many are engaged in virtual teams that often reorganize and have high turnover rates. This dispersion of work requires KMS that allows for effective sharing of the latest knowledge.[25,26]

Another issue is the shorter product and process life cycles in today's organizations.[26] This compresses the time window for capturing the lessons learned and knowledge created in the process and leaves the knowledge workers with little time to document and save their experiences. At the same time knowledge becomes obsolete much quicker. KMS need to be able to deal effectively with these circumstances.

The above concerns can be seen as aspects of a larger and overarching challenge, i.e., how to keep KMS updated and current. While many of today's organizations expect KMS to become major catalysts for innovations in terms of the ways in which businesses can be organized and conducted, there is plenty of IS research that indicate that such systems often fail when implemented in everyday knowledge work. In response, a distinguishable issue in KMS research is how to support knowledge work with IS in a successful way. It has been found that although the systems work technically and should function well in theory, they remain unused by the organizational members.[27] Following this, the development of systems with the capacity to bridge the knowing-doing gap in organizations has been recognized as a significant area of KMS research.

However, the imbalance between the desire for accurate content and the workload required to achieve this still appears to be a critical problem, leading to systems of little use for organizations in their knowledge application processes. It has been suggested that the problem stems from the fact that the requirements for KMS are fundamentally different from those of other types of IT and are thus not covered by existing IS design theories.

Markus et al. have identified three primary differences.[28] First, knowledge work processes requires that expert knowledge is adapted and/or contextualized to specific local conditions. Decision support systems and executive IS do not provide system features that can handle expert knowledge or contextualize translation rules. Resulting from this, DSS and expert systems inhibit creative problem finding and solution generation. While expert systems manage general expert knowledge, they fail to support contextual knowledge and the flexibility needed for process emergence. Second, these types of systems are all specifically designed for a known type of user, e.g., managers. Being designed for a particular type of user community, these systems are not well adapted to emergent work processes characterized by shifting user types having varying knowledge requirements. Third, knowledge workers have access to many different types of systems but since these systems often are isolated and not integrated into work practice, knowledge workers tend to manage their systems rather than getting the job done.

To circumvent these problems, it has been suggested that KMS should be integrated with or built into already existing applications since key to a successful KMS is to facilitate usage.[29] As knowledge work requires creativity in order to produce idiosyncratic and esoteric knowledge, knowledge work practice is untidy compared to operational or administrative business processes. Hence, KMS must be able to go beyond written instructions and official task descriptions, thus appreciating exceptions not only as something inevitable but as a necessity. Consequently, KMS must not be isolated but should be integrated into work practice. For the purpose of avoiding situations where knowledge workers manage their systems rather than getting the job done, developers must recognize sociotechnical issues associated with

disparity in work and benefit. In this way, KMS capable of attracting a critical mass of users can be developed. In addition, paying attention to unobtrusive accessibility and the adoption process may deepen developers' understanding of how support systems can be better integrated with both the day-to-day tasks of knowledge workers and their performance of the tasks.

CONCLUDING SUMMARY

In the 1990s there was a rather heated debate whether or not KM was a fad but this seems to have abated. Now, there is consensus that KM—at least as a pragmatic issue—is here to stay. With knowledge replacing economy of scale as business driver and with increasing portion of knowledge workers in today's organizations, knowledge management, and the need for IT support for it, is not likely to go away.

The strong focus on technology that we witnessed in early KM work has been compensated for and practitioners and researchers alike now have acknowledged that knowledge cannot exist outside the mind of a human being. Cultures that encourage and motivate individuals to share, combine, and reuse knowledge are recognized as equal, if not more, important as IT, even amongst technologists. IT is still likely to continue to play an important part, not as driver and single success factor but as catalyst, facilitator and enabler of social networks, virtual meeting places, and new discussion forums. One of the general lessons learned is that technology is important and useful but it should not be the driving force in KM work.

Several commentators have pointed to the fact that KMS in the late 1990s were discrete, stand-alone systems not aligned with the organizations' business processes. Such systems had to be explicitly attended to on top of ordinary tasks, thus adding to—not facilitating—the work to be carried out.[29] Newer KMS appear to be better integrated with existing business infrastructure and enterprise applications, thereby allowing employees to seamlessly apply organizational knowledge in whatever work they are engaged. However, there is still a need for development and research in this area.

On the theoretical side, no core theory on knowledge management has yet been developed, and KM may still be understood as an "umbrella construct," i.e., a broad and somewhat unclear label that is used to contain a whole variety of loosely connected issues.[30] Without a clear theoretical focus, some commentators argue, the original concept risks being eroded until it has no value and collapses, as researchers explore divergent paths and build isolated islands of knowledge. Spender[31] has argued strongly that KM and KMS research need a core theory that distinguishes them from other fields but at

Knowledge– Mobile

the same time is narrow enough to allow laypeople to recognize and understand what is and what is not a KMS. Not much work is currently to be found along such lines.

In their editorial introduction to the 2003 special issue on KM and IT in *IT and People*, Gray and Meister argue that KMS researchers are facing a bigger problem than did researchers of earlier organizational phenomena, since knowledge is neither new nor physically present and there is thus nothing concrete to point to. An independent core theory of KM and KMS is therefore needed, they argue.[32]

However, several future scenarios are possible. If the development towards more knowledge work continues, we may end up in the scenario predicted by Davenport and Grover where "every industry will view itself as knowledge-intensive."[4, p. 4] If everything is KM, will the concept then still be meaningful, and if every application is a KMS, will the term be useful? At the other end of the spectrum lies a scenario where KM becomes so diversified and scattered that for this reason is pointless to talk about KM and IT support for it. Where will we end up remains to be seen.

REFERENCES

1. Voelpel, S.; Dous, M.; Davenport, T. Five steps to creating a global knowledge-sharing system: Siemens' ShareNet. Acad. Manage. Execut. **2005**, *19* (2), 9–23.

2. Galliers, R.; Newell, S. Back to the future: From knowledge management to data management. Proceedings of European Conference on Information Systems 2001, Bled, Slovenia, June, 27–29, 2001; 609–615.

3. Cronin, B. Introduction. In *Information Management: From Strategies to Action*; Cronin, B., Ed.; Aslib: London, 1985; vii–ix.

4. Davenport, T.H.; Grover, V. Editorial: Special issue on knowledge management. J. Manage. Inform. Syst. **2001**, *18* (1), 3–4.

5. Swan, J.; Scarbrough, H.; Preston, J. Knowledge management—The next fad to forget people. Proceedings of European Conference on Information Systems 1999, Copenhagen, Denmark, June, 23–25, 1999; 668–678.

6. Maier, R. In *Knowledge Management Systems*, 2nd Ed.; Springer: Berlin, 2004.

7. Butler, T. From data to knowledge and back again: Understanding the limitations of KMS. Knowledge Process Management **2003**, *10* (3), 144–155.

8. Tiwana, A. In *The Knowledge Management Toolkit: Practical Techniques for Building Knowledge Management Systems*; Pearson Education: Upper Saddle River, NJ, 1999.

9. Sveiby, K.E.; Lloyd, T. In *Managing Know-How*; Bloomsbury: London, 1987.

10. Wiig, K.M. Management of knowledge: Perspectives of a new opportunity. In *User interfaces: Gateway or bottleneck?*, Bernold, T., Ed.; Gottlieb Duttweiler Institute: Zurich, 1988; 101–116.

11. Nonaka, I.; Takeuchi, H. In *The Knowledge-Creating Company: How Japanese Companies Create the Dynamics of Innovation*; Oxford University Press: Oxford, 1995.

12. Spender, J.-C. Making knowledge the basis of a dynamic theory of the firm. Strateg. Manage. J. **1996**, *17*, 45–62 Winter Special Issue.

13. Alavi, A.; Leidner, D. Review: Knowledge management and knowledge management systems: Conceptual foundations and research issues. MIS Q. **2001**, *25* (1), 107–136.

14. Wilson, T.D. The nonsense of knowledge management. Inform. Res. **2002**, *8* (1), paper no. 144. http://informationr.net/ir/8–1/paper144.html (accessed December 2008).

15. Tsoukas, H. The firm as a distributed knowledge system: A constructionist approach. Strateg. Manage. J. **1996**, (17), 11–25 Winter Special Issue.

16. Choo, C.W. In *The Knowing Organization*; Oxford University Press: Oxford, 1998.

17. Blackler, F. Knowledge, knowledge work and organizations: an overview and interpretation. Organ. Stud. **1995**, *16* (6), 1021–1046.

18. Swan, J.; Scarbrough, H. Knowledge management: Concepts and controversies. J. Manage. Stud. **2001**, *38* (7), 913–921.

19. Schultze, U. A confessional account of an ethnography about knowledge work. Manage. Inform. Syst. Quart. **2000**, *24* (1), 3–41.

20. Stenmark, D. Information vs. knowledge: The role of intranets in knowledge management. Proceedings of HICSS-35, Hawaii, January, 7–10, 2002.

21. Schultze, U.; Leidner, D. Studying knowledge management in information systems research: Discourses and theoretical assumptions. Manage. Inform. Syst. Quart. **2002**, *26* (3), 213–242.

22. Hansen, M.; Nohria, N.; Tierney, T. What's your strategy for managing knowledge?. Harvard Bus. Rev. **1999**, March–April, *77* (2), 106–116.

23. Hahn, J.; Subramani, M. A framework of knowledge management systems: Issues and challenges for theory and practice. Proceedings of International Conference on Information Systems 2000, Brisbane, Australia, December, 10–13, 2000; 302–312.

24. Levitt, B.; March, J.G. Organizational learning. Annu. Rev. Sociol. **1988**, *14*, 319–340.

25. Corso, M.; Martini, A.; Pellegrini, L.; Massa, S.; Testa, S. Managing dispersed workers: The new challenge in knowledge management. Technovation **2006**, *26* (5–6), 583–594.

26. Donnellan, B.; Fitzgerald, B. Developing systems to support organisational learning in product development organisations. Electron. J. Knowl. Manage. **2003**, *1* (2), 33–46.

27. Schultze, U.; Boland, R.J. Knowledge management technology and the reproduction of knowledge work practices. J. Strateg. Inform. Syst. **2000**, *9* (2–3), 193–212.

28. Markus, L.M.; Majchrzak, A.; Gasser, L. A design theory for systems that support emergent knowledge processes. Manage. Inform. Syst. Quart. **2002**, *26*, 179–212.

Knowledge–
Mobile

29. Stenmark, D.; Lindgren, R. System support for knowledge work: Bridging the knowing-doing gap. Intl. J. Knowl. Manage. **2006**, *2* (2), 46–68.

30. Hirsch, P.; Levin, D. Umbrella advocates versus validity police: A life-cycle model. Organ. Sci. **1999**, *10* (2), 199–212.

31. Spender, J.-C. Exploring uncertainty and emotion in the knowledge-based theory of the firm. Inform. Technol. People **2003**, *16* (3), 266–288.

32. Gray, P.H.; Meister, D.B. Introduction: Fragmentation and integration in knowledge management research. Inform. Technol. People **2003**, *16* (3), 259–265.

BIBLIOGRAPHY

General KM

1. Davenport, T.H.; Prusak, V. In *Working Knowledge: How Organizations Manage What They Know*; Harvard Business School Press: Boston, MA, 1997.

Knowledge Management Systems

2. In *Knowledge Management Systems: Theory and Practice,* Barnes, S., Ed.; Thomson learning: London, 2002.

3. Malhotra, Y. Why knowledge management systems fail? Enablers and constraints of knowledge management in human enterprises. In *Handbook on Knowledge Management 1: Knowledge Matters*; Holsapple, Ed.; Springer-Verlag: Berlin, 2002; 577–599.

4. Rubenstein, A.H.; Geisler, E. In *Installing and Managing Workable Knowledge Management Systems*; Greenwood Publishing Group Inc.: Westport, CT, 2003.

5. In *Knowledge Management Tools*; Ruggles, R.L., Ed.; Butterworth Heinemann: Boston, MA, 1997.

Location-Based Services

Ben Falchuk
Dave Famolari
Shoshana Loeb
Telcordia Technologies, Inc., Piscataway, New Jersey, U.S.A.

Abstract

Location-based services (LBSs) allow service providers to target customers and offer them services specifically tailored to where they are and what they need at a given moment in time and a given location in space. LBSs have the power to transform mobile services, making interactions more relevant, timely, and personal. Many factors contribute to successful LBSs, including positioning technologies, service policies, and content adaptation and personalization. Major communication providers, equipment providers, and application developers are actively supporting LBS standards development to encourage major roll outs of LBSs.

INTRODUCTION

Location-based services (LBSs) use the power of mobile networks to locate users and provide services specific to their present location. Imagine:

- You are about to call your boss, but when you highlight his or her name in your address book, you see that she or he is in a different time zone where it is the middle of the night. You decide to leave a voicemail instead.
- You are in a crowded theater and your phone automatically silences itself for all but the most urgent calls.
- You are wandering through the Museum of Natural History. As you pass each piece, exhibit-specific audio and video information is delivered to your mobile device.
- You are at the airport and your phone beeps to tell you that an old friend you have not seen in years is sitting at Gate 7 and looking for someone to have dinner with.

All of these scenarios (see Fig. 1 for illustration) are made possible by location-awareness and presence (e.g., see Internet Engineering Task Force or IETF.[11])—two concepts that are making their way into mobile devices and promising to enhance everything from social networking to marketing and advertising. Location-awareness enables a device (and the person carrying it) to be geographically located and presence allows a user to know the status of another user.

Mobile operators have been talking about LBSs since the end of the last decade but have yet to find ways to commercialize them successfully on large scales. An archetypal example of such earlier attempts includes services in which advertisers and individuals seeking social networking send information invites via Bluetooth. These services failed to gain much attraction because users did not like or trust them. Privacy and confidentiality of location information are important issues that must be addressed before consumers will be willing to adopt LBSs. With the greater adoption of Web-based and cellular services over the last few years, however, the general public appears more willing now to accept certain LBSs.

As discussed in the following section, many technologies can provide position fixes for mobile terminals. All vary depending whether the network or the edge device initiates the query and the degree to which each party participates in the positioning. Some technologies, such as the global positioning system (GPS) can operate completely independent and separate from the mobile operator. This enables third party LBS application development that can more quickly accelerate deployment and adoption of LBSs than solutions that are tightly controlled by the carrier.

The inclusion of GPS receivers in mobile handsets could jump-start LBS. ABI Research predicts that by 2011, there will be 315 million GPS subscribers for LBSs, up from a mere 12 million this year (see http://www.abiresearch.com). The mobile industry is now favoring applications, such as turn-by-turn directions and other navigation services, through which they bring functionality typically associated with in-car GPSs to the mobile device (see http://www.fiercewireless.com for details on such industry trends).

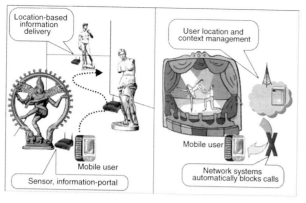

Fig. 1 Two conceptual notions of LBS, museum (left) and theatre (right).

SURVEY OF POSITIONING TECHNOLOGIES

This section outlines a variety of positioning technologies that form the basis of many LBSs. For more details, readers should refer to resources such as Kupper.[2]

GPS: The GPS is perhaps the most well-known positioning technology. It relies on a system of 24 or more geosynchronous satellites to broadcast references signals constantly to end devices, or GPS receivers. In addition to the satellites, GPS relies on monitoring stations placed on the ground at specific positions around the world; these stations control the operation and synchronization of the satellites by monitoring their orbits and tracking offsets between their internal clocks. To localize a GPS receiver in three dimensions, the receiver must be able to decode signals from four separate GPS satellites. The distribution of satellite orbits is therefore designed to ensure that every part of the earth is visible by at least four GPS satellites at any given time. GPS satellites transmit pilot codes that GPS receivers use to determine their range from the satellite. The satellites also transmit navigation information that helps the receiver determine the present position of the satellite as well as the satellite's clock offset. Using range measurements together with the locations of those satellites, a GPS receiver can determine its location in the neighborhood to within an accuracy of a few tens of meters. Various modifications and enhancements to the GPS can improve the position accuracy to within 10 m.

Although GPS is widely available, it suffers from a few drawbacks, the principle of which is the inability to receive satellite signals indoors and in high multipath environments. As a consequence, LBSs based on GPS positioning technologies may fail when there is no direct line of sight between the receiver and the GPS satellites. In addition, performing the initial synchronization of the GPS satellites can be time-consuming and can result in large "time to first fix," or TTFFs. Depending on the nature of the LBS, this value can be critical to the

usability and utility of the service. Another potential drawback of GPS for LBS in the cellular context is the reliance on devices with GPS receivers. These receivers add bulk and drain battery resources. However, manufacturers are increasingly integrating GPS chips into cellular handsets. In the United States, cellular service providers are required to meet so called E-911 regulations that require them to locate a cellular phone to within a few hundred meters for emergency purposes. To meet this need many providers have mandated that all their phones include GPS Locator chips that provide location assistance in case of emergency. These Locator chips are not fully functional GPS receivers and do not provide the capability to track users or support LBSs.

Enhancements to the GPS were designed to combat some of these drawbacks. In particular, carriers have begun implementing systems that assist the GPS by broadcasting additional reference signals to handsets. This technique is referred to as assisted-GPS (A-GPS), and carriers broadcast pilot signals from their fixed infrastructure that the terminal combines with GPS information to make a more accurate determination of its location. A-GPS addresses the inability to receive GPS signals indoors or without direct line of sight, and can significantly improve the accuracy of GPS position fixes in areas of high multipath such as urban areas.

Enhanced Observed Time Difference (E-OTD) and Uplink Time Difference of Arrival (U-TDoA): E-OTD and U-TDoA are positioning technologies that rely not on satellites, but on the cellular infrastructure for reference information. With E-OTD, the framing structure of the Global System for Mobile Communications (GSM) frame is used as a reference point to determine the flight times of GSM signals transmitted from the base station. As radio signals travel at the speed of light, a known quantity, flight times provide the terminal with the range from its present location to the base station. E-OTD, however, requires an additional element in the network to collect transmitted signals and compare them with those received by the terminal. This is the job of location measurement units (LMUs). LMUs are scattered throughout a provider's network and provide an additional set of measurements that can be used to determine offsets and to account for synchronization errors between the terminal and the base stations. E-OTD requires a good deal of synchronization between the terminal and a set of nearby base stations, between the LMU and the same set of base stations, as well as between the terminal and the LMU. This level of coordination can lengthen the initial time to acquire a position fix. To alleviate this issue, GSM operators tend to synchronize their LMUs periodically with nearby base stations. E-OTD does not require the terminal to make any ranging transmission to support the localization process and relies on terminal reception only. Thus, a terminal may remain in the idle mode while assisting in the localization process.

U-TDoA is similar in concept to E-OTD, however, it relies on the terminal to transmit ranging messages so that those signal arrival times may be measured at different LMUs and base stations. Thus, the transmitting and receiving responsibilities of the base stations and terminals are reversed in U-TDoA. In GSM systems, a mobile terminal can only transmit to one base station at a time, therefore LMUs are required to listen to the ranging transmission to correlate reception characteristics at different locations. In E-OTD, a single LMU is required, whereas in U-TDoA, multiple LMUs must be in range of the terminal and base stations. Also, as localization requires terminal transmissions, terminals must be in the active mode to participate in the localization process. Finally, dedicated software is required on the mobile terminals to support the localization process in E-OTD; however, as the terminal's only role in U-TDoA is the transmission of GSM data frames, no such software is required for U-TDoA positioning.

Observed Time Difference of Arrival (OTDoA): E-OTD and U-TDoA both rely on the GSM framing structure to derive timing estimates and ranges. OTDoA, however, is designed for CDMA (code division multiple access)-based cellular systems. OTDoA follows the same concepts as those of E-OTD and U-TDoA, namely to rely on transmitted signals to derive range estimates from known locations. OTDoA, differs because CDMA systems do not have a strictly synchronized framing structure as GSM and CDMA terminals are also capable of transmitting to multiple CDMA base stations simultaneously. Although the framing structure in CDMA is not synchronized, all CDMA base stations are synchronized and transmit a high-frequency pilot code that terminals can use to determine range and timing offsets accurately. A consequence of base station synchronization in CDMA is that LMUs are not needed. OTDoA operates in a similar fashion as that of E-OTD. Terminals decode pilot channel signals from nearby base stations to determine range estimates between its present location and the known locations of the base stations. Both systems provide roughly equivalent accuracy as well, and both systems require that the mobile terminals have dedicated software to assist in the localization process.

Ultrawideband: A few researchers and small companies (as well as the U.S. military) are looking at ultra wideband (UWB), as a promising location detection technology. UWB uses very short bursts of radio energy to perform precise ranging and synchronization measurements. The technology is extremely accurate (to within a few centimeter) and also requires very little power to operate. The technology has showed strong promise for performing indoor localization.

Wi-Fi positioning: Cellular and satellite positioning services generally perform worse indoors than they do outdoors. This limitation is principally due to the high multipath environment indoors that can affect timing measurements. During the mid-1990s, new wireless networking standards, collectively known as Wi-Fi, began to gain traction in homes and businesses. Today, Wi-Fi systems are widely deployed and provide an additional component for determining position. Wi-Fi networks are defined as wireless LANs and are generally small in range—in the order of up to 100 m in coverage. Although the indoor environment is not well suited for positioning technologies based on time difference arrival, the WLAN community has focused its positioning efforts on received signal strength. These systems estimate a terminal's position by comparing its received signal strength against previously recorded values at known locations. These techniques require a good deal of training to develop signal maps that serve as the reference basis for the positioning technology. This training involves taking a number of signal strength measurements at known locations and storing them in a database. When fulfilling a positioning request, the terminal sends the network its received signal strength information. The network consults the database and uses estimation and approximation algorithms to determine the location that provides the least estimation error. Wi-Fi positioning techniques attempt to tackle the problems caused by the indoor radio environment. Some systems, such as those commercially offered by Ekahau (see http://www.ekahau.com) offer accuracies in the order of a few meters. However, diligent training and maintenance are required to keep the signal maps updated. Also these signal maps can vary widely. Changes in the number of people present, the deployment of new access points, rearrangement of furniture, and differences in receiver sensitivities can all alter the signal maps and result in inaccurate readings.

TYPES OF LBSS

Due to the somewhat elusive definition of LBS in the academic literature, the scope of LBSs is large and opinions differ on what exactly comprises an LBS. This section lists some examples of LBS along with brief descriptions; subsequent sections present in more detail the functional components required to make these services a reality and the reader should explore the references for more specific information. The information below illustrates a wide range of LBSs—many more are possible:

- Navigation:

Knowledge— Mobile

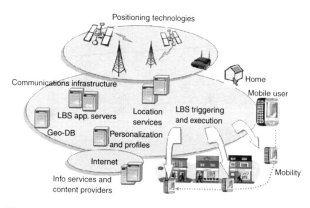

Fig. 2 LBS ecosystem.

- ○ Driving directions: e.g., sending turn-by-turn navigation directions to automobiles.
- ○ Traffic alerts: e.g., sending alerts to automotive users approaching heavy traffic areas.
- • Information:
  - ○ Advertising: coupons and sales, e.g., pushing information to mobile users about local stores and products, including redeemable coupons.
  - ○ Travel: location-based travel and tourist information, e.g., dialing a number may provide more historic information about a local monument.
  - ○ Search: e.g., searching for information that is relevant to a present location.
- • Tracking:
  - ○ Fleet-tracking: e.g., keeping track of service vehicles and their locations.
  - ○ People-tracking: e.g., keeping tabs on family members, getting notices when they roam out of predefined areas.
- • Emergency assistance and calling for mobile users.
- • Communication services options:
  - ○ Using dual mode (Wi-Fi and cellular) phones opportunistically according to prevailing local conditions.[3]
  - ○ Seamless session continuity between cellular and Wi-Fi networks.
- • Leisure and gaming:
  - ○ Finding "buddies," friends, and dates close to you at a given time.
  - ○ *Geocaching* and *geodashing*: "hide-and-seek" type gaming using GPS-enabled mobile devices.

LBS ECOSYSTEM

Providing end-to-end mobile LBS requires the coordination of many systems. Although to some extent each communication provider has their own infrastructure into which LBS functionality would be provisioned, there are certain largely agreed-upon functional requirements that all such systems share. This section describes

these high-level functions and puts them together in a simplified context. Fig. 2 shows that positioning technologies (e.g., cellular, satellite-based, Wi-Fi, or other) allow ongoing positioning of a mobile user. A core communications infrastructure hosts the application servers and other management servers [e.g., authentication, accounting—see 3rd generation partnership project (3GPP) IP multimedia subsystem (IMS) architectures] that together comprise LBS logic and delivers services to mobile users. The LBS may make use of other arbitrary information services in the core or in the Internet. Among other things, the geographic information systems or geographic databases (Geo-DBs) allow conversion of geographic coordinates, generation of addresses from coordinates, and layered map creation. A simple scenario is as follows: When a mobile user migrates from her home through an urban environment, e.g., her location is updated in core servers, such as those providing cellular service. At each such update LBS applications may be triggered; each service exploits the user's details, profiles, and location (perhaps filtered through a Geo-DB) and triggers some information delivery to the user (perhaps gathered from third party Internet-based content providers).

In a prototypical case the information relates to the stores nearby the user and personalizes the information to the specific user (perhaps by referring to a user-specific profile). See 3GPP for further rigorous LBS use-cases through the various LBS infrastructure components.

EMERGING SUPPORT IN STANDARDS BODIES

The notion of LBS is supported in several key geographic and wireless standards bodies (see Mopahatra and Suma[4] for details). The open mobile alliance comprises the world's leading communication providers; among its foci is the mobile location protocol (MLP) which is, "an application-level protocol for obtaining the position of mobile stations... independent of underlying network technology. The MLP serves as the interface between a Location Server and a Location Services Client" (cited from http://www.openmobilealliance.org). The IETF stewards a protocol called spatial location protocol which allows a client to "talk about" the spatial location of an Internet resource in a canonical way. The open geospatial consortium, comprised of over 200 companies and agencies, has defined a number of specifications that help with interoperability of LBS. These standards bodies—and others—have a keen focus on supporting LBS and have already provided valuable and relevant specifications.

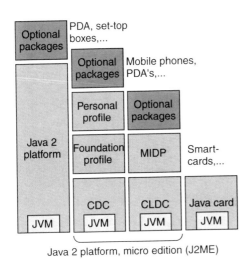

Fig. 3 Java stack highlighting layers related to mobile computing.

EMERGING SUPPORT IN MIDDLEWARE AND PROGRAMMING TOOLS

LBSs are typically delivered to, or executed upon, mobile handsets. Today's predominant mobile operating systems (OSs) include:

- Symbian
- Microsoft Windows Mobile
- Palm OS
- Linux

These OSs have a spectrum of capabilities to support LBS. Key to developing device-resident LBS applications for the mobile handsets is the availability of integrated development environments. Microsoft's *Visual Studio* and Sun's *Java Studio* (and *NetBeans Mobility Pack*) are two such environments, providing major support for mobile application development. Note that to implement a successful LBS on a device, a developer needs middleware and OS support not only for location application programming interfaces (APIs), but also for other important aspects of intelligent networked services such as communication stacks (e.g., transmission control protocol/IP (TCP/IP), Bluetooth), protocol stacks (e.g., HTTP), web services, and XML, to name only a few.

Software development kits (SDKs) offer the underlying support and APIs allow developers to write quickly source code that makes use of lower level LBS enablers, shielding the developer from their implementation complexity. Java 2 Platform, Micro Edition (J2ME), e.g., is a technical platform used for LBS implementations (especially on the client-side). Fig. 3 illustrates the architecture of the Java and J2ME stack. Standard device profiles and optional packages allow systematic cross-platform development of mobile Java applications. The figure shows that, for execution of Java upon a

mobile phone, the phone runs a Java Virtual Machine (JVM). The JVM runs according to a so-called Connected Limited Device Configuration (CLDC); this means that the JVM and its APIs are tailored to run on a certain set of limited capability devices. The Mobile Information Device Profile (MIDP) sits atop the CLDC and provides add-on APIs for the developer that remains compliant with CLDC; e.g., MIDP2.0 defines media, game, and messaging APIs for developers. Armed with these tools, the developer can more easily and effectively write cross-platform LBSs for mobile phones written in Java.

EXISTINGCOMMERCIAL TRENDS

This section outlines some commercial and grassroot trends by providing general descriptions and examples where possible. Although the service providers mentioned here may come and go over time, the themes they represent should be valid for much longer. Note that we are not interested here in cases in which online services are simply made available as wireless application protocol pages. For example, one of the web's most visited sites, eBay, makes its auction portal available via mobile devices. Such an initiative, however, does not exploit user-location in any deep way. Flash-point LBSs at the time of writing are mapping and directions, navigation, tourism, people- and fleet-tracking, trip planning, and real-time traffic information. These and others are outlined below.

People-Tracking and Personalized Services

Wireless people-tracking refers to the technique of locating an individual user in terms of geospatial coordinates (see previous sections for techniques) and exploiting this information in some useful way. While fleet-tracking via in-truck GPS-receivers is a common practice, offering value-adding LBS directly to mobile customers is seen by operators as a possible windfall of revenues. That is why peopletracking and related services are becoming very compelling—a *person* with a GPS receiver in hand cannot only be tracked but can also be offered information and m-commerce services at any moment in time for which they will pay a service fee. For years radio-frequency technologies have been used to ensure that criminals on probation remain inside the home; nowadays, cheaper GPS technologies allow some jurisdictions to track parolees on a very fine level with GPS "bracelets." In the commercial world, one trend sees middle-class families with wireless telephony services paying for child or family-tracking services from their providers. These services use location technologies such as GPS or cellular-based positioning to monitor if and when a child moves out of a specified region. If the child does break the region's virtual "barrier," the parent is notified. In 2006, *Verizon Wireless* began offering a similar service called *Chaperone* in which the child is given her own wireless phone that, in turn, enables several tracking modes for parents. In the same year, *Sprint Nextel* began offering a service called *Family Locator* that allows all family members to be tracked and monitored. These and other services typically require special equipment, mobile application software installation, and incur extra premiums on monthly bills.

Social networking applications such as dating and meet-up services have experienced something of a renaissance at the time of writing. Today's dating services can take advantage of ubiquitous Internet access, IM, and cellular networks. Many dating services now incorporate location information. The company *Meet-moi.com* allows daters to update not only their personal profiles but also their locations. Once the server understands the user location, it can send the user a list of other singles (and their short message service handles) that happen to be presently in the same geographic area. Messaging and meet-ups can then occur between the singles. *Proxidating.com* is a similar LBS dating service that relies on daters having Bluetooth receivers coming into range of each other and exchanging compatibility profiles. Other more technically advanced dating services will be able to infer singles' latitude/longitude coordinates seamlessly through a location service provider and offer a variety of meet-up possibilities.

With respect to automotive telematics, service providers can mine GPS receivers inside vehicles to glean useful information including vehicle location, trajectory, route and so on, and can then provide the driver with conditions that should be expected to encounter in the coming minutes (e.g., based on the car's trajectory). Such services are offered by major telecom and telematics providers. Adaptive route planning (navigation) is also a widespread LBS in which a vehicle's present location, destination, and road conditions in-between, are constantly monitored to provide an optimal journey.

Opportunistic M-Commerce

LBS allow service providers to find customers that are most likely to consume their services and to make the best use of *where they are* at a *given moment in time*. Loki.com is one of several services that deliver location-based information to a laptop independently from cellular network visibility. It achieves this by intermittently reporting the set of Wi-Fi access points that the laptop sees to its servers; the server then attempts to infer the user's location based upon a database of known access points (correlated to geo-locations). After this succeeds, Loki.com is able to pass the location

information along to third party plug-in modules that, in turn, provide various location-based information such as weather, traffic, and shopping bargains on a web browser toolbar. Elsewhere, most of the main online search and map providers (e.g., Google, Yahoo!) hold important LBS information. Not surprisingly, all enable mobile users to transmit their location and do "local searches." The results are the set of services matching the search query that are within some distance of the searcher's location (e.g., their zone improvement plan code or address). Searching for a local "pizza restaurant" or for local "movie listings" are prototypical examples.

Service providers are also turning to online video games as an outlet for LBS. Online games such as *World of Warcraft* and *Second Life* offer gamers rich three-dimensional environments in which their avatars interact with the environment and with other peers. *Microsoft's* 2006 purchase of *Massive* signals that in-game advertisements are deemed valuable; Massive specializes in technology that allows advertisers to inject dynamic logos and custom information onto virtual billboards in three-dimensional (online) video games. Though no fine-grain (or 1-to-1) billboard personalization has occurred at the time of writing, it is likely that eventually individual gamers will see virtual billboards that are targeted either directly to them or to small groups of players (who inhabit the same part of the world). Although these billboards will begin as static imagery, they could also constitute codes and coupons that unlock discounts on real-world or in-game goods and services.

Recreational and Grassroots

As GPS receivers have shrunk and become highly portable and affordable, more and more interesting grassroot uses of geospatial information have been demonstrated. Not all of these constitute services per se, but all show tremendous promise. Geocaching[5] is a social game played by a large number of users. Not unlike orienteering or hide-and-seek, the game is about navigating to and finding treasures located in various disparate regions. Once the treasure is found, the user gets to relocate parts of the treasure to some new position and challenge others to navigate to it. Though played largely as open source and free, there are obvious advertising possibilities for this sport. Geodashing is a game in which users armed with GPS receivers race to pass through a set of geospatial coordinates which together form a so-called dash. Finally, other grassroot use of GPS information and geospatial information includes GPS way-pointing and GPS drawings. In the former, users document interesting locations through text annotations, photos, and other links (e.g., to services); these can be used by other users as a sort of guidebook to local information. GPS drawing is an experimental phenomenon among conceptual artists who, with logging enabled on their GPS receivers, trace out (sometimes enormous) shapes on the earth and upload the logs to a server where they can be displayed (see Falchuk[6] for an architecture to support this in a systematic, large-scale fashion). Geotagging is the process by which imagery or photographs are tagged with geospatial coordinates. This is a specialization of photo tagging, given mass-market appeal most notably by Flickr.com and Zoomr.com.

There are several LBS possibilities in which location information is related to IM. A "where are my buddies" service for IM clients has gained in popularity. This service is available, e.g., as an open source plug-in to AOL's AIM and revolves around IM users receiving notification whenever one of their buddies registers a location that is less than some threshold distance away from their own. At the time of writing, similar services, with names like *Buddy Beacon* and *Boost Loopt*, were being offered by major telecom providers. Such a scenario is sometimes generally referred to as context-sensitive computing or location-aware computing.[7] At the writing, research has delivered several wireless context-based systems;[8] is a prototypical one. In context-sensitive systems, the computing platform gathers and understands aspects of the mobile user's surroundings (i.e., context), including but not limited to her location, activities, photographs taken, messages, etc. By correlating and aggregating user-context information, a deep understanding of user-needs can be inferred and as a result deeply targeted services can be offered by an LBS provider.

EXISTING AND FUTURE CHALLENGES

LBS creation is an ongoing research issue. Traditional intelligent network communication services have been designed and created on graphical SDKs emphasizing events and flow-control. IMS and implementations of location enablers must be programmatically integrated with services at creation-time. This LBS service creation tools have become more complex.[9] LBS SDKs have emerged from various vendors. It is thought that these tools must continue to improve to better support LBS development. Some of the salient issues include:

- Making LBS portable across devices; and
- Separating concerns of LBS creation and provisioning.

These issues and others are being considered by various standards and industry organizations (e.g., 3GPP, open mobile alliance, Europe-based *Information Society Technologies*—http://cordis.europa.eu/ist/).

Although LBSs attempt to provide users with value based on their present location, other geospatial attributes—such as the user's speed or acceleration—are also important. Research illustrates that as LBS becomes more peer-to-peer (i.e., services beneficial to one mobile user are located on another mobile user's platform) these attributes should come into play (e.g., see Falchuk and Marples[10]). Privacy is another flash-point in LBS; it has several dimensions:

- Users do not want providers to abuse the location or context information that they may have logged about them.
- Users should be allowed to remain anonymous from service providers and other users where possible.
- Effective identity and consent management are essential.

Detailed studies of these and other related issues can be found in the literature.[11,12]

CONCLUSION

LBSs have arrived and ongoing improvements to underlying protocols, equipment, and middleware will only make them more effective and profitable for communication providers. Although some challenges exist, it is widely believed that very soon almost all mobile users will rely on LBSs to get personalized information and service based upon their present location and context.

LINKS

1. 3rd generation partnership project (3GPP). Available at: http://www.3gpp.org/.
2. Java Platform Micro Edition, Sun Microsystems. Available at: http://java.sun.com/javame/index.jsp.
3. Microsoft, NET. Available at: http://www.microsoft.com/net/default.mspx.
4. AutoDesk location services (and Java SDK). Available at: http://www.autodesk.com.
5. Open mobile alliance (OMA) mobile location service enabler V1.0. Available at: http://www.openmobilealliance.org/release_program/mls_v1_0.html.
6. Internet Engineering Task Force (IETF). Available at: http://www.ieft.org.
7. Open Geospatial Consortium (OGC). Available at: http://www.opengeospatial.org/.
8. Microsoft Visual Studio. Available at: http://msdn.microsoft.com/vstudio.
9. Java NetBeans mobility pack. Available at: http://developers.sun.com.

REFERENCES

1. IETF RFC 3920. *Extensible Messaging and Presence Protocol (XMPP): Core Internet Engineering Task Force*.

2. Kupper, A. *Location Based Services*; John Wiley and Sons, Inc.: New York, NY, 2005.

3. Loeb, S.; Falchuk, B.; Eiger, M.; Elaoud, M.; Famolari, D.; Krishnan, K.R.; Lai, M.; Shallcros, D. Intelligent network-centric admission control for multi-network environments. In *IEEE International Symposium on Consumer Electronics (ISCE'06)*; St. Petersburg, Russia, May 28–1 and June 2006, IEEE: 296–301.

4. Mohapatra, D.; Suma, S. Survey of location based wireless services. In IEEE International Conference on Personal Wireless Communications (ICPWC'2005); New Delhi, India, Jan 23–25, 2005, IEEE: 358–362.

5. *Geocaching—The Official Global GPS Cache Hunt Site*. Available at: http://www.geocaching.com/.

6. Falchuk, B. Web application supporting large-scale collaborative GPS art. In Yao, J.T., Ed. Web Technologies, Applications, and Services, IASTED; Calgary, Canada, July 17–19, 2006, Acta Press.

7. Jones, Q.; Grandhi, S. P3 systems: putting the place back into social networks. IEEE Internet Comput. **2005**, 9 (5), 38–46.

8. Koolwaaij, J.; Tarlano, A.; Luther, M.; Nurmi, P.; Mrohs, B.; Battestini, A.; Vaidya, R. *Context watcher—sharing context information in everyday life In Yao, J.T., Ed. Web Technologies, Applications, and Services*; : Calgary, Canada, July 17–19, 2006, Acta Press., Ed.

9. Telcordia Technologies, Inc., *Converged Application Server (CvAS)*. Available at: http://www.telcordia.com.

10. Falchuk, B.; Marples, D. Ontology and application to improve dynamic bindings in mobile distributed systems. 2nd International IEEE/ACM Wireless Internet Conference;, ACM: Digital Library: Boston, Aug 2–5, 2006.

11. Kölsch, T.; Fritsch, L.; Kohlweiss, M.; Kesdogan, D. Privacy for profitable LBS. In *2nd International Conference on Security in Pervasive Computing*, Boppard, Germany, Apr 6–8, 2005; 168–178.

12. Stross, R. Cellphone as tracker: X marks your doubts. New York Times, Springer, Nov 19, **2006**.

Meta-Systems

G. Reza Djavanshir
Carey Business School, Johns Hopkins University, Baltimore, Maryland, U.S.A.

M. Jafar Tarokh
K.N. Toosi University of Technology, Tehran, Iran

Abstract

A meta-system, a type of system of system that is capable of dealing with emergent events, is described. The characteristics of such a system, its architecture and governance are also presented.

INTRODUCTION

The study of system-of-systems (SoS) has become a central research discipline. SoS is particularly gaining importance because of its tremendous and vast applications in engineering, infrastructure development, strategic management, and net-centric and extended organizational development, to name a few. However, despite all these applications, SoS is loosely defined and often misunderstood. Furthermore, the design and deployment of various types of systems, particularly extended net-centric organizations and globally networked supply chains, go beyond what is referred to in the literature as SoS; rather, they necessitate an understanding of meta-systems.

A meta-system is a viable SoS. By viable system, we mean a system capable of maintaining resilient existence[1] when it is dealing with unpredictable emergent events or threats from its uncertain environment. Therefore, in order for any SoS to be viable, it must be a meta-system. In this entry, we also emphasize calling the SoS the meta-system, for several reasons:

- The term SoS was originally used by Ackoff[2] in a different context, as he was trying to provide a system or a *set of concepts and definitions* to better define and describe systems. According to Ackoff, thus far, "The *concepts and terms* commonly used to talk about systems have not themselves been organized into a system. An attempt to do so is made here."
- It is the meta-system that has powerful mechanisms and structures that make SoS' architecture and integration possible and provides the necessary structure to deal with critical issues such as its complexity and unpredictable emergent events.[1,3,4]
- According to Keating,[5] "*It is the meta-system that structures the appropriate balance to relive the tensions, (i) autonomy of subsystems and the integration*

of the SoS as a whole, (ii) purposeful design and self-organization, (iii) focus on maintaining stability or pursuing change."
- Finally, SoS is indeed a meta-system.[6,7]

Therefore, in this entry, we emphasize calling the general SoS, and viable SoS in particular, with its real name, that is, the meta-system. We will attempt to provide a definition of meta-systems and their characteristics and properties.

Meta-systems are large-scale systems whose components are geographically distributed networked systems. The main objective of each individual component system is to serve the strategic goal and mission of the meta-system.

Component systems of the meta-system are semiautonomous heterogeneous enterprise systems composed of sociotechnical, human, organizational, hardware, and software elements. By semiautonomous, we mean that some degree of managerial flexibility or flexible control is provided to all the geographically distributed component systems for managing their local operations and program management. This includes issues such as maintenance, resource acquisitions, removal, or upgrades of distributed systems. The flexible control also enables the distributed components systems to balance tensions such as maintaining autonomous managerial functions while being an integral part of the entire meta-system.

A critical component of the meta-system is its centralized governance and support system (GASS), which guides, coordinates, and oversees the design, deployment, and operations of enterprise systems. Furthermore, various components of any meta-system often have predefined change, replacements, or transition strategies which require governance and support structures to formulate and implement new changes and prevent the meta-system from falling into unstable conditions.[8] The GASS also provides strategic architecture that articulates the meta-system's strategic goals, policies, and

Encyclopedia of Information Systems and Technology, DOI: 10.1081/E-EIST-120053802

Knowledge—
Mobile

operational standards, as well as the core capabilities needed to achieve them. The capabilities provided by the GASS also include managing crises, dealing with unpredictable complex emergent events, and responding to threats and opportunities in uncertain environments.

The design and operation of GASSs are based on three main networks, namely: 1) the *integrated communications and learning network* for information sharing, command and control signals; 2) the *infrastructures' network* which includes facilities, hardware and software platforms, and technological artifacts; and 3) the *institution's network* which includes organizations, people, centralized management, command, coordination, and control mechanisms. The GASS uses these three networks to provide the following critical functions:

- Formulate *overall* strategies (strategy architecting) and policies that define the meta-system's strategic goals and mission.
- Act as focal structures to steer the implementation of the overall strategy and provide regulative and consultative services.
- Ensure compliance with the adapted standards and policies.
- Formulate the required transition strategy for managing changes and controlling the transitions process.
- Balance operational tensions including local–central control and ensuring the meta-system's stable operations, and prevent the meta-system from falling into chaos.
- Gather and disseminate intelligence and useful information about the uncertain environment and identify possible threats and opportunities.

Therefore, defining and understanding the GASS as an integral part of the meta-system's design and operation is critical to its viable operations, particularly during unpredictable emergent events and the structural transitions of the meta-system.

This entry will be composed of five sections: Section 1 will provide an introduction, Section 2 will provide the definition of the meta-system and its characteristics, and Section 3 will provide the description of, and the rational for, a centralized GASS in the meta-system. The design and deployment of the meta-system are discussed in Section 4. Finally, Section 5 will provide a conclusion and recommendations for future research.

WHAT IS A META-SYSTEM?

Building on the definitions provided by Buede[9], Sage, Cuppan,[10] Keating,[11] Jamshidi,[12] Dagli and Kilicay-Ergin,[4] Eisner,[6] Kawalek and Wastell,[13] Martin,[14]

Beer,[1,3] Ashby,[15] and Djavanshir et al.,[7] we define the meta-system as follows:

The meta-system is a large-scale distributed system, comprised of distributed heterogeneous enterprise systems that are integrated and networked together by its GASS to accomplish a shared strategic goal.

The component meta-systems are enterprise systems composed of technological artifacts and organizational, managerial, human, and informational elements. These heterogeneous elements are integrated together to create capabilities and capacities for achieving a desired shared strategic goal (s). The meta-system structures and integrates these heterogeneous components through its governance structure, which is based on three networks: physical, social, and information.[4] However, to provide a comprehensive and robust definition of a meta-system in dealing with various complex emergent problems and uncertain environments, we expanded Daghli and Kilicay-Ergin's definition of three integrated networks (I3N) (the physical, social, and information networks) to include critical elements, such as: communications, information sharing, learning, knowledge accumulation mechanisms, and institutional elements that govern the dynamics of a meta-system's behaviors. Therefore, based on our studies of various literatures including Beer,[1,3] Ashby,[15] Keating,[5] Kawalek and Wastell,[13] Buede,[9] and Daghli and Kilicay-Ergin,[4] a meta-system should possess a system that governs and provides support services to all enterprise systems within the meta-system and, as we will discuss in this entry, it is the GASS contained in the meta-system that makes the meta-system viable. The GASS in the meta-system is created by the nexus of three networks: 1) an integrated communications and learning network for information and knowledge sharing, learning, command, and control signals; 2) an infrastructure network that includes facilities, hardware and software platforms, and technological artifacts; and 3) an institution's network such as organizations, people, management rules, command, coordination, and control mechanisms. These I3N are described as follows:

1. **Integrated communications and learning network** contains various multimedia communication networks, the Internet and Intranet, and learning channels providing information flows and knowledge sharing mechanisms that are essential to the meta-system's viable operations, particularly its effective functioning during uncertain and changing environments. This network carries signals, knowledge, and a constant exchange of information among the meta-system's components, which enables the meta-system to deal with emergent events, crises, threats, and opportunities. In addition, it facilitates the emergence of self-organizing structures during the system's perturbations and chaotic situations by

providing error detection, feedback, fault isolation, and correction.[5]

2. **Infrastructure network** includes all technological artifacts, hardware and software tools, platforms, supply chains, transmission grids, and other resources that support the functioning and operations of the meta-system.

3. **Institution's network** is composed of organizations, people, processes, and governance mechanisms that provide strategies, guidance, rules, policies, standardized interfaces, and operational protocols along with various regulative, normative, and cultural-cognitive elements that are necessary for the coherent integration and operation of the meta-system. A critical element in the institution's network is the GASS that coordinates and oversees the meta-system's design, integration, deployment, and operations to achieve its strategic goals.

Characteristics of the Meta-System

As we discussed in the previous section, the meta-system is comprised of I3N of various elements such as infrastructure, information, institutions, people, organizations, technological artifacts, and hardware and software platforms. In other words, the components of a meta-system are enterprise systems whose elements come from I3N, and the meta-system provides the synchronized integration of all the distributed enterprise systems, governing their operations by offering guidance, coordination, and overall strategy (strategy architecture). A critical task for the governance mechanism is to ensure the meta-system's stable operations to accomplish its strategic goal and mission. The governance mechanism also oversees the use of standardized interface protocols throughout the entire meta-system to ensure interoperability among its components. The meta-system also possesses specific characteristics that are described in the following section:

- **Heterogeneous elements:** The meta-system is comprised of various interdependent enterprise systems whose elements can include hardware and software platforms and technological artifacts, institutional elements such as people and processes, and infrastructures, information, and communications networks.
- **Semiautonomous enterprise systems:** The components of the meta-system are semiautonomous enterprise systems with operational and managerial autonomy;[4,16,17] however, they should operate under the governance and support mechanism of the meta-system to achieve their shared strategic goal and to avoid falling into unstable conditions. In the context of the meta-system, semiautonomy also means that enterprise systems are independently operable

systems on their own, but they are networked and integrated together to achieve the meta-system's strategic goal.[4] Therefore, enterprise systems exist for the purpose of serving the meta-system to achieve its mission (Luhmann, 2003 and Kauffman, 1994). In other words, although the desired outcomes expected from each enterprise system, along with the overall framework of the strategy (strategy architecture), are defined by the meta-systems, flexible-control is also provided to allow each enterprise system to manage its own local operations, detailing, and execution as part of the overall strategy. The semiautonomy of distributed enterprise systems also implies that these systems do not possess full independence from the meta-systems that govern them but rather the systems are integrated to achieve the meta-system's strategic goal and to prevent its operations from falling into chaos. For example, an enterprise system does not have the authority to make strategic decisions critical to the survival or failure of the meta-system, nor can an enterprise system make decisions that contradict the meta-system's overall strategy, interface standards, or protocols. However, depending on the mission, enterprise systems are autonomous in making tactical decisions and they are autonomous in managing their own programs and running their daily operations in terms of scheduling, maintenance, and resource acquisitions.

- **Topologically distributed enterprise systems:** Enterprise systems are also geographically dispersed at global, national, or local levels. These systems are linked to the GASS through integrated communications, institutions, and infrastructure networks with constant communication and the flow of resources, materials, information, and strategic decisions to achieve the meta-system's overall strategy and its goal (s).
- **Commensalism and symbiotic relationships:** Commensalistic and symbiotic relationships exist among enterprise systems and also between the meta-systems and all of their component systems. Commensalism and symbiotic relationships mean that intertwined, interdependent, or partially interdependent entities *use each other* (commensalistic relationship) and *help each other* (symbiotic relationship).[18]
- **Evolutionary self-producing process:** Meta-systems are developed through evolutionary and adaptive processes, where the components of the meta-system are modified, removed, added, or reconfigured in response to new requirements and changes, threats, or opportunities in the environment. Furthermore, as the environment evolves, the meta-system's requirements, boundaries, architecture, and configuration should change and coevolve as well to adapt to it. Therefore, the meta-system's requirements, configuration, and final design are always incomplete, and its

boundaries are in flux.[16] In addition, as we discussed in previous sections, the enterprise systems are created and integrated together by the meta-system, while the meta-system itself exists by means of its interacting enterprise systems. This process of the cocreation of the meta-system and its component enterprise systems results in the self-production (Autopoiesis) of the entire meta-system. In other words, as the environment evolves, the meta-system redesigns and reproduces itself to adapt and respond to new conditions in a coevolutionary manner. Coevolution means that as intertwined and interdependent entities adapt to their environment over time, they also coadapt to and coevolve with each other.[18] The coevolutionary processes within meta-systems also take place through communications and learning networks, as the enterprise systems interact with each other, exchange information, share knowledge, and coevolve. According to Dagli and Kilicay-Ergin,[4] when a component enterprise system is reconfigured without changing its interactions, links, or interfaces to other systems, the evolutionary transition process takes place. The coevolutionary transition of a meta-system starts in response to the evolution of the environment and to the shortcomings of existing policies, design, and technology options. By reexamining the current technologies, architecture, and design against the changed environment, gaps are identified, as are new requirements and technological options. Therefore, the system is recreated and the system is reproduced;[4] in other words, the meta-system reproduces itself with a new design in response to the continuously evolving environment and new requirements. The spiral process of self-reproduction (Autopoiesis) and transition of a meta-system from one state of design to another requires dynamically coevolving designs and architectures. However, the reproduction of a meta-system's new design should take place in a way that allows its *strategic framework* and *core architecture* to remain *invariant (homeostasis)*; otherwise, the resulting meta-system can be dysfunctional.

- **Emergence property**: There are two related forms of emergence properties in any adaptive system—Type I and Type II.[19] Type I is intentional and by design, where new capabilities, behaviors, and properties emerge from the process of structural interactions among the meta-system's components. Type II is the unintended consequence of not knowing about the emergence in advance.[5] This unpredictable behavior comes from the interactions of the meta-system within an uncertain and unpredictable environment. With respect to the unpredictable environment and the emergence of unintended consequences, the detailed design and specifications of a meta-system should not be specified in advance of its operation. Rather, the detailed knowledge and

information about the meta-system's design should be part of the design, operations, and implementation process. In other words, the system design should be based on the law of *minimum critical specifications*.[5] Otherwise, a detailed design and specifications would increase the system's complexity, which creates a structural sclerosis restricting the meta-system's agility, adaptability, and responsiveness to the evolving uncertain environment. This kind of sclerosis can result in unintended consequences, and it also restricts the meta-system's capacity to self-organize and self-produce based on the contextual information.

GOVERNANCE AND SUPPORT SYSTEM

Meta-systems possess a GASS that shapes and synchronizes the collective actions and integrations of the enterprise systems in the meta-system by providing strategy, direction, guidance, and coordination, as well as by overseeing the meta-system's operation in achieving its mission and objectives. In addition, the GASS is also responsible for balancing operational tensions within the meta-system and facilitating the emergence of self-organizing structures during the meta-system's perturbations.

Furthermore, the governance and support structure is in constant interaction with all distributed enterprise systems through the meta-system's I3N, which we discussed earlier in the entry, by flow of information sharing, resources and capital, and strategic decisions. However, it does not provide detailed strategic plans, nor does it manage the detailed and daily operations of its distributed enterprise systems. That is, loose-coupling or flexible control is provided to deal with the paradox of centralized power and control by encouraging semi-autonomous local operations of the enterprise systems within the framework of the meta-system's strategy (Well and Sage, 2009). In addition, meta-systems are complex constructs. Their complexities, coupled with the uncertainty of the environment, overwhelm the capacity of a centralized GASS to fully understand, control, or micromanage its distributed component enterprise systems. Therefore, the GASS should be loosely coupled with all distributed enterprise systems. In other words, the role of a GASS is not to get involved in the detailed management of its enterprise systems' operations but rather to provide strategic frameworks and guidance necessary to facilitate collaboration among its enterprise systems and to ensure stable operations and the emergence of self-organizing orders during unpredictable systems' perturbations.

In order to provide an effective response to opportunities, threats, and changes in its evolutionary

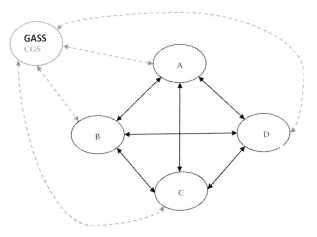

Fig. 1 Illustration of a governance structure.

environment, the meta-system must have a strategy architecture that manages the changes and transitions. However, the strategy architecture is not a detailed change plan; rather, it articulates the meta-system's mission and desired goals, providing a general framework and description of how the meta-system can accomplish its desired mission. The strategy architecture should be based on the assumption that the detailed information about a change is part of the change process. That is, it cannot be fully preidentified due to the lack of full information about uncertain future events. Therefore, flexibilities should be allowed in terms of the strategy's details and its execution and implementation.

Moreover, not every enterprise system has the means to create fair and balanced shared policies that meet the interests of all other enterprise systems. Therefore, a GASS is needed to resolve the operational tensions and suboptimizations at the local level, and to promote cooperative and coevolutionary behaviors among various geographically distributed enterprise systems. This system must also accomplish a common good among enterprise systems.[12,20] The need for a GASS is also articulated by DeRosa,[20] and can be summarized as follows:

1. Formulate, enforce, and manage common standards, particularly interoperability interface standards, throughout the entire meta-system.
2. Develop strategy architecture that defines the desired outcome to be achieved by the meta-system, as well as defines the capabilities expected from the enterprise systems in order to achieve the strategic goal. Component systems should collaborate to collectively provide the expected functional capabilities and capacities in achieving the meta-system's strategic goal and mission.
3. Facilitate the flow of information, capital, resources, and strategic attributes such as fitness rules and interface standards.

4. Facilitate the creation of a dynamic equilibrium that maintains the stability of the meta-system during internal and external changes and turbulence.[5] Dynamic stability is achieved through adjustments to changes, shifts, and disturbances.[5] (Skyttner, 1996). Therefore, during unstable, unpredictable emergent situations, a new order of behavior and structure emerges that allows the meta-system to maintain its stability. The GASS provides the necessary information, guidance, and coordination and it also encourages teamwork and communications that are required for self-organizing patterns to emerge out of chaotic situations.
5. Balance the tensions between local autonomy and centralized control; differentiations (diversity) and integration (stability); laissez-faire self-organization and detailed design and operational strategy; cooperation and competition; and individual enterprise system's self-interests (optimizing local benefits) and the achievement of the common good among all enterprise systems.[20] As shown in Fig. 1, the balancing point of all of these tensions is also dynamic; it changes as the meta-system's elements or environment evolve.[5]
6. Update and redefine the meta-system's fitness criteria (requirements) to avoid unstable or complex conditions. In high velocity changing environments ("fitness landscape"), design requirements ("fitness rules") should coevolve with the changing environment ("fitness landscape").

The meta-system's design requirements, its interface standards, or the overall fitness rules are shaped by the collective efforts of the meta-system's GASS in collaboration with enterprise systems. According to DeRosa,[20] the fitness criteria should coevolve with changes in the environment (fitness landscape); therefore, the GASS should constantly re-examine and redefine the fitness criteria. To do so, it should obtain feedback, update information, and make the necessary changes to the fitness criteria. The GASS creates policies and incentive structures, and it leverages a cooperative game approach to align the interests and functional operations of individual enterprise systems with the shared interests of all enterprise systems. This approach will, in turn, aid in the achievement of the meta-system's strategic goal. In cases where an individual component enterprise system pursues its own self-interests, the GASS should create conditions and incentives that benefit all enterprise systems.[12]

META-SYSTEMS' DESIGN AND FUNCTIONAL OPERATION

In previous sections we provided the definition and characteristics of the meta-system and we emphasized the importance of its GASS. We also showed that the design, deployment, and operations of the meta-system are based on three networks: 1) integrated communications and learning network; 2) infrastructure network; and 3) institution's network. These networks are built into the meta-system's design to provide the following critical functions:

- Monitor, govern, support, and maintain the meta-system's stable operations.
- Provide mechanisms for information and knowledge sharing, resource allocation, and flows of command and controls.
- Provide optimum alignment, allocation, and deployment of resources according to the dynamics of the meta-system's internal and external environments.
- Facilitate conflict resolution and balance the operational tensions between maintaining the status quo (homeostatic structure) and change (morphogenesis), detailed design, and self-organization.[5]
- Respond to threats and opportunities in an uncertain environment.
- Facilitate the emergence of self-organizing, stable order during the meta-systems' unpredictable perturbations.

The above-mentioned critical functions of the GASSs are performed by five interacting subsystems that support, govern, coordinate, guide, and oversee the operational functioning of enterprise systems.[1,3] These subsystems also identify and respond to opportunities, threats, and emergent events in the uncertain environment. The functionality possessed by each of these subsystems is described below.

An important question in the design and deployment of the meta-system is what form of internal architecture and design is needed to make it viable.[13] Beer's response to this question is based on the Law of Requisite Variety.[2] This law says that, for a system to be viable, the variety of regulator must be more than or equal to the variety of the regulated systems. By variety we mean the number of possible architectures and designs of a system. In the context of the meta-system design, this explains why meta-systems with detailed designs, or those with a large number of requirements, will have unintended consequences once their designs are deployed due to unpredictable changes in the environment or incomplete information about any future emergent event; in other words, the design of a meta-system can only be partially specified in advance.[5]

Hence, to ensure viability and the effective response of the meta-system to its uncertain and evolving environment, it must be designed with a minimum of critical requirements (regulations). In systems' design methodology, this concept of minimum critical regulations is known as minimum critical specification.[5,21,22] In this sense, maximum flexibility and agility of the meta-system is preserved, and therefore its maximum responsiveness to unpredictable perturbation is ensured.

In addition to the law of minimum requirement specifications, we believe there are two additional complementary issues that make the meta-system viable. These are: 1) standardized interconnectivities and interfaces; and 2) the modular design and deployment of the meta-system with the minimum possible connectivity.

Meta-System's Deployment and Maintenance

Thus far, we have described the characteristics, design, and functional operation of the meta-system. Now let us describe its deployment and maintenance processes. Let us assume that we are tasked with designing or redesigning one or more of the enterprise systems experiencing problems within a given meta-system. As shown in Fig. 2, the meta-system contains other enterprise systems along with the GASS that together are pursuing the meta-system's strategic goal and mission. The GASS is also providing guidance, strategy architecture, logistics, and supplies and is overseeing the redesign, upgrade, or replacement of the faulty enterprise system.

To understand how to diagnose fault, resolve the problem, or design and deploy the enterprise system, the GASS needs to understand the entire meta-system, including the structural interactions between the enterprise system to be replaced and other systems in the meta-system, as well as the environment or context of the meta-system.[9,14] The GASS must also re-examine the assumption, framework, and context of the problem in order to be effective in diagnosing and resolving the problem.

After the problem is resolved, the design and deployment of the new enterprise system may introduce new unintended problems (i.e., emergent behavior) as well. However, as we discussed, such unintended consequences or unpredictable emergent behaviors arise due to one of, or combinations of, the following issues:

- Systemic interactions among the meta-system's components or the meta-system itself with its unpredictable environment.
- Imperfect information about the environment or the context in which the meta-system is designed, deployed, and functions.

Fig. 2 Meta-system's evolutionary design and deployment.

- The bounded rationality of the human elements that designs, operates, governs, and supports the system.[23]

In addition to the introduction of potential emergent behavior, after the new enterprise system is deployed, the GASS should redesign or, it is better to say, reproduce itself (Autopoiesis) in order to adapt to and coevolve with new changes in the environment or the context of the meta-system. Additionally, in order for the upgraded meta-system to adapt to and coevolve with its changing environment, the deployment of the new enterprise system must be aligned "optimally" with the internal and external environment.

CONCLUSION AND RECOMMENDATIONS

In this entry we provided a definition of the meta-system and its main characteristics. A meta-system provides the structure, processes, and GASS that integrate and synchronize operational capabilities to create a viable SoS. The meta-system is comprised of GASS as well as networked enterprise systems consisting of people, technological artifacts, infrastructure, resources, communication and learning networks, organizations, and regulative, normative, and cultural cognitive institutions. Meta-systems coevolve with their changing environments (sometimes with high velocity) and in order to adapt to these changes, the meta-system's requirements and specifications are incomplete. Therefore, the coevolutionary process of transitioning and self-reproduction (Autopoiesis) of a meta-system from one state of design and operation to another requires dynamically coevolving architectures and system boundaries.

There are also commensalistic and symbiotic relationships among intertwined and interacting enterprise systems, meaning that they use and help each other, respectively, to survive. Furthermore, the meta-system and its enterprise systems not only collaborate, but also coevolve and cocreate each other as well.

We also emphasized the importance of a loosely centralized GASS that governs (not manages or rigidly controls) the overall design, deployment, and operation of the meta-system and prevents the meta-system from falling into chaos. The GASS also provides overall strategy (strategy architecture), policies, guidance, direction, and standard services that facilitate cooperative behaviors. Further, it supports the emergence of self-organizing behavior out of complex and chaotic situations.

For future research, it is recommended that the concepts of the GASS of meta-systems and the various degrees of autonomy of its component systems be examined and their governances also be studied. Additionally, the concept of the complex Autopoiesis SoS (self-production, where a whole exists for and is created by its parts and viceversa) can be used to further research and studies of meta-systems.

The authors would like to thank various members of the Johns Hopkins' Carey Business School for the insightful editorial work.

REFERENCES

1. Beer, S. *The Heart of Enterprise*; John Wiley: Chichester, England, 1979.
2. Ackoff, R.L. Toward a system-of-systems concept. Manag. Sci. **1971**, *17* (11), 661–671.
3. Beer, S. *Diagnosing the System for Organization*; John Wiley & Sons: Chichester, England, 1985.
4. Daghli, D.H.; Kilicay-Ergin, N. System of systems architecting. In *System of Systems Engineering, Innovation for the 21st Century*; Jamshidi, M., Ed.; John Wiley: Hoboken, NJ, 2009; 77–100.
5. Keating, C. Emergence in system of systems. In *System of Systems Engineering, Innovation for the 21st Century*; Jamshidi, M., Ed.; John Wiley: Hoboken, NJ, 2009; 169–217.
6. Eisner, H. *Essentials of Project and Systems Engineering Management*; John Wiley: Hoboken, NJ, 1997; p. 214.
7. Djavanshir, G.R.; Khorramshahgol, R.; Novitzki, J. *Critical characteristics of meta-systems: Toward defining metasystems governance characteristics*. IEEE, ITPro. 2009, May/June Issue, 31–34.
8. Klir, G. *Architecture of Systems Problem Solving*; Plenum Press: NewYork, NY, 1985; p. 305.
9. Buede, D.M. *The Engineering Design of Systems*, 2nd Ed.; *John Wiley: Hoboken, NJ*, 2009.
10. Sage, A.P.; Cuppan, C.D. On the systems engineering and management of systems and federation of systems. Inform. Knowled. Syst. Manag. **2001**, *2* (4), 325–345.
11. Keating, C., Rogers, R., Unal, R., Dryer, D., Sousa-Poza, A., Safford, R. Peterson, W. Rabadi, G. System of systems engineering. *Eng. Manag. J* **2003**;*15* (3): 36–45.
12. McCarter, B.G.; White, B.E. Emergence of SOS, socio-cognitive aspects. In *System of Systems Engineering, Principles and Applications*; Jamshidi, M., Ed.; CRC Press: Boca Raton, FL, 2009; 71–105.
13. Kawakek, P.; Wastell, D.G. A case study evaluation of the use of the viable system model in information systems development. In *Information Systems Evaluation Management*; Van Grembergen, W., Ed.; IRM Press: London, UK., 2002; 17–34.
14. Martin, J. The Seven Samurai of Systems Engineering: Dealing with the complexity of 7 interrelated systems. Proceedings of the INCOSE 14th Annual International Symposium, Toulouse, France, June 20–24, **2004**.
15. Ashby, W.R. *Introduction to Cybernetics*; Chapman and Hall: London, 1965.
16. Wells, GD., Sage, AP. Engineering of a System of Systems. *System of Systems Engineering*; John Wiley & Sons, Inc.: Chichester, England. 2009. 44–76.

17. Eisner, H.; Marciniak, J.; Mcmillan, R. Computer-aided system of systems (s2) engineering. *Systems, Man, and Cybernetics, 1991. Decision Aiding for ComplexSystems, Conference Proceedings., 1991* IEEE International Conference on IEEE **1991.**

18. Eisenhardt, K, Galunic DC. Coevolving at last a way to make synergies work. *Harvard Bus. Rev* **2000;** January--February *78* (1): 83–101.

19. Gharajedaghi J *System Thinking, Managing Chaos and Complexity: A Platform for Designing Business Architecture.* Butterworth-Heinemann: Woburn, MA; 1999.

20. DeRosa, J.K. Introduction. In *Enterprise Systems Engineering*; Rebovich, G., Jr., Whites, B. E., Eds.; CRC Press: Boca Raton, FL, 2011; 1–30.

21. Cherns, A. The principles of sociotechnical design. Hum. Relat. **1976**, *29* (8), 783–792.

22. Cherns, A. The principles of sociotechnical design revisited. Hum. Relat. **1987**, *40* (3), 153–161.

23. Simon, H. Bounded rationality and organizational learning. Org. Sci. **1991**, *2* (1), 125–134.

Mobile Ad-Hoc Networks

Jonathan Loo
Shafiullah Khan
School of Engineering and Information Sciences, Computer Communications Department, Middlesex University, London, U.K.

Ali Naser Al-Khwildi
Commission of Media and Communications (CMC), Jadreiah, Iraq

Abstract

This entry presents an overview of wireless networks and different aspects of mobile ad hoc network (MANET). The applications of MANETs are described with examples and how those applications work with different environments. Characteristic features are described. This entry also briefly covers the classification of MANETs.

INTRODUCTION

Wireless industry has seen exponential growth in the last few years. The advancement in growing availability of wireless networks and the emergence of handheld computers, personal digital assistants (PDAs), and cell phones is now playing a very important role in our daily routines. Surfing Internet from railway stations, airports, cafes, public locations, Internet browsing on cell phones, and information or file exchange between devices without wired connectivity are just a few examples. All this ease is the result of mobility of wireless devices while being connected to a gateway to access the Internet or information from fixed or wired infrastructure (called infrastructure-based wireless network) or ability to develop an on-demand, self-organizing wireless network without relying on any available fixed infrastructure (called ad hoc networks). A typical example of the first type of network is office wireless local area networks (WLANs), where a wireless access point serves all wireless devices within the radius. An example of mobile ad hoc networks (MANETs)[1] can be described as a group of soldiers in a war zone, wirelessly connected to each other with the help of limited battery-powered devices and efficient ad hoc routing protocols that help them to maintain quality of communication while they are changing their positions rapidly. Therefore, routing in ad hoc wireless networks plays an important role of a data forwarder, where each mobile node can act as a relay in addition to being a source or destination node.

WIRELESS NETWORKS

Wireless networks can be broadly categorized into two classes: infrastructure-based wireless networks and infrastructure-less wireless networks (ad hoc wireless networks). Infrastructure-based wireless networks rely on an access point, which is a device that acts as a bridge between the wired and wireless networks. With the help of such an access point, wireless nodes can be connected to the existing wired networks. Examples of infrastructure-based wireless networks are wireless networks set up in airports, offices, homes, and hospitals, where clients connect to the Internet with the help of an access point. Fig. 1 shows an infrastructure mode wireless network.

The other type of wireless networks does not rely on fixed infrastructure, and it is more commonly called an *ad hoc wireless network*. The word *ad hoc* can be translated as "improvised" or "not organized," which often has a negative meaning; however, in this context the sense is not negative, but it only describes the dynamic network situation. An ad hoc mode is used to connect wireless clients directly together, without the need for a wireless access point or a connection to an existing wired network. There are different examples of MANET in ad hoc mode such as building-to-building, vehicle-to-vehicle, ship-to-ship, etc.; they communicate with each other by relying on peer-to-peer routing. A typical ad hoc mode wireless network is shown in Fig. 2.

In wireless network communication, nodes communicate with other nodes via wireless channels. There are two important metrics that are used in the wireless networks: spectrum ranges and different radio frequencies. For example, IEEE 802.11a,[2] IEEE 802.11b,[3] and IEEE 802.11g[4] use a radio frequency of 5.15–5.35, 2.4–2.58, and 2.4–2.58 GHz, respectively. The signal

Knowledge–Mobile

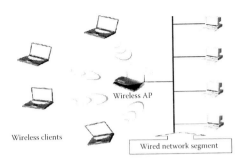

Fig. 1   Infrastructure mode wireless network.

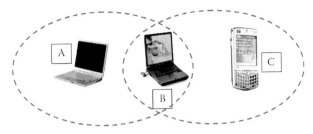

Fig. 3   Connectivity between nodes A, B, and C.

strength in a wireless medium decreases when the signal travels further beyond a certain distance, and it reduces to the point where reception is not possible.[5] Several medium access (MAC) layers are used in wireless networks to control the use of the wireless medium: Bluetooth MAC layer 802.15[6] and WLAN MAC layer 802.11.[3] The topology of the wireless network can be different with time because of the mobility feature. Besides the concept of mobility, another type of mobility is defined and well-studied. For example, in wireless networks, the hosts or subnets may be moved from one place to another. Traditional networks require reconfiguration of the IP address used by these hosts or subnets at the new place. A network enabled with mobile IP[7] allows these hosts or subnets to move without any manual IP address reconfiguration. The hosts can remain connected while they are moving around.

MOBILE AD HOC NETWORK

A *wireless ad hoc network* is a collection of two or more wireless devices having the capability to communicate with each other without the aid of any centralized administrator. Each node in a wireless ad hoc network functions as both a host and a router. The network topology is in general dynamic because the connectivity

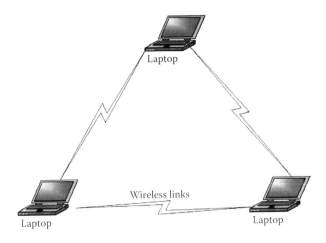

Fig. 2   Ad hoc mode wireless network.

among nodes may vary with time due to node mobility, node departures, and new node arrivals. Hence, there is a need for efficient routing protocols to allow the nodes to communicate.

Ad hoc nodes or devices should be able to detect the presence of other such devices so as to allow communication and information sharing. Besides that, it should also be able to identify types of services and corresponding attributes. Since the number of wireless nodes changes on the fly, the routing information also changes to reflect changes in link connectivity. Hence, the topology of the network is much more dynamic and the changes are often unpredictable as compared to the fixed nature of existing wired networks.

The dynamic nature of the wireless medium, fast and unpredictable topological changes, limited battery power, and mobility raise many challenges for designing a routing protocol. Due to the immense challenge in designing a routing protocol for MANETs, a number of developments focus on providing an optimum solution for routing. However, a majority of these solutions attain a specific goal (e.g., minimizing delay and overhead) while compromising other factors (e.g., scalability and route reliability). Thus, an optimum routing protocol that can cover most of the applications or user requirements as well as cope up with the stringent behavior of the wireless medium is always desirable.

However, there is another kind of MANET nodes called the *fixed network*, in which the connection between the components is relatively static; the sensor network is the main example for this type of fixed network.[8] All components used in the sensor network are wireless and deployed in a large area. The sensors can collect the information and route data back to a central processor or monitor. The topology for the sensor network may be changed if the sensors lose power. Therefore, the sensors network is considered to be a fixed ad hoc network.

Each of the nodes has a wireless interface and communicates with each other over either radio or infrared frequency. Laptop computers and PDAs that communicate directly with each other are some examples of nodes in an ad hoc network. Nodes in the ad hoc network are often mobile, but can also consist of stationary nodes, such as access points to the Internet. Semi-mobile nodes can be used to deploy relay points in areas where relay points might be needed temporarily. Fig. 3 shows a simple ad hoc network with three nodes. The outermost nodes are not within the transmitter range of each other. However, the middle node can be used to forward packets between the outermost nodes. Node B is acting as a router and nodes A, B, and C have formed an ad hoc network.

An ad hoc network uses no centralized administration. This ensures that the network would not collapse just because one of the mobile nodes moves out of the transmitter range of the other nodes. Nodes should be able to enter or leave the network as they wish. Because of the limited transmitter range of the nodes, multihops may be needed to reach other nodes. Every node wishing to participate in an ad hoc network must be willing to forward packets to other nodes. Thus, every node acts both as a host and as a router. A node can be viewed as an abstract entity consisting of a router and a set of affiliated mobile hosts. A router is an entity that, among other things, runs a routing protocol. A mobile host is simply an IP-addressable host or entity in the traditional sense.

Ad hoc networks are also capable of handling topology changes and malfunctions in nodes. They are fixed through network reconfiguration. For instance, if a node leaves the network and causes link breakages, affected nodes can easily request new routes and the problem will be solved. This will slightly increase the delay, but the network will still be operational.

MOBILE AD HOC NETWORK HISTORY

The history of wireless networks dates back to 1970s, and the interest has been growing ever since. Since the turn of the century, the interest has almost exploded, probably because of the fast-growing Internet. The tremendous growth of personal computers and the handy usage of mobile devices necessitate the need for ad-hoc connectivity.

The first generation goes back to 1972. At the time they were called PRNET (packet radio network). In conjunction with ALOHA (areal locations of hazardous atmospheres),[1] approaches for MAC control and a type of distance vector routing PRNET were used on a trial basis to provide different networking capabilities in a combat environment.

The second generation of ad hoc networks emerged in 1980s, when the ad hoc network was further enhanced and implemented as a part of the SURAN (Survivable Adaptive Radio Networks) project that aimed at providing ad hoc networking with small, low-cost, low-power devices with efficient protocols for improved scalability and survivability.[9] This provided a packet-switched network to the mobile battlefield in an environment without infrastructure.

In the 1990s, the concept of commercial ad hoc networks arrived with notebook computers and other viable communications equipment. At the same time, the idea of a collection of mobile nodes was proposed at several research conferences.

The IEEE 802.11 subcommittee had adopted the term "ad hoc networks" and the research community had started to look into the possibility of deploying ad hoc networks in other areas of application. Meanwhile, work was going on to advance the previously built ad hoc networks. Global mobile information systems (GloMo) and the NTDR (near-term digital radio) are some of the results of these efforts.[10] GloMo was designed to provide an office environment with Ethernet-type multimedia connectivity anywhere and anytime in handheld devices.

MOBILE AD HOC NETWORK DEFINITION

A clear definition of precisely what is meant by an ad hoc network is difficult to identify. In today's scientific literature, the term "ad hoc network" is used in many different ways. There are many different definitions that describe ad hoc networks, but only three are presented here. The first one is given by the Internet Engineering Task Force group,[11] the second one is given by National Institute of Standard and Technology,[12] and the final definition is given by the INTEC Research group.[13]

In MANETs, the wireless nodes are free to move and still connected using the multihop with no infrastructure support. The goal of mobile ad hoc networking is to support robust and efficient operation in mobile wireless networks by incorporating routing functionality into mobile nodes. Ad hoc networks have no fixed routers; all nodes are capable of movement and can be connected dynamically in an arbitrary manner. Nodes of these networks function as routers, which discover and maintain routes to other nodes in the network. Example applications of ad hoc networks are emergency search and rescue operations, meetings, and conventions in which a person wishes to make a quick connection for sharing information.

MANET APPLICATIONS AND SCENARIOS

With the increase of portable devices as well as progress in wireless communication, ad hoc networking is gaining importance because of its increasing number of widespread applications. Ad hoc networking can be applied anywhere at anytime without infrastructure and its flexible networks. Ad hoc networking allows the devices to maintain connections to the network as well

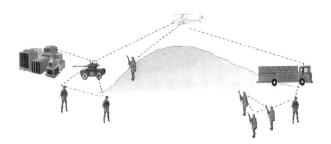

Fig. 4 Military application.

as easily adds and removes devices to and from the network. The set of applications of MANETs is diverse, ranging from large-scale, mobile, highly dynamic networks to small and static networks that are constrained by limited power. Besides the legacy applications that move from traditional infrastructure environment to the ad hoc context, a great deal of new services can and will be generated for the new environment. Typical applications include the following:

- Military battlefield: Military equipment now routinely contains some sort of computer equipment. Ad hoc networking can be very useful in establishing communication among a group of soldiers for tactical operations and also for the military to take advantage of commonplace network technology to maintain an information network between the soldiers, vehicles, and military information headquarters. Ad hoc networks also fulfill the requirements of communication mechanism very quickly because ad hoc network can be set up without planning and infrastructure, which makes it easy for the military troops to communicate with each other via the wireless link. The other important factor that makes MANET very useful and lets it fit in the military base is the fact that the military objects, such as airplanes, tanks, and warships, move at high speeds, and this application requires MANET's quick and reliable communication. Because of the information that transfers between the troops, it is very critical that the other side receives secure communication, which can be found through ad hoc networks. At the end, the primary nature of the communication required in a military environment enforced certain important requirements on ad

hoc networks, such as reliability, efficiency, secure, and support for multicast routing. Fig. 4 shows an example of the military ad hoc network.

- Commercial sector: The other kind of environment that uses an ad hoc network is emergency rescue operation. The ad hoc form of communications is especially useful in public-safety and search-and-rescue applications. Medical teams require fast and effective communications when they rush to a disaster area to treat victims. They cannot afford the time to run cabling and install networking hardware. The medical team can employ ad hoc networks (mobile nodes) such as laptops and PDAs and can communicate via the wireless link with the hospital and the medical team on-site. For example, a user on one side of the building can send a packet destined for another user on the far side of the facility, well beyond the point-to-point range of WLAN, by having the data routed from client device to client device until it gets to its destination. This can extend the range of the WLAN from hundreds of feet to miles, depending on the concentration of wireless users. Real-time communication is also important since the voice communication predominates data communication in such scenarios. Fig. 5 shows the ad hoc search-and-rescue application.

- Local level: Ad hoc networks can autonomously link an instant and temporary multimedia network using notebook computers or palmtop computers to spread and share information among participants at conferences, at meetings, or in classrooms. Another appropriate local level application might be in home networks, where devices can communicate directly to exchange information. Similarly, in other civilian environments such as taxicab, sports stadium, boat, and small aircraft, mobile ad hoc communications will have many applications.

- Personal area network (PAN): It is the interconnection of information technology devices within the range of an individual person, typically within a range of 10 m. For example, a person traveling with a laptop, a PDA, and a portable printer could interconnect them without having to plug anything in by using some form of wireless technology. Typically, this type of PAN could also be interconnected without wires to the Internet or other networks. A wireless personal area network (WPAN) is virtually a synonym of PAN since almost any PAN would need to function wirelessly. Conceptually, the difference between a PAN and a WLAN is that the former tends to be centered around one person while the latter is a local area network (LAN) that is connected without wires and serve multiple users.

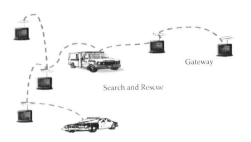

Fig. 5 Search-and-rescue application.

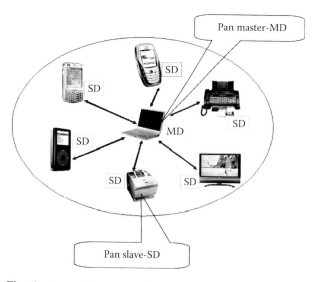

Fig. 6 Personal area network.

Bluetooth is an industrial specification for WPANs. A Bluetooth PAN is also called a *piconet* and is composed of up to eight active devices in a master–slave relationship (up to 255 devices can be connected in the "parked" mode). The first Bluetooth device in the piconet is the master, and all other devices are slaves that communicate with the master. A piconet has a range of 10 m that can reach up to 100 m under ideal circumstances, as shown in Fig. 6.

The other usage of the PAN technology is that it could enable wearable computer devices to communicate with nearby computers and exchange digital information using the electrical conductivity of the human body as a data network. Some concepts that belong to the PAN technology are considered in research papers, which present the reasons why those concepts might be useful:

- Small size of the device
- No need for huge power (lower power requirements)
- Not expensive
- Used specially for bodies and for sensitive information
- No methods for sharing data
- Networking can reduce function of input/output
- Allow new conveniences and services

AD HOC NETWORK CHARACTERISTICS

MANETs have the following features that are necessary to consider while suggesting or designing solutions for these types of networks:

- MANET has a feature of distributed operation because in MANET each node operates independently and there is no centralized server or computer

to manage this network. Instead this job is distributed among all operating nodes. Each node works with another node in cooperation to implement functions such as security and routing.

- MANETs have lower bandwidth capacity as compared with wired networks. MANETs can experience a problem of bit error rate and lower bandwidth capacity because end-to-end link paths are used by several nodes in the network. Also, the channel used for communication can be affected by other factors such as fading and interference.

- Another feature of MANET that can be used is energy in mobile devices. As all mobile devices will get their energy from batteries, which is a limited resource, whatever energy the mobile nodes have, it has to be used very efficiently.

- Security is the most important concern in MANETs because the nodes and the information in MANETs are not secured from threats, for example, denial of service attacks. Also, mobile devices imply higher security risks compared with fixed operating devices, because portable devices may be stolen or their traffic may insecurely cross wireless links. Eavesdropping, spoofing, and denial of service attacks are the main threats for security.

- In MANETs the network topology is always changing because nodes in the ad hoc network change their positions randomly as they are free to move anywhere. Therefore, devices in a MANET should support dynamic topology. Each time the mobility of node causes a change in the topology and hence the links between the nodes are always changing in a random manner. This mobility of nodes creates frequent disconnection; hence, to deal with this problem the MANET should adapt to the traffic and transmission conditions according to the mobility patterns of the mobile network nodes.

- A MANET includes several advantages over wireless networks, including ease of deployment, speed of deployment, and decreased dependences on a fixed infrastructure. A MANET is attractive because it provides an instant network formation without the presence of fixed base stations and system administration.

CLASSIFICATION OF AD HOC NETWORKS

There is no generally recognized classification of ad hoc networks in the literature. However, there is a classification on the basis of the communication procedure (single hop/multihop), topology, node configuration, and network size (in terms of coverage area and the number of devices).

Single-hop

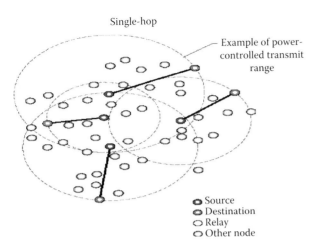

Example of power-controlled transmit range

● Source
◑ Destination
○ Relay
○ Other node

Fig. 7 Single-hop ad hoc network.

Classification According to the Communication

Depending on the configuration, communication in an ad hoc network can be either single hop or multihop.

Single-hop ad hoc network

Nodes are in their reachable area and can communicate directly, as shown in Fig. 7. Single hop ad hoc networks are the simplest type of ad hoc networks where all nodes are in their mutual range, which means that the individual nodes can communicate directly with each other, without any help of other intermediate nodes. The individual nodes do not have to be static; they must, however, remain within the range of all nodes, which means that the entire network could move as a group; this would not modify anything in the communication relations.

Multihop

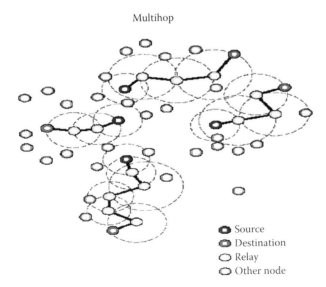

● Source
◑ Destination
○ Relay
○ Other node

Fig. 8 Multihop ad hoc networks.

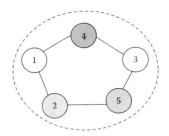

Fig. 9 Flat ad hoc network.

Multihop ad hoc network

This class in the literature is the most examined type of ad hoc networks. It differs from the first class in that some nodes are far and cannot communicate directly. Therefore, the traffic of these communication endpoints has to be forwarded by other intermediate nodes. Fig. 8 shows the communication path of far nodes as black lines. With this class also, one assumes that the nodes are mobile. The basic difficulty of the networks of this class is the node mobility, whereby the network topology is subjected to continuous modifications. The general problem in networks of this class is the assignment of a routing protocol. High-performance routing protocols must be adaptive to the fast topology modification.

Classification According to the Topology

Ad hoc networks can be classified according to the network topology. The individual nodes in an ad hoc network are divided into three different types with special functions: flat, hierarchical, and aggregate ad hoc networks.

Flat ad hoc networks

In flat ad hoc networks, all nodes carry the same responsibility and there is no distinction between the individual nodes, as shown in Fig. 9. All nodes are equivalent and can transfer all functions in the ad hoc network. Control messages have to be transmitted globally throughout the network, but they are appropriate for highly dynamic network topology. The scalability decreases when the number of nodes increases significantly.

Hierarchical ad hoc networks

Hierarchical ad hoc networks consist of several clusters, each one represents a network and all are linked together, as indicated in Fig. 10. The nodes in hierarchical ad hoc networks can be categorized into two types:

Knowledge—
Mobile

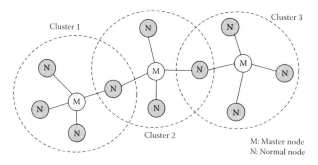

Fig. 10 Hierarchical ad hoc networks.

- Master nodes: Administer the cluster and are responsible for passing the data on to the other cluster.
- Normal nodes: Communicate within the cluster directly together and with nodes in other clusters with the help of the master node. Normal nodes are also called *slave nodes*.

One assumes that the majority of communication (control messages) takes place within the cluster and only a fraction between different clusters. During communication within a cluster, no forwarding of communication traffic is necessary. The master node is responsible for the switching of a connection between nodes in different clusters.

The no single point of failure is of great importance for a message to reach its destination. This means that if one node goes down, the rest of the network will still function properly. In the hierarchical approach, this is altogether different. If one of the cluster heads goes down, that section of the network will not be able to send or receive messages from other sections for the duration of the downtime of the cluster head.

Hierarchical architectures are more suitable for low-mobility cases. The flat architectures are more flexible and simpler than hierarchical ones; hierarchical architectures provide a more scalable approach.

Aggregate ad hoc networks

Aggregate ad hoc networks bring together a set of nodes into zones. Therefore, the network is partitioned into a set of zones as shown in Fig. 11. Each node belongs to two levels of topology: low-level (node-level) topology and high-level (zone-level) topology. Also, each node may be characterized by two ID numbers: node ID number and zone ID number. Normally, aggregate architectures are related to the notion of zone. In aggregate architectures, we find both intrazone and interzone architectures, which in turn can support either flat or hierarchical architectures.

Classification According to the Node Configuration

A further classification of ad hoc networks can be performed on the basis of the hardware configuration of the nodes. There are two types of node configurations: homogeneous networks and heterogeneous networks. The configuration of the nodes in a MANET is important and can depend very strongly on the actual application.

Homogeneous ad hoc networks

In homogeneous ad hoc networks, all nodes possess the same characteristics regarding the hardware configuration as processor, memory, display, and peripheral devices. Most well-known representatives of homogeneous ad hoc networks are wireless sensor networks. In homogeneous ad hoc networks, applications can proceed from certain prerequisites; for example, the localization is considerably facilitated by the presence of control components in each node, as shown in Fig. 12.

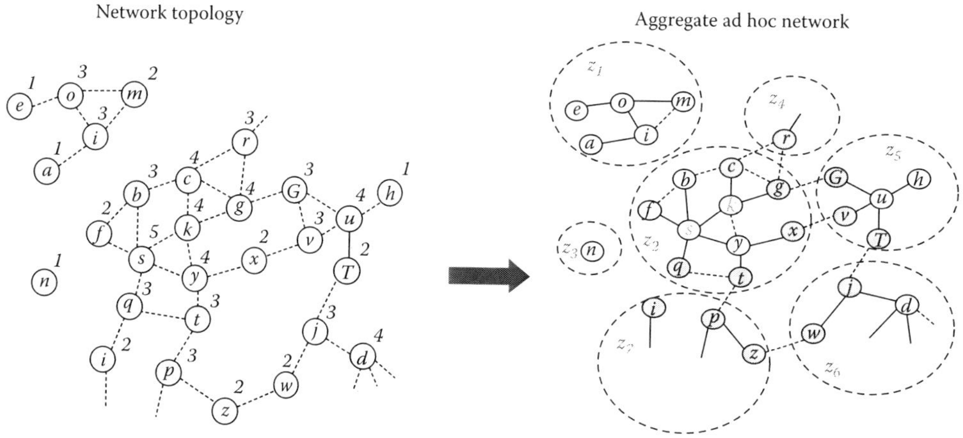

Fig. 11 Aggregate network architecture.

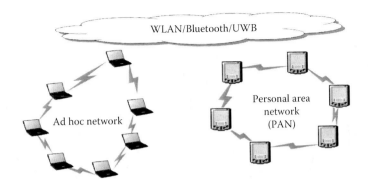

Fig. 12 Homogeneous networks.

Heterogeneous ad hoc networks

In heterogeneous ad hoc networks, the nodes differ according to the hardware configuration. Each node has different characteristics, resources, and policies. In ad hoc networks of this class, all nodes cannot provide the same services, as shown in Fig. 13.

Classification According to the Coverage Area

As shown in Fig. 14, ad hoc networks can be categorized, depending on their coverage area, into several classes: body area network (BAN), personal area network (PAN), local area network (LAN), metropolitan area network (MAN), and wide area network (WAN).[13,14] WAN and MAN are mobile multihop wireless networks presenting many challenges that are still being solved (e.g., addressing, routing, location management, and security), and their availability is not on immediate horizon.

A BAN is strongly correlated with wearable computers. The components of a wearable computer are distributed on the body (e.g., head-mounted displays, microphones, and earphones), and a BAN provides the connectivity among these devices. The communicating range of a BAN corresponds to the human body range, i.e., 1–2 m. As wiring around a body is generally cumbersome, wireless technologies constitute the best solution for interconnecting wearable devices. The PAN connects mobile devices carried by users to other mobile and stationary devices, while BAN is devoted to the interconnection of one-person wearable devices. A PAN has a typical communication range of up to 10 m. WPAN technologies in the 2.4–10.6-GHz band are the most promising technologies for the widespread PAN deployment. Spread spectrum is typically employed to reduce interference and utilize the bandwidth.[15]

In the last few years, the application of wireless technologies in the LAN environment has become increasingly important, and WLAN can be found in

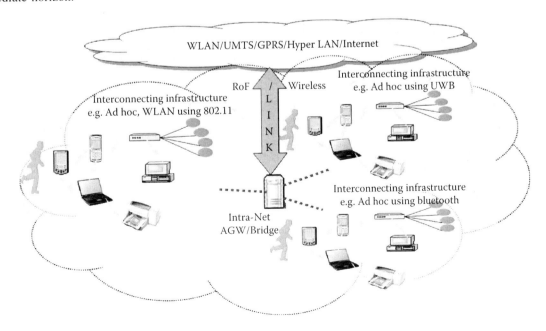

Fig. 13 Heterogeneous networks.

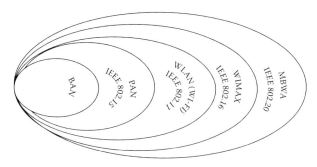

Fig. 14 Ad hoc network taxonomy according to coverage area.

different environments such as homes, offices, urban roads, and public places. WLAN, also called *wireless fidelity* (Wi-Fi), is than the wired LANs. Most of the personal computers, laptops, phones, and PDAs are capable of connecting to the Internet via WLAN. There are five major specifications in the WLAN family 802.11 namely 802.11a, 802.11b, 802.11g, and 802.11n. All use CSMA/CA (Carrier Sense Multiple Access with Collision Avoidance) for medium sharing which are standardized in 802.11c, 802.11d, 802.11e, and 802.11f.

WIMAX is based on the 802.16 IEEE standard and defined as a wireless MAN technology that will provide a wireless alternative to wire and digital subscriber line (DSL) for last mile broadband access. WIMAX has a communication range of up to 50 km, which also allows the users to get broadband connections without directly connecting to the base station, and provides shared data rates of up to 70 Mbps, which is enough bandwidth to support more than 60 T1 link and hundreds of home and office DSL connections. Likewise, WIMAX fully supports the quality of service. Finally, the last but not the least wireless technology called mobile broadband wireless access (MBWA) is approved by the IEEE standard board and defined as 802.20. The MBWA is similar to the IEEE 802.16e in that it uses Orthogonal Frequency Division Multiple Access (OFDMA), provides very high mobility, and has a shared data rate of up to 100 Mbps. At present, no operator has committed to the MBWA technology.

CONCLUSION

This entry has presented the overview of wireless networks and different aspects of MANET, such as: definition, application, classification, special features,

and various routing protocols. The applications of MANETs are described with examples and how those applications work with different environments. The MANET characteristic features are also pointed out such as distributed operation, lower bandwidth capacity, dynamic topology, and security. This entry also briefly covered the classification of MANETs in terms of communication procedure (single hop/multi hop), topology, (node configuration), and network size (coverage area and number of devices).

REFERENCES

1. Dressler, F. *Self-Organization in Ad Hoc Networks: Overview and Classification Technical Report 02/06*; Department of Computer Science 7 University of Erlangen.
2. Perkins, C.E. *Ad Hoc Networking*; Addison-Wesley: 2001.
3. Basagni, S.; Conti, M.; Giordano, S.; Stojmeovic, I. *Mobile Ad Hoc Networking;* Wiley-IEEE Press: 2004.
4. Gast, M. *802.11 Wireless Networks the Definitive Guide;* 2nd Ed.; O'Reilly Media: 2005.
5. Siva Ram Murthy, C.; Manoj, B.S. *Ad Hoc Wireless Networks Architectures and Protocols*; Prentice Hall: 2004.
6. Iiyas, M. *The Handbook of Ad Hoc Wireless Networks;* CRC Press: 2002.
7. Frodigh, M.; Johansson, P.; Larsson, P. Wireless ad hoc networking: the art of networking without a network. Erics. Rev. **2000**, (4), 248–263.
8. Kwak, B.-J.; Song, N.-O.; Miller, L.E. On the scalability of ad hoc networks. IEEE Commun. Lett. **2004**, *8* (8), 503–505.
9. Jubin, J.; Tornow, J.D. The DARPA packet radio network protocols. Proc. IEEE **1987**, *75* (1), 21–32.
10. Ramanathan, R.; Redi, J. A brief overview of ad hoc networks: challenges and directions. IEEE Commun. Mag. **2002**, *40* (5), 20–22.
11. Available at http://www.ietf.org/html.charters/wg-dir.html (Accessed July 2011).
12. Available at http://www.antd.nist.gov/ (Accessed July 2011).
13. *Wireless local area network hits the public* available at http://www.touchbriefings.com/pdf/744/wire041_vis.pdf (Accessed March 2011).
14. Chlamtac, M.C.; Jennifer, J.N. Mobile ad hoc networking: Imperatives and challenges. Elsevier Proc. Ad Hoc Networks **2003**, *1* (1), 13–64.
15. Abolhasan, M.; Wysocki, T.; Dutkiewicz, E. A review of routing protocols for mobile ad hoc networks. **2004**, *2* (1), 1–22.

Mobile Applications Development

Antonio Ghezzi
Department of Management, Economics and Industrial Engineering, Milan Polytechnic, Milan, Italy

Abstract
Emerging technological and strategic trends in the mobile telecommunications industry, including the evolution of mobile devices and their capability to process data and the rise in new types of contents, developers, and marketplaces, have determined a shift in the way mobile software applications are created and distributed. This entry will focus on providing a holistic view of the mobile application world, ranging from the business model analysis of the mobile application value networks, to how and by whom value is created and captured, as well as the main strategic and market implications and performances within this dynamic arena.

INTRODUCTION

The world of mobile applications is more than a multi-billion-dollar industry. It involves a plethora of intertwined actors, roles, and communities, which together create a world of seemingly endless business possibilities. The innovations in devices, such as smartphones and the network capabilities that enable fast and increased datatransfer have created an important new market for mobile content and services. Since this new market is rapidly growing in terms of both public and academic interest and revenues generated worldwide, it is very important that these aspects are thoroughly researched. Within this literature review, we will examine the development of mobile applications from several perspectives, but more notably, we will focus on the strategic perspective of the mobile application markets. From its emergence as the mobile portal of mobile network operators (MNOs) to the existing and dominating app stores, there has been a clear paradigm shift with many implications to a large number of players in the information and communications technology (ICT) sector.

The two-sided markets based on complex value networks are approached from both a high-level view, examining the business models, structure, and relationships within the ecosystems, and a more focused view, adopted by some of the key stakeholders in this industry. The goal of this contribution is to provide a comprehensive view of the main aspects, drivers, and currents within the mobile application marketplace, as well as of some real-life implications and results of this exploding playground.

TECHNOLOGY CREATING A NEW MARKET

The constantly accelerating development of technological capabilities of mobile devices, such as high-resolution screens, Internet connectivity, easy-to-use graphical interfaces, faster and smaller processors, provided subscribers with improved tools for content fruition.[1] Innovations in the fields of mobile devices and networks increased data-transfer and data-handling capacity and created a new competitive market for mobile content and services in the mobile industry.[2,3] Smartphones represent the fastest-growing segment of mobile devices, with more than 800 million smartphones sold in 2013,[4] 1.6 billion mobile broadband connections, and a projected 5.1 billion connections by 2017 with the existing calculated annual growth rate of 26%.[5] Global smartphone producers, such as Samsung, Apple, Nokia, LG, ZTE, and others, produce truly versatile multimedia computing devices, which enable the users to enrich their devices with mobile applications.[2] This evolution has enabled newcomers in the previously MNO-dominated industry to create a great disruptive effect and cause significant structural changes in the market by imposing and enforcing their own rules for the impending development of mobile applications. The implications of these changes not only concern the incumbent players, such as the MNOs, but also bring additional opportunities and constraints for a much larger set of existing and forthcoming players.[6]

BUSINESS MODEL PERSPECTIVE: A PARADIGM SHIFT

The mobile content market that emerged as MNOs started looking for new sources of revenues to cope

Encyclopedia of Information Systems and Technology, DOI: 10.1081/E-EIST-120049123

with the decline of usage of voice services and average revenue per user, and as a result, MNOs began to exploit their established position through the market making of multimedia digital content and services. With an uncontested bargaining power based on a large customer base; network infrastructure; brand identity; and a charging, billing, and accounting system, MNOs had dominance in the value-added services market.[1,2] The distribution paradigm mainly developed around the "Mobile Portal" model, which represented an interface through which mobile content & service providers (MCSPs), mobile technology providers (MTPs), media companies, web editors, and others were offering their products and services (such as games, video, and personalization options). The portal aggregated and displayed the offer of different services, and the customer could search, select, and purchase them through *Wireless Application Protocol* or *Short Message Service* billing, both of which were carried out by the MNOs themselves. Mobile portals were managed in a tightly constrained manner both upstream and downstream: customers were only able to access their operator's portal because of uniform resource locator restrictions or unsustainable extraportal data traffic fees. On the offer side, MCSPs, MTPs, and content owners were kept far away from the customer and were forced to accept nonincentivizing revenue sharing agreements, while MNOs took commission fees of + 50% on all value-added services and applications sold through them. MNOs have locked down and controlled the market while slowly developing and securing their value proposition, dubbing this approach the "walled garden" strategy.[1–3] At this point, it was thought that MNOs had assumed an impenetrable gatekeeper role. This resulted in the setting up of an alternative content, service, and application distribution paradigm that could actually jeopardize the MNOs' dominant position, breaking up the carrier-centric industry structure and opening the gates to a wide array of new entrants.[1]

Traditionally, in the mobile application industry, there were several actors intervening along the value chain, in which each actor has its own importance. Of late, this has changed with the arrival of software companies with new mobile phones and platforms, such as the iPhone and Android. As a result, because of the entry of the new players following different rules, the market structure and value chain are evolving, taking new shapes and forms.[6] The strategic implications of the paradigm shift will be described in the following text, but first, it is necessary to point out the characteristics of the "Apple Store" in order to see the main differences in the distribution process, which goes as follows: First, the developer uses development tools to build a mobile application—Software Development Kit (SDK) supplied by the platform owner along with third party tools. Second, the developer publishes its application on a portal, from which the consumers can download the application onto their mobile device. This model follows a mediated approach, where a third party (i.e., the application portal) plays an intermediary role between the service provider and the customer. This approach is different from the "walled garden" approach that was popular not long ago where MNOs were in charge of being the interface between customers and service providers.[6,7]

In a typical two-sided market, we find developers on one side and consumers on the other. In such a market, an increase or decrease on one side of the market induces a similar effect on the other side. In other words, in our specific case, as the number of consumers increases for a given platform, portal, or mobile device, the number of developers attracted to this platform, portal, or device will also increase. Similarly, as the number of developers, and thus the number of applications increase, the platform, portal, or mobile device will attract even more consumers. Contrary to the merchant mode, in which intermediaries acquire (digital) goods from sellers and resell them to buyers, multisided platforms allow affiliated sellers to sell directly to buyers. While the technical outlook of platforms refers to a hardware configuration, an operating system, and a software framework on which a number of services run, business models in platform markets aim to balance interests of all stakeholders to assess "a strategic fit." Successful two-sided markets can lead to a high volume of transactions and can thus be interesting for a middleman to charge a fee per sale. In the existing market, application portals play this role and charge 30% of the application retail price for each transaction.[1,8] So, on the one hand, developers have an incentive to develop for the most popular mobile devices using the most popular platform, and to publish their applications on the most popular portal in order to reach the largest number of consumers. On the other hand, consumers have an incentive to buy devices running a platform with many applications. This mechanism creates a positive feedback loop.[6]

The "Apple Store" model shows a number of significant differences if compared to the traditional mobile portal. From a technological point of view, application stores as mobile digital distribution platforms do not constitute a radical innovation, being quite similar to software libraries or marketplaces. However, the innovation lies in translating this computer-based and web-oriented nature in the mobile context: leveraging new smartphone features and capabilities, stores can be accessed from different networks (e.g., mobile, Wi-Fi, and fixedline), and are populated by digital content coming from external sourcing, which is integral to the success of this business model.[1,9]

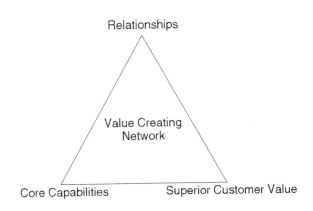

Fig. 1 Value-creating network model.

STRATEGIC IMPLICATIONS OF THE "APPLICATION STORE" BUSINESS MODEL

The shift in the mobile application store paradigm has inflicted several changes from the strategic perspective. Namely, there has been a transformation from a Service-as-a-Service (SaaS) model, which presents the embodiment of a one-sided market model for developing and delivering ICT services, wherein services flow in a linear fashion from independent software vendors (ISVs) to customers, with revenues flowing in the opposite direction to a Platform-as-a-Service (PaaS) one, a two-sided market model, wherein a platform mediates between the demand and supply side.[7] It has been argued that the main elements of leading platform providers' business logic are the following:

- Fostering a thriving ecosystem of internal and external complementary innovations and innovators;
- Influencing architectural design through open interfaces combined with core intellectual property assets;
- Balancing consensus and control strategies toward contributors of complementary innovations, and
- Reflecting this in the internal organization, for example, by adopting a systemic and neutral mindset that extends to the whole.[7,10]

This implies a structural change of the mobile phone industry from a value chain to a value network. Till date, the structure of the industry could best be described in terms of two relatively independent value chains for phone manufacturers and operators. With the addition of Internet compatibility and other functions, however, the structure of the mobile phone industry is gradually changing to a value network in which firms from a broad set of industries are interacting in the supply of a broad range of mobile Internet-related services. The concept of a value network is particularly relevant to network industries, such as the personal computer

and Internet, where a firm's internal processes are less important than the multiple ways in which firms and customers are connected to each other. Unlike value chains that connect multiple activities both within and between firms, value networks connect multiple buyers and sellers at a single node.[10–12]

The change from a value chain to a value network has important strategic implications for firms in the mobile phone industry. Apple's rapid dominance of the mobile market led to the emergence of a business model that weaves together Internet-enabled mobile devices with digital content, brought together within a closed proprietary platform or ecosystem.[9] Understanding network effects, creating a critical mass of users, and managing so-called multisided platforms are much more important issues in a value network than in a value chain. In particular, when multisided platforms are used to deal with different types of buyers and sellers through different pricing structures and information-sharing arrangements, the network is built upon the relationships, capabilities, and superior customer values of key firms and individuals within the value network (Fig. 1).

They are also known as "business ecosystems." Value networks or business ecosystems are a community of organizations, institutions, and individuals that impact the enterprise and its customers and suppliers, offering the potential to share risks and possibilities to generate economies of scale and scope, share knowledge, and facilitate learning, as well as shorten the time to market.[11–14]

It is argued that because of the compatibility between certain technologies, businesses that sell complementary products or services have to develop relationships with their allies. Thus, forming alliances, cultivating partners, and ensuring compatibility (or lack of compatibility) are critical business decisions, especially in the ICT sector where standards are an important issue. Relationships between the firms of an ecosystem are complex and show a mix of cooperation and competition, illustrating situations of competition.[12] Because of this, the frontiers of an ecosystem are unstable and keep changing depending on the interactions between member firms, their goals, and a wide number of strategic objectives and decisions.

COMPETITION DYNAMICS

The exponential growth and success of the market following the paradigm shift toward an "open garden" brought upon the industry a new level of dynamics and complexity. The competitive balance that was shaken by the mobile–web convergence and the alternative models it enables forced firms' value chains to transform into complex value networks, which imply new rules of the game.[1–3] Companies might engage in a form of partnership or alliance to overcome a weakness in the resources, to look for new competences through interorganizational learning, to search for approval and status, or to try to create new customer values through the synergistic combination of previously separate resources. Also, participating in various consortia allows firms to reduce uncertainty and risks when trying to promote a dominant design or platform.[12] To further confirm this, a study of 160 relationships among 92 companies has been conducted in order to examine the interrelations among MNOs, device manufacturers (DMs), web companies, and mobile platform and operating system vendors within this dynamic industry. The results found that more than half of the sample's relationships are shared by at least two different ecosystems. The studied ecosystems did not differ in terms of exclusive relationships, which suggest that competitive strategies are particularly relevant in the ecosystem-based view.[12] The authors also suggest that indirect competition is a clear characteristic of the business ecosystems.

MARKET IMPLICATIONS

The success of the new application store paradigm is apparent and proved not only by the exploding size of the app economy with 9.1 billion € from worldwide app sales, 10.5 billion € from app store subscriptions, licensing fees, *Application Programming Interface* (API) fees, etc., and 7.7 billion € of in-app advertising for 2013,[4] but also by the apparent trends of all the players involved including MNOs, DMs, and platform owners. Namely, there are observable trends moving from decentralized to centralized portals, device diversity, and portal integration, which, as practice has shown, are the paths toward harvesting benefits from this dynamic ecosystem.[6]

PRODUCT (APPLICATIONS) CONTEXT

Mobile applications can be categorized in different ways with respect to the preferred point of view. They can be business-to-business (B2B) or business-to-customer (B2C), depending on the targeted customers being businesses (to support internal processes) or individual customers, respectively. B2B apps can be further split into:

- Content-oriented apps fulfill individual needs for information, entertainment, communication, productivity, and socialization and include Twitter, instant messaging, e-mail, and social network clients for mobile phones.
- Marketing-oriented app—mostly used by companies for brand advertising or promotion.
- Service-oriented apps let users perform tasks—for example, checking a train schedule, booking theater tickets, or shopping at a mobile commerce platform.

There are many options for monetizing B2C apps, among which the most used are: 1) charging a fixed amount (paid apps); 2) free apps with reduced functionalities, which can be acquired by in-app purchases (freemium); or 3) paid apps with in-app purchases. Advertising is another option for monetizing mobile apps. In this model, ad space is sold in free apps that reach a large user base. Different monetizing options are assumed by companies and developers according to their business strategy and application type, as seen in the excerpt from the Distimo 2013 app market report on Fig. 2.[15]

Apart from the majority of the applications available and downloaded belonging to the free (or freemium) category, the sales are constantly increasing and the European app economy size comprising app-related products and services is expected to grow from 10.2 billion € in 2012 to a projected 14.9 billion € in 2016.[4]

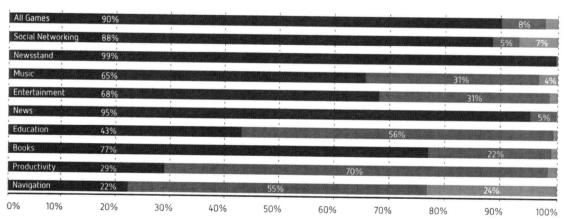

Fig. 2 Top 10 application categories in the order of largest revenue (from top to bottom), segmented by business model. Legend: Segments from left to right represent: Free apps with in-app purchases; Paid apps; Paid apps with in-app purchases.

CONTENT AS A VALUE DRIVER

Primary existence of companies is based on the value increase that they offer to customers utilizing the product or service. If these companies do not offer enough value for customers or the value is less than what the customer is willing to pay, the normal consequence is that the company exits from the markets, as Coase's law demonstrates.[13] For consumers, the appeal of the DMs hardware devices is closely linked with the variety of online content and services that are available to them. This market requires a continuous stream of innovation to sustain consumer interest. In opening up the platform to third-party developers, platform and application store owners have outsourced some of their software development to a global base of freelancers, thereby minimizing their own risk while developers create applications that may or may not be successful.[9] From the reviewed literature, it is apparent that ever since the creation of the mobile portals, and before, with most previous technologies and mediums—available and interesting content is what has proven to be the biggest success factor and has influenced the market's "decision" of whether that technology or medium will survive or not.[8,11] Although technology is basically a driver for new innovative services and business models (push-model), from a customer perspective, technology is only an enabler, and the main driver is the content itself and the most important value element for platform owners is earning revenues from applications hosted in the platform.[7] However simple this may look, application store and platform owners still face the classical chicken-or-egg problem of the platform creation business: attracting two different groups of customers who are dependent on one another, that is, to gain market shares, they need content desired by the customers, but to gain access to this content, significant market shares are required.

MNO PERSPECTIVE

The mobile telecommunication market has been shaken up by the arrival of new actors, such as Apple and Google.[3,6] As a consequence, the relatively well-established MNOs have had to rethink their position in the market if they wanted to participate in the growth of mobile telecommunication revenues.[1,3] However, with the existing market structure, MNOs do not hold a privileged position compared to mobile platform providers, such as Apple with iTunes.[3]

Reviewed literature argues that there is an opportunity for mobile operators to identify additional sources of revenue by exposing network functionalities through web-based service platforms.[3,7] Based on the analysis of various case studies, Gonçalves and Ballon[7] argue

that web services of mobile operators are decisively shifting from SaaS to PaaS models. However, these platforms incorporate fragmentation at several levels and are likely to face challenges in order to thrive. Mobile telecommunications networks and the Internet have evolved as disjoint worlds with regard to software applications and application development technologies. Mobile operators are now at crossroads of maintaining "dumb pipes"[3,7] that do not capture any value for the transactions made using their infrastructure. As large parts of the information technology industry are moving to a web service delivery model, there seems to be an opportunity for mobile operators to learn from these and their own experiences and adopt similar models by exposing network capabilities and combining these with online content and applications. Concurrent with this, MNOs seem to be bandwagoning on the application store model very quickly.

POSSIBLE MNO REACTIONS TO PARADIGM SHIFT

Four potential business models for emerging mobile service platforms are introduced in the work by Ballon and Walravens,[10] for which real-life cases are described and briefly analyzed. In the context of mobile service platforms, the crucial value-adding roles and key actors are identified, and from the different positions in the value network, they can assume the four business models are constructed and discussed along with the "gatekeeper" roles that can be assumed in each of them. From an MNO's perspective, it would be advisable to explore different possible models in order to avoid the "dumb-pipe" effect. Ballon and Walravens[10] present four different models, along with the real-life stakeholders who assume different roles. The models depict the major value-adding roles, as well as the value streams from and toward the user. Only direct revenue flows are indicated as it is still unclear how some indirect revenue models will come to fruition.

It is notable to mention that because constant improvement of hardware related to mobile computing opens new avenues for mobile application and service development,[3] there are possible avenues for MNOs. Broadcasting sports content has proved to be a popular strategy for driving the growth of the digital premium content marketplace earlier, and mobile service operators aim to enter the sports rights market. However, as the markets for live sports broadcasting are still dominated by established broadcasters, MNOs are facing significant barriers to access premium content, creating bottlenecks in the construction of business models.[8]

While moving to the now-dominant model, operators should adopt a platform mindset and incorporate the right balance of characteristics that guarantee platform adoption and avoid market and platform fragmentation. The biggest challenge to guarantee adoption seems to be posed by today's fragmentation of mobile operators' platforms.[7]

While the literature on ICT platforms has suggested that ICT service providers often have the discretion to make active design and strategic choices to become a platform or not, platform literature also suggests that the necessary competencies to succeed in services and in platform services are not aligned, and that there are specific contextual conditions under which platforms can thrive.[1,2,7] However, the question under what conditions platforms successfully thrive has remained largely unexplored up until now.

DEVELOPERS' PERSPECTIVE

Application developers are key players in the application value network, since they are the sole value-creating community that propels the entire industry. The shift from a "walled garden" to an "open garden" and a mobile application store has major implications on the developers or ISVs. The creation and distribution model of the mobile application store enables access and independence to third parties, following the self-publishing model.[2] Central to every development platform are the SDKs that enable third-party developers to build applications running for the platform. These kits usually include libraries, debuggers, and handset emulators,

among other useful development tools. Often platforms provide integrated development environments in order to facilitate the development process.[6] The self-publishing model follows the subsequent process: the developer uses the tools to build their mobile application, then they publish it on the portal, from which the consumer can download the app onto their mobile device. The platform owner facilitates an environment for application design, development, and delivery and allows application developers to provide a service to the end-customer and get revenues from it.[9] The developers only have to deal with the hosting (membership) charges and share the revenue with the platform owner (in most cases, 70% of the revenues go to the developer).

The most important benefits for developers include potential economies of scale in production and distribution costs, more predictable revenues, the development of software with lighter operating systems and hardware requirements, and shorter sales cycles.[9] The platform model also provides the developers a direct and continuous relationship between themselves and the consumer,[2,9] as well as built-in scalability, reliability, and security; built-in integration with web services and databases and support for collaboration among developers.[9] Contrary to popular perception, money is not the only motivator for mobile app developers—in fact, far from it. Revenues, in some form or other, are the goal for just 50% of mobile developers—53% of mobile developers are motivated by creativity or the sense of achievement, making this the most popular motivator. The fun of making an app is a motivator for 40% of

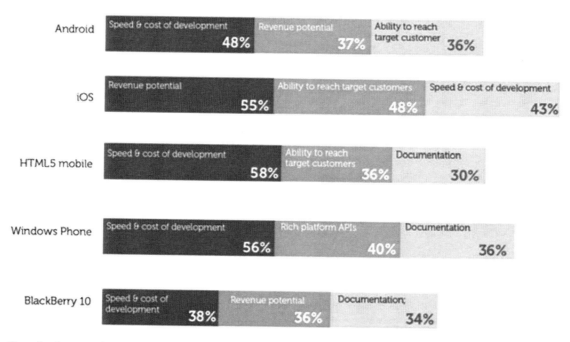

Fig. 3 How developers select a mobile platform: The top three most important platform criteria, by primary platform. Legend: Segments from left to right represent: Top choice; Second choice; Third choice.

mobile developers.[14] Looking at the criteria by which developers choose a platform (Fig. 3) also provide an interesting insight and possible success factors for application store owners.

Some platforms foster a developers' community, giving developers the means to communicate, share knowledge, and re-use other developers' code through case studies, blogs, and forums. A strong community around a platform gives developers a feeling of control over the platform and might be crucial to guarantee platform adoption. There is a never-ending cycle involved, as the presence of a community attracts more developers, which means more applications, which presumably attracts more customers, and the cycle goes on.[9] These communities also support the development phase and shorten timetomarket.

Still, the proliferation of proprietary stores based on different operator-device-OS combinations can increase app creation, design, and porting costs and also lengthen the timeto market. Moreover, raging competition can lower prices and profits and shrink the customer pool.[2,7] Another downside for developers is when they face the prospect of transferring platforms; the applications have to be made in a different language with a different SDK and API and, more often than not, they have to be made from the ground up. This is particularly important when taken into account that a survey of 6000 + mobile developers revealed that developers use 2.9 mobile platforms concurrently.[14] The data show that 84% of mobile developers are using iOS, Android, or HTML5 (mobile) as their primary platform, with developers preferring iOS (59%) over Android (49%) as their primary platform.[14]

Many developers face a dire power asymmetry and weak negotiating position with the portal owners because they can be easily replaced in an ever-growing and highly competitive marketplace. The majority of developers, who occupy a peripheral position in the network, can help neutralize power differentials by connecting with other developers in order to create a form of collective power. Developers generate work based on respect and recognition from their occupational communities, and become reliant on contacts. While developers simply exist as the "crowd" to the application portal owners, developers themselves rely upon these communities for support in surviving the harsh environment.[7] It will take a fundamental change in the pattern of competition to uproot the dominant platforms from their positions.[14]

CONCLUSIONS

The innovations in the fields of mobile devices and networks increased data-transfer and -handling capacity

and created a new competitive market for mobile content and services in the mobile industry. This evolution has enabled newcomers in the previously MNO-dominated industry to create a great disruptive effect and cause significant structural changes in the market by imposing and enforcing their own rules for the subsequent development of mobile applications. There has been a clear shift from one-sided to two- or multisided distribution platforms following the "Apple Store" model, going from a "walled garden" strategy to an "open garden" one, enabling self-publication by the application developers and a direct link to the consumers. Mobile application markets are successfully capturing value by serving as a mediator between the content creators and consumers by exploiting several monetizing approaches and revenue sharing models. The number of players within the industry and their complex interrelations within the value network imply that competitive strategies are often necessary in order to maintain sustainability. By exploiting crowdsourcing efforts in content creation and thus lowering design and creation costs, mobile application markets are able to capture substantial tangible benefits, and many intangible benefits too, thanks to improved brand reputation due to improved user experience and service levels. The success of the mobile application business models is evident, as the market size is within tens of billions of dollars and rapidly growing.

Despite the apparent benefits for the dominant players, the dynamic nature of the mobile application industry implies ever-changing conditions and factors for all of the players involved, from MNOs, DMs, and platform owners to the ISVs and application developers. It is thus very important to further research on how value is created and captured within the value networks, elaborating on possible business models, cooperation and competition strategies and implications of the complex network connections. There is still no consensus on the conditions for a successful business model or creating a "gatekeeper" role within such a vibrant field. Research efforts should also be directed in the direction of addressing the way content-creating communities are created and how they can be harnessed while overcoming the age-old chicken-or-egg problem.

REFERENCES

1. Ghezzi, A.; Balloco R; Rangone, A. How a New Distribution Paradigm Changes The Core Resources, Competences and Capabilities Endowment: The Case of Mobile Application Stores, Proceedings of the Ninth International Conference on Mobile Business (ICMB-GMR), Athens, Greece, Jun 13–15, Giaglis, G.; IEEE Computer Society Conference Publishing Services (CPS): Athens, Greece, 2010; 978-0-7695-4084-9/10, 33–42.

2. Cortimiglia, M.; Ghezzi, A.; Renga, F. Mobile applications and their delivery platforms. IT Prof. **2011**, *13* (5), 51–56.

3. Holzer, A.; Ondrus, J. Mobile application market: A mobile network operators' perspective. In *Exploring the Grand Challenges for Next Generation E-Business*, 1st Ed.; Sharman, R., Rao Raghav, H., Raghu, T. S., Eds.; Springer Berlin Heidelberg; Berlin, Heidelberg, Germany, 2011; Vol. 52, 186–191.

4. http://www.visionmobile.com/product/the-european-app-economy/.

5. http://www.atkearney.com/communications-media-technology/ideas-insights/the-mobile-economy-2013.

6. Holzer, A.; Ondrus, J. Mobile application market: A developer's perspective. Telemat. Inform. **2011**, *28* (1), 22–31.

7. Gonçalves, V.; Ballon, P. Adding value to the network: Mobile operators' experiments with Software-as-a-Service and Platform-as-a-Service models. Telemat. Inform. **2011**, *28* (1), 12–21.

8. Evens, T.; Lefever, K.; Valcke, P.; Schuurman, D.; De Marez, L. Access to premium content on mobile television platforms: The case of mobile sports. Telemat. Inform. **2011**, *28* (1), 32–39.

9. Bergvall-Kåreborn, B.; Howcroft, D. The Apple business model: Crowdsourcing mobile applications. Acc. Forum **2013**, *37* (4), 280–289.

10. Ballon, P.; Walravens, N. Competing Platform Models for Mobile Service Delivery: The Importance of Gatekeeper, Proceedings of the 7th International Conference on Mobile Business, Barcelona, Spain, Jul 7–8; IEEE Computer Society Conference Publishing Services (CPS): Barcelona, Spain, 2008; 978-0-7695-3260-8/08, 102–111.

11. Funk, J.L. The emerging value network in the mobile phone industry: The case of Japan and its implications for the rest of the world. Telecommun. Policy **2009**, *33* (1), 4–18.

12. Gueguen, G.; Isckia, T. The borders of mobile handset ecosystems: Is competition inevitable? Telemat. Inform. **2011**, *28* (1), 5–11.

13. Karvonen, J.; Warsta, J. In Mobile Multimedia Services Development - Value Chain Perspective, Proceedings of the Third International Conference On Mobile and Ubiquitous Multimedia, College Park, Maryland, USA, Oct 27–29; Association for Computer Machinery: New York, NY, USA, 2004; 1-58113-981-0/04/10, 171–178.

14. http://www.developereconomics.com/reports/q3-2013/.

15. http://www.distimo.com/download/publication/Distimo_Publication_-December_2013/EN/archive/.

Knowledge—Mobile

Mobile Business Models and Value Networks

Marcelo Nogueira Cortimiglia
Alejandro Germán Frank
Industrial Engineering Department, Federal University of Rio Grande do Sul, Porto Alegre, Brazil

Antonio Ghezzi
Department of Management, Economics and Industrial Engineering, Milan Polytechnic, Milan, Italy

Abstract

Business models and value networks have become buzzwords in strategic management and technology management fields. In particular, both constructs have been extensively applied to the analysis of rapidly changing and highly innovative telecommunications industry, yet there is no consensus on precisely what they represent or how to operationalize them. This entry reviews the literature on business models and value networks and presents examples of applications within the telecommunications industry. A working definition that integrates both concepts is suggested.

INTRODUCTION

The concepts of business models and value networks have attracted wide attention of late in the strategic management and technology management literatures.[1–3] In particular, business models have been extensively discussed in theoretical and applied works dealing with the telecommunications industry.[4–6] This trend is strongly related to the fact that the telecommunications industry is highly innovative and technology-intensive. In such an environment, players must constantly examine which are the main drivers of value creation and capture in their business. Similarly, the notion of a value network guiding the logic of value creation, delivery, and appropriation is particularly relevant for players operating in this industry, which is characterized by dynamic competitive scenarios where strategy making must be agile and responsive in order to cope with intense technologic, regulatory, competitive, and social change.[4]

However, although much has been written about business model and value networks and many attempts to define and operationalize the constructs have been made, a consensus on what they represent and how they can be operationalized has not been reached yet. This may be related to the fact that the concept of business models has emerged more or less independently in three different streams of literature (strategic management, technology management, and entrepreneurship),[2] or it may reflect the rather integrative and ad hoc use of these concepts by earlier authors, according to the objectives of each individual study. Whatever the reasons, it is striking that such useful and popular concepts still lack a unified, universally accepted definition.[2,3] Thus, in this entry we review the literature on business models and value networks, particularly as they are applied to the telecommunications industry.

This entry is structured in five sections. First, the main topic is introduced and its importance and relevance are discussed. The next section brings a brief review on the topic of Business Models from a historical evolution perspective, including a review of the main definitions and component dimensions proposed in the literature. The subsequent section includes a review on the topic of value networks. In the penultimate section, a number of examples of the use of the business model and value network concepts in the telecommunication industry are presented, followed by the proposition of an interpretative framework integrating both constructs that can be applied to the strategic analysis of and corporate-level decision making in the telecommunications industry in final section.

BUSINESS MODELS

Historical Evolution

The business model concept has much evolved since it first appeared in the business lexicon. Initially, it was used to describe, usually on empirical grounds and in a mostly informal way, the overall logic behind a firm or a business.[7] The understanding that different firms in the same industry could employ different business logics had been brewing among scholars of strategy since the 1980s, but this notion became relevant especially with the emergence of the Internet in the late 1990s.[1,2] At the time, it became obvious that the emerging e-business phenomenon allowed firms to articulate their business in new ways, using the Web to directly reach customers or establish partnerships, thus bypassing traditional intermediates, to conduct business operations more efficiently or even to create new products and services that would not make sense before the advent of the World Wide Web.[8] The business model concept thus appealed to entrepreneurs and business analysts interested in explaining how a business was articulated and how it operated in that new context.

At roughly the same time, the literature on technology management began to use the term business model to explain how a specific technology innovation would be marketed. This was due to the growing perception that the technology itself was not, in most cases, the main driver of successful innovation. It was necessary to explain how the technology created value for the customers, and also how the business would be able to capture part of that value to become sustainable. Similarly, the business model concept captured the internal and external activities (including the relationships with business partners) necessary to transform an invention into a successful innovation.[9]

These earlier uses of the business model concept mostly lacked coherence and formal structure. Thus, it was deemed more elusive than informative. Precisely for this reason, the business model construct has been criticized by influential authors as being murky or fuzzy.[10] Even so, it became highly popular with both academics and practitioners alike, mainly because of its usefulness from a practical point of view, its versatility, and intuitiveness. After all, business models actually serve a most useful purpose: to simplify the numerous variables that influence the way different businesses are structured and to present them in a coherent and unified form, allowing decision makers and managers to focus attention on the whole system that constitutes a business.

During the 2000s, scholars of technology management, entrepreneurship, and strategy began to systematically study that promising concept.[2,3,9] Consequently, a number of different definitions were proposed in that decade. Some of these definitions resorted to the simplicity that the concept evoked.[7,10] The general consensus at the time was that a business model should explicate why and how value is created, exchanged, and consumed in a network of interrelated actors.[1,8] Some authors even mentioned specific aspects of value proposition, positioning in the value network, and type of arrangement with the customers in order to generate value, but as a rule, not much was done in terms of analytical modeling or explaining causal relationships.[2,9]

More elaborate definitions followed. In a very influential work, Chesbrough and Rosenbloom[11] developed a functional definition of business model that recognized six functions that a working business model should attend to: articulate the value perspective; identify market segments; define the internal value chain and estimate costs and profits; describe the (external) value

network; and formulate the competitive strategy, that is, how the business model should evolve.

At the same time, much research was dedicated to identifying the building blocks of a business model, that is, what are its constituting elements and how they relate to each other and to the main objective of the business model, that is, explaining the logic behind a business. In fact, much of the early research was concentrated on proposing conceptual frameworks for business model design, analysis, and innovation in the form of meta-models. A widely cited literature review by Shafer et al.[12] came up with four major components: strategy formulation (including target market, value proposition and offering, revenue/pricing and identification of critical competences), value creation (resources, assets, processes, and activities), value capture, and value network (in particular, defining the relationships with suppliers, key partners, and customers). Moreover, Shafer et al.[12] propose the following integrative definition of business model: "a representation of a firm's underlying core logic and strategic choices for creating and capturing value within a value network."

The work by Shafer et al.[12] apparently captured the consolidation of the business model concept in the early 2000s. During the second half of the decade, most of the studies that described dimensions, components, or aspects that constitute a business model usually included dimensions or perspectives that were very similar to what the authors came up with: a value proposition perspective, which roughly described the offering in terms of products, services, and target market and proposed a narrative that explained on how this offering was valued by the customers; a value creation perspective, dealing with the internal and external mechanisms that allowed the firm to execute the value proposition; a value appropriation perspective, which informed how the firm would capture part of the created value; and a value delivery dimension, dealing with the external value network necessary to bring the offering to the customers, which included the key relationships and delivery channels accessed by the firm.

At the same time, a number of authors proposed classification schemes or typologies of business models. This approach is important because it generates insights on generic business models that are useful to a wide array of firms using a single unit of analysis. One of the first studies on business model typologies is that of Timmers[13] who proposed a framework for the classification of Internet-enabled business models. Another remarkable example is offered by Malone et al.[14] They start with a very simple operational definition of business models that describes what firms do and how they create value based on the combination of types of asset rights being sold (creators, distributors, landlords, and brokers) and types of assets transacted (financial, physical, intangible, and human). Then, the authors propose a typology of 16 possible business models built upon the combination of the four asset rights and types of assets. This typology is used to classify business models of existing firms, whose financial performances are assessed in order to identify whose business models generate the best results. However complete and generic the approach by Malone et al.[14] is, its main contribution was the demonstration that the business model concept can be used in a working typology and that it can be related to firm-level performance.

Business Models Today

Built upon the consolidated narrative of published literature reported in the previous section, the business model concept is now widely understood as an analytical model of how a business approaches value creation, delivery, and appropriation, including the choice of activities, resources, capabilities, and external relationships.[11] In other words, business models serve today a most useful purpose that is very akin to its original aims: to simplify the numerous variables that influence how businesses are structured and to present them in a coherent and unified form.[2,9] This allows all involved to share a common view of the business, including its strategic and operational parts as well as internal and external components.

A premise behind the logic of a business model is that value creation depends greatly on how the value proposition is formulated and enacted at the operational level.[11] Value proposition, in turn, should originate from top-level strategic choices regarding a firm's internal capabilities and resources and the challenges and opportunities detected in the external environment.[15] Thus, it may be argued that the business model concept operates at an intermediate, architectural level midway between strategic planning and operations.[12] In other words, a business model is how strategy is operationalized.[4,15] Given the overall strategic environment, a company chooses between different high-level strategic alternatives aimed at achieving and sustaining competitive advantage. Once the strategic directives are established, these can be implemented through a number of different business model alternatives, which focus on the creation and capture of customer value. In this context, the business model concept can be considered as a valuable tool for bridging the gap between strategy formulation/planning and implementation in the form of business processes and activities.[16] This is the most accepted interpretation till now of the relationship between business models and strategy.

Regarding the components of a business model, existing literature has not deviated much from what was established in the mid-2000s. For instance, Demil and Lecocq[17] describe a business model with three core components: resources and competences, organizational structure (including activities and relationships with external stakeholders), and value proposition (products and/or services, customers, and transactions). The components proposed by Demil and Lecocq[17] are related, respectively, to the notions of value creation, delivery, and proposition, while value capture derives from the choice of elements that define each specific business model.

The latest conceptual interpretation of business model by Habtay[18] encompasses five dimensions: strategy, value proposition, customer base, value network configuration, and revenue model, while that of Cortimiglia et al.[16] is built around five different dimensions: value proposition, value delivery, value appropriation, value networking, and value creation. Indeed, most other contemporary works on business modeling follow a similar structure, some emphasizing more on one aspect over the others according to the specific aims of each study. So, it seems that not much has changed since the seminal Ph. D. thesis by Osterwalder,[19] who further developed these four dimensions into nine generic business model parameters. This work later gave birth to the Business Model Canvas, a tool for business model design and analysis proposed by Osterwalder and Pigneur,[20] which is extremely popular with practitioners nowadays.

In the Business Model Canvas,[20] a business model is decomposed into nine interrelated parameters: value proposition, customer segments, information and distribution channels, customer relationships, key activities, key resources, key partners, cost structure, and revenue model. The value proposition block describes the products or services offered to the market, while the customer segment, customer relationships, and channels describe how value is actually delivered to clients. On the other hand, key activities, key resources, and key partners describe how the business creates the value proposition, while the cost and revenue structures explain how this value is captured by the business at hand. The Business Model Canvas has become extremely popular, particularly among practitioners and consultants, and is also widely used by academics.[4,16] However, the Canvas approach can be criticized for not explicating the causality logic behind the choices of elements.[16] In fact, most conceptual frameworks do not offer rules or guidelines to clarify how a change in one element within a dimension will impact the others. Moreover, it is also not clear how business model design relates to the overall strategy-making process.[15,16,21] Does a firm first analyze its internal resources and capabilities (value creation) and potential activities that partners may be responsible for (value networking) in order to define a concrete offering and a target market (value proposition) coupled with a revenue generation mechanism (value appropriation)? Or does a firm first define a value proposition and then search the environment for value creation alternatives?

These questions have been guiding a whole new stream of research on business models. Many scholars are now dedicated to understanding how business model design is conducted in both existing and new firms.[3] Consequently, the topic of business model evolution and innovation has risen in importance lately. It has long been recognized that business models are not static. In fact, most early approaches included remarks on how business models must adapt and change in response to dynamic environment conditions or, following a technology management venue, how business models must be loosely defined and easy to modify as new technologies were introduced and received by the target market. The topic of business evolution and change gained prominence through the numerous studies that described and analyzed the profound changes that affected the music and news industries of late.[1,3]

In a sense, the business model concept has always been seen as a more responsive construct than the overall firm strategy, a view that finds resonance in today's interpretations of the relationship between business models and strategy.[15] Similarly, the existing notion that experiments with business models may be a source of competitive advantage is inherently linked to the new interest in business model innovation. This topic remains an important venue for more research, as research in business model innovation is still mostly exploratory, and theoretical foundations have not yet been unequivocally established.[22,23]

VALUE NETWORKS

Hitherto, the main issues in business model research included approaches to internal cooperation and coordination and the level of vertical and horizontal integration.[1,15] However, as methodologies and ontologies for systematically mapping business models matured, the focus of business modeling shifted from the single firm to the entire value network.[4] The analysis of literature pertaining to value chains and value networks is of fundamental importance to this entry because it sheds light on the value creation processes and roles that are distributed throughout the network of relationships that make up a business model. In addition, to understand what is a value network facilitates the identification of the roles that are played in an industry or market.

The value network concept has its origins in the original value chain introduced by Porter,[24] which described the value-adding activities internal to the firm. The value chain perspective sees the firm as a series of

chained relevant activities, and posits that value is created through efficient resource allocation at these activities. Later, the value chain context was extended to the outside of the firm by introducing the notion of value system, meaning the larger stream of value-adding activities that include suppliers, delivery channels, and buyers at both extremes of a firm's value chain. It should be noted that the value chain does not give much importance to how value-adding activities are distributed along members, or how can resources be shared by or acquired from an external source. Although created for analyzing individual firms, the value chain construct was widely employed to investigate entire industries, especially in traditional manufacturing sectors.

At the end of the 1990s, with the combined emergence of the resource-based view of the firm and the strategic network bodies of literature, the value chain configuration was challenged. In particular, two new value configurations—or *logics for value creation*—appeared in the strategic management literature: the value network and the value shop.[25] While in the value chain logic the creation of value relies on efficient processes and routines focusing on the almost linear transformation of inputs into products, the other two configurations propose different approaches to value creation. In the value shop, value creation derives from the solution of unstructured (and sometimes unique) customer problems. In this sense, value creation depends strongly on a firm's resources and capabilities. In the value network logic of value creation, instead, value is created by connecting interdependent actors, usually with the help of mediating technologies. In this configuration, value creation is not the province of the single firm, but of the whole network. Financial services and telecommunications companies are good examples of firms that create value according to the value network logic.

Adopting a value network perspective requires business designers and decision makers to change the focus of their planning. Instead of considering the firm as the single most important unit of analysis, the examination of the relationships between a business enterprise and its partners, competitors, and clients has to come to the foreground. In this new paradigm, value is created, delivered, and appropriated through the network, and the role of the different members in each of these activities must be clearly specified when designing or analyzing a business model. The significance of the value network concept can be explained through the core competence[26] lens: as most firms narrow their set of core competences as a consequence of increasing market and environmental complexity, the only natural way to amplify a firm's value-creating capabilities is to associate with other firms.[8]

A distinctive aspect that must be considered when dealing with value networks is the role of information and communication technologies (ICT). Evidently, lower transaction costs due to automated systems and technologies eliminate much of the benefits associated with closed, integrated firms that are typical of the value chain paradigm.[8,9] Similarly, ICT also lower coordination and communication costs, facilitating the establishment and maintenance of alliances not only at the strategic level, but also at the operational level.[27] The most notorious technology behind the paradigmatic change in value creation logic is the Internet. The profound changes that characterized the traditional news industry until now exemplify the transformation from a value chain to a value network logic.[28] In this case, the biggest change came when the content creation activity, traditionally assigned to few internal critical assets, was challenged by the multiplicity of sources and delivery options made available by the Internet. However, the Internet is not the only technology that challenged the value chain logic. As it is shown in the next section, mobile phones also played a significant role.

BUSINESS MODELS AND VALUE NETWORKS IN THE TELECOMMUNICATIONS INDUSTRY

The business model and value network concepts have long been applied to the telecommunications industry. In fact, many of the academic works that first proposed a change of paradigm in the value creation logic from a chain-like structure where business models were connected sequentially to a network-like structure built upon multiple relationships that support value creation and appropriation were supported by empirical data from the telecommunications industry,[5] particularly the Internet and mobile sectors. Thus, special attention is given in this entry to previous researches featuring the business model and value network concepts circumscribed to the telecommunications industry, in particular within the mobile communications segment.

The first examples of research about business models and value networks applied to the telecommunications industry date from the early 2000s.[29–32] At the time, the mobile–Internet convergence that is in full act right now was still in its infancy, so there was still a striking difference between the Internet experienced at the desktops and mobile phones. Consequently, there was a relative level of separation between these two sectors. Studies that employed the concepts of business model and value network at the time usually described business models in terms of a logical architecture for the flow of products, services, and information in the mobile environment, which is organized accordingly in a network of interdependent actors.[30] Early attempts to apply the value network concept to the telecommunications industry were fairly descriptive, pointing out who were the main actors (technology platform vendors, infrastructure and equipment vendors, application platform vendors, application developers, content providers, content aggregators, mobile portal providers, mobile network operators[MNOs], and mobile service providers) and briefly sketching their business models as well as how these models related to each other.[29,30] Usually, the most studied mobile value networks were those articulated around the MNO, the business enterprise that effectively owns the final customer (the subscriber). Although the earlier studies on MNO-centered mobile value networks usually did not include a structured description of the relationships among actors, the list of players, and the highlighted importance of the MNO still remain valid today.

Just as MNOs dominated the research on value networks applied to the telecommunications industry, much of the early concern in terms of business models was also dedicated to the MNOs. In their study of MNOs' business models, for instance, Kallio et al.[33] proposed a business model framework originally with four operator-specific factors: Product Development Strategy, concerning value proposition and value creation mechanisms; Sales & Marketing Strategy and Servicing & Implementation Strategy, strongly related to the technological infrastructure for providing enabling services; and Value Creation Strategy, including revenue and profit generation as well as customer relationship issues. Moreover, the authors recognize four external factors that make up or directly impact an MNO business model: existing customer base, government policy and regulation, technological advancements and constraints, and relationship with other members of the value chain. The intriguing aspect in this business model conceptualization is the fact that it highlights components that are, at least theoretically, beyond the scope of the single firm. Moreover, it represents a working example of the business model construct adapted not to a single industry, but to a single type of player in an industry segment.

The study of MNO-centered mobile business models and value networks increased in popularity with the introduction of 3G mobile technologies, such as the Universal Mobile Telecommunications System adoption in Europe, in the early 2000s.[5] At the time, it was observed how the traditional 2G mobile telephony and basic dial-up Internet access value networks converged to form the 3G value network. The emergence of a new, complex value network involved the evolution from a linear, chained value-creating structure to another based on horizontal linkages and relationships. The 3G value network structure resulted from the convergence of mobile telephony, mobile data (including digital content and services) and Internet access, services, and digital content.[34] An important element introduced at the time was the enabler role, that is, firms that operate in the middle area between equipment, applications, and services such as middleware, content, and application service providers (ASPs). Moreover, the activities of content and application development and provision become separated, which created opportunities for new business models: intermediaries and content/application aggregators.[35]

One of the most influential analysis of mobile value networks outside the limited scope of MNOs is that of Barnes,[36] which highlights not only key players, but also their roles and the technologies involved. In his analysis, Barnes[36] argues that players in the mobile environment operate in two areas: services and infrastructure and content. To the services and infrastructure area, the following roles correspond: 1) mobile transport and transmission, where the main players are the telecommunication companies and network equipment vendors; 2) mobile services and delivery, involving players who provide and operate middleware infrastructure for supporting services like Internet connection, security, and payment; and 3) mobile interface and applications, which has the technology platform vendors, application developers, and mobile device vendors as main players. The content area includes the following roles: 1) content creation, with many possible players such as news agencies and entertainment companies (including players from outside the mobile arena, such as Internet-based firms); 2) content packaging, including activities of content edition, customization, and aggregation; and 3) market making, involving the promotion and sale of the content, where mobile portals (and, later, Internet portals) assume a central position.

Another useful description of the actors in the mobile business value network was proposed by Camponovo and Pigneur.[37] These authors see the mobile value network composed by primary and secondary players in five areas: technology, services, communication, regulation, and user. Technology players include device manufacturers and network equipment vendors as primary players, and device retailers, component makers, and platform vendors as secondary players. The services area includes application and content providers as primary players and payment agents, security solution providers, trusted third parties, advertising companies, and professional service providers as secondary players. MNOs and Internet service providers are considered primary communication players, while virtual operators and infrastructure management service providers are classified as secondary communication players. Finally, regulation players include governments, regulation authorities, and standardization groups, while players in the user area are further divided into business and consumer users; business users include firms operating in sectors where mobility is especially relevant, such as logistics or tourism, while consumer users include all individual customers of mobile products and services.

Furthermore, Camponovo and Pigneur[37] performed a complete analysis of these players' business models according to value proposition, target customers, core activities, business partners, and revenue flows, and provided some examples for each player category.

Another illustrative view of the mobile business value network is that of Pagiavlas et al.[38] The authors provide a process view of the value network that highlights five key components: infrastructure, operator/carrier, content, application, and portal. Actor and roles include device manufacturers and vendors, network service providers, software developers, system integrators, and Wireless ASPs in the infrastructure component; network operators and resellers in the operator/carrier component; information providers, aggregators, and distributors in the content component; developers for advertisement, entertainment, news, financial services, information, payments and security solutions in the application component; and content aggregators, horizontal portals, and vertical portals in the portal component. The authors stress that network operators not only dominate the key positions in the chain thanks to their ability to establish direct contact with the customer, but also highlight the challenges they face given the mobile–Internet convergence trend.

One of the few mobile business model propositions not limited to MNOs is that of Methlie and Pedersen.[39] The authors propose a business model construct for mobile services composed of three dimensions: revenue model, governance form, and service strategy. The service strategy dimension has two parameters: service value proposition, which can aim at mobility-specificity (uniqueness) or proposition breadth (scope), and market focus, where the choice is between the traditional focused or undifferentiated options. The governance form dimension describes how flows of information, resources, and goods are controlled by the parties involved: market-based governance, relational governance (implying open access to essential resources), and hierarchy (where access to the essential resources is closed or regulated by the operator). Finally, the revenue model dimension allows the choice between content-based versus transport-based revenue models.

By focusing on the central concepts of control (governance) and value within a business model, Ballon[40] proposed a design and analysis framework to model control and value proposition in business models related to innovative ICT products and services, which is especially adequate to the telecommunications industry. His four domains of business modeling correspond more or less to the four typical business model dimensions highlighted before: the value network (actors, roles, and relationships at the market level, that is, value delivery), the functional model (technical components, that is, value creation), the financial model (costs and revenues, akin to the value appropriation dimension), and the value proposition (characteristics of the offering). Each of these four domains is further detailed into three design parameters, and usual generic trade-offs for each parameter are suggested. Six of those, related to value network and functional architecture domains, are called control parameters, while the remaining six are referred to as value parameters.

For the value network domain, the parameters are: 1) combination of assets, relating to the hierarchies between actors, where the trade-off is between essential resources concentrated on or spread among multiple actors; 2) vertical integration, which details the way roles are assumed by the actors and whose values are either integrated or disintegrated; and 3) customer ownership, a parameter that explains the manner in which producing actors relate to consuming actors and whose possible trade-offs include intermediated versus direct customer ownership.

The functional model domain parameters are: 1) modularity of the design of systems, referring to their capability to operate as separate discrete and independent modules, which can be either modular or integrated; 2) distribution of intelligence, referring to the extent of distribution of processing power and functionality control among the architectures of systems, either centralized or distributed; and 3) interoperability, relating to the capability of system to function and exchange information with other systems and assuming either interoperable or stand-alone, or open versus proprietary solutions.

For the financial domain, the parameters are: 1) cost sharing model, where the trade-off is between concentrated versus distributed investments; 2) revenue model, whose value choices are mostly dependent on the application domain, but usually include the trade-offs between direct (consumer) and indirect (advertise) revenue or between content-based and transport-based revenue; and 3) revenue sharing model, relating to the presence or not of revenue sharing agreements between players.

For the value proposition domain, the parameters are: 1) positioning, referring to market choices on branding, segmentation, competition, and product or service attributes, where the main trade-off proposed is between complementary and substitutive products; 2) customer involvement, assumed as high, or intensive, versus low; and 3) intended value, referring to the strategies to achieve optimal value, usually one among operational excellence (price), product leadership (quality), and customer intimacy (lock-in).

Contemporary research on mobile value networks goes beyond listing actors and mapping their roles and relationships. Basole[41] maps the complexity of the multiple actors and relationships in the mobile ecosystem, drawing a network of nearly 7000 companies and over 18,000 relationships. In the context of business models for the

provision of mobile services, de Reuver et al.[42][2] show how organizational issues such as partner selection, network openness, orchestration of activities, management of relationship with partners, and outsourcing directly impact the division of roles among value network members. Similarly, they show how financial design issues such as pricing and division of investments, costs, and revenues affect acceptable risks, and how these two factors mediate profitability. Pagani and Fine[43] also propose a value network approach to study the mobile ecosystem, but concentrate on the changes brought by the diffusion of 3G technology. Using value network analysis, they map the driving forces involved in user adoption of innovative mobile services that make use of 3G technology and suggest guidelines for potential evolutionary scenarios for that industry. In a case study about the Japanese MNO market, Funk[44] also highlights the change from value chain to value network perspective and argues that till date the mobile industry was largely represented by only two main value chains: that of the MNO and that of the device manufacturers. With the emergence of the mobile Internet, the mobile environment has become highly dynamic and integrated with other business environments. This has impacted almost all business models in that. Finally, the author discusses the impacts of changing from a value chain to a value network perspective on issues like standard setting, policy making, and firm management. Not long ago, the diffusion of smartphones—with the consequent consolidation of mobile platform ecosystems and mobile application stores—has renewed the interest in the study of mobile value networks.[45,46]

In summary, it can be apprehended that both business models and value networks are valuable constructs to analyze the telecommunications industry, with all the technological, competitive, and regulatory changes that have characterized it till date. The business model construct is flexible enough that it can accommodate different perspectives, depending on the aims of each particular study. Similarly, the value network allows analysts to depict with precision the myriad of roles, players, relationships, and flows that characterize the contemporary landscape of telecommunication business. Taken together, these two concepts make up the basic toolbox of business researchers who wish to explore the telecommunications industry.

BUSINESS MODELS AND VALUE NETWORKS: AN INTERPRETATIVE FRAMEWORK

Following the review on business models and value networks and the discussion on the application of these concepts to the telecommunications industry, a summary conceptual model for jointly addressing both concepts is proposed. It considers the following definition of a

Knowledge—
Mobile

business model: a unit of analysis, in the form of an architectural system-wide logic comprising both the focal firm and its external stakeholders which translates the overall focal firm strategy into operational definitions focused on creating and delivering customer value and appropriate part of this value as revenues. This conceptual understanding is grounded in the theories of industrial organization, value chain, resource-based view, transaction costs economy, and industrial networks and is operationalized through five dimensions:

a. value proposition dimension, meaning the products and/or services offered and the logic through which these products and services create value for a specific target customer, including client selection, segmentation, and acquisition strategies;

b. value creation dimension, which describes the internal and external elements that determine how the value proposition is created and how it allows a unique strategic approach to the market, including key resources, processes, technologies, capabilities, and relationships;

c. value delivery dimension, which refers to how the business is articulated (internally and externally) in order to make the value proposition reach the target markets. It includes information and distribution channels as well as customer relationship;

d. value appropriation dimension, relative to how the business captures part of the value created and generates profit, including the parameters of revenue streams, revenue sharing mechanisms, investment model, and cost model; and

e. value network positioning, which describes how the elements and activities performed in the four previous dimensions are distributed among the focal firm and external partners, as well as the governance mechanisms that characterize the value network.

It is worth noticing that our proposed integrative framework purposely omits a strategy-related dimension because, in line with the existing dominant view in strategic literature, it considers business models as tools to select and implement strategy.[15] In other words, business models are a lower-level construct in comparison to firm strategy. Thus, a single strategy can be translated into different business models. In this view, the process of business model design and innovation becomes part of the strategy-making process. In rapidly changing environments, like that of the telecommunications industry, this process becomes extremely important in order to quickly sense and respond to disruptive change. Thus, such an integrative framework can be used to investigate the multiple, complex interrelationships between its constituting elements and the drivers of change both from the external environment and from the internal strategic actions. An example of the application of this

framework to analyze change and consequent business model response in the mobile telecommunication industry can be found in Ghezzi et al.[4]

CONCLUSION

In this entry, the popular concepts of business models and value networks were presented through a brief literature review discussing the state-of-the-art and promising research streams, like business model innovation. Moreover, the application of these concepts to the study of the telecommunications industry, with special emphasis on the mobile communications segment, was described. Finally, an interpretative framework that integrates both constructs was proposed; this framework can be applied to the strategic analysis of and corporate-level decision making in the telecommunications industry.

REFERENCES

1. Teece, D.J. Business models, business strategy and innovation. Long Range Plan. **2010**, *43*, 172–194.
2. Zott, C.; Amit, R.; Massa, L. The business model: Recent developments and future research. J. Manag. **2011**, *4*, 21–44.
3. George, G.; Bock, A.J. The business model in practice and its implications for entrepreneurship research. Entrep. Theo. Pract. **2011**, *35*, 83–111.
4. Ghezzi, A.; Cortimiglia, M.N.; Frank, A.G. Strategy and business model design in dynamic telecommunications industries: A study on Italian mobile network operators. Technol. Forecast. Social Change **2014**, *90*, 346–354.
5. Peppard, J.; Rylander, A. From value chain to value network: Insights for mobile operators. Eur. Manag. J. **2006**, *24*, 128–141.
6. Zhang, J.; Liang, X-J. Business ecosystem strategies of mobile network operators in the 3G era: The case of China Mobile. Telecommun. Policy **2011**, *35*, 156–171.
7. Magretta, J. Why business models matter. Harvard Bus. Rev. **2002**, *80*, 86–92.
8. Tapscott, D. Rethinking strategy in a networked world. Strategy + Bus. **2001**, *24*, 34–41.
9. Amit, R.; Zott, C. Value creation in e-business. Strateg. Manag. J. **2001**, *22*, 493–520.
10. Porter, M.E. Strategy and the internet. Harvard Bus. Rev. **2001**, *79*, 62–78.
11. Chesbrough, H.; Rosenbloom, R.S. The role of the business model in capturing value from innovation: Evidence from Xerox Corporation's technology spin-off companies. Ind. Corp. Change **2001**, *11*, 529–555.
12. Shafer, S.M.; Smith, H.J.; Linder, J.C. The power of business models. Busin. Horiz. **2005**, *48*, 199–207.
13. Timmers, P. Business models for electronic markets. J. Electron. Markets **1998**, *8* (2), 3–8.
14. Malone, T.W.; Weill, P.; Lai, R.K.; D'Urso, V.T.; Herman, G.; Apel, T.G.; Woerner, S.L. *Do some business*

models perform better than others? MIT Sloan Working Paper 4615-06, May 2006.

15. Casadesus-Masanell, R.; Ricart, J.E. From strategy to business models and onto tactics. Long Range Plan. **2010**, *43*, 195–215.

16. Cortimiglia, M.N.; Ghezzi, A.; Frank, A.G. Business model innovation and strategy making nexus: evidence from a cross-industry mixed-methods study. R&D Manag. **2015**, in press.

17. Demil, B.; Lecocq, X. Business model evolution: In search of dynamic consistency. Long Range Plan. **2010**, *43*, 227–246.

18. Habtay, S.R. A firm-level analysis on the relative difference between technology-driven and market-driven disruptive business model innovations. Creat. Innov. Manag. **2012**, *21*, 290–303.

19. Osterwalder, A. The business model ontology: A proposition in a design science approach. Doctoral Thesis on Management Informatics, Lausanne: Ecole des Hautes Etudes Commerciales, Universite de Lausanne, **2004**, p. 169.

20. Osterwalder, A.; Pigneur, Y. *Business Model Generation—A Handbook for Visionaires, Game Changers, and Challengers*; Wiley: New York, NY, 2010.

21. Hacklin, F.; Wallnöfer, M. The business model in the practice of strategic decision making: Insights from a case study. Manag. Dec. **2012**, *50*, 166–188.

22. Trimi, S.; Berbegal-Mirabent, J. Business model innovation in entrepreneurship. Intl Entrep. Manag. J. **2012**, *8*, 449–465.

23. Schneider, S.; Spieth, P. Business model innovation: Towards an integrated future research agenda. Intl J. Innov. Manag. *2013*, 17, 34.

24. Porter, M.E. *Competitive Advantage: Creating and Sustaining Superior Performance*; Free Press: New York, 1985; *576*.

25. Stabell, C.B.; Fjeldstad, Ø. D. Configuring value for competitive advantage: On chains, shops and networks. Strateg. Manag. J. **1998**, *19*, 413–437.

26. Hamel, G.; Prahalad, C.K. The core competence of the corporation. Harvard Busin. Rev. **1990**, *68*, 79–93.

27. Velu, C. Business model innovation and third-party alliance on the survival of new firms. Technovation **2015**, *35*, 1–11.

28. Swatman, P.M.C.; Krueger, C.; Van Der Beek, K. The changing digital content landscape: An evaluation of e-business model development in European online news and music. Internet Res. **2006**, *16*, 53–80.

29. Olla, P.; Patel, N.V. A value chain model for mobile data service providers. Telecommun. Policy, **2002**, *26*, 551–571.

30. Li, F.; Whalley, J. Deconstruction of the telecommunications industry: From value chains to value networks. Telecommun. Policy **2002**, *26*, 451–472.

31. Pateli, A.G.; Giaglis, G.M. Technology innovation-induced business model change: A contingency approach. J. Org. Change Manag. **2005**, *18*, 167–183.

32. Haaker, T.; Faber, E.; Bouwman, H. Balancing customer and network value in business models for mobile services. IntlJ. Mobile Commun. **2006**, *4*, 645–661.

33. Kallio, J.; Tinnilä, M.; Tseng, A. An international comparison of operator-driven business models. Bus. Process Manag. J. **2006**, *12* (3), 281–298.

34. Dunnewijk, T.; Hultèn, S. A brief history of mobile communication in Europe. Telemat. Informat. **2007**, *24* (3), 164–179.

35. Ghezzi, A.; Cortimiglia, M.N.; Balocco, R. Mobile content and service delivery platforms: A technology classification model. Info **2012**, *14* (2), 72–88.

36. Barnes, S.J. The mobile commerce value chain: Analysis and future developments. Intl J. Inform. Manag. **2002**, *22* (2), 91–108.

37. Camponovo, G.; Pigneur, Y. *Business Model Analysis Applied to Mobile Business.* In Proceedings of the 5th International Conference on Enterprise Information Systems, Angers, April 23–26, 2003.

38. Pagiavlas, N.; Marburger, P.; Stratmann, M.; Young, S. Mobile business—Comprehensive marketing strategies or merely IT expenses? A case study of the U.S. airline industry. J. Elect.. Comm. Res.. **2005**, *6* (3), 251–261.

39. Methlie, L.B.; Pedersen, P.E. Business model choices for value creation of mobile services. info **2007**, *9* (5), 70–85.

40. Ballon, P. Business modelling revisited: the configuration of control and value. info **2007**, *9* (5), 6–19.

41. Basole, R.C. Visualization of interfirm relations in a converging mobile ecosystem. J. Inform. Techn. **2009**, *24*, 144–159.

42. de Reuver, M.; Bouwman, H.; Haaker, T. *Capturing Value from Mobile Business Models: Design Issues That Matter.* In Proceedings of the 21st Bled eConference, Bled, Slovenia, June 15–18, 2008.

43. Pagani, M.; Fine, C.H. Value network dynamics in 3G-4G wireless communications: A systems thinking approach to strategic value assessment. J. Bus. Res. **2008**, *61* (11), 1102–1112.

44. Funk, J.L. The emerging value network in the mobile phone industry: The case of Japan and its implications for the rest of the world. Telecommun. Policy **2009**, *33* (1/2), 4–18.

45. Basole, R.C.; Karla, J. On the evolution of mobile platform ecosystem structure and strategy. Bus. Inform. Syst. Eng. **2011**, *3* (5), 313–322.

46. Cortimiglia, M.N.; Ghezzi, A.; Renga, F. Mobile applications and application stores: a strategy quick reference guide. IT Prof. **2011**, *13* (5), 51–56.

Knowledge—
Mobile

Mobile Data Security

George G. McBride
Senior Manager, Security and Privacy Services (SPS), Deloitte & Touche LLP, Princeton, New Jersey, U.S.A.

Abstract

In this entry, we review some of the many threats and risks that exist today to mobile devices of all shapes and sizes. From USB memory drives to laptops and from traditional mobile phones to smart phones, we discuss available controls and safeguards that can be implemented to reduce the overall level of mobile device risk, and we discuss tips to help audit and assess the overall security of an organization's mobile device infrastructure.

INTRODUCTION

Data breach. Information loss. Laptop theft. We typically don't go more than a few days without hearing about another loss of a laptop, a personal digital assistant (PDA), or perhaps even a USB memory drive. Was it social security numbers? Perhaps the medical history of several hundred thousand people? The strategic vision or initial public offering (IPO) plans of the company? Was the drive just lost or intentionally stolen? Most of the time, it doesn't even matter. Oftentimes, the results of the news hitting the newspapers or a popular website are enough to soil the reputation and image of the company, to cause the stock price to take a dip, and make you wonder if you should start checking the employment pages.

We live in a world where electronic information grows at a phenomenal rate. In 1982, my Commodore VIC-20 computer had less than 5 kilobytes (KB) of memory. In 1985, my Apple //GS computer came with a whopping 64 KB, which seemed to be an infinite source that could never be fully utilized. Today, with much larger programs and larger amounts of data, we're carrying 4 and 8 gigabytes (GB) USB memory drives, PDAs with 16 GBs, and laptops with 250 GB hard drives. Add a 1-terabyte (TB) portable USB hard drive and you can easily carry around all of the data that you could ever read or even need in a lifetime.

Many years ago when I worked for a large telecommunications firm, we had a policy that our laptops were to be securely cabled to a desk or permanent fixture in the office if we left them overnight. Being a dutiful corporate citizen, I left my laptop in the office one night secured to the desk and even had both keys with me. Early the next morning I returned to find an antitheft cable laying on the floor, its frayed end evidence that it had been cut off. Fortunately for me a piece of the cable had been left in the office; otherwise I would have had

to convince management and corporate security that I had actually secured the laptop.

Several months later, a person—likely innocent—told the police that he had purchased the laptop at a flea market for a few hundred dollars. Neither the lock still secured to the laptop nor the power-on BIOS password succeeded in stopping the purchaser from making a rational decision to pass on the purchase. When the purchaser called the computer manufacturer for some tips on how to remove the basic input/output system (BIOS) password and provided the computer serial number to the technician, the police were notified. When I left the firm several years later, the laptop was still in police custody as evidence.

This instance illustrates the difference between a deterrent and a preventative control. The cable deters a malicious person only to the point of choosing an easier target. Unfortunately, the easier targets had already been stolen that evening, and those that were cabled to the desk became fair game. Would a preventative control, such as locking the device inside a desk drawer, have been sufficient? What controls may have been sufficient to prevent the theft besides taking the laptop home with me, possibly exposing it to a different threat element?

The lesson here is that it is not just one safeguard that is the solution, but the deployment of a layered defense of carefully selected safeguards. Had the BIOS password not been installed, the laptop may never have been recovered as the purchaser easily could have booted up the laptop and installed any operating system without the need of help from the manufacturer. What is not known is whether the data stored on the hard drive was ever accessed. Although it appears that a financial motive existed to steal the laptop for later sale at a flea market and not to a competitor, it is only conjecture, and without a strong disk-based encryption to protect the data on the hard drive, we know that we didn't prevent the thief from accessing the data. This is the question that is often asked after the theft of a device

Encyclopedia of Information Systems and Technology, DOI: 10.1081/E-EIST-120046298

Knowledge– Mobile

that has stored any type of sensitive data, and it is a question that shouldn't matter when sufficient controls are deployed and you are comfortable, if not certain, that your data will be adequately protected.

BEFORE YOU CAN MEASURE THE RISKS

A number of risks should be considered when developing a program to secure mobile devices and data. One of the first constraints to measuring the risk to mobile data is evident when we look at a typical risk equation, which addresses the risk as a function of the asset(s) under consideration. However, most organizations do not know their asset base and consequently are challenged when calculating the risk of a device and especially of an infrastructure of tens of thousands of devices. Few organizations have an up-to-date and accurate asset inventory list. Fewer organizations have an accurate inventory of PDAs and smart phones in use. Add to that the devices that can be purchased by individuals, and you may feel that the task is impossible.

Some proven methods exist to understand the data population of mobile devices within the organization. I have seen surveys utilized as a successful tool to obtain a device count. I have seen reviews of inventory purchases, reviews of software installed on desktops (such as the synchronization software), and even a top-down approach of managers querying their teams for data. Each has its own merits and inherent flaws, but manages to get some of the data that will help determine statistically the count within the organization. Moving forward in this entry to the policy section, if you are having a difficult time determining the inventory, it may be necessary to strengthen the policy to reflect the requirements of the organization, such as allowing only firm-provided and firm-supported devices to be utilized and authorized to access and to store corporate information.

In addition to understanding the inventory count of the devices, it will be important to know the type of information that is at risk. For example, a data classification guide should exist to help associates within the firm have the knowledge to know who is responsible for classifying documents, how documents should be classified based on their content, and the effect to the firm if they are lost or stolen. The document should provide solid guidance on how to classify all documents and content such as web pages and e-mail that exist today and those that are created in the future.

A data inventory program is useful to know the types of data that exist within the organization and the relative amounts of data in each data classification category once they have been established. For example, it may be quite helpful to know that a particular organization in the firm does not access or manage sensitive documents and consequently incurs less of a risk than does a business unit that manages highly sensitive documents. The organization posing less of a risk may be addressed after the organizations with higher levels of risk have been addressed and may ultimately have fewer controls applied when addressed.

Finally, a data retention program may specify what data needs to be retained within the organization and establish schedules for regularly purging unnecessary or obsolete data. The data retention program, whether it addresses e-mail being archived from local message stores to a central server or it states that completed client engagement data must be securely and centrally archived and preserved, can actually reduce the amount of sensitive information stored on devices and the overall risk from those devices.

Wow. We've already discussed asset inventories, data classification, data inventories, and the benefits of a data retention program and we've barely scratched the surface of mobile data security. Unfortunately, if you start at the device security and focus exclusively on that, you'll reduce the risk, but you'll have avoided some areas that will have significant benefits not just with mobile devices, but throughout the entire organization. That being said, rather than embarking on a lengthy and focused process to build out the programs and then addressing mobile data security, I'd recommend a parallel approach that minimizes the threat imposed by mobile devices and addresses some of the risks discussed later in this entry, along with an approach that lays a solid foundation for information security by incorporating the programs mentioned earlier.

MOBILE DEVICES

Mobile data security refers to securing the data that is stored on or accessed by any type of mobile device from an old Palm Pilot 1000 or an Apple iPhone to a brand-new laptop. Some of the risks and controls that are discussed will also apply to simple devices such as USB memory sticks and external hard drives.

In general, several risks have been identified with mobile devices. Not surprisingly, not all risks are applicable to each device and even less surprising is that many of these risks exist with larger desktop computers that typically have more processing power, more storage, and higher bandwidth. What is not surprising is that these risks are manifested due to a lack of physical and logical controls that we can apply to those desktops. There is no guard or card key access to get to the laptop you thought you had left at your feet a few minutes ago. There is no corporate firewall or intrusion prevention system to protect your laptop while you are

Attack Vector	Controls and Safeguards								
	Auth	Encrypt	Config Mngt	Device AV	Device FW	Anti-Brute Force	Anti-SMS Spam	VPN or Tunnel	Remote Mngt & Control
Software			✓	✓	✓				
Connection Attack	✓				✓			✓	
Eaves-dropping								✓	
Loss	✓		✓			✓	✓		✓
Mobile Spam							✓		

Fig. 1 Controls vs. attack vectors.

accessing your e-mail using free wireless Internet access at the coffee shop. One of the themes of this entry is to extend those controls to the mobile devices or to offer compensating controls that offer different controls and safeguards that reduce the risk in a different but perhaps more practical manner. Fig. 1 highlights some of the controls that we'll discuss along with the attack vectors that they mitigate.

One of the most prevalent risks to mobile devices is the loss or theft of the device itself. Many years ago I left a phone charging cable in a very large hotel I was staying at and when I returned for my next stay, I stopped by the lost and found office to retrieve my cable. I was invited to look through several boxes of cables, where I ultimately found mine or at least one that looked like mine, as there were several. Although I was surprised at the number of charging and synchronization cables that were left in the hotel, I cannot believe to this day the shelves that were filled with laptops, mobile phones, smart phones, and Blackberry devices. Many times magazines and newspapers run stories about the lost and found departments at airports and the strange things that they contain. I'm forever amazed that people don't track their equipment down before it is sold for a small percentage of its true hardware value and before the new owner discovers the value of the software and data on the device.

Theft of mobile devices in public areas such as restaurants, airports, and other high-traffic areas continues to grow and pose a tremendous threat. Consider the case of the CEO of a large wireless and microelectronics manufacturer who had his laptop stolen moments after wrapping up a presentation to journalists. Was the laptop stolen for the hardware value, or for the sensitive data that a CEO's laptop was likely to contain that would be invaluable to competitors and potential customers who now had all of the pricing and design details that they may ever need? Although that is just

one of many high-profile cases that have been in the media, thousands of other cases illustrate that laptop and mobile device theft affects everybody.

Consider a device that isn't even stolen. A large-capacity memory stick filled to capacity can be copied in a few minutes. A hard drive can be removed from a computer and copied in a forensically sound manner that doesn't affect the system at all and, if left in suspend mode, would resume right where it had been suspended, and the owner would be none the wiser. There are many stories, likely some fact and some folklore, of business deals gone awry because somebody entered the hotel room of an executive and picked the safe to make a copy of the hard drive secured in that safe. Many mobile devices do not authenticate themselves or the system when synchronizing with a computer system, and it is often a matter of plugging the right cable into a device to be able to copy all the data from the device.

Wireless security continues to increase the risk of mobile devices. With devices moving from slower cellular transmission speeds to faster 3G speeds, data can be transmitted and received at high speeds. Many devices have very primitive, if any, firewalls or other controls built in to protect the device against attacks and threats from the service provider network. Many, but not all service providers restrict access from one device to another on their high-speed data networks and generally restrict traffic to travel between each device and some external endpoint. Do you know how the security has been configured within the service providers that you or your organization will be using?

Wireless risks also exist in the Wi-Fi spectrum. 802.11b continues to be the most popular, with other variants closely behind. Most of the modern mobile devices contain built-in wireless connectivity, which in some cases is configured to be on by default. Our devices, when enabled to transmit data over Wi-Fi, are susceptible to eavesdropping if the data is not encrypted, are susceptible to man-in-the-middle attacks with rogue access points that disable and then masquerade as the legitimate access point, and are susceptible to other malicious attacks that are possible when using a potentially untrusted connection medium.

A continued threat that has existed for quite a while as well is through an improperly configured Bluetooth radio component in a mobile device such as a smart phone. Bluetooth attacks have evolved to develop their own vocabulary including bluesnarfing, bluejacking, and bluebugging. Bluesnarfing involves a malicious individual gaining covert access to the device through a Bluetooth connection to transfer data such as calendar appointments or contacts from the device. Bluebugging is covertly issuing commands to the device to attempt eavesdropping or even to cause the device to dial a premium-rate telephone number and incur frighteningly high charges. Finally, bluejacking is an attack in which somebody sends an unsolicited short message service (SMS) or multimedia message service (MMS) message to an unwilling recipient in the form of a business card exchange that may contain an offensive message, perhaps an offensive image, or the link to download some Trojan from a website.

Going the way of the floppy drive, the infrared (IR) port on laptops and some older PDAs to facilitate printing and to synchronize data could pose a threat if it is misconfigured. In the unlikely event that a device still has an IR port, it should be disabled through an IT policy pushed down to a device in the operating system or system BIOS when not in use. Many firms provide a far more simple solution of applying a small piece of electrical tape over the IR sensor to prevent any data transmission.

Another risk stems from software that a malicious user is successful in loading into a mobile device. Whether it is in the form of a Trojan buried in a legitimate application, visiting a URL that results in the installation of the application, or causing the installation of the application on the host computer that is synchronized with a mobile device, once attackers can get software of their choice installed on a system, the system is generally considered to be compromised. Remember applications such as *Back Orifice* and *Sub7*, whose sole purpose was to provide a covert remote computer system control tool that the malicious user could use to have the target system execute any command or perform any function. Those and more advanced applications exist today.

Software threats exist in the PDA and Blackberry world as well. In 2006, Jesse D'Aguano demonstrated his proof-of-concept application called BBProxy that could be utilized to gain access to back-end system servers protected by an organization's firewalls through the use of a compromised Blackberry device. This tool, in conjunction with code executed on a Blackberry device, would provide access to the back-end systems and would also serve as a launch platform to identify other weaknesses and vulnerabilities within the corporate perimeter.

And finally, software threats exist with smart phones as well. The industry has seen some well-written proof-of-concept works and virus-like applications that propagate through Bluetooth or the calendaring program to infect other machines before very professionally deleting and wiping all data off of the device. A few companies have begun to offer complete monitoring software to track usage, location with *Global Positioning System* (GPS)-enabled phones, SMS, and phone call logs, and some of the deluxe software solutions record and then send the entire conversation back to a predefined e-mail address. Originally intended to identify cheating spouses and help protect children, the software could be installed surreptitiously on any compatible device without your knowledge as one of the program's strengths is typically its covert installation and operational capabilities.

One of the biggest threats to a firm's infrastructure is the introduction of unauthorized mobile devices that are typically only controlled via policy and awareness. Usually with the best and most honest of intentions, corporate associates may decide to utilize their own larger USB memory drive, their faster laptop, or their smart phone that works in the country that they will be visiting. With organizations moving toward utilizing encrypted USB memory drives; laptops with antivirus (AV), strong authentication, and encryption; and mobile devices that require authentication and encrypt all data on the device including memory cards, well-intentioned individuals would cause more harm than good in utilizing their own equipment and not that of their firms.

Complexity is often another contributing factor to the increase in risk of mobile devices. Multiply the number of permitted devices in the environment with the number of different configurations and parameters and the combinations are virtually unlimited. In addition, there is a certain element of uncertainty or mystery in how communications work. Take, for example, the security of a Blackberry device. Although the communications channels are well documented and have been assessed by independent third parties, a shroud of mystery surrounds the Research In Motion Network Operations Center (NOC) in Ottawa, Canada. If you refer to Fig. 2, it is evident that all e-mail communications to or from a Blackberry device travel through the NOC, but there is adequate protection through the use of Triple data encryption standard (DES) or advance encryption standard (AES) encryption to protect the message from eavesdropping.

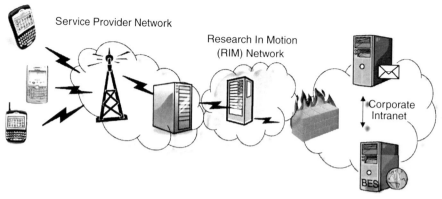

Fig. 2 Typical Blackberry infrastructure.

CONTROLS AND SAFEGUARDS

A number of controls and safeguards can be implemented that reduce and sometimes completely mitigate many of the risks that have been discussed. Unfortunately, many of the controls that are built into the operating system or device itself are sacrificed in the name of ease of use and by the request of executives who may not be sold on the need for the security controls or who place convenience ahead of security. Additionally, many individuals and small businesses lack the dedicated IT resources to administer and maintain the security features that are generally enabled just a few hours after the first time a smart phone or laptop is stolen or lost. Consider a small firm planning an IPO or focused on its first big product launch. Interested in enabling FileVault on their Mac OS X? Probably not. Concerned with turning the system firewall back on after disabling it to conduct the testing? Again, re-enabling the security features is unlikely to happen unless a timed feature automatically re-enables the firewall.

We've already discussed the development of a complete asset inventory of all mobile devices including PDAs, smart phones, and laptops. We've discussed the development of a data classification guide that provides a comprehensive and easy methodology for associates to categorize the data that they create or access, and we've reviewed the importance of an accurate data inventory program. Finally, we've discussed how a data retention program can ultimately reduce the amount of information that you are protecting as it is archived or redacted on a regular basis.

One of the best solutions to addressing the risks imposed by mobile devices is not a single control, but rather a collection of controls that form a defense-in-depth approach that incrementally increases security with each control and doesn't fail completely in the absence of one control. Recall my stolen laptop with a strong physical deterrent of the cable lock and the BIOS password-based authentication. The cable lock was

insufficient in protecting the device, but the BIOS password was the control that enabled its recovery. Having employed a third layer that included whole disk encryption would have sufficiently reduced the risk to the point of only wanting the laptop back to reformat, reconfigure, and then redeploy.

It is ironic that many firms in the past would deploy a laptop valued at several thousand dollars for the hardware, add licensed applications that may cost several thousand as well, and then not provide a cable lock for the device. Fortunately, many IT organizations today are beginning to deploy cable locks along with the laptops. For those that don't, it is recommended that the business units procure them for the associates. If you are protecting your own laptop, a $50 cable purchased at an office-supply or computer store will typically be sufficient and would be considered a worthy investment.

A software-based solution to recover laptops when the physical controls of locking the device fail comes from the growing sector of *call-home* type software. Whether it is a commercially available and centrally monitored solution that hides on a mobile device such as a laptop or smart phone, the software will contact a predefined system with information about the IP address that it currently has, perhaps some usage information, and on some devices with built-in cameras perhaps even send a picture back. Although this wouldn't be the first line of defense, publicly available anecdotes and news articles indicate that a modest investment up front to install and run the software on the system covertly may pay benefits if the device is stolen.

Training and awareness are important aspects of any information security program and the training aspects should include regular reminders of the mobile data security areas of the policy. The program should address the storage and transportation of mobile devices such as locking up a laptop in a car trunk or hotel safe when not in use, and should address logical security issues such as the installation of unauthorized software, the use of unauthorized devices, and the importance of not making changes to system and device configurations. Many other key areas of the firm's policy should also be part of the training and awareness program including defining personal liability in the event that associates are negligent in protecting the assets or intentionally defeat controls. Many companies today hold employees accountable for the replacement costs of laptops and devices when they are not secured and protected in accordance with the company policy.

A number of solutions address the typical confidentiality, integrity, and availability components of an information security policy. In addition, we'll also briefly discuss auditing as an additional control to support any investigative needs and accountability of users and their actions, both of which are notoriously weak in almost all PDAs.

Many of the following recommended controls and safeguards are those that are documented in the policy and those that we hope that our users follow. For many devices, whether an Apple Macintosh, a Microsoft Windows, a Microsoft Windows Mobile, or a Blackberry, many of the controls recommended in this section are available to be pushed down to the device in the form of IT policies. It is highly recommended to push the controls down to the user in the form of non-user-changeable local policies and not to rely on the end users to comply with corporate policies based on their recollection and will to comply.

The recommended solution is to identify all of the configuration options of the devices and the supporting infrastructure (such as Blackberry Enterprise Server, or BES) and then map those configurations and parameters to the existing corporate policy so that the implementation mirrors the corporate policy. These controls should be implemented prior to deployment to secure all devices as they are deployed and to help mitigate the necessity to *sell* the additional security, which will be seen as an unwelcome burden to the users when implemented post-deployment. How many times have you heard an administrator wish that a stronger or more secure control had been deployed at deployment time than having to now go through the return on investment, impact analysis, training and awareness programs, and more, just to increase the length of a password on a mobile device from six to eight characters?

The corporate policy should also address whether personal assets can be utilized to access or store corporate data. If an organization provides the associates with a password protected and encrypted USB memory drive, there should be a policy that prohibits the use of a personally owned USB memory drive. The use of personal PDAs, laptops, and computers at home should be addressed and not left ambiguous so that associates know exactly what is allowed and what is restricted. The mobile device policy should address the entire life cycle of the device from initial configuration and setup

to deployment and ultimately to decommissioning the device and preparing for the next user.

One of the easiest ways to protect the confidentiality and integrity of the data stored on any mobile device is to require some type of authentication to access the device. For laptops, users typically log in with their username and password pair to gain access. For handheld devices, users are usually prompted simply to enter a password, which is typically called a "pin" because it may be as short as four characters and may not require any specific complexity or special characters. Although some devices initiate a memory wiping of all data after an incorrect password is entered more than some predefined number of times, some simply increase the delay between password entries to slow down an attacker attempting to guess a valid pin or password.

One typical recommendation is to mirror the existing corporate policy (if it exists) or to utilize an industry best practice of a six- to eight-character password with some form of complexity, and an account lock-out or wipe after some number of incorrect attempts. Although a laptop may allow two or three sets of five password attempts with a 15-minute time-out between sets, that type of complexity may not be possible with a Blackberry or Microsoft Windows Mobile device and the device may automatically purge all of its content after some number of invalid attempts. I typically see many organizations utilizing the default setting of eight invalid attempts on a Microsoft Windows Mobile device or 10 invalid attempts on a Blackberry before automatically purging the memory.

Another important aspect of protecting the confidentiality and integrity of the data is to encrypt the data stored on the device as well as any add-on memory cards. These devices typically utilize the password or pin entered to log on or access the device as the decryption key and typically offer strong encryption in the form of Triple DES, AES, or elliptic curve cryptography to protect the data. A strong authentication requirement paired with a strong encryption algorithm is a great way to protect data stored on a USB memory device, many of which *enterprise class* devices have built in and run automatically when inserted into a laptop.

To protect the mobile device, especially when connected to a non-corporate network such as a service provider's 3G network or the Wi-Fi at a local coffee shop, a firewall and an automatically updating AV solution should be installed. The firewall should be configured to block unsolicited incoming traffic, and an optimal solution would transmit unsuccessful attempts and other pertinent events from the AV solution to a central location for monitoring and analysis. Equally important to protect the confidentiality and integrity of the data in transit to connect to the corporate network is the utilization of a virtual private network (VPN), which encrypts all traffic to the corporate network. It is important to note, however, that all traffic may not be protected. Some firms configure their client VPN to route all corporate traffic over the encrypted VPN tunnel while routing the non-corporate traffic such as banking information or personal e-mail over the unprotected Internet. Consumer-based solutions exist today to route unprotected traffic to a central location that decrypts the traffic and then sends the data along through the Internet. For either a one-time or monthly fee, these services protect data as it travels over a wireless (or wired) unsecured network such as a coffee shop or public Wi-Fi facility, but then send the data over the Internet.

ASSESSING AND AUDITING

One of the most important security aspects to consider is the inclusion of the mobile device infrastructure into the security assessment or audit schedule to identify vulnerabilities regularly and to develop plans to mitigate the identified risks. Additionally, the introduction or change of a mobile device infrastructure should trigger an assessment that includes the mobile device infrastructure.

Many vendors today produce excellent documentation highlighting the security features and configuration options of their devices. Industry standards such as ISO/IEC 27002 and those from the payment card industry provide some valuable guidance that can be applied to mobile devices. The U. S. National Institute of Standards and Technology also provides some guidance and recommendations that can be applied to bolster a firm's mobile device security program. In addition, the firm's corporate policy probably provides significant guidance for other devices that can be extrapolated and incorporated to develop a mobile device policy. These can serve as baseline documents to identify gaps and weaknesses from the audit and assessments that will be conducted.

Assessing the infrastructure will likely require a review of messaging servers, content servers, firewalls, authentication servers, and other devices that are integrated with and utilized by the mobile device infrastructure. They should be included in the regular assessment program if they are not already.

Any assessment should include a review of the policy infrastructure including policies, practices, standards, and guidelines, and should validate that they are being followed. The review should include the life cycle management of devices from how they are ordered to how they are shipped to a recycling firm (which had better include wiping of the data). The review should also be technical in nature and may include the use of tools such as packet sniffers to validate a vendor's claim of encryption or authentication and should test the effectiveness of important tools such as remote wiping in the event of an employee termination or loss of a device.

CONCLUSIONS

A few years ago an associate who left a large global financial institution sold his Blackberry on eBay. As an employee of the company, he had to buy his own device, so it was his, but it was maintained by the firm and configured to send and receive e-mail and to synchronize his corporate calendar, contacts, and other data. When he left the firm, he simply took it with him and decided to sell it on eBay. When the purchaser received it for approximately $15, he was surprised to find a treasure trove of information regarding upcoming transactions and activities, personal contact information of senior executives, and more. Needless to say, there was a lot of information on that device that could have been wiped remotely with a single command if the employee separation process and device decommissioning process had been integrated.

Laptops with sensitive data such as social security numbers, health information, and other personal information continue to be lost, stolen, and compromised. Without appropriate controls in place, companies wind up spending hundreds of thousands and many times tens of millions of dollars in notification and providing credit monitoring services to the affected customers. Ironically, the first thing that is done after the data breach is the implementation of the very controls that may have prevented it in the first place, so the money that could have been spent up front is spent after the breach. The only difference is the tens of millions of dollars in notification and monitoring costs, the regulatory fines, the unwanted publicity, and sometimes the opportunity for a few people to find another career.

Many times the controls that could have prevented the breach could have been implemented with minimal effort. Whether it is user resistance to those controls, a lack of funding, or a lack of knowledge or awareness on behalf of the end users or administrators, the problems are typically solvable utilizing the tools and mechanisms provided by the device vendors. Sometimes it requires a focus on gaining buy-in and sponsorship from executive management and sometimes it is simply an administrator configuring the device as it mirrors the corporate policy. It may be a long and arduous road to securing the infrastructure, but at the end of the day it is a road well taken.

By the way, has anybody seen where I left my Blackberry?

Network Management

Jianguo Ding
School of Informatics, University of Skovde, Skovde, Sweden

Ranganai Chaparadza
IPv6 Forum, ETSI-AFI, Berlin, Germany

Abstract

IT networks are evolving rapidly and have shown many new characteristics and are expected to support multiple emerging services. A variety of challenges in networks mean existing management approaches have to improve to match the new challenges and requirements. The techniques update so quickly that lots of new concepts and techniques bring confusions and challenges to users, even for professionals. This entry provides the overview of evolutions in network management and a deeper insight into network management, and provides a wide coverage of key technologies in network management including network management architectures and protocols, theories and techniques, the management of emerging networks, and autonomic and self-management, and related standard.

INTRODUCTION

Network management is facing new challenges, stemming from the growth in size, heterogeneity, pervasiveness, complexity of applications, network services, the combination of rapidly evolving technologies, and increased requirements from corporate customers.

Over decades ago, the classic agent-manager centralized paradigm was the prevalent network management architecture, exemplified in the Open Systems Interconnection standards (OSI) reference model, the Simple Network Management Protocol (SNMP), and the Telecommunications Management Network (TMN) management framework. The increasing trend towards enterprise application integration based on loosely coupled heterogeneous IT infrastructures forces a change in management paradigms from centralized and local to distributed management strategies and solutions that are able to cope with multiple autonomous management domains and possibly conflicting management policies. In addition, service oriented business applications come with end-to-end application-level quality of service (QoS) requirements and service-level agreements (SLA) that depend on the qualities of the underlying IT infrastructure.

More recently, requirements in network management and control have been amended by emerging network and computing models, including wireless networks, ad hoc networks, overlay networks, Grid networks, optical networks, multimedia networks, storage networks, the convergence of next generation networks (NGN), or even nan networks, etc. Increasingly ubiquitous network environments require new management strategies that can cope with resource constraints, multifederated operations, scalability, dependability, context awareness, security, mobility, and probability, etc. A set of enabling technologies are recognized to be potential candidates for distributed network management, such as policy-based management strategies, artificial intelligence (AI) techniques, probabilistic approaches, web-based techniques, agent techniques, distributed object computing technology, active networks technology, bio-inspired approach, or economic theory, etc. To bring complex network systems under control, it is necessary for the IT industry to move to autonomic management, context-aware management, and self-management systems in which technology itself is used to manage technology.[1]

Autonomic computing deals with the increasing difficulty of managing distributed computing systems, which become more and more interconnected and diverse, and software applications that go beyond corporate boundaries into the Internet. Autonomic computing anticipates systems consisting of myriads of interacting autonomous components that are able to manage themselves according to predefined goals and policies.

Context-aware systems management aims to take the availability of dynamically changing resources and services during a particular period of system operation into account. Management policies and automated mechanisms need to be able to adapt to dynamic changes such that they offer the best possible level of service to the user in the given situation.

Self-management capabilities include automated configuration of components, automated recognition of opportunities for performance improvement (self-optimization), automatic detection, diagnosis, and repair of local hardware and software problems, and automatic defense against attacks. The objective is to minimize the degree of external intervention, e.g., by human system managers, and, at the same time, to preserve the architectural properties imposed by its specification. The concept of self-configuration refers to a process in which an application's internal structure changes depending on its environment.

This entry documents the evolution of networks and network management solutions in network management paradigms, protocols, and techniques. It also investigates novel management strategies for emerging networks and services.

DEFINITION OF NETWORK MANAGEMENT

Definition

Network management is defined as the execution of the set of functions required for controlling, planning, allocating, deploying, coordinating, and monitoring the resources of a telecommunications network or a computer network, including performing functions such as initial network planning, frequency allocation, predetermined traffic routing to support load balancing, cryptographic key distribution authorization, configuration management, fault management, security management, performance management, and accounting management. Network management is to ensure the effective and efficient operations of a system within its resources in accordance with corporate goals. To achieve this, network management is tasked with controlling network resources, coordinating network services, monitoring network states, and reporting network status and anomalies. The objectives of network management are:

- Managing system resources and services: includes control, monitor, update, and report of system states, device configurations, and network services.
- Simplifying systems management complexity: is the task of management systems that extrapolates systems management information into a humanly manageable form. Conversely, management systems should also have the ability to interpret high-level management objectives.
- Providing reliable services: means to provide networks with a high QoS and to minimize system downtime. Distributed management systems should detect and fix network faults and errors. Network management must safeguard against all security threats.
- Maintaining cost consciousness: requires keeping track of system resources and network users. All network resource and service usage should be tracked and reported.

Another acceptable definition identifies network management as the activities, methods, procedures, and tools that pertain to the operation, administration, maintenance, and provisioning of networked systems.[2]

- Operation deals with keeping the network (and the services that the network provides) up and running smoothly. It includes monitoring the network to spot problems as soon as possible, ideally before users are affected.
- Administration deals with keeping track of resources in the network and how they are assigned. It includes all the "housekeeping" that is necessary to keep the network under control.
- Maintenance is concerned with performing repairs and upgrades—for example, when equipment must be replaced, when a router needs a patch for an operating system image, or when a new switch is added to a network. Maintenance also involves corrective and preventive measures to make the managed network run "better," such as adjusting device configuration parameters.
- Provisioning is concerned with configuring resources in the network to support a given service. For example, this might include setting up the network so that a new customer can receive voice service.

In short, network management involves the planning, organizing, monitoring, accounting, and controlling of activities and resources and to keep the network service available and correct.

Network Management Functions

A common way of characterizing network management functions is FCAPS—Fault, Configuration, Accounting, Performance, and Security.

Fault management

Fault management refers to the set of functions that detect, isolate, and correct malfunctions in a telecommunications network, compensate for environmental changes, and include maintaining and examining error logs, accepting and acting on error detection notifications, tracing and identifying faults, carrying out sequences of diagnostics tests, correcting faults, reporting error conditions, and localizing and tracing faults by examining and manipulating database information.

Fault management can typically be broken down into three basic steps, namely:[3]

- Fault detection:[4] the process of capturing online indications of disorder in networks provided by malfunctioning devices in the form of alarms. Fault detection determines the root cause of a failure. In addition to the initial failure information, it may use failure information from other entities in order to correlate and localize the fault.

- Fault isolation[5,6] (also referred to as fault localization, event correlation, and root cause analysis): a set of observed fault indications is analyzed to find an explanation of the alarms. This stage includes identifying the cause that leads to the detected failure in case of fault-propagation and the determination of the root cause. The fault localization process is of significant importance because the speed and accuracy of the fault management process are heavily dependent on it.
- Fault correction: is responsible for the repair of a fault and for the control of procedures that use redundant resources to replace equipment or facilities that have failed.

Configuration management

Configuration management refers to the process of initially configuring a network and then adjusting it in response to changing network requirements. An example is the configuration of various parameters on a network interface. The basic tasks of configuration management include:

- Facilitate the creation of controls
- Monitor and enforce baseline standards for specific hardware and software
- Store the configuration data and maintain an up-to-date inventory of all network components
- Log and report changes to configurations, including user identity

Network configuration management has to deal with detailed operation on network hardware configuration, network software configuration, and maintenance management.

Accounting management

Accounting management refers to gather usage statistics for users. Using the statistics, the users can be billed and usage quota can be enforced. The measurement of network utilization parameters enables individual or group uses on the network to be regulated appropriately. Such regulation minimizes network problems (because network resources can be apportioned based on resource capacities) and maximizes the fairness of network access across all users.

Performance management

Performance management refers to monitoring network utilization, end-to-end response time, and other performance measures at various points in a network. The results of the monitoring can be used to improve the performance of the network.

In network performance management, a set of functions evaluate and report the behavior of telecommunications equipment and the effectiveness of the network or network element. There are two central tasks involved in performance management: monitoring (performance analysis) and control (capacity planning). Monitoring consists of obtaining the utilization and error rates of current network links and network devices, collecting information about traffic (error rates, throughput, loss, utilization, collisions, volume, matrix), services (protocols, overhead, matrix, response time), and resources (CPU utilization, memory available, disk utilization, ports) and comparing this information with the normal and/or desirable values for each. Controlling consists of making baseline the utilization metrics and isolates any existing performance problems, taking actions to plan or modify network configurations and capacities to meet the desirable performance.

Security management

Security management refers to the set of functions that protects networks and systems from unauthorized access by persons, acts, or influences and that includes many subfunctions, such as creating, deleting, and controlling security services and mechanisms; distributing security-relevant information; reporting security-relevant events; controlling the distribution of cryptographic keying material; and authorizing subscriber access, rights, and privileges.

A security management subsystem, for example, can monitor users logging on to a network resource and can refuse access to those who enter inappropriate access. The basic tasks of security management include:

- Identify sensitive information or devices and access control to network resources by physical and logical means
- Implement a network intrusion detection scheme to enhance perimeter security
- Protect the sensitive information by configuring encryption policies
- Possibly respond automatically to security breaches and attempts with predefined operations

Management tools such as information classification, risk assessment, and risk analysis are used to identify threats, classify assets, and to rate system vulnerabilities so that effective control can be implemented.

Network–Programming

Expanded network management functions

The FCAPS model is useful for understanding the goals and requirements of network management, and also helps to build a foundation for understanding the significance of network management to compliance efforts. With the evolution of networks and related applications, there are some expanded network management functions, which include Service Level Agreement (SLA) management, change management, situation management (SM).

SLA Management. SLAs are based on fixed service and performance agreements between customers and suppliers and create transparency for both parties in terms of performance and costs. Specific SLAs are used to define the type, scope, and QoSs and to check that specifications are met. As SLAs also include potential sanctions for the event that agreed service parameters are not met, the specifications made in them have a significant effect on the commercial success of a company providing services for a customer. In the context of service-oriented architectures, the benefits of successful service-level management can be described as follows:[7]

- The number of conflict situations within supplier relationships can be reduced, resulting in enhanced customer satisfaction.
- The resources used in order to render the service (hardware, personnel, licenses) can be distributed at a detailed level by the provider and therefore used in such a way as to optimize costs.
- Problems can be identified speedily by service-level monitoring and the associated cause determined.

Costs can be made more transparent; on the one hand, the customer only wants to pay for services actually used while, on the other hand, plausible pricing can be guaranteed.

Change Management. Change Management is an IT Service Management discipline. The objective of Change Management in this context is to ensure that standardized methods and procedures are used for efficient and prompt handling of all changes to controlled IT infrastructure, in order to minimize the number and impact of any related incidents upon service. Changes in the IT infrastructure may arise reactively in response to problems or externally imposed requirements, e.g., legislative changes, or proactively from seeking imposed efficiency and effectiveness or to enable or reflect business initiatives, or from programs, projects, or service improvement initiatives. Change Management can ensure standardized methods, processes, and procedures are used for all changes, facilitate efficient and prompt handling of all changes, and maintain the proper balance between the need for change and the potential detrimental impact of changes.

Change Management would typically comprise the raising and recording of changes, assessing the impact, cost, benefit, and risk of proposed changes, developing business justification and obtaining approval, managing and coordinating change implementation, monitoring and reporting on implementation, reviewing and closing change requests.

Situation Management. SM is a goal-directed close-loop process of sensing, reasoning, perceiving, prediction, and affecting of event-driven dynamic systems, where evolving situations determine the overall behavior of the system.

The overall motivation for SM is achieving using the system a desired goal situation within the predefined limits. SM can improve the network management functions in modern dynamic networks and integrated IT systems.

SM as a management concept and technology is taking roots from disciplines, including situation awareness, situation calculus, and situation control. Critical aspects of SM include managing and controlling sources of information, processing real-time or near real-time streams of events, representing and integrating low-level events and higher level concepts, multisource information fusion, information presentations that maximize human comprehension, and reasoning about what is happening and what is important. Furthermore, commanders will require management support systems that include control over their current command options, prediction of probable situation evolutions, and analysis of potential threats and vulnerabilities.[8]

NETWORK MANAGEMENT ARCHITECTURE

Most network management architectures use the same basic structure and set of relationships. End stations (managed devices), such as computer systems and other network devices, run software that enable them to send alerts when they recognize problems (for example, when one or more user-determined thresholds are exceeded). Upon receiving these alerts, management entities are programmed to react by executing one, several, or a group of actions, including operator notification, event logging, system shutdown, and automatic attempts at system repair. Management entities can also poll end stations to check the values of certain variables. Polling can be automatic or user-initiated, but agents in the managed devices respond to all polls. Agents are software modules that first compile information about the managed devices in which they reside, then store this

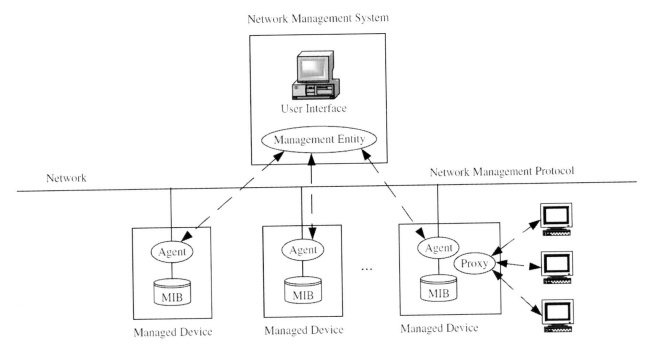

Fig. 1 The typical network management architecture.
Source: From Ding.[1]

information in a management database, and finally provide it (proactively or reactively) to management entities within network management systems (NMSs) via a network management protocol.

Networks, in essence, can be broadly classified as telecommunications networks and IP networks. Accordingly, current network management solutions have followed two general technical directions: the International Telecommunication Union -Telecommunication Standardization Sector's (ITU-T's) TMN for telecommunications networks and the Internet Engineering Task Force's (IETF's)

SNMP for IP networks. These two approaches adopt different standards, protocols, and implementations.

For the network management of telecommunications networks, it is derived from ITU M.3000 recommendation series building on OSI and is known as TMN. For IP networks, it is supported by IETF and based on SNMP, which has become the de facto standard in the management fields of IP networks. These two general models have thus adopted different standards and implementation methods, and are also designed for different network architectures.[9]

Well-known network management protocols include SNMP and Common Management Information Protocol (CMIP). Management proxies are entities that provide management information on behalf of other entities. Fig. 1 also depicts typical network management architecture.

TMN Management Architecture

TMN has been widely adopted to manage telecommunications networks, ranging from transportation backbones to access networks. The TMN provides a structured framework for enabling interconnectivity and communication across heterogeneous operating systems and telecommunications networks.

The TMN is defined in ITU M.3000 recommendation series, which cover a set of standards including CMIP, guidelines for definition of managed objects (GDMO), and abstract syntax notation one (ASN.1).

ITU M.3010 defines the general TMN management concepts and introduces several management architectures at different levels of abstraction: a functional architecture, a physical architecture, an information architecture, and a logical layered architecture (LLA). Fig. 2 presents the general relationship of a TMN to a telecommunication network.

Internet-Based Management Architecture

The Internet Standard Management Framework encompasses all of the technologies that comprise the TCP/IP network management solution. Current IP networks are often managed via SNMP, which is pushed by IETF as a specification, initially presented for the Internet. The SNMP Framework consists of a number of architectural components that define how management information is structured, how it is stored, and how it is exchanged using the SNMP protocol. The Framework also

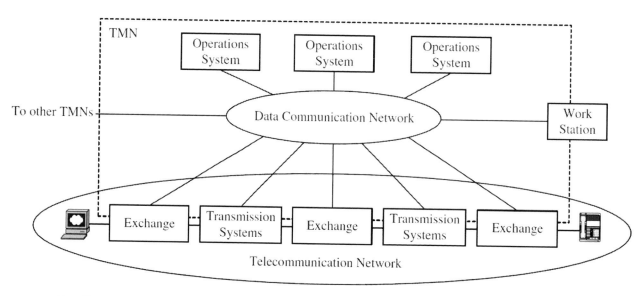

Note: The TMN boundary may extend to and manage customer/user services and equipment.

Fig. 2 General relationship of a TMN to a telecommunication network.
Source: From Ding.[1]

describes how the different components fit together, how SNMP is to be implemented in network devices, and how the devices interact.

SNMP consists of a small number of NMSs that interact with regular TCP/IP devices that are called managed nodes. The SNMP manager on the NMS and the SNMP agents on the managed nodes implement the

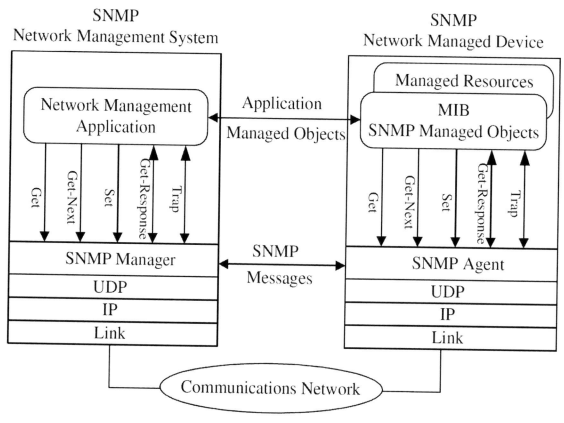

Fig. 3 SNMP protocol.
Source: From Ding.[1]

SNMP protocol allow network management information to be exchanged. SNMP applications run on the NMS and provide the interface to the human administrator, and allow information to be collected from the Management Information Bases at each SNMP agent (Fig. 3).[10]

Network Management Protocols

With the expansion of networks, the evolution of network architectures, and the increasing requirements for network management, the network management protocols also evolve consequently.

A typical management network system will make use of the management operation services to monitor network elements (NE). Management agents found on NE will make use of the management notification services to send notifications or alarms to the network management system.

Network management protocols are used to define how network management information is exchanged between network management services and management agents. Some popular network management protocols are discussed as follows:

1. The CMIP is the OSI specified network management protocol. Defined in ITU-T Recommendation X.711, ISO/IEC International Standard 9596-1. It provides an implementation for the services defined by the Common Management Information Service (CMIS) specified in ITU-T Recommendation X.710, ISO/IEC International Standard 9595, allowing communication between network management applications and management agents. CMIP also provides good security (support authorization, access control, and security logs) and flexible reporting of unusual network conditions.
2. SNMP is an "Internet-standard protocol for managing devices on IP networks. Devices that typically support SNMP include routers, switches, servers, workstations, printers, modem racks, and more.[11] An SNMP-managed network consists of managed devices, agents and NMS. Fig. 3 presents the SNMP protocol.
3. Other protocols for network management include: Internet Protocol Flow Information Export (IPFIX), the Network Configuration Protocol (NETCONF), Syslog, Ping, Trace route, and Terminal emulators, etc.

THEORIES AND TECHNIQUES FOR NETWORK MANAGEMENT

With the evolution of emerging networks and services, more challenges appear in managing the dynamic and complex networks. Thus some new theories and technologies are developed and designed for network management, such as policy-based network management, AI techniques for network management, graph-theoretic techniques for network management, probabilistic approaches for network management, and bio-inspired network management.[1]

Policy-Based Network Management

Policy-Based Network Management (PBNM) is that where the network management is accomplished based on policy.

Large-scale networks can now contain millions of components and potentially cross organizational boundaries. Components fail and so other components must adapt to mask these failures. New applications, services, and resources are added or removed from the system dynamically, imposing new requirements on the underlying infrastructure. Users are increasingly mobile, switching between wireless and fixed communication links. To prevent the operators from drowning in excessive detail, the level of abstraction needs to be raised in order to hide system and network specifics. Policies that are derived from the goals of management define the desired behavior of distributed heterogeneous systems and networks and specify means to enforce this behavior.

Policy provides a means of specifying and dynamically changing management strategy without coding policy into the implementation. Policy-based management has many benefits of delivering consistent, correct, and understandable network systems. The benefits of policy-based management will grow as network systems become more complex and offer more services (security service and QoS).

PBNM provides a means by which the administration process can be simplified and largely automated.[12]

Strassner defined PBNM as a way to define business needs and ensure that the network provides the required services.[13] In traditional network management approaches, such as SNMP, the usage of network management system has been limited primarily to monitoring status of networks. In PBNM, the information model and policy expressions can be made independent of network management protocols by which they are carried.

The most significant benefit of PBNM is that it promotes the automation of establishing management-level objectives over a wide range of systems devices. The system administrator would interact with the networks by providing high-level abstract policies. Such policies are device-independent and are stated in a human-friendly manner.

PBNM can adapt rapidly to the changes in management requirements via run-time reconfigurations, rather than reengineer new object modules for deployment. The introduction of new policies does not invalidate the correct operation of a network, provided the newly introduced policies do not conflict with existing policies. In comparison, a newly engineered object module must be tested thoroughly in order to obtain the same assurance.

For large networks with frequent changes in operational directives, policy-based network management offers an attractive solution, which can dynamically translate and update high-level business objectives into executable network configurations. However, one of the key weaknesses in a PBNM lies in its functional rigidity. After the development and deployment of a PBNM, the service primitives are defined. By altering management policies and modifying constraints, we have a certain degree of flexibility in coping with changing management directives.

AI Techniques for Network Management

Automation of network management activities can benefit from the use of AI technologies, including fault management, performance analysis, and traffic management.

Expert systems techniques

Expert systems try to reflect actions of a human expert when solving problems in a particular domain. The knowledge base is where the knowledge of human experts in a specific field or task is represented and stored. It contains a set of rules or cases with the knowledge about a specific task, that is, an instance of that class of problems. The inference engine of an expert system contains the strategy to solve a given class of problems using, for example, the rules in a particular sequence. It is usually set up to mimic the reasoning or problem-solving ability that the human expert would use to arrive at a conclusion. Rule-based, case-based, and model-based approaches are popular expert systems that are widely used in fault management.[14]

Machine learning techniques

Machine learning is a subfield of AI that is concerned with the design and development of algorithms and techniques that allow computers to "learn." In general, there are two types of learning: inductive and deductive.

Inductive machine learning methods extract rules and patterns out of massive data sets.

Machine Learning for Network Management can be used for anomaly detection and fault diagnosis, intrusion detection, network configuration, and optimization.

Artificial Neural Network (ANN) is to use computers to deal with a class of problems that are easily solved by the human brain, but which are not effectively treated with the exclusive utilization of conventional programming paradigms. ANN is appropriate in fault management since it can analyze patterns of common behavior over circuits, and/or can handle ambiguity, and incomplete data. For example, ANNs have been used for the purpose of fault localization.[15,16]

Graph-Theoretic Techniques for Network

Management Network management consists mainly of monitoring, interpreting, and handling events. In management, an event is defined as an exceptional condition in the operation of networks. Some problems are directly observable, while others can only be observed indirectly from their symptoms. Symptoms are defined as the observable events. However, a symptom cannot be directly handled; instead its root cause problem needs to be handled to make it go away. Relationships are essential components of the correlation, because problems and symptoms propagate from one object to another relationship. Graph-theoretic techniques are strong in modeling the interdependencies between network components and the symptoms of events, particularly in network fault management. The typical graph-theoretic techniques include causality graph model, dependency graph model, decision trees.

Probabilistic Approaches for Network Management

For evolving complex network system, uncertainty is an unavoidable characteristic, which comes from unexpected hardware defects, unavoidable software errors, incomplete management information, and dependency relationship between the managed entities. It is not always possible to build precise models in which it is evident that the occurrence of a given set of alarms indicates a fault on a given element (object). The knowledge of the cause–effect relations among faults and alarms is generally incomplete. The imprecision of the information supplied by specialists very often causes great difficulties. An effective management system in networks should deal with the uncertainty and suggest probabilistic reasoning for network management tasks.[17] Fuzzy logic and Bayesian networks are popular models for probabilistic fault management.

Bio-inspired Network Management

The properties of self-organization, evolution, robustness, and resilience are already present in biological systems. This indicates that similar approaches may be taken to manage different complex networks, which allows the expertise from biological systems to be used to define solutions for governing evolving communication networks. Ideal network applications are expected to be autonomous, scalable, adaptive to dynamic network environments, and simple to develop and deploy. In order to realize network applications with such desirable characteristics, various biological systems have already developed the mechanisms necessary to achieve the key requirements of evolving network applications such as autonomy, scalability, adaptability, and simplicity.

MANAGEMENT OF EMERGING NETWORKS AND SERVICES

More recently, requirements in network management and control have been amended by emerging network and computing models, including wireless sensor networks, ad hoc networks, overlay networks, grid networks, optical networks, multimedia networks, storage networks, the convergence of NGN, the clouds, or even nanonetworks, etc. Increasingly, ubiquitous network environments require new management strategies, which can cope with resource constraints, multifederated operations, scalability, dependability, context awareness, security, mobility, and probability, etc. To bring complex network systems under control, it is necessary for the IT industry to move to autonomic management, autonomic features in both the data and control planes of the network, context-aware management and self-management systems in which technology itself is used to manage technology. New theoretical approaches are needed in resolving the challenging problems in network management including network architectural reference models that incorporate autonomic and self-management principles.[18]

The network management tasks in emerging networks and services are identified as follows:

Mobility management

In dynamic wireless networks, such as wireless ad-hoc networks (WANET), the nodes may not be static in space and time. This will result in a dynamic network topology. Nodes can move freely and independently. Also some new nodes can join the network and some nodes may leave the network. Individual random mobility, group mobility, updating along preplanned routes

can have major impact on the selection of a routing scheme and can thus influence performance. Multicasting becomes a difficult problem because mobility of nodes creates inefficient multicast trees and inaccurate configuration of network topology.[9]

There are two distinct methods for mobility support in wireless ad-hoc networks:[19] mobile IP, and fast routing protocols. Mobile IP offers a pure network layer architectural solution for mobility support and isolates the higher layers form the impact of mobility. However, it does not work efficiently on a large-scale basis. Fast routing protocols are designed to cope with changes in the network topology. Routing in ad-hoc networks is basically a compromise between the method of dealing with fast topology changes and keeping the routing overhead to a minimum.

Routing management

Mobile wireless networks rely on a routing plane to fit with their dynamics and resource constraints. In particular, an ad-hoc routing protocol must be capable to maintain an updated view of the dynamic network topology while minimizing the routing traffic.

Dynamically changing network topology makes routing a complex issue and requires new approaches in the design of routing protocols for sensor networks.

Location management

Since there is no fixed infrastructure available for mobile wireless networks with nodes being mobile in the three-dimensional space, location management becomes a very important issue. For example, route discovery and route maintenance are some of the challenges in designing routing protocols. In addition, finding the position of a node at a given time is an important problem. This leads to the development of location aware routing, which means that a node will be able to know its current position. Some protocols have been proposed specifically for location management. They can be classified into two major categories, location-assisted[20] and zone-based protocols.[21] Location-assisted protocols take advantage of local information of hosts. In zone-based routing, the network is divided into several nonoverlapping regions (zones) and each node belongs to a certain zone based on its physical location.

RESOURCE MANAGEMENT

Emerging wireless networks use wireless medium to transmit and receive data. Nodes can share the same media easily. But wireless links have limited bandwidth and variable capacity. They are also error prone. In addition, most ad-hoc nodes have limited power supply and no capability to generate their own power. Energy efficient protocol design (e.g., MAC, routing, resource discovery) is critical for longevity of the mission. Bandwidth and energy are scarce resources in ad-hoc networks. The wireless channel offers a limited bandwidth, which must be shared among the network nodes. The mobile devices are strongly dependent on the lifetime of their battery.

Security Management

Emerging mobile networks are more vulnerable than fixed networks because of the nature of the wireless medium and the lack of central coordination. Wireless transmissions can be easily captured by an intruding node. A misbehaving node can perform a denial of service attack by consuming the bandwidth resources and making them unavailable to the other network nodes. It is also not easy to detect a malicious node in a multihop ad-hoc network and implement denial of service properly. In addition, in a multicasting scenario, traffic may pass through unprotected routers which can easily get unauthorized access to sensitive information (as in the case with military applications). Dynamic topology and movement of nodes in an ad-hoc network make key management difficult if cryptography is used in the routing protocol.

Scalability Management

In ad-hoc networks, overlay networks, and extendable networks, the management plane must be easy to maintain and must remain coherent, even when the ad-hoc network size is growing, when the network is merging with another one, or when it is splitting into different ones. Most of the routing algorithms are designed for relatively small wireless ad-hoc networks. However, in some applications (e.g., large environmental sensor fabrics, battlefield deployments, urban vehicle grids, etc.) the ad-hoc network can grow to several thousand nodes. For example, there are some applications of sensor networks and tactical networks, which require deployment of large number of nodes. For wireless "infrastructure" networks, scalability is simply handled by a hierarchical construction. The limited mobility of infrastructure networks can also be easily handled using Mobile IP or local handoff techniques. In contrast, because of the more extensive mobility and the lack of fixed references, pure ad-hoc networks do not tolerate mobile IP or a fixed hierarchy structure. Thus, mobility jointly with large scale becomes one of the most critical challenges in ad-hoc design.[22,23]

Reliability Management

Reliable data communications to a group of mobile nodes that continuously change their locations is extremely important particularly in emergency situations.[24] Contrary to wired lines, the wireless medium is highly unreliable. This is due to the variable capacity, limited bandwidth, limited battery power, attenuation and distortion in wireless signals, nodes motion, and prone to error. Thus, wireless systems must be designed with this fact in mind. Procedures for hiding the impairments of the wireless links from high-layer protocols and applications as well as development of models for predicting wireless channel behavior would be highly beneficial. Given the nature of mobile wireless networks, it is necessary to make the network management system survivable. This is due to the dynamic nature of such networks, as nodes can move in and out of the network and may be destroyed for various reasons such as battlefield casualties, low battery power, etc. Thus there should be no single point of failure for the network management system.

Integrated Management

A typical ad-hoc network is composed of various devices such as laptops, personal digital assistants, phones, and intelligent sensors. These devices do not provide the same hardware and software capabilities but they have to interoperate in order to establish a common network and implement a common task. Seamless roaming and handoff in heterogeneous networks, multiple radio integration and coordination, communication between wireless and wired networks and different administrative domains invoke WANET management systems to implement higher level integrated and cooperated policies. The network maintenance tasks are shared among the mobile nodes in a distributed manner based on synchronization and cooperation mechanisms.

Middleware is an important architectural system to support distributed applications. The role of middleware is to present a unified programming model to applications and to hide problems of heterogeneity and distribution. It provides a way to accommodate diverse strategies, offering access to a variety of systems and protocols at different levels of a protocol stack.

Recent developments in the areas of wireless multimedia and mobility require more openness and adaptivity within middleware platforms. Programmable techniques offer a feasible approach to avoid time-varying QoS impairments in wireless and mobile networking environments. Multimedia applications require open interfaces to extend systems to accommodate new protocols. They also need adaptivity to deal with varying levels of QoS from the underlying network. Mobility

Network-
Programming

aggravates these problems by changing the level of connectivity drastically over time.

Service Management

Incorporating QoS in emerging networks is a nontrivial problem because of the limited bandwidth and energy constraints. Designing protocols that support multiclass traffic and allows preemption, mobile nodes position identification, and packet prioritization are some of the open areas of research. In order to provide end-to-end QoS guarantee, a coordinated effort is required for multilayer integration of QoS provisioning. The success and future application of emerging wireless networks will depend on how QoS will be guaranteed in the future.

For example, emerging multimedia services demand high bandwidth. There are some challenges and problems that need to be solved before real-time multimedia can be delivered over wireless links in ad-hoc networks. The need for more bandwidth, less delay, and minimum packet loss are some of the criteria for high quality transmission. However, the current best-effort network architecture does not offer any QoS. Hence, in order to support multimedia traffic, efforts must be made to improve QoS parameters such as end-to-end delay, packet loss ratio and jitter.

AUTONOMIC MANAGEMENT, SELF-* MANAGEMENT AND CONTROL

Overview

Self-management

Self-management[25] is a new management paradigm that involves automation of management workflows as well as embedding decision-making entities in both the management plane and the fundamental end-to-end transport network architecture that react on observed events and state changes in order to "autonomically" adapt network resources' configuration to detected changes, new demands and incidents—with the goal of reducing human intervention and maintaining acceptable service quality and delivery. Self-Management includes various types of so-called Self-* features such as Self-Organization and the four functional areas mentioned below:

Self-configuration. Automated configuration of components and systems follows high-level policies. The configuration process can be more specifically defined as follows:

a. Installation: new installation of necessary components (OS, software, etc.)

b. Reconfiguration: reconfiguration of installed components to fit unique situations

c. Update: version management of applications or modification of components to correct defects. This also includes reinstallation when parts of the configuration files have been corrupted due to virus attack or system error.

Self-diagnosing and self-healing. System automatically detects, diagnoses, and repairs localized software and hardware problems. A system is self-healing to the extent that it monitors its own platform, detects errors or situations that may later manifest themselves as errors, and automatically initiates remediation. Fault tolerance is one aspect of self-healing behavior, although the cost constraints of personal computing often preclude the redundancy required by many fault-tolerant solutions.

Self-optimization. Components and systems continually seek opportunities to improve their own performance and efficiency. A system is self-optimizing to the extent that it automatically optimizes use of its own resources to ensure the optimal functioning with respect to the defined requirements. In a self-optimizing network, all these tasks (information collection, data analysis, configuration changes, and verification) should be accomplished automatically and the automation makes it easier and faster to respond to the network dynamics.

Self-protection. System automatically defends against malicious attacks or cascading failures. It uses early warning to anticipate and prevent system-wide failures. A system is self-protecting to the extent that it automatically configures and tunes itself to achieve security, privacy, function, and data protection goals. This behavior is of very high value to personal computing, which is exposed to insecure networks, an insecure physical environment, frequent hardware and software configuration changes, and often inadequately trained end users who may be operating under conditions of high stress. Security is one aspect of self-protecting behavior.

Context-aware and autonomic-management

A context-aware network is a form of computer network that is a synthesis of the properties of dumb network and intelligent computer network architectures. Dumb networks feature the use of intelligent peripheral devices and a core network that does not control or monitor application creation or operation. Such a network is to follow the end-to-end principle in those applications, which are set up between end peripheral devices with no control being exercised by the network. Such a network assumes that all users and all applications are of equal priority.

In general, context information can be static or dynamic and can come from different network locations, protocol layers, and device entities. Any conflict or undesired interaction must be handled by the independent applications. As such the network is most suited to uses in which customization to individual user needs and the addition of new applications are most important. The pure Internet ideal is an example of a dumb network.

An intelligent network, in contrast to a dumb network is most suited for applications in which reliability and stability are of great importance. The network will supply, monitor, and control application creation and operation.

A context-aware network is a network that tries to overcome the limitations of the dumb and intelligent network models and to create a synthesis that combines the best of both network models. It is designed to allow for customization and application creation while at the same time ensuring that application operation is compatible not just with the preferences of the individual user but with the expressed preferences of the enterprise or other collectivity which owns the network. The Semantic Web is an example of a context-aware network. Grid networks, pervasive networks, autonomic networks, application-aware networks, service-oriented networks all contain elements of the context-aware model.

A context-aware network is suited to applications in which both reliability and the need for system evolution and customization are required. It is finding great purchase in the development of enterprise system for business processes, customer relations management, etc. Service-oriented architectures, which are a specialization of the context-aware model, are the current trend in enterprise computing.[26]

So far, context-aware computing and self-managing systems are emerging independently. The application domains for which they are studied are different as well. The two approaches have several features in common. For example, both approaches aim at reducing human involvement: while context-aware computing aims at reducing the amount of explicit input a user should provide to computing systems, autonomous computing (self-management) aims at reducing the operational and maintenance cost of a system.

If one takes the conceptual framework of Kephart and Chess[27] as a reference framework of self-managing system, the sensing, actuating, and analysis component are typical components of context-aware computing. Much work has been done by the research community of context-aware computing to support context acquisition, context modeling, context representation, context reasoning, and context management. Researchers of autonomous computing can benefit a great deal by considering the usefulness of this work to develop self-managing systems.[28]

Software-Driven/Defined Networking, Network Function Virtualization, and Autonomic Management & Control of Networks and Services, as three Complementary Emerging Paradigms

Software-Driven/Defined Networking (SDN) is a networking paradigm involving the separation (decoupling) of the control plane software from the forwarding plane (the two planes have been traditionally coupled within a single closed box), enabling the control plane to run in centralized commodity servers.

The Autonomic Management & Control (AMC) paradigm involves customized control software (e.g., decision-making logic) that can be loaded at run-time into data plane nodes and also in the outer realm where the management and control planes run, and should be easily replaceable, thereby enabling the notion of "software-empowered networks". Such control-logics are meant to implement algorithms for intelligence (autonomics) in the capability of the control plane and the management plane to exhibit self-* features, such as self-configuration, self-healing, self-optimization, and so on. The control-logics (as software modules) that implement autonomic functions (i.e. decision-making logics) are targeted at flexible run-time loading and replacing of such modules wherever they may be required in the data-plane, the control-plane, or management plane. The network's decision-making capabilities are empowered by such dynamically loadable autonomics-related control-logics. Efforts to unify frameworks for AMC (realized through the ETSI AFI Generic Autonomic Network Architecture [GANA] Reference Model[29]) and SDN are underway in ETSI NTECH (Network Technology) AFI WG.[30,31] For example, GANA Functional Blocks for AMC enhance SDN with, e.g., GANA Knowledge Plane Decision Elements that can drive (as network intelligence enhancing applications) an SDN controller through the Northbound Interface of the SDN controller. More details on other enhancements to SDN by the ETSI AFI GANA Model can be found in Chaparadza et al.[31]

Network Functions Virtualization (NFV) is a network architecture that builds upon the success of virtualization techniques in information technology, to bring about the virtualization of network appliances (network functions) that traditionally have been deployable only as monolithic boxes. The resulting Virtualized Network Functions run as software in low-cost commodity servers. Efforts to unify frameworks for AMC (realized through the ETSI AFI GANA Reference Model[29]) and NFV MANO (Management and Orchestration) Architecture, are underway in ETSI NTECH AFI WG.[30,31]

Therefore, overall, relationships between the emerging complementary networking paradigms of AMC of Networks and Services, SDN and NFV are being established, and efforts to unify associated Reference Models have started, i.e., unification of the ETSI AFI GANA Model for AMC with SDN-enabling frameworks and ETSI NFV MANO architecture. The complementary aspects of the three Emerging Paradigms (AMC, SDN, NFV) must be expressed through Unified Reference Models and Standards. This is the reason why a newly launched Joint SDOs/Fora Initiative is addressing this subject, namely, the industry harmonization for unified standards for AMC of networks and services, SDN and NFV, as complementary emerging paradigms.[32]

Emerging Standards in Autonomics, Self-Management, and Control in the Evolving Networks and Future Internet

There are various groups in Standards Development Organizations (SDOs) that are developing standardized autonomics and self-management frameworks and architectures (including Future Network architectures). In Next Generation Mobile Networks (NGMN) and the 3rd Generation Partnership Project (3GPP) the concept of Self-Organizing Networks and the associated functions known as SON functions have been standardized for Long-Term Evolution (LTE i.e., 4G mobile networks). As noted in Agoulmine,[31] while reviewing various trends in automation in various network technologies, SON functions were specified for the Radio Access Network (RAN) where they apply. However, in NGMN and also in 3GPP, there is a growing need to develop similar automation functions (though some of the automation may not necessarily map to autonomicity) for the other network segments such as the backhaul and the core network segments, so as to have self-* operations in those segments as well. In IEEE there is a group called NGSON (Next Generation Service Overlay Networks) that has been attempting to address some limited scope of autonomics and self-management in networks. In ITU-T, Broadband Forum (BBF), TeleManagement Forum (TMF), and in some IETF WG(s) there are also some activities touching on the subject. European Telecommunications Standards Institute (ETSI) has a group called Autonomic Network Engineering for the Self-Managing Future Internet (AFI) that has a much broader scope on its activities on Standardization of Autonomics/Self-Management technologies than all the other various groups. It is widely understood that the field of Autonomics and Self-Management needs collaboration activities among the various standardization groups due to the complexity of the area (considering the need for testable, interoperable, and trusted autonomic systems). The ETSI AFI is therefore viewed as the growing focal point for Autonomics and Self-Management Frameworks, since ETSI AFI has liaisons with all the key standardization groups such as NGMN, ITU-T, 3GPP,

BBF, TMF, and is expected to establish liaisons with other groups.

In general, autonomics/self-management in the broader sense includes what has already been defined by Self-Organizing Networks (SON) for LTE (in 3GPP), and goes beyond SON to include other types of Self-* properties (apart from Auto-Discovery and Self-Configuration, Self-Diagnosing, Self-Healing/Self-Repair, and Self-Optimization), as well as design principles that help achieve advanced Decision-Making-Capabilities by the NE and Management Systems themselves.

The ETSI AFI is standardizing the Generic Autonomic Network Architecture (GANA) Reference Model for Autonomic Network Engineering, Cognition, and Self-Management.[25] GANA defines some Generic Functional Blocks and associated Reference Points and Characteristic Information that are specific to enabling Autonomics, Cognition, and Self-Management in a target architecture, when "instantiated" onto an implementation-oriented reference architecture such as the BBF architecture, NGN architecture, 3GPP architecture, etc. to create various types of Autonomicity-Enabled Reference Architectures. Some of the various Functional Blocks in the Reference Model would need to be implemented by OSS vendors, others by equipment manufacturers and others by network operators and service providers. Some of the Functional Blocks are bound to enhance or evolve EMSs or NMSs/OSSs. The generic Functional Blocks and Reference Points can also be applied in designing future network architectures that must exhibit self-management capabilities from the dawn (outset) of their design.

The GANA Model serves as a "blueprint model" that prescribes design and operational principles of "autonomic decision-making manager components/elements" called Decision Elements (DEs) responsible for "autonomic" management and adaptive control of resources. Autonomic Functions (AFs) include Auto-Discovery, Self-Configuration, Self-Diagnosing, Self-Healing/Self-Repair, Self-Optimization, and Self-Protection, etc., all of which must be performed by individual NEs and by the collaboration of NEs along an E2E path and in harmony with autonomic behaviors coordinated at EMS and NMS levels. Automation and Autonomicity (adaptive control of resources and behaviors) are the key aspects.

Network architects, researchers, and developers/implementers are the main users of GANA Reference Model, as they "refer" to the Reference Model when reasoning about or applying the concepts and principles defining the domain of autonomic communication, autonomic networking, autonomic and cognitive management and control—all as part of the "big-picture" of Self-Management.

Network–Programming

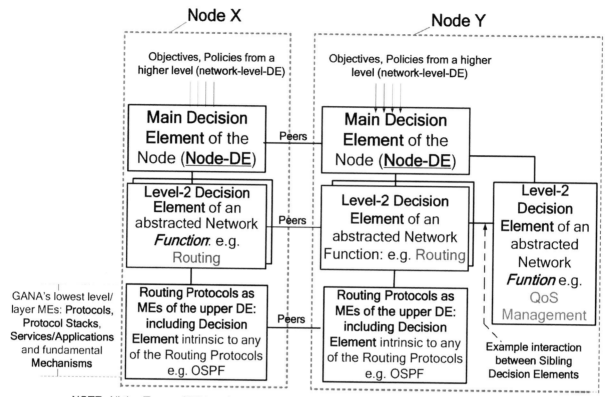

NOTE: All the *Types of DE Interfaces* depicted illustrate the need for *"node/device-intrinsic management"* and *"network-intrinsic management or in-network management"* in Self-Managing Future Networks

Fig. 4   GANA instantiation within a router, w.r.t. autonomic routing functionality.

The ETSI AFI GANA reference model

The Figs. 4 and below provide just snapshots of the Reference Model for selected key aspects. Fig. 5 provides an overview of some of the key aspects of the GANA Reference Model (specified in much more details in [2]). Fig. 5 presents an instantiation of GANA Model within a router, to illustrate instantiation (though not complete instantiation), with respect to autonomic routing as a working example. In general, self-manageability in GANA is achieved through instrumenting the NE (in Fig. 5, the case of routers) with autonomic DEs that collaboratively work together. DEs may form "peers" along a path within the fundamental E2E transport architecture. The DE-to-DE peers need not necessarily be hop-by-hop neighbors (i.e., being resident in on-link neighboring nodes) but the peer relationships may relate to e.g., border-relationships management in a heterogeneous network or may be related to some DEs in certain NE along an E2E path. The Reference Model defines a hierarchy of DEs, i.e., four basic levels of self-management (i.e., where control-loops can be introduced): the Protocol (GANA level-1), Function (GANA level-2), Node (GANA level-3), and Network (GANA level-4) levels. Each DE manages one or more lower-level DEs through a control loop. These lower-level DEs are therefore considered Managed Entities (MEs).

Over the control loop, the DE sends commands, objectives, and policies to an ME and receives feedback in the form of monitoring information or other type of knowledge. Each DE realizes some specific control-loop (s), and therefore, represents an "Autonomic Activity" or AF. Examples of AFs: Autonomic QoS Management-DE; Autonomic Security Management-DE; Autonomic Fault Management-DE; Autonomic Mobility Management-DE, etc.

The lowest level DEs are at the Protocol Level. They represent protocols, services, and other fundamental mechanisms, possibly already implemented in the network. Open Shortest Path First (OSPF), with its intrinsic control-loop can be considered an example of a Protocol Level DE. These DEs are managed by Function Level DEs such as the Routing Management DE, Monitoring DE, and QoS Management DE.

The Network Level DEs constitute the Functional Blocks of the Knowledge Plane (KP), together with Overlay Network for Information eXchange (ONIX) and Model-Based-Translation Service (MBTS). Clark et al.[34] define the KP as a pervasive system within the network that builds and maintains high-level models of what the network is supposed to do, in order to provide services and advice to other elements of the network. It is a distributed and decentralized construct within the Internet to gather, aggregate, and act upon information

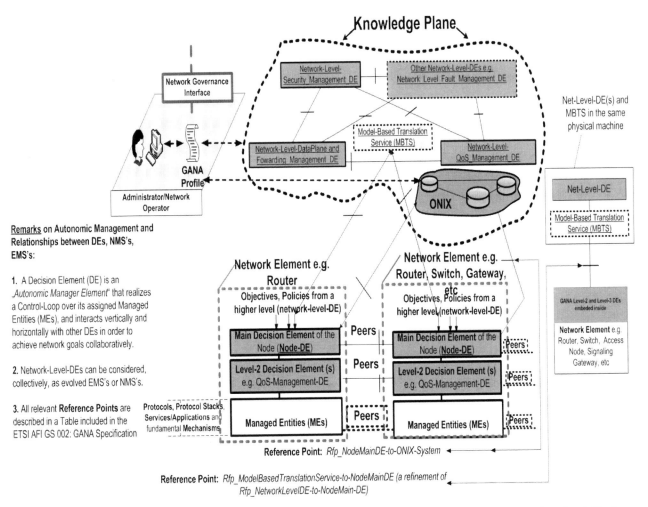

Fig. 5 Global view of GANA reference model (a simplified view: some of the reference points between functional blocks are omitted).

about network behavior and operation (citing Stephen Quirolgico et al.).[35]

On the Network Governance Interface, the network administrator can manage the operation of the whole autonomic network by authoring, validating, and submitting Policies, High-Level Network Objectives, and some Configuration-Data to the KP, all encapsulated together in the form of what is called a GANA Profile. This profile is then translated by the Network Level DEs and commands are issued to lower level DEs for enforcement. In addition to defining the abovementioned Functional Blocks, the GANA Reference Model also specifies Reference Points (a Summary Table of Reference Points is provided in the Specification). More details and further elaborations on the various aspects of the Reference Model are covered in the specification from ETSI AFI.[25]

Instantiations of the GANA Model onto Various Types of Reference Architectures to Enable Autonomicity

In the process of "instantiating the Reference Model", called GANA Instantiation, concrete device architectures and overall network architecture are instrumented with GANA Concepts and Principles by superimposing GANA DEs into node/device architectures and the overall network architecture, so that the DEs' behaviors can be further designed to perform autonomic management and adaptive control of the specific resources such as protocols, stacks, and mechanisms (i.e., Managed Entities) in that architecture. Therefore, the process of Instantiating the Reference Model by mapping, fusion and superposition of the conceptual building blocks takes as input a "Standardized Reference Architecture" such as ITU-T/TISPAN NGN architecture, or 3GPP LTE/EPC architecture, or BBF/ADSL FTTH architecture, etc. For example, introducing Autonomicity and Self-Management into the existing NGN architecture results in an "Autonomicity-enabled NGN architecture, having GANA concepts and principles fused into the node/device architectures and/or the overall network architecture." The same applies with an Autonomicity-Enabled BBF architecture or Autonomicity-Enabled 3GPP backhaul and core network architecture, Autonomicity-Enabled Mesh Architecture or Autonomicity-Enabled Future Network Architecture.

Achieving full-fledged Autonomics/Self-Management in current and future networks by instantiating the GANA Model onto a target architecture, requires enhancing both the Management Architecture and the Fundamental E2E Transport Architecture accordingly.[25]

In order to introduce or advance autonomicity in any type of reference network architecture, the following two actions and discussions need to be carried out so as to come up with an Autonomicity-Enabled Reference Architecture:

1. Instantiating Functional Blocks and Reference Points for Autonomicity/Self-Management from the GANA Reference Model from AFI[25] onto any target Reference Network Architecture and its Management Architecture.
2. Use the Instantiated Functional Blocks and Reference Points for Autonomicity/Self-Management from the Reference Model, to specify Autonomic Behaviors within the Management and the E2E Transport Architecture.

Benefits Brought to Various Stakeholders in the Instantiations of the ETSI AFI GANA Reference Model onto Various Architectures and Systems

The following are some of the benefits of progressing the work on transforming networks with autonomics (with some insight on how the various stakeholders benefit, see also Chaparadza et al.[36]

1. The work can easily apply architectural principles that enable enhancements of both the Management Architecture and the fundamental E2E architecture in a way that does not disrupt the current implementations, but rather gracefully evolves them.
2. The Modular Approach taken to defining the elements of the KP (see Fig. 2), such that there are clearly defined domains of the KP, such as Security Management, Fault Management, QoS Management, etc., and their interfacing, brings about benefits such as separation of issues of concern to enable the various modules to be designed, simulated, and validated. The corresponding Network-Level DEs that realize the domains of the KP can be designed to run various types of Self-Management Operations for the network and various types of Optimization

Algorithms. Various implementation options can be considered for the KP. For example, the validated behaviors and algorithms of Network-Level DEs may be used to evolve traditional EMS/NMS (OSSs) or, the DEs as well as the other elements of the KP may be implemented to run as standalone entities that interwork with traditional OSSs. Such an interworking can easily be implemented. In general, the ways to implement the KP can still be abstracted from an architectural specification level.

3. There are various technical benefits in applying the principles defined in the Reference Model for Autonomic Networking, Cognition, and Self-Management from AFI. The benefits include techniques and architectural principles that ensure that control-loops can be designed in a way that guarantees noncoupling and nonconflicting behaviors of AFs, so as to ensure Stability.
4. Methods for Knowledge Synthesis, Representation, and Presentation for the KP have also been captured in the Specification document of the GANA Reference Model from AFI.

Some of the benefits for Network Operators are:

• The Reference Model from AFI enables Policy-Control through the Network Governance Interface, as well as facilitating other mechanisms for supporting the Loading of Control-Strategies (executable runtime behavioral models) that can be pushed into the network i.e., into the autonomic manager elements/functions (particularly the DEs in the KP) by the operator and can be viewed as customized optimization behaviors/algorithms. Such executable run-time behavioral models enable more advanced control than use of policies, and are meant to be interpreted and executed by the DEs. Could this be viewed as programmability? Such subjects need further discussions.

• Policies are encapsulated by so-called GANA Network Profiles that also convey Goals/Objectives specified by the Operator as well as Configuration Data, and the Profiles are then pushed into the network as input to the Self-Managing Network. Translation Tools for translating High-Level business goals into technical objectives, profiles and policies pushed into the network would be used.

• Elements become Plug-n-Play, with Self-* features such as Self-Diagnosing, Self-Healing, Self-Optimization, etc., resulting in significant reduction in management complexity and human involvement in the Deployment, Operation, and Optimization of the network (thanks to autonomic operations ranging from Auto-Discovery, Self-Configuration, and other Self-* features that run from the Deployment phase (for a device and the network) through to the continuous Network Optimization phase).

Some of the benefits for Equipment Manufactures and OSS vendors are:

- KP entities (likely to be implemented to run in dedicated machines) can be developed by Manufacturers and/or OSS vendors. This could be further discussed.
- The place-holders for internal control-loops (inside a Network Element) depicted by the Reference Model enable to design and embed "node-local" Self-Management behaviors/algorithms, including node-local Self-Optimization, i.e., some degree of intelligence through the internal DEs that realize the internal control-loops. Example node-scoped Self-* behaviors that do not necessarily require collaboration/negotiation with other NE include: Plug-n-Play; Energy Savings through AFs; Autonomic Security Management (self-protection and self-defending behavior); Autonomic Fault-Management and Resilience (proactively and reactively), etc. Those network-element internal DEs (whether implemented to run as standalone run-time instances or merged as a single run-time entity) may need to participate in some "in-network" collaborative behaviors through DE-to-DE Peer communications that enhance the Control-Plane with exchanging some information (e.g., protocol or network-related events and statistics) or negotiation messages that enable the participating NE/nodes (possibly Hop-by-Hop along an E2E path) to perform some collaborative network optimization (i.e., possibly the "minimum" required). In some way, this can be viewed as realization of distributed control-loops spanning some NE within the E2E transport network. Enabling to realize distributed control-loops and possibly some basic optimization behaviors would need to be discussed by equipment manufacturers to see what sort of collaborative behaviors or enablers should be standardized. The types of distributed control-loops and the types of participating NE should be discussed and established.
- There are DE Algorithms that would provide Vendor Differentiation.

Some of the benefits for Algorithm developers and providers are:

- Various algorithms would be required to drive decision-making processes in an autonomic network. However, Algorithms per-se cannot be standardized, though there are some basic behaviors of AFs (DEs) that could be standardized. On the other hand, some optimization algorithms, for example, may be tailored to specific emergent resource and service topologies. The question is on how to facilitate the loading of various types of customized algorithms into the network and their use by the network to enhance DE behaviors. Would such facilitation be necessary in autonomic networks? Discussions are necessary. The role of algorithm providers can still be fulfilled by the different stakeholders, such as vendors, operators, and possibly research institutes and universities (in collaboration/partnerships with the various industry stakeholders).

CONCLUSION

The emerging networks and services have some of the following features: such as mobility, diffusion of heterogeneous nodes and devices, mass digitization, resource constraints, multifederated operations, scalability, dependability, context awareness, security, probability, new forms of user centered content provisioning, new models of service and the interaction with improved requirement in security and privacy. These features encourage new technologies and networking architectures and exhibit huge challenges to render robust services, security, and management.

Therefore new management standard, architectures, theory, and technologies should be investigated to match the current requirements to manage emerging networks and services. Furthermore a set of enabling technologies is recognized as potential candidates for network management and can be based on policy-based management strategies, AI techniques, probabilistic approaches, bio-inspired approaches, etc. The desire to keep complex network systems under control, it is necessary for the IT industry to move to autonomic management, context-aware management, and self-management systems in which technology itself is used to manage technology. To implement the autonomic and self-* management, a unified and common standard is needed to bridge heterogeneous architectures and system, and to support dynamic and emerging network services. AFI GANA reference model provides a prospect to support industrial applications on emerging network management.

REFERENCES

1. Ding, J. *Advances in Network Management*; CRC Press, Taylor & Francis Group, ISBN-10: 1420064525; ISBN-13: 978-1420064520, 2010.
2. Clemm, A. *Network Management Fundamentals*; Cisco-Press, ISBN: 1-58720-137-2, 2006.
3. ANSI T1.215 OAM&P—*Fault Management Messages for Interface between Operations Systems and Network Elements*, 1994.

Network-Programming

4. Boulouts, A.; Calo, S.; Finkel, A. Alarm correlation and fault identification in communication networks. IEEE Trans. Commun. **1994**; *42* (2–4), 523–533.

5. Bouloutas, A.T.; Calo, S.B.; Finkel, A.; Katzela, I. Distributed fault identification in telecommunication networks. J. Network Syst. Manag. **1995**, *3* (3), 295–312.

6. Kätker, S.; Geihs, K. A generic model for fault isolation in integrated management system. J. Network Syst. Manag. **1997**, *5* (2), 109–130.

7. Schmietendorf, A.; Dumke, R.; Reitz, D. SLA Management – Challenges in the Context of Web-service-based Infrastructures. Proceedings of the IEEE International Conference on Web Services, **2004**; 606–613.

8. Jakobson, G.; Lewis, L.; Matheus, C.J.; Kokar, M.M.; Buford, J.. Overview of situation management at SIMA 2005. Proceedings of IEEE Military Communications Conference, **2005** (MILCOM 2005), 1630–1636.

9. Mo, L.; Sandrasegaran, K. Network Management Challenges for Next Generation Networks. Proceedings of the The IEEE Conference on Local Computer Networks 30th Anniversary, **2005**; 593–598.

10. Kozierok, C.M. *The TCP/IP Guide: A Comprehensive, Illustrated Internet Protocols Reference*; No Starch Press: San Francisco, USA, ISBN 9781593270476, 2005.

11. Mauro, D.R.; Schmidt, K.J. *Essential SNMP*, 1st Ed.; O'Reilly & Associates: Sebastopol, CA, 2001.

12. Verma, D.C. Simplifying network administration using policy-based management. Network, IEEE, **2002**, 16, 20–26.

13. Strassner, J.S. *Policy-based Network Management: Solutions for the Next Generation*, ISBN: 1558608591, 9781558608597, Morgan Kaufmann, 2003.

14. Patel, A.; McDermott, G.; Mulvihill, C. *Integrating Network Management and Artificial Intelligence*; Integrated Network Management I, North-Holland, Amsterdam, 1989; 647–660.

15. Gardner, R.D.; Harle, D.A. Pattern Discovery and Specificaton Techniques for Alarm Correlation. Proceedings of Network Operation and Management Symposium (NOMS '98), IEEE communication society press: USA, **1998**; 713–722.

16. Wietgrefe, H. Investigation and practical assessment of alarm correlation methods for the use in GSM access networks. Proceedings of Network Operation and Management Symposium (NOMS'02), IEEE communication society press: USA, Stadler, R., Ulema, M., Eds.; **2002**; 391–404.

17. Ding, J. *Probabilistic Fault Management in Distributed Systems*; ISSN: 0178-9627, ISBN: 978-3-18-379110-1, VDI Verlag: Germany, 2008.

18. Ding, J.; Bouvry, P.; Balasingham, I. Management challenges for emerging wireless networks. In *Emerging Wireless Networks: Concepts, Techniques and Applications*; Makaya, C., Pierre, S., Eds.; ISBN: 9781439821350, ISBN 10: 1439821356, CRC press: 2012; 3–34.

19. Akyildiz, I.F.; McNair, J.; Ho, J.S.M.; Uzunalioglu, H.; Wang, W. *Mobility management in next-generation wireless systems*. Proceedings of the IEEE, **1999**; Vol. *87* (8), 1347–1384.

20. Hur, S.M.; Mao, S.; Hou, Y.T.; Nam, K.; Reed, J.H.. *A Location-Assisted mac Protocol for Multi-hop Wireless Networks*. In Wireless Communications and Networking Conference, WCNC , IEEE, *2007*; *322–327*, 11–15.

21. Chang, C.-Y.; Shih, K.-P.; Lee, S.-C.Zbp: A zonebased broadcasting protocol for wireless sensor networks. Wireless Pers. Commun. **2005**, *33* (1), 53–68.

22. Burgess, M.; Canright, G. Scalability of peer configuration management in partially reliable and ad hoc networks. In *Integrated Net-work Management*, **2003**. IFIP/IEEE Eighth International Symposium on, *2003*; 293–305, 24–28.

23. Ali, M.H.; Aref, W.G.; Kamel, I. *Scalability management in sensor-network phenomena bases*. International Conference on Scientific and Statistical Database Management. 91–100, **2006**.

24. Hallani, H.; Shahrestani, S.A. Improving the reliability of ad-hoc on demand distance vector protocol. WTOC, **2008**, *7* (7), 695–704.

25. Raz, D.; Juhola, A.; Serrat, J.; Galis, A.*Fast and Efficient Context-Aware Services*; John Wiley & Sons, Ltd., ISBN 0-470-01668-X, 2006.

26. ETSI GS AFI 002. *Autonomic network engineering for the self-managing Future Internet (AFI): GANA Architectural Reference Model for Autonomic Networking, Cognitive Networking and Self-Management.* This ETSI Specification is expected to be published by ETSI within the fourth quarter of 2012.

27. Kephart, J.O.; Chess, D.M. The vision of autonomic computing. Computer **2003**, *36* (1), 41–50.

28. Dargie, W. Contex and self-management. In *Context-Aware Computing and Self-Managing Systems*; ISBN 978-1-4200-7771-1, Taylor & Francis Group: Chapman & Hall/CRC, 2009; 1–14.

29. ETSI GS AFI 002: Autonomic network engineering for the self-managing Future Internet (AFI): GANA Architectural Reference Model for Autonomic Networking, Cognitive Networking and Self-Management. This ETSI Specification is publicly available since April 2013, http://www.etsi.org/deliver/etsi_gs/AFI/001_099/002/01.01.01_60/gs_afi002v010101p.pdf.

30. ETSI AFI Industry Specification Group: Autonomic network engineering for the self-managing Future Internet (AFI), http://portal.etsi.org/afi,and now AFI WG in NTECH, https://portal.etsi.org/NTECH/NTECH_AFI_ToR.asp.

31. Chaparadza, R.; Meriem, T.B.; Radier, B.; Szott, S.; Wodczak, M.; Prakash, A.; Ding, J.; Soulhi, S.; Mihailovic, A.. Proceedings of 2013 IEEE Globecom Workshops. In: *SDN enablers in the ETSI AFI GANA referencemodel for autonomic management & control (emerging standard), and virtualizationimpact*. IEEE Communication Society Press: Atlanta, Georgia, USA, December 2013. 818–823

32. Chaparadza R.; Menem T.B.; Strassner J.; Radier B.; Soulhi S.; Ding J.; Yan Z. Industry harmonization for unified standards on Autonomic Management & Control (AMC) of networks and services, SDN and NFV. *Proceedings of 2014 IEEE Globecom Workshops.* IEEE Communication Society Press: USA 2014; 155–160, ISBN: 978-1-4799-7470-2/14/.

Network-Programming

33. Agoulmine, N. *Autonomic Network Management Principles: From Concepts to Applications;* ISBN 978-0-12-382190-4, Elsevier; 2011.

34. Clark, D.D.; Partridge, C.; Ramming, J.C. A knowledge plane for the Internet. In *SIGCOMM*; 2003; 3–10.

35. Quirolgico, S.; Mills, K.; Montgomery, D. *Deriving Knowledge for the Knowledge Plane: Draft from National Institute of Standards and Technology Advanced Network Technologies Division Gaithersburg,* NIST (National Institute of Standards and Technology): USA, June 2003; 20899–28920.

36. Chaparadza, R.; Jokikyyny, T.; Ladid, L.; Ding, J.; Prakash, A.; Soulhi, S. *The diverse stakeholder roles to involve in Standardization of Emerging and Future Self-Managing Networks.* Proceedings of **2011** IEEE GLOBECOM Workshops pages 603 - 608, IEEE communication society press, ISBN: 978-1-4673-0039-1, **2011**.

Network Security

Bonnie A. Goins Pilewski
Christopher A. Pilewski
Senior Security Strategist, Isthmus Group, Inc., Aurora, Illinois, U.S.A.

Abstract

Network security is multifaceted. "Networking" itself is about the provision of access to information assets and, as such, may or may not be secure. "Network security" can be thought of as the provision of consistent, appropriate access to information and the assurance that information confidentiality and integrity are maintained, also as appropriate. Contrary to what may seem intuitive, network security is not simply a technology solution. It involves the efforts of every level of an organization and the technologies and the processes that they use to design, build, administer, and operate a secure network.

WHY IS NETWORK SECURITY ESSENTIAL?

An organization must have provisions for network security to protect its assets. Appropriate network security identifies and protects against threats to people, processes, technologies, and facilities. It can minimize or mitigate exposures to the organization that could be exploited by a knowledgeable insider or a malicious outsider. It suggests appropriate safeguards designed to promote long-term, continuous function of the environment. For some organizations, the law mandates it.

WHO IS RESPONSIBLE FOR NETWORK SECURITY?

Every employee, in every position and at every rank, is responsible for network security within an organization. In some cases, such as in a regulated environment, business or trading partners are also responsible for adherence to security strategies in place at the organization. Security responsibilities also extend to casual or temporary employees, such as part-time workers, interns, or consultants.

Role of Senior Management

Senior management is responsible for any security violations that occur in the environment and, by extension, any consequences the organization suffers as a result. To repeat: *senior management is responsible for any security violations that occur in the environment.* For many senior executives, this is a new concept. After all, how could an executive presume to know whether or not appropriate security is in place?

It is senior management's responsibility to support, promote, and participate in the security process, from conception to implementation and maintenance. Senior management can facilitate this obligation through: 1) active and continual participation in the security planning process; 2) communication of "the tone at the top" to all employees, vendors, and business and trading partners, indicating that security responsibilities rest organizationwide and that senior management will enforce this view unilaterally; 3) support of security professionals in the environment, through the provision of resources, training, and funding for security initiatives; and 4) the periodic review and approval of progress regarding security initiatives undertaken within the organization.

Many executives ask for methods to enhance their knowledge of the security space. Internal technology transfer, security awareness training, and self-study can all assist in expanding knowledge. The option also exists to contract with an appropriate consulting firm that specializes in executive strategy consulting in the security space.

Senior executives must also be prepared to communicate expectations for compliance to security responsibilities to the entire organizational community, through its approval of appropriate corporate security policies, security awareness training for employees, and appropriate support of its security professionals.

Role of the User

It is important to reiterate that all users share in the responsibility for maintaining the security of the organization. Typically, user responsibilities are communicated through a corporate security policy and security awareness program or materials. Users are always responsible for protection of the security of their credentials for

Encyclopedia of Information Systems and Technology, DOI: 10.1081/E-EIST-120046299

Network–Programming

access (i.e., passwords, userIDs, and tokens); maintenance of a clean workspace, to prevent casual removal of critical data or other resources from the desktop or workspace; protection of critical data and resources while they are in the user's possession (i.e., work taken offsite to complete and portable systems, such as laptops); vigilance in the environment, such as greeting strangers within their workspace and asking if they require help; reporting anything unusual in the environment, such as unexpected system performance; etc. Users may also have additional security responsibilities assigned to them.

Responsibilities must align with the user's ability to satisfy the requirement. For example, users responsible for shipping must not be held accountable to satisfy the responsibilities of a network administrator. Proper alignment of responsibilities to roles is essential for the organization to "function as advertised." An organization can facilitate this alignment by thoroughly and definitively documenting roles in the environment and outlining job function responsibilities for each. Job functions can then be aligned to security responsibilities. The personnel function also benefits from this elaboration and alignment.

Role of the Security Professional

The responsibilities of a security professional vary among organizations. Perhaps this can best be explained by the notion that security professionals come from diverse backgrounds and skill sets. Security professionals may have legal, compliance, management or business, or technical backgrounds; likewise, professionals may have experience across industries ranging from education to government, financials to manufacturing, healthcare to pharmaceuticals, or retail to telecommunications. Positions held by security professionals include management, compliance officer, security officer, litigator, network administrator, and systems analyst.

One responsibility that most organizations agree upon is that the security professional, or team of professionals, is responsible for the periodic reporting to senior management on the existing state of security within the organization, from both a business and technical perspective. To ensure this responsibility is carried out, the organization's existing state of security must be assessed; in some cases, such as in a regulatory environment, additional audits are performed as well.

Given that security professionals come from myriad backgrounds and skill sets, many have never performed assessments. Some organizations choose to outsource this activity; others train to conduct this activity in-house, as appropriate.

CHARACTERISTICS OF A SECURE NETWORK

Confidentiality

A secure network must have mechanisms in place to guarantee that information is provided only to those with a "need-to-know" and to no one else.

Integrity

A secure network must have mechanisms in place to ensure that data in the environment are accurately maintained throughout its creation, transmission, and storage.

Availability

A secure network must have mechanisms in place to ensure that network resources are available to authorized users, as advertised.

Accountability

A secure network must have mechanisms in place to ensure that actions taken can be tied back to a unique user, system, or network.

Auditability

A secure network must have controls in place that can be inspected using an appropriate security or audit method.

The organization itself must determine the priority of importance for the aforementioned security attributes. In some organizations, multiple security attributes are considered at the same priority level when making decisions about resource allocation and function.

A COMPREHENSIVE UNDERSTANDING OF NETWORK ARCHITECTURE

To properly design and implement a secure architecture, a comprehensive understanding of the network architecture is also essential. In many modern institutions, the network may be compared to a production line, where information, messages, and documents for all vital business processes are stored, viewed, and acted upon. To protect the network and the assets available on it, a security professional must clearly understand the: 1) hierarchical nature of the information assets that require protection; 2) structure of the network architecture itself; and 3) the network perimeter (i.e., the network's entry and exit points or portals, and the associated protection at these points).

Network–
Programming

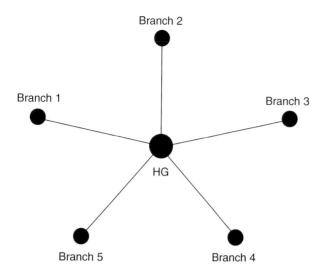

Fig. 1 Star topology WAN.

A "secure network" is simply a network that, by its design and function, protects the information assets available on it from both internal and external threats.

Network Architectures

A security professional can use a variety of sources to gain understanding of the network architecture. These include network diagrams, interviews, technical reports, or other exhibits. Each of these has its advantages and disadvantages.

Mapping and describing the network architecture can be a complicated endeavor. Network architectures can be described in a variety of terms. Many terms are, by their nature, relative and may have more than one meaning, depending upon the technology context in which they are used. Network professionals, when asked to describe their networks, will often begin by listing specific vendor-centric technologies in use at the site. This is not the most useful reference point for security professionals.

A reference point that nearly all institutions understand is the distinction between the LAN (local area network) and the WAN (wide area network). Although some might consider these terms outdated, they represent one of the few commonalities that nearly all network professionals understand consistently and agree with.

Both the LAN and the WAN can be accurately described using the following simple and empirical framework of three criteria: 1) locations; 2) links; and 3) topologies. Once the network architecture is clearly understood, the network perimeter can be investigated and properly mapped.

Wide area network

WANs can be mapped by first identifying, through listing or drawing, the physical locations that belong to the institution. Each building name and address should be listed. This may entail only a single building or may be a list of hundreds. Each location should be indexed in a useful way, using a numerical identifier or an alphanumeric designation. Conspicuous hierarchies should be noted as well, such as corporate or regional headquarters' facilities and branch offices.

The second step in mapping the WAN is to identify the links between locations, again by listing or drawing and then indexing. The level of link detail required can vary by specific assessment needs but, at a minimum, each link should be specifically identified and indexed. Many institutions may have redundant links between locations in failover or load-balancing configurations. Other institutions may have "disaster wiring" or dedicated phone lines for network management purposes that are intended for use only during emergency situations. To accurately map the WAN, every physical link of all types must be identified and indexed. Additional link data, such as carriers, circuit types, IDs, and speeds, can be of use for other purposes.

The third step in mapping the WAN is to identify the topology or topologies of the WAN. The topology represents the relationship between locations and links. The topology can be very simple or very complex, depending on the number of locations and links. An example of a simple topology would be a hub-and-spoke (or star) relationship between the headquarters of a regional business and individual branch offices. In this simple relationship, the headquarters represents a simple center of the network architecture. Other topologies may be much more intricate. A global organization can have independently operating national or regional centers, each with multiple satellite locations that connect through them. The regional centers of global organizations can connect only once to the global center. But more often, regional centers connect to more than one peer at a time in a partial mesh or full mesh topology. Accurately determining locations, links, and topologies will define the data security relationship(s) in the WAN.

Specific WAN topology examples illustrate the relationships between locations and links, and these are discussed further.

The hub-and-spoke, or star topology, WAN (see Fig. 1) has a clear center and has $(n - 1)$ connections for the n nodes it contains. Network traffic is aggregated at the center. If any branch needs to send information to any other branch, the information must flow through the HQ (headquarters) node. This configuration allows the HQ node to provide centralized services to the branches and to control the flow of information through the network.

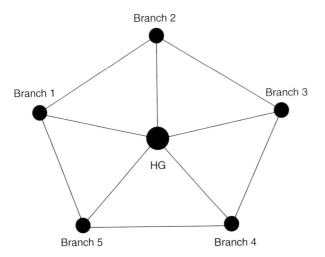

Fig. 2 Partial mesh topology WAN.

The partial mesh topology WAN (see Fig. 2) is similar to the star topology. There is still a clear center, but additional connections have been made between the individual branches. There can be any number of connections beyond $n - 1$ in a partial mesh. Unlike the star topology, branches can send and receive information to or from each other, without the information traversing the HQ center node. Many network designers use partial mesh topologies because they have desirable business continuity characteristics. In this partial mesh, any link (or any node) can be compromised and the others can continue to communicate. While these characteristics enable high availability, they complicate the security relationships between locations.

The full mesh topology WAN (see Fig. 3) can be thought of as the full extension of the partial mesh. In terms of data flow, there may be no clear center. Each branch has a direct connection to every other branch. There are $n \times (n - 1)$ connections in a full mesh. Full mesh topologies are rare in WANs because of the costs

of maintaining a large number of links. They are most often found when both high availability and high performance are needed. In full mesh topology WANs, individual traffic flows, and the associated security relationships, may be difficult or impossible to trace if complex routing metrics are used in the design.

Specific technologies common to WANs include leased circuits, Frame Relay, synchronous optical networking, and asynchronous transfer mode. Technologies such as ISDN, SMDS, X.25, and others are less common, but are still seen. The particular technology in use on an individual link is potentially of some interest for security purposes, but far more important is the completeness and accuracy of the WAN mapping itself (locations, links, and topologies). These determine the desired, and potentially undesired, information flow characteristics that define security relationships.

Local area network

LANs can be mapped similarly to WANs by first identifying, either through listing or drawing, the physical locations. In the case of LANs, the physical locations to be identified are usually data centers, server rooms, wiring closets, or other areas within a building where network equipment and cabling reside. A typical building will have at least one room where individual networks aggregate and at least one wiring closet per floor. Large buildings may have more of both. As with WANs, each location should be indexed in a useful way, through a numerical identifier or an alphanumeric designation. Hierarchies should be noted, such as data center, major closet, and minor closet. Older facilities may present special challenges because network equipment and cabling may have been positioned in any location possible at the time the network was built. These may include individual offices, janitorial closets, or even above suspended ceiling tiles.

The second step in mapping the LAN is to identify the links between locations, again by listing or drawing and then indexing. At minimum, each link should be specifically identified and indexed. Just as when WANs are mapped, redundant links should be mapped between locations in failover or load-balancing configurations. Supplemental link data, such as media type, speeds, or protocols, may be of use for other purposes.

The third step in mapping the LAN is identifying the topology or topologies in use. The topology of LANs can initially appear to be very different from WANs, but similarities do exist. LANs are typically confined to a single building or to a campus. The LAN can be mapped by determining the physical locations where network cable segments aggregate. Typically, a single room houses the switching core for a designated building. The switching core may be composed of a single

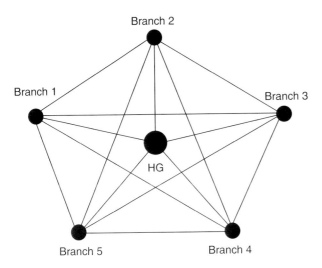

Fig. 3 Full mesh topology WAN.

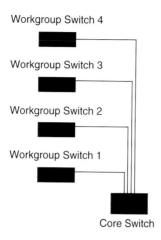

Fig. 4 Star topology LAN.

network switch or of multiple switches connected by high-capacity links. The switching core connects to individual workgroup switches that, in turn, connect to individual computers, servers, or other network devices. Often, several workgroup or closet switches connect to the switching core of the LAN. There may be one workgroup switch per floor of the building or several, depending on the building's size. These connections are typically arranged in the same hub-and-spoke (or star) relationship that characterizes many WANs. But like WANs, multiple connections between switches may be present and may form a partial mesh or a full mesh. Switched Ethernet of various speeds and on various physical media, such as unshielded twisted-pair cable or fiber optic cables, is the most common technology in use on a LAN. Other technologies, such as Token Ring or fiber distributed data interface, are still in use. Again, the specific technical characteristics of a particular LAN may be of note, but the architecture itself is of primary importance.

Wireless LANs

Wireless LANs merit special consideration because the LAN itself is not contained within the physical premises, or even on physical media. Wireless LANs reside in specific radio frequencies that may permeate building materials. Depending upon the design purpose of an individual wireless LAN, this may be desirable or undesirable. A number of tools and techniques (beyond the scope of this entry) exist to help a security professional detect and assess wireless LANs. A security professional must understand the relevance of the wireless LAN to the network architecture as a whole. Primary considerations include the existence and locations of wireless LANs and the termination points of individual wireless access points (WAPs). The termination points will determine the critical distinction between wireless LANs in use inside the network perimeter and wireless LANs in use outside the network perimeter.

Specific LAN topology examples illustrate the relationships between locations and links. There are similar relationships that exist in WANs, but they involve different components and often appear very different on network diagrams.

The hub-and-spoke or "star" topology LAN (see Fig. 4) has a clear center and $(n - 1)$ connections for the n nodes it contains (as was shown in the WAN example of the same topology). Although this LAN topology is not illustrated with a clear center, the network traffic is aggregated at the core switch. If any workgroup switch needs to send information to any other workgroup switch, the information must flow through the core switch. Centralized services to all clients on workgroup switches can be positioned on the core switch.

The partial mesh topology LAN (see Fig. 5) is similar to the star topology. There is still a clear center, but additional connections have been added between the individual workgroup switches. Network switches often use special protocols that select the best path for data to take, when more than one path exists. Network switches use various versions of Spanning Tree Protocol (STP) on *bridged* links; or a variety of routing protocols can be used on *routed* links, including RIP or OSPF. Multiple routing protocols can be used concurrently on the same network switch. The design goal is often the same as those in partial mesh WANs—high availability.

Full mesh topology LANs, as depicted in Fig. 6, are rarely found in practice. As in the WAN example, there are $n * (n - 1)$ connections in a full mesh. But because this topology facilitates both high availability and high performance, full mesh topologies are common in large network cores, such as those belonging to network providers.

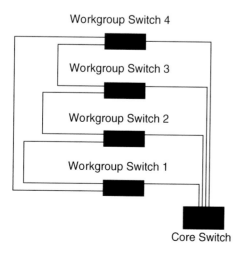

Fig. 5 Partial mesh topology LAN.

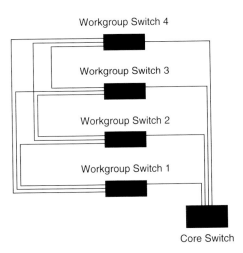

Fig. 6 Full mesh topology LAN.

Network perimeter

After mapping the LANs and WANs, the network perimeter can be defined and mapped. The network perimeter is the boundary where an organization's information leaves its immediate, direct control. As before, there may be a tendency to define the network perimeter in terms of technology products. Specific products are of interest, but the network perimeter should be defined by an organization's zone of authority. In more precise terms, the network perimeter should be thought of as the full set of entry points and exit points into and out of the network.

Defining the network perimeter this way will encompass many concepts familiar to security administrators, such as connections to Internet service providers (ISPs), and may also reveal aspects of the perimeter that are not routinely considered. Commonly understood network entry/exit points include ISP connections, remote access connections, virtual private networks (VPNs), and connections to business partners. Network entry and exit points that often go unexamined and unprotected include WAN and LAN components, such as links, server rooms, wiring closets, unrestricted network ports, and even computer workstations themselves.

Each entry and exit point should be documented and indexed, particularly the less obvious ones. After the network perimeter is properly assessed, appropriate safeguards can be evaluated for each entry and exit point. A common misconception in network security is that protecting against threats from the exterior is more important than protecting against threats from the interior. Both types must be addressed to make the network perimeter secure.

WHERE DOES NETWORK SECURITY START?

Identify Assets Requiring Protection

To apply security to any layer, the organization must determine the assets critical to its function. Arguably, all assets within the organization must be identified and categorized, to properly determine their criticality to the organization's function and to classify them accordingly. Classification of assets, particularly data and systems, instructs users on appropriate handling of the assets. This is essential if mistakes are to be avoided, such as the inappropriate dissemination of sensitive information. While all organizations consider their intellectual property as highly sensitive, regulated industries (e.g., healthcare and financials) also consider personally identifiable information of extreme importance and, therefore, sensitivity.

Organizations typically identify assets through the process of *business impact analysis* (BIA). Several methods exist to conduct a BIA; Disaster Recovery International (http://www.drii.org) presents a wealth of information to organizations engaged in this activity.

Identify threats to assets

To mount a successful defense of organizational assets, threats to those assets must be identified. Examples of threats typical to most environments include:

- *Malice. People might be motivated to harm an organization's assets by harboring anger toward management, coworkers, or the organization itself. A common theme among these individuals is the intent to do harm. An example of a malicious act is a network administrator opening an organization up to attack after notification of termination.*
- *Monetary gain.* Need or greed can also be a motivator for intrusion into a network. Many examples of the theft of intellectual or personal property, such as credit card numbers, are seen around the world.
- *Curiosity.* Human beings are curious by nature; many are equally clever. Curiosity can lead an individual to jeopardize assets, either knowingly or accidentally.
- *Accidents.* People make mistakes, despite best efforts. Accidents happen. Despite the fact that they are unintentional, accidents can cause harm to organizational assets and should be accounted for in security planning.
- *Natural disasters.* Weather-related and geographic emergencies must also be considered when planning for security. Data collected from the Federal Emergency Management Agency (FEMA) can assist the organization in assessing the threat from these disasters.

Identify countermeasures ("Safeguards") to threats

Once threats to the organization have been identified, it is important for the organization to take the next step and to design and implement appropriate countermeasures, which neutralize or minimize the threat. It is important to note that some threats pose more of a danger than others do; in additional, some threats have a greater likelihood of occurring within, or to, the organization. To properly identify whether the threats are manifested as exposures in the organization, an assessment should be undertaken.

Assess the environment

Assessment is typically done through "hunting" and "gathering." "Hunting" in this sense refers to the inspection of technology at its core ("intrusive assessment"). This is most often done through the use of software tools, both commercial-off-the-shelf (COTS) and open source. Security professionals who are experts in this area provide the most value for the organization through appropriate interpretation of information gathered both from tools and from research they have conducted in addition to the intrusive assessment. "Gathering" in this sense refers to the collection of data through documentation review, interviews, system demonstration, site visits, and other methods typically employed in nonintrusive assessments.

Nonintrusive assessment activities

Aspects of a security assessment that are evaluated through means other than direct manipulation and penetrative technology-based testing are considered "nonintrusive." Information is obtained through the review of previous assessments, existing policies and procedures, visits to the organization's sites, interviewing the organization's staff, and system demonstrations conducted by appropriate personnel. These assessment aspects are discussed in *Architecture: Secure*.

Nonintrusive assessment methods are very useful in gathering data surrounding people, processes, and facilities. Technology is also reviewed, although not at the granular level that can be attained through the use of software tools. An assessment method should be selected keeping the organization's business in mind. It is also highly advisable that a method recognized in the security space as a "best practice" be used. The National Security Agency (NSA), National Institute of Standards and Technology (NIST), and the International Organization for Standardization (ISO) all have security assessment methods that are easily adaptable to virtually any organization. All provide information that facilitates the building of a secure network environment.

Intrusive assessment activities

A number of activities might fall into the general description of intrusive assessment. These activities are loosely classified into two categories: 1) vulnerability scanning and 2) attack and penetration. The two can be employed individually, or attack and penetration can be employed as a complement to vulnerability scanning. Both activities help build a picture of an organization's network, servers, and workstations that is similar to the picture that an external attacker would develop.

Combining assessment activities to promote a holistic approach to security

As previously stated in this entry, effective organizational security can only be achieved by examining all aspects of the organization: its people, its processes, its facilities, and its technologies. There is little wonder, then, that to meet the objective of inspecting the organization in total, multiple assessment approaches must be used. Intrusive or tool-based discovery methods will not adequately address more subjective elements of the environment, such as people or processes. Nonintrusive discovery methods will not be sufficient to inspect the recesses of network and technology function. It is clear that if these approaches are used together and information gathered is shared among the security professionals conducting the assessments, a more global view of the organization's function, and by extension exposures to that function, is obtained. Again, while it is important to note that no particular approach, be it joint as suggested here, will identify 100% of the exposures to an organization, a more thorough and unified evaluation moves the organization closer to an optimal view of its function and the threats to that function.

- *Remediation definition. At a high level, remediation is defined as the phase where exposures to an organization are "fixed." These fixes are typically activities resulting in a deliverable, such as a policy, procedure, technical fix, or facility upgrade, that addresses the issue created by the exposure. Remediation and its characteristics are discussed in Architecture: Secure.*
- *Examples of remediation activities.* Remediation steps occur after completion of the assessment phases. Remediation activities for an organization might include security policy and procedure development; secure architecture review, design, and implementation; security awareness training; ongoing executive-level security strategy consulting and program development; logging and monitoring; and other remediation activities.

SUMMARY

Many factors combine to ensure appropriate network security within an organization. People, processes, data, technology, and facilities must be considered in planning, design, implementation, and remediation activities, in order to properly identify and minimize, or mitigate, the risks associated with each factor. Senior management must be clear in communicating its support of security initiatives to the entire organization. Additionally, security practitioners must be provided with the ability to succeed, through the provision of adequate resources, training, and budgetary support.

Open Standards

David O'Berry
Director of Information Technology Systems and Services, South Carolina Department of Probation, Parole and Pardon Services (SCDPPPS), Columbia, South Carolina, U.S.A.

Abstract

This entry offers scenarios, along with how and why a newer, quicker, more open standards process matters from a practical application standpoint.

From an information technology (IT) security perspective, the real world has changed so drastically in the last few years as to make an entry that describes "practical" thought processes with some real implementation considerations valid and therefore worth your time. This entry will not be like many of the entries in this encyclopedia in that it will ask you questions as well as proceed in a conversational style that may be disconcerting for some. Due to size restrictions, some concepts may simply be touched on while others may be more fully explored. To be clear, none of this is groundbreaking, and in reality there are probably very few original concepts that I will write about. What I am hoping to do is frame up the real world through a brief synthesis of existing ideas in hopes of encouraging a larger number of practitioners of our discipline to move back to some type of significant leadership role in this environment. Ultimately, instead of being herded, we can lead and be led by things that apply to what we are seeing right now instead of 5 or 10 years ago. In order for us to get to that point, we need to understand where we came from as well as some of the possible paths we have ahead of us.

WHAT MATTERS

All too often in IT, specifically in security, we get so inundated with the "wheres" and "hows" of something that we tend to lose sight of the real "whats" and "whys." Holistically speaking, the practice of security is one that everyone can subscribe to, but the realities of the world we live in is that practical application is something very few of us actually want to take on. Having said that, the real challenge that IT has had in the past, not specific to security, is a lack of customer-based leadership in what is going on at any given time. We have often allowed the vendor brain-trusts in one form or another to be the guiding light because, let's face it, in many cases those guys bring a lot of incredibly smart minds to the table, have patents, and do wizbang things that amaze us. An

unfortunate side effect of this is that we oftentimes allow ourselves to be cowed by them. They then get us in a situation and run a whole team of "ninja monkey engineers" at us that have every reason in the book why their product is far, far better than any other product and why we should buy only from them, asking us to barely give any consideration to what else is out there. In many cases this has even contributed to the concept of IT for IT's sake, which has then created tension between us and the business. What we have to remember is there are no IT projects—there are simply business projects with IT components. Yet, in the past, we have forgotten or at least strayed from that tenet that makes us ripe to be divided and conquered by vendors that need our dollars to survive.

Now, how often is the product by that single vendor you tested actually the best thing out there to solve the problem occurring in your organization? While the statistics vary depending on what source you reference, there is no question that far more products and companies are actual flops than successes. The reality is, that's how it's supposed to be really, because if everyone's idea was the best idea we would be left in intellectual gridlock. So what we have is a situation where more failures than successes are the true path to progress. The real problem is that instead of seeing this, we get this marketing blitz that tries to convince us to buy their product because their "ninja monkeys" actually get it right while these other vendors are supposedly just confused and bumbling around with no hope of finding salvation. Sound familiar?

It should sound familiar, because that is how the industry has worked for many years. That's certainly not a new thing and, especially in the initial phases of computing, was not necessarily a bad thing. However, as the stakes have been raised it has increasingly become evident that we have got to change our way of thinking. We cannot afford to wait anymore as these companies continue to slug it out to control what should be agile rapidly evolving open standards that we require to even have a remote chance of stepping away from the edge of the digital abyss at which we stand. What do I mean by that? Well, for starters we are in a digital ecosystem unlike anything

Encyclopedia of Information Systems and Technology, DOI: 10.1081/E-EIST-120046300

we have experienced at any point in human history. It is the concept of the "circle of life" but it is happening at warp factor nine and, to the chagrin of some, it is driven by users. Yeah, those horrible plankton-like creatures (joking here) are what feed the entire world because they are what matters. They are the iPhone Gremlins, Skype Monsters, Gmail Maggots, and Streaming Media Punks; those little malware-infested pod people are why we do what we do. These new generation of millennial "I GOTTA HAVE" end-users are a critical component of the engine that will drive the world economy forward in the next half century. Scary, isn't it? It does not have to be. At every turn we have to remember that business functions best based on efficiency, and these people that our industry has tended to look upon rather disdainfully at times are the lifeblood of each and every organization. That graphic artist that is so special that he has to have his own Mac is there for a reason, and it is to pay your salary, because in most cases what we do has no directly visible positive impact to the bottom line. That goes back directly to the purpose of IT and IT security as enablers for the business and not entities unto their own selves. I know what you are thinking and sure, we help the bottom line not become a negative, but let us be realistic: We know how hard that is to explain to people.

Why is that? Why does something that matter so much to individuals and companies seem so arcane? Why does it sometimes become such a chore to even attempt to provide a value proposition for what we do? For starters, it is hard to explain something that the world as a whole has taken very little vested interest in until it is almost too late. As a profession, you know that those of us who have been talking about the challenges coming have been in the minority quickly drowned out by the folks who tend to point to Y2K as some horrible failure because we did our jobs so well that nothing much happened. That may be counter-intuitive, but from a practical point of view, it

is often how the real world functions. Often these same professionals, as well as some of the vendors we deal with, get such tunnel vision that it looks to many of us like they have "Ostrich Syndrome" with heads so firmly buried there is no hope of illuminating the way to "truth." It sounds hopeless, but it is not. It just takes a different mentality and way of thinking that starts with customer-driven standards that move faster than the existing process. Going forward, it is my contention that standards-based interoperability is critical to network security with empowered users actively participating in driving those standards rather than passively allowing vendors to continue to control the process.

WHY IT MATTERS

Let us look at it in a different light for a moment. Do the various branches of the United States military usually wait for vendors to come tell them how and what they need to fight the next war? No, they do not. Instead they go to the vendors, they work together to determine what makes sense, and then put their combined knowledge and experience to use accomplishing incredibly important goals. For the most part, our industry operates almost completely opposite of that model usually driven by vendor's product cycles. The problem is now it is no longer practical to continue down that path. The reason the old way no longer works is that now we must contend with threat cycles that spin at a much more rapid pace than existing product cycles could ever hope to move. A simple graphical representation is given in Fig. 1.

What does that mean? Well, for one thing, by the time a product gets through a vendor's cycle and actually makes it to market, the real world needs of the customer have more than likely changed. So while we are waiting

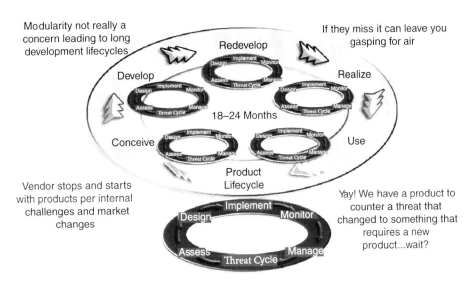

Fig. 1 Product cycle versus threat cycle: modular frameworks and standards required going forward.

through the starts, stops, and failures that I reference earlier as the standard way things progress, we are locked in a death-spiral as new problems hit. We all know that the real world issues stem from design challenges that often had security in the backseat (at best) early in the formative years. So now, the bolt-on thing keeps occurring over and over again, and vendors at times sell us bad code to protect worse code. But wait; there goes that counter-intuitive thing again. So how do we even begin to dig ourselves out of this situation? Well, the first step is to understand the gap between education and innovation in our society. We must also recognize that while luminaries from the vendors have generally led in the past, this does not have to be the case. In fact, it should not be the case in the majority of areas once we solve the education and communication aspect. We need to remember that open standards that evolve fairly rapidly are critical to this equalization of the customer/vendor relationship. They can contribute to a paradigm shift as entities of all sizes, from the incredibly large to the very small, are involved in a process that has too often been "big vendor and friends" only. I will touch on these topics plus some practical thought processes for design concepts in the next few pages.

STANDARDS—PART ONE: REVOLUTION, NOT EVOLUTION

I have discussed standards and their importance in the generic sense up until this point. Now I am going to discuss a couple of scenarios over the next few pages along with the how and why, in my opinion, a newer, quicker, more open standards process matters from a practical application standpoint.

We are all aware of the rapidly evolving security landscape and in many cases it stems from the confluence of vast amounts of computing power coupled with faster and faster ways of communicating. This creates some crazy good opportunities for businesses in all fields to leap forward and to really prosper. All facets of the economy have been affected by this "digital industrial revolution." It shows in many positive and also many negative ways. As with any revolution of sorts, there is collateral damage in many forms, and right now what we are dealing with is an older security posture with very new threats. Increases in bandwidth together with the ubiquity of attachment points left many people looking around trying to figure out how exactly to stem the flow of data to areas they were not prepared to protect in the early to mid-2000s. With that in mind, now we have to look at ways of gaining comprehensive distributed visibility across the enterprise while at the same time processing more security event-related information than people have the stomach to deal with at this point.

We all remember the intrusion detection system (IDS) scenario where at least one major pundit-filled analyst organization called the solution dead before it got fully implemented, based on false positives and what they felt was a uselessness of after the fact information. Of course, that gave way to the newest marketing phenomenon, intrusion prevention systems (IPS), and while that stays in effect today, many vendors initially just took their old IDS systems and called them IPS while giving them some blocking capabilities. This is a standard Marketing 101 trick: "Why invent when you can rename?" To be fair though, that is not a vendor only problem and in many cases IDS (when coupled with the proper configuration and education level) did, and still does, serve a purpose in many organizations. The challenge was also with organizations finding the people to run the systems or finding the money to educate on it. Both of those are not really vendor problems and so fall on organizations that see those types of things as just "line-item security issues" that can be cut the same as office supplies.

I grew up in a small individual computer world for the most part, starting back with the VIC 20 and Commodore 64, graduating to the Amiga and then the PC. When I look back I am always astounded at what we were able to accomplish back then on so little real estate versus what we can accomplish now with computers that simply dwarf those machines. As we began to connect those IBM PCs, the power of data-sharing really began to manifest itself and the world was a happy place. There was free flow of information, shared printers, and consolidated points of storage that did not cost millions of dollars. Businesses were in heaven and security was a real afterthought, because in the world of small disconnected PCs the mentality was far different than it had been working from the center out, the way mainframes functioned. Today, some organizations are swinging the pendulum back toward centralization with the thin client concept but we cannot ignore endpoint security. Infected endpoints can capture passwords and confidential data and mount attacks on critical systems. We really need trustworthy devices, whether through the use of hardware security like the trusted platform module (TPM), software security, or more likely a combination of the two.

While the concept of the "centrally distributed" computing model is fairly simple, what is not simple is the evolution and implementation of the idea. The seemingly contrary concepts of power at the edge and control at the center really make for a significant set of challenges. Addressing those things has often been the purview of the vendors and we have at times been forced to take a backseat and watch as each successive product has rolled out hoping for our chance to "get it right." The problem again comes back to the product cycle versus threat cycle issue and it has become more and more apparent over the last 10 years that the traditional vendor-centric model just cannot work without modifications. Enter open source and the concepts of development communities and others that now have different motives to create products and services. What that has created is a unique opportunity to potentially bring in the vendors we are used to dealing with and communities that are relatively new to create a workable yet completely untested paradigm shift to heterogeneous open interoperability.

STANDARDS—PART TWO: FOUNDATIONS FOR VISIBILITY

It is only relatively recently that there has there been real hope, in my opinion, for a fix to this situation that will *not* have to be brought on by a catastrophic failure that requires government intervention, regulations that will stifle innovation, and more fear and paranoia than is healthy for the participants in this global digital ecosystem. The old hardened perimeter is passé now with people calling for "deperimeterization" or whatever they choose to call it from week to week. "Defense in Depth" versus Mothra—many innocents in danger! So what is the real deal with the existing state? Well many companies have now recognized that security has to permeate what they do in order to have a chance at succeeding.

How permeation occurs is open to interpretation but the real problem comes in the fact that over the years very little heed has been paid to the security aspects of the frameworks and code that really are the foundation of the environment. First and foremost that has to be fixed, and organizations such as the International Information Systems Security Certification Consortium (ISC^2), Information Systems Security Association (ISSA), ISACA, and SANS are concerning themselves with at least discussing and possibly helping people to understand and hope to follow, test, and certify secure coding methodologies that will pay off in years to come. We even see large companies getting into the mix with Google, Microsoft, Sun, IBM, Oracle, and others preaching the virtues of writing good secure code while providing guidance within their own spheres of influence. The challenge is that in the interim we are not there and until we get there we need to bridge the risk gap in order for the digital ecosystem to continue to function properly.

To have a shot at really making a dent in the problem, we have to go back to standards, interoperability, and the leadership aspects that have been previously referenced. At this point organizations like the Trusted Computing Group (TCG) have in place various working groups that have responsibilities for many of the most at-risk areas of computing. The standard frameworks put forth by an organization like the TCG in an area like Network Access Control cannot really be overstated because the baseline security posture of many organizations is simply not where it needs to be. Going back to the ecosystem analogy, each of these organizations that are deficient can directly impact even the healthy organizations by becoming jump off points for attacks of various kinds. It is not unlike the human immune system in that a breach in one area threatens the entire organism. Another way to think about this is the "Digital Feudalism" concept and how in many of the older security models we have each gotten in our castles with our moats while peering out waiting for the horde to attack. Unfortunately, things have changed drastically and now the malware horde is even recruiting people within the castle to work from the inside out and we all know that it only takes one internal challenge (the horde recruiting one of your own) to make us vulnerable to all sorts of problematic issues.

From the design perspective it seems almost impossible to stop the threats without becoming restrictive to the point of complete uselessness. Throughout my career I have been down both roads (wide open and steel jaw shut) and I will tell you that with the new generations of users coming, and understanding what is really best for the businesses, there is no way to be closed up completely. One of my favorite lines in the movie *Jurassic Park* is where the scientist alludes to the fact that "nature will find a way" and that really holds true intentionally or unintentionally for both users and the people who want to take advantage of those users. All is not lost though, because over the past couple of years things in security have gotten markedly better on some fronts. The increasing adoption of Trusted Network Connect (TNC) standards should allow us to easily detect infected machines and raise the visibility from the edge. Microsoft's move to include TNC support in Windows Vista and Windows XP SP 3 and their publication of hundreds of Microsoft protocols on MSDN in early 2008 are positive moves that should be emulated by others. In Fig. 2, you see a logical mapping of real world capabilities that have now been vetted in whole or part by the Trusted Network Connect (TNC), Internet Engineering Task Force (IETF), as well as large multinational companies like Microsoft, Dell, Intel, Hewlett Packard, Symantec, and McAfee.

STANDARDS—TRIPLE PLAY: ENDPOINTS AND FLOWPOINTS AND THE THREAT STATE DATABASE

The challenge of the "power at the edge, control at the center" mantra is in how and where we deploy our

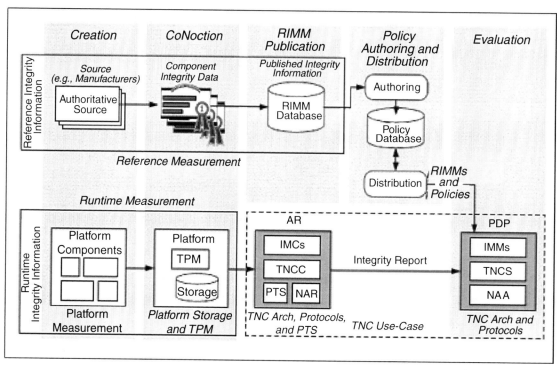

Fig. 2 A logical mapping of real-world capabilities that have now been vetted in whole or part by the TNC and the IETF.

protections. The "Endpoints and Flowpoints" concept is a fairly generic way of describing a defense in depth or "Flex Defense" concept that can adapt as we go to solve the many and varied attacks that we will continue to see. The best way to think about this is that you cannot dam the Mississippi River but you can dam some tributaries while you watch the Mississippi. What that means is that as endpoints come on the network we need to be able to take postures on them that we can then correlate with policies and behaviors. There have been some fascinating developments in this area, both in proprietary products and through open standards like IF-MAP. This new standard allows a wide variety of network security systems (NAC, IDS, DLP, etc.) to coordinate and communicate critical information, building a "Threat State Database" that shows the status of

all users, devices, and suspicious activity on the network (see Fig. 3).

By sharing this information, suspicious activity can be correlated with users to identify abnormal behavior and take corrective action. This sort of correlation and communication among network security devices using open standards is long overdue. Longer term, the standards-based participation of the endpoints themselves in the security of the network around them has to be carried forward in a way that they participate more in discerning what others are doing rather than being solely concerned with what they are doing locally. At every juncture, we need to be watching what is going on in the network with tools like sFlow in switches, NetFlow in switches and routers, developing SDKs for switches and routers that allow for open-source

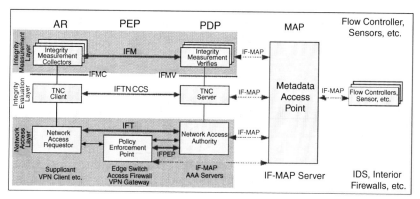

Fig. 3 The logical makeup of one available set of standards that could be used as a foundation.

innovation, and network visibility servers that can take in data to assist us in determining where we need to put our resources at any given point. While some of this has been around for a while, the deployment aspects of it have become a more complete picture as more and more companies seek to participate and are given that ability by the increased openness of many of the aspects of the community.

What we saw in the past with mostly signature-based mechanisms was an overwhelming of the networks ability to respond. Unlike the normal immune system in a human that generally only responds when a true threat exists, the various network visibility products in the past would simply inundate the security folks with warning after warning. It becomes the "boy that cried wolf" and then things simply begin to be ignored. In an analogy all of us can understand, we may respond to the first 5000 inconsequential Blackberry buzzes but that second 5000 have a high chance of not even raising an eyebrow. Instead, we need to be looking at visibility points along the way that then can trigger responses that begin to capture a lot more information at the first hint of trouble. Distributing some of that open reporting capability all the way out to the endpoint is where I think we will go because while the endpoints have clients on them that protect them, many times the challenge is how the proprietary systems often treat as nonexistent the warnings that come about violations that are not deemed critical. Host-based firewall data goes into the bit bucket from the view of the network as a whole, when it could possibly flow up into the centralized network visibility server to become part of an overlaid "threat state database." The evolution of something like this could be enterprise first, and eventually could be shared if the communication aspects continue to open up over the next few years. The SETI model with thousands of individual clients participating in a grid working on the distributed task of searching for extraterrestrial life makes a lot of sense going forward especially with the advent of technologies like Common Uniform Driver Architecture (CUDA) and the potential substantial extra processing power it brings. Looking at security in that light, we can see open source clients (there are already several out there for various capabilities) that could then become individual sensors from a network data perspective. This type of distributed peer review could then become an indicator on the network that gives some idea of the danger level based on what the individual clients see around them moreso than actually what they see on them. It would not be a stretch to consider weighting this input based on what we acknowledge to be "known good" endpoints or beacon/buoy machines on the network. The end goal would be to attempt to be able to create a "Federated Security" concept that gives us a whole picture of our enterprise (even a fuzzy one at first) but that allows us to quickly

focus the magnifying glass when an area becomes a concern (Robert Whiteley, Forrester Consulting). Eventually the feedback loop for the network needs to follow more along the concept of Boyd's Loop or OODA Loops that give us an overall more effective activity cycle than simply putting out fires. Refer back to Fig. 3 for an illustration of the logical makeup of one available set of standards that could be used as a foundation for this next iteration of network capability.

Basically in this environment, we are watching the sampled data at different points in the system and as heuristics continue to evolve, we can decide whether or not to focus the more intensive capabilities of the forensic aspect of that network on our trouble spots. With the proliferation of headless attack vectors like printers, iPods, and iPhones, there has to be a way of distributing the load of the visibility so that we have early warning indicators before things overwhelm the core. It has been proven that core defense simply does not work because of the drastic increase in bandwidth coming from the edge, the huge liability located in the endpoint including what data it sees and what it does with that data, and new valid "malware-like" software that serves valid business purposes while fraying the nerves of the security team. As we continue to move toward the evolution of more transient and distributed network security supplicants on these clients, we need to concern ourselves with network design that allows for the inclusion of this data in real time so that when it does get here we do not have to rip and replace yet again. Buying switches that are sFlow capable should be on the agenda while paying attention to both standards adherence in the past as well as roadmap postures for the future again comes to the forefront. Paying attention to how a router supports NetFlow and whether or not the company is really participating in the standards associated with communications in general should become a main criterion for our discussions. Recognizing how we are going to put that information to use and what we need to do in order to further the evolution of the industry needs to become a prime consideration if we are ever to get ahead of the curve.

STANDARDS: WHY DO THEY REALLY MATTER GOING FORWARD?

Simple concept: require standards. Right? Well, yes in theory. When we just say it out loud it sounds not only simple, but effective, and just plain makes sense. At the same time what we have found throughout the evolution of this industry and our profession is that the evolution of standards is nearly the sole domain of the vendors. If you think that seems backward then you are absolutely right. It goes directly back to both the "ninja monkeys" issue as well as the fact that the vendors have a ton of very smart people working for them. By no means am I saying that vendors are all evil, I am just saying that their goal is not an altruistic one by and large. Their goal, in most cases, is to make money for their business while doing no harm to the general public. That is a worthy goal and not one that I am condemning them for in the least. I am simply saying that it is not the goal of IT security, and awareness of their goals and objectives brings power to us and by the transitive property our organizations.

I wrote a brief column about this a few months back and will use some of that here because I have a real conviction about this topic (O'Berry, StateTech Magazine Jan/Feb 2008). I believe that what it really boils down to is that it is time for us to participate in the maturation of the industry instead of just watching as it evolves. One way to do that is to push vendors to abandon their proprietary technologies and demand they support open standards and frameworks. For the past decade, large companies have wagged the dog by manipulating, wasting time, and, in general, simply not allowing the industry to standardize in a timely manner. Some of the largest vendors have opted out of standardization efforts in hopes of forcing people to choose their technology, thereby locking out competitors and locking in customers. Many might say this is a valid business practice, and in the past it might well have been, based solely on a dollars-and-cents perspective. That era has passed, and the future should belong to open, nonproprietary, and scalable solutions because things are too important at this point to leave to simple market chance.

As mentioned earlier, security threats are evolving at an incredibly rapid pace today, which leaves us no real time for the old slow, painful, politics-filled standards process where the incumbent vendors drag their feet until they are forced to the table by market pressure. We have all witnessed the battles over standards such as OSPF, LLDP, IGMP, SMI-S, SFLOW, AVDL, and most recently Cisco NAC/TCG TNC/IETF NEA, and Microsoft NAP. From these various struggles, we have become familiar with the concept of vendor lock-in and defacto closed standards. Concurrently, the game and stakes have changed considerably for everyone involved and we are nearly overwhelmed at every turn by the complexity of handling security in our heterogeneous environments. The previous combination of factors creates a completely untenable situation for the entire "Digital Ecosystem" as a whole. It creates an environment where rapidly evolving user-driven open standards is possibly the only valid solution to step into the breach.

While the standards scenario is a seemingly obvious one, it has eluded our profession in many cases. What has instead happened in the past is at critical junctures where more pervasive open standards might take hold,

threatened vendors ramp up the attack, and their engineers and sale people keep coming fast and furious. That causes some of us to feel powerless and therefore give up. Those casualties within the practitioners creates additional gaps based on the silos that they attempt to keep us in and then the pendulum swings even further against the practitioners as those left are fighting increasing odds against not only vendors, but the pundits that tend to push those vendors for money. What we fail to realize is we do wield a great deal of influence if we band together. In my opinion, it is time to stand up as a profession with one voice and say to the vendors we support with our dollars, "do what is right." It is time to stand up and say that we will no longer allow the tail to wag the dog. At every juncture, we must demand aggressive support of open standards and push vendors to not only participate in organizations like The Open Group, OASIS, the Trusted Computing Group, and the IETF, but to also openly embrace and really contribute to organizations like them. To find our voice, we need to break through the communication silos that have been built around us and find new ways to share ideas and concepts with one another. Those different mechanisms exist now in many fragmented forms and new ones like demandstands.org are coming with the goal of pulling the various pieces together into some type of workable plan that will contribute to an overall global information system transformation.

In the meantime, we must question road maps and require that the vendors we choose to patronize are not only endorsing, but supporting and truly embracing open standards that will encourage the sharing of information, as well as the interoperability of heterogeneous pieces critical to our foundations. It is time for our profession to take a leadership role in our dealings with vendors and their products and interactions with one another. It is time for us to act before we are told we should do something by the very people who then want to sell us the tools to do it. It is time for a greater percentage of IT leaders to come from within the consumers of the technology rather than the purveyors. In order to do that we need to do our homework on each piece of our network to know what standards are necessary. In doing this we can take on various aspects of the product knowledge process collectively while making it clear what we will and will not stand for from the people we choose to do business with. At the same time, we need to consider stronger language in our contracts: "This procurement is contingent on adherence of this product to standard 'x, y, z' with the understanding that a lack of compliance by 'such and such date' will be grounds for a full refund of purchase price." Why do we need to take such an aggressive posture? At this point we have ubiquitous access from a steadily multiplying number of devices with rapidly evolving threats that increase in both numbers and complexity every day. The attackers have revolutionary new tools to deliver these threats. Considering all we are up against, we have no choice but to take issue with defacto standards and large vendors whose opposition to open standards kills us from an agility perspective. To put this in perspective we need to look at the network access control market and think about how many years it has been since a valid standard with multiple vendors supporting it has been in place. It is more than 2 years and yet it is still an issue. Why? Again, old standards processes where large vendors drag their feet are simply not reasonable any longer and at times step in the way of us protecting the shareholders and customers for each organization. It will not be long before the issue of public trust rears its head, which will at that point involve various governments stepping in and making life (by accident, of course) very difficult. Instead we need to get out ahead of that because the stakes are significantly higher now especially as it relates to data security. Earlier, standards adherence mostly centered on efficiency concerns but now it is systemic safety with each entity bearing a responsibility to the whole. That is a completely different level of responsibility and one that I do not believe vendors really want to truly acknowledge.

I briefly touched on the concept of "Endpoints and Flowpoints" and how with the incorporation of the new IF-MAP specification, we can really begin to have a valid shot to ingrain security as the network rapidly expands. We know the ways of the past simply did not scale and things had become nearly unmanageable with older technology. In order to move forward, adopting open standards based frameworks will be one of the most effective and efficient ways to get an agile, scalable, modular, distributed security architecture that is truly workable for the masses. Again, if we look at it with a human immune system concept in mind, basically we are all part of one organism in this digital ecosystem. Slow adoption and lip service to open standards, as previously mentioned, now not only affects efficiency, but also affects safety because if the extremities get an infection it can easily become systemic. While in the past we could just worry about the security of our organizations and even just the core of our organizations, this is no longer the case. Again, the practice of "Digital Feudalism" with the lords of the land retreating to their castles and pulling up the drawbridge while peering out from the throne room has seemed potentially reasonable in the past. Now, not so much because we realize the barbarian hordes (botnets, etc.) really can and are drafting our peasants, dogs, cats, etc., into service for use against us.

CONCLUSION

Contemplate this question: When the vast majority of the digital ecosystem is owned or completely broken

including the very drivers of the financial/economic food-chain, where will that leave the world as a whole?

Considering this question, and with everything I have written taken into consideration, from a "state of standards" perspective, you have to now ask yourself: "Why does the tail continue to wag the dog?" Do we deal with it just because it's always been this way? Are we going to let this state of existence continue? Can we afford to do that? From my perspective, that state of existence cannot and should not be acceptable going forward. Instead, as mentioned, a consolidated voice is required to make changes in how future critical standards evolve. Our future must include open security frameworks that allow plug-ins for innovation with rapidly evolving workable standards, not only requested but demanded. As individual practitioners we need to require legitimate road-maps, timelines, and milestones for standards in the products we use, while contractually requiring adherence by specifying when we expect open standards compliance and what the consequences are for failing on that front. Keep in mind that this is not being difficult no matter what a vendor or business unit says, because more rapid adoption of standard security frameworks opens the door for innovation both in our profession as well as the business as a whole. Blind adherence to a monoculture is neither feasible nor healthy going forward in any facet of our networks and businesses. Being in the security field, I am sure that those of you who have read this far realize that easier is not always better. Homogeneous is not practical at this point and each and every decision we make goes directly to the bottom line of our organizations, either positively or negatively. Our decisions are not made in a vacuum and there is no doubt that, in the future, things are likely to get tougher before they get better. With that in mind, we have to advance changes that matter at every opportunity we are given.

There are a great number of things that I have either just briefly touched on here or simply not mentioned because to do so would extend way past the scope of this entry. If you get nothing else from what I have written, then I hope that you realize that the information security field has changed rapidly over the last few years mostly because of just how young it is in the scheme of society, and it requires a much different mindset when looking at implementation principles going forward. As a profession, we need to think outside the box about how we can begin to affect changes to the old way of operating. Finally, we need to make sure we consider how we take things on, what we take on, how we lead, how we educate, how we drive, and then adhere to open standards, how we support groups like OASIS, The Open Group, and TCG, and how we support concepts like demandstandards.org while clarifying what we absolutely require of vendors. It is a tall order but one that I know we can fill if we communicate and support one another irrespective of old roles, titles, and predispositions going forward.

Penetration Testing

Chuck Bianco
IT Examination Manager, Office of Thrift Supervision, Department of the Treasury, Dallas, Texas, U.S.A.

Abstract

Penetration testing is not a be-all, end-all for security. Organizations must first perform risk assessments that determine the components of sound security policies and procedures. After the development, approval, and installation of security policies, organizations should install several control mechanisms to measure the success or failure of the risk analysis and security systems. One such control is a properly constructed penetration test.

WHAT IS A PENETRATION TEST?

Penetration testing involves examining the security of systems and architectures. It reviews the effectiveness of the security of the organization's Internet presence. This includes all the holes and information that might damage the organization. The tester uses one's creativity and resourcefulness to behave in the same manner as a hacker would.

The tester uses hacking tools and related techniques to challenge the efficiency and competence of the security design. The tester hopes to find problems before the hackers do and recommend fixes and solutions to identified vulnerabilities. Although penetration testing assesses security from the Internet side or the organization's network, it is not a full security assessment or a guarantee that your site is secure.

It is only a complement to a full range of security measures. Your company should already have a complete security policy based on a risk analysis of the data and items you need to protect. If you do not have a security policy in place, you may choose to use penetration testing to assist you in writing the security policy.

The penetration test is simply another security tool to assist in protecting your company's assets. There are several different types of penetration tests, depending on the depth of the test and the threats measured. Both outsiders and employees or trusted third parties can launch attacks on the company. The testing may be broad-based or narrow, depending on risk assessments, the maturity of security policies, prior testing histories, etc.

You may wish to test your systems from internal attacks or develop specialized penetration tests later.

WHY DO IT?

Many institutions offer Internet banking and related E-commerce activities. Some offer services through service bureaus and others offer the services on institution-run transactional websites. All institutions should ensure that they use all systems in a safe and sound manner. Intruders hack both institutions and service bureaus. These hacks place the assets of the institution in peril. The Federal Bureau of Investigation (FBI) claims that almost 60% of all business sites have been the victims of unauthorized access. Some companies have lost money. Many have been the victims of a denial-of-service (DoS) attack, in which a hacker sends more information than your system can handle. This causes your system to slow down or stop working. Examiners and auditors frequently find that the institution does not know whether or not it has suffered a security breach. According to the Computer Emergency Response Team (CERT) and the U.S. Department of Energy Computer Incident Advisory Center (CIAC), hackers invaded more than 25,000 sites in 2001.

Intrusions can lead to loss of money, data, and productivity. Hackers, spies, and competitors can all steal, regardless of whether or not an intrusion occurs. For example, hackers can take advantage of bugs in websites to gain unauthorized information. We have even discovered many examples where poorly designed websites allowed visitors access to unauthorized information. Therefore, even authorized visitors can copy information and can sell confidential customer information and strategic information to competitors. These attacks can damage the institution's reputation and expose it to legal action. The intruder can also install entrances for future activity, such as backdoors, Trojan horses, and program worms. A well-planned test reen-acts all such actions. Penetration testing will normally provide evidence of exposures before they occur. In the case of found Trojan horses and viruses, it will act as a detective control.

Encyclopedia of Information Systems and Technology, DOI: 10.1081/E-EIST-120046303

Penetration testing not only improves security but it also helps to train your staff about security breaches. It provides evidence of proper care and diligence in the event of lawsuits filed because of an intrusion. Moreover, penetration testing authenticates vendors' claims about their product features. We advise you to have the test performed by a disinterested third party. For example, if the tester recommends that you purchase his product after he completes the test, he may not recommend the most effective solution. He also may not find security weaknesses in his products. The testing must be impartial and provide a view of the entire security system.

All institutions that offer E-commerce products should perform annual penetration tests. In no way does this mean that an annual test is sufficient to ensure effective security. We believe that the institution should conduct such tests at least once per year and present the testing report of findings to the board of directors. However, the security plan must indicate how much penetration testing is sufficient. For many sites, an annual penetration test is the equivalent of having the security guard only check if someone locked the front gate after closing time about once a year. Many testers offer yearly contracts for regular testing, which most organizations find extremely helpful in keeping up with the number of exploits and holes published daily.

Institutions using service bureaus should insist on annual penetration testing of the service bureau. Ideally, the institution will take part in the penetration test. The service bureau should issue report findings to its client institutions. The institution should use this report to design a limited penetration test at the institution. An exception to this requirement occurs when the institution takes an active part in the penetration test of the service bureau.

COSTS

Costs of such tests can vary from as little as $2000 for targeted tests to several hundred thousand dollars. The risk assessment or Standard of Due Care Study and your security policy determine the extent of the test and necessary costs. Institutions will include penetration testing costs in cost/benefit studies as part of the business analysis decision.

LIMITS

The institution should carefully design the scope of the penetration test to protect the company from inadvertent downtime and loss of business due to a successful intrusion during the test. While it may also be impractical to allow the tester to have access to production systems, testing does not have to be perilous if done at low traffic times.

While the tester may be limited because the employees know about the penetration test, this knowledge only hampers penetration testing if the tester is also attempting to measure human security controls. Some testers prefer that company personnel know about the test in advance, so that the employees can tighten security before testing. For example, weekly penetration tests will cause the employees to apply patches the moment they come out, rather than waiting for a penetration test report showing they are not doing their jobs. Moreover, professional testers will notify the company as soon as they find any high risks and have them fixed immediately. They will still include the risks in the report, but the tester does not leave the company at risk during the testing and report-writing time.

The company must take great care to carefully design the limits and scope of the penetration test; yet, it must also allow the tester sufficient access to evaluate security effectiveness. The organization should define exactly what the tester can and cannot test. These requirements should go in the contract and be defined by IP addresses.

The test can include, but is not limited to, the following tools and techniques:[1]

- Network mapping and port scanning
- Vulnerability scanning
- Wardialing
- Sniffing
- Spoofing
- Session hijacking
- Various DoS and distributed DoS (DDoS) attacks
- Stack-based buffer overflows
- Password cracking
- Backdoors
- Trojan horses and rootkits

Disadvantages include the following:

- Penetration testing can cause severe line-management problems without the involvement of senior management.
- Penetration testing is a waste of time if it is the only security measure taken by the company.
- It is very expensive, especially if improperly planned.
- The tester can use the information he finds against you.

WHOM YOU SHOULD AVOID

Your institution should never enlist a convicted felon to test your security system.

WHAT YOU SHOULD TELL THE TESTER

- You should provide your institution's legal company name and address as well as the name of a contact person who they can always contact (day or night).
- You should also provide the limits and scope of the testing without denying the tester the opportunity to use his creativity. However, you must ensure that you instruct the tester that the testing should not damage anything and to document any problems caused or found.
- You should detail what systems or networks are off-limits and during what hours the testing will take place. Some experts suggest that you handle this like a firewall—list what you will allow and prohibit everything else. Be prepared to pay extra for testing at strange hours. Ensure that you have qualified employees on-site during those strange hours to reboot downed systems.
- You should also indicate if you own the transaction website or use an ISP.
- Specify whether you will allow social engineering attacks (deception, trickery, or coercion are at the heart of social engineering techniques). Many testers believe that social engineering attacks may do more harm than good because they affect employee morale. Therefore, you may wish to limit publication of the successful social engineering attacks or redact the names of employees the tester fooled into providing information.
- Specify whether you will allow DoS attacks. If you allow these attacks, schedule them for a non-operations time and have someone babysitting the network while the attack happens. However, never allow DDoS attacks, as they involve other companies; they always bring systems down and harm your Internet service provider and all routers in between.
- Specify whether the tester will cover his tracks or leave evidence on the system, such as text messages. The tester should never leave a backdoor program in your system. You may decide that a report of areas where the tester could have entered is sufficient.
- Specify exactly what the purpose of the test is:
  o Is it to get into your system, provide proof of successful entrance, and stop?
  o Will the tester place something on your system, such as a file or message, as proof that he gained entrance to the system?
  o Will you authorize the tester to gain system administrator privileges that allow him unlimited access to accounts?
  o Should the tester gain access to files or e-mail?
  o The tester should collect data indirectly by doing research on the Internet. This is mandatory for a penetration test. The Internet presence measures the footprints your employees leave on the Internet.
- Ask the tester to provide a list of things he or she will do to facilitate the test.
- Will the social engineering attacks be limited strictly to remote attacks, such as phone calls to employees, or will the hacker also conduct them in person? [In-person attacks include reviewing information in trash receptacles, posing as maintenance personnel, service bureau personnel, or employees of the institution, following employees into secured areas (tailgating), etc.] Many experts believe that on-site penetration testing is really auditing. Some companies have their employees perform the on-site social engineering tests in conjunction with the outside tester. Social engineering can also include e-mailing employees or inviting them to visit a certain website.
- Require that the tester indicates in his report how he got the data and if he believes your site is secured against the top-20 tools available in the world. Require that he give some examples of how he located these tools and which are those tools. It is not sufficient that your site is safe from the exploits these tools attempt. The tester should measure your network's response to each tool's unique signature or method. For example, some tools are poorly written and may accidentally bring down a network, even though that was not the intent of the tool. In this way, you determine if the tester just uses a commercial scanning tool, or if he really tries to hack into your system. Many experts believe that no one tool is more than 10% effective in penetration testing.

WHAT YOU SHOULD NOT TELL THE TESTER

You should not provide technical information that a hacker would not know in advance, such as information regarding:

- Firewalls
- Routers
- Filters
- Concentrators
- Configuration rules

WHAT YOU SHOULD DO BEFORE YOU FINALIZE THE CONTRACT

- You should determine the vendor's policy on hiring:
  o Obtain proof of liability insurance.
  o How long has the testing company been in business?
  o How long has the testing team been together?

- Ask for a description of the vendor's testing procedures. Avoid vendors who will not explain their entire testing procedure.
- Ask the vendor how you will reach them during the testing process. Avoid vendors you cannot reach at any time during the test.
- Ask the vendors about the dangers of DoS attacks. Avoid vendors who encourage DoS attacks without telling you how dangerous they are.
- Ask for and insist on merit examples of past work.
- Ask the vendor for redacted examples of his final product. Avoid a vendor who will not supply specific examples of his final product.
- Demand that the vendor sign a non-disclosure agreement. Avoid vendors who refuse to do so.
- Avoid vendors who offer refunds on security tests in cases of "secure networks." Professional security testers operate as a service and will not offer refunds in almost all cases.
- Have your contract reviewed by your attorney before signing.
- Acquire copies of files and data that the tester is able to access during the attacks. Specify whether these outputs will be paper or digital. Ask for traffic dumps, logs, and raw data. The tester should also provide the IP address from which the test is coming.

WHAT YOU SHOULD TELL YOUR STAFF

Try to limit the number of employees who know about the test to the technicians responsible for the networks and computer systems. Assign one employee as the Internal Trusted Agent (ITA). The tester and ITA will communicate with each other if needed during the test. Your employees should know that automated intrusion detection systems block out the tester's IP after a few seconds of scanning. They should not assume that all activity is part of the test. You could actually be under attack from a hacker. Ensure that the technicians know a scan is coming and from where.

WHAT THE TESTER SHOULD PROVIDE AT THE CONCLUSION OF THE TEST

The tester should provide both a brief executive summary (one or two pages) indicating test results, and a detailed listing of all findings and results and what methodology of attacks he used. He should indicate what weaknesses he found and include recommendations for improvement. He should write his report so that non-technical people understand it. At a minimum, the report should include the following items:

- What could be tested
- What was tested
- When and from where the test happened
- The performance effects on the test, and vice versa
- A detailed executive summary in non-technical terms that includes the good and bad
- The tools used for findings
- Information security findings
- Holes, bugs, and misconfigurations in technical detail with suggestions on fixing them
- Network map
- Any weaknesses discovered
- Passwords and logins discovered
- Specific firewall/router behavior findings against a list of attacks (not tools)

Your next move depends on his findings. If he finds many problems, you should begin by fixing the problems. You should also:

- Review all security policies and procedures.
- Ensure staff is trained in security.
- Determine if you need to conduct a full security assessment.
- Review corporate and disaster recovery planning.

Information technology has become ubiquitous due, in large part, to the extent of network connectivity. Telecommunication methodologies allow for the timely transport of information—from corner to corner, across the country, and around the globe. It is no surprise that this domain is one of the largest, because it encompasses the security of communication technologies, as well as the ever-expanding realms of the intranet, Internet, and extranet.

Firewalls, which continue to play an important role in protecting an organization's perimeter, are explored in this domain. Firewalls are basically barriers between two networks that screen traffic, both inbound and outbound, and through a set of rules, allow or deny transmission connections. In this domain, we compare the multiple aspects of the filtering devices.

While perimeter firewalls provide some level of protection, an organization's information, e.g., electronic mail, must still flow into and outside of the organization. Unfortunately, keeping these communication channels open allows for potential compromise. This domain covers the potential vulnerabilities of the free flow of information, and the protection mechanisms and services available. The computer viruses of the late 1980s appear tame compared with the rogue code that is rampant today. The networked globe allows for speedy replication. Malicious programs that take advantage of the weaknesses (or functionality) of vendor systems traverse the Internet at a dizzying speed. While companies are implementing defensive postures as fast as they can,

Network–Programming

in many instances, internal organizations lack the capacity or the tools to fortify their own infrastructures. In some cases, such as is documented in this domain, niche messaging vendors offer services to augment internal security, addressing threats such as e-mail spamming and malicious viruses. They also offer a 24-hour by 7-day monitoring capability and, in many instances, a preemptive notification capability that many organizations cannot accommodate with internal resources.

One of the most successful means of protecting data in transit is the use of encapsulation and encryption employed in virtual private networking. In this domain, we explore the concepts and principles of virtual private networks (VPNs), which allow for the transfer of private information across the public networks while maintaining the security of the data. With benefits that include the ability to do secure business with partners, offer new channels for goods and service delivery, and reach new markets at reduced costs, VPNs hold great promise. In this domain, we look at ways to evaluate, deploy, and leverage VPN technologies, as well as divulge the potential vulnerabilities inherent in those technologies.

Computer and communication technologies are rapidly evolving; devices are growing smaller and more functional; and at the same time, allowing the consumer more mobility, flexibility, and agility. Nowhere is this truer than in the wireless space. Moreover, wireless networks are more cost-effective, since installing and configuring cable and connected devices are not required. The desire to have access to information without the need to tether someone to a wired device is becoming a corporate mandate. And yet, the wireless world has its own set of vulnerabilities. In this domain, we address securing the wireless environment, at the physical layer, on the local area network and over the Internet.

ACKNOWLEDGMENTS

Many industry experts have contributed to this entry. Thanks to Chris Hare of Nortel Networks and Mike Hines of Purdue University. I am very grateful to those who made significant contributions. Hal Tipton of HFT Associates in Villa Park, California, and author of numerous IT security books; Clement Dupuis of CGI in Canada and moderator of the CISSP Open Study Guide Web Site; and Peter Herzog, moderator of the Open Source Security Testing Methodology Forum. The contents of this document are my own and do not represent those of any government agency. The Telecommunications, Network, and Internet Security domain encompasses the structures, transmission methods, transport formats, and security measures used to provide integrity, availability, authentication, and confidentiality for transmissions over private and public communications networks and media.

REFERENCE

1. http://www.cccure.org/modules.php?name=Downloads&d_op=view-downloaddetails&lid=9&ttitle=Domain_1.zip.

BIBLIOGRAPHY

1. Herzog, P. *The Open Source Security Testing Methodology Manual,* http://www.isecom.com.

Network–Programming

Pervasive Computing

Sian Lun Lau
Department of Computer Science and Networked Systems, Sunway University, Bandar Sunway, Malaysia

Abstract

Pervasive Computing is a research area that has been around since the 1990s. Also known as Ubiquitous Computing, the research area started short before 1990s and has gotten more attention since the introduction of Mark Weiser's well known publication—the Computer for the 21st century in 1991. It has brought researchers from various backgrounds—wireless communication, software engineering, human–computer interaction, engineers, etc.—to explore the potential of the vision presented by Mark. Since then the research has come a long way. Some of the envisioned scenarios, proof of concepts, and prototypes are beginning to emerge as commercially available products. Pervasive Computing will still continue to challenge researchers and industry to produce technology that hides complexity and explicit interaction to, on the one hand make computers invisible and disappear into the background, and on the other hand serves users through intuitive and unobtrusive manners to improve quality of life. In this entry, a brief history and important attributes about pervasive computing are presented. This is followed by a summary of example research activities since 1990s until today. A list of conferences and journals is also presented. The entry ends with a selection of example application areas of pervasive computing.

In the 20th century, one of the most significant technologies that have changed how we work and live is the modern computer. Fast forward to the present times, computers have become faster, smaller, and more accessible to everyone. The emergence of mobile computing devices has further revolutionized how computers work as well as how humans interact with computers. As mentioned in Krumm,[1] the change of human-modern computing relationships can be depicted (Fig. 1).

In the 1960s, computers were large and bulky systems, called mainframe computers. Users had to share the mainframe computers, commonly in an organization. Only as we entered into the 1970s, personal computers become increasingly common. Each user could have a computer dedicated to himself. Moving on from the personal computer era, we witness the beginning of the Pervasive Computing era. A user owns many devices—besides a personal computer, one may also own a mobile device or even embedded devices found in everyday equipment or appliances.

As we look at computers around us today, they demonstrate a few characteristics—firstly, devices are getting smaller and smaller, but not necessarily slower. A smartphone or a tablet is having the computational power and capacity similar to a personal computer some years back. Secondly, computers are no longer a terminal placed at the corner of a room. They have become more and more mobile, thanks to the decrease in size and improve technology. This also brings us to the third characteristic—connectivity. Computers are no longer just an island but are often interconnected via network. They allow users to access and process information from remote resources.

THE BEGINNING OF PERVASIVE COMPUTING

It is not easy to directly indicate when the above development began to take place. But the idea or the vision of Pervasive Computing begun somewhere in the 1990s. In 1991, the late Mark Weiser of Xerox PARC has presented the vision of pervasive computing, which he called "Ubiquitous Computing" (In literature, the terms "Pervasive Computing" and "Ubiquitous Computing" are often interchangeable) in his paper titled "The Computer for the 21st Century:"[2]

> The most profound technologies are those that disappear. They weave themselves into the fabric of everyday life until they are indistinguishable from it.
>
> …
>
> Therefore we are trying to conceive a new way of thinking about computers in the world, one that takes into account the natural human environment and allows the computers themselves to vanish into the background.

Mark Weiser anticipated the computers to be so ubiquitous one day that the users no longer need to consciously interact with a computer. Computers will

Encyclopedia of Information Systems and Technology, DOI: 10.1081/E-EIST-120048629

Network–
Programming

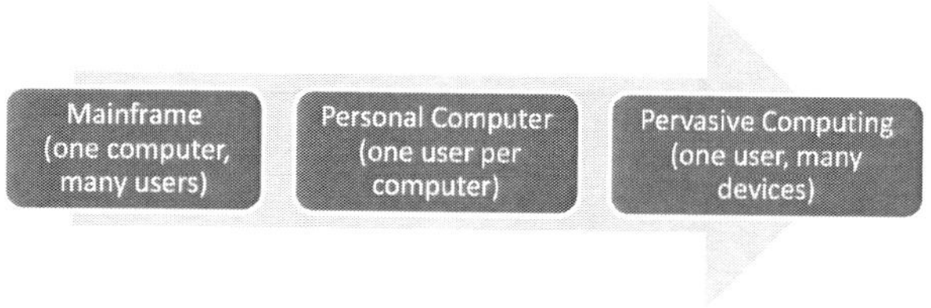

Fig. 1 The three eras of modern computing.

gradually become more invisible to their users. In this way, the interaction between a user and his computer may become more intuitive and ultimately natural. This changes not only how one interacts with a computer, but more importantly how computer scientists, together with others involved in pervasive computing related research, to innovate and develop newer technology that help to realize the vision.

From system point of view, Mark Weiser suggested the pervasive computing technology to be categorized into three parts: "cheap, low-power computers that include equally convenient displays, a network that ties them all together, and software systems implementing ubiquitous applications."[2] These three categories have since then been active research areas. In fact, the foundation of the research on pervasive computing was built based on different technologies started long before 1990s:[3] among them include distributed systems, mobile computing, wireless network, human computer/machine interaction, software architecture, automation technology, (wireless) sensor network, etc. The vision as well as the research of pervasive computing became a driving force to combine and integrate these different research areas into a system that enables future services that are invisible, intelligent, and unobtrusive.

The Name—Pervasive Computing

The research area of pervasive computing has different names in different communities. As mentioned above, ubiquitous computing became a well-known term among researchers since 1990s. Mark Weiser also mentioned calm and invisible computing in his widely quoted paper. Pervasive computing is a term used by another community, commonly stated as a term supported by IBM in the beginning of 2000s. Both terms are often seen as synonyms. In the European research contexts, the terms ambient intelligence (AmI) and ambient assisted living (AAL) are used (see http://www.aal-europe.eu/about/). The focus on AmI and AAL is very close to pervasive computing, but it emphasizes more on using pervasive technology to improve quality of everyday lives, particularly for the elderly and disabled communities.

Four Key Properties of Pervasive Computing

Stefan Poslad has summarized the key properties of pervasive computing as follows:[4]

1. Computers need to be connected, distributed, and transparently accessible: Computers in a pervasive computing environment should not only be always connected, but they are also distributed and open. The accessibility of any device or system should not be limited at any time. Therefore, communication between computers is no longer limited to the location, nor will the use of certain protocol or standards be a factor how communication may fail—the pervasiveness of these computers is ensured by enabling robust technologies that include openness, transparency, connectivity, and availability.

2. The interaction between human and computer needs to be more implicit and unobtrusive: Much of the human–computer interaction until beginning of year 2000s is still more explicit to a greater extent. As computers become more "invisible," this will also require the interaction to be made more implicit and unobtrusive. This may be achieved by either enabling newer techniques which require human to interact with computers in a more natural manner, or computers can take more proactive roles than human. Context-awareness[5] is one area that allows computers to "understand" the context or situation the user has in order to provide proactive responses.

3. Computers needs to behave and react autonomously: As mentioned earlier, computers may take a more proactive role in providing services. This is how autonomy gives more control and independence to a computer's actions. This can be achieved by setting the most suitable policies for computers to follow, or by applying artificial intelligence to help computers to behave, reach, and make decision adaptively, appropriate to the situation the users currently have. Such behavior will also help to reduce explicit interaction between human and computers.

4. Computers demonstrate a much higher level of ability in dynamic actions and interactions: By enabling the above few properties, computers are no longer portraying the passive nature as it used to be seen. Computers will be perceived as more intelligent, adaptive, dynamic, and efficient. They should only take charge when required and appropriate, and such level of ability will further increase the intuitiveness and unobtrusiveness of pervasive computing technology.

The Three Generations of Pervasive Computing Research Challenges

There had been three generations of Pervasive Computing research challenges since 1990.[6] The first 10 years focused more on *connectedness*. In order to make computers "disappear" and behave pervasively, researchers first worked on new technology that prepared the foundation of pervasive computing. Among them include advancement in electronics miniaturization, gate packaging, network connectivity with new wireless communication standards, and the growing Internet.[6] These technological advancements allowed devices in a pervasive computing environment to be always connected, often wirelessly. Devices have gradually become smaller and cheaper, but at the same time relatively fast and powerful for newer applications. This is also the phase where newer human–computer interaction has become more implicit than before.[6]

All these led to the next generation (early to mid-2000s), where the idea of awareness has become the focus. Researchers started investigating technology that allows devices to have the ability to capture information via sensors, often multiple sensors, to ultimately have the knowledge about the situation one may be in. Terms like context and situation awareness started to be observed in research.[5,7] Sensor-based recognition or knowledge representation and use of ontology to model semantic and knowledge, allowed awareness to be achieved, and through this awareness, adaptation and eventually autonomy can be demonstrated and achieved.

The third generation (mid-2000s to present) of pervasive computing is named the smartness generation. Indeed, pervasive computing, with its beginning in connectedness and awareness, has evolved to demonstrate how smart services or systems can be realized through exploitation of semantics of systems, services, and interactions. Researcher worked on techniques that allow systems to "understand" and "react" according to situations and actions. Such systems are seen as *highly complex, orchestrated, co-operative, and coordinated "ensembles of digital artifacts."*[6]

PROMINENT RESEARCH AND INVESTIGATIONS IN PERVASIVE COMPUTING

The First 10 Years

In the first 10 years of pervasive computing research, after the introduction of Mark Weiser's vision, many contributions were made by researchers in exploring different aspects of pervasive computing technology. In Xerox PARC Computer Science Laboratory (CSL), where Mark Weiser was based, a pervasive computing environment was built to investigate and demonstrate

the potential of the vision. Notable devices are the Parc-Tab, Parc Pad, and Liveboard.[8] The ParcTab is a palm (in-scale) computer that represents a pocket book or Wallet. The Parc Pad was designed to work as a pen-based notebook or an e-book reader. The Liveboard serves as a whiteboard with pen-based input and wall display. All these devices demonstrated how one can communicate with devices in a more intuitive manner (using the pen, for instance) and experience can be enhanced (i.e., easier retrieval or playback of previous discussion materials on the Liveboard). Moreover, context-awareness was also integrated, such as automatic tilting of the display if a change of device orientation was detected. All these devices and technology can be regarded as the forefather of current modern devices, as observed in tablets, smartphones, and smart displays.

At Olivetti Research in Cambridge, UK, the researchers developed the Active Badge system.[9] Users are provided with a badge to be worn or attached to objects. Diffuse infrared beacons were embedded into the badges, where each badge emitted signal that carries a unique ID. Sensors in the office environment were deployed to receive this signal to relate the ID to a certain location. This is one of the earliest location-based services demonstrated. In 1997, Olivetti Research developed the Active Bat system.[10] This system combined ultrasound and radio to achieve accurate three-dimensional positioning. The system was able to achieve an accuracy of about 3cm in a typical room, when sensors are installed at the distance of one sensor per ceiling tile.

There were also projects aiming to create smart devices. For example, in 1995, MIT Media Lab formed the Things That Think (TTT) consortium to investigate how the physical world can be integrated with the virtual world.[11] Projects like Oxygen and Tangible Bits explored innovative methods that allow users to interact and use devices or systems more intuitively and naturally. In University of Karlsruhe, miniature computers were embedded into everyday objects. One successful demonstration of the idea is the MediaCup.[12] The MediaCup is a cup integrated with multi sensors. Movements are detected as a person uses the cup, and this allowed capturing of contexts that explains the situation of the object.

The Second 10 Years

After this phase, during the next 10 years (2000–2010) the research in pervasive computing continued to grow. Research projects focused more on bigger or mobile systems. Another area of interest is the design of architecture and software system for pervasive computing. All these projects were built based on the outcome from the first 10 years since Mark Weiser's publication.

Microsoft Research is one of the institutions that have performed some prominent research. The RADAR project is one of the earliest example that utilizes WiFi Received Signal Strength Indication (RSSI) as data to perform indoor positioning.[13] This technique allows one to utilize commercially available WiFi access points to build WiFi RSSI signal maps. These maps will be used to enable recognition of a mobile computer's position in the building. The EasyLiving project built a smart room using architecture with the support of a middleware and different devices.[14] It has close similarity with Mark Weiser's ubiquitous computing vision. The system understands the physical space well so the interaction with human users can be more intuitive and richer.

Microsoft Research produced SenseCam, which is a small wearable computer.[15] It is capable of capturing images of the surrounding of its wearer using a fish-eyed camera. With these images, the system can extract contextual data about and around the wearer. This was demonstrated in the MyLifeBits project.[16] MyLifeBits is an experiment that logged the life of Gordon Bell. The digital artifacts captured in the experiment include literatures (articles, books, papers, letters, etc.), multimedia recordings (CDs, movies, lectures, etc.), and communications (phone calls, Internet messaging records). This project explored software and techniques that enable exploitation of logged items, such as easy annotations of activities, storage of huge amount of data, and ranking of similarity on logged items. Again, such project demonstrated how life in a pervasive computing-enabled environment may look like.

There were also several projects that looked into location-based services. Location can be considered as important information. Situational contexts often have correlation on location. Outdoor positioning is considered as matured with the Global Positioning System (GPS) outdoor location systems. Alternatives are such as location recognition based on Global System for Mobile Communications (GSM) cell transitions and GPS coordinates[17] and large scale location tracking project PlaceLab,[18] which its systems cover not only outdoor but also indoor locations using a combination of GPS, WiFi, GSM, and/or Bluetooth radio information.

Indoor positioning is another emerging research area in pervasive computing. Active Badge and RADAR have led the way in this area. Technology used for indoor positioning includes WiFi, Bluetooth, Radio Frequency Identification (RFID), or even ultra wide band (UWB). Common techniques used for WiFi-based positioning are triangulation using RSSI, angle of arrival (AOA), and time of arrival (TOA). The first two WiFi-based techniques require the knowledge of absolute locations of at least three access points, while the latter requires only two position measuring objects to enable

indoor positioning.[19,20] Bluetooth-based systems require installation of access points, which are less common compared to WiFi-based access points, to detect Bluetooth-enabled mobile devices or tags to estimate location of these devices/tags.[21] The RFID-based systems rely on active RFID technology with reference and tracking tags as well as RFID readers.[22] UWB-based technology exploits the characteristics of radio frequency (RF) in an indoor environment to filter reflected signals from the original signal.[23] Despite the high accuracy, UWB systems are very costly.

There were also a significant number of research projects working on pervasive computing middleware.[24] Middleware technology provides several advantages for the pervasive computing applications, such as interoperability, abstraction of functions (e.g., communication, information acquisition, management etc.), dynamic mediation (i.e., flexible discovery of functions/services), context management (acquisition of low level data as well as processing, interpretation, modeling, prediction, and fusion of contexts) and service adaptation. A few prominent middleware are Context Toolkit,[25] GAIA,[26] AURA,[27] and AMIGO.[28]

One of the core features in a pervasive computing environment is the ability to sense and perceive high level contexts from users and the surrounding environment. Context- and situation-awareness related research has also increased and undergone tremendous growth during this period of time. The definition from Dey[5]— "Context is any information that can be used to characterize the situation of an entity. An entity is a person, place, or object that is considered relevant to the interaction between a user and an application, including the user and applications themselves."—is commonly quoted and accepted as a general definition for context. The significance of context-awareness research in pervasive is the emphasis on acquisition of high-level contexts from raw data, such as translating raw GPS coordinates and interpret these coordinates as a location with certain level of semantics.

Wireless sensor network (WSN) related research is another area that also grew rapidly. Verdone et al. defines WSN as a network of nodes that sense information from the environment cooperatively, hence enabling the implicit interaction between users or devices and the surrounding environment.[29] The advantages of WSN include simple and ad-hoc setup of networks, suitable for hard-to-reach environment, flexible nature in setup and deployment, relatively cheap implementation cost (sensor nodes are usually designed as low cost devices).[30]

Common applications of WSN include tracking, monitoring, and controlling, usually applied in large areas. WSN may be seen as the source of data acquisition for a pervasive computing system. From home automation to plantation to battlefield scenarios, WSN can be seen as an attractive technology to provide useful sensor data for the interpretation of specific contexts that will enable appropriate automated action/reaction to be taken by the underlying pervasive computing system.

Wearable and mobile device have also undergone significant improvement since 2000. Their sizes have reduced and towards the year 2010, there were increasing number of such devices made available in the commercial market. Back in the beginning of 2000s, researchers began exploring activity recognition using sensors. The investigation of Bao and Intille is perhaps one of the most quoted example.[31] They used five sensor boards on different parts of the body, such as arm, wrist, knee, ankle, and waist. The custom-made sensor board consists of a biaxial accelerometer, four AAA batteries, and a memory card for storage. Another similar investigation was carried by Kern et al.[32] In his approach, 12 body-worn triaxial accelerometers were applied on the user's body. These investigations have shown that accelerometer-based activity recognition can provide an accuracy of up to around 90%.

Other sensors applied to enable such activity recognition includes Electrocardiogram (ECG),[33] heart rate monitor,[34] humidity, barometer, audio, And temperature.[35] Some of these research evolved into wearable wrist band, garments, or even integrated sensors on mobile phones. Particularly with the advancement and increasing popularity as well as availability of smartphones, there were also increasing number of researches using smartphone as a sensor and processing device towards 2010, such as Ravi et al.;[36] Lau and David;[37] Yang.[38]

Today and Towards the Future

Looking at where pervasive computing is today, it is indeed an exciting journey seeing how things have been conceptualized, emerged, demonstrated, and evolved. Today, we are already partially living in the vision of Mark Weiser. The ubiquity of smartphones and tablets is a sight we cannot avoid. Many carry more than one device with them. Among them, many also have connectivity and Internet everywhere they go. From 2010 onwards, wearable becomes part of the realized pervasive computing vision. Google glass (https://www.google.com/glass/start/) enabled its user to view and capture information almost seamlessly. A smart watch does more than telling time and receiving calls as well as notifications. Such developments are already evidence of how computers have slowly disappeared, and interaction with computers has become more easy, intuitive, and implicit.

From system and software point of view, modern software architectures will also mature and become popular. Service orientated architecture has been commonly investigated and applied to support pervasive computing systems. Peer-to-peer systems also contributed in making robust and large distributed system into working systems. Cloud computing is another important technology that leveraged on the improved connectivity and bandwidth, allowing users to move computing power from own devices to the "cloud." All these software technology allowed pervasive computing ideas to be implemented and demonstrated.

Rise of such devices and systems opens a new trend—big data. Pervasive computing itself provides the basis of connected devices, systems, and users. This basis offers tremendous amount of information—starting from sensor data to processed high level contexts, from conversation to posted messages on social media, and from traces left in using digital artifacts to habits learned by computers. All these enables big data technology to understand and detect useful patterns as well as "hints" that can reveal more implicit information one no longer can notice or recognize.

The sociotechnical fabric vision was proposed by Ferscha.[6] As computers disappear but become almost omnipresent, the exploitation social contexts based on pervasive computing technology is yet at its infancy. How humans interact with devices and hence with one another, and how that would lead to the understanding of the impact of such technology on the society, are interesting research areas for pervasive computing researchers to further investigate.

Research Conferences and Community

At the age of 20+, the research on pervasive computing is still vibrant and ongoing. As summarized in Krumm,[1] in the early stages, many of the works were published in the Association of Computing Machinery (ACM) Special Interest Group on Computer–Human Interaction (CHI) and ACM Symposium on User Interface Software and Technology (UIST) as well as Mobile Computing related conferences or workshops (e.g., Workshop on Mobile Computing Systems and Applications (WMCSA) (ACM HotMobile since 2007), and ACM MobiCom). In 2000, Karlsruhe University in Germany started the Ubiquitous Computing (UbiComp) conferences (http://ubicomp.org, the first conference was then named Handheld and Ubiquitous Computing [HUC] in 1999) to fill the conference vacuum in the area of pervasive computing. In 2002, the Pervasive Conference (http://www.pervasiveconference.org) had also taken off in Zurich. Both conferences have merged to continue as the ACM Joint Conference of Pervasive and Ubiquitous Computing (UbiComp) from 2013 onwards. The ACM MobiSys (started in 2003) is another venue for research work that focuses on mobile systems and applications.

The Institute of Electrical and Electronics Engineers (IEEE) community has also started the IEEE Annual Conference on Pervasive Computing and Communications (PerCom) (http://www.percom.org/) in 2003. It serves as a platform for researchers to publish their findings in the areas of pervasive computing and communications, including topics like wireless networking, mobile and distributed computing, sensor systems, RFID technology, and the ubiquitous mobile phone. Two other conferences that are equally interesting are the International Conference on Mobile and Ubiquitous Systems: Computing, Networking and Services (Mobiquitous) conference (http://mobiquitous.org/, started in 2004) and the International Conference on Mobile Computing, Applications, and Services (Mobi CASE) (http://mobicase.org/, started in 2009).

The wearable community has also its very own conferences that contribute to the pervasive computing research. The International Symposium on Wearable Computing (ISWC) (http://iswc.net/) focuses on state of the art research in wearable technologies (started in 1997). It is collocated with the Pervasive conference since 2011, and hence with the Pervasive and Ubiquitous conference (UbiComp) since 2012. The HotMobile workshop is also another venue for researchers to publish their findings on topics like wearable and mobile computing.

There are several prominent journals in the area of pervasive computing.[1] The early works were likely to be found in journals like IEEE Personal Communications and Springer's Personal & Ubiquitous Computing. In 2001, the IEEE Personal Communications evolved into two new publications, which are IEEE Pervasive Computing and IEEE Wireless Communications. The former is perhaps one of the top journals featuring state of the art research publications in the area of pervasive computing. Another journal worth mentioning is the Pervasive and Mobile Computing journal from Elsevier.

APPLICATION OF PERVASIVE COMPUTING

From the research and development in Pervasive computing since the 1990s, various application domains have been identified and demonstrated.

The advantages pervasive computing can bring include adaptation and automation. There are many areas where such advantages can be of use. For example, home automation can be implemented in a larger and intelligent scale. Systems react not only based on fixed thresholds but more flexible and intelligent where adaptations are done by learning from the occupants' habits and usage patterns. The same may apply to smart

building automation. Offices and public spaces may be monitored by pervasive devices and energy management can be optimized by understanding and proactively predicting future situations. Example projects are the Aware Home research at Georgia Institute of Technology (http://www.awarehome.gatech.edu) or inHaus at Fraunhofer Institute in Duisburg (http://www.inhaus.fraunhofer.de/en.html).

Such approaches will gradually be found everywhere. Imagine our cars have the ability to learn our driving and sitting patterns, adapting the offered functions according to situations we are in. Software systems extend its capacity and resources based on situations and demands, allowing suitable services to be offered and orchestrated just in time. Manufacturing systems knowing how to control the rate of productions, based on conditions specified in the configuration by the operators. Adaptive systems will assist and improve delivery of functions without implicit instruction from their users.

Other than using the learned situational information to provide suitable adaptation, one can also exploit this kind of information to allow pervasive computing systems to provide personalized services. Based on a user's preferences, or his history of usage and other usable information, a system can learn and build knowledge about the user. This knowledge will be essential in providing the most appropriate services based on the user's needs, situation, and preferences, known as personalized recommendation.

A common example is the personalized music player. The music player can automatically select the preferred songs to be played suitable to the likings of its user, and even recommend new songs suitably when required. Currently, there are already several online services offering such type of services, such as Last.fm, Pandora, Spotify, etc., all using Audioscrobbler as the music recommendation system. Another example is personalized training plans for sports training. Modeling of different training modules based on professional advice can be used to offer personalized training modules according to individual goals and current training conditions.

Another popular area where pervasive computing is investigated is the healthcare domain. Pervasive computing enables healthcare to benefit from the following aspects: Remote monitoring, Health monitoring, personal patients and carer assistance, etc. Pervasive technology can allow acquisition of patients' information such as activity, movement, intake of medication, and wellbeing. A pervasive health care system will utilize this information to understand the situation and health condition of the patients. For example, for chronic heart disease patients, remove monitoring using the 6 minute walk test (6MWT) via mobile devices and telemedicine middleware may allow doctors to be alerted when the outcome of the 6MWT demands their immediate attention.[39] With this possibility, patients no longer need to visit medical care institutions regularly in order to perform simple check-ups. There are also investigations in enabling support for medical professionals in a hospital setting. For example, Bardram & Christensen[40] presented their system that supports large-scale and long-range activities which may likely involve different parties such as clinicians and patients in a hospital.

Since the beginning of 2010s, consumer grade wearables have emerge in the market and it allows usage of small wearable devices to track different aspects of health-related information. For example, GPS and sensors-enabled watches are popular among athletes and joggers; such products are from the companies Suunto, Garmin, and Polar. There are even services that allow users to upload their exercise logs to portals to allow sharing with friends or even like-minded people. Such capabilities are then extended to smart phones or small "pods" that can be installed e.g., in running shoes. There are also upcoming products, such as Emotiv EPOC (https://emotiv.com/epoc.php) or Melon (http://www.thinkmelon.com/) that measure emotion, iHealth (http://www.ihealthlabs.com/blood-pressure-monitors/wireless-blood-pressure-wrist-monitor/) and H^2 (http://www.h2care.com/) that measure blood pressure, and GoBe (http://healbe.com/) that measures blood pressure, calories. All this technology will help to change how people live and take care of their health.

With the ability to use small and connect devices to sense and acquire contexts such as location, movement, etc., pervasive computing has opened new opportunities in mobility and transportation. In recent years, more services offer consolidation of transportation or travelling information with almost real time updates. Most recent successes are such as Waze (https://www.waze.com/) and Moovit (http://www.moovitapp.com/) has changed how people travel and commute. Similarly, such tracking also enhances services like travel assistance/guide,[41,42] logistic tracking,[43] and car2X applications.[44]

Beyond Today

Many of the current research areas will become the future of pervasive computing. One particular area that will become more and more popular is the Internet of Things (IoT). With the maturing technology and availability of small miniature networked computing devices, IoT will be increasingly popular in various application domains. May it be used in a home environment, or a large cooperate building, or even in a plantation environment, IoT will allow stake holders to access desired information conveniently and maximize the potential these information and their interpreted outcome may bring.

The increase of information to be collected will also demand newer techniques for data acquisitions, processing, and also analysis as well as manipulation. A term that has received attention since a few years ago is Big Data. An aspect of pervasive computing that focuses on interpreting contexts and detecting trends as well as anomalies will continue to grow in the Big Data movement. The scope of such research is no longer restricted to a small to moderate size of participants and devices, but may go beyond a city, region, or even country. This will further challenge researchers in the pervasive computing to rethink and innovate ways to implement pervasive computing systems that will cater to such growth and trends.

CONCLUSION

Since the bold introduction of Mark Weiser's vision, we observed exciting and vibrant growth in the research area of pervasive computing since the 1990s. The development of this area, particular in the last decade is phenomenal. Systems, techniques, and mobile devices are strong evidence how far and successful pervasive computing has demonstrated its potential. The road ahead remains challenging but promising, seeing different communities, including researchers, industry and even governments, will continue to contribute in this area to bring more technology into our everyday life.

REFERENCES

1. Roy, W.Adrian, F.;Jakob, B.; Marc, L.; Bernheim, B.A. J.; Alex, S.T.; Aaron, Q.;Shwetak, P.; Alexander, V.; Anind, K.D.; John, K. *Ubiquitous Computing Fundamentals*. CRC Press: Boca Raton, London, New York, 2009.
2. Weiser, M. The computer for the 21st century. Scient. Am. **1991**, *265* (3), 94–104.
3. Chalmers, D. *Sensing and Systems in Pervasive Computing*. Springer London: London, 2011, Available at: http://link.springer.com/10.1007/978-0-85729-841-6 (accessed November 2014).
4. Poslad, S. *Ubiquitous Computing: Smart Devices, Environments and Interactions*. Wiley, 2009, Available at: http://books.google.com.my/books/about/Ubiquitous_Computing.html?id=knfGIltq86kC&pgis=1 (accessed November 2014).
5. Dey, A.K. Understanding and Using Context. Person. Ubiquit. Comp. **2001**, *5* (1), pp. 4–7. Available at: http://dl.acm.org/citation.cfm?id = 593570.593572 (accessed October 2014).
6. Ferscha, A. 20 Years past Weiser: What's next? IEEE Pervasive Comput. **2012**, *11* (1), 52–61. Available at: http://ieeexplore.ieee.org/lpdocs/epic03/wrapper.htm?arnumber = 6072200 (accessed November 2014).

7. Schilit, B.; Adams, N.; Want, R. Context-aware computing applications. Mobile Comput. Syst. Appl. **1995**, 85–90. Available at: http://ieeexplore.ieee.org/lpdocs/epic03/wrapper.htm?arnumber = *512740*.

8. Want R.; Schilit B.N.; Adams N.I.; Gold R.; Petersen K.; Goldberg D. The Parctabparctab Ubiquitousubiquitous Computingcomputing Experimentexperiment. The parctab ubiquitous computing experiment. Imielinski-Want TRoy, KorthSchilit HBill N.. In *Mobile Computing SE—2. The Kluwer International Series in Engineering and Computer Science.* Imielinski T., Korth H., Eds.; Springer U.S.: New York. 1996; pp. 45–101. Available at: http://dx.doi.org/10.1007/978-0-585-29603-6_2.

9. Want R.; Hopper A.; Falcão V.; Gibbons J. The active badge location system. *ACM Trans. Inform. Syst.* **1992**; *10* (1): 91–102. Available at: http://portal.acm.org/citation.cfm?doid = 128756.128759.

10. Harter, A.; Hopper, A.; Steggles, P.; Ward, A.; Webster, P. In *Proceedings of the 5th annual ACM/IEEE international conference on Mobile computing and networking—MobiCom '99.* ACM Press: New York, NY, USA, 1999; 59–68. Available at: http://dl.acm.org/citation.cfm?id = 313451.313476 (accessed November 2014).

11. MIT Media Lab. *Things That Think Consortium.* Available at: http://ttt.media.mit.edu/ (accessed November 2014).

12. Gellersen, H.-W.; Beigl, M.; Krull, H. The mediaCup: Awareness technology embedded in an everyday object. In *Handheld and Ubiquitous Computing SE—30. Lecture Notes in Computer Science*; H.-W. Gellersen, Ed.; Springer Berlin Heidelberg, 1999; 308–310. Available at: http://dx.doi.org/10.1007/3-540-48157-5_30.

13. Bahl, P.; Padmanabhan, V.N. RADAR: An in-building RF-based user location and tracking system. In *Proceedings IEEE INFOCOM 2000. Conference on Computer Communications.* Nineteenth Annual Joint Conference of the IEEE Computer and Communications Societies (Cat. No.00CH37064). IEEE, 2000; 775–784, Available at: http://ieeexplore.ieee.org/articleDetails.jsp?arnumber = 832252 (accessed September 2014).

14. Brumitt B.; Meyers B.; Krumm J.; Kern A.; Shafer S.A. EasyLiving: Technologies for Intelligent Environments. In: *HUC '00 Proceedings of the 2nd international symposium on Handheld and Ubiquitous Computing.* Berlin, HeidelbergSpringer-Verlag Berlin Heidelberg; 2000, 12–29, Available at: http://dl.acm.org/citation.cfm?id = 647986.743885 (accessed November 2014).

15. Hodges, S.; Williams, L.; Berry, E.; Izadi, S.; Srinivasan, J.; Butler, A.; Smyth, G.; Kapur, N.; Wood, K. Sense-Cam: A Retrospective Memory Aid. In Proceedings of the 8th International Conference on Ubiquitous Computing. Lecture Notes in Computer Science. Orange County, CA: Springer Berlin Heidelberg, **2006**; 177–193.

16. Gemmell, J.; Bell, G.; Lueder, R. MyLifeBits: A personal database for everything. Commun. ACM Personal Inform. Manag. **2006**, *49* (1), 88–95.

17. Nurmi, P.; Koolwaaij, J. Identifying meaningful locations. In 2006 Third International Conference on Mobile and Ubiquitous Systems: Networking & Services. IEEE, 2006; pp. 1–8. Available at: http://ieeexplore.ieee.

18. LaMarca, A.; Chawathe, Y.; Consolvo, S.; Hightower, J.; Smith, I.; Scott, J.; Sohn, T.; Howard, J.; Hughes, J.; Potter, F.; Tabert, J.; Powledge, P.; Borriello, G.; Schilit, B. Place lab: device positioning using radio beacons in the wild. In PERVASIVE'05 Proceedings of the Third international conference on Pervasive Computing, Gellersen, H.-W., Want, R., Schmidt, A., Eds.; . Lecture Notes in Computer Science. Berlin, Heidelberg: Springer Berlin Heidelberg, 2005; 116–133.

19. Hightower, J., Borriello, G.Location systems for ubiquitous computing. Computer **2001**, *34* (8) 57–66.

20. Gu, Y.; Lo, A.; Niemegeers, I. A survey of indoor positioning systems for wireless personal networks. IEEE Commun. Surv. Tutor. **2009**, *11* (1), 13–32. Available at: http://ieeexplore.ieee.org/articleDetails.jsp?arnumber=4796924 (accessed November 2014).

21. Kawakubo, S.; Chansavang, A.; Tanaka, S.; Iwasaki, T.; Sasaki, K.; Hirota, T.; Hosaka, H.; Ando, H. *Wireless Network System for Indoor Human Positioning.* In 1st International Symposium on Wireless Pervasive Computing. IEEE, 2006; 1–6. Available at: http://ieeexplore.ieee.org/articleDetails.jsp?arnumber = 1613611 (accessed November 2014).

22. Ni, L.M.; Patil, A.P. LANDMARC: *Indoor Location Sensing Using Active RFID.* In Proceedings of the First IEEE International Conference on Pervasive Computing and Communications. (PerCom 2003). IEEE Comput. Soc, 2003; 407–415. Available at: http://ieeexplore.ieee.org/articleDetails.jsp?arnumber=1192765 (accessed November 2014).

23. Zhang, Y.; Liu, W.; Fang, Y.; Wu, D. Secure localization and authentication in ultra-wideband sensor networks. IEEE J. Select. Areas Commun. **2006**, *24* (4), 829–835. Available at: http://ieeexplore.ieee.org/articleDetails.jsp?arnumber=1618808 (accessed November 2014).

24. Schiele, G.; Handte, M.; Becker, C. Pervasive computing middleware. In *Handbook of Ambient Intelligence and Smart Environments SE —8*, Nakashima, H., Aghajan, H., Augusto, J., Eds., Springer U.S.: New York. 2010; 201–227. Available at: http://dx.doi.org/10.1007/978-0-387-93808-0_8.

25. Dey, A.; Abowd, G.; Salber, D. A conceptual framework and a toolkit for supporting the rapid prototyping of context-aware applications. Human-Comp. Interact. **2001**, *16* (2), 97–166. Available at: http://www.informaworld.com/openurl?genre=article&doi=10.1207/S15327051HCI16234_02&magic=crossref||D404A21C5BB053405B1A640AFFD44AE3.

26. Román, M.; Hess, C.; Cerqueira, R.; Ranganathan, A.; Campbell, R.H.; Nahrstedt, K. Gaia: A middleware platform for active spaces. ACM SIGMOBILE **2002**, *6* (4), 65–67. Available at: http://dl.acm.org/citation.cfm?id = *643550.643558* (accessed November 2014).

27. Garlan, D.;Siewiorek, D.P.;Smailagic, A.;Steenkiste, P. Project aura: Toward distraction-free pervasive computing. IEEE Pervas. Comput. **2002**, *1* (2), 22–31. Available at: http://ieeexplore.ieee.org/articleDetails.jsp?arnumber=1012334 (accessed November 2014).

28. Jouve, W. et al. Building Home Monitoring Applications: From Design to Implementation into The Amigo Middleware. In 2007 2nd International Conference on Pervasive Computing and Applications. IEEE, 2011; 231–236. Available at: http://ieeexplore.ieee.org/articleDetails.jsp?arnumber = 4365445 (accessed November 2014).

29. Verdone, R.; . Dardari, D.; Mazzini, G.; Conti, A. *Wireless Sensor and Actuator Networks*; Elsevier: 2008, Available at: http://www.sciencedirect.com/science/article/pii/B9780123725394000014 (accessed November 2014).

30. Bhattacharyya, D.; Kim, T.; Pal, S. A comparative study of wireless sensor networks and their routing protocols. Sensors 2010, *10* (12), 10506–105023. Available at: http://www.mdpi.com/1424-8220/10/12/10506/htm (accessed November 2014).

31. Bao, L.; Intille, S.S. Activity recognition from user-annotated acceleration data. In *Pervasive computing,* Springer Berlin: Heidelberg,. 2004, 1–17.

32. Kern, N.; Schiele, B.; Schmidt, A. Recognizing context for annotating a live life recording. Person. Ubiquit. Comput. 2006, *11* (4), 251–263. Available at: http://www.springerlink.com/index/10.1007/s00779-006-0086-3 (accessed April 2011).

33. Jatobá, L.C.; . Grossmann, U.; Kunze, C; Ottenbacher, J.; Stork, W.Context-aware mobile health monitoring: Evaluation of different pattern recognition methods for classification of physical activity. In Engineering in Medicine and Biology Society, 2008. EMBS 2008. 30th Annual International Conference of the IEEE, 5250–5253. IEEE, 2008.

34. Tapia, E.M. et al. Real-Time Recognition of Physical Activities and Their Intensities Using Wireless Accelerometers and a Heart Rate Monitor. 2007 11th IEEE International Symposium on Wearable Computers, 2007; 1–4. Available at: http://ieeexplore.ieee.org/lpdocs/epic03/wrapper.htm?arnumber = 4373774

35. Lester, J.; Choudhury, T.; Borriello, G. A practical approach to recognizing physical activities. *In Pervasive Computing.* Springer: Berlin-Heidelberg, 2006, 1–16.

36. Ravi, N.; Dandekar, N.; Mysore, P.; Littman, M.L. Activity recognition from accelerometer data. In IAAI'05 Proceedings of the 17th conference on Innovative applications of artificial intelligence. AAAI Press: 2005; 1541–1546. Available at: http://dl.acm.org/citation.cfm?id = 1620092.1620107 (accessed November 2014).

37. Lau, S.L.; David, K. Movement recognition using the accelerometer in smartphones. In *Future Network and Mobile Summit 2010.* Florence, Italy, 2010, pp. 1–9.

38. Yang, J. Toward physical activity diary: Motion recognition using simple acceleration features with mobile phones. In Proceedings of the 1st international workshop on Interactive multimedia for consumer electronics, ACM. 2009, 1–10.

39. Lau, S.L.; König, I.; David, K.; Parandian, B.; Carius-Düssel, C.; Schultz, M. Supporting patient monitoring using activity recognition with a smartphone. In 7th International Symposium on Wireless Communication Systems (ISWCS), 2010; 810–814.

40. Bardram, J.; Christensen, H. Pervasive Computing Support for Hospitals: An overview of the Activity-Based Computing Project. IEEE Pervas. Comput. 2007, *6* (1), 44–51. Available at: http://ieeexplore.ieee.org/lpdocs/epic03/wrapper.htm?arnumber = 4101141 (accessed November 2014).

41. Cheverst, K.; Davies, N.;Mitchell, K.;Friday, A.; Efstratiou, C. Developing a context-aware electronic tourist guide: Some issues and experiences. Computing. 2002, *2* (1), 17–24.

42. Yang, W.-S.; Hwang, S.-Y. iTravel: A recommender system in mobile peer-to-peer environment. J. Syst. Software 2013, *86* (1), 12–20. Available at: http://www.sciencedirect.com/science/article/pii/S0164121212001768 (accessed December 2014).

43. Oliveira, R.R. et al. SWTRACK: An intelligent model for cargo tracking based on off-the-shelf mobile devices. Exp. Syst. Appl. 2013, *40* (6), 2023–2031. Available at: http://www.sciencedirect.com/science/article/pii/S0957417412011359 (accessed December 2014).

44. Flach, A. et al. Pedestrian Movement Recognition for Radio Based Collision Avoidance: A Performance Analysis. In 2011 IEEE 73rd Vehicular Technology Conference (VTC Spring). Budapest, Hungary, 2011; 1–5.

Network–
Programming

PKI: Public Key Infrastructure

Harry B. DeMaio
Cincinnati, Ohio, U.S.A.

Abstract

This entry discusses encryption as a form of security, mostly focusing on public key infrastructures (PKIs). After a detailed examination of encryption, public-key encryption, and PKI, the author discusses how well PKI satisfies the needs of today. Although PKI is viewed as a possible approach, the author discusses whether it is the best choice as well as how to actually make PKI a "cost-effective reality."

In the history of information protection, there has been an ongoing parade of technologies that loudly promises new and total solutions but frequently does not make it past the reviewing stand. In some cases, it breaks down completely at the start of the march. In others, it ends up turning down a side street. Is public key infrastructure (PKI) just another gaudy float behind more brass bands, or is there sufficient rationale to believe that this one might make it? There are some very good reasons for optimism in this case, but optimism has been high before.

To examine PKI, one needs to know more than just the design principles. Many a slick and sophisticated design has turned embarrassingly sour when implemented and put into application and operational contexts. There are also the questions of economics, market readiness, and operational/technological prerequisites, all of which can march a brilliant idea into a blind alley.

APPROACH AND PRELIMINARY DISCUSSION

We'll start with a short review of the changing requirements for security. Is there really a need, especially in networking, that didn't exist before for new security technologies and approaches?

- We'll (very) briefly describe encryption, public-key encryption, and PKI.
- We'll see how well PKI satisfies today's needs from a design standpoint.
- We'll look at what's involved in actually making PKI a cost-effective reality.
- Finally, we'll ask whether PKI is an exceptional approach or just one of many alternatives worth looking at.

CHANGING WORLD OF NETWORKED SYSTEMS

First, a few characteristics of yesterday's and today's network-based information processing need to be considered. If the differences can be summed up in a single phrase, it is "accelerated dynamics." The structure and components of most major networks are in a constant state of flux—as are the applications, transactions, and users that traverse its pathways. This has a profound influence on the nature, location, scope, and effectiveness of protective mechanisms.

Table 1 illustrates some of the fundamental differences between traditional closed systems and open (often Internet-based) environments. These differences do much to explain the significant upsurge in interest in encryption technologies.

Clearly, each network is unique, and most display a mix of the preceding characteristics. But the trends toward openness and variability are clear. The implications for security can be profound. Security embedded in or "hard-wired" to the system and network infrastructure cannot carry the entire load in many of the more mobile and open environments, especially where dial-up is dominant. A more flexible mode that addresses the infrastructure, user, work station, environment, and data objects is required.

An example: envision the following differences:

- A route salesperson who returns to the office work station in the evening to enter the day's orders (online batch)
- That same worker now entering on a laptop through a radio or dial-up phone link those same orders as they are being taken at the customer's premises (dial-up interactive)
- Third-party operators taking orders at an 800/888 call center
- Those same orders being entered by the customer on a website
- A combination of the preceding

Encyclopedia of Information Systems and Technology, DOI: 10.1081/E-EIST-120046791

Table 1 Open vs. closed networks

	Legacy/closed network	Modern open network
User environments	Known and stable	Mobile/variable
End points	Established	Dynamic/open
Network structure	Established/known	Dynamic/open
Processing	Mainframe/internally distributed	Multisite/multienterprise
Data objects	Linked to defined process	Often independent

The application is still the same: order entry. But the process is dramatically different, ranging from batch entry to Web-based electronic commerce.

In the first case, the infrastructure, environment, process, and user are known, stable, and can be well controlled. The classic access control facility or security server generally carries the load.

In the second (interactive dial-up) instance, the employee is still directly involved. However, now there is a portable device and its on-board functions and data, the dial-up connections, the network, the points of entry to the enterprise, and the enterprise processes to protect if the level of control that existed in the first instance is to be achieved.

The third instance involves a third party, and the network connection may be closed or open.

The fourth (Web-based) approach adds the unknowns created by the customer's direct involvement and linkage through the Internet to the company's system.

The fifth, hybrid scenario calls for significant compatibility adjustments on top of the other considerations. By the way, this scenario is not unlikely. A fallacious assumption in promoting web-based services is that one can readily discontinue the other service modes. It seldom happens.

Consider the changes to identification, authentication, and authorization targets and processes in each instance. Consider monitoring and the audit trail. Then consider the integrity and availability issues. Finally, the potential for repudiation begins to rear its ugly head. The differences are real and significant.

EVOLVING BUSINESS NETWORK

Remember, too, that most network-based systems in operation today have evolved, or in many cases, accreted into their existing state—adding infrastructures and applications on demand and using the technology available at the time. Darwin notwithstanding, some of the surviving networks are not necessarily the fittest. In most of the literature, networks are characterized as examples of a specific class—open-closed, intranet-extranet, LAN-WAN-Internet, protocol-X or protocol-Y.

Although these necessary and valuable distinctions can be used to describe physical and logical infrastructures, remember that when viewed from the business processes they support supply chain, order entry, funds transfer, and patient record processing. Most "business process" networks are technological and structural hybrids.

The important point is that today security strategy and architecture decisions are being driven increasingly by specific business requirements, not just technology. This is especially true in the application of encryption-related techniques such as PKI. Looking again at the earlier order entry example, the application of consistent protective mechanisms for a hybrid order entry scenario will undoubtedly require compatibility and interoperability across platform and network types unless the entire system is rebuilt to one specification. This seldom happens unless the enterprise is embarking on a massive reengineering effort or deploying major application suites such as the SAP AG R/3 or PeopleSoft.

Disintegration and Reintegration of Security Mechanisms

To be effective, a protective mechanism must appropriately bind with the object and the environment requiring protection. In open networks, the connection, structure, and relationship of the components are more loosely defined and variable. Therefore, the protective mechanisms must be more granular, focused, and more directly linked to the object or process to be protected than was the case with legacy systems. Formerly, protection processes operated primarily at a "subterranean plumbing" level, surfacing only in password and authorization administration and log-ons. Now the castle moat is being supplemented with "no-go" zones, personal bodyguards posted at strategic spots, food tasters, and trusted messengers.

Encryption mechanisms fit this direct, granular requirement often ideally, since they can protect individual files, data elements (including passwords), paths (tunneling and virtual private networks), and manage access management requirements. (Identification and authentication through encryption is easier than authorization.) But saying that encryption is granular is not the same as saying that a PKI system is interoperable, portable, or scalable. In fact, it means that most encryption-related systems today are still piece parts, although some effective suites such as Entrust are in the market and several others, such as IBM SecureWay and RSA/SD Keon, are just entering.

This "disintegrated" and specialized approach to providing security function creates a frustrating problem for security professionals accustomed to integrated suites. Now the user becomes the integrator or must use a third-party integrator. The products may not integrate well or even be able to interface with one another. At the 1999 RSA Conference in San Jose, CA, the clarion call for security suites was loud and clear.

Encryption Defined

Encryption is a process for making intelligible information unintelligible through the application of sophisticated mathematical conversion techniques. Obviously, to be useful the process must be reversible (decryption). The three major components of the encryption/decryption process are as follows:

1. *The information stream in clear or encrypted form.*
2. *The mathematical encryption process*—the algorithm. Interestingly, most commercial algorithms are publicly available and are not secret. What turns a public process into a uniquely secret one is the encryption key.
3. *The encryption key.* The encryption key is a data string that is mathematically combined with the information (clear or encrypted) by the algorithm to produce the opposite version of the data (encrypted or clear). Remember that all data on computers is represented in binary number coding. Binary numbers can be operated upon by the same arithmetic functions as those that apply to decimal numbers. So by combining complex arithmetic operations, the data and key are converted into an encrypted message form and decrypted using the same process and *same key—with one critical exception.*

Before explaining the exception, one more definition is required. The process that uses the *same key* to decrypt and encrypt is called *symmetric* cryptography. It has several advantages, including exceptional speed on computers. It has a serious drawback. In any population of communicating users (n), in order to have *individually unique* links between each pair of users, the total number of keys required is n (n + 1)/2. Try it with a small number and round up. If the population of users gets large enough, the number of individual keys required rapidly becomes unmanageable. This is one

(but not the only) reason why symmetric cryptography has not had a great reception in the commercial marketplace in the last 20 years.

The salvation of cryptography for practical business use has been the application of a different class of cryptographic algorithms using *asymmetric* key pairs. The mathematics is complex and is not intuitively obvious, but the result is a *pair of linked keys* that must be used together. However, only one of the pair, the private key, must be kept secret by the key owner. The other half of the pair—the public key—can be openly distributed to anyone wishing to communicate with the key owner. A partial analogy is the cash depository in which all customers have the same key for depositing through a one-way door, but only the bank official has a key to open the door to extract the cash. This technique vastly reduces the number of keys required for the same population to communicate safely and uniquely.

ENTER PKI

If the public key is distributed openly, how do you know that it is valid and belongs with the appropriate secret key and the key owner? How do you manage the creation, use, and termination of these key pairs. That is the foundation of PKI. Several definitions follow:

> The comprehensive system required to provide public-key encryption and digital signature services is known as the *public-key infrastructure* (PKI). The purpose of a public-key infrastructure is to manage keys and certificates.
>
> —Entrust Inc.
>
> A public-key infrastructure (PKI) consists of the programs, data formats, communications protocols, institutional policies, and procedures required for enterprise use of public-key cryptography.
>
> —Office of Information Technology, University of Minnesota
>
> In its most simple form, a PKI is a system for publishing the public-key values used in public-key cryptography. There are two basic operations common to all PKIs:
>
> 1. Certification is the process of binding a public-key value to an individual organization or other entity, or even to some other piece of information such as a permission or credential.
> 2. Validation is the process of verifying that a certificate is still valid.
>
> How these two operations are implemented is the basic defining characteristic of all PKIs.
>
> —Marc Branchaud

Digital Certificate and Certificate Authorities

Obviously, from these definitions, a digital certificate is the focal point of the PKI process. What is it? In simplest terms, a digital certificate is a credential (in digital form) in which the public key of the individual is embedded along with other identifying data. That credential is encrypted (signed) by a trusted third party or certificate authority (CA) who has established the identity of the key owner (similar to but more rigorous than notarization). The "signing key" ties the certificate back to the CA and ultimately to the process that bound the certificate holder to his or her credentials and identity proof process.

By "signing" the certificate, the CA establishes and takes liability for the authenticity of the public key contained in the certificate and the fact that it is bound to the named user. Now total strangers who know or at least trust a common CA can use encryption not just to *conceal* the data but also to *authenticate* the other party. The *integrity* of the message is also ensured. If you change it once encrypted, it will not decrypt. The message *cannot be repudiated* because it has been encrypted using the sender's certificate.

Who are CAs? Some large institutions are their own CAs, especially banks (private CAs). There are some independent services (public CAs) developing, and the government, using the licensing model as a take-off point, is moving into this environment. It may become a new security industry. In the Netherlands, KNB, the Dutch notary service, supplies digital certificates.

As you would expect, there has been a move by some security professionals to include more information in the certificate, making it a multipurpose "document." There is one major problem with this. Consider a driver's license, which is printed on special watermarked paper, includes the driver's picture, and is encapsulated in plastic. If one wished to maintain more volatile information on it, such as the existing make of car(s), doctor's name and address, or next of kin, the person would have to get a new license for each change.

The same is true for a certificate. The user would have to go back to the CA for a new certificate each time he made a change. For a small and readily accessible population, this may be reasonable. However, PKI is usually justified based on large populations in open environments, often across multiple enterprises. The cost and administrative logjam can build up with the addition of authorization updates *embedded in the certificate.* This is why relatively changeable authorization data (permissions) are seldom embedded in the certificate but rather attached. There are several certificate structures that allow attachments or permissions that can be changed independently of the certificate itself.

To review, the certificate is the heart of the PKI system. A given population of users who wish to intercommunicate selects or is required to use a specific CA to obtain a certificate. That certificate contains the public-key half of an asymmetric key pair as well as other indicative information about the target individual. This individual is referred to as the "distinguished name"—implying that there can be no ambiguities in certificate-based identification—all Smiths must be separately distinguished by ancillary data.

Where Are Certificates Used?

Certificates are used primarily in open environments in which closed network security techniques are inappropriate or insufficient for any or all of the following:

- Identification/authentication
- Confidentiality
- Message/transaction integrity
- Nonrepudiation

Not all PKI systems serve the same purposes or have the same protective priorities. This is important to understand when one is trying to justify a PKI system for a specific business environment.

How Does PKI Satisfy Those Business Environment Needs?

Market expectation

As PKI becomes interoperable, scalable, and generally accepted, companies will begin to accept the wide use of encryption-related products. Large enterprises such as government, banks, and large commercial firms will develop trust models to easily incorporate PKI into everyday business use.

Existing reality

It is not that easy. Thus far, a significant number of PKI projects have been curtailed, revised, or temporarily shelved for reevaluation. The reasons most often given include the following:

- Immature technology
- Insufficient planning and preparation
- Underestimated scope
- Infrastructure and procedural costs
- Operational and technical incompatibilities
- Unclear cost–benefits

Apparent Conclusions about the Marketplace

PKI has compelling justifications for many enterprises, but there are usually more variables and pitfalls than anticipated. Broadside implementation, though sometimes necessary, has not been as cost-effective. Pilots and test beds are strongly recommended.

A properly designed CA/registration authority (RA) administrative function is always a critical success factor.

CERTIFICATES, CA, AND RA

How do they work and how are they related?

First look at the PKI certificate lifecycle. It is more involved than one may think. A digital certificate is a secure and trustworthy credential, and the process of its creation, use, and termination must be appropriately controlled.

Not all certificates are considered equally secure and trustworthy, and this is an active subject of standards and industry discussion. The strength of the cryptography supporting the certificate is only one discriminating factor. The degree to which the certificate complies with a given standard, X.509, for example, is another criterion for trustworthiness. The standards cover a wide range of requirements, including content, configuration, and process. The following is hardly an exhaustive list, but it will provide some insight into some of the basic requirements of process.

- *Application*—How do the "certificate owners to be" apply for a certificate? To whom do they apply? What supporting materials are required? Must a face-to-face interview be conducted, or can a surrogate act for the subject? What sanctions are imposed for false, incomplete, or misleading statements? How is the application stored and protected?
- *Validation*—How is the applicant's identity validated? By what instruments? By what agencies? For what period of time?
- *Issuance*—Assuming the application meets the criteria and the validation is successful, how is the certificate actually issued? Are third parties involved? Is the certificate sent to the individual or, in the case of an organization, some officer of that organization? How is issuance recorded? How are those records maintained and protected?
- *Acceptance*—How does the applicant indicate acceptance of the certificate? To whom? Is non-repudiation of acceptance eliminated?
- *Use*—What are the conditions of use? Environments, systems, and applications?
- *Suspension or Revocation*—In the event of compromise or suspension, who must be notified? How? How soon after the event? How is the notice of revocation published?

- *Expiration and Renewal*—Terms, process, and authority?

Who and What Are the PKI Functional Entities That Must Be Considered?

Certification authority

- A person or institution who is trusted and can vouch for the authenticity of a public key
- May be a principal (e.g., management, bank, or credit card issuer)
- May be a secretary of a "club" (e.g., bank clearing house)
- May be a government agency or designee (e.g., notary public, Department of Motor Vehicles, or post office)
- May be an independent third party operating for a profit (e.g., VeriSign®)
- Makes a decision on evidence or knowledge after due diligence
- Records the decision by signing a certificate with its private key
- Authorizes issuance of certificate

Registration authority

- Manages certificate life cycle, including Certificate Directory maintenance and Certificate Revocation List(s) (CRL) maintenance and publication.
- Thus can be a critical choke point in PKI process and a critical liability point, especially as it relates to CRLs.
- An RA may or may not be CA.

Other entities

- *Other Trusted Third Parties*—These may be service organizations that manage the PKI process, brokers who procure certificates from certificate suppliers, or independent audit or consulting groups that evaluate the security of the PKI procedure.
- *Individual Subscribers.*
- *Business Subscribers*—In many large organizations, two additional constructs are used:

1. *The Responsible Individual* (RI)—The enterprise certificate administrator.
2. *The Responsible Officer* (RO)—The enterprise officer who legally assures the company's commitment to the certificate. In many business instances, it is more important to know that this certificate is backed by a viable organization that will accept liability than to be able to fully identify the actual certificate holder. In a business transaction, the fact

that a person can prove he or she is a partner in Deloitte & Touche LLP who is empowered to commit the firm usually means more than who that person is personally.

PKI policies and related statements include the following:

- Certificate policy
- Named set of rules governing certificate usage with common security requirements tailored to the operating environment within the enterprise
- Certificate practices statement (CPS)
- Detailed set of rules governing the CA's operations
- Technical and administrative security controls
- Audit
- Key management
- Liability, financial stability, due diligence
- CA contractual requirements and documents
- Subscriber enrollment and termination processes

Certificate Revocation List

Of all the administrative and control mechanisms required by a PKI, the CRL function can be one of the more complex and subtle activities. The CRL is an important index of the overall trustworthiness of the specific PKI environment. Normally it is considered part of the RA's duties. Essentially, the CRL is the instrument for checking the continued validity of the certificates for which the RA has responsibility. If a certificate is compromised, if the holder is no longer authorized to use the certificate, or if there is a fault in the binding of the certificate to the holder, it must be revoked and taken out of circulation as rapidly as possible. All parties in the trust relationship must be informed. The CRL is usually a highly controlled online database (it may take any number of graphic forms) at which subscribers and administrators may determine the currency of a target partner's certificate. This process can vary dramatically by the following:

- *Timing/frequency of update.* Be careful of the language here. Many RAs claim a 24 hours update. That means the CRL is refreshed every 24 hours. It does not necessarily mean that the total cycle time for a particular revocation to be posted is 24 hours. It may be longer.
- *Push-pull.* This refers to the way in which subscribers can get updates from the CRL. Most CRLs require subscribers to pull the update. A few private RAs (see the following text) employ a push methodology. There is a significant difference in cost and complexity and most important the line of

demarcation between an RA's and the subscriber's responsibility and liability. For lessened liability alone, most RAs prefer the pull mode.

- *Up link/down link.* There are two transmissions in the CRL process: the link from the revoking agent to the CRL and the distribution by the CRL to the subscribing universe. Much work has been exerted by RAs to increase the efficiency of the latter process, but because it depends on the revoking agency, the up link is often an Achilles' heel. Obviously, the overall time is a combination of both processes, plus file update time.
- *Cross-domain.* The world of certificates may involve multiple domains and hierarchies. Each domain has a need to know the validity status of all certificates that are used within its bounds. In some large extranet environments, this may involve multiple and multi-layer RA and CRL structures. Think this one through very carefully and be aware that the relationships may change each time the network encompasses a new environment.
- *Integrity.* One major way to undermine the trustworthiness of a PKI environment is to compromise the integrity of the CRL process. If the continued validity of the certificate population cannot be assured, the whole system is at risk.
- *Archiving.* How long should individual CRLs be kept and for what purposes?
- *Liabilities and commitments.* These should be clearly, unambiguously, and completely stated by all parties involved. In any case of message or transaction compromise traceable to faulty PKI process, the RA is invariably going to be involved. Make very sure you have a common understanding.

As you might expect, CAs and RAs come in a variety of types. Some of the more common include the following:

- *Full-service public CA* providing RA, certificate generation, issuance, and life-cycle management. Examples: VeriSign, U.S. Postal Service, TradeWave
- *Branded public CA* providing RA, certificate issuance, and lifecycle management
- *Certificates generated by a trusted party*, e.g., VeriSign, GTE CyberTrust. Examples: IDMetrix/*GTE CyberTrust*, Sumitomo Bank/*VeriSign*
- *Private CAs* using CA turn-key system solutions internally. Examples: ScotiaBank (*Entrust*), Lexis-Nexis (*VeriSign On-Site*)
- *IBM Vault Registry*

There are also wide variations in trust structure models. This is driven by the business process and network architecture:

Network–Programming

- Hierarchical trust (a classical hierarchy that may involve multiple levels and a large number of individual domains)
- VeriSign, Entrust
- X.509v3 certificates
- One-to-one binding of certificate and public key
- Web of Trust (a variation on peer relationships between domains)
- PGP
- Many-to-one binding of certificates and public key
- Constrained or Lattice of Trust structures
- Hybrid of hierarchical and web models
- Xcert

There are several standards, guidelines, and practices that are applicable to PKI. This is both a blessing and a curse. The most common are listed in the following text. Individual explanations can be found at several websites. Start at the following site, which has a very comprehensive set of PKI links—http://www.cert.dfn.de/eng/team/ske/pem-dok.html. This is one of the best PKI link sites available.

- X.500 Directory Services and X.509 Authentication
- Common Criteria (CC)
- American National Standards Institute (ANSI) X9 series
- Department of Defense Standards
- Trusted Computer System Evaluation Criteria (TCSEC), Trusted Software Development Methodology (TSDM), Software Engineering Institute Capability Maturity Model (SEI CMM)
- Internet Engineering Task Force (IETF) RFC—PKIX, PGP
- S/MIME, SSL, IPSEC
- SET
- ABA Guidelines
- Digital Signatures, Certification Practices
- FIPS Publications 46, 140-1, 180-1, 186

CA/RA targets of evaluation

To comprehensively assess the trustworthiness of the individual CA/RA and the associated processes, Deloitte & Touche developed the following list of required evaluation targets:

- System level (in support of the CA/RA process and certificate usage if applicable)
- System components comprising a CA/RA environment
- Network devices
- Firewalls, routers, and switches
- Network servers
- IP addresses of all devices

- Client work stations
- Operating systems and application software
- Cryptographic devices
- Physical security, monitoring, and authentication capabilities
- Data object level (in support of the CA/RA process and certificate usage)
- Data structures used
- Critical information flows
- Configuration management of critical data items
- Cryptographic data
- Sensitive software applications
- Audit records
- Subscriber and certificate data
- CRLs
- Standards compliance where appropriate
- Application and operational level (repeated from earlier)
- Certificate policy
- Named set of rules governing certificate usage with common security requirements tailored to the operating environment within the enterprise
- CPS
- Detailed set of rules governing the CA operations
- Technical and administrative security controls
- Audit
- Key management
- Liability, financial stability, and due diligence
- CA contractual requirements and documents
- Subscriber enrollment and termination processes

How Well Does PKI Satisfy Today's Open Systems Security Needs?

In a nutshell, PKI is an evolving process. It has the fundamental strength, granularity, and flexibility required to support the security requirements outlined. In that respect, it is the best available alternative. But wholesale adoption of PKI as the best, final, and global solution for security needs is naïve and dangerous. It should be examined selectively by business process or application to determine whether there is sufficient "value-added" to justify the direct and indirect cost associated with deployment. As suites such as Entrust become more adaptive and rich interfaces to ERP systems such as the SAP R/3 become more commonplace, PKI will be the security technology of choice for major, high-value processes. It will never be the only game in town. Uncomfortable or disillusioning as it may be, the security world will be a multi-solution environment for quite a while.

What Is Involved in Making PKI a Cost-Effective Reality?

The most common approach to launching PKI is a pilot environment. Get your feet wet. Map the due diligence and procedural requirements against the culture of the organization. Look at the volatility of the certificates that will be issued. What is their life expectancy and need for modification? Check the interface issues. What is the prospective growth curve for certificate use? How many entities will be involved? Is cross-certification necessary? Above all else, examine the authorization process requirements that must co-exist with PKI. PKI is not a full-function access-control process. Look into the standards and regulations that affect your industry. Are there export control issues associated with the PKI solution being deployed? Is interoperability a major requirement? If so, how flexible is the design of the solutions being considered?

CA PILOT CONSIDERATIONS

Type of Pilot

- *Proof of concept*—May be a test bed or an actual production environment.
- *Operational*—A total but carefully scoped environment. Be sure to have a clear statement of expectations against which to measure functional and business results.
- *Inter-enterprise*—Avoid this as a start-up if possible. But sometimes it is the real justification for adopting PKI. If so, spend considerable time and effort getting a set of procedures and objectives agreed upon by all of the partners involved. An objective third-party evaluation can be very helpful.
- Examine standards alternatives and requirements carefully—especially in a regulated industry.

- Check product and package compatibility, interoperability, and scalability *very carefully*.
- Develop alternative compatible product scenarios. At this stage of market maturity, a Plan B is essential. Obviously not all products are universally interchangeable. Develop a backup suite and do some preliminary testing on it.
- Investigate outsourced support as an initial step into the environment. Although a company's philosophy may dictate an internally developed solution, the first round may be better deployed using outside resources.
- What are the service levels explicitly or implicitly required?
- Start internally with a friendly environment. You need all the support you can get, especially from business process owners.
- Provide sufficient time and resources for procedural infrastructure development, including CA policy, CPS, and training.
- Do not promise more than you can deliver.

Is PKI an Exceptional Approach or Just One of Many Alternatives Worth Looking At?

The answer depends largely on the security objectives of the organization. PKI is ideal (but potentially expensive) for extranets and environments in which more traditional identification and authentication are insufficient. Tempting as it may be, resist the urge to find the *single solution*. Most networked-based environments and the associated enterprises are too complex for one global solution. Examine the potential for SSL, SMIME, Kerberos, single sign-on, and virtual private networks (VPNs). If you can make the technical, operational, and cost-justification case for a single, PKI-based security approach, do so. PKI is a powerful structure, but it is not a religious icon. Leave yourself room for tailored multi-solution environments.

Network–
Programming

Portable Computing Environments

Phillip Q. Maier
Vice President, Information Security Emerging Technology & Network Group, Inovant, San Ramon, California, U.S.A.

Abstract

The use of portable computing presents very specific data security threats. For every potential threat, some countermeasure should be implemented to ensure the company's proprietary information is protected. This involves identifying the potential threats and implementing the level of protection needed to minimize these threats. By providing a reasonably secure portable computing environment, users can enjoy the benefits of portable computing and the organization can remain competitive in the commercial marketplace.

Today's portable computing environment can take on a variety of forms: from remote connectivity to the home office to remote computing on a standalone microcomputer with desktop capabilities and storage. Both of these portable computing methods have environment-specific threats as well as common threats that require specific protective measures. Remote connectivity can be as simple as standard dial-up access to a host mainframe or as sophisticated as remote node connectivity in which the remote user has all the functions of a workstation locally connected to the organization's local area network. Remote computing in a standalone mode also presents very specific security concerns, often not realized by most remote computing users.

PORTABLE COMPUTING THREATS

Portable computing is inherently risky. Just the fact that company data or remote access is being used outside the normal physical protections of the office introduces the risk of exposure, loss, theft, or data destruction more readily than if the data or access methods were always used in the office environment.

Data Disclosure

Such simple techniques as observing a user's remote access to the home office (referred to as shoulder surfing) can disclose a company's dial-up access phone number, user account, password, or log-on procedures; this can create a significant threat to any organization that allows remote dial-up access to its networks or systems from off-site. Even if this data or access method isn't disclosed through shoulder surfing, there is still the intermediate threat of data disclosure over the vast amount of remote-site to central-site communication

lines or methods (e.g., the public phone network). Dial-up access is becoming more vulnerable to data disclosure because remote users can now use cellular communications to perform dial-up access from laptop computers.

Also emerging in the remote access arena is a growing number of private metropolitan wireless networks, which present a similar, if not greater, threat of data disclosure. Most private wireless networks don't use any method of encryption during the free-space transmission of a user's remote access to the host computer or transmission of company data. Wireless networks can range in size from a single office space serving a few users to multiple clusters of wireless user groups with wireless transmissions linking them to different buildings. The concern in a wireless data communication link is the threat of unauthorized data interception, especially if the wireless connection is the user's sole method of communication to the organization's computing resources.

All of these remote connectivity methods introduce the threat of data exposure. An even greater concern is the threat of exposing a company's host access controls (i.e., a user's log-on account and static password), which when compromised may go undetected as the unauthorized user accesses a system under a valid user account and password.

Data Loss and Destruction

Security controls must also provide protection against the loss and destruction of data. Such loss can result from user error (e.g., laptop computers may be forgotten in a cab or restaurant) or other cause (e.g., lost baggage). This type of data loss can be devastating, given today's heavy reliance on the portable computer and the large amount of data a portable computer can contain. For this reason alone some security practitioners would prohibit the use of portable computers, though increased popularity of portable computing makes this a losing proposition in most organizations.

Other forms of data loss include outright theft of disks, copying of hard disk data, or loss of the entire unit. In today's competitive business world, it is not uncommon to hear of rival businesses or governments using intelligence-gathering techniques to gain an edge over their rivals. More surreptitious methods of theft can take the form of copying a user's diskette from a computer left in a hotel room or at a conference booth during a break. This method is less likely to be noticed, so the data owner or company would probably not take any measures to recover from the theft.

Threats to Data Integrity

Data integrity in a portable computing environment can be affected by direct or indirect threats, such as virus attacks. Direct attacks can occur from an unauthorized user changing data while outside the main facility on a portable user's system or disk. Data corruption or destruction due to a virus is far more likely in a portable environment because the user is operating outside the physical protection of the office. Any security-conscious organization should already have some form of virus control for on-site computing; however, less control is usually exercised on user-owned computers and laptops. While at a vendor site, the mobile user may use his or her data disk on a customer's computer, which exposes it to the level of virus control implemented by this customer's security measures and which may not be consistent with the user's company's policy.

Other Forms of Data Disclosure

The sharing of computers introduces not only threats of contracting viruses from unprotected computers, but also the distinct possibility of unintended data disclosure. The first instance of shared computer threats is the sharing of a single company-owned portable computer. Most firms don't enjoy the financial luxury of purchasing a portable computer for every employee who needs one.

In order to enable widespread use of minimal resources, many companies purchase a limited number of portable computers that can be checked out for use during prolonged stays outside the company. In these cases, users most likely store their data on the hard disk while working on the portable and copy it to a diskette at the end of their use period. But they may not remove it from the hard disk, in which case the portable computer's hard disk becomes a potential source of proprietary information to the next user of the portable computer. And if this computer is lost or misplaced, such information may become public. Methods for protecting against this threat are not difficult to implement; they are discussed in more detail later in this entry.

Shared company portables can be managed, but an employee's sharing of computers external to the company's control can lead to unauthorized data disclosure. Just as employees may share a single portable computer, an employee may personally own a portable that is also used by family members or it may be lent or even rented to other users. At a minimum, the organization should address these issues as a matter of policy by providing a best practices guideline to employees.

DECIDING TO SUPPORT PORTABLES

As is the case in all security decisions, a risk analysis needs to be performed when making the decision to support portable computers. The primary consideration in the decision to allow portable computing is to determine the type of data to be used by the mobile computing user. A decision matrix can help in this evaluation, as shown in Table 1. The vertical axis of the decision matrix could contain three data types the company uses: confidential, sensitive, and public. Confidential data is competition-sensitive data that cannot be safely disclosed outside the company boundaries. Sensitive data is private, but of less concern if it were disclosed. Public data can be freely disclosed.

The horizontal axis of the matrix could be used to represent decisions regarding whether the data can be

Table 1 Decision matrix for supporting portable computers

Data classification	Portable computing not permitted	Control strategy Portable computing with stringent safeguards	Portable computing with minimal safeguards	Portable computing with few safeguards
Company confidential	Recommended action	Not permitted	Not permitted	Not permitted
Company sensitive	Recommended action	Recommended action	Not permitted	—
Public data	—	—	Recommended action	Recommended action

Table 2 Portable computing threats and protection measures

	Data					
	Disclosure		Loss/destruction		Integrity	
Threats	Authentication disclosure	Transmission disclosure	Direct theft	Indirect theft	Virus	Malicious tampering
Protections	One-time passwords	Encryption	Software controls	Physical controls	Antivirus software	Software access controls
		Hardware control	Encryption	Color-coded disks	Physical control procedures	
			Encryption			

used for portable computer use and the level of computing control mechanisms that should be put in place for the type of data involved. (The data classifications in Table 1 are very broad; a given company's may be more granular.) The matrix can be used by users to describe their needs for portable computing, and it can be used to communicate to them what data categories are allowed in a portable computing environment.

This type of decision matrix would indicate at least one data type that should never be allowed for use in a mobile computing environment (i.e., confidential data). This is done because it should be assumed that data used in a portable computing environment will eventually be compromised even with the most stringent controls. With respect to sensitive data, steps should be taken to guard against the potential loss of the data by implementing varying levels of protection mechanisms. There is little concern over use of public data. As noted, the matrix for a specific company may be more complex, specifying more data types unique to the company or possibly more levels of controls or decisions on which data types can and cannot be used.

PROTECTION STRATEGIES

After the decision has been made to allow portable computing with certain use restrictions, the challenge is to establish sound policies and protection strategies against the known threats of this computing environment. The policy and protection strategy may include all the ideas discussed in this entry or only a subset, depending on the data type, budget, or resource capabilities.

The basic implementation tool for all security strategies is user education. Implementing a portable computing security strategy is no different; the strategy should call for a sound user education and awareness program for all portable computing users. This program should highlight the threats and vulnerabilities of portable computing and the protection strategies that must be implemented. Table 2 depicts the threats and the potential protection strategies that can be employed to combat them.

User Validation Protection

The protection strategy should reflect the types of portable computing to be supported. If remote access to the company's host computers and networks is part of the portable computing capabilities, then strict attention should be paid to implementing a high-level remote access validation architecture. This may include the use of random password generation devices, challenge/response authentication techniques, time-synchronized password generation, and biometric user identification methods. Challenge/response authentication relies on the user carrying some form of token that contains a simple encryption algorithm; the user would be required to enter a personal ID to activate it. Remote access users are registered with a specific device; when accessing the system, they are sent a random challenge number. Users must decrypt this challenge using the token's algorithm and provide the proper response back to the host system to prove their identity. In this manner, each challenge is different and thus each response is unique. Although this type of validation is keystroke-intensive for users, it is generally more secure than one-time password methods; the PIN is entered only into the remote users' device, and it is not transmitted across the remote link.

Another one-time password method is the time-synchronized password. Remote users are given a token device resembling a calculator that displays an eight-digit numeric password. This device is programmed with an algorithm that changes the password every 60 seconds, with a similar algorithm running at the host computer. Whenever remote users access the central host, they merely provide the existing password followed by their personal ID and access is granted. This method minimizes the number of keystrokes that must be entered, but the personal ID is transmitted across the remote link to the host computer, which can create a security exposure.

A third type of high-level validation is biometric identification, such as thumb print scanning on a hardware device at the remote user site, voice verification, and keyboard dynamics, in which the keystroke timing is figured into the algorithm for unique identification.

The portable computer user validation from off-site should operate in conjunction with the network security firewall implementation. (A firewall is the logical separation between the company-owned and managed computers and public systems.) Remote users accessing central computing systems are required to cross the firewall after authenticating themselves in the approved manner. Most first-generation firewalls use router-based access control lists (ACLs) as a protection mechanism, but new versions of firewalls may use gateway hosts to provide detailed packet filtering and even authentication.

Data Disclosure Protection

If standalone computers are used in a portable or mobile mode outside of the company facility, consideration should be given to requiring some form of password user identification on the individual unit itself. Various software products can be used to provide workstation-level security.

The minimum requirements should include unique user ID and one-way password encryption so that no cleartext passwords are stored on the unit itself. On company-owned portables, there should be an administrative ID on all systems for central administration as necessary when the units return on-site. This can help ensure that only authorized personnel are using the portable system. Although workstation-based user authentication isn't as strong as host-based user authentication, it does provide a reasonable level of security. At the least, use of a commercial ID and password software products on all portables requires that all users register for access to the portable and the data contained on it.

Other techniques for controlling access to portables include physical security devices on portable computers. Though somewhat cumbersome, these can be quite effective. Physical security locks for portables are a common option. One workstation security software product includes a physical disk lock that inserts into the diskette drive and locks to prevent disk boot-ups that might attempt to override hard-disk-resident software protections.

In addition to user validation issues (either to the host site or the portable system itself), the threat of unauthorized data disclosure must also be addressed. In the remote access arena, the threats are greater because of the various transmission methods used: dial-up over the public switched telephone network, remote network access over such media as the Internet, or even microwave transmission. In all of these cases, the potential for unauthorized interception of transmitted data is real. Documented cases of data capture on the Internet are becoming more common. In the dial-up world, there haven't been as many reported cases of unauthorized

data capture, though the threat still exists (e.g., with the use of free-space transmission of data signals over long-haul links).

In nearly all the cases, the most comprehensive security mechanism to protect against data disclosure in these environments is full-session transmission encryption or file-level encryption. Simple Data Encryption Standard (DES) encryption programs are available in software applications or as standalone software. Other public domain encryption software such as Pretty Good Privacy is available, as are stronger encryption methods using proprietary algorithms. The decision to use encryption depends on the amount of risk of data disclosure the company is willing to accept based on the data types allowed to be processed by portable computer users.

Implementing an encryption strategy doesn't need to be too costly or restrictive. If the primary objective is protection of data during remote transmission, then a strategy mandating encryption of the file before it is transmitted should be put in place. If the objective is to protect the file at all times when it is in a remote environment, file encryption may be considered, though its use may be seen as a burden by users, both because of the processing overhead and the potentially extra manual effort of performing the encryption and decryption for each access. (With some encryption schemes, users may have to decrypt the file before using it and encrypt it again before storing it on the portable computer. More sophisticated applications provide automatic file encryption and decryption, making this step nearly transparent to the user.) Portable computer hardware is also available that can provide complete encryption of all data and processes on a portable computer. The encryption technology is built into the system itself, though this adds to the expense of each unit.

A final point needs to be made on implementing encryption for portable users, and that is the issue of key management. Key management is the coordination of the encryption keys used by users. A site key management scheme must be established and followed to control the distribution and use of the encryption keys.

VIRUS PROTECTION IN A PORTABLE ENVIRONMENT

All portable or off-site computers targeted to process company data must have some consistent form of virus protection. This is a very important consideration when negotiating a site license for virus software. What should be negotiated is not a site license per se, but rather a use license for the company's users, wherever they may process company data. The license should include employees' home computers and as well as

Table 3 Portable computing security checklist

- Remove all data from hard disk of company-owned portables before returning them to the loan pool office.
- Leave virus-scanning software enabled on portable computers.
- If it is necessary to use company data on home computers, install and use virus-scanning software.
- Use company-supplied color-coded ("red") disks to store all data used outside the company.
- If no virus-scanning software is available on external computers, virus scan all red disks before using them on company internal computers.
- Physically protect all company computing resources and red disks outside of the facility. (Remember that the value of lost data could exceed that of lost hardware.)
- Be aware of persons watching your work or eavesdropping when you work at off-site locations.
- Report any suspicious activity involving data used in an off-site location. (These might involve data discrepancies, disappearances, or unauthorized modifications.)
- Remote access (dial-up) guidelines
- If dial-up facilities are to be used, register with the information security office and obtain a random password token to be used for obtaining dial-up access.
- Encrypt all company-sensitive data files before transferring them over dial-up connections in or out of the central facility.
- Report when you no longer require dial-up access and return your password-generating token to the security office.

company-owned portables. If this concept isn't acceptable to a virus software vendor, then procedures must be established in which all data that have left the company and may have been processed on a nonvirus-protected computer must be scanned before it can reenter the company's internal computing environment. This can be facilitated by issuing special color-coded diskettes for storing data that are used on portables or users' home computers. By providing the portable computer users with these disks for storage and transfer of their data and mandating the scanning of these disks and data on a regular basis on-site, the threat of externally contracted computer viruses can be greatly reduced.

CONTROLLING DATA DISSEMINATION

Accumulation of data on portable computers creates the potential for its disclosure. This is easily addressed by implementing a variety of procedures intended to provide checks against this accumulation of data on shared portable computers. A user procedure should be mandated to remove and delete all data files from the hard disk of the portable computer before returning it to the company loan pool. The hardware loaning organization should also be required to check disk contents for user files before reissuing the system.

THEFT PROTECTION

The threat of surreptitious theft can be in the form of illicit copying of files from a user's computer when unattended, such as checked baggage or when left in a hotel room. The simplest method is to never store data on the hard disk and to secure the data on physically secured diskettes. In the case of hotel room storage, it is common for hotels to provide in-room safes, which can easily secure a supply of diskettes (though take care they aren't forgotten when checking out).

Another method is to never leave the portable in an operational mode when unattended. The batteries and power supply can be removed and locked up separately so that the system itself is not functional and thus information stored on the hard disk is protected from theft. (The battery or power cord could also easily fit in the room safe.) These measures can help protect against the loss of data, which might go unnoticed. (In the event of outright physical theft, the owner can at least institute recovery procedures.) To protect against physical theft, something as simple as a cable ski lock on the unit can be an effective protection mechanism.

USER EDUCATION

The selection of portable computing protection strategies must be clearly communicated to portable computer users by means of a thorough user education process. Education should be mandatory and recurring to ensure that procedures, tools, and information are provided to portable users. In the area of remote access to on-site company resources, such contact should be initiated when remote users register in the remote access authentication system.

For the use of shared company portable computers, this should be incorporated with the computer check-out process; portable computer use procedures can be distributed when systems are checked out and agreed to by prospective users. With respect to the use of noncompany computers in a portable mode, the best method of accountability is a general user notice that security guidelines apply to this mode of computing. This notification could be referenced in an employee nondisclosure agreement, in which employees are notified of their responsibility to protect company data, on-site or off-site. In addition to registering all portable users, there should be a process to revalidate users in order to maintain their authorized use of portable computing resources on a regular basis. The registration process and procedures should be part of overall user education on the risks of portable computing, protection mechanisms, and user responsibilities for supporting these procedures.

Table 3 provides a sample checklist that should be distributed to all registered users of portables. It should be attached to all of the company's portable computers as a reminder to users of their responsibilities. This sample policy statement includes nearly all the protection mechanisms addressed here, though the company's specific policy may not be as comprehensive depending on the nature of the data or access method used.

SUMMARY

The use of portable computing presents very specific data security threats. For every potential threat, some countermeasure should be implemented to ensure the company's proprietary information is protected. This involves identifying the potential threats and implementing the level of protection needed to minimize these threats. By providing a reasonably secure portable computing environment, users can enjoy the benefits of portable computing and the organization can remain competitive in the commercial marketplace.

Network–Programming

Programming Languages

D.E. Stevenson
School of Computing, Clemson University, Clemson, South Carolina, U.S.A.

Abstract

Programming languages are first and foremost languages and hence they can be understood in terms of our knowledge of natural and other formal languages. The concept of algorithm (although not called such) begins with constructive Euclidean geometry. We start there and consider the development of programming languages not as a subject in itself but a natural outgrowth of the requirements to concisely describe computations through language. We start with a short history of constructive and algebraic mathematics. We then introduce the structural theory of de Sassure and Chomsky to describe the various parts of a contemporary programming language. Our goal is not to be technically deep but to explain the thinking behind the various parts of the language development process.

Note to the Reader. This entry assumes that the reader has significant programming experience with at least one higher-level language. We assume the reader has experience with writing and interpreting recursive functions and implementing graph structures.

Goal. After reading this entry, the reader should be prepared to read more technical presentations of computing languages, including graduate textbooks.

Purpose. Our purpose is to provide information technology professionals with insights needed to understand, evaluate, and use contemporary language systems in information technology. Our intent is to use the least technical language consistent with the subject.

Our story. Languages are used to convey information among individuals of a community. No language springs completely formed from thin air; computing and programming have a long history that we explore. To understand the technical details we explore the structure of language using the structuralist theory of de Saussure and Chomsky. With this background we can study the detailed structure of programming languages.

PART I: PRINCIPLES OF LANGUAGE AS APPLIED TO COMPUTING

Introduction

We cannot hope to survey all of the programming languages nor all of the various concepts that have been developed since 1954, the year FORTRAN I appeared. What we can do is explain to programmers how such languages are designed and the broad overview of how they are implemented.

Before going on, let us agree on the use of certain words. Like any technical subject, the study of programming language has a large, complex technical vocabulary. Different authors use words differently, so we need to agree on the informal (nontechnical) meaning of several terms (see Fig. 1).

Context

Algorithms are developed by **humans** to **compute** a **solution** to a **problem**. Algorithms are comprised of representations and transformations. A **programming language** encodes these representations and transformations. A programming language is any notation that can instruct a computer how to compute after translation. (Because machine language has no translator, only an interpreter, we do not consider it a programming language.) Computers compute, by which we mean that computers **follow a set of rules** in the computer's **instruction set** to produce a representation of a solution. For this entry, we have in mind the von Neumann model, that is, we do not include multicore, multimemory, quantum, or analog computers. Such computers have a **memory** and a **central processing unit** that follows the **program** produced from the programming language **compiler**. The **instruction set** is a set of operations that the computer's central processing unit can perform. The compiler **transforms** algorithms written in the programming language into memory layout and sets of instructions from the instruction set. A computer may have **external** devices attached to it; these devices have their own programming requirements.

The purpose of language is to transmit information from one entity to another. We can use a modified Shannon–Weaver (Fig. 2) diagram to visualize the process. There is a source message—call it a program—constructed in a source language. It must be encoded, interpreted, and then decoded into a target language

Encyclopedia of Information Systems and Technology, DOI: 10.1081/E-EIST-120048641

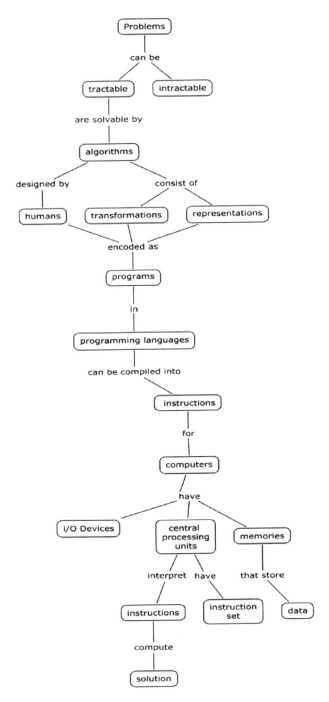

Fig. 1 Concept map.

Concept Map

Concept maps are graphical tools for organizing and representing knowledge – technically, directed acyclic graphs. They include concepts, usually enclosed in circles or boxes of some type, and relationships between concepts indicated by a connecting line linking two concepts. Words on the line, referred to as linking words or linking phrases, specify the relationship between the two concepts. The natural order is to read the graph top-down and left to right.

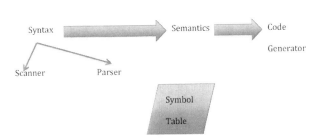

Fig. 2 Information form of programming languages.

message—output. We replace the "channel" in the original Shannon–Weaver diagram (Fig. 3) by an "interpreter."

We are interested in programming languages used to encode algorithms into programs, although the same concepts hold for any formal language-based system. Algorithms have four components: data representation, data storage, transformations, and the ordering of executions to transform data. Notice the recursion! Our approach is to describe programming languages in terms of our understanding of natural and formal languages

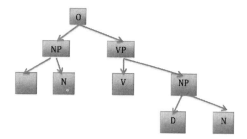

Fig. 3 Shannon–Weaver model.
Source: From Weaver.[9]

and using the information model as the fundamental mechanism.

Linguistics is the study of natural language, but the more general study of language is semiotics.[1] Semiotics is the study of signs and symbols and their interpretation (use). There are three major themes in semiotics: syntax, which includes orthography (spelling) and grammar; semantics, which deals with meaning; and pragmatics, which deals with how a language is used. Programming languages are formal languages with formal syntax. The use of the term *semantics* is somewhat an abuse of language: In general use, the term is strictly applied to single words. Semantics of programming languages is discussed at an appropriate time. Informally, in programming languages we mean how constructs are translated. Pragmatics represents cognitive and metacognitive processes of the group and is not necessarily formal; in effect, pragmatics equals "current best practice."

A SHORT HISTORY

In order to make sense of the subject, it is worthwhile to consider a short history of the development of formal languages. The reader is urged to read Gleick's *The Information*.[3] The first historical find of an arithmetical nature is a fragment of a table: The broken clay tablet Plimpton 322 (Larsa, Mesopotamia, ca. 1800 BCE) contains a list of "Pythagorean triples" that was laid out like a spreadsheet. The appropriate place, then, to discuss programming languages is the origins of algorithmic thinking and notations.

Constructive Mathematics

India and Mesopotamia are the birthplace of arithmetic. While the Greeks were primarily interested in logical relationships, Eratosthenes and Menaechmus were interested in constructing solutions. The Islamic mathematicians were interested in the computation of values. The best known of these mathematicians is Abū ʿAbdallh Muḥammad ibn Mūs al-Khwrizmī (c. 780–850)

who introduced algebraic techniques for solving linear and quadratic equations. Al-Khwrizmī is also credited with introducing the term *al-jabar*, which is transliterated to *algebra*. Modern algebraic notation evolved through the seventeenth century and extended with the development of the Calculus in the eighteenth century. Theorem 5 of Newton's *Principia* is the algorithm we know today as "Newton's Method for Finding Roots." Newton and his contemporaries develop many tabular methods for various operations in order to compute values of derivatives and integrals. Modern numerical analysis is built around Taylor's theorem. Concomitantly, other forms of computation were developed such as logical notations and constructive geometry to name two. The modern computer allows us to compute a broad range of elements.

L. E. J. Brouwer, in his 1907 dissertation, adopted the notion that mathematical objects exist if and only if they can be constructed by algorithms. There are several branches of such constructive mathematics. We take Church's, Turing's, and Markov's view, which is that constructive mathematics is essentially recursive functions. The modern version of this idea is due to Per Martin-Löf. His thinking is most obvious in strongly-typed functional languages. Every object in a computation has a representation, and the class it belongs to is called a type. So, for example, 123 is not just three characters but it represents something of "integer type"; but then again DXXIII is the same object with a different name. Following Martin-Löf[7] "A type is defined by describing what we have to do in order to construct an object of that type." A full development of Martin-Löf theory leads naturally to functional notations.

The Lambda Calculus and Turing Machines

Two important theoretical ideas were proposed in the 1930s: the lambda calculus by Alonzo Church and the Turing machine by Alan Turing.

Alonzo Church and the Lambda Calculus

The period 1880–1940 was an active one for mathematics—it was having a crisis of confidence. The foundations of mathematics were brought into question by Russell's Paradox: Informally it states that one cannot have a set of all sets. One of the questions this raised was exactly how recursive functions worked in terms of variable binding and substitution. Space prohibits describing the theory in full.

The major operational ideas of the lambda calculus are a fundamental part of programming languages. All functional languages such as LISP, ML, and OCAML have a construct called an anonymous function—a function with no name—which is just lambda expressions. Most other common languages hide this by requiring all functions (and subroutines) to have a name. We are all familiar with the functional schema:

Name (arg$_1$, ..., arg$_n$) Body.

One of Church's insights was an understanding of *binding* and *scope*. Church laid out the scope and binding rules we use today. But he also realized that *name* was just a binding for the remainder of the statement. Thus, in the lambda calculus,

Name : = λ(arg$_1$, ..., arg$_n$) Body

where ": = " means "equal by definition." But how do we make sense of these symbols?

We introduce three new concepts: evaluation, application, and rewriting. Evaluation means ordering the calculations, application is the use of a function, and rewriting is obvious. For example, suppose we have "add by one" or *incr : = λ (n)(n + 1)*.

Incr (3)	Apply "incr" to 3
(λ (n)(n + 1)) (3)	Substitute "incr's" definition
(3 + 1)	Apply lambda's semantics: substitute and apply " + " to its arguments (3,1)
4	Rewrite as "4"

Alan Turing and the Turing Machine

In 1928, the German mathematician reminded researchers of a problem, originally posed by Gottfried Leibniz, known in German as the Entscheidungsproblem (in English, "decision problem"). The problem asks for an algorithm that takes as input statements of a first-order logic and answers "Yes" or "No" according to whether the statement is universally valid (true in every structure satisfying the axioms). In 1936 and 1937, Alonzo Church and Alan Turing, respectively, published independent papers showing that a general solution to the Entscheidungs problem is impossible.

Turing reformulated an earlier proof by Kurt Gödel's (1931) on the limits of proof and computation, replacing Gödel's universal arithmetic-based formal language with the formal and simple hypothetical devices that became known as Turing machines. In modern terms, think of a computer with a very simple instruction set and an indefinitely long linear storage. Basically, the CPU can read and write a very simple alphabet (0, 1, blank) and move to an address one higher or one lower than its current location. Even with such a simple machine, Turing was able to prove that some such machine would be capable of performing any conceivable mathematical

computation if it were representable as an algorithm. He also introduced a "Universal Machine" (Universal Turing machine), with the idea that such a machine could perform the tasks of any other machine, or in other words, is provably capable of computing anything that is computable.

These two theoretical results are the basis of the theory of computation and play a key role in the development of algorithms and programming languages.

Short History of Programming Languages

The evolution of programming languages begins in the mid-1850s and continues to the present day. Even more fascinating is the claim that there are 2,500 programming languages.[4]

Programming languages from the beginning

We recognize Augusta Ada King, Countess of Lovelace (10 December 1815–27 November 1852), as the world's first programmer and programming language inventor. She documented all her work on Babbage's "Engines" and developed a notation for programming. But even she stood on the shoulders of giants: Leibniz provided a machine design in 1671 (constructed in 1673) and was a champion of the binary system. Algebraic and logical notations expanded more or less intuitively until Church and Turing introduced the Church–Turing conjecture: "Every effectively calculable function (effectively decidable predicate) is general recursive".[5] In 1963, John McCarthy wrote a seminal paper "A basis for a mathematical theory of computation" that cemented this relationship with programming languages.[6]

Historical development of computer languages beginning with FORTRAN, ALGOL, LISP, and COBOL focused on algorithmic information needed: 1) to describe representation of information structures in computer memory, 2) to specify fundamental operational "algebras," and 3) to prescribe operational order. ALGOL, FORTRAN, and COBOL represent imperative languages, so-called because they are based on a command-style paradigm. LISP is the original functional language, being based on the idea that every computation is a function that returns a value. Logic languages, a third major language group, arrived in 1972 when Prolog became available. Logic languages are based on the concept that a program is a proof of a theorem.

Language developments are based on the experiences and needs of the using community. The concept of object-oriented languages began with Simula-67, a discrete-event simulation language that naturally used objects in modeling. This led eventually to Smalltalk and today's object-oriented languages. Objects became a major paradigm for design with languages such as Java so that today object-oriented programming systems abound in all problem areas.

As another example, E. Dijkstra analyzed the concept of the "goto" construct and showed that the unrestricted use of the "goto" construct was bad practice; current languages such as Java do not have the "goto" among its constructs. The programming language syntax does not have the goto, but the machine language does. This shows that programming languages can be used to control the use of machine capabilities.

Between 1965 and 2000, computing hardware also radically changed, leading eventually to the supercomputers and multicore (multiple CPUs). Hardware changes made programming languages evolution inevitable. The Cray I and Cray II computers required FORTRAN to introduce constructs that enabled the programmer to control parallel computation. In 2012, the frontier is multi-core. NVIDIA's CUDA was specifically designed to take advantage of multiple cores.

Language zoo

From the beginning of language design, there have been different paradigms on how the features of the language should be presented. The ongoing discussions are often called the "Language Wars," which leads to the "Language Zoo." This entry cannot describe each language in the Zoo or even do justice to the unique paradigms in use. But we do not have to. The Church–Turing conjecture means that any programming language that can implement recursion is equivalent to any other such language. So why are there so many programming languages? It has to do with the fact that the human mind works using mental models in symbolic systems. For that reason, the next section explores semiotics, how humans process language.

Keeping it all straight: Language and meta-language

Before proceeding, it is necessary to make a distinction between a "programming language" and "the language used to describe the programming language." The former is called the object language and the latter is called the meta-language. We will drop the term "object" unless required by context to differentiate the two. In the classroom, English (or the local native language) is the meta-language because it is used to describe how the object programming language being taught operates.

So why does it matter? Let us take the C programming language as an example. The C compiler can be written in C. So C as the object language is described by the C used as a meta-language. So a programming language that can serve as its own meta-language is bootstrap-able. As another example, there are several

notations used to describe programming language grammars. Is there just one notation that can describe them all? According to the Church–Turing conjecture: no, there are many such languages.

PART II: SEMIOTICS AND PROGRAMMING LANGUAGES

In Part I, we have explored many of the ideas and experiences that have gone into programming language evolution. We look at the more general issue of the technical qualities of all language. While linguistics is the study of natural language, we abstract to all languages and use semiotics as our framework.

LANGUAGE FROM THE SEMIOTICS VIEWPOINT

We are interested in language as a formal system of signs governed by formal grammatical rules to communicate meaning. This is known as the structuralist view of language, introduced by Ferdinand de Saussure, and remains foundational for most approaches to language study today. Noam Chomsky, who defines language as a particular set of sentences that can be generated from a particular set of rules, helped popularize the structuralist view in computing languages. Chomsky's hierarchy is a categorization of computing languages and the problems they can solve.

We use language to maintain or transmit information, and language must be interpreted to recover this information. The interpreter's function is to convey every semantic and pragmatic element that the source-language utterance carries to target-language utterance. ("Interpreter" has many different technical meanings. We use the most general meaning: it takes in a source sentence and outputs sentences in the target language.) Information must be preserved in this process. Whether human or computer, the interpreter will take in a complex concept from one language, choose the most appropriate vocabulary in the target language to faithfully render the source message in a completely equivalent target message.

Semiotics proposes that languages are composed of three elements: syntax, semantics, and pragmatics. Syntax is comprised of orthography and grammar, which specifies the form of correctly formed words and sentences in the language, respectively. Semantics gives the meaning of the individual words by associating the word with its meanings. Pragmatics, on the other hand, is not mathematically rigorous. Pragmatics explains how the language is used in practice—think of common, everyday conversation as pragmatics.

The Shannon–Weaver Mathematical Model, 1949

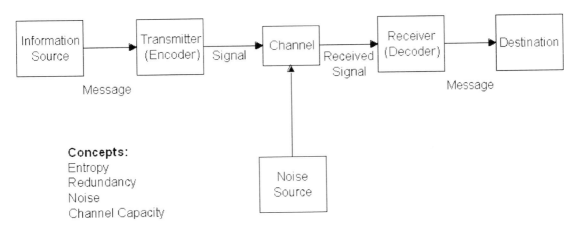

Fig. 4 Transformational generative grammars.

Network–
Programming

Syntax

Syntax deals with the form of words and sentences. In order to do this, the compiler has to recognize words, associate words with definitions, determine the classification of the words, and relate the words by their classification by predetermined relationships in the grammar.

Words: Orthography, lexicon, and vocabulary

A word is a single distinct conceptual unit of language. In every language, there are rules governing orthography, rules for the formation of proper words—Chinese is an example of a symbolic language in which each word has a distinct symbol: English has 26 characters, Chinese over 20,000. A lexicon is a set of words in a language and a vocabulary is a lexicon, each word of which has one or more definitions associated with it.

Grammar

Grammars are bodies of rules that describe the structure of "sentences" in the language.

Formal grammars are prescriptive rules that delineate the entire language, and the development of a programming language grammar is based on the structures we want to incorporate in the language.

There are many notations that have arisen for specifying orthography and grammars in programming languages. There are many stable programs to specify these elements that remove the tedious coding involved in implementing these elements. The original—still available and highly regarded—programs were *YACC* and *LEX*. Conceptually, these are formulated in the same way through the use of productions and grammars in formal languages or automata. Rather than exploring

these, we will examine the underlying concept of a transformation based on pattern matching (see Fig. 4).

Semantics

Semantics is concerned with the meanings of expressions. There are a number of branches of semantics in human speech that we will not explore. In programming languages there have been three standard models to semantics: 1) axiomatic (connotative), uses mathematical logic to specify meaning; 2) denotational uses recursive structures to show how values are computed; and 3) operational constructs a specification of an abstract machine that acts as the interpreter. Operational came first and is the most intuitive: Most programmers of the time were assembler-level programmers and could design a machine that would give the "usual" meaning to a construct. Axiomatic came as the desire for high quality, logically correct programs became important. In axiomatic semantics, we are interested in the assertions (inferences) we can make based on the algebraic rules of the language. Axiomatic views develop the abstract meaning or intension of a term, which forms a principle determining which objects or concepts it applies to. Denotational semantics refers to the object or concept to which a term refers, or the set of objects for which a predicate is true. Christopher Strachey and Dana Scott developed denotational semantics from recursive function theory.[8]

Pragmatics

The essence of the usability of language is pragmatics. Have you ever wondered why there are so many programming languages? Have you wondered why it is so hard to learn a completely different programming language? The answer is pragmatics. This is the cause of the "language wars." Try this experiment. Use your search engine on the exact term "language wars." It is not just programming languages that have such problems.

What is the difference between semantics and pragmatics? In the C programming language, there are two obvious ways to implement the thought "increment the value (named by the variable *x*)by 1." One way is to write "*x* + + "and a second way is to write "*x* + *1*." The semantics are completely different: The value of *x* is changed in the former and not the latter. We decide which form to use based on our pragmatic needs at the time. But the two forms are pragmatically useful.

Holistic Summary of Language and Language Learning

Language is used to transmit information between the sender and the receiver. In our context, there are two classes of receivers: computers and humans. Computers have defined formal semantics, which we discuss at the appropriate time. Passing information from human to human by means of a formalized computer program is the subject of this section. Passing meaning from one human to another means we have to understand a bit of psychology.

Cognition and Metacognition

Cognition is the mental process of acquiring knowledge and understanding through thought, experience, and the senses. Metacognition is awareness and understanding of one's own thought processes—this is often said to be "cognition about cognition." In our context, language acquisition is a cognitive process while the realization that one does not understand a sentence is a metacognitive process. Metacognition relates to our knowing strategies to approach problems and control on our thinking ("Is this right?"). These strategies often play a seminal role in programming design. "Structured programming" of the 1970s is a strategy of writing programs with no uncontrolled transfer of control ("goto"). Metacognition increases with experience leading to expertise.

What do cognition and metacognition have to do with programming?

Firstly, language acquisition is a cognitive process. While programming language syntax is formal and perhaps easier to learn than a natural language, the semantics and pragmatics are often byzantine. On the other hand, mastering the pragmatics is a metacognitive task, for example, transferring strategies from one language to another.

Programming language texts that focus on built-in structures and features are primarily cognitive in nature, providing the semantic symbol knowledge. On the other hand, texts that focus on algorithms—especially language implementation independent ones—are metacognitive in nature because they provide strategies. It is important to realize that a certain level of expertise with languages is required to understand and assimilate algorithms.

Role of pseudocode

Pseudocodes are informal languages often used to describe algorithms so that any programmer, regardless of programming language experience, can read and understand the intent of the algorithm. One common use for pseudocodes is in textbooks. Programmers use pseudocode to "sketch out" an algorithm in varying levels of detail without strictly adhering to a formal syntax. Another use is to use the pseudocode as a draft mechanism, much as one might write several drafts for a technical paper with each draft more specific and closer to the ultimate implementation form. Pseudocode is a natural product of our cognitive and metacognitive use of language in problemsolving.

SURFACE DETAILS OF COMPUTER LANGUAGES

Chomsky[2] developed the idea that each sentence in a language has two levels of representation: 1) the surface language and 2) the deep language. The deep structure represented the core semantic relations of a sentence and can be mapped to the surface structure via transformations. Strictly speaking, Chomsky's concept of natural language is to convert the deep structure to the surface structure using transformations. In programming languages, we have the inverse: We are presented with a surface sentence and must transform it to the deep structure.

The surface language, which behaves according to the syntax rules, is the visible language that we read. The deep structure captures the semiotic relationships in the surface language and in our context the deep structure is a graph. In order to simplify the presentation of the technical details of implementing a computer language, we think of the transformation as occurring in three steps: 1) user-written code (surface language) is rewritten into a data structure (deep structure); 2) then a series of graph transformations from the source language to the target language; and finally 3) writing the final graph into interpreter/machine usable form. The graph formations in step 2 represent the translation of the source semantics to target semantics via the interpreter. Step 3, in effect, is a reverse translation between the semantics of the interpreter to the syntax recognized by the interpreter. This section describes many surface structures found in programming languages.

Surface Features

This section is organized into subsections: 1) types and operations; 2) memory operations; and 3) control operations.

Types

Data representations and transformations are, technically speaking, algebras. Algebraic structure refers to a set of objects; transformations are "functional rules"; and relations are "logical rules."

The most familiar of these algebras is the integers with two operations: addition and multiplication. Remember, though, that the computer's integers are **not** the same as the formal mathematical integers and this is a metacognitive correction we must make when computing. For example, there is a maximum computer integer—call it *maxint*—and *maxint* + *maxint* is meaningless because the result is not predictable on must modern machines. There are many algorithms for integer operations. The actual bit value for *maxint* + *maxint* depends on which algorithms are used and hence the value is unpredictable.

There are many formal ways to present algebra systems but the most common mechanism for computing is the Martin-Löf type system.

A type consists of a set of constants, operations on those constants, and relations on those constants. Each operation or relation has a *signature* that gives the number and types of the arguments (arity). A common computer type is the 32-bit integers (but the size is set by the hardware). In this case the constants range from -2^{32} to $2^{31}-1$ with the usual operators (+, −, *, /, mod) and relations (=, $\neq$, <, >, $\leq$, $\geq$). We immediately notice that there are more negative constants than positive ones; therefore, $-(2^{32}) = 2^{32}$ in the arithmetic integers but the value is unrepresentable in 32-bit integers. This is just the tip of the iceberg, which is why there are both cognitive and metacognitive adjustments to be made when programming: you expect the numbers to work the way they always did in grade school, but they don't.

A type system maps values and expressions into types. The type system also defines how the types themselves interact.

From the programming language designers' standpoint, then, the rule is simple: For every type, one must be able to represent the constants and have algorithms for each of the operators and relations. Some of the types are predefined by the compiler and whatever else is needed requires "user-types."

Variables and bindings

The reader undoubtedly knows the difference between mathematical variables and programming language variables: We solve for mathematical variables for values but we use programming variables to store values. A value is *bound* to a variable. Variables have both a *type* and a *scope*. A variable's type defines what types of constants can be stored in a variable and the scope of a variable is the time the variable is defined and its value is available in memory.

A word about scope. Scope rules originally came from quantifiers in logic. The concept is simple: A variable's value is "available" from the beginning of its scope to the end. In practice, this is not so simple. Typical programming practice has several different scopes:

- Language definition
- Compiler implementation
- Library implementation
- Compile time (there could be several here)
- Run time

Names that are not predefined must be declared for type in many (but not all) modern languages. In terms of syntax, such declarations are a sublanguage; this means that it appears under very specific rules.

Memory operations

During the execution of a program, we can follow its computation by looking at the state of the program. The state of a program is the list of all the variables (including, perhaps, operating system variables, program counter, registers) and their current value. The state of a program is changed by the assignment of a different value to some variable, hardware/software interrupts, and keyboard keystrokes to name just a few. During declaration, a name is assigned to a memory location; this location is called an *l-value*. The value stored in the memory location is called the *r-value*. These terms come from the usual syntax for assignments:

l-value = r-value

with pointers being a type of *l-value* and a legal constant of the type of the variable.

Let *lvalueof (x)* return *x*'s l-value and *rvalueof (x)* its r-value. We would like the following identity to be true:

rvalueof (lvalueof (x)) = x = lvalueof (rvalueof (x))

This is not true in most languages (try it in your favorite language). The right hand side of this expression is what we mean by associative memory.

Control operations

The difference between the practice of (nonconstructive or Platonic) mathematics and the practice in computing is that the values in computing must be constructed. Foundationally, we want to know what is the minimum set of operations that are needed to control these algorithms and constructions. There are three: conditionals, iterations, and invocations (call-return).

Conditionals. Conditional statements are composed to three things: a logical value and two sets of statements. This is the first nonintuitive construct we have encountered, primarily since it does not normally occur in usual mathematics. We can use this to illustrate the whole thought process for compiling.

Syntax: *if* (expression) *then* statement-1 *else* statement-2 *fi*

If, then, else, and *fi* are known as "keywords." In most modern languages, keywords are symbols that look like variables but cannot be used as variables. The parentheses are known as "grouping symbols." The expression indicates that any valid pattern recognized by the "expression recognizer" is acceptable. Statement-1 and statement-2 are similar to expression but rather a pattern recognized by the "statement recognizer." The output of the pattern recognizer for such a statement is (IF tree (expression) tree (statement-1) tree (statement-2)). Notice that *then, else,* and *fi* are not represented because they have no semantic value. The *if* has been replaced by the IF statement, indicating a semantic value/function.

Semantics. The informal semantics of this statement can be expressed by the following statements. "Evaluate the expression and convert to a Boolean value (either *true* or *false)*. If the value is *true*, then arrange that statement-1 is executed and statement-2 is not. Similarly, if *false*, then statement-2 is executed and statement-1 is not." Regardless of what form of semantics we use (algebraic, denotational, operational), the informal meaning of the statement must be translated to the formal.

Pragmatics. The pragmatics of the if-statement is when and how one uses such a statement. Since in programming we are always working with values, the if-statement can be used to prevent errors such as dividing by zero, checking sort order, controlling formatting as simple examples.

Iteration. Iteration is a "looping" construct that causes a series of statements to be executed repeatedly.

There are two general forms, one that stops at the end of a count and one that stops when a particular Boolean value is *true*.

Invocation and Packaging. Programming would not be practical if we did not have a way of packaging statements in such a way as to reuse the packaged code.

Functions and subroutines. Most languages borrow from the mathematical notation of *name (argument₁, …, argumentₙ)*. This notation is used in two ways: 1) to invoke the code; and 2) to define the code that should be executed. In practice, the term *function* implies that a value is returned and *subroutine* implies no value is returned. Here we will use the term *routine* unless the distinction is needed.

Defining functions and subroutines. Definition is the association of a signature (head) such as *name (argument₁, …, argumentₙ)* with a body of code. Depending on the particular language, the body may contain other definitions or executable code such as iterations, conditionals, and assignments. Originally, the desire was that the code should act as if it were substituted in place of the head—for technical reasons, this does not work well in practice.

Binding argument names. How the arguments in the head and the body are bound is specific to the language. In the simplest case, the arguments must be single variables and those names are taken as the value holders in the body. There can be many more complex rules.

Invoking a routine. Most languages interpret a head without an accompanying body declaration as a routine invocation. That is, we expect the computation to jump to the body of the routine (which must be previously defined), execute the body, and then return to the point of invocation.

Other Packaging Issues. While routines are the most common packaging concept, many languages have more: 1) structured data; 2) objects; and 3) file structures.

Structured data. Structured data is defined in terms of primitive types (the provided types) and other structured data, for example, a program that processes a file of addresses into mailing labels. Each address has five fields: name, street address, city, state, zip code. The data for these are "packaged together" as a unit.

Objects. One can think of objects as an extended form of structures. Objects act like algebras in that the object definition includes constants, functions, and relations.

Many applications naturally lend themselves to object-oriented concepts.

Files. Since programs are written and stored, there is a question of how the files may be organized. Some languages will only accept one definition per file; others will accept any number. In current systems, files, networks, and so forth are primarily the purview of the operating system. Therefore, the interface is established and the programming language works within that framework. Some languages have extensive file operations as part of their language (COBOL, PL/I) or none at all (C).

Application interfaces. The 1960 ALGOL Report mentions that the main purpose of programming languages is to develop libraries of programs for applications. Many of the innovations by object-oriented languages and strict typing languages were initiated by the difficulties in accomplishing the purpose. An application programming interface (API) is a software specification that defines an interface by which software components communicate. An API may include specifications for routines, data structures, and variables. In other words, APIs are algebra specifications.

Summary

Not surprisingly, our familiarity with various programming languages is through the surface languages presented to the programmer. How much work the programmer has to do and how much the programming language must do is the decision of the using community. But our total understanding of any particular language includes the association of semantics and pragmatics to the surface constructs. This means that our understanding of the exact workings of the language is filtered.

DEEP STRUCTURE OF PROGRAMMING LANGUAGES

The parser converts the surface structure of the program into an equivalent deep structure. These structures go by

many names (parse tree, abstract parse tree, annotated parse tree) in the literature but we will use directed acyclic graph to encourage the reader to visualize programs as graphs. The language LISP was originally developed to accomplish the tree transformations so its input is in the form of a linearized tree.

Most parsers have two components: a **scanner** (or lexer) and the **parser** proper. The scanner reads the input character by character, forms individual words, and constructs a token consisting of the input word and its type. The parser takes the tokens and applies rule patterns that make up the language's grammar. As described in Fig. 5, the "parse tree" is formed based on the substitution rules used. Both the scanner and parser rules typically are developed from automata and/or formal language principles. There are many tools that can be used to develop both the scanner and the parser so there is little reason to hand-code them.

Diagramming Sentences as Parse Trees

A diagram is a graphical picture of the relationships of the words of a natural language sentence. If you were fortunate enough to have a teacher who required extensive diagramming exercises you can skip this section. This section is for those who were not so fortunate.

English grammar is not about words per se, but about parts of speech and how these parts function in the sentence. There are eight parts of speech in English from which we can construct complicated sentences. Unfortunately, many words have many possible ways they could be used making the understanding context sensitive. In formal languages, where every word has a type, we use type as part of speech.

As an example, consider the sentence "man bites dog." This has the form of "noun verb noun" and has a simple diagram of "noun | verb /noun." Now consider the simple assignment statement "x = 1." This has the form "variable = constant." Now, rather than putting this into diagram form, we put in into the form of a tree with the operator at the root, which linearizes as "(= variable constant)."

We now have enough information to understand the entire surface to deep structure transformation. The scanner reads the program and classifies each word as

Fig. 5 Simple example of a grammar.

A simple example illustrating the generation of a simple declarative sentences are formed. In this example, S is a sentence, D is a determiner, N a noun, V a verb, NP a noun phrase, and VP a verb phrase.

S := NP VP	NP := D N	NP := N
VP := V NP	VP := V	

Our lexicon is simple: (1) dog and food are each nouns; (2) the is a determiner; and (3) ate is a verb.

Example. The dog ate the food.

Derivation.

S	Start with S
NP VP	Use "NP VP" as substitute for "S"
D N VP	Use "D N" as substitute for "NP"
D N V NP	Use "V NP" as substitute for "VN"
D N V D N	Use the lexicon to substitute for letters
The dog ate the food	Final form. We have generated the target sentence

Fig. 6 Schematic of implementation.

to its type (part of speech). It pairs the symbol and its type together into a token. The parser takes the tokens and recognizes patterns. For each recognized pattern there is an associated processing statement that transforms the graph. This process continues (assuming no errors) until the entire text is read and transformed. This final graph is the deep structure.

Deep Structure Manipulations

There are three standard ways to describe the manipulation of deep structures: algebraic/axiomatic, denotational, and operational. The author believes that the denotational is the most natural (your taste may differ), partially because it is based on functional programming (actually the other way around) and partially because it more naturally fits the manipulation of natural and formal languages.

IMPLEMENTATION STRUCTURE

This section discusses how all the concepts can be used to design an implementation. There are many tools available for syntax operations. These tools make it possible to put together an ad hoc command language in short order. A common approach to implementations for portable languages such as *C* or *Java* is to "bootstrap": the compiler is written in itself and a "throw-away"

code generator is constructed for the first version (see Fig. 6).

This section is organized to coincide with the syntax, semantics, and pragmatics theme used throughout. The first subsection describes the implementation of dictionaries ("symbol table"), which handles the duties of lexicography. In the syntax subsection we look at orthography, lexicography, vocabulary lookup, and grammars. The outcome of the syntax operation is a graph. The next subsection describes operations on graphs to implement both semantics and pragmatics. Finally, we discuss code generation.

Symbol Tables and the Handling of Dictionary Duties

We all know what dictionaries are, and as the world becomes more integrated, dictionaries fulfill the need for exact understanding of words. Historically in compilers, the dictionary is called a "symbol table." We will stick with dictionary because it is the exact metaphor we want and something we can go look at for insights.

Dictionary

Dictionaries are sets of entries, with each entry a pair (key, entries). The key could be a single word or more complicated, such as a phrase. Considering a simple program, every word is a symbol and hence a key. Any key can have multiple definitions, or unique definitions

Table 1 BNF grammar for Ol' faithful

1	<E > eof	Return (value (E))
2	<E > : = <T > + <E >	Loc1 = value (T); Loc3 = value (E); Return (Loc1 + Loc3);
3	<E > : = <T >	Return (value (T))
4	<T > : = <F > * <T >	Loc1 = value (F); Loc3 = value (T); Return (Loc1*Loc3);
5	<T > : = <F >	Return (value (F))
6	<F > : = (E)	Return (value (E))
7	<F > : = Any (integer)	Return (value (integer))

in different contexts. Some symbols—call them grammatical symbols—need not be in the dictionary: parentheses in most languages have no semantics so they can be resolved by the scanner. Be that as it may, conceptually every symbol has a dictionary entry.

Scope, context, and binding

Most languages allow for a symbol to be defined multiple times in a program provided it is uniquely defined in scope. Most scope delineations are in the programmer's control and indicated in using special constructs: definitions of function heads or *begin...end* type constructs. How and where scopes may be used is defined in the grammar and in the semantics routines.

Binding refers to the association of a definition with a key. A formal definition of scope is the time between when an entry is bound to a symbol and when it is unbound.

Algorithms

Any searchable list can be used to implement a dictionary. At this point, the choice is strictly a data structure/algorithm choice. Any vocabulary of more than 100 words should be a hash table. There are many APIs for hash table maintenance: choose your favorite.

Table 2 Recursive descent algorithm example

Expansion	Rule	Value
E eof		7
T + E eof	<E > : = <T > + <E >	1 + 6 = 7
F + E eof	<T > : = <F >	1
1 + E eof	<F > : = 1	1
1 + T eof	<E > : = <T >	6
1 + F * T eof	<T > : = <F > * <T >	2 * 3 = 6
1 + 2 * T eof	<F > : = 2	2
1 + 2 * F eof	<T > : = <F >	3
1 + 2 * 3 eof	<F > : = 3	3

Grammars: Orthography and Structure

The actual process for orthography and grammar checking is similar. Traditionally, programming languages were designed for English speakers and hence the characters were the standard ASCII alphabet. Grammars are due to the work in the 1950s and 1960s, notable by the researchers in computability and computational linguistics. In 1965, Donald Knuth published a paper "On the Translation of Languages from Left to Right" that pulled together the disparate approaches to grammars. This has led to a plethora of tools for constructing programs to do both scanners and parsers. In this section, we present a unified discussion of how to think about designing input for these programs.

The essence of a design is the definition of a set of rules all having the same form variously known as Backus Normal Form, Backus Naur Form, or BNF. BNF can be interpreted either bottom-up or top-down. It is somewhat more natural for humans to interpret it top-down, while bottom-up is generally more efficient given a proper formulation of the grammar:

<symbol > := expression {actions};

Table 1 shows "Ol' Faithful" as a BNF table. It is called "Ol' Faithful" because it seems to appear in every textbook with the intent of capturing all syntactically correct integer statements that include " + " and "*." The grammar as written in Table 1 BNF Grammar for Ol' Faithfulis a language and therefore needs an

```
Put 'E eof' as workstring
Do
    Start at the front of the string.
    Find first Nonterminal in workstring.
    Replace Nonterminal with each right hand side.
    While there are Nonterminals.
Does one of the generated strings match the input?
    YES? Accept
    NO? Reject
```

interpreter.

As an example (Table 2), we show the generation of the string "1 + 2*3 eof" using the recursive descent algorithm. A recursive descent parser is a set of mutuallyrecursive procedures where each such procedure usually implements one of the production rules of the grammar. The pattern of the rule must match before the action can be executed.

This concludes the tutorial part on syntax. Industrial-strength programming languages are much more complex and the rules are correspondingly more complex.

Comparing Semantics and Pragmatics

In many texts the term *pragmatics* is not used, pragmatic issues are mixed in with semantics. Since we are
studying the whole idea of developing and implementing
a programming language, this is the time to show how
they occur. Programming languages are formal languages; hence, a semantics is provided when an
interpretation or model is specified. So, for example,
when the statement "$x + 1$" is encountered, semantics
tells us how to make the types match and how to compute the answer.

On the other hand, the principles governing appropriate "conversational" moves are called pragmatics. A
pragmatic treatment of a feature of the use of a language explains the feature in terms of general principles
governing an appropriate manner of expressing thoughts
rather than in terms of a semantic rule. The rule that a
variable should be initialized before it is used is a pragmatic rule not a semantic one.

The take-home message is that the syntax defines the
surface structure of the language but the semantics and
pragmatics define the interpreter. Unfortunately, the
term *interpreter* connotes a type of program; where
there may be confusion, we will use the term *PL interpreter* to mean the general concepts and just *interpreter*
where the programming language system is meant.

Programming Language Interpreter Design

The PL-interpreter takes the syntax trees that represent
the (raw) program and transforms it to a final tree. This
final tree drives the output. The PL-interpreter can be
simple or complex. Interpreting a single DOCTYPE
(yes, it requires an interpreter) to produce text can be
simple; compiling code for a heterogeneous supercom-
puter can be quite complex.

The design of an interpreter is again patternbased. In
this case, the patterns are based on the format of a
graph. The most complicated graphs occur when significant optimization is required. Although the rules can be
mixed in various passes over the graph, it is conceptually easier to think of many multiple passes each
addressing one issue. For example, the documentation
for gcc lists 23 passes (http://gcc.gnu.org/onlinedocs/
gcc-2.95.3/gcc_14.html on 29 Mar 2012). These passes
perform various actions such as external name declarations, including linkages for library routines, and
optimizing operations, for example. The various passes
may produce files that will be included later as well as
the so-called object file.

While production level compilers produce programs
that are processed and set into loadable form, one could
also produce programs that are input to another compiler. This can be done in several ways. Source-to-
source compilers (transcompiler or transpiler) transform
the input language into a source program for another
language to be compiled on the same machine. If the
target language is on another type machine, then the
process is called cross-compiling. Either approach is the
fastest way of producing a new compiler.

An intermediate form of this approach is used by the
GNU compilers. Simplistically, GNU compilers are two
separate programs: a front end and a back end. The
front end is a source-specific parser that produces an
abstract syntax tree of the source program. This tree is
passed to the back end, which is common to the GNU
line. The back end produces the machine code for a particular machine.

A third approach is used by Java. The java compiler
produces codes for an interpreter known as the Java virtual machine (JVM). The JVM is similar to the series of
interpreters in the forth line. Forth input is written in
postfix style making it possible to bypass a complicated
parsing/semantics phase.

SUMMARY AND THE FUTURE

Summary

The purpose of any language is to communicate information from a sender to a receiver. For programming
languages, the information required is that needed to
pass an algorithm from human to machine. Programmers
use the source language to encode the algorithm. To
encode an algorithm, we need information about representation of data, available operations, and the
sequencing of operations. At this time (June, 2012),
there are at least 2,500 programming languages extant.
But based on the Church–Turing conjecture, these 2,500
languages are isomorphic in the sense that they can
each be used to encode recursive functions.

Learning a programming language is a metacognitive
task, while using a language is a cognitive one. When
we learn a language, we must master three aspects: syntax, semantics, and pragmatics. Syntax deals with the
surface language: how the language appears to the
writer through orthography and grammar. Semantics is
the meaning of particular symbols. Semantics comes in
two sorts: predefined and userdefined. For the most part,
programming language textbooks focus on syntax and
the semantics of predefined symbols. Pragmatics is how
the language is used—perhaps the clearest examples are
application program interfaces.

Most textbooks do not distinguish among syntax,
semantics, and pragmatics. Because of this, a learner of
a new language—even ones as close as C and C + + —
may find the switch difficult. By and large, orthography
is common among various languages if the standard
ANSI character set is used. Grammars pose the major

immediate obstacle, since it defines the surface language—however, learning successive languages should be easier. One would hope that the semantics of the arithmetic operators would be the same. However, once we consider types other than the standard for which a universal vocabulary is available there are plenty of opportunities for confusion. New pragmatics is the most difficult of all because the learner must use a new way of writing and thinking.

History Repeated

For deep understanding of programming languages, it pays to examine the evolution of expression. At the core of each language is a machine, often called a virtual machine. Though the term is greatly extended now, its original meaning indicated the data and functions that were the base on which the language began. The original virtual machine was not so virtual: it was a very rudimentary operating system through the first and second generations. Programming in the late 1950s and early 1960s was accomplished using assemblers. But assembler language programming is very error prone: Large systems were difficult to develop and maintain.

The answer to this engineering and economic problem has been the Language Zoo. Researchers and practitioners both searched for ways to avoid known deficiencies in current languages. By 1965, there were seven standard languages: Algol-60, APL, COBOL, FORTRAN, Jovial, LISP, and SNOBOL. FORTRAN and COBOL were the dominant commercially used languages. Algol was the lingua franca of research along with APL, LISP, and SNOBOL. Jovial was used for U.S. Military applications. Each of these languages had a different semiotics: For example, Lisp is built on recursive functions and SNOBOL was based on pattern matching. From these the 2,500 sprang. For most commercially viable languages, layers of changes were added to some previous language. The introduction of structured programming in the 1970s removed the GOTO construct, making for more easily comprehended programs with fewer bugs.

Occasionally, a completely new paradigm is developed and becomes popular. Smalltalk-80 introduced object-oriented capabilities. Software engineers have developed significant improvements to the software engineering processes by using object-oriented concepts to match with models of problems. The actual viability of C + + came from the fact that there are very few internal changes necessary to C to implement C + + . In effect, C + + was hidden in C from Day 1.

The Future

What will the future programming languages look like? What features will they have? What will the next languages look like?

The answer is that we do not know yet. The emphasis on semiotics, information, and (meta)cognition is a conscious attempt to show the reader that programming languages are a natural development of hardware, development methodology, and paradigm preferences. The most obvious candidate for disruptive programming languages is quantum computing.[10] Quantum computing is disruptive because it and classical computers have fundamentally different memory representation and operations.

This should not be surprising: the same disruptions occurred in the mid-1980s when multi-instruction multiple-datastream (MIMD) computers became available. The languages of the day simply could not take advantage of the capabilities of the hardware. This was mainly due to the many different models of computing that have been developed. Throughout this entry we have only investigated the single von Neumann machine model. In the MIMD world, the interconnection among the individual machines eliminates any standard computing model. Who knows what quantum computing and beyond will bring.

For More Information

The Internet provides detailed information concerning available programming languages. Wikipedia has entries including languages organized by types that organize languages into 43 categories. Eric Levenez's website contains a graph of 50 prominent languages over time and how they are related to one another.

REFERENCES

1. Chandler, D. *Semiotics-The Basics*, 2nd Ed.; Routledge: New York, NY, 2007.
2. Chomsky, N. *Aspects of the Theory of Syntax*; MIT Press: Cambridge, MA, 1965.
3. Gleick, J. *The Information: A History, A Theory, A Flood*; Vintage: New York, NY, 2012.
4. Kinnersly, W. The Language List, http://people.ku.edu/~nkinners/LangList/Extras/langlist.htm (accessed June 2012).
5. Kleene, S. *Introduction to Metamathematics*; Van Nostrand: New York, NY, 1952.
6. Mccarthy J A Basis for a Mathematical Theory of Computation). In: *Computer Programming and Formal Systems*. North-Holland: North Holland Publishing Co., 1963.
7. Bengt, N.; Petersson, K.; Smith, J.M. *Programming in Martin-Löf 's Type Theory*; Oxford University Press: Oxford, UK, 1990.

8. Stoy, J.E. Denotational Semantics: *The Scott-Strachey Approach to Programming Language Theory*; MIT Press: Cambridge, MA, 1981.

9. Weaver, W.; Claude, E.S. *The Mathematical Theory of Communications*; University of Illinois Press: Urbana-Champaign, IL, 1963.

10. Yanofsky, N.S.; Mirco, A.M. *Quantum Computing for Computer Scientists*; Cambridge University Press: Cambridge, U. K., 2008.

Resources: Measurement and Management

Greg Schulz
StorageIO Group, Stillwater, Minnesota, U.S.A.

Abstract

Good decision making requires timely and insightful information. Key to making informed decisions is having insight into information technology (IT) resource usage and services being delivered. Information about what IT resources exist, how they are being used, and the level of service being delivered is essential in identifying areas of improvement to boost productivity and efficiency and to reduce costs. This entry identifies metrics and techniques that enable timely and informed decisions to boost efficiency and meet IT service requirements.

In this entry you will learn:

- Why metrics and measurements are important for understanding how resources are used
- How to ensure that required resources are available
- Key tenets of metrics and benchmarks for different use scenarios

Metrics reflect information technology (IT) resource usage across different dimensions, including performance, availability, capacity, and energy (PACE), for active and inactive periods over different time frames. IT resources can be described as being either active or performing useful work or inactive when no work is being performed. In keeping with the idea that IT data centers are information factories, metrics and measurements are similar to those for other factories. Factories in general, and highly automated ones, in particular, involve costly resources and raw goods being used to create valuable goods or services, all of which need to be measured and tracked for effective management.

The overall health and status of the equipment, steady supply of raw materials, energy or power supply, and quality of service are constantly measured for timely management decisions to be made. For example, in an electrical power plant, control rooms or operations nerve centers closely monitor different aspects of the facility and its resources, including fuel supply and cost, production schedules or forecasts, boilers, exhaust air scrubbers, water chillers and associated pumps, turbines, and transmission status.

At a higher level, the generating power plant is being are used to manage generation supply proactively in order to meet current and predicted demand as well as to aid in future planning and maintenance purposes and to support customer usage and billing systems.

IT data centers are measured to gauge the health, status, efficiency, and productivity of resource usage to delivering a given level of service. Several types of metrics and measurements, ranging from component level to facility-wide, serve different purposes, and audiences at various times. Metrics and measurements feed management tools, graphical user interfaces, dashboard displays, e-mail and other notification mechanisms, frameworks and other monitoring tools, with key performance indicators. Metrics and measurements provide insight about what is occurring, how resources are being used and the efficiency of that usage, and the quality of service. Metrics and measurements of resources include performance, availability, capacity and energy for servers, storage, networks, and facilities to meet a given level of service and cost objectives. Measurements can be used for real-time reactive and proactive monitoring and management of resources, event correlation for problem diagnosis and resolution, and for planning and analysis purposes, as shown in Fig. 1.

There are different points of interest for different audiences at varying times during a product or technology life cycle, as shown in Fig. 1. For example, a vendor's engineers use comparative or diagnostic measurements at the component and system levels during research and development and during manufacturing and quality assurance testing. Performance and availability benchmarks, along with environmental power, cooling, and other metrics, are used for comparison and competitive positioning during the sales cycle. Metrics are also used on an ongoing basis to assess the health and status of how a technology is performing to meet expectations.

In the typical data center, a different set of metrics is used than what a vendor utilizes during design and manufacture. For example, instead of a detailed component focus, data center personnel generally take a more holistic view. That is, for a storage system, they may focus on the total amount of power being used, performance in terms of input/output operations per second (IOPS) or bandwidth, and available capacity in a given footprint.

Encyclopedia of Information Systems and Technology, DOI: 10.1081/E-EIST-120053840

Resources–
Six Sigma

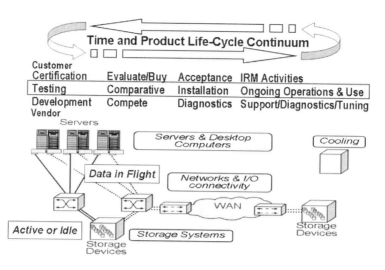

Fig. 1 Metrics and measurements points of interest—the big picture.

Additional detailed information is generally available, such as how a storage system is performing at the disk drive or other component levels. Similarly, vendors often have additional built-in measurement and diagnostic capabilities—sometimes hidden from customer access—that provide additional insight into activities and events for performance or troubleshooting purposes. Another example from a facilities perspective is the total power being used for the data center measured independently of work being performed or data being stored or even the type and quantity of IT resources such as servers, storage, and networking devices.

Electrical power usage will vary depending on the type of device, its design, and low-power features such as intelligent power management, adaptive voltage scaling, or adaptive power management. A device may require more power at start-up or power-up than when running in a steady state. Less power is generally needed when doing minimum or no work, and even less power when in a low-power (idle, standby, or sleep) mode.

A common example is a workstation or laptop computer using power management; the amount of power can be varied depending on the activity. When active, power management features in the workstation operating system software can speed up or slow down the process to vary energy consumption. Other steps that can be taken on a workstation or laptop computer include dimming or turning off monitors, turning off or reducing power on disk drives, or entering a standby sleep mode, or going into hibernation in addition to being completely powered off. Note that on a laptop computer, standby mode enables fairly rapid resumption of work or activity but draws less power running in normal mode.

Standby mode draws more power than when the computer is in hibernation mode, which, in turn, draws more power than if the device is completely powered off. In hibernation the device appears to be drawing no power; however, a very small amount of power is being used. The energy efficiency benefits of putting a laptop computer into standby or hibernation mode along with leveraging other power management features are most commonly used to maximize the amount of time work that can be done when running on battery power.

A server is basically either busy doing work or is idle. Likewise, a networking device is generally supporting movement of data between users and servers, between servers and other servers, between servers and storage, or between storage devices on a local, metropolitan, or wide-area basis. Storage devices support active work including movement of data to satisfy input/output (I/O) operations such as read and write requests as well as storing data. Consequently, storage devices can be measured on an active or working basis as well as on the ability to store information over long periods of time.

Not all storage devices should be compared on the same active-or-idle workload basis. For example, magnetic tape devices typically store inactive data offline and consume power only when data is being read or written. By comparison, magnetic hard disk drives are generally always spinning, ready or already performing work in data center storage systems.

DATA CENTER-RELATED METRICS

There are many different sources of metrics and measurements in a typical IT data center. Metrics can be focused on activity and productivity, usually reported in terms of performance and availability, along with resource usage and efficiency. Consequently, metrics can reflect active work being done to deliver IT services in a given response time or work rate as well as indicate how IT resources are being used. IT equipment can be active or inactive. Data storage can be considered active when responding to read and write requires or I/O operations, and how much data is being stored can be measured independent of activity. Consequently, different types of storage need to be compared on different bases.

For example, magnetic tape used for offline archival and backup data can be measured on an idle or inactive basis, such as capacity (raw, usable, or effective) per watt in a given footprint, data protection level, and price. While capacity is a concern, online active storage for primary and secondary data, including bulk storage, needs to be compared on an activity-per-watt basis along with how much capacity is available at a given data protection level and cost point to meet service-level objectives.

Metrics are available from a variety of sources in a data center. Different metrics have meaning to various groups, and multiple similar metrics may be collected by server, storage, and networking groups as well as separate metrics by facilities personnel.

Some common key attributes of all these measurements are that they are:

- Applicable to the function or focus area of various persons using the metrics
- Relevant to a given point or period in time for real-time or historical purposes
- Reproducible over different scenarios and relevant time periods
- Reflective of the work, activity, or function being performed

For servers, useful metrics include application response time, I/O queues, number of transactions, web pages or e-mail messages processed, or other activity indicators as well as utilization of central processing units (CPUs), memory, I/O or networking interfaces, and any local disk storage. Availability can be measured in terms of planned and unplanned outages or for different time frames such as prime time, nights, and weekends, or on a seasonal basis.

A common focus, particularly for environments looking to use virtualization for server consolidation, is server utilization. Server utilization does provide a partial picture; however, it is important to look also at performance and availability for additional insight into how a server is running. For example, a server may operate at a given low utilization rate to meet application service-level response time or performance requirements. For networks, including switches, routers, bridges, gateways, and other specialized appliances, several metrics may be considered, including usage or utilization; performance in terms of number of frames, packets, IOPS, or bandwidth per second; and latency, errors, or queues indicating network congestion or bottlenecks.

From a storage standpoint, metrics should reflect performance in terms of IOPS, bandwidth, and latency for various types of workloads. Availability metrics reflect how much time, or what percent of time, the storage is available or ready for use. Capacity metrics reflect how much or what percent of a storage system is being used. Energy metrics can be combined with performance, availability, and capacity metrics to determine energy efficiency. Storage system capacity metrics should also reflect various native storage capacities in terms of raw, unconfigured, and configured capacity. Storage granularity can be assessed on a total usable storage system (block, file, and object/cas) disk or tape basis or on a media enclosure basis—for example, disk shelves enclosure or individual device (spindle) basis. Another dimension is the footprint of the storage solution, such as the floor space and rack space and may include height, weight, width, depth, or number of floor tiles.

Measuring IT resources across different types of resources, including multiple tiers, categories, types, functions, and cost (price bands) of servers, storage, and networking technologies, is not a trivial task. However, IT resource metrics can be addressed over time to address PACE to achieve a given level of work or service delivered under different conditions.

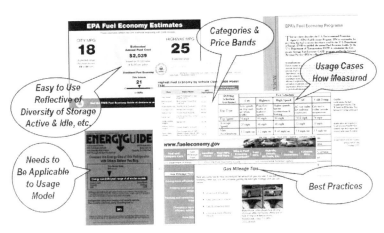

Fig. 2 Metrics and measurements for different categories, uses, and activities.

It is important to avoid trying to do too much with a single or limited metric that compares too many different facets of resource usage. For example, simply comparing all IT equipment from an inactive, idle perspective does not reflect productivity and energy efficiency for doing useful work. Likewise, not considering low-power modes ignores energy-saving opportunities during low-activity periods. Focusing only on storage or server utilization or capacity per given footprint does not tell how much useful work can be done in that footprint per unit of energy at a given cost and service delivery level.

Fig. 2 shows an example of what can be done with metrics and measurements and what continues to be refined. Why should one compare IT resources to automobiles? Because both consume energy to do some amount of useful work, some carry cargo or passengers over long distances while others do frequent start-and-stop operations, some are always in use while others sit at rest consuming no power for extended periods of time. Both involve different types and categories of vehicles to address different tasks or functions.

You are probably familiar with comparisons of automobile miles per gallon for city and highway driving, but the U.S. Environmental Protection Agency (EPA) also provides breakdowns for different categories, price bands, and tiers of vehicles, from trucks and buses to automobiles. In addition, these vehicles are compared under various scenarios, such as city start-and-stop versus highway driving, highway driving at high speed, and highway driving with the air conditioning turned on.

While not 100% applicable, the comparison of different vehicles and useful work to energy consumed does have an interesting resemblance to similar comparisons of IT resources and is certainly food for thought. In fact, the EPA is currently working with the IT industry (vendors, customers, analysts, and consultants) to extend its Energy Star™ program, which already addresses consumer appliances and some consumer electronics including workstation and laptops. By the time you read this, the EPA should have in place the first specifications for Energy Star servers and be on its way to defining follow-on server specifications as well as specifications for Energy Starstorage and data centers. (Note that while the fuel economy estimates and Energy Star are both EPA programs, they are overseen by a different division within the EPA.)

The EPA is not alone in working on energy efficiency metrics. Other countries around the world are also looking into new metrics to support emission tax schemes and other initiatives.

DIFFERENT METRICS FOR DIFFERENT AUDIENCES

What metrics and measurements are needed depend on the audience that will use them. For example, manufacturers or software developers have different needs and focus areas than sales and marketing departments. IT organizations may need data on the macro or "big picture" view of costs, energy usage, number or type of servers, amount of storage capacity, or how many transactions can be supported, among others. Needed metrics also vary at different times, including during development, manufacture and quality assurance, sales and marketing, customer acquisition and installation, integration testing, and ongoing support.

Metrics encompass PACE consumption along with general health and status, including the effectiveness of a solution. Given various usage scenarios, metrics address IT resources when being used to process work or move data as well as how data is stored when not in use. From the standpoint of power, cooling, floor space, and environment (PCFE), IT resources need to be monitored in terms of effective work along as well as how much data can be stored in a given footprint for a given level of service and cost.

Fig. 3 shows on the left various points of focus for metrics, ranging from facilities at the bottom to business and application centered at the top. Various types of metrics and measurements are available in the different categories that feed to infrastructure resource management (IRM) monitoring, notification, logging, reporting, and correlation and analysis tools as shown on the right of Fig. 3.

From a PCFE standpoint, metrics such as energy consumption, cost, heat generated, and carbon dioxide (CO_2) emissions need to be made available. IT resources need to be measured and looked at while considering many factors, including activity or inactivity, environment, applications, compute or I/O centric, the amount of data being stored (storage centric) versus the amount being processed (server centric), and geographic location (which determines energy rates, availability, and emissions).

A server-centric environment may use energy to power and cool servers compared to storage and other IT equipment. An environment that has a larger ratio of storage capacity and I/O operations with less compute or server resources may show a lower percentage of power used for servers and more for storage (disk and tape). Keep in mind that these are averages, and typical environments and "actual mileage will vary" depending on the factors specific to a situation.

Establishing a baseline set of measurements is important for many reasons, including establishing normal and abnormal behavior, identifying trends in usage or

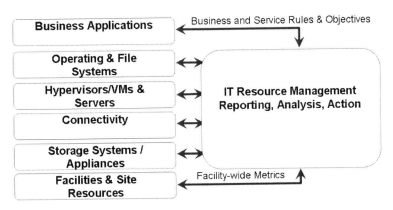

Fig. 3 IT Resource and service points of interest for metrics and measurement.

performance patterns, as well as for forecasting and planning purposes. For example, knowing the typical IOP rates and throughput rates for the storage devices, as well as the common error rates, average queue depths, and response times, will allow quick comparisons and decisions when problems or changes occur.

Baselines should be established for resource performance and response time, capacity or space utilization, availability and energy consumption. Baselines should also be determined for different application work scenarios in order to know, for example, how long certain tasks normally take. Baseline IRM functions, including database maintenance, backups, virus checking, and security scans, can be used to spot when a task is taking too long or finishing too fast, both of which could indicate a problem. Another example is that high or low CPU utilization compared to normal could indicate an application or device error resulting in excessive activity or blocking work from being done.

For planning purposes, resource usage and other key performance indicators can be plotted as shown in Fig. 4 to show available resource capacity limits, thresholds for acceptable service delivery, actual usage, availability or performance, and trends. Establishing thresholds, which are usually less than the actual physical limits of the equipment, is useful for managing

service delivery to a given response time or a particular performance or availability level.

For example, to meet a specific performance response time, servers or storage performances may be kept at less than full performance capacity; or resource usage can be targeted, based on experience and historical baselines, below a certain percent utilization to ensure acceptable service delivery at a specific cost point.

From a forecasting and planning perspective, baseline comparisons can be used to determine or predict future resource usage needs while factoring in business and application growth. The benefit is that with a resource usage and performance capacity plan, the right amount and type of resources can be made available in a timely and cost-effective manner when needed. By combining capacity planning across servers, storage, networks, and facilities, different groups can keep each other informed on when and where resources will be needed to support server, storage, and networking growth.

Table 1 lists several metrics pertaining to electivity usage with descriptions and comments, including how to convert or translate a known metric to get an unknown value. For example, if you know the number of watts of power a device is using, you can determine the number of amps by dividing watts by known voltage. Similarly, if you do not know the number of watts for a device but

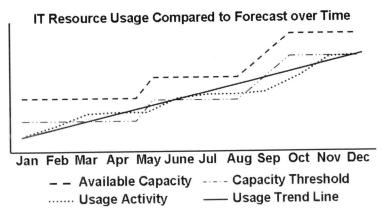

Fig. 4 Measuring and comparing IT resource usage over time.

Table 1 Some power, cooling, floor space, and environmental or IT-related metrics

Term	Description	Comments
AC	Alternating current	Type of electicity commonly used for most electrical or electronic devices.
Amps	Watts/volts	The flow rate of electricity, e.g., 144 watts/ 12 volts = 12 amps.
Annual kWh	kWh × 24 × 365	Amount of energy used in kilowatts in 1 year.
Bandwidth	Bytes per second	The quantum of data that is moved in 1 second. Used for measuring storage system as well as network data in-flight performance
Btu/hour	Watts × 3.413	Heat generated in 1 hour from using energy, in British thermal units. 12,000 Btu/hour equates to 1 ton of cooling.
CO_2 emission	On average, 1.341 lb per kilo-watt-hour of electricity generated	The amount of average CO_2 emissions from generating an average kilowatt-hour of electricity.
DC	Direct current	Electicity used internally by IT equipment after conversion from AC.
Hz	Hertz	Frequency of electricity, such as 60 Hz (60 cycles per second) in North America or 50 Hz in other parts of the world.
IOPS	Input/output operations per second	Measure of the number of I/O operations, transactions, file requests, or activity in 1 second.
Joule	1 watt per second	Rate at which energy is used per second. One watt-hour is equivalent to 3,600 joules. 1 kWh represents 3,600,000 joules, or 1,000 joules per second.
kVA	Volts × amps/ 1,000 or kW/ power factor	Number of kilovolt-amperes.
kW	kVA × power factor	Efficiency of a piece of equipment's use of power.
Latency	Response time	How long work takes to be performed.
MHz or GHz	Megahertz or gigahertz	An indicator of processor clock speed.
Power factor (pf)	Efficiency of power conversion	How effectively power is used and converted by power supplies. Power supplies that are 80% efficient or better may be referred to as "80-plus."
U or rack unit (RU)	1 U = 1.75 inches	Electronic Industry Alliance (EIA) metric describing height of IT equipment in racks, units, or cabinets.
Valve Anti-Cheat	Volts AC	The amount of AC volts that are being used.
Volt-amperes (VA)	Volts × amps	Power can be expressed in volt-amperes.
Volts or voltage	Watts/amps	The amount of force on electrons as a measurement of electricity (AC or DC).
Watt	Amps × volts or multiple Btu/hr × 0.293	Unit of electrical energy power to accomplish some amount of work.

you are given the number of Btu, simply divide the number of Btu by 0.293; for example, 1000 Btu × 0.293 = 293 W. Metrics such as IOPS per watt are calculated by dividing the number of IOPS per second by the number of watts of energy used. Similarly, megahertz per watt or bandwidth per watt is found by dividing the number of megahertz or amount of bandwidth by the energy used.

Some metrics are measured and others are derived from measured metrics or are a combination of different metrics. For example, a storage system may report the number of I/O operations on a read and write basis along with the amount of data read and written. A derived metric is created by dividing bandwidth by number of I/O operations to get average I/O size. Similarly, if number of I/O operations and average I/O size are known, bandwidth can be determined by multiplying I/O rate by I/O size. Different solutions will report various metrics at different levels of detail. Similarly, third-party measurement and reporting tools, depending on data source and collection capabilities, will vary in the amount of detail that can be reported.

Bytes are counted using different schemes including binary base 2 and decimal base 10 (see Table 2). Networks traditionally have been measured in bits per second, whereas storage and related I/O are measured in bytes per second. These are sometimes referred to as "little b" (bits) and "big B" (bytes). Also shown in Table 2 are various abbreviations, including those of the international system of units (SI).

Intuitively, energy would be measured in terms of joules per second to parallel activity metrics per second. Generally speaking, however, electrical power is measured and reported on a kWh basis, in alignment with how utilities bill for power use. For example, if a device consumes 1000 watts on a steady-state basis for 1 hour, it will consume 1 kWh of energy or 3,600,000 joules.

Table 2 IRM counting and number schemes for servers, storage, and networks

	Binary number of bytes	Decimal number of bytes	Abbreviations
Kilo	1,024	1,000	K, ki, kibi
Mega	1,048,576	1,000,000	M, Mi, bebi
Giga	1,073,741,824	1,000,000,000	G, Gi, gibi
Tera	1,099,511,627,776	1,000,000,000,000	T, Ti, tebi
Peta	1,125,899,906,842,620	1,000,000,000,000,000	P, Pi, pebi
Exa	1,152,921,504,606,850,000	1,000,000,000,000,000,000	E, Ei, exbi
Zetta	1,180,591,620,717,410,000,000	1,000,000,000,000,000,000,000	Z, Zi, zebi
Yotta	1,208,925,819,614,630,000,000,000	1,000,000,000,000,000,000,000,000	Y, Ui, yobi

Metrics can be instantaneous burst or peak based, or they may be sustained over a period of time, with maximum, minimum, average, and standard deviation noted along with cumulative totals. These metrics can be recorded and reported by different time intervals, for example, by hour, work shift, day, week, month, or year.

IT technology manufacturers provide information about electrical energy consumption and/or heat (Btu/hour) generated under a given scenario. Some vendors provide more information, including worst-case and best-case consumption information, whereas others provide only basic maximum breaker size information. Metrics published by vendors and that should be visible on equipment may include kilowatt (kW), kV, amps, Valve Anti-Cheat, or British thermal units. Missing information can be determined if the other factors are available. For example, if a vendor supplies Btu/hour, the number of watts can be found by multiplying Btu/hour times 0.293. As an example, a device that produces 1000 Btu/hour, uses 293 watts.

Other metrics that can be obtained or calculated include those related to recycling, emissions, air flow, and temperature. Other metrics pertain to server CPU, memory, I/O, and network utilization, capacity usage, and performance of local or internal storage. A compound metric is derived from multiple metrics or calculations. For example, IOPS per watt can be determined when base metrics such as IOPS and watts are known; these can be used to determine a metric for activity per energy consumed.

Application metrics include number of transactions, e-mail messages, files, photos, videos, or other documents processed. Metrics for data protection include amount of data transferred in a given time frame, number of successful or failed backup or data protection tasks, how long different jobs or tasks take, as well as other error and activity information. Configuration management information includes how many of different types of servers, storage, networking components, software, and firmware, along with how they are configured.

These and other metrics can indicate a rate of usage as a count or percentage of a total such as server CPU measured from zero to 100% busy. Percent utilization gives a relative picture of the level of activity of a resource, percent utilization by itself does not indicate how service is being delivered or of the PCFE impact. For example, a server running at 50% utilization may consume less power than at 85%, yet, at 85%, application response time and performance may decrease in a nonlinear fashion. Performance of servers, storage, and networks typically degrade as more work is being done, hence the importance of looking at response time and latency as well as IOPS or bandwidth as well as percent utilization and space used.

MEASURING PERFORMANCE AND ACTIVE RESOURCE USAGE

Generally speaking, as additional activity or application workload (including transactions or file accesses) is performed, I/O bottlenecks will cause increased response time or latency. With most performance metrics, including the throughput, the higher the value the better it is; however, with response time, the lower the latency the better it is. Fig. 5 shows the impact as more work is performed (dotted curve): I/O bottlenecks increase and result in increased response time (solid curve). The specific acceptable response time threshold will vary by applications and service-level agreement requirements. As more workload is added to a system with existing I/O issues, response time will increase correspondingly (as shown in Fig. 5). The more severe the bottleneck, the faster the response time will deteriorate. Eliminating bottlenecks allows more work to be performed while maintaining response time at acceptable service-level threshold limits.

To compensate for poor I/O performance and to counter the resulting negative impact to IT users, a common approach is to add more hardware to mask or move the problem. If overconfiguring to support peak workloads and prevent loss of business revenue, excess storage capacity must be managed throughout the nonpeak periods, adding to data center and management costs. The resulting ripple effect is that now more storage needs to be managed, including allocating storage network ports, configuring, tuning, and backing up data.

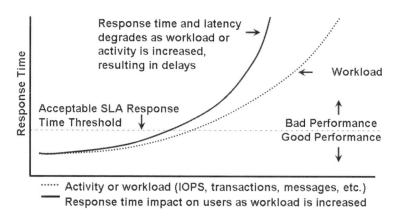

Fig. 5 I/O response time performance impact.

Storage utilization well below 50% of available capacity is common. The solution is to address the problem rather than moving and hiding the bottleneck elsewhere (rather like sweeping dust under the rug).

Another common challenge and cause of I/O bottlenecks is seasonal and/or unplanned workload increases that result in application delays and frustrated customers. In Fig. 6, a seasonal workload is shown, with seasonal spikes in activity (dotted curve). Fig. 6 can represent servers processing transactions, file, video, or other activity-based work, networks moving data, or a storage system responding to read and write requests. The resulting impact to response time (solid curve) is shown in relation to a threshold line of acceptable response time. The threshold line is calculated based on experience or expected behavior and represents the level at which, when work exceeds that point, corresponding response time will degrade below acceptable. For example, peaks due to holiday shopping exchanges appear in January, then drop off, and then increase again near Mother's Day in May.

Thresholds are also useful from a space capacity basis—for example, on servers, determining that particularly applications can run statistically at up to 75%

utilization before response time and productivity suffer. Another example would be establishing that storage capacity utilization to meet performance needs for active data and storage is 70%, while near-line or offline storage can be utilized at a higher rate. It is important to note that the previous threshold examples are just that—examples—and actual thresholds will vary. Check application or system software as well as with hardware manufacturers for guideline and configuration rules of thumb.

For activity-based IT data center measurements, that is, where useful work is being done, activity per unit of energy metrics are applicable. In everyday life, a common example of activity or useful work per energy used is miles per gallon for automobiles or miles per gallon per passenger for mass transit including commercial aviation. Examples of data center useful work and activity include data being read or written, transactions or files being processed, videos or web pages served, or data being moved over local- or wide-area networks.

Activity per watt of energy consumed can also be thought of as the amount of work per energy used. A reciprocal is amount of energy per unit of work performed. Activity per watt can be used to measure

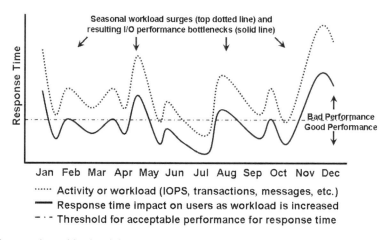

Fig. 6 I/O bottlenecks from peak workload activity.

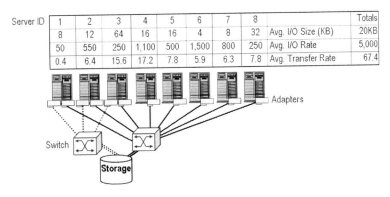

Server ID	1	2	3	4	5	6	7	8		Totals
	8	12	64	16	16	4	8	32	Avg. I/O Size (KB)	20KB
	50	550	250	1,100	500	1,500	800	250	Avg. I/O Rate	5,000
	0.4	6.4	15.6	17.2	7.8	5.9	6.3	7.8	Avg. Transfer Rate	67.4

Fig. 7 Examples of server, storage, and network being measured.

transient or flow-through networking and I/O activity between servers and storage devices, or between user workstations and an application server. Common examples of work per energy used are MHz per watt, IOPS, transactions, bandwidth or video streams per watt, storage capacity per watt, or miles per gallon. All indicate how much work is being done and how efficiently energy is being used to accomplish that work. This metric applies to active workloads or actively used and frequently accessed storage and data.

Fig. 7 shows a simple example of eight servers and their average storage I/O activity. In the example, some servers are single attached and some are dual attached over different paths for redundancy to Fibre Channel or Ethernet storage. Activity-based measurements can occur at the server via third-party or operating system utility-based tools, via application-specific tools, or benchmark and workload simulation tools, via various tools.

As an example, assume that when server number seven is actively doing work, the energy used is 800 watts, and that energy yields 800 IOPS (8 kbytes) or 1 IOPS per watt on average. The more IOPS per watt of energy used, the better it is. Of course, this example does not include networking or switch use, or storage system activity. If, say, the storage consumes on average 1200 watts when doing active work, the number of kbytes per second from each of the servers can be totaled to determine bandwidth per watt of energy for the storage system. In this example, the storage system at average active energy consumption of 1200 watts,

yields about 57.5 kbytes per watt or about 4.17 IOPS per watt.

For LAN and SAN networks, the process involves determining the amount of power used by a switch and then the amount being used per port. For example, the switches shown in Table 3 consume 1600 watts each in total, but only 50 watts per port (32-port switch). Without factoring in activity (for example, the number of frames, packets, IOPS, or bandwidth) to support the previous example, 15 ports are needed yielding (15 × 50 watts) 750 watts.

Adding up the energy used for the servers, network, and storage along with activity or work being performed provides a more granular view of the efficiency and productivity of the data center. Note that the above example does not consider whether the servers are fully utilized, what the response time or latency is per I/O operation, or what the time duration or period is. For example, the values shown in Table 3 may represent 24-hour averages, or they could represent a prime-time work shift. Also not factored into the above simple example is the amount of cooling required to remove heat, the density or footprint, or the usable capacity.

In Fig. 8, at the application server, energy is used to perform work, including running applications, processing transactions, supporting e-mail or exchange users, handling I/O operations, etc. On the far right, storage systems take in data written by servers and respond to read requests. Some of the data may be active, either being both read and written or updated, some of the data may be read-only or static reference or look-up data, whereas other data may be offline and inactive,

Table 3 Activity metrics server, storage, and networking example

Server	1	2	3	4	5	6	7	8	Total
Average watts per server	800	800	800	800	800	800	800	800	6,400
I/O size (kbytes)	8	12	64	16	16	4	8	32	
I/O rate per second	50	550	250	1,100	500	1,500	800	250	5,000
Bandwidth (kbytes per second)	400	6,600	16,000	17,600	8,000	6,000	6,400	8,000	69,000
IOPS per watt	0.1	0.7	0.3	1.4	0.6	1.9	1.0	0.3	
Bandwidth per watt	0.5	8.3	20.0	22.0	10.0	7.5	8.0	10.0	

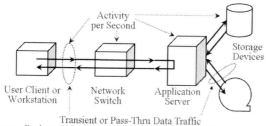

Fig. 8 Bandwidth per second for transient data in-flight and storage systems.

including previous backup or archives for compliance or long-term data preservation.

Activity per watt can also be used to measure the amount of data moved to and from storage devices by servers or between other storage systems. Fig. 8 shows activity being performed per unit of energy in several locations, including transactions being requested by a user or client workstation resulting in network traffic. In the middle of Fig. 8, network traffic, including frames or packets per second, IOPS, transactions or bandwidth per second, passes through a switch that consumes energy to move data between the client on the left and the server on the right. Activity per watt is calculated as work (IOPS) divided by energy used (watts).

Note that when using an activity-per-energy measurement, it is important to know whether the energy consumed is just for the equipment or if it also includes cooling. Note also that activity per watt should be used in conjunction with another metric such as how much capacity is supported per watt in a given footprint. Total watts consumed should also be considered, along with price, to achieve a given level of service for comparative purposes.

Bandwidth per watt should not be confused with capacity per watt, such as terabytes of storage capacity space. This latter metric refers to the amount of data moved per second per energy used. Bandwidth per watt also applies to transient and flow-through networking traffic. It is also used for measuring the amount of data that can be read or written from a storage device or server, such as Mbytes per second per watt of energy for network traffic or switch.

IOPS per watt represents the number of I/O operations (read or write, random or sequential, small or large) per unit of energy in a given time frame for a given configuration and response time or latency level. Examples include SPEC and SPC-1 IOPS per watt or other workloads that report I/Os or IOPS.

Multiple metrics can and should be considered. It is important, however, to look at them in the context of how and where they are being used. For example, a fast solid-state disk (SSD) will have a high IOPS and low power consumption per physical footprint compared to a

traditional disk drive. However, a SSD will usually also have a lower storage capacity and may require different data protection techniques compared to regular disk storage. Furthermore, while SSD may be more expensive on a capacity basis, on an IOPS-per-footprint basis, the SSD can have a lower cost per transaction, IOP, or activity performed than regular disk, albeit with less space capacity.

Exercise caution in combining too many different metrics in an attempt for a normalized view. The risk is that different metrics can cancel each other and lose their reflective value. An example of marketing magic is along the lines of (capacity * IOPS)/(watts * space). The challenge with marketing numbers is that their purpose is usually rooted in making sure that a particular vendor's technology looks more favorable than others rather than actual applicability.

For example, marketing may not factor in bandwidth versus I/O-intensive applications or the cost and applicable data-protection level. Another issue with "magic" metrics, like the one in the previous example, is that they can be mistakenly used to try and measure different types, tiers, and categories of storage. Another common mistake is to use raw disk drive numbers for theoretical performance, rather than combined storage controller and disk drive performance based on industry standard or other acceptable benchmarks. For true comparison purposes, look at applicable metrics relevant to the task and reflective of the function for which the resource will be used.

MEASURING CAPACITY AND IDLE RESOURCE USAGE

Capacity metrics are important in data centers in many different technology domains. A variation of capacity-based measurements, briefly touched on previously, is idle or inactive resource usage. One scenario of idle usage is a server assigned to support an application that is inactive during certain periods. For example, a server is busy doing work for 12 hours of the day and then, other than supporting some IRM or data maintenance functions, is idle until the next day.

Another variation is storage that is allocated and has data written to it for storage purposes, yet the data is not regularly accessed. An example is reference or static data, also known as persistent data, that does not change but is written to disk and seldom, if ever, read. To help optimize PACE use, inactive data can be moved to offline storage such as magnetic tape. Once written to tape, the storage does not require power to be stored. Some disk drive-based solutions are replacing or coexisting with tape and optical-based storage solutions for near-line storage of inactive data. For online and active disk storage, performance is an important metric, along with availability, capacity, and energy use; near-line and offline disk based storage has a lesser focus on performance.

For space capacity-based storage and, in particular, storage for idle data including backup targets or archiving solutions involving data de-duplication, there is a tendency to measure in terms of de-duplication ratios. Ratios are a nice indicator of how, for a given set of data, the data and its footprint can be reduced. Data movement or ingestion and processing rate, which is the rate at which data can be reduced, is a corollary metric for data-reduction ratios. Data-reduction rates, including compression rates, can indicate how much data can be reduced in a given window or time frame.

The amount of equipment per rack or the number of cabinets per footprint reflects IT resource density in a given footprint. This is a compound metric that can look at the total power consumption of all equipment installed in a given rack or cabinet footprint. The metric can also factor in the amount of resource space and capacity available or the number of servers or storage devices. A caveat in using this type of metric is to be sure to include the height of the rack or equipment cabinets. Variations of this metric can be the amount of resources, including performance IOPS or bandwidth, capacity, data protection, number of servers or network ports, per "U" or rack unit. Another variation is to base the footprint on floor space in square feet or meters while keeping in mind that some equipment utilizes deep, wide, or other nonstandard cabinets. Metrics can be obtained by measuring intelligent power distribution units and power management modules in the cabinets or from the individual components in a rack or cabinet. Another factor with regard to footprint is how much weight in addition to power and cooling is required or supported, particularly when shifting equipment.

Still another metric variation looks at the amount of storage capacity per watt in a given footprint. This is useful for inactive and idle storage. This metric is commonly used by vendors, similar to how dollar per capacity ($/GB) is often used, for comparing different storage technologies. One issue with this metric is whether it is considering the capacity as raw (no data protection configuration such as mirroring, no file system or volume formatting) or as allocated to a file system or as free versus used. Another issue with this metric by itself is that it does not reflect activity or application performance or effectiveness of energy per unit of capacity to support a given amount of work—for example, watt per tape cartridge when the tape is on a shelf versus when the tape is being written to or read. Another concern is how to account for hot spare disk drives in storage arrays. Also, the metric should account for data offline as well as data online and in use.

A point of confusion can exist around the use of Mbyte, Gbyte, Tbyte, or Pbyte per watt when the context of bandwidth or capacity is missing. For example, in the context of bandwidth, 1.5 Tbyte per watt means that 1.5 Tbytes per second are moved at a given workload and service level. On the other hand, in the context of storage space capacity, 1.5 Tbyte per watt means that 1.5 Tbytes are stored in a given footprint and configuration. The takeaway is not to confuse use of bandwidth or data movement with storage space capacity when looking at Tbyte or Pbyte and related metrics per watt of energy.

MEASURING AVAILABILITY, RELIABILITY, AND SERVICEABILITY

Availability can be measured and reported on an individual component basis, as a sum of all components, or a composite of both. A balanced view of availability is to look at the big picture in terms of end-to-end or total availability. This is the view that is seen by users of the services supported by the storage network and its applications.

The annual failure rate (AFR) is the association between mean time between failures (MTBF) and the number of hours a device is run per year. AFR can take into consideration different sample sizes and time in use for a device. For example, a large sample pool of 1,000,000 disk drives that operates 7×24 hours a day (8760 hours a year) with 1000 failures has an AFR of 8.76%. If another group of similar devices is used only 10 hours a day, 5 days a week, 52 weeks a year (2600 hours) with the same sample size and number of failures, the AFR is 2.6%. MTBF can be calculated from AFR by dividing the total annual time a device is in use by the AFR. For the previous example, MTBF = 2600/2.6 = 1000. AFR is useful for looking at various size samples over time while factoring in duty or time in use for availability comparison or other purposes.

There can be a cost associated with availability that needs to be understood to determine availability objectives. Vendors utilize terms such as five nines, six nines, or higher to describe their solution's availability. It is important to understand that availability is the sum of all components and their configuration. Seconds of downtime per year is calculated as $100\% \times [(100\ N)/100]$, where N is the desired number of 9s of availability as shown in Table 4. Availability is the sum of all components combined with design for fault isolation and containment. How much availability you need and can afford will be a function of your environment, application and business requirements, and objectives.

Availability is only as good as the weakest link in a chain. In the case of a data center, that weakest link

Table 4 Availability expressed as number of 9s

Availability (%)	Number of 9s	Amount of downtime per year
99	0	3.65 days/year
99.9	1	8.77 hours/year
99.99	2	52.6 minutes/year
99.999	3	5.26 minutes/year
99.9999	4	31.56 seconds/year
99.99999	5	3.16 seconds/year
99.999999	6	∫ second/year

could be the applications, software, servers, storage, network, facilities and processes, or best practices. Virtual data centers rely on physical resources to function; a good design can help eliminate unplanned outages to compensate for individual component failures. A good design removes complexity while providing scalability, stability, ease of management, and maintenance as well as fault containment and isolation.

APPLYING VARIOUS METRICS AND MEASUREMENTS

The importance of these numbers and metrics is to focus on the larger impact of a piece of IT equipment including its cost and energy consumption, and factoring in cooling and other hosting or site environmental costs. At a macro or "big-picture" level, the energy efficiency of an IT data center can be measured as a ratio of power being used for heating, ventilating, and air conditioning (HVAC) or cooling and power for IT equipment independent of actual work being done or data being stored. An example is the metric called **power usage effectiveness (PUE)**, and its reciprocal, **data center efficiency (DCiE)**, being put forth by the Greengrid industry trade group.

PUE is defined as the total facility power divided by total IT equipment (excluding HVAC). This provides a gauge of how effectively electrical power is being used to power IT equipment. DCiE is the reciprocal PUE and is defined as 1/PUE or total IT equipment power consumption divided by total facility power (including HVAC) × 100%. PUE can range from 1 (100% efficiency) to infinity. For example, a PUE of 3, the equivalent of a DCiE of 33%, indicates that about 70% of power being consumed by a data center is used for non-IT equipment.

Another metric being put forth by the Greengrid is **Data Center Productivity (DCP)**, which considers active or useful work being done per energy being consumed. DCP is a very generic and broad metric that will take time to evolve and define what determines work or activity across different types, tiers, and categories of

servers, storage, and networking devices. In the near term, a subset example of DCP could be considered to be activity per watt of power.

Another metric or series of metrics attempts to look at the total impact of the emissions and environmental health and safety footprint over the entire life of an IT resource. These could have focus on only the time frame an IT organization owns and operates the equipment, or they could be cradle-to-grave metrics that also factor in vendor manufacturing and materials, green supply chain, and ecosystem, through acquisition, installation, and use until final disposition and recycling.

Questions that arise with an emissions metric is whether it is only for CO_2 and emissions-related tax accounting purposes or whether it is designed to provide a complete picture of the impact on environmental health and safety. Does the footprint or impact include associated IRM tasks and overhead, including data protection, backup, business continuity, disaster recovery and associated software running on different servers? Other issues to consider include whether the emissions footprint is based on averages or on a specific location and energy fuel source.

A simple emissions footprint can be determined by multiplying the number of watts used for a device plus applicable watts associated with cooling the equipment times 1.341 per kWh used to derive the number of CO_2 tons/kWh of electricity used. For example, if a device consumes 1200 watts plus 600 watts (1.8 kWh) for cooling, the average hourly average emissions is 2.413.8 lb of CO_2 or about 10.57 tons of CO_2 per year. Note that 1.341 lb/kWh is an average and will vary by location, depending on energy costs and fuel source. Another note is that this simple calculation does not take into consideration the actual amount of carbon, which may be taxed separately under some emission tax schemes.

SOURCES FOR METRICS, BENCHMARKS, AND SIMULATION TOOLS

Metrics and measurements can be obtained from many different sources, including external probes or analyzers, built-in reporting facilities, and add-on third-party data collection and reporting tools. Sources for information include event, activity, and transaction logs and journals as well as operation system and application-based tools. Vendors of servers, storage, and networking solutions also provide varying degrees of data collection and reporting capabilities. Metrics can also be obtained from facilities monitoring tools, power conversion, and distribution units, computer room air conditioners, and other points within the data center, including security and event logs or alerts. For example, temperature and air flow data can be used to determine conflicts between hot and cold zones or areas of confluence, or how much energy is being consumed and how effectively it is being converted.

IT equipment power, cooling, footprint, and environmental metrics, including basic power requirements, can be found on equipment labels or nameplates. Other sources of equipment PCFE metrics include vendor documentation such as site installation and planning guides or vendor websites that may also include sizing and configuration tools or calculators. Note that equipment nameplate values may exceed the actual power and cooling requirements for the equipment, as these values have a built-in safety margin; for a more accurate assessment, review vendor specification documents.

Performance testing and benchmarks have different meanings and different areas of focus. There is testing for compatibility and interoperability of components. There is performance testing of individual components as well as testing of combined solutions. Testing can be very rigorous and thorough, perhaps beyond real-world conditions; or testing can be relatively simple, to verify data movement and integrity. What is the best test for your environment depends on your needs and requirements. The best test is one that adequately reflects your environment and the applications' workload and can be easily reproduced.

SUMMARY

Virtual data centers require physical resources to function efficiently and in a green or environmentally friendly manner. Thus it is vital to understand the value of resource PACE usage to deliver various IT services.

Understanding the relationship between different resources and how they are used is important to gauge improvement and productivity as well as DCiE. For example, while the cost per raw terabyte may seem relatively inexpensive, the cost for I/O response time performance needs to be considered for active data.

Having enough resources to support business and application needs is essential to a resilient storage network. Without adequate storage and storage networking resources, availability and performance can be negatively impacted. Poor metrics and information can lead to poor decisions and management. Establish availability, performance, response time, and other objectives to gauge and measure performance of the end-to-end storage and storage–networking infrastructure. Be practical, as it can be easy to get caught up in the details and lose sight of the bigger picture and objectives.

Additional key points include:

- Balance PACE and PCFE requirements to various levels of service.
- Compare resources "apples to apples," not "apples to oranges."
- Look at multiple metrics to get a multidimensional view of resource usage.
- Use caution in applying marketing-focused "magic" metrics that may not reflect reality.
- Metrics and measurements can be obtained and derived from many different sources.
- Use metrics and link to business and application activity to determine resource efficiency.
- Establish baseline metrics and profiles to compare current use with historical trends.

Resources–
Six Sigma

Root Cause Analysis and Troubleshooting Techniques

Gary G. Jing
TE Connectivity, Shakopee, Minnesota, U.S.A.

Abstract

Troubleshooting is a fundamental technique that everyone should acquire. It is rooted in the various techniques collectively referred to as cause–effect analysis (root cause analysis or RCA) but with significant differences. Both utilize cause–effect relationships as the key to finding solutions. However, troubleshooting is usually more short-term oriented, focusing on what is wrong (where and how), while RCA is more long-term oriented, focusing on why (for long-term solutions). The intent of this article is to clarify some common points of confusion, including the true meaning of root cause and RCA, the difference between RCA and troubleshooting, and techniques and tools for RCA and troubleshooting.

INTRODUCTION

The term "root cause" is frequently used in our professional life, and occasionally in our social and personal lives as well. "Have you found the root cause yet?" is a common question we hear people ask. We care about it because when we run into problems, we believe that identifying and addressing root cause will help us resolve the problem more effectively and/or thoroughly.

Given that root cause analysis (RCA) is an old subject, somewhat familiar to many people, one might assume that they would generally have a clear mind on it. Yet, surprisingly, this is often not the case. RCA frequently tops the list of tools people want to learn more about. Many professionals do not feel confident about it and want to see some light shed upon it.

This article summarizes and expands upon a series of publications[1–3] on the subject, and will address the following topics:

- The true meaning of root cause
- The true meaning of RCA
- Techniques to find the leverage point for high return on investment (ROI)
- The difference between RCA and troubleshooting
- Techniques generic for RCA
- Techniques unique for troubleshooting

There are several concepts introduced in this publication that make it unique. Some are simple and powerful, yet not widely known.

- Root Cause: There is NO true root cause in an absolute sense. So-called root cause is what is subjectively chosen to serve in that role. This subjectivity is the source of conflict and confusion about the best strategy and criteria to apply to consistently achieve high-quality RCA outcomes.
- RCA: The purpose of RCA is not to find the "true" root cause per se, since there is none. The purpose of RCA is to find the leverage point that maximizes ROI. There are some unique techniques to help differentiate the potential "root causes" so that one can set priority to actions.
- Troubleshooting: There are strong connections as well as differences between RCA and Troubleshooting. Both rely on cause–effect relationships to find answers. The difference is that RCA is more long-term oriented (focusing on why), while troubleshooting is more short-term oriented for quick turnaround, (focusing on what, where, and how). Focusing on RCA when the need is troubleshooting diminishes ROI, which can cause frustrations, while focusing on troubleshooting when the need is RCA reduces the long-term effectiveness.
- Techniques: There are a series of generic techniques from simple to complex to span the whole spectrum of RCA need. Meantime, there are some unique techniques that are especially suitable for troubleshooting. Is/Is Not Comparative Analysis, Relationship Diagram, and Fault Tree Analysis (FTA) are some examples. FTA is similar to RCA using a root cause tree (RCT) but the goals are different. FTA is focused on troubleshooting to identify what, where, and how; RCT is focused on identifying why, for long-term solutions. The outcomes between the two can be quite different.

THE TRUE MEANING OF ROOT CAUSE

There are a lot of publications and programs explaining tools/methods to do RCA, yet very few of them explain

Encyclopedia of Information Systems and Technology, DOI: 10.1081/E-EIST-120049147

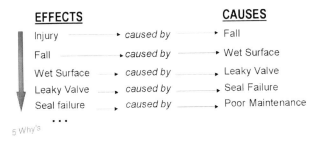

Fig. 1 An example of chain of causation.

or explore the true meaning of root cause. The term "root cause" appears to be simple but is quite misleading and confusing.

Many people who use the term "root cause" are unaware of the larger context of this concept. When asked what root cause means to them, some typical responses are: "It is what is really happening"; "it is the one thing that causes everything else"; "it is the switch that when flipped, turns the light on," etc. Better yet, "it is the originator of the problem."

With these types of descriptions, many people imply that there is one specific thing that is the originator of the problem, and that this origination is somewhat "absolute," meaning unconditional and not relative. This "absolute" originator is what people usually consider as the root cause.

The books on RCA often fail to give clear descriptions of the concept of root cause. For example, although RCA is a must-have tool category, most Six Sigma books only explain the specific tools themselves without exploring the true meaning of "root cause." Even the encyclopedic quality book, *Juran Quality Handbook*,[4] does not have an entry for root cause. One exception is the *Six Sigma Black Belt Handbook*, by McCarty et al.,[5] which provides a list of tenets that "underpin the belief that root causes can be fixed to improve processes," citing that "they are must-be accepted beliefs" for Six Sigma to reliably succeed. This is a rare case.

Concept of Chain of Causation

Although not many quality or Six Sigma books go very far in exploring the true meaning of "root cause," the nature of the cause–effect relationship and "root cause" have been widely explored at the philosophical level throughout human history, outside the technology and engineering arena. Some discussions of these subjects can be traced back to the Aristotle and Socrates era. The following argument is widely recognized in the philosophical world: "The nature of a cause-effect relationship forms an infinite chain of causation. Any event is both a cause and an effect at the same time. It is an effect of its upstream events and a cause of its downstream events. One can continue to identify causes to

the causes without ending. The only way to force an end to the chain is to attribute the cause to 'God' or God's creation, although this doesn't provide any practical help in solving a given problem."

A possible explanation of why nobody touches upon the true meaning of root cause is that god's creation belongs to the religious, nonscientific world. Some people do recognize the infinite nature of causation, but do not want to cross the line between science and religion. This amounts to a kind of taboo. The rest of the majority simply do not know.

God's creation was formally attributed as the ultimate end of the chain of causation through the introduction of teleological causality in the Hegelian dialectic. Alexada Spirkin provided a good summary of the concept of the infinite chain of causation in his *Dialectical Materialism*:[6]

> An important feature of causality is the continuity of the cause-effect connection. The chain of causal connections has neither beginning nor end. It is never broken. It extends eternally from one link to another. And no one can say where this chain began or where it ends. It is as infinite as the universe itself. There can be neither any first (that is to say, causeless) cause nor any final (i.e., inconsequential) effect. If we were to admit the existence of a first cause we should break the law of the conservation of matter and motion. And any attempt to find an "absolutely first" or "absolutely final" cause is a futile occupation, which psychologically assumes a belief in miracles.

To summarize the philosophy of the infinite chain of causation (or causality) again, there is no fixed, absolute "true" root cause per se. The so-called root cause in practice is something subjectively chosen to serve in the "root cause" role. It is a moving target. RCA is not about finding the "true" root cause; it is about how to select the one out of many that benefits the objective the most.

Although this concept is well established in the philosophical world and is self-evident when people are truly objective, it is not widely recognized in the engineering world. In fact, it was somewhat shocking to many people when they were first exposed to this concept. Dean L. Gano helped introduce the concept to the engineering world with his book, *Apollo Root Cause Analysis—A New Way Of Thinking*.[7] Fig. 1 illustrates an example used in that book. As easily seen, the chain can go on and on with no ending. He designated Chapter 2 to introduce the chain of causation concept. Yet, he warned, "because this book challenges conventional wisdom, it may not validate your existing belief system."

Cause–Effect Network

Although individual cause–effect relationships form chains of causation, a single chain of causation can

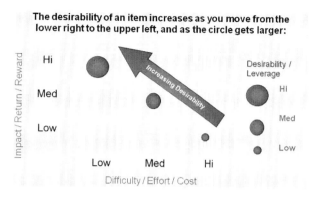

Fig. 2 ROI chart.

hardly provide a complete picture of the cause–effect relationship. In reality a single effect may have multiple causes jointly affecting it, thus forming multiple trailing chains; so may a cause have multiple effects in parallel. A collection of multiple parallel chains may merge and/or split, forming a cause–effect network, infinite at both ends. In this case, a specific problem event is simply a knot in the network. There are some techniques to deal with cause–effect networks, which will be discussed in later sections of this article.

THE TRUE MEANING OF RCA

With the infinite chain of causation concept in mind, one of the major challenges for people is how to know when and where to stop "drilling down" and conclude that they have reached a "root cause" out of the infinite layers of cause and effect. This is the wisdom that differentiates an adult from a 2 year old, and an expert from a novice.

Many articles in the quality literature highlight one key goal of RCA, which is to identify and eliminate

the noncritical causes out of many likely causes. In order to do that, one needs to study the strength of the cause–effect relations, deselecting the weak ones, while keeping the ones with high impact. While this is one of the interests of cause–effect analysis, it is insufficient.

The clue resides in the typical business mindset. The ultimate goal of RCA should be to select something that yields high ROI, that is, high return with low cost. That is how most businesses make decisions. It is also how people apply RCA, often subconsciously and without realizing it. Thus, in practice, RCA is about ROI calculation, intentionally or unintentionally. Although ROI calculation may not be openly claimed or recognized as a key goal when performing RCA, it is likely what going through people's minds, perhaps subconsciously, when choosing root cause. The noncritical causes usually do not generate high ROI. Much can be said about the ROI mindset. ROI has two main dimensions, cost and return, as shown in Fig. 2. The ideal is to achieve low cost and high return simultaneously but this is not always possible. Ultimately, the ratio of return to cost is the deciding factor, the higher the better.

Fig. 3 shows a framework depicting the relationship of problem-cause-effect-solution. It is revised from Wessel' 98.[8] According to this framework, a problem is shown along with its causes and effects and the two types of solution approaches. Solutions aimed at mitigating the effects are adaptive or reactive in nature; while those aimed at the causes are corrective and preventive in nature. The general idea is to shift attention to the cause side when possible, since preventive solutions are usually (but not always) associated with higher return. When people apply this approach, the original cause will become the new problem (or focus), which has new cause (s) and associated new solutions. This drives the continuous shift of attention to the new cause (s), which is the focus of the 5-Why's technique. Note that during this continuous process, solutions that were corrective or preventive become adaptive or reactive now, as causes become effects of their own causes. This highlights the fact that roles are relative and are moving targets. Without ROI in mind, it is hard to decide when to stop the chase.

Although it is generally true that the cause side solutions are usually associated with higher returns, there are certainly exceptions. Importantly, the costs associated with the cause side solutions are usually higher too and at least some cost components are always higher. This is usually not recognized by people, resulting in the major fallacy of thinking the deeper the better, as well as in the common dilemma of not knowing when to stop. In contrast, people are frequently stuck with short-term solutions without understanding the deeper causes for the problem. The truth is that deeper is not necessarily better, and

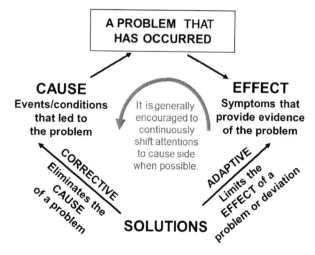

Fig. 3 Problem-cause-effect-solution framework.

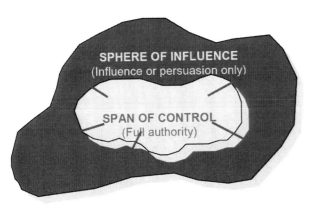

OUTSIDE, UNCONTROLLED ENVIRONMENT

Fig. 4 Sphere of influence.

choosing when to stop is much easier if people are conscious of the costs and returns.

To better understand this mentality, let us take a look at the cost structure of RCA. The cost of a solution (solution cost) has at least two components—the cost to search for the cause and solution (research cost), and the cost to implement the solution (implementation cost). The research cost will always go higher the deeper we go, while implementation cost may vary significantly. The trick is to find a solution that has significantly lower implementation cost, to offset the research cost and get a low solution cost overall:

$$\text{Solution cost} \downarrow = \text{research cost} \uparrow + \text{implementation cost} \downarrow\downarrow$$

When a cause has a low solution cost and high return, it is a good candidate to serve as the root cause. Yet research is a risky business and before the right cause is found, everything is unknown. It requires experience, functional expertise, intuition, and, sometimes, belief to succeed. Because of this, in many cases people do not want to or can not afford to take the risk. They will settle on less fundamental causes, at least to keep the research cost low.

ROI assessment can be internal (self), external (customer), short-term, or long-term oriented. The results can be very different. These differences tend to be overlooked. In many cases, short-term solutions are chosen due to cost constraints. Also, ROI may change over time, as does root cause. To make the fix long-lasting and organizationally sustainable, all parties' (stakeholders') interests need to be considered and balanced. Because of these inherent differences, many CAPA (corrective and preventive action)-like action plans ask for both short-term and long-term solutions.

TECHNIQUES TO FIND THE LEVERAGE POINT FOR HIGH ROI

There are three keys to help identify high ROI solutions. They are:

1. The Leverage Point Principle
2. The Pareto Principle (80–20 rule)
3. The Span of Control/Sphere of Influence Principle

Generally speaking, it is much more rewarding to focus on the causes that have high leverage or high frequency and are within the span of control. These causes should be the first to be considered as the root causes.

The leverage point refers to the causes that cost less to fix but affect more, with higher impact. The Pareto principle has a similar intent. A handful of "vital few" has greater impact than the "trivial many." That is the mindset of the 80–20 rule—80% of problems are caused by 20% of causes. It is easy to see how the leverage point and Pareto principles affect ROI. But it may be harder to see the link between the span of control and ROI.

Regarding span of control, people's influence can be roughly grouped into three zones as shown in Fig. 4. At the center is a core area within which people have full control. It is called the span of control. Outside the central core area, people have some influence but not full control. It is called the sphere of influence. Outside the sphere of influence is the area over which people have no influence whatsoever. The span of control/sphere of influence principle prescribes that people should operate within the span of control as much as possible. If it is not possible, people should try to operate within the sphere of influence while always avoiding operation outside of it. The point behind this mindset is that the causes within the span of control usually provide the highest leverage or ROI and the zone outside the sphere of influence gives no leverage and no ROI at all.

In practice, the span of control principle can be used to identify where to stop drilling-down the chain of causation and to select the preferred root causes to work on. Ideally, the root causes should be situated within the span of control; at worst, within the sphere of influence. If all of the causes that may interact with each other are within the span of control, usually it is safe to stop drilling-down the chain (s) and to treat them as the root causes. By the same token, if a cause is outside the sphere of influence, it is also a good indication to stop drilling, because working beyond that generates no returns. That is not to say that people should always give up in this case, because the influence boundaries may be expandable. The focus then needs to be shifted to expanding the influence boundaries to enclose the cause outside the sphere of influence. In practice, the sphere of influence is frequently the dominating factor in root cause selection.

One engineer with a strong engineering mindset had a hard time adopting the span of control mindset. He made the following counter argument: "When you lose your key at night, you look for it where it is most likely to be at, not limiting yourself only to where you can see, e.g., under the street lights, etc. If it's likely to be in the dark area, you need to look in the dark area." This is a typical outside-of-influence scenario. In this case, the most rewarding action is to expand the sphere of influence by bringing in flashlights to assist in the search.

Case Studies of Root Cause Concept Applications

Two famous RCA cases, the Jefferson Memorial Preservation and the John Snow Cholera Breakout Investigation, can be used to demonstrate how the three keys have been used intuitively or unintentionally to help investigators land on root causes that generate high ROI. After the two case studies, Six Sigma trainees who enter the program confused always walk away enlightened and excited, dealing with RCA with newfound confidence. The Quality Minutes video produced by Juran Institute contains some brief video clips for the two cases. The study here is from a specific angle, looking for clues for the three keys.

Case 1: Jefferson Memorial preservation case

Here is the synopsis for the case:

The U. S. Park Service noticed that the Jefferson Memorial monument deteriorated faster than other monuments. They investigated the problem with the "5-Why's" and formed a chain of causation:

- Why does it deteriorate faster? Because it gets washed more frequently.
- Why is it washed more frequently? Because it has more bird droppings.
- Why more bird droppings? Because more birds are attracted to the monument.
- Why more birds? Because there are more fat spiders in and around the monument.
- Why more spiders? Because there are more midgets flying in and around the monument in the evening.
- Why more midgets? Because the monument illumination attracts more midgets.

The list can keep going, on and on. Multiple events at various stages can be declared as the root causes and, thus, various solutions can be sought after, to break the chain of causation. For example, people can treat the

bird droppings as the root cause and focus on their removal or prevention through alternative measures, such as coating the surface of the monument with water-resistant coatings, etc. Or, they can focus on the removal and prevention of spider infestations caused by the presence of midgets, through pesticizing spiders. Or, they can try different lighting features, such as color, intensity, location, and pattern, to make it less attractive to midgets, etc. The solution chosen by the Park Service was to turn on the lighting one hour later in the evening. This simple act allegedly reduced 90% of the bird-dropping problem.

A lot can be said about this simple yet magical solution. The biggest advantage of it over others is really the high ROI, although the people who selected it may not realize it that way. The illumination, in this case, is not the absolute originator of the problem, but it is both a high leverage point and fully within the span of control of the park service, and, therefore, is a wonderful choice of root cause.

Worth noting is the common observation that ROI is usually a concern of the private sector. The public sector, that is, government functions, usually is not as sensitive to and motivated by ROI. The same is generally true for scientific research. Scientists usually are inclined to seek and identify more fundamental level causes. In this case study, it is very likely that researchers would try to have a better understanding of why and how this particular site is more attractive to midgets. This knowledge may lead to ways to alter lighting features to reduce the attraction. They might even attempt to change the midgets themselves to reduce their attraction to the light. While this approach may be more scientific, it may not provide as high ROI and may be outside the span of control of the Park Service. Taking into consideration all three criteria, leverage point, Pareto principle, and, especially, the span of control, the solution of choice, delaying the lighting by 1 hour, is a clear winner.

Case 2: 1854 London cholera epidemic case

There was a famous cholera breakout in 1854, London, where 127 people died in three days. Dr. John Snow, a preeminent physician then, and a legendary figure in the history of public health, closely monitored the breakout and made a breakthrough observation. He was able to trace the source of the breakout back to a particular water pump on Broad Street, using his famous Snow Map (a concentration map, see Fig. 5). Because of this, he was able to contain the breakout by removing the handle of the pump. "For his persistent efforts to determine how cholera was spread and for the statistical mapping methods he initiated, John Snow is widely

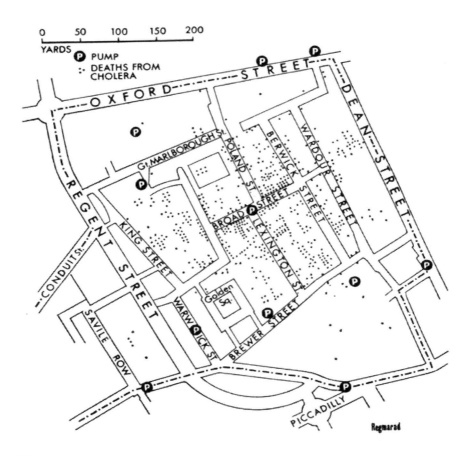

Fig. 5 The snow map.

considered to be the father of modern epidemiology"—citation from *Old News* by Vachon.[9]

"He found out that the addresses of the cholera epidemic victims clustered around the Broad Street pump. He found out through interviews that the great majority of the victims had used the Broad Street pump as their source of drinking water. While Dr. Snow did not know what had caused the epidemic in the first place, he was able to succeed in persuading the local community leaders (parish guardians) to remove the pump handle. The epidemic ended immediately!" For people who want to know more details about John Snow and this famous breakout, the Department of Epidemiology of (University of California, Los Angeles) has a wonderful, dedicated webpage for it: http://www.ph.ucla.edu/epi/snow.html.

Interestingly, at that time, people had no idea about cholera. Dr. Snow examined the water under a microscope and found that it contained "white, flocculent particles." He suspected it was the cause, but nobody believed him and he moved no further. He was only able to isolate the source without understanding of what it really is. Another scientist from the same era, Italian scientist Filippo Pacini, was credited as the discoverer of cholera. So, clearly, Snow was not anywhere close to identifying the true "root cause" of cholera. Yet, he was able to get a handle on the problem, literally, the handle of the pump, which is the high leverage point of the breakout. The pump handle is a good visual illustration of what the leverage point is really about. Fig 6 shows what now stand on London's Broadwick Street (then Broad Street), the John Snow Memorial and Pub. Note that the pump is without its handle.

Fig. 6 John snow memorial and pub on Broadwick Street, London.

Resources—
Six Sigma

It is worth noting that the fundamental root cause of the cholera breakout went beyond the cholera itself. The poor living conditions of that Soho neighborhood of London were the more fundamental cause of the series of breakouts there. The following is a description from *Soho—A History of London's Most Colourful Neighborhood* by Summers[10]: "By the middle of the 19th century, Soho had become an insanitary place of cowsheds, animal droppings, slaughterhouses, grease-boiling dens, and primitive, decaying sewers. And underneath the floorboards of the overcrowded cellars lurked something even worse—a fetid sea of cesspits as old as the houses, and many of which had never been drained. It was only a matter of time before this hidden festering time-bomb exploded."

In fact, the 1854 breakout was not the only breakout, nor the first. There was a series of cholera breakouts starting in 1831. Reports show that nothing was done about the living conditions there 1 year after the famous 1854 breakout. So if Dr. Snow was to concentrate on the more fundamental root causes of the problem, it would be beyond his sphere of influence as a physician. It would not be a choice with high ROI, at least no quick returns for the breakout. Even for the choice of removing the pump handle, he still needed to expand his sphere of influence through persuasion of the local community leaders (parish guardians) to adopt the idea.

POPULAR RCA TOOLS AND GENERIC TROUBLE SHOOTING TECHNIQUES

This section introduces selected tools to cover the whole spectrum of generic RCA need. It also introduces a unique practice and technique: a weighting system, to differentiate and prioritize potential root causes. It prevents loss of focus over many equally important causes.

Although many tools can be used to identify root causes, the following five are some of the most popular ones that cover the whole spectrum from simple to complex. The five popular tools are (from simple to complex):

- Is/is not comparative analysis.
- 5-Why's—Good for digging deep, yet with narrow focus.
- Fishbone Diagram (Cause–Effect Diagram)—Good for investigating broadly, yet not too deeply, the causes for a single effect.
- RCT—A tree structure diagram that begins with undesirable effects (UDEs) and drills down to root causes. It is a combination of the Fishbone and the

5-Why's and allows studying the interactions among causes.
- Cause and effect matrix (X–Y matrix)—Used to quantify and prioritize the impacts of a group of causes (X's) on a group of effects (Y's) through a numerical ranking. It is originally intended to handle multiple effects.

Some of the tools are so popular that most people are familiar with them, for example, the 5-Why's and the Fishbone. The following discussion will focus on highlighting some aspects that are usually overlooked.

Is/Is Not Comparative Analysis

Is/is not analysis is a comparative analysis method. It has not been formally classified as a cause–effect analysis tool. But, it can certainly provide insight into the details of what's happening, and it has frequently been used to investigate root causes when the cause–effect relationships are broad but not deep.

Fig. 7 (a) shows a sample template for is/is not analysis. There are fancier versions for this, but the key components are the same. They generally focus on the six "WH's", What, Why, How, Where, When and Who, the basic dimensions to identify and describe things. These basic things appear to be simple but allow people to zoom in on the problem to get visibility and clarity on details. As shown in Fig. 7 (b), by this method, the problem can be quickly narrowed in on and defined in clear relief by a process of segregation, or, to put it another way, by dividing and conquering.

Some firms use is/is not exclusively as the primary problem solving tool. They have standardized the descriptions into eight categories and added additional components such as brief sections for potential causes and cause testing. The eight categories are as follows:

1. What items have the problem?
2. What's wrong with the item?
3. Where was the item located?
4. Where was the problem located?
5. When was the problem first noticed?
6. How does the problem repeat?
7. When in the process or lifecycle was the problem seen?
8. How big is the problem?

Many people like this tool a lot after the first exposure, since it is straightforward and intuitive, not high-tech, yet very effective in discovering and organizing a lot of details. Some organizations consider it the first step in every RCA effort.

Problem Statement:			
	Is	Is Not	Differences and Changes
What	What is the specific object hat has the defect? What is the specific defect?	What similar objects could have the defect but do not? What other defects could be observed but are not?	
Where	Geographically? Physically on the part?	Where, when, and what size could the defect have been but it was not?	
When	When was the defect first observed? When since then? When in the product life cycle?		
Size	How many objects with the defect? How many defects per object? Size of defect? Trend?		

A

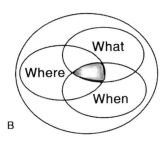

B

Fig. 7 Is/is not template.

5-Why's

The 5-Why's technique is good for digging deep, yet with narrow focus. The 5-Why's is essential to develop the chain of causation, as illustrated in Fig. 1, and is a no-brainer to most people. Again, what might be unclear to many people is what has been discussed earlier, how to decide when and where to put an end to the chain.

Fishbone Diagram (Cause–Effect Diagram, Ishikawa Diagram)

Fishbone is good for investigating broad, yet not too deep, causes for a single effect. This is a popular tool, very good for investigating a large number of causes. A major limitation is that the relationships among the causes are not readily seen and interactions among them

will be missing. To identify and diagram interactions requires RCT tools.

One problem many people have with this tool is that it will identify a bunch of causes or potential root causes. People may get lost regarding what to focus on in the next step. Thus, prioritizing the causes becomes a needed step. Sometimes people use a cause–effect matrix to formally do that. But, in this application, the matrix only uses single output criteria for the evaluation, which is not what the matrix was originally designed for.

One unique practice is to do the evaluation and prioritization right on the fishbone diagram. This is an extra value-added step. This technique employs a unique weighting system to reflect the ROI mindset in the assessment. As shown in Fig. 8, the weighting system has two dimensions, opportunity, which represents returns, and controllability, which represents costs. The

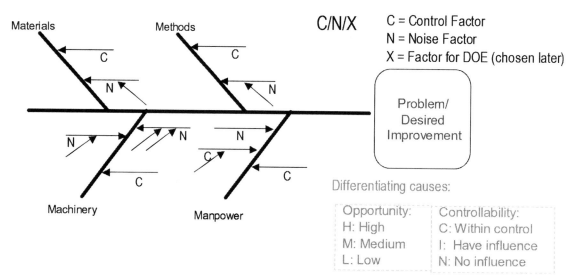

Fig. 8 Fishbone with weighting categories.

assessment can be done either categorically or numerically. Certainly, more or different criteria can be used for this assessment, such as those used in FMEA (Failure Mode and Effect Analysis): severity and frequency, etc. But opportunity and controllability are among the ones having the most leverage. This practice can help in clarifying and visualizing the focus of the next step in problem solving. Causes with high opportunity and within the span of control get the highest priority. An additional value-added practice is to highlight high priority items in red or circle them.

The fishbone diagram can be linked to the affinity diagram. The affinity diagram is used for open-minded brainstorming using post-it notes to capture ideas, one per note, then grouping the free-flowing ideas into categories by physically moving around and reorganizing the post-its. While the fishbone is more rigidly structured, usually having recommended categories to go by (as shown in Fig. 9), the affinity diagram is less structured, more free-flowing, not constrained by pre-set categories, and is a better format to use during the

brainstorming stage. Fundamentally, the two diagrams are the same. The biggest advantage of the affinity diagram is the flexibility to regroup ideas to create better, more relevant categories. When no categories are prescribed or pre-selected, sometimes people create an affinity diagram first, and then turn it into a fishbone diagram.

RCT

RCT is a tree-structured diagram that begins with UDEs and drills down to root causes. In a way, RCT is a combination of the fishbone diagram and the 5-Why's, which facilitates both broad and deep analysis. The way they are combined also allows studying the interactions among causes.

RCT is the most sophisticated and complex method of cause–effect analysis. Similar tools with mutations include FTA, event tree analysis, current/future reality tree, etc. RCT can be presented in a formal or less formal format. Fig. 10 shows a formal tree structure, a

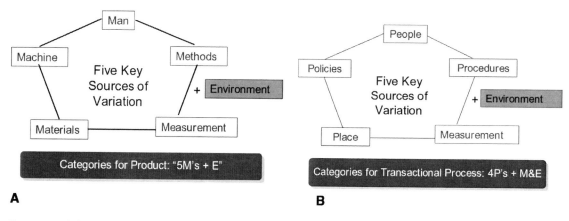

A   **B**

Fig. 9 Recommended cause categories for fishbone.

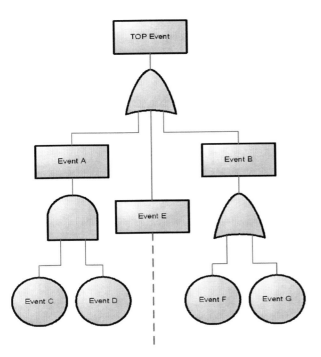

Fig. 10 RCA example.

fault tree. In this case, formal notations (called gates) are used to show the relationships. But this is not always needed. When the relationship is simple, like an "or" relationship, for example, no gate is necessary.

The biggest advantage of this tool is that it can study and present the interrelationships among causes. The most common relationship is the "or" relationship, meaning either cause A or B alone can lead to effect C. Sometimes the relationship is an "and," meaning causes A and B together are needed to produce effect C. Other relationships may occur as well, although they are hardly used. For example, one cause A may have multiple standalone effects, B and/or C. Sometimes, multiple causes need to occur in sequence to generate an effect. Sometimes the "or" relationship is exclusive. Sometimes some causes are conditional. All of the relationships, although many are not commonly used, can be captured as shown in Table 1. The RCT format provides sufficient flexibility to allow people to study and present all of these types of relationships.

To make the tree focused and concise, it is advisable to focus on UDEs for each event/cause. The key points are:

- UDEs are negative on their own merit
- No further explanation is needed on why
- Effects are negative at face value

One point of confusion for beginners is deciding how to initiate the tree. While officially it is recommended to start from the top UDE and add branches along the

Table 1 Formal notation for various relationships

	AND Gate If all input events occur, the output event will occur		**Priority AND Gate** Output event occurs if all events occur in the right order from left to right
	OR Gate If any input event occurs, the output event will occur		**Exclusive OR Gate** Output event occurs if one, but not both of the two input events occurs
	Event Any higher level event that is a result of lower level events		**Inhibit Gate** Input produces output when conditional event occurs
	Basic Event The lowest level event. The limiting resolution in our analysis.		**Conditional Event** Used with inhibit gate

Resources— Six Sigma

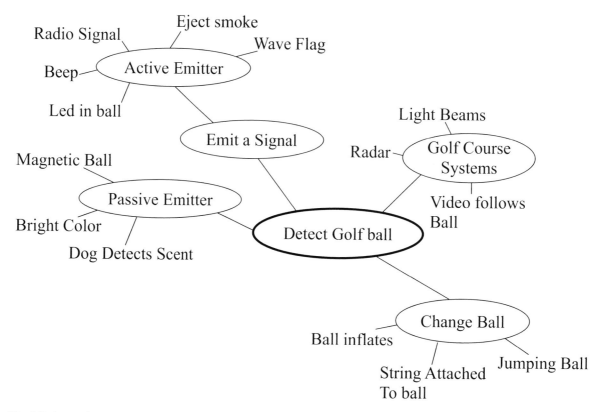

Fig. 11 Mind mapping example.

way, there are actually multiple approaches for doing this.

1. Top-down approaches
   - Complete fishbone first. If further analysis is needed, turn the bone structure 90 degrees counterclockwise to form the initial tree, study the (and, or) relationship among the existing causes, and then expand from there.
   - Perform mind mapping to generate ideas, study relationships among items, consolidate items, and rearrange them in tree structure. Fig. 11 shows an example mind map. It is equivalent to a free-flow RCT, without showing the relationships.
   - Perform 5-Whys on each of the first layer causes; repeat "horizontally" to exhaust all possible first layer causes and form multiple chains in parallel; study the relationship across the chains and consolidate when needed; repeat the same process at each layer.
2. Bottom-up approach
   - Complete affinity diagram to generate and organize ideas. Connect and consolidate groups into tree structure.

One limitation with top-down approaches is that when the tree is directly drawn on paper, it is difficult and inefficient to make changes, especially when

rearranging relationships. It is strongly recommended to use post-it notes to capture events/causes to avoid this problem. Alternatively, a bottom-up approach has some advantages. It allows generating and capturing thoughts without restriction prior to putting them in order.

Once again, the decision of when and where to stop drilling down is a common concern when using this tool. The sphere of influence criterion can help assess ROI. The point where a cause crosses a control boundary (i.e., the sphere of influence or span of control) is generally a good place to stop.

In the spirit of continuous improvement, it is acceptable to customize tools to incorporate more useful information that may help analysis. Besides generating the traditional cause–effect relationships, another thing that can be done is to differentiate and group the causes through the previously described weighting system and color coding. An example is shown in Fig. 12. With this type of notation, readers can quickly and easily identify in the diagram the key causes to be focused on in the next step. Those highlighted with the letters "H" and "C" and colored in red are the ones that should be further explored first. They are highlighted by circling them as well. Most applications in practice miss this type of value-added assessment and information.

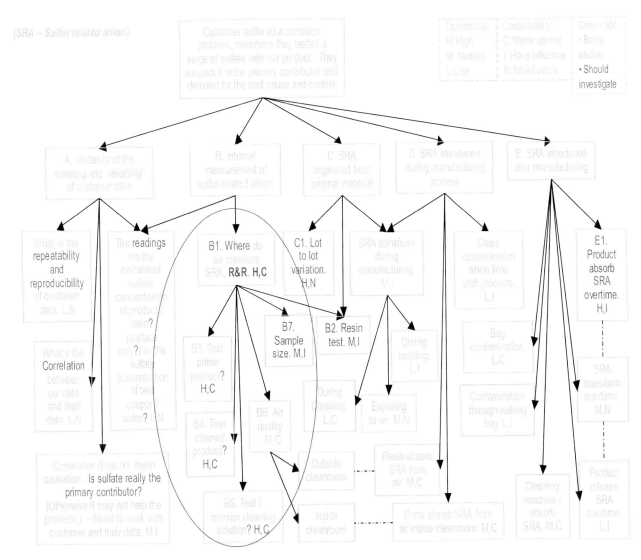

Fig. 12 Example of RCT with weighting categories.

Table 2 Example of cause–effect matrix

Rating of Importance to Customer	10	6	9	8		
	1	2	3	4		
PROCESS INPUTS	Efficiency	Commonality	Yield (accuracy)	Change Implementation	TOTAL	%
1 Customer Input	8	6	8	8	252	11.36%
2 Equipment Specs	8	5	10	8	264	11.90%
3 Bill of Materials	7	5	10	5	230	10.37%
4 # of Revisions	8	6	10	8	270	12.17%
5 Label Documentation	8	2	8	9	236	10.64%
6 Drawings	5	3	2	2	102	4.60%
7 Pre Meeting	5	5	2	2	114	5.14%
8 Ownership	8	10	8	8	276	12.44%
9 Approval Cycles	8	8	5	8	237	10.69%
10 Delays	8	8	5	8	237	10.69%
					2218	

Table 3 Example of cause–effect matrix with objective scores

Weight	0.1	0.5	1	3	5	0.138	1	-2	1	-2			
Material	# of Adjustment Entry/Total	Added Quantity/Total	Subtracted Quantity/Total	Added $/Total	Subtracted $/Total	Overall	Added Quantity/Consumption	Subtracted Quantity/Consumption	Added $/Consumption	Subtracted $/Consumption	Rank Without Consumption Info	Rank by Subtracted $	Overall Rank
Input Variables - Materials													
830R25	**0.001**	**0.000**	**0.001**	**0.000**	**0.027**	**0.138**		**-2.840**		**-2.840**	**11**	**4**	**1**
225	0.001	0.000	0.036	0.000	0.013	0.102	0.028	-2.807	0.028	-2.807	18	17	2
7500-0585-03	0.007	0.020	0.037	0.003	0.004	0.076	0.358	-0.317	0.357	-0.316	28	51	3
01-001638	0.004	0.000	0.003	0.042	0.184	1.050	0.011	-0.036	0.011	-0.036	1	1	4
01-006154	0.005	0.004	0.010	0.008	0.014	0.108	0.183	-0.244	0.157	-0.209	15	15	5
4002-5973-02	0.002	0.002	0.006	0.004	0.012	0.081	0.102	-0.202	0.102	-0.202	24	20	6
01-004488	0.003	0.001	0.005	0.009	0.061	0.337	0.027	-0.134	0.027	-0.134	2	2	7
8100-0100-01	0.012	0.009	0.000	0.067	0.000	0.206	0.564		0.564		7	403	8
200	0.003	0.009	0.034	0.005	0.013	0.117	0.071	-0.135	0.071	-0.135	13	18	9
7500-0585-07	0.003	0.024	0.017	0.008	0.004	0.071	0.258	-0.092	0.258	-0.092	30	52	10
1032-047	0.018	0.052	0.000	0.014	0.000	0.069	0.570		0.569		32	403	11
PKG-782	0.017	0.131	0.000	0.009	0.000	0.096	0.530		0.530		20	403	12
01-009871	0.002	0.002	0.005	0.018	0.030	0.212	0.072	-0.083	0.071	-0.084	6	3	13
01-009644-17C0	0.001	0.000	0.001	0.006	0.017	0.103	0.047	-0.107	0.046	-0.103	17	11	14
9700-7036-01	0.003	0.004	0.002	0.049	0.018	0.241	0.141	-0.037	0.141	-0.037	4	8	15
01-001651	0.003	0.003	0.005	0.015	0.020	0.152	0.073	-0.070	0.073	-0.070	9	7	16
160	0.001	0.000	0.001	0.000	0.016	0.079		-0.095		-0.094	25	13	17
01-018514	0.016	0.034	0.000	0.073	0.000	0.238	0.203		0.203		5	403	18
01-021524	0.001	0.001	0.003	0.008	0.016	0.109	0.062	-0.069	0.047	-0.071	14	12	19
01-009897	0.003	0.002	0.008	0.003	0.011	0.076	0.029	-0.076	0.029	-0.077	27	21	20
01-021554	0.001	0.000	0.002	0.001	0.012	0.069	0.013	-0.073	0.014	-0.087	31	19	21

Cause and Effect Matrix (X–Y Matrix)

X–Y matrix is primarily used to quantify and prioritize the impacts of a group of causes (input variables, X's) on a group of effects (output variables, Y's) through numerical ranking. This tool was originally intended to handle multiple effects. Because of this, the X–Y matrix is a tool that can be used to analyze and evaluate the relationships in a cause–effect network.

As shown in Table 2, a typical X–Y matrix lists input variables (X, causes) to the left and output variables (Y, effects) at the top. It contains two sets of numerical evaluations: the impact of individual X's on individual Y's in the middle part of the matrix and the weight or importance of individual Y's on the top part of the matrix. The final score, shown in the "total" column, is the weighted summation ("sumproduct" function in Excel) of he individual impact multiplied by weight for each X. It represents the impact of an individual X on all Y's overall.

Most of the time the impact scores are subjective, but they may, in some cases, be objective as well. Table 3 shows a unique example of objective scores, where impacts are the % contribution of each of the X's (materials) to specific Y's ($, quantities, or # of entries). They are all based on actual values.

Some people like to use the X–Y matrix to formally prioritize the causes generated by the fishbone, as a separate step. Unfortunately, even when people perform this additional step, they do not necessarily connect the output explicitly to ROI. Also, using the matrix for a single criterion (i.e., single Y) evaluation defeats the original intent of the matrix structure.

X–Y matrix represents one of three major scoring schemas existing for multivariate-multi-response scenarios, typically in matrix format. The other two are the schema used for FMEA and the original Pugh matrix. The weighted summation schema is widely used in many forms with mutations. For example, the core of quality function deployment, also called house of quality (HOQ), is built around the X–Y matrix. Just the layout is transposed, outputs listed to the left and inputs listed on the top.

Tools Specifically Good For Trouble Shooting

As mentioned earlier, there are strong connections as well as differences between RCA and troubleshooting. They both rely on cause–effect relationships to find solutions. The difference is that RCA is more useful for the pursuit of long-term gains, while troubleshooting is more useful for quick, short-term solutions. Troubleshooting usually focuses on what is wrong (specifically where or how), while RCA usually focus on why it is wrong. To perform RCA when the need is troubleshooting dilutes both efficiency and effectiveness, which can bring frustration to the pursuit of a practical solution. While all of the discussions on identifying root causes

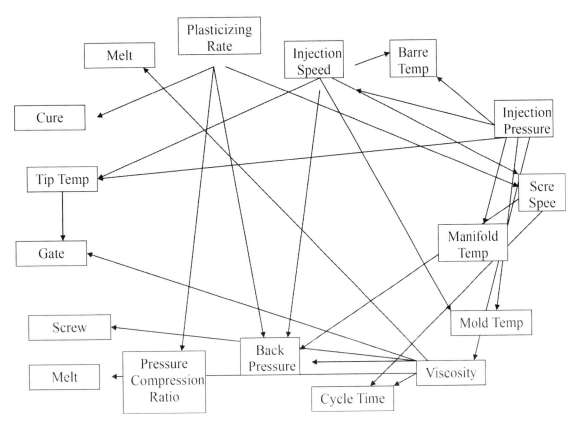

Fig. 13 Example of relationship diagram.

remain valid here, it is important to remember that the ROI for troubleshooting is short-term oriented.

There are some unique techniques that are especially good for troubleshooting. Three tools are typically handy as examples:

- Is/is not comparative analysis
- Relationship diagram
- FTA

Is/is not comparative analysis has already been discussed indepth. The important point is that the purpose of this analysis is not to go deep. It is well-suited to the pursuit of short-term, quick-fix solutions.

Fig. 13 shows an example of a relationship diagram. In this case, the effects of molding factors upon each other are shown. This tool graphically shows the interconnections and interactions between all related parties. With the arrows shown, one can trace back to the origination side and forward to the receiving side. The party that has more arrows going out is likely to be at the upstream origination side; the ones having more arrows going in are more likely to be at the downstream receiving side. The tool was originally used by law enforcement to investigate crimes. Because it is quite effective in zooming in on suspects, it was adopted for other uses, typically investigation-related.

FTA and RCT analysis are performed similarly, but they have different goals. FTA aims at troubleshooting to determine what, where, and how to find short-term solutions; RCT aims at why, to find long-term solutions. With these different goals, the outcomes may be quite different. A typical FTA for troubleshooting purposes may focus on the decomposition or breakdown of the product or object only, from assembly to sub-assembly, to components. The idea is that if we can verify a certain subset (e.g., sub-assembly) works well, we can eliminate this area and focus on other areas for root causes. In a way, it is doing segregation by following the product structure.

CONCLUSION

Most people have not thought much about the deeper meaning of "root cause" and therefore are not very clear on when and where to stop searching for root causes. Events in the universe form an infinite chain of causation, where no absolute root cause exists until you reach "God." There is no true absolute root cause per se. So-called root causes are what people subjectively choose to serve in the role of origination. The task to find the root cause is really the task to decide when and where to terminate the chain of causation. The key resides in the business mindset, ROI. There are three keys that can help us land on appropriate root causes with high ROI,

the leverage point, the Pareto principle, and the sphere of influence.

Here is a good RCA framework and problem-solving mentality.

1. Identify as many potential factors/causes to the problem as possible. In many cases, this process is based on experience or expert opinions. A structured approach with a big picture view will help avoid omissions.
2. Establish differentiation among the causes based on ROI. A quick easy way is to assess opportunity and controllability. The purpose of the first two steps is to establish hypotheses.
3. Seek objective data evidence to verify the hypotheses. If no existing data is available, perform experiment (s) (DOE) to generate new data.

There are five popular tools that can meet the full spectrum of requirements for cause–effect analysis. From simple to complex, they are as follows:

- Is/is not comparative analysis.
- 5-Why's—Good for digging deep, yet with narrow focus.
- Fishbone Diagram (Cause–Effect Diagram)—Good for investigating broad, yet not too deep, causes for a single effect.
- RCT—A diagram that begins with UDEs and works back to root causes and core problems. It is a combination of the Fishbone Diagram and the 5-Why's and allows studying the interactions among causes.
- Cause and Effect Matrix (X–Y Matrix)—Used to quantify and prioritize the impacts of a group of causes (X's) on a group of effects (Y's) through a numerical ranking. It was originally designed to handle multiple effects.

There are strong connections as well as differences between RCA and troubleshooting. They both rely on cause–effect relationships to find solutions. The difference is that RCA is more useful for the pursuit of long-term gains (focusing on why), while troubleshooting is more useful for finding quick turnaround, short-term solutions (focusing on what, where, and how). The following are some unique techniques that are especially good for troubleshooting.

- Is/is not comparative analysis
- Relationship diagram
- FTA

ACKNOWLEDGMENT

The author likes to thank Dr. David Hurd for providing feedback and polishing the language.

REFERENCES

1. Jing, G. Digging For The root cause. Six Sigma Forum Mag. **2008**, *5*, 19–24.

2. Jing, G. Flip the switch—Root cause analysis can shine the spotlight on the origin of a problem. Qual. Progr. **2008**, *10*, 50–55.

3. Jing, G. Understand the true meaning of root cause. *IQPC Webcast*, August, **2010**. http://www.sixsigmaiq. com/video.cfm?id = 917 (accessed February 2013).

4. Juran, J.M. *Juran's Quality Control Handbook*, 4th Ed.; McGraw-Hill: 1988.

5. McCarty, T.; Lorraine, D.; Michael, B.; Praveen, G. *Six Sigma Black Belt Handbook*; McGraw-Hill Professional: New York, NY, 2004; p. 16.

6. Spirkin, A. *Dialectical Materialism*; Progress Publishers: Moscow, 1983.

7. Gano, D.L. *Apollo Root Cause Analysis—A New Way Of Thinking*; Apollonian Publications: Kennewick, WA, 1990.

8. Wessel, D. An ounce of prevention. Qual. Progr. **1998**, *12*.

9. Vachon, D. Snow blames water pollution for cholera epidemic. Old News **2005**, *16* (8), 8–10.

10. Summers, J. *Soho—A History of London's Most Colourful Neighborhood*; Bloomsbury Pub. Ltd.: London, 1989; 113–117.

Search Engines

Randolph Hock
Online Strategies, Vienna, Virginia, U.S.A.

Abstract

This entry provides an overview of Web search engines, looking at the definition, components, leading engines, searching capabilities, and types of engines. It examines the components that make up a search engine and briefly discusses the process involved in identifying content for the engines' databases and the indexing of that content. Typical search options are reviewed and the major Web search engines are identified and described. Also identified and described are various specialty search engines, such as those for special content such as video and images, and engines that take significantly different approaches to the search problem, such as visualization engines and metasearch engines.

INTRODUCTION

Web search engines, for the public at large, have come to be perhaps the most frequently used computer services for locating information. To some degree the same is true for many researchers, information professionals, and others. To most effectively and efficiently utilize these services, some understanding of the structure, make-up, content, features, and variety and breadth of these services is essential. This entry addresses those various aspects including just what is meant by "search engines," the components of a search engine, and typical search features, and it provides a profile of the major general Web search engines and a look at specialty search engines, visualization engines, and metasearch engines.

WHAT IS MEANT BY "SEARCH ENGINES?"

The term "search engines" can have a variety of meanings, in the broadest sense referring to any computer program that facilitates the searching of a database. In the context of library and information science, however, the term has come to primarily refer to "Web search engines," that is, those services on the Web that allow searching of a large database of Web pages and other Web content by word, phrase, and other criteria. (For this discussion, hereafter, "search engines" will be taken to refer to "Web search engines.") A certain level of ambiguity becomes apparent, however, when it is realized that what is often referred to as a "search engine" is often a reference to the overall service that is provided, beyond just a search of Web sites. ("Google" is thought of not as just the searching part of the Google enterprise, but the many added features and content as well.) It is often impossible and unproductive to discuss the narrower "searching" part without discussing the broader range of services. That ambiguity in terminology is a result and artifact of the history of search engines but recognition of the ambiguity is necessary for an understanding of the current nature of such services.

Search engines vary in a number of ways and most could be considered to fall into one of the following four categories: General Web Search Engines (which have the purpose of searching a large portion of all pages that exist on the Web), Specialty Search Engines (which focus on searching a specific kind of document, file type, or source from a particular subject or geographic region), Visualization Search Engines (which furnish diagrams, images, or other "visuals" to show relationships among the items in a particular set of retrieved items), and Metasearch Engines (which gather together the search results on a specific topic from multiple search engines).

COMPONENTS OF A SEARCH ENGINE

General Web search engines and specialty search engines can be considered to have four major components that correspond to the steps required to create the service: 1) the identification and gathering of the material (Web pages, etc.) to be included in the engine's database; 2) an indexing program and the corresponding generated indexes; 3) the searching and ranking algorithms; and 4) the user interface.

Identifying Material to Be Included

Search engines identify those Web pages (and other items) to be included in the service's database by two means: "crawling" and "submissions" of pages. The first, "crawling" consists of having programs ("crawlers"

Encyclopedia of Information Systems and Technology, DOI: 10.1081/E-EIST-120043725

or "spiders") that on an ongoing basis scan the Internet to identify new sites or sites that have changed, gather information from those sites, and feed that information to the search engine's indexing mechanism. The crawlers start by examining pages that the service already knows about and looking there for "new" links (links that the service does not already know about). When such links are identified, the pages to which the links led are likewise examined for "new" links, and so on. More popular Web sites (such as those that have lots of links to them) may be crawled more thoroughly and more frequently than less popular sites.

The second way search engines identify new items to be added to the database is by having Web site owners (or others) "submit" sites or pages. Most engines provide a form by which this can be done. Search services maintain their own policies as to whether submitted (or for that matter, pages identified by crawling) will indeed be added to the database, particularly looking to exclude unacceptable content (spam, sexually explicit material, etc.)

Search Engine's Index and Indexing Program

After a new or changed page is identified by the search engine's crawler, the page will typically be indexed under virtually every word on the page (up to some usually undisclosed limit). In addition to text words, other parts or characteristics of the page may also be indexed, including the URL (Uniform Resource Locator, the "Web address"), parts of the URL, links, metadata found in the "head" of the document, the URLs of links on the page, image filenames, words in linked text, etc. By identifying and indexing these pieces of data (pieces or characteristics of the Web page or other type of indexed document, such as an Excel file), they become searchable "fields," thereby allowing users to use those fields to increase the quality of their search. The search system may also "derive" additional fields, such as language, by analysis of the document.

The Search Engine's Retrieval and Ranking Algorithms

By narrow definition, the actual search "engine" is the search service's retrieval program, that is, the program that identifies (retrieves) those pages in the database that match the criteria indicated by a user's query. That identification function is necessarily supplemented by another important and more challenging program that is used to determine the order in which the retrieved records should be displayed, based on measures that try to identify which retrieved records (pages, etc.) are likely to have the highest relevance in respect to the user's query.

This "relevance-ranking" algorithm usually takes many factors into account.

Exactly what factors go into the relevance ranking process varies, but they include: use of keywords in titles, text, headings, etc.; popularity of the sites (how many and which sites link to the site); words used in anchors (clickable text); internal links (how many and what kind of links within the larger site point to the page); quality of links leading out to other pages (whether they point to high quality pages) and so on.[1]

The success or the failure of the relevance ranking algorithm is critical to the user's perception of the search engine, the user's continued use of that system, and the commercial success of the engine.

The Interface Presented to the User for Gathering Queries

This interface that the user typically sees includes the home page of the search service and other pages (such as an advanced search page) that present search options to the users and accept the users' search queries, as well as the search results page. The search service can choose to have their page focus almost exclusively on "search" (as with Google) or be a more general, wide-reaching "portal" page, providing much more than just searching capabilities. (The "portal" dilemma for search services will be discussed in more detail later.)

Regardless of what other services and information are provided on the service's homepage, the "searching" part usually consists of a single search box plus links to an advanced search page and to other searchable databases that are made available by the service (images, video, news, etc.). Usually there are also links to "help" screens, etc. While the simplicity of a single search box appeals to the less experienced user, it also usually provides substantial, but not obvious, capabilities for extensive searching sophistication, such as the potential for using Boolean logic and "prefixes" (e.g., "title:") to perform field searching and other functions. The advanced search page much more explicitly lays out the possibilities to the user, providing a menu-based approach to utilization of features.

The Portal Dilemma

From the early days of search engines, search engine providers have wrestled with the decision as to whether to make their home page one that focuses almost exclusively on "search" or one that provides a variety of added services such as news, weather, etc., the latter approach often referred to as a "portal." From its beginning, before it was even a "search engine" and was just a directory, Yahoo! preferred the portal approach. Alta-Vista, a leading search engine in the 1990s, went back and forth between the two extremes, a situation which may have contributed to its demise. Google was, from the beginning, almost purely a "search engine" and the simplicity of its interface was undoubtedly one factor in its rapid rise in popularity. Search services tend to "cover their bets" however, by providing alternatives. Yahoo! provides a Google-like option at search.yahoo. com and Google provides a personalizable Yahoo-style page with its iGoogle portal page.

Searching Options Typically Provided

All leading search engines provide a range of user accessible options that permit the user to modify their search queries in ways that can improve both the precision and the recall of their search results. Which specific options are provided varies from engine to engine, but there are several that are fairly typical (and some that are unique to a particular engine). The most typical options include Boolean operations, phrase searching, language specification, and specifying that only those pages are retrieved for which the search term appears in a particular part (field) of the record such as the title, URL, or links. Since engines now cover other document types beyond just pages written in Hyper-Text Markup Language (HTML), with several engines, users can also narrow their search to a specific file format (Web pages, Adobe Acrobat files, Excel files, etc.). Most engines also provide an option to filter "adult content" material.

Boolean logic

In the context of Web searching, "Boolean logic" refers to the process of identifying those items found in the database that contain a particular combination of search terms. It is used to indicate that a particular group of terms must all be present (the Boolean "AND"), that any of a particular group of terms is acceptable (the Boolean "OR"), or that if a particular term is present, the item is rejected (the Boolean "NOT"). (See the entry, Boolean Algebras [ELIS Classic], p. 660.)

Engines usually provide two different ways to qualify a query with Boolean operations: 1) the option of applying a syntax directly to what is entered in the search box and 2) menu options on an advanced search page. Using the menus can be thought of as "simplified Boolean" and, depending upon the structure of the advanced search page, may or may not provide the precision achievable by the use of syntax in the main search box. (For example, the ability to apply "OR"s to more than one of the concepts included in the query may be done in the main search box but may not be allowed for on the advanced search page.)

The exact syntax used varies with the search engine. All major engines currently automatically apply an "AND" between your terms, so when the following is entered:

prague economics tourism

what will be retrieved is what more traditionally would have been expressed as: prague AND economics AND tourism.

Very precise search requirements can be expressed using combinations of the operators along with parentheses to indicate the order of operations. For example:

(grain OR corn OR wheat) (production OR harvest) Oklahoma 1997

At various times, search engines have allowed the use of symbols (+, &, −, etc.) instead of words (AND, OR, NOT) and indeed, for the "NOT" most search engines currently suggest the use of a minus sign in front of the term. Some search engines require the use of parentheses around "nested" (OR'ed) terms, some do not.

For details on Boolean syntax for any search engine, the help pages for that engine should be consulted. There are also Web sites, such as Search Engine Showdown from Greg Notess (http://www.searchengineshowdown.com) that summarize the syntax (and other features) for all major engines.

The alternative to using syntax to apply Boolean is the use of menus on an advanced search page. There, for example, you may find a pull-down menu, where, if you choose the "all the words" option, you are requesting the Boolean AND. If you choose the "any of the words" option from such a menu, you are specifying an OR. There is usually also a box for excluding terms (NOT).

Phrase searching

Phrase searching is an option that is available in virtually every search engine, and almost always uses the same syntax, the use of quotation marks around the phrase. For example, searching on "Red River" (with the quotation marks) will assure that you get only those pages that contain the word "red" immediately in front of the word "river." Of all search engine techniques, this is widely regarded as one of the most useful and easiest for achieving higher precision in a Web search. It is also useful for such things as identifying quotations and identifying plagiarism.

Title searching

Title searching, that is, limiting your retrieval to only those items (pages) that have a particular term or combination of terms in their title, is one example of "field searching," as referred to earlier. It is also another example of a technique that can yield very high precision in a search. Most search engines use the "intitle:" prefix and/or the "allintitle:" prefix for the syntax for title searching ("allintitle:" allows specifying that more than one term be included in the title, not necessarily in any particular order).

URL, site, and domain searching

Search engines typically index Web pages (and other document types) by both the overall URL and by the segments of the URL. This facilitates the finding of any document that comes from a particular domain or part of a domain (also a specific site or part of a site). Doing a search in which results are limited to a specific site allows one, in effect, to perform a search of that site. Even for sites that have a "site search" box on their home page, more complete results can often be found by using this technique than by using the site's own search feature. "inurl:," "allinurl:," and "site:" are the prefixes commonly used.

The term, "Domain searching" is sometimes used to refer to the above process and the use of the term, "Domain," points out that this approach can be used to limit retrieval to sites having a particular top-level domain, such as: gov, edu, uk, ca, or fr. This could be used, for example, to identify only Canadian sites that mention tariffs, or to only get educational sites that mention biodiversity.

Link searching

There are two varieties of "link" searching. In the more common variety, one can search for all pages that have a hypertext link to a particular URL, and in the other variety, one can search for words contained in the linked text on the page. In the former, you can check, for example, which Web pages have linked to your organization's URL. In the second variety, you can see which Web pages have the name of your organization as linked text. Either variety can be very informative in terms of who is interested in either your organization or your Web site. Also, if you are looking for information on an organization, it can sometimes be useful to know who is linking to that organization's site.

This searching option is available in some search engines on their advanced page and/or on the main page with the use of prefixes. (usually "link:"). Engines may allow you to find links to an overall site, or to a specific page within a site.

Language searching

Although all of the major engines allow limiting retrieval to pages written in a given language, they differ in terms of which languages can be specified. The 40 or so most common languages are specifiable in most of the major engines. Though some engines provide a pre-fix option for searching for languages, more typically one would go to the engine's advanced search page to narrow to a language.

Date searching

Searching by the date of Web pages is an obviously desirable option, and most major engines provide such an option. Unfortunately, because of lack of clear or reliable information on a page regarding when the page itself was initially created, the date on which the content of the page was created, or even when the content on the page was significantly modified, it is often impossible for a search engine to assign a truly "reliable" date to a Web page. As a "workaround," engines may take the date when the page was last modified or may assign a date based on when the page was last crawled by the engine. For searching Web pages, users should be aware of this approximation and its effect on precision when using the date searching option that is offered by most search engines (usually on their advanced search page). (On the other hand, for some of the other databases an engine may provide, such as news, the date searching may be very precise.)

Searching by file type

For most of the 1990s, most search engines only indexed and allowed searching of regular HTML pages. In the crawling process (or for submitted pages) when the engine's indexing program encountered a link that led to another type of document, such as an Adobe Acrobat (pdf), or Excel (xls) file, the link was ignored. Starting with Adobe Acrobat files, other file types were fairly rapidly added to the corpus of "indexable" pages. This not only increased the breadth of resources available to the searcher, but also provided the capability for the searcher to limit retrieval by type of file. Limiting to Adobe Acrobat files provides documents more suited to printing. Narrowing to PowerPoint files can provide convenient summaries of a topic. Limiting to Excel files can often enable a greater focus on statistics.

Search Results Pages

As well as providing enhanced searching capabilities, search engines also enhance the content of results pages, beyond presenting just a listing of the Web page results that match the user's query. At the same time they search their Web database, they may automatically search the other databases they have, such as news, images, and video, and on search pages may automatically provide links to the matching items from those additional databases. Some search engines may search additional "reference" resources, such as dictionaries, encyclopedias, maps, etc., and likewise display matching content from those sources.

Resources— Six Sigma

As well as displaying such supplemental content on results pages, search engines may also provide suggestions for ways in which the user might further qualify search criteria. This is done by suggesting related, narrower, or broader topics. Some engines also provide links to narrow the search by file type, language, or type of site (weblog, forum, commercial, or noncommercial, etc.)

Specific options may also be offered on results pages for each retrieved item. Some engines keep a copy of each page they have indexed and provide a link to that "cached" page. This is particularly useful if, in the time since the page was indexed, the page was removed, is not available because of a server problem, or has changed in a way such that the term the user searched for is no longer on the page.

With records for pages that are not in the language of the search engine interface, there may be an option to translate the record (for example, if the user is using an English language version of Google and a page is in French or if the user is using the French version and the page is in English). Click on the "translate" link to receive a machine translation of the page. As with other machine translations, what you get may not be a "good" translation, but it may be an "adequate" translation, adequate in that it will give you a good idea of what the page is talking about. Also keep in mind that only "words" are translated. The translation program cannot translate words you see on a page that are actually "images" rather than "text."

One feature offered on search results pages by all of the major engines is a spell-checker. If you misspelled a word, or the search engine thinks you might have, it graciously asks something like "Did you mean?" and gives you a likely alternative. If it was indeed a mistake, just click on the suggested alternative to correct the problem.

Search results pages will usually display links labeled as "Sponsor Results," "Sponsored Links," etc.—These are "ads" for Web sites and are there because the Web site has paid to appear on the search engine's results pages. Major engines keep these sponsor sites clearly identifiable by, for example, putting them in a blue background, or to the side of the page. Searchers should remain aware that it is the presence of these ads that makes the existence of search engines possible.

The Search Engine Leaders—Post-2000

Popularity of various search engines can change fairly quickly. In the early and mid-1990s, a list of the most popular engines included, among others, AltaVista, Hotbot. Excite, InfoSeek, and Lycos (Yahoo! was still primarily a directory, and though it had a search engine function, for that function it made use of, at various times, AltaVista's and Google's databases.)

By the latter part of the 2000s the following were the leaders: Google, Yahoo!, MSN/Windows/Live Search, AOL, and Ask. (in that order). Those five search engines represented 94 percent of all (U.S.) searches.[2] (Brief profiles of the engines just mentioned are given below.)

Google

Google, which emerged as a company in 1998, grew very rapidly, its growth attributed largely to the simplicity of its interface, the lack of advertisements on the home page, and the quality of its relevance ranking (that fact significantly affected by Google's patented Page Rank program).[3] Google rather quickly went beyond "search" and began providing additional features and content, some of the enhancements emerging from within the Google organization and some (such as its e-mail service, Gmail) being patterned after such services already offered by its competitors. By the late 2000s, Google claimed more of the search market than all of its competitors combined and was offering a broad range of search services and a number of services not directly related to search.

For its Web search offerings, Google provides all of the typical search options (Boolean, field searching, etc.) plus some unique searching features, the latter including numeric range searching (e.g., China history 1850 to1890), and synonym searching (e.g., ~cars). As well as the searching of Web pages, Google also offers searches of databases of images, maps, news, products, video, groups, books (Google Book Search), journal articles (Google Scholar), and blogs. Some of these search offerings are very similar to corresponding services offered by Google's competitors, but some, such as "Google Book Search," were original and regarded by many as "ground-breaking" and even in some cases, controversial. (Google Books Search is a major book digitalization project, in cooperation with major publishers and libraries.) The search features provided with each of these databases is typically tailored to the specific nature of that kind of content.

Many of Google's Web search features are features that were already found on other search engines, but for which Google provided significant enhancements. One example is Google Language Tools. Many search engines have provided a translation option that allows retrieved items from a number of non-English languages to be translated, using programs such as SYSTRAN's Babel Fish. In 2007, Google enhanced its own translation feature by allowing the user not just to translate a specific result, but to input a search in the user's own language, then have Google automatically translate the search terms, perform the search, and then deliver results in both languages. Translations are done using Google's own statistical translation technology.

As it grew, Google rather rapidly redefined itself to be much more than a "search engine," adding services that went beyond "search" and even beyond usual Web site content. Some services had a direct relationship to "search," such as Google News Alerts, Google's financial portal ("Google Finance"), the Google Toolbar for Web browsers, a desktop search tool for searching the content of one's own computer, and Google's own Web browser ("Chrome"). Some of the services Google began to offer included types of things that already existed as "portal" features in other search services. These offerings included a customizable portal page (iGoogle) with Google's own calendar and notebook and links to a variety of other content such as newsfeeds. Among other services are Gmail (a Web-based e-mail service), Google Earth (imagery and related geospatial content for the entire Earth, as well as the Moon and the sky) and Google Talk (an instant messaging service). One of the manifestations of "Web 2.0" is the availability of user-accessible software that is resident on the Web, rather than on the user's own computer. (The term, "Web 2.0," refers not to an actual "version" of the Web, but to the fact that the nature of the Web, by the middle of the first decade of the 20th century, had changed from being primarily a place to go to find information to being a place that was much more personal, interactive, and collaborative, with the Web as a "platform" where programs are provided, used, and shared.) Google has moved very much in the Web 2.0 direction, providing Picasa (a photo-sharing and editing service), SketchUp (a computer-aided design, CAD, program), Google Docs (a collaborative spreadsheet, word-processor, and presentations program), and Sites (for creating Web sites). Google also offers "mobile" services (including mobile search, maps, text messaging, Gmail, etc.), an enterprise version of Google's search engine, and a custom search engine that allows a user to have a search box (on their own Web site or as a page on Google) that delivers a search of only the user's own selection of Web sites.

Yahoo!

Yahoo! was among the earliest Web sites that had the purpose of leading users to specific content on the Web. In the beginning, Yahoo! was exclusively a "Web directory," a categorized list of selected Web sites. By 2000, however, it had begun a transformation to a portal site, having, in addition to the directory, over three dozen links to news, services, and other resources provided by Yahoo and its affiliates, including pages for shopping, auctions, phone numbers, a calendar, and more. From its earliest days, the Yahoo! homepage contained a search box, but results for that search came from a search of the directory, and later a search of Web databases from other search providers.

Yahoo!'s directory function became less and less central and in 2004 Yahoo! created its own database of Web pages. Though emphasis on "search" continued to increase and the emphasis on the directory declined significantly, Yahoo!'s main image continued to be that of a portal, with the emphasis on the wide range of other services provided by Yahoo! and its partners, including Yahoo!'s highly popular e-mail service and its sections on autos, finance, games, groups, health, job listings, maps, real estate, travel, and over 50 other content areas.

In the area of Web search, Yahoo! currently provides typical Web search features such as Boolean and field searching, though a continued absence of a link on its main page to its advanced search page, reinforces the impression of Yahoo!'s preference for a portal focus over search focus. It's personalized portal page, My Yahoo!, is judged by some to be the most popular portal on the Web.[4]

In addition to Web search, Yahoo! offers searching of the following databases: news, images, video, maps, local (businesses), shopping, audio, jobs, Creative Commons, people (phone numbers and addresses), and travel reservations search.

MSN/Live search

Microsoft has made several attempts since the mid-1990s to produce a Web search engine that is competitive with Google and Yahoo!. The attempts, made available primarily through Microsoft's MSN portal, have gone by a variety of names, including Microsoft Search, MSN Search, Windows Live, and, in 2008, Live Search (live.com). Search features have varied considerably and have at times been less robust than those of its competitors. Live Search presented some innovative features such as a design that allowed continuous scrolling through search results, but it, like some other features in the MSN search products, was short-lived. The 2008 version provided the typical Boolean and field searching options, plus some additional options such as "prefer:" by which the user can adjust the ranking weight for search terms, and "feed:" and "hasfeed;" which identify Web sites that contain RSS links on the user's chosen topic. In addition to the search for Web pages, Live Search also offers searches for images, video, news, maps, health information, local (businesses), products, and travel.

AOL

AOL Search is the search engine found on AOL's main portal page and is also available at search.aol.com. The search is provided in conjunction with Google and Web search results come from the Google database (but are typically fewer in number than when the search is done on Google itself). AOL Search also provides options for searching images (using Google), video ("Powered by TRUVEO"), news, shopping, jobs, maps, movies, music, personals, travel, and yellow pages.

Ask

Ask, which was formerly AskJeeves, underwent a number of significant changes as it changed from the "question and answer" format of the original AskJeeves. Ask created a substantial Web database with fairly typical search functionality, though missing some features such as an OR Boolean function. In 2008, the company underwent a reorganization which produced some doubts among those who watch search engines as to Ask's commitment to "search." As well as its Web search, with Ask you can also search databases of images, news, maps, businesses, shopping, TV listings, events, videos, recipes, and blogs. Results pages for Web searches automatically incorporate results from multiple databases and provide a "binoculars" icon for previewing results without leaving the results page.

Other general search engines

There are a number of other general Web search engines, including GigaBlast, Exalead, and others. Exalead (http://www.exalead.com/search), from France, incorporates a number of features unavailable in other current search engines, including truncation ("words starting with"), phonetic spelling, approximate spelling, and NEAR. These are important to note because they are reflective of a level of sophistication of search techniques a bit closer to those found in commercial search services such as Lexis/Nexis, Factiva, and DIALOG, but not found in Web search engines.

Specialty Search Engines

Over the years, a variety of search engines have appeared that could be classified as "specialty" search engines. Among these there have been attempts to create search engines that focus on a particular topic or geographic location. In most cases, an examination of these showed that what was provided was more of a "directory" of selected sites than a broad ranging crawler-based search of Web pages for the specific topic or locality. On the other hand, there have been many successful attempts to produce search engines that provide searching for a particular format or type of document, such as images, video, blogs, forums, etc.

News

Searching of news databases is available from all the general Web search engines. There are numerous other Web sites that specialize in searching news content. Each of these have varying degrees of searchability, and from the research perspective it is important to note that the coverage can vary significantly, especially in regard to the number of news sources included, the time span for the content of the database, and the languages covered. Among the better-known news search engines are: NewsNow, Silobreaker, NewsExplorer, RocketNews, Topix.net, World Press Review Online, and NewsTin.

Images

The most commonly encountered image search engines are those that are included as databases provided by the general Web search engines, including Google, Yahoo!, Live Search, AOL, and Ask. As well as subject searching, most of these engines allow for Boolean, and narrowing by size, coloration, site, and adult-content filtering. On Google's advanced image search page you can also narrow to news or photo content, or those that appear to include faces. Flickr (flicker.com), an image sharing Web site, has also gained extensive popularity as an image search engine. The extensive tagging of photos by Flickr users makes millions of images searchable. PicSearch provides an extensive collection of images from the Web and in addition to the above search criteria also allows narrowing to animated images. There are also image search engines such as Corbis, Fotosearch, and Stock. XCHNG which enable users (for a fee) to have use of photos from commercial photographers and photo archives.

Video

As with image searching, searching for video is available from major search engines, including Google, Yahoo!, Live Search, and AOL. Extensive searching of videos produced by individuals, as well as commercial video, is available from YouTube, the leading video-sharing site. Depending upon the search engine, options are provided for searching by Boolean, language, duration, domain/site/source, format, popularity, aspect ratio, and resolution, plus filtering for adult-content. Some video search engines specialize in video from TV, including news programs, interviews, etc. These include Blinkx (free) and TVEyes (fee-based). Both of these utilize voice-recognition technologies to create searchable transcripts for their video content.

Forums

Content found in forums (discussion groups, groups, newsgroups, etc.) can be utilized for a number of applications, ranging from hobbies to tracking terrorist activities, and there are search engines that specialize in finding this category of document. Among the search engines that provide such access to forums from multiple sources across the Web are BoardReader and OMGILI. (There are a number of other places where groups can be searched, such as Google, Yahoo!, Topica, Delphi Forums, but those sites focus on searching only the content that is hosted on their own Web sites.)

Other specialty search engines

There are still other categories of specialty search engines, including those for searching blogs and RSS feeds (examples: Technorati, IceRocket, Bloglines, and Google Blog Search), for searching podcasts (examples, Podcastdirectory.com, and Podcast.com), and for searching for information on people (examples, pipl Search, Infobel, Yahoo People Search, Intelius, and PeopleFinders).

Visualization Engines

Visualization search engines are Web sites (or programs) that provide a very different "look" (literally) at search results. Instead of the traditional linear, textual list of retrieved items, results are shown on a map that spatially shows conceptual connections. Most current visualization engines utilize not a database of their own, but borrow one from other engines (such as Google, or Yahoo!) or other sites such as Amazon.com. Visualization has been, and continues to be, an area of extensive research and there are several sites that demonstrate various visualization approaches. The type of conceptual and visual mapping done by these sites can be especially useful for quickly exploring the concept possibilities, directions, and terminology for a particular search. It presents a "connect the dots" approach, enabling understanding relationships among the concepts found in various search results—rather than just browsing lists of results. Among the leaders in this area are Kartoo, TouchGraph, and Grokker, and Quintura.

Metasearch Engines

The term "metasearch engine" (or "metasearch site") usually refers to Web sites that search multiple search engines in a single search. The degree of overlap (or lack thereof) between search engine results is something that professional searchers frequently consider and allow for as they search and searching more than one engine is a widely encouraged technique. Metasearch engines have been available since the 1990s and include sites such as Dogpile, Clusty, Ixquick, Mamma, Search.com, and many others. Each of these may provide additional benefits beyond just a compilation of results from more than one engine, for example, the "clustering"

(categorization) of retrieved results, a feature that may not be provided by the target engines themselves. However, users should be aware of several shortcomings that may be encountered with these tools: 1) Most of the current metasearch engines do not cover the largest major engines, particularly Google and Yahoo!, which tend to block queries from metasearch engines; 2) Metasearch engines typically only return the first 10–20 results from any of the "target" engines; 3) Metasearch engine results often discard useful and search-relevant information found on the actual search engine's results pages; 4) Metasearch sites, even if they do cover the largest engines, may be required by those engines to show paid listings first; and 5) Metasearch engines typically do not allow application of many of the search features available in the target engines themselves.

Metasearch engines should be distinguished from "comparison search" sites, such as Zuula.com and Twingine (twingine.no) which provide more of a side-by-side comparison of actual results from the target engines.

CONCLUSION

Web search engines have evolved significantly since they were first introduced in the early 1990s. The basic concept has remained the same, but the quality of results, the size of their databases, and the types of material that they include have increased dramatically. The total number of general Web search engines "in the race" has decreased and at present is dominated by one service, Google. Where the field of players has expanded is in the area of specialty search engines which focus on a specific type of Web "document." What has evolved even more dramatically is the "mission" of search services, which particularly in the case of Google, has gone far beyond "search." With advancing technologies, increasing interactiveness of the Web, and a more and more Internet-centered society, users can expect continued, fast-paced innovation.

REFERENCES

1. Sullivan, D. Ranking the SEO ranking factors. In *Search Engine Land*. Available at: searchengineland.com/ranking-the-seo-ranking-factors-10890.php (accessed April 2009).

2. *Nielsen//Netratings Announces August U.S. Search Share Rankings*. NetRatings, Inc., New York, NY (accessed September 2007). Available at: http://www.nielsen-netratings.com/pr/pr_070919.pdf.

3. Vise, D.; Malseed, M. In *The Google Story*; Bantam Dell: New York, NY, 2005; 37–40.

4. Web Trends: The Top Ten Most Popular Portals on the Web. February **2008**, About.com. Available at: http://

webtrends.about.com/od/webportals/a/topten_portals.htm (accessed April 2009).

BIBLIOGRAPHY

1. Search Engine History. Available at: http://www. searchenginehistory.com.

2. Search Engine Showdown. Available at: http://www. searchengineshowdown.com.
3. Vise, D.; Malseed, M. *The Google Story*; Bantam Dell: New York, NY, 2005.

Semantic Web: Applications

Kieron O'Hara
Wendy Hall
Intelligence, Agents, Multimedia Group, University of Southampton, Southampton, U.K.

Abstract

The "semantic web" is a vision of a web of linked data, allowing querying, integration, and sharing of data from distributed sources in heterogeneous formats, using ontologies to provide an associated and explicit semantic interpretation. This entry describes the series of layered formalisms and standards that underlie this vision, and chronicles their historical and ongoing development. A number of applications, scientific and otherwise, academic and commercial, are reviewed. The SW has often been a controversial enterprise, and some of the controversies are reviewed, and misconceptions defused.

INTRODUCTION

The semantic web (SW) is an extension, in progress, to the World Wide Web (WWW), designed to allow software processes, in particular artificial agents, as well as human readers, to acquire, share, and reason about information. Whereas the WWW consists largely of documents, which are generally created for human consumption, the SW will be a web of data, making them more amenable for computers to process.[1] The data will be processed by computer via semantic theories for interpreting the symbols (hence: *semantic* web). In any particular application, the semantic theory will connect terms within a distributed document set logically, and thereby aid interoperability.

For instance, people use a lot of data in daily interactions, viewing bank statements, or digital photographs, or using diaries or calendars. But this does not constitute a web of data, because the data are neither exported from the applications in which they are stored or were created, nor linked to other relevant data. In a genuine web of data, such data could be used seamlessly in a number of applications. For example, one could view one's photographs (which will contain a time stamp) in one's calendar, which would then act as a prompt to suggest what one was doing when they were taken. The data that one uses would be to some extent freed from the constraints of particular applications, and instead could be interlinked and reused creatively.

As another example, Web services can now be accessed and executed via the Web, but because the Web does not provide much information-processing support, services must be specified using semiformal languages and, as with information retrieval, humans need to be kept in the loop. Web services described using SW techniques should provide support for autonomous agents and automatic systems.[2]

The world of linked information is a very unstructured, "scruffy" environment. The amounts of information that systems need to deal with are very large indeed. Furthermore, systems must pull together information from distributed sources, where representation schemes can be expected to be highly heterogeneous, information quality variable, and trust in information's provenance hard to establish. SW technology needs to be based on standards that can operate in this heterogeneous information world.

The SW therefore requires two types of information standard to operate. First, it requires common formats for integrating information from these diverse sources. Second, it needs a language to express the mapping between the data and objects in the real world, in order to allow a seamless understanding of a distributed set of databases. Hence, for instance, we could signal that a database containing a column *zip code* and another database with a column labeled *ZC* were actually both referring to the same concept with their different labels, and by creating such a semantic link, we could then start to reason over both databases in an integrated fashion. Such semantic links are often obvious to humans, but not to computers. A key formalism here is the *ontology*, which defines the concepts and relationships that we use in particular applications. Ontologies are central to the SW vision, as providing the chief means by which the terms used in data are understood in the wider context.[1,3]

THE AIM OF THE SEMANTIC WEB

The aim of the SW is to shift the emphasis of reasoning from documents to data, for three reasons. First, it will facilitate data reuse, often in new and unexpected contexts. Second, it will help reduce the amount of

Encyclopedia of Information Systems and Technology, DOI: 10.1081/E-EIST-120043686

Resources–
Six Sigma

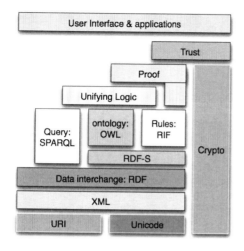

Fig. 1 The layered view of the semantic web.
Source: From Berners-Lee, Hall, et al.[6]

relatively expensive human information processing. Third, it will release the large quantity of information, not accessible as of now, that is stored in relational databases (RDBs) by making it directly machine-processable.[4]

This implies that RDB objects must be exported to the Web as first-class objects, which in practice entails mapping them onto a consistent system of resource identifiers—called Universal Resource Identifiers (URIs). The SW itself is a suite of languages and formalisms designed to enable the interrogation and manipulation of representations that make use of URIs.[1]

It is hoped that the SW will exhibit the same *network effects* that promoted the growth of the WWW. Network effects are positive feedback effects connected with *Metcalfe's Law* that the value of a network is proportional to the square of the number of users/members. The more people share data that can be mapped onto URIs, the more valuable that data is. As value increases, more agents join the network to get the benefits, and include information that they own in the network which further increases its value. This, like the WWW model, is radically different from other models of the value of information, wherein value is dictated by *scarcity* (copyright, intellectual property restrictions, etc). In decentralized networks like the Web, the value of information is dictated by *abundance*, so it can be placed in new contexts, and reused in unanticipated ways.

This is the dynamic that enabled the WWW to spread, when the value of Web documents was seen to be greater in information-rich contexts. One initiative to support the development of the SW is the creation of a discipline of *web science*, which is intended to exploit study of both technical and social issues to predict such matters with more accuracy.[5,6]

If the SW is to grow in an analogous way, more data have to be exposed to the Web that can be mapped onto URIs. In practice, this means that the data must be

exposed in the resource description framework (RDF), an agreed international standard whose role in the SW is described here[7]; in particular, it can be used not only to assert a link between two resources, but also to name (and therefore make explicit) the relationship that links them. RDF is the language of choice for reuse, because it is a relatively inexpressive language compared to other formalisms used in the SW (see Fig. 1 for a pictorial representation of the layers of formalisms required for the SW vision—expressivity increases as we ascend the diagram). The importance of RDF in this model is dictated by the so-called principle of least power, which states that the less expressive the representation language, the more reusable the data.[8]

The importance of growth is such that a stage can be reached when reuse of data—one's own or that of other people—is facilitated. There would ideally be so much information exposed in RDF that the contexts into which one's own data can be placed would be rich enough and numerous enough to increase its value significantly. RDF represents information as a subject–predicate–object triple; each of whose component parts is a URI. If the objects, resources, or representations referred to by the URIs are defined in ontologies, then this enables the interoperability at which the SW aims.

Hence another vital component in the SW is the development and maintenance of ontologies. These must be endorsed by the communities that use them, whether they are large-scale, expensive ontologies developed as a result of a major research effort, or relatively ad hoc creations intended to support small-scale collaboration.

Ontologies can also play an important role in bringing (representatives of) two or more communities together for a common purpose, by expressing a common vocabulary for their collaboration, onto which the terms of each discipline can be mapped. Such collaborative efforts are extremely important for reuse of content.[3]

This is not to say that search and retrieval on the existing Web is not of high quality; the methods pioneered by Google and others work very well. Nevertheless, keyword-based search techniques are vulnerable to a number of well-known flaws. Individual words can be ambiguous. A document can refer to a topic of interest without using the keyword. Keywords are language-dependent. Information distributed across several documents cannot be amalgamated by keyword search. And even though PageRank and related algorithms for search produce impressive results, the user still needs to read manually through the ordered list of retrieved pages, and inspect their content to determine relevance to his/her inquiry. This involvement of the user is a hindrance to scalability.

The SW should make more accurate querying possible, using ontologies to help with problems of ambiguity and unused keywords, and data linking to query across distributed datasets. Furthermore, it should be able to go beyond the existing search with respect to the three issues of reuse, automation, and exploitation of RDBs, as well as search and retrieval, the addition of information processing support to the Web will help promote other functions such as Web services and knowledge management.

COMPONENTS OF THE SEMANTIC WEB

At one level, the SW is a complex of formalisms and languages; each doing a different job in the representation of information, as shown in Fig. 1. Each formalism is an internationally agreed standard, and the composition of the functions these formalisms serve supports semantically enabled reasoning on data.

At the bottom of this diagram stands the URIs that identify the resources about which the SW provides reasoning capabilities.[9] The universality of URIs is extremely important—i.e., it is vital that whatever naming convention is used for URIs is adopted globally, so as to create the network effects that allow the SW to add value. Interpretation of URIs must also be consistent across contexts. In other words, when we *dereference* URIs (i.e., when we locate the resource to which the URI refers), we should always get the same object. If these conditions about URI naming schemes are met, then making an association between a URI and a resource means that different people can refer or link to it consistently in their conversations. The other basic formalism, Unicode, is an industry standard that allows computers to represent text in different writing systems.

The next layer up, eXtensible Markup Language (XML), is a language to mark up documents, and a uniform data exchange format between applications.[10] It allows the insertion of user-defined tags into documents that provide information about the role that the content plays. So, for instance, XML allows one to write a document describing a book, and also to *annotate* the document with machine-readable *metadata* to indicate, e.g., who the authors of the book are.

RDF[7] is a very minimal knowledge representation framework for the Web, which uses a basic subject–predicate–object structure, with the twist that it assigns specific URIs to its individual fields—including in the predicate position, and thereby identifying a relationship between the entities identified by the connected nodes. This use of URIs allows us to reason not only about objects but also about the relationships between them. XML is a meta-language that provides a uniform framework for mark-up, but it does not provide any way of getting at the *semantics* of data; RDF is the first step toward semantics.

The resource description framework schema (RDFS, sometimes known as RDF(S)[11]) gives greater scope for

sharing information about individual domains; whereas RDF is a data interchange language that lets users describe resources using their own vocabularies, and makes no assumptions about the domains in question. RDFS provides a basic set of tools for producing structured vocabularies that allow different users to agree on particular uses of terms. An extension of RDF, it adds a few modeling primitives with a fixed meaning (such as class, subclass and property relations, and domain and range restriction).

A key component for SW applications is the *ontology*. Ontologies[3] are shared conceptualizations of a domain that are intended to facilitate knowledge and information sharing by coordinating vocabulary and allowing basic inference of inheritance and attributes of objects. Several initiatives are developing ontologies, particularly in a number of sciences, which means that the scientists are likely to be among the important early adopters of SW technology. RDFS is an important step toward the SW vision, as the addition of modeling primitives makes it a basic ontology representation language.

However, greater expressivity is likely to be required in the development of more complex ontologies, and the World Wide Web Consortium (W3C) has issued a Web Ontology Language (OWL[12]) in multiple versions that allows ontologies to be not only represented but also checked for logical properties such as consistency. The three species of OWL are: 1) OWL Full, containing all the OWL primitives, allowing arbitrary combination of those primitives with RDF and RDFS (allowing changes in meaning even of predefined OWL or RDF primitives), but also providing so much expressive power as to make the language undecidable (i.e., it cannot be guaranteed that a computation using the full expressive power of OWL Full will be completed in a finite time); 2) OWL DL, which restricts application of OWL's constructors to each other, and corresponds to a decidable *description logic*, but which is not fully compatible with RDF; and 3) OWL Lite, which sacrifices even more expressive power to facilitate implementation and reasoning.[12] This set of relations affects the downward compatibility of the SW layer diagram—the only version of OWL that is downward compatible with RDF and RDFS (i.e., so that any processor for that version of OWL will also provide correct interpretations of RDFS) is OWL Full, which is undecidable.[13,14]

All varieties of OWL use RDF for their syntax, and use the linking capabilities of RDF to allow ontologies to be distributed—ontologies can refer to terms in other ontologies. Such distributivity is a key property for an ontology language designed for the SW.[15]

OWL supports some kinds of inference, such as subsumption and classification, but a greater variety of rules and inference is needed. Hence, work is ongoing on the Rule Interchange Format (RIF), which is intended to allow a variety of rule-based formalisms, including

Horn-clause logics, higher-order logics, and production systems, to be used.[16] Various insights from Artificial Intelligence (AI) have also been adapted for use for the SW, including temporal (time-based) logic, causal logic, and probabilistic logic.[1]

Having represented data using RDF and ontologies, and provided for inference, it is also important to provide reliable, standardized access to data held in RDF. To that end, a special query language SPARQL (pronounced "sparkle"), which became a W3C recommendation in January 2008, has been designed.[17] Logic and proof systems are envisaged to sit on top of these formalisms to manipulate the information in deployed systems.[1]

A very important layer is that of *trust*.[18] If information is being gathered from heterogeneous sources and inferred over, then it is important that users are able to trust such sources. The extent of trust will of course depend on the criticality of the inferences—trust entails risk, and a risk-averse user will naturally trust fewer sources.[19,20] Measuring trust, however, is a complex issue.[21] A key parameter is that of provenance, a statement of: 1) the conditions under which; 2) the methods with which; and 3) the organization by which, data were produced. Methods are appearing to enable provenance to be established, but relatively little is known about how information spreads across the Web.[22]

Related issues include respect for intellectual property, and the privacy of data subjects. In each case the reasoning abilities of the SW can be of value, and initiatives are under way to try to exploit them.[23] Creative commons[24] is a way of representing copyright policies and preferences based on RDF to promote reuse where possible (the existing standard copyright assumptions are more restrictive with respect to reuse). And research into the policy aware web is attempting to develop protocols to allow users to express their own privacy policies, and to enable those who wish to use information to reason about those policies.[25] Cryptography protocols to protect information will also play an important role, as shown in Fig. 1.

ADDITIONAL FACTORS IN SEMANTIC WEB DEVELOPMENT

Infrastructure

Another important part of SW development is the infrastructure that supports it. In particular, if data are to be routinely published to the Web in RDF format, there must be information repositories that can store RDF and RDFS. These *triple stores* (socalled because they store the RDF triples) must provide reasoning capabilities as well as retrieval mechanisms, but importantly must be *scalable*. Examples of triple stores include JENA,[26] 3store,[27,28] and Oracle 11g.[29] OWLIM is a repository

that works as a storage and inference layer for the Sesame RDF database, providing reasoning support for some of the more expressive languages of the SW, RDFS, and a limited version of OWL Lite.[30,31]

Reasoners

As representation in the SW is more complex than in previous technologies, so is reasoning. The area of SW reasoning has been the focus of much research, in order to infer the consequences of a set of assertions interpreted via an ontology. In such a context, inference rules need clear semantics, and need to be able to cope with the diverse and distributed nature of the SW.

There are a number of important issues of relevance in this area: 1) Under what conditions is negation monotonic (i.e., the addition of new facts does not change the derivation of not-p), or nonmonotonic (including negation as failure, deriving not-p from the failure to prove p)?; 2) How should we handle conflicts when merging rule-sets?; 3) "Truth" on the Web is often dependent on context—how should a reasoner represent that dependence?; 4) How should scalability be balanced against expressivity?; 5) Logic often assumes a static world of given "facts," but how should it be adapted to the SW, a much more dynamic space where propositions are asserted and withdrawn all the time?; and 6) The heterogeneous nature of the SW means that data in the SW are of varying trustworthiness; how should a reasoner deal with variable reliability? None of these questions has a "correct" answer, but any SW reasoning system needs to address them.

There has been a lot of research on SW reasoning, but an important desideratum is that a reasoner should support the W3C recommended formalisms, in particular supporting OWL entailment at as high a level as possible, and SPARQL querying. Examples include: Jena, an open source SW framework for Java, with a rule-based inference engine;[32] Pellet, a sound and complete OWL-DL reasoner;[33] and KAON2, an infrastructure for managing ontologies written in OWL-DL and other SW rule languages.[34] For a short review of the problems and prospects for SW reasoning, see Fensel.[35]

Bootstrapping

Bootstrapping content for the SW is one more important issue. Sufficient content is required for the hoped-for network effects to appear. There are initiatives to generate data in RDF and to expose it on the Web as a vital first step. The DBpedia[36] is based on the Web 2.0 community-created encyclopedia Wikipedia, and is intended to extract structured information from Wikipedia allowing much more sophisticated querying. Sample queries given on the DPpedia Web site include a list of people influenced by Friedrich Nietzsche, and the set of images of American guitarists. DBpedia uses RDF, and is also interlinked with other data sources on the Web. When accessed in late 2007, the DBpedia dataset consisted of 103 million RDF triples. Other examples of linked data applications include the DBLP bibliography of scientific papers,[37] and the GeoNames database that gives descriptions of millions of geographical features in RDF.[38]

Even if RDF began to be published routinely, there is still a great deal of legacy content on the Web, and to make this accessible to SW technology some automation of the translation process is required. Gleaning Resource Descriptions from Dialects of Languages (GRDDL) allows the extraction of RDF from XML documents using transformations expressed in Extensible Stylesheet Language Transformations (XSLT) an extensible stylesheet language based on XML. It is hoped that such extraction could allow bootstrapping of some of the hoped-for SW network effects.[39]

Annotating documents and data with metadata about content, provenance, and other useful dimensions (even including relevant emotional reactions to content[40]) is also important for the effort to bring more content into the range of SW technologies.[41] Multimedia documents, such as images, particularly benefit from such annotation.[42] Again, given the quantities of both legacy data, and new data being created, methods of automating annotation have been investigated by a number of research teams in order to increase the quantity of annotated data available without excessive expenditure of resources.[41,43,44]

The Social Context: Web Science

The SW vision has been delineated with some care by the W3C, and as has been seen involves an intricate set of connections between a number of formalisms, each of which is designed to do a certain job. As described in the next section, that vision has altered and gained complexity over time.

In general, there are severe complications in the mapping between the microlevel engineering of Web protocols, and the macrolevel social effects that result from large-scale use of the Web. The combination of scales, effects, and phenomena involved is too large to be easily covered by a single discipline, even computer science. The social interactions enabled by the Web place demands on the Web applications underlying them, which, in turn, put requirements on the Web's infrastructure. However, these multiple requirements are not well understood so far.[45] Social studies tend to regard the Web as a given, whereas the Web is rather a world changeable by alterations to the protocols underlying it. Furthermore, the Web changes at a rate that is at least

equal and may be faster than our ability to observe and analyze it.

The SW is a development bringing the Web vision to a new level of abstraction, yet the existing state of our knowledge of the Web and its relation to off-line society leaves a number of questions unanswered about how it will impact at a large scale. In particular, it is unknown what social consequences there might be of the greater public exposure and sharing of information that is so far locked in databases. Understanding these consequences is important, partly because the developers of the SW want to build a technology that is not harmful to society thanks to emergent social effects, and partly because it is important that the SW goes with the grain of society, in order that it be effective in real-world situations.[5]

To this end, in 2006, the Web Science Research Initiative (WSRI) was set up as a joint venture by the Massachusetts Institute of Technology and the University of Southampton to foster the interdisciplinary study of the Web in its social and technical context. WSRI's role includes crafting a curriculum for study across the various relevant disciplines; Berners-Lee[6] gave a detailed review of the wide range of scientific and social-scientific research that is likely to be relevant, including graph and network theory, computer science, economics, complexity theory, psychology, and law.

HISTORY AND INTELLECTUAL BACKGROUND

The vision of a web of data was always implicit in the ideas underlying the development of the WWW, and was articulated by Sir Tim Berners-Lee at the first WWW conference in 1994. Berners-Lee is well known as the inventor of the WWW in 1989–1991, and has been a leading figure in the development of the SW. As well as holding chairs at the Massachusetts Institute of Technology, United States, and the University of Southampton, United Kingdom, Berners-Lee is the director of the W3C, which he founded in 1994.

A key moment in the development, and public perception, of the SW was an entry written for *Scientific American* by Berners-Lee, James A. Hendler, and Ora Lassila in 2001.[46] This entry postulated the next stage of the WWW explicitly as one where data and information, as well as documents, are processed automatically, and envisaged a world where intelligent agents were able to access information (e.g., from calendars, gazetteers, and business organizations) in order to undertake tasks and planning for their owners.

This vision of automation of a series of routine information processing tasks had not emerged in 2008. The article's agent-oriented vision distracted attention from the main point of the SW, the potential of a web of linked *data* (as opposed to documents) with shared

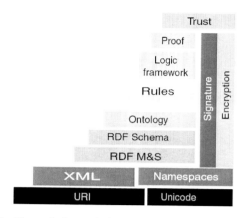

Fig. 2　The early layered view of the Semantic Web.

semantics. Hence, in 2006, Berners-Lee, together with Nigel Shadbolt and Wendy Hall, published another article in the IEEE journal *Intelligent Systems*, which made that point explicitly, and argued that the agent-based vision would only flourish with well-established data standards.[1]

The *Scientific American* article painted a very enticing picture, but its key message was less to do with the agents and more to do with the semantic information infrastructure that Berners-Lee and colleagues were advocating. Indeed, the infrastructure will be used for many knowledge management purposes, not only in allowing agents to communicate. The agent-focused rhetoric of the article has prompted some to argue that the SW is a restatement of the program of AI in the 1960s and 1970s, and will share its perceived failures. We address this question in the section titled "Controversies."

In 2001 (and before), the conceptualization of the various formal layers of the SW was as shown in Fig. 2, with a fairly straightforward cascade up from URIs to XML and namespaces, to RDF and RDFS, through ontologies to rules, logic, proof, and trust (the diagram has been widely distributed, but see, e.g., Berners-Lee).[47] Comparison with Fig. 1 shows how the details of the SW layers have had to be amended over time as implementation has continued. The requirements for expression of ontology-related information have led to an extra complexity from that envisaged in 2001, while the criticism of the SW vision based on the *Scientific American* article has led to a realization that not only the expressive formalisms need to be in place, but also tools and methods need to be created to allow use of SW technologies to integrate smoothly into organizations' standard information workflows (e.g., Shadbolt, Vargas-Vera, Golbeck and Alani[1,44,48,49]). This led to a top layer, User Interface, being added to the Fig. 2 structure at a later date.

Where intelligent agency has appeared—and there exist several applications, including shopbots and auction bots—it has tended to be handcrafted and unable to interact with heterogeneous information types. This is largely because of a lack of well-established scalable standards for information sharing; however, progress is being made toward that goal, especially via the painstaking committee-based standards development processes instituted by the W3C. These standards are crucial for the SW to "take off," and for the hoped-for network effects of a large number of users to emerge.[1]

The SW vision has been implemented by standard bodies, such as the Internet Engineering Task Force (IETF) as well as the W3C (the W3C is responsible for standards specific to the WWW), which have orchestrated efforts together with the user community to develop the languages at various levels to share meaning. Once standards are set by the W3C, they are called *recommendations*, acknowledging the reality that with the decentralization of the Web, and a lack of a central authority, standards cannot be enforced. The first RDF standard was specified in 1997 and became a W3C recommendation in 1999, and thereby providing a minimal knowledge representation language for the Web with the clear backing of the nascent SW community.

Fixed standards for expressing ontologies appeared later in the process, with RDFS and OWL becoming recommendations in 2004. OWL evolved from other ontology language efforts, including Ontology Inference Layer (OIL)[50] and DARPA Agent Markup Language (DAML)[51] whose merged product, DAML + OIL, was the most important predecessor to OWL.[52] In January 2008, the query language SPARQL became a W3C recommendation, while the RIF was under development in mid-2008.

Fig. 3, created in 2003, illustrates Berners-Lee's vision of the pattern of SW development using the visual metaphor of a tide flowing onto a beach (this diagram is widely available, but see Connolly).[53] From top to bottom in the diagram are the various layers of the SW diagram, from trust and proof down to data exchange and mark-up. From left to right come the various stages in a rough lifecycle from research to deployment: the first stage is a blue-sky research project; the second is the production of a stable system or formalism that is not a standard; the best aspects of these systems are then used as the bases for W3C standards, and the final stage is one of wide deployment. Hence, for instance, early ontology efforts like Cyc and description logics led to efforts such as DAML and OIL, which in turn helped create OWL. Wide deployment of OWL then results in a so-called web of meaning.

The "sea" of research and deployment approaches from the bottom left of Fig. 3 to the top right, as the "tide" comes in. Hence, in 1998, various formalisms were in place for all the various levels of representation of the SW, but only XML was a Web standard and beginning to be used widely. By 2003, OWL and RDFS were close to their final forms, and RDF was beginning

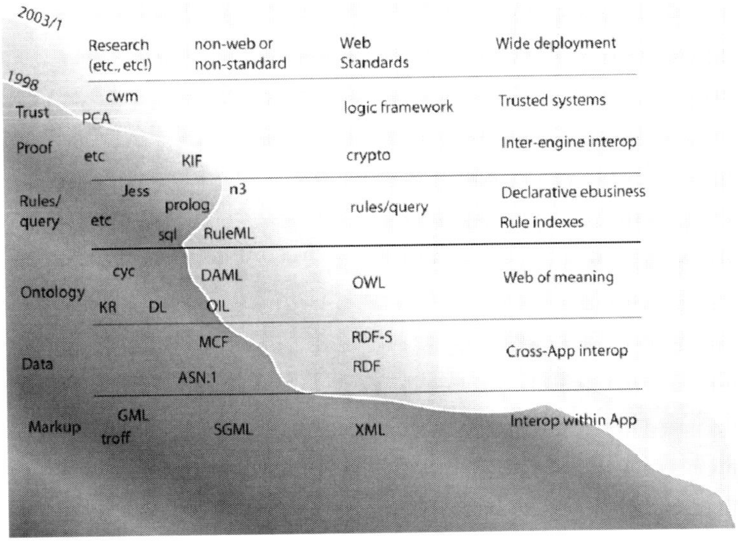

Fig. 3 A representation of the progress of semantic web development.

to be used widely for cross-application interoperability. At the time of writing, the "tide" has advanced further to the right, so work is ongoing on rule language RIF, and query language SPARQL became an official W3C recommendation in 2008. Meanwhile, OWL is being used more frequently by ontology builders.

The SW's history to date is largely one of standard-setting. However, it has also been argued that, analogous to other systems that have spread quickly and grown exponentially, what is needed is a "killer app" (i.e., an application that will meet a felt need and create a perception of the technology as "essential"). Less ambitiously, the SW's spread depends not only on having an impressive set of formalisms, but also software tools to use information represented in those formalisms.[49] The SW is clearly not, at the time of writing, an information resource in routine use. Nevertheless, there are some applications where SW technologies are serving valuable purposes, and we review some of these in the next section.

APPLICATIONS AND SYSTEMS

Properties of Systems

In general, SW projects tend to exhibit a few constant features. They generate new ontologies for the application domain (for example, art, or computer science), and use them to interrogate large stores of data, which could be legacy data or freshly harvested. Hence, a body of evidence is building up that ontologies have an important role in mediating the integration of data from heterogeneous sources.

Furthermore, the results of SW projects are generally presented using custom-built interfaces. This hints at a very important research area, which is the development of scalable visualizers capable of navigating the graph of connected information expressed in RDF. As can be seen, the importance of applications and user interfaces was made clear in the latest version of the layered SW diagram (Fig. 1).

In this section we will look at active SW successes, focusing on application areas and types, then commercial/real-world systems, before finally looking at some of the more successful academic efforts as judged by the SW development community itself.

Application Areas

There are areas where the SW is already an important tool, often in small focused communities with pressing information-processing requirements and various more or less common goals. Such communities can function as early adopters of the technology, exactly as the high-energy physics discipline played a vital role in the development of the WWW. A series of case studies and use cases is maintained in w3.org's Web site.[54]

The most important application for SW technology is *e-science*, the data-driven, computationally intensive pursuit of science in highly distributed computational environments.[55] Very large quantities of data are created by analyses and experiments in disciplines such as particle physics, meteorology, and the life sciences. Furthermore, in many contexts, different communities of scientists will be working in an interdisciplinary manner, which means that data from various fields (e.g., genomics, clinical drug trials, and epidemiology) need to be integrated. Many accounts of distinct and complex systems (e.g., the human body and the environment) consist of data brought from disciplines varying not only in vocabulary, but also in the scale of description; understanding such systems, and the way in which events at the microscale affect the macroscale, and *vice versa*, is clearly an important imperative. Many scientific disciplines have devoted resources to the creation of large-scale and robust ontologies for this and other purposes. The most well known of these is the *gene ontology*, a controlled vocabulary to describe gene and gene product attributes in organisms, and related vocabularies developed by open biomedical ontologies.[56] Others include the protein ontology, the cell cycle ontology, Medical Subject Headings (MeSH, used to index life science publications), systematized nomenclature of medicine (SNOMED), and AGROVOC (agriculture, forestry, fisheries, and food).

E-government is another potentially important application area, where information is deployed widely, and yet is highly heterogeneous. Government information varies in provenance, confidentiality, and "shelf life" (some information will be good for decades or even centuries, while other information can be out-of-date within hours), while it can also have been created by various levels of government (national/federal, regional, state, city, and parish). Integrating that information in a timely way is clearly an important challenge (see, for instance, a pilot study for the United Kingdom's Office of Public Sector Information, exploring the use of SW technologies for disseminating, sharing, and reusing data held in the public sector.[57])

Commercial Activity

There are an increasing number of applications that allow a deeper querying of linked data. We have already discussed DBpedia,[36] DBLP,[37] and GeoNames.[38] Commercial applications are also beginning to appear. Garlik[58] is a company seeking to exploit SW-style technologies to provide individual consumers with more power over their digital data. It reviews what is held about people, harvesting data from the open Web, and represents this in a people-centric structure. Natural Language Processing is used to find occurrences of people's names, sensitive information, and relations to other individuals and organizations. Declaration of interest: Wendy Hall is chair of the Garlik Advisory Board. Twine[59] is intended to enable people to share knowledge and information, and to organize that information using various SW technologies (also, like Garlik, using Natural Language Processing). Twine's developer Nova Spivack has coined the term "knowledge networking" to describe the

process, analogous to the Web 2.0 idea of "social networking."

The increasing maturity of SW technology is being shown by the growing number of successful vendors of SW technology. We have already seen OWLIM,[31] which was developed by Ontotext, a semantic technology lab focused on technologies to support the SW and SW services based in Sofia, Bulgaria, and Montreal, Canada; Ontotext has been and is a partner in a number of major SW research projects.[60] Ontoprise, based in Karlsruhe, Germany, is a software vendor for implementing SW infrastructure in large, distributed enterprises; its products include OntoBroker, which provides ontology support using the W3C recommended languages OWL, RDFS and SPARQL, and Semantic MediaWiki +, a collaborative knowledge management tool.[61] Asemantics, with offices in Italy, Holland, and the United Kingdom, uses a combination of Web 2.0 paradigms with SW technologies such as XML and RDF. The SW technologies are powerful representational tools but are often perceived as hard to use and search, so Asemantics attempts to exploit the perceived usability of Web 2.0 to present data in more widely accepted formats.[62]

Academic Work: The Semantic Web Challenge

Much of the major work in the SW has been carried out in the academic sphere, and in funded research projects between academic and commercial partners, and is reported in journals and conferences (see end of entry for a list of the more importance conferences). Any review of academic work in this field will inevitably be selective; for the purposes of this entry we will focus on a particular effort to nurture applications, the *Semantic Web Challenge*.

The SW Challenge was created in 2003, and associated with the International Semantic Web Conference (ISWC) of that year. Since then it has become an annual competition to create an application that shows SW technology in its best aspects, and which can act as a "benchmark" application. Hence, the SW Challenge gives us a series of illustrative applications thought by researchers' peers to constitute best SW practice.[63]

To meet the criteria for the Challenge, a tool or system needs to meet a number of requirements,[64] which provide a useful characterization of the expectations governing an SW system, and are suggestive of the expected properties of SW applications. For instance, it should use information from sources that are distributed and heterogeneous, of real-world complexity and with diverse ownership. It should assume an open world, and that the information is never complete, and it should use some formal description of the meaning of the data. Optional criteria include a use of data in some way other than the creators intended, use of multimedia, and use of devices other than a PC. Applications need not be restricted to information retrieval, and ideally the system would be scalable in terms of the amount of data used and the number of distributed components cooperating. All these criteria indicate areas where SW systems would be expected to have an advantage.

The winners of the SW Challenge to date are as follows.

2003: CS AKTive Space (University of Southampton), an integrated application that provides a way to explore the U. K. Computer Science Research domain across multiple dimensions for multiple stakeholders, from funding agencies to individual researchers, using information harvested from the Web, and mediated through an ontology.[65]

2004: Flink (Vrije Universiteit Amsterdam), a "Who's Who" of the SW that allows the interrogation of information gathered automatically from Web-accessible resources about researchers who have participated in ISWC conferences.[66]

2005: CONFOTO (appmosphere Web applications, Germany), a browsing and annotation service for conference photographs.[67]

2006: MultimediaN E-Culture Demonstrator (Vrije Universiteit Amsterdam, Centre for Mathematics and Computer Science, Universiteit van Amsterdam, Digital Heritage Netherlands and Technical University of Eindhoven), an application to search, navigate, and annotate annotated media collections interactively, using collections from several museums and art repositories.[68]

2007: Revyu.com (Open University), a reviewing and rating site specifically designed for the SW, allowing reviews to be integrated and interlinked with data from other sources (in particular, other reviews).[69]

CONTROVERSIES

The SW vision has always generated controversy, with a number of commentators being highly skeptical of its prospects. Let us briefly review some of the disputed issues.

The Semantic Web as "Good Old-Fashioned Artificial Intelligence"

One view holds that the SW is basically a throwback to the project to program machine intelligence, which was jokingly christened by John Haugeland "GOFAI" (good old-fashioned AI). This proved impossible: so much of human intelligence is implicit and situated that it was too hard a problem to write down everything a computer needed to know to produce an output that exhibited human-like intelligence. For instance, if a human is told about a room, further explanations that a room generally

has a floor, at least three walls, usually four, and a ceiling, and some method of ingress that is generally but not always a door, are not required. But a computer needs to be told these mundane facts explicitly—and similarly every time it is introduced to a new concept.[70]

One attempt to work around this problem is the Cyc project, set up in 1984, which aims to produce a gigantic ontology that will encode all common-sense knowledge of the type about the room given above, in order to support human-like reasoning by machines.[71] The project has always aroused controversy, but it is fair to say that over two decades later, GOFAI is no nearer. The implicit nature of commonsense knowledge arguably makes it impossible to write it all down.

Many commentators have argued that the SW is basically a re-creation of the (misconceived) GOFAI idea, that the aim is to create machine intelligence over the Web, to allow machines to reason about Web content in such a way as to exhibit intelligence.[72,73] This, however, is a misconception, possibly abetted by the strong focus in the 2001 *Scientific American* article on an agent-based vision of the SW.[46] Like many GOFAI projects, the scenarios in that article have prominent planning components. There is also continuity between the AI tradition of work on formal knowledge representation and the SW project of developing ontologies.

The SW has less to do with GOFAI as with context-based machine reasoning over content (and the provision of machine-readable data on the Web). The aim is not to bring a single ontology, such as Cyc, to bear on all problems (and therefore implicitly to define or anticipate all problems and points of view in the ontology definition), but rather to allow data to be interrogated in ways that were not anticipated by their creators. Different ontologies will be appropriate for different purposes; composite ontologies can be assembled from distributed parts (thanks to the design of OWL); and it is frequently very basic ontologies (defining simple terms such as "customer," "account number," or "account balance") that deliver large amounts of content. It is, after all, a matter of fact that people from different communities and disciplines can and do interact without making any kind of common *global* ontological commitment.[1,6,74]

Indeed, we can perhaps learn from the experience of hype and reaction that accompanied the development of AI. There has been a great deal of criticism of AI, but much has been learned from AI research and some AI methods and systems are now routinely exploited in a number of applications. The same may be expected of the SW. We should not expect to wake up one morning with the SW implemented and ready for use. Rather, a likelier model is that SW technologies will be incorporated into more systems "behind the scenes" wherever methods are needed to deal with signature SW problems (large quantities of distributed heterogeneous data).

Arguments for and against Ontologies

The importance of ontologies for the SW has been another point of friction with those who believe the program unrealistic. Ontologies are seen as expensive to develop and hard to maintain. Classification of objects is usually done relative to some task, and as the nature of the task changes, ontologies can become outdated. Classifications are also made relative to some background assumptions, and impose those assumptions onto the resulting ontology. To that extent, the expensive development of ontologies reflects the worldview of the ontology builders, not necessarily the users. They are top-down and authoritarian, and therefore opposed to the Web ethos of decentralization and open conversation. They are fixed in advance, and so they don't work very well to represent knowledge in dynamic, situated contexts.[75–77]

Furthermore, say the critics, the whole point of the Web as a decentralized, linked information structure is that it reflects the needs of its large, heterogeneous user base, which includes very many people who are naïve in their interactions. The infrastructure has to be usable by such people, which argues for simplicity. The rich linking structure of the existing Web, combined with statistically based search engines such as Google, is much more responsive to the needs of unsophisticated users. The SW, in contrast, demands new information mark-up practices, and corporations and information owners need to invest in new technologies. Not only that, but the existing statistical methods will scale up as the number of users and interactions grows, whereas logic-based methods such as those advocated by the SW scale less well (cf., e.g., Zambonini).[78]

Folksonomies

One development as part of the so-called Web 2.0 paradigm (of systems, communities, and services that facilitate collaboration and information-sharing among users) that has drawn attention in this context is that of the "folksonomy." Folksonomies have arisen out of the recent move to allow users to "tag" content on Web 2.0 sites such as the image-sharing site Flickr, and the video-sharing site YouTube. Having seen content, users are allowed to tag it with key words, which, when the number of users has become large enough, results in a structure of connections and classifications emerging without central control. Their promoters argue that folksonomies "really" express the needs of their users (since all the structure has arisen out of their user-based classifications), whereas ontologies "really" express the needs of authorities who can "impose" their views from the top-down.[76]

However, folksonomies are much less expressive than ontologies; they are basically variants on keyword searches. A tag "SF" may refer to a piece of science fiction, or to San Francisco, or something else from the user's private idiolect. Indeed, that ambiguity arises even if we make the unrealistic assumption of a monoglot English user community. Once we realize speakers of other languages will use a system, then there are further possible ambiguities—for instance, in German "SF" might refer to the Swiss television station Schweizer Fernsehen.

Resolving This Controversy

When a community is large enough and the benefits clear, then a large-scale ontology building and maintenance program is justified. In a note, Berners-Lee argues that such conditions will be perhaps more frequently encountered than skeptics believe. On the very broad assumptions that the size of an ontology-building team increases as the order of the log of the size of the ontology's user community, and that the resources needed to build an ontology increase as the order of the square of community size, the cost per individual of ontology building will diminish rapidly as user community size increases. Of course, these assumptions are not intended to be deeply realistic, so much as indicative of how the resource implications diminish as the community increases in size. Berners-Lee's moral: "Do your bit. Others will do theirs."[74]

Even so, not all ontologies need to be of great size and expressive depth. Certainly, the claim that has been made that the SW requires a single ontology of all discourse on the model of Cyc, but this is not backed up by the SW community. Such an ontology, even if possible, would not scale, and in a decentralized structure like the Web its use could not be enforced. We should rather expect a lot of use of small-scale, *shallow* ontologies defining just a few terms that nevertheless are widely applicable.[74] Experience in building real-world SW systems often shows that expectations about the cost and complexity of the ontologies required are overblown, and the ontology-building process can be relatively straightforward and cheap.[79]

For example, the machine-readable friend-of-a-friend (FOAF) ontology is intended to describe people, their activities, and their relations to other people. It is not massively complex, and indeed publishing an FOAF account of oneself is a fairly simple matter of form-filling (using the FOAF-a-matic tool).[80] But the resulting network of people (showing their connections to other people) has become very large indeed. A survey performed in 2004 discovered over 1.5 million documents using the FOAF ontology.[81]

With respect to Folksonomies, it is important to note that ontologies and folksonomies serve different purposes. Folksonomies are based on word tags, whereas the basis for ontology reference is via a URI. One of the main aims of ontology definition is to *remove* ambiguity—not globally, for this may well be impossible, but rather within the particular context envisaged by the developer (see the section on "Symbol Grounding"). Folksonomies will necessarily inherit the ambiguity of the natural language upon which they are based. And while folksonomies emerge from data-sharing practices, it is not necessarily the case the ontologies are authoritarian; rather, the latter should ideally be *rationalizations* of existing sharing practice. This does entail departure from prevailing practice, but not necessarily of great magnitude. Indeed, a strong possibility is to use cheaply gathered folksonomies as starting points for ontology development, gradually morphing the Web 2.0 structures into something with greater precision and less ambiguity.[82]

Symbol Grounding

An important aspect of the SW is that URIs must be interpreted consistently. However, terms and symbols are highly variable in their definitions and use through time and space. The SW project ideally needs processes whereby URIs are given to objects, such that the management of these processes is by communities and individuals, endorsed by the user community, who ensure consistency. This URI "ownership" is critical to the smooth functioning of the SW.[1]

But the process of *symbol grounding* (i.e., ensuring a fixed and known link between a symbol and its referent) is at best hard, and at worst (as argued by Wittgenstein, for instance) impossible.[83,84] Meanings do not stay fixed, but alter, often imperceptibly. They are delineated not only by traditional methods such as the provision of necessary and sufficient conditions, but also by procedures, technologies, and instrumentation, and alter subtly as practice alters.

Any attempt to fix the reference of URIs is a special case of symbol grounding, and is consequently hard to do globally. It is certainly the case that attempting to resist the alteration in community practices and norms, and reformulation of meanings of terms, would be doomed.

Yorick Wilks has argued that since much knowledge is held in unstructured form, in plain text, automatic Natural Language Processing techniques, statistically based, can be used to "ground" meanings of terms for the SW.[73] Berners-Lee, however, maintains that the SW is necessarily based on logic and firm definitions (even if those definitions were imperfect, or highly situated and task-relative), not words, use patterns and statistics.

Wilks's point is that the aim of defining terms in logic is too idealistic, and anyway depends on false assumptions about ordinary word meaning. Berners-Lee's counterargument is, in effect, that though meanings are not stable, they can be stable *enough* relative to individual applications and in particular contexts to allow the SW approach to work.

CONCLUSION

The SW has been somewhat misunderstood in some commentaries. Its aim is not to force users to accept large ontologies remote from data-sharing practice imposed by shadowy authorities. Neither is it intended to produce a theory of all discourse, or to reproduce GOFAI. Rather, it is intended to shift the emphasis of the Web from being a web of documents to a web of linked *data*. It is the development of formalisms and technologies facilitating the creation, sharing, and querying of linked data using sharable ontologies to establish common interpretations. For this reason, an alternative name for the SW is the *web of linked data*.

The SW is a work in progress. As it stands, the "buy in" to the SW has not yet produced the desirable network effects, although several disciplines are enthusiastic early adopters of the technology (e.g., the e-science community). And there are still several important research issues outstanding. It is not yet known how best to: 1) query large numbers of heterogeneous information stores at many different scales; 2) translate between, merge, prune, or evaluate ontologies; 3) visualize the SW; and 4) establish trust and provenance of the content.

As complex technologies and information infrastructures are developed, there is a dynamic feedback between requirements, analysis, engineering solutions, and hard-to-predict global behavior of human, machine, and hybrid systems. Understanding how basic engineering protocols governing how computers talk to each other can result in social movements at a very different level of abstraction is very hard, yet essential to realizing the SW vision. Indeed, such understanding, the defining purpose of the discipline of *Web Science*, is essential to ensuring that *any* Web-based information structure is beneficial.[5]

ACKNOWLEDGMENTS

The authors would like to thank Tim Berners-Lee, Nigel Shadbolt, James A. Hendler, Daniel J. Weitzner, Harith Alani, Marcia J. Bates, and an anonymous referee for helpful comments and discussions.

Resources—
Six Sigma

REFERENCES

1. Shadbolt, N.; Hall, W.; Berners-Lee, T. The Semantic Web revisited. IEEE Intell. Syst. **2006**, *21* (3), 96–101.

2. Fensel, D.; Bussler, C.; Ding, Y.; Kartseva, V.; Klein, M.; Korotkiy, M.; Omelayenko, B.; Siebes, R. Semantic Web application areas. In 7th International Workshop on Applications of Natural Language to Information Systems (NLDB 2002), Stockholm, Sweden, June, 27–28, 2002; http://www.cs.vu.nl/~ronny/work/NLDB02.pdf (accessed July 2008).

3. Fensel, D. In *Ontologies: A Silver Bullet for Knowledge Management and Electronic Commerce*; 2nd Ed. ; Springer: Berlin, 2004.

4. Berners-Lee, T. In *Relational databases on the Semantic Web;* 1998 http://www.w3.org/DesignIssues/RDB-RDF.html (accessed December 2007).

5. Berners-Lee, T.; Hall, W.; Hendler, J.; Shadbolt, N.; Weitzner, D. Creating a science of the Web. Science **2006**, *313* (5788), 769–771.

6. Berners-Lee, T.; Hall, W.; Hendler, J.A.; O'Hara, K.; Shadbolt, N.; Weitzner, D.J. A framework for Web Science. Found. Trends. Web Sci **2006**, *1* (1), 1–134.

7. Klyne, G.; Carroll, J.J.; McBride, B. In *Resource Description Framework (RDF): Concepts and abstract syntax* 2004 http://www.w3.org/TR/rdf-concepts/ (accessed December 2007).

8. Berners-Lee, T. In *Principles of design;* 1998 http://www.w3.org/DesignIssues/Principles.html (accessed December 2007).

9. Berners-Lee, T.; Fielding, R.; Masinter, L. In *Uniform Resource Identifier (URI): Generic syntax* 2005 http://gbiv.com/protocols/uri/rfc/rfc3986.html (accessed December 2007).

10. Bray, T.; Paoli, J.; Sperberg-McQueen, C.M.; Maler, E.; Yergeau, F. In *Extensible Markup Language (XML) 1.0,* 4th Ed.; 2006, http://www.w3.org/TR/xml/ (accessed December 2007).

11. Brickley, D.; Guha, R.V.; McBride, B. In *RDF vocabulary description language 1.0: RDF Schema;* 2004, http://www.w3.org/TR/rdf-schema/ (accessed December 2007).

12. McGuinness, D.L.; van Harmelen, F. OWL Web Ontology Language overview, 2004. http://www.w3.org/TR/owl- features/ (accessed December 2007).

13. Antoniou, G.; van Harmelen, F. In *A Semantic Web Primer*; MIT Press: Cambridge, MA, 2004.

14. Dean, M.; Schreiber, G.; Bechhofer, S.; van Harmelen, F.; Hendler, J.; Horrocks, I.; McGuinness, D.L.; Patel-Schneider, P.F.; Stein, L.A. In *OWL Web Ontology Language Reference,* 2004, http://www.w3.org/TR/owl-ref/ (accessed December 2007).

15. Smith, M.K.; Welty, C.; McGuiness, D.L. In *OWL Web Ontology Language guide,* 2004, http://www.w3.org/TR/owl-guide/ (accessed December 2007).

16. Boley, H.; Kifer, M. In *RIF basic logic dialect,* 2007 http://www.w3.org/TR/rif-bld/ (accessed December 2007).

17. Prud'hommeaux, E.; Seaborne, A. In *SPARQL query language for RDF;* 2007, http://www.w3.org/TR/rdf-sparql-query/ (accessed December 2007).

18. Golbeck, J. Trust on the World Wide Web: A survey. Found. Trends Web Sci. **2006**, *1* (2), 1–72.

19. Bonatti, P.A.; Duma, C.; Fuchs, N.; Nejdl, W.; Olmedilla, D.; Peer, J.; Shahmehri, N. Semantic Web policies—a discussion of requirements and research issues. The Semantic Web: Research and Applications; 3rd European Semantic Web Conference 2006 (ESWC-06), Budva, Montenegro, 2006; Sure, Y., Domingue, J., Eds.; Springer: Berlin, 2006.

20. O'Hara, K.; Alani, H.; Kalfoglou, Y.; Shadbolt, N. Trust strategies for the Semantic Web. Workshop on Trust, Security and Reputation on the Semantic Web; 3rd International Semantic Web Conference (ISWC 04), Hiroshima, Japan, 2004; http://eprints.ecs.soton.ac.uk/10029/ (accessed December 2007).

21. Golbeck, J.; Hendler, J. Accuracy of metrics for inferring trust and reputation in Semantic Web-based social networks. *Engineering Knowledge in the Age of the Semantic Web*; Proceedings of 14th International Conference, EKAW 2004, Whittlebury Hall, U. K., 2004; Motta, E., Shadbolt, N., Stutt, A., Gibbins, N., Eds.; Springer: Berlin, 2004; 116–131.

22. Groth, P.; Jiang, S.; Miles, S.; Munroe, S.; Tan, V.; Tsasakou, S.; Moreau, L. In *An architecture for provenance systems* http://eprints.ecs.soton.ac.uk/13216/1/provenanceArchitecture10.pdf, 2006 (accessed December 2007).

23. O'Hara, K.; Shadbolt, N. In *The Spy in the Coffee Machine: The End of Privacy As We Know It*; Oneworld: Oxford, 2008.

24. http://creativecommons.org/about/.

25. Weitzner, D.J.; Hendler, J.; Berners-Lee, T.; Connolly, D. Creating a policy-aware Web: Discretionary, rule-based access for the World Wide Web. In *Web and Information Security*; Ferrari, E., Thuraisingham, B., Eds.; Idea Group Inc: Hershey, PA, 2005.

26. http://jena.sourceforge.net/.

27. http://sourceforge.net/projects/threestore.

28. Harris, S.; Gibbins, N. 3store: Efficient bulk RDF storage. Proceedings of the 1st International Workshop on Practical and Scalable Systems, Sanibel Island, FL, **2003**, http://km.aifb.uni-karlsruhe.de/ws/psss03/proceedings/harris-et-al.pdf (accessed December 2007).

29. http://www.oracle.com/technology/tech/semantic_technologies/index.html.

30. http://www.ontotext.com/owlim/.

31. Kiryakov, A.; Ognyanov, D.; Manov, D. OWLIM: A pragmatic semantic repository for OWL. *Web Information and Systems Engineering–WISE 2005 Workshops*; Proceedings of the Workshop on Scalable Semantic Web Knowledge Base Systems at WISE 2005, New York, November, 2005; Dean, M., Guo, Y., Jun, W., Kaschek, R., Krishnaswamy, S., Pan, Z., Sheng, Q. Z., Eds.; Springer: Berlin, 2005; 182–192 http://www.ontotext.com/publications/ssws_owlim.pdf (accessed July 2008).

32. McBride, B. Jena: Implementing the RDF model and syntax specification. *Proceedings of the 2nd International Workshop on the Semantic Web: SemWeb 2001*; World Wide Web Conference 2001, Hong Kong, May, 2001; Decker, S., Fensel, D., Sheth, A., Staab, S., Eds.; 2001; Vol. 40, CEUR-WS, http://sunsite.informatik.rwth-

aachen.de/Publications/CEUR-WS/Vol-40/mcbride.pdf (accessed July 2008).

33. Sirin, E.; Parsia, B.; Cuenca Grau, B.; Kalyanpur, A.; Katz, Y. Pellet: A practical OWL-DL reasoner. J. Web Semant. **2007**, *5* (2), 51–53.

34. http://kaon2.semanticweb.org/.

35. Fensel, D.; Van Harmelen, F. Unifying reasoning and search to Web scale. IEEE Internet Comput **2007**, *11* (2), 94–96 (sic).

36. Auer, S.; Bizer, C.; Kobilarov, G.; Lehmann, J.; Cyganiak, R.; Ives, Z. DBpedia: A nucleus for a Web of open data. In Proceedings of the 6th International Semantic Web Conference 2007, Busan, South Korea, 2007; http://iswc2007.semanticweb.org/papers/715.pdf (accessed December 2007).

37. http://www4.wiwiss.fu-berlin.de/dblp/.

38. http://www.geonames.org/.

39. In *Gleaning Resource Descriptions from Dialects of Languages (GRDDL)*; 2007,Connolly, D., Ed.; http://www.w3.org/TR/grddl/ (accessed December 2007).

40. Schröder, M.; Zovato, E.; Pirker, H.; Peter, C.; Burkhardt, F. W3C emotion incubator group report, 2007. http://www.w3.   org/2005/Incubator/emotion/XGR-emotion/ (accessed December 2007).

41. In *Annotation for the Semantic Web*; Handschuh, S., Staab, S., Eds.; IOS Press: Amsterdam, 2003.

42. Troncy, R.; van Ossenbruggen, J.; Pan, J.Z.; Stamou, G.; Halaschek-Wiener, C.; Simou, N.; Tsouvaras, V. In *Image annotation on the Semantic Web*, 2007, http://www.w3.org/2005/Incubator/mmsem/XGR-image-annotation/ (accessed December 2007).

43. Handschuh, S.; Staab, S.; Ciravegna, F. S-CREAM— Semi-automatic CREAtion of Metadata. *Knowledge Engineering and Knowledge Management: Ontologies and the Semantic Web*; Proceedings of 13th International Conference, EKAW 2002, Sigüenza, Spain, 2002; Gómez-Pérez, A., Benjamins, V. R., Eds.; Springer: Berlin, 2002; 358–372.

44. Vargas-Vera, M.; Motta, E.; Domingue, J.; Lanzoni, M.; Stutt, A.; Ciravegna, F. MnM: Ontology-driven semi-automatic and automatic support for semantic markup. *Knowledge Engineering and Knowledge Management: Ontologies and the Semantic Web*; Proceedings of 13th International Conference, EKAW 2002, Sigüenza, Spain, 2002; Gómez-Pérez, A., Benjamins, V. R., Eds.; Springer: Berlin, 2002; 379–391.

45. Hendler, J.; Shadbolt, N.; Hall, W.; Berners-Lee, T.; Weitzner, D. Web Science: An interdisciplinary approach to understanding the World Wide Web. Commun. ACM **2008**, *51* (7), 60–69.

46. Berners-Lee, T.; Hendler, J.; Lassila, O. The Semantic Web. Sci. Am. **2001**, http://www.sciam.com/article.cfm? articleID = 00048144-10D2-1C70-84A9809EC588EF21 (accessed December 2007).

47. Berners-Lee, T. Foreword. In *Spinning the Semantic Web: Bringing the World Wide Web to its Full Potential*; Fensel, D., Hendler, J., Lieberman, H., Wahlster, W., Eds.; MIT Press: Cambridge, MA, 2003; xi–xxiii.

48. Golbeck, J.; Grove, M.; Parsia, B.; Kalyanpur, A.; Hendler, J. New tools for the Semantic Web. *Knowledge Engineering and Knowledge Management: Ontologies*

and the Semantic Web; Proceedings of 13th International Conference, EKAW 2002, Sigüenza, Spain, 2002; Gómez-Pérez, A., Benjamins, V. R., Eds.; Springer: Berlin, 2002; 392–400.

49. Alani, H.; Kalfoglou, Y.; O'Hara, K.; Shadbolt, N. Towards a killer app for the Semantic Web. *The Semantic Web*; Proceedings of the International Semantic Web Conference 2005, Hiroshima, Japan, 2005; Gil, Y., Motta, E., Benjamins, V. R., Musen, M. A., Eds.; Springer: Berlin, 2005; 829–843.

50. Fensel, D.; Horrocks, I.; van Harmelen, F.; Decker, S.; Erdmann, M.; Klein, M. OIL in a nutshell. *Knowledge Engineering and Knowledge Management: Methods, Models and Tools*; Proceedings of 12th European Knowledge Acquisition Workshop (EKAW 2000), Juan-les-Pins, France, October, 2000; Dieng, R., Corby, O., Eds.; Springer: Berlin, 2000; 1–16 http://www.cs.vu.nl/~ontoknow/oil/downl/oilnutshell.pdf (accessed July 2008).

51. http://www.daml.org/about.html.

52. Patel-Schneider, P.; Horrocks, I.; van Harmelen, F. Reviewing the design of DAML + OIL: An ontology language for the Semantic Web. In Proceedings of the 18th National Conference on Artificial Intelligence (AAAI02), Edmonton, Canada, 2002, http://www.cs.vu.nl/~frankh/postscript/AAAI02.pdf (accessed December 2007).

53. Connolly, D. In *Semantic Web update: OWL and beyond*; 2003, http://www.w3.org/2003/Talks/1017-swup/all.htm (accessed December 2007).

54. http://www.w3.org/2001/sw/sweo/public/UseCases/.

55. Hendler, J.; de Roure, D. E-science: The grid and the Semantic Web. IEEE Intell. Syst. **2004**, *19* (1), 65–71.

56. http://www.geneontology.org/.

57. Alani, H.; Dupplaw, D.; Sheridan, J.; O'Hara, K.; Darlington, J.; Shadbolt, N.; Tullo, C. Unlocking the potential of public sector information with Semantic Web technology. In Proceedings of the 6th International Semantic Web Conference 2007, Busan, South Korea, 2007; http://iswc2007.semanticweb.org/papers/701.pdf (accessed December 2007).

58. https://www.garlik.com/index.php.

59. http://www.twine.com/.

60. http://www.ontotext.com/index.html.

61. http://www.ontoprise.de/index.php?id = 134.

62. http://www.asemantics.com/index.html.

63. http://www.informatik.uni-bremen.de/agki/www/swc/index.html.

64. http://challenge.semanticweb.org/.

65. Schraefel, m.m.c.; Shadbolt, N.R.; Gibbins, N.; Glaser, H.; Harris, S. CS AKTive Space: Representing computer science on the Semantic Web. In *Proceedings of WWW 2004*; New York, 2004 http://eprints.ecs.soton.ac.uk/9084/ (accessed December 2007).

66. Mika, P. Flink: Semantic Web technology for the extraction and analysis of social networks. J. Web Semant **2005**, *3* (2), http://www.websemanticsjournal.org/papers/20050719/document7.pdf (accessed December 2007).

67. Nowack, B. CONFOTO: A semantic browsing and annotation service for conference photos. *The Semantic Web*; Proceedings of the International Semantic Web Conference 2005, Hiroshima, Japan, 2005; Gil, Y., Motta, E.,

Benjamins, V. R.; Musen, M. A., Eds.; Springer: Berlin, 2005; 1067–1070.

68. Schreiber, G.; Amin, A.; van Assem, M.; de Boer, V.; Hardman, L.; Hildebrand, M.; Hollink, L.; Huang, Z.; van Kersen, J.; de Niet, M.; Omelayenko, B.; van Ossenbruggen, J.; Siebes, R.; Taekema, J.; Wielemaker, J.; Wielinga, B. MultimediaN e-culture demonstrator, 2006. http://www.cs.vu.nl/~guus/papers/Schreiber06a.pdf (accessed December 2007).

69. Heath, T.; Motta, E. Revyu.com: A reviewing and rating site for the Web of data. In Proceedings of the 6th International Semantic Web Conference 2007, Busan, South Korea, 2007; http://iswc2007.semanticweb.org/papers/889.pdf (accessed December 2007).

70. Haugeland, J. Understanding natural language. J. Philos. 1979, 76, 619–632.

71. Lenat, D.B. Cyc: A large-scale investment in knowledge infrastructure. Commun. ACM 1995, 38 (11), 32–38.

72. Jones, K.S. What's new about the Semantic Web? Some questions. SIGIR Forum 2004, 38 (2), http://www.sigir.org/forum/2004D/sparck_jones_sigirforum_2004d.pdf (accessed December 2007).

73. Wilks, Y. The Semantic Web: Apotheosis of annotation, but what are its semantics?. IEEE Intell. Syst. 2008, 23 (3), 41–49.

74. Berners-Lee, T. The fractal nature of the Web, 2007. http://www.w3.org/DesignIssues/Fractal.html (accessed December 2007).

75. Pike, W.; Gahegan, M. Beyond ontologies: Toward situated representations of scientific knowledge. Intl. J. Hum. Comput. Stud. 2007, 65 (7), 674–688.

76. Shirky, C. Ontology is overrated: categories, links and tags, 2005. http://www.shirky.com/writings/ontology_overrated.html (accessed December 2007).

77. Stevens, R.; Egaña Aranguren, M.; Wolstencroft, K.; Sattler, U.; Drummond, N.; Horridge, M.; Rector, A. Using OWL to model biological knowledge. Intl. J. Hum. Comput. Stud. 2007, 65 (7), 583–594.

78. Zambonini, D. In The 7 (f)laws of the Semantic Web; 2006, http://www.oreillynet.com/xml/blog/2006/06/the_7_flaws_of_the_semantic_we.html (accessed December 2007).

79. Alani, H.; Chandler, P.; Hall, W.; O'Hara, K.; Shadbolt, N.; Szomsor, M. Building a pragmatic Semantic Web. IEEE Intell. Syst. 2008, 23 (3), 61–68.

80. http://www.ldodds.com/foaf/foaf-a-matic.

81. Ding, L.; Zhou, L.; Finin, T.; Joshi, A. How the Semantic Web is being used: An analysis of FOAF documents. In Proceedings of the 38th International Conference on System Sciences, 2005; http://ebiquity.umbc.edu/_file_directory_/papers/120.pdf (accessed December 2007).

82. Mika, P. Ontologies are us: A unified model of social networks and semantics. J. Web Semant. 2007, 5 (1), 5–15.

83. Harnad, S. The symbol grounding problem. Physica D 1990, 42, 335–346, http://users.ecs.soton.ac.uk/harnad/Papers/Harnad/harnad90.sgproblem.html (accessed December 2007).

84. Wittgenstein, L. In Philosophical Investigations; Basil Blackwell: Oxford, 1953.

BIBLIOGRAPHY

1. Antoniou, G.; van Harmelen, F. In A Semantic Web Primer; MIT Press: Cambridge, MA, 2004.

2. Berners-Lee, T. In Weaving the Web: The Past, Present and Future of the World Wide Web by Its Inventor; Texere Publishing: London, 1999.

3. Berners-Lee, T.; Hall, W.; Hendler, J.A.; O'Hara, K.; Shadbolt, N.; Weitzner, D.J. A framework for web science. Found. Trends Web Sci. 2006, 1 (1), 1–134.

4. Berners-Lee, T.; Hall, W.; Hendler, J.; Shadbolt, N.; Weitzner, D. Creating a science of the Web. Science 2006, 313 (5788), 769–771.

5. Berners-Lee, T.; Hendler, J.; Lassila, O. The Semantic Web. Sci. Am. 2001, http://www.sciam.com/article.cfm?articleID = 00048144-10D2-1C70-84A9809EC588EF21 (accessed December 2007).

6. Fensel, D. In Ontologies: A Silver Bullet for Knowledge Management and Electronic Commerce; 2nd Ed.; Springer: Berlin, 2004.

7. Fensel, D.; Hendler, J.; Lieberman, H.; Wahlster, W. In Spinning the Semantic Web: Bringing the World Wide Web to its Full Potential; MIT Press: Cambridge, MA, 2003.

8. Shadbolt, N.; Hall, W.; Berners-Lee, T. The Semantic Web revisited. IEEE Intell. Syst. 2006, 21 (3), 96–101.

9. There are several important annual conferences for the SW community, including: the World Wide Web Conference (WWW); the International Semantic Web Conference (ISWC—pronounced Iss-wick); the European Semantic Web Conference. These conferences preserve their proceedings online.

10. The World Wide Web Consortium's Semantic Web activity page is at http://www.w3.org/2001/sw/, and contains references to interviews, manifestos and statements by key SW developers. It also maintains a useful site of case studies and use cases at http://www.w3.org/2001/sw/sweo/public/UseCases/. For Web Science, see http://webscience.org/.

Semantic Web: Languages, Tools, and Standards

Valentina Janev
Sanja Vraneš
Mihajlo Pupin Institute, Belgrade, Serbia

Abstract

The term "Semantic Web" (SW) refers to Sir Tim Berners-Lee's vision of the Web of Linked Data (called also the Web of Data) as an extension of the conventional Web. In the time since the SW's initial conception, the W3C SW Activity Group has accepted numerous Web technologies as standards or recommendations. However, in order to make the Web of Data a reality, and push large-scale integration of, and reasoning on, data on the Web, huge amounts of data must be made available in a standard format, reachable and manageable by SW tools. Therefore, the SW community has delivered a wide range of software frameworks that support the Linked Data life cycle including the extraction, storage, interlinking, enrichment, quality analysis, publishing, and exploitation phases. This entry gives an overview of the state-of-the-art SW knowledge representation mechanisms, SW tools, SW services technologies, SW application domains, as well as a projection of the future trends based on the current major open issues.

INTRODUCTION

The term "Semantic Web (SW)" refers to Sir Tim Berners-Lee's vision of the Web of Linked Data (called also the Web of Data) as an extension of the conventional Web. The conventional Web was first proposed by Tim Berners-Lee in 1989 and further refined by him and Robert Cailliau at the European Laboratory for Particle Physics in 1990. The Internet evolution from Web to SW consists of several phases commonly known as Web 1.0, Web 2.0, Web 3.0, and beyond. Web 1.0, which lasted from 1990 to 2002, was mainly devoted to establishing a back end. Although the Web 1.0 phase marks the early Internet days and is characterized by static Hyper Text Markup Language (HTML) Web pages and passive consumption, Web 2.0 (the social Web) aims to facilitate creativity, collaboration, and sharing among users. The next stage, Web 3.0 (the "web of data," since 2006), focuses on meanings, connecting knowledge, and putting everything to work in ways that enable computers and people better cooperation.[1] To make the Web of Data a reality, and push large-scale integration of, and reasoning on, data on the Web, huge amounts of data must be made available in a standard format, reachable and manageable by SW tools. Furthermore, the relationships among data should be made available, thus creating a collection of interrelated datasets (see Fig. 1, retrieved from http://linkeddata.org/) on the Web also referred as Linked Data.[2,3]

The further development of the Internet toward the SW influenced and changed the information technology (IT) market structure in a way that besides the major IT providers (*IBM, ORACLE, Microsoft, SAP*), new semantic technology vendors appear such as *Ontoprise, OpenText, Intellidimension, Topquadrant, Racer Systems,* and others. These software companies along with universities, IT research organizations, and government agencies are actively involved into the SW standardization activities conducted by few international standardization organizations and thus participate in development and implementation of the SW standards. Most relevant standardization organizations for the SW field are the World Wide Web Consortium (W3C) (http://www.w3.org/), the Institute of Electrical and Electronics Engineers Standards Association (http://standards.ieee.org/), the Organization for the Advancement of Structured Information Standards (OASIS) (http://www.oasis-open.org/), and the Object Management Group (http://www.omg.org/).

This entry aims at providing an overview of processes, standards, and tools involved in the realization of Sir Tim Berners-Lee's vision of the Web of Linked Data as well as some background information relevant for understanding the SW technologies. Additionally, it analyses the maturity of SW technologies and possibilities for building real-world applications. In the concluding section, some open issues such as stability of SW languages, interoperability issues, and scalability of SW applications are discussed.

BACKGROUND

The conventional Web is based on HTML, Extensible Markup Language (XML) (http://www.w3.org/XML/), and XHTML Web documents. HTML is a

Encyclopedia of Information Systems and Technology, DOI: 10.1081/E-EIST-120048807

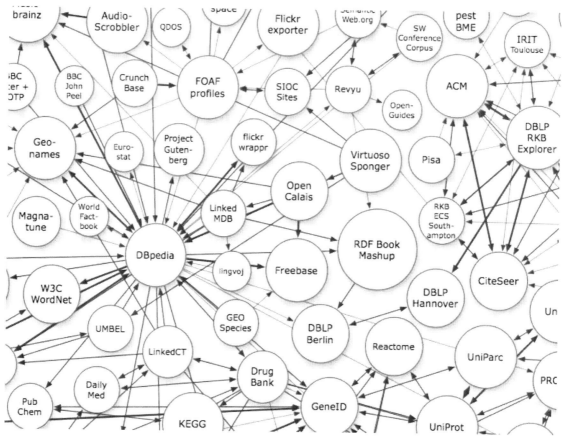

Fig. 1 Part of the linking open (LOD) data project cloud diagram.

nonproprietary format based upon the Standard Generalized Markup Language (ISO 8879:1986 SGML), an ISO-standard technology for defining generalized markup languages for documents published on the World Wide Web. HTML documents can be created and processed by a wide range of tools, from simple plain text editors to sophisticated WYSIWYG (i.e., WhatYou See Is What You Get) authoring tools.

XML is a generic markup language for describing the structure of data. Unlike in HTML, neither the tag set nor the semantics of XML are fixed. XML can thus be used to derive markup languages by specifying tags and structural relationships. XML is, by now, the foremost data representation format for the Web and for semistructured data in general. The term "XML document" is used to denote a hierarchically structured content represented with XML conventions. Since its development in 1996 from the W3C XML Working Group, it has been adopted in a stupendous number of application domains, ranging from document markup (XHTML, http://www.w3.org/TR/xhtml2/) over video annotation and music libraries to Extensible Stylesheet Language Transformations (XSLT) style sheets. Additionally, XML is adopted for serialization of (semantically) richer data representation formats such as Javascript Object Notation and Resource Description

Framework (RDF). Therefore, XML is not only a standard for representing data but it is also a family of standards (some in progress) for information management that includes query languages such as Xpath, XQuery, and Xcerpt; programming interfaces such as Simple Application Programming Interface (API) for XML (SAX) and Document Object Model and Web services standards such as Simple Object Access Protocol (SOAP) and Web Services Description Language (WSDL). XHTML Web documents have HTML tags, XML tags, and plain text and are fully oriented toward visual presentation and keyword search, which makes it appropriate for humans but much less for accesses by software applications.

SW KEY TECHNOLOGIES

The vision of the SW is that of a worldwide distributed architecture where data and services easily interoperate. In the time since the SW's initial conception,[1] the W3C SW Activity Group has accepted numerous Web technologies as standards or recommendations (see Table 1). In an attempt to structure and relate these technologies, Tim Berners-Lee presented several versions of the SW architecture that layered them into a so-

Table 1 W3C key technologies

Description	Date of publication
The general goal of RDF (Resource Description Framework, http://www.w3.org/RDF/) is to define a mechanism for describing resources that make no assumptions about a particular application domain, nor defines the semantics of any application domain. RDF provides interoperability between applications that exchange machine-understandable information on the Web and emphasizes facilities to enable automated processing of Web resources.	2004-02-10
RDF Schema (RDFS) is a declarative language used for the definition of RDF schemas. RDF defines a framework in which independent communities can develop vocabularies that suit their specific needs and share vocabularies with other communities. In order to share vocabularies, the meaning of the terms must be specified in detail. The descriptions of these vocabulary sets are called RDF Schemas. A schema defines the meaning, characteristics, and relationships of a set of properties, and this may include constraints on potential values and the inheritance of properties from other schemas	2004-02-10
SPARQL Query Language for RDF is as a standard language for querying RDF data. Besides querying, SPARQL could be used for data integration from multiple distributed, heterogeneous data sources. A query in SPARQL consists of two parts: the result construction part (head) and the retrieval part (body). SPARQL supports four different querying forms: SPARQL SELECT, SPARQL ASK, SPARQL CONSTRUCT, and SPARQL DESCRIBE.	2008-01-15
OWL 2 Web Ontology Language is one of the most popular ontology languages. OWL facilitates greater machine interpretability of Web content than that supported by XML, RDF, and RDF Schema (RDF-S) by providing additional vocabulary along with a formal semantics. OWL has three increasingly expressive sublanguages: OWL Lite, OWL DL, and OWL Full. The last two languages are based on Description Logics (DL), as well as last version OWL 2. OWL 2 extends the previous version of OWL with a small but useful set of features (EL, QL, and RL) that enable effective reasoning.	2009-10-27
SKOS (Simple Knowledge Organization System Reference) provides a common data model for sharing and linking knowledge organization systems via the Web, as well as a lightweight, intuitive language for developing and sharing new knowledge organization systems.	2009-08-18
RDFa (Resource Description Framework in Attributes) in XHTML is a specification for attributes to express structured data in any markup language, as well as a technique to augment the visual information on the Web with machine-readable hints.	2008-10-14
RIF Rule Interchange Format a standard for exchanging rules among rule systems, in particular among Web rule engines. Known rule systems fall into three broad categories: first-order, logic-programming, and action rules. Therefore, RIF serves to define syntactic mappings from one rule language to RIF dialects and back. The RIF Working Group defined only two logic dialects, the Basic Logic Dialect (RIF-BLD) and a subset, the RIF Core Dialect, shared with RIF-PRD, the Production Rule Dialect (RIF-PRD). Other dialects are expected to be defined by the various user communities.	2010-06-22
POWDER Protocol for Web Description Resources provides means for individuals or organizations to describe a group of resources through the publication of machine-readable metadata.	2009-09-01
GRRDL (Gleaning Resource Descriptions from Dialects of Languages) specification introduces markup based on existing standards for declaring that an XML document includes data compatible with the Resource Description Framework (RDF) and for linking to algorithms (typically represented in XSLT), for extracting this data from the document.	2007-09-11

called stack of increasingly expressive languages for metadata specification (http://www.w3.org/2001/sw/). To represent information on the Web in the form of a graph, the SW uses the RDF as a general-purpose language. To ensure interoperability between applications that exchange machine-understandable information, RDF describes information in terms of objects ("resources") and the relations between them via the RDF Schema, which serves as a meta-language or vocabulary to define properties and classes of RDF

Table 2 RDF specific domain vocabularies/ontologies

Domain	Technology	Date of publication
Government	ORG (an organization ontology, http://www.w3.org/TR/2012/WD-vocab-org-20120405/) is a core ontology for organizational structures, aimed at supporting linked-data publishing of organizational information across a number of domains.	W3C WD, 2012-04-05
Government	DCAT (Data Catalog Vocabulary, http://www.w3.org/TR/2012/WD-vocab-dcat-20120405/) is an RDF vocabulary designed to facilitate interoperability between data catalogs published on the Web.	W3C WD, 2012-04-05
Government	The RDF Data Cube Vocabulary, http://www.w3.org/TR/vocab-data-cube/. The model underpinning the Data Cube vocabulary is compatible with the cube model that underlies SDMX (Statistical Data and Metadata eXchange), an ISO standard for exchanging and sharing statistical data and metadata among organizations.	W3C WD, 2012-04-05
Health Care and Life Sciences	SWAN (Semantic Web Applications in Neuromedicine, http://www.w3.org/TR/hcls-swan/) ontology is an ontology for modeling scientific discourse and has been developed in the context of building a series of applications for biomedical researchers, as well as extensive discussions and collaborations with the larger bio-ontologies community.	W3C Note, 2009-10-20
Media	Ontology for Media Resources (http://www.w3.org/TR/mediaont-10/) defines a core set of metadata properties for media resources, along with their mappings to elements from a set of existing metadata formats.	W3C Recommendation, 2012-02-09
Multidomain	VoID (The Vocabulary of Interlinked Datasets, http://www.w3.org/TR/void/) is an RDF Schema vocabulary that provides terms and patterns for describing RDF datasets and is intended as a bridge between the publishers and users of RDF data.	W3C Note, 2011-03-03
Multidomain	PROV-O (Provenance, http://www.w3.org/TR/prov-o/) family of specifications defines various aspects that are necessary to achieve the vision of interoperable interchange of provenance information in heterogeneous environments such as the Web.	W3C WD, 2012-07-24
Multidomain	EARL (The Evaluation and Report Language, http://www.w3.org/TR/EARL10-Schema/) defines a vocabulary for expressing test results. It enables any person, software application, or organization to assert test results for any test subject tested against any set of criteria. The test subject might be a Website, an authoring tool, a user agent, or some other entity. The set of criteria may be accessibility guidelines, formal grammars, or other types of quality assurance requirements.	W3C WD, 2011-05-10
Multidomain	The Dublin core (DC, http://dublincore.org/) standard includes a standard set of meta tags that are used to track objects in a library collection, making the collection objects searchable in a standard manner. Dublin Core Metadata Element Set has been standardized as ISO Standard 15836:2009.	Version 1.1 2012-06-14
Multidomain	FOAF (Friend of a Friend, http://xmlns.com/foaf/spec/) is a dictionary of named properties and classes using W3C's RDF technology that collects a variety of terms; some describe people, some groups, and some documents.	Version 0.98 2010-08-09
Multidomain	SIOC (SemanticallyInterlinked Online Communities, http://rdfs.org/sioc/spec/) provides the Semantic Web ontology for representing rich data from the Social Web in RDF.	W3C Submission, 2007-06-12

resources. To avoid ambiguity, the RDF Schema uses uniform resource identifier (URI) references for naming. URI reference is a string that represents, for instance, the name or address of an abstract or physical resource on the Web. Furthermore, since every SW resource has a unique URI, it is possible to establish links among existing models, reuse existing models, and build new models upon them, thus creating a network of ontologies and enabling the development of large-scale SW applications.

RDF/OWL VOCABULARIES AND ONTOLOGIES

The next layer on top of the RDF/RDFS (RDF Schema) data model serves to formally define domain models as shared conceptualizations, also often called ontologies.[4] This means that ontology is a description (formal specification) of the concepts and relationships that are of interest for humans or machine agents. Studer, Benjamins, and Fensel[5] define the ontology as "a formal, explicit specification of a shared conceptualization." Roughly, ontologies correspond to generalized database schemes made up of concepts, and the relations between them, that are relevant for a specific domain of knowledge. However, an ontology not only provides a database scheme for storing metadata but also facilitates

Table 3 Main SWS conceptual models and languages

Description	Date of publication
OWL-S (Semantic Markup for Web Services, http://www.w3.org/Submission/OWL-S/) is an ontology of services composed of three main parts: the service profile for advertising and discovering services; the process model, which gives a detailed description of a service's operation; and the grounding, which provides details on how to interoperate with a service, via messages.	W3C Submission, 2004-11-22
WSMO (Web Service Modeling Ontology, http://www.w3.org/Submission/WSMO/) provides a conceptual framework and a formal language for semantically describing all relevant aspects of Web services in order to facilitate the automation of discovering, combining, and invoking electronic services over the Web.	W3C Submission, 2005-06-03
WSDL (Web Services Description Language, http://www.w3.org/TR/wsdl) provides a model and an XML format for describing Web services. It enables one to separate the description of the abstract functionality offered by a service from concrete details of a service description such as "how" and "where" that functionality is offered.	2007-06-26
SAWSDL (Semantic Annotations for WSDL and XML Schema, http://www.w3.org/TR/sawsdl/) a set of extension attributes for the Web Services Description Language and XML Schema definition language that allows the description of additional semantics of WSDL components, for example, input and output message structures, interfaces, and operations.	2007-08-28
SOAP (Messaging Framework, http://www.w3.org/TR/soap12-part1/) is a lightweight protocol intended for exchanging structured information in a decentralized, distributed environment. It consists of the SOAP processing model, the SOAP extensibility model, the SOAP underlying protocol binding framework, and the SOAP message construct that defines the structure of a SOAP message.	2007-04-27
WSML (Web Service Modeling Language, http://www.w3.org/Submission/WSML/) provides a formal syntax and semantics for the Web Service Modeling Ontology WSMO. WSML consists of a number of variants based on these different logical formalisms (Description Logics, First-Order Logic, and Logic Programming), namely, WSML-Core, WSML-DL, WSML-Flight, WSML-Rule, and WSML-Full. WSML-Core corresponds with the intersection of Description Logic and Horn Logic.	W3C Submission, 2005-06-03
SML (Service Modeling Language, http://www.w3.org/TR/sml/) provides a rich set of constructs for creating models of complex services and systems. Depending on the application domain, these models may include information such as configuration, deployment, monitoring, policy, health, capacity planning, target operating range, service level agreements, and so on.	2009-05-12
SA-REST (Semantic Annotations for REST, http://www.w3.org/Submission/SA-REST/) is a poshformat to add additional metadata to (but not limited to) REST API descriptions in HTML or XHTML	W3C Submission, 2010-04-05

semantic content annotation, that is, assigning semantics to a set of knowledge sources (documents) and the definition of rules that are both tractable by machines and understandable for humans. Therefore, ontologies are nowadays very often used for building integrated inter- and intraorganization business services, and to make the search and retrieval both efficient and meaningful. Table 2 points to some of the vocabularies/ontologies under consideration by W3C. As a result of the Open Government Initiative (http://opengovernmentinitiative.org/), the government domain has emerged as one of the promising application areas for SW technologies (e.g., see also http://data.gov.uk/).

After standardizing RDF and the ontology layer, the SW research community's primary efforts in the past few years have been focused on standardizing technologies for SW services and provisioning technologies and tools that enhance interoperability and availability of content on the SW. This latter effort involves the development of rule languages, rule exchange languages, and engines that enhance reasoning, improvement of ontology languages, invention of new knowledge representation formalisms, and elaboration

of methods and tools for publishing linked data on the Web.[6]

SEMANTIC WEB SERVICES TECHNOLOGIES

"Semantic Web services" (SWS) were proposed in order to pursue the vision of the SW presented whereby intelligent agents would be able to exploit semantic descriptions in order to carry out complex tasks on behalf of humans. Activities related to SWS have involved developing conceptual models or ontologies, algorithms, and engines that could support machines in semi-automatically or automatically discovering, selecting, composing, orchestrating, mediating, and executing services.[7] The main principles and conceptual models proposed thus far are OWL-S, Web Service Modeling Ontology (WSMO), Semantic Annotations for WSDL (SAWSDL), and SOAP (see also Table 3). Due to the evolution of the research different definitions of the main SWS tasks can be found in literature. The W3C Web Services Glossary (http://www.w3.org/TR/ws-gloss/) includes the following entries related to SWS tasks:

crawling, discovery, matching, ranking, selection, composition, orchestration, choreography, mediation, invocation, grounding, lifting, and lowering. The architectural model for developing software out of reusable and distributed services is often referred to as Service-Oriented Architecture (SOA).

SW TOOLS

In literature and in practice, SW tools are named by using different keywords: ontology design/management/maintenance tools, semantic data management and integration platforms,[8,9] RDF triple storage systems, Web services, SOA middleware platforms, semantic annotation tools, content indexing and categorization tools, semantic search and information retrieval technologies,[10] Natural Language Processing (NLP), linguistic analysis and text mining algorithms, collaboration and other social networking technologies, knowledge visualization/presentation technologies, ontology mediated portals, ontological querying/inference engines, rule-based engines, ontology learning methods, ontology reasoners, etc. Analyzing the functionalities of more than 50 SW tools provided by 30 different commercial vendors and open source communities, Janev[11] established the following classification of key semantic technology segments: semantic modeling and development, semantic annotation, semantic data management and integration, semantic search and retrieval, semantic collaboration including portal technologies, learning, and reasoning. Exploring the business value of semantic technologies provided by 50 commercial companies, Davis et al.[15] identified the following four major functions: discover, acquire, and create semantic metadata; represent, organize, integrate, and interoperate meanings and resources; reason, interpret, infer, and answer using semantics; and provision, present, communicate, and act using semantics.

Within the LOD2 project, the LOD2 Stack (see http://stack.lod2.eu/) was delivered as a platform of integrated software tools and components enabling corporations, organizations, and individuals to employ *Linked Data* technologies with minimal initial investments. Software tools from 15 different research and commercial organizations provide functionalities for extraction of RDF data from different formats and Relational Database Management System (RDBMS), storing /querying RDF data, manual revision/authoring, interlinking/fusing information, classification/enrichment, quality analysis, evolution/repair, and searching/browsing/exploration (See Table 4). In an attempt to structure the processes that are supported by the Linked Data tools, Auer et al.[2] introduced the Linked Data life cycle, as is presented in Fig. 2. The LOD processes can be defined as follows:

- **Extraction** is an activity that obtains RDF data from different structured and unstructured sources (databases, files).
- **Storage** activity refers to storing RDF datasets in a database.
- **Authoring** is an activity of manual revision of RDF data or content. The authoring tools should completely hide the technicalities of the RDF, RDFS, or OWL data models from end users, thus realizing WYSIWYG for the authoring of knowledge bases.
- **Interlinking** activity is used for creating links between datasets such as mappings between different ontologies. Semiautomatic learning or/and supervised learning algorithms can be used for automatically suggesting interlinking methods and parameters.
- **Enrichment** activity can include the annotation of a document with metadata, the assignment of RDF classes to instances (i.e., the enrichment of RDF instances with upper level ontologies).
- **Analysis** activity is responsible for content and context analysis. The purpose of such an activity can be to evaluate the quality of the content/context withrespectto certain metrics (e.g., regency and trustworthiness among others). Additionally, quality assessment activity is responsible for assessing/analyzing the quality of a dataset.
- **Evolution/repair** activity aims at the automatic maintenance of RDF/OWL knowledge models. A combination of schema enrichment and ontology repair steps can be used for this purpose.
- **Exploration** activity might be a querying and/or visualization activity. A querying activity refers to the execution of queries on a repository or set of repositories via a SPARQL End Point. A visualization activity refers to the visual presentation of a dataset (e.g., CubeViz, http://aksw.org/Projects/CubeViz.html, is a tool for graphical representation of RDF Data Cube models).

Additionally, we can define the following processes that are relevant for tracking provenance on the SW:

- **Transformation** activity includes operations on RDF datasets like merging two datasets, cleaning, or transformation between different formats. During this process the RDF dataset can be modified.
- **Publication** activity refers to the publication of RDF datasets originating from different sources (e.g., databases) on the Web. The RDF datasets can be either uploaded in the cloud (e.g., the LOD cloud at http:// lod2.openlinksw.com/sparql) or registered by a portal (e.g., http://PublicData.eu).

Besides the LOD2 project, there are other projects such as Linked Open DataAround-The-Clock (http:// latc-project.eu/) and PlanetData (http://www.planet-data.

Table 4 LOD processes and tools[a]

Functionalities	LOD2 stack components	Other tools
Extraction of RDF data from structured sources	D2R, Virtuoso Sponger, Triplify	Ontotext WMF
Extraction of RDF data from unstructured sources, annotation, semantic entity extraction and recommendation, reconciliation with DBpedia	DBpedia Spotlight, PoolParty PPX, Zemanta LODGRegine	GATE, UIMA, SemTag, OntosMiner, Mondeca ITM, Ontotext WMF, Ontotext Semantic Biomedical Tagger
Storing/querying RDF data/Semantic Web middleware	Virtuoso	ORACLE 11G, SESAME, OntoBroker, OWLIM, Jena
Manual revision/authoring/semantic modeling	OntoWiki, PoolParty PPT	OntoStudio, TopBraid Composer
Interlinking/fusing information	Silk, Limes	Ontotext KIM Platform
Classification/enrichment	DL-Learner	Aleph ILP Programming system
Quality analysis/evolution/repair	ORE	LINK-QA, Pellet
Searching/browsing/exploration	Sindice, Sig.ma, SPARQL-ED, iSPARQL, LinkedGeoData Browser/Editor	SWSE, Swoogle, Watson, SemanticMiner, Ontotext FactForge, PowerAqua
Semantic portals/cataloguing/publishing	OntoWiki, CKAN	Semantic MediaWiki

[a]A comprehensive list of appropriate Webof data tools, frameworks, and libraries is available at http://esw.w3.org/topic/SemanticWebTools.

eu/) funded by the European Commission with the aim to provide tools and data sets that can speed up the publishing and consumption of Linked Data.

SW APPLICATION DOMAINS

The scientific literature lacks survey analyses of business applications of semantic technologies. In the "The Technology Roadmap of the SW" white paper the authors deliver a comprehensive analysis maturity, applicability, and adoption of the SW technologies[13] based on a survey conducted with selected experts from industry and academia. Using the Gartner Hype Cycle Curve

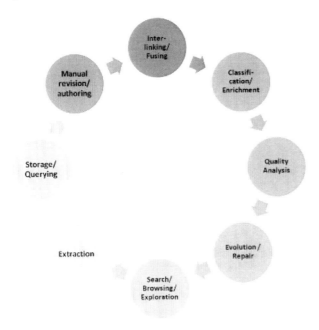

Fig. 2 The linked data life cycle.
Source: From LOD2 project page, http://stack.lod2.eu/.

(http://en.wikipedia.org/wiki/Hype_cycle), they present expert opinions, that is, results of estimation of years to mainstream adoption for different SW technologies and applications both from the researchers' and the business point of view. They found out that "research community considers that developments from the past 10 years have resulted in some tools and standards, which are reliable and mature enough to be transferred to industry and successfully integrated into SW applications. The developers' community, however, is not yet fully aware of the availability of such tools, which, consequently, has to be promoted further, together with the innovative functionalities they can provide to software applications." In the "The Semantic Web Awareness Barometer,[14]" the authors use statistical methods to summarize the results of the survey and the Chi-Square test to compare expert opinions from industry and academia. The analysis indicated that

> the expectations in Semantic Web technologies were very high in both groups. Generally both groups believe that organisational culture is not yet ready for the Semantic Web. Additionally, application-oriented participants believe that Semantic Web technologies are too complex. On the contrary, research-oriented participants believe that the lack of success stories, a lack of quality of available software, the problem of quantifying the benefits, the costs of implementation and the general heterogeneity of information are the biggest obstacles to the application of Semantic Web technologies.

The scientific literature regarding the classification of SW application domains is as follows. In a technology assessment report based on findings from 35 semantic technology early adopters from many different verticals, Davis et al.,[15] identified the following application areas: infrastructure and integration, managing risk, customer-facing services, output management, smart

Table 5 Semantic Web technologies' application domains

Goal	Application/service description	Example tool
Data integration	Services for retrieving, merging, and storing of data originated in heterogeneous, expanding set of corporate/public data sources using ontologies and Web services.	*OpenLink's Virtuoso* (http://virtuoso.openlinksw.com/), a middleware and database engine.
Service integration	Web services with the aims to augment service integration, i.e., discovery, composition, ranking, selection, and mediation of services.[16]	*WSMX* (http://www.wsmx.org/) is a component-based execution environment for WSMO that aims to support the discovery, composition, mediation, selection, and invocation of Web services based on a set of user's requirements. WSMX is also a reference architecture of OASIS Semantic Execution Environment Technical Committee.
Semantic Search/ Semantic content discovery	Services that aim to augment and improve traditional search results by using not just words but concepts and logical relationships.	*SIG. MA* (http://sig.ma/) is a search application built on top of *Sindice* (Semantic Web index, sindice.com) that aggregates heterogeneous data gathered on the Web of Data into a single entity profile using Semantic Web data consolidation techniques.
Information extraction and Semantic annotation	Services that enable assigning unambiguous meaning to resources (e.g., assigning types to single terms or semantic relations to pairs of terms) in order to enable a more efficient discovery mechanism.	*DBpedia Spotlight* (http://spotlight.dbpedia.org/) is a tool for annotating mentions of DBpedia resources in text, providing a solution for linking unstructured information sources to the Linked Open Data cloud through *DBpedia* (dbpedia.org).
Natural language interfaces	Applications that provide natural, human-like interaction with the computer.	*Watson* (http://www-03.ibm.com/innovation/us/watson/) is a question-answering system that utilizes NLP technology to interpret the question and extract key elements such as the answer type and relationships between entities. Watson is based on the *DeepQA* software architecture and has been applied in healthcare and finance domains.
Social networks	Technologies that are used to help people track, discover, and share content around topics they are interested in, thus forming social networks.	*OntoWiki* (http://ontowiki.net/) is a semantic collaboration software that provides support for agile, distributed knowledge engineering scenarios. *Onto Wiki* uses RDF in the first place to represent information. For human users, *Onto Wiki* allows to create different views on data, such as tabular representations or maps. For machine consumption it supports various RDF serializations as well as RDFa, Linked Data, and SPARQL interfaces.
Publishing linked open data	Technologies aimed at data publishers (e.g., national and regional governments, companies, and organizations) wanting to make their data open and available.	*CKAN* (http://ckan.org/) is a powerful data management system that makes data accessible—by providing tools to streamline publishing, sharing, finding, and using data.

products and services, design and manufacture, research, input management, supplier facing processes, intelligence, and security. Analyzing the time to mainstream adoption of semantic technologies in different business applications from practitioners' point of view, European researchers[13] found that the most mature business application areas were bioinformatics, knowledge management, and e-learning. Business areas with less than 5 years of mainstream adoption were B2B (Business-to-Business) and B2C (Business-to-Customer), while the duration to mainstream adoption for e-government applications was estimated to be more than 5 years. Looking at the business areas of early adopters registered in the W3C collection of SW Case Studies and Use Cases,

Janev and Vraneš[12] found that 36% of the early adopters were public institutions and that 47% of them implemented e-government principles using semantic technologies. Further, 12% of them were applications in the health sector and exactly the same share had the applications in the IT industry, and then follow with less than 10% the applications in the telecommunications sector, life sciences (pharmaceutical industry), broadcasting services and library services, while only 2% were finance applications. Additionally, the authors compiled a list of the most mature application areas of semantic technologies (see Table 5).

Table 6 RDF resources available in the LOD cloud

Domain	Thesaurus/vocabulary/ontology
Agriculture	AGROVOC—Agriculture Vocabulary published for the first time in the early 1980s by the Food and Agriculture Organization of the United Nations, http://aims.fao.org /
Agriculture	NALT—National Agricultural Library Thesaurus, United States Department of Agriculture, http://agclass.nal.usda.gov/
Social science	TheSoz—Thesaurus for the Social Sciences, http://www.gesis.org/en/services/research/thesauri-und-klassifikationen/social-science-thesaurus/
Environment	GEMET—General Multilingual Environmental Thesaurus, http://eionet.europa.eu/gemet
Economy	STW—Thesaurus for Economics, http://zbw.eu/stw/versions/latest/about
Aeronautics and space science	NASA—National Aeronautics and Space Administration Taxonomy, http://nasataxonomy.jpl.nasa.gov
Geography	GeoNames—Worldwide geographical database, http://www.geonames.org/
Health care and life sciences	MeSH—National Library of Medicine's controlled vocabulary thesaurus, http://www.nlm.nih.gov/mesh
Health care and life sciences	DO—Standardized ontology for human diseases, http://www.disease-ontology.org/
Health care and life sciences	SNOMED CT—the Systematized Nomenclature of Medicine Clinical Terms, http://www.ihtsdo.org/snomed-ct/, owned and administered by the International Health Terminology Standards Development Organisation.
Health care and life sciences	GO—Gene Ontology, http://www.geneontology.org/

For more info, please see http://www.w3.org/2001/sw/wiki/SKOS/Datasets.

Data and Service Integration

Ontologies (see Table 2) and RDF resources (see Table 6) are the backbone of the SW, a semantic-aware version of the World Wide Web. They provide reference models for data and process integration as well as knowledge sharing between systems and people in ways that facilitate machine reasoning and inference.

Considering the most often used languages and formalisms for building ontologies, we found out that most of the domain-specific, business process, and geospatial ontologies were based on the RDFS, OWL-Lite, F-logic,[17] and Web Service Modeling Language (WSML) Flight knowledge representation language. As our analysis previously showed, ontology-based approaches to service and data integration are slowly considered as an alternative for existing approaches of SOA and RDBMS-based data integration.

Semantic Search and Content Discovery

Considering the applicability of SW technologies for search and content discovery, we can distinguish three different use scenarios of utilization of SW technologies:

- Meaningful search in domain-specific applications, for example, discovery and retrieval of geospatial information or indexing, cataloging, or searching for biomedical and health-related information and documents
- Visual search, navigation, and querying of large public interlinked datasets within the Web of Data (e.g.,

see tools such as the SW indexing engine *Sindice* at http://www.sindice.com/, the Semantic Information MAshup *SIG. MA* at http://sig.ma/, or the *VisiNav* system at http://visinav.deri.org/).
- Hybrid search as a search method that supports both document and knowledge retrieval via the flexible combination of ontology-based search and keyword-based matching

SW approaches proved their advantages in domain-specific applications on the search side. Considering the knowledge extraction side, the focus of research has moved from semiautomatic annotation and text-based topic discovery to semantic knowledge extraction from multimodal data sources.[18] Comparing the SW search and metadata service engines such as *Sindice*, *SWSE* (http://swse.deri.org/), *Swoogle* (http://swoogle.umbc.edu/), and *Watson* (http://kmi-eb05.open.ac.uk/Watson-WUI/) with the traditional ones such as *Google* and *Yahoo*, we conclude that the traditional search engines mainly search for unlimited topics in unstructured contents, while semantic search engines search for limited/unlimited topics in structured/unstructured contents. In order to improve the search and become a real knowledge engine, *Google* introduced an enhancement known as *Knowledge Graph* (http://www.google.com/insidesearch/features/search/knowledge.html), a massive graph of real-world things and their connections.

Semantic Annotation

Semantic annotations are machine-processable tags that are associated with a word, phrase, text, picture, or video with the aim to describe that portion of data uniquely. SW annotation systems utilize text/video processing approaches to assign semantics, expose the annotations as linked data, and to create links to contextually relevant resources on the Web (e.g., *DBpedia*). The semantics of words differ from domain to domain, and therefore efficient semantic annotation requires domain learning or manual domain specification in a form of taxonomy.

Natural Language Interfaces

Natural language search interfaces aim at hiding the formality of an ontology-based knowledge base as well as the executable query language from end-users by offering an intuitive and familiar way of query formulation. Two types of ontology-based QA systems exist: Natural Language Interfaces to structured data (databases and multiple and heterogeneous SW sources, e.g., *PowerAqua*) and QA over free text (e.g., *Watson*). *PowerAqua*'s main advantage "with respect to current state of the art approaches is its deep exploitation of the massively distributed and heterogeneous SW resources to drive, interpret and answer the users' requests" (http://technologies.kmi.open.ac.uk/poweraqua/). Watson query answering system, for instance, uses NLP to analyze (prior to the competition) the vast amounts of unstructured text (encyclopedias, dictionaries, news articles, etc.) that may provide evidence in support of the answers to the questions.

Social Networks

Social network technologies such as wiki-based systems and social tagging systems aim at interactive information sharing, facilitating interoperability, user-centered design, and improving the collaboration on the World Wide Web. The basic features of social networking sites are profiles, friends' listings and commenting, messaging, discussion forums, blogging, media uploading, and sharing. From the SW perspective, one of the limitations of the social network technologies is that metadata that is added to the Web content is based on freely chosen keywords (folksonomies) instead of a controlled vocabulary thus producing ambiguity in the meaning of words or phrases on the Web. Therefore, research efforts during the last several years have been devoted to bridging the gap between the Web 2.0 and SW paradigms and to developing and implementing SW tools and technologies into Social Web applications.

Publishing Linked Open Data on the Web

Linked Open Data (LOD) is a growing movement for organizations to make their existing data available in a machine-readable format. Although in the past governments have been protective over the data they collect, citing national security and citizen privacy as reasons, recently they (especially the United States of America and the United Kingdom) have been taking active part in the Open Government Data initiative. The process of integrating public data into the LOD cloud can be implemented with the LOD2 tools discussed earlier.[19]

CONCLUDING REMARKS

Although many SW-related technologies have emerged or have been elaborated in the last few years and have already been adopted in corporate environments, a lot still has to be done until Berners-Lee's vision of the SW becomes a reality.[6]

Investigating the adoption of the SW technologies by enterprises, Davis et al.[15] identified the following major open issues: scalability and run-time support, interoperability between different knowledge organization schemas, data synchronization between OWL/RDF-based knowledge bases and the traditional persistence mechanisms, migration from traditional to semantic-enabled technologies. Herein, we will discuss the future development of SW technologies from the following perspectives: i) availability of content; ii) interoperability; iii) standardization and stability of SW languages; iv) scalability; and v) large-scale adoption.

Availability of Content

The process of online conversion of the existing unstructured contents on the Web into a format understandable by computers is not a trivial and not generally solvable task. However, we have to note here that the majority of content on the Web is generated dynamically, for example, exported from RDBMS. When the content stored in RDBMS is exported into RDFS, the problem of consistency and synchronization appears, because the RDF store should be updated each time the RDBMS is updated. Therefore, it is a recent trend to use the RDBMS as a SW endpoint and SPARQL + SPARQL/Update for ontology-based read and write access to relational data.

Heterogeneity and Interoperability Issue

One of the most challenging and important tasks of the SW ontology engineering is the integration of ontologies with the purpose of building a common ontology for all Web sources and consumers in a domain. The available ontologies often exhibit different conceptualizations of similar or overlapping domains, thus leading to the interoperability problem. The problem could be overcome by detecting semantic relations between concepts, properties, or instances of two ontologies, that is, ontology matching. Due to the increasing number of methods available for schema matching/ontology integration, the Ontology Alignment Evaluation Initiative (see http://oaei.ontologymatching.org/) was started with the aim to compare systems and algorithms on the same basis and to allow anyone to draw conclusions about the best matching strategies. The recent and future trends in overcoming schema heterogeneity between linked semantic repositories, that is, ontology matching consider using reasoning languages (e.g., Distributed Description Logics) to reason about ontology alignments in distributed environments.

Standardization and Stability of Languages

While the W3C makes extensive efforts to define and standardize the upper layers of the W3C SW architecture model that refers to logic, inference, and reasoning, the research communities come out with new SW languages (as was presented earlier). Reasoning is a distinctive feature of the SW. The advanced reasoning tools and technologies are mainly delivered by open source communities, while the contemporary commercial SW development frameworks offer integration with few years old reasoning engines such as *Pellet*, *KAON2*, or *Jess*.

Scalability of SW Applications

The scalability issue was identified very early in the SW research and adequately addressed. However, despite the huge number of SW applications today, advanced SW technologies such as reasoning under open-world assumptions are hardly applicable in real-time on Web scale.

Large-Scale Adoption

The problem of widespread adoption of SW technologies in situations where existing Web technologies already proved useful still exists. In our opinion, additional investments are needed to mature SW technologies, especially to optimize the querying and reasoning strategies. Concepts and methods already proven in information retrieval (e.g., the *MapReduce* approach introduced by *Google*) and data base processing should be adopted to improve the performance of distributed systems and achieve scalable distributed reasoning. Instead of competing, the SW should integrate features from other similar research communities, that is, the Social Web and the Pragmatic Web (http://www.pragmaticweb.info/). While the SW promotes "cooperation through shared models of knowledge," the Pragmatic Web "does not rely merely on shared models of knowledge, but also on shared ways of socially cultivating the ways of representing knowledge."[20] Thus, the relevant topics of future investigation and development include ontology negotiations, the integration of contextual ontologies, and developing pragmatic patterns for defining issues such as communication, information, and tasks.

ACKNOWLEDGMENTS

The research presented in this paper is partly financed by the European Union (FP7 LOD2 project, Pr. No: 257943; FP7 GeoKnow, Pr. No: 318159), and partly by the Ministry of Science and Technological Development of Republic of Serbia (SOFIA project, Pr. No: TR-32010).

REFERENCES

1. Berners-Lee, T.; Hendler, J.; Lassila, O. *The Semantic Web. Scientific American*, May **2001**, http://www.sciam.com/article.cfm?id = the-semantic-web

2. Auer, S.; Buhmann, L.; Dirschl, C.; Erling, O.; Hausenblas, M.; Isele, R.; Lehmann, J.; Martin, M.; Mendes, P.; van Nuffelen, B.; Stadler, C.; Tramp, S.; Williams, H. Managing the Life-cycle of Linked Data with the LOD2 Stack. In Proceeding of 11th International Semantic Web Conference, Springer: Berlin Heidelberg, Boston, MA, USA, Nov 11–15, 2012; pp. 1–16; **2012**.

3. Heath, T.; Bizer, C. Linked data: Evolving the web into a global data space. In *Synthesis Lectures on the Semantic Web: Theory and Technology* (1st Ed.); Morgan & Claypool: 2011; Vol. 1, 1–136.

4. Gruber, T.R. A translation approach to portable ontology specification. Knowl. Acquisit. **1993**, *5* (2), 199–220. Retrieved from http://tomgruber.org/writing/ontolingua-kaj-1993.htm

5. Studer, R.; Benjamins, V.R.; Fensel, D. Knowledge engineering: principles and methods. Data Knowl. Eng. **1998**, *25*, 161–197.

6. Bizer, C.; Heath, T.; Berners-Lee, T. Linked data—The story so far. Intl J. Semant. Web Inform. Syst. **2009**, *5* (3), 1–22.

7. McIlraith, S.A.; Cao Son, T.; Zeng, H. Semantic web services. IEEE Intel. Syst. **2001**, *16* (2), 46–53.

8. Cardoso, J. The semantic web vision: Where are we? IEEE Intel. Syst. September/October **2007**, *22* (5), 22–26.

9. d'Aquin, M.; Motta, E.; Sabou, M.; Angeletou, S.; Gridinou, L.; Lopez, V.; Guidi, D. Toward a new generation of semantic web applications. IEEE Intel. Syst. **2008**, *23* (3), 20–28.

10. Mangold, C. A survey and classification of semantic search approaches. Int. J. Metadata Semant. Ontol. **2007**, *2* (1), 23–31.

11. Janev, V. A comparison and critical assessment of cutting edge semantic web products and technologies. In *Semantic Web and/or Web 2.0: Competitive or Complementary?* S. Vraneš (Ed.), Academic mind: Belgrade, Serbia, **2008**; pp. 148–165.

[12] Janev V, Vraneš S. Applicability assessment of semantic web technologies. *Inform. Process. Manag* **2011**;*47*(4):507–17

13. Cuel, R.; Delteil, A.; Louis, V.; Rizzi, C. The Technology Roadmap of the Semantic Web. KnowledgeWeb White paper, FP6-507482, **2007**. Retrieved from http://knowledgeweb.semanticweb.org/o2i/menu/KWTR-whitepaper-43-final.pdf

14. Pellegrini, T.; Blumauer, A.; Granitzer, G.; Paschke, A.; Luczak-Rösch, M. Semantic Web Awareness Barometer 2009 - Comparing Research- and Application-oriented Approaches to Social Software and the Semantic Web. In *Proceedings of I-KNOW '09 and I-SEMANTICS '09*, A. Paschke, H. Weigand, W. Behrendt, K. Tochtermann, T. Pellegrini (Eds.); Graz, Austria: J. UCS.

15. Davis, M.; Allemang, D.; Coyne, R. *Evaluation and Market Report. IST Project 2001-33052 WonderWeb*: Ontology Infrastructure for the Semantic Web, **2004**.

16. Pedrinaci, C.; Domingue, J.; Sheth, A. *Semantic web services. In Handbook of Semantic Web Technologies*, Vol. 2 – *Semantic Web Applications*; J. Dominique, D. Fensel, J. Hendler (Eds.); Springer, **2010**. Retrieved from http://knoesis.wright.edu/library/download/Semantic_Web_Services-Formatted.pdf

17. Kifer, M. Rules and ontologies in F-logic. Reason. Web **2005**, 22–34.

18. Ahmed, A.; Arnold, A.; Coelho, L.P.; Kangas, J.; Sheikh, A.-S.; Xing, E.; Cohen, W.; Murphy, R.F. Structured literature image finder: Parsing text and figures in biomedical literature. J. Web Semant. **2010**, *8* (2–3), 151–154.

19. Janev, V.; Milošević, U.; Spasić, M.; Milojković, J.; Vraneš, S. Linked open data infrastructure for public sector information: Example from Serbia. In Proceedings of the I-SEMANTICS **2012** Posters & Demonstrations Track. S. Lohmann, T. Pellegrini (Eds.); CEUR Workshop Proceedings, **2012**; Vol. *932*, pp. 26–30.

20. Alani, H.; Hall, W.; O'Hara, K.; Shadbolt, N.; Szomszor, M.; Chandler, P. Building a pragmatic semantic web. IEEE Intel. Syst. May/June **2008**, *23* (3), 61–68.

SIM: Society for Information Management

Leon Kappelman
Information Technology and Decision Sciences Department, University of North Texas, Denton, Texas, U.S.A.

Abstract

Since 1968, the Society for Information Management (SIM) has inspired the minds of the most prestigious information technology (IT) leaders in the industry. Highly regarded as the premier network for IT leadership, SIM is a community of thought leaders who share experiences and rich intellectual capital, and who explore future IT direction.

VISION

The vision of Society for Information Management (SIM) is to be recognized as the community that is most preferred by information technology (IT) leaders for delivering vital knowledge that creates business value and enables personal development.

MISSION

SIM is an association of senior IT executives, prominent academicians, selected consultants, and other IT thought leaders; it is built on the foundation of local chapters who come together to share and enhance their rich intellectual capital, for the benefit of its members and their organizations. SIM members strongly believe in and champion:

- The alignment of IT and business as a valued partnership.
- The creation and sharing of best practices.
- The effective, efficient, and innovative business use of information technology to continuously bring to market valuable products and services.
- IT management and leadership skills development that enables our members growth at each stage of their career.
- The replenishment and education of future IT leaders including a strong role in influencing university curriculums and continuing education.
- Working with the IT industry to shape its direction.
- Policies and legislation that stimulate innovation, economic development, healthy competition, and IT job creation.
- Serving our communities and the industry through giving and outreach.

WHAT DOES SIM OFFER?

Recognizing the unique needs of the industry, SIM collects the intellectual capital of IT leaders nationwide and offers the resources you need to do business better, including:

- **Face-to-face meetings/networking**—Annual SIMposium conference, advance practices council meetings, regional leadership forums, chapter meetings, working groups, communities of interest, and CIO roundtables bring you face-to-face with other key industry executives to share knowledge and network about topics pertinent to IT leaders.
- **Online tools**—On-demand webinars and archived webcasts, an online library featuring nearly fifty white papers, working group deliverables, past conference presentations, and much more to bring best practices of other IT leaders straight to your desktop.
- **Publications**—*SIM News*—a compilation of association news, articles of interest, interviews, and industry insights—and *MIS Quarterly Executive*—a quarterly publication dedicated to publishing high-quality articles, case studies, and research reports.
- **More resources/programs**—SIM offers a wealth of knowledge with these resources and more. Visit http://simnet.org for additional information.

INSIDE SIM

Strategic direction for the organization is provided by SIM's elected executive board. SIM's standing committees are key to developing initiatives that fulfill the strategic goals of the association. Supporting the organization and fulfilling day-to-day management responsibility is SIM's professional staff.

Resources– Six Sigma

Encyclopedia of Information Systems and Technology, DOI: 10.1081/E-EIST-120053820

Six Sigma

Christine B. Tayntor
Writer, Cheyenne, Wyoming, U.S.A.

Abstract

Although the term *Six Sigma* has become synonymous with highly efficient, customer-focused companies that have reduced costs while increasing customer satisfaction, at its most fundamental, Six Sigma is a measurement of quality. A process that operates at the Six Sigma level has so few defects that it is nearly perfect.

DEFINING SIX SIGMA

Six Sigma has its origins in statistics, and, in fact, the term is a statistical one. A statistician would explain that in addition to being the 18th letter of the Greek alphabet, sigma (σ) is the symbol for standard deviation. The same statistician would point out that a process that is at the Six Sigma level has six standard deviations between its process center and the upper and lower specification limits. In simpler terms, that process produces only 3.4 defects per million opportunities. If that sounds close to perfection, it is.

While there is no denying the statistical origin of Six Sigma or the fact that statistical analysis plays an important role in many companies' implementation of Six Sigma, it has become more than a simple measurement of defects. The term is now used to encompass concepts and tools, all of which are designed to help achieve the goal of nearly perfect processes, in many cases without relying on heavy-duty statistics.

MORE THAN STATISTICS

Six Sigma is more than statistics. While its objectives are to reduce variation and prevent defects, it has also become a management philosophy that includes in its credo the need for fact-based decisions, customer focus, and teamwork.

If this sounds like *déjà vu*, yet another productivity program *du jour* that will be supplanted next year, the results Six Sigma companies have achieved should dispel the skepticism. While some previous quality and productivity initiatives promised great benefits but frequently failed to deliver them, Six Sigma delivers. Streamlined processes and less rework result in lower costs. Add them to improved customer satisfaction, and

the effect on the bottom line can only be positive. This is the power of Six Sigma.

How great can the improvement be? To put Six Sigma in perspective, most companies operate between three and four sigma. As shown in Table 1, a four sigma process has greater than 99% accuracy. While that might appear acceptable, consider the third column in Table 1. Four sigma processes have 6210 defects per million, compared to 3.4 for Six Sigma. If it took only 1 minute to correct each defect, a four sigma company would spend $103^1/_2$ *hours* in error correction compared to less than $3^1/_2$ *minutes*. Even at minimum wage, the difference is significant. Most defects, of course, require far more than a minute to correct.

More significantly, many are never corrected but instead are found by customers. While not all customers will return a defective product and demand a replacement, it is a rare one that will ignore poor quality. For the company that permitted defective products to ship, the result may be thousands of dollars of lost future sales.

NOT JUST PRODUCTS

Although Six Sigma had its origin in manufacturing, it also applies to service industries. A defect is a defect. Whether a customer receives the wrong sized widget or an incorrect answer to an inquiry, the result is the same: dissatisfaction, increased costs to correct the error, and potential lost sales.

Six Sigma companies focus on far more than the measurement and elimination of defects. For them, Six Sigma is the way they do business. It permeates their corporate culture and becomes one of the things that defines them and differentiates them from their competition.

Encyclopedia of Information Systems and Technology, DOI: 10.1081/E-EIST-120053842

Table 1 Comparison of sigma levels three through six

Sigma level	Percent correct	Number of defects per million opportunities	Lost time per century
3	93.3193	66,807	3½ months
4	99.3790	6,210	2½ days
5	99.9767	233	30 minutes
6	99.99966	3.4	6 seconds

Six Sigma is built on a foundation that includes the following tenets:

- Prevent defects
- Reduce variation
- Focus on the customer
- Make decisions based on facts
- Encourage teamwork

DEFECT PREVENTION

One way in which Six Sigma differs from previous quality initiatives is in its insistence that the way to eliminate defects is through prevention rather than correction. This is an important distinction. While it may seem that the results—zero defect products—appear the same to the customer, there is a fundamental difference between the philosophies of correction and prevention, just as there is a fundamental difference between fire fighting and fire prevention. Classic quality control inspected *products* to find the defects, then corrected them. Six Sigma analyzes the *process* to determine what causes the defects then changes the process to prevent them. As shown in Table 2, the effect of prevention is widespread and permanent.

Although the difference may not be immediately apparent to the customer, prevention of defects has a positive effect on the company's bottom line. That is because the cost of poor quality (COPQ) has been eliminated. Although some companies equate COPQ with warranty work and the cost of returned products, both of those are the result of customer-detected defects. Because the objective is to identify defects before they leave the factory, the COPQ should also include the following elements related to internal detection.

- *Scrap or waste:* the product or material that cannot be used or sold.
- *Rework:* the effort required to correct an error.
- *Inspection:* the cost of performing quality control.

- *Reporting:* the effort involved in developing and reviewing reports.

While many companies focus on the first two components, the cost of inspection and reporting can exceed scrap and rework, particularly in service processes. Sometimes whole organizations spring into existence to monitor quality. In other cases, employees develop informal methods of detecting and correcting defects before they reach quality control and can be reported. These processes are often referred to as "a hidden factory."

The COPQ can be significant. The need to reduce it was, in fact, the impetus for Motorola's initiating a Six Sigma program in 1979. For a four sigma company, the COPQ is estimated to be between 15% and 25% of sales; whereas for a six sigma company, it is less than 1% of sales. Reducing the COPQ can have a measurable effect on the bottom line. This is the reason Six Sigma companies place such a high emphasis on preventing rather than correcting defects. By "mistake-proofing" a process, defects are eliminated, and the COPQ is greatly reduced.

REDUCED VARIATION

The second Six Sigma tenet is to reduce variation, or—to explain it in another way—to increase consistency. This is one way to prevent defects. Consistency is important because it is predictable. And what is predictable can be perfected. As shown on Fig. 1, although it might appear that the dart player on the left is the better one, because they hit the bull's eye once, a Six Sigma company would prefer the consistency of the player on the right. Although they have never hit the bull's eye, and in fact have never even come close, this player's aim is consistent. Whatever they are doing wrong that keeps them from hitting the bull's eye is unvarying. As such, it can be corrected.

Table 2 Comparison of Six Sigma and quality control

	Action taken	Action is on	Effect is	Effect is on	Need to repeat
Quality control	Inspect	Product	Correction of error	One product	Constantly
Six Sigma	Analyze	Process	Prevention of defect	All products	None

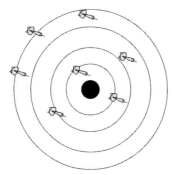

Hitting the bull's eye once isn't good enough. This player shows too much variation.

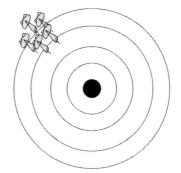

Although this player never hit the bull's eye, the consistency of dart placement means that a "process shift" could result in consistent bull's eyes.

Fig. 1 Which player is better? A pictorial representation of variation.

As detailed in "More than Statistics," for a Six Sigma company, the next steps would be to examine the process (i.e., throwing darts) to determine what has caused the defect (i.e., not hitting the bull's eye) and then change the process to eliminate the defect. Perhaps the player is holding the dart too high. Perhaps they did not considered the effect of the wind. Perhaps

their eyesight is not perfect. In any case, with training or improved tools (glasses), they should be able to hit the bull's eye consistently.

Consistent, on-target results are the goal of every company. Six Sigma helps them get there.

CUSTOMER FOCUS

Six Sigma companies spend a lot of time talking about—and to—customers. Whether they are external customers, the ones who buy the products or services the company sells, or internal ones, such as a department that uses a service another department provides, customers are the focal point of all activities. This is in direct contrast to many companies' focus on the bottom line. Six Sigma companies know that satisfying customers and increasing profits are not mutually exclusive but, rather, that increased profits are a direct result of having a strong customer focus. That is one of the reasons why eliminating defects is so important. Customers want— and deserve—perfect products and services.

Six Sigma projects begin by listening to the *voice of the customer*. That means learning what customers need and which of those requirements are most important to them. But concern for the customer does not end when requirements are identified and the project is initiated. The entire project life cycle is characterized by constant communication, and it is much more than delivering periodic status reports. This is genuine two-way communication, ensuring that customers are a part of the

process and that the results will satisfy their requirements.

The reason for such a high level of customer focus is simple: without the customer, there is no need for the company itself to exist.

FACT-BASED DECISIONS

One of the hallmarks of a Six Sigma company is its insistence that decisions are based on facts. Although a project may be initiated because someone says, "*I think* we could improve our process by doing...," no action would be taken until the project team can state, "*We know* that our process will be improved if we...." Intuition and *gut feel* are second to incontrovertible facts. As detailed in "More than Statistics," getting from *I think* to *we know* requires an analysis of both the current process and the reason why the change is necessary or desirable. Although these analyses can be performed concurrently, neither can be neglected.

It is important to understand exactly how a process is operating before making any changes. That may sound basic, and it is, but all too often in the rush to show progress in solving a problem, companies fail to understand exactly what it is that they are changing before they begin to implement the modification. The result of this failure can be unexpected side effects or, in Six Sigma terms, defects.

Consider the Monster Cracker Manufacturer. When its best-selling crackers emerged from the oven apparently undercooked, the intuitive response would have been to raise the temperature of the oven. Instead, the company analyzed the entire cracker-making process and discovered that the problem was caused by excess humidity in the mixing room. Had the oven been adjusted rather than reducing the amount of liquid in the batter, the result would have been crackers that still did not meet the company's—or the customer's—standards.

Similarly, it is important to ensure that the change being made is the right one. This is a corollary to focusing on the customer. Before beginning any process changes, a Six Sigma company knows that it is essential to understand what the customer *really* wants, not simply the project team's perception of the customer's needs. A defect-free product is of no value if it is not one the customer will buy.

Like customer focus, the reason for insisting on fact-based decisions is simple. By having all the facts before making any change, a Six Sigma company eliminates the rework and waste caused by solving the wrong problem.

TEAMWORK

It is not insignificant that the previous paragraphs described the process of moving from *I think* to *we know*, because teamwork is one of the characteristics of Six Sigma companies. Just as they recognize the importance of working on the right projects, these companies realize that the ability to understand what is currently happening, to determine what is causing the variation, and to develop methods of preventing defects requires having the right people working together to solve the problem. Individual heroics are much less important than the work that is accomplished by having the right group of people working together, sharing knowledge and expertise.

Although the corporate hierarchy does not disappear in a Six Sigma company, it is of little importance when a team is formed. This is why many meetings begin with the admonition to *check titles at the door*. Team members are selected and valued because of their knowledge and expertise, not their position on an org chart.

Similarly, departmental rivalries and functional silos that discourage sharing of information have no place in a Six Sigma company. Because most processes span departmental boundaries, with one department providing input to a process and another using the output, teams are almost always cross-functional. The objective is to assemble the right group of people so that decisions are indeed fact based rather than being dependent on incomplete knowledge or assumptions.

Teams are, quite simply, the mechanism Six Sigma companies use to eliminate defects.

TOOLS AND TRAINING

Because one of their primary goals is to reduce variation, it is logical that Six Sigma projects would use a standard process and set of tools, rather than relying on each team to develop its own problem-solving techniques. Not only does this increase consistency, but it also reduces the time—and cost—of teams' reinventing processes.

Six Sigma projects are divided into five phases, with recommended tools for each phase. "More than Statistics" describes the phases, tools, and overall process in detail.

Because Six Sigma companies recognize that training is a necessity rather than a luxury if their employees are to understand both the philosophy of Six Sigma and the best ways to implement that philosophy,

there are three levels of formal training programs: 1) Green Belt; 2) Black Belt; and 3) Master Black Belt. Green Belt courses, which consist of up to 2 weeks of training, provide basic knowledge of the concepts and tools. Black Belts are given in-depth training, normally an additional 4 weeks, with more emphasis on the statistical analysis tools, while Master Black Belts receive specialized training in the statistical tools, enabling them to guide and mentor Black Belts on their projects.

Unlike many corporate training programs, these culminate in employee certification. Typically, participants may not attend training unless they are part of a team with an approved project. The reason for this stipulation is the understanding that learning is more effective when it includes applying concepts to *real-world* problems rather than simply using classroom examples. Having a project turns theory into practice. This approach has the added benefit of getting projects completed, because certification occurs only after the project is finished and the students can demonstrate both knowledge of the Six Sigma problem-solving process and that they used the tools in their project.

A STRATEGY, NOT AN INITIATIVE

Six Sigma is often described as a strategy rather than an initiative. Although that may seem like semantics, it is not. Webster defines an initiative as an "introductory step," while a strategy is a "careful plan or method." The distinction is an important one. Six Sigma is more than a beginning or a first step. With its emphasis on analysis and fact-based decisions, it provides a method for improving a company.

To do that, three things must be right: the right *people* must be working on the right *problem* in the right *way*.

DESIGN FOR SIX SIGMA (DFSS): THE LOGICAL EXTENSION TO SIX SIGMA

Six Sigma is a strategy and a highly effective one. It does, however, have limitations. Even when applied rigorously,

Table 3 Comparison of six sigma and DFSS

	Action taken	Timing of action	Action is on	Effects are	Effects is on	Need to repeat
Six Sigma	Analyze	At any point in the lifecycle of the process/product	Any portion of existing process	Prevention of defects	All products	None
DFSS	Design	Before the process/product is initially developed	Entirely of new process	Prevention of defects, increased quality, increased customer satisfaction	All products	None

companies have discovered that they are not reaching their goal of having six sigma processes, but in fact rarely exceed a sigma level of 4.5. This represents 1350 defects per million opportunities, a number that is still too high for most companies. The reason for this shortfall is that traditional Six Sigma focuses on improving existing processes. While there is no denying the benefit to be derived from reducing variation and eliminating defects in existing processes, this may not be enough.

Classic Six Sigma assumes that the fundamental design of the process being optimized is a good one. It may not be. As Chowdhury states, "80 percent of quality problems are unwittingly designed into the product."[1] In that case, because the Six Sigma process begins after design is complete, it may be impossible to correct all of the problems and achieve the company's goal of near-perfection.

DFSS tackles this problem by starting earlier in the process. As its name implies, it focuses on the *design* of the product or service. Using statistical methodologies and tools, DFSS has as its goal ensuring that the design fully meets the customers' requirements and results in a product that can be manufactured at the six sigma level.

Information technology (IT) professionals are familiar with the Five Ps (prior planning prevents poor performance). DFSS is the ultimate embodiment of those Five Ps. Table 3 illustrates the difference between classic Six Sigma and DFSS.

Although DFSS is a powerful methodology, it should be noted that it is not applicable to all situations. There are many projects that are better suited to classic Six Sigma. The strengths of DFSS are best applied to the development of new products or the major reengineering of existing ones. Classic Six Sigma and DFSS are complementary strategies. A successful company will employ both.

APPLYING SIX SIGMA TO SYSTEM DEVELOPMENT

Although it is doubtful that any IT manager would deny the importance of reducing defects, increasing customer satisfaction, and operating more efficiently, many IT departments have not adopted Six Sigma. While there are a number of reasons, there are also two misconceptions that are frequently associated with Six Sigma and system development. The first is that, because Six Sigma has its basis in statistical analysis, it can be applied only to manufacturing or engineering processes and that it has little or no relevance to the system development life cycle and the IT department in general. The second is that IT cannot use Six Sigma techniques unless the entire company has adopted the Six Sigma philosophy. Both ideas should be debunked.

NO RELEVANCE TO IT

There is some irony to the belief that Six Sigma applies to engineering processes but not to IT, because system development is sometimes referred to as software engineering. The truth is that the use of Six Sigma's disciplined approach and tools benefits service organizations as well as manufacturing processes. Both the tools and the techniques can increase the probability of successful system development by ensuring that the "three rights" are in place.

1. *The right people are involved.* Too often, projects fail either because all stakeholders are not represented or because they join the team too late to participate in the definition of requirements. With its emphasis on teamwork and the clear identification of customers, Six Sigma mitigates this problem. As explained in "More than Statistics," the definition of *customer* is broad and can include everyone who touches a product or process. Having these groups as active participants means that the right people are involved and helps to ensure the next *right*.

2. *The right problem is solved.* Although meant as a joke, there is some truth to the classic cartoon that shows an IT manager speaking to his staff. "You start coding," he says. "I'll find out what they want." Six Sigma tools provide a clear way to identify not just the customer's requirements, but also

the impact that a proposed solution will have on those requirements. Stringent use of the tools will help the team focus on the system components with the greatest value and will assist in separating nice-to-have features from those that are essential. In manufacturing terms, IT will produce the right product.

3. *The right method is employed.* Just as they can for a process on the manufacturing shop floor, Six Sigma tools can be used to assist the IT department in evaluating its processes and procedures to

determine where there is variation, why defects occur, and how to prevent them. If, for example, projects are consistently over budget, the use of Six Sigma techniques will help IT uncover the root cause and correct it. Following Six Sigma principles will ensure that decisions are fact based and risks such as modifying the wrong part of the process are avoided.

ALL OR NOTHING

The second misconception is that IT cannot benefit unless the entire company has adopted Six Sigma.

While there is no denying that it is easier for IT to implement Six Sigma processes if the remainder of the company has embraced the philosophy, there are benefits to be derived from employing the tools and incorporating the process into system development, even if the corporation as a whole is not a Six Sigma company. This entry describes ways in which Six Sigma tools can improve various aspects of system development. These tools are designed to be used in any IT department.

Six Sigma has applicability in software engineering. The techniques for ensuring that customer requirements are understood, that the impact of proposed changes is measured and evaluated, and that the development process is made more reliable will benefit all IT departments. The reasons for adopting these techniques are clear. Fewer defects, faster delivery, and increased customer satisfaction will result in a more effective IT department, one with enhanced value to the corporation.

REFERENCE

1. Subir, C. *Design for Six Sigma*; Dearborn Trade: Chicago, IL, 2005; p. 9.

SOA: Service-Oriented Architecture

Glenn Cater
Director, IT Risk Consulting, Aon Consulting, Inc., Freehold, New Jersey, U.S.A.

Abstract

The concept of service-oriented architecture (SOA) has been around in various forms for some time, but the SOA model has really become popular of late because of advances in web technology, web services, and standards. Although the concept of an SOA is not tied to a specific technology, in most cases SOA now refers to a distributed system using web services for communication. Other examples of SOA architectures are primarily based upon remote procedure calls, which use binary or proprietary standards that cause challenges with interoperability. Web services solve the problems of interoperability because they are based upon eXtensible Markup Language (XML), by nature an interoperable standard. Significant effort is being put into developing security standards for web services to provide integrity, confidentiality, authentication, trust, federated identities, and more. Those security standards will be the focus of this entry, which will cover XML, XML encryption, XML signature, Simple Object Access Protocol (SOAP), Security Assertion Markup Language (SAML), WS-Security, and other standards within the WS-Security family.

INTRODUCTION

So what is a service-oriented architecture (SOA)? SOA is an architectural model based on independent (or loosely coupled) services, with well-defined interfaces designed in such a way as to promote reuse. SOA fits extremely well with an architecture based on web services, which by nature meet the definition of loose coupling and well-defined interfaces. For instance, as an example of a service in SOA, imagine a user directory that is accessible via web services. In this example, the interface may specify functions, or methods, that include searching the directory (searchDirectory), password resets (resetPassword), updating user information (updateUser), and adding and removing users (addUser, removeUser). As long as the interface is adequately defined, the consumer of the service does not need to know how the service is implemented to use it. Fig. 1 illustrates a simplified SOA.

Fig. 1 shows that each service is reasonably independent and has a well-defined purpose. The idea behind SOA is that, provided the services and their interfaces are designed well, they can be combined in different ways to build different types of applications. For example, the order-processing service may be accessible from both the public website for placing orders and the internal website for sales and marketing purposes. Services expose their functionality through industry standard web service interfaces described using the Web Services Description Language (WSDL), which is discussed later in this entry.

In the simple example mentioned earlier, there is no security shown on Fig. 1. To add security to this picture some of the following need to be addressed:

- Network security, operating system security (server hardening), application security, and physical security
- Transport security, typically via the use of secure sockets layer (SSL)
- Web service security, through the use of the Web Service-Security family (WS-*) of standards for securing web services messages
- Utilizing other WS-Security extensions to provide trust relationships between the company, the payment provider, and the shipping provider

Web services and Web Services Security standards make heavy use of eXtensible Markup Language (XML). XML has revolutionized data exchange because of its simplicity and power. As a simple, human-readable, text format XML has facilitated data exchange between applications and businesses even across dissimilar systems.

The remainder of this entry discusses web services and the methods used to secure applications and data in an SOA environment. XML, XML encryption, XML signature, simple object access protocol (SOAP), security assertion markup language (SAML), and Web Services Security standards will also be covered as part of this entry.

Encyclopedia of Information Systems and Technology, DOI: 10.1081/E-EIST-120046795

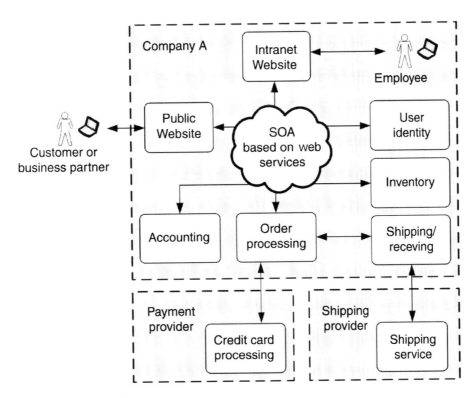

Fig. 1 Simplified SOA example.

FOUNDATIONS FOR WEB SERVICES AND WEB SERVICES-SECURITY

Web services and Web Services Security are based upon a number of standards that should be understood to some extent by a security practitioner. The idea is to provide an overview of the relevant standards here and how they fit together. Then for some of the more complex standards, we will delve into more detail in later sections.

eXtensible Markup Language

XML is the basic building block on which all the other web services standards and Web Services Security standards are built. XML is a free, open standard recommended by the World Wide Web Consortium (W3C) as a method of exchanging data using a simple text-based format. The fact that XML is a simple, human-readable format and works across heterogeneous systems makes it perfect for web services and SOAs for which the

```
<?xml version="1.0"?>
<Person>
    <First_Name>John</First_Name>
    <Last_Name>Doe</Last_Name>
    <Eye_Color>Hazel</Eye_Color>
    <Height>5'10"</Height>
    <Date_Of_Birth>February 21, 1982</Date_Of_Birth>
</Person>
```

Fig. 2 Simple XML example.

service and the consumer (client) may be on different platforms.

The example in Fig. 2 is a snippet of XML describing a person. This simple example shows how XML can be easily read by a human being. The structure of the XML clearly identifies this as data related to a person (see the person element in Fig. 2). So in addition to exchange of data, the XML gives some understanding of what the data represents.

XML extensions

Although not really important for the understanding of how XML relates to Web Services Security, there are some extensions to XML that should be included for completeness.

XML schema is an important extension that allows the structure of XML to be defined similar to the way in which an SQL database schema is defined. Among other things, XML schema specifies what the structure of the XML should be, such as the order in which elements appear, how many of each element is allowed, and the data types. XML schema is useful for creating specifications and for automatically validating the correctness of XML.

XML also has the concept of "XML namespaces." XML namespaces provide a way to avoid naming conflicts. For example, imagine that there are two different definitions of an employee in XML; to differentiate them XML namespaces can be used. The way this is

SOA–
Vulnerability

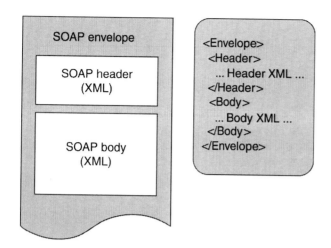

Fig. 3 A SOAP message.

done is by prefixing the name with a namespace prefix, for example <abc:Employee >, where abc is the namespace prefix that contains a definition of the employee type.

Other extensions exist that provide powerful ways to extract and query data in an XML message. These extensions are called XPath and XQuery. XPath provides a way to reference parts of the XML structure, whereas XQuery is a powerful query language that allows queries to be written against the XML data, similar to SQL, which is the query language for relational databases.

Simple Object Access Protocol

SOAP is an important messaging protocol that forms the basis for the web services protocol stack. SOAP messages are designed to be independent of a transport protocol, but are most often transmitted via HTTP or HTTPS when used with web services. SOAP messages are not tied to the HTTP protocol, however, and may also be used in message queuing systems, sent through e-mail, or via other transport mechanisms.

The SOAP standard is based upon XML and defines the structure of messages that can be passed between systems. Messages defined in SOAP have an envelope, a header, and a body as shown in Fig. 3. The SOAP header allows for the inclusion of security elements such as digital signatures and encryption within the message. Although security elements are not restricted only to the header, it is used heavily with WS-S standards to transmit security information with the message.

There are two primary messaging modes used by SOAP—"document" mode and remote procedure call (RPC) mode. Document mode is good for one-way transmission of messages, in which the sender submits the SOAP message but does not expect a response. RPC mode is more commonly used and is a request–response

model in which the sender submits the SOAP request and then waits for a SOAP response.

WSDL and UDDI

The WSDL and Universal Description, Discovery, and Integration (UDDI) standards allow a consumer of a web service to understand how to find a web service and how to use that service. This includes the following:

Discovery of basic information about the service such as the service name

Where to find the service, including network endpoints and protocol used

How to call the service (the service contract)

WSDL is essentially metadata in the form of XML that describes how to call a web service. There is a security concern with the protection of the WSDL data, because if it falls into the wrong hands it can expose information about your network. The WSDL metadata may be stored as an XML file, but is often available via a URL on the same application server where the web service is hosted. The WSDL should be made available only to authorized users of the service. Later in this entry, we will discuss how security policy requirements are included in WSDL.

UDDI is different in that it defines a standard for a directory of web services. This allows other applications or organizations to discover the WSDL for a web service that meets their need. Businesses publish the WSDL for their web service in the directory so that it can be easily discovered by others. UDDI directories can be hosted publicly on the Internet or internally within corporations to allow services to be discovered dynamically. Security of UDDI directories must be maintained to prevent man-in-the-middle attacks, by which a fake web service could be published in place of a real one. UDDI builds upon other Web Services Security standards to ensure integrity and trust for the data within the directory, which is particularly important for publicly accessible directories.

XML Signature

XML signature provides for integrity and authentication of XML data through the use of digital signatures and can be applied not only to XML but to any digital content. The primary use within Web Services Security is to sign XML messages to ensure integrity and to prove the identity of the signer. Fig. 4 shows an informal

```
<Signature ID?>
  <SignedInfo>
    <CanonicalizationMethod/>
    <SignatureMethod/>
    (<Reference URI? >
      (<Transforms>)?
      <DigestMethod>
      <DigestValue>
    </Reference>)+
  </SignedInfo>
  <SignatureValue>
  (<KeyInfo>)?
  (<Object ID?>)*
</Signature>


? = Zero or One Occurrence
+ = One or More Occurrences
* = Zero or More Occurrences
```

Fig. 4 Informal XML signature syntax.

representation of the XML signature syntax. The details are removed to reveal the basic structure. Unfortunately, a more complete explanation of how digital signatures work is beyond the scope of this discussion.

XML signature is itself represented as XML, as Fig. 4 shows. The structure contains the following elements:

- Signature is the containing element that identifies that this is a digital signature.
- SignedInfo contains the references to, and digests of, the data that is digitally signed.
- CanonicalizationMethod refers to the way the SignedInfo element is prepared before the signature is calculated. The reason for this is because different platforms may interpret data slightly differently (e.g., carriage returns <CR > versus carriage return/line feeds <CRLF >), which would cause signatures to compute differently on different platforms.
- SignatureMethod refers to the algorithm used for signature generation or validation, for example, *dsa-sha1*, which refers to the use of the DSA algorithm with the SHA-1 hashing function.
- The reference element is complex, but in a nutshell it refers to the data being signed, which is either part of the same XML data, or a uniform resource identifier (URI) that refers to external data, such as a document, web page, or other digital content. In addition, the reference element defines transforms that will affect the content prior to being passed to the digest

for computing the hash (via DigestMethod). The resultant hash value is stored as DigestValue.

- SignatureValue is the actual computed signature value. Rather than digitally signing the actual content, the signature is computed over SignedInfo so that all the references, algorithms, and digest values are digitally signed together, which ensures the integrity of the data being signed.
- KeyInfo enables the recipient to obtain the key needed to validate the signature, if necessary. This structure is fairly complex and is described in more detail under XML encryption.
- The object element contains arbitrary XML data that can be referenced within SignedInfo. It can also include a manifest element, which provides an alternate list of references, where the integrity of the list itself is validated, but the integrity of the actual items will not invalidate the signature. The purpose of such a list might be to include an inventory of items that should accompany the manifest. It also defines a SignatureProperties element by which other properties of the signature are stored such as the date and time the signature was created.

The XML signature standard defines three types of digital signatures, which are enveloped, enveloping, and detached. An enveloped signature refers to a signature on XML data, whereby the signature element is contained within the body of the XML. Enveloping signatures contain the XML content that is being signed, and this is where the object element is used to contain the data that is signed. Finally, the detached signature type signs content that is external to the XML signature, defined by an URI, which may be external digital content, but can also include elements within the same XML data such as sibling elements. Fig. 5 provides an example of a detached signature.

As discussed earlier, XML signature allows any type of digital content to be signed, and there are uses for XML signature that go beyond the scope of Web Services Security. However, this overview of XML signature is intended to provide a foundation for understanding how it relates to Web Services Security.

XML Encryption

By design, XML is a plain text format with no security built in. XML encryption provides data confidentiality through a mechanism for encrypting XML content that relies on the use of shared encryption keys. Fig. 6 shows an informal representation of the XML encryption syntax. The details are removed to simplify explanation of the structure symmetric encryption keys. Standard key exchange techniques based on public-key cryptography provide secrecy for the shared key. Typically the shared

```
<Signature Id="MySignature"
  xmlns="http://www.w3.org/2000/09/xmldsig#">
<SignedInfo>
  <CanonicalizationMethod
    Algorithm="http://www.w3.org/TR/2001/REC-xml-c14n-20010315"/>
  <SignatureMethod
    Algorithm="http://www.w3.org/2000/09/xmldsig#dsa-sha1"/>
  <Reference URI="http://www.company.com/file.doc">
    <Transforms>
      <Transform
        Algorithm="http://www.w3.org/TR/2001/REC-xml-c14n-20010315"/>
    </Transforms>
    <DigestMethod
      Algorithm="http://www.w3.org/2000/09/xmldsig#sha1"/>
    <DigestValue>j90j2fnkfew3...</DigestValue>
  </Reference>
</SignedInfo>
<SignatureValue>GFh8fw3greU...</SignatureValue>
<KeyInfo>
  <KeyValue>
    <DSAKeyValue>
      <P>...</P><Q>...</Q><G>...</G><Y>...</Y>
    </DSAKeyValue>
  </KeyValue>
</KeyInfo>
</Signature>
```

Fig. 5 XML signature example.

key is included within the XML message in an encrypted form, is referenced by name or URI, or is derived from some key exchange data. Symmetric encryption keys are used to encrypt data for performance reasons because public-key encryption can be very slow in comparison.

```
<EncryptedData Id? Type? MimeType? Encoding?>
  <EncryptionMethod/>?
  <ds:KeyInfo>
    <EncryptedKey>?
    <AgreementMethod>?
    <ds:KeyName>?
    <ds:RetrievalMethod>?
    <ds:*>?
  </ds:KeyInfo>?
  <CipherData>
    <CipherValue>?
    <CipherReference URI?>?
  </CipherData>
  <EncryptionProperties>?
</EncryptedData>

? = Zero or One Occurrence
+ = One or More Occurrences
* = Zero or More Occurrences
```

Fig. 6 Informal XML encryption syntax.

Fig. 6 shows an informal representation of the XML encryption syntax. The details are removed to simplify the explanation of the structure.

Like XML signature, XML encryption is itself represented as XML, as Fig. 6 shows. The structure contains the following elements:

- EncryptedData is the containing element that identifies that this is encrypted data.
- EncryptionMethod defines the encryption algorithm that is used to encrypt the data, such as Triple-DES (3DES). This is an optional element and if it is not present, then the recipient must know what algorithm to use to decrypt the data.
- ds:KeyInfo contains information about the encryption key that was used to encrypt the message. Either the actual key is embedded in encrypted form or there is some information that allows the key to be located or derived.
- EncryptedKey contains an encrypted form of the shared key. As mentioned previously, this key will typically be encrypted using public-key cryptography. There may be multiple recipients of a message, each with their own encrypted key element.
- AgreementMethod is an alternate way of deriving a shared key by using a method such as Diffie–

```
<EncryptedData xmlns='http://www.w3.org/2001/04/xmlenc#'
  Type='http://www.w3.org/2001/04/xmlenc#Element'/>
  <EncryptionMethod
    Algorithm='http://www.w3.org/2001/04/xmlenc#tripledes-cbc'/>
    <ds:KeyInfo xmlns:ds='http://www.w3.org/2000/09/xmldsig#'>
      <ds:KeyName>John Doe</ds:KeyName>
    </ds:KeyInfo>
  <CipherData><CipherValue>F59E7F12</CipherValue></CipherData>
</EncryptedData>
```

Fig. 7 Example of an XML-encrypted message.

Hellman. Providing key agreement methods means that the key does not need to be previously shared or embedded within the EncryptedKey element.

- ds:KeyName provides another way of identifying the shared encryption key by name.
- ds:RetrievalMethod provides a way to retrieve the encryption key from a URI reference, either contained within the XML or external to it.
- ds:* refers to the fact that there is other key information, such as X.509v3 keys, PGP keys, and SPKI keys that can be included.
- CipherData is the element that contains the actual encrypted data, either with CipherValue as the encrypted data encoded as base64 text or by using CipherReference to refer to the location of the encrypted data, in the XML or otherwise.
- EncryptionProperties contains additional properties such as the date and time the data was encrypted.

Fig. 7 shows an example of an XML-encrypted message. The encrypted data is clearly visible in the CipherValue element.

This basic overview of the XML encryption standard helps to give some background on how data confidentiality can be achieved with XML; however, there is much more detail than can be covered here.

The XML signature and XML encryption standards together form the basic security building blocks upon which the rest of the WSS standards rely.

SECURITY ASSERTION MARKUP LANGUAGE

Security assertion markup language (SAML) is a standard framework based on XML for communicating user identity, user entitlements, and user attributes between organizations or entities in separate security domains. SAML builds upon XML signature and XML encryption to provide integrity, confidentiality, and authentication of SAML assertions.

SAML allows an entity or organization to vouch for the identity of an individual, via a SAML assertion (a portable XML authentication token). The SAML assertion can be presented as proof of identity to another entity provided a trust relationship has been established between the two parties. This can be important for SOAs for which services are located within separate companies or security domains. This concept is really the basis of federated identity, which insulates organizations from the details of authentication and identity management within other organizations.

SAML attempts to solve several problems:

- Web single sign-on—by which a user can sign into one website and then later sign into a second related website using the credentials (a SAML assertion) provided by the first site.
- Delegated identity—by which credentials supplied to an initial website or service can be utilized by that service to perform actions on behalf of the user. An example is a travel website, which can pass the user identity to other services to perform airline, hotel, and car rental reservations.
- Brokered single sign-on—by which a third-party security service authenticates the user. The credentials provided by the third-party security service can then be used to authenticate to multiple websites.
- Attribute-based authorization—by which attributes about the user are placed into the SAML assertion. These attributes are then used to make authorization decisions. For example, user "John Doe" has level "director" in the "human resources" department; based upon these attributes he is allowed certain access to the human resources systems.

Within the SAML assertion will be some information about a user's identity, such as the user's e-mail address, X.509 subject name, Kerberos principal name, or an attribute such as employee identification number. For privacy purposes, SAML 2.0 introduced the concept of pseudonyms (or pseudorandom identifiers), which can be used in place of other types of identifiers, thereby hiding personal identification information such as an e-mail address. SAML provides two main ways to confirm the subject's identity. One way is referred to as "holder of key," where the sender of the message (the subject) typically holds the key that was used to digitally sign the message. The other confirmation method is referred to as "sender vouches," which means that the

SOA–Vulnerability

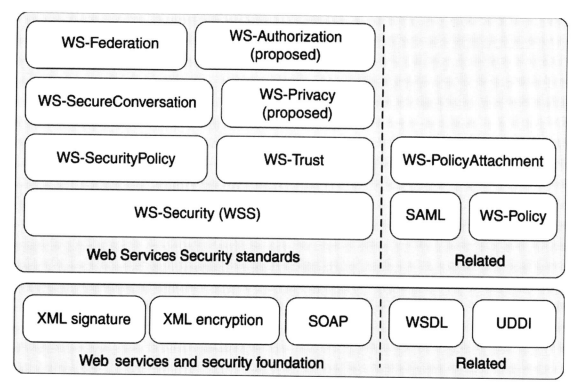

Fig. 8 WS-S standards.

digital signature on the message was created by a trusted third party.

This description of SAML is intended to provide some understanding of where it fits within SOAs. By leveraging trust relationships between service providers, SAML provides loose coupling and independence with respect to user identity. SAML is also referenced by the WS-S standards as a type of security token.

WEB SERVICES SECURITY STANDARDS

To gain an understanding of how all the Web Services Security protocols fit together, refer to the illustration in Fig. 8. This diagram shows how XML signature, XML encryption, and SOAP form the foundation of the stack, with the other Web Services Security standards building upon them. Other standards, such as WSDL, UDDI, SAML, WS-Policy, and WS-PolicyAttachment are listed down the right-hand side of Fig. 8 that have relationships to the security standards, but are not specifically security standards themselves.

It is clear from Fig. 8 that the WS-Security protocol suite is complex, which can serve to discourage adoption of these standards into an SOA, particularly for application developers whose job is complicated by these security protocols. This complexity can lead to a reliance on SSL and firewall policies to provide point-to-point security for SOAP messages. Fortunately, tools are available to simplify the integration of security into web services and SOA.

WS-Security

The WS-Security standard, also referred to as WSS: SOAP Message Security, specifies extensions to SOAP

```
<S11:Envelope>
  <S11:Header>
    <wsse:Security>
      (<wsse:UsernameToken>|
       <wsse:BinarySecurityToken>|
       [..XML Token..])*
      <ds:Signature>
        ...
        <ds:Reference URI="#MsgBody">
        ...
      </ds:Signature>*
      <xenc:ReferenceList>
        <xenc:DataReference URI="#MsgBody"/>
      </xenc:ReferenceList>*
    </wsse:Security>
  </S11:Header>
  <S11:Body>
    <!-- XML Encrypted Body -->
    <xenc:EncryptedData Id="MsgBody">
      ...
      <xenc:CipherData>
    </xenc:EncryptedData>
  </S11:Body>
</S11:Envelope>
```

Fig. 9 A SOAP message with WS-S extensions.

that provide message integrity, message confidentiality, and message authentication. WS-Security leverages XML signature to ensure that the integrity of the message is maintained and XML encryption to provide confidentiality of the message. Security tokens are supported for authentication purposes to provide assurance that the message originated from the sender identified in the message.

There are three categories of security tokens that are defined by WS-Security: username tokens, binary security tokens, and XML tokens. Each of the security tokens supported by WS-Security fits within one of these categories. Examples of security tokens are usernames and passwords (UsernameToken), Kerberos tickets (Binary-SecurityToken), X.509v3 certificates (BinarySecurity-Token), and SAML (XML Token). The WS-Security header is designed to be extensible to add additional security token types.

Fig. 9 shows where the WS-Security SOAP extensions appear within the header of the SOAP message.

The example in Fig. 9 shows that the structure of a SOAP message is altered when WS-Security extensions are added. It also shows how the security tokens, XML signature, and XML encryption fit within the WS-Security (wsse) header. The receiver of a message with WS-Security extensions processes the extensions in the order they appear in the header, so in this case the signature is verified on the message body and then the message is decrypted.

The following five types of tokens are discussed in version 1.1 of the standard:

- Username token, which is the most basic type of token. A UsernameToken contains a username to identify the sender and it can also contain a password as plain text, a hashed password, a derived password, or an S/KEY password. Obviously, the use of plain-text passwords is strongly discouraged.
- X.509 token, which is a BinarySecurityToken, identifies an X.509v3 certificate that is used to digitally sign or encrypt the SOAP message through the use of XML signature or XML encryption.
- Kerberos token, which is also a BinarySecurityToken, includes a Kerberos ticket used to provide authentication. Ticket granting tickets (TGT) and service tickets (ST) are supported.
- SAML token, which is an XML token, provides a SAML assertion as part of the SOAP security header.
- Rights expression language (REL) token, which is an XML token, provides an ISO/IEC 21000 or MPEG-21 license for digital content. This type of token is used for communicating the license to access, consume, exchange, or manipulate digital content.

WS-Security allows for the inclusion of time stamps within the SOAP security header. Time stamps can be required (see WS-Policy and WS-SecurityPolicy) to determine the time of creation or expiration of SOAP messages.

In addition, WS-Security defines how to add attachments to SOAP messages in a secure manner by providing confidentiality and integrity for attachments. Support for both multipurpose Internet mail extension (MIME) attachments and XML attachments is provided.

SOAP messages and attachments may be processed by different intermediaries along the route to the final recipient, and WS-Security allows parts of messages to be targeted to different recipients to provide true end-to-end security. There is an important distinction between point-to-point security technologies such as SSL and end-to-end security in which there are multiple intermediaries. A possible scenario is that one intermediary might need to perform some processing on a message before passing the message along; however, some parts of the message are confidential and intended only for the final recipient. SSL would not provide the necessary security in this scenario.

WS-Policy and WS-SecurityPolicy

The WS-Policy standard by itself is not directly related to security. Its purpose is to provide a framework for describing policy requirements in a machine-readable way. A policy might describe communication protocols, privacy requirements, security requirements, or any other type of requirement. WS-SecurityPolicy builds upon the WS-Policy framework to define security policies for WS-Security, WS-Trust, and WS-SecureConversation.

The following types of assertions are available within WS-SecurityPolicy:

- Protection assertions (integrity, confidentiality, and required elements), which define which portions of a message should be signed or encrypted and which header elements must be present.
- Token assertions, which specify the types of security tokens that must be included (or not included), such as UsernameToken, IssuedToken (third-party-issued token, e.g., SAML), X509Token, KerberosToken, Spnego-ContextToken (used with WS-Trust), SecurityContext-Token (external), SecureConversationToken (used with WS-SecureConversation), SamlToken, RelToken, Https-Token (requires use of HTTPS).
- Security-binding assertions, which define requirements for cryptographic algorithms, time stamps, and the order of signing and encrypting; whether the signature must be encrypted or protected and whether signatures must cover the entire SOAP header and body.

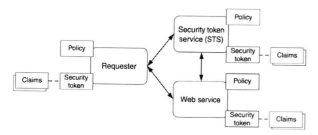

Fig. 10 WS-Trust security model.

- WS-Security assertions, which indicate which aspects of WS-Security must be supported within the message.
- WS-Trust assertions, which define policy assertions related to WS-Trust.

There is a related standard, called WS-PolicyAttachment, that defines attachment points within WSDL at which security policies can be defined. This provides a mechanism for describing the security policy associated with a web service along with the web service interface definition.

WS-Trust

WS-Trust builds upon WS-Security and WS-Policy to define mechanisms for issuing, renewing, and validating security tokens. The WS-Trust model has many similarities to Kerberos, and there are direct analogies such as the delegation and forwarding of security tokens. Of course WS-Trust is designed to work over web services and with many types of security tokens, such as X.509, Kerberos, XML tokens, and password digests. WS-Trust can also extend to trust relationships over the Internet, whereas Kerberos is more suited to providing trust within intranet-type scenarios. WS-Federation, discussed later in this entry, builds upon these principles and adds mechanisms to provide a framework for implementing identity federation services.

In the WS-Trust model shown in Fig. 10, the web service has a policy that defines what security tokens are required to use the service (via WSDL). To access the web service, the requester needs a valid security token that the web service understands. To obtain a valid security token, the requester may directly request a token from the security token service (STS), via a RequestSecurityToken request. Assuming the requester adequately proves its claims (via digital signatures) to the STS and meets the STS policy, the STS will respond with a RequestSecurityTokenResponse containing a new token signed by the STS. This new token will be in a format the web service understands, even if the client and web service support different authentication mechanisms. For example, say the client understands X.509 certificates only and the web service understands SAML

only, then the STS can issue a SAML token for the requester to present to the web service.

WS-Trust addresses the issue of trust in the security tokens by providing mechanisms for brokering trust relationships through the use of one or more STSs. Trust is established through relationships between the requester and an STS, between the web service and an STS, and between STSs. So the web service need not directly trust the requester or the STS it uses to accept security tokens, as long as there is a trust relationship between the requester's STS and the web service's STS.

WS-SecureConversation

The WS-SecureConversation standard builds upon WS-S and WS-Trust to define the concept of a security context, or session between services. Establishing a security context aims to alleviate some of the potential security problems with WS-S, such as message replay attacks and support for challenge–response security protocols.

There are three different ways to establish the security context.

- An STS (see WS-Trust) is used, whereby the initiator requests the STS to create a new security context token.
- The initiator is trusted to create the security context itself and sends it along with a message.
- A new security context is created via a negotiation between participants, typically using the WS-Trust model.

An advantage of WS-SecureConversation is that it optimizes multiple secure web service calls between services by performing the authentication step only once for the conversation, by reducing message size with the use of a small context identifier, and by performing only fast symmetric cryptography (using the shared secret keys). WS-SecureConversation uses public-key cryptography to derive shared secret keys for use with the conversation.

WS-Federation

WS-Federation builds upon WS-Security, WS-Policy, WS-SecurityPolicy, WS-Trust, and WS-Secure Conversation to allow security identity and attributes to be shared across security boundaries. As its name suggests, WS-Federation provides a framework for implementing federated identity services.

WS-Federation defines certain entities.

- Principal is an end user, an application, a machine, or another type of entity that can act as a requester.

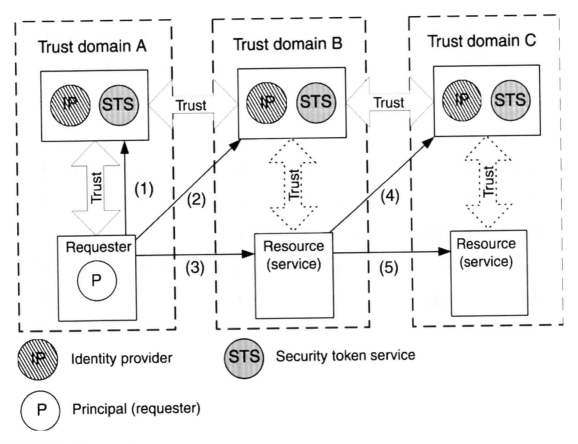

Fig. 11 WS-Federation example.

- STS, as defined in WS-Trust, issues and manages security tokens such as identity tokens and cryptographic tokens. The STS is often combined with an identity provider role as STS/IP.
- Identity provider is a special type of STS that performs authentication and makes claims about identities via security tokens.
- Attribute service provides additional information about the identity of the requester to authorize, process, or personalize a request.
- Pseudonym service allows a requester (a principal) to have different aliases for different services and optionally to have the pseudonym change per service or per log-in. Pseudonym services provide identity mapping services and can optionally provide privacy for the requester, by utilizing different identities across providers.
- Validation service is a special type of STS that uses WS-Trust mechanisms to validate provided tokens and determine the level of trust in the provided tokens.
- Trust domain or realm is an independently administered security space, such as a company or organization. Passing from one trust domain to another involves crossing a trust boundary.

These services can be arranged in different ways to meet different requirements for trust, from simple trust scenarios through to quite complex trust scenarios. The example in Fig. 11 illustrates a fairly complex scenario in which the requester first requests a token from the STS/IP it trusts: 1) The security token is then presented to the resource's STS to request a token to access the resource; 2) Assuming the requester's token is valid, the resource's STS will issue a new token, which is then presented to the web resource to request access; 3) The web service resource at some point needs to perform work on behalf of the principal, so it queries another STS/IP in a separate security domain to obtain a delegated security token; 4) Assuming the web service has the appropriate proof that it is allowed to perform delegation, the STS/IP will issue a security token; 5) This delegated security token is then presented to the resource on behalf of the principal. The chain of trust between the requester and the resource in trust domain C can be followed in Fig. 11.

WS-Federation introduces models for direct trust, direct brokered trust, indirect brokered trust, delegated trust, and federated trust relationships. Other services can be added to the picture, such as attribute and pseudonym services for attribute-based authorization, role-based authorization, membership, and personalization. Pseudonym services store alternate identity information, which can be used in cross-trust domain scenarios to support identity aliases and identity mapping.

WS-Federation also describes a way for participants to exchange metadata such as the capabilities, security requirements, and characteristics of the web services that form the federation. This exchange of metadata is achieved through the use of another standard called WS-MetadataExchange, which builds primarily upon WSDL and WS-Policy.

WS-Authorization and WS-Privacy (Proposed Standards)

As these standards are not yet published, they are mentioned here just for completeness. WS-Privacy is a proposed standard language for describing privacy policies for use with web services. The standard is intended for use by organizations to state their privacy policies and to indicate their conformance with those policies. WS-Authorization is a proposed standard for how to describe authorization policies for web services using a flexible authorization language. The standard will describe how authorization claims may be specified in a security token and validated at the endpoint.

WS-I Basic Security Profile 1.0

With the large number of WS-* security standards, vendors are implementing them at different times, and not all of the options are common from one vendor's system to the next. WS-I Basic Security Profile 1.0 is intended to provide a baseline for WS-Security interoperability among different vendor's products. The idea is that if the products conform to the Basic Security Profile 1.0, then they should be interoperable at least to some level. This can be important when implementing SOAs with products from different vendors, such as Sun's Java J2EE, BEA Weblogic, and Microsoft's .NET platform.

The Basic Security Profile 1.0 supports a good number of security extensions, including Kerberos, SAML, X.509, and username tokens and support for SSL transport-layer security (HTTPS).

PUTTING IT ALL TOGETHER

Now that we have covered the suite of Web Services Security standards, we can apply this knowledge to the problem of securing an SOA based on web services.

It is important to note that traditional security principles should form the basis of a secure SOA. The environment in which the systems are running should be managed appropriately to ensure that the organization's security policies are satisfied, and that regulatory requirements placed on the organization are being met.

This includes attention to network security, operating system security, application security (including the web services infrastructure), and physical security. Security risk assessments, threat analysis, vulnerability scanning, and penetration testing techniques should be used to validate the security of the SOA services, platforms, and related systems.

To perform a thorough security assessment, the following types of questions should be asked:

- What does the overall SOA look like?
- Who are the intended consumers of the service (s)?
- How are the services discovered by consumers? Is WSDL or UDDI used?
- What interactions occur between consumers and services and between services?
- Are any of the services or consumers on untrusted networks?
- What types of data are passed between consumers and services at various points?
- Is data integrity or confidentiality required at any point within the SOA?
- Does data flow through multiple intermediaries?
- Is there a need to provide end-to-end security for certain types of data?
- What are the authentication and authorization requirements for each of the services?
- Is the authorization based upon roles or attributes?
- Is data privacy a concern?
- What security technologies, such as X.509, Kerberos, or SAML, are available?
- Are multiple security domains involved? Is there a need for cross-domain trust relationships?
- Are there different web services technologies, such as J2EE, Weblogic, or .NET, in use that might cause issues with protocol support or interoperability? If so, is the WS-I Basic Security Profile 1.0 supported?
- Threat analysis—what potential threats are there to the infrastructure, such as malicious attacks, insider threats, information disclosure, disasters, message replay attacks, or denial-of-service (DoS)?

The following summarizes the types of threats that apply to SOA and mechanisms to mitigate the threats:

- Information disclosure (confidentiality)—Use of XML encryption within WS-Security can provide data confidentiality. End-to-end message confidentiality can also be handled with XML encryption.
- Message tampering—Message tampering could be used to remove XML, add XML, or otherwise alter data or cause some unintended behavior within the application. XML signatures can be used to ensure the integrity of messages.
- Message injection—Message injection may be used to cause some unintended behavior within the

application. Authentication mechanisms and input validation within the service can help to mitigate this issue.

- Message replay—WS-SecureConversation provides mechanisms to prevent this kind of attack, but otherwise, message identifiers or time stamps can be used to prevent message replay.
- Authentication—Authentication is provided by XML signatures and security tokens such as Kerberos, X.509 certificates, and SAML, or even username tokens. These methods are supported by WS-Security and WS-Trust.
- Authorization—Authorization can be role based or attribute based. The web services platform will typically provide some form of authorization capability, but for more advanced authorization needs, the application will have to include explicit authorization checks.
- Service availability—Disasters, whether natural or human-made, need to be planned for by ensuring that an adequate disaster recovery strategy is in place. Other malicious attacks such as DoS can affect the network, operating system, or application. Dealing with DoS attacks is beyond the scope of this entry, however.
- Token substitution—Attempts to substitute one security token for another can be prevented by ensuring that digital signatures provide integrity over all the security critical portions of the message, including security tokens.

Once a risk assessment is completed, and the security requirements are understood, decisions need to be made about how to secure the SOA environment. Risks are normally rated in terms of impact and likelihood and should be prioritized,for example, into high-risk, medium-risk, and low-risk categories. Security measures can then be chosen to mitigate the risks and meet security requirements, based on a cost–benefit analysis.

General security principles should be followed when choosing security measures, such as:

- Ensuring the confidentiality, integrity, and availability of data and services
- Defense in depth
- Principle of least privilege
- Minimizing the attack surface
- Promoting simplicity rather than complexity

At the network level, firewall policies can be applied to limit access to web services, because SOAP messages are transmitted via HTTP, typically on Transmission Control Protocol (TCP) port 80, or via HTTPS on TCP port 443. Internet-facing servers should have access restricted just to the port that the service is listening on. Firewall policies can form the first line of defense by

reducing the available attack surface. Other standard techniques, including DMZ architecture, security zones, and intrusion detection/prevention, can reduce risk at the network level and provide defense in depth.

At the transport level, web services are often secured through the use of SSL, via the HTTPS protocol, and policies can be applied through WSDL to ensure that web services are secured with SSL. The use of SSL should definitely be considered, particularly because it is a well-understood protocol, although it is important to understand that SSL provides only point-to-point encryption and that other techniques need to be applied if the security of the SOAP messages is to be maintained beyond the SSL session.

At the message level, XML is by nature a text-based standard, so data confidentiality and integrity are not built in. SOAP messages and attachments may be processed by different intermediaries along the route to the final recipient, and WS-Security allows parts of messages to be targeted to different recipients. This is an important distinction between point-to-point security technologies, such as SSL, and end-to-end security, which WS-Security supports. XML encryption can provide end-to-end data confidentiality via public-key cryptography and shared symmetric-key cryptography, whereas XML signature can meet data integrity and message authentication needs.

Other issues exist when dealing with trust relationships and cross-domain authentication. The WS-Trust and WS-Federation standards provide a technical foundation for establishing trust for SOAs. Organizational security policies and regulatory requirements should define the security requirements that need to be placed on interactions with customers and business partners. These security requirements can be used as a basis for determining the security mechanisms that need to be used to provide an appropriate level of trust, such as encryption strength or method of authentication (X.509 digital certificates, SAML, Kerberos, etc.). However, trust between organizations goes beyond technical implementation details and also needs to be addressed by contractual obligations and business discussions.

CONCLUSION

The WS-S family provides an essential set of standards for securing SOAs; however, the number and complexity of the standards is a definite problem. This complexity can serve to discourage the adoption of these standards into an SOA, particularly for application developers, whose job is complicated by security needs. These standards are also evolving and new security standards are being developed, so expect the SOA security landscape to evolve over time.

SOA–
Vulnerability

Fortunately vendors are providing new tools to simplify the integration of WS-Security standards into web services. These tools can help by hiding many of the lower-level details from security practitioners and architects. Expect these tools to evolve over time as SOA and web services become more mature. At this time, however, it is still not an easy task to integrate WS-Security standards into web services.

For the security practitioner, standard security principles can be leveraged to assist in guiding architects and developers in selecting appropriate mechanisms to secure SOAs.

BIBLIOGRAPHY

1. *IBM developerWorks Web Services Standards Documentation,* http://www.ibm.com/developerworks/webservices/standards.

2. *Microsoft MSDN Documentation on WSE Security and WCF Security,* http://msdn2.microsoft.com/en-us/library/default.aspx.

3. *OASIS Standards for WS-Security, WS-Trust, WS-Secure Conversation, WS-Federation, UDDI and SAML,* http://www.oasis-open.org/specs/index.php.

4. *Security in a Web Services World: A Proposed Architecture and Roadmap,* http://msdn2.microsoft.com/enus/library/ms977312.aspx.

5. *W3C Standards for XML, XML Encryption, XML Signature, SOAP, WSDL, WS-Policy and WS-PolicyAttachment,* http://www.w3.org/.

Social Networking: Legal, Privacy, and Security Issues

Jessica Keyes
New Art Technologies, Inc., New York, New York, U.S.A.

Abstract
This entry presents legal barriers easily overlooked in social networking. Privacy issues are discussed, as well as potential breaches of security.

Do these facts concern you?

- When you buy a Microsoft Kinect, you bring into your home or office a telescreen that can recognize who's in the room and interpret body language.
- A joint effort by a British university and a Canadian security company will bring to a theater near you the ability to monitor facial expressions.
- Cisco commissioned a survey of 2600 workers and information technology (IT) professionals in 13 countries. Twenty percent of the IT leaders said that their relationships with their employees were dysfunctional—demonstrating a disconnect among IT, employees, and policies.
- A recent survey of 1100 mobile workers found that 22% had breached their employers' strict smartphone policies when using nonmanaged personal smartphones to access corporate information.
- One in eight malware attacks is accomplished via a Universal Serial Bus (USB) device, according to Avast Software, a security firm.
- The U.S. Department of Defense estimates that more than a hundred foreign intelligence organizations have attempted to break into U.S.-based networks (governments, universities, and businesses). Every year, hackers steal enough data to fill the Library of Congress many times over.
- A virus may be transmitted by any connected device, for example, MP3 players, cameras, fax machines, and even digital picture frames. In 2008, the Best Buy chain found a virus in the Insignia picture frames it sold.
- Companies outsourcing data storage (to a cloud) are responsible for any data breached. Make sure your cloud or data service provider is investigated carefully.
- Cybercriminals are getting smarter. They invented poisoned search results, rogue anti-viruses (AVs), social networking malware, malicious advertisements, and even built-in instant messaging clients that notify criminals when their "marks" have logged onto their online bank accounts.

Social networking raises some issues concerning content use, infringement, defamation, attribution, tort liability, privacy, and security. While most of these issues relate to public social networking sites such as Facebook and LinkedIn, most are also relevant to internal social software engineering, particularly if public platforms are integrated into the toolsets.

WEBSITE LEGAL ISSUES

Defamation and other torts—Wikis, blogs, workspaces, and other IT facilities provide ample opportunities for defamation (harming the reputation of another by making a false statement to a third person). These resources should be monitored for possible defamation and other tort liabilities. Examples of damages arising from torts include intentional infliction of emotional distress, interference with advantageous economic relations, fraud, and misrepresentation.

Trademarks—Trademark or service mark notices should be notably displayed wherever required. If a mark has been registered with the U.S. Patent and Trademark Office (http://www.uspto.gov/), the "registered" (®) symbol should be displayed; otherwise, the trademark (™) or service mark (℠) symbol should be displayed. Organizations should be vigilant in protecting their trademarks and service marks, and equally vigilant in preventing infringements on the marks of others. Content that resides on an organization's servers should be audited to ensure no trademark infringement is taking place.

Copyrights—Copyright is a form of protection provided to the authors of "original works of authorship" including literary, dramatic, musical, artistic, and other types of intellectual works such as software, both published and unpublished. The 1976 Copyright Act

SOA–Vulnerability

Encyclopedia of Information Systems and Technology, DOI: 10.1081/E-EIST-120053822

generally gives the owner of a copyright the exclusive right to reproduce the copyrighted work, prepare derivative works, distribute copies or audio recordings of the copyrighted work, perform the copyrighted work publicly, and display the copyrighted work publicly. A copyright protects the form of expression rather than the subject of the writing. For example, a description of a machine could be copyrighted, but doing so would only prevent others from copying the description; it would not prevent others from writing their own descriptions or from making and using the machine.

It is important for organizations to audit data residing in their social networks to make sure that any content, data, and information is not violating copyrights of other individuals or organizations. One example is dynamically accessing Google and downloading research results to a social network. Because Google's content is copyrighted to Google, you would need to take care not to violate any copyrights. Using third-party content without permission can result in both criminal and civil liability, including treble damages and attorney fees under the U.S. Copyright Act. Essentially, the best tactic is to periodically review network content to screen for possible copyright violations.

Computer Fraud and Abuse Act (CFAA)—Most organizations provide their employees with PCs capable of wireless Internet access. Many companies and home users have installed wireless Internet connectivity. It is not usual for people to seek out unsecured "hot spots," as these wireless connections are known. Several computer equipment manufacturers have developed inexpensive, small hot-spot locaters for this purpose. The CFAA makes it punishable for whoever intentionally accesses a computer without authorization. Organizations must develop very clear policies warning employees against using corporate-supplied PCs in this manner.

Corporate content—Not long ago, a Congressman made a secret trip to Iraq. Upon arrival, he tweeted a message that he had just landed. His trip was no longer a secret. While we have not focused on the use of Twitter as a social software engineering tool, we expect Twitter or its corporate equivalent, Yammer to be used. Because these systems enable almost instantaneous communication with an entire network of people within and outside an organization, users must be very careful about exactly what they communicate.

DEVELOPING YOUR EPOLICY

It is important that the organization develop an ePolicy that addresses how employees use email, Internet access, and all social networking activities. The policy should be comprehensive, appear in the employee handbook,

and be reviewed with all new employees. It is also a good idea to refresh the memories of all employees annually by sending an e-mail, instructing them to review the ePolicy. The policy should be stored on the corporate intranet, and one staff member should be assigned as the main point of contact for the ePolicy, if questions or problems arise. Some points to address in an ePolicy include

- Whether employees may use the Internet for personal use.
- Whether external social networking services such as Facebook, LinkedIn, and Yammer may be used.
- Notice that e-mail is monitored (if it is not, it should be). Let employees know that the e-mail and social networking systems they use are owned by the organization, and they can expect that management or designated staff may access e-mail, workspaces, blogs, wikis, etc.
- Descriptions of the types of content that can be maintained within internal or external social networking site, e.g., copyrighted materials.
- Netiquette policies for using e-mail and social networking websites.
- Details of corporate discrimination and sexual harassment policies, particularly as they relate to online environments.
- The expectation that individual employees will respect the privacy of the individuals whose information they may access, and use all available security methods to preserve the integrity and privacy of information within their control.
- A directive that specifies that employees are not to engage in any activity that alters or damages data, software, or other technological-related resources belonging to the organization or to someone else; compromise another individual's ability to use technological-related resources; or intentionally disrupt or damage corporate technology resources.
- A stipulation that individuals who observe potential abuse are expected to report it for appropriate resolution.

SECURITY ISSUES

In 2008, Cisco commissioned a study on security in the workplace. The study findings will probably not surprise you:

- One of five employees altered security settings on work devices to bypass IT policy to access unauthorized web sites. More than half said they simply wanted to access the sites; a third indicated that the sites they accessed "were no one's business." Seven out of ten IT professionals said employee access of unauthorized applications and websites ultimately resulted in as many as half of their companies' data loss incidents. This belief was most common in the United States (74%) and India (79%).

- Two of five IT pros dealt with employees accessing unauthorized parts of a network or facility. Of those who reported this issue, two-thirds encountered multiple incidents in the past year, and 14% encountered it monthly.
- One in four employees admitted verbally sharing sensitive information with nonemployees such as friends, family, and even strangers. When asked why, the most common answers included, "I needed to bounce an idea off someone," "I needed to vent," and "I didn't see anything wrong with it."
- Almost half of the employees surveyed share work devices with others, including nonemployees without supervision.
- Almost two out of three employees admitted using work computers daily for personal use. Activities included music downloads, shopping, banking, blogging, and participating in chat groups. Half of the employees used personal e-mail to reach customers and colleagues; only 40% said such use was authorized by IT.
- At least one in three employees left computers logged on and unlocked when they left their desks. They also tended to leave laptops on their desks overnight, sometimes without logging off, creating potential for theft and allowing unauthorized access to corporate and personal data.
- One in five employees stored system log-ins and passwords in their computers or wrote the information and left it on their desks, in unlocked cabinets, or pasted on the front of their computers.
- Almost one in four employees carried corporate data on portable storage devices outside the office.
- More than one in five employees allowed nonemployees to roam around offices unsupervised. The study average was 13%; 18% allowed unknown individuals to "tailgate" behind employees into corporate facilities.

As you can see, information systems (ISs) are vulnerable to many threats that can inflict various types of damage, resulting in significant losses. This damage can range from errors harming database integrity to fires destroying entire systems centers. Problems can arise from inside the company (employees) to the more common scenario such asoutsiders intent on harm. All manner of hardware and software is at risk, including mobile devices. In 2010, we all awoke to the news that iPad users' e-mail addresses and device user identifications (IDs) were exposed. In 2009, security experts identified 30 security flaws in the software and operating systems of smartphones. Also in 2010, two European university researchers extracted an entire database of text messages (including deleted messages) from an iPhone using a corrupt website they controlled.

Losses from these exploits can stem, for example, from the fraudulent actions of supposedly trusted employees, outside hackers, or careless data entry. An organization should develop an ISs security program to implement and maintain the most cost-effective safeguards to protect against deliberate or inadvertent acts, including

1. Unauthorized disclosure of sensitive information or manipulation of data
2. Denial of service or decrease in reliability of critical IS assets
3. Unauthorized use of systems resources
4. Theft or destruction of system assets

An extremely detailed checklist of best practices for security has been compiled by the U.S. Department of Defense. It covers access control, confidentiality, integrity, availability, non-repudiation, protection, detection, reaction to incidents, configuration management, vulnerability management, personnel security, physical security, and security awareness and training. All of these topics should be reviewed before initiating any social software engineering program from setting the parameters for its use. The checklist should also be used on a periodic basis to ensure the security of the social software engineering platform on an ongoing basis. The organization should develop an IS security plan to meet the following goals:

1. Achieve data integrity levels consistent with the sensitivity of the information processed.
2. Achieve systems reliability levels consistent with the sensitivity of the information processed.
3. Comply with applicable state and federal regulations.
4. Implement and maintain continuity of operations plans consistent with the criticality of user information processing requirements.
5. Implement and follow procedures to report and act on IS security incidents.

Organizations should conduct periodic security reviews to ensure that

1. Sufficient controls and security measures are in place to compensate for any identified risks associated with the program/system or its environment.
2. The program/system operates cost effectively and complies with applicable laws and regulations.
3. The information in the program/system is properly managed.

SOA–Vulnerability

4. The program/system complies with management, financial, IT, accounting, budget, and other appropriate standards.

Two types of security assessments of computer facilities must be conducted periodically: risk assessments and security reviews. A risk assessment is a formal, systematic approach to assessing the vulnerability of computer assets, identifying threats, quantifying potential losses from threat realization, and developing countermeasures to eliminate or reduce threats and potential losses. Risk assessments should be conducted whenever significant modifications are made to the system.

The three major IT security components are management controls, operational controls, and technical controls. The *management controls* address matters deemed managerial. The *technical controls* are security measures that should be implemented on systems that transmit, process, and store information. The *operational controls* address security measures implemented by employees that directly support the technical controls and processing environment.

Management controls are necessary to manage a security program and its associated risks. They are non-technical techniques, driven by policy and process, and are intended to meet IT protection requirements. Program security policies and system-specific policies are developed to protect sensitive information, transmitted, stored, and processed within system components. Program security policies are broad and are developed to establish a security program and enforce security at the program management level. System-specific security policies are detailed and developed to enforce security at the system level. The information, applications, systems, networks, and resources must be protected from loss, misuse, and unauthorized modification, access, and compromise. All organizations that process, store, or transmit information must develop, implement, and maintain IT security programs, to ensure protection of their information. The program security policy establishes the program, assigns the appropriate personnel, and outlines the duties and responsibilities of all individuals in the program.

Operational controls focus on controls implemented and executed to improve the security of a particular system. Media controls address the storage, retrieval, and disposal of sensitive materials that should be protected from unauthorized disclosure, modification, and destruction. Media protection is composed of two security requirements: computer output controls and electronic media controls. Computer output controls apply to all printout copies of sensitive information, and specify that all printout copies of sensitive information should be clearly marked. Electronic media controls should encompass all the controls of printout materials;

however, procedures must be established to ensure that data cannot be accessed without authorization and authentication from electronic media that contain sensitive information.

All personnel with responsibilities for the management, maintenance, operations, or use of system resources and access to sensitive information should have the appropriate management approvals. Organizations should institute personnel security procedures to specify responsibilities of the security personnel and users involved in the management, use, and operation of systems. The IT staff must be alert and trained in offensive and defensive methods to protect the organization's information assets. Adequate staffing and key position back-up are essential in maintaining a secure environment. Personnel security also includes establishing and maintaining procedures for enforcing personnel controls, including

- Determining appropriate access levels (logically and physically)
- Ensuring separation of duties (logically and physically) to prevent compromise of system data and attempts to thwart technical controls
- Conducting security training and providing awareness tools for all staff
- Issuing and revoking IDs and passwords

Technical controls focus on security controls that the computer system executes, and they rely on the proper configuration and functionality of the system. The implementation of technical controls always requires significant operational considerations. Technical controls should be consistent with the management of security within the organization. When updating a security plan, the organization should refer to the security issues and questions, as shown, in Table 1 to ensure its plan remains current.

WEB SERVER SECURITY

Securing the operating system that runs the web server is the initial step in providing security for the server. The web server software differs only in functionality from other applications that reside on computers. However, because the web server may provide public access to the system along with organization-wide access, it should be configured securely to prevent it and the host computer from being compromised by intruders.

One precaution to take when configuring a web server is to never run the Web service as a root or administrative user (super user). Web services or applications should never be located at the root of a directory structure. They should be in a component-specific subdirectory to provide

Table 1   Internet security: Checklist of issues to address

1. Describe the functions (data transfer, forms-based data entry, browser-based interactive applications, etc.) the Internet will perform.
2. Describe your application categories and how they are integrated with your production systems (information access = hypertext, multimedia, soft content, and data; collaboration = newsgroups, shared documents, videoconferencing; transaction processing = Internet commerce and links to IT applications).
3. What communication protocols are in use? FTP, HTTP, telnet, or a combination?
4. How do you control access, identification and authorization (I&A), sensitive or private information, no repudiation, and data integrity?
5. Are firewalls or proxy servers present? If so, describe the software used.
6. Is data encryption used? Is it hardware or software based?
7. What application languages (HTML, XML, JavaScript, etc.) are used? Are they static, semidynamic, or dynamic?
8. What database connectivity or application program interfaces are in place?
9. Do you have separate web servers? Describe the hardware and software.
10. Describe the controls in effect for shared resources, including password protection, user groups, smartcards, biometrics, data encryption, callback systems, virus scanners, vulnerability scanners, and intelligent agents.
11. Are user logons and passwords challenged frequently via a multilevel protection scheme? Do you allow synchronization of passwords for a single sign-on?
12. Are passwords changed regularly? How often? Is change system-controlled or manual?
13. How many people have administrative rights to the application, telecommunications, and web servers? Are these rights separated by function, or can a single person access all servers?
14. Are Internet application files and data files backed up? How often?
15. Is a contingency plan in place? Has it been tested? How often is it updated?

optimum access management. The Web service should be run with the permissions of a normal user to prevent the escalation of privilege if the web server were compromised. Also, the file system of the web server (directories and files) should be configured to prevent write access for any users other than authorized employees who require such access. Other precautions and secure configuration issues to consider when configuring a public web server are

- The web server should be on a separate local area network separated from other production systems by a firewall configuration or demilitarized zone (DMZ).
- The web server should never have a trust relationship with any other server that is not also an Internet-facing server or server on the same local network.
- The web server should be treated as an untrusted host.
- The web server should be dedicated to providing Web services only.
- Compilers should not be installed on the web server.
- All services not required by the web server should be disabled.
- The web server should utilize the latest vendor software, including hot fixes and patches.

A Web browser is usually a commercial client application used to display information requested from a web server. It should be a standard browser approved for use within the system environment. Because of the security holes in scripting languages such as JavaScript and ActiveX (Microsoft), it is recommended that all

scripting languages not required for official systems operation be disabled within the browser.

Network security addresses requirements for protecting sensitive data from unauthorized disclosure, modification, and deletion. Requirements include protecting critical network services and resources from unauthorized use and security-relevant denial-of-service conditions.

Firewalls provide greater security by enforcing access control rules before connections are made. These systems can be configured to control access to or from the protected networks, and are most often used to shield access from the Internet. A firewall can be a router, a personal computer, or a host appliance that provides additional access control to the site. The following firewall requirements should be implemented:

- Firewalls that are accessible from the Internet are configured to detect intrusion attempts and issue an alert when an attack or attempt to bypass system security occurs.
- Firewalls are configured to maintain audit records of all security-relevant events. The audit logs are archived and maintained in accordance with applicable records retention requirements and security directives.
- Firewall software is kept current with the installation of all security-related updates, fixes, and modifications, as soon as they are tested and approved.
- Firewalls should be configured under the "default deny" concept. This means that activation of a service or port must be approved for specific use. By

**SOA–
Vulnerability**

default, the use of any service or communications port without specific approval is denied.

- Only the minimum set of firewall services necessary for business operations is enabled, and only with the approval of IT management.
- All unused firewall ports and services are disabled.
- All publicly accessible servers are located in the firewall, DMZ, or an area specifically configured to isolate these servers from the rest of the infrastructure.
- Firewalls filter incoming packets on the basis of Internet addresses to ensure that any packets with internal source addresses received from external connections are rejected.
- Firewalls are located in controlled access areas.

Routers and switches provide communication services that are essential to the correct and secure transmission of data on local and wide area networks. The compromise of a router or switch may result in denial of service to the network and exposure of sensitive data, which can lead to attacks against other networks from a single location. The following best-practice solutions should be applied to all routers and switches throughout an application environment:

- Access to routers and switches is password-protected in accordance with policy guidance.
- Only the minimum set of router and switch services necessary for business operations is enabled and only with the approval of IT management.
- All unused switch and router ports are disabled.
- Routers and switches are configured to maintain audit records of all security-relevant events.
- Router and switch software is kept current by installing all security-related updates, fixes, and modifications, as soon as they are tested and approved for installation.
- Any dial-up connections via routers must be performed by a method approved by IT management.

All systems should use AV utilities or programs to detect and remove viruses and other malicious codes. The AV software must be kept current with the latest available virus signature files installed. AV programs should be installed on workstations to detect and remove viruses in incoming and outgoing e-mail messages and attachments, and also actively scan downloaded files from the Internet. Workstation and server disk drives should be routinely scanned for viruses. The specific restrictions outlined below should be implemented to reduce the threat of viruses on systems:

1. Traffic destined to inappropriate websites should not be allowed.
2. Only authorized software should be introduced on systems.

3. All media should be scanned for viruses before introduction to the system. This includes software and data from other activities and programs downloaded from the Internet.
4. Original software should not be issued to users but should be copied for use in copyright agreements. At least one copy of the original software should be stored according to configuration management controls.

Table 2 outlines the topics of a systems security plan. During development of a security plan, the following questions should be asked and answered:

1. Does the plan address the logical and physical security of the system?
2. Does the logical security include password protection, data encryption (if applicable), and access profiles, to preclude access to data by unauthorized personnel?
3. Does the logical security allow supervisory intervention if needed (determined case by case)?
4. Are negotiable documents or authorizations stored securely?
5. Does the physical security address both equipment security and building security?
6. Does the physical security address safety and environment issues?
7. Does the security plan address data and application back-up procedures?
8. Does the security plan include disaster preparedness and recovery procedures? (They may appear in a separate plan.)
9. If a department or organization-wide security plan exists is the point where the system security plan stops and the organization plan takes over (and vice versa) delineated clearly?
10. Does the logical security include separation of duties among functions to prevent potential fraud situations?

PROTECTING MOBILE DEVICES

Many people ignore security policies pertaining to their smartphones. They seem not to realize how they may be exposing themselves, their companies, and their companies' stakeholders to harm. While mobile devices cannot be totally secured, certain measures afford some measure of security:

1. Do not use hotel wireless networks to access sensitive information.
2. Hotel wired networks are often open to eavesdropping. All packets for a set of rooms, a floor or

Table 2 Systems security plan

Topic Outline

1. Scope—Describe site, giving location, configuration, operations, processing supported, and identify IT units and applications covered by plan
2. Definitions—Explain terms that may not be familiar to all readers
3. Overall security assessment—Discuss policies and practices, addressing assignment of security responsibilities, personnel security clearance policies, audit reports, and training; also assess current activities and plans for next year
4. Site plan and equipment schematic diagrams
5. Obtain the following information for each sensitive application system: date of last system evaluation, date of last system certification or recertification, date of next evaluation or recertification
6. Summary of risk analysis reports
7. Continuity plan (s)
8. Summary of security reviews for all processing platforms in use
9. Training needs with action schedules
10. Other supporting documents (terminal security rules, local security procedures, user handbooks, etc.)

Policies and Procedures

1. Physical security of resources
2. Equipment security to protect equipment from theft and unauthorized use
3. Software and data security
4. Telecommunications security
5. Personnel security
6. Continuity plans to meet critical processing needs during short- or long-term interruption of service
7. Emergency preparedness
8. Designation of IT security officer or manager

several floors, or even an entire hotel can be seen by all other systems on the network. Unprotected packets are prime targets for capture, analysis, and data extraction. A company should invest in wireless broadband equipment for employees who must travel and bring their work with them.

3. Encrypt all data on a device in case it is stolen or lost—a common occurrence. Better yet, store information on the server or in the cloud, not on the device.
4. Configure devices to block external snooping. Firewalls are required and are available for many handheld devices.
5. Backup critical information. This sounds obvious, but employees on the road may neglect to do this. If the organization does not have a mobile-accessible back-up server, use a cloud service such as Microsoft Skydrive (skydrive.login.com).
6. Do not start a laptop with a USB device attached. This can result in direct loading of malware ahead of antivirus software.
7. Secure all wireless access points. Strong, mixed passwords should be used and changed frequently.

SOA–Vulnerability

Social Networking: Tools

Jessica Keyes
New Art Technologies, Inc., New York, New York, U.S.A.

Abstract

This entry presents the wide variety of tools available to support social software engineering. Three methodologies are available when making a platform decision: 1) off-the-shelf; 2) mashup; and 3) build your own. This entry provides information to start you moving in a direction that is the most suitable for your organization.

Most professionals, when they think of social networking at all, think in terms of Facebook and Twitter. Chief Information Officers (CIOs) see great potential in these sorts of tools. IBM conducted a worldwide study of 2500 CIOs in late 2010. The collective take on collaboration tools is that they must be institutionalized to meet the demands of business. Surprisingly, as we will shortly show, and with some effort, all of these tools can be institutionalized to enhance the productivity of the software engineering discipline. Based on the popularity of these types of tools among consumers, it is no wonder that a variety of such tools are geared to specific business disciplines.

TOOLS THAT PROVIDE NETWORKING CAPABILITIES

Salesforce.com, the enterprise customer relationship management giant, has begun to provide social networking capabilities. Its new Chatter service is available on Salesforce's real-time collaboration cloud. Users establish profiles and generate status updates that may be questions, bits of information and/or knowledge, or relevant hyperlinks. All of this information is then aggregated and broadcast to coworkers in their personal networks. Essentially, a running feed of comments and updates flow to those in a particular network. Employees can also follow colleagues throughout a company, not just in their own personal networks, enabling cross-organizational knowledge sharing. Toward that end, Chatter also provides a profile database that users can tap into to find needed skills for a particular project. Chatter is accessible via desktop or mobile.

Like Salesforce.com, more than a handful of well-known software companies have developed collaboration tools, all for a fee. Oracle's Beehive provides a spate of tools such as instant messaging, e-mail, calendaring, and team workspaces. Microsoft's SharePoint is heavily used within IT departments. Microsoft's Lync Server product that permits users to communicate from anywhere via voice, video, or document share is also becoming a contender. One of the first companies to dabble in the collaborative market—indeed they created it—was Lotus. Now owned by IBM, Lotus Notes brings together a wide array of tools: instant messaging, team rooms, discussion forums, and even application widgets.

A wide variety of free tools are available, which may be adapted for various purposes. LinkedIn has been widely used to provide networking capabilities for business people. A relevant feature is the LinkedIn group that may be created for any purpose, with permission required to join. Thus, project teams can make use of the already developed facilities LinkedIn provides. For example, the Tata Research Development and Design Centre (TRDDC) was established in 1981 as a division of Tata Consultancy Services Limited, India's largest information technology (IT) consulting organization. TRDDC is currently one of India's largest research and development centers for software and process engineering. TRDDC has its own membership-by-request LinkedIn group. It is very easy to create a members-only LinkedIn group for a particular project, which can be limited to specific members, as shown in Fig. 1.

Of all the collaborative tools available, particularly those that are free, wikis are the most commonly used. Zoho.com provides a wide range of tools, including chats, discussions, meetings, and projects, but it is their wiki tool I will focus on. Fig. 2 is a wiki I created to store all the artifacts for a typical project, i.e., project plan, systems requirement specifications, analysis documents, etc. Fig. 3 shows the project plan artifact in wiki form. Note the ability to post comments.

Twitter, a social networking application made famous by celebrities who tweet hourly updates on what they are doing (eating lunch, shopping, etc.), has morphed into an enterprise social networking application called

Encyclopedia of Information Systems and Technology, DOI: 10.1081/E-EIST-120053821

SOA–Vulnerability

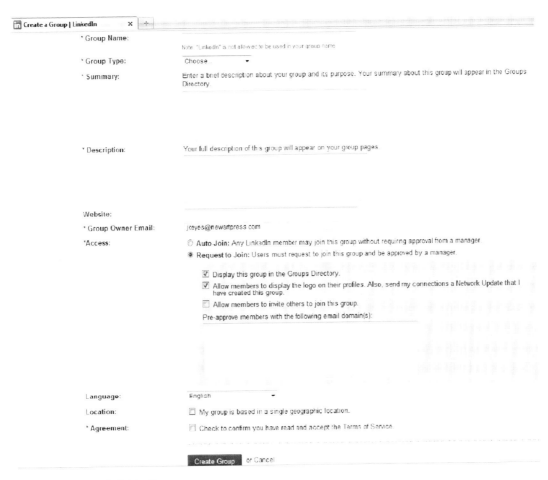

Fig. 1 Creating members-only LinkedIn group.

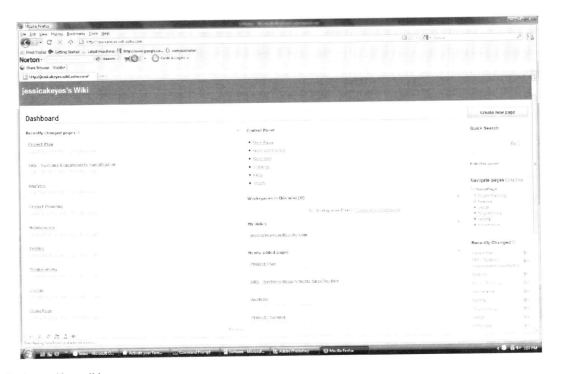

Fig. 2 Project artifact wiki.

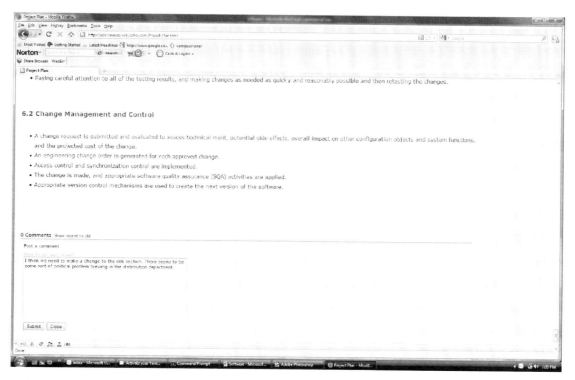

Fig. 3 Project plan wiki demonstrating ability to include comments.

Yammer. With the ability to integrate with tools such as SharePoint, Yammer provides a suite of tools including enterprise microblogging, communities, company directories, direct messaging, groups, and knowledge bases. SunGard employees actually started using Yammer on their own to share information about projects they were working on. Now, Yammer has been rolled out to all 20000 + employees. Much of what Yammer offers is free with its basic service. A gold subscription provides such corporate niceties as security controls, administrative controls, broadcast messages, enhanced support, SharePoint integration, keyword monitoring, and virtual firewall solutions. Yammer can be used by the software development team to interactively discuss any aspect of a project, as shown in Fig. 4.

Project groups have used wikis in some creative ways: writing personal research and making comments on others' research, asking questions, posting links to resources that may be of interest to others in the group, adding details for upcoming events and meetings, letting each other know about activities, adding comments to other team members' information and pages, and recording minutes of meetings in real-time. One may expect that use of these sorts of ad hoc discussion tools would degenerate into chaos. In truth, this rarely happens—even in social networks of anonymous users. Anderson[1] talks about the fact that the largest wiki of all, Wikipedia, is fairly resistant to vandalism and ideological battles. He stresses that the reason is "the emergent behavior of a Pro-Am [professional and amateur] swarm

of self-appointed curators." This group of curators has self-organized what Anderson terms the most comprehensive encyclopedia in history—creating order from chaos. Welcome to the world of "peer production."

WIKIS IN ACTION

Intellipedia (https://www.intelink.gov/wiki) is an online system for collaborative data sharing used by the United States intelligence community (IC). It consists of three different wikis with different levels of classification: Top Secret, Secret, and Sensitive But Unclassified. The levels used by individuals with appropriate clearances from the 16 agencies of the IC and other national-security-related organizations, including Combatant Commands and other federal departments. The wikis are not open to the public.

Intellipedia includes information on the regions, people, and issues of interest to the communities using its host networks. Intellipedia uses MediaWiki, the same software used by the Wikipedia free-content encyclopedia project. Officials say that the project will change the culture of the U. S. IC, widely blamed for failing to "connect the dots" before the September 11, 2001 attacks.

The Secret version predominantly serves Department of Defense and Department of State personnel, many of whom do not use the Top Secret network on a day-to-day basis. Users on unclassified networks can access

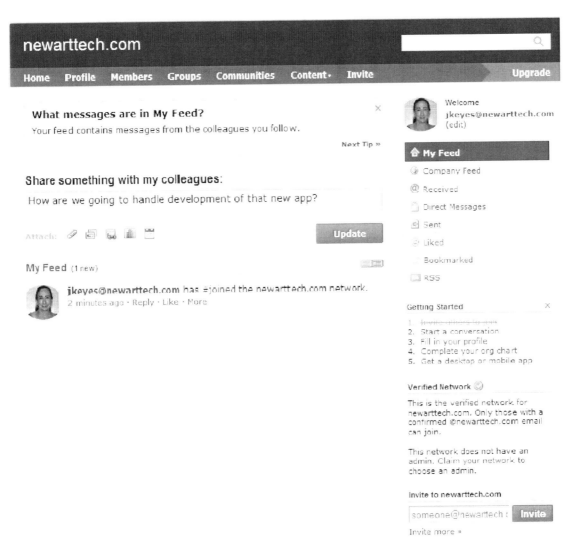

Fig. 4 Dynamic discussion using Yammer.

Intellipedia from remote terminals outside their workspaces via a virtual private network, in addition to their normal workstations. Open Source Intelligence (OSINT) users share information on the unclassified network.

Intellipedia was created to share information about some of the most difficult subjects facing U. S. intelligence and bring cutting-edge technology into its ever-more-youthful workforce. It also allows information to be assembled and reviewed by a wide variety of sources and agencies, to address concerns that prewar intelligence did not include robust dissenting opinions about Iraq's alleged weapons programs. Some view Intellipedia as risky because it allows more information to be viewed and shared, but most agree that the result is worth the risk.

The project was greeted initially with a lot of resistance because it runs counter to past practices that limited the pooling of information. Some encouragement has been necessary to spur contributions from the traditional IC. However, the system appeals to the new generation of intelligence analysts because this is how they like to work, and it represents a new way of thinking.

The wiki provides so much flexibility that several offices throughout the community use it to maintain and transfer knowledge about daily operations and events. Anyone with access to read it has permission to create and edit articles. Because Intellipedia is intended as a platform for harmonizing the various views of the agencies and analysts of the IC, Intellipedia does not enforce a neutral point of view policy. Instead, viewpoints are attributed to the agencies, offices, and individuals participating, with the hope that a consensus view will emerge.

During 2006 and 2007, Intellipedia editors awarded shovels to users to reward exemplary wiki "gardening" and encourage others in the community to contribute. A template with a picture of the limited-edition shovel (actually a trowel) was created to place on user pages for Intellipedians to show their gardening status. The

SOA–
Vulnerability

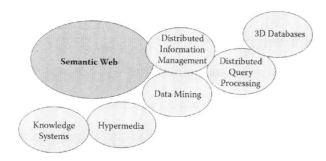

Fig. 5 Semantic web.

handle is imprinted: "I dig Intellipedia! It's wiki wiki, baby." The shovels have now been replaced with mugs bearing the tag line "Intellipedia: it's what we know." Different agencies have experimented with other ways of encouraging participation. For example, Central Intelligence Agency managers have held contests for best pages and awarded prizes such as free dinners.

Chris Rasmussen, a knowledge management (KM) officer at the Defense Department's National Geospatial Intelligence Agency (NGA), argues that "gimmicks" like the Intellipedia shovel, posters, and handbills encourage people to use Web 2.0 tools like Intellipedia, and they are effective low-tech solutions, and using them is easy to promote. Also, Rasmussen suggests that social software-based contributions should be written in an employee's performance plan.

MEANING-BASED COMPUTING

Even before the advent of social networking, the shear amount of data needed to be processed by a worker was overwhelming. Researchers and writers talked about information overload decades ago. Now data arrives from many more directions, much of it unstructured and unordered (e-mail, IM, video, audio, etc.). Wall Street technologies have a solution for such data overload. They make use of powerful computers to speed-read news reports, editorials, company websites, blogs, posts, and even Twitter messages. Intelligent software then parses all the input and figures out what it means for the markets. If only we could have a smart software like this for our IT-oriented blog, wiki, discussion group, and other types of messages!

Autonomy.com is a leader in the movement toward finding a way to add a sort of autonomy to this disorganized chaos of data. Termed meaning-based computing, the goal is to give computers the ability to understand the concepts and context of unstructured data, enabling users to extract value from the data where none could be found earlier. Meaning-based computing systems understand the relationships between seemingly disparate pieces of data and perform complex analyses of such data, usually in real-time. Key capabilities of

meaning-based computing systems are automatic hyperlinking and clustering that enable users to connect to documents, services, and products that are linked contextually to the original text. The ability to collect, analyze, and organize data automatically to achieve this end requires these computer systems to extract meanings. Autonomy's meaning-based computing platform known as Intelligent Data Operating Layer (IDOL) is capable of processing any type of information from any source. IDOL can aggregate hundreds of file formats including voice, video, document management systems, e-mail servers, web servers, relational database systems, and file systems.

Google's most recent plans for "augmented humanity" will most certainly give Autonomy.com something to think about. According to Google CEO Eric Schmidt, Google knows pretty much everything about us: "We know roughly who you are, roughly what you care about, roughly who your friends are." Schmidt sees a future in which people simply don't forget anything because the computer (read that Google) remembers everything. Some of these abilities are already available if you use Google tasks, contacts, calendar, and documents. Your searches are stored and accessible by Google. If you use Google e-mail and chat, this data lives on Google servers as well. Google's plan is to be able to suggest what you should do based on what your interests or knowledge requirements are. It intends to use this knowledge to suggest ideas and solutions that you may have found, if you performed your own analysis. Some writers are comparing this eventuality as a clone or "your own virtual you".[2] Coupled with Google's new voice synthesizer that can replicate an individual voice, it's not much of a stretch to find that one day you will go on vacation and your clone will give your team a call to set up a project meeting.

SEMANTIC WEB

Google cloning is actually an extension of technology that exists today. Tim Berners-Lee, the inventor of the World Wide Web and HTML, also came up with the idea of a semantic web as shown in Fig. 5. The semantic web represents a synthesis of all corporate and external data, including results from data mining activities, hypermedia, knowledge systems, etc. It uses a common interface that makes data easily accessible by all (e.g., suppliers, customers, employees).

The semantic web is sometimes called the defined web, and serves as an ultimate repository of all content and knowledge on the web. It uses Extensible Markup Language (XML), a formalized version of HTML, to tag information on intranets, extranets, and the Internet. Tim Berners-Lee explains the semantic web as follows:

Fig. 6 Using Second Life to host conference.

At the doctor's office, Lucy instructed her semantic web agent through her hand-held web browser. The agent promptly retrieved information about mom's *prescribed treatment* from the doctor's agent, looked up several lists of *providers*, and checked for the ones *in-plan* for mom's insurance within a *20-mile radius* of her *home* and with a *rating* of *excellent* or *very good* on trusted rating services. It then began trying to find a match between available *appointment times* (supplied by the agents of individual providers through their websites) and Pete's and Lucy's busy schedules.

Hewlett-Packard's Semantic Web Research Group frequently circulates items of interests such as news articles, software tools, and links to websites; they are called snippets or information nuggets.[3] Because e-mail is not the ideal medium for this type of content, the group had to find a technique for decentralized, informal KM. They began a research project to create a system capable of aggregating, annotating, indexing, and searching a community's snippets. The required characteristics of this for this system include:

Ease of use and capture.

Decentralized aggregation. Snippets will be in a variety of locations and formats. It will be necessary to integrate them and perform a global search of the results.

Distributed knowledge. Information consumers should be able to add value by enriching snippets at the point of use by adding ratings, annotations, etc.

Flexible data model. Snippets are polymorphic. The system should be able to handle e-mail, web pages, documents, text fragments, images, etc.

Extensible. It should be possible to extend snippet data schema to model the changing world.

Inferencing. It should be possible to infer new metadata from old. For example, a machine should "know" that a snippet about a particular HP Photosmart model is about a digital camera.

Some have suggested that blogs make ideal tools for this type of content and KM. However, today's blogging tools offer only some of the capabilities mentioned. Traditional blogging has many limitations but the most important one is that metadata is used only for headline syndication in a blog. Metadata is not extensible, not linked to a risk-flexible data model, and incapable of supporting vocabulary mixing and inferencing.

The researchers, therefore, looked to the semantic web for a solution. As discussed previously, the premise of the semantic web is that data can be shared and reused across applications, enterprises, and community boundaries. RSS1.0 (web.resource.org/rss/1.0) is a semantic web vocabulary that provides a way to express and integrate with rich information models. The semantic web standard Resource Description Framework specifies a web-scale information modeling format (http://www.w3.org/RDF). Using these tools, researchers devised a prototype (http://www.semanticblogging.org/blojsom-hp/blog/default/) for creating what they called a semantic blog. The prototype has some interesting searching capabilities. For example, snippets can be searched via their own attributes ("I'm interested in snippets about HP") or via the attributes of an attached blog entry ("I'm interested in snippets captured by Bob").

VIRTUAL WORLDS

Perhaps the most interesting of all social-based community software is Linden Labs' Second Life (http://www.secondlife.com). While Second Life is used primarily for such fun activities as fantasy role-playing (pirates, Goths, science fiction, etc.), the software has a serious side.

In 2008, IBM's Academy of Technology held a virtual world conference and annual meeting in Second Life, as shown in Fig. 6. The virtual meeting conference space had room for breakout sessions, a library, and areas for community gathering.

IBM estimates that the return on investment for the virtual world conference was about $320,000 and that the annual meeting cost one-fifth that of a real-world event (http://work.secondlife.com/en-US/successstories/case/ibm/). Just think of the possibilities. Project team members near and far can use Second Life to hold virtual but tactile team meetings and even work with end users.

KM TOOLS

KM has been defined as the identification and analysis of available and required knowledge and the subsequent planning and control of actions to develop these into "knowledge assets" that will enable a business to generate profits and/or increase its competitive position. The major focus of KM is to identify and gather content from documents, reports, and other sources and be able to search such content for meaningful relationships. A variety of business intelligence, artificial intelligence, and content management methodologies and tools constitutes the framework under which KM operates. While we will discuss the relationship of KM, social networking, and software engineering in more depth later, it is worthwhile to briefly address the best-known KM construct now.

Individual groups who share knowledge about a common work practice over time, while not part of a formally constituted work team, are considered "communities of practice" (CoPs) that generally cut across traditional organizational boundaries. They enable individuals to acquire new knowledge faster. They may also be called communities of interest if the people share an interest in a common task but do not necessarily perform the work on a daily basis. For example, in one government agency, a group of employees who were actively involved in multiparty, multi-issue settlement negotiations began a monthly discussion group during which they explored process issues, discussed lessons learned, and shared tools and techniques. CoPs can be more or less structured, depending on the needs of the membership.

CoPs provide mechanisms for sharing knowledge throughout one organization or across several organizations. They lead to improved networks of organizational contacts, supply opportunities for peer-group recognition, and support continuous learning, all of which reinforce knowledge transfer and contribute to better results. They are valuable for sharing tacit (implicit) knowledge. To be successful, CoPs require support from organization (s). However, if management closely controls their agendas and methods of operation, they are seldom successful. This issue is more applicable to CoPs within organizations.

CoPs can be used virtually anywhere within an organization: within one organizational unit or across organizational boundaries, with small or large groups of people, in a single or multiple geographic locations. They can also be used to bring together people from multiple companies, organized around a profession, shared roles, or common issues. They create value when tacit information, if shared, produces better results for individuals and the organization. CoPs are also valuable in situations where knowledge is constantly gained and shared, which is beneficial to the accomplishment of an organization's goals.

CoPs serve a number of purposes. Some develop best practices, some create guidelines, and others meet to share common concerns, problems, and solutions. They can connect in different ways: personally, in small or large meetings, or electronically. These virtual CoPs are called VCoPs.

VCoPs (as well as face-to-face CoPs) need a way to capture their collective experiences for online examination. Daimler AG does this via its Engineering Book of Knowledge (EBOK) system that provides best practice information on almost every issue related to the manufacture of cars. Tech CoPs share knowledge related to various car processes by consolidating the information into the EBOK system.

CoPs provide a great amount of what academics called social capital that provides the motivation and commitment required to populate knowledge stores such as EBOK. CoP has historically been used for small team interaction. More recently, some organizations are attempting to use it for large group interventions, although some dispute whether this can be effectively done at all. In experiments, up to 300 people were brought together within a CoP to work through organizational issues. While it would be unusual for a software engineering effort to involve such large populations, it would not be out of the question to have to develop a system in which team members and stakeholders, together, approached this number. A variety of CoP-based designs apply to groups of this size. The World Café is perhaps the best known and most popular example of them all; others are Open Space Technology, Participative Design, and Wisdom Circles.

The World Café (http://www.theworldcafe.com/) describes its process as an innovative yet simple methodology for hosting conversations. These conversations link and build on each other as people move among groups, cross-pollinate ideas, and discover new insights into the questions and issues raised. As a process, the World Café can evoke and make visible the collective intelligence of any group, thus increasing capacity for effective action in pursuit of a common aim.

In a face-to-face environment, the way to do this is simple. Tables allow seating for a series of conversational rounds lasting from 20 to 45 minutes, each of which intends to tackle a specific question. Participants are encouraged to write, doodle, or draw key ideas and themes on the tablecloths, as shown in Fig. 7. At the end of each round, one person remains at the table as the host and the others travel to new tables. The hosts welcome the newcomers and share the table's conversation so far. The newcomers share what they discussed from the tables they've already visited and so on. After the last round, participants return to their individual tables to integrate all the information. At the end of the

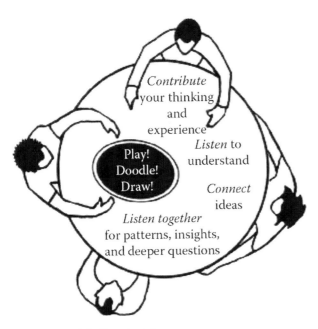

Fig. 7 World Café methodology.

session, everyone shares and explores emerging themes, insights, and learning. The process serves to capture the collective intelligence of the group.[4]

Visiting the World Café's website demonstrates how the construction was modified to suit the online environment. One output of this type of brainstorming session might be a "tag cloud" or visual depiction of user-generated tags based on discussions. Tags are usually single words, usually listed alphabetically. The importance of a tag is shown by font sizes or colors as shown in Fig. 8.

Tag clouds were popularized by websites such as Flickr and Technorati. They actually serve a very useful purpose for software engineers by providing methods to classify, organize, and prioritize the results of meetings. Because individual tags may be hyperlinks, it is possible to tag clouds to store increasingly granular levels of information. Perhaps the best-known cloud tag generator is Wordle (http://www.wordle.net/create).

MASHUPS

Web developers have long been engaged in what is known as service composition—the practice of creating value-added services by reusing existing service components. Mashups represent an emerging paradigm of Web 2.0 that enables developers and very talented end users to create new web-based applications and services, which address specific needs and interests. *Mashup* implies fast integration. This is achieved by using open APIs and data sources to produce enriched results that were not necessarily the original reasons for producing the raw source data. Mashup tools generally support visual wiring of GUI widgets, services, and components together.

Some tech leaders have discontinued their mashup tool offerings (Microsoft's Popfly in 2009 and Google's Mashup Editor in 2009). However, Yahoo Pipes (http://pipes.yahoo.com/pipes/) is still supported. As Yahoo describes it:

> Pipes is a free online service that lets you remix popular feed types and create data mashups using a visual editor. You can use Pipes to run your own web projects, or publish and share your own web services without ever having to write a line of code. You make a Pipe by dragging preconfigured modules onto a canvas and wiring them together in the Pipes Editor. Each Pipe consists of two or more modules, each of which performs a single, specific task. For example, the Fetch module will retrieve a feed URL, while the Sort module will re-order a feed based on criteria you provide (you can find a complete list of available modules in the documentation). You can wire modules together by clicking on one module's output terminal and dragging the wire to another module's input terminal. Once the terminals are wired together, the output from the first module will serve as input to the second module. In addition to data feeds, Pipes also lets you add user input fields into your Pipe. These show up at runtime as form fields that users of your Pipe can fill in.

JackBe Corporation is a privately held software provider of enterprise mashup software. JackBe's flagship product is an enterprise mashup platform called Presto (http://www.jackbe.com/products/), with support for

Fig. 8 Tag cloud.

Microsoft SharePoint. JackBe launched its Enterprise App Store product in July 2010 as a platform for creating internal enterprise application stores. Enterprise App Store is aimed at non-developers, allowing them to create new business applications and share them with other users. JackBe is a founding member of the Open Mashup Alliance (OMA) that promotes enterprise mashup interoperability and portability. JackBe was the original contributor and continues to be a key supporter of OMA's Enterprise Mashup Markup Language (EMML), an XML markup language for creating enterprise mashups. These software applications consume and "mash" data from variety of sources, often performing logical or mathematical operations, as well as presenting data. Mashed data produced by enterprise mashups is presented in graphical user interfaces as mashlets, widgets, or gadgets. EMML is an open language specification promoted by OMA. EMML is fairly easy to understand and use because it is a derivative of the now-familiar XML. For example, the EMML code below joins Yahoo! News, Financial News, and Reuters feeds.

```
<merge inputvariables = "$YahooRSS,
$FinancialNewsRss,
  $ReutersRSS"
  outputvariable = "$NewsAggregate"/ >
```

EMML provides a common command to invoke any publically accessible web service or website using the <directinvoke > operation. The following code shows how this operation can be used to access the Google Finance web page and retrieve the financial information for the ticker through the web clipping feature provided by EMML. Web Clipping converts the HTML result of any URI into XHTML and gives you a clip of the required content from the web page:[5]

```
<foreach variable = "value" items = "$itemNames/
records/record" >
  <template expr = " http://finance.google.com/
finance?q = {$ticker}" outputvariable =
"wholeURL"/ >
  <!- invoke the Google Finance web page that has
stock information - >
  <directinvoke outputvariable = "clipresult"
endpoint = "$wholeURL"/ >
  <assign fromexpr = "$clipresult//xhtml:div
[@class = 'g-section sfe-break-bottom-8']"
```

```
outputvariable = "clipresult2"/ >
  <assign fromexpr = "$clipresult2//xhtml:h3/
string ()" outputvariable = "$company"/ >
  <assign fromexpr = "$clipresult//xhtml:span
[@class = 'pr']" outputvariable = "clipresult3"/
>
  <assign fromexpr = "$clipresult3//xhtml:span/
string ()" outputvariable = "$price"/ >
  <assign fromexpr = "$clipresult//xhtml:div
[@id = 'price-change'] outputvariable =
"clipresult4"/ >
  <assign fromexpr = "$clipresult4//xhtml:span
[@class = 'chg']/string ()" outputvariable =
"change"/ >
</foreach >
```

Detailed documentation for EMML can be found on the OMA website (http://www.openmashup.org/omadocs/v1.0/index.html).

CONCLUSION

As you can see, a wide variety of tools are available to support social software engineering and you can choose from three methodologies when making a platform decision: 1) off-the-shelf; 2) mashup; and 3) build your own. This entry has provided information to start you moving in a direction that is the most suitable for your organization.

REFERENCES

1. Anderson, C. *The Long Tail*; Hyperion: New York, NY, 2006.
2. Elgan, M. How Google plans to clone you. Computerworld **2010**. http://www.computer world.com/s/article/9199638/.
3. Cayzer, S. Semantic blogging and decentralized knowledge management. Commun. ACM **2004**, *47* (12), 47–52.
4. Raelin, J. A. *Work-Based Learning: Bridging Knowledge and Action in the Workplace*; Jossey-Bass: San Francisco, 2008.
5. Viswanathan, A. *Mashups and the Enterprise Mashup Markup Language (EMML)*. Dr. Dobb's: The World of Software Development. April 12, 2010. http://deepakalur.wordpress.com/2009/09/24/omg-we-launched-oma-and-emml/.

Software Development Lifecycles: Security Assessments

George G. McBride
Senior Manager, Security and Privacy Services (SPS), Deloitte & Touche LLP, Princeton, New Jersey, U.S.A.

Abstract

With events, such as buffer overflows, Structured Query Language code injection, and arbitrary code injection, we are faced with a continuous flood of vulnerability and threat information for our systems, our applications, and our networks. Whether the information comes from a customer, an employee, or an auditing or assessment firm, organizations are continuously addressing the endless cycle of vulnerability and threat identification, measurement of risk, and the implementation of some appropriate corrective action (also referred to as a *control*). Surely, there must be some measures that organizations can take when developing software to proactively address security and in turn reduce potentially negative publicity and the costs of development and ongoing maintenance for themselves and their customers.

INTRODUCTION

This entry discusses how organizations that are involved with the development of software systems can build security, reliability, and resiliency into their applications. In addition, readers of this entry will also understand areas that should be reviewed during an audit or assessment of a typical software development life cycle (SDLC). The software engineering field has several equally viable and applicable SDLC methodologies depending upon the business, industry, type of application, and experience of the development team. This entry provides recommendations, best practices, and areas to review during an audit or an assessment for any and all of the SDLC methodologies. Finally, every effort has been made to ensure that whether you develop in house or outsource the development of software systems, each aspect of this entry will be relevant to you.

This entry focuses on the following areas:

- The need for secure and reliable software
- Development environments, including physical and logical security, source code management, auditing, authentication, authorization, and access control to source and run-time code
- Common security challenges to all SDLC methodologies
- Security with purchased, open-sourced, and proprietary code embedded in applications under review
- Security in the requirements and definition phases
- Security in the software systems design phase and how Formal Methods can help secure the design
- Security in the implementation and coding phases, including source code review tools

- Security in the integration and testing phases including module and unit testing and integration
- Security during installation and deployment phases
- Security in the lifecycle maintenance mode, including software updates, obsolescence, and decommissioning
- Security through third-party solutions, and whether they hinder or help the overall software solution

One of the first questions that any fiscally minded manager may ask is "Why?" Why would any company choose to spend additional funds, accept longer development cycles, and possibly require additional personnel to develop code more securely when customers are already buying the software as is? Perhaps the thought is that the initial code will be developed and shipped, and then security features will be implemented as incremental updates over the product's lifecycle, thus ensuring a first-to-market strategy. Perhaps the thought is that nobody will notice the absence of security features, or that the security features will not be required as the software is not mission critical, or will not be associated with any sensitive data.

Whether the use of the software exceeds its programmers' original expectations, whether it is run on a platform on which it was not originally intended to run, or whether the system receives input data from systems and processes that were designed years later, there is little in today's system design that developers can trust or assume.

Finally, one of the strongest reasons for building security into today's products during the development cycle (and not post-deployment) is cost savings or cost avoidance, depending on your view. For the consumers, whether it is an individual or a business, there are costs associated with applying patches, hot fixes, updates, or

Encyclopedia of Information Systems and Technology, DOI: 10.1081/E-EIST-120046744

service packs. Connection charges to receive the patches, time taken away from other activities, business disruption, building install packages for the patch, regression testing, and increased network bandwidth are just some of the additional "costs" to the purchaser. The companies that produce software with security defects have costs as well. In addition to making sure that their own infrastructure maintains the latest patches and updates for their applications and operating systems, they also incur costs associated with the management of the software vulnerabilities in their own applications. Longer maintenance cycles, additional personnel, additional testing, additional patches, and the erosion of the company's base or brand name are all additional costs borne by the manufacturer.

Performing an internal code walkthrough during the design phase, discovering a vulnerability, making a few changes to a few lines of code and updating the documentation (if that is even necessary) could take as little as a few minutes. Having the help desk field calls from concerned customers who believe that there is a security vulnerability, logging the issue into a database, having a quality assurance associate duplicate the problem, opening up the code, reviewing the code, updating the code, updating the documentation, packaging the update, maintaining the new version, shipping it out, and then fielding calls from customers wondering why the patch just disabled some other application, will cost a lot more. In today's environment, it is not a matter of *if* the costs will be incurred; it is a matter of when and how much. Nobody can argue money can be saved by fixing an undocumented feature (a software bug) or vulnerability after the first vulnerability is detected and the product is already in the hands of the customers.

Likewise, there are several reasons why security features (and other features, such as privacy, reliability, resiliency to disasters, etc. that will be discussed later) are not typically incorporated in the systems that are still being developed today. Lack of awareness continues to be the reason most given as to why vulnerabilities continue to exist in code. Even with all of the advertisements, supporting applications, magazines, books, and announcements seen today, software developers often feel that they are not at risk for a number of reasons, such as assumed external controls, assumed validated input and so on. Security features, similar to any other feature or requirement, cost money to implement, time to design, code, and test, and may be considered too restrictive to the application from an end-user experience.

Why not just build security features into applications today? Why not just run some tools and ensure that every software bug, whether security related or not, is mitigated? Software design is an inherently complex process, with multiple programming languages, development methodologies, and development environments.

Owing to continually evolving development and compiler aids, oftentimes there are an infinite combination of inputs and platforms to run on, which further amplifies design complexity. However, it is not an impossible task, and the remainder of this entry highlights the activities that a development organization can undertake to increase the security and reliability of its applications.

SOFTWARE DEVELOPMENT LIFE CYCLE

There are a number of SDLC models in use today. Waterfall, spiral, rapid application design, joint application design, and prototyping are five of the more common models used by programmers and software engineers when developing software projects. The model chosen is typically dependent on the size of the project (either the team or the size of the expected code base), the amount of time available, how firm the requirements are, and the background, familiarity, and experience of the design company and its employees. Although any model is capable of producing secure code, without strong controls, some models may be more disposed to producing less secure code. For example, the waterfall model maintains strong gates between each of the development cycles, whereas the rapid prototyping methodology usually involves several iterations between end-users (or the marketing organization) and the development team to reach an agreement on the look, feel, and high-level functionality of the application. Once an agreement has been reached and the requirements have been defined, the prototype is supposed to be discarded and the development efforts are begun from scratch, based on the requirements developed during the prototyping activities. How many organizations do you believe actually do that?

SOFTWARE DEVELOPMENT SECURITY FUNDAMENTALS

The guiding principles of the software development process should be documented in a hierarchically arranged and integrated set of policies, practices, standards, and procedures. This policy framework should document many aspects of the SDLC, such as the following:

- A policy that states that the prototyping development methodology will be utilized in all customized software development efforts
- A practice that defines how a particular code is commented
- A standard that identifies the permitted programming languages or development environments

- A procedure that provides step-by-step instructions on how to conduct a code review or generate a software build.

It has been my experience through many audits and assessments that the policy framework might exist, but may be antiquated and not used because it adds no value to the overall process. An up-to-date, well-maintained policy framework provides the foundation and guiding principles for defining how software is developed securely, efficiently, and within company standards. In the event of a disaster, an up-to-date policy framework could be utilized to support recovery operations. Additionally, a policy framework is required to support auditing activities, ISO certification, and other compliance-related activities. The need for a SDLC policy framework is inevitable. Why not ensure that your framework is tup to date and complete now, and use it to drive development activities, rather than completing it after the fact to prepare for an audit?

The waterfall model is one of the most documented and most structured development methodologies available and will be used as an example throughout this entry. There are several phases of the waterfall model, including:

- Business case and conceptual requirements definition
- Functional requirements and specifications definition (what it needs to do from a business perspective)
- Technical requirements and specifications definition (what it needs to do from a technical perspective)
- Design and architecture of the system
- Coding
- Unit and system test
- Implementation and deployment
- Maintenance
- Decommissioning of software systems

A typical software design team has several coders, one or more architects or software engineers, some quality assurance personnel, a team leader, a project manager, user representatives (sometimes marketing personnel), and sometimes a secretary or recorder who is responsible for taking notes and minutes. Typically missing from most teams is a security consultant or advocate who can offer guidance, support, and advice on security issues throughout the SDLC. In the absence of that advocate, this entry provides introductory advice the development team can use to add some baseline security functionality to the next release.

Securing the Foundation

One of the most commonly overlooked areas is physical security, and it is important to cover a few basic concepts in this entry. At a very high level, we should be concerned about the physical security of the developer's workstations, as well as the security of the source code repositories, build machines, source code back-up, and so on. As any lawyer will tell you, the more that you protect your intellectual property, the easier it will be in court to prosecute somebody who has inappropriately gained access to it. If you leave your code stored on several developers' machines, burned on CDs lying around, and printouts of code in the development labs, opposing counsel will always ask "How valuable could it have been?"

If you can perform a thorough physical review, conduct one from top to bottom. If you cannot, at a minimum, the following should be done:

- Ensure that back-up tapes of source code, sample data, and design documents are conducted regularly and properly secured
- Take the clean desktop policy to heart and ensure that all electronic media and paper copies are properly secured at each developer workstation
- Review the physical security of the server room (and perhaps of the developers if they are co-located in a single area) to include access controls, logging, environmental controls, guest access, etc.

Likewise, a team of information technology (IT) security professionals should conduct a thorough assessment of the logical security of the infrastructure. Although a description of that assessment is beyond the scope of this entry, at a minimum, the following questions should be answered:

- What are the back-up procedures? For example, how often is the development environment, source code, and compiled code backed up? Where are they stored? Who has access to the back-up media?
- Have any tapes been restored to validate the back-up process?
- Is there a business continuity and disaster recovery plan to detail how restoration and development activities will continue in the event of an incident?
- How are logical access controls managed for the source code, executable build systems, and test systems? Who approves the access list? When was it last reviewed?
- Have unnecessary services been turned off on the servers and workstations? Are updates and security patches regularly applied?
- How do the developers authenticate to the servers? Is traffic encrypted? Are clear text protocols used (such as Telnet)? If developers are using X Windows, has the configuration been reviewed?
- Are the developers and the development infrastructure segmented from the corporate network? A great

SOA–
Vulnerability

way to add an additional layer of logical security is to segment the development environment from the rest of the company via a firewall with well-designed policies permitting only the required traffic.

- Are the access logs to the servers, firewalls or routers (if applicable), and workstations reviewed for security events and investigated when required?

Now that the environment where the software will be developed has a secure baseline, we can focus our attention on the foundation of the development activities themselves. As part of that foundation, developers should have a minimum baseline of knowledge or awareness of security vulnerabilities, coding best practices, and industry trends and best practices.

There are numerous resources available, including Web sites, magazines devoted to information security, training programs, and organizations that offer specialized classes and seminars. Several security training organizations have offered classes in the past, magazines have published excellent articles on building security into the SDLC, and several excellent books have been published detailing specific vulnerabilities and how to avoid them, as well as how to develop a methodology to improve the reliability and security of software systems. Finally, numerous Web sites, online articles, and Web-based seminars have offered free, relevant, and very timely advice on how to produce secure software.

As a further reason to help encourage the development of secure code, senior management may wish to consider rewarding developers who reduce the number of security vulnerabilities within their code, or perhaps rewarding quality assurance personnel who discover vulnerabilities prior to deployment. In any event, it is important to ensure that all team members are educated and aware of the resources that are available to them, and have the commitment from management to allow them the time and resources to learn.

The education process should not be a one-time effort, but instead built into the overall SDLC to ensure that each team member's skills are continually honed and enhanced. Additionally, new attack vectors (where and how attacks originate) and new vulnerabilities are regularly announced. Keeping abreast of specific language, software development kits (SDKs), and development environment vulnerabilities can be accomplished through vendor training, subscriptions to vulnerability announcement mailing lists, and subscription services, as well as through participation in industry and user groups.

Vulnerabilities are many and diverse. Structured Query Language and XML code injection, buffer overruns, race conditions, improper storage of cryptographic keys, format string errors, cross site scripting, and poor usability leading to the user disabling some security features are just a few of the vulnerabilities that must be

mitigated in today's code. If designers and coders are not aware of the range of vulnerabilities, they may not be able to avoid them. If quality assurance personnel are not aware of the different types of vulnerabilities, they cannot test for them and alert the coding team. Continuous awareness and training sessions for all team members must be a requirement and part of each associate's annual review process.

Conceptual Design

After the organization has a basic security awareness foundation, it is time to form the team to begin the first step, which is typically conceptual design. As I re-read this entry, I noted that I have said that each SDLC phase was the "most important" from a security perspective. Let us consider the conceptual phase that really sets expectations for the overall functionality of the application. Security personnel at this phase should be providing guidance based on known threats, vulnerabilities, risks, and available and potential controls. Although not necessarily driving the end result, security input early on can help define what can and cannot be done. As an example, and I am not making this up, an organization wanted to develop an application that required real-time access to a critical system on our company's intranet for Internet users. Although it could have been done securely with the addition of numerous and costly controls, designing a tiered DMZ infrastructure allowed the development team to implement multiple other features, delighting the sales and marketing team and making the IT security organization even happier.

Technical and Functional Requirements

The next step in the SDLC is the formulation of the functional and technical requirements. As noted previously, these are sometimes completed in parallel or combined. For the sake of this entry, we will discuss the functional and technical requirements as a single phase. As a very simple example, consider the functional requirement that the application "must read input on a text file outputted by another program" and a technical requirement that the application "must read standard ASCII comma delimited text, fields up to 256 characters, with a record size limited only by the storage capacity." What happens when the format is not comma delimited, or when the fields have 50,000 characters? We typically do not put the negative cases in the requirements documents, but that is how we typically get into trouble with buffer overflows, unchecked inputs, and so on. Defining and understanding the entire range of inputs (not just what is expected) and defining the requirements for responding to all input, whether expected or not, are paramount to system security.

During the technical and functional requirement phases, it is imperative that the security consultant provides inputs and direction regarding the security requirements. Although it is unwieldy to add the requirement to check for buffer overflows, unchecked inputs, and so on at every input requirement, it is necessary to capture the overall requirement that all input will be checked and validated prior to processing. In addition, there will likely be several key areas that will be detailed in this requirements section that will need to be incorporated into the application.

Depending on the system under development, there are likely numerous privacy requirements that must be incorporated into the final system. The source of the privacy requirements may come from any number of sources, including:

- Health Insurance Portability and Accountability Act (HIPAA) of 1996
- Gramm–Leach–Bliley Act of 1999
- European Privacy Directive
- Canadian Privacy Act
- The development organization and end customer's privacy standards.

The privacy requirements will typically drive how information is stored, how it must be transmitted, back-up requirements (such as requiring encryption), how long data can be retained, how and with whom it may be shared, and how it must be destroyed. Finally, privacy requirements will drive the business continuity and security requirements that are discussed next.

In addition to privacy requirements, there will likely be disaster recovery and business continuity requirements that will need to be incorporated into the application. If the system is going to support a critical business process or perhaps be one, failover, redundancy, and back-up features will likely be included in the overall requirements. Specifications as to the types of back-ups, transaction logs, parameters of system heartbeats to support hot-swappable capabilities, and perhaps how the system manages the fail-over process will be part of the requirements. As part of the requirements phase, security consultants must be tasked with identifying the relevant regulations that will influence the application and provide input based on those regulations and industry best practices. To accomplish that, an understanding of the customer base, including where they will use the application and what it will be used for, will be needed so as to incorporate the applicable requirements for that region or industry.

The security requirements will also influence how the system traverses the remainder of the SDLC. There will be many security requirements that will be part of the system. Validating all input, authentication, encryption of data in transit and rest, and authorization must be addressed. Roles and corresponding responsibilities must be defined and be flexible and granular enough to ensure that "least privilege" concepts are met while not interfering with the day-to-day activities of the system.

One of the most comprehensive efforts to identify the requirements from a security perspective is the development of a threat and vulnerability matrix, or an attack vector. Through this exercise, commonly undertaken as part of a risk assessment, comes the understanding of the threats, vulnerabilities, and computed risks that a software system will face upon deployment. Vulnerabilities of the host operating system, auxiliary systems, threats to industries where the application may be deployed, its target (and potential) audience, and mitigating controls that may be placed into effect alongside the system are examples of inputs to the threat and vulnerability matrix. By developing an attack vector of what segments or functions of the system are likely to be vulnerable, special attention can be paid to those areas to ensure a strong resiliency to attack. It must be noted that threats, vulnerabilities, and controls are continually changing, and it would be negligent to ensure that the software is resilient to attack only at the areas identified in the threat vectors. The attack vector approach should only be used to ensure that the segments most likely to be attacked have sufficient controls and that all functions of the application enjoy a similar level of protection.

One can also consider conducting a risk assessment of the proposed system. Knowing that a commonly-accepted definition of the value of risk is Risk (System) = (Threats × Vulnerabilities)/Controls, we can compute the value of risk, and then, as the project moves from the design phase to coding and implementation phases, the value of risk can be continuously measured and monitored, and reduced as necessary to achieve a sufficiently low level. Noting that the risk equation cited earlier is defined as a function, we can compute the risk of any or all components of the system depending on our area of interest or review.

Significant events must be logged. Questions to be answered include what is logged, the location to which it is logged, what happens when the log fills up (i.e., does the system halt, or does it overwrite the oldest log data?), whether the logs are stored locally or remotely, and whether they can be centrally monitored. Access to the logs and control of the logging configuration are equally important, as either could afford a malicious user the opportunity to hide the tracks of an attack. It is the responsibility of the security consultant to ensure that minimum standards of logging (as well as other security-sensitive areas) as identified in any corporate policies are incorporated into the system's requirements.

SOA–
Vulnerability

Databases require particular attention, as they are typically the stores of the data processed by systems. Ensuring that default and system accounts are disabled unless the functionality is required, and then changing passwords of required system accounts, would be ideal requirements. Setting strong passwords on system accounts so they are resilient against long-term, brute force attempts should be a requirement as well. Requirements should include encrypting at the database level, defining authorization for read, write, and deletions, as well as how the database is to be accessed through the software system, that is, through the databases console or other third-party applications.

System Design

In the design phase, the functional and technical requirements are used to architect a system at a high level by decomposing it into functions, modules, libraries, etc. Participants in the design phase should have a thorough understanding of the hardware requirements (if applicable) of the system and should develop a design that is sufficiently robust to withstand attack when implemented on noncompliant hardware with drivers that were not validated or on operating systems that have never been updated or patched. In many commercial software development projects, it is impossible to predict the target platform hardware, operating system, other applications or services on the system, and so on. Systems that do not make assumptions about trusting the operating system, hardware, and other applications will fare better than those that blindly accept all inputs or transactions. Just like in real life, systems should trust, but verify.

At the design phase, the developers should be aware of the available controls and should be designing the system to maximize their use, while including additional controls to mitigate all threats and vulnerabilities previously identified during the threat and vulnerability discovery or risk assessment phases. Finally, the designers should include built-in mechanisms that regularly check for updates to the system and are able to receive and install those updates regularly and easily.

Coding

When the coding phase is initiated, a solid set of requirements should exist that highlights the technical and functional requirements of the system. These should include security requirements. The coding personnel should know they have the additional responsibility of implementing features, functions, and attributes of the system with security functionality in mind, even when it is not explicitly defined in the requirements. Care should be taken to review requirements with the

marketing organization, sales group, end users, or end customer when the organization that is responsible for coding has not been part of the entire SDLC.

Development efforts should utilize a source code management system that is adequately secured to protect source code assets from unauthorized access, disclosure, modification, or deletion. User account management, logging, and auditing should be carefully managed and regularly reviewed to ensure that personnel have access only to the data they need for their work and that they are authorized to access. Change control and configuration management are two important programs that support security requirements and are likely supported by features within the source code management system.

The coding phase introduces a number of areas that must be considered, including the complexity of the system, the application development language, the integrated development environment (IDE), the use of SDKs, and use of code libraries. The use of code libraries and SDKs introduces new challenges to the SDLC, as the source code may not always be available to the development team for review, and usually only provides the defined interfaces, such as how to call the application and what each function does. Its resiliency to a buffer overflow attack may not be known and may need to be tested in a black-box fashion detailed later in this entry.

Although the number of tools available for Web-based applications exceeds that available for traditional executable applications, there are many tools that integrate with IDEs to provide immediate feedback when they suspect potential security coding vulnerabilities. Just as a word processor highlights misspelled words as the user types, applications are available to highlight potential errors in the code that could be compromised. Although this solution should not be considered the sole control during the coding process, it is a very strong and successful approach. Doing a Web-based search for application coding vulnerability scanners will highlight some of the tools that are available commercially or through open source efforts. Although some are significantly better than others, cost, vendor preference, programming language, and IDE are factors that will drive the decision-making process. Many of these products have complementary products that provide similar testing features on the compiled or Web-enabled applications after they are installed. Typically, although not a requirement, IDE-based programs serve the needs of developers, whereas the tools used to scan executables or Web-based applications are used by auditors, assessors, and quality assurance personnel.

During the coding phase, code reviews should be conducted to provide peer review and feedback. The subject of many books and articles, code reviews are simply an opportunity for software coders to share their code with other coders to solicit their feedback, comments, and insights. Typically not focusing solely on security vulnerabilities, a code review serves to identify inefficiencies, areas of potential code re-use, logic errors, and suggestions for cleaner or more robust code. For critical interfaces and processes, a larger team may be deployed to include other members of the SDLC team, such as designers and quality assurance personnel.

"Formal methods" is a software engineering process in which mathematical and logical proofs are used to "prove" that the software is correct, or does what the requirements specify that it should do. The formal-methods approach provides additional insights for validating software, although it is typically time and resource intensive, as it is often quite a challenging effort with only a few automated tools to provide assistance. Finally, the formal-methods approach can be used to prove that code handles inputs as intended and properly rejects code that is incorrectly formatted or is invalid.

"Secure by default" is a term we hear quite often these days; it refers to the initial values of the various settings, parameters, and configurations. For example, consider a program that advertises that it securely uploads files to a remote server on a nightly basis over the Internet. Unless the operator knows that it is possible to enable the "secure copy" option, the program may utilize the traditional file transport protocol that sends the account information and data in clear text. With the secure copy option enabled, the transfer is significantly more secure. "Secure by default" initially enables the security features of the system and thus increases the overall security. End users must indicate that they do not want the default level of security by disabling or reducing the security controls.

Finally, the code must be documented. Although one can argue that secure code can be developed without documentation, best practices require that source code be commented and that sufficient documentation exists to detail how the code was developed in support of the requirements. In the event of vulnerability announcements in time to come, commented code can support reviews and investigations as to which code may need to be redeveloped.

A common security error that originates in the coding phase is the use of test data that is real customer data. Although using data that is valid and representative of real-word situations, it is important to note that, in many instances, using customer data for coding and testing procedures may be in violation of federal regulations stipulating that data must be protected. There are several ways to accomplish testing without using such data, including creating entirely random data, manually populating a test database, or using algorithms like as one-way hashes to mask the data used in testing. Creating artificial data can leave testers without the invalid or unchecked data that may often exist in real-life data. The SDLC team should utilize a dataset that contains both sufficient valid and invalid data to test exception cases that will inevitably be encountered in operation.

System and Unit Test

The test phase should be the last line of defense for discovering security vulnerabilities, not the front line. Using the test phase to catch vulnerabilities in the code base not only increases costs to correct the code, but detracts from the other responsibilities of the quality assurance personnel who are also reviewing documentation, installation, operation, interfaces with other systems and processes, as well as the logic of the application.

As noted during the previously discussed coding phase, there are several applications that are available to review and test the code for not only logic errors, but for security vulnerabilities as well. If the quality assurance personnel have been involved with the project from the earliest stages, test plans, test cases, expected results, and areas of concern should have been identified and documented. Code utilized as part of an SDK or that is received as precompiled will have to be reviewed as well. These reviews can use black-box testing, a term that is applied to testing code when you have no insight into the source code and can only supply different inputs (some within the interface parameters and some that are not), to ensure that the output is as expected.

Finally, there are many applications available to quality assurance personnel that provide support in automated testing. Applications that can learn expected responses, offer scripting, accept various forms of input, and automatically capture and flag suspect results can be utilized to reduce the time and resources required for testing, or more importantly, to allow the testers to investigate suspect and questionable results.

Deployment

The SDLC continues after the software has been designed and coded, as efforts begin to package, ship, deploy, and implement the software. Depending upon whether the software is a customized software solution or a commercial off-the-shelf solution (COTS), the involvement of the vendor will vary. During the initial deployment, quality assurance and design personnel should be closely supporting the help desks to provide guidance and, most importantly, to identify trends and patterns that may indicate vulnerability. In addition, Web-casts, alerts to customers, awareness training for employees, and so on. may be useful mechanisms for informing and educating users about the secure operation and management of the system. Finally, the system's documentation may require updates and

SOA–Vulnerability

clarifications based on feedback from the help desk to ensure clarity and understanding of the security features.

The installation package is created to facilitate the installation of the software. Proper testing should be performed to ensure that the installation doesn't introduce additional vulnerabilities (such as network-based installation packages that may introduce specialized services to support the installation); the latest documentation should be provided to the customers as well. Finally, customers should be made aware of mechanisms for receiving updated software packages and documentation as they become available.

Depending upon contractual requirements for customized software development, as the system moves into deployment, the release version of the source code may be transferred into "escrow" or may be transferred to the procuring organization itself. Although the escrow contract may dictate how the software is to be transferred and stored, appropriate measures must be taken to protect the data while in storage and transit, while still providing access to authorized users. The storage and management of cryptographic keys will need to be planned and agreed upon by the development firm, the end customer organization, and the escrow organization (when appropriate).

Software System Maintenance

Once the software system begins to ship, the maintenance mode typically begins. Vendors usually offer several years of support for each release for COTS-based packages, whereas the support for customized software is generally dictated by contractual terms. In any event, the vendor will typically receive input from:

- Customers who have uncovered potential security vulnerabilities
- Security research firms who are continually reviewing and dissecting applications and operating systems of all types
- Vulnerability announcements from the manufacturers of the IDEs, SDKs, and the compilers and language developers
- Continued quality assurance testing efforts that may uncover existing vulnerabilities while testing new features and updates

It will be critical to the organization's reputation and customer service to be able to accept and acknowledge vulnerability information and to be able to validate that information before issuing updates that mitigate the vulnerability in a reasonable time. There are a number of competing factors regarding disclosure. Some believe in "full disclosure," which is the release of vulnerability information as soon as it is made available. The

argument for full disclosure says "If I find vulnerability in a software package, everybody should know about it to provide an opportunity to implement additional controls." The argument against full disclosure is that as those with malicious intent become aware of the vulnerability, the clock begins to tick for the development of malware, viruses, and Trojans that will exploit that vulnerability. As a compromise, *de facto* standards have emerged that highlight recommended timelines, communications, and interactions between the discoverer of the vulnerability and the manufacturer of the vulnerability. COTS applications that must run on various platforms and multiple operating system versions may require lengthier timeframes (sometimes 30 days or more) to include regression testing, documentation, and packaging, whereas open sourced applications (and some commercial applications as well) have taken just a few hours to release a patch.

Decommissioning

Although the decommissioning phase can be as simple as clicking on "Uninstall," the removal of associated data and other configuration information is of the most concern. For example, if the application is uninstalled, then application data (which can be contained in anything from text files to relational databases) as well as configuration information (such as cryptographic keys and stored user names and passwords) must be deleted. Additionally, any adjunct services that were installed must be removed unless they are required by other applications. This is often a tricky task as the user must guess if any other installed applications require that particular service. Secured or not, it is not prudent to leave a service running when it is no longer needed.

During decommissioning or uninstalling, the user must be presented with options for what should be done with application data, cryptographic data, or user account information. If the user requests deletion of the data, then the user should be informed that data is not truly "deleted" and may be easily recovered with readily available tools. The uninstall function should provide recommendations on how to securely delete the data if it is considered sensitive. If application data is to be retained for use or for back-up purposes in time to come, appropriate security controls should be instituted to protect the data.

CONCLUSION

With security research firms paying a bounty to receive previously unannounced vulnerability information to boost the awareness of their firms and their credibility, and with malicious individuals paying a bounty to be the first to generate exploit code, it is critical for software development firms to incorporate timely and efficient mechanisms for managing security vulnerabilities from discovery through delivering an update. Freelancers, white-hat, gray-hat, and black-hat hackers have devoted careers to reviewing, disassembling, reverse engineering, and trying every combination and permutation of inputs and configurations in an attempt to find the one scenario where the system crashes, releases some private information in an error message, or allows some arbitrary code to run.

Software development is a customized process with many equally valid options for how to reach the end state. Programming languages, styles, environments, platforms, and designing and coding experience are all variables that will ultimately shape the end result, including how it operates, how it interfaces with other components, and how it works on various hardware and system platforms.

Through the development and use of a continually-updated policy framework, the development team will have the basic information of how software must be developed in the organization. Equally important is the continual training and awareness of the entire team of existing threats, vulnerabilities, industry best practices, and most importantly, regulations, that they must be aware of and compliant with. It is important to note that many tasks in this entry, particularly those of developing a strong policy framework and awareness, must be continually updated. Vulnerabilities and threats continue to change. New ones are added, and older ones are mitigated regularly. Having a program in place to develop software that is resilient in the face of vulnerabilities of the present as well as the time to come will allow a company to survive. Having a program in place to update its software in a timely manner when security issues arise will allow a company to build customer confidence and thrive.

The delivery of a secure software package is the goal of every development organization. Perhaps a realistic goal is to develop software in which the known security vulnerabilities are mitigated, or have sufficient controls in place, and the discovered vulnerabilities are managed in a timely and professional manner.

SOA– Vulnerability

Steganography

Mark Edmead
President, MTE Software, Inc., Escondido, California, U.S.A.

Abstract

The word *steganography* comes from the Greek, and it means covered or secret writing. As defined today, it is the technique of embedding information into something else for the sole purpose of hiding that information from the casual observer. Many people know a distant cousin of steganography called watermarking—a method of hiding trademark information in images, music, and software. Watermarking is not considered a true form of steganography. In stego, the information is hidden in the image; watermarking actually adds something to the image (such as the word *confidential*), and therefore it becomes a part of the image. Some people might consider stego to be related to encryption, but they are not the same. We use encryption—the technology to translate something from readable form to something unreadable—to protect sensitive or confidential data. In stego, the information is not necessarily encrypted, only hidden from plain view.

Of late there has been an increased interest in steganography (also called stego). We have seen this technology mentioned during the investigation of the 9/11 attacks, where the media reported that the terrorists used it to hide their attack plans, maps, and activities in chat rooms, bulletin boards, and websites. Steganography had been widely used long before these attacks and, as with many other technologies, its use has increased due to the popularity of the Internet.

One of the main drawbacks of using encryption is that with an encrypted message—although it cannot be read without decrypting it—it is recognized as an encrypted message. If someone captures a network data stream or an E-mail that is encrypted, the mere fact that the data is encrypted might raise suspicion. The person monitoring the traffic may investigate why and use various tools to try to figure out the contents of the message. In other words, encryption provides confidentiality but not secrecy. With steganography, however, the information is hidden; and someone looking at a JPEG image, for instance, would not be able to determine if there was any information within it. So, hidden information could be right in front of our eyes and we would not see it.

In many cases, it might be advantageous to use encryption and stego at the same time. This is because, although we can hide information within another file and it is not visible to the naked eye, someone can still (with a lot of work) determine a method of extracting this information. Once this happens, the hidden or secret information is visible for him to see. One way to circumvent this situation is to combine the two—by first encrypting the data and then using steganography to hide it. This two-step process adds additional security. If someone manages to figure out the steganographic system used, he would not be able to read the data he extracted because it is encrypted.

HIDING THE DATA

There are several ways to hide data, including data injection and data substitution. In data injection, the secret message is directly embedded in the host medium. The problem with embedding is that it usually makes the host file larger; therefore, the alteration is easier to detect. In substitution, however, the normal data is replaced or substituted with the secret data. This usually results in very little size change for the host file. However, depending on the type of host file and the amount of hidden data, the substitution method can degrade the quality of the original host file.

In the article "Techniques for Data Hiding," Walter Bender outlines several restrictions to using stego:[1]

- The data that is hidden in the file should not significantly degrade the host file. The hidden data should be as imperceptible as possible.
- The hidden data should be encoded directly into the media and not placed only in the header or in some form of file wrapper. The data should remain consistent across file formats.
- The hidden (embedded) data should be immune to modifications from data manipulations, such as filtering or resampling.
- Because the hidden data can degrade or distort the host file, error-correction techniques should be used to minimize this condition.

Encyclopedia of Information Systems and Technology, DOI: 10.1081/E-EIST-120046745

Table 1 Eight-bit pixel

1	1	0	0	1	1	0	1

- The embedded data should still be recoverable even if only portions of the host image are available.

STEGANOGRAPHY IN IMAGE FILES

As outlined earlier, information can be hidden in various formats, including text, images, and sound files. In this entry, we limit our discussion to hidden information in graphic images. To better understand how information can be stored in images, we need to do a quick review of the image file format. A computer image is an array of points called pixels (which are represented as light intensity). Digital images are stored in either 24- or 8-bit pixel files. In a 24-bit image, there is more room to hide information, but these files are usually very large in size and not the ideal choice for posting them on websites or transmitting over the Internet. For example, a 24-bit image that is 1024 × 768 in size would have a size of about 2 MB. A possible solution to the large file size is image compression. The two forms of image compression to be discussed are lossy and lossless compression. Each one of these methods has a different effect on the hidden information contained within the host file. Lossy compression provides high compression rates, but at the expense of data image integrity loss. This means that the image might lose some of its image quality. An example of a lossy compression format is Joint Photographic Experts Group (JPEG). Lossless, as the name implies, does not lose image integrity and is the favored compression used for steganography. GIF and BMP files are examples of lossless compression formats.

A pixel's makeup is the image's raster data. A common image, for instance, might be 640 × 480 pixels and uses 256 colors (8 bits per pixel).

Fig. 1 Unmodified image.

Fig. 2 Image to be hidden in Fig. 1.

In an 8-bit image, each pixel is represented by 8 bits, as shown in Table 1. The 4 bits to the left are the most-significant bits (MSB), and the 4 bits to the right are the least-significant bits (LSB). Changes to the MSB will result in a drastic change in the color and the image quality, while changes in the LSB will have minimal impact. The human eye cannot usually detect changes to only 1 or 2 bits of the LSB. So if we hide data in any 2 bits in the LSB, the human eye will not detect it. For instance, if we have a bit pattern of 11001101 and change it to 11001100, they will look the same. This is why the art of steganography uses these LSBs to store the hidden data.

PRACTICAL EXAMPLE OF STEGANOGRAPHY AT WORK

To best demonstrate the power of steganography, Fig. 1 shows the host file before a hidden file has been introduced. Fig. 2 shows the image file we wish to hide. Using a program called Invisible Secrets 3, by NeoByte Solution, Fig. 2 is inserted into Fig. 1. The resulting image file is shown in Fig. 3. Notice that there are no visual differences to the human eye. One significant difference is in the size of the resulting image. The size of the original Fig. 1 is 18 kb. The size of Fig. 2 is 19 kb. The size of the resulting stego-file is 37 kb. If the size of the original file were known, the size of the new file would be a clear indication that something made the file size larger. In reality, unless we know what the sizes of the files should be, the size of the file would not be the best way to determine if an image is a stego carrier. A practical way to determine if files have been tampered with is to use available software products that can take a snapshot of the images and calculate a hash value. This baseline value can then be periodically checked for changes. If the hash value of the file changes, it means that tampering has occurred.

Fig. 3 Image with Fig. 2 inserted into Fig. 1.

PRACTICAL (AND NOT SO LEGAL) USES FOR STEGANOGRAPHY

There are very few practical uses for this technology. One use is to store password information on an image file on a hard drive or web page. In applications where encryption is not appropriate (or legal), stego can be used for covert data transmissions. Although this technology has been used mainly for military operations, it is now gaining popularity in the commercial marketplace. As with every technology, there are illegal uses for stego as well. As discussed earlier, it was reported that terrorists use this technology to hide their attack plans. Child pornographers have also been known to use stego to illegally hide pictures inside other images.

DEFEATING STEGANOGRAPHY

Steganalysis is the technique of discovering and recovering the hidden message. There are terms in steganography that are closely associated with the same terms in cryptography. For instance, a steganalyst, like his counterpart a cryptanalyst, applies steganalysis in an attempt to detect the existence of hidden information in messages. One important—and crucial—difference between the two is that in cryptography, the goal is not to detect if something has been encrypted. The fact that we can see the encrypted information already tells us that it is. The goal in cryptanalysis is to decode the message. In steganography, the main goal is first to determine if the image has a hidden message and to determine the specific steganography algorithm used to hide the information. There are several known attacks available to the steganalyst: stego-only, known cover, known message, chosen stego, and chosen message. In a stego-only attack, the stego host file is analyzed. A known cover attack is used if both the original (unaltered) media and the stego-infected file are available. A known message attack is used when the hidden message

is revealed. A chosen stego attack is performed when the algorithm used is known and the stego host is available. A chosen message attack is performed when a stego-media is generated using a predefined algorithm. The resulting media is then analyzed to determine the patterns generated, and this information is used to compare it to the patterns used in other files. This technique will not extract the hidden message, but it will alert the steganalyst that the image in question does have embedded (and hidden) information.

Another attack method is using dictionary attacks against steganographic systems. This will test to determine if there is a hidden image in the file. All of the steganographic systems used to create stego images use some form of password validation. An attack could be perpetrated on this file to try to guess the password and determine what information had been hidden. Much like cryptographic dictionary attacks, stego dictionary attacks can be performed as well. In most steganographic systems, information is embedded in the header of the image file that contains, among other things, the length of the hidden message. If the size of the image header embedded by the various stego tools is known, this information could be used to verify the correctness of the password guessed.

Protecting against steganography is not easy. If the hidden text is embedded in an image, and the original (unaltered) image is available, a file comparison could be made to see if they are different. This comparison would not be able to determine if the size of the image has changed—remember, in many cases the image size does not change. However, the data (and the pixel level) does change. The human eye usually cannot easily detect subtle changes—detection beyond visual observation requires extensive analysis. Several techniques are used to do this. One is the use of stego signatures. This method involves the analysis of many different types of untouched images, which are then compared to the stego images. Much like the analysis of viruses using signatures, comparing the stego-free images to the stego images may make it possible to determine a pattern (signature) of a particular tool used in the creation of the stego-image.

SUMMARY

Steganography can be used to hide information in text, video, sound, and graphic files. There are tools available to detect steganographic content in some image files, but the technology is far from perfect. A dictionary attack against steganographic systems is one way to determine if content is, in fact, hidden in an image.

Variations of steganography have been in use for quite some time. As more and more content is placed on Internet websites, more corporations—as well as individuals—are looking for ways to protect their intellectual properties. Watermarking is a method used to mark documents, and new technologies for the detection of unauthorized use and illegal copying of material are continuously being improved.

REFERENCE

1. Bender, W.; Gruhl, D.; Morimoto, N.; Lu, A. Techniques for data hiding. IBM Syst. J. **1996**, February, *35* (3–4), 313–336.

BIBLIOGRAPHY

1. Great introduction to steganography by Duncan Sellars, http://www.cs.uct.ac.za/courses/CS400W/NIS/papers99/dsellars/stego.html.
2. Neil F. Johnson's Web site on steganography. Has other useful links to other sources of information, http://www.jjtc.com/Steganography/.
3. Another good site with reference material and software youcan use to make your own image files with hidden information, http://stegoarchive.com/.
4. Lewis, R. Steganography, http://www.sans.org/infosecFAQ/covertchannels/steganography3.htm.
5. Bartel, J. Steganalysis, http://www.sans.org/infosecFAQ/encryption/steganalysis2.htm.

VNC Systems: Virtual Network Computing Systems

Chris Hare
Information Systems Auditor, Nortel, Dallas, Texas, U.S.A.

Abstract

This entry discusses what virtual network computing (VNC) is, how it can be used, and the security considerations surrounding VNC. The information presented does get fairly technical in a few places to illustrate the protocol, programming techniques, and weaknesses in the authentication scheme. However, the corresponding explanations should address the issues for the less technical reader.

A major issue in many computing environments is accessing the desktop or console display of a different graphical-based system than the one you are using. If you are in a homogeneous environment, meaning you want to access a Microsoft Windows system from a Windows system, you can use applications such as Timbuktu, pcAnywhere, or RemotelyPossible.

In today's virtual enterprise, many people have a requirement to share their desktops or allow others to view or manipulate it. Many desktop-sharing programs exist aside from those mentioned, including Microsoft NetMeeting and online conferencing tools built into various applications.

The same is true for UNIX systems, which typically use the X Windows display system as the graphical user interface. It is a simple matter of running the X Windows client on the remote system and displaying it on the local system.

However, if you must access a dissimilar system (e.g., a Windows system from a UNIX system) the options are limited. It is difficult to find an application under UNIX that allows a user to view an online presentation from a Windows system using Microsoft PowerPoint. This is where Virtual Network Computing (VNC), from AT&T's United Kingdom Research labs, enters the picture.

WHAT IS VNC?

The VNC system, or VNC, was developed at the AT&T Research Laboratories in the United Kingdom. VNC is a very simple graphical display protocol allowing connections from heterogeneous or homogeneous computer systems.

VNC consists of a server and a viewer, as illustrated in Fig. 1. The server accepts connection requests to display its local display on the viewer.

The VNC services are based on what is called a *remote framebuffer* or RFB. The framebuffer protocol simply allows a server to update the framebuffer or graphical display device on the remote viewer. With total independence from the graphical device driver, it is possible to represent the local display from the server on the client or viewer. The portability of the design means the VNC server should function on almost any hardware platform, operating system, windowing system, and application.

Support for VNC is available for a number of platforms, including:

- Servers:
  - UNIX (X Window system)
  - Microsoft Windows
  - Macintosh
- Viewers:
  - UNIX (X Window System)
  - Microsoft Windows
  - Macintosh
  - Java
  - Microsoft Windows CE

VNC is described as a thin client protocol, making very few requirements on the viewer. In this manner, the client can run on the widest range of hardware. There are a number of factors distinguishing VNC from other remote display systems, including:

- VNC is stateless, meaning you can terminate the session and reconnect from another system and continue right where you left off. When you connect to a remote system using an application such as a PC X Server and the PC crashes or is restarted, the X Window system applications running terminate. Using VNC, the applications remain available after the reboot.
- The viewer is a thin client and has a very small memory footprint.

SOA–Vulnerability

Encyclopedia of Information Systems and Technology, DOI: 10.1081/E-EIST-120046801

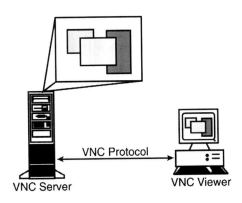

Fig. 1 The VNC components.

- VNC is platform independent, allowing a desktop on one system to be displayed on any other type of system, including Java-capable web browsers.
- It can be shared, allowing multiple users the ability to view and share a single desktop at the same time. This can be useful when needing to perform presentations over the network.
- And, best of all, VNC is free and distributed under the standard GNU General Public License (GPL).

These are some of the benefits available with VNC. However, despite the clever implementation to share massive amounts of video data, there are a few weaknesses, as presented in this entry.

HOW IT WORKS

Accessing the VNC server is done using the VNC client and specifying the IP address or node name of the target VNC server as shown in Fig. 2.

The window shown in Fig. 2 requests the node name or IP address for the remote VNC server. It is also possible to add a port number with the address. The VNC server has a password to protect unauthorized access to the server. After providing the target host name or IP address, the user is prompted for the password to access the server, as seen in Fig. 3.

The Microsoft Windows VNC viewer does not display the password when the user enters it, as shown in Fig. 4. However, the VNC client included in Linux systems does not hide the password when the user enters it. This is an issue because it exposes the password for the

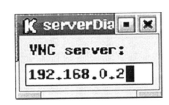

Fig. 2 The X windows VNC client.

Fig. 3 Entering the VNC server password.

server to public view. However, because there is no user-level authentication, one could say there is no problem. Just in case you missed it, *there is no user-level authentication*. This is discussed again later in this entry in the section entitled "Access Control."

The VNC client prompts for the password after the connection is initiated with the server and requests authentication using a challenge–response scheme. The challenge–response system used is described in the section entitled "Access Control."

Once the authentication is successful, the client and server then exchange a series of messages to negotiate the desktop size, pixel format, and the encoding schemes. To complete the initial connection setup, the client requests a full update for the entire screen and the session commences. Because the client is stateless, either the server or the client can close the connection with no impact to either the client or server.

Actually, this entry was written logged into a Linux system and using VNC to access a Microsoft Windows system that used VNC to access Microsoft Word. When using VNC on the UNIX- or Linux-based client, the user sees the Windows desktop as illustrated in Fig. 5.

The opposite is also true—a Windows user can access the Linux system and see the UNIX or Linux desktop as well as use the features and functionality offered by the UNIX platform (see Fig. 6). However, VNC is not limited to these platforms, as mentioned earlier and demonstrated later.

However, this may not be exactly what the Linux user was expecting. The VNC sessions run as additional displays on the X server, which on RedHat Linux systems default to the TWM Window Manager. This can be changed; however, that is outside the topic area of this entry.

SOA– Vulnerability

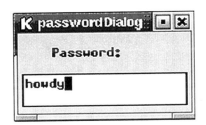

Fig. 4 The UNIX VNC client displays the password.

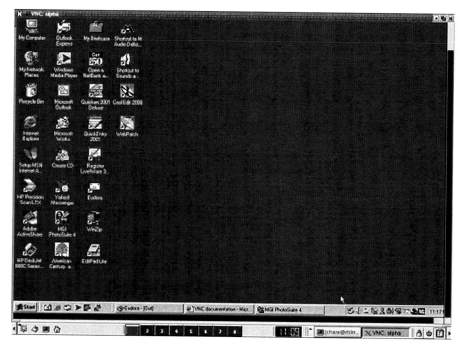

Fig. 5 The windows desktop from Linux.

NETWORK COMMUNICATION

All network communication requires the use of a network port. VNC is a connection-based TCP/IP application requiring the use of network ports. The VNC server listens on two ports. The values of these ports depend on the access method and the display number.

The VNC server listens on port 5900 plus the display number. WinVNC for Microsoft Windows defaults to display zero, so the port is 5900. The same is true for the Java-based HTTP port, listening at port 5800 plus the display number. This small and restrictive web server is discussed more in the section entitled "VNC and the Web."

If there are multiple VNC servers running on the same system, they will have different port numbers because their display number is different, as illustrated in Fig. 7.

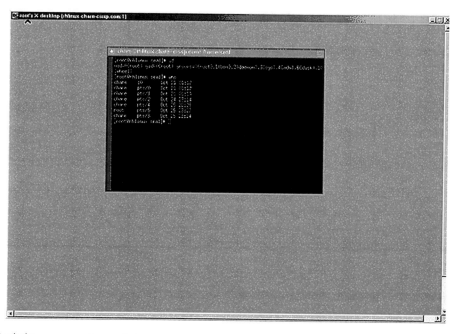

Fig. 6 The TWM window manager from windows.

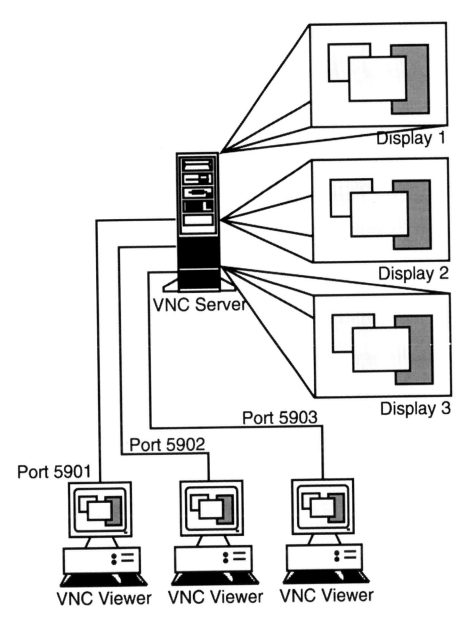

Fig. 7 Multiple VNC servers.

There is a VNC server executed for each user who wishes to have one. Because there is no user authentication in the VNC server, the authentication is essentially port based. This means user chare is running a VNC server, which is set up on display 1 and therefore port 5901. Because the VNC server is running at user chare, anyone who learns or guesses the password for the VNC server can access chare's VNC server and have all of chare's privileges.

Looking back at Fig. 6, the session running on the Linux system belonged to root as shown here:

```
[chare@rhlinux chare]$ ps -ef | grep vnc
root20368 10 23:21 pts/100:00:00 Xvnc :
  1 -desktop X -httpd/usr/s
chare20476204360 23:25 pts/
```

```
300:00:00 grep vnc
[chare@rhlinux chare]$
```

In this scenario, any user who knows the password for the VNC server on display 1, which is port 5901, can become root with no additional password required. Because of this access control model, good-quality passwords must be used to control access to the VNC server, and they must be kept absolutely secret.

As mentioned previously, the VNC server also runs a small web server to support access through the Java client. The web server listens on port 58xx, where xx is the display number for the server. The HTTP port on the web server is only used to establish the initial HTTP connection and download the applet. Once the applet is running in the browser, the connection uses port 59xx.

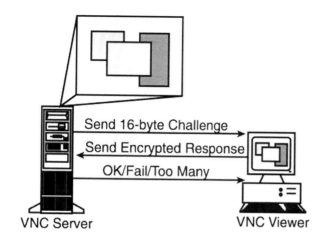

Fig. 8 The VNC authentication challenge–response.

The section entitled "VNC and the Web" describes using the VNC Java client.

There is a third mode, where the client listens for a connection from the server rather than connecting to a server. When this configuration is selected, the client listens on port 5500 for the incoming connection from the server.

ACCESS CONTROL

As mentioned previously, the client and server exchange a series of messages during the initial connection setup. These protocol messages consist of:

- Protocol Version
- Authentication
- ClientInitialization
- ServerInitialization

Once the ServerInitialization stage is completed, the client can send additional messages when it requires and receive data from the server.

The protocol version number defines what level of support both the client and server have. It is expected that some level of backward compatibility is available because the version reported should be the latest version the client or server supports. When starting the VNC viewer on a Linux system, the protocol version is printed on the display (standard out) if not directed to a file.

Using a tool such as tcpdump, we can see the protocol version passed from the client to the server (shown in bold text):

```
22:39:42.215633 eth0 < alpha.5900 > rhlinux.
  chare-cissp.com.1643:
P 1:13(12) ack 1 win 17520 <nop,nop,times
  stamp 37973 47351119 >
```

```
4500 0040 77f0 0000 8006 4172 c0a8 0002
c0a8 0003 170c 066b 38e9 536b 7f27 64fd
8018 4470 ab7c 0000 0101 080a 0000 9455
02d2 854f 5246 4220 3030 332e 3030 330a
E^@ ^@ @ w.. ^@^@. .^F A r.... ^@^B
....^@^C ^W^L ^F k 8.. S k j` d..
..^X D p. . | ^@^@ ^A^A ^H^J ^@^@.. U
^B.... O R F B 0 0 3. 0 0 3^J
```

and then again from the server to the client:

```
22:39:42.215633 eth0 > rhlinux.chare-cissp.
com.1643
> alpha.5900: P 1:13(12) ack 13 win 5840 <nop,
nop,time
stamp47351119 37973 > (DF)
  4500 0040 e1b5 4000 4006 d7ac c0a8 0003
  c0a8 0002 066b 170c 7f27 64fd 38e9 5377
  8018 16d0 d910 0000 0101 080a 02d2 854f
  0000 9455 5246 4220 3030 332e 3030 330a
E^@ ^@ @. ... @^@ @^F. ..... ... ^@^C
.... ^@^B ^F k ^W^L ^¿ ` d.. 8.. S w
..^X ^V.. ..^P ^@^@ ^A^A ^H^J ^B.. ... O
^@^@. . U R F B 0 0 3. 0  0  3^J
```

With the protocol version established, the client attempts to authenticate to the server. The password prompt shown in Fig. 3 is displayed on the client, where the user enters the password.

There are three possible authentication messages in the VNC protocol:

1. *Connection Failed.* The connection cannot be established for some reason. If this occurs, a message indicating the reason the connection could not be established is provided.
2. *No Authentication.* No authentication is needed. This is not a desirable option.
3. *VNC Authentication.* Use VNC authentication.

The VNC authentication challenge–response is illustrated in Fig. 8.

The VNC authentication protocol uses a challenge–response method with a 16-byte (128-bit) challenge sent from the server to the client. The challenge is sent from the server to the client in the clear. The challenge is random, based on the existing time when the connection request is made. The following packet has the challenge highlighted in bold:

```
14:36:08.908961 < alpha.5900 > rhlinux.chare-
cissp.com.
2058: P 17:33(16) ack 13 win 17508 <nop,nop,
timestamp
800090 8590888 >
  4500 0044 aa58 0000 8006 0f06 c0a8 0002
  c0a8 0003 170c 080a ae2b 8b87 f94c 0e34
  8018 4464 1599 0000 0101 080a 000c 355a
```

```
0083 1628 0456 b197 31f3 ad69 a513 151b
195d 8620
E^@ ^@ D.. X ^@^@..^F ^O^F.... ^@^B
.... ^@^C ^W^L ^H^J..+.... ..L ^N 4
..^X D d ^U..^@^@ ^A^A ^H^J ^@^L 5 Z
^@.. ^V ( ^D V.... 1.... I. .^S ^U^[
^Y] ..
```

The client then encrypts the 16-byte challenge using Data Encryption Standard (DES) symmetric cryptography with the user-supplied password as the key. The VNC DES implementation is based upon a public domain version of Triple-DES, with the double and triple length support removed. This means VNC is only capable of using standard DES for encrypting the response to the challenge. Again, the following packet has the response highlighted in bold:

```
14:36:11.188961 < rhlinux.chare-cissp.com.2058 >
alpha.5900: P 13:29(16) ack 33 win 5840
<nop,nop,timestamp 8591116 800090 > (DF)
     4500 0044 180a 4000 4006 a154 c0a8 0003
     c0a8 0002 080a 170c f94c 0e34 ae2b 8b97
     8018 16d0 facd 0000 0101 080a 0083 170c
     000c 355a 7843 ba35 ff28 95ee 1493 caa7
     0410 8b86
     E^@ ^@ D ^X^J @^@ @^F..T.... ^@^C
     .... ^@^B ^H^J ^W^L .. L ^N 4 ..+....
     ..^X ^V... ... ^@^@ ^A^A ^H^J ^@.. ^W^L
     ^@^L 5 Z x C.. 5.. ( .... ^T.. ....
^D^P....
```

The server receives the response and, if the password on the server is the same, the server can decrypt the response and find the value issued as the challenge. As discussed in the section "Weaknesses in the VNC Authentication System" later in this entry, the approach used here is vulnerable to a man-in-the-middle attack, or a cryptographic attack to find the key, which is the password for the server.

Once the server receives the response, it informs the client if the authentication was successful by providing an *OK*, *Failed*, or *Too Many* response. After five authentication failures, the server responds with *Too Many* and does not allow immediate reconnection by the same client.

The *ClientInitialization* and *ServerInitialization* messages allow the client and server to negotiate the color depth, screen size, and other parameters affecting the display of the framebuffer.

As mentioned in the "Network Communication" section, the VNC server runs on UNIX as the user who started it. Consequently, there are no additional access controls in the VNC server. If the password is not known to anyone, it is safe. Yes and no. Because the password is used as the key for the DES-encrypted response, the password is never sent across the network

in the clear. However, as we will see later in the entry, the challenge–response method is susceptible to a man-in-the-middle attack.

VNC Server Password

The server password is stored in a password file on the UNIX file system in the ~/.vnc directory. The password is always stored using the same 64-bit key, meaning the password file should be protected using the local file system permissions. Failure to protect the file exposes the password, because the key is consistent across all VNC servers.

The password protection system is the same on the other supported server platforms; however, the location of the password is different.

The VNC source code provides the consistent key:

```
/*
●We use a fixed key to store passwords, because we
assume
●that our local file system is secure but
nonetheless
●don't want to store passwords as plaintext.
*/
unsigned char fixedkey[8] =
{23,82,107,6,35,78,88,7};
```

This fixed key is used as input to the DES functions to encrypt the password; however, the password must be unencrypted at some point to verify authentication.

The VNC server creates the ~/.vnc directory using the standard default file permissions as defined with the UNIX system's umask. On most systems, the default umask is 022, making the ~/.vnc directory accessible to users other than the owner. However, the password file is explicitly set to force read/write permissions only for the file owner; so the chance of an attacker discovering the password is minimized unless the user changes the permissions on the file, or the attacker has gained elevated user or system privileges.

If the password file is readable to unauthorized users, the server password is exposed because the key is consistent and publicly available. However, the attacker does not require too much information, because the functions to encrypt and decrypt the password in the file are included in the VNC source code. With the knowledge of the VNC default password key and access to the VNC server password file, an attacker can obtain the password using 20 lines of C language source code.

A sample C program, here called attack.c, can be used to decrypt the VNC server password should the password file be visible:

```
#include <stdio.h>
#include <stdlib.h>
```

```
#include <string.h>
#include <sys/types.h>
#include <sys/stat.h>
#include <vncauth.h>
#include <d3des.h>
main ( argc, argv)
     int argc;
     char **argv;
{
   char *passwd;
   if (argc < = 1)
     {
     printf ("specify the location and name of a
VNC
     password file/n");
     exit (1);
     }
   /* we might have a file */
   passwd = vncDecryptPasswdFromFile (argv[1]);
   printf ("passowrd file is%s\n," argv[1]);
   printf ("password is%s\n," passwd);
   exit (0);
}
```

Note: Do not use this program for malicious purposes. It is provided for education and discussion purposes only.

Running the attack.c program with the location and name of a VNC password file displays the password:

```
[chare@rhlinux libvncauth]$./attack $HOME/.vnc/
passwd
passowrd file is/home/chare/.vnc/passwd
password is holycow
```

The attacker can now gain access to the VNC server. Note, however, this scenario assumes the attacker already has access to the UNIX system.

For the Microsoft Windows WinVNC, the configuration is slightly different. Although the methods to protect the password are the same, WinVNC uses the Windows registry to store the server's configuration information, including passwords. The WinVNC registry entries are found at:

- *Local machine-specific settings:*
  HKEY_LOCAL_MACHINE\Software\ORL
  \WinVNC3\
- *Local default user settings:*
  HKEY_LOCAL_MACHINE\Software\ORL
  \WinVNC3\Default
- *Local per-user settings:*
  HKEY_LOCAL_MACHINE\Software\ORL
  \WinVNC3\ *<username>*
- *Global per-user settings:*
  HKEY_CURRENT_USER\Software\ORL\WinVNC3

The WinVNC server password will be found in the local default user settings area, unless a specific user defines his own server. The password is stored as an individual registry key value as shown in Fig. 9.

Consequently, access to the registry should be as controlled as possible to prevent unauthorized access to the password.

The password stored in the Windows registry uses the same encryption scheme to protect it as on the UNIX system. However, looking at the password shown in Fig. 9, we see the value:

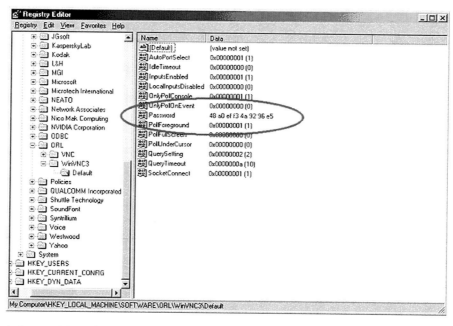

Fig. 9   WinVNC windows registry values.

```
48 a0 ef f3 4a 92 96 e5
```

and the value stored on UNIX is:

```
a0 48 f3 ef 92 4a e5 96
```

Comparing these values, we see that the byte ordering is different. However, knowing that the ordering is different, we can use a program to create a binary file on UNIX with the values from the Windows system and then use the earlier attack.c program to determine the actual password. Notice that because the password values shown in this example are the same, and the encryption used to hide the passwords is the same, the passwords are the same.

Additionally, the VNC password is limited to eight characters. Even if the user enters a longer password, it is truncated to eight. Assuming a good-quality password with 63 potential characters in each position, this represents only 63^8 possible passwords. Even with this fairly large number, the discussion thus far has demonstrated the weaknesses in the authentication method.

RUNNING A VNC SERVER UNDER UNIX

The VNC server running on a UNIX system uses the X Window System to interact with the X-based applications on UNIX. The applications are not aware there is no physical screen attached to the system. Starting a new VNC server is done by executing the command:

```
vncserver
```

on the UNIX host. Because the VNC server program is actually written in Perl, most common problems with starting vncserver are associated with the Perl installation or directory structures.

Any user on the UNIX host can start a copy of the VNC server. Because there is no user authentication built into the VNC server or protocol, running a separate server for each user is the only method of providing limited access. Each VNC server has its own password and port assignment, as presented earlier in the entry.

The first time a user runs the VNC server, he is prompted to enter a password for the VNC server. Each VNC server started by the same user will have the same password. This occurs because the UNIX implementation of VNC creates a directory called. vnc in the user's home directory. The. vnc directory contains the log files, PID files, password, and X startup files. Should the user wish to change the password for the VNC servers, he can do so using the vncpasswd command.

VNC Display Names

Typically the main display for a workstation using the X Window System is display 0 (zero). This means on a system named *ace*, the primary display is ace:0. A UNIX system can run as many VNC servers as the users desire, with the display number incrementing for each one. Therefore, the first VNC server is display ace:1, the second ace:2, etc. Individual applications can be executed and, using the DISPLAY environment variable defined, send their output to the display corresponding to the desired VNC server.

For example, sending the output of an xterm to the second VNC server on display ace:2 is accomplished using the command:

```
xterm –display ace:2 &
```

Normally, the vncserver command chooses the first available display number and informs the user what that display is; however, the display number can be specified on the command line to override the calculated default:

```
vncserver :2
```

No visible changes occur when a new VNC server is started, because only a viewer connected to that display can actually see the resulting output from that server. Each time a connection is made to the VNC server, information on the connection is logged to the corresponding server log file found in the $HOME/.vnc directory of the user executing the server. The clog file contents are discussed in the "Logging" section of this entry.

VNC as a Service

Instead of running individual VNC servers, there are extensions available to provide support for VNC under the Internet Super-Daemon, inetd and xinetd. More information on this configuration is available from the AT&T Laboratories website.

VNC AND MICROSOFT WINDOWS

The VNC server is also available for Microsoft Windows, providing an alternative to other commercial solutions and integration between heterogeneous operating systems and platforms. The VNC server under Windows is run as a separate application or a service. Unlike the UNIX implementation, the Windows VNC server can only display the existing desktop of the PC console to the user. This is a limitation of Microsoft Windows, and not WinVNC. WinVNC does not make

Fig. 10 WinVNC system tray icons.

the Windows system a multiuser environment: If more than one user connects to the Windows system at the same time, they will all see the same desktop.

Running WinVNC as a service is the preferred mode of operation because it allows a user to log on to the Windows system, perform their work, and then log off again.

When running WinVNC, an icon as illustrated in Fig. 10 is displayed. When a connection is made, the icon changes color to indicate there is an active connection.

The WinVNC properties dialog shown in Fig. 11 allows the WinVNC user to change the configuration of WinVNC. All the options are fully discussed in the WinVNC documentation.

With WinVNC running as a service, a user can connect from a remote system even when no user is logged on at the console. Changing the properties for WinVNC when it is running as a service has the effect of changing the service configuration, also known as the default properties, rather than the individual user properties. However, running a non-service mode WinVNC means a user must have logged in on the console and started WinVNC for it to work correctly. Fig. 12 illustrates

accessing WinVNC from a Linux system while in service mode.

Aside from the specific differences for configuring the WinVNC server, the password storage and protocol-level operations are the same, regardless of the platform. Because there can be only one WinVNC server running at a time, connections to the server are on ports 5900 for the VNC viewer and 5800 for the Java viewer.

VNC AND THE WEB

As mentioned previously, each VNC server listens not only on the VNC server port but also on a second port to support web connections using a Java applet and a web browser. This is necessary to support Java because a Java applet can only make a connection back to the machine from which it was served. Connecting to the VNC server using a Java-capable web browser to:

```
http://ace:5802/
```

loads the Java applet and presents the log-in screen where the password is entered. Once the password is provided, the access controls explained earlier prevail. Once the applet has connected to the VNC server port, the user sees a display resembling that shown in Fig. 13.

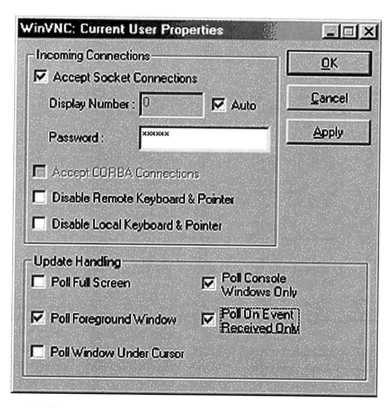

Fig. 11 The WinVNC properties dialog.

SOA–
Vulnerability

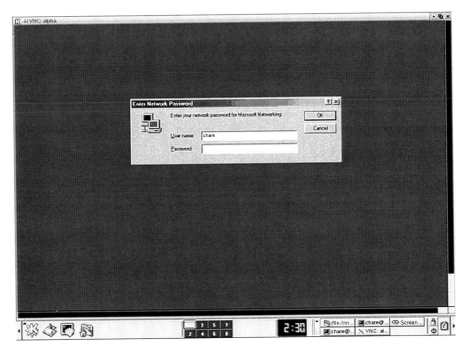

Fig. 12 Accessing WinVNC in service mode.

With the Java applet, the applications displayed through the web browser can be manipulated as if they were displayed directly through the VNC client or on the main display of the workstation.

LOGGING

As with any network-based application, connection and access logs provide valuable information regarding the operation of the service. The log files from the VNC server provide similar information for debugging or later analysis. A sample log file resembles the following. The first part of the log always provides information on the VNC server, including the listing ports, the client name, display, and the URL:

```
26/10/01 23:25:47 Xvnc version 3.3.3r2
26/10/01 23:25:47 Copyright © AT&T Laboratories
Cambridge.
```

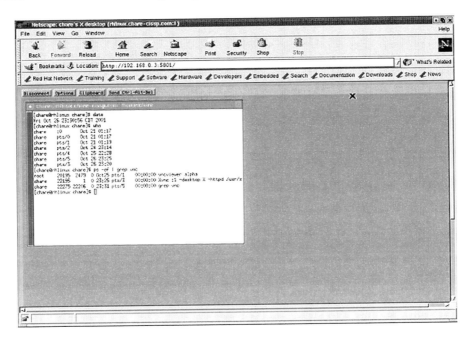

Fig. 13 A VNC connection using a Java-capable web browser.

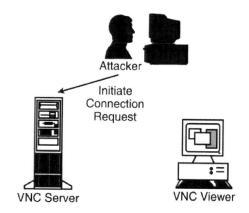

Fig. 14 Attacker opens connection to VNC server.

```
26/10/01 23:25:47 All Rights Reserved.
26/10/01 23:25:47 See http://www.uk.research.
att.com/
  vnc for information on VNC
26/10/01 23:25:47 Desktop name `X' (rhlinux.
chare-cissp.com:1)
26/10/01 23:25:47 Protocol version supported
3.3
26/10/01 23:25:47 Listening for VNC connections
on TCP port 5901
26/10/01 23:25:47 Listening for HTTP connections
on TCP port 5801
26/10/01 23:25:47 URL http://rhlinux.chare-
cissp.com:5801
```

The following sample log entry shows a connection received on the VNC server. We know the connection came in through the HTTPD server from the log entry. Notice that there is no information regarding the user who is accessing the system—only the IP address of the connecting system:

```
26/10/01 23:28:54 httpd: get `` for 192.168.0.2
26/10/01 23:28:54 httpd: defaulting to `index.
vnc'
26/10/01 23:28:56 httpd: get `vncviewer.jar' for
192.168.0.2
26/10/01 23:29:03 Got connection from client
192.168.0.2
26/10/01 23:29:03 Protocol version 3.3
26/10/01 23:29:03 Using hextile encoding for
client 192.168.0.2
26/10/01 23:29:03 Pixel format for client
192.168.0.2:
26/10/01 23:29:03 8 bpp, depth 8
26/10/01 23:29:03 true colour: max r 7 g 7 b 3,
shift r 0 g 3 b 6
26/10/01 23:29:03 no translation needed
26/10/01 23:29:21 Client 192.168.0.2 gone
26/10/01 23:29:21 Statistics:
26/10/01 23:29:21 key events received 12,
pointer events 82
26/10/01 23:29:21 framebuffer updates 80,
```

```
rectangles 304, bytes 48528
26/10/01 23:29:21 hextile rectangles 304, bytes
48528
26/10/01 23:29:21 raw bytes equivalent 866242,
compression ratio
17.850354
```

The log file contains information regarding the connection with the client, including the color translations. Once the connection is terminated, the statistics from the connection are logged for later analysis, if required.

Because there is no authentication information logged, the value of the log details for a security analysis are limited to knowing when and from where a connection was made to the server. Because many organizations use dynamic host configuration protocol for automatic IP address assignment and IP addresses may be spoofed, the actual value of knowing the IP address is reduced.

WEAKNESSES IN THE VNC AUTHENTICATION SYSTEM

We have seen thus far several issues that will have the security professional concerned. However, these can be alleviated as discussed later in the entry. There are two primary concerns with the authentication. The first is the man-in-the-middle attack, and the second is a cryptographic attack to uncover the password.

Random Challenge

The random challenge is generated using the rand (3) function in the C programming language to generate random numbers. The random number generator is initialized using the system clock and the existing system time. However, the 16-byte challenge is created by successive calls to the random number generator, decreasing the level of randomness on each call. (Each call returns 1 byte or 8 bits of data.)

This makes the challenge predictable and increases the chance an attacker could establish a session by storing all captured responses and their associated challenges. Keeping track of each challenge–response pair can be difficult and, as discussed later, not necessary.

Man-in-the-Middle Attack

For the purposes of this illustration, we will make use of numerous graphics to facilitate understanding this attack method. The server is system S, the client is C, and the attacker, or man in the middle, is A. (This discussion ignores the possibility the network connection

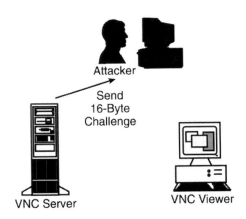

Fig. 15   Server sends challenge to attacker.

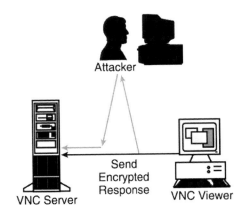

Fig. 17   Attacker and client send encrypted response.

may be across a switched network, or that there are ways of defeating the additional security provided by the switched network technology.)

The attacker A initiates a connection to the server, as seen in Fig. 14. The attacker connects, and the two systems negotiate the protocols supported and what will be used. The attacker observes this by sniffing packets on the network.

We know both the users at the client and server share the DES key, which is the password. The attacker does not know the key. The password is used for the DES encryption in the challenge–response.

The server then generates the 16-byte random challenge and transmits it to the attacker, as seen in Fig. 15. Now the attacker has a session established with the server, pending authorization.

At this point, the attacker simply waits, watching the network for a connection request to the same server from a legitimate client. This is possible as there is no timeout in the authentication protocol; consequently, the connection will wait until it is completed.

When the legitimate client attempts a connection, the server and client negotiate their protocol settings, and the server sends the challenge to the client as illustrated in Fig. 16. The attacker captures the authentication

request and changes the challenge to match the one provided to him by the server.

Once the attacker has modified the challenge, he forges the source address and retransmits it to the legitimate client. As shown in Fig. 17, the client then receives the challenge, encrypts it with the key, and transmits the response to the server.

The server receives two responses: one from the attacker and one from the legitimate client. However, because the attacker replaced the challenge sent to the client with his own challenge, the response sent by the client to server does not match the challenge. Consequently, the connection request from the legitimate client is refused.

However, the response sent does match the challenge sent by the server to the attacker; and when the response received from the attacker matches the calculated response on the server, the connection is granted. The attacker has gained unauthorized access to the VNC server.

Cryptographic Attacks

Because the plaintext challenge and the encrypted response can both be retrieved from the network, it is possible to launch a cryptographic attack to determine the key used, which is the server's password. This is easily done through a brute-force or known plaintext attack.

A brute-force attack is the most effective, albeit time-consuming, method of attack. Both linear cryptanalysis, developed by Lester Mitsui, and differential cryptanalysis, developed by Biham and Shamir, are considered the two strongest analytic (shortcut) methods for breaking modern ciphers; and even these have been shown as not very practical, even against Single-DES.

The known plaintext attack is the most advantageous method because a sample of ciphertext (the response) is available as well as a sample of the plaintext (the challenge). Publicly available software such as *crack* could

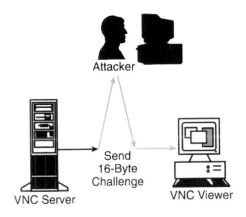

Fig. 16   Attacker captures and replaces challenge.

be modified to try a dictionary and brute-force attack by repeatedly encrypting the challenge until a match for the response is found. The nature of achieving the attack is beyond the scope of this entry.

Finding VNC Servers

The fastest method of finding VNC servers in an enterprise network is to scan for them on the network devices. For example, the popular nmap scanner can be configured to scan only the ports in the VNC range to locate the systems running it:

```
[root@rhlinux chare]# nmap -p "5500,5800-5999"
192.168.0.1-5
Starting nmap V. 2.54BETA29 (www.insecure.org/
nmap/)
All 201 scanned ports on gateway (192.168.0.1)
are: filtered
Interesting ports on alpha (192.168.0.2):
(The 199 ports scanned but not shown below are in
state: closed)
Port State Service
5800/tcp open vnc
5900/tcp open vnc
Interesting ports on rhlinux.chare-cissp.com
(192.168.0.3):
(The 199 ports scanned but not shown below are in
state: closed)
Port State Service
5801/tcp open vnc
5901/tcp open vnc-1
Nmap run completed — 5 IP addresses (3 hosts up)
scanned in 31 seconds
[root@rhlinux chare]#
```

There are other tools available to find and list the VNC servers on the network; however, nmap is fast and will identify not only if VNC is available on the system at the default ports but also all VNC servers on that system.

Improving Security through Encapsulation

To this point we have seen several areas of concern with the VNC environment:

- There is no user-level authentication for the VNC server.
- The challenge–response system is vulnerable to man-in-the-middle and cryptographic attacks.
- There is no data confidentiality built into the client and server.

Running a VNC server provides the connecting user with the ability to access the entire environment at the privilege level for the user running the server. For example, assuming root starts the first VNC server on a UNIX system, the server listens on port 5901. Any connections to this port where the remote user knows the server password result in a session with root privileges.

We have seen how it could be possible to launch a man-in-the-middle or cryptographic attack against the authentication method used in VNC. Additionally, once the authentication is completed, all the session data is unencrypted and could, in theory, be captured, replayed, and watched by malicious users. However, because VNC uses a simple TCP/IP connection, it is much easier to add encryption support with Secure Sockets Layer (SSL) or Secure Shell (SSH) than, say, a telnet, rlogin, or X Window session.

SSH is likely the more obvious choice for most users, given there are clients for most operating systems. SSH encrypts all the data sent through the tunnel and supports port redirection; thus, it can be easily supported with VNC. Furthermore, although VNC uses a very efficient protocol for carrying the display data, additional benefits can be achieved at slower network link speeds because SSH can also compress the data.

There are a variety of SSH clients and servers available for UNIX, although if you need an SSH server for Windows, your options are very limited and may result in the use of a commercial implementation. However, SSH clients for Windows and the Apple Macintosh are freely available. Additionally, Mindbright Technology offers a modified Java viewer supporting SSL.

Because UNIX is commonly the system of choice for operating a server, this discussion focuses on configuring VNC with SSH using a UNIX-based system. Similar concepts are applicable for Windows-based servers, once you have resolved the SSH server issue. However, installing and configuring the base SSH components are not discussed in this entry.

Aside from the obvious benefits of using SSH to protect the data while traveling across the insecure network, SSH can compress the data as well. This is significant if the connection between the user and the server is slow, such as a PPP link. Performance gains are also visible on faster networks, because the compression can make up for the time it takes to encrypt and decrypt the packets on both ends.

A number of extensions are available to VNC, including support for connections through the Internet superserver inetd or xinetd. These extensions mean additional controls can be implemented using the TCP Wrapper library. For example, the VNC X Window server, Xvnc, has been compiled with direct support for TCP Wrappers.

More information on configuring SSH, inetd, and TCP Wrappers is available on the VNC website listed in the "Bibliography" section of this entry.

SUMMARY

The concept of thin client computing will continue to grow and develop to push more and more processing to centralized systems. Consequently, applications such as VNC will be with the enterprise for some time. However, the thin client application is intended to be small, lightweight, and easy to develop and transport. The benefits are obvious—smaller footprint on the client hardware and network, including support for many more devices including handheld PCs and cell phones, to name a few.

However, the thin client model has a price, and in this case it is security. Although VNC has virtually no security features in the protocol, other add-on services such as SSH, VNC, and TCP Wrapper, or VNC and xinetd provide extensions to the basic VNC services to provide access control lists limited by the allowable network addresses and data confidentiality and integrity.

Using VNC within an SSH tunnel can provide a small, lightweight, and secured method of access to that system 1000 miles away from your office. For enterprise or private networks, there are many advantages to using VNC because the protocol is smaller and more lightweight than distributing the X Window system on Microsoft Windows, and it has good response time even over a slower TCP/IP connection link. Despite the security considerations mentioned in this entry, there are solutions to address them; so you need not totally eliminate the use of VNC in your organization.

BIBLIOGRAPHY

1. CORE SDI advisory: weak authentication in AT&T's VNC, http://www.uk.research.att.com/vnc/archives/2001-01/0530.html.
2. VNC Computing Home Page, http://www.uk.research.att.com/vnc/index.html.
3. VNC Protocol Description, http://www.uk.research.att.com/vnc/rfbproto.pdf.
4. VNC Protocol Header, http://www.uk.research.att.com/vnc/rfbprotoheader.pdf.
5. VNC Source Code, http://www.uk.research.att.com/vnc/download.html.

SOA–
Vulnerability

VPNs: Virtual Private Networks

James S. Tiller
Chief Security Officer and Managing Vice President of Security Services, International Network Services (INS), Raleigh, North Carolina, U.S.A.

Abstract

The goal of this entry is to introduce virtual private networks, and explain their surge in popularity as well as the link to existing advances in Internet connectivity, such as broadband. Then, the security experienced with legacy remote access solutions is compared with the realized security the industry has adopted. This is an opportunity to look beyond the obvious and discuss the huge impact this technology is having on the total security posture of organizations. The problem is so enormous that it is difficult to comprehend—a "can't see the forest for the trees" syndrome.

It is no surprise that virtual private networks (VPNs) have become tremendously popular among many dissimilar business disciplines. Regardless of the vertical market or trade, VPNs can play a crucial role in communication requirements, providing flexibility and prompt return on investment when implemented and utilized properly. The adoption of VPNs has been vast and swift; and as technology advances, this trend will only increase. Some of the popularity of VPNs is due to the perceived relative ease of implementing the technology. This perceived simplicity and the promise of cheap, limitless access have created a mad rush to leverage this newfound communication type. Unfortunately, these predominant characteristics of VPNs have overshadowed fundamental security flaws that seem to remain obscure and hidden from the sales glossies and product presentations. This entry is dedicated to shedding light on the security risks associated with VPNs and the misunderstanding that VPNs are synonymous with security.

It is crucial that the reader understands the security limitations detailed herein have almost nothing to do with VPN technology itself. There are several types of VPN technologies available—for example, IPSec, SSL, and PPTP, to mention a few—and each has advantages and disadvantages depending on the requirements and implementation. In addition, each has various levels of security that can be leveraged to accommodate a mixture of conditions. The insecurity of VPNs as a medium and a process is being discussed, and not the technical aspects or standards.

What is being addressed is the evaluation of VPNs by the general consumer arrived at from the sales paraphernalia flooding the market and the industry's products claiming to fulfill consumers' needs. Unfortunately, the demand is overwhelming, and the development of sufficient controls that could be integrated to increase the security lags behind what is being experienced. The word "security" appears frequently when VPNs are being discussed, which typically applies when defining the VPN itself—the protection of data in transit. Unfortunately, the communication's security stops at the termination point of the VPN, a point where security is paramount.

ONE THING LEADS TO ANOTHER

The popularity of VPNs seems to have blossomed overnight. The ability to remove the responsibility of maintaining a dedicated line for each contiguous remote user at the corporate site and leverage the existing Internet connection to multiplex a greater number of connections previously unobtainable has catapulted VPN technology.

As with many technological combinations, one type may tend to feed from another and reap the benefits of its companion's advances. These can materialize as improvements or options in the technologies and the merger of implementation concepts—a marriage of symbiotic utilities that culminate to equal more than attainable alone. Cell phones are an example of this phenomenon. Cell phones support digital certificates, encryption, e-mail, and browsing, among other combinations and improvements. The wireless community has leveraged technologies normally seen in networking that are now gaining attention from their use in another environment. Cell phone use is more robust and the technology used is employed in ways not originally considered. It is typically a win–win situation.

The universal embracement of VPNs can be attributed to two primary changes in the communication industry: global adoption of Internet connectivity and inexpensive broadband Internet access. These contemporary transformations and the ever-present need to

Encyclopedia of Information Systems and Technology, DOI: 10.1081/E-EIST-120046387

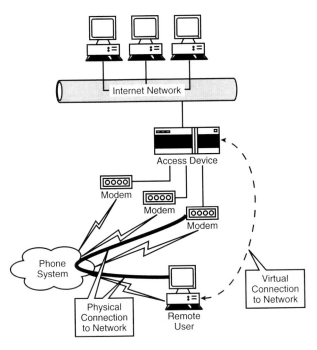

Fig. 1 Standard remote access via modems.

support an increasing roaming user community have propelled VPN technologies to the forefront of popularity.

ROAMING USERS

Roaming is characterized by the natural progression from early networks providing services to a captive

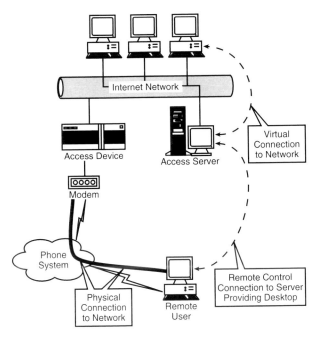

Fig. 2 Standard remote access via modems using remote control or remote desktop.

population and allowing those same services to be accessible from outside the normal boundaries of the network. Seemingly overnight, providing remote access to users was paramount and enormous resources were allocated to providing it.

Initially, as shown in Fig. 1, modems were collected and connected into a common device that provided access to the internal network, and, of course, the modems were connected to phone lines that ultimately provided the access. As application requirements grew exponentially, the transmission speed of modems increased modestly and change was on the horizon. The first wave of change came in the form of remote desktops, or in some cases, entire systems. As detailed in Fig. 2, a user would dial in and connect to a system that could be either remotely controlled or export the desktop environment to the remote user. In both cases, the bandwidth required between the remote user and the core system was actually reduced and the functionality was amplified. Cubix, Citrix, and PC Anywhere became the dominant players in providing the increased capabilities, each with its own requirements, advantages, and cost.

Performance was realized by the fact that the remote access server on the internal network had very high access speeds to the other network resources. By using a lightweight protocol to control the access server, or to obtain desktop imagery, the modem connection had virtually the same feel as if on the actual network. It was at this point in the progression of remote access that having the same look and feel of the internal network had become the gauge to which all remote access solutions would be measured. From this point forward, any differences or added inconveniences would diminish the acceptance of a remote access solution.

INTERNET ADOPTION

The Internet's growth has been phenomenal. From the number of people taking their first steps on the Net, to the leaps in communication technologies, Internet utilization has become increasingly dense and more populated. The Internet has become a requirement for business and personal communications rather than a novelty or for simple amusement. Businesses that were not associated in some way with the Internet are now attempting to leverage it for expansion and increase client satisfaction while reducing costs. It is not uncommon for an organization to include an Internet connection for a new or existing office as a default installation.

In contrast, early adopters of dedicated Internet connections, as a rule, had a single access point for the entire organization. As depicted in Fig. 3, remote offices

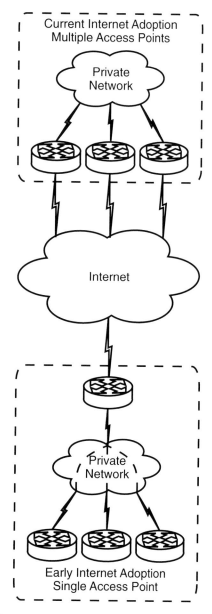

Fig. 3 Internet access through one central point compared to the several typically seen now.

could get access by traversing the wide area network (WAN) to the central location at which the Internet was accessible. This very common design scenario was satisfactory when Internet traffic and requirements were limited in scope and frequency. As the requirements for Internet access grew, the number of connections grew in direct proportion, until the WAN began to suffer. Shortly thereafter, as the costs for direct connectivity declined and the Internet became more and more a part of business life, it became an essential tool and greater access was needed.

The Internet has become an indispensable utility for successful businesses, and the volume of Internet traffic coursing through internal networks is astounding. The need for information now greatly outweighs the cost of

Internet connectivity. Hitherto, Internet connections had to be validated and carefully considered prior to implementation. Today, the first question is typically, "How big a pipe do we need?" not "Where should we put it?"

The vast adoption of the Internet and acceptance of it as a fundamental requirement has resulted in the increased density and diversity of the Internet. Organizations now have several access points and leverage them to reduce load on other internal networks and provide increased performance for internal users as well as provide service redundancy. By leveraging the numerous existing connections, an organization can implement VPN technology to enhance communication, while using a service that was cost-justified long before the inclusion of VPNs.

BROADBAND

Before the existence of high-speed access to the Internet that is standard today, there were typically only modems and phone lines that provided painfully slow access. There were, of course, the few privileged users who had ISDN available to them that provided some relief. However, access was still based on modems and could be a nightmare to get to work properly. The early adopters of remote access used modems to obtain data or services. As the Internet became popular, modems were used to connect to an Internet service provider (ISP) that provided the means for accessing the Internet. In either case, the limited speed capabilities were a troubling constant.

Today's personal and home access to the Internet can reach speeds historically realized only with expensive lines that only the largest companies could afford or obtain. At present, a simple device can be installed that provides a connection to the ISP and leverages Ethernet to connect to the host PC in the home or small office. Today, access is provided and controlled separately from the PC and rarely requires user intervention. The physical connection and communication medium are transparent to the user environment. Typically, the user turns on the computer and the Internet is immediately available. This is in stark contrast to the physical connection associated with the user's system and the modem, each working together to become the signal termination point and assuming all the responsibilities that are associated with providing the connection.

As with many communication technologies (especially with regard to modem-based remote access), a termination point must be supplied to provide the connection to the remote devices or modems. With dial-up solutions, a modem (virtual or physical) is supplied for the remote system to dial into and establish communications. A similar requirement exists for broadband, whether for cable modems or for xDSL technologies: a termination point must be supplied to create a connection for the remote devices at the home or office.

The termination point at the core—with regard to the adoption of VPNs—has become one of the differentiating factors between broadband and modems. To provide remote dial-up access for employees, a single modem could be installed in a server—or workstation for that matter—and a phone line attached. The remote user could be supplied with a modem, the phone number, and the use of some basic software; a connection could be established to provide ample access to the system and services.

In contrast, broadband implementations are more complicated and considerably more expensive; thus, today, only service providers implement this type of technology. An example is Internet cable service; not too many companies have access to the cable infrastructure to build their own internal remote access solution. Broadband is not in use for point-to-point remote access solutions. Therein lies the fundamental appeal of VPNs: a way to leverage this advanced communication technology to access company resources.

Not only is the huge increase in speed attractive because some of the application requirements may be too great for the limited bandwidth provided by modems, but also the separation of the technology from the computer allows for a simplified and scalable integration. Under these circumstances, broadband is extremely attractive for accessing corporate resources. It is one thing to have broadband for high-speed Internet browsing and personal excursions, but it is another to have those same capabilities for business purposes. Unfortunately, as described earlier, broadband technologies are complex and infeasible for a non-service-provider organization to implement for internal use. The result is a high-speed communication solution that only provides Internet access—that is, until that advent of VPNs.

EXTENDED ACCESS

As communication capabilities increased and companies continued to integrate Internet activities into everyday procedures, the creation of VPN technology to merge the two was critical. Dial-up access to the Internet and broadband provide access to the Internet from nearly anywhere and with high speeds. Both allow global access to the Internet, but there is no feasible or cost-effective way to terminate the connection to the company headquarters. Since broadband access was intimately associated with the Internet and direct-dial solutions were ineffective and expensive, the only foreseeable solution was to leverage the Internet to provide

private communications. This ultimately allowed organizations to utilize their existing investment in Internet connectivity to multiplex remote connections. The final hurdle was to afford security to the communication in the form of confidentiality, information integrity, access control, authentication, auditing, and, in some cases, nonrepudiation.

The global adoption of the Internet, its availability, and the increased speeds available has exceeded the limitless access enjoyed with dial-up. With dial-up, the telephone system was used for establishing communications—and telephones are everywhere. The serial communication itself was carried over a dedicated circuit that would be difficult to intercept for the everyday hacker and therefore relatively secure. Now that the Internet is everywhere, it can be used to duplicate the availability that exists with the telephone network while taking advantage of the increased speeds. Granted, if a modem is used to connect to the Internet, the speed is not realized and the phone system is being used to connect, but locally; the Internet is still being used for the common connection medium. Even with dial-up remote access, this was a huge leap in service because many corporate-provided remote access solutions could be difficult to connect to from overseas. If not restricted by policy, cost became an issue because phone equipment and systems were not of the quality that exists today, and long-distance transmissions would hinder the connection. In contrast, there are tens of thousands of ISPs worldwide that can provide access to the Internet, not including the very large ISPs that provide phone numbers globally. Finally, in addition to the seemingly endless supply of access points, there are companies that act as a central point for billing and management for hundreds of ISPs worldwide. From the users' viewpoint, there is one large ISP everywhere on the globe.

The final hurdle was to provide the communication protection from in-transit influence or exposure as had occurred with old remote access over the phone network. VPN technology was immediately used to fill this gap. With the advent of expanded communication capabilities and the availability of the Internet, the ever-expanding corporate existence could be easily supported and protected during transit.

CONNECTED ALL THE TIME

Earlier, a remote user could dial into a modem bank at headquarters and access services remotely with little concern for eavesdropping, transmission interception, or impersonation. From the perspective of the hosting site, layers of security could be implemented to reduce exposure. Authentication, dial-back, time limitations, and access restrictions were employed to increase control

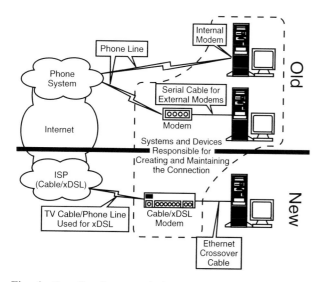

Fig. 4 Broadband removed the user and system from the establishment of the connection.

over the communication and decrease exposure to threats. These protection suites were made possible primarily because of the one-on-one aspect of the communication; once the connection was established, it could be easily identified and controlled. As far as the communication itself, it was relatively protected while traversing the public phone system over dedicated circuits.

Because broadband technology can utilize Ethernet to allow connectivity to the access device, the computer simply has to be "on" for Internet communications (see Fig. 4). This represents a huge change from traditional modem access, where the computer was responsible for establishing and maintaining the connection. However, with typical broadband the connection is sustained at the access device, allowing Internet connectivity, regardless of the state of other systems on the Ethernet interface. The Ethernet interface on the computer does not require a user to initialize it, know a phone number, or be concerned about the connection. All these options are controlled by the operating system; even the IP address is automatically assigned by the ISP, reducing the interaction with the user even further. Now the responsibility for Internet connectivity rests solely on the access device, freeing the user and the user's computer from the need to maintain the connection. The end system is simply a node on a network.

Computers that are connected to the access device are connected to the Internet with little or no protection. It is very common for a broadband provider to install the cable or line and an Ethernet interface in the computer and directly connect the system with no security modifications. This results in basic end-systems with no security control being connected directly to the Internet for extended periods of time. The difference is tremendous. Instead of a fleeting instance of a roaming user on

the Internet dialing up an ISP, the IP address, type of traffic, and even the location of the computer are exposed to the Internet for extended periods of time. When compared with the direct remote user dial-up support for corporations, the exposure is staggering. The obvious difference is that the user is connected to the Internet, whereas the dial-up service provided by the company was pointtopoint.

It is widely accepted that when a system is connected to the Internet, regardless of the type, it is exposed to a colossal number of threats. It is also accepted that the greater the length of continuous time the connection is established, the greater the exposure or the risk of being found and targeted. Firewalls are usually placed on networks that have dedicated Internet connections, but they are not usually seen on hosts that have intermittent connections to the Internet. One of the reasons can be the nature of the connection—it is much more difficult to hit a moving target. But the reality is that this can be misleading, and roaming systems can be accosted in the same way as a system with a dedicated connection. In short, dial-up access to the Internet exposes the system to threats, and dedicated connections are exposed to the same threats as well, but with increased risk that can typically be attributed to duration. Whether connected all the time or some of the time, by broadband or modem, if you are on the Internet you are exposed to attack; it just so happens that when connected all the time, you are a sitting duck, not a flying one.

ACCESSING CORPORATE NETWORKS

VPN technology is the final catalyst for allowing remote users to gain access to corporate resources by utilizing the Internet. This was a natural progression; the Internet is everywhere. Like the phone system, the higher bandwidth connections are becoming the norm, and VPN technology is securing the transmission with encryption techniques and authentication.

Much of VPN's success has been attributed to the advent and availability of broadband technologies, because high-speed access was great for browsing and getting bigger things off the Internet faster, but that is about all. Almost overnight the bandwidth typically associated with personal access, such as 32K or even 56K modems, to the Internet was increased 100 times. The greater access speeds attained by moving away from the public phone system and modems to dedicated broadband connectivity were quickly followed by rash of excitement; however, at the same time, many wanted the service to access corporate resources. As the excitement wore off from the huge leap in access speeds, many turned their eyes on ways to use this for remote

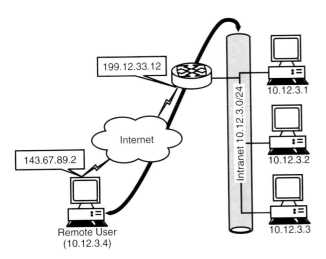

Fig. 5 Attacker must attempt access to corporate data directly, the most difficult path.

access. It is at this point that VPN technology took off and absorbed the technical community.

Remote client software was the first on the scene. A product package included a device that was connected to the Internet at the corporate site and the client software that was loaded on the roaming system, resulting in remote access to corporate resources over the Internet. A great deal of time and money was invested in remote access solutions, and that continues today. In concert with remote client-based access, the rush to VPNs was joined by DSL and cable modem replacements that provided the VPN termination, once again relieving the client system from the responsibility of the communication. VPNs are now a wildfire being pushed across the technical landscape by a gale-force wind of broadband access.

Once unbridled access to the corporate network was available, it was not uncommon for remote sites or users to copy or open data normally maintained under the protection of elaborate firewalls and other protection suites provided at the corporate site. For many implementations, VPNs are used to run applications that would normally not be available on remote systems or require expensive resources and support to provide to employees at remote offices. In short, VPNs are being used for nearly everything that is typically available to a system residing on the internal network. This is to be expected, considering that vendors are selling the technology to do just that—operate as if on the internal network. Some solutions even incorporate Microsoft's Windows Internet Naming Service (WINS) and NetBIOS capabilities into their products to allow Domain browsing for systems and resources as if at the corporate site.

In essence, VPNs are being implemented as the panacea to integrate remote activities into internal operations as seamlessly as possible. The end product is data and applications being run from systems well outside the confines of a controlled environment.

OPEN ENDED

Fundamentally, the service afforded by a VPN is quite simple: protect the information in transit, period. In doing so, various communications perks can be realized. A good example is *tunneling*. To accommodate protected communications as seamlessly as possible, the original data stream is encapsulated and then transmitted. The encapsulation procedure simplifies the protection process and transmittal of the datagram. The advantage that arises is that the systems in the VPN communicate as if there were no intermediary. An example, shown in Fig. 5, is a remote system that creates a datagram that would operate normally on the internal network; instead, it is encapsulated and forwarded over the Internet to a system at the corporate office that deencapsulates (and decrypts, if necessary) the original datagram and releases it onto the internal network. The applications and endsystems involved are typically never the wiser.

The goal for some VPN implementations is to provide communications for remote users over the Internet that emulates intranet services as closely as possible. Many VPN solutions are critiqued based on their capabilities to allow services to the client systems that are usually only available internally. With the adoption of broadband Internet access there is less stress on pure utilitarian aspects normally seen with dial-up solutions, where various limitations are assumed because of the limited bandwidth. To allow for the expanded communication requirements, many VPN solutions integrate into the environment in a manner that remains transparent not only to the user, but also to the applications that utilized the connection. Therefore, the protection realized by the VPN is extended only to the actual transport of data—exactly its purpose.

For the most part, prior to encapsulation or encryption, anything goes, and the VPN simply protects the transmission. The connection is protected but that does not equate to the communication being protected. To detail further, systems on internal networks are considered a community with common goals that are protected from the Internet by firewalls and other protection measures. Within the trusted community, data flows openly between systems, applications, and users; a VPN simply augments the process and protects it during transmission over the Internet. The process is seamless and transparent, and it accommodates the traffic and application needs. The result is that data is being shared and utilized by shadowy internal representations of the remote systems.

ACCESS POINTS

Having internal services wholly available to systems residing on internal networks is expected. The internal network is typically a controlled, protected, and monitored environment with security policies and procedures in place. As services and data are accessed internally, the exposure or threat to that communication is somewhat known and accepted at some level. Most organizations are aware of security threats on internal networks, but have assumed a level of risk directly proportional to the value or impact of loss if they were to be attacked. Much of this is attributed to simple population control; they assume greater risk to internal resources because there are fewer people internally than on the Internet, interaction is usually required (hence, a network), and each system can be monitored if desired. Basically, while some statistics tell us that internal networks are a growing source of attacks on corporate data, organizations feel confident that they can control what lies within their walls. Even organizations that do not have security policies and may consider themselves vulnerable will always assume that there is room to grow and implement security measures as they see fit. Nevertheless, the Internet represents a much greater threat in the eyes of many organizations, and this may be a reality for some organizations; each is different. The fundamental point is that the Internet is an unknown and will always be a threat, whereas certain measures can be taken—or the risk can be accepted—more readily on an internal network. In any case, internal networks are used to share information and collaborate to support or grow a business, and it is that open interaction people want from home over the Internet.

VPN technology is a total contradiction of the assumed posture and reach of control. The internal network, where applications, services, and data reside, is considered safe by virtue of firewalls, procedures, and processes overseen by administrators focused on maintaining security in some form or another. However, the nature of VPN negates the basic postulation of corporate security and the understood security attitude. Attackers who may have been thwarted by hardened corporate firewalls may find remote VPN clients much easier targets that may provide the same results.

On the whole, administrators are constantly applying security patches, updating processes, and performing general security maintenance on critical systems to protect them from vulnerabilities. Meanwhile, these vulnerabilities remain on end-user systems, whose users are much less likely to maintain their systems with the same integrity. In the event that an advanced user were to introduce a comprehensive protection plan, many remote systems do not run enterprise-class operating systems and are inherently insecure. Microsoft's

Windows 95 and 98 platforms are installed on the majority of personal or end-user class systems and are wellknown for limited security capabilities and overall robustness. Therefore, fundamental flaws weaken any applied security in the system.

The collision of the attributes that contribute to a common VPN implementation result in the cancellation of applied security infrastructure at the corporate site. Nearly every aspect of Internet-facing protection is invalidated the minute a user connects to corporate with a VPN. A single point of protection applies only if the protected network does not interact with the volatile environment being evaded.

ENVELOPE OF SECURITY

To fully grasp this immense exposure, envision a corporate network segmented from the Internet by an arsenal of firewalls and intrusion detection systems, and even suppose that armed guards protect the building housing a private community of systems. Assume that the data on the network is shared and accessed in the open while on the internal network. Each system participating is protected and controlled equally by the establishment.

Now, take one of the systems to an uncontrolled remote location and build a point-to-point connection with modems. The remote computer is still isolated and not connected to any untrusted systems other than the phone system. The communication itself is relatively anonymous and its interception would be complicated, if discovered. However, as we see in VPNs, encryption can be applied to the protocol over the phone system for added protection.

Next, take the same system at the remote location and connect it to the Internet and establish a VPN to the corporate network. Now the system is exposed to influences well beyond the control realized when the computer was at the corporate office; still, the same access is being permitted.

In the three foregoing examples, degradation in security occurs as the computer is removed from a controlled environment to a remote location and dial-up access is provided. The risks range from the system being stolen to the remote chance of the transmission being captured while communicating over the telephone network, but the overall security of the system and the information remain relatively protected. However, when the remote computer is placed on the Internet, the exposure to threats and the risk of operation are increased exponentially.

In the beginning of the example, the systems reside in an envelope of protection, isolated from unauthorized influences by layers of protection. Next, we stretch the envelope of protection out to the remote dial-in system;

understandably, the envelope is weakened, but it certainly exists in nature to keep the information sheltered. The remote dial-in system loses some of the protection supplied by the fortified environment of corporate and is exposed to a finite set of threats, but what is more important is that the envelope of security for the corporate site had not been dramatically affected.

In reality, the added risks of allowing remote systems to dial in directly are typically associated with unauthorized access, usually gained through the phone system. Corporate provides phone numbers to remote users to gain access and those same numbers are accessible from anywhere on the planet. Attackers can easily and quickly determine phone number ranges that have a high probability of including the target remote access numbers. Once the range is known, a phone-sweeping or "war-dialer" program can be employed to test each number with little or no intervention from the attacker. However, there are many factors that still manage to keep these risks in check. Dial-back, advanced and multilayered authentication, extensive logging, time constraints, and access constraints can combine to make a formidable target for the attacker. With only a single point of access and the remote system in isolation, the security envelope remains intact and tangible. The degree of decay, of course, is directly related to the security of the single point of access at corporate and the level of isolation of the remote system.

In the last scenario, where the employment of a VPN provides corporate connectivity over the Internet, the security is perceived to be very high, if not greater than or equal to dial-up access solutions. Why not? They appear to have the same attributes and arguably the same security. In dial-up solutions, the communication is relatively protected, the system providing termination at corporate can be secured, and authentication measures can be put in place to reduce unauthorized access. VPNs, too, have these attributes and can be exercised to acquire an inclusive security envelope.

Unfortunately, the VPN offers a transparent envelope, a security façade that would not normally exist at such intensity if VPNs were not so accomplished as a protocol. The corporate-provided envelope is stretched to a breaking point with VPNs by the sheer fact that the remote system has gained control of the aspect of security and the employment of protection. It will become very clear that the envelope of security is no longer granted or managed by corporate, but rather the remote system is now the overseer of all security—locally and into corporate.

A remote system connects to the Internet and obtains an IP address from the ISP to allow communication with the rest of the Internet community. Somewhere on the Internet is a VPN gateway on the corporate network that is providing access to the internal network. As the remote system establishes the VPN to share data, a host

of vulnerabilities are introduced that can completely circumvent any security measures taken by corporate that would normally be providing the security envelope. It is at the point of connecting to the Internet where the dramatic tumbling of realized security takes place, and the remote system becomes the judge, jury, and possibly the executioner of corporate security.

The remote system may have employed a very robust VPN solution, one that does not allow the host system to act as a router or allow the forwarding of information from the Internet into the private network. To take it one step further, the VPN solution may employ limited firewalling capabilities or filtering concepts to limit access into the internal network. Nonetheless, the protection possibly supplied by the VPN client or firewall software can be turned off by users, ultimately opening them up to attack. In the event that a package can be implemented in which the user cannot turn off the protection suite, it can be assumed that a vulnerability will arise that requires a patch to remedy.

This scenario is extremely common and nearly an everyday occurrence for firewall and perimeter security administrators simply attempting to keep up with a limited number of firewalls. Given the lack of attention normally seen in many organizations toward their firewall maintenance, one can only imagine the disintegration of security when vulnerabilities are discovered in the remote system's firewall software.

VULNERABILITY CONCEPTS

To fully understand the extremity of the destruction of perceived corporate security made available by ample amounts of technology and processes, it is necessary to know that the remote system is open and exposed to the Internet. In some cases, as with broadband, the exposure is constant and for long periods of time, making it predictable—an attacker's greatest asset.

The Internet is a sea of threats, if nothing else, simply because of the vast numbers of people and technologies available to them to anonymously wreak havoc on others, especially those unprepared. There are several different types of attacks that are for different uses and affect different layers in the communication. For example, denial-of-service (DoS) attacks are simply geared to eliminate the availability of a system or service—a purely destructive purpose. DoS attacks take advantage of weaknesses in low-level communication attributes, such as protocol vulnerability, or higher-level weaknesses that may reside in the application itself. Some other attacks have very specific applications and are designed for particular situations to either gain access or obtain information. It is becoming more and more common to see these attacks taking advantage of application

SOA–
Vulnerability

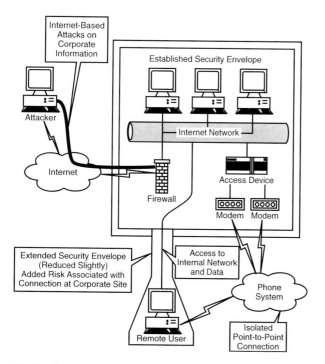

Fig. 6 Attacker must attempt access to corporate data directly, the most difficult path.

errors and quirks. The results are applications specifically engineered to obtain system information, or even to remotely control the host system.

Trojans have become very sophisticated and easy to use, mostly because of huge weaknesses in popular operating systems and very resourceful programmers. A typical system sitting on the Internet can have a Trojan installed that cannot only be used to gain access to the system, remotely control portions of the host system,

obtain data stored locally, and collect keyboard input, but can also notify the attacker when the host system is online and ready for access. In some cases, information can be collected offline and sent to the attacker when the Internet connection is reestablished by the victim. It is this vulnerability that represents the worst-case scenario and, unfortunately, it is commonplace for a typical home system to be affected.

In a case where the Trojan cannot be installed or implemented fully, an attacker could gain enough access, even if temporarily, to collect vital information about the targeted system or user, ultimately leading to more attacks with greater results. It can be argued that anti-virus programs and host-based firewall applications can assist the user in reducing the vulnerabilities and helping in discovering them—and possibly eradicating them. Unfortunately, the implementation, maintenance, and daily secure operation of such applications rests in the hands of the user. Nevertheless, it is complicated enough protecting refined, highly technical environments with dedicated personnel, much less remote systems spread all over the Internet.

A STEP BACK

Early in the adoption of the Internet, systems were attacked, sometimes resulting in unauthorized access and the loss of data or the disclosure of proprietary information. As the threats became greater, increasingly more sophisticated, and difficult to stop, firewalls were implemented to reduce the direct exposure to the attack. In combination, systems that were allowing certain services were hardened against known weaknesses to further the overall protection. Furthermore, these hardened specific systems were placed on isolated networks, referred to as DMZs, to protect the internal network from attacks launched from them or weaknesses in their implementation. With all these measures in place, hackers to this day continue to gain astounding access to internal systems.

Today, a firewall is a fundamental fixture in any Internet-facing connection, and sometimes in huge amounts protecting vast numbers of systems and networks. It has become the norm, an accepted fact of Internet life, and an expensive one as well. Protecting the internal systems and resources from the Internet is paramount and enormous work and finances are usually dedicated to supporting and maintaining the perimeter.

It is reasonable to state that much of the protection implemented is to protect proprietary data or information from dissemination, modification, or destruction. The data in question remains within the security envelope created by the security measures. Therefore, to get to the information, an attacker would have to penetrate,

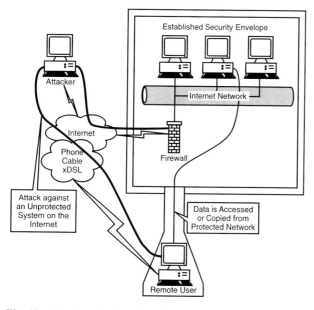

Fig. 7 Attacker obtains data from a much less protected point on the Internet.

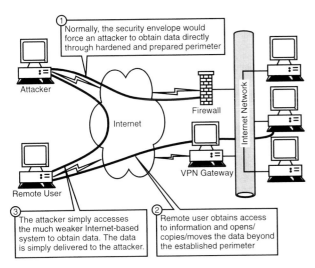

Fig. 8 Data is accessed by a system exposed to vulnerabilities and various risks associated with the Internet.

circumvent, or otherwise manipulate operational conditions to obtain the data or the means to access it more directly (see Fig. 6).

With the advent of VPNs, the remote system is permitted a protected connection with the corporate data, inside the enclave of known risks and threats. It is assumed that the VPN protects the communication and stretches the security outward from the corporate to the remote location. Unfortunately, this assumption has overlooked an essential component of VPNs—the Internet. Now, as shown in Fig. 7, an attacker can access corporate data on a system completely exposed and in control of a common user—not under the protection of technology or experience found at the corporate site.

From the attacker's viewpoint, the information is simply on the Internet, as is the corporate connection; therefore, the access process and medium have not changed, just the level of security. The result is that the information is presented to the attacker, and direct access through a much more complicated path is not required. If it were not for the Internet connection, the remote hosts would have increased functionality, speed, and protection compared with legacy remote access with modems. Regrettably, the Internet is the link to the extended functionality as well as the link to ultimate insecurity.

Logically, this is a disaster for information security. We have invested monumental amounts of time, research, and money into the evolution of security and the mitigation of risk associated with connecting to a global, unrestricted network. We have built massive walls of security with bricks of technology ranging from basic router filtering, firewalls, and intrusion detection systems to system hardening, DMZs, and air-gaps. Now that we have a plethora of defense mechanisms pointed at the Internet, we are implementing an alternative route

for attackers, leading them away from the traps and triggers and pointing them to our weakest points.

The concept of alternative forms and directions of attack when faced with considerable fortifications can be likened to medieval warfare. Castles were constructed with enormous walls to thwart intruders. Moats were filled, traps were laid, and deadly focal points were engineered to halt an attack. In some of these walls, typically under the surface of the moat, a secret gateway was placed that allowed scouts and spies out of the castle to collect information or even supplies to survive the siege. It is this reality that has repeated itself—a gateway placed facing the world to allow allies access into the stronghold. The differentiating factor between what is being seen now and ancient warfare is that long ago the kingdom would not permit a general, advisor, or any person outside the walls who could have information valuable to the enemy.

In stark contrast, today, people from every level in the corporate chain access information outside the protected space. This is equivalent to sending a general with attack plans through the gateway, out of the castle, so he can work on the plan in his tent—presumably unprotected. It does not take much effort for an attacker to pounce on the general and collect the information that would normally require accessing the castle directly. In reality, a modern-day attacker would have so much control over the victim that data could be easily modified or collected in a manner that would render the owners oblivious to their activities. Fig. 8 clearly depicts the evolution of the path of least resistance.

Disappointingly, the complicated labyrinthine safeguards we have constructed are squarely pointed at the enemy; meanwhile, we are allowing the information out into the wild. The result is that the finely honed and tuned wall of protection is reduced to almost nothing. Where a small set of firewalls protected information on internal networks at a single entry point, there now exist thousands of access points with no firewalls. Not only have we taken a step back but also the problem reduced by firewalls has increased in scale. Early in Internet adoption a single Internet connection with a firewall would suffice. Today, organizations have several Internet connections with complicated protection measures. With the addition of VPNs for remote systems and small home offices, organizations have thousands of Internet connections beyond reasonable control.

CASE IN POINT

Late one Friday, I received a phone call from a friend who worked for a large national construction company as a chief engineer. Calls from him were typical when his computer was acting up or a fishing trip was being planned for the weekend. However, this call started very unusually. He stated that he thought he had been hacked—his hard drive runs late into the night and the newly loaded BlackIce was logging a great deal of unknown traffic. I knew he used a cable modem and a VPN to work from home, either at night or during the day, to avoid traffic and general office interruptions. I was also aware that he used Windows 98 as an operating system and standard programs to complete his work. Additionally, he left his computer on all the time—why not?

Completely convinced that he had been attacked, I told him not to touch the computer and to start a sniffer using another computer on his home network to see what was going over the wire. In a few minutes, communications were started between his computer and an Internet-based host. It was clear, after looking at the traffic more clearly, that his system was being accessed. Between his experiences, log files from various software he had installed on the system, and previous experiences with other friends in his shoes, I assumed that his system was accessed. I had him unplug the Ethernet from the cable modem and asked how serious could the issue be—in other words, what was on the box that someone would want or appreciate getting.

After a short discussion, it appeared that the hacker was accessing all the bid packages for building projects all over the United States, each encrusted with logos, names, contact information, competition analysis, schedules, and cost projections. It was my friend's job to collect this information and review it for quality control and engineering issues. Further discussions proved that he knew when he last accessed the data based on work habits and general memory. It was at this point that he told me this had been going on for some time and he just got around to calling me. He wanted to try antivirus programs and freeware first so that he would not bother me with a false alarm. Subsequently, we collectively decided to access the system to try to determine what was accessed and when.

The first thing we found was BackOrifice with basic plug-ins, which led me to believe that this may not have been intentionally directed at him, but rather someone wanting to play with a wide-open Windows system sitting on the Internet. We started checking files for access times; many were accessed in the middle of the night several weeks prior. More investigation turned up hidden directories and questionable e-mails he had received sometime before. At this point, I simply stopped and told him to assume the worst and try to think of anything else that may have been on his system. It turned out that a backup of his TurboTax database—not password protected—was on the system along with approved human resource documents for employees in his department who had received a raise of late.

The entire phone conversation lasted about 3 hr—that's all it took. I suspect that the call to his manager was much more painful and felt much longer. But was it his fault? His company provided him the Internet connection and the VPN software, and access from home was encouraged. It seemed logical to him and his manager. He needed access to the Internet for research, and he typically got more done at home than at the office. However, an unknown assailant on the Internet, who could be either a hired gun to get the information or a script-kiddie who stumbled into a pot of gold, accessed extremely sensitive information. In either case, it was out there and could have an impact on the business for years.

SOLUTIONS

There is, of course, no easy solution to the security dilemma that is presented by the implementation of VPNs. Even with sophisticated technology, organizations still cannot stop hackers. They continue to access systems in heavily protected networks with apparent ease. Much of this can be attributed to poor design, gaps in maintenance, improper configuration, or simple ignorance. In any case, with focused attention on the perimeter, unauthorized access is still happening at an alarming rate. Given this scenario of hundreds if not thousands of remote computers on the Internet, what can be done to protect them? Simply stated, if an internal network cannot be protected when the best efforts are thrown at the problem, there is little hope of protecting the masses at home and on the road.

As with any sound security practice, a security policy is crucial to the protection of information. Specifying data access limitations and operating parameters for information exchange can greatly reduce the exposure of information. In other words, if a certain type of information is not needed for remote work, then remote access systems should not provide access to that information or system. By simply reducing the breadth of access provided by the remote access solution, data can be inherently protected. The practice of limiting what is actually accessible by remote users has materialized in the form of firewalls behind VPN devices seemingly protecting the internal network from the VPN community. Unfortunately, this design has enormous limitations and can limit the scalability of the VPN in terms of flexibility of access. Another eventuality is the inclusion of filtering methods employed in the VPN access device. Filters can be created to control traffic that is injected into the internal network, and in some cases filters can be associated with actual authenticated users or groups.

No matter how access is restricted, at some point a remote user will require sensitive information and anyone implementing services for users has been faced with that "special case." Therefore, technology must take over to protect information. Just as we look to firewalls to protect our internal networks from the Internet, we must look to technology again to protect remote systems from relaying proprietary information into the unknown. The application of host-based protection software is not entirely new, but the growing number of attacks on personal systems has raised awareness of their existence. However, these applications are point solutions and not a solution that is scalable, flexible, or centrally controlled or managed to maintain security. In essence, each user is responsible for his or her realized security posture.

CONCLUSION

VPNs can be enormously valuable; they can save time, money, expand access, and allow organizations ultimate flexibility in communications. However, the private link supplied by a VPN can open a virtual backdoor to attackers. Organizations that permit sensitive data to traverse a VPN potentially expose that information to a plethora of threats that do not exist on the protected internal network.

There are many types of VPN products available, all with their own methods of establishing the connection, maintaining connectivity, and providing services usually found on the internal network. Unfortunately, if the remote system is not involved in dedicated communications with the central office via the VPN, the system can be considered extremely vulnerable.

The Internet has grown to permeate our lives and daily activities, but there has always been a line drawn in the sand by which separation from total assimilation can be measured. Firewalls, modems, routers, filters, and even software such as browsers can provide a visible point of access to the Internet. As technology becomes more prevalent, the demarcation between the Internet and private networks will begin to blur. Unfortunately, without proper foresight, the allocation of security measures and mitigation processes will not keep up with advances in information terrorism. If not properly planned and controlled, seemingly secure alternative routes into a fortification can negate all other protection; a castle's walls will be ineffective against an attack that does not come directly at them.

Vulnerability Management

Park Foreman
Austin, Texas, U.S.A.

Abstract

Vulnerability management is the detailed, cyclical process of identifying and remediating weaknesses in an information technology system. It includes skills, processes, standards, and technologies combined to appropriately address the most relevant vulnerabilities in the target environment. While many standards and technologies exist, their selection and application are unique to the organization and threat environment.

INTRODUCTION

Vulnerability management (VM) is the detailed, cyclical process of identifying and remediating weaknesses in an information technology system. The scope of the IT system includes technologies, processes, people, standards, policies, and strategies. In most cases, technologists tend to focus on vulnerabilities in technologies as this resides in their comfort zone. However, the successful exploitation of vulnerabilities in other areas can be equally or more devastating. For example, an improperly or insufficiently trained staff member may be vulnerable to certain types of social engineering attacks that will give unauthorized persons access to the organization.

VM is a continuous process that must evolve and adapt to a constantly changing environment. This subject can be regarded as a subset or style of risk management that is focused on evaluating weaknesses. Threats, although a component of assessing priorities, are not central to the management of vulnerabilities. Instead, threats should be considered a central component of threat management or more broadly, risk management.

This entry will discuss the fundamental components of a VM program and the resources needed to define and implement it. The reader will gain a clear, structured understanding of what actions are necessary to plan and execute this function in an organization. The program participants who will naturally adapt the foregoing description to their needs will ultimately determine the priorities of each step.

RISK MANAGEMENT AND VULNERABILITIES

In risk management, evaluations must be made on the degree or severity of the risk and the impact should be risk realized. Once the risk is well understood and quantified, the process of prioritization must take place. These priorities are then used to allocate resources to address the risks. General examples of priority assessments based on impact are as follows:

- No significant risk probability or impact; no remediation necessary
- Minor probability or impact; mid- to long-term remediation
- Moderate probability or impact; immediate to mid-term remediation
- Severe probability or impact; immediate/urgent remediation

Based on these assessments in risk management, the organizational leadership can choose to accept, mitigate, reduce, or avoid the risk. These same options are available in VM. The relationship between risk management and VM can be identified by similar assessments of vulnerabilities. Specific factors that are taken into consideration of vulnerabilities are:

- Ease of exploitation—This is the ease with which a vulnerability can be exploited to achieve unintended behavior of a computer system. The vulnerability may have varying levels of exploitability:
- Easy: A vulnerability is easily exploited by someone with readily available tools and little to no experience in executing an attack. Such vulnerabilities are often exploited through predefined scripts or programs that need only be provided the location of the target system. The users of such systems are commonly referred to as script kiddies.
- Medium: This type of exploitation requires someone with more detailed knowledge of computer systems and the tools available to launch the attack. The configuration and operation of these tools is generally more complex and may require more technical knowledge of the target.

Encyclopedia of Information Systems and Technology, DOI: 10.1081/E-EIST-120048617

- Difficult: This vulnerability exploitability level is generally reserved for the more advanced attacker that may use multiple complex tools and perform several steps of attack to eventually reach the desired target.
- Exposure to exploitation—Exposure describes the accessibility of the vulnerability by the attacker. If performing the attack requires the attacker to be authenticated to the system, then it is considered less vulnerable than if an unauthenticated user can perform the attack. However, it is also possible that some attacks can be used to target a vulnerability using the available credentials of an authenticated user. For example, a cross-site request forgery attack can be used to exploit a vulnerability in a system to which a user is actively authenticated.
- Impact of exploitation—The impact of the exploitation is value attributed to what ill effects can be realized in the target system. This value can be monetary, physical safety, reputational, or anecdotal. In all cases, the final result is typically monetary or related to human safety. Frequently, anecdotal values are applied such as high, medium, and low. The problem with anecdotal values is that the impact can change over time and location. Unless the values are aligned with specific circumstances under which the value was determined, it is easy to lose sight of the changing vulnerability level.
- Cost/ease of remediation—An important part of the decision-making process in remediation is the cost and complexity. If a complex system must be completely rewritten to remediate a low-impact vulnerability, it may not be desirable to take any action. Alternatively, some severe vulnerabilities can be cost-effectively remediated through the application of a software patch that has no adverse impact on the operation of the system.
- Value of target asset—Also relevant to the decision process in addressing vulnerabilities is the value of the target system. If the system is of little value to the organization and the cost of remediation is high, it may not be a worthy investment. However, if the system is critical to the continued operation of the enterprise and exploitation of the vulnerability has a severe impact, then management should apply a high priority to remediation.

These factors and others are used individually or in a combined formula to make decisions about the overall severity of the vulnerability and to determine the appropriate remediation priority.

PROGRAM FORMATION PROCESS

Forming a VM program involves several seminal steps that require considerable effort with complexity that extends beyond the technical realm. These steps are as follows:

- Establish a VM policy—Having a clearly defined policy is essential. This policy will set the business requirements for identifying and remediating vulnerabilities. The policy will also establish the responsibility for these steps and overall program governance.
- Determine the scope of the program—Understanding which targets are to be assessed and how many is essential to determining the cost and the parties to be involved in the process. Additionally, understanding the nature of the targets will determine the kinds of assessments performed. In some cases, assessing operating systems and commercial off-the-shelf software will require a different technology and process than assessments of in-house software.
- Identify the key participants—All of the scanning, review, and remediation will require multiple participants throughout the organization based on the previous step. The owners of networks, systems, and applications will have to review the identified vulnerabilities and remediate them.
- Establish technology and process—Technology and process are tightly bound. By identifying the technology in conjunction with process development, the effectiveness of the program can be optimized.
- Develop program governance model—The overall program will have to be monitored to ensure that it continues to meet the needs of a changing threat environment. The changes to this environment are caused by new systems, new vulnerabilities, new business initiatives, and a changing organization. All of these things affect the overall attack surface of the organization. The program will have to remain aligned with these changes.
- Implement the system—Implementation will vary by environment. It may include acquisition and deployment of hardware, software, personnel, and network equipment. Training and consulting activities might also be a significant component. All of this is done in conjunction with the next step, the operational process.
- Institute operational process—The detailed process of monitoring and maintaining the VM system and remediating the vulnerabilities is phased in during implementation. Small steps starting at some appropriate point and expanding outward are generally recommended.

**SOA–
Vulnerability**

OPERATIONAL PROCESS

The operational process for VM, like many IT processes, is cyclical. The cyclical nature is essential since vulnerabilities are constantly changing. So too do the operating environment and external threats change. Environmental conditions can have a large impact on the prioritization of scanning and remediation activities. These and other factors must be taken into account in the following four process steps.

Perform Assessment

Vulnerability assessments can be both a technical and an artistic practice. A vulnerability scanner can check a computer system for known vulnerabilities. The identification of "soft" vulnerabilities that can be found in operating processes, training programs, and business strategies require the skills of people.

Technical vulnerability assessments can be automated to follow a schedule or passively identify vulnerabilities based on monitored events. Different technologies exist to achieve each.

The scheduling of active vulnerability scans is generally done with a dedicated host connected to a network or specialized software installed on several production systems. The former is more typical in a large organization that cannot allow for the installation of software on a production system due to regulatory or compatibility concerns. The latter approach can be very cost effective and require less dedicated hardware provided that the scanning activity does not interfere with the operation of the production system.

Dedicated hardware can either be active scanningoriented or passive. Similar to or as part of an intrusion detection system, network traffic can be inspected for behavior suggesting vulnerabilities in the source or destination. This approach can yield cost-effective security devices performing multiple functions. There are limits to the capabilities of these systems since some vulnerabilities may exist that cannot be revealed by network traffic. This may be particularly true for exploits that are performed using physical access to the device.

Alternatively, active scanning hardware and software can be used to conduct several activities on the network directed at a range of hosts.

Review Results

Once vulnerabilities are identified, the priorities of these vulnerabilities require review and decisions. The review begins with an evaluation of the vulnerability scores assigned during the assessment. These scores are but one component of the prioritization process. Other items that must be considered are as follows:

- Criticality of the system—The importance of the system, software, or service to the operation of the business and utility to customers.
- Asset value—The monetary value of the asset that will be affected by exploitation of the vulnerability.
- Complexity and impact of remediation—Remediation itself can have a significant impact on the system and consequently the organization.
- Cost of remediation—All activities have a cost. Personnel and potentially external consultants are needed to perform some remediation activities. These personnel not only spend time working on remediation but may also, in the process, be reallocated from other important functions thus incurring additional costs.

With the information gathered and assessment of the results complete, priorities are then assigned to the vulnerabilities. Those priorities are then scheduled accordingly in the planning phase.

Formulate Remediation Plan

Once priorities have been established in the review of vulnerabilities, resources must be allocated and scheduled. This schedule can be as simple as an overnight application of patches to a system or extensive software development and testing requiring numerous resources and time.

Monitor Remediation

As in any project management function, some amount of monitoring is required to ensure the successful treatment of risks. Regular reports from remediation teams are needed to gauge the progress and continued relevance of the vulnerability. Since the environment changes over time, some vulnerabilities need not be remediated. This can happen, for example, in the decommissioning of a system where the vulnerability is no longer present.

In other cases, vulnerabilities may be severe but easily patched. Yet the complexity of individual roles in the organization may result in the failure to address a simple patch action. Reviewing subsequent vulnerability assessment results should reveal such failures. Over time, the same vulnerability on the same system should not appear outside of the planned remediation period.

GOVERNANCE

As any information security program, VM requires some level of governance. Since the operating environment is constantly changing, the approach to each step in the operating and implementation processes may need

SOA–
Vulnerability

to change. New business models emerge and some are eliminated. This has an impact on the efficacy of methods for deploying and operating VM tools, personnel, and processes. "…governance will drive more consistent results and greater reliability. Without this step, the program runs the risk of atrophy and degradation."[11]

Activities in the governance process include:

- Conduct regular reviews of vulnerability reports. A summary report of the vulnerabilities found and a comparison with reports from previous cycles can be instructive about the changing security posture.
- Evaluate the worst performing remediation sources. Sometimes some incentive needs to be applied to personnel to maintain compliance with remediation policies. When vulnerabilities go unremediated beyond the allowable time according to policy, it is useful to increase the visibility of these risks. A top10 list of the networks or systems with the most severe vulnerabilities is also a good tool for similar results.
- Equally useful is to give positive recognition for exception compliance. By identifying the best performers, good behavior is encouraged. Those who are doing the right things should be examined for their instructive value.
- Another important performance monitor is trend analysis. Faults in processes or systems can occur slowly and go unnoticed. To address this problem, trend analysis is used to make an early identification of an impending problem. Escalation may be required when the trend for a particular network or business area seems to rise in vulnerability count or score.

TECHNOLOGY

Vulnerability assessment technology comes in multiple flavors designed for various deployment strategies. These strategies are largely the result of restrictions imposed by the business-operating model. Factors such as the distribution of facilities and organization of infrastructure have a major influence on the technology choices made. Cost and efficiency are also ever-present factors in any decision. Next we will discuss the variety of technology and the unique features and issues of each.

There are four common, industry-accepted approaches to VM technology:

1. Active Scanning—Technology assets are scanned or local scans are initiated over a network connection.
2. Passive Assessment—System, network, and application behavior is monitored passively for the identification of vulnerabilities.

3. Hybrid—This term refers to a combination of assessments and dedicated scanning devices. This approach is generally selected with network or financial limitations so require it.
4. Inference—Behavioral analysis is performed on system logs, configuration management files, and other data sources already collected.

One or more of these approaches can be used in the vulnerability assessment process. In some cases, a single approach may not sufficiently identify vulnerabilities in the target systems necessitating the use of multiple methods. When implementing vulnerability assessment technologies, there are three general models used: hardware appliances, user-supplied hardware/virtualization, and agents[2]

Hardware Appliance Model

The hardware appliance model is exactly that, hardware with built-in software to perform the desired vulnerability scans. The devices are typically placed throughout a network and report back to a central server. The scanning appliances are usually a complete but simple computer system. A typical design has an operating system, supporting software modules, and the specialized code written by the developers to perform scans and communicate results. Some vendors use open-source tools and others will use commercial operating systems and components.

One major advantage of a hardware-based system is that the vendors will have in-depth knowledge about the configuration of the host. They take responsibility for the maintenance and stability of that configuration. Any failure of the software to perform as advertised should be addressed in the client–vendor relationship.

In most designs, each scanner will report back to a central server. The vulnerability and compliance information collected will be transmitted back to the server for analysis and reporting. Devices will also receive assessment instructions over the network. Those instructions may be delivered by polling, on-demand connection, or through reverse polling.

Polling is the process of taking a poll of the vulnerability scanners associated with a central server. Each scanner is typically contacted through a Transmission Control Protocol (TCP) port with special authentication methods that keep the entire conversation encrypted. The devices that are polled may be only those for which the server has a job prepared or in progress. The server checks the status to see if any data is available or if the unit is ready to accept a job. This approach can be cumbersome but has the advantage of only requiring a connection originating from the server. In some cases, not all scanners are polled unless there is scheduled work, which can result in not knowing the status of a scanner until that time. Most vendors that poll will poll all scanners. Reverse polling is the process whereby each scanner contacts the server on a regular basis. Should there be a job scheduled for the scanner, it would then be provided. The same strong authentication and encryption methods apply. The scanner will send the results of the scan back to the central server either during the scan or at the conclusion depending on the software designer's choice. This approach has the added advantage of allowing the scanner to complete a local job even if the connection with the server is lost. The scan results may simply be cached until a connection can be re-established.

User Supplied Hardware and Virtualization

Similar to the appliance approach, the distinction is that you provide your own hardware to support the vulnerability tool. This is obviously very common with open-source products such as Nessus™ (Nessus is a trademark of Tenable Network Security, Inc.). Most vendors prefer not to offer a software-only solution because they are difficult to support on a large user-base with large variations in the hardware. A well-controlled hardware platform will provide more consistent performance and predictable behavior enabling vendors to squeeze out all the necessary performance for the product and meet customer expectations. This will become more apparent later when we discuss the operating details of a vulnerability assessment tool.

A solution more palatable to vendors is a virtual machine version of their products. The hardware environment is more predictable and manageable in a virtual machine because it is abstracted and controlled by the underlying hypervisor. Precise specification can be made for the amount of memory, CPU, network connections, and other hardware elements to be made available to the product. Also, the OS version and configuration is controlled by the vendor, which eliminates errors in configuration and provides more predictable, supportable behavior.

Agents

Once operating systems improved memory and process handling capabilities, agents developed to enhance the functionality of systems and people without requiring their direct involvement. The key distinction between an agent and a utility is that an agent can accept a set of instructions or parameters and then continuously and autonomously pursue the results. An agent is more than a tool. It is an assistant. The capabilities of vulnerability agents are relatively simple in comparison to what has been envisioned by systems designers.

Agent architecture

Agents typically execute one or more services in the background of a system with system privileges sufficient to carry out its purpose. These services normally consume very little CPU resources except when requested to perform a major task. There are usually at least two services running at any given time with other services running depending on the architecture of the product. Vulnerability assessment agents are inextricably linked to the audit of the target whereas appliances can be used for more than one audit method.

One service listens on the network for configuration and assessment instructions from a controlling server. This same service or additional service may be used to communicate assessment results back to the server. The second service is the one that performs the actual vulnerability assessment of the local host and in some cases of adjacent hosts on the network.

The basic capabilities of an agent include the following:

- Autonomous—They do not require constant input and operation by another system or individual.
- Adaptive—They respond to changes in their environment according to some specified rules. Depending on the level of sophistication, some agents are more adaptive than others.
- Distributed—Agents are not confined to a single system or even a network.
- Self-updating—Some consider this point to not be unique to agents. For VM, this is an important capability. Agents must be able to collect and apply the latest vulnerabilities and auditing capabilities.

A VM agent is a software system tightly linked to the inner workings of a host that recognizes and responds to changes in the environment that may constitute a vulnerability. VM agents function in two basic roles. First, they monitor the state of system software and configuration vulnerability. The second function is to perform vulnerability assessments of other nearby systems on behalf of a controller. By definition, agents act in a semiautonomous fashion. They are given a set of parameters to apply to their behavior and carry out those actions without further instruction. An agent does not need to be told every time it is to assess the state of the machine on which it is hosted. It may not even be necessary to instruct the agent to audit other adjacent systems.

Unlike agents, network-based vulnerability scanners are typically provided detailed instructions as to when and how to conduct an audit. The specifics of each audit are communicated every time one is initiated. By design, agents are loosely coupled to the overall VM system so they can minimize the load and dependency on a single server.

The detection of local host vulnerabilities is sometimes carried out by performing an audit of all configuration items on the target host in a single, defined process in a specific time window. An alternative approach is to monitor the configuration state of the current machine continuously. When a change is made, the intervening vulnerability assessment software evaluates the change for vulnerabilities and immediately reports the change to the management server.

Vulnerability Assessment Approaches

Active scanning

Active scanning involves using software that can generate packets on the network to actively engage the targets to detect their presence and vulnerabilities. It is a more complex but highly scalable approach that is the most popular today. The scanner is connected to the network just as any other host. The position of the scanner relative to the targets is critical in getting the best results. We will talk more about this later.

Active scanning essentially emulates the behavior of hackers to discover targets with one critical difference. Hackers use tools and techniques designed to conceal their activities whereas legitimate active scanning tools do not. Scanners also can perform some of the exploits to determine susceptibility. The degree to which these exploits are performed depends on options selected in the scan configuration. Most products avoid using exploits that might have adverse effects on the target without specific selection by the administrator in the scan configuration. Furthermore, it should be understood that most commercial tools are designed to detect vulnerabilities, not exploit them. Although they can be used as part of a penetration test, there are other, more appropriate tools to complete such a task.

Advantages and Disadvantages

Some key advantages of active scanning are as follows:

- Highly scalable because scanning takes place from a central or distributed location of the security architect's choice and does not require software installation on the targets.
- The technology can provide a hacker's view of the network and targets so the vulnerability manager can have a realistic view of their risks in the production environment.
- Potential to support any networked device, that is, not limited to compatible platform for an agent.

The process of assessing vulnerabilities has three phases: discovery, reconnaissance, and white box testing. The discovery process entails identifying all hosts connected to a particular network or Internet Protocol (IP) address range as specified in the scan configuration. Reconnaissance is a process whereby the hosts are profiled for the type, version, and passively detectable vulnerabilities. This is done through creative use of protocols and analysis of application behavior.

White box testing is performed when the scanner is given special information and credentials to access details of the host, which are generally reserved for trusted entities. This is also known as an internal check or authenticated check.

The difference between surface and internal checks is obviously significant not only in the way they obtain information but in the value and quality of that information. Establishing an authenticated connection to a host and perusing its configuration will yield more detailed data. Although the information tells us a lot about the host, it does not typically represent the view of an attacker who performs reconnaissance on an unknown host. Therefore, although valuable from an analysis standpoint, many attacks take place by probing the host from the view of an outsider and therefore information that can be obtained in the same fashion is often more relevant.

Passive assessment

Passive network analysis involves installing a piece of equipment on a network switch to listen to a copy of the traffic and analyze it for vulnerabilities. This is similar in functional design to an intrusion detection system or a sniffer. A piece of hardware with a network port is connected to the network switch carrying the traffic to be examined. A command on the network switch sends a copy of much of the switch traffic to that physical port where the analyzer can read it. Alternatively, a network tap can be used to inspect traffic in a single physical network connection. That connection may carry large amounts of consolidated traffic from multiple networks.

The analyzer looks for several things that can reveal vulnerabilities. The IP addresses, network and application protocols, and general communication patterns are all checked for anomalies or attributes that reveal an exploitable flaw.

Port mirroring, also called switched port analyzer (SPAN) by Cisco, is a commonly available technology in modern network switches. The network administrator has the option of specifying ingress traffic only, egress traffic only, or both. An alternative approach to SPAN is a tap. A tap is precisely what it sounds like, a physical installation into a network connection that allows a passive analyzer to see the traffic. The passive analysis approach has several advantages:

- The analyzer does not interact with the network to discover hosts and their related vulnerabilities. Only the interface through which the user accesses the software to get reports is active.
- Little to no testing is required to be certain there is no negative impact on the network or hosts. Since the technology is completely passive, little verification is required. Even if the device physically fails, it is not placed in-line where it would have to handle the bits on the wire.
- The discovery process takes place continuously. New hosts are revealed as soon as they are connected to the network and begin communicating. In contrast to the active scanning and agents, vulnerabilities may not be known until the next scan cycle.
- Hidden hosts can be discovered that do not listen for active probing traffic on the network. Instead, these hosts only communicate by initiating conversation on the network and can therefore only be detected passively.
- Since routing protocols and other network information are also visible to the traffic analyzer, it may also be able to map the topology of the network and use this information to create a picture of the attack surface of a more complex network. This type of information can also be obtained by authenticated active scans and by providing configuration data to specialized tools.

Some disadvantages to this technology are as follows:

- The device typically must be installed on the switch that carries the traffic to be monitored. Remote monitoring of a network is often not practical over a busy wide area network connection. This will limit the number of locations that can be scanned. If your organization requires monitoring on a broad geographic scale, this may not be the right technology.
- There is limited visibility into vulnerabilities. Many of the vulnerabilities that can be detected with a host agent or active, authenticated network scan cannot be detected by analyzing network traffic.

Overall, passive analysis may not see as many vulnerabilities on systems but they function 24 hours a day and provide network topology information that would otherwise be unavailable. Changes to the environment on the network and hosts would be detected first using the passive analysis method if those vulnerabilities have a network footprint.

Hybrid methods

In some cases, active scanning is insufficient for the identification of vulnerabilities. In other instances, passive assessment is limited in what can be detected. As a result a combination of methods is used and referred to as a hybrid configuration. For example, a server farm whose traffic passes through a single access point might be more efficiently monitored for vulnerabilities using passive methods. This decision might be made if the mission critical nature of the servers and limits of available network bandwidth do not allow for the added load of active scanning. However, desktop computers and some file servers distributed throughout the organization benefit from active scanning technology. So a hybrid approach is called for.

Inference method

Related to passive assessment, inference involves inspection of back-end logs, databases, and infrastructure management data sources to infer vulnerabilities. This approach has virtually no impact on the organization but is limited in the scope of the vulnerabilities that can be identified. However, logging systems could be combined in a hybrid-approach to detect vulnerabilities using an agent on a local host and logged in a central system. Those vulnerabilities can then be included in the inference scanning process.

Definitions

Vulnerability—A weakness in the software or hardware that allows use of product beyond its design intent with an adverse effect on the software, system, or data. Small errors in design decisions can lead to major failures in production. In many instances, the design of an application reflects a naive view of how the application might be used.

Exposure—The revelation of information about a system that can be used to assist an attacker in exploiting one or more vulnerabilities. The version number of an application is an example of data that may reveal potential vulnerabilities. Knowledge of a vulnerability or potential vulnerability can be considered an exposure. It is information that is generally not necessary for the user population to have since it is not the intended function of the owner of the system.

Target—A host, application, virtual host, or group of hosts that is in range of a scanning device and is designated for vulnerability assessment. When performing a scan, the scanner is directed at a target by its IP address, group of IPs, or name. A target is simply the subject of a scan. It may be specified or discovered automatically.

Discovery—A phase in the scanning process that finds targets connected to the network segment in a specified range.

Scan Configuration—The set of parameters used to create a planned scanning event. This may include IP address range, ports, dates and times, bandwidth limits, credentials, or special checks to perform.

Vulnerability Check—Exactly what it sounds like, a particular set of items to check on a target that may reveal the presence of a vulnerability.

Compliance Check—Similar to a vulnerability check, this does not necessarily discover a vulnerability but a failure to comply with established company policy. For example, if passwords are required to be at least 10 characters long, the compliance check will generate an event to record instances where the password is outside of the requirement, in this case shorter than 10 characters.

Security Posture—The net resulting security state of the security state of a host, network, or organization based on the factors affecting that state.

Attack Vector—Akin to a vulnerability, an attack vector is the basic strategy used by a miscreant to compromise a system. This includes the exploitation of one or more vulnerabilities or design deficiencies.

Common Vulnerabilities and Exposures (CVE)—CVE is a list of common names for vulnerabilities that are publicly known and provided by the MITRE Corporation at cve.mitre.org. This is a popular list of vulnerabilities used as a reference when analyzing and remediating vulnerabilities. It is not the only source available nor should it be considered complete. But it does bring a degree of standardization to the identity of vulnerabilities.

Scanner—A vulnerability scanner in the form of software or hardware that performs vendor and user-designated checks. Scan configurations are sometimes used to specify which scanner will perform the checks.

Audit—The scanning of one or more targets to determine the vulnerabilities present.

Vulnerability Assessment—This is a synonym for audit; commonly referred to as an assessment.

Reporting

As with any complex system, monitoring requires reporting that is aligned with the intended outcome. Vulnerability reporting takes place at three levels: 1) governance; 2) operational monitoring; and 3) execution.

At the governance level, reports are used to monitor the effectiveness of the processes in achieving the desired risk management objectives. These reports are typically used to determine if systems, processes, and policies are producing positive results. For example, a governance report may reveal trends in vulnerability types and their severities. Such reports can be used to identify either problems in policies, processes, or technologies in the VM system or other areas that are not directly related but may be the cause of vulnerabilities. For example, an application development team may be using poor coding practices that results in an increase in vulnerabilities. Therefore, scanning and remediation are not the underlying cause of the problem.

Operational monitoring reports are focused on staff performance to service levels and compliance with policies related to managing vulnerabilities. The speed and effectiveness of remediation is measured, for example, by showing the amount of time required to remediate critical vulnerabilities. Such remediation times should remain below a certain threshold that is usually established in a service level agreement or security policy. Audit reports for operational monitoring are used to determine the operational performance of the vulnerability scanning components. For example, it may be important to know: when are active vulnerability scans scheduled? Did the last scan succeed? Were any errors generated? What was the scan performance over time?

General categories of execution reports include discovery/inventory reports, profile reports, and audit reports.

Discovery or inventory reports are used to identify the assets in a network and align the assets with an inventory usually obtained from a configuration management database (CMDB). This is highly beneficial in the risk management process because it helps identify the vulnerability risk as it is aligned to the value of an asset. This assumes that the CMDB or other data source has been maintained and includes the value of the asset in terms of replacement cost and business impact cost.

Audit reports are detailed reports usually consisting of lists of vulnerabilities by asset or target. These lists are usually sorted by severity, asset value, or both. The owners and/or operators of these assets review these reports to verify that they are operating within the risk requirement levels established in IT security policy. The details are also used to prioritize the work effort in remediation. An example of such a report is shown in Fig. 1.

Summary reports are generated for management review to assess the current state of the IT environment. Those reports are typically provided at the manager, senior manager, or global leadership level. Such reports are used to assess the effectiveness of the staff, processes, and adherence to policy objectives. Such reports contribute to the governance process and can be used to identify missing or defective resources. Summary reports are typically used for vulnerability and remediation trend analysis. Fig. 2 illustrates a trend report by network that might be used in the governance process.

SOA–
Vulnerability

Vulnerability Assessment Report: XYZ Segment

Scan Date: 1 January 2020

Vulnerability	Asset	Value	Severity	Owner
Weak administrator password	db1.xyz.com	25000	High	Joe Admin
Default web server credentials	ww3.xyz.com	15000	High	Jill Admin
Cross Site Scripting vuln.	www.xyz.com	45000	Medium	Business Unit Mgr

Fig. 1   Vulnerability assessment report.

Fig. 3 is a remediation report indicating a number of vulnerabilities remediated and the number of new vulnerabilities introduced.

The profile reports seek to provide an understanding of the environment in terms of architecture. Quantity, criticality, and the value of an asset are shown in the context of architectural or business area. It can be very instructive, for example, to quantify the number of critical hosts residing in a public-facing environment versus noncritical hosts. A similar metric indicating how many hosts are deployed overall for back office purposes versus direct revenue generation is helpful to understand the amount of administration and monitoring necessary to maintain different aspects of the business. It also provides an opportunity for senior management to see if the assets by category are appropriately aligned with business priorities.[3]

COMMON VULNERABILITY SCORING SYSTEM

An open standard for scoring vulnerabilities is the Common Vulnerability Scoring System (CVSS). CVSS uses metrics with specific criteria for assigning a value to each characteristic of a vulnerability. The metrics are grouped into categories:

- Base Metrics—These are metrics that remain constant with a vulnerability over time. For example, the access vector metric takes into account the fact that local network access may be required to exploit the vulnerability.
- Temporal Metrics—These metrics represent attributes of a vulnerability that change over time. An example is the exploitability of a vulnerability. If there is no known exploit, the score for this metric will be low. Later, when an active tool is released to the public

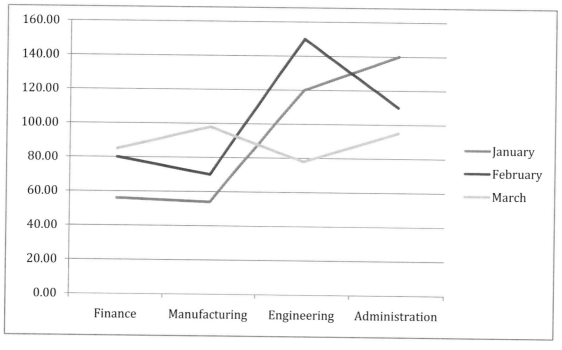

Fig. 2   Vulnerability trend report.

Network Name	Manufacturing Division				Contact		Joe Armistice	
	Vulnerabilities Discovered | Remediated							
	Severe		High		Medium		Low	
January	12	8	14	12	52	33	70	65
February	10	7	16	10	55	48	77	63
March	8	5	18	14	69	52	90	50
Year-to-Date	35	22	62	40	210	161	240	210

Fig. 3 Vulnerability remediation report.

enabling exploitation, the temporal metric will have a higher score.

• Environmental Metrics—These metrics are an assessment of the environment in which the vulnerability is present. It will vary by organization and details of the implementation of IT components supporting the vulnerability. One factor is the distribution of prevalence of the vulnerability in the infrastructure.

SECURITY CONTENT AUTOMATION PROTOCOL

The Security Content Automation Protocol (SCAP[4]) is a suite of specifications that standardize the format and nomenclature by which software flaw and security configuration information is communicated, both to machines and humans. SCAP is a multipurpose framework of specifications that support automated configuration, vulnerability and patch checking, technical control compliance activities, and security measurement. Goals for the development of SCAP include standardizing system security management, promoting interoperability of security products, and fostering the use of standard expressions of security content.

SCAP utilizes software flaw and security configuration standard reference data. This reference data is provided by the National Vulnerability Database (NVD), which is managed by National Institute of Standards and Technology (NIST) and sponsored by the Department of Homeland Security.

SOURCES OF VULNERABILITY INFORMATION

There are numerous sources of information on vulnerabilities available publicly. These sources vary greatly in their details and speed of publication. It is beneficial to use multiple sources of information to decrease the probability that some vulnerabilities will go unchecked.

Commercial products are the most industryconnected and motivated to deliver timely information. They are driven by the threat of competition and the ability of customers to switch. Some useful sources are as follows:

US-CERT—The United States Computer Emergency Readiness Team provides clear, high-level information about vulnerabilities and patches. One can subscribe to the alerts mailing list. More information: http://www.us-cert.gov.

Security Focus—This commercial site publishes a robust, searchable database of vulnerabilities. It provides for subscription to mailing lists of related information in specific, selectable subject areas. More information: http://www.securityfocus.com.

NVD—Run by NIST, this system has many components that are searchable and have links to useful tools. It is naturally aligned with the database of CVE from the Mitre Corporation. The vulnerability search engine is the most relevant tool that can be used to search for specific vulnerabilities. It does not provide new vulnerability alerting but does retrieve vulnerability information if you already know the CVE number or operating system or other relevant key words. The NVD also supports protocols such as SCAP. More information: http://nvd.nist.gov.

CONCLUSION

VM is a critical component of an information security management system. It involves processes, technologies, training, and management of people to be successful. As with any operational function, oversight and governance are required. The VM program must stay "fresh" and aligned with a constantly changing threat environment.

SOA–
Vulnerability

Vulnerabilities are discovered, analyzed, and remediated constantly.

In addition to newly emerging vulnerabilities, changes to the operating environment can reintroduce vulnerabilities thus undoing the work previously accomplished. This makes it necessary to perform vulnerability checks repeatedly over an appropriate time frame. This can mean that in some cases, the vulnerability assessment process can be as dynamic as the environment itself. It will require an adaptive architecture that has a minimal impact on the production environment.

Considerable analysis and review of the state of the environment both technically and strategically will assist in establishing an appropriate VM architecture. Relevant reporting and review processes with constant vigilance will yield longer-term consistent results. Motivational factors related to identifying and remediating vulnerabilities often bear consideration when designing processes and policies. Well-formed policies will help keep the system and process owner's priorities aligned with the risk management objectives of the company and the VM program.

REFERENCES

1. Foreman, P. *Vulnerability Management*; CRC Press: New York, NY, 2010; Ch. 6, 186.
2. Foreman, P. *Vulnerability Management*; CRC Press: New York, NY, 2010; Ch. 4, 61–79.
3. Foreman, P. *Vulnerability Management*; CRC Press: New York, NY, 2010, Ch. 7.
4. NIST Special Publication 800-126r2; 1 http://csrc.nist.gov/publications/PubsSPs.html#SP-800-126-Rev.%202

W3C: World Wide Web Consortium

Terrence Brooks
iSchool, University of Washington, Seattle, Washington, U.S.A.

Abstract

The World Wide Web Consortium (W3C) is the organization that leads the development of standards for the Web. Sir Tim Berners-Lee, the founder and director of the W3C, envisions a linked network of information resources that guides Web standards development and points the way toward the creation of a Semantic Web. This entry describes the pioneering role of Berners-Lee in the development of the Web, the accomplishments and vision of the W3C, and the development of the Semantic Web.

INTRODUCTION

This entry introduces the World Wide Web Consortium (W3C) by outlining the pioneering role of Sir Tim Berners-Lee in the creation of the Web and Web browsers, the development process employed by the W3C community to construct Web standards, and the vision and development of the Semantic Web.

In 2007, the W3C was an international consortium with more than 400 members. Berners-Lee leads a team of about 60 researchers and engineers who are located primarily in three institutions: the Massachusetts Institute of Technology Computer Science and Artificial Intelligence Laboratory (MIT/CSAIL); the European Research Consortium in Informatics and Mathematics, Nice, France; and Keio University, Japan.

The W3C is the leading organization in the development of Web standards and general guidelines for Web development. Its general mission is the development of Web standards and protocols that maximize benefits for the greatest number of people. While the process model of the W3C is consensual agreement and cooperation, it lacks any means to coerce the adoption of its standards and protocols.

Since 1994, the W3C has published more than 90 Web standards called W3C recommendations. By building applications that comply with W3C recommendations, a Web developer supports the community of users and software that promote the sharing of information and platform independence. Berners-Lee and the W3C can justifiably be credited with inventing the World Wide Web, pioneering the development of the Web browser, and developing the protocols that make sharing information possible.

THE VISION OF THE W3C

The ultimate motivation of the W3C springs from the vision of Berners-Lee for the Web, and has been variously expressed as the W3C motto: "To lead the World Wide Web to its full potential by developing protocols and guidelines that ensure long-term growth for the Web," or more simply "Leading the Web to its full potential..." This vision privileges the notions of interoperability and device independency, and suggests a public network where information can be easily shared among strangers, and is not confined to a specific application software suite or a particular vendor's products. The essence of the W3C vision is that a document or program that follows W3C specifications should work identically across different applications and different computers. To "work identically" in this context means that the essential information or functionality is preserved, while conceding that presentation issues such as the size of the display device, color options, accessibility accommodations, and so on, may introduce variability.

The vision of the W3C is displayed by its future of the Web document[1] which claims that the Web is for:

- *Everyone* (regardless of culture, abilities, etc.).
- *Everything* (applications and data stores, and on devices ranging from power computers with high-definition displays to mobile devices to appliances).
- *Everywhere* (from high to low bandwidth environments).
- *Diverse mode of interaction* (touch, pen, mouse, voice, assistive technologies, computer to computer).
- *Enable computers to do more useful work* (through advanced data searching and sharing).

To complement its advocacy of interoperability and device independence, the W3C also promotes

W3C–
XML

accessibility. Accessibility refers to the degree that application software is sympathetic to people with disabilities, but also in a more general sense, the degree to which applications can be used in environments degraded by noise, lighting, etc.

THE SEMANTIC WEB

Residing behind the W3C's vision of the Web as networked personal and corporate information is the more ambitious vision of the Web as a network of semantics. An early statement of this particular vision of the Semantic Web appeared in the Scientific American.[2] This entry sketched a Web network of publicly available documents that possessed semantics structured as metadata. These metadata were to be harvested mechanically and manipulated by inference tools to solve ad hoc everyday problems such as finding the office hours of the closest doctor, the cheapest available tickets for the theater, and so on. The subtitle of the Scientific American article summarizes this vision of a Semantic Web: "A new form of web content that is meaningful to computers will unleash a revolution of new possibilities."

This original description of the Semantic Web was refined[3] by suggesting the difference between the Web of public HTML documents destined to be displayed in Web browsers, and a web of structured data that would be amenable to mechanical harvest. Theoretically, these two Webs would coexist and even overlap as HTML documents destined for display in Web browsers might also contain structured metadata. An example technology that could be used in this way would be Resource Description Framework (RDF) attributes. Examples of the data that exist on the Web and that could be harvested mechanically might be calendar data, travel arrangements, photograph descriptions, and financial transactions.

The vision of the Semantic Web as a web of linked open data has come to dominate. The result might be called a web of data, where islands of semantics exist; that is, pools of structured documents on the open Web that could be harvested mechanically. Current efforts are now focusing on linking common data points that are related but exist in different semantic islands on the Web. In summarizing the achievements and challenges of constructing the Semantic Web, Ivan Herman[4] gives a voice to the shift of the Semantic Web from a single huge, central ontology organizing all knowledge, which would be unmanageable if not impossible to construct. Instead he described the use of numerous ontologies and vocabularies, such as Friend of a Friend and Dublin Core that would capture local richness and encourage the discovery of new relationships among data. The

challenge of such architecture is linking disparate data points together.

The Linking Open Data project[5] centralizes the increasingly common construction of resources that are available for the mechanical harvest of structured information. The following enumerates some of the structured data available on the Web, which are, in effect, islands of semantics that might be linked together:

- IgentaConnect (http://www.ingentaconnect.com/) offers bibliographic metadata storage and has more than 200 million RDF triplets available.
- RDFS/OWL Representation of WordNet (http://wordnet.princeton.edu/) has 150MD of RDF/XML available for download. WordNet facilitates the browsing of meaningfully related words and concepts.
- "Département/canton/commune" is available from the French Statistical Institute and represents statistical surveys on population, employment, wages, prices, business, economy, and French national accounts.
- Geonames Ontology and Data has information on 6 million geographical features.
- RDF Book Mashup makes information about books, their authors, reviews, and online bookstores available on the Semantic Web. Information drawn from sources such as Amazon, Google, and Yahoo can be integrated into the Semantic Web.
- dbpedia is a community effort to extract structured information from Wikipedia and link this information to other sources of structured information.

Semantic Web Case Studies and Use Cases[6] list descriptions of systems that have been deployed in industry that use Semantic Web techniques.

HISTORICAL HIGHLIGHTS OF THE W3C

The invention of the World Wide Web in 1989 was a by-product of Berners-Lee's solution to a document sharing problem at CERN (European Organization for Nuclear Research). He proposed a global hypertext project of linked documents to help people coordinate their work during large project development. To manifest his vision he created the first World Wide Web server and the first browser/client called "World Wide Web." This early Web browser was first offered to CERN in December 1990 and then to the Internet at large in the summer of 1991.

During the period of 1991 to 1993, Berners-Lee extended the development of the Web by constructing basic technologies such as Uniform Resource Identifiers (URIs), Hypertext Transfer Protocol, and Hypertext Markup Language (HTML). As an early model of community development, Berners-Lee's technological initiatives were modified by feedback from the nascent Web community. In 1994 Berners-Lee founded the W3C at MIT/CSAIL where he is a senior research scientist.

The beginnings of the World Wide Web can be found in the proposal "Information Management: A Proposal"[7] placed by Berners-Lee before CERN's governing board. Its ambition was to solve the information management problems of large projects by utilizing the idea of a hypertext, which had been pioneered by Nelson.[8] Such a hypertext featured human-readable information linked together in ad hoc and unconstrained ways, thus promoting the discovery of hitherto unrecognized parallels or points of convergence among disparate texts.

In September 1992 Berners-Lee gave an invited presentation to the Computing in High Energy Physics 92 conference, where he claimed that the "W3 project merges networked information retrieval and hypertext to make an easy but powerful global information system...W3 now defines the state of the art in networked information retrieval, for user support, resource discovery and collaborative work." In 1993 the CERN W3 software suite appeared in the public domain.

The first W3C recommendation, for Portable network graphics, appeared in October 1996. Within several years, major recommendations were issued that were foundational for the growth and development of the Web. These included the recommendation for HTML 4.0 in December 1997, which added tables, scripting, and style sheets. These features permitted authors to create significantly more expressive Web content. And in February 1998, the recommendation for XML 1.0 appeared. XML provided a platform for a host of following recommendations and has evolved into a universal language of the Internet.

The following enumerates some of the important historical achievements of the W3C:

- The portable network graphics recommendation in October 1996 provides a cross-platform graphics format.
- The cascading style sheets recommendation of December 1996 laid the foundation for a uniform strategy for adding style (e.g., fonts, colors, spacing) to Web pages.
- The Web accessibility initiative of February 1997 promoted accessibility of the Web through four primary areas of work: technology, tools, education and outreach, and research and development.
- The HTML 4.0 recommendation of December 1997 added new features to Web publishing such as tables, scripting, style sheets, internationalization, and accessibility.

- The XML 1.0 recommendation of February 1998 introduces the fundamental technology that would become an influential Web standard.
- In August 2000, the scalable vector graphics recommendation introduced two-dimensional graphics and graphical applications in XML.
- XML schema recommendation of May 2001 provided a standard method of architecting XML vocabularies.
- Web services activities introduce a fundamental protocol for Web services in January 2002.
- In May 2003, the W3C adopted a royalty-free patent policy and encouraged the development of open standards.
- Two fundamental protocols of the Semantic Web, RDF and Web ontology language (OWL) were introduced in February 2004.
- In March 2004, VoiceXML promoted the use of interactive voice response applications to Web-based development and content delivery.
- The W3C mission of universal access was promoted in February 2005 with the introduction of the character model recommendation. The goal of the character model recommendation was the ease of use of the Web regardless of language, script, writing system, and cultural conventions.
- The mobile Web initiative of May 2005 set the mission of making Web access from a mobile device as simple as Web access from a desktop device.
- In November 2005, the Semantic Web for health care and life sciences interest group deployed standardized Semantic Web specifications for the medical industry.

This historical listing illustrates the foundational role of the W3C in designing specifications and protocols that foster the sharing of information. The culmination of the worldwide sharing of information is expressed in the vision of the Semantic Web.

MEMBERSHIP OF THE W3C

The W3C brings together a diverse group of stake holders to achieve its mission of developing Web standards and protocols. As of 2008 there were more than 400 members of the W3C representing more than 40 countries. Approximately 37% of these members are American and about 9% are from the United Kingdom. The stake holders of the W3C represent many different types of organizations with the largest category being consultants and systems integrators, followed by the university research and development category, and the general software companies' category. Other categories of members include vendors of technology products and services, content providers, corporate users, research laboratories, standards bodies, and governments.

W3C–
XML

ACTIVITIES OF THE W3C

The activities of the W3C manifest themselves as various kinds of groups. Working groups focus on technical developments, interest groups focus on nontechnical issues, and coordination groups focus on the communication among related groups.

The following is an overview of some of the leading activities of the W3C:

- XML activities represent a core set of technologies around which orbit a number of working groups that are focused on development in the areas of extensible stylesheet language, efficient XML interchange, XML binary characterization, XML processing model, and XML linking, query, and schema.
- Graphics activities focus on the development of scalable vector graphics (SVG) technologies.
- The HTML activities group works on the evolution of this standard language of the Web. The current goal is to evolve HTML into an XML-based markup language and thereby ease its use with other markup languages.
- Internationalization activities work to ensure that the W3C's formats and protocols are amenable to all of the world's languages, writing systems, character codes, and local conventions.
- Math activities facilitate the use and presentation of mathematics on the Web.
- Mobile Web activities are working to overcome fundamental interoperability and usability problems associated with mobile Web access. They attempt to integrate the key players in the mobile area: authoring tool vendors, content providers, handset manufacturers, browser vendors, and mobile operators.
- Multimodal interaction activities target the ability of Web users to dynamically switch to the most appropriate mode of interaction. Ideally, a multimodal Web application would permit users to input data via speech, handwriting, and keystrokes, and receive output via displays, prerecorded and synthetic speech, audio, and various haptic displays.
- Patent policy activities alert the W3C community about developments in the legal and standards environment.
- Rich Web client activities focus on Web-based applications that extend the user experience on the Web beyond static HTML. Often these applications support compound documents that combine multiple formats such as Extensible Hypertext Mark-up Language, SVG, Synchronized Media Integration Language (SMIL), and XForms.
- Security group activities focus on the security context of Web applications that prevent surfers on the Web from being deceived and defrauded.

- Semantic Web activities focus on the creation of a universal medium for the exchange of data. Ideally both personal information and enterprise applications would be smoothly integrated creating a global sharing of commercial, scientific, and cultural data.
- Style activities focus on style components of Web pages. This group is working to extend style to other types of documents such as XML, SVG, and SMIL.
- Synchronized multimedia activities focus on choreographing multimedia presentations where audio, video, text, and graphics are combined in real time. A Timed Text working group is working in designing formats for streaming text synchronized with other timed media.
- Ubiquitous Web applications activities focus on enabling value-added services and business models for ubiquitous networked devices.
- Voice browser activities aim at technologies for capturing and producing speech and managing the dialog between user and computer.
- Web content accessibility initiative (WAI) focuses on accessibility to the Web resources, while the WAI technical group focuses on the technical aspects in three areas: Web content, user agent, and authoring tool accessibility.
- Web services activities promote the technology of Web services as a standard means of interoperability between different software applications running on a variety of platforms and frameworks. This group is designing the infrastructure, architecture, and core technologies for Web services.
- XForms activity focuses on the use of Web forms for the collection and distribution of information.

New areas of interest and activity are incorporated into the W3C by a recommendation development process.

RECOMMENDATION DEVELOPMENT PROCESS

The W3C strives to create high-quality standards for the Web though the strategy of community consensus. The general public is encouraged to join the members of the W3C in coming to consensus of Web standards and protocols. A new development begins with expressions of interest in a topic, and perhaps a workshop that brings interested persons together for the exchange ideas and information. Next, a proposal for a new activity describes the scope and duration of the project, as well as working groups, interest groups, and coordination groups that will carry out the work. As the development work proceeds, candidate specifications and guidelines cycle in revision and review as they advance to recommendation status. This may be a long process that may ultimately lead to a success recommendation, or may result in the abandonment of the proposal. As successful proposals near completion, a W3C advisory committee finally examines the mature proposal and issues a recommendation.

CONCLUSION

The W3C has had a major influence on the creation of the World Wide Web, arguably the most important public information utility of our age. It has taken as its mission the development of the Web in the manner of consensus building with the aim of creating the greatest benefit for the greatest number. As the Web grows in size and sophistication, more and more Semantic Web applications are appearing.

REFERENCES

1. About W3C: Future, http://www.w3.org/Consortium/future.

2. Berners-Lee, T.; Hendler, J.; Lassila, O. The Semantic Web. Sci. Am. **2001**, May, 29–37.

3. Shadbolt, N.; Hall, W.; Berners-Lee, T. The Semantic Web revisited. IEEE Intell. Syst. **2006**, May/June, *21* (3), 96–101 http://eprints.ecs.soton.ac.uk/12614/1/Semantic_Web_Revisited.pdf (accessed June 2008).

4. Herman, I. State of the Semantic Web. In 2008 Semantic Technology Conference, San Jose, CA, May, 18–22; http://www.w3.org/2008/Talks/0518-SanJose-IH/HTML/Overview.html (accessed May 2008).

5. Linking Open Data project, http://esw.w3.org/topic/SweoIG/TaskForces/CommunityProjects/LinkingOpenData.

6. Semantic Web case studies and use cases, http://www.w3.org/2001/sw/sweo/public/UseCases/.

7. Berners-Lee, T. Information management: a proposal. http://www.nic.funet.fi/index/FUNET/history/internet/w3c/proposal.html (accessed December 2007).

8. Nelson, T. *Literary Machines*; The report on, and of, Project Xanadu concerning word processing, electronic publishing, hypertext, thinkertoys, tomorrow's intellectual… including knowledge, education and freedom. Mindful Press: Sausalito, CA, 1981.

Web Retrieval and Mining

Carlos Castillo
Yahoo! Research, Barcelona, Spain

Ricardo Baeza-Yates
Barcelona Media Innovation Centre, Yahoo! Research, Barcelona, Spain

Abstract

The advent of the Web in the mid-1990s followed by its fast adoption in a relatively short time, posed significant challenges to classical information retrieval methods developed in the 1970s and the 1980s. The major challenges include that the Web is massive, dynamic, and distributed. The two main types of tasks that are carried on the Web are searching and mining. Searching is locating information given an information need, and mining is extracting information and/or knowledge from a corpus. The metrics for success when carrying these tasks on the Web include precision, recall (completeness), freshness, and efficiency.

INTRODUCTION

Information retrieval is the area of computer science concerned with the representation, storage, organization, and access to documents.

Documents, in this definition, are understood in a broad sense, and include Web pages and other contents available on the Web. The Web is a unique medium for information dissemination, characterized by low entry barriers, low publishing costs, high communication speeds, and a vast distribution network.

Most methods for information retrieval were developed in the 1970s and 1980s for relatively small and coherent collections, such as the ones found in traditional libraries. The Web poses significant challenges to these methods, being massive, dynamic, and distributed.[1]

Web information retrieval (Web IR) or Web search, differs significantly from traditional information retrieval. The two main differences are the scale and nature of the collections being processed. Web search includes topics such as Web crawling, indexing and querying, adversarial Web IR issues, and Web distributed systems and evaluation metrics. Another relevant topic is Web data mining, which includes the analysis of the content, structure, and usage of the Web. In the following, we focus on these two topics: Web search and Web data mining. Our coverage of details and bibliography is by no means complete, and the interested reader is referred to Baeza-Yates and Ribeiro-Neto[2] and Chakrabarti.[3]

WEB SEARCH

Web search is the main application of Web IR, and a very successful one. From the user's point of view, a short query consisting of a few keywords is written in a search box, and the search engine displays in return a short list, typically of 10–20 Web pages that are considered relevant to the query issued and expected to be high-quality documents.

The two main goals in a search are precision and recall, and they are, to a certain extent, competing goals.

Precision is defined as the fraction of relevant results contained in the result set, or in a part of the result set. For instance, if 3 out of 10 results for a query are relevant, the precision is 30%.

Recall is defined as the fraction of relevant results in a set, compared with the total number of pages on the Web that would be relevant for this query. Of course, the total number of pages on the Web relevant for a particular query is an unknown quantity, but for popular query terms it can be estimated using sampling techniques.

An information retrieval system can have high recall at the expense of precision, simply by returning more results, and high precision at the expense of recall, by removing results for which the algorithm is unsure about their relevance. The design of effective algorithms for search seeks a balance among these two extremes, and in the Web the focus is on precision as recall cannot be measured, only estimated.

In the case of Web search there is a third goal that is freshness. The Web changes continuously and the copy of the Web that the search engine has can become stale very quickly. The three goals: precision, recall, and freshness are sometimes mutually exclusive and introduce three-way trade-offs,[4] as depicted in Fig. 1. These trade-offs create the possibility of several niche markets apart from general Web search, including: vertical search, over a particular subset of pages; archive search, over several snapshots of

Encyclopedia of Information Systems and Technology, DOI: 10.1081/E-EIST-120043706

Fig. 1 Trade-offs of different search engines.

the Web; and news search, over Web sites that change with very high frequency.

An additional consideration in search engine design is efficiency. Large Web search engines have to deal with a large volume of queries and search huge data collections, so even large amounts of computational resources can be insufficient. Successful algorithms for Web search avoid consuming too many resources per query or per document.

From the point of view of the search engine, Web search occurs in two main phases. The first phase is off-line, with a certain periodicity or by permanent incremental maintenance. It includes crawling the Web to download pages and then indexing them to provide fast searches. The second phase is done online, and corresponds to the process of querying and ranking, which consists of building a ranked list of results using the index for a particular query. These phases are depicted in Fig. 2 and explained in more detail in the rest of this section.

Web Crawling

A Web crawler is a system that automatically downloads pages from the Web following a set of predefined rules. A Web crawler receives as input a starting set of URLs that constitutes a "seed set," and a set of rules to follow. The crawler first downloads the pages from the seed set, extracts the links found in such pages, and then follows those links recursively while certain criteria are met.

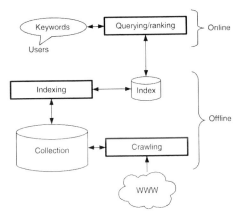

Fig. 2 Phases of Web search.

Crawling the Web is a required step for many Web IR applications.

Aside from Web search, Web crawlers are multipurpose systems that can be used for a variety of tasks, including finding and reporting "broken links" or other coding errors, and computing statistics about the Web.

The most important design constraint of Web crawlers is that they must avoid disrupting the Web servers they interact with. While downloading Web pages, the crawler is using the resources of others, and thus it must keep its resource consumption as low as possible. Web crawler designers and operators must take every possible step to control the frequency of visits to sites and keep them to a minimum. Also, the authors of Web sites have to ultimately decide which part, if any, of their sites can be visited by crawlers. This is done by using the robots exclusion protocol.[5]

After downloading the pages, they have to be processed to be used by the search engine or other application. HTML is the main language for coding documents on the Web, but there are many other formats present, including PDF, plain text, plus the document formats used by popular text-processing software such as Microsoft Word or OpenOffice. These formats have to be converted to a single representation before they can be used.

The importance of freshness is another aspect of the crawler's operation. The Web is very dynamic, and it changes continuously; this means that by the time the crawler has finished collecting a set of pages, many of the pages it has downloaded have already changed.[6] Crawling the Web, to a certain extent, resembles watching the sky at night:[2] the light we see from the stars has often taken thousands of years to reach our eyes. Moreover, the light from different stars has taken different amounts of time, so what we see is not a snapshot of the sky at any given moment, present or past. It is a combination of images from different times. The same happens with the collection of Web pages crawled by a search engine.

The Web pages that are not directly accessible by following links, but require the user to enter a query in an online form (e.g., enter an author's name to retrieve bibliographic data), constitute the "hidden Web."[7] Searching this content is challenging for search engines. In most cases, large information providers generate "crawler-friendly" pages for better indexing by search engines, but other forms of collaboration may arise in the future, including exposing an interface for querying the local database to the search engine.

Indexing

After collecting pages, the next step is to create an index to enable fast searches over the downloaded

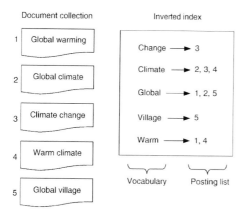

Document collection

Inverted index

Vocabulary   Posting list

Fig. 3   Example of an inverted index.

pages. The first step toward indexing a large collection is to consider an appropriate logical view of the content. The most used logical view for this task is the "bag of words" model,[8] in which each document is represented as a multiset containing all its keywords, disregarding the order in which they appear.

To produce this logical view, text normalization operations are applied to the original texts. These operations include tokenization, stopword removal, and stemming.

Tokenization is the process by which a text is separated into words. This is trivial in Western languages, but harder to do in other languages such as Chinese.

Stopwords are functional words that do not convey meaning by themselves, such as articles and prepositions. The removal of stopwords reduces the amount of data processing and the size of the index, and also improves the retrieval accuracy of information retrieval systems.

Stemming is the extraction of the morphological root of a word. This allows us to search for "housing" and retrieve results that include "house" or "houses."

After the text normalization operations have been applied, most search systems build an index, a data structure designing to accelerate the process of retrieving documents containing a given query. The most prevalent type of such structure is an inverted index. In Fig. 3, an example of an inverted index for a collection of five toy documents (each of them having two words) is shown.

An inverted index is composed of two parts: a vocabulary, containing all the terms in the collection, and a posting list, which contains references to the documents (s) in which each word of the vocabulary appears. An inverted index is a powerful tool for the search engine, enabling very fast response times. In the example of Fig. 3, if we search for "global AND climate" in the inverted index, the task is basically to intersect the set of pages containing "global" {1, 2, 5} with the set of pages containing "climate" {2, 3, 4}, obtaining as a result the set {2}. If these lists are sorted, their

intersection can be computed very quickly. This is how a basic inverted index works. There are many techniques for providing faster search or reducing the space occupied by the index. For example, if phrase or proximity search is needed, the exact positions where the term appears in a document must be also encoded in the posting list. The interested reader is referred to Baeza-Yates and Ribeiro-Neto[2] and Witten et al.[9] for an overview of indexing techniques.

Another aspect is that large search engines achieve high response times by means of parallelization. In this case, the index has to be divided in some way, and each piece of the index has to be given to a different physical computer. There are two main strategies for this partitioning. One is to give each machine a set of documents, the other one is to give each machine a set of terms.[10]

Querying and Ranking

Most search engines receive queries expressed as a set of keywords. Scalable question answering systems, in which users express their information need by means of a question, have remained elusive to researchers in particular because many natural language processing algorithms still require a prohibitive amount of computational power for Web-scale collections.

Typical queries are very short, between two and three keywords each. After receiving a query, the search engine uses its inverted index (or indexes) to build a page with results that is shown to users. To a certain extent, the problem of finding a set of pages that are related to the query is the "easy" part, given that for most broad queries there are thousands or millions of documents that are potentially appropriate. The most difficult challenge is to find among those documents, a small subset of the best 10 or 20. This is the problem of ranking.

Ranking has two main aspects: relevance and quality. The dimension of relevance indicates how related is the retrieved document to the user intention. The dimension of quality indicates how good is the document by itself. Search engines try to produce results for a given query that are both relevant for the query and have high quality. One of the main techniques to do fast ranking is to use partial evaluation techniques, such that only the top ranked answers are computed, and the rest of the answer is computed incrementally as the user demands it.

Relevance

Given that the search engine cannot understand the meaning of the queries nor of the documents, it must resort to statistical methods to compare queries to documents. These statistical methods allow the search engine to provide an estimation on how similar the query is to each document retrieved, which is used as an approximation of how relevant is the document for the query.

The vector space model[8] is the most used framework for measuring text similarity. It represents each document as a vector in a high-dimensional space, in which each dimension is a term, and the magnitude of each component of the vector is proportional to the frequency of the corresponding term, and inversely proportional to the document frequency of the term in the collection.

Differences in document size have to be taken into account for the similarity measure between documents, so the angle between documents is used instead of, for instance, the Euclidean distance between them. For instance, the angle between the documents "global warming" and "warming warming global global" is zero (so the documents are equivalent according to this metric), the angle between the documents "global warming" and "global climate" is 45° (under a simple weighting scheme), and the angle between the documents "global warming" and "climate change" is 90°. For normalization purposes, the cosine of such angle is the standard way of expressing this similarity metric.

Information retrieval systems usually do not apply the vector space model naïvely, as it has significant weaknesses. By itself the vector space model does not take relationships among terms into account. For instance, strictly speaking the cosine similarity between the "global warming" and "climate change" is zero, and the cosine similarity between "global warming" and "strawberry ice cream" is also zero; but clearly the first pair of concepts have a closer relationship than the second pair. Two methods that can be applied to overcome this problem are query expansion and latent semantic indexing.

Query expansion consists in adding related words to the queries, and the same technique can be applied to documents. For instance, this could convert automatically "global warming" into "global world warming climate" and "climate change" into "climate warm cold change global." The specific words that are added can be obtained from different sources, including co-occurrence in the collection. In the case of the Web, there are rich sources of information to obtain words related to a document. The main one is anchor text, that is, the text contained in the links pointing to the present document. This is a very important feature in the ranking computed by most modern search engines. A second source of information is social book-marking sites that allow users to associate tags to documents.

Latent semantic indexing[11] consists in projecting the vectors representing queries (and documents) into a different, and usually smaller, space. This technique is based on principal component analysis and attempts to group automatically terms into the main "concepts" representing multiple weighted terms.

Quality

Search engines are designed to extract a set of features from the documents they index, and use those features to assert what is the quality of a given document. Quality is hard to define and of course hard to estimate using statistical measures. However, certain textual features from documents, including content length, frequencies of some words, features about the paragraphs, etc. tend to be correlated with human assessments about document quality.[12]

Apart from the content of the pages themselves, on the Web, a rich source of information for inferring quality can be extracted from links. Links on the Web tend to connect topically related pages,[13] and they often imply that the target document has an acceptable or high level of quality. Thus, they can be used for finding high-quality items in the same way as academic citations can partially characterize the importance of a paper. The same considerations as for academic citations apply: not all of the links imply endorsement,[14] some pages attract many citations for other reasons aside from quality, and citation counts can be inflated by self-citations or citations that point to errors; among other problems.

There are two classic link analysis algorithms to obtain quality metrics for Web pages: PageRank and HITS. For a survey of their variants, and other methods, see Borodin et al.[15]

The PageRank algorithm[16] defines the importance of a page in a recursive manner: "a page with high PageRank is a page referenced by many pages with high PageRank." Despite the definition being recursive, it is possible to compute PageRank scores using results from Markov chain theory. In brief, the wanderings of a "random surfer" are simulated, in which a person browses the Web by following links at random. The PageRank score of a page is roughly proportional to the amount of expected visits the random surfer will do to each page.

The hyperlink-induced topic search (HITS) algorithm[17] is another method for ranking Web pages. It starts by building a set of pages related to a topic by querying a search engine, and then expands this set by using incoming and outgoing links, by crawling the Web or by querying a search engine again. Next, two scores for each page are computed: a *hub score* and an *authority score*.

As shown in Fig. 4, a page with a high hub score is a page that links to many pages with a high authority score. A page with a high authority score is a page linked by many pages with a high hub score. Again,

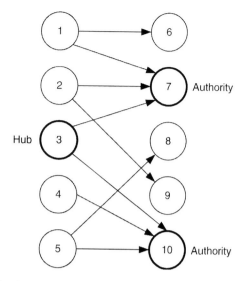

Fig. 4 A graph with one page with high hub score (number 3) and two pages with large authority scores (numbers 7 and 10).

despite the apparent circularity of the definition, both hub and authority scores can be computed efficiently by an iterative computation.

Another source of information for ranking pages on the Web is usage data. A page that is visited frequently and/or for long periods by users may be more interesting than a page that is not. This information can be obtained by the search engine by providing a client-side add-on such as a toolbar, or by instrumenting the search engine result pages to capture click information.

Ranking manipulation

Visits from search engines are an important source of traffic for many Web sites. Given that in the case of commercial ventures on the Web, traffic is strongly correlated with sales volume, there is a significant economic incentive for obtaining high rankings on search engines. These incentives may lead Web page authors to use deceptive techniques for achieving high rankings.[18] These deceptive techniques are known on a whole as search engine spam.

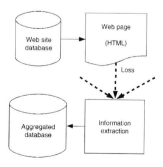

Fig. 5 Information loss when extracting content from the Web.

There are many types of search engine spam: inserting many keywords on Web pages, linking nepotistically among pages, providing different contents to the search engine than to users (also called "cloaking"), among others; for a survey of these methods, Gyöngyi.[19]

Search engine spam has been an important issue for search engines for a number of years, and it is not likely to be solved in the near future. Web spam damages search engines' reputation as it exploits and weakens the trust relationship between users and search engines.[19] Spamming has become so prevalent that without countermeasures to identify and remove spam, the quality of search engine results would be very poor.[20]

WEB MINING

Web mining is the application of data mining techniques to find patterns on data downloaded from the Web. Based on the main source of data they use, these techniques can be broadly classified as Web content mining, Web link mining, and Web usage mining.

Content Mining

Web content mining is the extraction of knowledge from the textual content of Web pages. The main challenge here is that HTML, while designed initially to be a language for logical formatting, is actually used as a language for physical formatting. Logical formatting describes document structure, such as paragraphs and headings, while physical formatting describes visual attributes like font sizes, colors, and spacings. With logical formatting, it would be easier to extract information than with the present physical formatting.

In general, the Web sites that are rich in information are built using "dynamic pages" that are generated on demand, in response to a user click or query. These pages are created by querying a local database, formatting the results as HTML, and then displaying such results to the user.

For example, let us consider a Web site about movies being shown in theaters. This Web site may present the movies on a tabular form with the titles, ratings, and show times, for instance. A Web search engine or other information provider interested on doing Web information extraction must read this table and reconstruct the original schema based on it. For example, it must find out that the first column contains the movie title, the second column the rating, and the third column the show times. This is easy for a human but it is hard to do it automatically. Most of the time, some information is lost, as depicted in Fig. 5.

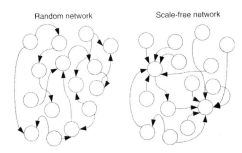

Fig. 6 Difference between a random network and a scale-free network.

Information extraction systems use clues from the page's formatting and structure, domain knowledge, and training examples, among other sources of information, to map HTML fragments to tuples in relations. They can also use methods for detecting the page template and isolating navigational areas that do not contribute content. The systems that do this task are informally known as "content scrapers" and they can be quite accurate, especially when restricted to particular domains. For a survey of information extraction methods, Kayed and Shaalan.[21]

Other aspects of content mining besides information extraction are content classification, sentiment analysis, and duplicated pages detection.

Content classification in general looks at statistics obtained from the Web pages to classify their contents. In many cases, this is done to find out what is the topic the contents are about. In other cases, content classification is used to extract document properties such as the genre of the document, or whether it expresses more opinions or more facts, or to evaluate how well-written a document is. In all cases, a statistical description of the document is created, and then a machine learning algorithm takes that description and a set of training labels to construct a model able to separate automatically the classes.[22,23]

Sentiment analysis, including "intention mining," is the task of finding what is the sentiment or intention of the author of a document. Specifically, it can be used to determine if a certain fragment is expressing a negative or positive opinion. This is very important given the large amount of product and service reviews available on Web pages, blogs, or forums. These reviews are typically very short, usually no more than a few paragraphs. The techniques of sentiment classification include the analysis of the frequency of certain terms,[24] with the aid of parts-of-speech taggers or other natural language processing tools.

Finally, there is a significant amount of duplicate content on the Web. According to Broder et al.,[25] roughly one-third of the pages on the Web are duplicates or near duplicates of another page, and present studies have confirmed this trend. Finding near-duplicate content[26] is important for efficiency reasons, to avoid downloading and indexing many times the same pages. It is also important to filter out plagiarism, so that the original page gets ranked high, and not the copies.

Link Mining

The overall structure of the Web differs significantly from the one exhibited by random networks. The most salient difference is that, while on a random network most of the nodes have a degree (number of connections) close to the average, in networks such as the Web, the distribution of the degree is very skewed. The networks that have this property are called scale-free networks.

Fig. 6 depicts a random network and a scale-free network with the same number of nodes and edges. In a scale-free network, a few nodes attract more of the in-links. This can be explained by "rich-get-richer" processes[27] in which having many links gives a better chance of attracting new links, increasing the disparity in the number of connections over time.

At a macroscopic level, looking at the properties of the network as a whole, we can describe the Web in terms of the strongly connected components on it. A strongly connected component is a part of a graph in which all pairs of nodes can reach each other (in both directions) by following links. The Web exhibits a very large strongly connected component (CORE), other components that are reachable to/from it by directed links (IN and OUT, respectively), and pages that cannot be reached at all from the CORE, which are called ISLANDS. Minor components such as TENDRILS and TUNNEL can also be identified. This description is called the bow-tie structure of the Web[28] given its shape, depicted in Fig. 7.

PageRank and HITS could be considered simple link mining techniques. More elaborated link analysis can be used for finding similar pages, communities, or detection of Web spam based in links.

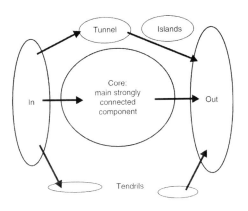

Fig. 7 Bow-tie structure on the Web.

Usage Mining

Usage data on the Web is abundant and valuable. Web site administrators can capture usage data by enabling logging on their Web servers, and they can enrich such data by instrumenting their internal links. There are several free software packages available that can do sophisticated analysis of access logs and can discover, for instance, typical browsing paths. This is of particular importance for retailers and other e-commerce Web sites that can use this information to drive the design of their Web sites, improving the user experience and/or increasing their sales volume.

Search engines have access to the queries written by the users, and the pages they selected after seeing the list of results (and the pages they did not select). Data from user search sessions can be used to increase the relevance of the results.[29] Interesting relationships can be inferred by looking at users, queries, and pages. We can observe, for instance, that similar users tend to issue similar queries, that similar pages show up as results for related queries, and so on.

Usage data is increasingly valuable for search engines. Privacy issues arise in the confluence of the legal and technical aspects associated to this data collection, and both users and search engine have incentives for maintaining and enforcing the secrecy of this data.

CONCLUSIONS AND PRESENT TRENDS

As we have seen, Web retrieval methods differ from standard information retrieval methods, and can adapt to the large-scale, open, and distributed nature of the Web. For the future, two topics that are attracting a significant research effort are the mobile Web and the semantic Web.

The Mobile Web is the Web that is accessible and used through portable devices. Today, the capabilities of most mobile cell phones are well beyond just making phone calls. Many include Web-browsing software, and a growing fraction of the activity on the Web is carried through these devices, including browsing, searching, and even producing content (e.g., in the case of cell phones equipped with cameras). A challenge here is to provide users of portable devices with an experience that takes into account their geographical location and their present activity.

The Semantic Web[30] is a vision of the future of the Web, in which the Web contents can be read and understood by both humans and software agents. This will enable information integration and sharing without losing information. Several technologies enable the semantic Web, ranging from simple markup languages as the Extensible Markup Language to other languages that describe relationships among objects, classes, and properties. On top of these layers, applications will be able to analyze and, later, to reason about the contents and to extract knowledge from them.

REFERENCES

1. Arasu, A.; Cho, J.; Garcia-Molina, H.; Paepcke, A.; Raghavan, S. Searching the web. ACM Trans. Internet Technol. **2001**, *1* (1), 2–43.
2. Baeza-Yates, R.; Ribeiro-Neto, B. In *Modern Information Retrieval*; Addison-Wesley: New York, NY, 1999.
3. Chakrabarti, C. In *Mining the Web: Analysis of Hypertext and Semi Structured Data*; Morgan Kaufmann: San Francisco, CA, 2002.
4. Kobayashi, M.; Takeda, K. Information retrieval on the web. ACM Comput. Surv. **2000**, *32* (2), 144–173.
5. Koster, M. In *A standard for robot exclusion,* 1996, http://www.robotstxt.org/wc/robots.html.
6. Ntoulas, A.; Cho, J.; Olston, C. What's new on the web?: The evolution of the web from a search engine perspective. Proceedings of the 13th conference on World Wide Web; ACM Press: New York, NY, 2004; 1–12.
7. Raghavan, S.; Garcia-Molina, H. Crawling the hidden web. Proceedings of the 27th International Conference on Very Large Data Bases, Morgan Kaufmann: Rome, Italy, September, 2001; 129–138.
8. Salton, G. In *Introduction to Modern Information Retrieval (McGraw-Hill Computer Science Series)*; McGraw-Hill: New York, NY, 1983.
9. Witten, I.H.; Moffat, A.; Bell, T.C. In *Managing Gigabytes: Compressing and Indexing Documents and Images*; Morgan Kaufmann: San Francisco, CA, 1999.
10. Tomasic, A.; Garcia-Molina, H. Performance of inverted indices in shared-nothing distributed text document information retrieval systems. PDIS '93: Proceedings of the Second International Conference on Parallel and Distributed Information Systems, IEEE Computer Society Press: Los Alamitos, CA, 1993; 8–17.
11. Deerwester, S.; Dumais, S.T.; Furnas, G.W.; Landauer, T. K.; Harshman, R. Indexing by latent semantic analysis. J. Am. Soc. Inform. Sci. **1999**, *41* (6), 391–407.
12. Richardson, M.; Prakash, A.; Brill, E. Beyond pagerank: Machine learning for static ranking. Proceedings of the 15th international conference on World Wide Web, Edinburgh, Scotland, May, 2006; ACM Press, 707–715.
13. Davison, B.D. Topical locality in the web. Proceedings of the 23rd annual international ACM SIGIR Conference on Research and Development in Information Retrieval, Athens, Greece, July, 2000; ACM, 272–279.
14. Haas, S.W.; Grams, E.S. Page and link classifications: Connecting diverse resources. Proceedings of the third ACM conference on Digital libraries, Pittsburgh, PA, June, 1998; ACM Press, 99–107.
15. Borodin, A.; Roberts, G.O.; Rosenthal, J.S.; Tsaparas, P. Link analysis ranking: Algorithms, theory, and experiments. ACM Trans. Internet Technol. **2005**, *5* (1), 231–297.

16. Page, L.; Brin, S.; Motwani, R.; Winograd, T. *The page-rank citation ranking: Bringing order to the Web, Technical report;* Stanford Digital Library Technologies Project, 1998.

17. Kleinberg, J.M. Authoritative sources in a hyperlinked environment. J. ACM **1999**, *46* (5), 604–632.

18. Gori, M.; Witten, I. The bubble of web visibility. Commun. ACM **2005**, *48* (3), 115–117.

19. Gyöngyi, Z.; Garcia-Molina, H. Web spam taxonomy. First International Workshop on Adversarial Information Retrieval on the Web, Chiba, Japan, May, 2005; 39–47.

20. Henzinger, M.R.; Motwani, R.; Silverstein, C. Challenges in web search engines. SIGIR Forum **2002**, *36* (2), 11–22.

21. Kayed, M.; Shaalan, K.F. A survey of web information extraction systems. IEEE Trans. Know. Data Eng. **2006**, *18* (10), 1411–1428.

22. Dumais, S.; Chen, H. Hierarchical classification of web content. Proceedings of the 23rd annual international ACM SIGIR conference on Research and development in information retrieval, Athens, Greece, July, 2000; ACM Press, 256–263.

23. Chakrabarti, S.; Dom, B.; Agrawal, R.; Raghavan, P. Scalable feature selection, classification and signature generation for organizing large text databases into hierarchical topic taxonomies. VLDB J. **1998**, *7* (3), 163–178.

24. Pang, B.; Lee, L.; Vaithyanathan, S. Thumbs up?: Sentiment classification using machine learning techniques. *EMNLP '02*: Proceedings of the ACL-02 conference on Empirical methods in natural language processing, Association for Computational Linguistics: Philadelphia, PA, 2002; July, 79–86.

25. Broder, A.Z.; Glassman, S.C.; Manasse, M.S.; Zweig, G. Syntactic clustering of the web. Comput. Netw. ISDN Syst. **1997**, *29* (813), 1157–1166.

26. Fetterly, D.; Manasse, M.; Najork, M. Detecting phrase-level duplication on the world wide web. *SIGIR '05*: Proceedings of the 28th annual international ACM SIGIR conference on Research and development in information retrieval, ACM Press: New York, NY, 2005; 170–177.

27. Barabási, A.L.; Albert, R. Emergence of scaling in random networks. Science **1999**, *286* (5439), 509–512.

28. Broder, A.; Kumar, R.; Maghoul, F.; Raghavan, P.; Rajagopalan, S.; Stata, R.; Tomkins, A.; Wiener, J. Graph structure in the web: Experiments and models. Proceedings of the Ninth Conference on World Wide Web, ACM Press: Amsterdam, Netherlands, May 2000; 309–320.

29. Baeza-Yates, R. Applications of web query mining. Proceedings of the 27th European Conference on IR Research, *ECIR 2005, volume 3408,* Springer: Santiago de Compostela, Spain, March 2005; 7–22.

30. Berners-Lee, T.; Hendler, J.; Lassila, O. The semantic web. Scientific American **2001**, *284* (5), 34–43.

BIBLIOGRAPHY

1. Information Retrieval methods, in general, and Web Search, in particular, is discussed in Chapter 13 of the book by Baeza-Yates and Ribeiro-Neto[2]. A textbook by Chakrabarti[3] deals with several topics related to Web Mining.

2. Sahami, M.; Mittal, V.; Baluja, S.; Rowley, H. The happy searcher: Challenges in web information retrieval. 8th Pacific Rim International Conference on Artificial Intelligence, volume 3157 of Lecture Notes in Computer Science, Auckland, New Zealand, August, 2004; Springer: Berlin/Heidelberg, 3–12.

W3C–
XML

Web Services

John W. Rittinghouse
Tomball, Texas, U.S.A.

James F. Ransome
Cisco Systems, Santa Clara, California, U.S.A.

Abstract

This entry examines some of the web services delivered from the cloud. It reviews Communication-as-a-Service (CaaS), and explains some of the advantages of using CaaS. Infrastructure is also a service in cloud land, and there are many variants on how infrastructure is managed in cloud environments. When vendors outsource Infrastructure-as-a-Service (IaaS), it relies heavily on modern on-demand computing technology and high-speed networking. It provides some vendors who provide Software-as-a-Service (SaaS), such as Amazon.com, with their elastic cloud platform. The entry then presents implementation issues, the characteristics, benefits, and architectural maturity level of the service. Outsourced hardware environments (called platforms) are available as Platforms-as-a-Service (PaaS). The case study of Mosso (Rackspace) is offered to examine key characteristics of a PaaS implementation.

As technology migrates from the traditional on-premise model to the new cloud model, service offerings evolve almost daily. Our intent in this entry is to provide some basic exposure to where the field is from the perspective of the technology, and give you a feel for where it will be down the road.

Web service offerings often have a number of common characteristics, such as a low barrier to entry, where services are offered specifically for consumers and small business entities. Often, little or no capital expenditure for infrastructure is required from the customer. While massive scalability is common with these types of offerings, it's not always necessary. Many cloud vendors have yet to achieve massive scalability because their user base generally does not require it. Multitenancy enables cost and resource sharing across the (often vast) user base. Finally, device and location independence enables users to access systems regardless of where they are, or what device they are using. Now, let's examine some of the more common web service offerings.

COMMUNICATION-AS-A-SERVICE (CAAS)

CaaS is an outsourced enterprise communications solution. Providers of this type of cloud-based solution (known as CaaS vendors) are responsible for the management of hardware and software required for delivering Voice over IP (VoIP) services, Instant Messaging (IM), and video conferencing capabilities to their customers. This model began its evolutionary process from within the telecommunications (Telco) industry, not unlike how the SaaS model arose from the software delivery services sector. CaaS vendors are responsible for all of the hardware and software management consumed by their user base. CaaS vendors typically offer guaranteed quality of service (QoS) under a service-level agreement (SLA).

A CaaS model allows a CaaS provider's business customers to selectively deploy communications features and services throughout their company on a pay-as-you-go basis for service (s) used. CaaS is designed on a utility-like pricing model that provides users with comprehensive, flexible, and (usually) simple-to-understand service plans. According to Gartner,[1] the CaaS market is expected to total $2.3 billion in 2011, representing a compound annual growth rate of more than 105% for the period.

CaaS service offerings are often bundled, and may include integrated access to traditional voice (or VoIP) and data, advanced unified communications functionality such as video calling, web collaboration, chat, real-time presence and unified messaging, a handset, local and long-distance voice services, voice mail, advanced calling features (such as caller ID, three-way and conference calling, etc.), and advanced private branch exchange (PBX) functionality. A CaaS solution includes redundant switching, network, Points of Presence and circuit diversity, customer premises equipment redundancy, and wide area network (WAN) fail-over, which specifically addresses the needs of their customers. All

Encyclopedia of Information Systems and Technology, DOI: 10.1081/E-EIST-120053835

VoIP transport components are located in geographically diverse, secure data centers for high availability and survivability.

CaaS offers flexibility and scalability that small and medium-sized business might not otherwise be able to afford. CaaS service providers are usually prepared to handle peak loads for their customers by providing services capable of allowing more capacity, devices, modes, or area coverage, as their customer demand grows. Network capacity and feature sets can be changed dynamically, so functionality keeps pace with consumer demand, and provider-owned resources are not wasted. From the customer's perspective, there is very little to virtually no risk of the service becoming obsolete, since the service provider's responsibility is to perform periodic upgrades or replacements of hardware and software to keep the platform technologically current.

CaaS requires little to no management oversight from customers. It eliminates the business owner's need for any capital investment in infrastructure, and it eliminates expense for ongoing maintenance and operations overhead for infrastructure. With a CaaS solution, customers are able to leverage enterprise-class communication services without having to build a premises-based solution of their own. This allows those customers to reallocate budget and personnel resources to where their business can best use them.

Advantages of CaaS

From the handset found on each employee's desk to the PC-based software client on employee laptops, to the VoIP private backbone, and all modes in between, every component in a CaaS solution is managed 24/7 by the CaaS vendor. As we said previously, the expense of managing a carrier-grade data center is shared across the vendor's customer base, making it more economical for businesses to implement CaaS than to build their own VoIP network. Let's look as some of the advantages of a hosted approach for CaaS.

Hosted and managed solutions

Remote management of infrastructure services provided by third parties once seemed an unacceptable situation to most companies. However, with enhanced technology, networking, and software, the attitude has changed. This is, in part, due to cost savings achieved in using those services. However, unlike the "one-off" services offered by specialist providers, CaaS delivers a complete communications solution that is entirely managed by a single vendor. Along with features such as VoIP and unified communications, the integration of core PBX features with advanced functionality is managed by one

vendor who is responsible for all of the integration and delivery of services to users.

Fully Integrated, Enterprise-Class Unified Communications

With CaaS, the vendor provides voice and data access and manages local area network/wide area network (LAN/WAN), security, routers, e-mail, voice mail, and data storage. By managing the LAN/WAN, the vendor can guarantee consistent QoS from a user's desktop across the network and back. Advanced unified communications features that are most often a part of a standard CaaS deployment include:

- Chat
- Multimedia conferencing
- Microsoft Outlook integration
- Real-time presence
- "Soft" phones (software-based telephones)
- Video calling
- Unified messaging and mobility

Providers are constantly offering new enhancements (in both performance and features) to their CaaS services. The development process and subsequent introduction of new features in applications is much faster, easier, and more economical than ever before. This is, in large part, because the service provider is doing work that benefits many end users across the provider's scalable platform infrastructure. Because many end users of the provider's service ultimately share this cost (which, from their perspective, is miniscule compared to shouldering the burden alone), services can be offered to individual customers at a cost that is attractive to them.

No capital expenses needed

When a business outsources their unified communications needs to a CaaS service provider, the provider supplies a complete solution that fits the company's exact needs. Customers pay a fee (usually billed monthly) for what they use. Customers are not required to purchase equipment, so there is no capital outlay. Bundled in these types of services are ongoing maintenance and upgrade costs, which are incurred by the service provider. The use of CaaS services allows companies the ability to collaborate across any workspace. Advanced collaboration tools are now used to create high-quality, secure, adaptive work spaces throughout any organization. This allows a company's workers, partners, vendors, and customers to communicate and collaborate more effectively. Better communication allows organizations to adapt quickly to market changes and to build a competitive advantage. CaaS can also accelerate decision making within an organization. Innovative unified communications capabilities (such as presence, IM, and rich media services) help ensure that information quickly reaches whoever needs it.

Flexible capacity and feature set

When customers outsource communication services to a CaaS provider, they pay for the features they need when they need them. The service provider can distribute the cost services and delivery across a large customer base. As previously stated, this makes the use of shared feature functionality more economical for customers to implement. Economies of scale allow service providers enough flexibility that they are not tied to a single vendor investment. They are able to leverage best-of-breed providers such as Avaya, Cisco, Juniper, Microsoft, Nortel, and ShoreTel more economically than any independent enterprise.

No risk of obsolescence

Rapid technology advances, predicted long ago and known as Moore's law,[2] have brought about product obsolescence in increasingly shorter periods of time. Moore's law describes a trend he recognized that has held true since the beginning of the use of integrated circuits (ICs) in computing hardware. Since the invention of the integrated circuit in 1958, the number of transistors that can be placed inexpensively on an integrated circuit has increased exponentially, doubling approximately every two years.

Unlike IC components, the average life cycles for PBXs and key communication equipment, and systems range anywhere from 5 to 10 years. With the constant introduction of newer models for all sorts of technology (PCs, cell phones, video software and hardware, etc.), these types of products now face much shorter life cycles, sometimes as short as a single year. CaaS vendors must absorb this burden for the user by continuously upgrading the equipment in their offerings, to meet the changing demands in the marketplace.

No facilities and engineering costs incurred

CaaS providers host all of the equipment needed to provide their services to their customers, virtually eliminating the need for customers to maintain data center space and facilities. There is no extra expense for the constant power consumption that such a facility would demand. Customers receive the benefit of multiple carrier-grade data centers with full redundancy—and it's all included in the monthly payment.

Guaranteed business continuity

If a catastrophic event occurred at your business's physical location, would your company disaster recovery plan allow your business to continue operating without a break? If your business experienced a serious or extended communications outage, how long could your company survive? For most businesses, the answer is "not long." Distributing risk by using geographically dispersed data centers has become the norm today. It mitigates risk and allows companies in a location hit by a catastrophic event to recover as soon as possible. This process is implemented by CaaS providers because most companies don't even contemplate voice continuity if catastrophe strikes. Unlike data continuity, eliminating single points of failure for a voice network is usually cost-prohibitive because of the large scale and management complexity of the project. With a CaaS solution, multiple levels of redundancy are built into the system, with no single point of failure.

INFRASTRUCTURE-AS-A-SERVICE (IAAS)

According to the online reference Wikipedia, IaaS is the delivery of computer infrastructure (typically a platform virtualization environment) as a service.[3] IaaS leverages significant technologies, services, and data center investments to deliver IT as a service to customers. Unlike traditional outsourcing, which requires extensive due diligence, negotiations ad infinitum, and complex, lengthy contract vehicles, IaaS is centered around a model of service delivery that provisions a predefined, standardized infrastructure, specifically optimized for the customer's applications. Simplified statements of work and à la carte service-level choices make it easy to tailor a solution to a customer's specific application requirements. IaaS providers manage the transition and hosting of selected applications on their infrastructure. Customers maintain ownership and management of their application(s) while off-loading hosting operations and infrastructure management to the IaaS provider. Provider-owned implementations typically include the following layered components:

- Computer hardware (typically set up as a grid for massive horizontal scalability)
- Computer network (including routers, firewalls, load balancing, etc.)
- Internet connectivity (often on OC 192 backbones [An Optical Carrier (OC) 192 transmission line is capable of transferring 9.95 gigabits of data per second.])
- Platform virtualization environment for running client-specified virtual machines

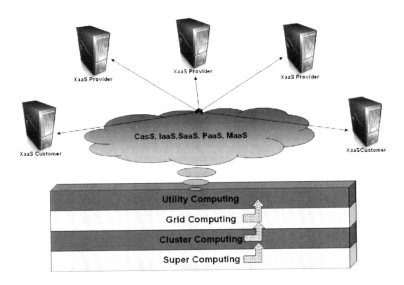

Fig. 1 Building blocks to the cloud.

- SLAs
- Utility computing billing

Rather than purchasing data center space, servers, software, network equipment, etc., IaaS customers essentially rent those resources as a fully outsourced service. Usually, the service is billed on a monthly basis, just like a utility company bills customers. The customer is charged only for resources consumed. The chief benefits of using this type of outsourced service include:

- Ready access to a preconfigured environment that is generally ITIL-based[4] (The Information Technology Infrastructure Library [ITIL] is a customized framework of best practices designed to promote quality computing services in the IT sector.)
- Use of the latest technology for infrastructure equipment
- Secured, "sand-boxed" (protected and insulated) computing platforms that are usually security monitored for breaches
- Reduced risk by having off-site resources maintained by third parties
- Ability to manage service-demand peaks and valleys
- Lower costs that allow expensing service costs instead of making capital investments
- Reduced time, cost, and complexity in adding new features or capabilities

Modern On-Demand Computing

On-demand computing is an increasingly popular enterprise model in which computing resources are made available to the user as needed.[5] Computing resources that are maintained on a user's site are becoming fewer and fewer, while those made available by a service

provider are on the rise. The on-demand model evolved to overcome the challenge of being able to meet fluctuating resource demands efficiently. Because demand for computing resources can vary drastically from one time to another, maintaining sufficient resources to meet peak requirements can be costly. Overengineering a solution can be just as adverse as a situation where the enterprise cuts costs by maintaining only minimal computing resources, resulting in insufficient resources to meet peak load requirements. Concepts such as clustered computing, grid computing, utility computing, etc., may all seem very similar to the concept of on-demand computing, but they can be better understood if one thinks of them as building blocks that evolved over time and with techno-evolution to achieve the modern cloud computing model we think of and use today (see Fig. 1).

One example we will examine is Amazon's Elastic Compute Cloud (Amazon EC2). This is a web service that provides resizable computing capacity in the cloud. It is designed to make web-scale computing easier for developers and offers many advantages to customers:

- Its web service interface allows customers to obtain and configure capacity with minimal effort.
- It provides users with complete control of their (leased) computing resources, and lets them run on a proven computing environment.
- It reduces the time required to obtain and boot new server instances to minutes, allowing customers to quickly scale capacity as their computing demands dictate.
- It changes the economics of computing by allowing clients to pay only for capacity they actually use.
- It provides developers the tools needed to build failure-resilient applications and isolate themselves from common failure scenarios.

Amazon's Elastic Cloud

Amazon EC2 presents a true virtual computing environment, allowing clients to use a web-based interface to obtain and manage services needed to launch one or more instances of a variety of operating systems (OSs). Clients can load the OS environments with their customized applications. They can manage their network's access permissions, and run as many or as few systems as needed. In order to use Amazon EC2, clients first need to create an Amazon Machine Image (AMI). This image contains the applications, libraries, data, and associated configuration settings used in the virtual computing environment. Amazon EC2 offers the use of preconfigured images built with templates to get up and running immediately. Once users have defined and configured their AMI, they use the Amazon EC2 tools provided for storing the AMI by uploading the AMI into Amazon S3. Amazon S3 is a repository that provides safe, reliable, and fast access to a client AMI. Before clients can use the AMI, they must use the Amazon EC2 web service to configure security and network access.

Using Amazon EC2 to run instances

During configuration, users choose which instance type (s) and OS they want to use. Available instance types come in two distinct categories, Standard or High-CPU instances. Most applications are best suited for Standard instances, which come in small, large, and extra-large instance platforms. High-CPU instances have proportionally more CPU resources than random-access memory, and are well suited for compute-intensive applications. With the High-CPU instances, there are medium and extra large platforms to choose from. After determining which instance to use, clients can start, terminate, and monitor as many instances of their AMI as needed by using web service Application Programming Interfaces (APIs) or a wide variety of other management tools that are provided with the service. Users are able to choose whether they want to run in multiple locations, use static IP endpoints, or attach persistent block storage to any of their instances, and they pay only for resources actually consumed. They can also choose from a library of globally available AMIs that provide useful instances. For example, if all that is needed is a basic Linux server, clients can choose one of the standard Linux distribution AMIs.

Amazon EC2 Service Characteristics

There are quite a few characteristics of the EC2 service that provide significant benefits to an enterprise. First of all, Amazon EC2 provides financial benefits. Because of Amazon's massive scale and large customer base, it is an inexpensive alternative to many other possible solutions. The costs incurred to set up and run an operation are shared over many customers, making the overall cost to any single customer much lower than almost any other alternative. Customers pay a very low rate for the compute capacity they actually consume. Security is also provided through Amazon EC2 web service interfaces. These allow users to configure firewall settings that control network access to and between groups of instances. Amazon EC2 offers a highly reliable environment, where replacement instances can be rapidly provisioned.

When one compares this solution to the significant up-front expenditures traditionally required to purchase and maintain hardware, either inhouse or hosted, the decision to outsource is not hard to make. Outsourced solutions like EC2 free customers from many of the complexities of capacity planning, and allow clients to move from large capital investments and fixed costs to smaller, variable, expensed costs. This approach removes the need to overbuy and overbuild capacity to handle periodic traffic spikes. The EC2 service runs within Amazon's proven, secure, and reliable network infrastructure and data center locations.

Dynamic scalability

Amazon EC2 enables users to increase or decrease capacity in a few minutes. Users can invoke a single instance, hundreds of instances, or even thousands of instances, simultaneously. Of course, because this is all controlled with web service APIs, an application can automatically scale itself up or down depending on its needs. This type of dynamic scalability is very attractive to enterprise customers because it allows them to meet their customers' demands without having to overbuild their infrastructure.

Full control of instances

Users have complete control of their instances. They have root access to each instance, and can interact with them as one would with any machine. Instances can be rebooted remotely using web service APIs. Users also have access to console output of their instances. Once users have set up their account and uploaded their AMI to the Amazon S3 service, they just need to boot that instance. It is possible to start an AMI on any number of instances (or any type) by calling the *RunInstances* API that is provided by Amazon.

Configuration flexibility

Configuration settings can vary widely among users. They have the choice of multiple instance types, OSs, and software packages. Amazon EC2 allows them to select a configuration of memory, CPU, and instance storage that is optimal for their choice of OS and application. For example, a user's choice of OSs may also include numerous Linux distributions, Microsoft Windows Server, and even an OpenSolaris environment, all running on virtual servers.

Integration with other Amazon web services

Amazon EC2 works in conjunction with a variety of other Amazon web services. For example, Amazon Simple Storage Service (Amazon S3), Amazon SimpleDB, Amazon Simple Queue Service (Amazon SQS), and Amazon CloudFront are all integrated to provide a complete solution for computing, query processing, and storage across a wide range of applications.

Amazon S3 provides a web services interface that allows users to store and retrieve any amount of data from the Internet at anytime, anywhere. It gives developers direct access to the same highly scalable, reliable, fast, inexpensive data storage infrastructure Amazon uses to run its own global network of web sites. The S3 service aims to maximize benefits of scale and to pass those benefits on to developers.

Amazon SimpleDB is another web-based service, designed for running queries on structured data stored with the Amazon Simple Storage Service (Amazon S3) in real time. This service works in conjunction with the Amazon Elastic Compute Cloud (Amazon EC2) to provide users the capability to store, process, and query data sets within the cloud environment. These services are designed to make web-scale computing easier and more cost-effective for developers. Traditionally, this type of functionality was provided using a clustered relational database that requires a sizable investment. Implementations of this nature brought on more complexity and often required the services of a database administer to maintain it.

By comparison to traditional approaches, Amazon SimpleDB is easy to use and provides the core functionality of a database (e.g., real-time lookup and simple querying of structured data) without inheriting the operational complexity involved in traditional implementations. Amazon SimpleDB requires no schema, automatically indexes data, and provides a simple API for data storage and access. This eliminates the need for customers to perform tasks such as data modeling, index maintenance, and performance tuning.

Amazon SQS is a reliable, scalable, hosted queue for storing messages as they pass between computers. Using Amazon SQS, developers can move data between distributed components of applications that perform different tasks without losing messages or requiring 100% availability for each component. Amazon SQS works by exposing Amazon's web-scale messaging infrastructure as a service. Any computer connected to the Internet can add or read messages without the need for having any installed software or special firewall configurations. Components of applications using Amazon SQS can run independently, and do not need to be on the same network, developed with the same technologies, or running at the same time.

Amazon CloudFront is a web service for content delivery. It integrates with other Amazon web services to distribute content to end users with low latency and high data transfer speeds. Amazon CloudFront delivers content using a global network of edge locations. Requests for objects are automatically routed to the nearest edge server, so content is delivered with the best possible performance. An edge server receives a request from the user's computer and makes a connection to another computer called the origin server, where the application resides. When the origin server fulfills the request, it sends the application's data back to the edge server, which, in turn, forwards the data to the client computer that made the request.

Reliable and resilient performance

Amazon Elastic Block Store (EBS) is yet another Amazon EC2 feature that provides users powerful features to build failure-resilient applications. Amazon EBS offers persistent storage for Amazon EC2 instances. Amazon EBS volumes provide "off-instance" storage that persists independently from the life of any instance. Amazon EBS volumes are highly available, highly reliable data shares that can be attached to a running Amazon EC2 instance and are exposed to the instance as standard block devices. Amazon EBS volumes are automatically replicated on the back end. The service provides users with the ability to create point-in-time snapshots of their data volumes, which are stored using the Amazon S3 service. These snapshots can be used as a starting point for new Amazon EBS volumes and can protect data indefinitely.

Support for Use in geographically disparate locations

Amazon EC2 provides users with the ability to place one or more instances in multiple locations. Amazon EC2 locations are composed of Regions (such as North America and Europe) and Availability Zones. Regions consist of one or more Availability Zones, are geographically dispersed, and are in separate geographic areas or countries. Availability Zones are distinct locations that are engineered to be insulated from failures in other Availability Zones and provide inexpensive, low-latency network connectivity to other Availability Zones in the same Region.[6] For example, the North America Region may be split into the following Availability Zones: Northeast, East, SouthEast, NorthCentral, Central, SouthCentral, NorthWest, West, SouthWest, etc. By launching instances in any one or more of the separate Availability Zones, you can insulate your applications from a single point of failure. Amazon EC2 has a SLA that commits to a 99.95% uptime availability for each Amazon EC2 Region. Amazon EC2 is currently available in two regions, the United States and Europe.

Elastic IP (EIP) addressing

EIP addresses are static IP addresses designed for dynamic cloud computing. An EIP address is associated with your account and not with a particular instance, and you control that address until you choose explicitly to release it. Unlike traditional static IP addresses, however, EIP addresses allow you to mask instance or Availability Zone failures by programmatically remapping your public IP addresses to any instance in your account. Rather than waiting on a technician to reconfigure or replace your host, or waiting for Domain Name System to propagate to all of your customers, Amazon EC2 enables you to work around problems that occur with client instances or client software by quickly remapping their EIP address to another running instance. A significant feature of EIP addressing is that each IP address can be reassigned to a different instance when needed. Now, let's review how the EIP works with Amazon EC2 services.

First of all, Amazon allows users to allocate up to five EIP addresses per account (which is the default). Each EIP can be assigned to a single instance. When this reassignment occurs, it replaces the normal dynamic IP address used by that instance. By default, each instance starts with a dynamic IP address that is allocated upon startup. Since each instance can have only one external IP address, the instance starts out using the default dynamic IP address. If the EIP in use is assigned to a different instance, a new dynamic IP address is allocated to the vacated address of that instance. Assigning or reassigning an IP to an instance requires only a few minutes. The limitation of designating a single IP at a time is due to the way Network Address Translation (NAT) works. Each instance is mapped to an internal IP address and is also assigned an external (public) address. The public address is mapped to the internal address using NAT tables (hence, NAT). If two external IP addresses happen to be translated to the same internal IP address, all inbound traffic (in the form of data packets) would arrive without any issues. However, assigning outgoing packets to an external IP address would be very difficult because a determination of which external IP address to use could not be made. This is why implementors have built in the limitation of having only a single external IP address per instance at any one time.

Mosso (Rackspace)

Mosso, a direct competitor of Amazon's EC2 service, is a web application hosting service and cloud platform provider that bills on a utility computing basis. Mosso was launched in February 2008, and is owned and operated by Rackspace, a web hosting provider that has been around for some time. Most new hosting platforms require custom code and architecture to make an application work. What makes Mosso different is that it has been designed to run an application with very little or no modifications. The Mosso platform is built on existing web standards and powered by proven technologies. Customers reap the benefits of a scalable platform for free. They spend no time coding custom APIs or building data schemas. Mosso has also branched out into cloud storage and cloud infrastructure.

Mosso cloud servers (MSC) and files

MCS came into being from the acquisition of a company called Slicehost by Rackspace. Slicehost was designed to enable deployment of multiple cloud servers instantly. In essence, it touts capability for the creation of advanced, high-availability architectures. In order to create a full-service offering, Rackspace also acquired JungleDisk, an online backup service. By integrating JungleDisk's backup features with virtual servers that Slicehost provides, Mosso, in effect, created a new service to compete with Amazon's EC2. Mosso claims that these "cloud sites" are the fastest way for customers to put their site in the cloud. Cloud sites are capable of running Windows or Linux applications across banks of servers numbering in the hundreds.

Mosso's *Cloud Files* provide unlimited storage for content by using a partnership formed with Limelight Networks. This partnership allows Mosso to offer its customers a content delivery network (CDN). With CDN services, servers are placed around the world and, depending on where you are located, you get served via the closest or most appropriate server. CDNs cut down on the hops back and forth to handle a request. The chief benefit of using CDN is a scalable, dynamic storage platform that offers a metered service, by which customers pay only for what they use. Customers can manage files through a web-based control panel or programmatically through an API.

Integrated backups with the CDN offering implemented in the Mosso services platform began in earnest with Jungle Disk version 2.5 in early 2009. Jungle Disk 2.5 is a major upgrade, adding a number of highly requested features to its portfolio. Highlights of the new version include running as a background service. The background service will keep running even if the Jungle Disk Monitor is logged out or closed. Users do not have to be logged into the service for automatic backups to be performed. There is native file system support on both the 32-bit and 64-bit versions of Windows (Windows 2000, XP, Vista, 2003, and 2008), and Linux. A new download resume capability has been added for moving large files and performing restore operations. A time-slice restore interface was also added, allowing restoration of files from any given point-in-time where a snapshot was taken. Finally, it supports automatic updates on Windows (built-in) and Macintosh (using Sparkle).

MONITORING-AS-A-SERVICE (MAAS)

MaaS is the outsourced provisioning of security, primarily on business platforms that leverage the Internet to conduct business.[7] MaaS has become increasingly popular over the last decade. Since the advent of cloud computing, its popularity has grown even more. Security monitoring involves protecting an enterprise or government client from cyber threats. A security team plays a crucial role in securing and maintaining the confidentiality, integrity, and availability of IT assets. However, time and resource constraints limit security operations, and their effectiveness, for most companies. This requires constant vigilance over the security infrastructure and critical information assets.

Many industry regulations require organizations to monitor their security environment, server logs, and other information assets to ensure the integrity of these systems. However, conducting effective security monitoring can be a daunting task because it requires advanced technology, skilled security experts, and scalable processes—none of which come cheap. MaaS security monitoring services offer real-time, 24/7 monitoring and nearly immediate incident response across a security infrastructure—they help to protect critical information assets of their customers. Prior to the advent of electronic security systems, security monitoring and response were heavily dependent on human resources and human capabilities, which also limited the accuracy and effectiveness of monitoring efforts. Over the years, the adoption of information technology into facility security systems, and their ability to be connected to security operations centers (SOCs) via corporate networks, has significantly changed that picture. This means two important things: 1) The total cost of ownership (TCO) for traditional SOCs is much higher than for a modern-technology SOC; and 2) achieving lower security operations costs and higher security effectiveness means that modern SOC architecture must use security and IT technology to address security risks.

Protection against Internal and External Threats

SOC-based security monitoring services can improve the effectiveness of a customer security infrastructure by actively analyzing logs and alerts from infrastructure devices around the clock and in real time. Monitoring teams correlate information from various security devices to provide security analysts with the data they need to eliminate false positives (A false positive is an event that is picked up by an intrusion detection system and perceived as an attack but that in reality is not.), and respond to true threats against the enterprise. Having consistent access to the skills needed to maintain the level of service, an organization requiring enterprise-level monitoring is a huge issue. The information security team can assess system performance on a periodically recurring basis and provide recommendations for improvements as needed. Typical services provided by many MaaS vendors are described below.

Early detection

An early detection service detects and reports new security vulnerabilities shortly after they appear. Generally, the threats are correlated with third-party sources, and an alert or report is issued to customers. This report is usually sent by e-mail to the person designated by the company. Security vulnerability reports, aside from containing a detailed description of the vulnerability and the platforms affected, also include information on the impact the exploitation of this vulnerability would have on the systems or applications previously selected by the company receiving the report. Most often, the report also indicates specific actions to be taken to minimize the effect of the vulnerability, if that is known.

Platform, control, and services monitoring

Platform, control, and services monitoring is often implemented as a dashboard interface (A dashboard is a floating, semitransparent window that provides contextual access to commonly used tools in a software program.), and makes it possible to know the operational status of the platform being monitored at any time. It is accessible from a web interface, making remote access possible. Each operational element that is monitored usually provides an operational status indicator, always taking into account the critical impact of each element. This service aids in determining which elements may be operating at or near capacity or beyond the limits of established parameters. By detecting and identifying such problems, preventive measures can be taken to prevent loss of service.

Intelligent log centralization and analysis

Intelligent log centralization and analysis is a monitoring solution based mainly on the correlation and matching of log entries. Such analysis helps to establish a baseline of operational performance and provides an index of security threat. Alarms can be raised in the event an incident moves the established baseline parameters beyond a stipulated threshold. These types of sophisticated tools are used by a team of security experts who are responsible for incident response once such a threshold has been crossed and the threat has generated an alarm or warning picked up by security analysts monitoring the systems.

Vulnerabilities detection and management

Vulnerabilities detection and management enables automated verification and management of the security level of information systems. The service periodically performs a series of automated tests for the purpose of identifying system weaknesses that may be exposed over the Internet, including the possibility of unauthorized access to administrative services, the existence of services that have not been updated, the detection of vulnerabilities such as phishing, etc. The service performs periodic follow-up of tasks performed by security professionals managing information systems security and provides reports that can be used to implement a plan for continuous improvement of the system's security level.

Continuous system patching/upgrade and fortification

Security posture is enhanced with continuous system patching and upgrading of systems and application software. New patches, updates, and service packs for the equipment's OS are necessary to maintain adequate security levels and support new versions of installed products. Keeping abreast of all the changes to all the software and hardware requires a committed effort to stay informed, and to communicate gaps in security that can appear in installed systems and applications.

Intervention, forensics, and help desk services

Quick intervention, when a threat is detected, is crucial to mitigating the effects of a threat. This requires security engineers with ample knowledge in the various technologies and with the ability to support applications as well as infrastructures on a 24/7 basis. MaaS platforms routinely provide this service to their customers. When a detected threat is analyzed, it often requires forensic analysis to determine what it is, how much effort it will take to fix the problem, and what effects are likely to be seen. When problems are encountered, the first thing customers tend to do is pick up the phone. Help desk services provide assistance on questions or issues about the operation of running systems. This service includes assistance in writing failure reports, managing operating problems, etc.

Delivering Business Value

Some consider balancing the overall economic impact of any build-versus-buy decision as a more significant measure than simply calculating a return on investment (ROI). The key cost categories that are most often associated with MaaS are: 1) service fees for security event monitoring for all firewalls and intrusion detection devices, servers, and routers; 2) internal account maintenance and administration costs; and 3) preplanning and development costs.

Based on the TCO, whenever a customer evaluates the option of an in-house security information monitoring team and infrastructure compared to outsourcing to a service provider, it does not take long to realize that establishing and maintaining an in-house capability is not as attractive as outsourcing the service to a provider with an existing infrastructure. Having an in-house security operations center forces a company to deal with issues such as staff attrition, scheduling, around the clock operations, etc.

Losses incurred from external and internal incidents are extremely significant, as evidenced by a regular stream of high-profile cases in the news. The generally accepted method of valuing the risk of losses from external and internal incidents is to look at the amount of a potential loss, assume a frequency of loss, and estimate a probability for incurring the loss. Although this method is not perfect, it provides a means for tracking information security metrics. Risk is used as a filter to capture uncertainty about varying cost and benefit estimates. If a risk-adjusted ROI demonstrates a compelling business case, it raises confidence that the investment is likely to succeed because the risks that threaten the project have been considered and quantified. Flexibility represents an investment in additional capacity or agility today that can be turned into future business benefits at some additional cost. This provides an organization with the ability to engage in future initiatives, but not the obligation to do so. The value of flexibility is unique to each organization, and willingness to measure its value varies from company to company.

Real-Time Log Monitoring Enables Compliance

Security monitoring services can also help customers comply with industry regulations by automating the collection and reporting of specific events of interest, such as log-in failures. Regulations and industry guidelines often require log monitoring of critical servers to ensure the integrity of confidential data. MaaS providers' security monitoring services automate this time-consuming process.

PLATFORM-AS-A-SERVICE (PAAS)

Cloud computing has evolved to include platforms for building and running custom web-based applications, a concept known as Platform-as-a-Service. PaaS is an outgrowth of the SaaS application delivery model. The PaaS model makes all of the facilities required to support the complete life cycle of building and delivering web applications and services entirely available from the Internet, all with no software downloads or installation for developers, IT managers, or end users. Unlike the IaaS model, where developers may create a specific OS instance with homegrown applications running, PaaS developers are concerned only with web-based development and generally do not care what OS is used. PaaS services allow users to focus on innovation rather than complex infrastructure. Organizations can redirect a significant portion of their budgets to creating applications that provide real business value instead of worrying about all the infrastructure issues in a roll-your-own delivery model. The PaaS model is thus driving a new era of mass innovation. Now, developers around the world can access unlimited computing power. Anyone with an Internet connection can build powerful applications, and easily deploy them to users globally.

The Traditional On-Premises Model

The traditional approach of building and running on-premises applications has always been complex, expensive, and risky. Building your own solution has never offered any guarantee of success. Each application was designed to meet specific business requirements. Each solution required a specific set of hardware, an OS, a database, often a middle-ware package, e-mail and web servers, etc. Once the hardware and software environment was created, a team of developers had to navigate complex programming development platforms to build their applications. Additionally, a team of network, database, and system management experts was needed to keep everything up and running. Inevitably, a business requirement would force the developers to make a change to the application. The changed application then required new test cycles before being distributed. Large companies often needed specialized facilities to house their data centers. Enormous amounts of electricity also were needed to power the servers as well as to keep the systems cool. Finally, all of this required the use of fail-over sites to mirror the data center so that information could be replicated in case of a disaster. Old days, old ways—now, let's fly into the silver lining of today's cloud.

The New Cloud Model

PaaS offers a faster, more cost-effective model for application development and delivery. PaaS provides all the infrastructure needed to run applications over the Internet. Such is the case with companies such as Amazon.com, eBay, Google, iTunes, and YouTube. The new cloud model has made it possible to deliver such new capabilities to new markets via the web browsers. PaaS is based on a metering or subscription model, so users pay only for what they use. PaaS offerings include workflow facilities for application design, application development, testing, deployment, and hosting, as well as application services such as virtual offices, team collaboration, database integration, security, scalability, storage, persistence, state management, dashboard instrumentation, etc.

Key Characteristics of PaaS

Chief characteristics of PaaS include services to develop, test, deploy, host, and manage applications to support the application development life cycle. Web-based user interface creation tools typically provide some level of support to simplify the creation of user interfaces, based either on common standards such as HTML and JavaScript or on other, proprietary, technologies. Supporting a multitenant architecture helps to remove developer concerns regarding the use of the application by many concurrent users. PaaS providers often include services for concurrency management, scalability, fail-over, and security. Another characteristic is the integration with web services and databases. Support for Simple Object Access Protocol and other interfaces allows PaaS offerings to create combinations of web services (called mashups) as well as having the ability to access databases and reuse services maintained inside private networks. The ability to form and share code with ad-hoc, predefined, or distributed teams greatly enhances the productivity of PaaS offerings. Integrated PaaS offerings provide an opportunity for developers to have much greater insight into the inner workings of their applications and the behavior of their users, by implementing dashboard-like tools to view the inner workings based on measurements such as performance, number of concurrent accesses, etc. Some PaaS offerings leverage this instrumentation to enable pay-per-use billing models.

SOFTWARE-AS-A-SERVICE (SAAS)

The traditional model of software distribution, in which software is purchased for and installed on personal computers, is sometimes referred to as Software-as-a-Product. SaaS is a software distribution model in which applications are hosted by a vendor or service provider and made available to customers over a network, typically the Internet. SaaS is becoming an increasingly prevalent delivery model, as underlying technologies that support web services and service-oriented architecture (SOA) mature and new developmental approaches become popular. SaaS is also often associated with a pay-as-you-go subscription licensing model. Meanwhile, broadband service has become increasingly available to support user access from more areas around the world.

The huge strides made by Internet Service Providers (ISPs) to increase bandwidth, and the constant introduction of ever more powerful microprocessors coupled with inexpensive data storage devices, is providing a huge platform for designing, deploying, and using software across all areas of business and personal computing. SaaS applications also must be able to interact with other data and other applications in an equally wide variety of environments and platforms. SaaS is closely related to other service delivery models we have described. International Data Corporation (IDC) identifies two slightly different delivery models for SaaS.[8] The hosted application management model is similar to an Application Service Provider (ASP) model. Here, an ASP hosts commercially available software for customers and delivers it over the Internet. The other model is a software on demand model where the provider gives customers network-based access to a single copy of an application created specifically for SaaS distribution. IDC predicted that SaaS would make up 30% of the software market by 2007 and would be worth $10.7 billion by the end of 2009.

SaaS is most often implemented to provide business software functionality to enterprise customers at a low cost, while allowing those customers to obtain the same benefits of commercially licensed, internally operated software without the associated complexity of installation, management, support, licensing, and high initial cost.[9] Most customers have little interest in the how or why of software implementation, deployment, etc., but all have a need to use software in their work. Many types of software are well suited to the SaaS model (e.g., accounting, customer relationship management, e-mail software, human resources, IT security, IT

service management, video conferencing, web analytics, web content management). The distinction between SaaS and earlier applications delivered over the Internet is that SaaS solutions were developed specifically to work within a web browser. The architecture of SaaS-based applications is specifically designed to support many concurrent users (multitenancy) at once. This is a big difference from the traditional client/server or ASP based solutions, which cater to a contained audience. SaaS providers, on the other hand, leverage enormous economies of scale in the deployment, management, support, and maintenance of their offerings.

SaaS Implementation Issues

Many types of software components and applications frameworks may be employed in the development of SaaS applications. Using new technology, found in these modern components and application frameworks, can drastically reduce the time to market and cost of converting a traditional on-premises product into a SaaS solution. According to Microsoft,[10] SaaS architectures can be classified into one of four maturity levels whose key attributes are ease of configuration, multitenant efficiency, and scalability. Each level is distinguished from the previous one by the addition of one of these three attributes. The levels described by Microsoft are as follows.

- **SaaS Architectural Maturity Level 1—Ad-Hoc/ Custom.** The first level of maturity is actually no maturity at all. Each customer has a unique, customized version of the hosted application. The application runs its own instance on the host's servers. Migrating a traditional non-networked or client-server application to this level of SaaS maturity typically requires the least development effort and reduces operating costs by consolidating server hardware and administration.
- **SaaS Architectural Maturity Level 2—Configurability.** The second level of SaaS maturity provides greater program flexibility through configuration metadata. At this level, many customers can use separate instances of the same application. This allows a vendor to meet the varying needs of each customer by using detailed configuration options. It also allows the vendor to ease the maintenance burden by being able to update a common code base.
- **SaaS Architectural Maturity Level 3—Multitenant Efficiency.** The third maturity level adds multitenancy to the second level. This results in a single program instance that has the capability to serve all of the vendor's customers. This approach enables more efficient use of server resources without any

apparent difference to the end user, but ultimately this level is limited in its ability to scale massively.

- **SaaS Architectural Maturity Level 4—Scalable.** At the fourth SaaS maturity level, scalability is added by using a multitiered architecture. This architecture is capable of supporting a load-balanced farm of identical application instances running on a variable number of servers, sometimes in the hundreds or even thousands. System capacity can be dynamically increased or decreased to match load demand by adding or removing servers, with no need for further alteration of application software architecture.

Key Characteristics of SaaS

Deploying applications in a SOA is a more complex problem than is usually encountered in traditional models of software deployment. As a result, SaaS applications are generally priced based on the number of users that can have access to the service. There are often additional fees for the use of help desk services, extra bandwidth, and storage. SaaS revenue streams to the vendor are usually lower, initially, than traditional software license fees. However, the trade-off for lower license fees is a monthly recurring revenue stream, which is viewed by most corporate CFOs as a more predictable gauge of how the business is faring quarter to quarter. These monthly recurring charges are viewed much like maintenance fees for licensed software.[11] The key characteristics of SaaS software are the following:

- Network-based management and access to commercially available software from central locations rather than at each customer's site, enabling customers to access applications remotely via the Internet.
- Application delivery from a one-to-many model (single-instance, multitenant architecture), as opposed to a traditional one-to-one model.
- Centralized enhancement and patch updating that obviates any need for downloading and installing by a user. SaaS is often used in conjunction with a larger network of communications and collaboration software, sometimes as a plug-in to a PaaS architecture.

Benefits of the SaaS Model

Application deployment cycles inside companies can take years, consume massive resources, and yield unsatisfactory results. Although the initial decision to relinquish control is a difficult one, it is one that can lead to improved efficiency, lower risk, and a generous return on investment.[12] An increasing number of companies want to use the SaaS model for corporate applications such as customer relationship management, and those that fall under the Sarbanes-Oxley Act compliance umbrella (e.g., financial recording and human resources). The SaaS model helps enterprises ensure that all locations are using the correct application version and, therefore, that the format of the data being recorded and conveyed is consistent, compatible, and accurate. By placing the responsibility for an application onto the doorstep of a SaaS provider, enterprises can reduce administration and management burdens they would otherwise have for their own corporate applications. SaaS also helps to increase the availability of applications to global locations. SaaS also ensures that all application transactions are logged for compliance purposes. The benefits of SaaS to the customer are very clear:

- Streamlined administration
- Automated update and patch management services
- Data compatibility across the enterprise (all users have the same version of software)
- Facilitated, enterprise-wide collaboration
- Global accessibility

As we have pointed out previously, server virtualization can be used in SaaS architectures, either in place of or in addition to multitenancy. A major benefit of platform virtualization is that it can increase a system's capacity without any need for additional programming. Conversely, a huge amount of programming may be required in order to construct more efficient, multitenant applications. The effect of combining multitenancy and platform virtualization into a SaaS solution provides greater flexibility and performance to the end user. In this entry, we have discussed how the computing world has moved from stand-alone, dedicated computing to client/ network computing, and on into the cloud for remote computing. The advent of web-based services has given rise to a variety of service offerings, sometimes known collectively as XaaS. We covered these service models, focusing on the type of service provided to the customer (i.e., communications, infrastructure, monitoring, outsourced platforms, and software).

SUMMARY

In this entry, we have examined the various types of web services delivered from the cloud. Having the ability to leverage reusable software components across a network has great appeal to implementors. Today, the most common and successful example of cloud computing is SaaS, but other functions, including communication, infrastructure, and platforms, are also core components of cloud computing. Because of the extremely low barriers to entry, offerings have been made available to consumers and small businesses, as well as mid-sized and large enterprises. This is a key differentiator from many SOA offerings, which will be covered next.

REFERENCES

1. Gartner Press Release, Gartner Forecasts Worldwide Communications-as-a-Service Revenue to Total $252 Million in 2007. August **2007** (accessed January 2009).
2. Moore, G.E. Cramming more components onto integrated circuits. Electron. Mag. **1965**, *4*, (accessed January 2009).
3. http://en.wikipedia.org/wiki/Infrastructure_as_a_Service (accessed January 2009).
4. Bon, J.V. The Guide to IT Service Management, Vol. I; Addison-Wesley: New York, NY, 2002; 131.
5. http://searchdatacenter.techtarget.com/sDefinition/0,, sid80_gci903730,00.html# (accessed January 2009).
6. http://developer.amazonwebservices.com/connect/entry. jspa?externalID = 1347 (accessed January 2009).
7. http://en.wikipedia.org/wiki/Monitoring_as_a_service (accessed January 2009).
8. Software as a Service Threatens Partner Revenue and Profit Streams, New Partners Emerging, IDC Research Shows, from http://www.idc.com/getdoc.jsp?contain erId = prUS20884007, *20 Sep* **2007**, (accessed January 2009).
9. http://en.wikipedia.org/wiki/Software_as_a_service (accessed January 2009).
10. http://www.microsoft.com/serviceproviders/saas/ saasplatform.mspx (accessed January 2009).
11. Traudt, E.; Konary, A. Software as a Service Taxonomy and Research Guide, IDC, http://www.idc.com/getdoc. jsp?containerId = 33453&pageType = PRINT FRIENDLY#33453-S-0001, **2005** (accessed January 2009).
12. http://searchnetworking.techtarget.com/generic/0,295582, sid7_gci1164670,00.html (accessed January 2009).

Web Services: Security

Lynda L. McGhie
Information Security Officer (ISO)/Risk Manager, Private Client Services (PCS), Wells Fargo Bank, Cameron Park, California, U.S.A.

Abstract

This entry discusses a core set of security functions that must be addressed in any successful security infrastructure. Web services security is introduced, defined, and discussed within the framework of the technology and tools that are already in place within a particular environment and how one can use the security control capabilities within Web services technologies to provide similar functionality.

INTRODUCTION

IT security professionals are challenged to keep abreast of constantly evolving and changing technology and, thus, new and complex security solutions. Often, it is impossible to implement new security control mechanisms concurrently with the implementation of new technology. One challenge most often facing Information Systems Security Organizations (ISSOs) is the competition with other business and IT departments for a share of IT budgets. Another is the availability of resources to include trained security architects, engineers, and administrators. In many large and complex organizations, the IT organization and hence the security support functions are often fragmented and spread throughout the enterprise to include the lines of business. This is a good thing because it increases awareness and builds support for the untenable task at hand, yet it most often results in the ongoing implementation of a very fragmented security infrastructure and company security posture.

Security is typically not brought into the beginning of any project, application, or systems development life cycle. More often, security is asked to sign off just prior to implementation. How then does the ISSO catch up with or stay abreast of the constantly changing IT and business environment while ensuring that the enterprise is secure and security support services are optimized and effective? This entry looks at that challenge with regard to Web services and suggests a roadmap or a blueprint for integrating Web services security into an existing enterprise security strategy, policies, architecture, and access management function. A primary goal is to ensure that the above support components are designed to smoothly integrate new technology and applications without a great demand on resources or disruption. Another goal is to optimize previous and existing investments, yet be able to smoothly integrate new solutions.

Web services introduces a whole new set of standards, capabilities, vocabulary, and acronyms to learn and relate back to existing threats, vulnerabilities, and security solutions. The entry discusses a core set of security functions that must be addressed in any successful security infrastructure. Web services security is introduced, defined, and discussed within the framework of the technology and tools that are already in place within a particular environment and how one can use the security control capabilities within Web services technologies to provide similar functionality.

It is hoped that by framing legacy functionality and its associated toolset in light of introducing a new technology, standards, and functionality, the discussion will have a solid baseline and point of reference, resulting in greater understanding and utility.

This entry focuses on Web security services standards—what they are and what they do. Security should be applied only when and to the extent required, and the security architecture design should be as simplistic as possible and require as few resources to maintain as possible. To the extent feasible, access controls should be based on group-level policies, and individual access rules should be the exception rather than the norm. Remember that baseline security policies and access control requirements should originate from company business requirements and corporate threat profiles, *not* from technology. In this case, technology *is not* the driver. Sure, security tools are evolving fast and furiously, and for those of us who have been in security for some time, we finally have the wherewithal to actually do our jobs, but we need to stay in check and *not* over-design a Web services security solution that over delivers on the baseline requirements.

This entry concludes with a discussion of changes to firewalls and traditional external perimeter controls, as well as Web services threat models. It also looks at the evolutionary aspects of the legal framework now so intrinsic to any enterprise security program.

W3C-XML

Encyclopedia of Information Systems and Technology, DOI: 10.1081/E-EIST-120046397

Web services security introduces a whole new set of security capabilities and functionality. Web services have been slow to take off and evolve. Standards have existed for several years and have really matured, and for the most part vendors are aligned and in agreement. There are a few vendor alliances and a minimal number of groups with differing approaches, although more or less in agreement. This is different from what was seen in the past when other service-oriented infrastructures were proposed (e.g., CORBA and DCE). This alone will enhance the potential for success with Web services standards. Companies have been slow to move toward embracing Web services for various reasons: up-front investments, the newness of the technology, and also the maturity of the security solutions. Nowadays, companies are moving from point-to-point or service-to-service internal applications to enterprise-wide and externally facing, many-to-many implementations.

When the World Wide Web (WWW) was first introduced, it was viewed more as an Internet tool and certainly *not* as a production-worthy system within the enterprise. First uses included internal reporting, where data was transported from legacy applications to the Web environment for reporting. A later use was in browser GUI front-end-to-legacy applications. Still later as security became more robust and layered or defense-in-depth security architectures enabled the acceptance of greater risk within the Internet and Web application environments, Web-based applications began to move to DMZs (protected networks between the internal corporate network and the Internet). Eventually, these applications moved out to the Internet itself. Today e-business applications are served from customer-facing portals on the Internet, and many companies conduct their entire business this way, communicating with partners, supply chains, and customers.

With Web services, this evolution will continue and become more cost-effective because application development will become easier, more standardized, and the time to market for applications will greatly decrease. Along with this will come reusable services and functionality and a more robust set of capabilities than has ever been seen before in the application space. However, the road to Web services security will be a scary ride for the ISSO team.

In further examining the capabilities and solutions for Web services security, remember that the same vulnerabilities exist. The exploits may take a slightly different path, but the overall security solutions and functions do not change—that is, threat and vulnerability management, alert and patch management, and crisis management. Keep in mind some of the same baseline security tenets in going forward, including protecting data as close to the data as possible. Where possible, use the native capabilities within the operating system or vendor product, and strive to use a dedicated security product as opposed to building individual security solutions and control mechanisms into each application. There are differing approaches to doing this today within Web services, and this entry examines some of the choices going forward.

As Web services security standards continue to coalesce, vendors align, products evolve, and vendors either merge, get bought out, or fall by the wayside, the number of directions, solutions, and decisions decreases. But that does not change the complexity of the problem, or get us any closer to the right solution set for each company's unique set of today's requirements. How each company solves this problem will be unique to its business vertical, customer, and stakeholder demands, existing IT infrastructures and investments, resource availability, and business posture and demand.

One needs to choose from the resultant set of vendors and decide on looking at suites of products and functionality from a single vendor (Microsoft, BEA Systems, IBM, etc.) or adding third-party vendors to the mix, such as Netegrity, Sanctum, and Westbridge. ISSOs will traditionally approach this dilemma by reducing the number of products to support and administer separately. They will be looking for front-end provisioning systems and back-end integrated and correlated audit systems. They will also strive to reduce some of the security products, hoping that vendors combine and add functionality such as network firewalls, moving to incorporate application layer functionality. However, in the Web services security space, there is a need for new products because the functionality one is trying to secure is new, and existing products *do not* address these problems or have the capability to secure them.

Okay, there is a new technology, and for once there is agreement on a set of standards and solutions and therefore fewer choices to make and vendors to select, but how does one decide? If there is a heavy investment in one vendor and that vendor is in one or more alliances, it makes sense to join up there. If one is an agnostic or has some of everything, the decision becomes more difficult. This author suggests that you inventory your legacy, document your direction, and conduct a study. Look at a business impact analysis based on where integrated business processes are going at your company in the future. Which applications will be invested in, and which will be sun-setting?

PROFITING FROM PREVIOUS SECURITY INVESTMENTS

Current security investments, particularly at the infrastructure layer, are still necessary, and enhancements there should continue with the goal of integrating to a common, standard, and single architecture.

The same components of a well-planned and well-executed security implementation need to remain and be enhanced to support Web services. Unfortunately, as Web services standards continue to evolve, as applications migrate to Web services, and as vendors and partners adopt differing standards, approaches, and directions, the ISSO's job gets more difficult and more complex. There will be some false starts and undoubtedly some thrown away, but nevertheless it is best to get an early start on understanding the technology and how it will be implemented and utilized in a particular environment. And finally, how it will be integrated and secured in your environment. Most likely, one will need to support a phased Web services security implementation as tools and capabilities become available and integrate. One might be balancing and straddling two or more security solution environments simultaneously, while keeping in mind the migration path to interface and eventually integrate to a single solution.

Investments in security infrastructure are still of value as a baseline framework and a springboard to Web services security. Also, look to augmentation through people, process, and other technology to determine what to keep, what to throw away, and what to adapt to the new and emerging environment. Do not count on having fewer security products or capabilities in the future, but certainly do count on automating a lot of today's manual processes.

Looking then to understanding the new through the old, we now consider and address the basic components and security imperatives embodied in a typical security model:

- *Confidentiality*: Data or information is not made available or disclosed to unauthorized persons or processes.
- *Integrity*: The assurance that data or information has not been altered or destroyed in an unauthorized manner.
- *Availability*: Data or information is accessible and useable upon demand by an authorized person.

- *Authentication*: The verification of credentials presented by an individual or process in order to determine identity.
- *Authorization*: To grant an individual permission to do something or be somewhere.
- *Audit*: Collects information about security operating requests and the outcome of those requests for the purposes of reporting, proof of compliance, non-repudiation, etc.

Table 1 compares today's Web security tools, standards, and capabilities to the new Web service security capabilities with respect to the model.

In migrating a security toolset, one will be using many of these control mechanisms together, and hopefully as one's company becomes more standardized to Web services, one will leave some of these behind. Nevertheless, existing investments are salvageable and still need to be augmented with people, processes, and technology, as well as a combination of technical, physical, and administrative controls.

WEB SERVICES APPLICATIONS

A Web services application is an application that interacts with the world using XML for data definition, WDSL for service definition, and SOAP for communication with other software. Web services application components operate across a distributed environment spread across multiple host systems. They interact via SOAP and XML. Other services include UDDI-based discovery (Web services directory) and SAML-based federated security policies.

WEB SERVICES

- A stack of emerging standards that define protocols and create a loosely coupled framework for

Table 1 Web security tools, standards, and capabilities versus new Web service security capabilities

Security functionality	Traditional standards and solutions	Web services security solutions	Protective goals
Confidentiality	SSL, HTTPS, IPSec, VPN	XML encryption	Can prying eyes see it?
Integrity	OS hardening, ACLs, configuration/change/patch management	XML signature	Was it altered before I got it?
Authentication	Username/passwords, tokens, smart cards, LDAP, AD, digital certificates, challenge-response, biometrics	SAML, XACML	Are you who you say you are?
Authorization	ACLs, RBACs, LDAP, AD, OS, etc.	SAML, XACML	Are you allowed to have it?
Audit	Logging, monitoring, scanning, etc.	Logging, monitoring, scanning, etc.	Can I prove what happened?

W3C–XML

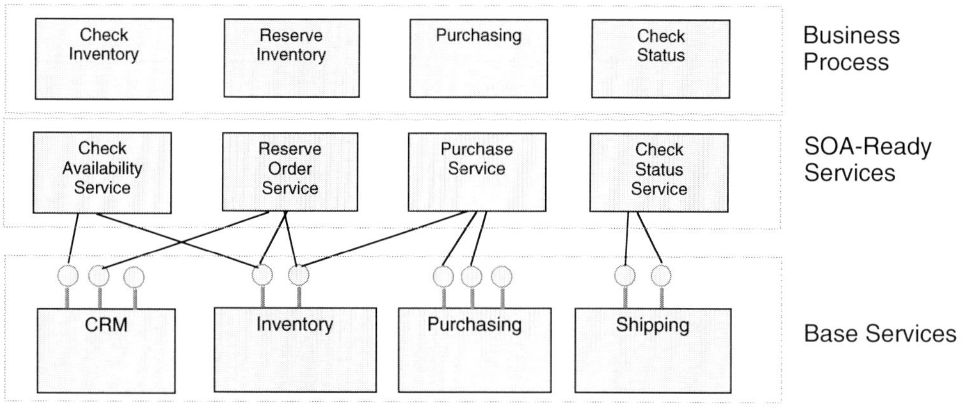

Fig. 1 Service-oriented architecture.

programmatic communication among disparate systems (The Stencil Group)

- An emerging architectural model for developing and deploying software applications (The Stencil Group)
- Self-contained, modular applications that can be described, published, located, and invoked over a network—generally, the World Wide Web (IBM)

SERVICE-ORIENTED ARCHITECTURES

Service-Oriented Architectures (SOA) is a development in distributed computing, wherein applications call other applications over a network. Functionality is published over the network, utilizing two distinct principles: the ability to find the functionality and the ability to connect to it. In Web services architecture, these activities correspond to three distinct roles: Web services provider, Web services requestor, and Web services broker.

SOA is a process and an architectural mindset that enables a type of IT structure to be put in place. It requires significant coordination and integration throughout the enterprise, to include IT and business organizations. SOA is a continuous process that changes the way IT technologies are developed and used. One of the benefits of SOA is that an organization does not have to change all of its applications right away to derive a benefit. Companies can pursue a strategy of making some of their applications services-oriented and gradually migrating future applications. Often, a significant ROI is attained at all levels. Because SOA is all about reuse, the first project often yields a positive ROI.

Fig. 1 defines and illustrates the interaction and interface of SOA layered components.

SIMPLE OBJECT ACCESS PROTOCOL

Simple Object Access Protocol (SOAP) provides the definition of XML-based information that can be used

for exchanging structured and typed information between peers in a decentralized, distributed environment.

SOAP is fundamentally a stateless, one-way message exchange paradigm, but applications can create more complex interaction patterns (e.g., request/response, request/multiple responses, etc.) by combining such one-way exchanges with features provided by an underlying protocol or application-specific information. SOAP is silent on the semantics of any application-specific data it conveys, as it is on issues such as the routing of SOAP messages, reliable data transfer, firewall traversal, etc. However, SOAP provides the framework by which application-specific information can be conveyed in an extensible manner. Also, SOAP provides a full description of the required actions taken by a SOAP node on receiving a SOAP message.

A SOAP message is basically a one-way transmission between SOAP nodes—from a SOAP sender to a SOAP receiver—but SOAP messages are expected to be combined by applications to implement more complex interaction patterns, ranging from request/response to multiple, back-and-forth "conversational" exchanges.

CONFIDENTIALITY

When data is stored, access control or authorization can potentially suffice for protection; but when data is in transit, encryption is often the most appropriate way to ensure confidentiality. Remember that decisions regarding what technology to use and in what layer of the OSI stack to place security may or may not be a function of technology, but may be more associated with the business process being addressed and the sensitivity and criticality of the information processed. Secure Socket Layer (SSL) can be used if the SOAP request is bound to HTTP or IPSec at the network layer. XML encryption enables confidentiality across multiple SOAP messages

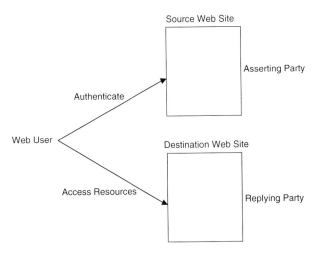

Fig. 2 Authentication and authorization.

and Web services. If SSL is used alone, there is a gap at each endpoint.

DIGITAL SIGNATURES AND ENCRYPTION

Digital signatures perform a key role in Web services, including non-repudiation, authentication, and data integrity. The XML signature is a building block for many Web security services technologies.

This functionality has been provided previously for Web applications utilizing S/MIME and PKCS#7. Public key cryptography standards (PKCS) is a voluntary standard (created by RSA and others). The W3C Digital Signature Working Group ("DSig") proposes a standard format for making digitally signed, machine-readable assertions about a particular information resource. Prior to XML signatures, PKCS could digitally sign an XML document, but not in a standardized DML format. It was also not possible to sign just a portion of a document. Binding a signature to a document already existed for e-mail using S/SMIME, therefore enabling the recipient to verify the integrity and non-repudiation of the signer.

AUTHENTICATION AND AUTHORIZATION

Secure Assertion Markup Language (SAML) defines a framework for exchanging security information between online business partners. More precisely, SAML defines a common XML framework for exchanging security assertions between entities. SAML's purpose is to define, enhance, and maintain a standard XML-based framework for creating and exchanging authentication and authorization information. SAML is different from other security systems, due to its approach of expressing assertions about a subject that other applications within a network can trust. These assertions support specific

entities, whether or not those entities are individuals or computer systems. These entities must be identifiable within a specific security context, such as human who is a member of a workgroup or a computer that is part of a network domain. An assertion can be defined as a claim, statement, or declaration. This means that assertions can only be accepted as true subject to the integrity and authenticity of the entity making the assertion (entity making claim/assertion must have authority). If one can trust the authority making the assertions, the assertion can be accepted as true with the same level of certainty as any other certification authority can be trusted. Additionally, SAML defines a client/server protocol for exchanging XML message requests and responses.

SAML is concerned with access control for authenticated principals based on a set of policies (see Fig. 2). There are two actions that must be performed with respect to access control in any enterprise system: 1) making decisions about access control based on a set of policies, and 2) enforcing those decisions at the system level; SAML provides two functions: policy decision point and policy enforcement point.

SAML is critical to the ability to deliver Web services applications because it provides the basis for interoperable authentication and authorization among disparate systems, and it supports complex workflows and new business models. The adoption of SAML by vendors of operating systems, identity and access management systems, portals, and application servers will simplify security integration across heterogeneous environments (Gartner IGG-05282003-02).

EXTENSIBLE ACCESS CONTROL MARKUP LANGUAGE

Extensible Access Control Markup Language (XACML) is being produced by the OASIS standards body to define an XML vocabulary to express the rules on which access control decisions are based. XACML enables interoperability across differing formats, enabling single sign-on, etc. XACML defines both architecture and syntax. The syntax is a means of defining how various entities process these XACML documents to perform access control:

- Defines rules to allow access to resources (read, write, execute, etc.) (more granular, defines XML vocabulary)
- Defines the format of the rules (rules for making rules) (policies)
- Policy exchange format between parties using different authorization rules (interoperability across disparate formats for SSO)

W3C–
XML

- Access control: ACLs and RBACs = syntax and architecture
- Authentication, confidentiality, integrity, and privacy

Focus on deploying Web services security and management infrastructures, as opposed to building application-based security. Much of Web services security can be implemented external to the application. Enterprises should plan to deploy a Web services management system or a security infrastructure that remains centralized, that is available for distributed Web services applications, and that is managed outside the application by the security management system and the ISSO. The benefit of this approach is that security services and capabilities are bundled together in a single Web services architecture rather than within stovepipe applications utilizing different standards, mechanisms, products, implementations, and configurations.

SECURITY MANAGEMENT AND PROVISIONING

With SOA, the challenge is to configure, maintain, and deploy consistent security policies across the Web services infrastructure. Web services are created and used many times over by many applications written and supported by many different programmers. Programs, other services, or human beings can execute these services from many places within the network. Security management and provisioning systems offload the security burden from developers and ensure consistent security application and management. Many systems calling Web services do not have the mapping capabilities to associate and authenticate requestors and repliers. Security Management Systems can provide this interface and mapping to META directories (AD, LDAP, native, etc.).

Complexity has traditionally been the enemy of security. A centralized security model utilizing common security policies and toolsets reduces the complexity and moves the security responsibility into the hands of the security professional. Centralized identity management and provisioning also provides for a single repository for authorized objects to the enterprise. It enables changes to be dynamically applied across the Web services enterprise for quick termination of accounts or dynamic change to move objects from one group policy to another.

LIBERTY ALLIANCE PROJECT AND PASSPORT

Today's administrative and business environment calls for information sharing on an unprecedented scale, from government to business to citizen. Sharing and interoperating among agencies, businesses, and governments around the world create opportunities to simplify processes and unify work, as well as improve the overall performance of government. Secure interoperability, based on identity management solutions, enables substantial cost savings, streamlined processes, and faster communication of vital information to the benefit of governments and citizens of all nations. At the core of this revolution is the concept of identity management and the need for a standard that is open, interoperable, and decentralized. In addition, it must allow for privacy safeguards across all sectors.

The Liberty Alliance Project was established to address this need, and to tackle the twin issues of standards and trust. The Liberty Alliance is ushering in federated identity implementations that allow the public sector to find substantial benefits, including:

- Improved alliances, both within governments and between governments, through interoperability with autonomy
- Faster response time for critical communications
- Cost avoidance, cost reduction, and increased operational efficiencies
- Stronger security and risk management
- Interoperability and decreased development time

. NET PASSPORT

Passport is a suite of services for authenticating (signing in) users across a number of applications. The suite includes the Passport single sign-in service and the Kids Passport service.

.NET Passport Single Sign-In Service

The Passport single sign-in service solves the authentication problem for users by allowing them to create a single set of credentials that will enable them to sign in to any site that supports a Passport service (referred to as "participating sites").

Passport simplifies sign-in and registration, lowering barriers to access for the millions of users with Passport accounts today. The objective of the Passport single sign-in service is to help increase customer satisfaction by allowing easy access without the frustration of repetitive registrations and forgotten passwords.

As a part of the single sign-in service, if a user chooses to, he can store commonly used information in a Passport profile and, at his option, transmit it to the participating sites he visits. This reduces the barriers to acquiring customers because new users are not required to retype all of their information when they register at a new site. It also enables the sites they visit to customize and enhance their experience without having to prompt them for user information.

WEB SERVICES THREAT MODELS

Gartner predicts that by 2005, Web services will have reopened 70% of the attack paths against Internet-connected systems that were closed by network firewalls in the 1990s. Web services applications bypass traditional perimeter defenses and firewalls, and communicate through them over Hypertext Transport Protocol (HTTP) port 80 or Simple Mail Transport Protocol (SMTP). The threat then enters the protected internal network through the firewall and enters the application/Web services environment. The same attack scenarios that we have been seeing apply here as well:

- Traditional identity attacks, "Web services enabled":
  o Identity spoofing
  o Eavesdropping
  o Man-in-the-middle attack
- Content-borne attacks:
  o SQL injection, LDAP injection, Xpath injection
- Operational attacks:
  o XML denial-of-service
  o Malicious or inadvertent attack

EVOLUTION OF FIREWALLS

Traditional network firewalls protect the physical boundaries of a network (category 1). The functionality provided by network firewalls is starting to expand to move up the OSI stack toward the application layer (category 2). There is a distinction between application level firewalls (category 3) and XML firewalls (category 4), and some situations may require some or all of these solutions.

Network Firewalls: Category 1

A network-level firewall sits at the doorstep of a private network as a guard and typically provides the following services:

- Monitors all incoming traffic
- Checks the identity of information requestors trying to access specific company resources
- Authenticates users based on their identities, which can be the network addresses of the service requesters or the security tokens
- Checks security and business policies to filter access requests and verify whether the service requestor has the right to access the intended resource

- Provides for encrypted messages so that confidential business information can be sent across the untrusted Internet privately

Application Firewalls: Category 2

Application-level firewalls will be required to provide edge shielding of servers running Web services exposed applications. They will focus on a small number of protocols—mainly HTTP and SMTP in the Web services world—and require a high degree of application awareness to filter out malicious XML constructs and encapsulations.

Such firewalls will be embedded in servers or act in conjunction with traditional firewalls, in much the same way that gateway-side content inspection is implemented today. Software-based solutions will not be successful on general-purpose Internet servers, but will be embedded in appliances or at the network level.

Application firewalls work in an interesting way: by learning what well-formed traffic to and from an application looks like and identifying the unexpected. To do this, Web application firewalls must inspect packets at a deeper level than ordinary firewalls. As with intrusion detection systems (IDSs), this is not a plug-and-play service; one must calibrate application firewalls carefully to reduce false positives without letting sneaky attacks through.

XML Firewalls: Category 3

XML firewalls can be used to protect corporations against the unique dangers and intrusions posed by Web services. These firewalls can examine SOAP headers and XML tags, and based on what they find, distinguish legitimate from unauthorized content. This entry now takes a look at how XML firewalls work, which vendors make them, and whether they are right for your organization today.

Traditional firewalls protect a network's perimeter by blocking incoming Internet traffic using several different means. Some block all TCP ports except for port 80 (HTTP traffic), port 443 (HTTPS traffic), and port 25 (e-mail traffic). Some ban traffic from specific IP addresses, or ban traffic based on the traffic's usage characteristics.

The problem with these firewalls when it comes to Web services is that, as a general rule, many Web services are designed to come in over port 80. So even if the service is a malicious one, the firewall will let it through. That is because traditional firewalls cannot filter out traffic based on the traffic's underlying content—they can only filter on the packet level, *not* the content level. That is where XML firewalls come in. They are designed to examine the XML content of the

Table 2 Contracts and legal issues

What was agreed to?	Data security and Internet security
When was it agreed to?	Time-stamping
Who agreed to it?	Certificate security and private key security
Proof: trustworthy audit trails	System security, LAN internal security, and LAN perimeter security

incoming traffic, understand the content, and based on that understanding, take an action—for example, letting the traffic in or blocking it.

XML firewalls typically work by examining SOAP message headers. The header may have detailed information put there specifically for the firewall to examine; and if so, the firewall can take an action based on that information. Even if the header does not have this information, XML firewalls can still take actions based on what is in the header. The header, for example, might have information about the recipients of the message, about the security of the overall message, or about the intermediaries through which the message has passed.

In addition, XML firewalls can look into the body of the message itself and examine it down to the tag level. It can tell if a message is an authorized one or is coming from an authorized recipient. If a federated ID system is involved, it can examine the SAML security token, and see if it trusts the token's creator, and then take action based on that—for example, blocking traffic, sending it to a secure environment where it can be further examined, or allowing it to pass through.

XML firewalls have other methods of protection as well. They can understand metadata about the Web service's service requestor as well as metadata about the Web service operation itself. They can gather information about the service requestor, such as understanding what role the requestor plays in the current Web service request. XML firewalls can also provide authentication, decryption, and real-time monitoring and reporting.

WEB SERVICES AND TRUST MODELS

The Web services trust framework ensures integrity in the authentication process, trusting who is vouching for whom. Good-faith trust is what contracts are about, and trust enters into a multitude of contractual arrangements. Through the Web services trust framework, the ebXML (electronic business XML) collaboration protocol profile and the agreement system enable one to make that kind of contractual arrangement machine-readable. One is agreeing to certain aspects of the interaction that one is

going to have on a technical level, on a machine-machine level. Trust is built by explicitly specifying what it is one is going to do.

CONTRACTS AND LEGAL ISSUES

What are the compelling legal issues driving security within Web services? Be sure to consult with a legal professional throughout the life cycle of Web services development projects. In legal matters relating to Web services, being technically astute without being legally savvy could be trouble if the legal implication of a technical vulnerability is unknown—that is, in today's environment where end-to-end security may not be technically feasible or not deployed (see Table 2). What security is required to contract online? Take a minimalist view.

A contract can be defined as a promise or a set of promises the law will enforce. A contract does not depend on any signature; it depends on the will of the contracting parties. Also, some feel that a digital signature in itself is not analogous to an ink signature. Some claim that it is more difficult to forge ink on a paper signature repeatedly than steal an unsecured private key on a PC (but there is ongoing debate regarding this).

This is a can of worms and obviously left to the legal experts. It is important to note that the technical experts must confer with understanding regarding the risk, the value of the transaction or application, and the legal implications of binding contracts and holistic security. Enterprises must ensure and be able to demonstrate due diligence when conducting business on the Internet utilizing Web services.

CONCLUSION

While Web services attempt to simplify application security architectures and bundles with integrated standards, there are still many pieces that must be consciously designed and applied to equal a secure whole. Web services offers a lot of promise to developers of Web-based e-business applications or even the enhancement of traditional interfaces to legacy or even distributed systems. There is a bigger benefit to using this technology than not using it. However, security is still an issue and a challenge, and one needs to be aware of the potential security problems that might occur.

Holes, fillers, new standards, and solutions create a beacon with a clear and ever-resounding message: Proceed with caution!

WiMAX Networks: Security Issues

Mohamad Badra
College of Technological Innovation, Zayed University, Dubai, United Arab Emirates

Sherali Zeadally
College of Communication and Information, University of Kentucky, Lexington, Kentucky, U.S.A.

Abstract

The Worldwide Interoperability for Microwave Access (WiMAX) technology is based on the IEEE 802.16 standard which offers flexible fixed and mobile wireless solutions along with long-distance high-bandwidth and broadband services. It combines the economic and technological advantages of different transmission technologies to provide a context-aware, adaptive, and ubiquitous service access. Security is one of the major problems that arise at the radio link level between WiMAX nodes. We first briefly present the security of WiMAX access systems as defined in the IEEE 802.16 standards. Then we discuss various security issues that arise in WiMAX infrastructures. We present and discuss several proposed security approaches aimed at achieving an adaptive, scalable, rapid, easy-to-manage, and secure WiMAX service access.

INTRODUCTION

Wireless communication systems (fixed and mobile) have constantly evolved since the introduction of the radio telephone systems. Wireless systems started as pure analog systems to be later converted to digital as with Global System for Mobile communications (GSM). The switch to digital technology has led to the development and emergence of different types of communication systems. These systems have traditionally been circuit-switched but have gradually become packet switched (such as Fourth generation [4G] technologies).

The main application of wireless communication systems was the telephone system but in recent years, they have gradually been deployed in extending local area networks (LANs) wirelessly with the introduction of wireless LAN. This technology provides Internet access to users wirelessly while technologies such as Enhanced Data rates for GSM Evolution enabled users to connect to the Internet through its cellular telephone systems by establishing mobile networks. Technological advances in third generation (3G) technologies allowed Wi-Fi technology to become an extension of not only to LANs but also to mobile networks especially with the emergence of the IEEE 802.11n[1] standard and the introduction of smart mobile devices.

To extend wireless accessibility from LAN to WAN, various design architectures that integrate wireless LANs with cellular networks have been proposed in the literature. In addition, we have also witnessed the introduction of technologies such as Long-Term Evolution (LTE) and WiMAX that enable WAN access from LANs. LTE and WiMAX technologies enable Internet protocol (IP)-based communications between wireless LANs and cellular networks. Increased transmission speeds (see Fig. 1) by LTE and WiMAX technologies have also fueled their fast adoption and deployment as alternative technologies for high-speed Internet access.

The number of users of International Mobile Telecommunications-2000 (IMT-2000) mobile communication services that was launched in October 2001 has already reached about 2.1 billion subscribers in the world at the end of 2012. IMT-2000 supports a variety of advanced multimedia services such as video communications and high speed Internet access. Since the inception of IMT-2000, 4G technologies have emerged and continue to be widely adopted in various parts of the world because of their superior performance (as shown in Fig. 1). The development process of new mobile systems consists of developing the requirements they are expected to meet, providing solutions that satisfy these requirements, demonstrating that each technology satisfies the requirements, as well as building international consensus through the standardization activities. Fig. 1 summarizes some of the recent advances in wireless communication technologies with respect to the generation of the mobile communication systems, transmission speed (Kilo/Mega/Giga bits per second), switching technology, and mobile and fixed technology.

W3C–
XML

Encyclopedia of Information Systems and Technology, DOI: 10.1081/E-EIST-120048801

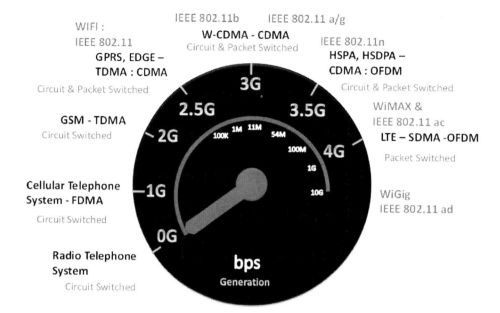

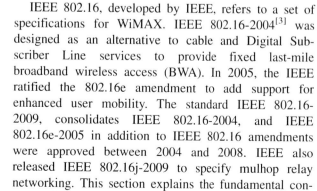

EDGE: Enhanced Data rates for GSM Evolution
FDMA: Frequency Division Multiple Access
GPRS: General Packet Radio Service
GSM: Global System for Mobile Communications
HSDPA: High-Speed Downlink Packet Access
HSPA: High Speed Packet Access

OFDM: Orthogonal Frequency-Division Multiplexing
SDMA: Space-Division Multiple Access
TDMA; Time Division Multiple Access
WiFi: Wireless Fidelity
WiGig: Wireless Gigabit Alliance
WiMAX: Worldwide Interoperability for Microwave Access

Fig. 1 Evolution of wireless technologies.

WiMAX OVERVIEW

The WiMAX technology, based on the IEEE 802.16 Air Interface Standard,[2] has evolved significantly over the last few years. WiMAX has been widely deployed in a variety of network environments and for several applications such as last mile broadband services and has converged with both Internet and 4G infrastructures. The convergence between WiMAX and LTE allows operators to provide multi-mode networks. In fact, WiMAX descends from Wi-Fi rather than from cellular technologies, whereas LTE is backward compatible with existing GSM and 3G networks.

IEEE 802.16, developed by IEEE, refers to a set of specifications for WiMAX. IEEE 802.16-2004[3] was designed as an alternative to cable and Digital Subscriber Line services to provide fixed last-mile broadband wireless access (BWA). In 2005, the IEEE ratified the 802.16e amendment to add support for enhanced user mobility. The standard IEEE 802.16-2009, consolidates IEEE 802.16-2004, and IEEE 802.16e-2005 in addition to IEEE 802.16 amendments were approved between 2004 and 2008. IEEE also released IEEE 802.16j-2009 to specify mulhop relay networking. This section explains the fundamental concepts of WiMAX technology, including its topologies, and discusses the evolution of the IEEE 802.16

standard. In 2012, IEEE released IEEE Standard 802.16-2012, a revision of IEEE Std 802.16-2009 that consolidates material from IEEE Std 802.16j-2009 and IEEE Std 802.16h-2010. The standard IEEE 802.16-2012 also incorporates IEEE Std 802.16m-2011 and supersedes as well as makes obsolete IEEE Std 802.16-2009, IEEE Std 802.16j-2009, IEEE Std 802.16h-2010, and IEEE Std 802.16m-2011.

The standard IEEE 802.16-2012[2] specifies the air interface, including the medium access control (MAC) layer and the PHYsical (PHY) layer, of combined fixed and mobile point-to-multipoint BWA systems providing multiple services.

The motivations for the deployments of WiMAX include high-performance and cost effective broadband wireless network access. While the most obvious advantage of WiMAX is to make high quality, long-range data, and voice communications affordable, there are also other major benefits including the following:

- *Installing and maintaining flexibility*: Installation of a WiMAX system by end-users is fast and easy and eliminates the terminal cabling costs. It extends to rural areas where wires are hard to install.
- *Ease of use*: WiMAX is easy for novice and expert users alike, eliminating the need of a significant knowledge to take advantage of WiMAX.

- *Transparency*: WiMAX is transparent to a user network, allowing applications to work in the same way as they do in wired LANs and mobile networks.
- *Scalability*: WiMAX is designed to be simple or complex; they range from networks suitable for a small number of nodes to full infrastructure-based networks of thousands of nodes and a large PHY area by adding relay stations (RSs) to extend coverage and to provide users roaming capabilities between different areas.
- *Improved Quality of Service (QoS)*: WiMAX supports several classes of services to provide *QoS* and to handle delay-sensitive and loss tolerant interactive applications such as video conferencing and streaming.
- *Support of various applications*: WiMAX has been developed to provide higher data rates for supporting various types of applications such as streaming media, interactive gaming, Voice over IP, and video conferencing.

As previously mentioned, WiMAX has been developed to support higher data rates, coverage, availability, and mobility. However, there are some constraints introduced by WiMAX, especially the shared medium, interference, and to the signal. Consequently, WiMAX security becomes harder to maintain compared to wired networks. In WiMAX, it is possible for an attacker to snoop on confidential communications or modify them to gain access to the network much more easily than wired networks. The temptation for unauthorized access and eavesdropping is also possible because an attacker could easily access the underlying communications medium. Other security issues are mostly because of the lack of PHY protection of the wireless network access or the radio transmissions. WiMAX handles security issues such as authentication, key exchange, and confidentiality by establishing secure connections between subscriber/mobile station (SS/MS) and the base station (BS). The encryption is achieved by using symmetric-key algorithms such as triple data encryption standard (3DES) whereas the key exchange could be established by deploying RSA-based certificates.

The rest of the entry presents a more detailed description of the various WiMAX standards from a

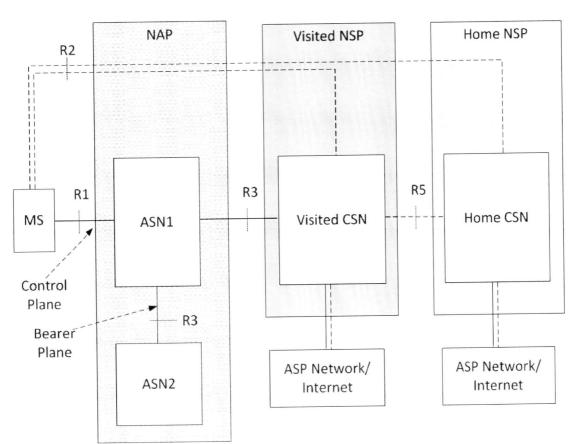

NAP: Network Access Provider
ASN: Access Service Network
MS: Mobile Station

ASP: Application Service Provider
CSN: Connectivity Service Network

Fig. 2 The WiMAX network reference model.[4]

security perspective; challenges and possible attacks in WiMAX; WiMAX infrastructure security including authentication, authorization, and access control; confidentiality and privacy; and key management and establishment.

WiMAX ARCHITECTURE AND TOPOLOGIES

The WiMAX architecture supports sharing of the network with a wide variety of business models, namely, network access provider (NAP) and network service provider (NSP). The NAP provides WiMAX radio access infrastructure to one or more NSPs.

A WiMAX network reference model consists of several functional and logical entities and interfaces between those entities (Fig. 2), namely, SS/MS, BS, Access Service Network (ASN), ASN gateway (ASN-GW), and connectivity service network (CSN).[4]

- A SS/MS is a communication device that provides connectivity to a WiMAX network to deliver high-speed data, voice, and multimedia. WiMAX enables the simultaneous support for both mobile WiMAX and fixed WiMAX enabled through universal serial bus adapter, smart phones, PC card, etc.
- The BS is the entity that ensures the connectivity over the air interface to the MS and manages access to the operator network. It acts as a RS in the multi-hop relay topology to forward the packets from one hop to another hop in the network.
- An ASN is defined as a set of network functions providing radio access to WiMAX subscribers. These functions mainly include network discovery and selection, connectivity between the SS and the CSN, QoS and policy management for admission control, radio resource management, intra-ASN mobility, paging, and location management.
- An ASN-GW is placed at the edge of the ASN for mapping the radio bearer to the IP network. It includes multiple functions such as bearer plane; authentication, authorization, and accounting (AAA); context and profile management; service flow authorization; paging; and radio resource and handover management.
- A CSN is defined as a set of network functions that provide IP connectivity services to the WiMAX subscribers. A CSN typically consists of several network elements such as routers, AAA proxy/servers, policy and admission control servers, content service gateways, interworking gateways, and user databases. A CSN can ensure multiple functions such as Internet access, WiMAX subscriber billing and interoperator settlement, inter-CSN tunneling for roaming, inter-ASN mobility, and connectivity to WiMAX services.

The WiMAX network reference model contains reference points R1–R8 representing the interface between different WiMAX functional entities.

- R1: Reference point between MS and ASN implementing the protocols and procedures over the air interface.
- R2: Reference point between the MS and CSN implementing the protocols and procedures associated with authentication, authorization, and IP host configuration management.
- R3: Reference point between ASN and CSN supporting AAA, policy enforcement, and mobility management capabilities.
- R4: Reference point between ASN and ASN for managing SS mobility across ASNs.
- R5: Reference point for internetworking between home and visited NSP.
- R6: Reference point for communications between BS and ASN-GW within a single ASN.
- R7: Reference point used for coordination between the data plane and the control plane in ASN-GW.
- R8: Reference point between BSs connected to the same ASN-GW for ensuring fast and seamless handover.

The WiMAX MAC layer is a connection-oriented architecture and supports a variety of applications and services mapped to connections. In other words, an application establishes a connection with the BS that assigns a unique connection ID (CID) to the connection for requesting bandwidth, associating QoS parameters, routing data, and other actions associated with the application service. WiMAX communications use two types of messages: management messages and data messages. Management messages are mainly used to maintain wireless links and to negotiate security parameters between SS and BS, whereas data messages are used to carry the data to be transmitted over wireless links.

WiMAX supports several network topologies including point-to-multipoint, multi-hop relay, and mobile.

- A point-to-multipoint topology consists of a central BS providing network access to subscribers. This topology is commonly used to enable the delivery of last mile wireless broadband access.
- A multihop relay topology is used to extend BS reach and coverage for WiMAX networks by permitting SS/MS to relay traffic by acting as RS.
- A mobile topology consists of multiple BSs collaborating to provide optimized handover with low latencies and to facilitate handoffs of MS between BS coverage areas.

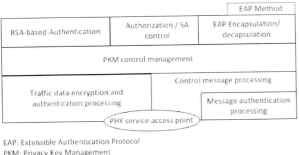

EAP: Extensible Authentication Protocol
PKM: Privacy Key Management
PHY: Physical layer
SA: Security Association

Fig. 3 WiMAX Security sub-layer.

WiMAX SECURITY ESSENTIALS

The 802.16 standard specifies a security sublayer below the MAC layer providing authentication, secure key exchange, and encryption. It also specifies the security association (SA), which is a shared set of security parameters that a BS and its SS/MS share in order to support secure communications.

Security Association

A SA has a unique IDentifier (SAID) and includes several security parameters such as traffic encryption keys (TEKs), X.509 certificate, and cipher block chaining (CBC) initialization vectors (IVs). The communications between a BS and one or more of its SSs are secured depending on the SA the BS shares with those SSs.

There are three defined types of SAs: primary, static, and dynamic. A primary SA is established during the SS initialization process. Static SAs are provisioned within the BS and are only initiated if the SS intends to use a new service and are dynamically terminated. Dynamic SAs are dynamically created and terminated by the BS and are provided to the SS as required in response to the initiation and termination of a specific service flow. Both static and dynamic SAs may be shared by multiple SSs.

There are two types of SA used by IEEE 802.16: data SA and authorization SA. The data SA consists of several components, namely, a 16-bit SA identifier (SAID), two TEKs for data encryption, two 2-bit key identifier one for each TEK, TEK lifetime, a 64-bit IV for each TEK, encryption algorithm (e.g., advanced encryption standard (AES) in Counter with CBC-MAC (CCM) mode), hash message authentication code (HMAC) digest, and the type of SA. The exact content of the SA is dependent on the SA's cryptographic suite, which is a pairing of data encryption and authentication algorithms. The authorization SA consists of an X.509 certificate identifying the SS, a 160-bit authorization key (AK), an AK lifetime, a key encryption key (KEK)

used in distributing the TEKs, and a downlink and uplink HMAC key.

WiMAX Security Sub-Layer

The IEEE 802.16-21012 standard describes a security sub-layer to provide security to the subscribers and to the network as well. The WiMAX security sublayer (Fig. 3) has two protocols: i) an encapsulation protocol to secure packet data by negotiating a set of supported cryptographic suites; and ii) a privacy key management (PKM) protocol to securely convey keying materials from the BS to the SS and to help the BS enforce conditional access on the services provided by the network.

Moreover, the security sublayer (Fig. 3) consists of several layers such as the PKM control management for controlling all security components, traffic data encryption/authentication processing for encrypting/decrypting and for authenticating the traffic data, RSA-based authentication for performing RSA-based authentication using X.509 digital certificates, extensible authentication protocol (EAP) encapsulation/decapsulation for providing the interface with the EAP layer, and EAP and EAP method protocol[5] for implementing EAP-based authorization that is negotiated by the SS and the BS.

WiMAX Security Model

The WiMAX security model consists of three phases: authentication, key management, and encryption of data traffic.

Authorization phase

The first feature of the authorization phase is to grant authenticated SSs access to the network. The authorized SS uses PKM to request from the BS an SA's traffic keying material. The authentication is established by using either the RSA authentication protocol (support is mandatory in PKMv1 and is optional in PKMv2) or the extensible authentication protocol (EAP) (enabled by PKMv2 only and is optional).

The two versions of PKM differ in various aspects. PKMv1 initially specified by IEEE802.16-2009 only allows unilateral authentication, where the SS is authenticated by the BS, but not vice versa. PKMv2 is described in IEEE802.16-2012 with mutual authentication enabled between the BS and the SS. It is worth noting that for data encryption, PKMv1 uses 3DES and AES whereas PKMv2 uses the same algorithms in addition to AES in CCM, CBC, and Counter (CTR) modes. For data integrity, PKMv1 uses HMAC whereas PKMv2 uses HMAC and cipher-based MAC (CMAC).

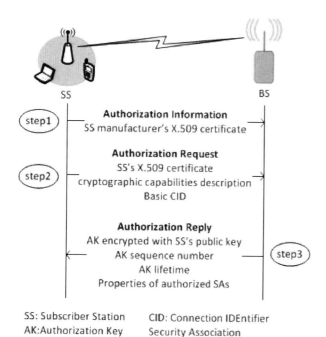

Fig. 4 PKMv1 Exchange.

PKMv1. The SS starts the PKMv1 authorization process (Fig. 4, step 1) by sending an authentication information message to its BS to get the AK. This message includes the SS manufacturer's X.509 certificate. Next, the SS sends an authorization request (step 2) including the manufacturer-issued X.509 certificate of SS, a description of the cryptographic capabilities supported by DD, and the SS's Basic CID.

Upon receipt of the authorization request, the BS verifies the SS's identity, determines the encryption algorithm and protocol support it shares with the SS, activates an AK and encrypts it with the SS's public key, and sends it back to the SS in an authorization reply message (step3). The authorization reply message also includes an AK sequence number to distinguish between successive generations of AKs, the lifetime of

AK, the SAIDs and the properties of SAs for which the SS is authorized to access.

PKMv2. The PKMv1 authentication is unilateral where the SS is authenticated by the BS but not vice versa. To ensure mutual authentication, IEEE802.16-2012 describes PKMv2, which supports two authentication modes: EAP-based and RSA-based authentication.

We describe here the RSA-based authentication, which is initiated by SS by sending a PKM-request (PKM-REQ) with Auth Info as a message type (Fig. 5). This request contains the SS manufacturer's X.509 certificate. The SS then sends a PKM-REQ with an RSA-request message type (PKMv2 RSA-request) to request for the pre-primary authorization key (pre-PAK) and the SAIDs. This request includes the manufacturer-issued X.509 certificate of SS, a description of the cryptographic capabilities supported by SS, and the SS's basic CID and a 64-bit random number.

Upon receipt of the PKMv2 RSA-request message, the BS verifies the SS's identity, determines the encryption algorithm and protocol support it shares with the SS, generates an pre-PAK, and encrypts it with the SS's public key, and sends it back to the SS in an PKMv2 RSA-Reply message. This message also includes the BS's digital certificate, a PAK sequence number to distinguish between successive generations of PAKs, the lifetime of PAK, a 64-bit random number, the random number received from the SS, the SAIDs and properties of SAs for which the SS is authorized to access, and the signature of the BS over all the attributes of RSA reply message. The additional parameters (e.g., the signature of the BS and the random number received from the SS) allow for mutual authentication. At this point, the SS and the BS generate the PAK from the pre-PAK and derive the encryption and MAC keys and perform a three-way handshake as described later.

Key hierarchy

When the SS attempts to join the WiMAX network, the SS and the BS negotiate many critical parameters during the network entry process such as the supported authorization policy that can be RSA only authorization, EAP only authorization, or EAP authorization after RSA authorization.

The key derivation process is different for the two versions of the PKM protocols and according to the selected authorization policy. In fact, the RSA-based authorization process produces the pre-PAK (Fig. 6) whereas the EAP-based authentication process establishes the master session key (MSK). All other keying material is generated from pre-PAK and/or MSK.

It is worth noting that EAP is used in conjunction with an operaor-selected EAP method that requires a

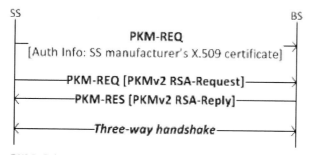

Fig. 5 PKMv2 RSA-based authentication.

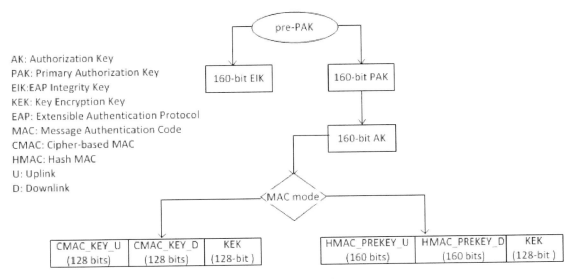

Fig. 6 Key derivation from PAK generated during RSA-based authentication.

logical authentication server entity. The standard IEEE 802.16-2012 does not actually specify any EAP method. However, the following EAP methods could be used:

- Extensible authentication protocol-transport layer security (EAP-TLS) for X.509-based authentication.
- Authentication and key agreement (EAP-AKA) for the subscriber identity module (SIM) based authentication.
- EAP-Tunneled TLS for the Microsoft-Challenge Handshake Authentication Protocol (MS-CHAPv2).

All key derivations are based on the Dot16KDF algorithm as defined in the standard IEEE802.16-2012. The pre-PAK is used as an input to Dot16KDF to generate the PAK whereas the MSK is truncated to 160 bits to derive the pairwise master key (PMK). Based on the selected authentication process, AK will then be derived from either the PAK or the PMK.

When an EAP-based authentication is initiated after a RSA mutual authorization has occurred, the EAP messages are protected using EAP integrity key that is derived from pre-PAK. In this case, the AK is derived from both the PAK and the PMK.

Other keys are established as a result of a successful authentication:

- **Key encryption key** (KEK): derived from AK and is used to encrypt the traffic encryption key (TEK) during the TEK exchange, group KEK (GKEK), and all other keys sent by the BS to the SS in a unicast message.
- **Traffic encryption key**: generated by the BS and transmitted to the SS encrypted with the KEK. It is used to encrypt WiMAX data messages.
- **Group traffic encryption key** (GTEK): generated by the BS and transmitted to the SS encrypted with the

GKEK. It is used to encrypt multicast traffic between a BS and SSs belonging to the multicast group.

- **Group KEK** (GKEK): generated by the BS and transmitted to the SS encrypted with the KEK. There is one GKEK per group SA. This key is used to encrypt the GTEKs sent by the BS to the SSs in the same multicast group.

The standard IEEE 802.16-2012 describes two message authentication code (MAC) modes for message authentication and integrity control: hashed MAC (HMAC) and cipher-based MAC (CMAC). The MAC keys used to generate HMAC or CMAC values are generated as follows. There is a different key for uplink (MAC-mod_KEY_U) and downlink (MAC-mod_-KEY_D) derived from the AK.

Three-way handshake. After the key derivation, a three-way handshake is performed (with PKMv2) to confirm the mutual possession of the AK by both the BS and the SS. The BS starts this handshake by sending a SA-TEK-challenge message including a random number, a sequence number for the new AK, the AK's IDentifier (AKID), and the key lifetime. This challenge message is protected by HMAC or CMAC tuple (e.g., HMAC_KEY_D).

Next, the SS replies with a request message that includes (in addition to the parameter received in the BS's challenge message): a random number generated by the SS, the cryptographic suites supported by the SS and the SS's security capabilities. This message is protected by HMAC or CMAC tuple (e.g., HMAC_KEY_L). Finally, the BS validates the received request message. If the validation is successful, the BS sends a response message back to SS. Otherwise, the BS ignores the message and the SS resends its request

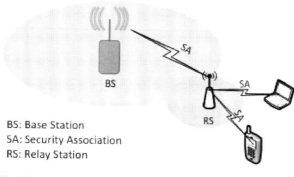

BS: Base Station
SA: Security Association
RS: Relay Station

Fig. 7 Multi-Hop Relay Security Architecture in WiMAX.

message up to a predefined time interval until its maximum number of retransmissions is reached.

Encryption of data traffic phase

During this phase, SS and BS use the TEK and the cryptographic suite negotiated during the authentication phase to encrypt/decrypt their MAC protocol data unit. The standard IEEE802.16-2012 specifies the following data encryption methods: 3DES, AES in CCM, CBC, and CTR modes.

Multihop Relay Security Architecture

As previously indicated, the standard IEEE 802.16-2012 specifies a multihop relay networking having design principles that are similar to the cellular network. This standard also describes the use of RS to relay traffic and to extend the BS's reach and coverage for WiMAX networks. Moreover, the relay architecture supports users' roaming between different areas and enhances the user throughput and the capacity of access networks (Fig. 7).

IEEE 802.16-2012 defines a security mechanism called security zone (SZ) dedicated to the multihop relay topology. A SZ usually consists of a multihop relay BS (MR-BS) acting as a master relay and several RSs have a trusted relationship and share a security context to protect the relay management messages.[6] A RS can join the SZ after being successfully authenticated by the MR-BS, which will deliver to the authenticated RS the SZ's key material.

Two security modes, centralized and distributed, are specified for protecting the relay management messages. The centralized model[7] is based on the key management between the MR-BS and the SS. Consequently, RSs simply forward the relay management messages destined for the next hop in the network without performing any security operation over those messages. The distributed mode incorporates the authentication and key management between the MR-BS and the access RS and between the access RS and the SS in which the authenticated key established between the

MR-BS and the SS is securely transmitted by the MR-BS to its access RS.

ATTACKS AND THREATS TO WiMAX SECURITY

In this section, we examine some of the threats to the security of WiMAX at both the PHY and MAC layers. The attackers usually focus on compromising the radio links between WiMAX nodes to attack the network. The standard IEEE 802.16-2012 has been developed with a special attention to the security concerns. However, WiMAX is still vulnerable to various attacks and threats mainly because of the open nature of the wireless medium.

The standard IEEE-802.16-2012 includes the procedure for entering, registering, and initializing a new SS or a new node to the network. These procedures consist of several phases, namely, the phase "Authorize SS/RS and perform key exchange." However, some other phases will take place before authenticating the SS and before performing the key exchange such as negotiating basic capabilities and consequently, important and critical negotiated parameters are transmitted in clear text and are subject to alteration and falsification by attackers.

PHY Layer Attacks

Radio frequency (RF) jamming attacks

A problem related to all wireless technologies is RF jamming attacks. Jamming is the process of introducing a powerful RF signal to overwhelm the spectrum being used by the system or to significantly reduce the signal to noise ratio.[8] RF jamming is classified as a denial of service (DoS) attack.[9]

Scrambling attacks

Scrambling attacks affect all wireless systems. These attacks can selectively scramble management messages to affect the normal operation of the network. They essentially consist of injecting RF interference during the transmission of the management messages thereby forcing the targeted nodes to retransmit those messages.

Ranging attacks

IEEE802.16-2012 describes a management connection called initial ranging connection, in which power adjustment, timing offset estimation, and synchronization between the BS and the SS within a cell are done during the initial ranging process.[10] An attacker can manipulate the ranging messages to affect a single SS or the entire network. Several relevant attacks are found in literature such as RNG-RSP DoS attack, RNG-RSP downgrading attack, and RNG-RSP water torture attack.[10]

Power saving attacks

IEEE802.16-2012 includes a power-saving feature to maximize operational efficiency and to prolong the battery life of mobile devices. This is achieved with the mobile device functioning in sleep or idle mode.[10] Sleep mode is a state during which the MS turns off various functions thus becoming unavailable for prenegotiated periods of time. Several relevant attacks[11,12] take the advantage of sending unauthenticated traffic indication messages and repeatedly sending them to a sleeping mobile device will exhaust the energy resources of the mobile device.

Handover attack

IEEE802.16-2012 includes a feature allowing a BS to transmit a neighbor advertisement message (MOB_NBR-ADV) at a periodic interval in order to identify the network and define the characteristics of a neighboring BS to a potential MS seeking handover.[9] Since the integrity of the neighbor's advertisement message is not protected, the attacker can change it by falsifying information about neighboring BSs and impeding the handover process. The real danger of this attack is the potential to associate SS with a malicious BS.[13]

MAC Layer Threats

As previously discussed, some important and critical parameters, such as the supported PKM versions, the supported authorization policies, and the MAC modes are negotiated before the BS and the SS/RS start their encryption over exchanged messages. Consequently, an attacker can forge messages containing altered information about the security capabilities of the legitimate SS. In this case, the BS and the SS are vulnerable to man-in-the-middle attacks. For example, an attacker may downgrade the encryption to the lowest available (e.g., DES-CBC) or the supported PKM version to a previous version.

In the case of PKMv1, only the SS is authenticated to the BS. Consequently, a rogue BS may impersonate a legitimate BS and causes DoS for the legitimate users because the MS will disconnect. This is also the case when SS is seeking to perform a handover during which the legitimate SS will disconnect from its current BS when trying to connect to a rogue BS.

The attacker also has the options of manipulating other important messages.[9] For example, the attackers can manipulate the neighbor's advertisement message to advertise nonexisting BS to potential SS seeking initial network entry or handover and then to disconnect the legitimate SS from its current serving BS. This attack is similar to the handover attack described earlier.

Other possible attacks include interleaving and replay attacks. An interleaving attack consists of two rounds as described in Altaf et al.[14] During the first round, an attacker impersonating a legitimate SS sends an authorization request message. The attacker will start a second round aiming at using the valid SS as an oracle to construct an authorization acknowledgement message on behalf of the SS.[14]

Attacks on multicast/broadcast rekeying algorithm (MBRA)

The standard IEEE 802.16-2012 includes secure multicast protocols for the multicast/broadcast service (MBS). For example, the BS uses MBRA (i.e., using PKMv2 group-key-update-command messages) for updating and transmitting traffic keying material simultaneously to all the SSs of a given group. By using MBS mode, the BS can transmit data encrypted with keys (i.e., GKEK) that are shared with all the members of the same group. After the registration and authorization phases, every SS will send a PKMv2 key request to the BS, which replies with a PKMv2 key reply conveying the GTEK encrypted with the GKEK shared between the BS and that SS. Any member of the group can decrypt the traffic generated by the BS in the MBS mode. Any SS member of the group can masquerade as if it is the BS and the other members will not be able to determine if a message (that is symmetrically encrypted with the GTEK) is generated by the BS or by a malicious SS member of the group. For example, a malicious node can manipulate MBRA to distribute its own fake GTEK using the GKEK shared with the group's members to update their active GTEK. As a result, the other group's members will not be able to decrypt future traffic received from the BS.[15]

Another attack known as GTEK theft of service attack[15] can take place when new members join the group. The BS transmits the currently active GTEK to these new members so that they can decrypt not only future traffic, but also the traffic transmitted after activating the current GTEK in case the new members stored the transmitted traffic during the GTEK's lifetime. In other words, backward and forward secrecy cannot be provided here.

Concerns related to privacy and identity protection

During the authentication process of PKM, both the SS and the BS exchange their digital certificates in clear text (without any encryption). Therefore, security parameters flowing in the network could potentially be logged, archived, and searched. Certificates usually link the identity of the owner of a certificate to the public key. Hence, an eavesdropper may learn who is reaching the network, when, and from where, and then track users by correlating the client's identity to the location of the connection. The tracking of the location is a serious security issue for WiMAX subscribers because the WiMAX access medium is open to eavesdroppers and the mobility is a reasonable service. The EAP-TLS authentication method can be used to protect the user's identity because it supports a two-phase negotiation with the first phase used to establish a TLS with only BS authentication and the second phase used to deliver, among others, the SS credentials.

Countermeasures and Security Solutions for WiMAX

There are no perfect solutions to address all of the threats and vulnerabilities described earlier. However, some solutions and countermeasures found in the literature for dealing with the WiMAX threats are analyzed in the following text.[9]

It is possible to prevent jamming attacks by combining cryptographic mechanisms with PHY-layer parameters, but cryptographic solutions are assumed to be time consuming.[16] In Barbeau and Laurendeau,[17] the author indicates that resilience to jamming could be augmented by increasing the power or the bandwidth of signals using spreading techniques. The author proposes monitoring anomalies in performance criteria in order to detect scrambling attacks.

To prevent attacks that may occur before the authorization phase such as DoS and ranging attacks, technical security approaches should be implemented, especially during the initial network entry. In Naseer et al.,[13] the authors propose deploying the Diffie–Hellman key exchange algorithm to protect the critical traffic being exchanged during the process of initial network entry. Another solution described in Tan et al.[11] proposes using a modified version of Diffie–Hellman to protect against DoS and man-in-the-middle attacks.

Several solutions have been proposed to improve the security PKMv2 protocol, such as in Xu and Huang[18] and Altaf et al.[19] where the authors introduced the use of timestamps to avoid replay attacks. In Rahman and Kowsar,[20] the authors propose replacing the authorization procedure in PKMv2 with Diffie–Hellman as a key exchange method to generate the TEK.

To address the problems of MBRA, Kambourakis et al.[21] proposes unicasting the GTEK to each member of the same group so that the GTEK is sent encrypted with KEK instead of GKEK. In order to reduce the complexity and cost of this solution, the authors in Xu et al.[22] describe a solution that includes mechanisms to refresh keys and to provide forward and backward secrecy. In Huang and Chang,[23] MBS groups are divided into a larger number of subgroups, so every group member will have the same GTEK in addition to the sub group key encryption keys of the other subgroups. Finally in Kambourakis et al.,[21] the authors proposed an approach based on asymmetric encryption methods and on the assumption that each group's member has a public key. According to this approach, every member will acquire a different secret decryption key so that other members cannot decrypt messages being sent to this member. As a result, the protocol deals effectively with insider attacks and provides both backward and forward secrecy.[15]

Karen et al.[24] propose the use of client device's security such as personal firewalls, policy enforcement, antimalware software, and host-based intrusion detection and prevention systems to enhance the system security posture. By properly securing client devices, we enforce protection against compromising the system.

Finally, it would be possible to use smart cards to overcome the vulnerabilities of the storage of private and shared keys. In fact, without using secure devices such as smart cards, unauthorized access can be easily established to SS to retrieve confidential and personal data stored on it. A smart card is a portable and tamper-resistant device that provides data security, data integrity, and personal privacy and supports mobility. Furthermore, major application areas (including mobile communications) use smart card to convey the user's subscription and identification information as well as to provide the user's identity for network access.

CONCLUSION

The proliferation and adoption of WiMAX networks have increased exponentially as wireless services become more popular over the last few years. In this entry, we introduce WiMAX security architectures and requirements. Then we discussed some important security threats and attacks at the WiMAX sublayers (i.e., PHY and MAC layers) that can result in sniffing, falsifying, and hijacking sensitive and critical data/management messages. After highlighting the possible security attacks on WiMAX, we also presented countermeasures that can improve WiMAX security and reduce the risks inherent to WiMAX systems. Given the major WiMAX benefits, WiMAX networks have tremendous potential to continue to be a viable, successful communication technology if the vulnerabilities and threats associated with this communication technology are addressed.

ACKNOWLEDGMENTS

We thank the reviewers for their useful comments, which have helped us improve the quality and presentation of this entry. We would also like to thank Molly Pohlig and the editor-in-chief for their encouragement and support during the preparation of this entry.

REFERENCES

1. *IEEE 802.11n: Wireless LAN Medium Access Control (MAC) and Physical Layer (PHY) specifications Amendment 5: Enhancements for Higher Throughput.* ANSI/IEEE Std 802.11n-2009, IEEE, October 2009.

2. IEEE 802.16-2012 (08/2012) *IEEE Standard for Air Interface for Broadband Wireless Access Systems.*

3. 802.16-2004, I. S. *IEEE Standard for Local and Metropolitan area networks Part 16: Air Interface for Fixed Broadband Wireless Access Systems.*

4. Ahmadi, S. *Mobile WiMAX: A System Approach to Understanding the IEEE 802.16m Radio Access Network;* Elsevier Inc.: USA., 2011.

5. Aboba, B.; Blunk, L.; Vollbrecht, J.; Carlson, J.; Levkowetz, H. *Extensible authentication protocol (EAP).* IETF RFC 3748, June 2004. http://www.ietf.org/rfc/rfc3748.txt.

6. Huang CT, Huang CT. Secure mutual authentication protocols for mobile multi-hop relay WiMAX networks against rogue base/relay stations. *ICC* **2011**, 1–5 doi: 10.1109/icc.2011.5963292.

7. Liu, H. Next-generation wireless standards and their integration with the internet. In *Emerging Wireless Technologies and the Future Mobile Internet;* Raychaudhuri, D., Gerla, M., Eds.; Cambridge University Press: United Kingdom, 2011.

8. Simon, M.K.; Omura, J.K.; Scholtz, R.A.; Levitt, B.K. *Spread Spectrum Communications Handbook;* McGraw-Hill: United States, 2001.

9. Kolias, C.; Kambourakis, G.; Gritzalis, S. Attacks and countermeasures on 802.16: Analysis and assessment. IEEE Commun. Surv. Tutor. **2013**, 15 (1), 487–514.

10. Mahmoud, H.; Arslan, H.; Ozdemir, M. Initial Ranging for WiMAX (802.16e) OFDMA. MILCOM 2006, 1–7 doi: 10.1109/MILCOM.2006.302240.

11. Han, T.; Zhang, N.; Liu, K.; Tang, B.; Liu, Y. *Analysis of Mobile WiMAX Security: Vulnerabilities and Solutions.* The proceedings of The 5th IEEE International Conference on Mobile Ad Hoc and Senor Systems, 2008.

12. Ibikunle, F. Security Issues in Mobile WiMAX (IEEE 802.16e). MWS'09 Proceedings of the 2009 IEEE conference on Mobile WiMAX, 2009; 117–122.

13. Naseer, S.; Younus, M.; Ahmed, A. Vulnerabilities Exposing IEEE 802.16e Networks to DoS Attacks: A Survey. Software Engineering, Artificial Intelligence, Networking, and Parallel/Distributed Computing, 2008. SNPD '08. Ninth ACIS International Conference, Aug 6–8, 2008; 344–349.

14. Altaf, A.; Javed, M.Y.; Ahmed, A. Security Enhancements for Privacy and Key Management Protocol in IEEE 802.16e-2005. Proc. IEEE ACIS Intl Conf. Software Eng., Artificial Intelligence, Networking, and Parallel/Distributed Computing (SNPD), Aug 2008.

15. Kambourakis, G.; Konstantinou, E.; Gritzalis, S. Revisiting WiMAX MBS security. Comp. Mathem. Appl. **2010**, 60 (2), 217–223.

16. Proano, A.; Lazos, L. Packet-hiding methods for preventing selective jamming attacks. IEEE Trans. Dependable Sec. Comp. **2012**, 9, 101–114.

17. Barbeau, M.; Laurendeau, C. Analysis of threats to WiMAX/802.16 security. In *Mobile WiMAX: Toward Broadband Wireless Metropolitan Area Networks, ser.* Wireless Networks and Mobile Communications Series; 2007; 347–362.

18. Xu, S.; Huang, C. Attacks on PKM Protocols of IEEE 802.16 and Its Later Versions. Wireless Communication Systems, 3rd International Symposium on Wireless Communication Systems, 2006; 185–189.

19. Altaf, A.; Javed, M.Y.; Ahmed, A. Security Enhancements for Privacy and Key Management Protocol in IEEE 802.16e-2005. Proceeding IEEE ACIS International Conference Software Engineering, Artificial Intelligence, Networking, and Parallel/Distributed Computing (SNPD), 2008.

20. Rahman, M.S.; Kowsar, M.M.S. WiMAX security analysis and enhancement. 12th International Conference on Computers and Information Technology, **2009**; 679–684.

21. Kambourakis, G.; Konstantinou, E.; Gritzalis, S. Revisiting WiMAX MBS security. Comp. Mathem. Appl. **2010**, 60 (2), 217–223.

22. Xu S.; Huang C-T.; Matthews M.M. Secure multicast in WiMAX. *J. Networks N. Am.* **2008**; *3* (2): 48–57.

23. Huang, C.; Chang, L. Responding to security issues in WiMAX networks. IT Prof. **2008**, 15–21.

24. Karen, S.; Tibbs, C.; Sexton, M. Guide to securing WiMAX wireless communications recommendations of the national institute of standards and technology. NIST Special Pub. 2010, Available at: http://csrc.nist.gov/publications/nistpubs/800-127/sp800-127.pdf

WLANs: Wireless Local Area Networks: Design

Suresh Singh
Portland State University, Portland, Oregon, U.S.A.

Abstract

Wireless local area networks along with cellular networks, connected to high-speed networks, allow users with portable devices and computers to be connected with communication networks and service providers.

INTRODUCTION

A proliferation of high-performance portable computers combined with end-user need for communication is fueling a dramatic growth in wireless LAN technology. Users expect to have the ability to operate their portable computer globally while remaining connected to communications networks and service providers. Wireless LANs and cellular networks, connected to high-speed networks, are being developed to provide this functionality.

Before delving deeper into issues relating to the design of wireless LANs, it is instructive to consider some scenarios of user mobility.

1. A simple model of user mobility is one where a computer is physically moved while retaining network connectivity at either end. For example, a move from one room to another as in a hospital where the computer is a hand-held device displaying patient charts and the nurse using the computer moves between wards or floors while accessing patient information.
2. Another model situation is where a group of people (at a conference, for instance) set up an ad hoc LAN to share information as in Fig. 1.
3. A more complex model is one where several computers in constant communication are in motion and continue to be networked. For example, consider the problem of having robots in space collaborating to retrieve a satellite.

A great deal of research has focused on dealing with physical layer and **medium access control (MAC)** layer protocols. In this entry we first summarize standardization efforts in these areas. The remainder of the entry is then devoted to a discussion of networking issues involved in wireless LAN design. Some of the issues discussed include routing in wireless LANs (i.e., how does data find its destination when the destination is mobile) and the problem of providing service guarantees to end users (e.g., error-free data transmission or bounded delay and bounded bandwidth service).

PHYSICAL LAYER DESIGN

Two media are used for transmission over wireless LANs, IR and RF. RF LANs are typically implemented in the industrial, scientific, and medical ISM frequency bands 902–928 MHz, 2400–2483.5 MHz, and 5725–5850 MHz. These frequencies do not require a license allowing the LAN product to be portable, i.e., a LAN can be moved without having to worry about licensing.

IR and RF technologies have different design constraints. IR receiver design is simple (and thus inexpensive) in comparison to RF receiver design because IR receivers only detect the amplitude of the signal not the frequency or phase. Thus, a minimal of filtering is required to reject interference. Unfortunately, however, IR shares the electromagnetic spectrum with the sun and incandescent or fluorescent light. These sources of modulated IR energy reduce the signal to noise ratio of IR signals and, if present in extreme intensity, can make the IR LANs inoperable. There are two approaches to building IR LANs.

1. The transmitted signal can be focused and aimed. In this case the IR system can be used outdoors and has an area of coverage of a few kilometers.
2. The transmitted signal can be bounced off the ceiling or radiated omni directionally. In either case, the range of the IR source is 10–20 m (i.e., the size of one medium sized room).

RF systems face harsher design constraints in comparison to IR systems for several reasons. The increased demand for RF products has resulted in tight regulatory constraints on the allocation and use of allocated bands. For example, in the United States it is necessary to

Encyclopedia of Information Systems and Technology, DOI: 10.1081/E-EIST-120043948

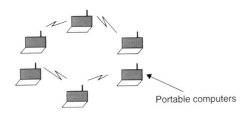

Fig. 1 Ad hoc wireless LAN.

implement spectrum spreading for operation in the ISM bands. Another design constraint is the requirement to confine the emitted spectrum to a band, necessitating amplification at higher carrier frequencies, frequency conversion using precision local oscillators, and selective components. RF systems must also cope with environmental noise that is either naturally occurring, e.g., atmospheric noise, or man-made, e.g., microwave ovens, copiers, laser printers, or other heavy electrical machinery. RF LANs operating in the ISM frequency ranges also suffer interference from amateur radio operators.

Operating LANs indoors introduces additional problems caused by multipath propagation, Rayleigh fading, and absorption. Many materials used in building construction are opaque to IR radiation resulting in incomplete coverage within rooms (the coverage depends on obstacles within the room that block IR) and almost no coverage outside closed rooms. Some materials, such as white plasterboard, can also cause reflection of IR signals. RF is relatively immune to absorption and reflection problems. Multipath propagation affects both IR and RF signals. The technique to alleviate the effects of multipath propagation in both types of systems is the same use of aimed (directional) systems for transmission enabling the receiver to reject signals based on their angle of incidence. Another technique that may be used in RF systems is to use multiple antennas. The phase difference between different paths can be used to discriminate between them.

Rayleigh fading is a problem in RF systems. Recall that Rayleigh fading occurs when the difference in path length of the same signal arriving along different paths is a multiple of half a wavelength. This causes the signal to be almost completely canceled out at the receiver.

Because the wavelengths used in IR are so small, the effect of Rayleigh fading is not noticeable in those systems. RF systems, on the other hand, use wavelengths of the order of the dimension of a laptop. Thus, moving the computer a small distance could increase/decrease the fade significantly.

Spread spectrum transmission technology is used for RF based LANs and it comes in two varieties: direct sequence spread spectrum (DSSS) and frequency hopping spread spectrum (FHSS). In a FHSS system, the available band is split into several channels. The transmitter transmits on one channel for a fixed time and then hops to another channel. The receiver is synchronized with the transmitter and hops in the same sequence; see Fig. 2A. In DSSS systems, a random binary string is used to modulate the transmitted signal. The relative rate between this sequence and user data is typically between 10 and 100; see Fig. 2B.

The key requirement of any transmission technology is its robustness to noise. In this respect, DSSS and FHSS show some differences. There are two possible sources of interference for wireless LANs: the presence of other wireless LANs in the same geographical area (i.e., in the same building, etc.) and interference due to other users of the ISM frequencies. In the latter case, FHSS systems have a greater ability to avoid interference because the hopping sequence could be designed to prevent potential interference. DSSS systems, on the other hand, do exhibit an ability to recover from interference because of the use of the spreading factor Fig. 2B.

It is likely that in many situations several wireless LANs may be collocated. Since all wireless LANs use the same ISM frequencies, there is a potential for a great deal of interference. To avoid interference in FHSS systems, it is necessary to ensure that the hopping sequences are orthogonal. To avoid interference in DSSS systems, on the other hand, it is necessary to allocate different channels to each wireless LAN. The ability to avoid interference in DSSS systems is, thus, more limited in comparison to FHSS systems because FHSS systems use very narrow subchannels (1 MHz) in comparison to DSSS systems that use wider subchannels (e.g., 25 MHz), thus, limiting the number of wireless LANs that can be collocated. A summary of design issues can be found in Bantz and Bauchot.[1]

MAC LAYER PROTOCOLS

MAC protocol design for wireless LANs poses new challenges because of the inbuilding operating environment for these systems. Unlike wired LANs (such as the Ethernet or token ring), wireless LANs operate in strong multipath fading channels where channel characteristics

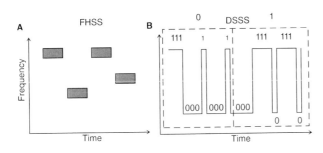

Fig. 2 Spread spectrum.

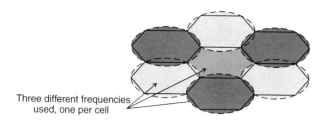

Fig. 3 Cellular structure for wireless LANs note frequency reuse.

can change in very short distances resulting in unreliable communication and unfair channel access due to capture. Another feature of the wireless LAN environment is that carrier sensing takes a long time in comparison to wired LANs; it typically takes between 30 and 50 μs,[2] which is a significant portion of the packet transmission time. This results in inefficiencies if the carrier sense multiple access (CSMA) family of protocols is used without any modifications.

Other differences arise because of the mobility of users in wireless LAN environments. To provide a building (or any other region) with wireless LAN coverage, the region to be covered is divided into cells as shown in Fig. 3. Each cell is one wireless LAN, and adjacent cells use different frequencies to minimize interference. Within each cell there is an access point called a **mobile support station** (MSS) or base station that is connected to some wired network. The mobile users are called **mobile hosts (MHs)**. The MSS performs the functions of channel allocation and providing connectivity to existing wired networks; see Fig. 4. Two problems arise in this type of an architecture that are not present in wired LANs.

1. The number of nodes within a cell changes dynamically as users move between cells. How can the channel access protocol dynamically adapt to such changes efficiently?
2. When a user moves between cells, the user has to make its presence known to the other nodes in the

cell. How can this be done without using up too much bandwidth? The protocol used to solve this problem is called a handoff protocol and works along the following lines: a switching station (or the MSS nodes working together, in concert) collects signal strength information for each MH within each cell. Note that if a MH is near a cell boundary, the MSS node in its cell as well as in the neighboring cell can hear its transmissions and determine signal strengths. If the MH is under the coverage of MSS M1 but its signal strength at MSS M2 becomes larger, the switching station initiates a handoff whereby the MH is considered as part of M2's cell (or network).

The mode of communication in wireless LANs can be broken in two: communication from the mobile to the MSS (called *uplink* communication) and communication in the reverse direction (called *downlink* communication). It is estimated that downlink communication accounts for about 70–80% of the total consumed bandwidth. This is easy to see because most of the time users request files or data in other forms (image data, etc.) that consume much more transmission bandwidth than the requests themselves. In order to make efficient use of bandwidth (and, in addition, guarantee service requirements for real-time data), most researchers have proposed that the downlink channel be controlled entirely by the MSS nodes. These nodes allocate the channel to different mobile users based on their requirements using a protocol such as TDMA. What about uplink traffic? This is a more complicated problem because the set of users within a cell is dynamic, thus making it infeasible to have a static channel allocation for the uplink. This problem is the main focus of MAC protocol design.

What are some of the design requirements of an appropriate MAC protocol? The IEEE 802.11 recommended standard for wireless LANs has identified almost 20 such requirements, some of which are discussed here (the reader is referred to Chen,[3] for further details). Clearly any protocol must maximize throughput while minimizing delays and providing fair access to all users. In addition to these requirements, however, mobility introduces several new requirements:

1. The MAC protocol must be independent of the underlying physical layer transmission technology adopted (be it DSSS, FHSS, or IR).
2. The maximum number of users can be as high as a few hundred in a wireless LAN. The MAC protocol must be able to handle many users without exhibiting catastrophic degradation of service.
3. The MAC protocols must provide secure transmissions because the wireless medium is easy to tap.

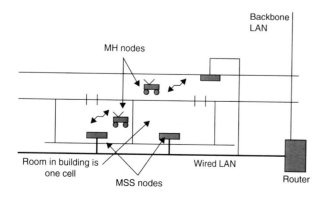

Fig. 4 Inbuilding LAN (made up of several wireless LANs). MH, mobile host; MSS, mobile support station.

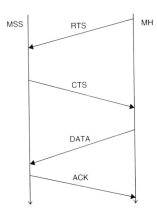

Fig. 5 CSMA/CA and four-way handshaking protocol.

4. The MAC protocol needs to work correctly in the presence of collocated networks.
5. It must have the ability to support ad hoc networking (as in Fig. 1).
6. Other requirements include the need to support priority traffic, preservation of packet order, and an ability to support multicast.

Several contention-based protocols exist that could be adapted for use in wireless LANs. The protocols being looked at by IEEE 802.11 include protocols based on **CSMA**, polling, and TDMA. Protocols based on CDMA and FDMA are not considered because the processing gains obtained using these protocols are minimal while, simultaneously, resulting in a loss of flexibility for wireless LANs.

It is important to highlight an important difference between networking requirements of ad hoc networks (as in Fig. 1) and networks based on cellular structure. In cellular networks, all communication occurs between the MHs and the MSS (or base station) within that cell. Thus, the MSS can allocate channel bandwidth according to requirements of different nodes, i.e., we can use centralized channel scheduling for efficient use of bandwidth. In ad hoc networks there is no such central scheduler available. Thus, any multi-access protocol will be contention based with little explicit scheduling. In the remainder of this section we focus on protocols for cell-based wireless LANs only.

All multi-access protocols for cell-based wireless LANs have a similar structure; see Chen.[3]

1. The MSS announces (explicitly or implicitly) that nodes with data to send may contend for the channel.
2. Nodes interested in sending data contend for the channel using protocols such as CSMA.
3. The MSS allocates the channel to successful nodes.
4. Nodes transmit packets (contention-free transmission).
5. MSS sends an explicit ACK for packets received.

Based on this model we present three MAC protocols.

Reservation-TDMA

This approach is a combination of TDMA and some contention protocol (see packet reservation multiple access PRMA in Goodman).[4] The MSS divides the channel into slots (as in TDMA), which are grouped into frames. When a node wants to transmit, it needs to reserve a slot that it can use in every consecutive frame as long as it has data to transmit. When it has completed transmission, other nodes with data to transmit may contend for that free slot. There are four steps to the functioning of this protocol:

a. At the end of each frame, the MSS transmits a feedback packet that informs nodes of the reservation of slots (and also which slots are free). This corresponds to Steps 1 and 3 from the preceding list.
b. During a frame, all nodes wishing to acquire a slot transmit with a probability p during a free slot. If a node is successful it is so informed by the next feedback packet. If more than one node transmits during a free slot, there is a collision and the nodes try again during the next frame. This corresponds to Step 2.
c. A node with a reserved slot transmits data during its slot. This is the contention-free transmission (Step 4).
d. The MSS sends ACKs for all data packets received correctly. This is Step 5.

The reservation TDMA RTDMA protocol exhibits several nice properties. First and foremost, it makes very efficient use of the bandwidth, and average latency is half the frame size. Another big benefit is the ability to implement power conserving measures in the portable computer. Since each node knows when to transmit (nodes transmit during their reserved slot only) it can move into a power-saving mode for a fixed amount of time, thus increasing battery life. This feature is generally not available in CSMA-based protocols. Furthermore, it is easy to implement priorities because of the centralized control of scheduling. One significant drawback of this protocol is that it is expensive to implement.[5]

Distributed Foundation Wireless MAC

The CSMA/CD protocol has been used with great success in the Ethernet. Unfortunately, the same protocol is not very efficient in a wireless domain because of the problems associated with cell interference (i.e., interference from neighboring cells), the relatively large amount of time taken to sense the channel[6] and the hidden terminal problem.[7,8] The proposal is based on a CSMA/collision avoidance (CA) protocol with a four-way handshake; see Fig. 5.

The basic operation of the protocol is simple. All MH nodes that have packets to transmit compete for the channel by sending ready to transmit (RTS) messages using non-persistent CSMA. After a station succeeds in transmitting a RTS, the MSS sends a clear to transmit (CTS) to the MH. The MH transmits its data and then receives an ACK. The only possibility of collision that exists is in the RTS phase of the protocol and inefficiencies occur in the protocol, because of the RTS and CTS stages. Note that unlike R-TDMA, it is harder to implement power saving functions. Furthermore, latency is dependent on system load making it harder to implement real-time guarantees. Priorities are also not implemented. On the positive side, the hardware for this protocol is very inexpensive.

Randomly Addressed Polling

In this scheme, when a MSS is ready to collect uplink packets it transmits a READY message. At this point all nodes with packets to send, attempt to grab the channel as follows:

a. Each MH with a packet to transmit generates a random number between 0 and P.
b. All active MH nodes simultaneously and orthogonally transmit their random numbers (using CDMA or FDMA). We assume that all of these numbers are received correctly by the MSS. Remember that more than one MH node may have selected the same random number.
c. Steps a and b are repeated L times.
d. At the end of L stages, the MSS determines a stage (say, k) where the total number of distinct random numbers was the largest. The MSS polls each distinct each random number in this stage in increasing order. All nodes that had generated the polled random number transmit packets to the MSS.
e. Since more than one node may have generated the same random number, collisions are possible. The MSS sends a ACK or NACK after each such transmission. Unsuccessful nodes try again during the next iteration of the protocol.

The protocol is discussed in detail in Chen and Lee[2] and a modified protocol called group RAP (GRAP) is discussed in Chen.[3] The authors propose that GRAP can also be used in the contention stage (Step 2) for TDMA and CSMA-based protocols.

NETWORK LAYER ISSUES

An important goal of wireless LANs is to allow users to move about freely while still maintaining all of their connections (network resources permitting). This means that the network must route all packets destined for the mobile user to the MSS of its cell in a transparent manner. Two issues need to be addressed in this context:

• How can users be addressed?
• How can active connections for these mobile users be maintained?

Ioanidis et al.[9] propose a solution called the IPIP IP-within-IP protocol. Here each MH has a unique IP address called its home address. To deliver a packet to a remote MH, the source MSS first broadcasts an address resolution protocol (ARP) request to all other MSS nodes to locate the MH. Eventually some MSS responds. The source MSS then encapsulates each packet from the source MH within another packet containing the IP address of the MSS in whose cell the MH is located. The destination MSS extracts the packet and delivers it to the MH. If the MH has moved away in the interim, the new MSS locates the new location of the MH and performs the same operation. This approach suffers from several problems as discussed in Teraoka and Tokoro.[10] Specifically, the method is not scaleable to a network spanning areas larger than a campus for the following reasons:

1. IP addresses have a prefix identifying the campus subnetwork where the node lives; when the MH moves out of the campus, its IP address no longer represents this information.
2. The MSS nodes serve the function of routers in the mobile network and, therefore, have the responsibility of tracking all of the MH nodes globally causing a lot of overhead in terms of message passing and packet forwarding.[11]

Teraoka and Tokoro,[10] have proposed a much more flexible solution to the problem called virtual IP (VIP). Here every MH has a VIP address that is unchanging regardless of the location of the MH. In addition, hosts have physical network addresses (traditional IP addresses) that may change as the host moves about. At the transport layer, the target node is always specified by its VIP address only. The address resolution from the VIP address to the IP address takes place either at the network layer of the same machine or at a gateway. Both the host machines and the gateways maintain a cache of VIP to IP mappings with associated time-stamps. This information is in the form of a table called *address mapping table* (AMT). Every MH has an associated *home gateway*. When a MH moves into a new

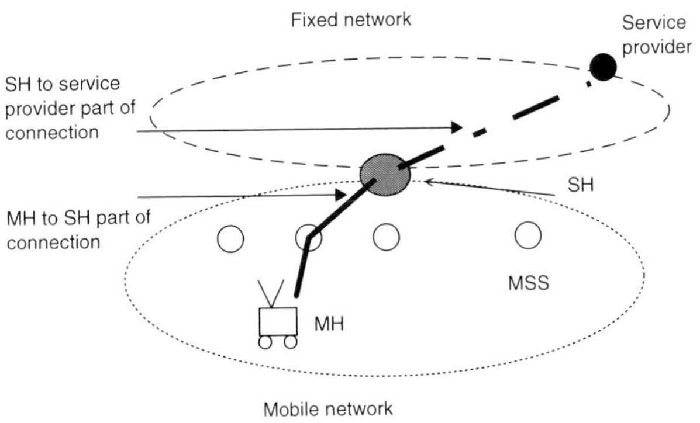

Fixed network

Service provider

SH to service provider part of connection

MH to SH part of connection

SH

MSS

MH

Mobile network

Fig. 6 Proposed architecture for wireless networks.

subnetwork, it is assigned a new IP address. It sends this new IP address and its VIP address to its home gateway via a *VipConn* control message. All intermediate gateways that relay this message update their AMTs as well. During this process of updating the AMTs, all packets destined to the MH continue to be sent to the old location. These packets are returned to the sender, who then sends them to the home gateway of the MH. It is easy to see that this approach is easily scaleable to large networks, unlike the IPIP approach.

Alternative View of Mobile Networks

The approaches just described are based on the belief that mobile networks are merely an extension of wired networks. Other authors[12] disagree with this assumption because there are fundamental differences between the mobile domain and the fixed wired network domain. Two examples follow:

1. The available bandwidth at the wireless link is small; thus, end-to-end packet retransmission for TCP-like protocols (implemented over datagram networks) is a bad idea. This leads to the conclusion that transmission within the mobile network must be connection oriented. Such a solution, using virtual circuits (VCs), is proposed in Ghai and Singh.[11]
2. The bandwidth available for a MH with open connections changes dynamically since the number of other users present in each cell varies randomly. This is a feature not present in fixed high-speed networks where, once a connection is set up, its bandwidth does not vary much. Since bandwidth changes are an artifact of mobility and are dynamic, it is necessary to deal with the consequences (e.g., buffer overflow, large delays, etc.) locally to both, i.e., shield fixed network hosts from the idiosyncrasies of mobility as well as to respond to changing bandwidth quickly without having to rely on end-to-end control. Some other differences are discussed in Singh.[12]

A Proposed Architecture

Keeping these issues in mind, a more appropriate architecture has been proposed in Ghai and Singh,[11] and Singh.[12] Mobile networks are considered to be different and separate from wired networks. Within a mobile network is a three-layer hierarchy; see Fig. 6. At the bottom layer are the MHs. At the next level are the MSS nodes, (one per cell). Finally, several MSS nodes are controlled by a **supervisor host (SH)** node (there may be one SH node per small building). The SH nodes are responsible for flow control for all MH connections within their domain; they are also responsible for tracking MH nodes and forwarding packets as MH nodes roam. In addition, the SH nodes serve as a *gateway* to the wired networks. Thus, any connection setup from a MH to a fixed host is broken in two, one from the MH to the SH and another from the SH to the fixed host. The MSS nodes in this design are simply connection endpoints for MH nodes. Thus, they are simple devices that implement the MAC protocols and little else. Some of the benefits of this design are as follows:

1. Because of the large coverage of the SH (i.e., a SH controls many cells) the MH remains in the domain of one SH much longer. This makes it easy to handle the consequences of dynamic bandwidth changes locally. For instance, when a MH moves into a crowded cell, the bandwidth available to it is reduced. If it had an open FTP connection, the SH simply buffers undelivered packets until they can be delivered. There is no need to inform the other endpoint of this connection of the reduced bandwidth.
2. When a MH node sets up a connection with a service provider in the fixed network, it negotiates some quality of service (QoS) parameters such as bandwidth, delay bounds, etc. When the MH roams into a crowded cell, these QoS parameters can no longer be met because the available bandwidth is smaller. If the traditional view is adopted i.e., the mobile networks are extensions of fixed networks then these QoS parameters will have to be renegotiated each time the bandwidth changes (due to roaming). This is a very expensive proposition because of the large number of control messages that will have to be exchanged. In the approach of Singh,[12] the service provider will never know about the bandwidth changes since it deals only with the SH that is accessed via the wired network. The SH bears the responsibility of handling bandwidth changes by either buffering packets until the bandwidth available to the MH increases (as in the case of the FTP example) or it could discard a fraction of real-time packets (e.g., a voice connection) to ensure delivery of most of the packets within their deadlines. The SH could also instruct the MSS to

allocate a larger amount of bandwidth to the MH when the number of buffered packets becomes large. Thus, the service provider in the fixed network is shielded from the mobility of the user.

Networking Issues

It is important for the network to provide connection-oriented service in the mobile environment (as opposed to connectionless service as in the Internet) because bandwidth is at a premium in wireless networks, and it is, therefore, inadvisable to have end to end retransmission of packets as in TCP. The proposed architecture is well suited to providing connection-oriented service by using VCs.

In the remainder of this section, we look at how VCs are used within the mobile network and how routing is performed for connections to MHs. Every connection set up with one or more MH nodes as a connection endpoint is routed through the SH nodes and each connection is given a unique VC number. The SH node keeps track of all MH nodes that lie within its domain. When a packet needs to be delivered to a MH node, the SH first buffers the packet and then sends it to the MSS at the location of the MH or to the predicted location if the MH is between cells. The MSS buffers all of these packets for the MH and transmits them to the MH if it is in its cell. The MSS discards packets after transmission or if the SH asks it to discard the packets. Packets are delivered in the correct order to the MH (without duplicates) by having the MH transmit the expected sequence number (for each VC) during the initial handshake (i.e., when the MH first enters the cell). The MH sends ACKs to the SH for packets received. The SH discards all packets that have been acknowledged. When a MH moves from the domain of SH1 into the domain of SH2 while having open connections, SH1 continues to forward packets to SH2 until either the connections are closed or until SH2 sets up its own connections with the other endpoints for each of MH's open connections (it also gives new identifiers to all these open connections). The detailed protocol is presented in Ghai and Singh.[11]

The SH nodes are all connected over the fixed (wired) network. Therefore, it is necessary to route packets between SH nodes using the protocol provided over the fixed networks. The VIP appears to be best suited to this purpose. Let us assume that every MH has a globally unique VIP address. The SHs have both a VIP as well as a fixed IP address. When a MH moves into the domain of a SH, the IP address affixed to this MH is the IP address of the SH. This ensures that all packets sent to the MH are routed through the correct SH node. The SH keeps a list of all VIP addresses of MH nodes within its domain, and a list of open VCs for

each MH. It uses this information to route the arriving packets along the appropriate VC to the MH.

TRANSPORT LAYER DESIGN

The transport layer provides services to higher layers including the application layer, which includes connectionless services like user datagram protocol (UDP) or connection-oriented services like TCP. A wide variety of new services will be made available in the high-speed networks, such as continuous media service for real-time data applications such as voice and video. These services will provide bounds on delay and loss while guaranteeing some minimum bandwidth.

Variations of the TCP have been proposed that work well in the wireless domain. These proposals are based on the traditional view that wireless networks are merely extensions of fixed networks. One such proposal is called I-TCP[5] for indirect TCP. The motivation behind this work stems from the following observation. In TCP, the sender times out and begins retransmission after a timeout period of several hundred milliseconds. If the other endpoint of the connection is a MH, it is possible that the MH is disconnected for a period of several seconds (while it moves between cells and performs the initial greeting). This results in the TCP sender timing out and transmitting the same data several times over, causing the effective throughput of the connection to degrade rapidly. To alleviate this problem, the implementation of I-TCP separates a TCP connection into two pieces, one from the fixed host to another fixed host that is near the MH and another from this host to the MH (note the similarity of this approach with the approach in Fig. 6). The host closer to the MH is aware of mobility and has a larger timeout period. It serves as a type of gateway for the TCP connection because it sends ACKs back to the sender before receiving ACKs from the MH. The performance of I-TCP is far superior to traditional TCP for the mobile networks studied.

In the architecture proposed in Fig. 6, a TCP connection from a fixed host to a MH would terminate at the SH. The SH would set up another connection to the MH and would have the responsibility of transmitting all packets correctly. In a sense this is a similar idea to ITCP except that in the wireless network VCs are used rather than datagrams. Therefore, the implementation of TCP service is made much easier.

A problem that is unique to the mobile domain occurs because of the unpredictable movement of MH nodes (i.e., a MH may roam between cells resulting in a large variation of available bandwidth in each cell). Consider the following example. Say nine MH nodes have opened 11 Kbps connections in a cell where the available bandwidth is 100 Kbps. Let us say that a tenth

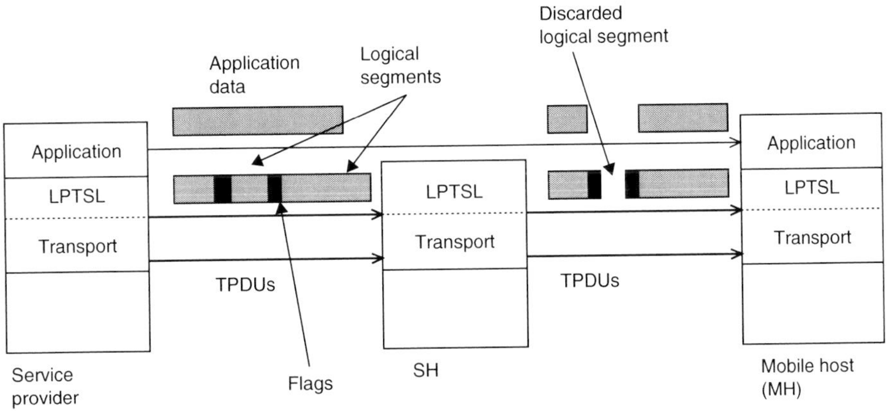

Fig. 7   LPTSL, an approach to handle dynamic bandwidth variations.

MH M10, also with an open 11 Kbps connection, wanders in. The total requested bandwidth is now 110 Kbps while the available bandwidth is only 100 Kbps. What is to be done? One approach would be to deny service to M10. However, this seems an unfair policy. A different approach is to penalize all connections equally so that each connection has 10 Kbps bandwidth allocated.

To reduce the bandwidth for each connection from 11 to 10 Kbps, two approaches may be adopted:

1. Throttle back the sender for each connection by sending control messages.
2. Discard 1 Kbps data for each connection at the SH. This approach is only feasible for applications that are tolerant of data loss (e.g., real-time video or audio).

The first approach encounters a high overhead in terms of control messages and requires the sender to be capable of changing the data rate dynamically. This may not always be possible; for instance, consider a teleconference consisting of several participants where each mobile participant is subject to dynamically changing bandwidth. In order to implement this approach, the data (video or audio or both) will have to be compressed at different ratios for each participant, and this compression ratio may have to be changed dynamically as each participant roams. This is clearly an unreasonable solution to the problem. The second approach requires the SH to discard 1 Kbps of data for each connection. The question is, how should this data be discarded? That is, should the 1 Kb of discarded data be consecutive (or clustered) or uniformly spread out over the data stream every 1 sec? The way in which the data is discarded has an effect on the final perception of the service by the mobile user. If the service is audio, e.g., a random uniform loss is preferred to a clustered loss (where several consecutive words are lost). If the data is compressed video, the problem is even more serious because most random losses will cause the encoded

stream to become unreadable resulting in almost a 100% loss of video at the user.

A solution to this problem is proposed in Seal and Singh,[13] where a new sublayer is added to the transport layer called the *loss profile transport sublayer (LPTSL)*. This layer determines how data is to be discarded based on special transport layer markers put by application calls at the sender and based on negotiated loss functions that are part of the QoS negotiations between the SH and service provider. Fig. 7 illustrates the functioning of this layer at the service provider, the SH, and the MH. The original data stream is broken into *logical segments* that are separated by markers (or flags). When this stream arrives at the SH, the SH discards entire logical segments (in the case of compressed video, one logical segment may represent one frame) depending on the bandwidth available to the MH. The purpose of discarding entire logical segments is that discarding a part of such a segment of data makes the rest of the data within that segment useless, so we might as well discard the entire segment. Observe also that the flags (to identify logical segments) are inserted by the LPTSL via calls made by the application layer. Thus, the transport layer or the LPTSL does not need to know encoding details of the data stream. This scheme is being implemented at the University of South Carolina by the author and his research group.

CONCLUSIONS

The need for wireless LANs is driving rapid development in this area. The IEEE has proposed standards (802.11) for the physical MAC layer protocols. A great deal of work, however, remains to be done at the network and transport layers. There does not appear to be a consensus regarding subnet design for wireless LANs. Our work has indicated a need for treating wireless LAN subnetworks as being fundamentally different from fixed networks, thus resulting in a different subnetwork and transport layer designs. Efforts are under way to validate these claims.

DEFINING TERMS

CSMA: Protocols such as those used over the Ethernet.
MAC: Protocols arbitrate channel access between all nodes on a wireless LAN.
MH nodes: The nodes of wireless LAN.
SH: The node that takes care of flow control and other protocol processing for all connections.

REFERENCES

1. Bantz, D.F.; Bauchot, F.J. Wireless LAN design alternatives. IEEE Netw. **1994**, *8* (2), 43–53.
2. Chen, K.-C.; Lee, C.H. In *RAP: a novel medium access control protocol for wireless data networks, IEEE GLOBECOM 1993, Houston, TX, Nov 29Dec 2, 1993*; IEEE Press: Piscataway, NJ, 1993; 1713–1717.
3. Chen, K.-C. Medium access control of wireless LANs for mobile computing. IEEE Netw. **1994**, *8* (5), 50–63.
4. Goodman, D.J. Cellular packet communications. IEEE Trans. Commun. **1990**, *38* (8), 1272–1280.
5. Barke, A.; Badrinath, B.R. *I-TCP: indirect TCP for mobile hosts*; Tech. Rept. 1994, DCS-TR-314Dept. Computer Science, Rutgers University: Piscataway, NJ, 1994.
6. Glisic, S.G. 1-Persistent carrier sense multiple access in radio channel with imperfect carrier sensing. IEEE Trans. Commun. **1991**, *39* (3), 458–464.
7. Tobagi, F.; Kleinrock, L. Packet switching in radio channels: Part I carrier sense multiple access models and their throughput delay characteristic. IEEE Trans. Commun. **1975**, *23* (12), 1400–1416.
8. Tobagi, F.; Kleinrock, L. Packet switching in radio channels: Part II the hidden terminal problem in CSMA and busyone solution. IEEE Trans. Commun. **1975**, *23* (12), 1417–1433.
9. Ioanidis, J.; Duchamp, D.; Maguire, G.Q. *IPbased protocols for mobile internetworking*, ACM SIGCOMM, Zurich, Switzerland, Sept 36, 1991; ACM Press: New York, 235–245.
10. Teraoka, F.; Tokoro, M. *Host migration transparency in IP networks: the VIP approach*, ACM SIGCOMM, San Francisco, Sept 13–17, 1993; ACM Press: New York, 45–65.
11. Ghai, R.; Singh, S. An architecture and communication protocol for picocellular networks. IEEE Pers. Commun. Mag. **1994**, *1* (3), 36–46.
12. Singh, S. Quality of service guarantees in mobile computing. J. Comput. Commun. **1996**, *19* (4), 359–371.
13. Seal, K.; Singh, S. Loss profiles: A quality of service measure in mobile computing. J. Wirel. Netw. **1996**, *2* (1), 45–61.

FURTHER INFORMATION

A good introduction to physical layer issues is presented in Bantz and Bauchot[1] and MAC layer issues are discussed in Chen.[3] For a discussion of network and transport layer issues, see Singh[12] and Ghai and Singh.[11]

WLANs: Wireless Local Area Networks: IEEE 802.11

José Antonio Garcia-Macias
CICESE Research Center, Esenada, Mexico

Leyla Toumi
Software Systems Research Laboratory (LSR-IMAG), National Center for Scientific Research (CNRS)/National Polytechnic Institute of Grenoble (INPG), Grenoble, France

Abstract

The IEEE 802.11 is a standard for wireless LANs.

802.11 STANDARD

The IEEE ratified the original 802.11 specification in 1997 as the standard for wireless local area networks (WLANs). That version of 802.11 provides for 1 and 2 Mbps data rates and a set of fundamental signaling methods and other services. Some disadvantages with the original 802.11 standard are the data rates that are too slow to support most general business requirements. Recognizing the critical need to support higher data transmission rates, the IEEE ratified the 802.11b standard for transmissions of up to 11 Mbps. With 802.11b (also known as WiFi), WLANs are able to achieve wireless performance and throughput comparable to wired 10 Mbps ethernet. 802.11a offers speeds of up to 54 Mbps, but runs in the 5 GHz band, so products based on this standard are not compatible with those based on 802.11b.[1] Several task groups are working on further developments for the 802.11 standard, as shown in Table 1.

Like all 802.x standards, 802.11 focuses on the bottom two layers of the open system interconnection reference model, the physical, and the data link layers. In fact, the standard covers three physical layer implementations: direct sequence (DS) spread spectrum, frequency hopping (FH) spread spectrum, and infrared (IR). A single media access control (MAC) layer supports all three physical layer implementations, as shown in Fig. 1. We will further discuss the two ISO layers that the 802.11 standard deals with.

802.11 ARCHITECTURE

Each computer (mobile, portable, or fixed) is referred to as a station in 802.11. Mobile stations access the LAN during movement. The 802.11 standard defines two modes: infrastructure mode and *ad hoc* mode. In infrastructure mode (Fig. 2), the wireless network consists of at least one access point (AP) connected to the wired network infrastructure and a set of wireless end stations.

This configuration is called a basic service set (BSS). An extended service set (ESS) is a set of two or more BSSs forming a single sub-network. Two or more ESSs are interconnected using a DS distribution system. In an ESS, the entire network looks like an independent BSS (IBSS) to the logical link control (LLC) layer; this means that stations within the ESS can communicate or even move between BSSs transparently to the LLC. The DS can be thought of as a backbone network that is responsible for MAC level transport of MAC service data units. The DS, as specified by 802.11, is implementation independent; therefore, the DS could be a wired 802.3 Ethernet LAN, an 802.4 token bus LAN, an 802.5 token ring LAN, a fiber distributed data interface metropolitan area network, or another 802.11 wireless medium. Note that while the DS could physically be the same transmission medium as the BSS, they are logically different because the DS is solely used as a transport backbone to transfer packets between different BSSs in the ESS. An ESS can provide gateway access for wireless users into a wired network such as the Internet. This is accomplished via a device known as a portal. The portal is a logical entity that specifies the integration point on the DS where the 802.11 network integrates with a non 802.11 network. If the network is an 802.x, the portal incorporates functions that are analogous to a bridge, i.e., it provides range extension and the translation between different frame formats.

The *ad hoc* mode (also called peer-to-peer mode or an IBSS) is simply a set of 802.11 stations that communicate directly with one another without using an AP or any connection to a wired network in *ad hoc* networks (see Fig. 3), there is no base and no one gives permission to talk; these networks are spontaneous and can be

Encyclopedia of Information Systems and Technology. DOI: 10.1081/E-EIST-120043907

W3C–XML

Table 1 Activities of the task groups working on the 802.11 standard

Task group	Activities
802.11	Initial standard, 2.4 GHz band, 2 Mbps
802.11a	High speed PHY layer in the 5 GHz band, up to 24 or 54 Mbps
802.11b	High speed PHY layer in the 2.4 GHz band, up to 11 Mbps
802.11d	New regulatory domains countries
802.11e	MAC enhancements: multimedia, QoS, enhanced security
802.11f	Interaccess point protocol for AP interoperability
802.11g	Higher data rate extension in the 2.4 GHz band, up to 22 Mbps
802.11h	Extensions for the 5 GHz band support in Europe

set up rapidly, but are limited both temporally and spatially.

PHYSICAL LAYER

The three physical layers originally defined in the 802.11 standard included two spread spectrum radio techniques and a diffuse IR specification. The radio-based standards operate within the 2.4 GHz ISM (industrial, scientific, and medical) band. These frequency bands are recognized by international regulatory agencies, such as the FCC (United States), ETSI (Europe), and the MKK (Japan) for unlicensed radio operations. As such, 802.11 based products do not require user licensing or special training. Spread spectrum techniques, in addition to satisfying regulatory requirements, boost throughput and allow many unrelated products to share the spectrum without explicit cooperation and with minimal interference.

The original 802.11 wireless standard defines data rates of 1 and 2 Mbps via radio waves using FH spread

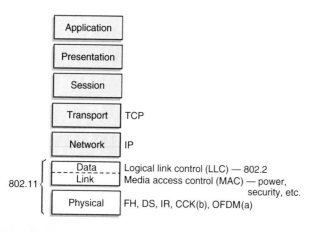

Fig. 1 The 802.11 standard and the ISO model.

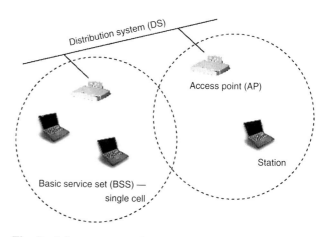

Fig. 2 Infrastructure mode.

spectrum or direct sequence (DS) spread spectrum. It is important to note that these are fundamentally different transmission mechanisms and will not interoperate with each other. DS has a more robust modulation and a larger coverage range than FH, even when FH uses twice the transmitter power output level. FH gives a large number of hop frequencies, but the adjacent channel interference behavior limits the number of independently operating collocated systems. Hop time and a smaller packet size introduce more transmission time overhead into FH, which affects the maximum throughput. Although FH is less robust, it gives a more graceful degradation in throughput and connectivity.

Under poor channel and interference conditions, FH will continue to work over a few hop channels a little longer than over the other hop channels.

DS, however, still gives reliable links for a distance at which very few FH hop channels still work. For collocated networks (APs), DS gives a higher potential throughput with fewer APs than FH, which has more APs. The smaller number of APs used by DS lowers the infrastructure cost.

DATA LINK LAYER

The data link layer within 802.11 consists of two sublayers: LLC and MAC. 802.11 uses the same 802.2 LLC and 48 bit addressing as other 802.x LANs,

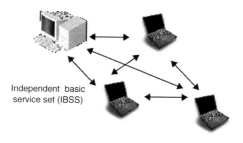

Fig. 3 *Ad hoc* mode.

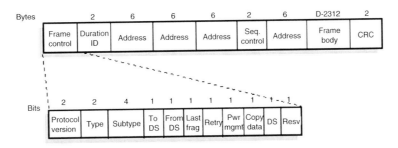

Fig. 4 Standard 802.11 frame format.

allowing for very simple bridging from wireless to wired networks, but the MAC is unique to WLANs.

Of particular interest in the specification is the support for two fundamentally different MAC schemes to transport asynchronous and time-bounded services. The first scheme, distributed coordination function (DCF), is similar to traditional legacy packet networks. The DCF is designed for asynchronous data transport, where all users with data to transmit have an equally fair chance of accessing the network. The point coordination function (PCF) is the second MAC scheme. The PCF is based on polling that is controlled by an AP.

The basic access method, DCF, is drawn from the family of carrier sense multiple access with collision avoidance (CSMA/CA) protocols. The collision detection (CD)mechanism as used in the (CSMA/CD) protocol of ethernet cannot be used under 802.11 due to the near/far problem: to detect a collision, a station must be able to transmit and listen at the same time, but in radio systems the transmission drowns out the ability of the station to hear a collision. So, 802.11 uses

CSMA/CA, under which collisions are avoided by using explicit packet acknowledgment (ACK) to confirm that the data packet arrived intact.

802.11 supports three different types of frames: management, control, and data. The management frames are used for station association and disassociation with the AP, timing and synchronization, and authentication and deauthentication. Control frames are used for handshaking during a contention period (CP), for positive ACK during the CP, and to end the contention-free period (CFP). Data frames are used for the transmission of data during the CP and CFP, and can be combined with polling and ACKs during the CFP. Fig. 4 shows the standard 802.11 frame format.

REFERENCE

1. Nobel, C. Making 802.11 standards work together. eWeek, July 19, **2000**.

WLANs: Wireless Local Area Networks: Security

Franjo Majstor
EMEA Senior Technical Director, CipherOptics Inc., Raleigh, North Carolina, U.S.A.

Abstract

Wireless communication represents a wide area of radio technologies, as well as protocols on a wide scope of transmission frequencies. Although initially used in venues where traditional wired networks were previously unavailable, the flexibility of wireless communication, together with the adoption of the 802.11, standard has driven wireless communication to rapidly move into the information technology environment in the form of the so-called "wireless local area networks" (WLANs). This entry aims to give information security practitioners a quick overview of WLAN technology and an in-depth view of the present security aspects of the same technology. Likewise, it presents possible solutions and directions for subsequent developments.

WLAN TECHNOLOGY OVERVIEW

Wireless local area networking technology has existed for several years, providing connectivity to wired infrastructures where mobility was a requirement for specific working environments. Early networks were based on different radio technologies and were nonstandard implementations, with speeds ranging between 1 and 2 Mbps. Without any standards driving wireless local area network (WLAN) technologies, the early implementations of WLAN were relegated to vendor-specific implementation, with no provision for interoperability, thus inhibiting the growth of standards-based WLAN technologies. Even WLAN is not a single radio technology, but is represented by several different protocols and standards, all of which fall under the 802.11 umbrella of the Institute of Electrical and Electronics Engineers (IEEE) standards.

Put simply, WLAN is, from the network connectivity perspective, similar to the wired local area network (LAN) technology with a wireless access point (AP) acting as a hub for the connection stations equipped with WLAN networking cards. As to the absence of wires, there is a difference in communication speed among the stations and AP, depending on which particular WLAN technology or standard is used for building the data wireless network.

802.11 Alphabet

WLAN technology gained its popularity after 1999 through the 802.11b standardization efforts of the IEEE, but it is not the only standard in the 802.11 family. Others are 802.11a, 802.11g, and 802.11i or 802.1x. For information security practitioners, it is important to understand the differences between them, as well as to know the ones that have relevant security implications on wireless data communications. What is interesting to mention before we demystify the 802.11 alphabet is that particular letters (a, b, g, etc.) were assigned by the starting time of development of the particular standard. Some of them, however, were developed and accepted faster than the others, so here they will be described in the order of importance and the scope of usage instead of alphabetical order.

- *802.11b*. The 802.11b standard defines communication speeds of 1, 2, 5, and 11 Mbps at a frequency of 2.4 GHz, and is the most widely accepted WLAN standard at present with a large number of vendors producing 802.11b devices. The interoperability of the devices from different vendors is ensured by an independent organization originally called the Wireless Ethernet Compatibility Alliance (WECA), which identifies products that are compliant with the 802.11b standard with "Wi-Fi" (Wireless Fidelity) brand. Not so long ago, WECA renamed itself as Wi-Fi Alliance. From a networking perspective, the 802.11b standard offers 11 (United States), 13 (Europe), or 14 (Japan) different channels, depending on the regional setup, although only three of those channels are nonoverlapping channels. Each of the channels could easily be compared to an Ethernet collision domain on a wired network, because only stations, which transmit data on nonoverlapping channels, do not cause mutual collisions; also, each channel is very similar in behavior to a wired Ethernet segment in a hub-based LAN environment.
- *802.11a*. In 1999, the IEEE also ratified another WLAN technology, known as 802.11a thatoperates at a frequency of 5 GHz and has eight nonoverlapping channels, compared to three in 802.11b, and offers

Encyclopedia of Information Systems and Technology, DOI: 10.1081/E-EIST-120046401

W3C–
XML

data speeds ranging from 6 Mbps up to 54 Mbps. Despite its speed, it is far from the level of acceptance of 802.11b due to several reasons. There are fewer vendor offers on the market and Wi-Fi interoperability testing has not yet been done. IEEE 802.11a operates at a different frequency than 802.11b and is not backward-compatible with it. Due to different frequency allocations and regulations in different parts of the world, 802.11a might be replaced in the near future by 802.11g as a new compromise solution.

- *802.11g.* 802.11g is the latest entrant to the WLAN standardization efforts; it tries to achieve greater communication speeds at the same unlicensed frequency as 802.11b (i.e., 2.4 GHz), and also tries to be backward-compatible with it. However, 802.11g is not a ratified standard and there are no products offered by any of the vendors on the market. Due to practical reasons and the delays in 802.11g standardization efforts, vendors are also offering dual-band devices that are operating at both 2.4 GHz and 5 GHz, thus offering a flexible future migration path for connecting stations.

As mentioned above, there are multiple other "letters" of the alphabet assigned to 802.11—802.11d defines world mode and additional regulatory domains, 802.11e defines quality-of-service mechanisms, 802.11f is used as an inter-AP protocol, and 802.11h defines dynamic frequency selection and power control mechanisms—but all are beyond the scope of this entry. Others, such as 802.11i and 802.1x, however, are very important from a security perspective and will be discussed in more detail in the sections on the security aspects of WLANs and upcoming developments.

WLAN SECURITY ASPECTS

Considering that it does not stop at the physical boundaries or perimeters of a wired network, wireless communication has significant implications on the security aspects of modern networking environment. WLAN technology has, precisely for that reason, built in the following mechanisms, which are meant to enhance the level of security for wireless data communication:

- Service set identifier (SSID)
- Device authentication mechanisms
- Media access control (MAC) address filtering
- Wired Equivalent Privacy (WEP) encryption

Service Set Identifier

The SSID is a mechanism similar to a wired-world virtual local area network identity tag that allows the

logical separation of WLANs. In general, a client must be configured with the appropriate SSID to gain access to the WLAN. The SSID does not provide any data-privacy functions, nor does it authenticate the client to the AP.

SSID is advertised in plaintext in the AP beacon messages. Although beacon messages are transparent to users, an eavesdropper can easily determine the SSID with the use of an 802.11 WLAN packet analyzer or by using a WLAN client that displays all available broadcasted SSIDs. Some AP vendors offer the option to disable SSID broadcasts in the beacon messages, but the SSID can still be determined by sniffing the probe response frames from an AP. Hence, it is important to understand that the SSID is neither designed nor intended for use as a security mechanism. In addition, disabling SSID broadcasts might have adverse effects on Wi-Fi interoperability for mixed-client deployments.

Device Authentication

The 802.11 specification provides two modes of authentication: open authentication and shared key authentication. Open authentication is a null authentication algorithm. It involves sending a challenge, but the AP will grant any request for authentication. It is simple and easy, mainly owing to 802.11 compliancy with handheld devices that do not have the central processing unit (CPU) capabilities required for complex authentication algorithms. Shared key authentication is the second authentication mode specified in the 802.11 standard. Shared key authentication requires that the client configure a static WEP shared key, and involves sending a challenge and then receiving an encrypted version of the challenge. Most experts believe that using shared key authentication is worse than using open authentication and recommend turning it off. However, shared key authentication could help deter a denial-of-service (DoS) attack if the attacker does not know the correct WEP key. Unfortunately, other methods of launching DoS attacks are available.

It is important to note that both authentication mechanisms in the 802.11 specifications authenticate only wireless nodes and do not provide any mechanism for user authentication.

MAC Address Authentication

MAC address authentication is not specified in the 802.11 standard, but many vendors support it. MAC address authentication verifies the client's MAC address against a locally configured list of allowed addresses or against an external authentication server (AS). MAC authentication is used to augment the open and shared key authentications provided by 802.11, further reducing

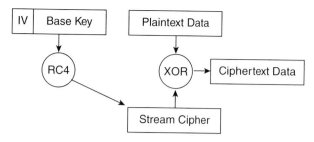

Fig. 1 The WEP encryption process.

the likelihood of unauthorized devices accessing the network.

However, as required by 802.11 specification, MAC addresses are sent in the clear during the communication. A consequence for WLANs that rely only on MAC address authentication is that a network attacker might be able to bypass the MAC authentication process by "spoofing" a valid MAC address.

WEP Encryption

All the previous mechanisms addressed access control, whereas none of them have thus far addressed the confidentiality or integrity of the wireless data communication. WEP, the encryption scheme adopted by the IEEE 802.11 committee, defines for that purpose the use of a symmetric key stream cipher RC4 that was invented by Ron Rivest of RSA Security Inc. A symmetric cipher uses the same key and algorithm for both encryption and decryption. The key is the one piece of information that must be shared by both the encrypting and decrypting endpoints. RC4 allows the key length to be variable, up to 256 bytes, as opposed to requiring the key to be fixed at a certain length. The IEEE specifies that 802.11 devices must support 40-bit keys with the option to use longer key lengths. Several vendors support 128-bit WEP encryption with their WLAN solutions. WEP has security goals of confidentiality and integrity but could also be used as an access control mechanism. A node that lacks the correct WEP key can neither send nor receive data from an AP, and also should neither be able to decrypt the data nor change its integrity. The previous statement is fully correct in the sense that the node that does not have the key can neither access the WLAN network nor see or change the data. However, several cryptography analyses listed in references have explained the possibility that, given sufficient time and data, it is possible to derive the WEP key due to flaws in the way the WEP encryption scheme uses the RC4 algorithm.

WEP Vulnerabilities

Because WEP is a stream cipher, it requires a mechanism that will ensure that the same plaintext will not

generate the same ciphertext (see Fig. 1). This is the role of an initialization vector (IV), which is concatenated with the key bytes before generating the stream cipher. The IV is a 24-bit value that the IEEE suggests, although does not mandate, to be changed with each frame. Because the sender generates the IV with no standard scheme or schedule, it must be sent unencrypted with the data frame to the receiver. The receiver can concatenate the received IV with the WEP key it has stored locally to decrypt the data frame.

The IV is the source of most problems with WEP. Because the IV is transmitted as plaintext and placed in the 802.11 header, anyone sniffing a WLAN can see it. At 24 bits long, the IV provides a range of 16,777,216 possible values. Analysts at the University of California, Berkeley, found that when the same IV is used with the same key on an encrypted packet (known as an IV collision), a person with malicious intentions could capture the data frames and derive information about the WEP key. Furthermore, cryptanalysts Fluhrer, Mantin, and Shamir (FMS) have also discovered inherent shortcomings in the RC4 key-scheduling algorithm. They have explained shortcomings that have practical applications in decrypting 802.11 frames using WEP, using a large class of weak IVs that can be generated by RC4, and have highlighted methods to break the WEP key using certain patterns in the IVs. Although the problem explained by FMS is pragmatic, the most worrying fact is that the attack is completely passive; however, it has been practically implemented by AT&T Labs and Rice University[1] and some tools are publicly available on the Internet (e.g., Airsnort).

Further details about WEP weaknesses are explained in depth in the references, but for information security practitioners, it is important to understand that the 802.11 standard, together with its presentWEP implementation, has security weaknesses that must be taken care of when deploying WLAN networks.

WLAN SECURITY SOLUTIONS

Major security issues in WEP include the following. First, it does not define the key exchange mechanism. Second, it has implementation flaws with the use of static keys. An additional missing security element from the present security 802.11 feature set is the lack of individual user authentication. Information security practitioners should be aware of this and look for solutions appropriate to their environments. A proposal jointly submitted to the IEEE by Cisco Systems, Microsoft, and other organizations introduced a solution for the above issues using 802.1x and the Extensible Authentication Protocol (EAP) to provide enhanced security functionality. Central to this proposal are two main elements:

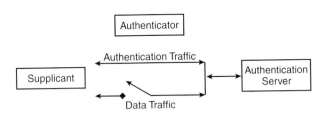

Fig. 2 The 802.1x port access control mechanism.

- EAP allows wireless clients that may support different authentication types to communicate with different back-end servers such as Remote Access Dial-In User Service (RADIUS)
- IEEE 802.1x, a standard for port-based network access control

IEEE 802.1x Protocol

The 802.1x is a port-based security standard protocol developed by the IEEE 802.1 working group for network access control in wired networks. Its major role is to block all the data traffic through a certain network port until the client user authentication process has been successfully completed. In essence, it operates as a simple switch mechanism for data traffic, as illustrated in Fig. 2.

Extensible Authentication Protocol

The EAP is a flexible authentication protocol specified in RFC 2284 that rides on top of another protocol, such as 802.1x or RADIUS. It is an extension of the Point-to-Point Protocol that enables the support of advanced authentication methods, such as digital certificates, MD-5 hash, or one-time password (OTP) mechanisms. Layers of 802.1x and EAP methods are illustrated in Fig. 3.

Dynamic Key Exchange Mechanisms

Each of the EAP protocols, except EAP-MD5, provides a solution to WEP security problems by tying the dynamic key calculation process to an individual user

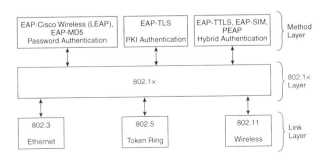

Fig. 3 EAP and 802.1x layers.

authentication. With the EAP mechanism, each individual user obtains its own unique dynamic WEP key that is changed every time the user connects to an AP. Alternatively, it could also be recalculated based on the timeout defined on the AS.

EAP-MD5

EAP-MD5 (Message Digest 5) is the easiest of the EAP authentication schemes and provides only user authentication. The user authentication scheme employed is a simple username/password method that incorporates MD5 hashing for more secure authentication. It provides neither a mutual authentication nor a method for dynamic WEP key calculation; hence, it still requires manual WEP key configuration on both sides, clients as well as on the wireless AP.

EAP-Cisco Wireless or Lightweight Extensible Authentication Protocol

EAP-Cisco Wireless, also known as Lightweight Extensible Authentication Protocol (LEAP), is an EAP method developed by Cisco Systems. Based on the 802.1x authentication framework, EAP-Cisco Wireless mitigates several of the weaknesses by utilizing dynamic WEP key management. It supports mutual authentication between the client and an AS, and its advantage is that it uses a simple username/password mechanism for providing dynamic per-user, per-session WEP key derivation. A wireless client can only transmit EAP traffic after it is successfully authenticated. During user login, mutual authentication between the client and the AS occurs. A dynamic WEP key is then derived during this mutual authentication between the client and the AS, and the AS sends the dynamic WEP key to the AP. After the AP receives the key, regular network traffic forwarding is enabled at the AP for the authenticated client. The credentials used for authentication, such as a log-on password, are never transmitted in the clear, or without encryption, over the wireless medium. Upon client log-off, the client association entry in the AP returns to the nonauthenticated mode. The EAP-Cisco Wireless mechanism also supports dynamic re-keying based on the predefined timeout preconfigured on the AS. The disadvantages of the EAP-Cisco Wireless method is that, although it is based on an open standard, it is still proprietary and its authentication mechanism is limited to static usernames and passwords, thus eliminating the possible use of OTP user authentication.

EAP-TLS

The EAP Transport Layer Security (TLS), as defined in RFC 2716, is a Microsoft-supported EAP authentication method based on the TLS protocol defined in RFC 2246. TLS is the Internet Engineering Task Force (IETF) version of Secure Socket Layer used in most Web browsers for secure Web application transactions. TLS has proved to be a secure authentication scheme and is also available as an 802.1x EAP authentication type. TLS utilizes mutual authentication based on X.509 certificates. Because it requires the use of digital certificates on both the client and the authentications server side, it is the most secure method for user authentication and dynamic per-user, per-session WEP key derivation that also supports OTP user authentication. EAP-TLS security superiority over any of the other EAP methods is, at the same time, its weakness, because it is overkill to require the establishment of a public key infrastructure (PKI) with a certificate authority to distribute, revoke, and otherwise manage user certificates just to be able to use layer 2 WLAN connectivity. This is the main reason why TLS has resulted in the development of hybrid, compromised solutions, such as EAP-Tunneled TLS (TTLS) and Protected EAP (PEAP).

EAP-TTLS

The EAP-TTLS protocol is an 802.1x EAP authentication method that was jointly authored by Funk Software and Certicom, and is presently an IETF draft RFC. It uses server-side TLS and supports a variety of authentication methods, including passwords and OTPs.

With the EAP-TTLS method, the user's identity and password-based credentials are tunneled during authentication negotiation, and are therefore not observable in the communications channel. This prevents dictionary attacks, man-in-the-middle attacks, and hijacked connections by wireless eavesdroppers. In addition, dynamic per-session keys are generated to encrypt the wireless connection and protect data privacy. The AS can be configured to re-authenticate and thus re-key at any interval, a technique that thwarts known attacks against the encryption method used in WEP.

Protected EAP

Protected EAP (PEAP) is another IETF draft developed by RSA Security, Cisco Systems, and Microsoft. It is an EAP authentication method that is—similar to EAP-TTLS—designed to allow hybrid authentication. It uses digital certificate authentication for server-side only, whereas for client-side authentication, PEAP can use any other EAP authentication type. PEAP first establishes a secure tunnel via server-side authentication, and then uses any other EAP type for client-side authentication, such as OTPs or EAP-MD5 for static password-based authentication. PEAP, by using only server-side EAP-TLS, addresses the manageability and scalability

shortcomings of EAP-TLS for user authentication. It avoids the issues associated with installing digital certificates on every client machine as required by EAP-TLS, so the clients can select the method that best suits them.

EAP-Subscriber Identity Module

The EAP subscriber identity module (SIM) authentication method is an IEEE draft protocol designed to provide per-user/per-session mutual authentication between a WLAN client and an AS, similar to all the previous methods. It also defines a method for generating the master key used by the client and AS for the derivation of WEP keys. The difference between EAP-SIM authentication and other EAP methods is that it is based on the authentication and encryption algorithms stored on the Global System for Mobile (GSM) communications SIM card, which is a smart card designed according to the specific requirements detailed in the GSM standards. GSM authentication is based on a challenge–response mechanism and employs a shared secret key, which is stored on the SIM and otherwise known only to the GSM operator's Authentication Center. When a GSM SIM is given a 128-bit random number as a challenge, it calculates a 32-bit response and a 64-bit encryption key using an operator-specific algorithm. In GSM systems, the same key is used to encrypt mobile phone conversations over the air interface.

EAP Methods Compared

It is obvious that a variety of EAP methods try to solve WLAN security problems. All of them, with the exception of the EAP-SIM method specific to GSM networks and EAP-MD5, introduce solutions for user authentication and dynamic key derivation, by using different mechanisms of protection for the initial user credentials exchange and different legacy user authentication methods. The feature of EAP method comparison is shown in in Table 1.

VPN AND WLAN

Combining IP Security Protocol-Based VPN and WLAN

Because a WLAN medium can carry IP over it without any problems, it comes easily as an idea for solving all security problems of WEP to simply run the IP Security Protocol (IPSec) over the WLAN. Although the fairly standardized and security-robust IPSec-based solution could certainly help improve the security of communication over WLAN media, IPSec also has its own limitations. WLAN media can carry any type of IP traffic, including broadcast and multicast, whereas IPSec is

Table 1 The EAP methods compared

			EAP-Cisco		
	EAP-MD5	EAP-TLS	Wireless	EAP-TTLS	PEAP
Dynamic WEP key derivation	No	Yes	Yes	Yes	Yes
Mutual authentication	No	Yes	Yes	Yes	Yes
Client certificate required	No	Yes	No	No	No
Server certificate required	No	Yes	No	Yes	Yes
Static password support	Yes	No	Yes	Yes	Yes
OTP support	No	Yes	No	Yes	Yes

limited to unicast traffic only. Hence, if it is necessary to support multicast application over WLAN, IPSec does not represent a viable solution. Although it is possible to run IPSec encryption algorithms like Data Encryption Standard (DES) or 3DES in hardware, it is very seldom the case that client personal computers are equipped with the additional IPSec hardware accelerators. That means that IPSec encryption is done only in the software, limited by the speed of the personal computer CPU, which certainly represents a bottleneck and thus reduces the overall speed of communication over WLAN media (in particular on low-CPU handheld devices). IPSec authentication mechanisms support pre-shared keys, RSA digital-signatures, and digital certificates, which are all flexible options, but only digital certificates are the most scalable and robust secure option, which requires establishment of PKI services. If PKI services are already established, the same security level could also be achieved with EAP-TLS. The EAP-TLS method avoids all the limitations of IPSec with regard to the overall solution. Last but not the least, running IPSec on user personal computers most of the time requires, depending on the operating systems, additional software installation plus loss of user transparency, and it keeps the device protected only while the IPSec tunnel is established. Overall, IPSec-protected WLAN communication could possibly solve WLAN security problems, but it is not always applicable and requires an examination of its benefits and disadvantages before being deployed.

FUTURE DIRECTIONS

The IEEE has formed a task group i that is working on the 802.11i protocol specification to solve the security problems of the WEP protocol and provide a standardized way of doing so. The solution will most probably come in multiple phases with initial help for already-known problems, up to the replacement of the encryption scheme in the WEP protocol.

Temporal Key Integrity Protocol

The Temporal Key Integrity Protocol (TKIP) aims to fix the WEP integrity problem and is intended to work with existing and legacy hardware. It uses a mechanism called fast-packet re-keying, which changes the encryption keys frequently and provides two major enhancements to WEP:

1. A message integrity check (MIC) function on all WEP-encrypted data frames
2. Per-packet keying on all WEP-encrypted data frames

The MIC (Fig. 4) augments the ineffective integrity check value (ICV) of the 802.11 standard and is designed to solve the following major vulnerabilities of IV reuse and bit flipping. For initialization vector/base key reuse, the MIC adds a sequence number field to the wireless frame so that the AP can drop frames received out of order. For the frame tampering/bit flipping problem, the MIC feature adds an MIC field to the wireless frame, which provides a frame integrity check not vulnerable to the same mathematical shortcomings as the ICV.

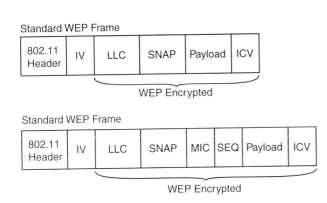

Fig. 4 Message Integrity Check: MIC.

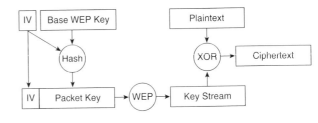

Fig. 5 The TKIP encryption process.

TKIP (Fig. 5) is using advanced hashing techniques, understood by both the client and the access point, so that the WEP key is changed on a packet-by-packet basis. The per-packet key is a function of the dynamic base WEP key.

The Wi-Fi Alliance has accepted TKIP as an easy, software-based upgrade, an intermediate solution for WEP security issues, and has established a new certification program under the name of Wi-Fi Protected Access (WPA). On the side of TKIP for WEP encryption improvement, WPA also covers user authentication mechanisms relaying on 802.1x and EAP.

Advanced Encryption Standard

In essence, all of the above-mentioned proposals do not really fix the WEP vulnerabilities, but when combined with packet re-keying, significantly reduce the probability that an FMS[2] or Berkeley attack will be effective. Flaws still exist with RC4 implementation but are more difficult to compromise because there is less traffic with identical keys. Standards bodies are investigating the use of the Advanced Encryption Standard (AES) as a possible alternative to RC4 in future versions of 802.11 security solutions. AES is a replacement for DES and uses the Rijndael algorithm, which was selected by the U.S. Government to protect sensitive information. However, the standardization of AES to solve encryption problems is still under discussion, without any commercially available products in the market today. As standards continue to develop, many security experts recommend using the IPSec standard that has been deployed in global networks for more than 5 years as an available alternative.

SUMMARY

WLAN technology based on 802.11 standards plays an important role in today's modern networking; and although it has its advantages in rapid and very flexible deployment, information security practitioners should be aware of its security weaknesses. Multiple proposals are on the scene to address major flaws in the WEP security protocol with different mechanisms for cryptographic integrity checks, dynamic key exchange, and individual user authentication. It is important to understand what security functionalities they offer or miss. Although IPSec virtual private network technology deployed over

WLANs is also an optional solution, it requires additional hardware and, hence, creates additional costs in addition to its limitations. Of the multiple EAP proposals for per-user/per-session dynamic WEP key derivation, it is expected that EAP-TTLS or PEAP will be the predominant solutions in the near future, assuming that either solution gets ratified. As the short-term solution for 802.11 security problems, an alliance of multiple vendors has decided to adopt the TKIP solution as a sufficient fix for existing WEP vulnerabilities under the name of Safe Secure Networks, even before its final approval by the IEEE 802.11i standards body. The Wi-Fi Alliance has adopted a similar scheme for its vendor interoperability testing under the name of WPA. Together they predict a bright future for safer WLAN deployment.

REFERENCES

1. *AT&T Labs and Rice University paper, Using the Fluhrer, Mantin, and Shamir Attack to Break WEP,* August 2001, http://www.cs.rice.edu/~astubble/wep/wep_attack.pdf.
2. Fluhrer, S.; Mantin, I.; Shamir, A. *Weaknesses in the Key Scheduling Algorithm of RC4,* http://www.cs.umd.edu/~waa/class-pubs/rc4_ksaproc.ps.

BIBLIOGRAPHY

1. Aboba, B.; Simon, D. *PPP EAP TLS Authentication Protocol,* RFC 2716, October 1999.
2. Andersson, H.; Josefsson, S.; Zorn, G.; Simon, D.; Palekar, A. *Protected EAP Protocol (PEAP).* IETF Internet Draft, draft-josefsson-pppext-eap-tls-eap-05.txt (accessed September 2002).
3. Blunk, L.; Vollbrecht, J. *EAP PPP Extensible Authentication Protocol (EAP),* RFC 2284, March 1998.
4. Bovison, N.; Goldberg, I.; Wagner, D. *Security of the WEP Algorithm,* http://www.isaac.cs.berkeley.edu/isaac/wep-faq.html.
5. Greem, B.C. *Wi-Fi Protected Access,* http://www.wi-fi.net/opensection/pdf/wi-fi_protected_access_overview.pdf (accessed October 2002).
6. Funk, P.; Blake-Wilson, S. *EAP Tunneled TLS Authentication Protocol (EAP_TTLS).* IETF Internet Draft, draft-ietf-pppext-eap-ttls-01.txt (accessed February 2002).
7. *SAFE: Wireless LAN Security in Depth,* White paper from Cisco Systems, http://www.cisco.com/warp/public/cc/so/cuso/epso/sqfr/safwl_wp.htm.

XML and Other Metadata Languages

William Hugh Murray
Executive Consultant, TruSecure Corporation, New Canaan, Connecticut, U.S.A.

Abstract

HyperText Markup Language (HTML) and similar metadata languages have given us levels of interoperability that were not dreamed of a decade ago. As the number of interoperable systems on the Internet has risen linearly, the value to the users has risen exponentially. EXtensible Markup Language (XML) promises us another order-of-magnitude increase in that interoperability. Not only will it help create interoperability between clients and servers on the Internet, but it will also improve interoperability among arbitrary objects and processes wherever located. By conserving and communicating the meaning and intent of data, it will increase its utility and value. Not since the advent of Common Business-Oriented Language (COBOL) has there been a tool with such promise; this promise is far more likely to be realized and may be realized on a grand scale.

When the author was a beardless boy, he worked as a punched-card machine operator. These were primitive information processing machines in which the information was stored in the form of holes punched in paper cards. Although paper was relatively cheap by historical standards, by modern standards it was very expensive storage. For example, a gigabyte of storage in punched paper would fill the average room from floor to ceiling, wall to wall, and corner to corner. It was dear in another sense, that is, there was a limit to the size of a record. A "unit record" was limited to 80 characters when recorded in Hollerith code. This code in this media could be read serially at about 10–15 characters per second. In parallel, it might be read at 8–12 thousand characters per minute.

As a consequence, application designers often used very dense encoding. For example, the year in a date was often stored as a single digit and two digits when the application permitted it. This was the origin of the famous Y2K problem. As the Y2K problem resolved, it was often thought of as a programming logic problem. That is, the program would not process years stored as four digits and might interpret 2000 as being earlier than 1999 rather than later. However, it was also a quality of data problem. When the year was encoded as one or two digits, information was often permanently lost. In fixing the problem, one often had to guess what the real data was.

The meaning of a character in a punched-card record was determined by its position in the record. For example, an account number might be recorded in columns 1 to 8 of the card. Punched-card operators of large stable applications could often understand the records from that application by looking at the color of the card and determine what information was stored in which columns by looking at the face of the card where the fields were delineated and identified. When dealing with small or novel applications, one often had to refer to a "card layout" recorded on a separate piece of paper and stored in a binder on the shelf. Because this piece of paper was essential in understanding the data, its loss could result in the loss of the ability to comprehend the data.

The name of the file was often encoded in the color of the card, and the name of the field in its position in the card. The codebook might have been printed on the face of the card or it might have been stored separately. In any case, it was available to the operators, but not to the machine. That is, the data about the data was not machinereadable and could not be used by it.

This positional encoding of the meaning of information and separate recording of its identity on a piece of paper carried over into early computer programming. Therefore, when starting to resolve the Y2K problem, one could not rely on the machine to identify where instances of the problem might appear, but had to refer to sources external to the programs and the data.

METADATA

In modern parlance, this data about the data is called metadata. Metadata is used to permit communication about the data to take place between programs that do not otherwise know about each other. Database schemas, style sheets, tagged languages, and even the data definition section of Common Business-Oriented Language (COBOL) are all examples of metadata. Because storage is now both fast and cheap, modern practice calls for the storage of this metadata with the data that it

Encyclopedia of Information Systems and Technology, DOI: 10.1081/E-EIST-120046751

W3C–XML

describes. In many applications and protocols, the metadata is transmitted with the data. A good example is electronic data interchange (EDI), in which fields carry their meaning or intended use in tags.

Good practice says that one never stores or moves the data without the metadata. Preferred security practice says that the metadata should be tightly bound to the data, as in a database, so as to resist unintended change and to make any change obvious. In object-oriented computing, the data, its meaning, and all of the operations that can be performed upon it may be bound into a single object. This object resists both arbitrary changes and misunderstanding.

Tagged Languages

One form of metadata is the tag. A tag is a specially formatted field that contains information about the data. It is associated with the data to which it refers by position, that is, the tag precedes the data. Optionally but often, the tag refers to everything after it and before a corresponding end tag.

XML is a tagged language. In this regard, it is similar to HTML, EDI, and SGML. A tag is a variable that carries information about the data with which it is contextually associated. A tag is metadata. To a limited degree, tags are reserved words. Only limited reservation is required because, as in these other tagged languages, tags are distinguished from data by some convention. For example, tags can be distinguished by bracketing them with the left and right pointing arrows, <tagname>, or beginning them with the colon, :tagname. Each tag has an associated end tag that is similarly distinguished, for example, by beginning the end tag with the left pointing arrow followed by a slash, </tagname> or the colon followed by the letter "e," :etagname. The use of end tags eliminates the need for a length attribute for the data. Tags are often nested. For example, the tags for name and address may appear inside a tag for name and address.

A tagged language is a set of tag definitions. Such a set, language, dialect, or schema is defined in a Document Type Definition object. This schema can be encapsulated in the object that it describes, or it can be associated with it by reference, context, or default. These language definitions can be, and usually are, nested. This provides maximum functionality and flexibility but may cause confusion.

The concept of "markup" comes from editing and publishing. The author submits a document to the editor who "marks up" the text to communicate with both the author and the printer or composer. One early tagged language was the Generalized Markup Language, perhaps the prototypical markup language. However, the concept of markup suggests something that is done in a

separate step to add value or information to the original. Many of the tagged languages called markup languages are really not markup languages in that special sense.

As with most languages, tagged languages provide for special usage. They provide for special vocabularies that may be meaningful only in a special context. For example, the meaning of the word "security" is different when used in financial services than when it is used in information technology. Similarly, EDI uses a number of different vocabularies, including X12, EDIFACT, TRADACOMS, which are applicable only in their intended applications.

The eXtensible Markup Language

XML is a language for describing data elements. It describes the attributes of the data and identifies its intended meaning and use. It consists of a set of tags that are associated with each data element and a description that decodes the tag. Keep in mind the analogies of a database schema and a record layout. Also keep in mind the limitations of these languages. Think of the analogy of HTML; as HTML says this is how to display or print it, XML says these are its attributes and this is what it means. XML is not magic.

XML is an open language. That is why it is called extensible. Of course, all programming languages are extensible to some degree or another. The dynamic HTML bears only a family resemblance to the HTML of a decade ago. Browsers are dynamically extensible through the use of plug-ins and the Dynamic Object Model (DOM). Modern HTML is dynamically extensible, extensible on-the-fly. The capabilities of the interpreter are dynamically extended through the use of plug-ins, applets, and similar mechanisms.

The owner of the object in which XML is used is permitted to define arbitrary tags of their own choice and embed their definition in the object. The meaning and attributes of a new tag are described in old tags. XML is a dialect of the Standard Generalized Markup Language, developed by IBM and adopted as an ISO standard. XML is the parent of a number of dialects, including cXML (Commerce XML), VXML (Voice XML), and even MSXML (Microsoft XML). There can be dialects for industries, applications, and even services. However, the value of any dialect is a function of the number of parties that speak it.

XML is a global language. That is to say, it has global schemas that go across enterprises, industries, and even national boundaries. These schemas represent broad prior agreement between users and applications on the meaning and use of data. The scope of the vocabulary of XML can be contrasted to that of programming languages such as COBOL where the data description is usually limited to an enterprise and often to a single program, where the base set of verbs is common across enterprises but there are no common nouns.

XML implements the concept of namespaces. That is, it provides for more than one agreement between a name and its meaning. The intended namespace is indicated by the name of the space, followed by a colon in front of the tagname (<ns:tagname >). There can be broad agreement on a relatively small vocabulary with many special vocabularies used only in a limited context.

XML is a declarative language. It makes flat statements. These statements are interpreted; they are not procedural. It says what is rather than what to do. However, one must keep in mind that tagnames can encapsulate arbitrary definitions that are the equivalent of arbitrary procedures.

XML is an interpreted language. Like BASIC, Java, and HTML, it is interpreted by an application. However,

to provide for consistency and to make XML-aware applications easier to build, most will use a standard parser and a standard definition or schema.

It is recursive. The XML schema, the object that defines XML, is written in XML. It can include definitions by reference. For example, it can reference definition by uniform resource locator (URL). Indeed, because it increases the probability that the intended definition of the tag will be found, this style of use is not only common, but also frequently recommended. Of course, from the perspective of the owner of the data, this is safe; it ensures the owner that the tags will be interpreted using the definitions that the owner intended. From the perspective of the recipient of the data, it may simply be one more level of indirection (i.e., sleight of hand) to worry about. The good thing about this is that URLs begin with a domain name. (Keep in mind that,

Table 1 The E Wallet: An example

A good example of the use of metadata in communication is the E-wallet application. Its owner uses the e-wallet to store and use electronic credentials. These include things such as name and address, user IDs and passwords, credit card numbers, etc. Because all of this information is sensitive to disclosure, it is usually stored in a database. The database can hide the data and associate it with its metadata, its intended meaning and use. Alternatively, the data could be stored in a flat file using tags for the metadata and file encryption to hide the data in storage when not in use.

The user employs the E-wallet application to present the credentials in useful ways. For example, suppose that the user has decided to make a purchase from an online merchant. After making a selection, the user presses the checkout button on the screen and is presented with the checkout screen. This screen asks for the name and billing address, name and shipping address, and charge information. The user invokes the E-wallet application to complete this screen.

The E-wallet presents the data stored in it and the user clicks and drags it to the appropriate fields on the checkout screen. The user knows what information to put in what places on the screen because the fields are labeled. These labels are put on the screen using HTML. While they are visible to the user, they are not visible to the E-wallet application. Therefore, the user must do the mapping between the fields in the E-wallet and those on the checkout screen. Although this process is flexible, it is also time-consuming. Although it ultimately produces the intended results, it relies on feedback and some intermediate error correction. When the screen is completed to the user's satisfaction, the user presses the Submit button. At this point, the screen is returned to the merchant where the merchant's computer verifies it further and might initiate another round of error correction.

If, in addition to labeling the fields on the screen with HTML, the merchant also labeled them with XML, then an XML-aware E-wallet could automatically complete part of the checkout screen for the user. If the checkout screen requests billing information, the E-wallet will look to see if it has the information to complete that section. In the likely case that it has more than one choice, it will present the choices to the user and the user will choose one. When the screen is completed to the user's satisfaction, the user will press the Submit button. When the screen is returned to the merchant, the data is suitably labeled with his XML so that his XML-aware applications and those of his trading partners (e.g., his credit card transaction service) can validate the data.

The use of XML has not changed the application or its appearance to the user. It has not changed the data in the application or its meaning. It has simply facilitated the communication between XML-aware applications. It has made the communication between the applications more automatic. Data is stored where it is supposed to be, controlled as it is supposed to be, and communicated as it is supposed to be. The applications behave more automatically and the opportunity for error is reduced. Notice that the applications of some merchants, most notably Amazon, achieve the same degree of automation. However, they do it at the cost of replicating the data and storing it in the wrong place, that is, user data is stored on the merchant system. This can and has led to compromises of that data. While one might argue that the data is better protected on the merchant's server than on the customer's client, the aggregation of data across multiple users is also a more attractive target.

Just as there are multiple browsers, there will be multiple E-wallet applications. As the requirement for the browser is that it recognizes HTML, the requirement for the E-wallet is to speak the same dialect of XML as the merchant's application. To make sure that it speaks the same dialect of XML as the merchant, the E-wallet may speak multiple XML dialects, similar to the way that browser applications speak multiple encryption algorithms.

Notice that the merchant's application could request information from the user's E-wallet that it does not display on the screen and which the user does not intend to provide. The user relies on the behavior of his application, the E-wallet, to send only what he authorizes.

As the merchant's application might attempt to exploit the E-wallet or its data, the user might attempt to alter the tags sent by the merchant in an attempt to dupe the merchant. The merchant relies on his application to protect him from such duping.

W3C-XML

while domain names are very reliable, they can be spoofed.) While it is possible, even usual, for the meaning of the metadata to be stored in a separate object, local definition may override the global definition.

It supports "typed" data, that is, data types on which only a specified set of operations is legal. However, as with all properties of XML-defined data, it is the application, not the language itself that prevents arbitrary operations on the data. For example:

```
<simpleType name="nameType">
  <restriction base="string">
  <maxLength value="32"/>
  </restriction>
</simpleType>
```

sets the maximum length of "nameType" equal to 32. Similar metadata could impose other restrictions or define other attributes such as character set, case, set or range of valid values, decimal placement, or any other attribute or restriction.

XML and other tagged metadata languages are not tightly bound to the data. That is to say, anyone who is privileged to change the data may be privileged to change the metadata. Anyone who is privileged to change the tag can separate it from the data. This loose binding can be contrasted with a database in which changing the metadata requires a different set of privileges than changing the data itself (see Table 1).

XML Capabilities and Limitations

Every tool has both capabilities, things that it can do, and limitations. The limitations may be inherent in the very concept of the tool (e.g., screwdrivers are not useful for driving nails) or they may be implementation induced (e.g., the handle of the screwdriver is not sufficiently bound to the bit). The tool may not be suitable for the application (e.g., the screwdriver is too large or too small for the screw). One does not use Howitzers to kill flies. This section discusses the capabilities, uses, misuses, abuses, and limitations of XML and similar metadata languages.

XML is metadata. It is data about data. Its role is similar to that of the schema in a database. Its fundamental role is to carry the identity, meaning, and intent of the data. It is neither a security tool nor is it intrinsically a vulnerability. From a security point of view, its intrinsic role is to support communication and reduce error. The potentially hostile or threatening aspects of XML are not those unique to it, but rather those that it shares with other languages and metadata, tagged and otherwise; a language that usually communicates truth can be used to lie.

People have been using and living with HTML for almost a decade. As XML is defined in XML, so is HTML 4.0, the vocabulary known as XHTML. (Recursion is often confusing and sometimes even scary.) People have been using EDI tags for almost a generation. Although they are now a subset of XML, all of our experience with them is still valid.

Perhaps the aspect of XML that is the source of most security concerns is that it is used with "push" technology, that is, the tags that describe the data come with the data. Moreover, the schema for interpreting the data may also be included. All of this often happens without much knowledge or intent on the part of the recipient or user. However, the meaning will be interpreted on the receiving system. Although it causes concern, it is as it should be. Only the sender of the data knows the intended meaning.

The fundamental responsibility for security in XML rests with the interpreter. As the browser hides the file system from HTML, the application must hide it from XML. As the browser decides how the HTML tag is to be rendered, so the application decides on the meaning of the XML tag. However, in doing so, it may rely on a called parser to help it deal with the tags. To the extent that the application relies on the parser, it must be sure that the one that it is using is the one that it expects.

Table 2 Web mail: An example

"Web mail" turns normal two-tier client/server e-mail into a three-tier client/server application. Perhaps the most well-known example is Microsoft's Hotmail. However, other portals such as Excite and Yahoo! have their own implementations. Many Internet service providers have an implementation that permits their mail users to access their post office from an arbitrary machine, from behind a firewall (that permits HTTP but restricts mail), or from a public kiosk.

In Web mail, the message is actually decoded and handled on the middle tier. Then the message is displayed to the user on his workstation by his Web browser. In one implementation, the middle tier failed to recognize the tags and simply passed them through to the Web browser. An attacker exploited this capability to use the browser to pop up a window labeled as the Web mail log-on window with prompts for the username and passphrase. Although mature users would not respond to a log-on prompt that they were not expecting, novice users did. Although all applications behaved as intended, the attacker used them to produce a result that duped the user. Web mail enabled the tags to escape the mail environment where they were safe, merely text, into the browser environment in which they were rendered in a misleading way.

This exploit illustrates an important characteristic of languages like XML that is easy to overlook when discussing them: they are transparent to the end user. The end user does not even know that they exist, much less what they say, how they carry meaning to the user system, the user's application, or to users themselves.

While normal practice permits a program to rely on the environment to vouch for the identity of a called program, good security practice may require that the application validates the identity of the parser, even to the extent of checking its digital signature.

Similar to many interpreted languages, XML can call escape mechanisms that permit it to pass instructions to the environment or context in which the user or receiver expects it to be interpreted. This may be the most serious exposure in XML, but it is not unique to XML. Almost all programming or data description languages include such an escape mechanism. These escape mechanisms have the potential to convert what the user thinks of as data into procedure (see Table 2).

While most of the use of such mechanisms will be benign, they have the potential to be used maliciously. The escape mechanisms included in Word, Excel, and Visual Basic have been widely exploited by viruses to get themselves executed, to get access to storage in which to place replicas, and to display misleading information to the user.

WORLD WIDE WEB SECURITY

While XML will have many applications other than the World Wide Web, this is the application of both interest and importance. As discussed, XML does little to aggravate the security of the Web. It is true that it can be used to dupe both users and applications. However, the vulnerabilities that are exploited can as easily be exploited using other languages or methods. By making the intent and meaning of the data more explicit, it may facilitate intelligence gathering.

On the other hand, it has the potential to improve communication and reduce errors. XML is being used to extend the capabilities of web clients and servers so as to increase the security of their applications. While these capabilities might be achieved in a variety of other ways, they are being implemented using XML. That they are being implemented using a metadata language demonstrates one value of such languages. These implementations have the potential to bring to security many of the advantages of metadata languages, including interoperability that is both platform and transport independent. However, keep in mind that these definitions are about the use of XML for security rather than about the security of XML.

Control of Access to XML Objects

One such application is the control of access to documents or arbitrary objects stored on web servers in a manner that is analogous to the control of access to database objects. In client/server applications, XML can be analogous to an SQL request. That is, it is used to specify the data that is being requested. As the database server limits access to the data that it stores and serves up, the server responding to an XML request can control access to the data that it serves.

In SQL, the fundamental object of request and control is a table. However, most database servers will also provide more granular control. For example, they may provide for discretionary access control over rows, columns, or even cells. Many can exercise control over arbitrary combinations of data called views. Notice that discretionary access control over the data is a feature of the database manager rather than of the language or schema. Notice also that the data is bound to the schema only when it is in a database manager. Once the data is served up by the database manager, trusted paths and processes may be required to preserve its integrity.

In XML, as in HTML, the fundamental object of access control is the document. For this purpose, the document is analogous to the database table. Almost all servers can restrict access to some pages. While this capability is rarely used, many provide discretionary access control to pages, that is, the ability to grant some users access to a page while denying it to others. For example, the Apache Web server permits the manager to grant or restrict access to named documents to specified users, user groups, IP addresses, or address/user pairs. Notice that as a database administrator can exercise more granular access control by naming multiple views of the same data, so too can the administrator of a server exercise more granular control by creating multiple documents.

However, tags are used to specify more granular objects than documents. This raises the possibility of more granular access control. As a database manager may provide more granular access control than a table, a server may provide more granular access control than a page. If it is going to do this at all, it can do it to the level of any tagged object. While administratively one might prefer large objects, from the perspective of the control mechanism, one tag looks pretty much like any other. Damiani et al.[1] have demonstrated such a mechanism.

Process-to-Process Authentication

On the web, particularly in E-commerce applications, it is often necessary for a client process to demonstrate its identity to a server process. These *bona fides* are often obtained from a trusted third party or parties. Such a demonstration may involve the exchange of data in such a way that the credentials cannot be forged or replayed. The protocols for such exchanges are well worked out. These protocols lend themselves to being described in structured data. In XML, such exchanges involve two schemas: one for the credentials themselves and another for requesting them.

A dialect of XML, authXML, has been proposed for this application. It defines formats for data to assert a claim of identity and for evidence to support that claim.

Process-to-Process Integrity

Similarly, in E-commerce applications, it is necessary to be able to digitally sign transactions so as to demonstrate their origin and content. This requires tags for the transaction itself, the signature, and the certificate. S^2ML, the Security Services Markup Language, provides a common language for the sharing of security services between companies engaged in B2B and B2C transactions.

RECOMMENDATIONS

1. *Identify and tag your own data.* Keep tags with your data. Although useful and used for communication, metadata is primarily for the use of the owners of the data.
2. *Bind your metadata to your data.* Use database managers, access-controlled storage, encryption, trusted applications, trusted systems, and trusted paths.
3. *Verify what you rely on.* This is the fundamental rule of security in the modern networked world. If relying on an object description, then be sure that you are using that description. If you are relying on an object not to have a script hidden in it, then be sure to scan for scripts.
4. *Accept tags only from reliable sources.* Do not place more reliance on tags from a source than you would on any other data from that source. While you might reject data without tags from a source, do not accept data with tags where you might not accept the data without the tags.
5. *Reject data with unexpected tags.* Do not pass the tags on. Do not strip them off and pass the data on.
6. *Include tags in logs and journals.* Not only will this improve the integrity and usability of the logs and journals, but it will improve accountability.
7. *Use the security tags where indicated and useful.*
8. *Communicate these recommendations to application developers and managers in appropriate standards, procedures, and enforcement mechanisms.* Although these measures are essential to the safe use of metadata, their use and control is usually in the hands of those with other priorities.
9. *Focus on the result seen by the end user.* After all is said and done, the security of the application will reside in what the end user understands and does.

CONCLUSION

HyperText Markup Language (HTML) and similar metadata languages have given us levels of interoperability that were not dreamed of a decade ago. As the number of interoperable systems on the Internet has risen linearly, the value to the users has risen exponentially. EXtensible Markup Language (XML) promises us another order-of-magnitude increase in that interoperability. Not only will it help create interoperability between clients and servers on the Internet, but it will also improve interoperability among arbitrary objects and processes wherever located. By conserving and communicating the meaning and intent of data, it will increase its utility and value. Not since the advent of Common Business-Oriented Language (COBOL) has there been a tool with such promise; this promise is far more likely to be realized and may be realized on a grand scale.

However, as with any new tool, the value of XML will depend, in large part, on one's skill in using it. As with any idea, its value will depend on one's understanding of it. As with any new technology, its value may be limited by fear and ignorance.

As with any new tool, one must understand both its capabilities and its limitations. Few things in information technology have caused as many problems as using tools without proper regard for their limitations.

Although the use of XML will often be outside the purview of the information security professional, hardly anyone else will be concerned about its limitations, misuse, or abuse. If the enterprise suffers losses because of limitations, misuse, or abuse, it is likely to hold us accountable. If the fundamental idea should become tarnished because of such limitations, misuse, or abuse, we will all be poorer for it.

REFERENCE

1. Damiani, E.; di Vimercati, S.; De, C.; Paraboschi, S. Design and implementation of an access control processor for XML documents. Computer Networks: The International Journal of Computer and Telecommunications Networking **2000**, *33* (1–6), 59–75 http://www9.org/w9cdrom/419/419.html.

W3C–XML

Index

Firewalls, 1047–1048
First generation computers
  Colossus computers, 179
  Harvard Mark I computer, 179
  International Business Machines Corporation
    (IBM), 179
  Lorenz SZ40/42 machine, 179
  two data streams, 179
Fisher iris data, 360–361
Fisher's data set, 407–408
Fixed channel allocation schemes, 155
Flash user interface, 197
Flat-fading channels, 150
Flexible querying
  components, 541
  definition, 541
  evaluation mechanism, 541–542
  linguistic quantifiers, 545–546
  weighted queries, 541–544
Folding@home, 171
Forensic analysis, see Analysis, cyberforensics
  goals, 357
  known unknowns, 358
  NN, see Neural networks (NN)
  objective function, 357
  syntactic methods, search engine problem,
    366–370
  unknown unknowns, 358
  unsupervised learning, see Unsupervised
    learning
Forensic imaging, 281
Forensic models, 403
Forensic Toolkit, 462, 463
Forensic Tool Kit (FTK), 287
FORmula TRANslation (FORTRAN), 755
Forward error correction (FEC), 72
Fossil fuels, 569–570
Fourth-generation computers
  Apple I and II, 181
  IBM PC, 181
  LSI, 181
  Micro Instrumentation Telemetry Systems
    Altair 8800, 181
  microprocessor, 181
Free and Open Source Software movement,
  175
Frequency division duplex (FDD), 151
Frequency division multiple access (FDMA),
  151
Frequency hopping spread spectrum (FHSS), 8
Frequency-selective channels, 150
FTK, see Forensic Tool Kit (FTK)
FTP, see File transfer protocol (FTP); File
  Transfer Protocol (FTP)
Functional configuration audit (FCA), 266
Functional domain databases
  Conserved Domains Database, 120
  Pfam, 121
  PROSITE, 120
  Simple Modular Architecture Research Tool
    (SMART), 121
Fusion layer, 363
Fuzzy associative mechanisms
  associated descriptors, 546
  clustering for documents, 547–548
  fuzzy categorizations, 546
  fuzzy ontologies, 546
  fuzzy pseudothesauri, 546
  fuzzy thesauri, 546–547
Fuzzy ontologies, 546
Fuzzy pseudothesauri, 546
Fuzzy set theory, IRSs, 532
  cross-language retrieval, 533
  current trends, 533
  improved string searching algorithms, 533

inconsistency, 535
multicriteria decision-making (MCDM), 532
performance measures, 548
retrieval models, 535–536; see also Fuzzy
  associative mechanisms
retrieval status value (RSV), 534
term recent semantics, 534
uncertainty, 534
vagueness and imprecision, 533–534
Fuzzy thesauri
  associations between terms, 546–547
  broader term (BT), 546
  keyword connection matrix, 547
  narrower relationships, 547
  narrower term (NT), 546
  reason, 546
  synonym link, 547

GAAPs, see Generally Accepted Accounting
  Principles (GAAPs)
Gartner Enterprise Architecture Framework,
  482
GAs, see Genetic Algorithms (GAs)
Gaussian minimum shift keying (GMSK), 145
GenBank, 116, 118
GeneCards, 118
Gene-centric databases
  Transcriptional Regulatory Element Database
    (TRED), 118
  TRANSFAC, 119
Gene Expression Omnibus (GEO), 119
Generally Accepted Accounting Principles
  (GAAPs), 510
3rd generation partnership project (3GPP), 834
Generic Autonomic Network Architecture
  (GANA)
  Autonomic Functions (AFs), 893
  blueprint model, 893
  Decision Elements (DEs), 893
  emerging standards, 893
  ETSI AFI GANA reference model, 894–895
  instantiations, 895–896
  reference model, 893
  stakeholders benefit, 896–897
Genetic Algorithms (GAs), 46
Genome-centric databases
  Ensembl, 119–120
  National Center for Biotechnology
    Information, 119
  UCSC Genome Browser, 120
GeoDA software, 557
Geoexploration systems, 557
Geographical information systems (GIS), 757
Geographic information systems/geographic
  databases (Geo-DBs), 834
Geographic information systems (GIS)
  applications, 558
  books, 559
  certification, 558
  computer-based system, 551
  definition, 551–552
  educational institutions, 554–555
  ESRI, 555
  future, 558
  GIS Day, 558–559
  history, 551
  Idrisi software, 555–556
  MAPINFO, 556–557
  overview, 551
  software packages, 555
  spatial autocorrelation, 557–558
  state of the art in 2008, 552–553
  synopsis, 551
  tool vs. science, 552
Geographic resources analysis support system
  (GRASS), 552
Geography markup language, 557–558

Geometric correction, 670
Geospatial information, 836–837
GFS, see Google File System (GFS)
GIS, see Geographic information systems
  (GIS)
Global dynamics, 254
Global mobile information systems (GloMo),
  850
Global positioning system (GPS), 87, 91,
  95, 96
  LBS application development, 831
  positioning technologies, 832
Global Positioning System (GPS), 341, 877
Global System for Mobile Communications
  (GSM), 924
Global System for Mobile Communications
  (GSM) frame, 832
Global Systems for Mobile Communication
  (GSM), 136
Globus Alliance, 188
Globus Toolkit, 188
God and Golem, Inc., 292
Gold image VM, 215
Google
  Android Market, 195
  Android Software Development Kit,
    194–195
  application programming interfaces (APIs),
    195
  Dalvik virtual machine (VM), 195–196
  Linux kernel, 194
  major components, 195
  services and systems, 195
  T-Mobile G1, 195
Google™, 107
Google Analytics, 297
Google Docs, 166
Google File System (GFS), 98
Google Gears, 167
Google Glass, 107
Governance, enterprise architecture
  Control Objectives for Information
    Technology (CobIT), 481
  creation, 481
  discovery, 481
  implementation, 481
  Information Technology Infrastructure
    Library (ITIL), 481
  International Organization for
    Standardization/International
    Electrotechnical Commission (ISO/IEC)
    27002, 481
  layering, 482
Governance and support system (GASS)
  definition, 840
  managing crises, 840
  meta-systems, 840
  strategic architecture, 839–840
GPS, see Global positioning system (GPS)
Gradient boosting, 350
Graphical interface, 448–449
Graphical user interfaces (GUIs), 32, 33
Graphic types
  age distribution chart, 305
  bar chart, 305
  bubble chart, 305, 306
  classic pie chart, 304–305
  heat map, 306, 307
  line chart of continuous variable distribution,
    305
  map visuals, 305–306
  points to be considered, 304
  scatterplot for correlations, 305, 306
  time series line charts, 305